MERRY'S CRICKET CLUB HOTEL

THE COMPLETE ILLUSTRATED HISTORY OF
AUSTRALIAN CRICKET

THE COMPLETE
ILLUSTRATED HISTORY OF
AUSTRALIAN CRICKET

JACK POLLARD

VIKING

Viking
Penguin Books Australia Ltd
487 Maroondah Highway, PO Box 257
Ringwood, Victoria 3134, Australia
Penguin Books Ltd
Harmondsworth, Middlesex, England
Viking Penguin, A Division of Penguin Books USA Inc.
375 Hudson Street, New York, New York 10014, USA
Penguin Books Canada Limited
10 Alcorn Avenue, Toronto, Ontario, Canada M4V 3B2
Penguin Books (N.Z.) Ltd
182-190 Wairau Road, Auckland 10, New Zealand

First published by Penguin Books Australia Ltd 1992
Revised edition published by Penguin Books Australia Ltd 1995

10 9 8 7 6 5 4 3 2 1

Typeset in Sabon by Midland Typesetters, Maryborough, Victoria
Printed and bound through Bookbuilders Limited, Hong Kong

National Library of Australia
Cataloguing-in-Publication data

Pollard, Jack, 1926- .
The complete illustrated history of Australian cricket.

Rev. ed.
Bibliography
Includes index.
ISBN 0 670 90329 9.

1. Cricket - Australia - History. 2. Cricket - Australia - History -
Pictorial works. 3. Cricket - Australia - Records. I. Title.

796.3580994022

CONTENTS

FOREWORD *by Matthew Engel*

The English winter of 1962–63 was the coldest in memory. The snow fell on Boxing Day and stayed until March. There were regular power cuts. At school, we went on cross-country runs every sports afternoon; it was all we could do.

But on those bitter mornings, as a pale sun struggled to get over the horizon, our transistor radios picked up news from what seemed like a different planet, much nearer the sun, rather than just the far side of this one.

The ABC team of the day were not men who painted word pictures the way John Arlott did; they were more clipped, more statistical, more factual. But they said enough. And the image they painted of this sun-drenched cricketing land remained with me for two decades, until I packed for my first-ever trip to Australia – reporting the 1982–83 tour – and wondered to myself whether I might at some point want a sweater. I knew nothing of southerly busters, the wind blowing into the old MCG press box or, heaven help us all, Hobart. I learned. Yet that fascination with Australia, begun that dreadful English winter, has never dimmed. It never does for any cricket-besotted Englishman.

The philosopher David Stove explained the fact that Australia beat England at cricket more often than not by noting: 'Whereas Australians hate the Poms, the Poms only despise the Australians.' It is a great line but not one that does full justice to this strange relationship.

Jardine was an exception. Every stuck-up, tight-bottomed MCC tie-wearing Englishman I have ever known has been humanised by contact with the straightforwardness of Australian cricket and Australian life. And one gets just as astonished by seeing how much even the most stereotyped Ocker is moved by the gentler, more sentimental English side of the game. It is a sort of marriage: each partner bringing out traits in the other's character that would otherwise remain submerged.

If something had gone wrong with history, and the French or Germans had got to the southern continent first, there would still be cricket in England. But it would be an infinitely poorer, more marginal game, perhaps no more than a pastime, a curiosity like the obscure old games still played in a few rural pubs: ringing-the-bull and knur-and-spel.

Of course, Australia has given the game Trumper, Bradman, Harvey, Lillee, Warne and the rest of the heroes Jack Pollard celebrates. But more than that: it has given cricket a sense of purpose, of combat, that has kept the game great.

Sometimes it seems prudent from an English point of view to let the Australians keep winning. When Mike Gatting's team won the Ashes at the MCG, the Melbourne *Sun*, as it then was, managed to all but censor the news, sticking it on a distant inside page, as though it were indeed a knur-and-spel contest. There have been other times, when a floodlit one-day game is displaying cricket at its most superficial, most raucous and most forgettable, when one starts to fear for the Australian game.

But here we have a country that failed to notice that railway trains running on different gauges have some difficulty getting from one place to another, that cannot – even in 1995 – agree on the matter of daylight saving times. In the winter, Melbourne is obsessed by a game that baffles Sydney and vice versa. It was cricket (and perhaps, more particularly, Bradman) that did more than anything to create the Australian identity that is now such a strong and vibrant force in the world.

And cricket's roots run deep throughout Australia: at weekends in the cities where the scorecards are filled with names like Minelli and Chang and Papadopoulos; on the stony ground of every country town where Nolanesque figures still play as night falls under the gum trees; and in the hearts and minds of the people. I believe it will be so forever.

MATTHEW ENGEL
Editor, *Wisden Cricketers' Almanack*

INTRODUCTION

Writing an accurate history of Australian cricket is a task beset with pitfalls for the author. Changes in the rules and conditions of play throughout the past 192 years mean it is not always possible to find definitive reports of early matches.

The matches described in this book go back to 1803, but the early ones cannot be supported by official scores. The authority for Australian cricket, the Board of Control, was formed in 1905, and scores preceding that date – involving 11 white tours of England, one white tour of South Africa, and an English tour by an Aboriginal team – have to be taken from independent sources. These do not always agree. For instance, three authorities quote fewer matches being played by the 1878 team – *Wisden* says 40, Boyle & Scott 37 and A.B. Rae 37 – but I consider the 41 quoted by manager John Conway in his book on the tour to be correct. The original schedule contained 37 matches but four times, when three-day matches finished early, additional one-day matches were played.

Even today Australia usually only sends official scorers on tours of England and for other tours relies on scoresheets provided by India, Pakistan, South Africa, the West Indies and New Zealand to supplement managers' reports. There have been several instances where scores handed over by our host countries have not added up!

Happily, cricket is blessed with some remarkably accurate reference books. *Wisden's Almanacks* (begun in 1864), the books by Roy Webber and Bill Frindall, and the Marylebone Cricket Club's *Cricket Scores and Biographies*, begun in 1862 by Frederick Lillywhite and carried on through 15 editions by Arthur Haygarth and F.S. Ashley-Cooper, are invaluable sources for all cricket histories.

For Australian writers, there is also *Cricket Walkabout*, Professor John Mulvaney's account of the 1868 tour of England by 13 Aborigines; P.E. Reynolds's description of the first white tour in 1878; the four books by Clarence P. Moody who pioneered use of the term 'Test match', and won universal acceptance of the first 38 England v. Australia matches that he judged to be Tests; the cricketers' guides put out by Henry F. Boyle and David Scott between 1879 and 1884; the *Australian Cricketers' Guide* by H. Biers and William Fairfax (1856–9); and W.J. Hammersley's *Cricketers' Register for Australasia* (1861–4). State year books have often proved unreliable, with errors taking years to correct once they creep in.

Although the records from all these sources have, in the statisticians phrase, been sanctified by time, I must admit to an uneasy feeling about several. I am not sure the Tasmania v. Victoria match in 1851 should be accepted as Australia's initial first-class encounter. The Victorians were not the best in their colony, though they might have been the best in the Port Phillip area, while the Tasmanians were taken only from select clubs like the Derwent and the side was not fully representative of the colony. Moreover, the match was over in two days (although there was then no official rule regarding length of first-class matches). The honour of staging the initial first-class match seems to me to belong more correctly to the 1856 match in Melbourne between New South Wales and Victoria, when all the best players from these colonies appeared.

Another match that continues to cause problems among historians is the England v. Australia Test in Melbourne, the scheduled Third Test of the 1971–72 series. The captains tossed and Illingworth, winning, put Australia in, but before players or umpires could take the field rain fell and continued until the third day when the match was abandoned. Administrators added an additional Test to the itinerary, which became known as the Seventh Test.

Although not a ball was bowled, the Australian Board ruled that the Melbourne Test should count in their players' records. By including it, Johnny Gleeson reached the mark that qualified him for the Board's Provident Fund payment – 30 Tests. But logically, the players in the Australian team have all been credited with a Test they did not deserve and took no part in.

Far more justifiable to be called Tests were the 16 Super Tests played by the Packer rebels during the two years of World Series Cricket. None of these matches – ten in Australia, one in New Zealand, and five in the West Indies – is recognised as first-class.

Similarly, the Board refuses first-class status to the 22 matches in 1985–86 and 1986–87 by Australian rebel teams, or those played by any of the international teams in the 16 years of the South African anti-apartheid ban. All respected cricket statisticians have ignored this absurd ruling and include South African performances by the Chappells, Benaud, Gooch, Gleeson, Francis, Hughes etc. in their career records.

Conditions of play have varied continually since the first cricket in Australia in 1803. Five runs were awarded for hits over the boundary before 1907–08, with the players then changing ends, and hits right out of the ground were rewarded with six. Since then all hits on the full over the boundary have counted as six runs. Only since 1985 in England v. Australia Tests have no balls and wides not scored from been counted against the bowlers' analyses.

Intervals have varied also. Before 1905 there were no tea breaks in England, but tea was taken out and served to the players in the Tests of 1899 and 1902. Since 1905 tea has been a regular feature and lasts 20 minutes. The luncheon interval, usually 40 minutes, has been a part of Tests since 1876–77, while the pre-lunch session of play has varied between 1 hour 30 minutes and 2 hours 30 minutes, and is now set at two hours.

In England before 1926 all Tests were limited to three days. From 1930 to 1938 this was extended to four days, and from 1948 to five. In Australia the Tests of 1876–77 were restricted to four days, the 1878–79 Tests to three days. Captains in the 1881–82 series had the right to ask for an extra day if required. Between 1882–83 and 1936–37 all Tests in Australia were played to a finish, with the exception of the final Test in 1891–92 which was limited to six days but was completed in any case in four. From 1946 to 1958–59 Australian Tests were limited to six days but since 1960–61 all Tests have been fixed at five. There have been five 'timeless' Tests between England and Australia: the 1912 match lasted four days, 1926 four days, 1930 went into the sixth day, but with no play possible on that day, and the 1934 and 1938 timeless Tests were both over in four days.

In England an over has consisted of four (1880 to 1888), five (1890 to 1899) or six balls (1902 to the present). In Australia the Test over has consisted of four balls (1876–77 to 1887–88), six balls (1891–92 to 1920–21), eight balls (1924–25), six balls (1928–29 to 1932–33), eight balls (1936–37 to 1978–79) and six balls since then.

The follow-on was originally compulsory in both England and Australia when teams finished their first innings with a deficit of 100 runs. This was decreased to 80 runs in 1854, then increased to 120 runs in 1894–95, but since 1907–08 enforcing the follow-on has been optional in Australia. England made the follow-on margin 200 runs in 1964 and Australia made the 200-run deficit optional from 1970–71.

Before 1926 there were no regulations on covering pitches. From 1926 pitches could be completely covered before play began but no part of the pitch could be covered after that. From 1934 to 1956, the entire pitch could be covered before play began but after the first ball was bowled only the 3ft 6in in front of the popping crease could be covered. This move to protect the bowlers' approach runs against rain was continued from 1961 to 1968, but the rest of the pitch could only be completed covered when play was suspended for the day. Since 1981 English pitches have been completely covered as soon as play is suspended. In Australia from 1920–21 to 1946–47 the whole of the pitch could be covered before the start of a Test, but only the pitch ends after play began. Since 1950–51 it has been obligatory to protect the whole pitch against rain at all times.

There have been other variations in the law allowing the captain to take a new ball, from 200 runs to 50 overs, 65 overs, then 75 overs, but since 1979–80 85 overs has been standard in Australia.

Finally, I must explain my use of the description 'English' attached to touring teams. Between 1903–04 and 1974–75 the Marylebone Cricket Club sponsored the team tours to Australia. The players involved received letters beginning 'The MCC invites you to join its team'. I am well aware that the teams in that period should be described as 'MCC teams', but to Australian cricket followers they were called English teams and for the sake of simple linguistics I have used English instead of MCC. Similarly I refer to the Board of Control in my text, instead of the full Australian Board of Control for International Cricket; from 1980, when David Richards took over, its name became the Australian Cricket Board.

JACK POLLARD
Sydney, 1995

Acknowledgement: The author and publishers would like to thank Charlie Wat for his help in compiling the scorecards in this book, and for his meticulous checking of the statistics throughout.

CHAPTER ONE

A START
AMONG THE COWPATS

Cricket was sixty-nine years old in America, and had firm footholds in Canada, Scotland and India, when Captain James Cook discovered the east coast of Australia in 1770. Irish cricket was recovering well from Cromwell's edict of 1656 that all bats, stumps and balls should be burned. In England the dominance of the Hambledon Club on a strip of heathland known as Broadhalfpenny Down in Hampshire had waned and a party of cricketers from Kent and Surrey had become arbiters of the laws of cricket through their Star and Garter Club in Pall Mall. A group of diners, drinkers and gentlemen from that club played regularly at Islington, in the London suburbs, under the banner of the White Conduit Club. By the time Captain Phillip sailed into Botany Bay in 1788 with the First Fleet, influential members of the White Conduit Club had sounded out Thomas Lord on whether he would care to establish an exclusive ground with greater privacy than the open fields at Islington and nearer to the centre of London.

Lord secured the lease of his first ground on part of the Portman family's vast Marylebone estate and by May 1787, when Governor Phillip was reserving a large area of the new city of Sydney, including the Domain and Hyde Park, to become known as Phillip's Common, the first match was played by the Marylebone club. Sixteen years after Lord's first opened and fifteen years after white Australia was established, cricket was reported in Australia.

The *Sydney Gazette and New South Wales Advertiser*, founded in March, 1803 – largely to announce prison sentences, the capture of rum smugglers, court decisions and restrictions on stock thieves – published the first report of cricket in the colony in its issue of 8 January 1804, when it said that 'in favourable weather the

Spectators ring the Hyde Park pitch where Australian cricket began at the beginning of the 19th century, with St James' church in the distance. Watercolour by T.H. Lewis. (Dixson Gallery, Sydney)

amateurs of cricket have scarce lost a day in the past month'. This sets the first Australian game of cricket at least as early as the southern summer of 1803–04, though the editor of the *Gazette*, a convict named George Howe – born in the Caribbean island of St Kitt's – was clearly no cricket lover and would not have given earlier reports on the game any preference over stories about pastimes such as cockfighting.

There was in those early years intense rivalry for the limited recreational space available. The main military barracks in Sydney was situated in what is now known as Wynyard Square, between Barrack and Jamieson streets, and when this space was not being used for parade ground drills, cricketers snatched the chance for brief practices. To play a full match they had to go out beyond the end of Phillip's Common to an area known as St George's Field, the present site of Sydney Cricket Ground.

The main arena for organised sport, variously known as the 'Common', the 'Exercising Ground', the 'Cricket Ground' and the 'racecourse', was given the name Hyde Park in 1810 by Governor Macquarie, and there Australia's first horse races and cricket matches were held. Later, as new streets developed and reduced the size of Hyde Park, the cricketers were forced to move closer to Sydney Harbour, to what was known as The Domain, a sloping area of reclaimed scrubland that soon became such a popular area

An early match in the Sydney Domain, cricket's headquarters after Hyde Park became too crowded. (Mitchell Library, *Sydney*)

for walkers the cricketers found themselves unwelcome. The first inter-colonial matches were held on The Domain but even when they enclosed the playing area the cricketers could not legally charge for admission. This, plus the lack of flat ground suitable for pitches, started a search for a better home for Sydney cricket.

Cricket spread to Tasmania in 1825, when a team of free settlers played a side from the Hobart garrison, to Victoria in 1838 when a team made up of the founders of the Melbourne Cricket Club played a military XI, to South Australia in 1839 when a match was held on Thebarton Cricket Ground between Eleven Gentlemen of Royal Victoria Independent Club and Eleven Gentlemen of Adelaide, to Western Australia in 1846 when a team of tradesmen engaged on building Government House played the Perth Cricket Club, and to Queensland in 1846 when the *Moreton Bay Courier* recorded a match in Brisbane between eleven working men and an equal number of gentlemen. There were earlier reports of club meetings and talks about buying equipment but these were the first dates on which scores of matches were kept in the colonies concerned.

Importing equipment from England and securing copies of the latest *Laws of Cricket* proved a major obstacle to early clubs. Some of the gear used was locally crafted from native trees and Australian produced leather. Changes in the laws, such as the advent of roundarm and then overarm bowling, took a long time to reach

3

Australia and many settlers preferred to stick to the old laws to which they were accustomed. Thus visiting sides in Australia were honoured with first innings of matches long after English teams had adopted the idea of tossing before matches.

From the start the colony governors encouraged cricket as a valuable influence in entertaining even the most recalcitrant convicts and sustaining their links with England. The policy of making free grants of land to colonists with respectable beginnings also brought in hundreds of squatters and their families well aware of how cricket matches were conducted. The gold rushes of the 1840s accelerated this influx. Many of those who arrived and immediately left their ships for the goldfields were the products of English public schools and universities, with experience in fine cricket teams. At one time no less than seven cricketers who had played for Oxford or Cambridge were said to be working as sugar planters in the Mackay district of Queensland. Some of them stayed only a year or two, but some remained for the rest of their lives and their inclusion in local teams proved a major boost for Queensland cricket.

Early matches between the colonies were tense, argumentative affairs, with discussion over alleged chuckers, umpiring decisions, preparation of wickets and playing hours enduring long after the sun went down. Contemporary accounts of matches accused players of cowardice, bribing umpires and other forms of cheating no modern reporter would dare raise.

An illustration from the London Tatler *magazine in the 1830s showing Australian cricketers arriving from their farms for a match in the bush.* (Mitchell Library, *Sydney*)

Despite the presence of unsavoury toughs attracted by big betting –
and sometimes welshing – the male citizens of Sydney and Melbourne attended inter-colonial games in their top hats and gloves
and the ladies wore their best finery, mingling with garrison officers
strutting about in their colourful uniforms, their medals glinting.
Large regimental bands played during breaks in play and champagne
flowed in such quantities visiting teams invariably returned home
limp and seedy. Inter-colonial trips usually had to be made in small
coastal ships that reacted badly to gales and heavy seas.

When they began, players in inter-colonial matches fielded
without boots in stockinged feet, on dusty and lumpy outfields from
which cow and goat dung had just been cleared. Ground staff used
wooden rollers and water had to be carried in buckets to the areas
from which captains would select their batting pitches. The desire
to win was so intense, rows over finer points frequently followed
players from the field into the tent in which they changed and later
to their hotels. Additionally, the police were unwilling to protect
players from the gambling vagabonds who jumped the fence and
struck them cowardly blows with sticks or umbrellas.

For captains a recurring hazard was the players who failed to turn
up. They often travelled long distances to matches on ill-defined
roads and when a dray, coach or horse broke down there was nothing
they could do to inform their captains. Landholders who fielded
private teams generally used Aboriginal labourers to make up their
teams but they were seldom among those originally selected.

Personalities just as unusual and colourful as any who appeared
in England at the time studded Australian cricket. England had
'Silver Billy' Beldham, William Hogsflesh and Edward ('Lumpy')
Stevens, but Australia had John Rickards, who bowled his fast
roundarmers with such success between 1833 and 1835 he was
known as the 'Australian Lillywhite'. Captain Edward Ward,
deputy director of the Mint, later Major-General Sir Wolstone-
holme Ward – an eccentric in all he did – took guard with his
buttocks facing the bowler and peered at him from behind his left
shoulder. Ward always batted wearing a monocle. Another character
was Henry Fysche Gisborne, son of a House of Commons MP who
arrived in 1830 and invariably played his cricket in a top hat. He
was appointed a magistrate in 1836 and wore the same hat in court.
Another oddity was Tom Lewis, who felt he had to hit every ball
and not let one get past him, even to the extent of hurling his bat
at wide deliveries.

On the Sydney Domain the crowds' favourite was John James McKone, our finest exponent of the grubber. He took 10 for 36 in a match-winning display in New South Wales' first match against Victoria in 1856, and in three matches for his colony did not once allow a ball to leave the ground.

The most remarkable bowling figures in all Australian first-class cricket, however, were achieved by Gideon Elliott, a Surrey professional lured to Australia by the gold rushes. In February 1858 Elliott took 9 wickets for 2 runs for Victoria against Tasmania at Launceston; 17 of his 19 overs were maidens. Tasmanians considered Elliott's roundarmers foul play, educated as they were in the pure underarm style.

One of Tasmania's outstanding bowlers, fiery Tom Hogg, was no-balled for lifting his arm above the shoulder in his first senior match. Hogg, one of 11 children whose father died in his thirties, said the umpire was ignorant of the laws that then applied and stalked from the field, but when he appeared in the Tasmanian side Hogg restricted himself to roundarm. In 1866 he took 5 for 13 and 5 for 4 against Victoria. The enforced alterations to Hogg's action produced a style that defied erudite description. The Melbourne *Telegraph* said he strolled to the crease and 'seemed to take the ball from behind his right ear and perform a little legerdemain with it behind his back before launching it'.

Although similarly restricted by umpires who failed to keep up with law changes, Gideon Elliott was luckier than Hogg. He was allowed to play in eight inter-colonial matches for Victoria, and his 48 wickets cost only 4.93 runs apiece. Against New South Wales he took 7 for 27 and 3 for 7 in 1855–56, 5 for 17 in 1857–58, and 6 for 23 in 1859–60. This earned him enough fame to ensure his success as a publican.

Elliott often bowled in tandem with Thomas Wentworth Wills, the first outstanding Australian-born cricketer. Wills was born at Molonglo Plains in New South Wales but was sent to England to be educated, polishing his cricket talents at Rugby School, Kent, the MCC and in one match for Cambridge University. His ten seasons in first-class cricket brought 121 wickets at 10.09 and 602 runs at 12.28. He took five wickets in an innings 14 times in a period in which that was a rare feat, and confessed to cheating occasionally by throwing when umpires were not looking. Test captain Tom Horan, in one of his 'Felix' columns for the *Australasian*, described Wills as 'the W.G. Grace of Australian cricket'.

When the Melbourne-based firm of caterers and restaurateurs, Felix Spiers and Nicholas Pond, looking for novel ways to promote their business, brought the first England cricket team to Australia in 1862, Wills began to travel with the tourists and then play for their opposition, who were invariably in need of assistance. Spiers and Pond were meticulous men. They sent their staff man, Mallam, to England to sign up players for the tour and in October, 1861, when they learned Mallam had been successful, wrote to Dick Wardill, then secretary of the Melbourne Cricket Club, asking him if he could get a grandstand ready for the Englishmen's appearance. In the days before builders' unions had to be taken into account when planning construction, Wardill complied, although he had only two months before the first match.

Mallam, instructed to offer English players £150 each, plus fares and expenses for the 50,000-kilometre trip, found England's best cricketers in Birmingham for a Players of the North v. Players of the South match. Over dinner he explained the planned Australian tour to them, but one of the most influential men at the table, George Parr, doubted if £150 was a fair reward for such a long trip to terrain completely unknown to the players. Parr had taken over the All England XI when its founder, William Clarke, died in 1855, and in 1859 had taken the side to America. Success of that tour led to a team captained by another Nottinghamshire cricketer, Richard Daft, touring America in 1861.

Parr's North of England colleagues agreed £150 was an inadequate fee, but back in London the Surrey secretary William Burrup helped Mallam sign a strong team of South of England professionals under the captaincy of Surrey's skipper, Heathfield Stephenson. Mallam made a special trip to Dublin to persuade Charles Lawrence to join the side, a wonderful thing later for Australian cricket. The first English team was H.H. Stephenson (Captain), W. Caffyn, C. Lawrence, W. Mortlock, T. Sewell, G. Griffith and W. Mudie from Surrey, T. Hearne from Middlesex, E. Stephenson and R.I. Iddison from Yorkshire, G. Bennett from Kent and G. Wells from Sussex.

Spiers, the promoter, owned the Royal Hotel and Café de Paris in Bourke Street, haunt of Melbourne's stage stars. Pond had the Piazza Hotel. Their friend George Selth Coppin, dynamic impresario of the Australian theatre, was filled with enthusiasm for the forthcoming tour, and while the English team travelled to Australia in the six-masted steamship *Great Britain*, Coppin chaired a

The first England team to Australia, with William Caffyn holding the ball in the middle row. The man in the top hat is William Mallam, who negotiated the tour for restaurateurs Spiers and Pond. (MCG Museum)

Arrival of the first English team, captained by H.H. Stephenson, at the Café de Paris, Bourke Street, Melbourne, 1861. (MCG Museum)

committee that picked the Victorian players to oppose England in their first match.

More than 10,000 people assembled at the Melbourne dock to greet the Englishmen, who were paraded through streets lined with cheering well-wishers to the Café de Paris. The players sat on the roof of a coach pulled by four superb greys. Stunned by the welcome, Stephenson said that after 62 days at sea the prospect of facing 22 opponents in their first match was daunting – teams of more than 11 players were a common answer to sides of differing skills – and asked for the Victorian team to be reduced to 15. Coppin's committee compromised and cut the Victorian side to 18.

The Englishmen were surprised at the strength of Victorian cricket, which already boasted 70 clubs, and amazed by the tour promotion. For the opening match at the lavishly decorated Melbourne Cricket Ground on New Year's Day 1862 each man was issued with a helmet-style sun hat and a sash for his waist in the same colour as the ribbon on his hat. These colours were shown beside each man's name on the scorecards to provide quick identification. The stand, with accommodation for 6000, had been completed and the entire ground was circled by bright marquees and advertising slogans. Publicans brought in hundreds of cases of beer and one enterprising house painter offered use of his ladder for a few pennies a time to those who wanted to watch from the trees.

The *Melbourne Herald* estimated that more than 15,000 people watched the start of play, but others thought that when the customers from shooting galleries, hurdygurdies and refreshment stalls were counted the crowd would have been much larger. There were six ducks in the Victorian Eighteen's first innings of 118, with the Victorian captain, George Marshall – born in Nottingham, where he had several professional engagements including a period with the Duke of Sutherland's private team – top-scoring with 27. William Caffyn made 79 in England's 305 in reply. There were ten ducks in the Victorian Eighteen's second innings of 92 and the match ended early on the fourth day, with England winners by an innings and 96 runs.

More than 45,000 people attended the match, which ended with the ground not far from full. The takings more than covered Spiers' and Pond's costs for the entire tour. Typically, they had additional entertainment ready for the crowd when stumps were drawn and acted on George Coppin's suggestion that they launch the first balloon flight seen in Australia, to fly over the MCG. The balloon carried a large portrait of Queen Victoria and all the English players on the outside and remained aloft for 35 minutes, drifting all over Melbourne before the balloonists, Mr and Mrs Brown, brought it down in Albert Street. Memorable celebrations followed that night at the Cricketers' Hotel in Swanston Street, where George Marshall was landlord.

Spiers and Pond sent the Englishmen 300 kilometres out into the scrub to play Twenty-Two of the Ovens Valley at Beechworth, a journey that introduced them to rough trips in which apparently only the driver could see the road. They went back and forth: to Sydney in a tiny, pitching and rolling coastal boat; by coach across the Blue Mountains to Bathurst, the oldest settlement in the west; down to Tasmania by sea; and back to Melbourne, where they rounded off the tour with a draw against Twenty-Two of Victoria.

In the main cities the colony governor and his entourage attended their matches. The country towns usually sent out bands to accompany the Englishmen's coach for the last few miles. Good performances by any of the tourists invariably attracted generous collections among spectators. The continuous round of champagne breakfasts, lunches and after-the-match banquets caught up with the tourists when they were beaten by a combined Twenty-Two of New South Wales and Victoria in mid-February on the Sydney Domain. The player mainly responsible for this defeat was one of Australian cricket's forgotten heroes, George Moore.

Moore, born at Ampthill in Bedfordshire in 1820, ran a confectionery shop in the Maitland district north of Sydney, where his right-hand roundarm slows and medium-pacers dominated local cricket. He travelled to Sydney three times to play for New South Wales, making his debut in first-class matches against Victoria in 1871 when he was a few weeks short of his fiftieth birthday. He took 4 for 22 from 83 deliveries against Stephenson's team, helping the Twenty-Two to win by 2 wickets after England scored 60 and 75. George's brother James and James's sons William and Leon all played for New South Wales, but the most famous cricketer in the family was George's grandson Charlie Macartney. George made his final appearance for New South Wales in 1873–74 when he was 52 years 325 days old, and he remains Australia's oldest mainland cricketer, junior only to Tasmania's John Marshall, who played his last game at 58.

Stephenson's first English team's only other loss on their 14-match Australian tour was the second last game, when they succumbed by three wickets to Twenty-Two of Castlemaine. England made 80 and 68, Castlemaine 54 and 18 for 96. England won six matches in all, five against Twenty-Twos and one against Eighteen, and had four draws.

Spiers and Pond made a profit of £11,000 on the tour after all expenses, including the agreed £150 per man, and gave each tourist a hundred-sovereign bonus. They let the players keep the gate for the Melbourne match between Surrey and the Rest of the World in which the six Surrey players had the help of five locals in opposing six team-mates from other counties plus five locals. The World XI won by six wickets. Spiers and Pond also gave the Englishmen half the proceeds of their last match, a draw against Twenty-Two of Victoria. The English players refused an offer of £1200 to stay for a further month, mainly because of county commitments at home.

The romantic suggestion that Anglo-Australian cricket owes its origin to Spiers and Pond turning to the English cricketers when novelist Charles Dickens rejected their invitation to tour is untrue. Dickens, whose work often mentions cricket, did not have dealings with Spiers and Pond until June 1862, when they met him in London and invited him to make an Australian lecture tour for £10,000 as a sequel to their cricket venture. Dickens's letters show that he vacillated for six months before he turned down their offer at Christmas 1862, admitting he was greatly tempted to go.

*   *   *

George Parr changed his mind about visiting Australia when he heard of the hospitality and generous payments the first side received. Roger Iddison reported he did not think much of the Australian standard of play but 'they're a wonderful lot of drinkin' men'. In 1863–64 Parr accepted an invitation from the Melbourne Cricket Club to captain and select the second English team to Australia. He chose 12 players who were far more representative of English cricket than the previous team.

William Caffyn was the only member of Parr's team who also toured in Stephenson's side, although Charles Lawrence had remained in Melbourne when the first team went home, accepting £200 a year to coach at Sydney's Albert club. Parr's other players were Alfred Clarke, J. Jackson, R.C. Tinley (all Notts players), Julius Caesar, Tom Lockyer and Caffyn of Surrey, a trio from Cambridgeshire, T. Hayward, R. Carpenter and G. Tarrant, Yorkshireman George Anderson, and the team's sole amateur, Gloucestershire all-rounder Dr Edward Mills Grace, brother of the legendary Dr W.G. Grace.

In August of 1863 in London Edgar Willsher was no-balled six times in succession for raising his arm above the shoulder in the first display of overarm bowling. Playing for England against Surrey at The Oval, Willsher stormed from the field after umpire John Lillywhite no-balled him for the sixth time. By then experienced cricketers all regarded overarm bowling as fair but Lillywhite believed it was his duty to no-ball Willsher. But for the second English tour of Australia the visitors and locals still bowled underarm and roundarm, with Dr E.M. Grace preferring lobs delivered with either style.

The Englishmen had a fortnight's practice in Melbourne after a 61-day voyage from England. The team stayed at the Cricketers' Hotel, owned by George Marshall, and it soon became apparent that he bore financial responsibility for the tour and that the Melbourne Cricket Club had simply guaranteed Marshall the use of their ground. Marshall's role as organiser of the tour was badly received in Sydney, where the leading cricketers remained angry about his behaviour in inter-colonial matches with Victoria. Charles Lawrence wrote to Parr before he left England, offering him alternative terms for a tour devised in Sydney but Parr refused and suggested Lawrence contact Marshall. Tom Wills described Lawrence's attempt to arrange a separate tour as an insult to all Victorian players and proposed that Parr's team by-pass Sydney and Maitland.

The second English tour began on 1 January, 1864, when Marshall faced the first ball for a Victorian Twenty-Two before a crowd of 15,000 spectators. From that moment the tour was labelled a 'continuous ovation', with spectators applauding every action of the touring players, whom Marshall had decked out in bow-ties and red-spotted shirts. The Twenty-Two made 145, England 176, and then the Twenty-Two reached 143 in the second knock. Tinley followed his first-innings bowling of 11 for 52 with 8 for 63. Left to score 114 to win, England moved to 4 for 105 by six o'clock, expecting the match to be played out, but with England only nine short of victory the umpires drew stumps and called the match a draw.

Four country matches followed, Parr's XI defeating Twenty-Twos in Bendigo, Ballarat, Ararat and Maryborough thanks to 'Spider' Tinley consistently baffling batsmen with his lobs. Tinley took 98 wickets in the four matches, with the match hauls of 27, 23, 26 and 22. His success continued in the five matches that followed in New Zealand. Tinley's dominance, in fact, gave the Englishmen unexpected free days and allowed them to try their luck on the goldfields.

Parr's tour was spoiled by persistent trouble with erysipelas, an inflammation of the skin that kept him off the field but allowed him to continue negotiations with Charles Lawrence for some matches in New South Wales. Parr finally accepted Lawrence's guarantee of £1600 plus expenses and 20 per cent of the gate takings after £2000 had been deducted to cover Lawrence's costs. The negotiations went on until the end of February and Parr did not take his players on to the Sydney Domain until 16 March. Play lasted a remarkable nine days because of breaks caused by rain. The Twenty-Two mastered Tinley in their first innings of 137, but on a soaked pitch could not handle Jackson in the second. Jackson, who had the disconcerting habit of blowing his nose in such noisy fashion he was known as 'Foghorn', took 9 for 20, restricting the Twenty-Two to 50. England lost six wickets scoring the 60 required to win.

This match attracted 20,000 spectators and the hard fight by the locals ensured big crowds for the two other matches against New South Wales Twenty-Twos. The first was drawn with honours even but the decisive third match was again upset by rain. The Twenty-Two made only 68 in their first innings but England fared little better with 75.

1844. ASSOCIATION CRICKET GROUND.   KERRY PHOTO. SYDNEY.

The Sydney Cricket Ground soon after the New South Wales Cricket Association moved there from Redfern, when it was known as the Association Ground. (National Library of Australia)

In the crowd watching George Tarrant strain every sinew to secure pace in the New South Wales second innings was a schoolboy named Frederick Spofforth, whose joy was unconfined when Tarrant scattered the stumps. It was Tinley however who again proved the best of Parr's bowlers, finishing with a match-winning 10 for 33 in the Twenty-Two's total of 83. Three English wickets fell cheaply, with 77 wanted for victory. Lawrence made every run scored difficult but England scraped home with nine batsmen out. Lawrence finished with 6 for 48.

Still excited by the closeness of their win the Englishmen boarded the steamer *Wonga Wonga* to return to Melbourne. A large crowd waved them off at the wharf but they had barely cleared Sydney Harbour when they collided with the yacht *Viceroy*. The *Viceroy* sank quickly and the captain of the *Wonga Wonga* lowered a lifeboat to pick up the *Viceroy*'s passengers. George Parr lost his head, rushed below to gather up mementoes of the tour, and then tried to board the lifeboat, only to be told in rough language to keep out of the way.

All the *Viceroy*'s passengers were saved and the *Wonga Wonga* limped back to Sydney for repairs. At the dock it was discovered that 'Foghorn' Jackson, who had enjoyed a long farewell banquet, had slept through the collision. The team boarded another ship for Melbourne two days later and rounded off their tour with matches

13

in Geelong, Maryborough, Ballarat and on the Melbourne ground. Of the 16 matches they played Parr's team won 10 and drew six. Tinley finished with 171 wickets at an astonishing 3.71 runs each. Carpenter headed the batting averages with 399 runs at 22.11.

The tour made £7000 profit out of which all the players except Grace received £250, plus money from collections and all their cricket equipment, which they sold. They returned home laden with gifts, leaving Edward Grace, who remained to visit friends, and William Caffyn, who stayed to take a £300-a-year job as the Melbourne Cricket Club's professional coach and ground bowler for members. Caffyn's fiancée joined him in Melbourne and after a glittering wedding she was able to exploit her skills as a hairdresser. Her husband's 13 years coaching in Melbourne and Sydney had a profound influence on Australian cricket.

Roundarm bowling, introduced by Christina Willes to get round her long hooped skirt, had become legal in 1835 and overarm bowling in 1864. Caffyn, in the midst of the controversy the new style had created in Melbourne, was unimpressed by an action that abolished the underarm shooter, a delivery he had seen create havoc. 'Oh, those shooters at Lord's,' Caffyn wrote. 'One or two balls high as your head, then one in the ribs, and then a shooter! No wonder we were greeted with a volley of applause when we stopped one.'

Caffyn saw vast improvement in Australian cricket between his visits in 1862 and 1864. The leading clubs in Melbourne and Sydney now fielded very capable teams. Players practised more diligently, and showed an eagerness to travel to country towns and even to other colonies for games. Carlton, Warwick, Albert, National, East Sydney and the Currency clubs had tense struggles for supremacy in Sydney, while the Melbourne club knew it had a tough match on its hands when it played Richmond, East Melbourne, Geelong or South Melbourne. Country centres like Ballarat and Maitland fielded teams that matched those in the big cities.

Teams coached by Caffyn and Lawrence played some fascinating matches in the 1860s. Caffyn made 121, his highest score in Australia, for Melbourne against Richmond, but it was not until he moved to Sydney's Warwick club that the marked difference in their approach became clear. At the Warwick club Caffyn stressed the need to play forward, especially on rough pitches. At the Albert club Lawrence demonstrated the merit in playing back. Both encouraged natural aggression or instinctive stonewalling according to temperament and both taught by example in the nets.

The syndicate operating the Albert Ground in the Sydney suburb of Redfern opened it for business in October, 1864, and when that year's Victoria v. New South Wales match was abandoned in a Victorian protest against the players' behaviour the previous year in Sydney, the Albert club sent a peace-making team to Melbourne. Tasmania, Queensland and Western Australia lacked communicators of the Caffyn–Lawrence calibre, despite migrants with cricket training at English schools and universities arriving almost daily.

Between them Lawrence and Caffyn transformed playing standards in the ten years between the 1864 tour by Parr's team and the third English team's visit in 1873 under Dr W.G. Grace, the best-known Englishman of his time. American bowlers had despaired of getting him out on his 1872 US tour, and the Melbourne Cricket Club was elated when, after prolonged bartering, he agreed to bring a team to Australia. He was a unique drawcard, a tall, black-bearded man of 25, with powerful wide shoulders, a flair for gamesmanship, and unlimited confidence in the athleticism he applied to cricket.

Dr Grace's English team of 1873–74. (Jack Pollard Collection)

Grace's visit came two years after the Marylebone Cricket Club issued an edict from Lord's on the qualifications of county cricketers. The MCC acted at the request of county officials worried about players like Roger Iddison (Yorkshire and Lancashire) playing for more than one county. Acceptance of the MCC edict ended independent touring elevens from England and firmly installed the MCC as the arbiter of English cricket. From then on invitations for the MCC to send teams overseas poured into Lord's, but it was not until England visited Australia in 1903–04 that the MCC took full responsibility for tours.

Grace was therefore very much in charge of his team's visit and its dealings with the syndicate of clubs that made the tour possible. The East Melbourne and South Melbourne clubs put up £1750 between them, the Melbourne club £2000, with Melbourne club president Tom Hamilton holding the guarantees. Hamilton had to pay Grace £1500, plus all expenses for himself and his wife. The professionals in Grace's team received £170 each. A cloud fell over the visit when Dick Wardill, secretary of the Victorian Cricketers' Association who originally suggested the approach to Grace, suicided by throwing himself into the Yarra River after admitting to absconding with £7000 from the Victoria Sugar Company, but by the time Grace's team arrived in December, 1873, 52 days after leaving England, the scandal of Wardill's death had passed.

Grace's team comprised W.G. Grace, J.A. Bush, F.H. Boult, W.R. Gilbert, A. Greenwood, R. Humphrey, H. Jupp, J. Lilly-white, M. McIntyre, W. Oscroft, J. Southerton and G.F. Grace, W.G.'s fifth and youngest brother. The professionals – Oscroft, Greenwood, Southerton and McIntyre – had a large number of bats in their luggage which they expected to sell to Australians at a huge profit. They did not object when it was found the Melbourne Cricket Club had booked them into a different hotel to the amateurs.

On their first afternoon in Melbourne a crowd of 7000 wildly applauded the Englishmen when they arrived at a South Melbourne club match. Within a few minutes an umpire's decision upset spectators and a big section of the crowd jumped the fence and play had to be abandoned after a prolonged demonstration. Grace was assured the incident was a rarity but wrote that it proved a foretaste of 'experiences that fell our lot'. This was a valid comment because the playing standards of Australian cricket had left umpiring standards a long way behind.

English cricket had no difficulty handling on-the-field disputes because all her umpires were paid, but in Australia, where umpires had to be conscripted and there was no trade union or governing body, bad decisions were frequent. W.G., a master gamesman, took full advantage of this. When one of his players, Bush, was bowled first ball, W.G. replaced the bails and explained that batsmen always had trial balls. W.G. left the field only for the sharpest nicks into the 'keeper's gloves and stayed put when a fieldsman caught him inside the field and then fell over the chains marking the boundary. But he made many recommendations helpful to Australian cricket and never complained when subjected to even the harshest journeys. Not the least of his improvements was to give a pitch three or four days rolling instead of picking out the strip to be used on the morning of the match.

There was a sensation in the very first match when Bransby Beauchamp Cooper, born in India and educated in England, made 84 and helped Eighteen of Victoria to reach 266. Cooper had at one time partnered W.G. in a stand of 283 for the Gentlemen of the South v. Players of the South, Cooper scoring 100, W.G. 180. Against Victoria Grace took 10 for 58 with the ball but managed only 23 and 51. Forced to follow on after a first innings of 132, Grace's XI were beaten by an innings and 21 runs. W.G. blamed himself for this inglorious start through not taking the ball earlier.

The organising syndicate put Grace and his players through a gruelling round of country matches, all against Twenty-Twos, at Ballarat, Stawell and Warrnambool, on pitches W.G. described as 'execrable', before sending them by sea to Sydney to play Eighteen of New South Wales. They were beaten by ten wickets at Stawell on a dust-bowl of a pitch covered by flies, after which W.G. lectured his players about drinking during matches.

England's match against the Eighteen of New South Wales was one of the most important played on the Albert Ground at Redfern, a completely enclosed ground where every spectator paid to watch, built by a private company. Grace's high opinion of the ground was not shared by the New South Wales Cricket Association, which had been founded in 1859. The NSWCA had been forced to move to the ground because it could not charge for admission to matches on The Domain, a public park. At the Albert Ground, however, they found themselves faced with high rentals.

Grace's first appearance on the Albert Ground brought his initial encounter with the rising young bowling sensation Fred Spofforth, but it was Joe Coates, a professional from Huddersfield, who swept aside the English batting, finishing with 6 for 29 in an innings of 92. Grace's cousin, William Pocock, was among the batsmen who contributed handy scores for the home team and they made 127.

THE ALBERT GROUND DURING THE LATE INTERNATIONAL CRICKET MATCH, ENGLAND V. NEW SOUTH WALES.

The Albert Ground in Redfern, Sydney, the first Australian ground that could charge admission money. The site is now a government housing development. (Jack Pollard Collection)

17

England's batting again collapsed in their second innings of 90. Left to score 56 to win, the New South Wales Eighteen lost nine wickets getting them, to win by eight wickets. The excitement in the crowd reached a peak each time Grace went cheaply.

Through townships under floodwaters or covered in dust from drought W.G. took his men to play often farcical cricket. W.G. rode on the engine of the train that took them into Bathurst, went shooting for kangaroos, duck and quail, and apart from excessive speechmaking ('altogether overdone in Australia') had a marvellous time. For the fourteenth match he found himself on an open field covered by stones at Kadina on South Australia's Yorke Peninsula. There was not a blade of grass to be seen and when Grace asked for the location of the pitch he was told he was standing on it. A bushel of pebbles had to be cleared away before play could begin. England's 64 enabled them to win by an innings and nine runs, Twenty-Two of Kadina mustering only 42 and 13.

This farce completed Grace's programme for the Melbourne syndicate and allowed him to accept an offer of £110, plus half the gate receipts, from the South Australian Cricket Association to play the first international match on Adelaide Oval. The SACA, formed in 1872, had worked for a year to get Adelaide Oval in shape for its opening on 13 December 1873, with a match between Colonial- and British-born association members which, with a concert, raised £60 and enabled the SACA to clear most of its debts.

Adelaide Oval in April, 1874, during the match between W.G. Grace's touring team and Twenty-Two of South Australia. (South Australian Archives)

The coach that took the Englishmen on the 18-hour drive from Kadina to Adelaide was driven by a man named Hill, who said his son Clem was a promising cricketer, but he could not get the team to Adelaide Oval until 4 p.m. on the day they had to play. The SACA persuaded the government to declare a half-holiday on the second day, and England won by seven wickets, scoring 108 and 3 for 38 against 63 and 82 by the local Twenty-Two.

The SACA set an important precedent for this match by charging admission for the first time at Adelaide Oval, which some argued was public parkland. By making a small profit (£100) in efficiently staging the match the SACA showed they were ready to join New South Wales, Victoria and Tasmania in inter-colonial competition.

Over the tour, in their 15 matches W.G.'s team won ten, lost three and had two draws. Veteran Melbourne professional Sam Cosstick summed up: 'Bar W.G., we're as good as they are, and some day we'll lick 'em with eleven.'

The presence of Grace's team created a 'cricket mania' that inspired Australia's first women's match in the Victorian mining town of Bendigo. The parade to the ground by what the *Bendigo News* called a 'bevy of beauties' received more space than their cricket, although the full scorecard was published and showed that The Blues defeated The Reds by 21 runs.

Grace, of course, continued to play against Australians to the turn of the century, but his cousin Walter Raleigh Gilbert was not as lucky. Gilbert, hero of England's eight-wicket win over Twenty-Two of Tasmania in March, 1874, with his 8 for 47 in the Twenty-two's second innings, played 108 first-class matches alongside W.G. for Gloucestershire and made a living as secretary of the United All England XI. In 1886, after becoming the professional for East Gloucestershire, he went to prison for 28 days for stealing half a sovereign from a member's clothing in the dressing-room.

Gilbert's family packed him off to Calgary in Canada, where he died in 1924 after 38 years in exile. The Graces had his name expunged from the scoresheets of the East Gloucestershire club. A long succession of *Wisden* editors agonised over how he should be reported in the *Almanack*. Some ignored his existence, a curious fate for a batsman who had made 205 not out for an England XI against Cambridge University at Fenner's. In 1934, he was restored as 'Gilbert, W.R.' and in 1935 as an amateur, 'Mr W.R. Gilbert'.

CHAPTER TWO
TEST MATCHES BEGIN

James Lillywhite's fourth English touring team, which introduced Test cricket to Australians, had to play without a regular 'keeper because Pooley (third from top, centre) was in prison in New Zealand. (Jack Pollard Collection)

Australian cricket reached maturity in the first few weeks of 1877. On 15 and 16 January that year James Lillywhite's English touring team was held to a draw in an 11-a-side match by New South Wales in Sydney, after three defeats by 15-man teams from Victoria and New South Wales. The drawn match against New South Wales was the first of four English tours played on level terms. The previous 58 matches involving English tourists saw the visitors opposed to sides of 22, 18 or 15 players or in exhibition matches where Englishmen figured in both teams.

The drawn match in Sydney ended with the home side requiring 48 runs to win, with four wickets left. The Australians were convinced they would have made the runs, given more time. The Englishmen were just as strongly of the view that they would have taken four wickets without conceding 48 runs. A match on level terms between All Australia and All England was suggested to Lillywhite, who agreed to add it to his tour programme after England completed an eight-match tour of New Zealand.

Lillywhite left it to his tour manager John Conway to arrange the big match while the Englishmen were in New Zealand. Conway, 35, a shrewd, enterprising journalist, had been born at Fyansford on the outskirts of Geelong and had learned his cricket at Melbourne Church of England Grammar School. At 19 Conway had played for Eighteen of Victoria against Heathfield Stephenson's XI in the first-ever international cricket match in Australia, taking 4 for 60 with roundarm deliveries and scoring one run. He developed into a sound batsman, brilliant slips field and, as captain of South Melbourne, a crafty tactician.

Conway was a splendid judge of cricket talent, the first to spot the promise of players such as Jack Blackham and Tom Horan, who had become local heroes through their exploits in Victorian teams. He was solely responsible for selection of the first Australian XI but listened to the views of knowledgeable cricket fans like show-business entrepreneur George Coppin, donor of trophies for competition among Melbourne clubs. Generally Conway opted for players of good sense whom he judged would be reliable under severe tension.

Conway contacted players of his choice direct, ignoring the existing administrative bodies, the Victorian Cricketers' Association and the New South Wales Cricket Association, which had yet to win players' support. Twenty-three years before federation of the Australian colonies, Conway was not impeded by fellow selectors, arguments over players' religions or social status, nor by a national board of control. The NSWCA was far from impressed by his endeavours, however, and passed the following resolution:

It has been publicly notified that a game is about to be played between All England and a combined eleven of New South Wales and Victoria. This association desires to place on record that game has been arranged without any reference to the association, and cannot be recognised as a match in which chosen representatives of New South Wales take part.

John Conway, sole selector and organiser of Australia's first Test team, overcame some unexpected withdrawals. (MCG Museum)

Conway was aware that both the Sydney and Melbourne associations were desperate for funds and would try to take some of the profits if they were brought into the promotion. Their disapproval was the least of his problems. The champion all-rounder Edwin Evans declined to play because of his duties as a government inspector of land selections (Melbourne *Punch* immediately awarded Evans a white feather). Fred Spofforth, the demoniacal fast bowler whose glare was said to frighten out some batsmen, originally agreed to join his Sydney colleagues Dave and Ned Gregory, Nat Thompson, Tom Garrett and Charles Bannerman, but withdrew when he learned that his friend Billy Murdoch would not be his wicket-keeper. Spofforth had spent many childhood hours bowling to Murdoch at the 'Pigeon Ground' in Balmain's Gladstone Park and he could not conceive of anyone keeping wicket better than Murdoch.

Spofforth's withdrawal weakened the Australian team but it also provided the match with unexpected publicity. The *Australasian* commented:

Spofforth, apparently believing his success was due to his wicket-keeper

21

and not his own merit, and fearing he would be shorn of his lustre if another was behind the stumps, has declined to play unless his own special wicket-keeper is picked.

Conway was aware of the combination Spofforth and Murdoch had developed but he had been a Jack Blackham fan from the day he first saw him in a Melbourne journalists' social match, and he steadfastly stood by Blackham's selection even when it became known that Blackham had only joined South Melbourne after failing to win a place in Carlton's first XI. With the Australian players assembling in Melbourne, Conway received a telegram from Spofforth's replacement, left-arm swing bowler Frank Allan, which said Allan could not spare the time to play. Allan had made a habit of attending the Warrnambool Agricultural Show and said he preferred to join friends there than play for Australia.

The match at Melbourne Cricket Ground from 15 to 19 March 1877 was recognised as the first Test match, but in fact was a contest between professionals from four English counties touring Australia on a guarantee of £150 apiece during the English winter and a mixture of leading Sydney and Melbourne cricketers, all unpaid. Six of the 11 players who appeared under the label 'All Australia' had been born overseas – one at Dacca, India, one in Ireland and four in England. The 'All England' line-up included five Yorkshiremen, three from Sussex, two from Nottinghamshire and one from Surrey. Tom Garrett, son of a Sydney politician, played in the Australian team aged 18 years 232 days and in 1992 remained the youngest Australian to play against England. James Southerton appeared for England at 49 years 119 days, and is still the oldest Test cricketer on debut.

One of Conway's problems was that he could not induce Australia's most experienced cricketer, Bransby Beauchamp Cooper, to practise. Cooper regarded practice as a form of slavery that gentlemen avoided and remained true to that tradition of English amateurs who let the professionals do the hard work in the field and all stock bowling. Born in India, educated at Rugby School, he had assisted Middlesex and Kent as a hard-hitting right-hand batsman, figuring in some fine partnerships with W.G. Grace for the Gentlemen against the Players. Cooper was widely expected to captain the Australians, but when Conway left it to the team they elected the Sydney Audit Office boss and father of three, Dave Gregory. This was a major coup for Gregory in a side in which Victorians outnumbered Sydneyites and inter-colonial jealousy was high.

Gregory, then 31, had the presence of a natural leader, erect in bearing, 6 ft 2 in (187 cm) tall and weighing 14 st 4 lb (90.7 kg). He had made dramatic progress since leaving St James Church of England School in Sydney at 15 and asking the governor, Sir William Denison, to give him the job Denison had promised him at the school's Speech Day. He was a man who never stooped, took pride in his trim waistline and beard, and was never seen the worse for liquor. One of his first tasks was to introduce English-born James Robart Hodges, 21, to his team-mates. Hodges, the late replacement for Frank Allan, was a fast-medium left-arm bowler on trial at Richmond club but had not played for Victoria.

The East Melbourne club threatened legal action against Conway and Lillywhite, claiming their ground had been booked for the same dates as the All England v. All Australia match at the MCG. Conway finally agreed to pay East Melbourne £230 compensation and allow 500 East Melbourne members free admission so the big game would go ahead.

The Englishmen endured a stormy crossing from New Zealand, arriving in Melbourne the day before play began with their players all suffering from sea-sickness. They were without their only specialist wicket-keeper, Ted Pooley, who was in jail in Christchurch. Pooley had been arrested and charged with causing malicious damage to a pub after coaxing a New Zealander to bet on the England v. Eighteen of Christchurch match. Pooley claimed he could predict what every Christchurch batsman would score and offered to pay one shilling for every score he got wrong if he received £1 for each score he got right. Wager accepted, Pooley wrote nought against every Christchurch player's name and made a tidy profit as half the Christchurch team failed to score. Police blamed Pooley for the disturbance that followed.

Behind the Australians lay 73 years of steady improvement in their cricket standards since the first match had been reported in the *Sydney Gazette* in January 1804, just 16 years after the beginning of white settlement on the island with the arrival of the First Fleet. From humble beginnings in Sydney's Hyde Park amid the droppings of garrison troops' horses and later among the cowpats on the slopes of Sydney Domain, cricket had progressed to splendid grounds in each colony's biggest settlement, and from inter-colonial matches to games against English touring teams.

*　　*　　*

Australia's first Test captain, Dave Gregory. Father of 16 children, he prided himself on his beard, his erect posture, ability to hold his liquor, and his expertise with NSW government accounts. (Jack Pollard Collection)

The Ballarat XI at the time Test cricket began, with an interesting mixture of white and black players. (Mitchell Library, *Sydney*)

The first inter-colonial match – at Launceston on 11 and 12 February 1851, between a combined northern and southern Tasmanian side and a team from Port Phillip styling themselves 'Victoria' – produced a surprise three-wicket win for Tasmania. Befuddled by the rigours of crossing Bass Strait in the tiny SS *Shamrock* and excessive banqueting on arrival, the Victorians scored only 82 and 57. Tasmania made 104 and 7 for 37. The Tasmanian triumph was attributed to the tactical acumen of their captain John Marshall, then 55 and sporting a beard that hadn't been cut since his teens. Marshall played for Tasmania in the third Tasmania v. Victoria inter-colonial match three years later, retiring at 58 as Australia's oldest-ever first-class cricketer.

Convicts working in road gangs were transferred to help prepare cricket fields for these matches and governors loaned horses to pull rollers over ground on which garrison troops drilled. Tasmania, flushed by the discovery of gold and the influx of wealthy landholders and young aristocrats from England, was perhaps the first colony to introduce pads and gloves for batsmen and certainly the first to use spring-handled bats from English makers. Tasmanian players wore white breeches and scarlet jackets, and were forbidden to smoke on the field. Their major problem was in achieving harmony in teams fielding commoners who kept shops or pubs, herdsmen with convict ancestry, serving officers, bankers like Marshall and noblemen who had taken up large areas of land without paying for them.

Tasmanians regarded Victoria's inclusion of bowlers using the new style of roundarm bowling as foul play and for two years refused to play against Victoria because it had professionals in its teams. These were the ground bowlers retained by Melbourne clubs to bowl whenever members felt in need of a practice bat. The Victorians argued that teams without their professionals would not be the best available.

Tasmanians are extremely fortunate that history has judged the 1851 match in Launceston between 'Combined Tasmania' and the 'Port Phillip Bay XI' as Australia's initial first-class match. The honour of staging that match belongs more appropriately to the first Victoria v. New South Wales game in Melbourne in 1856. This match stemmed from an advertisement in the *Argus* in 1855 in which the Melbourne Cricket Club challenged any team in the colonies for a stake of £200-a-side. A Sydney group called the 'Inter-colonial Committee', set up by William Tunks – a publican turned road-builder, born in the Nepean district in 1816 – found they had to raise £181 to go to Melbourne to accept this challenge. Of this £134 would be needed for sea passages, £12 for gear and other incidentals, and £35 to meet hotel and food bills in Melbourne. Just over £173 was raised in collections run by leading Sydney players, and the other £8 was carried forward as a deficit which a return match in Sydney would recover. The host teams were to take all the gate-money in their own cities.

The New South Wales team sailed to Melbourne without one of their best players, William Rutter of Parramatta, who was to follow on a later ship. On the morning of the match when Rutter had not appeared, the side replaced him with Richard Driver, the Sydney solicitor who had put £72 into the match fund. Driver was not expected to contribute runs or take wickets, but when he went in at number ten in the New South Wales first innings, he scored 18, equal top score for the match.

New South Wales enjoyed a splendid moral triumph before a ball was bowled by refusing to play for money and insisting that the honour of playing was reward enough for gentlemen. Apart from Driver none of them had any money anyway, but the Victorians recoiled as if they had insulted a virtuous guest. The visitors then called on Driver's legal skills when they found that Victoria wanted to toss for first innings. Driver ridiculed the idea. There was a law as old as cricket itself, he said, that gave visiting sides the right to decide who batted first.

Invited to bat, Victoria made only 63 and 28 in their two innings.

The coaches who brought dramatic improvement in Australian cricket: Charles Lawrence, top, and William Caffyn. Both accepted offers to remain after touring Australia in English teams. (Jack Pollard Collection)

John James McKone, a tricky fast underarm bowler adept at the Sydney grubber, took 5 for 11 in Victoria's second innings. Driver's contribution lifted New South Wales's first innings to 76, and they only had to score 16 to win in their second attempt. They lost seven wickets getting them, their captain George Gilbert showing them how to deal with attacks of the jitters by scoring seven priceless runs. Gilbert was yet another cousin of W.G. Grace.

Now Australia was to face England in the first of all cricket Tests, but with little public expectation that they would do well, although years of work in the nets under the coaching of Caffyn and Lawrence had achieved dramatic improvements.

Refreshment tents circling the ground were well patronised before a ball was bowled. Spectators in their finest clothes gossiped under the elms, with the ladies juggling their parasols. High in the branches small boys looked down on Union Jacks and the Melbourne Cricket Club flag.

Gregory won the toss and chose to bat. He sent in the untidily bearded Nathaniel Thomson and morose, unsmiling Charles Bannerman – born at Woolwich, Kent in 1851 – to open Australia's innings. Thomson, 37, was considered a stubborn, cagey cricketer, Sydney-born, with six seasons in the New South Wales team behind him.

Play began at 1.05 p.m. on 15 March, 1877, in front of less than 1000 spectators, a stark contrast to the capacity crowd that had packed every vantage point of the Melbourne Cricket Ground for England's Australian debut in 1862. Lillywhite handed the ball to 34-year-old Alfred Shaw, a bearded, roly-poly Nottingham all-rounder whose mastery of line and length made him the most economical bowler of his time. Bowling with a tie neatly knotted around his neck and a black sash about his bulging waist, Shaw delivered more overs than he conceded runs throughout his 33-year career. Four-ball overs allowed him to continue playing in first-class matches until he was 51.

Bannerman, in his tenth innings in seven first-class matches, took a single from Shaw's second ball, the first run in Test cricket. Thomson also nudged away a single from rangy Yorkshireman Allen Hill before Hill scattered his stumps with the score on two. Tom Horan, a free settler from Middleton, Ireland, joined Bannerman and when lunch was taken between 2 and 2.40 p.m. they were still together. Some accounts say Armitage dropped Bannerman before he reached ten but in fact Armitage did not get his hands to the ball, which hit him on the stomach. England's fielding was obviously disrupted by having to use John Selby as substitute for 'keeper Pooley.

Australia lost Horan, caught by Hill off Shaw for 12, with the score on 40. One run later Dave Gregory was run out. The batsmen that followed hung on desperately, sensing that Bannerman had the measure of the bowling at the other end. Cooper went for 15 to a shooter from Southerton, who also dismissed Midwinter. Ned Gregory came and went for Test cricket's first duck. Bannerman responded by hitting ten off Armitage's first over. Frustrated, Armitage resorted to lobs, attempting to go over Bannerman's head on to the bails. Commentators unaccustomed to this delivery said they could not have been reached with a clothes prop.

Irishman Tom Horan, dropped from the Second Test despite a useful performance in the First Test, later became a Test captain, batting in coloured pads 100 years before Packer adopted coloured gear. (Age, Melbourne)

All Bannerman's runs were made in front of the stumps. He never cut or glanced, but he drove powerfully on both sides of the wicket and, unlike other batsmen of that time, frequently moved down the wicket to the pitch of the ball. His mood throughout was poised and determined and when play ended at 5 p.m. on the first day he was 126 not out, Australia 6 for 166. Bannerman had treated the disconcerting pace of Ulyett and Hill like slow bowling.

Although the English bowlers Shaw, Hill, Southerton, Lillywhite and Emmett sustained their accuracy, Bannerman moved to 165 the next day before a fast, rising ball from Ulyett split the second finger of his right hand and forced him to retire. Australia were then 7 for 240 and Bannerman had batted for four hours 45 minutes, hitting 15 fours. For more than a century there have been cricket buffs keen to support Bannerman's 165 undefeated in conditions no one had ever before experienced as the greatest innings of all time. Statistician Bill Frindall calculated that Bannerman contributed 67.3 per cent of his team's runs, still the highest individual proportion in a Test innings.

Shaw's figures demonstrated the high calibre of England's bowling in Australia's innings of 245, for he conceded only 51 runs in 55.3 overs, 34 of them maidens, and took three wickets. The seven bowlers used delivered 85 maidens and stand-in 'keeper John Selby allowed only eight sundries. Lillywhite had to dig deep into his long experience in captaincy to dislodge Bannerman's dour partners.

Australia's fielding and bowling reached a high standard when England batted, and after Jupp (63) and Charlwood (36) provided

27

Australia's First Test heroes: left-arm bowler Tom Kendall, top, whose seven wickets in the final innings brought victory and opening batsman Charles Bannerman, who made an epic 165 before retiring hurt. (Jack Pollard Collection)

a sound start the innings foundered before Midwinter's skilful medium-pace. Only a bold 35 not out by England's no. 9 batsman Hill took them to within 49 runs of Australia's score. Midwinter's 5 for 78 came from 54 overs. By now spectators were flooding into the ground as news spread around Melbourne of the tense struggle.

Shaw bowled England into a winning position by taking 5 for 38 in Australia's second innings of 104, completing the match with 50 maidens in his 89.3 overs. Bannerman batted with his split finger heavily strapped and made four. Paddy Horan was the sole Australian to reach 20. Midwinter (17) and Kendall (17 not out) batted doggedly, but only a last wicket stand of 29 by Kendall and Hodges took the score past 100.

The beer tents were crowded now for the climax, spectators thick in the trees, as Hill and Greenwood began England's chase for the 154 needed. Tom Kendall brought shouts of joy echoing round the ground when he had Hill caught by Thomson before a run had been scored. England never recovered. Supported by Midwinter, whose 19 overs cost only 23 runs, Kendall cleverly exploited the flight and variety he had learned in his native Bedford.

At 4 for 22, Ulyett and Selby lifted English hopes by adding 40. Kendall bowled Ulyett for 24 and Hodges had Selby caught by Horan for 38, and England collapsed to be all out for 108, giving Australia victory by 45 runs on the fourth morning. By taking 14 wickets between them Kendall and Midwinter made vital contributions, but the win belonged to Bannerman and his unbeaten 165.

Dave Gregory, who had made only four runs in the two knocks, praised the good sense and fighting temperament of his team, but the *Argus* said Gregory's captaincy proved the difference between evenly matched sides. Gregory commented: 'Willie Caffyn taught me all I really know about cricket.' He hadn't wasted the hours spent in Caffyn's hairdresser's chair having his beard trimmed.

Despite their opposition to the match, the Victorian Cricketers' Association presented the Australians with gold medals to commemorate their win. Dave Gregory received a slightly larger medal for keeping his team alert and competitive in the field. A collection among spectators for Bannerman realised £83 7s 6d, and a whip-round for Kendall and Blackham yielded £23 5s 0d each. Melbourne *Punch* could not resist a jibe at the three bowlers who declined to take the field:

When bowling cracks of little mind
Prove beggars upon horses,
Australia is compelled to find
Fresh strength and new resources.

For Allan, Evans, Spofforth
She does not care a snuff,
Since Kendall, Mid and Hodges proved
Themselves quite enough.

So patriotic A., E., S.,
Next time, 'tis we will strike;
Henceforth go play with babes,
For like should mate with like.

The Sydney *Daily News* welcomed Australia's victory as epoch-making, a powerful reminder to leaders of the game at Lord's and The Oval that cricket was thriving in the colonies. 'It may console them to know that the English race is not disintegrating in a distant land on turf where lately the black fellow hurled his boomerang,' the *News* added.

None of the Englishmen in the First Test received mementoes of the historic occasion, but at a gathering of cricket followers in the Cricketers' Hotel in Swanston Street, Melbourne, Conway announced that a return Test would be played on the Melbourne ground from 31 March to 4 April 1877, with the entire gate receipts going to the Englishmen. This was received as great news in the pub that had been founded years before by George Marshall, the wicket-keeper from Nottingham who had been the first captain of Victoria in inter-colonial matches. Marshall had died of 'softening of the brain' nine years before the First Test.

Australia's win in the First Test guaranteed larger audiences for the return. With Pooley still in prison in New Zealand, the Englishmen had only 11 fit players but they had shaken off the sea-sickness that affected their first Test performance. Conway strengthened All Australia by bringing in Spofforth for Ned Gregory, Murdoch for Horan and Thomas Joseph Dart Kelly for B.B. Cooper. The Melbourne Cricket Club's members' enclosure was packed when Dave Gregory again won the toss and once more decided to bat. A brass band was present to play during intervals and a surprisingly large number of schoolchildren attended. Kelly's

MELBOURNE CRICKET GROUND
1877

The Melbourne Cricket Ground at the time of the first Test in 1877 with the entire ground staff at work in the middle. (MCG Museum)

red, white and blue blazer and matching sash shone like a beacon from the players' seats.

Bannerman and Thomson opened again for Australia. John Selby kept wicket for England in the first session, but after lunch handed the gloves to Henry Jupp who did the job for the rest of the match. Hill dismissed Bannerman at 29 and Thomson at 30, and by bowling at a lively pace in right-arm roundarm style also had Blackham and Garrett out by lunch. On a firm, true pitch, Australia could not recover and only Midwinter's pugnacious 31 lifted the total to 122. The run outs that sent back Murdoch for three and Hodges for two hastened Australia's collapse.

Spofforth had not changed his preference for Murdoch behind the stumps, but he bowled very fast from the start of England's innings with Blackham standing right up on the stumps. In his third over, Blackham took a delivery that lifted and brilliantly stumped Shaw. Spofforth never again criticised Blackham's 'keeping. Kendall bowled Jupp and at the end of the day England were 2 for 7.

Australia bowled steadily and accurately at the start of the second day before a series of dropped catches demoralised both bowlers and fieldsmen. The bowlers wilted and were collared. From 5 for 88, England's middle order hit out freely, Ulyett (52), Emmett

(48) and Hill (49) taking the score to 261.

With his team in trouble at 139 runs behind, Dave Gregory promoted himself to open the innings with Thomson. They put on 88 in a brave stand, reducing the arrears to 51, and thereafter aggressive batting right down the order built up the Australian total to 259. Bannerman's 30 took only 18 minutes and Kelly's 35 included eight successive scoring shots for four. Left to score 121 to win, England were 3 for 9 at lunch on the fourth day. The next two wickets added 67 but with half the English side out for 76 Australia still appeared sure to win.

George Ulyett, whose career as an opening batsman for England and Yorkshire produced 20,823 runs and 18 centuries, came in at no. 5 and soon realised the pitch was ideal for batting and the outfield very fast. Batting boldly, he lifted England to within nine runs of victory with a glorious 63. Hodges, who caught Ulyett brilliantly off Spofforth, found after England had won by four wickets that big cricket can be harsh on young players. After taking six wickets in his first two Tests at the age of 21, bootmaker Hodges was not seen again in a Test team, and has never rated a mention in *Wisden* until 1993, when it was discovered he had been born in England on 11 August 1855, and christened James Robart. His family settled in Melbourne in 1856, but he never played for Victoria, returning to the Capulet XI in Collingwood juniors after his Test appearance.

Thomas Joseph Dart Kelly, whose cricket blazers 'shone like beacons' in his two Test appearances. (Jack Pollard Collection)

The Australians had clearly demonstrated in the first two Tests that they were little inferior to the more experienced English players. Their performance encouraged Conway to seek the support of the leading players to organise the first tour of England by a white Australian team in the northern summer of 1878, ten years after an Aboriginal team organised by Charles Lawrence had played 47 matches in England in 99 playing days.

Conway wrote to likely tourists personally, informing them that they would be required to sign an agreement with other players who made the trip, under which they would be asked to play matches around the Australian colonies before they left to help raise funds for the tour fares and expenses. Each player had to put up £50, three times the fare to England, to become a partner to this agreement. If further capital was required and approved by a majority of the partners, each player would be asked for a further contribution. The partners were entitled to examine a financial statement of receipts and disbursements after each match. At the end of the tour all profits were to be distributed evenly among the players and manager.

James Lillywhite acted as the Australians' agent in England and when they received the programme of matches he had lined up the Australians were amused to find so many of them were against fifteens and eighteens. Only 15 of the proposed 37 matches were first-class. Lillywhite had not been able to fill in all the dates available and he had not been able to arrange a Test match, and his itinerary involved frequent trips from one end of England to the other.

The lack of a single Test match was the result of disquiet among amateur stalwarts at Lord's that the Australians would want a share of the gate receipts from their matches and fear among English professionals that Australians threatened their livelihood. None of those involved in the organisation appreciated the public interest in international matches, nor were they aware of the standard Australia had already reached.

Conway chose Spofforth, Murdoch, Garrett and Charles Bannerman from New South Wales, and Blackham, Allan, Boyle, Kendall and Horan from Victoria, but was disappointed when the reliable Sydney batsman Ned Sheridan opted out because of the death of his mother. Conway considered that nobody from Western Australia or South Australia was good enough but to spread the team's representation he telegraphed the gifted Tasmanian John Arthur about joining the team. Two days after he received the telegram Arthur died. His father had played for Tasmania, as had his brother George, and John had been the first to score a century in a North v. South Tasmania match. Cause of his death was confused. The *Launceston Examiner* said he died of 'brain fever', the *Hobart Mercury* blamed pleurisy and Arthur's death certificate gave the cause of death as 'inflammation of the brain'. His place in the Australian team went to George Bailey, a Hobart banker, who had learned cricket in Ceylon, where he was born, and had advanced his skills at private schools in England.

Bailey and the Melbourne contingent assembled in Sydney on 2 November 1877. They all agreed not to play against each other until the team returned from England, although this reduced public interest in that summer's inter-colonial matches. Conway said he had arranged to secure Billy Midwinter's services in England whenever Midwinter's commitments to the Gloucestershire county side permitted.

All the team wanted Thomson to join them but he pulled out, apparently unable to afford £50. Conway chose Charles Bannerman's brother Alick to replace him, although Alick had never appeared in inter-colonial cricket. For reasons best known to himself Alick gave varying years for his birth, including 1854, 1856 and 1859. The Association of Cricket Statisticians and Historians believes 1854 is most likely, which means he was 23 in 1878.

Alick Bannerman was not among the eleven players Conway sent to Brisbane on 3 November for their first match. The boredom of the long, smoky train trip was soon forgotten when Brisbane fans greeted them at the station with a brass band and took them in an open carriage through the streets to a welcoming banquet. Play began on the Prince of Wales' birthday at Eagle Farm in the presence of the governor, Sir Arthur Kennedy, and his daughter, plus about 4000 spectators. From the start the Australian XI outclassed their Eighteen opponents, who scored 58 and 68 against the Australians' 149, Charles Bannerman contributing 74. Champagne flowed freely in the vice-regal tent.

Nat Thomson, a tough, seasoned professional who opened for Australia in the first two Tests, but could not afford to join the first white tourists in England.
(Jack Pollard Collection)

The *Brisbane Courier*'s account of the match said Kendall and Allan bowled 'Serpentine slows', with Blackham as watchful as a 'Crimean Sergeant'. Charles Bannerman drove the ball in 'low, parabolic curves'. Kendall was the bowling star of the match, taking 13 for 35 in the two Brisbane innings, including one batsman he clean bowled with one of his 'spiral permeators'. The Australians followed this innings victory with an overwhelming win on the Darling Downs, against Twenty-Two of Toowoomba.

Back in Sydney they met a strong Sydney Fifteen on the Albert Ground. Conway expected 12,000 spectators, as the Australians' opposition included Ned Gregory and Phillip Sheridan, and other players experienced in inter-colonial matches, but only 200 turned up for the entire match. Charles Bannerman again top-scored for the Australians with 83. Horan made 37. The Sydney Fifteen were unable to handle Spofforth, only George Geary, 29, and his brother John Geary, 21, offering resistance. Spofforth's match bag was 19 for 108. Crowd support was similarly lacking for matches in Maitland and Newcastle where the mastery of Charles Bannerman, Kendall and Spofforth produced further easy wins.

They then sailed for Adelaide to play Eighteen of South Australia before the biggest audience of their home tour. Spofforth assured the Australian victory by nine wickets by taking 17 for 125. Horan made 34 and 26 not out, Charles Bannerman 25 and 44 not out.

At Melbourne, against a strong combination of 15 leading Sydney and Melbourne players, the Australians were left to score 113 in the fourth innings to win. They wanted only one run when the last man, Kendall, went to the crease, but Edwin Evans bowled him for a duck to produce the first tie in big cricket in Australia. Boyle's 10 for 29 in the Combined Fifteen's second innings and Sheridan's 38 in the Combined Fifteen's first innings were the features of a badly attended match. A bigger crowd turned out in Bendigo for the Australians' easy win over a local Twenty-Two.

On 3 January, 1878, the Australians sailed from Melbourne to New Zealand for seven matches, carrying all their cricket gear in a large canvas bag marked 'Australian XI', which they took turns in lumping from ships and trains. Conway fitted them out in pillbox hats and coloured sashes. They won five, drew one and lost one of their New Zealand matches, the first against Twenty-Two of Invercargill after Charles Bannerman scored 128 during the first appearance by an Australian side in New Zealand. They had a draw against Twenty-Two of Dunedin, defeated Twenty-Two of Oamaru by 43 runs, lost by three wickets against Fifteen of Canterbury, defeated Twenty-Two of Wellington by nine wickets and finished with an innings and 38 run-win over Twenty-Two of Napier and by an innings and 25 runs against Twenty-Two of Auckland.

Off the New Zealand coast their tiny steamer sustained heavy punishment in a gale that appeared likely to wreck the ship. Clinging to his bed and listening to waves batter the ship, Spofforth asked Charles Bannerman, an expert swimmer, whom he would save if the boat foundered. Bannerman said he would save his brother Alick, Murdoch and Spofforth.

'What about the Victorians?' said Spofforth.

'Let them drown – you don't think I'd risk my life for them?' said Bannerman.

There was a setback on their return to Sydney, when the players chosen to appear against them for the return Combined Fifteen match refused the terms offered. Several members of the Combined Fifteen said they objected to comments made about them by Australian players. Finally Conway negotiated match fees that suited the Combined Fifteen and apologised for any abusive comments his players had uttered. The publicity this generated produced a crowd of 10,000 spectators for the start of play on the Albert Ground on 22 February.

Frank Allan, who had dropped out of the New Zealand part of the tour because of sciatica, rejoined the Australian side in Sydney and when the Combined Fifteen batted immediately struck form. His 9 for 26 from 39.2 overs included 27 maidens, and had the Combined Fifteen out for only 78.

The fielding by the Australian XI reached a standard reporters said had never been equalled in Sydney, even by touring English teams, but occasional boos greeted outstanding interceptions that prevented fours. Most of the crowd clearly shared the view of the Victorian and New South Wales administrative bodies that the Australian XI were money-hungry opportunists who could not be regarded as a genuine national side.

The Australians led by 47 on the first innings and had to make 104 to win in the final innings. At two minutes to six, with time for only one more over, the scores were level. Tom Garrett bravely lifted Evans's third ball over a fieldsman to win the match by four wickets. There were no cheers or applause, just an eerie silence as the players left the field.

Three more matches in Victoria wound up the team's programme in Australia. They defeated Twenty-Two of Geelong, drew against Twenty-Two of Ballarat and had a sound win over an Eighteen chosen from the leading Melbourne clubs before returning to Sydney for a farewell dinner.

By then Conway and Dave Gregory had agreed to omit Kendall from the touring team. He had taken 102 wickets at a cost of only 6.26 each on the 20-match spin round Australia and New Zealand, figures only surpassed by Spofforth (281 wickets at 4.10) and Garrett (103 wickets at 3.28) and was obviously among the best left-arm bowlers in the world, capable of turning the ball each way with a delivery style that was difficult to read. But his drinking and lack of discipline had caused incidents on the warm-up tour that Gregory did not want repeated in England.

Kendall's omission left Gregory with only four main bowlers on the tour of England – Spofforth, Boyle, Garrett and Allan – and strengthened the idea that the trip was a presumptuous venture. The batting looked reasonably strong, with Charles Bannerman scoring 748 runs at 24.28 in the warm-up matches, Horan 644 at 23.23 and Dave Gregory 459 at 20.19. The proceeds of the warm-up tour disappointed both Conway and Gregory, but it gave Gregory a chance to drill his players into a splendid fielding side.

CHAPTER THREE

THE FIRST WHITE TOURS

International cricket developed from the interchange of touring teams between England and Australia. England began the idea of teams touring abroad in 1859 by sending a side of 12 professionals on the terrible voyage across the Atlantic for an eight-match tour, for which each man received £90. However it was really the visits to Australia by the English teams under H.H. Stephenson (1861–62), George Parr (1863–64), W.G. Grace (1873–74) and James Lillywhite (1876–77), and the series of Australian tours that started in 1878 that ushered in cricket between nations.

The 1878 Australian tour of England demonstrated that English players did not hold ascendancy over the rest of the world, although England laid down the laws of play. The tour showed that English cricketers could be subjected to pressures that inhibited their skills, and at the same time opened up a whole new panorama of high-level contests between the best available cricketers.

When the Australians sailed from Sydney for San Francisco in the *City of Sydney*, with 116 other passengers, there were less than a dozen people on the wharf to see them off. The Australian public rated their mission a silly gamble, a cheeky exercise likely to flop. Some of the team thought so little of their chances of playing matches that would make money they paid their return fares in advance to ensure they would not be stranded in England.

They boarded a train in San Francisco on 27 April for the long journey across America on the Central Pacific Railway to New York, which they reached a week later. Surprisingly, members of America's St George Cricket Club helped load their gear on the *City of Berlin* for manager John Conway, who had preceded them to England by way of the Suez Canal and met them at Liverpool on

The first white Australian team to tour England, in 1878 (L to R): back, J. Conway, G.H. Bailey, W.C.V. Gibbes (Treasurer), F.E. Allan; centre, H.F. Boyle, W.L. Murdoch, T. Horan, D.W. Gregory (Captain), A. C. Bannerman, F.R. Spofforth; front, T.W. Garrett, C. Bannerman and J.M. Blackham. (MCC Library)

13 May. They travelled immediately to Nottingham for their first match. Billy Midwinter, fresh from matches with W.G. Grace in the Gloucestershire county team, joined the other Australians as they drove through the Nottingham streets in a bus drawn by four splendid greys and led by a band. All the way to their hotel the streets were lined with people eager to see them. Local aldermen, the sheriff and the region's lacemakers and weavers were surprised to find they were not all black.

At the Maypole Hotel they drank bumpers of champagne after the mayor's welcoming speech and within two hours of arrival were practising at the Trent Bridge ground. They had three days' practice on sloppy, rain-saturated pitches and without exception the form of all 12 players was very poor. Conway knew he could fill in if a player was injured, and he had been able to secure the services of a Melbourne medical student, H.N. Tennant, as a substitute in minor matches, but they were all aware that the programme they faced would fully test their toughness.

Lillywhite said the Australians could win half the matches he had arranged, provided the differences between Victorian and New South Wales members were minimised. Players who had come on the tour expecting some of the easy pickings English professionals enjoyed in Australia were disappointed to find that those same

English players resented their presence and feared them as a threat to the meagre pay they received from county clubs.

Confusion among Nottingham residents over the colour of the Australian players was understandable. They had been keen supporters of the Australian Aboriginal team that toured England in 1868 and posters advertising the novelty sports demonstrated by the Aborigines between cricket matches hung in the Trent Bridge pavilion. Locals still recalled their amazement watching Dick-a-Dick dodge cricket balls thrown at him from a few yards away and the Aborigines' skill with spears and boomerangs.

These white Australians were extremely fit from their long warm-up schedule of matches and daily shipboard callisthenics, tough, gnarled-handed men without a pound of excess fat on them, but over the next four months even they had to marvel at the heavy programme the 1868 Australian Aboriginal team had completed. The Aborigines had played 47 matches between May and October, winning 14, losing 14 and leaving 19 drawn. They were on the field 99 out of a possible 126 playing days, and appeared in 15 counties. They played 11 of their matches in September and six in October, in bitterly cold conditions, a far more gruelling experience to men brought up in the sun than anything encountered by the white Australian sides that followed. They had no tea breaks and lunch usually was taken between 2 and 3 p.m. for 35 minutes. There

The Australian Aboriginal team who toured England ten years before the first white team, shown after practising in Melbourne with coach Tom Wills, far left. (MCG Museum)

were no arrangements for the Aborigines to take lunch and they simply queued at the refreshment tents and took their chances with the public. At York they were even barred from the refreshment tent.

There were many similarities between the black and white tours. Although they were ten years apart, both teams had to endure calls for them to abandon their trips, the Aborigines from the Protection Board who claimed they would be prone to disease and likely to be killed off in a foreign climate, the whites by cricket followers who argued that they simply were not good enough to take on top English cricketers. Both had enormous difficulty attracting matches when they first arrived in England but both were blessed by strong, gutsy leadership. Charles Lawrence, assisted by William Shepherd, a former Surrey professional who travelled with the Aborigines as their umpire and played in seven matches, supplied the captaincy and management skills for the Aboriginals. John Conway and tough-thinking Dave Gregory did the same for the white players. Both teams lost key players during their tours, the blacks when King Cole died of tuberculosis, the whites when a conflict of interests cost them the services of the player with most experience in English conditions.

Star of early Aboriginal cricket Johnny Mullagh, who averaged 23.65 runs an innings on the 1868 English tour. (MCG Museum)

Eight of the 12 white cricketers Conway introduced at the Nottingham dinners celebrating their arrival wore fashionable beards. Dave Gregory's glistening dark red beard won the honours but the beards sported by Horan, Boyle and Blackham were studied with awe. The full team comprised:

• *David William Gregory* (Captain), 33, born at Fairy Meadow, New South Wales, on 15 April, 1845, 6 ft 2 in. Right-hand middle-order batsman, right-arm fast roundarm bowler. Chief of the Sydney Audit Office.
• *Francis Erskine Allan*, 29, born at Allansford, Victoria, on 2 December, 1849, 6 ft. Tail-end left-hand batsman, left-hand high-armed roundarm bowler, splendid slips field. Melbourne civil servant.
• *Henry Frederick Boyle*, 31, born at Sydney, New South Wales, on 10 December, 1846, 6 ft. Lower-order right-hand batsman, right-hand fast-medium roundarm bowler, excellent close-in field, Melbourne civil servant.
• *William Lloyd Murdoch*, 23, born at Sandhurst, Victoria, on 18 October, 1854, 5 ft 10 in. Stylish right-hand middle-order batsman, reserve wicket-keeper. Sydney solicitor.

Australia's first cricket captain Dave Gregory, right, with batsman Alick Bannerman, with whom he made the pioneer tour of England in 1878. (Mitchell Library, Sydney)

• *Charles Bannerman*, 26, born at Woolwich, Kent, on 23 July, 1851, 5 ft 10 in. Excellent right-hand opening batsman, fine outfield, occasional bowler. Professional cricketer.

• *Alexander Chalmers Bannerman*, 24, born at Paddington, Sydney, on 21 March, 1854. 5 ft 5 in. Noted stonewaller. Right-hand opening batsman, right-hand medium-pace roundarm bowler. Brother of Charles. New South Wales Government Printing Office employee.

• *George Herbert Bailey*, 24, born at Colombo, Ceylon, on 29 October, 1853, 5 ft 10 in. Lower-order right-hand batsman, fast right-hand roundarm bowler, deep field specialist. Tasmanian banker.

• *John McCarthy Blackham*, 23, born at North Fitzroy, Victoria, on 11 May, 1854, 5 ft 9 in. Brilliant wicket-keeper, stubborn right-hand defensive batsman. Bank clerk in Melbourne.

• *Thomas William Garrett*, 20, born at Wollongong, New South Wales, on 26 July, 1858, 5 ft 11 in. Lower-order right-hand batsman, right-arm fast-medium bowler. A noted sprinter, whose speed in the field excited spectators. Clerk of Sydney's Supreme Court.

• *Thomas Patrick Horan*, 24, born at Middleton, County Cork, Ireland on 8 March, 1854, 5 ft 10 in. Defensive middle-order right-hand batsman, right-hand fast-medium roundarm bowler. Noted tactician. Victorian civil servant and freelance journalist.

• *Frederick Robert Spofforth*, 24, born at Balmain, New South Wales, on 9 September, 1853, 6ft 2in. Right-hand lower-order batsman, right-arm fast-medium overarm bowler of rare subtlety and hostility. Bank officer in Sydney.

• *William Evans Midwinter*, 26, born at St Briavels, Gloucestershire, on 19 June, 1851, 6 ft. Right-hand middle-order batsman, accurate right-hand medium-pace bowler, outstanding outfieldsman. Noted billiards player. First international cricket commuter. Played for Victoria and Gloucestershire each year. Worked as goldmi' er, butcher, publican.

Even Conway was not aware that Midwinter owed Gloucestershire his services and he was included in the Australian Eleven from the first match in the belief he would be with the team for the entire tour. He had been promised benefit matches in Sydney and Melbourne if he returned with the team.

The first match turned out disastrously, with the Australians all out for 63, Shaw taking 5 for 20. Shivering in silk shirts in weather that demanded heavy sweaters, the Australians skidded over damp, windswept grass, wishing they were back in the Australian sun. Notts were dismissed for 153, and on the second day 10,000 turned up to watch Australia score the 90 they needed to avoid an innings defeat. Eight batsmen failed to reach double figures and the innings ended at 76, leaving Notts winners by an innings and 14 runs.

Australia's setback at Nottingham in their first outing on English soil left fans unprepared for an amazing upset. Despite their heavy defeat the Australians' hosts at Trent Bridge treated them to a sumptuous banquet and commiserated with them about their ill-luck in encountering such appalling weather.

There was no similar warmth in the Australians' reception in London, where on 27 May, 1878, they began their second match against the Marylebone Cricket Club. On a showery morning, after a night of heavy rain, they drove in their brake through large puddles from their Covent Garden hotel to Lord's. Like most Australians they were disappointed at first sight of the game's headquarters, which they found lacked many of the facilities of the Melbourne and Sydney grounds. Less than 1000 spectators watched the opening of the match.

The general belief that the match would result in an easy MCC win appeared justified when W.G. Grace cracked the first ball of the match for four. Midwinter immediately struck a telling blow for Australia when he moved quickly round from fine leg to catch Grace off the second ball at square leg, clearly aware that the doctor enjoyed that shot early in his innings. This clever dismissal was still under discussion in the crowd when Allan bowled Clem Booth for a duck. Hornby appeared to be caught behind by Murdoch, substituting for Blackham who was ill, but a confident appeal was rejected. At 2 for 25 Gregory replaced Allan with Spofforth and a dramatic change came over the match. In 23 balls, Spofforth took six wickets for four runs, including a hat-trick with the first three deliveries of his fifth over which removed Hearne, Shaw and Vernon.

Brilliant Australian fielding accompanied this incredible spell by the bowler the English historian Harry Altham labelled the greatest of all time. With the MCC all out for 33, onlookers crowded to the gate to get a close look at the players who had managed it. Most of them believed reality would return in MCC's second innings, a view that the Australian batsmen strengthened by struggling to a total of 41 in their first innings. Only Midwinter (10) reached double figures against bowling of sustained hostility from Shaw, 5 for 10, and Morley, 5 for 31.

The original demon bowler, Fred Spofforth, from the Sydney suburb of Balmain, a match-winner who toured England five times with Australian teams. (Jack Pollard Collection)

The crowd had increased to around 10,000 as word of the spectacular cricket spread around London by the time MCC began their second innings. The latecomers were not disappointed. Murdoch dropped W.G. Grace off the first ball, then Spofforth bowled him with the second. Grace's obvious discomfort at both deliveries, ending with his bails on the turf after a wonderful, fast break-back, inspired a storm of applause that continued until Grace reached the pavilion. A.J. Webbe, a notoriously stubborn fighter, followed, but with his third ball Spofforth had him for a duck. Ridley came in but Boyle quickly removed his leg stump and when he bowled Booth MCC were 4 for 1.

Boyle hit the stumps six times as MCC succumbed for a total of 19 and had an analysis of 6 for 3 from 8.1 four-ball overs. Spofforth's 4 for 16 came from nine overs and between them the two Australians bowled eight maidens in their 17.1 overs. Left to score 12 runs to win, Australia made them with the loss of Charles Bannerman's wicket, to win by nine wickets in an astonishing three hours 40 minutes against the cream of English cricket.

This legendary victory proved more important to Australian and international cricket than any Test triumph. For it opened up the sport to countries outside England and encouraged the wise men at Lord's to continue with a policy of sending teams overseas. After years of dour county championship matches, English cricket could offer exciting games involving other countries. The *London Globe* said: 'Seldom in the annals of modern cricket has so small a score been made as by the MCC yesterday, and never was so severe a humiliation inflicted individually and collectively on the members of the club.'

Murdoch had dropped the only chance put down by the Australians in a wonderful fielding display, the only ball misfielded by the Australians in two innings. There could be no dispute at the manner of dismissal of England's best batsmen as 14 had been clean bowled and nobody had been run out or leg-before-wicket. The only excuse that could be offered for the MCC was that Hornby had been badly hurt and forced to leave the field when hit by a vicious Spofforth delivery when he opened the MCC's second innings. Hornby resumed using W.G. Grace as a runner, but made only a single. Seven MCC batsmen were out first ball, four to second balls.

Among the crowd who watched Horan make the winning hit through the slips were Sir Charles Du Cane, former governor of Tasmania, who had often joined southern Tasmanian cricketers in the nets in the years when they helped pioneer inter-colonial cricket; Queensland MP the Hon. Leslie Thorne; Mr De Pass and Colonel Ward, of the Melbourne Cricket Club; and the hoteliers Spiers and Pond, who had sponsored the first English team to Australia 16 years earlier.

London opened its heart to the Australians: 'The reputation of the Colonial Eleven is made, and they will be welcomed with enthusiasm wherever they now appear,' said the *Globe*. 'The MCC Eleven was as good a one as could be found to represent London and England, and probably nearly as good as the club has ever turned out. Yet its best batsmen were bowled over one after another as if they were novices.'

Punch magazine greeted the Australians' win with:

> The Australians came down like a wolf on the fold,
> The Marylebone cracks for a trifle were bowled;
> Our Grace before dinner was very soon done,
> And Grace after dinner did not get a run.

The newspaper *Home News* predicted that the Australians would be very difficult to beat. 'Their fielding is the admiration of all who behold it,' the paper said, 'they have among them many excellent bats, but their great strength is in their bowling. Their bowlers have long enjoyed peculiar soubriquets indicative of their powers. Left-handed Allan is known as the "Crouching Panther" or "Bowler of the Century"; Boyle is described as the "very devil"; but Spofforth as the "demon bowler" carries off the palm. His delivery is quite appalling; the balls thunder in like cannon shot; yet he has the guile when seemingly about to bowl his fastest to drop in a "slow" which is generally fatal to the batsman.' Altham noted that Spofforth never overdid his power of spin, always aiming at just enough to beat the bat, but concluded his consummate gift was in concealing his changes of pace.

The Australians had another weapon Englishmen took a long time to notice – the presence of Boyle, the original suicide fields-man, a few metres from the bat, ready to make catches from the defensive stroke when Spofforth bowled his fast off-breaks. By the end of the tour the position was known as 'Boyley's mid-on', later to become familiar as 'silly mid-on' and today as the 'bat-pad' position.

By the time the players went to the English Derby the day after their celebrated win over MCC, the vacant dates for the rest of the Australians' tour had all been filled. Large audiences attended all subsequent matches, ensuring a splendid profit from the players' investments. Outstanding wins followed over Yorkshire and Surrey. They won by six wickets over Yorkshire at Huddersfield, where Spofforth took 4 for 30 and 5 for 31 in Yorkshire innings of 72 and 73. At The Oval they beat Surrey by five wickets, with Spofforth taking 8 for 52 and 3 for 42. Only two gate-keepers were on duty at The Oval and they were quite unable to contain the 40,000 spectators who burst through fences and gates and rushed out on to the field. Conway grabbed his top hat and collected entrance money in it but half the crowd still got in without paying.

The team's success had a curious effect on matches designed as social occasions against eighteen and twenty-two opponents. They found leading batsmen and bowlers eager to get a close look at their technique. Eighteen of Hastings fielded Lord Harris and the Hon. Ivo Bligh, both future England captains, Frank Penn and Charles Absolom from the Kent side, who both toured Australia in English teams, plus James and Henry Phillips from the Sussex XI, and John and Charles Noble, from the Surrey county staff. The Eighteen scored 131 and 82, Australia 260, Bailey contributing 106, one of the two Australian centuries of the tour. The Eighteen of Yeadon and District fielded 17 professionals from Yorkshire, Lancashire and Derbyshire, including the England players Edmund Peate and Richard Barlow, dour Test cricketers but amiable men. The Leicestershire professional Arnold Rylott appeared against the Australians eight times.

The Eighteen of Hunslet included a Yorkshire fast bowler named Arthur Motley who admitted he threw every ball and laughed at his luck in never being no-balled. Dave Gregory threatened to call off the match when a ball from Motley cannoned off Horan's chest on to the stumps. Motley was taken from the attack but the Australians later allowed him to bat.

Boyle's endurance throughout the tour repeatedly amazed his team-mates. He took a delight in sitting out in the wind – or even a snowfall – next to the team's coach drivers. He was responsible for the most incredible feat of the tour when he took seven wickets in eight deliveries against Eighteen of Elland. Allan commented that if three wickets from successive deliveries was worth a hat, then Boyle's display deserved a full suit of clothes. He despatched batsmen so quickly they had trouble padding up fast enough to take

The first Tasmanian to play for Australia, banker George Bailey, a free wristy batsman of style, who made 106 against Eighteen of Hastings during the tour. (Rick Smith)

their turn at the wicket. Impatient spectators hollered 'Send in a man', at which another shouted 'Send in three or four – one's no use.' Spofforth scattered the stumps eight times in taking ten wickets in the second innings of this match.

By the eleventh match of the tour, against Middlesex at Lord's, Midwinter had decided to remain with the Australians and forsake his ties with Gloucestershire. On the morning of the match Conway went to The Oval to inform W.G. Grace Midwinter would not be joining the Gloucestershire team for their match there against Surrey, but instead would play for Australia at Lord's. The news angered Grace, who lost his temper, and accused Conway and his team of being a lot of sneaks who had enticed Midwinter to deny his native county. Bitter words were exchanged and Conway insisted Midwinter had reached his decision alone. Conway then took a cab to Lord's, where Midwinter was padding up to open the Australian innings with Alick Bannerman.

Shortly afterwards Grace arrived with the Gloucestershire amateur James Bush, who had been a member of Grace's team in Australia in 1873–74. Further argument followed before Midwinter walked out of the room with his bag. 'That Grace lost his temper and sadly forgot himself there can be no doubt, while the indecision of Midwinter, who did not seem to know his own mind for two minutes together, cannot be too strongly deprecated,' wrote Tom Horan later in the *Australasian*. 'Nothing can justify Grace's passion and language, nor his conduct in coming to Lord's and almost forcibly leading away the captive Midwinter.'

Gloucestershire's claim on Midwinter was based on the fact that he was born at St Briavels in the Forest of Dean in Gloucestershire, but his family moved to Cirencester in the Cotswolds, 80 kilometres to the east, soon after his birth. When Billy was nine his father, William John Midwinter, joined a group of unemployed workers from the Forest of Dean who decided to try their luck on the Australian goldfields. They arrived in 1861. Midwinter senior, then 38, failed to find gold but he took a job as a butcher at Sandhurst, where Billy began his long friendship with Harry Boyle. Together they cleared land for a cricket pitch on what was known as Sydney flat, on the Bendigo goldfields. Billy left the Sydney Flat CC to play for the Bendigo First XI at the age of 13.

The Australians' row with W.G. Grace had been simmering for weeks. His 'kidnapping' of Midwinter brought it to a heated climax. The Australians vigorously objected when Grace and W.R. Gilbert were each paid £60 expenses for playing against them for the Gentlemen of England, arguing that the Gentlemen were an all-amateur side. They were told that W.G. and his brothers, G.F. and E.M. Grace, were always paid for playing. The Australians' share from the match with the Gentlemen at Prince's Ground, Chelsea, London, was also hit when police refused to move against a full-house audience for fear of a disturbance. More than 14,000 onlookers paid one shilling admission, a further 5000 2s 6d, and the rest 5s for reserved seats, but the majority of those in the reserved section paid the lower prices. Beaten by an innings and one run, the Australians went on to Lord's only to be told by W.G. Grace after the Midwinter arguments that 'You haven't the ghost of a show against Middlesex.'

Frank Allan, in his account of the tour, later serialised in Melbourne, said that when W.G. bundled Midwinter into his carriage and departed for The Oval, Dave Gregory, Conway and Midwinter's lifelong friend Harry Boyle hired another carriage and gave chase right across London. Outside The Oval gates a further altercation occurred before the Australians returned empty-handed to Lord's. Allan, who replaced Midwinter in the side, bowled Australia to victory by 98 runs in taking 7 for 38 and 6 for 76, despite a brilliant innings of 113 by the Hon. Edward Lyttelton,

Early Australian cricket heroes at a Sydney Cricket Ground reunion (L to R): Dave Gregory, Fred Spofforth, Hugh Massie, Alick Bannerman and Tom Garrett. (SCG Archives)

the only century scored against the tourists. With Gregory disturbed perhaps by the pre-match clashes with W.G. Grace, Lyttelton scored the majority of his runs with the square cut, without a fieldsman at deep third man to prevent them becoming boundaries.

The joy over their defeat of Middlesex multiplied when news reached the Australian dressing-room that Surrey, whom the Australians had beaten by five wickets, had defeated Gloucestershire by 16 runs. The team management agreed they would not play the scheduled match against Gloucestershire until W.G. apologised. Nasty letters passed between Gloucestershire and the Australians before W.G. wrote an apology that did not include Conway. The Australians refused to accept it until finally W.G. sent the following letter to Dave Gregory:

Dear Sir.
I am sorry that my former expression of regret to the Australians has not been considered satisfactory. Under the circumstances, and without going further into the matter, I wish to let bygones be bygones, and I apologise again and express my extreme regret to Conway, Boyle, and yourself, and through you to all the Australian cricketers, that in the excitement of the moment, I should have made use of unparliamentary language to Mr Conway. I can do no more, but assure you that you will meet a hearty welcome and a good ground at Clifton.

Yours truly, W.G. Grace

Midwinter, who injured his hand in the match with Surrey at The Oval, had a miserable season in which all form left him. Left without a twelfth man, the Australians proudly refused to borrow fieldsmen from opposing sides, although their fatigue became so great one or two had to be awakened to take their turn to bat. In the seventeenth match of the tour they met Leicestershire, the first side to agree to a match and the only club that had agreed to pay them a lump sum. But the great form the Australians had shown from the second match of their tour turned Leicestershire's gamble into a profit of £500 and attracted the best crowds of the tour.

'On such a beautiful wicket one of us should make a century,' Charles Bannerman said. Set 209 to win, the Australians immediately attacked, Bannerman hitting boundaries from the first three balls he faced. He went on to a thrilling 133, hitting 97 of them in boundaries. In all he hit nine singles, nine twos, three threes, 23 fours and one five, to record the initial century by an Australian in England. His innings did not draw a false stroke and ended only when he was run out by a substitute fieldsman. Spectators lured by expectations of devastating Australian bowling cheered the runs the strokemaking Bannerman provided instead.

The antagonism of English professionals towards the Australians emerged just before a match at The Oval against a Professional XI. The professionals, who normally played for a match fee of £10, demanded £20 each. Conway refused this increase on the advice of the Surrey committee and a second-string professional side replaced the one originally announced. The game proved a thriller.

The Australians were dismissed for 77 and 89 thanks to fine bowling by Edward Barratt. Spofforth had six Professionals out for a duck in their first innings including a hat-trick. In the second innings when the Professionals wanted only 19 to win, with five wickets left, the batsmen crumbled and Australia won by eight runs.

This took the Australians to Clifton for the long-awaited clash with Gloucestershire in a confident mood. Gloucestershire, the reigning county champions, had never been beaten on their home ground but Spofforth's 7 for 49 and 5 for 41 soon changed that. Leading by 71 after the first innings, Australia scored the 17 needed for a ten-wicket victory early on the second morning.

Overall on the tour, the expected arguments between Victorian and New South Wales members of the Australian team failed to emerge. The batting lacked experience on damp pitches once Midwinter left, though Charles Bannerman and Murdoch matched any Englishman in stroke play. Alick Bannerman's stonewalling could hold up the most hostile bowling, while Tom Horan could be relied on to hammer anything loose for boundaries. 'The other seven are worth only 30 runs between them,' wrote one English critic.

There was no disagreement, however, about Blackham's wicket-keeping, only unanimous approval that it was superior to anything previously seen in England. Day after day he stood up to the stumps to take the fastest deliveries from Spofforth, Allan, Boyle and Garrett, seldom conceding byes, and often bringing off stumpings that provided extra pressure for even the best batsmen.

With Blackham in such form and Gregory providing alert, firm captaincy, the Australian fielding was far superior to all bar the top English teams. Their throwing was a revelation, reaching a standard unknown in England, and every man knew misfielding on the ground would incur their captain's displeasure. Spofforth's masterly bowling was well supported by that of Boyle, Allan and Garrett and gave them an advantage in the field. Contemporary accounts of their tour repeatedly pay tribute not only to their resolution and discipline but also to their smart appearance and unfailing punctuality. With the sad fate of Tom Kendall in mind, not one member of the team was seen the worse for liquor.

After four gruelling months touring England and Scotland, the Australians returned home via America and Canada, where they played a further six matches. The impatience they had shown in England with some umpiring decisions finally brought trouble in the match at Niceton, on 3–5 October 1878, against a Philadelphia XI. The Australians were dumbfounded when the umpires applauded every run scored by Philadelphia and when Blackham had a stumping appeal rejected with the batsman three or four paces down the pitch, Dave Gregory led his players from the field in protest. In the dressing-room American officials told Conway the cheque they had given him that morning would be dishonoured unless the Australians continued the match. Gregory took the team back on the field, much to the relief of 10,000 spectators, and the match was played out to a draw.

In Canada a thief stole many of their tour souvenirs such as gold watches and medals, as well as large amounts of cash, while they were out fielding against Twenty-Two of Montreal. Charles Bannerman scored another century in this match (125), the first by an Australian in Canada, but that did not lessen the players' depression at the loss from their dressing-room of so many tour treasures.

In contrast to their dismal send-off, on their return to Australia they sailed up Sydney Harbour to a tumultuous welcome, with dozens of launches and small boats tooting. Cheering crowds lined the shore and there was a big band honking away on the wharf. They were driven through streets decorated with flowers to Sydney Town Hall in a large four-horse coach. Similar welcomes greeted them in Melbourne and Adelaide, when they played their last few matches.

Spofforth took all the honours on this first overseas tour by an Australian cricket team, with an amazing 764 wickets in all matches at an average cost of 6.08 runs. He began with 281 wickets on the warm-up tour of Australia, took 326 wickets in England, 69 in America and Canada, and 88 in the final matches after the team

W.C.V. Gibbes, mystery man revealed on Australia's 1878 tour. (Jack Pollard Collection)

returned. The batting prize went to Charles Bannerman, the first Australian to score centuries in three overseas countries, and the only batsman to exceed 1000 runs in the team's matches.

In the final match of the tour, George Bailey broke his arm fielding against New South Wales while throwing the ball back to Blackham, the bone snapping like a pistol shot. It was the only severe injury sustained in 41 matches by this tough group, who had 19 victories, seven losses and 15 draws in a tour that virtually opened up international cricket for all who could reach the required standard.

Throughout the long tour Dave Gregory was at pains in his many speeches to explain that the tour was the idea of one man, John Conway, and had gone ahead despite opposition from administrators in Australia. 'We shall forever be grateful to him; but for him the majority of us would never have been seen in England,' Gregory told guests at a Manchester dinner attended by the Duke of Manchester. 'He had to work hard to put it together but he has done so with more success than any of us could have anticipated.'

In 1994, 116 years after that first tour, I discovered that the Australian team had had two managers, not just Conway. Dave Gregory had invited his friend William Gibbes to be the team's treasurer. Gibbes, an accountant with the Equity Division of the New South Wales Supreme Court, handled all the tour finances and proved overseas tours viable, but for more than a century remained unidentified.

At a time when a large home cost a few hundred pounds in Australia, every player in the Australian team received £750 from the 1878 tour. Years later some of the team leaked to reporters that they had actually received £1040 each and that the team had approved an additional 7.5 per cent to Conway for his tireless negotiations. When news of the payments spread there can have been few aspiring cricketers in Australia who did not intensify their practising.

The New South Wales Cricket Association president Richard Driver helped Dave Gregory, Tom Garrett and Charles Bannerman draft a letter to the colony premier Sir Henry Parkes. In it they asked for their full salaries as public servants for the 15 months they had been away, as their tour had brought prestige and future benefit to the colony. Parkes rejected the request on 'principles that ought to be impartially applied', leaving Garrett and Bannerman without wages for the period, like 11 of their team-mates.

CHAPTER FOUR
THE SYDNEY RIOT

George Robert Canning was a top-class forcing right-hand batsman, a brilliant field, and a useful right-hand fast roundarm bowler, who had his first net at Lord's in 1862 at the age of 11 and learned to love the ground. His celebrated sound judgement saw the Marylebone Cricket Club, which had its headquarters at Lord's, control the administration of cricket and give it a unique place in society. Despite a sharp temper, he was a fearless upholder of cricket's standards of behaviour.

From a rich and influential family who educated him in the Tory tradition, he still sympathised with professional cricketers in their efforts to secure a fair and reasonable living from the game. Above all the laws of cricket were his passion and he always insisted they were laws, not rules. 'Rules are made to be broken, but laws are made to be kept,' he said.

He was born at St Anne's in Trinidad on 3 February, 1851, attended Eton from 1868 to 1870 when he captained the First XI, and Oxford University from 1871 to 1874, winning Blues in three of his four years, and from 1871, when he was appointed county captain, virtually controlled all cricket in Kent for half a century. He became the fourth Lord Harris in 1872, six years before he took the fifth English cricket team to Australia in the southern summer of 1878–79.

Harris's team was an all-amateur outfit chosen by his friend Isaac Donnithorne Walker, a long-time stalwart of the Middlesex county club which used Lord's for home games. The Melbourne Cricket Club invited Walker, the best of seven brothers from Southgate, London, with an unrivalled record in club cricket, to visit Australia at its expense, but Walker had only just selected the side when his

Lord Harris at the crease, wearing slatted pads, black tie and a winged collar. He did more than any other cricketer to uphold dignified standards.
(MCC Library)

51

Lord Harris's 1878–79 English team to Australia (L to R): back, F. Penn, A.J. Webbe, C.A. Absolom, S.S. Schultz, L. Hone; centre, F.A. McKinnon, A.N. Hornby, Lord Harris, H.C. Maul, G. Ulyett; front, A.P. Lucas, V.P.F.A. Royle, T. Emmett. They lost the only Test of the tour in Melbourne. (MCG Museum)

brother Arthur died, forcing Isaac to drop out.

Lord Harris judged the team to be short on bowlers that could be relied on for long spells in the heat, a chore not relished by amateurs accustomed to ground bowlers carrying out such work for the equivalent of a labourer's wages. He therefore brought in the tough Yorkshiremen Tom Emmett, a left-hand roundarm fast bowler who had just handed over the county captaincy to Lord Hawke, and his clubmate George Ulyett, the right-hand fast roundarm bowler known as 'Happy Jack', to handle the hard bowling load. The Melbourne club still advertised the side as 'The Gentlemen of England', despite the presence of these two front-rank professionals.

Ulyett and Emmett travelled second-class in the ship to Australia, the amateurs first-class, and throughout England's Australian stay they were booked into inferior hotels to the amateurs. Australians unaccustomed to the English habit of asking professionals to change in different rooms to amateurs, and to take the field by different gates, were shocked at the treatment of Ulyett and Emmett but neither made a fuss about it. Both had to get through a prodigious amount of work.

The Englishmen began their programme of 13 matches in December in Adelaide, at the same time as the first Australian team under Dave Gregory was receiving its triumphant welcome home in Sydney. From the start the lack of a regular wicket-keeper left Lord Harris's side handicapped. They were exposed to the growing strength of Australian batting whenever Emmett or Ulyett rested because they had only one other bowler who could sustain any degree of accuracy, the Essex slow right-hand roundarmer Alfred Lucas. Further, they found all their Australian opponents in a highly combative mood, fired up by the exploits of Gregory's team in England. Lord Harris discovered that fieldsmen who could be relied on at home to hold their catches dropped far too many in the demanding Australian conditions. They lost three of their five first-class matches.

This was the second tour of Australia by an English team sponsored by the Melbourne Cricket Club. The club had been founded in 1838 when Melbourne itself was only three weeks old, by five gentlemen who signed the foundation document and paid one guinea each to make it legal. Their five guineas bought two bats and balls, and with them club members played their first cricket match one week later on a paddock that is now the site of the Royal Mint in William Street. Despite defeat in the initial inter-colonial match in Launceston at the hands of Tasmania, the club's influence expanded rapidly. The club settled on its third home in Richmond Paddock, where R.C. Bagot, who also designed Flemington racecourse, designed a picturesque ground for members.

The Melbourne club had sponsored the visit by the third English team, led by Dr W.G. Grace, in 1873–74. In 1878 the presence in Australia of such a group of wealthy, well-bred amateurs as Lord Harris captained confirmed the club's position as Australia's leading cricket club 27 years before Australia's controlling body was formed and 22 years before the colonies were federated into one nation. Understandably, the Melbourne club's investment gave its senior members hope that the club might eventually take over the administration of all Australian cricket, just as the Marylebone CC had done at Lord's with English cricket.

Lord Harris's team was just as appealing to socialites as it was to cricket fans. It included Francis Alexander McKinnon, a Scottish Highland chief educated at Cambridge, the Reverend Vernon Fanshawe Royle of Oxford University and Lancashire, Alexander Josiah Webbe, legendary cricketing missionary from Oxford and Middlesex, Leland Hone, of Rugby and Cambridge and one of a noted family of Irish cricketers, Charles Alfred Absolom, of Cambridge and Kent, Frank Penn, of Canterbury, Cambridge and later Kent president, Albert Neilson Hornby, of Harrow and Lancashire, Sandford Spence Schultz of Cambridge and Lancashire who later changed his name to Storey when he realised the German 'Schultz' caused offence, and Alfred Perry ('Bunny') Lucas, of Cambridge, Surrey, Middlesex and Essex.

Adelaide Oval at the time of the visit by Lord Harris's English team. They beat Eighteen of South Australia. (National Library of Australia)

Lord Harris's team began their 13-match Australian tour with a three-wicket win over an Eighteen of South Australia that included a 19-year-old off-spinner named George Giffen, and moved to the major engagement of their programme in the third match at East Melbourne against an Australian XI. This later became recognised as the third Test match. England found the bowling of Spofforth, who took 13 wickets for 110 runs in the match, too much for them, and Australia won by ten wickets. Spofforth bowled Royle and McKinnon had Emmett caught for Test cricket's first hat-trick. Thomas Kelly was the only player in the Australian team who had not toured England the previous year but he had played in the second Test in Melbourne in 1877. Kelly, who had migrated from County Waterford at the age of 19 after a brief sojourn playing cricket in Bristol with the Grace family, was notable for his spectacular red, white and blue blazer, which he wore with a matching sash. Kelly contributed 10 runs to Australia's score while George Bailey, the man he had replaced, watched from the stands with his injured arm in a sling.

Lord Harris hired one of the umpires from the Test match, George Coulthard, to accompany his players to Sydney to stand in the match against New South Wales on 24 January. Coulthard was a Carlton club Australian Rules football star who worked as a ground bowler for the Melbourne Cricket Club and at 22 was one summer away from his introduction to inter-colonial cricket with the Victorian team. He umpired in the match in which New South Wales defeated the tourists by five wickets, with Murdoch continuing his advance as a batsman by scoring 70 and 49. Coulthard also went to Bathurst for a drawn game against a local Eighteen before going to Sydney for the return match against New South Wales.

There was heavy betting on this match from the start of play, with gamblers in the stands ignoring signs warning them of fines or imprisonment. Following Australia's win in the Test, punters invested heavily on New South Wales, but England took a 90-run first-innings lead and forced New South Wales to follow on. With the New South Wales total on 19, Coulthard gave Murdoch run out for 10. Immediately angry spectators jumped the fence and rushed on to the pitch.

There is conflict about who was hit in the wild demonstration that followed. Tom Horan, a model of accuracy in his 'Felix' columns in the *Australasian*, maintained until he died that Lord Harris was *not* hit across the back by a stick or whip as some accounts reported. Horan said that only umpire Coulthard was hit across the back. Whether he was protecting Lord Harris or Coulthard no one knew, but it was unanimously agreed that 'Monkey' Hornby had his shirt torn from his back. Hornby wrestled with the man responsible and amid confusion carried a man to the pavilion. Trustees and members of the English team rushed to protect Hornby from a mob intent on rescuing his prisoner. Coulthard came off unhurt and after a lot of pushing and shoving all the Englishmen reached the dressing-room safely.

A.N. ('Monkey') Hornby had his shirt torn from his back protecting Lord Harris in the Sydney riot. (MCC Library)

Attendants cleared the ground after half an hour, but Dave Gregory refused to make any attempt to resume play until Coulthard was replaced. Lord Harris refused, arguing that all his fieldsmen who had a good view of the run-out believed it was a fair decision. Lord Harris expressed his anger at later allegations that Coulthard had bet on the match result.

Two attempts to get the players back on to the field failed. Lord Harris was intent on occupying the pitch if he could, apparently in an attempt to prevent New South Wales claiming the match on a forfeit, but his presence at the centre of the ground only provoked demonstrators to fresh waves of catcalling. After play was abandoned for the day the *Sydney Morning Herald* said the riot had been stimulated by two English players calling the first wave of demonstrators 'sons of convicts'.

The second umpire, Edmund Barton, later Prime Minister of Australia, considered Coulthard's decision perfectly fair and defended the Englishmen's behaviour. He scoffed at the suggestion that the professionals Emmett and Ulyett were responsible for the 'sons of convicts' call, but there were many at the ground who claimed to have heard it. Readers wrote to the *Herald* saying the comment had 'spread like wildfire' around the ground, inflaming the mob. The *Australasian* found it strange that the three policemen on duty at the ground remained outside the fence throughout the disturbance.

Ned Kelly's gang raided Jerilderie on the same day as the Sydney riot, but received little space from newspapers more concerned with lawlessness at the cricket.

Lord Harris apparently spent the Sunday rest day that followed writing his account of events to Isaac Walker in London and, when parts of the letter appeared in the London *Daily Telegraph*, Anglo-Australian cricket relations slumped to an all-time low. 'Lord Harris is a pretty good cricketer, but we cannot congratulate him on his appearance in print,' 'Felix' said in the *Australasian*. 'His version of the treatment he received at the hands of the "howling mob" in Sydney is certainly not written in good taste, nor does it evince those finer sentiments of good feeling and tact that we might expect in an English gentlemen and a peer of the realm . . . Lord Harris owns to a "*sly kick or two*", but as he came out of the howling mob safe and sound after 30 minutes detention, and afterwards remained for an hour and a half on the ground, it is evident the noble cricketer did not incur as much danger as he would imply. Victorian cricketers have experienced rougher treatment more than once on Sydney fields, but they took it like men, and the Victorian press, though it denounced the rowdyism of their cousins over the border, did not exhibit the vindictiveness and bad taste displayed by the English press in commenting on this case.'

Dave Gregory's intransigence in refusing to get the match restarted on the Saturday – the match was played out on the Monday – is puzzling until his record of objecting to umpiring decisions both in England and America is recalled. He was a bluff, dominant figure, quite unlike his brother Ned who prepared the Sydney pitch, a jolly man full of chuckles who enjoyed taking touring English cricketers fishing on Sydney Harbour. The personality clash between Lord Harris and Dave Gregory cost Sydney a Test match, for his Lordship refused to keep his team in Sydney for the return match against the Combined XI and instead took them back to Melbourne for another match against Victoria.

A famous quartet watching a match in Melbourne after their return from England in 1878 (L to R): Frank Allan, Tom Horan, Jack Blackham and Harry Boyle. (Jack Pollard Collection)

The Sydney match wound up with England winners by an innings and 41 runs after they dismissed New South Wales for 49 runs, but amid all the publicity about the Saturday riot, Ulyett's feat in taking four wickets with successive balls was sadly overlooked. Rioters were fined £2, plus 25 shillings costs, in the Sydney Police Court, where Richard Driver revealed that a Victorian bookmaker had been banned for life from the SCG.

The riot deprived Dave Gregory of a fitting farewell in his last first-class match. His record as Australia's first cricket captain deserved better. He was a man's man who never wore dentures or glasses, played the flute, and prided himself on his posture and the condition of his beard, a man who kept in step with companions on long bush walks. His first wife, Mary Ann Hutchings, died in 1890 after providing him with 13 children. Two years later he married Lillis Leslie MacMillan, who bore him three more.

The fame that began when Dave and his brothers Charles and Ned defeated the crack Victorians Tom Wills, John Conway and Sam Cosstick by famous runs in a renowned match at the Albert Ground in April, 1871, never inflated Dave. He remained unruffled, just as he had when the three Gregorys prevailed over the Victorians for a stake of £100 before 5000 spectators, scoring 24 and 30 against 21 and 28. Dave Gregory's three Tests yielded 60 runs at 20.0 and he did not bowl. In 41 first-class matches, he made 889 runs at 14.57 and took 29 wickets at 19.06.

The *Bulletin* magazine said the tour by Lord Harris's team lost £6000 for the Melbourne Cricket Club, largely because their wine bill exceeded that sum. At the team's farewell dinner in Melbourne Lord Harris was full of praise for his hosts, and said he considered Australia's bowling superior to England's, with the batting even.

When he arrived home, he said that within a few years the best Australian side would match England's best, but deplored the betting on Australian cricket, and scoffed at the notion that England's professional umpires were dishonest or inferior to Australia's amateur umpires. The fledgling New South Wales Cricket Association were so angered at this they sent a letter to the London *Daily Telegraph*, which said the NSWCA and other Australian bodies strongly disapproved of betting at cricket matches and stressed that the Sydney press and public had condemned the demonstrators:

Lord Harris, by what we feel to be a most ungenerous suppression of these facts, has led the British public to believe that in New South Wales 'a party of gentlemen travelling through the colonies for the purpose of playing a few friendly games of cricket should have been insulted and subjected to indignities', while the press and inhabitants of Sydney neither showed surprise, indignation nor regret.

We cannot let a libel so unfounded as this pass without challenge. The country upon which such a reproach could be fastened would be unworthy of a place among civilised communities, and the imputation is especially odious to Australians.

The letter added that the betting men to whom Lord Harris referred were not members of the New South Wales Cricket Association, but the demonstration did remind the association of the problems associated with using grounds it did not own. The association shared its Sydney ground with sports such as professional footrunning and cycling, which encouraged betting and often had huge sums riding on their results. Australian magazines had for years published the rules for cricket gambling, which in England went back as far as 1730, when the Prince of Wales played cricket for big side-bets. Lord Frederick Beauclerk boasted he annually earned £600 betting on cricket.

The Melbourne Cricket Club could confidently sponsor Australian tours by English teams because, right from the first day international cricket was staged at the club's ground, large crowds attended. But the betting fraternity had to be accommodated at the Sydney Association Ground – later to become the SCG – because the ground was seldom full and every single spectator was valuable to the association.

Two years of international competition on level terms had helped create a fast-growing pool of talent in the Australian colonies. The retirements of Dave Gregory, Charles Bannerman, Tom Horan and George Bailey were hardly felt at all. Bannerman wanted to concentrate on his new job as the £150-a-year coach at the Melbourne Cricket Club, Horan sought to pursue his career in journalism, and Bailey was keen to develop his job in banking. Tom Garrett dropped out temporarily to complete his legal studies and graduate as a solicitor.

Despite the animosity they knew existed at Lord's because of the rough treatment of Lord Harris's players in the Sydney riot, the leading players decided to press ahead with a second Australian tour of England in 1880. The colonial associations supported this tour and Harry Boyle, as chief selector and provisional captain of the tourists, was able to make a thorough assessment of form. Invited players subscribed to a new tour fund and appointed George

The team that represented Australia in the only Test of the 1880 English tour (L to R): back, F.R. Spofforth, T.U. Groube, W.A. Giles (Assistant manager), G.E. Palmer, G. Alexander (Manager); centre, H.E. Boyle, G.J. Bonnor, W.H. Moule, W.L. Murdoch (Captain), J. Slight, A.C. Bannerman; front, J.M. Blackham, P.S. McDonnell, A.H. Jarvis. (MCG Museum)

Alexander, a dashing batsman, handy change bowler and a hard-working fieldsman from the Melbourne club, as player-manager. Alexander had distinguished himself while the first Australian team was away by scoring 75 and taking 5 for 64 in a display that enabled Victoria to defeat New South Wales in Melbourne.

The second Australian team included five players from the first: Murdoch, Boyle, Spofforth, Blackham and Alick Bannerman. Newcomers included burly Arthur ('Affie') Jarvis, at 19 the first South Australian chosen for Australia, who kept wicket so could provide relief for Blackham and had a splendid record as a forceful batsman, 'Joey' Palmer, who had demoralised Lord Harris's side in Melbourne with his off-breaks, and Percy McDonnell, George Bonnor, Tom Groube, Harry Moule and James Slight.

McDonnell was born in the London suburb of Kensington but was taken to Melbourne by his parents at the age of three. He was educated at St Patrick's Jesuit College in Melbourne, where he recorded some remarkable scoring feats, showing little fear of bowlers right from his start in junior teams. He went into the Victorian team at the age of 17, failing to score in each innings against New South Wales. He was only 19 when chosen to tour England for the first time.

Bonnor was a bearded giant from the western New South Wales town of Bathurst, 6 ft 6 in (1.98 metres) tall, and 16 stone (107 kg), known as 'The Colonial Hercules' and 'The Australian Giant'. He made some of the longest hits in the history of cricket but despite the enormous power he could impart to the ball when he connected, preferred to be known as a scientific batsman with a copybook array of strokes.

In the warm-up matches before they left Australia, Will Murdoch quickly emerged as the tourists' main batting hope. After his graduation from Sydney University, he followed his brother Gilbert into law and, free from examinations, developed into a superb right-hand batsman who could combine artistry with power. The better the bowling the more he enjoyed batting, and he became one of the finest exponents of the 'dog shot', in which he lifted his front pad and glanced the ball away before it reached his rear pad.

Murdoch's intelligence and happy nature had a marked effect on his team-mates from the day they boarded the *Garonne* in March, 1880, and set sail for England via the Suez Canal. Boyle's planning had them fitted out with blue and white blazers that looked like artists' smocks and they were called on for daily callisthenics. The manner in which Murdoch charmed the ladies during dances on board was magical to a country-bred lad like Bonnor. Before they cleared the Suez Canal, the team had a meeting at which they voted to depose Boyle as captain and replace him with Murdoch. They did this in the knowledge that Murdoch's bonhomie was more likely to win them friends in England than Boyle's rustic, taciturn approach. Alexander had been warned before the voyage began that Lord Harris would refuse to meet them and would not help in securing matches.

The Australians arrived on 13 May, 1880, only to be told that all the leading counties had already filled their fixture lists. Nobody had expected them. Lord Harris sent a message denouncing the lack of prior consultation but offered to try and organise matches in London if the Australians would make a declaration that they were touring for pleasure and would only accept expenses. Murdoch refused to give such an undertaking.

Will Murdoch playing his famous 'dog shot', in which he lifted his leg to glance the ball.

Forced to advertise for matches, the Australians were confined to the north of England and the Midlands, mainly taking on local teams against the odds. They did not get a single match at Lord's. They were not really tested by any of the counties and even their two matches against Yorkshire were not approved by the county committee. Manager Alexander wrote to the *Sporting Life* news- paper challenging both the Gentlemen and the Players to matches with all profits to go to the Cricketers' Fund, for destitute or injured players. The challenge met with no response despite an article in the magazine *London Society* reminding English professionals of the number of their colleagues who had returned from Australian tours with hundreds of pounds to their credit.

Denied access to Lord's, the Australians held their first practice on Mitcham Green, where Bonnor demonstrated his amazing hitting powers by striking a ball 147 yards 2 feet (135 metres). James Southerton, who had played in the first of all Tests in Melbourne, owned a Mitcham pub, and was so bemused by Bonnor's blow he went out and carefully measured the distance. Bonnor said he did not regard the hit as one of his longest.

Restricted to only nine first-class matches, in a programme that eventually included 26 games against the odds, the Australians needed all Murdoch's good humour to suppress the idea of packing up and going home. The damage the Sydney riot had done to their reputations as gentlemen was demonstrated almost daily. They were left in no doubt that county secretaries were snubbing them when

George Bonnor, who hit some of the longest sixes ever seen on English grounds. He made five tours of England. (MCG Museum)

counties who claimed their fixture lists were closed provided matches for a Canadian team that arrived weeks after them.

At a conference with Murdoch and Alexander, W.G. Grace and Surrey secretary C.W. Alcock, Lord Harris said Lord's was fully booked for the entire summer and all the best amateurs were scattered all over the country. When Alcock offered The Oval for an Australia v. England match it was agreed to play it on dates originally set aside for Australia to play Sussex.

Just before the international match Australia played an England XI at Scarborough. Towards the end of Australia's first innings, a fast right-hand bowler named Joseph Frank came on and to the Australians' amazement was not no-balled although he threw every delivery. Murdoch protested to the umpire, who told him to mind his own business. In Australia's second innings, Alick Bannerman drew away from the crease after one delivery from Frank. Fieldsmen called to Frank to bowl down the stumps, which he did. Murdoch again protested about Frank throwing but play proceeded after the umpire ruled Bannerman not out. Later in the Australian innings Frank broke Spofforth's finger with another obvious throw.

The injury to Spofforth forced Australia to include Alexander in the team for the international match, which became recognised as the first Test played in England. All three Graces played for England, the first instance of three brothers appearing in the same Test. Before play began W.G. and Murdoch had a bet for a sovereign on who would top-score. London cricket fans paid the Australians a big tribute by crowding into The Oval in droves on the first day, 6 September 1880, and 20,814 spectators were present to watch Boyle bowl the first ball to W.G. Among the seven Australian newcomers to international cricket were two 19-year-olds, Palmer and McDonnell.

On a perfect pitch Palmer and Boyle failed to provoke a false stroke from the Grace brothers, W.G. and E.M., and it was from Alick Bannerman, with his medium-paced right-hand round-armers, that E.M. Grace hit a catch to Alexander. At lunch England were 1 for 167, with W.G. 82, and he reached his century soon after the interval. This set up a big England total. W.G. put on 120 with 'Bunny' Lucas before he was out for 152, and by the end of the first day England were 8 for 410.

That night a drizzling rain fell on the ground. Play began only five minutes late at 11.05 a.m. but Australia were batting by 11.40 and were immediately in difficulty on the wet pitch against Morley and Steel. At lunch Australia were 9 for 126 and destined to follow on. Although Boyle hit out bravely for 36 not out, the innings finished at 149, leaving Australia with a 271-run deficit.

Bonnor's dismissal in this innings remained the talk of English cricket for generations. Bonnor skied a ball from Alfred Shaw at which he had a lash so high the batsmen had turned for their third run before G.F. Grace caught it, a wonderful piece of judgement by a fieldsman who made a duck in each innings. A Mr Frederick Gale chained the distance of Bonnor's hit with two of The Oval ground staff and measured it at 115 yards. When team-mates sympathised with Bonnor in the Australian dressing-room, he said: 'Hard luck, nothing. I should have hit the perisher.'

The Australians made an appalling start in their second innings, losing Boyle, who had been sent in to protect the leading batsmen while the pitch dried, run out with the score on eight. Bannerman and Groube quickly followed and at 3 for 14 Australia's position appeared hopeless. McDonnell joined Blackham and hit with exciting freedom until the total reached 97 and McDonnell left for 43. At stumps Australia were 6 for 170, still 101 runs behind, and Murdoch, who had batted for two and a half hours, was 79 not out.

On the third morning Bonnor's stand with Murdoch looked highly promising, but after adding 38 runs for the seventh wicket they were parted when Bonnor took an enormous swish at a straight delivery from A.G. Steel and was bowled for 16. At 8 for 187 Alexander joined Murdoch in a partnership worth 52, during which Murdoch reached his century. When Alexander left for 33, the Melbourne barrister Harry Moule joined Murdoch in preventing an innings defeat. Moule made 34 in a last-wicket stand worth 88, leaving Murdoch unbeaten on 153 and just one run ahead of W.G.'s first innings of 152. Murdoch wore the sovereign W.G. gave him for winning their bet on his watch chain for the rest of his life.

Faced with the apparent formality of scoring 57 runs to win, England's batsmen were soon in disarray against inspired bowling from Boyle and Palmer. G.F. Grace was out for a 'pair', Lucas was caught behind, Lyttelton was bowled, Barnes caught at mid-on, and E.M. Grace bowled second ball. At 5 for 31, the great W.G. came through the gate and strode imperiously to the crease. His opening bowlers spent, and without Spofforth, Murdoch was forced to watch the famous batsman calmly pick up the runs needed for a five-wicket English victory.

Murdoch and his great friend Dr W.G. Grace photographed at Sheffield Park after Murdoch settled in England. (MCG Library)

With this defeat the Australians justly felt aggrieved over the absence of Spofforth, but their brave showing in the international earned them invitations to play six further matches in the last month of their tour.

Murdoch's 153 not out in the international match was the only century of Australia's tour and allowed him to head the first-class averages with 465 runs at 25.83. Percy McDonnell was next with 418 runs at 23.22. Joey Palmer easily headed Australia's wicket-takers with 80 first-class wickets at 11.12. Spofforth took 46 wickets in only five matches at 8.60, Boyle 39 wickets at 15.79. Blackham's wicket-keeping once again proved superior to anything England could match and by the end of the tour he attracted the curious criticism from English clergymen that he had eliminated the need for their normal fielding position in village matches, long stop, behind the 'keeper on the boundary.

Bonnor was the personality English crowds loved, a golden-haired Adonis of vast proportions, sensitive enough to bring tears to his own eyes when he sang Irish ballads. W.G. called Bonnor 'a model of physical beauty', and in every match in which he encountered Bonnor took great joy in baiting him to have a barndoor swing at the ball. Bonnor would keep his head down, playing orthodox cricket for several overs, but eventually W.G.'s taunts would get to him and he would open those vast shoulders. He hit 26 sixes on the tour, many of them the longest ever seen on the grounds concerned, and there was a strong feeling in the Australian side that he could forsake all attempts at refined, disciplined batting and hit out from the moment he took guard. There was no denying that his prodigious hitting could completely demoralise an attack.

Bonnor pleaded with Murdoch to put him earlier than no. 7 but Murdoch took a fiendish delight in saying: 'What's the good of putting you in early – you're only a plodder.'

The Australians enjoyed telling the story of George Bonnor walking down the street of his native Bathurst with his family on one of his rare visits home. Locals watched the mountains of flesh that represented the Bonnor family coming towards them until somebody spotted George and asked: 'Who's that little bloke with the Bonnors?' Asked to name the best batsmen in the world, George Bonnor considered the question carefully. 'W.G. must be first and Murdoch second,' he replied. 'After that I would prefer not to comment.'

Bonnor watched in disbelief when Charles Inglis Thornton,

regarded as the greatest hitter of all time with blows of 152 yards, 162 yards and 168 yards to his credit, batted against the Australians. 'Call yourself a hitter,' said Bonnor. 'My sister could hit the ball further than you!' Thornton took this slur on his reputation calmly. 'You should bring her over to England and marry her off to Louis Hall [the famous Yorkshire stonewaller],' said Thornton. 'You could then expect them to produce the perfect batsman of the future.'

The catch made by G.F. Grace to dismiss Bonnor in the international match at The Oval in 1880 proved to be George Grace's last great feat. He caught a cold sleeping on a damp bed a few days later, developed pneumonia, and died within a few days. He had scored 6906 first-class runs but his best years were thought to be all ahead of him, and he was expected to multiply his total of eight first-class centuries quickly.

Harry Boyle, round-arm bowler responsible for many Australian victories, also invented the silly mid-on fielding position, originally called 'Boyle's mid-on'. (SCG Archives)

All the four matches Australia lost on that 1880 tour were played while Spofforth was recovering from his broken finger. They won 21 matches and had 12 draws in addition to the four defeats. They were so badly hit by injuries they had to use countrymen W.A. Giles and J. Macdonald in some matches. Although they lost the match that counted most, they increased the public's interest in big matches, and fully deserved the £1100 they received as their share of the Test receipts. They also succeeded in healing wounds that lingered after the infamous Sydney riot. At their farewell dinner at the Mansion House before London's Lord Mayor, Murdoch paid special tribute to Lord Harris's generosity and to the late G.F. Grace.

Between them three Australian bowlers dismissed 909 of the 967 batsmen faced in England. Despite his injury Spofforth did well enough on the warm-up tour in Australia and in the ten matches the team played on the way home to finish with 763 wickets from all games at a cost of only 5.49 each, with 391 of his wickets falling in England. Boyle took 411 wickets on the tour, and Palmer 533. In the pre-tour matches in New Zealand they won six, drew three and lost one match. Their sole loss was to Twenty-Two of Wanganui, and they avenged their defeat three years earlier by Canterbury. Murdoch won a bet that he would score more runs than the entire Canterbury team.

Bannerman's absence from the 1880 tour after his splendid trip in 1878 puzzled Englishmen, but not Australians. His old teammate W.H. Cooper said: 'Charlie's liking for drinking and gambling was his downfall, a fate that has befallen many cricketers.'

CHAPTER FIVE

AN ENGLISH GAMBLE

Alfred Shaw, who bowled the first ball in Test cricket in the 1877 Melbourne match and in a career that lasted 40 years never bowled a single wide. He took 100 wickets in an English season nine times.
(MCC Library)

Three hard-nosed English professional cricketers paid for the sixth England team's tour of Australia in the summer of 1881–82. They studied the Australian custom of team members putting up funds to pay for fares and splitting profits on return, and decided instead to gamble on a tour they sponsored themselves. All three had had first-hand experience of overseas touring.

They were an oddly assorted threesome: James Lillywhite, junior, who had gone with W.G. Grace to Australia in 1873–74 and sponsored his own Australian tour in 1876–77, but in his fortieth year was too old to do anything on tour except 'umpire, hit a few fourers and bowl a few slow-medium left-arm overs'; Alfred Shaw, right-arm medium-pace bowler of remarkable accuracy who had made two tours of America and been a member of Lillywhite's team to Australia five years earlier; and Arthur Shrewsbury, England's principal professional batsman, who had been to America in the team led by Richard Daft in 1879.

Shaw and Shrewsbury had engineered a strike by Notts players for more pay from the match against Australia in Nottingham in 1880, which ended when the Notts secretary 'Hellfire' Jack Holden was forced to increase the home professionals' fees from £6 to £20. While the row over fees progressed, Shaw, Lillywhite and Shrewsbury were finalising selections for their Australian tour. They had appointed John Conway as their advance agent and on the basis of the matches he had booked offered their players £225 each to tour.

Conway booked them anywhere he believed a profit was possible, and the Englishmen found themselves at Maitland, Newcastle, Orange, Bathurst, Parramatta, Cootamundra, Windsor, Stanmore, Dunolly and Ballarat as well as playing major matches in Sydney,

Melbourne and Adelaide. With four matches in America and eight in New Zealand added, it made for an arduous trip.

The nine players selected to join the three sponsors on the tour were G. Ulyett, W. Bates, T. Emmett, E. Peate from Yorkshire, R. Pilling and R. Barlow from Lancashire, W.H. Scotton and J. Selby from Notts, and the nomadic Billy Midwinter, who in 1880 had made 137 not out for Lord's ground staff against Leicestershire. Shrewsbury suffered a severe bout of bronchitis just before the team sailed and was doubtful for a time, but ten days after the team left for America he sailed direct to Australia via Suez.

George Ulyett, known to fellow cricketers as 'Happy Jack' because of his cheery Yorkshire wit, toured Australia five times. (MCG Museum)

Receipts in America were so disappointing Shaw had problems paying for the team's passage to Australia, but they moved through the first twelve matches in Australia with encouraging results. In the thirteenth match, against Victoria in Melbourne, 20,000 attended the second day. Although England won a match that featured heavy betting among spectators, there were accusations that two English players had been paid £100 each to throw the match. It was alleged that one had intentionally dropped a catch and that Midwinter had been beaten up because he refused to join the conspiracy. Shaw held an inquiry into the charges but found they were unsupported.

Midwinter played for England in all four Tests that summer. England drew the First and Fourth Tests, and Australia won the Second and Third to take a surprise 2–0 win from a series in which she introduced six new Test players: William Cooper, George Giffen, Edwin Evans, Hugh Massie, George Coulthard and Sam Jones. Horan and Giffen recorded Australia's first century partnership in Tests, 107 for the fifth wicket in the First Test, Horan going on to 124 in four hours. Cooper's leg-breaks accounted for nine wickets in the First Test, Palmer's off-breaks 20 wickets in the Second and Third Tests, but the most memorable feat of the season was Percy McDonnell's 147 in the Fourth Test, when he and Alick Bannerman put on 199 in a total of 260.

While the Englishmen were away for their seven matches in New Zealand between the First and Second Tests, Billy Murdoch became the first Australian to score more than 300 runs in a first-class match by batting for two days to 321 against Victoria in Sydney. He gave only one chance, at 120, and hit 38 fours, nine threes, 41 twos and 60 singles off ten Victorian bowlers. His score remained the highest in Sydney until the 1920s, when Bradman made 340 not out against Victoria at the age of 20, and 452 not out against Queensland at 21.

The sixth English team to tour Australia won eight of their 14 matches against the odds, lost three and drew three. Ulyett was the best of the English batsmen, with 1424 runs at 33.11, and Peate the best bowler with 264 wickets at 5.84. Pilling kept wicket economically without matching Blackham's standards.

The tour enhanced the reputation of Shrewsbury, the Geoffrey Boycott of the 1880s, who proved a model of efficiency on wet or damaged wickets. The trip also cured a long-standing problem he had had over never being able to sleep soundly away from his home in Nottingham. He returned to England a great player, improved by international competition just as Australia's Murdoch had been.

The amazing Midwinter not only completed the tour for England, taking useful wickets and scoring handy runs, but he rejoined Victoria for inter-colonial matches in 1882–83! He told the *Sydney Mail* he objected to being called an Anglo-Australian and insisted that he was Australian to the core, but the paper would have none of it. 'Are we to endure another season of vagueness from this very slippery cricketer?' the paper asked.

George Giffen, champion all-rounder who first won fame with the third Australian team to tour England in 1882. He returned for further tours in 1884, 1886 and 1893. (Adelaide Advertiser)

The rise of Jarvis and Giffen should have alerted Victorian selectors not to take South Australian cricket lightly but they erred badly in sending an inferior side to play South Australia in Adelaide in March, 1882. Norwood bowler Jack Quilty hit the stumps six times, taking 9 for 55 in the match. Jack Noel's 65 in their second innings helped South Australia to a 31-run win. The innings started unsuccessful moves to have Noel included in the third Australian team to tour England in 1882, but in 27 innings for the colony it proved to be Noel's best score. South Australians had to be content with George Giffen as their sole representative in the touring team.

Giffen, born in Adelaide, started his career with Norwood club but switched to West Adelaide. His job as a postman kept him out of doors and he matured into a tough, nuggety, wide-shouldered figure who seldom carried an excess gram of flesh. He turned his off-breaks out of a vast fist, and performed with excessive enthusiasm whether bowling, fielding or batting. An observant, intelligent cricketer, he developed on classical lines into one of the great all-rounders.

Giffen's first trip to England was in an Australian side some rate the finest ever sent there and certainly the outstanding Australian line-up of the nineteenth century. The rustic, sometimes primitive batting techniques of other Australian teams disappeared in a team that worked skilfully for their runs. In Alick Bannerman they had a stonewalling opener on whom to base long innings, with hitters Massie, McDonnell and Bonnor to follow, and the cultivated Murdoch ready to steady an innings. Horan and Sam Jones provided ideal middle-order aggression before opposing bowlers reached the tail. The bowling included four of the most consistent wicket-takers of all time: Boyle, Spofforth, Palmer and Garrett. They were disciplined, athletic and alert to every signal from the captain Murdoch or their matchless 'keeper, Blackham. Jarvis was unlucky to be left behind when it was decided to use Murdoch as Blackham's deputy.

Arthur Jarvis, who served as Jack Blackham's understudy for many years, was rated the second great Australian wicket-keeper. After Blackham retired he kept with distinction against Stoddart's English team. (MCC Library)

By the 1880s most bush towns boasted of their pitches, and cricket was described as the national game. There were some excellent displays in club cricket. In the 1881–82 season Sam Morris, a coloured batsman born in Hobart of West Indian migrants lured by the gold rushes, scored 280 for Richmond against St Kilda in Melbourne. In Adelaide, George Giffen made 158 at better than a run a minute for Norwood against the Kent club. In Sydney Alick Bannerman made 111 and 104 not out for Carlton against the Albert club. For all cricketers, however, the great prize was a trip to England. Stricken by sunstroke during the last Test against Shaw's English team in Melbourne, Percy McDonnell made sure he would not miss the 1882 trip by being carried aboard the *Assam*.

Unlike cricketers in Australian teams a century later who went by air in two days, the players enjoyed a long, relaxing voyage to England. It was enlivened by receptions in their honour in Melbourne and Adelaide, a day's spectacular fishing during refuelling in King George Sound, WA, where they filled eight buckets with fish (Boyle winning the sweep for the best catch with five dozen), followed by nightly concerts and fancy-dress shows as they cruised to Ceylon and on through the Suez Canal. Blackham sang 'Genevieve' with a tenderness that had tears streaming down Bonnor's face, following up with 'See My Grave's Kept Green'. Murdoch and manager Beal, the youngest-ever to hold the job at 27, were Bones and Tambo in an hilarious black-and-white-minstrel show and, fittingly, Spofforth appeared as Mephistopheles on fancy-dress nights. The only concern was that McDonnell remained in a weak condition that puzzled the ship's doctors.

Bonnor kept everyone amused with his appearances as a Roman soldier and he won useful cash for himself by betting a fellow

Australia's 1882 tourists in England, the first to defeat an English team in England. This victory at The Oval created the Ashes legend. (MCG Museum)

passenger he could throw a cricket ball 100 yards or more on the first day the *Assam* arrived in England. The wager was settled at Raglan Barracks, Devonport, when Bonnor made a throw of 104 yards. Bonnor was not impressed as he had throws of 120 yards and 131 yards to his credit in Australia.

In their opening match Massie, the last man chosen, gave the Australians a wonderful start by scoring 206 in three hours, savaging a highly rated Oxford University attack. The weight of his driving and cutting spreadeagled fieldsmen in a display that began with the first ball. His second century came while only 12 runs were scored by team-mates at the other end, after making his first hundred by lunch in a total of 145. This innings, ranked among the finest ever played at the Christ Church ground, set up an Australian win by nine wickets.

Murdoch surpassed even that wonderful innings by scoring 286 not out in the second match against Sussex at Brighton, where Australia made 643, the highest total to that time in a first-class match. Australia won by an innings and 355 runs, Palmer chiming in with a hat-trick. No touring team could have hoped for a more satisfying start.

They were in danger in the next match against the Orleans club at Twickenham after being caught on a rain-soaked pitch replying to Orleans' first innings of 271. Out for 75 and forced to follow on they were 9 for 240 when time ran out, with Murdoch on 107 not out after a lovely innings. Bonnor made one hit clean out of the ground and over several houses for six but W.G. Grace bowled him next ball.

After ten weeks without defeat the Australians suffered their first loss against Cambridge University Past and Present when the Studd brothers, J.E.K., C.T., and G.B., scored 297 of the 393 runs Cambridge made in the match. Charles Thomas Studd made 118 in the first innings and took eight wickets in a match Cambridge won by six wickets. Horan blamed Murdoch for not bowling Giffen earlier in the Cambridge first innings and two bad decisions by umpire Heathfield Stephenson. R.C. Ramsay, who spent most of his life farming in Queensland, took seven Australian wickets in their second innings. Bonnor made 66 out of the total 79 in half an hour and hit the ball right out of the large Portsmouth ground four times.

Undeterred by this defeat the Australians then had a sequence of 14 wins in 19 matches. They won three of their five matches against Yorkshire – the other two were drawn – and had wins over fancied sides such as Lancashire, Middlesex, Gloucestershire and the Gentlemen. Their only setback came when Blackham was injured against Middlesex and byes reached 29, top score in the Middlesex total of 104. Horan made centuries against Gloucestershire and a United XI.

Bonnor kept delighting crowds by hitting massive sixes. At The Oval against the Gentlemen he made 74 and three of his ten fours cleared the boundary. At the time only hits right out of the ground counted six and those that went into the crowd like this brought only four runs. Australia reached 334 with Bonnor cursing his ill luck. Then a brilliant bowling effort from Giffen forced the Gentlemen to follow on. Thirteen of Giffen's 31 overs were maidens and after clean bowling W.G. Grace, W.W. Read, C.T. Studd and E.F.S. Tylecote, he finished with 8 for 49. Sam Jones clinched a great triumph for the Australians by holding a spectacular catch on the long-on boundary high in his left hand. The margin of an innings and one run against such strong opposition and their oustanding record throughout the tour took the Australians back to The Oval at the end of August for the sole international match of the tour in confident mood.

Australian hopes soared when England's selectors – Lord Harris, Frederick Burbidge and the Walker brothers Isaac and Vyell – omitted Arthur Shrewsbury. Most of the Australians also felt Lord Harris should have been England's captain instead of 'Monkey' Hornby, who had led too many sides beaten by Australia and always had problems facing Spofforth.

Murdoch won the toss, but Australia quickly lost this advantage when Ulyett uprooted Massie's leg stump before a capacity crowd with the third ball of his second over. Encouraged by the ecstatic applause this brought, England fielded brilliantly and there were some superb saves. At 1 for 20 England's bowlers produced 20 successive maidens. At 6 for 30, Blackham and Garrett put on 18, but none of the Australians handled the left-arm bowling of Peate and Barlow with any confidence and after 80 overs Australia were all out for 63. Barlow had 5 for 19 from 36 overs but the Australians offered no excuses for their ineptitude against him on a pitch soaked by two days of steady rain. Spofforth sustained his hostility for 36.3 overs and was rewarded with 7 for 41 in the England innings of 101, a lead of 38.

Next morning heavy rain fell as the Australians travelled to the

Hugh Hammon Massie, aggressive opening batsman whose 55 out of 66 scored while he was at the crease played a vital part in Australia's victory in the Ashes Test at The Oval. (Jack Pollard Collection)

71

The Bannerman brothers, Alick, left, and Charles. Faced with a crisis in which one of them had to be run out, Charles deliberately ran out Alick, saying he was more valuable to Australia.
(Mitchell Library, *Sydney*)

ground. Just after noon the umpires decided the pitch was fit to play, but with sawdust filling the bowlers' footmarks and a soft, slippery ball in their hands, conditions were far from ideal, with fieldsmen slithering about in the mud. The Australians realised that this period in which the pitch dried out gave them the chance to swing the match. Bannerman defended grimly while Massie went after the bowling. They wiped off the deficit and put Australia in front.

Massie, in a wonderful show of attacking cricket, reached 50 out of 61 in only 45 minutes before the pitch began to take spin. Steel bowled Massie around his leg for 55 with the score on 66. Hornby repeatedly changed the bowling to prevent the Australians settling and quickly dismissed Bannerman, Horan, Bonnor and Giffen before a slight shower removed the spite from the pitch and allowed Murdoch to add invaluable runs.

Joined by Sam Jones after Blackham had become Peate's third victim, Murdoch edged the ball to leg. The Australians took a single. Jones wandered out of his crease, Lyttelton flicked the ball to W.G., who whipped off the bails and appealed for a run out. Jones later said he was 'gardening' – patting down a bump in the pitch – when W.G. appealed but umpire Thoms gave Jones out. The Australians later contended that they distinctly heard Thoms say: 'As you claim it, Sir, Out!' Murdoch immediately challenged the decision but Thoms refused to change it. There was no doubt in the Australian dressing-room about W.G.'s lack of ethics in the dismissal, however, and the players were still simmering with disapproval when the innings ended on 122, leaving England only 85 to win.

Bell's Life commented: 'It was strict cricket, but it was taking advantage of a young player's thoughtlessness.' The incident fired up the Australian team. George Giffen described in his book *With Bat and Ball* how Spofforth strode up and down the Australian dressing-room in the ten minutes between innings like a caged lion, declaring 'this thing can be done', until he had the Australians ready to die to right the injustice that had been done as they filed down the pavilion steps.

On a chilly autumn afternoon Hornby decided to open the last innings himself with Grace, but at 15 Spofforth removed Hornby's stumps with a vicious break-back. Barlow followed, only to meet the same fate with the very first ball. At 2 for 15 the tenseness of the struggle gripped the crowd, who remained grimly silent for the next half-hour as Grace and Ulyett put on 36 runs. Then with only

34 runs needed and eight fine batsmen left to get them, the England team lost their nerve.

At 51, Ulyett played for Spofforth's break-back but the ball remained straight, nicking the edge of Ulyett's bat for Blackham to take the catch. Two runs later Grace failed to get to the pitch of the ball as he tried to drive Boyle and hit a catch to Bannerman at mid-off. Lyttelton hit a splendid four immediately he joined Lucas and the score crept to 50 as the struggle for the match intensified. Boyle and Spofforth bowled like men inspired as maiden followed maiden until 12 had been bowled in succession. Then Spofforth whispered to Murdoch and Bannerman deliberately misfielded a shot from Lyttelton which took him to the end facing Spofforth. Four more maidens followed before a deadly break-back scattered Lyttelton's stumps. The sound of the ball smacking into Blackham's gloves as he stood right up on the stumps subdued the crowd.

Sam Jones, whose run out by W.G. Grace in the Ashes Test at The Oval fired Australia's desire to win. (MCC Library)

With 20,000 spectators concentrating on every ball, not one Australian fumbled or lost confidence, fielding safely as Boyle and Spofforth continued to bowl with laser-beam accuracy. Maurice Read, who had made a promising 19 not out in the first innings, was completely beaten by Spofforth's second ball and departed, his stumps awry. England was 6 for 70 with 15 runs still needed, and then Spofforth bowled Steel for a duck.

England's hopes now rested with 'Bunny' Lucas, Barnes, one of the best professionals of the period, and Studd, who had twice made a century against Australia. Five runs were added before Lucas played on against Spofforth, leaving England at 8 for 75, still ten short of their target. Studd, who according to 'Buns' Thornton had been walking round the pavilion with a blanket over his head, went to the crease, but his nerves were never tested as he did not have to face a ball.

Boyle made the first ball of his twentieth over pop up suddenly and Barnes was caught by Murdoch at point off his glove. England 9 for 75. Peate then decided to settle the issue and took two from a risky shot to leg off Spofforth's thirty-seventh over. The second ball almost bowled him and undeterred he took a mighty flail at the next, only to be bowled. Australia had won by seven runs and England had sustained her first defeat at home when at full strength.

Horan later wrote that in the desperate excitement of the last half-hour a spectator died from a heart attack and several others fainted. One man gnawed off part of his umbrella handle and one

Edmund Peate, who opened the bowling for England in the Ashes Test of 1882, and was last man out as Spofforth clinched Australia's victory by seven runs. (MCC Library)

of the scorers was so unsteady he wrote 'Geese' instead of 'Peate' on the scoresheet. The crowd greeted the end in stunned silence and then let out a huge roar, hundreds breaking over the fence in a wild rush to get close to the players who had achieved this incredible victory. Spofforth was carried shoulder-high to the pavilion, with Studd, who had not faced a ball, trudging forlornly behind. In the dressing-room Spofforth danced and jigged. He had taken 14 wickets for 90 runs in the match, bowled ten maidens in his last 11 overs, and taken four wickets for two runs from his final seven deliveries. His figures were not bettered by an Australian at Lord's until Bob Massie took 16 for 137 in 1972.

When he was asked why he did not give a proven strokemaker like Studd the strike Peate said: 'Mr Studd was so nervous I did not feel I could trust him to score a single run.' The Surrey secretary C.W. Alcock said that in the crisis English batsmen noted for their calmness had shivered as if from cold. Boyle was highly praised by players on both sides for the support he gave Spofforth. He conceded only 19 runs in his 20 overs, 11 of them maidens, and took three vital wickets, never allowing the English batsmen any relief when they got through a Spofforth over.

Murdoch's skilful application of pressure, Blackham's magnificent wicket-keeping, the brilliance of Alick Bannerman's fielding close to the batsmen and the hitting by Massie that brought the runs Australia's bowlers needed, all attracted lavish praise. But it was Spofforth who made it all possible on a pitch that ideally suited him. The subtlety of his bowling confused many onlookers, some of whom claimed he bowled at express pace, others that he was mostly a medium-pacer. *Punch* paid tribute to him in these lines:

> Well done, Cornstalks, whipt us
> > Fair and square.
> Was it luck that tripped us?
> > Was it scare?
> Kangaroo land's 'Demon' or our own
> > Want of devil, coolness, nerve, backbone.

Bell's Life said, 'Though England for the first time had to lower her colours to Australia at home, we were beaten by a magnificent eleven, before whose prowess it was no disgrace to lose.' The *Sporting Times* published a mock obituary five days after Australia's triumph, written by Reginald Brooks, son of the editor of *Punch*, which began the legend of 'The Ashes'.

> In Affectionate Remembrance
> of
> ENGLISH CRICKET
> which died at The Oval
> on
> 29th August, 1882
> Deeply lamented by a large circle of
> Sorrowing Friends and Acquaintances
> R.I.P.
> N.B. – The body will be cremated and the
> Ashes taken to Australia.

Tom Garrett, one of only three bowlers used by Australia's captain Billy Murdoch, in the 1882 win at The Oval against England. (Jack Pollard Collection)

Nothing on the rest of the Australians' tour could match the excitement of The Oval Test, and the players went through eight matches with a strong sense of anti-climax, coupled with regret that there were not two or even four Tests in the series. Bonnor provided one of the tour highspots with a devastating show of hitting against I Zingari at Scarborough, scoring 122 not out in 105 minutes, with 16 fours and four enormous sixes.

Sydney Pardon wrote in *Wisden* that W.G. Grace, then in his thirty-fifth year, had planned to retire to his medical practice at the end of that summer, but that the Australians defeat of England had revived his ambitions as a cricketer. W.G.'s doctorate was never a courtesy title as some cynics suggested. He completed his studies despite a dislike for scholarship and each winter in England carried through the duties of a country doctor. He hired a locum to run his practice in the cricket season.

Australia's success was completed in conditions foreign to most of them. Only around a dozen of their 38 matches were played on hard or firm pitches, and most were badly upset by rain in a summer which cost them seven whole days through bad weather. They still won 23 matches, drew 11, and lost only four despite the disruption to their bowling caused by the loss of crack bowler Joey Palmer, who missed the last 13 matches.

Four Australian batsmen – Murdoch, Horan, Massie and Bannerman – scored more than 1000 runs on the tour. Murdoch topped the averages with 1711 runs at 30.55, a performance critics acknowledged as unrivalled even by W.G. Grace. Palmer managed

Eugene ('Joey') Palmer,
whose 132 wickets on the
1882 English tour included
a hat-trick againt Sussex.
(MCG Museum)

to capture 138 wickets despite his injury, averaging 12.54 runs per wicket. Three other Australians took more than 100 wickets, Garrett 128 at 13.74, Boyle 144 at 11.68, and Spofforth 188 at 12.13, Spofforth confirming his place as the greatest living bowler. The sole disappointment was young Sam Jones who scored only 370 runs in 32 innings at an average of 11.93, but he may have had as big an influence on the tour as any of his team-mates by providing the motivation that led to a historic victory in the only Test.

The Australians had benefited throughout their tour by the arrangements made for them weeks before their arrival. This was done by the MCC secretary, Henry Perkins, who convinced county committees there was money to be made from these colonials and filled their fixture book from the middle of May for the following four months. None of the county secretaries appeared concerned by the condition that Australia receive half the gate takings.

The only hiccup was at Nottingham where 'Hellfire' Jack Holden refused to serve them lunch because they were professionals and suggested they try the refreshment tent for a beer and a sandwich alongside the Notts professionals. When Beal explained that all the other counties provided lunch for his players, Holden refused to listen. 'Say no more,' Holden shouted. 'I will positively hear no more!' Beal laughed and said, 'But you have had all the say yourself.'

The Australians came away from that Notts match with £238 profit, plus an apology from the Notts committee for the lack of lunch. They were not surprised to learn some months later that Notts had dispensed with Holden's services. They returned home via America after a series of matches against the odds in New York and Philadelphia. They had been away eight months when they arrived back in Australia. The *Bulletin* said that in the days that followed it 'rained dinners' for the team in the capital cities. In Melbourne they were given a torchlight procession and each player was awarded a medal. They had won the match that counted at The Oval, a test of nerve that assured the future of all international cricket.

CHAPTER SIX
IVO'S ASHES FIDDLE

Reginald Shirley Watkinson Brooks' mock obituary of English cricket was only a small item tucked away among advertisements on an inside page of the *Sporting Times*. It was intended as a harmless bit of fun but to the surprise of the author was taken seriously at Lord's by the traditionalists who safeguarded the honour of English cricket. They suggested to the Melbourne Cricket Club that further Anglo-Australian contests were desirable. The Melbourne club was glad to comply and brought the seventh English team to Australia for four months in the summer of 1882–83.

The English team was captained by the Honourable Ivo Francis Walter Bligh, 23-year-old second son of the sixth Earl of Darnley from Cobham in Kent, the cradle of English cricket. Bligh, after attending prep school at Cheam, distinguished himself at Eton and Cambridge, where he was awarded a Blue for cricket as a freshman. He played in the MCC side captained by Edward Lyttelton that defeated the first Australian team in a single innings match at Lord's in 1878. In 1879 he made 113 not out for Cambridge against Surrey, and in 1880, when he made 1013 runs at 30.69, he scored 105 for Kent against Surrey at The Oval. Handsome and wealthy, he was a pillar of English amateurism and from the time he got the job of leading a mixture of amateur and professional cricketers to Australia he pledged to bring back the Ashes.

Bligh's vice-captain was Edmund Tylecote, a wicket-keeper-batsman for Oxford University, Kent and Bedfordshire, who had first attracted interest at Lord's with an innings of 404 not out for Clifton School. The six other amateurs in the team were W.W. Read of Surrey, A.G. Steel of Lancashire, and four from Middlesex, C.T. Studd, G.B. Studd, G.F. Vernon, and C.F.H. Leslie. The four

The Hon. Ivo Bligh's English team which claimed to have recaptured the Ashes in Australia after winning two of the first three Tests. But Australia won the Test added to the itinerary to share the rubber. (MCG Museum)

professionals were F. Morley and W. Barnes of Notts, W. Bates of Yorkshire, and R.G. Barlow from Lancashire. The Melbourne club persuaded George Alexander to manage the English team after the club advertised the job without response.

The team left in two groups which met at Suez aboard the mail steamer *Peshawur* only two weeks after The Oval Test, and weeks before the Australians completed their English tour. Among their fellow passengers was the multi-millionaire Australian landowner and philanthropist William Clarke. The ravishing Florence Rose Morphy, daughter of a Gold Commissioner from Beechworth, Victoria, was one of Clarke's staff, with the job of caring for his children and teaching them music.

The *Peshawur* was about 250 kilometres out of Colombo when it collided with a fully rigged barque, later identified as the *Glenroy*. The ships limped back to Colombo locked together, with the passengers badly shaken. Fred Morley was knocked out and sustained a broken rib. Later Bligh injured his arm in a shipboard game and had it in a sling for six weeks. He recovered in time to lead England to a 2–1 victory in the three scheduled Tests. The teams won one Test each in Melbourne in December and January and England took the decider in Sydney by 69 runs. Big crowds at all three matches more than covered the Melbourne Cricket Club's investment on the tour.

The Ashes urn and the velvet bag Melbourne ladies claimed was not grand enough to carry the celebrated ashes. (MCC Library)

Bligh stayed at the Sydney home of the Paddington Cricket Club secretary J.H. Fletcher in Ocean Street, Woollahra, and when England won the Test Fletcher's wife Annie made him a velvet bag in which he could carry the Ashes home. Bligh enjoyed the joke and in accepting Annie's bag at a dinner for his players challenged an 'All Australia' XI to a match.

At Brisbane in the next part of the tour England defeated Eighteen of Queensland by an innings and 154 runs and Eighteen of Wide Bay and Burnett by an innings and 58 runs. These heavy defeats helped Queensland cricket as they led to the appointment of Sydney all-rounder Ned Sheridan as a coach in Brisbane.

Back in Sydney an 'All Australia' XI, strengthened by the addition of Billy Midwinter and Edwin Evans, beat Bligh's team by four wickets in the fixture that had been added to their original programme. Some noted cricket historians, England's Harry Altham among them, believe this levelled the series at 2–2 and that Australia thus retained the Ashes, but when Bligh got to Melbourne for the final tour match against Victoria he raised no objections when

Florence Morphy and her lady friends said the velvet bag was an inappropriate container for the Ashes and offered to get him something grander. The ladies bought a silver urn, which they filled with ashes. Argument over whether they burnt a stump or a set of bails to get the ashes has never been resolved.

Bligh proposed to Florence Morphy and after the tour was completed went home to tell his father of her acceptance. The Ashes were reported to have gone with him, but it seems more likely that he left them and the urn in Melbourne, knowing he would move all Florence's belongings to England after their wedding in 1884.

Bligh's seventh English team won four and lost three of their matches on level terms, and won five and drew five of their matches against the odds. They were so popular the Melbourne Cricket Club ended the tour with a cash surplus that allowed it to pay £2100 off its debts for two grandstands. Murdoch pulled off the coup of the summer when he sent Bonnor in to open with Alick Bannerman. Bonnor responded with an 87 that included some of the biggest hits ever seen in Sydney.

Bonnor was unimpressed. 'You won't catch me going in first again with Alick,' he said. 'It's "Come on Bon, are you asleep?" and then it's "Go back, you fool!". And when you've done everything he's called for, he comes down the pitch and reads the Riot Act at you.' Bonnor left the ground pursued by a wealthy widow out from England. Somehow he escaped her attentions, for he never married.

The Blighs' first child was born in Melbourne before they returned to England, where Bligh became the eighth Lord Darnley in 1900. When he died in 1927, his will never mentioned the Ashes, but Florence presented them to the MCC, who have retained them at Lord's. Many replicas have been made but the original Ashes urn has only once left Lord's – in 1988 when an England v. Austalia match was staged in Sydney as part of Australia's Bicentenary celebrations and the urn was lent to the organisers to help promote the game.

The Ashes have remained the symbol of supremacy between England and Australia cricket teams since 1882, but they were completely forgotten in the ten years following Ivo Bligh's Australian tour. In 1894, the South Australian sportswriter Clarence P. Moody published a book, *Australian Cricket and Cricketers*, in which he set out to establish which matches played in the early years between England and Australia should be rated as Tests. Moody did the job so well his list was universally accepted and has remained unchallenged. Moody revived the Ashes story, which originally had only been a jest Reginald Brooks expected to be quickly forgotten. Ten years after Moody's book appeared 'Plum' Warner, England's captain, decided on *How We Recovered the Ashes*, as the title for his book on the 1903–04 Australian tour and gave the 'Ashes' the status of a spiritual trophy.

Rowland Bowen argued in his magazine *Cricket Quarterly* that a term with such phoney origins should best be discarded. Bowen said the public knew when the regular England v. Australia matches were played that the Ashes would not change hands. 'It began as a joke, then because of an historical mistake became a fetish, and it is time it was abolished,' said Bowen.

In 1982, an article in the English magazine *Cricketer* reported that one of Lord Darnley's servants had confessed to spilling the Ashes when he upset the urn whilst cleaning. With the original ashes scattered across the carpet, the servant had burnt some twigs and replaced them. The Marylebone Cricket Club refused to comment on the authenticity of the ashes in the urn now kept in the Imperial Cricket Museum across a passage from the Long Room. Florence, the Dowager Countess of Darnley, died at Henley-on-Thames in 1944.

Ivo Bligh's cricket career was relatively brief, owing to ill-health. He played in 47 first-class matches for Kent and in his four Tests he made only 62 runs at an average of 10.33. After his successful Australian tour, he devoted himself to restoring the family estate at Puckle Hill, Cobham, to its former elegance, taking over from a grumpy father who had allowed the property to run down. During the First World War the Blighs threw their family home open to Australian soldiers recuperating from their war wounds.

A sketch of Florence Morphy at the time of her marriage to the Hon. Ivo Bligh, later Lord Darnley. On his death she presented the Ashes urn to the MCC at Lord's, where it has remained. (MCC Library)

The Blighs' romance made Australian cricket highly popular within social circles and throughout the 1880s attendances at inter-colonial matches in Sydney and Melbourne became fashion parades that regularly attracted crowds of 20,000. Newspapers and magazines of the period were full of photographs of wealthy young women in their finery at big cricket matches. Women's cricket, which had had its Australian origins at Bendigo in 1874, may have been short of participants but there was no shortage of fashionable women in the main grounds in Sydney and Melbourne.

The major development of the 1880s, however, was in schools and junior matches. Most headmasters made cricket an obligatory subject, following the example of English universities and public schools who cited cricket as a source of the British Empire's strength. Boyle and Scott's *Cricketers' Guide* published in 1882–83 reported that crowds of 10,000 were not uncommon at Melbourne junior cricket matches. In Adelaide, a new grandstand was opened at Adelaide Oval in 1882 at a cost of £3093, but that same year the SACA refused Jesse Hide's request for an £18 per annum increase in salary, a decision that ended Hide's five-year sojourn in South Australia.

The South Australians began their match against Victoria on 24 March, 1883, full of confidence engendered by the colony's advances in cricket, but they found 'Joey' Palmer and Harry Boyle virtually unplayable on a mud-heap and were all out for 23, the lowest score ever in inter-colonial cricket. John Noel scored 18 of South Australia's runs. Seven batsmen failed to score. Victoria made 200 in reply, enough to win by an innings and 98 runs. Boyle took 4 for 6 and 4 for 28, Palmer 5 for 16 and 5 for 28 in what the Adelaide *Register* called 'a fiasco for South Australian cricket'. The SACA lost £112 on the trip.

Cricket flourished in country areas in all the colonies with the introduction of matting that could be laid over lumpy ground, a development later improved with the introduction of concrete over which the matting was laid. The Sydney sporting weekly, the *Referee*, gave credit for the invention of matting to F.J. Ironside, the organiser of junior cricket in Sydney, who was hard-pressed to find pitches for all the boys who wanted to play. The ground on Moore Park was so uneven Ironside got the idea of laying down strips of matting, made from coconut fibre by prisoners in Darlinghurst Jail, at £6 each. Soon every country town had its matting pitch.

The New South Wales government appointed a trust to administer Sydney Cricket Ground and the New South Wales Cricket Association quickly found it had no exclusive rights to the ground. Other sports such as rugby and professional cycle racing were given dates wanted by the NSWCA, which increased its problems by deferring all grade cricket when big matches were staged in Sydney. Desperate for funds and without a ground of its own the NSWCA had no authority to prevent leading players from joining further English tours.

Australian touring teams by then had become an exclusive club for players who zealously guarded their own interests and the end-

H.J.H. ('Tup') Scott, who contributed 102 to Australia's 551 against England at The Oval in 1884, including a stand of 207 with Murdoch. (MCG Museum)

of-tour payouts. One player who managed to break into the side was Dr Henry James Herbert ('Tup') Scott, who had the support of the powerful Melbourne Cricket Club and was highly recommended as a future star by Sam Cosstick, the Melbourne club's ground bowler. Scott was born in the Melbourne suburb of Toorak in 1858 and headed the St Kilda club's first-grade averages while he was still at Wesley College. He studied engineering initially at Melbourne University but switched to medicine after two years. At 23, he moved to the East Melbourne club while still practising most days at the MCG.

At Melbourne in December 1883 Scott helped Victoria pull off a magnificent win over New South Wales after New South Wales scored 412 in their first innings. Horan batted with his customary pluck for 126 and with Scott contributing 114 not out, Victoria took a first-innings lead of eight runs. On a worn pitch Midwinter then took 7 for 54, bundling New South Wales out for 143. Left to score 136 to win, Victoria lost seven wickets reaching their target. This innings won Scott a place in the 1884 Australian team to England after Evans, Horan and Garrett dropped out and Massie had retired to club cricket.

Billy Midwinter, English-born all-rounder, who appeared in 12 Tests, eight for Australia and four for England, travelling between England and Australia. (Jack Pollard Collection)

Having taken time to rest their leading players and to take stock of some exciting inter-colonial displays, Australia was back in England some fourteen months after Bligh's team completed their Australian tour. They followed the same procedure as the three earlier teams, each man entering into an arrangement with his teammates whereby they put up a nominated sum to fund the tour and agreed to share all profits and losses. No national control body or colony association was involved and the side was managed by George Alexander, of the Melbourne Cricket Club, who was on his second trip to England.

The Australian team comprised Murdoch, Bannerman, Blackham, Boyle and Spofforth, who had been on all three earlier tours, Bonnor who, with McDonnell, Palmer, and Midwinter, was on his third tour, George Giffen who was on his second tour, and the newcomers 'Tup' Scott and William Cooper. They left behind some classy cricketers, including the left-hander Harry Moses, who scored 149 for Fifteen of New South Wales in one of the Australian team's pre-tour matches. Moses was then 26 and at the peak of his powers, but preferred to stay at home and concentrate on his career in banking, wine-making and dog-breeding.

Cooper, one of the major hopes in the Australian attack because of the leg-breaks he turned big distances, was an amazing cricketer. He only took up the game at the age of 27 on the advice of a doctor who urged him to get more exercise, played himself into the Victorian team within three years, and in 1882–83 was appointed sole selector of colony teams by the Victorian Cricketers' Association. Teams Cooper selected beat New South Wales, England and South Australia in successive matches, all by an innings. Most Victorians believed that inside Cooper's balding head lay a masterly tactical machine.

Cooper gave support to this view when he took 15 wickets for 194 runs for the Australians against Fifteen of South Australia en route to England. Later on the voyage, however, he collided with Alick Bannerman during a game of shinty and severely damaged the third finger of his bowling hand – his spinning finger – as he crashed into an engine-room skylight. The ship's surgeon failed to mend the finger and in London Queen Victoria's surgeon, Sir James Paget, said the finger injury would have been easier to cure had Cooper broken a bone. A long rest was all that could be recommended for the torn ligaments. Cooper played only six matches, leaving unanswered the notion that his wide turn would have been unplayable.

W.H. Cooper, the sensational Melbourne leg-spinner expected to be a match-winner in England unfortunately injured his hand on the voyage and played in only six matches. (Illustrated News)

The Australians opened their tour on 12 May 1884 by scoring 212 against Lord Sheffield's XI at Sheffield Park, winning by an innings and six runs. This started a tradition of Australian sides opening their tours under his lordship's patronage. With Cooper reduced to helping Alexander with the team's accounts, the side faced a long, ambitious programme with only 11 fit players. Alexander appeared five times to rest weary bowlers. Murdoch had not kept in practice as a wicket-keeper and this threw a heavy burden on Blackham.

England won the three-Test series 1–0. Lord Harris refused to play in the First Test at Old Trafford because the selectors included the notorious 'chucker' John Crossland in the English team. He returned for the Second and Third Tests when Crossland was omitted. After rain produced a draw at Old Trafford, Australia lost the first Test ever played at Lord's, thanks to a unique catch. Murdoch fielded for W.G. Grace when Grace injured a finger and when 'Tup' Scott was 75 Murdoch caught Scott off Steel's bowling, the first catch by a substitute in a Test. Murdoch made 211, the first double century in a Test in the drawn Third Test at The Oval during which he put on 207 with Scott (102).

The fourth Australian team to tour England in 1884 (L to R): back, J.M. Blackham, H.J.H. Scott, an unidentified umpire, W. Midwinter, P.S. McDonnell, W.H. Cooper; centre, G.F. Giffen, H.F. Boyle, W.L. Murdoch (Captain), G.J. Bonnor, G.E. Palmer; front, A.C. Bannerman, F.R. Spofforth. (MCG Museum)

The London newspaper the *World* summed up the tour accurately when it said the Australians' matches made all others played in England that summer appear tame and insipid. 'The Australians make their own terms, insist on them, not always gracefully, and they play too obviously for the money's sake,' said the *World*. 'It should be made clear to them that if they visit England to make money, they must rank, with others in same condition, as professionals. English professionals are sore at this point, and it is for the Australians themselves to decide between their pride and their pocket.'

The 1884 Australians steadfastly refused to be labelled and none of the players who followed them in national touring teams wanted to be regarded as 'amateurs' or 'professionals' but simply as 'cricketers'. The 1884 side were outstanding entertainers. With only 11 fit players, they won 18 of their 32 matches, lost seven and drew seven in a programme that for the first time consisted of only 11-a-side matches. The tour ended happily with a match between Smokers and Non-Smokers in which the players from both sides mingled. Bonnor made 124 out of the 156 scored while he was at the crease, hitting 14 boundaries and a six. All proceeds of this match went to the fund for old cricketers on hard times.

Spofforth topped the Australian bowling averages with 216 wickets at 12.23, followed by Palmer with 132 dismissals at 16.14. Between them they enabled Australia to make up for the loss of Cooper. Murdoch (1378 at 30.62), McDonnell (1225 at 23.55) and Giffen (1052 at 21.04) all made more than 1000 runs, and Scott had his stumps disturbed only ten times in 51 innings to score 973 runs on his first tour. Giffen took 82 wickets at 19.78 in addition to scoring more than 1000 runs.

Somehow Australia had completed her first four tours of England without a specialist left-handed batsman who could counter deliveries that shrewd English professionals turned across right-handers' legs. Indeed it was a tremendous compliment to Australia's pioneer tourists for Lord Harris to assess standards of English and Australian cricket as 'about equal' after watching the 1884 Australians rout the South of England at The Oval in the final tour match.

Lord Harris's views on the unabated exploitation of England v. Australia matches was not recorded, but he must have been shocked to learn that the eighth English team to Australia was to be jointly sponsored again by English professionals James Lillywhite, Alfred Shaw and Arthur Shrewsbury. This team travelled to Australia with Murdoch's returning team only four days after the English tour ended. Shaw and Shrewsbury had invested profits from the 1881–82 trip in a bat-making and sports equipment business whose products they could sell at high prices in Australia. The advance agents for these trips had become very important and in planning their 1884–85 Australian tour the English again hired the best available man, John Conway, to negotiate terms and dates weeks before their arrival.

Six players refused £300 each to tour – W.W. Read, E.J. Diver, R. Pilling, M. Sherwin, R.G. Barlow and W. Wright – before the sponsors, who each invested £450 on the venture, settled on a team comprising W. Barnes, W. Bates, A. Shrewsbury, J. Briggs, G. Ulyett, W.H. Scotton, J.M. Read, W. Flowers, J.M. Lillywhite, W. Attewell, R. Peel and J. Hunter, with Alfred Shaw as manager, only willing to play in minor matches.

George Giffen, seen demonstrating his bowling action, made his place among the great all-rounders secure by taking 82 wickets and scoring 1052 runs for the 1884 Australians. (SACA Archives)

Conway was apprehensive about how Barnes would handle the alcohol that flowed freely at after-the-match banquets, as Barnes's drunkenness had brought frequent reprimands from the Notts committee. Carpeted for one escapade Barnes looked carefully at each committeeman. 'How many of you could make a hundred, drunk or sober?' he asked. Barnes was to make 21 first-class centuries before the booze prematurely ended his career.

On the voyage out Shaw and Ulyett, after sight-seeing around Cairo, hired two Arabs to row them to their ship's anchorage. Half-way out the Arabs stopped rowing and refused to go on without further payment. Ulyett threw one man into the sea and rowed to the ship himself with the Arab swimming alongside.

The Englishmen found the newly appointed South Australian Cricket Association secretary John Creswell in a co-operative mood when they reached Adelaide for the start of the tour. Creswell was desperate to give Adelaide a Test match and to fulfil this wish later in the tour had to agree to extortionate terms for all three of the Englishmen's matches in Adelaide.

The eighth English tour of Australia began on 31 October 1884 on Adelaide Oval, where an even 100 from Ulyett and 52 from Shrewsbury lifted England to a total of 239, enough to defeat Fifteen of South Australia by three wickets after fine bowling by Flowers (7 for 54), Attewell (7 for 61) and Peel (6 for 52). The attendance at this match and one that followed immediately at Norwood, in the Adelaide suburbs, was very poor and the SACA lost heavily on both. England drew against Eighteen of South Australia at Norwood and immediately went to Melbourne by sea, Creswell having secured signed contracts for the Test.

When the members of Murdoch's fourth Australian team (1884) to England heard of the fees Conway had negotiated for the Englishmen, they refused to play against them unless they received more pay. The leading Australian players wanted excess gate receipts to go into their own pockets rather than to colony associations after the Englishmen had been paid. None of Murdoch's players therefore was available for the tourists' match on level terms against Victoria in Melbourne from 14 November because the Victorian Cricketers' Association refused to meet their terms, and England had a hollow win by 118 runs. England scored 202 and 150, Victoria 146 and 88, with Flowers taking 8 for 31 in the final innings against a makeshift Victorian side.

The ill-feeling between the 1884 Australian team and the tourists continued and all the 1884 Australians refused to play for New South Wales against the Englishmen in Sydney. England again won convincingly against a reconstructed New South Wales team, but the promoters were delighted when 30,000 spectators turned up for the three days' play. New South Wales' makeshift side led England by 74 runs on the first innings, scoring 184 to 110, but Attewell (5 for 19) bundled New South Wales out for 44 in their second innings. England lost six wickets scoring the 119 needed to win.

Test cricket returned on 12–16 December 1884, in Adelaide. Only members of Murdoch's 1884 side in England were considered for the Australian team, which made a bright start when McDonnell scored his second successive Test century (124) in a total of 243, Bates tying down the other Australian batsmen with a commendable 5 for 31. England took a 126-run lead because of Scotton's 82, Ulyett's 68 and a brilliant 134 from Barnes on a very tricky Adelaide pitch.

SACA secretary Creswell had persuaded the government to declare a public holiday for the opening day of this Test, but with the admission charge at two shillings, less than 5000 spectators turned up, under half the number expected. Creswell reduced admission to one shilling and sent a team of messenger boys to newspaper offices to spread the news. More than 10,000 attended the second day's play, when a violent dust storm struck the ground. Fieldsmen had to lie flat on the turf to avoid suffocation.

Murdoch refused to allow either Shaw or Shrewsbury to umpire and the inexperienced local umpire Ian Fisher had both sides shaking their heads in disbelief over some of his decisions. On the Sunday rest day rain flooded Adelaide Oval. While the pitch was wet McDonnell made 83 to go with the first innings century, but Billy Murdoch, who was on his honeymoon following his marriage to heiress Jemima Watson four days before the Test began, failed again when Peel scattered his stumps. George Giffen, with 47 on his home ground, held England up for a time before Australia were out for 191, Peel taking 5 for 51. England scored the 67 required for the loss of two wickets for a handsome eight-wicket victory after having all the worst of the pitch. After paying each side the agreed £450 for the match, the SACA lost £271 on the venture, but was widely praised for the first-class staging of the game.

Shaw and Murdoch remained at loggerheads. Shaw argued that when the Australians built up their splendid profits on the last tour of England the professionals appeared for only £10 per man. Now

Percy McDonnell, who in the 1884–85 Australian summer became the first batsman to score centuries in successive Tests by scoring 124 in the first Test held in Adelaide. (MCG Museum)

it was the Australians' turn to return the favour and let England's players make some money. Murdoch disagreed and demanded half the profits from all matches between his players and the tourists. Shaw offered him 30 per cent of the profits and then £30-a-man but Murdoch would not accept either.

Four up-country matches against the odds, all of them drawn, followed at Maryborough, Bendigo, Ballarat and Benalla. The Australian public believed good sense would prevail by the time of the next Test in Melbourne. The Murdoch team stuck to their demand for half the gate, however, and the Victorian Cricketers' Association announced that a completely new Australian team would play in the Test. W. Bruce, A.H. Jarvis, A.P. Marr, S. Morris, H. Musgrove, R.J. Pope, W.R. Robertson, J.W. Trumble and J. Worrall all made their Test debuts for Australia, alongside Sam Jones and Tom Horan. This ended the unique run of J.M. Blackham, who had played for Australia in all the first 17 Tests.

Sam Morris became the first coloured man to play for Australia, because of his West Indian parentage, a record he retains 108 years later. Dr Rowley Pope, the Sydney doctor who travelled the world as medical adviser and unpaid baggagemaster for Australian teams, also played in this Test after making his debut for New South Wales a few weeks earlier. Horan, honoured with the captaincy, made this bitter attack on Murdoch's team in the *Australasian*:

Sam Morris, the only coloured man to play for Australia, got his chance in the 1884–85 Melbourne Test when the top team refused the playing fees offered. (Age, Melbourne)

On all sides their action as a team has been condemned in the strongest possible terms. The public desire to see the best team in Australia meet the Englishmen, but rather than please the public these men prefer to vent their spite by doing all in their power to keep the pounds out of the pockets of our English professional visitors who make their living by playing cricket. They have done all they can to destroy the good feeling between English and Australian cricketers and to injure the good name Australia deservedly enjoys for extending kindness and generous welcome to visitors. They have shown no manliness, no courtesy, no spark of kindly feeling whatever to our English friends.

The new-look Australian team Horan led suffered a massive defeat at Melbourne, England winning by ten wickets despite plucky first-innings batting by Horan (63), John Trumble (59) and wicket-keeper Jarvis (82). Lancashire left-hander Johnny Briggs made 121 of England's first innings of 401. Australia followed on after scoring 279 in reply and managed only 126 in their second innings, Barnes taking 6 for 31. The Victorian Cricketers' Association temporarily disqualified Blackham, Boyle, Bonnor, McDonnell, Palmer and Scott. In Sydney Spofforth expressed disgust at the action of these former team-mates.

Meanwhile country towns continued to strongly support England's matches in the six matches against the odds before England met the powerful New South Wales team. Candello, population 200, raised a £300 guarantee to stage the match between England and a local Twenty-Two. Every farmer from 20 miles around turned up. There were 150 buggies at the match and a further 600 rode in on horseback, happy to pay the 2s 6d admission charge. At Moss Vale England made 432 by batting from noon on Wednesday until 4 p.m. on Thursday, and then dismissed the local Twenty-Two for 14, Peel taking 18 for 7.

The 1884 Australians still refused to play when New South Wales played against England. Despite rain, 7000 spectators watched the first day and 10,000 attended the second day, but after New South Wales had been dismissed for 60 in response to England's 205, only 1000 appeared on the final day when England won by an innings. England then won three matches against Twenty-Twos in Brisbane, Maryborough and Gympie, where Scotton won 250 gold-mine shares for making top score.

By the time they returned to Sydney for the Third Test against Australia on 20 February, the English team had dispensed with Conway as their advance agent and publicist and replaced him with C.W. Beal, who had managed the 1882 Australians in England. This helped improve relations between the tourists and Murdoch, who had been feuding bitterly with Conway. Murdoch had given up big cricket in protest against the Victorian and New South Wales associations' refusal to pay his players half the gate, and retired to his law practice at Cootamundra – a sad loss for Australian cricket. Four of the players he had led on the 1884 English tour and in the boycott of the Melbourne Test joined him, giving up their careers rather than back down on the principle of what they believed was justice.

Hugh Massie returned to captain Australia, and only four of the make-shift side that played in Melbourne retained their places – Horan, Jones, Jarvis and Trumble. Five others from the Melbourne Test – Morris, Pope, Marr, Musgrove and Robertson – were not seen again in Tests. England's hopes of winning the Third Test disappeared, however, when Barnes, the most successful bowler of the tour, quarrelled with his captain Shrewsbury and refused to bowl in either innings.

A hailstorm covered the turf like snow at lunch on the first day, and when play resumed Australia's batsmen found Attewell and Flowers unplayable on the sodden pitch. Edwin Evans and Tom Garrett resumed next morning with Australia on 9 for 101 and put on 80 priceless runs for the last wicket. England finished 48 behind when Horan found a spot left by Spofforth's follow-through and took 6 for 40 with his fast right-hand roundarmers. Steady bowling from Attewell, who had 36 maidens in his 58 overs and Bates (5 for 24), supported by fine fielding, restricted Australia to a lead of 214. Fortunes fluctuated throughout the last day, until Evans brilliantly caught Flowers for 56 with England only six short of victory.

Blackham became Australia's fourth captain in as many matches when he took over the team for the Fourth Test in Sydney in mid-March, after England had played four more up-country matches against the odds. Spofforth bowled very fast without taking wickets but Giffen pitched into the rough he created to take 7 for 117 and have England out for 269. Bonnor then played the innings of his life, scoring 113 in one 85-minute period and five times hitting the ball into the crowd. He did not make a mistake until he was 99 and batted 115 minutes for his 128. After overnight rain England had a choice of pitches for their second innings but decided to bat on the same strip on which Australia had made 309 and were dismissed for 77. Australia lost two wickets scoring the 38 needed to win, levelling the series.

Arguments over umpires and the suspension of key players disrupted the Fifth Test, on 21–25 March. Australia were forced to bring in Victorians F.G. 'Paddy' McShane and Frank Walters to make up their side. Horan took over the captaincy again when Blackham was ruled out. Shrewsbury won the match for England with a chanceless 105 not out as Horan tried eight bowlers, England winning by an innings and 98 runs. One London paper hailed England's success in the series as 'Proof that professionals are always better to rely on than amateurs'. The Australian papers disagreed and pointed out that Ulyett made only 19 in his last six Test innings, due to his fondness for Australian beer.

The Englishmen returned home with pleasant memories after 34 matches. They won six and lost two of their eight matches on level terms and had 10 wins and 16 draws in games against the odds in a six-month tour that took them through the fierce heat of tropical Australia, provided regular adventures with flies and mosquitoes, and produced a strange fear of koalas in Flowers. They endured the arid plains, gaunt gums, wild coastal voyages, bought pineapples for a penny each in Brisbane, dived fully clothed into the Clarence River to dodge the sun and went home with their agreed £300 per man. The three sponsors made £150 each for their trouble, a disappointment they attributed to the boycott by Murdoch's men. The only player hurt was Johnny Briggs, kicked by a wild horse and sent flat on his face. The pipe he was smoking at the time ripped into the roof of his mouth.

At the end of the 1886–87 season Fred Ironside organised Sydney's first women's cricket matches between the Siroccos, captained by Nellie Gregory, and the Fernleas, led by Nellie's sister Lilly. The first match at the Association Ground on 8 March, 1886, ended in a draw, with the Fernleas, 41 and 8 for 93, four runs away from an outright win over the Siroccos, who made 83 and 54. Encouraged by this success – 1000 spectators raised £215 for charity – Ironside staged a return on 7 April, 1886. This time the Siroccos won by four wickets before 3500 spectators. Nellie Gregory was the star of the match with 12 wickets and scores of 35 and 47 not out. Fernleas made 63 and 53, Siroccos 86 and 6 for 65.

Nellie Gregory, one of the famous cricketing family which lived at the Sydney Cricket Ground. (SCG Archives)

CHAPTER SEVEN
DISCORD BRINGS DECLINE

Former Test player John Hodges refused to continue as an umpire in the Fifth Test of the 1884–85 series because of complaints over his decisions. (MCG Museum)

The Melbourne Cricket Club's golden chance to become the ruling body of Australian cricket faltered through the failure of the 1886 team in England. This fifth tour of England by Australia was again sponsored by the Melbourne club, captained by the Melbourne CC's nominee Dr Henry ('Tup') Scott, and managed by Major Ben Wardill, secretary-manager of the club. Had the team returned after glorious success or a strong showing, the Australian public, the media and the players would have granted Melbourne similar status to that enjoyed in England by the Marylebone Cricket Club.

The tour matches consistently attracted large audiences and overshadowed county cricket, but the triumphs the Australian public craved were not forthcoming. Scott's team won only nine of their 38 matches, and the tour became part of Australian cricket's dismal record in the second half of the 1880s. This slump was particularly evident in poor attendances at big matches in Australia.

At the completion of the Australian tour funded by Shaw, Lilly-white and Shrewsbury in 1884–85, Australia had won nine of the 21 Tests played, England eight, and four had been drawn, but England won nine of the next ten Tests and lost only one because, as English cricket historian Harry Altham said, the great strength of Australian cricket was sapped for year after year by internal argument.

As the initial heroes of Australian cricket, the great men who had given the country such a spectacular entry into big cricket, disappeared, disputes over match fees and who should govern the game, inter-colonial rivalry, and even physical conflict among representative players brought failures on the field.

The Melbourne Cricket Club did not help in assembling the side for Scott to captain. They foolishly insisted on an all-amateur team, which prevented seasoned Test players like Alick Bannerman, a paid coach, from touring. They made little effort to get Murdoch to leave his bush legal practice, and none at all to prevent Percy McDonnell losing his pay and seniority at the Victorian Education Department while he was away. These players would have been invaluable to a team comprising H.J.H. Scott, G. Giffen, S.P. Jones, G.E. Palmer, G.J. Bonnor, J.W. Trumble, A.H. Jarvis, J. McIlwraith, J.M. Blackham, W. Bruce, T.W. Garrett, E. Evans and F.R. Spofforth.

Bruce was the sole success among the four newcomers to England, with Evans, Trumble and McIlwraith disappointing. The bowlers lacked hostility, and when Spofforth injured his hand trying to stop a Lord Harris drive, took constant punishment. Giffen virtually stood alone, heading both the batting and bowling averages, and had a wonderful spell in which he took 40 wickets in five innings.

Billy Bruce, a success in the 1886 team to visit England. (MCC Library)

Bonnor, injured in July, only appeared occasionally in the last two months of the tour. His boots, on display in a shop window in The Strand, aroused more discussion than his social blunders. When guests at a party laughed because he had never heard of Dr Johnson, Bonnor jumped to his feet and said: 'I come from a great country where you can ride a horse 60 miles a day for three months and never meet a soul who has heard of Dr Johnson either.'

Friction among the players developed before their first match, and Scott frequently had to adjudicate in their disputes. 'The cares of leadership affected Scott's run-getting, for quarrels between his players were many, and he did not have sufficient strength to cope,' said cricket historian Arthur Haygarth. 'Tup' Scott gained his nickname from his fondness for taking twopenny sightseeing rides on London buses.

Australia lost their first match to Lord Sheffield's XI, and the third to Surrey. They beat the Gentlemen in the sixth match but by the time of the first Test at Manchester, on 5–7 July, 1886, both manager Wardill and supporter Dr Rowley Pope had been forced to play in minor matches because of players' injuries.

England had to fight hard to win the First Test by four wickets, but won the Second and Third tests by wide margins. Shrewsbury made 164 in the Second Test and W.G. Grace 170. Beaten 3–0 in the Tests and seven times on tour, Australia fielded like novices. Shrewsbury was dropped in the slips and should have been stumped by Blackham during his 161-run stand with Barnes at Lord's, and Grace was dropped four times before he reached 100 at The Oval. In his thirty-eighth year Grace made 812 runs in 19 innings against

Edwin Evans, in his prime the most highly rated cricketer in Australia, unfortunately left his debut in England until too late in his career and was one of the failures of the 1886 tour. (Jack Pollard Collection)

the Australians, success that stimulated him to go on to a further decade of record-breaking scoring, a decade in which he altered the whole conception of batting. He had revolutionised accepted standards of batting in the first 20 years of his career. Now in middle age he continued the prodigious feats that made him the focus of an empire's devotion to cricket and in the process made W.G. the best-known Englishman of his time.

England introduced another great player against Scott's team, George Alfred Lohmann, who at 21 bowled right-hand roundarm above medium-pace with accuracy and subtlety beyond his years. His 12 wickets for 104 runs (7 for 36 and 5 for 68) was responsible for Australia's defeat at The Oval by an innings and 217 runs, the biggest margin by either side to that time. Lohmann's triumph in Spofforth's last Test in England robbed Spofforth of a spectacular farewell, but his figures on five tours provided eloquent evidence of Spofforth's unique stature as a bowler:

Year	Wickets	Average
1878	97	11.00
1880	40	8.40
1882	157	13.24
1884	201	12.75
1886	89	17.17

(These figures are for first-class matches only, and on the 1878 tour represent less than half the matches he played. In 1886 he missed three months through injury.)

Scott received a hammering for his captaincy from Australian critics, but he never spared himself on the tour, resting only once in the 38 matches. He preferred to bat in the middle of the order, but opened the batting 16 times. He scored two of his four first-class centuries in England and made 2244 of his 2863 runs there. He was seen no more in big cricket after the 1886 tour, remaining in London to take degrees at the Royal College of Surgeons and the Royal College of Physicians when his team sailed home. Thereafter he preferred the life of a country doctor, renowned for his generosity in not pressing needy patients to pay their bills. The people of Scone, New South Wales, named the Scott Memorial Hospital after him.

Ben Wardill told English players that the Melbourne Cricket Club would fund the next English tour of Australia in 1886–87, and offered contracts to leading players to join the tour. Lillywhite, Shaw and Shrewsbury, alert to the money-making chances such a tour represented, arranged their own, cleverly exploiting the English professionals' resentment over being forced to accept £10 a match for games that saw the Australians walk away with hundreds of pounds. Wardill tried to argue that the Melbourne CC had priority over private sponsors, but conceded defeat when the Marylebone Cricket Club refused to pick a touring side for him. Lillywhite, Shaw and Shrewsbury had the advantage of a coup achieved by their new Australian advance agent, former Victorian player John Tennent, who had replaced John Conway. Tennent secured exclusive rights to play on the Sydney Cricket Ground, where much of the tour profit was made. This checkmated Wardill but by outwitting him the tour promoters created mistrust within the Melbourne Cricket Club.

Arthur Shrewsbury, the Geoffrey Boycott of his day, had made a financial killing from his first venture as a joint promoter of an English tour of Australia in 1884–85, but the 1886–87 tour did not do so well. (MCC Library)

Shaw was honoured by having the English team carry his name, Shrewsbury captained the side and Lillywhite umpired. This was Lillywhite's fifth visit to Australia, the fourth for Bates and Shaw, the third for Barnes, Barlow, Scotton and Shrewsbury, and the second for Briggs, Flowers and Read. They were all elated that they no longer faced rough sea trips to and from Adelaide, and could instead join the Melbourne–Adelaide railway, even though this involved a six-hour wait at Bordertown and two hours at Dimboola. The new men were the classic stylist William Gunn, George Lohmann and wicket-keeper Mordecai Sherwin, who preferred the tour to a winter keeping goal for Notts County soccer team.

The tour was badly promoted, with Shrewsbury too busy selling bats and discovering the extent of the Nottingham lace business in Australia to give cricket interviews, and several of England's big games clashed with inter-colonial fixtures. Additionally, the Melbourne Cricket Club's members felt the English tour belittled their club. Shrewsbury even wrote to his manager back in Nottingham to recruit Dick Pougher for a tour to Australia the following summer in a bid to thwart Wardill's attempts to stage the postponed 1887–88 tour.

The all-professional ninth English tour of Australia began on 30 October, 1886, with a match against Fifteen of South Australia in Adelaide, and ended on 26 March, 1887, with a similar match on the same ground, and included two Tests on a 29-match programme. The itinerary took England to 19 country towns, some of them remote, which helped develop cricket but did little for tour profits when Tennent's speculations turned sour.

Johnny Briggs, whose 121 in the 1884–85 Melbourne Test had given England victory by ten wickets against the new-look Australian side, returned in 1886. (MCC Library)

Percy McDonnell took over the Australian captaincy in the Tests, inheriting a rebellious lot. His players were full of inter-colonial jealousies, enmity towards England's professionals and given to throwing punches during arguments. McDonnell, son of barrister Morgan McDonnell, attorney-general in two Victorian governments, was the only Australian cricket captain who could read Greek poets in their original language. He sympathised with Aristotle's logic and chuckled at *Lysistrata*, and in the First Test of 1886–87 became the first captain to win the toss and then invite the opposition to bat.

His reasoning proved sound as the rain-affected Association Ground – as the SCG was called at the time – wicket suited Test debutants Turner and Ferris and England were all out for 45, one of the lowest totals in Anglo-Australian cricket. Turner took 6 for 15, Ferris 4 for 27, but their coup was as much due to some remarkable catching as it was to the bowling. Spofforth took two astonishing catches, which McShane and Garrett matched.

Despite this collapse England recovered to win the match in an astounding turn-around. Australia appeared to have the match in hand on 4 for 76 at the start of the second day, but lost six wickets for 43 runs and achieved a lead of only 74. England's second innings ended at 184, leaving Australia 111 to win. Moses and Midwinter took the score to 80 before the seventh wicket fell, but an inspired spell by Billy Barnes (6 for 28) got England home by 13 runs. Shrewsbury wrote this account of it to his sister Amelia:

We have just finished a match against Combined Australia and I don't think that in the time I have played cricket I ever played in a match that was literally pulled out of the fire as this one was . . . All our players in Australia's last innings worked and fielded like a high machine, every man thinking it was on their individual efforts the result depended. Some of the Australian players did not take their defeat gracefully . . . and I wish that Colonial teams could bear licking with the same graceful manner as they can a win.

The Englishman Barnes became involved in an argument with McDonnell which ended when he took a tremendous swipe at McDonnell's face, missed, and smashed his fist into a wall. The injury caused him to miss the rest of the tour. Spofforth also missed with a haymaker aimed at Barlow, leaving honours for fisticuffs about even. Shrewsbury had more success than the pugilists when he signed an agreement with ground boss Phillip Sheridan for exclusive use of the Association Ground in 1887–88.

Spofforth, Australia's first great modern bowler, suffered the ignominy of being dropped from Australia's team for the Second Test at the age of 34. He needed only six wickets to claim 100 Test victims, having taken 94 at 18.41 and 853 first-class wickets altogether at 14.95.

He went off to England and married his Derbyshire sweetheart. Her father owned the Star Tea Company and Spofforth soon became a director. Between 1889 and 1891 Spofforth played occasionally for Derbyshire and in 1889 took 15 for 81 in a match against Yorkshire. In 1896, he took 11 for 100 at Wembley Park in London against the Australians. As managing director of the tea company, he continued to top the bowling averages for Hampstead Cricket Club in London, and when he died at Long Dutton, Surrey, in 1926, aged 73, he left £164,000, a fortune at that time.

Spofforth was not the only notable absentee from the Second Test in 1886–87. Blackham missed a place in a team that saw five changes, his place going to little-known Sydney wicket-keeper Fred Burton. Solicitor Reginald Allen, 19-year-old Sydney colt John Cottam, George Giffen's brother Walter, and the big hitter from Gawler, South Australia, Jack Lyons, also made their Test debuts.

None of the newcomers could master Lohmann, who hit the stumps five times in his first-innings bag of 8 for 35. Australia were out for 84 chasing England's 151, and all the expertise of Turner (9 for 93 in the match) and Ferris (9 for 140) could not prevent Australia's defeat by 71 runs.

John James Lyons, one of the most punishing hitters Australia ever sent to England, which he toured three times. He once made 158 in an hour, including 32 from six balls. (MCC Library)

The tour lost money, largely because of the lack of support from the Melbourne Cricket Club, but also because of an indifferent public. Less than 1000 watched each day's play in a fabulous Smokers v. Non Smokers match at East Melbourne in which the best Victorians played on the same teams as the Englishmen. On the same day more than 20,000 watched a professional cycling race on Melbourne Cricket Ground.

Shrewsbury had formed a close friendship with Phillip Sheridan, a good-humoured Irishman who had migrated to Australia in 1849 at the age of 15. Sheridan was one of the original trustees of Sydney Cricket Ground and ran the ground as secretary from 1877 until his death in 1910. He was renowned for his wit and his rich fund of cricket stories, and his determination to make the Sydney ground the best in the world. Shrewsbury could not have had a more influential ally than Sheridan, who had as many friends at Lord's as he had in the New South Wales parliament.

There were some intriguing casualties among the players tried in the Tests against Shrewsbury's 1886–87 team. Cottam, an outstanding talent, went off to the Kalgoorlie goldfields to get rich, got typhoid fever instead, and died. Reg Allen found himself too busy in his legal practice for big cricket, became a founder of the leading law firm Allen, Allen and Hemsley, and was an Australian Jockey Club committeeman for 30 years. Wicket-keeper Burton settled in New Zealand, where he became a leading umpire.

In February, 1887, Midwinter and the popular black man Sam Morris combined to give Victoria victory over South Australia at the MCG. Midwinter took 5 for 22 while Morris took 5 for 21 at the other end. Morris became groundsman at South Melbourne that year and held the job for 30 years until he went blind. Midwinter, 36, retired to his Melbourne hotel after 12 Test appearances – eight for Australia, four for England – but tragedy dogged him. His daughter Elsie died in 1888, his wife in 1889, followed three months later by his son Albert. Normally jovial, Midwinter broke down from these setbacks and was committed to Kew Asylum. He died in 1890 at 39, bereft of reason and paralysed from the waist down, after talking with Harry Boyle in a rare period of lucidity. Haygarth wrote: 'May the death of no other cricketer who has taken part in great matches be like his.'

None of Australia's top players wanted an English tour in 1887, believing that hostility among English professionals would pass in a cooling-off season. The Australian summer of 1887–88 saw highly promising newcomers straining for recognition. After the emergence of Ferris and Turner in New South Wales, Victoria produced George Henry Steven Trott, known as Harry, who turned right-arm leg-breaks sharply and was the eldest of three talented brothers, and a gawky, loose-limbed off-break bowler who leapt high in his delivery stride called Hugh Trumble, younger brother of Test player John. South Australia reckoned that in John James Lyons they had a hitter whose power rivalled Bonnor, who had become a commercial traveller and could not be found by his colony selectors.

A powerful figure had appeared in Perth with the formation of the Western Australian Cricket Association in November, 1885 – John Charles Horsey James, son of the Reverend J.H. James. He was educated at Rugby and Oxford and was elected as the first WACA president. James spent his early weeks in office explaining the needs of cricketers to ignorant Perth council members. At a time when Test cricket was established in the east the WACA regarded the delivery of a water barrel with handles attached as a coup. In March, 1887, James convened a meeting to assess the prospects of sending a team to the colonies in the east. Seven months later the WACA appointed W.V. Duffy as the colony's first coach, on a salary of £100 a year, with the specific task of lifting the west's playing standards to match those in the east.

The 1887–88 season proved disastrous for big cricket in Australia with two English teams touring simultaneously. Ben Wardill went ahead with the Melbourne Cricket Club-funded tour by a largely amateur side, and Shrewsbury, Shaw and Lillywhite also brought out a side, captained by C.A. Smith, later Sir Aubrey Smith, the celebrated film actor. Both teams suffered heavy financial losses. Shaw, Shrewsbury and Lillywhite were asked to call off their tour but refused to do so.

The side sponsored by the Melbourne Cricket Club was captained initially by the Honourable Martin Bladen, who had played for Eton and Cambridge and had captained Yorkshire since 1883. After five matches his father died and he returned to England to become Lord Hawke. The Middlesex right-hand amateur batsman George Frederick Vernon, who played rugby five times for England, took over the captaincy just after recovering from a nasty fall on the voyage to Australia. Statisticians dubbed Vernon's team the tenth to visit Australia.

Vernon's tenth English team and Smith's eleventh English team travelled to Australia in the same ship, the *Iberia*, and they all landed in Adelaide on 25 October, 1887. Vernon's team began their programme of 26 matches in Adelaide against South Australia with a 71-run win. Wardill toured country towns arranging fixtures for them until just before they arrived. Vernon's team was A.E. Stoddart, T.C. O'Brien, A.E. Newton, W.W. Read, M.P. Bowden, R. Abel, J. Beaumont, J.T. Rawlin, W. Bates, R. Peel and W. Attewell.

Smith's team began with a draw against Eighteen of Parramatta. His team comprised C.A. Smith, J. Brann, L.C. Docker, J.M. Read, A.D. Pougher, G. Ulyett, R. Pilling, G.A. Lohmann, J.M. Preston, J. Briggs and W. Newham, plus the promoters Lillywhite and Shaw. Wardill attempted to stay out of the way of the opposing tour whereas Shrewsbury tried to prove his team was superior by playing and beating the same opponents as Vernon's team by a bigger margin. The public stayed away from matches on the clashing tours, judging it to be essentially English rivalry.

The two English teams combined to play a Test match against All Australia on 10 February, 1888, when five of Vernon's players joined six from Shrewbury's party in a side captained by Walter Read. They met a highly experienced XI led by McDonnell and defeated them by 126 runs on a sodden Sydney pitch. Staged to celebrate Australia's centenary, this remains the worst attended of all Tests, with only 1973 people watching three days' play. Two days were washed out. Shrewsbury alone mastered atrocious conditions and his 44 took England to 113 in their first innings. Australia's 42 in reply was the lowest in an Australian Test. Peel took 5 for 18 and 5 for 40 for England, Turner 5 for 44 and 7 for 43 for Australia, in a match that yielded only 250 runs.

The Melbourne Cricket Club lost £2000 on the tour by Vernon's team, a loss that hurt the club at a time when the entire Australian banking industry was in trouble. Shaw, Lillywhite and Shrewsbury lost £2400 on their tour and while Vernon's players sailed home Shrewsbury took his team to New Zealand for three matches he hoped would rescue tour finances. The results were disappointing and he sent the bulk of his team home convinced the New Zealand gatekeepers had swindled him, as their receipts were below crowd figures. Shrewsbury wrote to Shaw, then back in England, explaining that he had been unable to pay nine of his players. According to Peter Wynne-Thomas' book *Give Me Arthur*, Shrewsbury listed these amounts owed to his side: W. Newham £146; G. Brann £189, G.A. Lohmann £80; M. Read £100; J. Briggs £60; R. Pilling £55; J.M. Preston £45; A.D. Pougher £75; G. Ulyett £73.

Shrewsbury was optimistic that a rugby football tour of Australia and New Zealand, which he had organised to immediately follow the cricket tour, would more than cover the cricket-tour losses and he told Shaw he would cable him the money to pay the cricketers as it came in from the football matches. Shrewsbury persuaded five players from the cricket team to remain in Australia, which saved him their fares to England.

All the players on the football tour were paid, fully justifying protests by the English Rugby Union that the tour breached the laws of amateurism. Docker, Stoddart, Brann, C. Aubrey Smith and Newham stayed behind to play football and were joined by 15 leading rugby players from England, all but one of them from the north. They included four internationals and were far from representative of British rugby but on this pioneer tour of Australasia the British rugby side were too experienced for their opponents from leading public schools. They won 14 of their 16 games in Australia and drew the other two.

Scoring in rugby matches differed in New South Wales and Queensland, with NSW referees awarding two points for a try, compared with one in Queensland. Points for goals also varied. Another extraordinary feature of the tour was that the British team played more Australian Rules matches than rugby matches, winning nine and losing ten. Shrewsbury was very disappointed in the results from the Australian Rules matches as he believed rugby players would adapt well to that code. In all, Shrewsbury was only able to cable £350 home to Shaw towards the money owed the cricketers – about half the required sum.

The 1888 ventures by Lillywhite, Shaw and Shrewsbury showed an £800 loss on the Australian football tour to add to the £2400 loss from the cricket tour. Shrewsbury had to find £1600 of this instead of £1070 under the trio's agreement because Lillywhite had already gone broke. For all three their four Australian tours had proved a financial liability.

An unknown batsman named Ken Burn hit a fine 99 not out in Tasmania's total of 405 against Vernon's XI. Sam Jones made 134 for the Australian XI. George Giffen scored 203 for South Australia against Vernon's team after an unknown vandal flooded the pitch. The watering made batting so easy the Englishmen refused to play the match out and left to catch their boat for Melbourne, leaving the game drawn.

Vernon's team won six, lost one and drew one of their 11-a-side matches, and won three and drew 13 of their matches against the odds. The highlight of their tour was an innings of 285 in six hours by Andrew Stoddart on a matting wicket against Eighteen of Melbourne. Aubrey ('Gunboat') Smith's team won five and lost two of their seven matches on level terms, and in matches against the odds won seven and lost eight. Shrewsbury later disclosed that this team's tour would never have occurred had he known that Lillywhite was broke.

That summer belonged to Charles Bias Turner, known by then as 'The Terror', whose 106 first-class wickets for New South Wales cost only 13.59 each, setting a record that has never been equalled in an Australian season. Turner's victims included 91 English batsmen and 15 Victorians. On the batting side, in the Sydney match between New South Wales and Victoria, Harry Moses scored 297 not out in NSW's total of 576, running out of partners when within reach of Murdoch's record 321.

Turner's success sparked the ambitions of country cricketers in every colony, strengthening the tradition that Australia can always rely on bush talent to fill important roles in the national team. Turner had established himself as Spofforth's replacement by practising alone for hours at a time in Bathurst, in New South Wales mid-west, 210 kilometres from Sydney on the Macquarie River. He had the huge hands of a country boy, and although he was slightly below average height, had an immensely powerful back that allowed him to defy coaches and deliver his off-breaks with a front-on action. At Bathurst Grammar School he failed to win a place in the First XI. He took a job in stables servicing Cobb & Co coaches, rising at 4 a.m. to harness horses. This allowed

Four of the players in Australia's 1888 team in England (L to R): J.D. Edwards, John Lyons, Alick Bannerman and Jack Blackham. (SACA Archives)

102

him to spend the rest of the day bowling at a single stump.

Turner became a renowned expert in judging how pitches would play wherever his travels with the Australian team took him. At home he understood why Phillip Sheridan had imported Merri Creek soil from Victoria for the SCG after its success at the Melbourne Cricket Ground, and he knew how badly Merri Creek wickets played after heavy rain. Few could adjust as cleverly to a Merri Creek 'sticky', and no bowler ever made the switch from matting to grass so easily. In the 1890s when Bulli soil replaced Merri Creek soil in the preparation of Sydney wickets, Turner alone of the topline bowlers noted the change.

The Australians returned to England in the northern summer of 1888 determined to call themselves amateurs and to be treated as amateurs, however galling that appeared to English professionals. They had little sympathy for professionals who refused to rebel against the injustices of their employment, and remained what Wilfred Rhodes called 'VIPs on very low wages'.

The sixth Australian team had only Blackham, Boyle and Alick Bannerman left from the pioneer side that had established the country's international reputation. Only the London-born captain Percy McDonnell, Boyle, Bonnor, Jarvis, Jones and Bannerman could get runs on wet pitches. Newcomers Harry Trott, Jack Lyons, Jack Worrall and John Edwards were accustomed to hard, dry wickets. The bowling depended entirely on Ferris and Turner, with erratic spinner Trott the only other bowler likely to get good players out.

The team again signed a shared promotional contract, and was managed by Claude Beal, who had to keep secret a doctor's diagnosis soon after arrival that Sam Jones had smallpox. Had it become known that such an infectious disease had struck the team, the entire tour could have been ruined.

There were two vital withdrawals before the side left. George Giffen refused an invitation to tour because his brother Walter was not picked, and Harry Moses refused to go because the bank of which he was a director was in trouble. Moses, who married a wealthy member of the Friend family, had lent the bank a lot of his wife's money. With the entire Australian banking industry under threat, he stayed home to protect that investment.

Defection of these two outstanding players weakened the Australian batting and, more importantly, robbed McDonnell of a bowler (Giffen) who could be used to rest Ferris or Turner. When

Charles Turner, top, and James Ferris, who had to do virtually all the bowling on Australia's 1888 English tour. Turner took 314 wickets, Ferris 220, and nobody else reached 50 wickets. (MCG Museum)

Jones fell ill, Beal was forced to recruit the colourful all-rounder 'Sammy' Woods to help the team. Woods, then only 21, had just made a fine start with Cambridge University after outstanding displays for Sydney Grammar School and Brighton College in Sussex, for whom he had taken 14 wickets for 27 runs, all bowled, in 1886. At school in Sydney he once took seven wickets in successive deliveries, and as he matured to a powerful 6 ft 1 in and 13 st 6 lb it was obvious to all that Woods was a born fast bowler, but his commitments at Cambridge rationed his matches for Australia to the Tests.

With Jones dangerously ill for weeks, Beal erred in not finding a supporting bowler for Ferris and Turner. Jack Worrall should have been given more work early in the tour to develop his right-arm off-breaks. Initially there was time to bring a replacement from Australia, but under the system in which the team was picked there was no information on who might be available. Instead McDonnell was left with virtually a two-man attack.

John Ferris bowled left-arm swingers at the start of each innings, moving the ball either way at a lively pace, when the ball became worn reverting to left-arm spinners. Turner bowled off-breaks throughout, varying his pace cleverly from a uniform medium-pace, extracting exceptional nip from the pitch, and never wasting time despite his workload. Harry Altham rated them cricket's most successful bowling partnership:

To those who regard 1000 overs in a season as more than flesh and blood can stand, the record of Ferris and Turner in 1888 will come as a revelation. They knew that unless they got the enemy out, Australia would continue to field. Bowl they had to, and bowl they did. Together they took 534 wickets or just 405 more than the rest of the team put together, and this against the flower of English batting with hardly a rest day for 20 weeks.

Only two Australian batsmen made 20 in the opening match of the tour against C.I. Thornton's XI on 7–8 May at Norberry Park, Surrey, but Australia won easily, Ferris and Turner taking all 20 wickets for 161 runs. At Old Trafford against Lancashire Ferris took 8 for 41 in the first innings. At Stoke against an English XI Turner had 9 for 15 in the first innings, with seven of the victims clean bowled and the other men run out. At Hastings against an England XI Turner's match figures were 17 for 50, with 14 batsmen cleaned bowled and two lbw. In the tour's 40 matches, the great duo's figures were:

	Balls	Maidens	Runs	Wickets	Average
C.T.B. Turner	10 359	1 222	3 492	314	11.38
J.J. Ferris	8 890	998	3 103	220	14.23

Turner's feat in delivering more than 10,000 balls by bowling virtually unchanged overshadowed the performance of the leading English wicket-taker George Lohmann, who in a wet summer took 209 wickets at 10.90. Turner created such widespread interest he was taken to Woolwich Arsenal to have the speed of his bowling delivery scientifically measured. He was found to deliver the ball at 55 miles an hour, which was a long way short of speedsters like Surrey's Tom Richardson, but a very brisk pace indeed for a bowler who turned his off-breaks so sharply.

Australia won the First Test on a mudheap at Lord's on 16 and 17 July by 61 runs, with Turner and Ferris taking 18 wickets between them. Batting weaknesses showed up more as the Australians' tour progressed. They were no match for England on a hard, fast Oval pitch in the Second Test, England levelling the series with an innings and 137-run win. Australia never recovered from the loss of McDonnell in the first over of the match to Lohmann.

Harry Trott, a moderate success in the 1888 Australian team to England, returned a much improved player for three further tours, in 1896 as captain. (MCC Library)

Australia had a sequence of five successive losses leading up to the final Test, but when rain fell for two days before play began were given an even chance of winning, such was the awe in which Ferris and Turner were held. Facing England's 182 after clever wet weather batting by W.G. Grace (38), Billy Barnes (24) and Frank Sugg (24), Australia failed to avoid the follow-on by 11 runs. Australia lost six wickets for seven runs in their second innings, giving England the rubber with an innings and 21-run win by lunch on the second day.

The sixth Australian team to England played 40 matches, all on level terms, won 19, lost 14 and drew seven, a record which might have been even worse had the two-man attack not bowled on so many wet pitches. McDonnell (1393 at 22.83), Bonnor (1204 at 19.73) and Harry Trott (1212 at 19.23) were the batsmen to score 1000 runs, although Turner produced an innings of 103 against Surrey at The Oval. McDonnell hit a marvellous 82, the innings of the tour, against North of England at Old Trafford, but was not seen again in Tests. Australia lost five of the six Tests in which he was captain, but his wide experience of uncovered pitches on four English

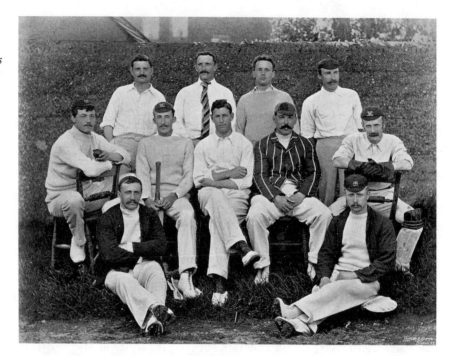

Sydney-born Sammy Woods, with the Somerset team he captained for years with great gusto. Seconded to assist the 1888 Australians in England, he had only moderate success in the three Tests. (MCC Library)

tours made him one of Australia's best batsman on wet pitches.

One of Australia's major disappointments on this tour was in not getting the best out of Sammy Woods. He bowled only four overs in the first Test, 32 in the second and 18.1 in the third, and his five wickets cost 24.20 each. With the bat he averaged only 6.1 in six innings. These were poor returns from a man acknowledged as one of the finest all-rounders in cricket, a mountain of a man who excelled at beagling, fox-hunting, billiards and soccer and who played rugby for England. His wit matched his versatility. When he clean-bowled W.G. Grace, he watched the notorious gamesman depart and said, 'I shouldn't go, doctor, there's still one stump standing.'

The players returned home to find that a sensational cricketer had arrived in Adelaide in one-time miner Ernie Jones. Playing district cricket for the North Adelaide club, Jones had had one knock of 70 runs out of the 80 scored while he was at the crease in 35 minutes, his first 50 taking only 12 minutes. But it was as a bowler that South Australian hopes for Jones rested. He had a physique of hard-muscled shoulders, legs and arms that convinced officials he would prove a classy pace bowler if his action could be improved. Bowling off a long run, he rushed at the stumps like a runaway train and let the ball go at speeds that terrified his wicket-keepers as much as opposing batsmen. Byes ran quickly into the twenties because of Jones's erratic deliveries, and in one club match reached 48!

Club cricket was flourishing in all colonies but the controlling bodies remained short of funds. The Victorian Cricketers' Association decided that it could not afford two matches against New South Wales in 1889–90 and asked for just one. The New South Wales Cricket Association would not agree and inter-colonial cricket fell into disarray until the Melbourne Cricket Club agreed to stage two matches. Early in January, 1889, New South Wales won the first in Melbourne by six wickets to stretch their winning sequence over Victoria to six, but three weeks later in Sydney they suffered a sensational reversal. Set to make only 76 to win, New South Wales failed by 12 runs, thanks to clever bowling by Hugh Trumble (6 for 43) and Jack Worrall (4 for 19).

Trumble continued this outstanding bowling in December, 1889, in two incident-studded matches. George Giffen refused to leave the crease when given out by the umpire in the first of these at the Adelaide Oval. George's bowling had taken a battering in Victoria's first innings of 320, finishing with 1 for 108. A confident appeal for leg before was dismissed before he scored. At nine he fell down as a ball rapped his pads. With the Victorians appealing for lbw, George struggled to his feet. The fieldsmen then noticed that a bail had fallen off and appealed for hit wicket. The umpire ruled the lbw appeal not out but allowed the hit wicket appeal. George refused to leave, claiming the ball was dead and that the second appeal could not be made. The Victorians played on under protest and won the match by 18 runs but weeks of acrimonious letter-writing between the VCA and the SACA followed and the Victorians even asked Lord's for a ruling.

In January, 1890, Joseph Coleman Davis, a delegate to the New South Wales Cricket Association from the Albert Club in Sydney – and the editor of the Sydney sporting weekly, the *Referee*, for more than 50 years – took a NSW team to New Zealand for seven matches. This followed up earlier visits to New Zealand by Australian touring teams and in 1883–84 by a Tasmanian team which had won two and drawn three of their five matches with New Zealand provincial sides. Davis's New South Wales team included Sam Jones, whose century had just helped New South Wales to a first-innings total of 349 and a four-wicket win in Sydney over Victoria, and Sydney Thomas Callaway, a vigorous right-arm fast bowler and useful right-hand middle-order batsman.

Davis's team were undefeated, winning six matches and playing a draw with Auckland. Callaway, a tall, heavily moustached figure, took 54 wickets on the tour at an average cost of only 7.07 runs each and found New Zealand pitches so much to his liking he returned to live there permanently after playing in three Tests for Australia.

Although Horan called the 1880s a period of 'cricket decadence' in Australia, this criticism really only applied to the shambles to which international matches had deteriorated. The public showed their disgust with players unwilling to represent their country unless the price was right by staying away from the Tests. Bickering between associations and star players over match payments did not reach the bush or affect cricket in the suburbs of growing cities. Plenty of exciting cricket kept pushing gifted players forward.

In Sydney, Dr Percy Charlton won a place in the colony side with quality right-hand batting and bowling for the Belvidere club. Sydney Edward Gregory, son of the Sydney Cricket Ground curator and former Test cricketer Ned, honoured his famous family by winning a colony berth from the South Sydney club. In Tasmania Ken Burn, who had so nearly scored a century against Vernon's English tourists, continued to thrill spectators. In Adelaide, George Giffen, Jack Lyons and a newcomer named John ('Dinny') Reedman did enough to earn an invitation for South Australia to play its inaugural match against New South Wales in Sydney. In Melbourne Dr John Barrett and big-hitting Frank Walters forced their way into the Victorian team.

Tasmanian Ken Burn, chosen as a wicket-keeper for the 1890 tourists in Australia's worst selection blunder, had never kept in his life. (Ric Smith)

Harry Boyle considered all of them when he was made manager and joint selector, with Blackham and Turner, for the 1890 team to England. Billy Murdoch, after missing 15 Tests and two English tours, had once more made himself available. Giffen again refused to go and finally this team was picked for the seventh tour: W.L. Murdoch, G.H.S. Trott, F.H. Walters, H. Trumble, J.M. Blackham, E.J.K. Burn, Dr J.E. Barrett, J.J. Lyons, C.T.B. Turner, S.E. Gregory, J.J. Ferris, P.C. Charlton and S.P. Jones. The team suffered an early setback when Burn joined their ship in Adelaide, and announced he could not fill the deputy wicket-keeper's role as he had never kept wicket in his life. Boyle and Blackham had mistaken him for another Tasmanian, John Burn. The players decided to take Burn anyway, shrugging off the worst selection blunder of them all.

CHAPTER EIGHT
LORD SHEFFIELD'S GIFT

The slump in public support for Tests in Australia and the scornful newspaper criticism of leading players did not apply in England, where large, well-behaved crowds that disdained to shout profanities watched most of the 1890 touring side's matches. The team was a poor mixture of largely unsuccessful newcomers and faded veterans, lacking batting depth and with only two high-class bowlers, but on the days they fielded well remained a competitive outfit.

Murdoch showed only glimpses of his former class as he slowly recovered from his long lay-off, but he remained tremendously popular with everyone he met. He was an unrivalled *bon viveur* with a vast appetite for food and drink, a man who in C.B. Fry's phrase 'could enjoy a Klondike bar or a Mansion House dinner'. He ran the Australian team in the style of the landlord of a popular country pub, ensuring his men mixed with their opponents, and issuing instructions with phrases all his own. Instead of telling the team the umpires were waiting, he would call, 'The white coats are out, boys.'

The team played 38 matches, all against 11-a-side, and sustained 16 defeats, winning 13, and leaving nine unfinished, but county treasurers were delighted with the gates they attracted. From the opening match of the tour at Sheffield Park, where Ferris and Turner produced victory by dismissing Lord Sheffield's XI for 27 and 130, their reception was warm, with no expense spared.

Lord Sheffield was notoriously camera-shy. This sketch of him in Australia in 1893–94 is the only known picture of him. (MCG Museum)

Henry Holroyd North, the third Earl of Sheffield, born in London on 18 January, 1832, entertained the first seven Australian touring teams in a lavish manner. One of the early tour rituals was for each team to be photographed on the lawn in front of the lovely wrought-iron verandah at Sheffield Park.

Ferris took 12 for 88 in the first match at Sheffield Park, and followed with 7 for 42 in the next match against Warwickshire, where he bowled unchanged with Turner. This set the pattern for the entire tour, with defeat imminent if batsmen survived the Ferris–Turner attack. Charlie Turner took 215 wickets at 12.47 on the tour, Jack Ferris 215 wickets at 13.20. Hugh Trumble was next-best bowler with 53 wickets at 21.47. Harry Trott, whose leg-breaks had promised so much, managed only 23 wickets at 26.52.

Newcomers had no chance to learn the vagaries of uncovered pitches as the itinerary unfolded at a hectic pace. Barrett's batting lacked style but he showed pluck and patience as a left-handed stonewaller. Frank Walters was a failure, Sam Jones lacked his former distinction, Trott consistently disappointed, Syd Gregory's exciting innings were erratic, and only Ken Burn and Jack Lyons improved. For the first time since Anglo-Australian matches began Australia lost its big advantage in wicket-keeping, England's Gregor McGregor matching Blackham and showing the enterprise he displayed in his rugby matches for Scotland.

The days of the touring representative sides had passed, and the Australians were surprised by the improvement in county championship standards. From haphazard beginnings in 1873, it had developed into an outstanding competition. Lord Harris and his colleagues at Lord's had improved the wages of professionals and removed their social constraints and by liaising with headmasters had made dozens of amateurs from public schools keen to play for their counties.

Yorkshire (twice), MCC, Notts, South of England and The Players (twice) all beat Australia before the First Test, from 21 to 23 July 1880 at Lord's, but the public ignored forecasts of a one-sided match by turning up in force. With England leading by 41 runs on the first innings, Barrett won a niche in cricket history by batting right through Australia's second innings for an unbeaten 67, the first time this had been done in Tests. Set to score 136 to win, England won by seven wickets. W.G. Grace, whose fumbles in the field aroused guffaws, made sure of England's triumph with 75 not out after being dropped on 44.

Barrett cost Australia a chance of winning the Second Test at The Oval in mid-August when he threw wildly after a clean pick-up at cover with the last pair at the crease and the scores level. The two over-throws that resulted gave England victory. The Third Test at Old Trafford was abandoned because of rain, England winning the rubber 2–0.

Murdoch left Australian cricket to join Sussex after the 1890

Australian tour and Ferris went to Gloucestershire, losses team-mates considered calamitous for Australian cricket. The English selectors showed they agreed by including them in the England team that toured South Africa in 1891–92 under Walter Read's captaincy. Both played for England in the only Test, England winning by 189 runs. Ferris had 13 for 91 in the match. Murdoch took over as Sussex captain in 1893 and remained in the job until 1899. Between 1901 and 1904 he played in the London Counties XI with his old friend W.G. Grace. In 1904 at the age of 49 he made 140 for The Gentlemen, against The Players.

Murdoch went out of Australian cricket amid accusations at home that the 1890 team he led in England was a drunken one in which brawling was common. Popular Harry Boyle was reported to have been decked by the burly Jack Lyons in one dust-up. In the resulting flurry of charge and counter-charge, Murdoch's feat in heading the Australian tour batting averages for the fourth time in five trips to England was forgotten. The *Bulletin* magazine commented:

The Australian cricketer in England, batting the day after a banquet, sees at least two balls approaching. One is dead on the wicket. He smites at the other and sees four bails flying about, two wicket-keepers looking the other way, two prostrate and two erect stumps. Then he retires to two pavilions, makes 22 excuses, and another cable about bad luck and wet wickets is despatched. The Australians always bat on a wet wicket after a banquet.

The financial disasters suffered by both English touring teams in 1887–88 gave the Australian public a three-year respite from international cricket and a chance to concentrate on domestic competitions. Large crowds attended club and inter-colonial matches. Richard Cashman, in his notable study of cricket crowds *Have A Go, Yer Mug*, found that an average of 5853 spectators per day, or 26,340 a match, went to New South Wales v. Victoria games on the Sydney Cricket Ground in the ten seasons between 1890–91 and 1900–01. When dramatic events were forecast for club matches, crowds up to 10,000 were customary.

Revenue from these domestic matches strengthened the colony associations financially but they remained wary of ventures involving seasoned Test players, whom they regarded as greedy, money-grubbing pests. New faces who might push the old guard out of the Australian XI were warmly greeted.

Ned Gregory, curator responsible for Sydney Cricket Ground's first Test wickets, designer of a wonderful scoreboard, and head of a noted cricket family. (SCG Trust)

At the Sydney ground the Gregory family flourished in a cottage dividing the no. 1 and no. 2 fields, known as 'Gregory's Cottage'. After looking after the complex for soldiers from the nearby Victoria Barracks and then for the East Sydney Club and subsequently the Civil Service Club, Ned Gregory remained when the New South Wales Cricket Association took over. Ned watched its transformation from the Civil and Military Ground to the Association Ground and finally to the Sydney Cricket Ground. At his cottage Ned experimented with making cricket bats from Moreton Bay fig trees, and there in 1870 his son Sydney was born, destined to become the first Australian to follow his father into the Test team.

Thanks to committeemen with influential contacts in the stricken banking industry, the Melbourne Cricket Club slowly recovered from the £500 overdraft it had been left with after sponsoring the tour by Vernon's English team. Bob McLeod, first of three brothers to play for Victoria, took 7 for 107 and scored 87 when Victoria had a shock six-wicket win over NSW at Melbourne in 1891–92. A month later Frank Walters made 112 to set up a Victorian win in Sydney by an innings and 115 runs.

Victorian claims to colonial supremacy were shattered, however, by a fine team from South Australia that included George Giffen, Joe Lyons, Affie Jarvis, Jack Noel and Walter Giffen. In January, 1891, South Australia scored 472 to defeat Victoria, 220 and 190, by an innings and 62 runs in Melbourne. George Giffen made 237 and took 12 wickets on a perfect batting strip, a feat welcomed in Adelaide by a special civic reception and the presentation to George of a purse full of sovereigns.

Western Australia and Queensland lagged behind NSW, Victoria and South Australia, and the stormy waters of Bass Strait made Tasmania too remote for regular matches against mainland sides. In Brisbane, the colourful Arthur Coningham continually gave cricket fans something to cheer about. He followed his 43 in a total of 116 against Melbourne Cricket Club in 1890 in Melbourne with a unique knock for 26 runs in a mid-week match for the Stanleys against the Alberts in Brisbane. His seven scoring shots produced 6,4,5,5,3,2,1 and his 26 were all the runs his team scored in an innings without extras!

Melbourne at the end of the 1890s was abuzz about the visit of the divine Sarah Bernhardt for a fee of £20,000. Tickets for her performance were so scarce they had to be auctioned. Excitement was high in other sports too. A crowd of 32,595 attended the 1890

Australian Rules grand final on Melbourne Cricket Ground when the Melbourne club admitted footballers for the first time to an oval previously used only by cricketers and in November Carbine won the Melbourne Cup from 38 competitors carrying 10 st 5 lb.

Victorian cricketers at the time were accustomed to regular visits from James ('Dimboola Jim') Phillips, a skilful right-hand batsman and right-arm medium-pace bowler who strengthened the prestigious Melbourne Cricket Club team. Phillips, born at Pleasant Creek near Adelaide in 1851, lived in the hamlet that gave him his nickname until an age when cricketers thought about retiring. He first played for Victoria in 1885–86, aged 34, and in 1893 made 165 for Players of Melbourne against Melbourne. He travelled to and from England for many years and appeared for the Marylebone Cricket Club from 1888 to 1893 and for Middlesex from 1890 for nine seasons. He had a top score of 85 in 17 matches for Victoria, six times taking five wickets in an innings, with a best analysis of 7 for 20 against New South Wales in 1890.

Back in England Lord Sheffield, recalling how much he had enjoyed the heat of Constantinople during a three-year diplomatic stint there, decided to escape the rigours of an English winter by bringing a cricket team to Australia in 1891–92. He corresponded with

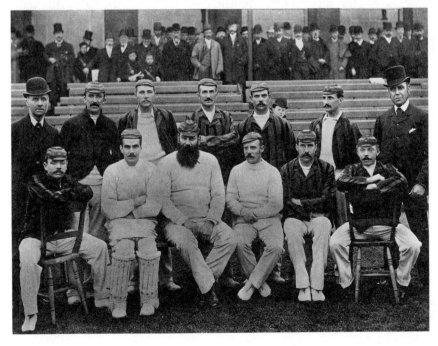

The English team Dr W.G. Grace brought to Australia for Lord Sheffield in 1891–92 succeeded in attracting big crowds back to cricket. (Mitchell Library, *Sydney*)

Australian Test hero Harry Boyle, who encouraged him to carry out the scheme, but to make sure he brought Dr W.G. Grace to ensure the box-office success of his team. His lordship was in his sixtieth year and regarded as one of the world's richest men. He had spent a fortune restoring Sheffield Park, where it was customary for him to stage lunches for 300 people in the honour of touring Australian teams. He explained his approach to the tour in this letter to the Melbourne *Leader*:

I have long waited to see your country and your cricket, and as I was compelled by my failing health to take a long sea voyage and spend the winter away from England, it occurred to me that if it was convenient for you in Australia to see us, I could combine a visit for health with a visit of English cricketers.

Fears that Australian clubs might consider a tour by Lord Sheffield's team a disruption to Australian domestic cricket proved false among an Australian public who held a man of such prominence in awe. Lord Sheffield wrote to Arthur Shrewsbury inviting him to join the team and seeking his advice on the tour outlook. Shrewsbury declined to go but went to the trouble of drawing up a prospective budget for the tour. For 21 weeks in the colonies, Shrewsbury calculated that a team of 13 would cost £6800 for the trip, the main costs being £1300 in return passages, £3250 in salaries for the 13 players at £250 each, and £859 in hotel charges at an average cost of nine shillings a day. This budget even included items such as the hiring of bands at the team's eight main matches at £10 per day, tips for stewards on the ships to and from England at £2 per player or £26 each way, plus £100 for the agent who would arrange the team's matches in advance and help promote them before the team arrived.

The Tasmanian cricket historian Ric Finlay, after a detailed search of Lord Sheffield's venture, said that his lordship was strongly urged to make the trip by old friends in the diplomatic corps who were concerned at the long delay by Australia towards federation and the effect this would have on British investments in the colonies. Lord Sheffield's friends at Lord's, Lord Darnley and Lord Harris, concerned over reports of declining cricket standards in Australia, believed an English tour would end the slump.

Both Lord Sheffield's professional advisors, Shrewsbury and Alfred Shaw – who by then had joined his lordship's personal staff – warned him of the heavy additional expenditure that would occur if he included amateurs in the touring team. They pointed out that when Lord Harris's team was in Australia in 1878–79, the expenses of each amateur was double that of the professionals, largely because of the amateurs' high wine bills.

Shrewsbury said the presence of Dr W.G. Grace in the team would improve tour takings by about £1500–2000 as a new generation of cricketers had sprung up who would be anxious to see him. Lord Sheffield immediately wrote to Grace, who politely refused to join the tour on the grounds that his fee would be too high. Lord Sheffield then invited Grace to Sheffield Park and after a meeting there in March, 1891, Grace agreed to make his second tour of Australia for a fee of £3000, plus all expenses for himself, his wife and two children, and the cost of employing a locum to run Grace's medical practice while he was away. The total cost to Lord Sheffield just for Grace was around £5000.

The New South Wales Cricket Association granted the tour its patronage as soon as it learned Dr Grace would tour. The Victorian Cricket Association, still smarting from the losses of the 1887–88 English teams, only agreed to particpate in the tour if Lord Sheffield travelled with the team. After a meeting with his advance agent Frank Illingworth at Sheffield Park, Lord Sheffield also promised to include matches in Tasmania, Queensland and New Zealand.

George Gunn joined Shrewsbury in turning down the tour but William Attewell, George Lohmann, Johnny Briggs, Robert Peel and Robert Abel all accepted £300, plus expenses 'exclusive of wine and cigars', to join the tour. To this hard core of professionals, Lord Sheffield added the amateurs Octavius Radcliffe, Gregor McGregor, George Bean, John Sharpe and Hylton Philipson. Lord Sheffield emphasised that none of the amateurs had a financial interest in the tour. He had budgeted for expenditure of £11,000 and any receipts above that amount would be divided evenly among the team's professionals.

Lord Sheffield enjoyed bands and he hired a full complement to play at London's Albert Dock as the *Arcadia* steamed out with the strongest cricket team England had ever sent abroad. The famous explorer H.M. Stanley was on board, heading for a four-month lecture tour of Australia. Ben Wardill met the *Arcadia* when she berthed at Albany, Western Australia. There Lord Sheffield quickly explained that, because of his aversion to speech-making, responsibility for the twenty speeches he was scheduled to make on the tour would be taken over by W.G. Grace. As his team disembarked from the *Arcadia* Grace said jokingly: 'If I had known I would have to make so many speeches I would not have come.'

Wardill wrote to John Portus, secretary of the NSWCA, explaining that he would have to apologise to all the mayors who had expected to entertain Lord Sheffield that his health would not stand it. The letter added that his lordship had offered to pay for a trophy to the value of 150 guineas for competition between Victoria, South Australia and New South Wales and asked Portus for suggestions how such a competition should be conducted.

In between practising for their first match in Adelaide against South Australia, the Englishmen watched South Australia play Victoria, and were lucky to witness one of the great all-round feats of Australian cricket. George Giffen batted seven hours for 271 and then claimed 9 for 96 and 7 for 70. W.G. watched carefully and commented: 'You have one of the best all-round men in the world. If we are lucky enough to get rid of him we will get on very well.' Giffen had a top score of 49 in the Tests and only in the Second Test, when he took ten wickets, did he make a major contribution to Australia's display.

England began splendidly on 20 November, 1891, by defeating South Australia in Adelaide by an innings and 62 runs. Attewell took 11 wickets and Briggs, Read and Stoddart scored half-centuries. The team went by train to Melbourne while Lord Sheffield travelled by sea, and the *Argus* said there was 'a wild storm of cheering when the heavily bearded face of old Grace the warrior appeared on the platform'. The tourists were thrust into coaches with the horses decorated in Lord Sheffield's colours – gold, crimson and dark violet – and paraded through the city. At the Melbourne Cricket Ground a band played 'A Fine Old English Gentleman' as W.G. stepped down with his wife and children.

The Australian newspapers took delight in describing Grace's bulk. One paper said he had the same powerful chest as on his previous visit but it had slipped down a bit. The *Bulletin* expressed shock at the size of W.G.'s feet: 'He could get two pound a week and tucker merely to walk about in the grasshopper districts and kill off the pest.' Grace took his amateurs to the Oriental Hotel while the professionals went to the inferior Sheahan's Treasury Hotel and throughout the tour the two groups were accommodated separately, assembling together for matches, practice sessions and receptions.

At the tea interval in the match against Victoria, W.G. was on

Although overweight, W.G. Grace remained a formidable cricketer whether bowling or batting, drawing big crowds where he appeared.
(MCC Library)

a century and when the players went for the twenty-minute break he refused to go off. The Victorians moved towards the gate but the crowd supported W.G. who continued to 159 out of 284. Lord Sheffield arrived at the ground to watch Grace's century and between innings he was taken out on the pitch to inspect the wicket. This was the first sight most Australians had had of him and this is how the *Australasian* reported the event:

His Lordship is genial, jovial, hearty and a thorough sportsman, cricket being his special hobby. He cares little for vanity of wearing apparel, but dresses himself for comfort and in a style all his own. He wore an Alpine hat carrying the colours of his eleven, roomy nankeen trousers, and a dark-blue shooting jacket. A newspaper parcel was in one pocket and a warm-tinted handkerchief in the other. He chatted merrily with all and sundry who were presented to him, and when he made his tour of the ground the crowd cheered him, recognising a fine old English gentleman who had always been the first to welcome 'our boys' on English soil.

Behind his affable, consistently warm exterior Lord Sheffield was, in fact, seething over the treatment he had received in Adelaide from the South Australian Cricket Association secretary John Creswell. The Englishmen's itinerary included a Test in Adelaide, and to make sure of it Creswell had threatened to withdraw the South Australian members of the Australian team, George Giffen and Jack Lyons, if it did not go ahead. Lord Sheffield told Creswell he had his Test but refused to have anything further to do with him. He even asked the SACA to appoint a temporary secretary he could deal with instead of Creswell.

After defeating Victoria by an innings and 107 runs, England continued in outstanding form by beating New South Wales in Sydney by four wickets. The New South Wales captain Harry Moses objected to the Englishmen using Dennis Cotter, a wicket-keeper who had played for Victoria, as their travelling umpire. This held up the start of play for an hour until both sides agreed Alfred Shaw should umpire in Cotter's place. Turner took 6 for 45 and 5 for 77 for a NSW side in which only Moses (55) made runs against Briggs and Attewell.

Turner at the time was the hero of the Carlton club, for whom he once dismissed the entire Albert club for ten. The overall superiority of the Carlton and Belvidere clubs killed the Sydney public's interest in club cricket. On 11 January, 1893, the *Referee*

Heavily bearded W.G. Grace sits on the steps at Government House in Sydney, accompanied by Australia's Test stars and their wives. John Ferris is holding a rifle for some reason. (Mitchell Library, Sydney)

said: 'Anyone with international ambitions must join the Carltons to have a chance of selection.'

Blackham, elected captain by team-mates for the first six-ball-over Test match in Australia, led his team to a resounding win in Melbourne after a long series of defeats, thanks to opening partnerships of 84 and 60 by Alick Bannerman and Jack Lyons. Bannerman's return gave Australia's batting a steadiness – he was at the crease 435 minutes for 45 and 41 – lacking in his absence and allowed the rapidly maturing Lyons to attack. England put on a marvellous batting display, scoring only 54 runs fewer in eight hours 20 minutes batting than Australia scored in 13 hours. Left to make 213 in 150 minutes to win, England went for the runs instead of settling for a draw. W.G. delighted the crowd with innings of 50 and 25. Bob McLeod, in his Test debut, took 5 for 55 in England's first innings and Turner had 5 for 51 in the second.

At a time when bankers were suiciding and Victoria faced the worst depression in its history, 75,000 paid to watch the Test. The Melbourne Cricket Club granted free use of the MCG in appreciation of the hospitality Lord Sheffield had given so many Australians at Sheffield Park. Lord Sheffield's cheque from the match reached £2600 which made nonsense of Shrewsbury's forecast £500 profit. The first-day crowd of 25,000 had only ever been exceeded by one match in England at that point. Australia's team for this match, chosen for the first time by a selection panel comprising George Giffen, Jack Blackham and C.T.B. Turner (one from each colony), won on merit after both sides sustained injuries. Turner was in bed all the first day, Moses strained a leg, and Briggs and Bean both cut their hands.

After six more bush matches, W.G. gave Blackham a stern warning as the teams assembled in Sydney for the second Test. 'If you play Moses, I'll not allow you a substitute,' said W.G. This was fair enough as Moses was still hobbling because of the injury sustained in Melbourne, but to the public W.G.'s attitude was that of an inflexible, unsportsmanlike opponent desperate for success.

Australia gambled by including Moses and at 3 for 63 at lunch on the first day he was quickly called to the crease. He batted well but when his leg broke down again he was not offered a runner. Lohmann took 8 for 58 to have Australia out for 145 and when England batted at the end of the first day Moses limped from end to end, fielding in the slips. The next day he could not field at all. Amid growing hostility from the crowd, W.G. finally allowed the ageing Tom Garrett to field in Moses's place after pointedly telling the much fitter, fleet-footed Syd Gregory he would not be required.

Some newspapers said W.G. allowed Garrett on to the field on instructions from Lord Sheffield. Others claimed W.G. made the gesture on his own initiative, but there was no doubt that spectators' desire for a match played on even terms and their growing anger over Australia fielding a man short had officials worried when Garrett ran on to the ground.

England took a 162-run lead when Abel carried his bat through their first innings for 132 not out, the first Englishman to achieve the feat in Tests. Abel batted 5 hours 25 minutes and when Australia lost Harry Trott before stumps on the second day an English win looked certain, with Moses unable to bat. Despite this Australia produced a wonderful display of batting on the third day, with Lyons (134) and Bannerman (91) putting on 174 for the second wicket. At stumps Australia were 101 in front at 3 for 263.

Australia added a further 36 runs without loss on the fourth morning before rain drenched the pitch. Left-hander Billy Bruce cast caution aside as he swung lustily at virtually every ball and, with luck, reached 72 before Briggs finished the innings off with a hat-trick, dismissing Walter Giffen, Syd Callaway and Blackham with successive balls. Rain came again before stumps with England, chasing 230 to win, on 3 for 11. Notwithstanding a splendid 59 from Stoddart, England never mastered Turner (4 for 46) and Giffen (6 for 72) on the fifth day, although the pitch rolled out well. Bannerman had batted for 15 hours in the two Tests in a legendary display of stonewalling. He made only 67 in the entire second day of the Second Test, and his 91 in 448 minutes remains one of the slowest knocks in all first-class matches. Asked about the relative merits of Bannerman and Syd Gregory, William Attewell said: 'I don't have to pick the Australian team but as a bowler I'd say put out Bannerman by all means – it's more than we could do.'

Bannerman's performance failed to arouse any wish for a collection among spectators, but Lord Sheffield rewarded Abel for his first-innings century with a cheque for £50. Jack Lyons lost a bet that he would score 200 runs in the Test when he outlayed two £50 notes at odds of 20 to 1, but he recovered his money with a £10 to £100 wager that he would beat Abel's 132 in his second innings.

On the fourth morning Bob McLeod had learned that his brother Norman had died in Melbourne. The Australians wore black armbands, and after scoring 18 runs in Australia's second innings McLeod left on the Melbourne train. This compelled Blackham to ask W.G. for another substitute and when Blackham suggested Ernest Hutton, a Melbourne University student who played for Victoria, W.G. replied: 'Is he a better field than McLeod?' Blackham conceded that Hutton was superior to McLeod so W.G. told him to get somebody else. Blackham decided on Harry Donnan, who had been dropped after the First Test in Melbourne.

Despite his occasional tantrums, Grace was the reason for record crowds and a great revival in Australian cricket. Lord Sheffield left him to run the tour and the organisers gave W.G. little rest. He confessed surprise that newspapers should condemn the NSW governor, the Earl of Jersey, for excluding the English professionals from an invitation for the team to attend Government House on the Sydney rest day during the Second Test – this was the way professionals were always treated in England, the way the pros expected to be treated.

Grace's sportsmanship overshadowed his fits of pique. When George Giffen caught and bowled Attewell to take Australia to 2–0 in the three-match series and give Australia the Ashes for the first time in ten years, Grace was quick to congratulate Blackham and his players. The *Argus* reported that there were unprecedented scenes: 'Straw hats, a popular summer gear in Sydney, were thrown in the air a thousand at a time. The ladies who crowded the reserve smashed their parasols on the seats and battered umbrellas were kicked about the lawns. The crowd howled and yelled and cheered themselves hoarse, and it was some time before they left the ground.'

Four matches against odds followed before the next match on level terms, the return with the powerful New South Wales side. By then Lord Sheffield had decided that the banqueting and the heat on the mainland was too much for him and had departed for Hobart, where he took an entire floor of the most expensive Hobart hotel and spent his days talking to derelicts in the streets and the park near his hotel. When one of his players was served with a £500 writ for allegedly assaulting a Sydney barmaid, Lord Sheffield settled the claim for £90.

Centuries from Maurice Read (106) and Lohmann (102) took England to a first-innings score of 414 against New South Wales. When England fielded, W.G. abused umpire E.J. Briscoe for disallowing a catch. Briscoe strode from the field and refused to return even after W.G. apologised. After a long delay, Charles Bannerman replaced Briscoe. England won by seven wickets after Syd Gregory confirmed his great potential with a stirring 93 not out. A farewell outing for the English players and a banquet that night in their honour were cancelled by irate local officials after this match, with Lord Sheffield still absent in Hobart and W.G. unwilling to give another speech.

At Adelaide in the final match of the tour, the Third Test, England batted first on a splendid pitch, and with Stoddart scoring 134 and Peel 82, the total reached 499. On the second afternoon rain transformed the pitch and W.G. angered the umpires by demanding that they inspect the playing surface every fifteen minutes. Briggs took full advantage of the conditions and had Australia out for 100 and 169, taking 6 for 49 and 6 for 87, to give England victory by an innings and 230 runs.

W.G. played in all 29 tour matches and adjusted his batting order to ensure as many people as possible saw him bat, but there was a lot of friction with his own players because of his large tour fees. He came to blows with Stoddart in Adelaide. 'When W.G. lost two Tests in a row he lost his temper, and he kept on losing it to the end of the tour,' said the *Australasian*. 'He developed a capriciousness strongly to be deprecated.' The *Sydney Mail* said there was a disposition among the rougher class of spectators to 'hoot and snarl' at Grace.

The colonies spent the 150 guineas Lord Sheffield gave for the development of Australian cricket on this trophy, the Sheffield Shield, which was first competed for in 1892–93. (Jack Pollard Collection)

Despite all the irritations of a tour he did not want to make originally, W.G. retained a great affection for Australia and the progress of Australian cricket. He regretted the disappearance of the Albert Ground at Redfern in Sydney, missed the wooden pavilion in Melbourne and the luscious grapes that climbed over it. 'And where is that famous well into which a bucket was lowered and players drank copious drafts of icy cold water?' he asked. His major plea to Australians was to improve their standard of umpiring, which he said was deplorable.

Lord Sheffield seemed content that expenses for the tour blew out to £16,000, which was £2700 more than receipts. Informed that the revised estimate of £11,000 for the tour costs had proved far too low, Arthur Shrewsbury said Lord Sheffield would have been more than £3000 better off if he had not taken W.G. Grace and also would have had a better team. 'I warned him about the amount of wine the amateurs would drink and that Grace himself would drink enough to sink a ship,' Shrewsbury said.

Lord Sheffield spent his final hours in Australia handing out cheques for charities and presenting Ben Wardill with five solid silver dessert pieces of the finest design and workmanship. Among the beneficiaries of his generosity were a group seeking to buy a tombstone for Aboriginal cricketer Johnny Mullagh. His lordship was still glowing about the warmth of his Australian reception when he posted Wardill a cheque for 150 guineas from Naples to be spent 'on the advancement of Australian cricket'.

Aware that the 150 guineas would be forthcoming, Wardill had tried all through the summer of 1892–93 to get agreement among the colonies about how it should be spent. Victoria simply wanted the money divided three ways with New South Wales and South Australia, whereas New South Wales and South Australia favoured a trophy for competition among the three colonies. Wardill himself preferred to boost club competitions with the money and preferred three trophies for the best clubs in Adelaide, Melbourne and Sydney. Wardill sent the cheque for safe-keeping to Sydney Cricket Ground trustee Phillip Sheridan, an unhappy choice since Sheridan had feuded with the NSWCA since 1877.

Years of argument about the need for a national cricket control body had seen the formation of the Australasian Cricket Council in Sydney's Oxford Hotel on 13 September, 1892. New South Wales and Victoria each had four delegates at this meeting, South

Australia two. Tasmania and Queensland sent letters regretting their inability to attend. Nobody thought of inviting Western Australia. The council's name left the way open for New Zealand to join later.

The council's main aims were to regulate and control all international tours, to arrange inter-colonial matches, to amend and interpret the laws of cricket, and to settle disputes between associations represented on the council. With no money available from the colonial associations, which were all hard-pressed even to pay the costs involved in sending a team from one mainland capital to another, it was difficult to envisage how the council would overcome the leading players' unanimous objection to its formation.

Richard Teece and John Portus were elected chairman and secretary, with Victor Cohen and J.M. Gibson also representing New South Wales, R.W. Best, H.H. Budd, W. Kelleher and D.A. Madden represented Victoria, and the South Australian delegates were G. Mostyn Evan and A. Robinson. Evan held proxy votes for G.O. Whitridge and SACA secretary John Creswell. Most of the council's first meeting was devoted to a proposed 1893 Australian tour of England, to which they appointed Cohen manager.

Late in the afternoon of the first meeting the council came to the problem of Lord Sheffield's 150 guineas and how best to spend it. When Victoria asked that the money be split between the three colonies, an angry debate followed, which ended when South Australia moved an amendment that the money be spent on a shield, to be held by the premier colony for the year. This amendment was passed by five votes to four and a committee appointed to draw up rules for the Sheffield Shield competition overnight.

Next day, during a boozy cruise round Sydney Harbour, the committee presented a draft of rules for the new competition. They made a terrible mess of it, agreeing in effect to a competition in which the Shield was held by the winner of the first match between any two of the three colonies. The holder retained the Shield until it was beaten. Under these rules South Australia became the first winner of the Shield by defeating New South Wales at Adelaide in December, 1892. The next match, between Victoria and New South Wales, had no bearing on the Shield as neither held it, but when South Australia travelled to Melbourne and lost to Victoria on 4 January, 1893, they also lost the Shield they had held for only 14 days.

By mid-January, when it became obvious that the foundation rules were absurd, the council delegates altered them so that the

Shield went to the colony with the best performance each season in all inter-colonial matches. Victoria, which had opposed spending Lord Sheffield's 150 guineas on such a trophy, thus became the first official winners. At this point Sheridan handed his Lordship's cheque to John Portus, the council secretary, and Portus called for tenders from jewellers. Originally, it was intended to have a figure of Lord Sheffield on top, but when the council accepted the design of Melbourne jeweller Phillip Blashki from 21 tenders, they decided to replace the portly frame of his lordship with the bosomy figure of Victory, a symbol of success in Greek mythology.

In England the decisive defeat of Lord Sheffield's strong team in the first two Tests changed attitudes to Australian cricket overnight. English counties welcomed manager Cohen's request for matches, regardless of any disruption they might cause to the county programme. Lord Hawke's condemnation of Australian matches as money-making ventures for sham-amateurs was not shared by Lord Sheffield's players, nor by the county secretaries eagerly awaiting the takings Australia's next tour of England would produce.

George Giffen wrote in his book *With Bat and Ball* that the Australasian Cricket Council upset all Australia's leading players by instructing the selectors of the 1893 Australian team to England – Giffen, Blackham, Turner, Lyons, Harry Trott and Alick Bannerman – to include the former Queenslander, Arthur Coningham, who was then playing in New South Wales. The Council was having trouble convincing the MCC hierarchy at Lord's that it was fully representative of Australian cricket, and apparently believed that by including a player from Queensland it would demonstrate that it represented the majority of Australian colonies. Coningham's inclusion would be a memorable one for the Australians – and not just on account of his cricket.

CHAPTER NINE

PRANKSTER CONINGHAM

Harry Graham was only a little man of 5 ft 6 in and weighing 9 st 7 lb, but few men have driven a cricket ball as hard as he did in his prime. He was all animation at the crease, perpetually aggressive, eager to play shots all round the wicket, never allowing the bowler's reputation to curb his vigour. More than any of his team-mates he demonstrated the revival in Australia's cricket standards on the 1893 tour of England, although he was then only 22 years old.

Harry Graham, a dashing Victorian who scored centuries on his debut in Tests in both England and Australia. (MCG Museum)

Graham was born in the Melbourne suburb of Carlton and attended Berwick Grammar School, where he was fortunate to have a headmaster, Edward Vieusseux, who advised all-out attack. Throughout his 14 years in big cricket, Harry tried to follow Vieusseux's tuition and most of his nine centuries were batting classics.

Graham was known as the 'Little Dasher' from the time he came into the South Melbourne First XI. He became involved in many big stands with Harry Trott, and earned his first English tour with a series of dazzling knocks for Victoria in 1892–93, especially his 86 not out against South Australia on the Melbourne Cricket Ground. There have been few more nimble-footed batsmen than Graham, who astonished George Giffen in that match by jumping down the pitch to well-flighted balls, driving them confidently to the fence. He was similarly assured against fast bowling and was one of the fastest runners between wickets in Australia's cricket history. He could field anywhere with rare skill but because of his Dean Jones-like speed was probably most valuable in the deep. On two tours of England he developed his skill batting on wet pitches and became one of the best of Australia's batsmen after rain.

Syd Gregory, Harry Trott, Charlie Turner, Alick Bannerman, Hugh Trumble, Jack Lyons and Jack Blackham were all virtually

The 1893 Australian team to England (L to R): back, R.W. McLeod, J.J. Lyons, H. Trumble, W. Bruce, G.H.S. Trott; centre, A. Coningham, G. Giffen, J.M. Blackham, C.T.B. Turner, W.F. Giffen; front, A.H. Jarvis, A.C. Bannerman, S.E. Gregory, H. Graham. (Jack Pollard Collection)

automatic selections given their outstanding records. Affie Jarvis went as Blackham's deputy behind the stumps after some splendid batting for South Australia. Robert McLeod became the first of the McLeod brothers to tour England, and Melbourne left-hand batsman Billy Bruce made his second tour. With Harry Moses unavailable yet again, the controversial selections were Walter Giffen and Arthur Coningham. Walter Giffen lacked the form to justify selection but George would not go without him so with George's magnificent record in colony matches in mind, the selectors passed over more gifted players than Walter and included him. Coningham's inclusion came as the direct instruction from the Australasian Cricket Council.

In a hot, dry English summer Blackham did little to develop Coningham into the opening bowler the team urgently needed. Coningham, married on the day the team sailed from Sydney, played in only 16 of the Australians' 36 matches. He showed rich promise with his fast-medium left-arm deliveries, but in a season when William Lockwood, Arthur Mold and Tom Richardson troubled Australia with their speed, Blackham denied Coningham a fair chance.

Coningham's eccentric make-up probably contributed to Blackham's handling of him, but the entire team resented Coningham being in the side. He was immensely attractive to women and when he failed to win regular selection absented himself from the team without notice. When he did play he proved a prankster who could make Merv Hughes look like a choir boy. At Blackpool on a bitterly cold day he gathered some sticks together and lit a fire to keep himself warm at the fall of a wicket. In the first match of the tour against Lord Sheffield's XI at Sheffield Park he walked the length of the pitch on his hands, both legs aloft, when Trumble caught W.G. Grace off his bowling for 63.

Arthur Coningham, first player chosen from the Queensland team to tour England, was born in Melbourne. He was a gifted left-arm pace bowler, and an incorrigible prankster. (QCA Archives)

Despite his unpopularity Coningham won the admiration of team-mates when he dived fully clothed into the Thames and saved a boy who appeared likely to drown. His versatility was remarkable, for not only was he a powerful swimmer but he was a first-rate pigeon shooter and often made money gambling on his billiards skills, as well as having a successful background as a footballer and an oarsman.

The team suffered from major problems at the top, with an inexperienced manager unable to deal diplomatically with disputes that are inevitable on long tours, and a highly strung, consistently edgy captain in Blackham. Manager Vic Cohen, the first not chosen by the players, was regarded as an Australasian Cricket Council spy whom players kept at a distance. In moments of tension Blackham buried his head under a towel in the dressing-room and talked about black omens and events his team considered superstitious nonsense.

Tour matches passed off happily enough after the loss in the first match to Lord Sheffield's XI in May, to wins over Lancashire, Oxford and Cambridge universities, the Players, Kent and the North of England. However, in one game Blackham's reluctance to bring on George Giffen until it was too late caused a midfield clash that became so nasty Trumble felt obliged to step in as Blackham and Giffen raised their fists. In a period when covers were not used, rain often gave slow bowlers a few hours of creating havoc which Blackham missed.

In a rain-influenced match against Gloucestershire, Giffen batted regally for 180 as Australia reached 503 and then took 7 for 11, with the county routed for 41, all this against a team that included W.G. Grace and former Australian star John Ferris. An eight-wicket win over Sussex in two days, with Trott taking 9 for 83 and Turner 7 for 78, and eventually a morale-boosting win over Yorkshire, took the Australians into the First Test at Lord's from 17 to 19 July.

England introduced one of their great Test batsmen, F.S. Jackson,

Although nerveless behind the stumps, Jack Blackham proved a highly agitated captain on the 1893 tour, incapable of hiding his distress from team-mates and burying his head under towels in the change room. (MCG Museum)

a cocksure product of Harrow and Cambridge with unbending confidence in his own brilliance. Australia missed three catches that would have deflated him on his way to a handsome 91 on debut, but Shrewsbury overshadowed even this innings by scoring 106 to become the first batsman to score 1000 runs in Tests, and the first to score three centuries for England. With Australia chasing 334, Graham joined Gregory at 5 for 75.

The two youngest players in the Australian team then produced a memorable recovery, running superbly between wickets and vigorously attacking the bowling. They put on 142 in 100 minutes before Gregory left for 57. Partnered by Bruce, Graham saved the follow-on, and repeatedly sparked applause from spectators with his glorious drives. The audience rose to applaud him all the way back to the pavilion when he was out for 107, the first Australian since Charles Bannerman to reach a century in his debut innings.

England led by 63, and when Shrewsbury and George Gunn put on 172 for the second wicket in the second innings, defeat looked likely for Australia. But rain held up play on the last day and Australia escaped with a draw. Apart from Graham's debut century, the match was notable because of the umpiring of Australian 'Dimboola Jim' Phillips, who had previously umpired Tests in Australia and later in South Africa.

Blackham seldom slept the night before big matches, publicly abused respected players for their failures, and converted the Australian dressing-room into a den of gloom. When hiding his head in a towel provided no solution he took a hansom cab and rode about near the ground. However, none of his tensions showed in his calm, resolute displays behind the stumps, although in an era of little padding he continued to take hard knocks.

W.G. Grace (68) and Stoddart (83) set England on the way to victory in the Second Test at The Oval with an opening stand of 151. Shrewsbury's 66 and Jackson's 103 took the England total to 483. Giffen's 7 for 128 was commendable in an attack without any pace. Australia followed on after collapsing for 91 through the wiles of Briggs (5 for 34), and lost by an innings and 43 runs despite some bright batting by Trott (92), Gregory (42) and Graham (53).

Australian critics savaged the team's conduct when news of the defeat reached Sydney and Melbourne. 'What a night the Australians must have had previous to the Test match,' said the *Bulletin*. 'Eleven catches were dropped off Stoddart's batting.' One fan wrote to the *Sydney Mail* alleging that the teetotallers in the Australian team were worn out from doing the heavy work for their drunken team-mates. One *Bulletin* contributor said the team's problem was that they were unable to find an effective pick-me-up after a night's celebration.

Blackham lacked the authority to discipline even chronic misbehaviour. The culprits escaped punishment when factions within the team resorted to fisticuffs on a rail trip in Sussex that left a compartment spattered with blood by the time the train reached Brighton. Rewards for outstanding performances were non-existent, and there was nobody within the team with whom players could discuss problems with their technique.

Coningham and McLeod bowled unchanged in both innings against Liverpool and District in an impressive display of stamina and accuracy. Coningham took 9 for 100 and McLeod 10 for 56 in the match. Nevertheless, Coningham was not considered for the Tests and McLeod looked far less effective without Coningham as a foil.

Despite all their problems Australia still arrived at Old Trafford for the Third Test on 24–26 August, following a win over Gloucestershire, with a chance to level the series and take the Ashes home. For the home side, Lockwood had succumbed to an injury, and Jackson and Peel were not released by Yorkshire, but lack of aggressive captaincy let a weakened England escape with a draw. Australia made 203 and 236, England 243 and 4 for 118. Gunn's 102, the first century in an Old Trafford Test, gave England a 39-run first-innings lead which seemed likely to be enough to provide a win when Australia were 9 for 200, but Turner and Blackham added 36 for the last wicket to see Australia safe. When Turner dislocated a finger during this stand W.G. Grace pulled the finger back into place.

Andrew Stoddart, whose opening stand of 151 with W.G. Grace helped England win the Second Test at The Oval in 1893, the only Test to produce a result. Stoddart made 83. (MCC Library)

Blackham's uninspiring leadership was matched by his decline as a wicket-keeper. In four completed innings England's totals were improved by 100 sundries, 72 of them byes, and 28 leg-byes. One correspondent commented that Blackham was still capable of snapping up a brilliant catch in his old style, but hard knocks were no longer to his liking.

Seven members of the 1893 team scored more than 1000 runs, with Graham heading the averages. Apart from that famous century at Lord's, he had a top score of 219 against Derbyshire in four hours. He hit 34 fours and did not give a chance against a county not then ranked first-class. Bannerman made 105 in this match, in which Trott took nine wickets, Australia winning by an innings. The

Robert McLeod, first of the McLeod brothers to play for Australia, suffered from deafness that occasionally embarrassed him.
(MCG Museum)

audacious Lyons joked on the voyage to England that he would 'dazzle them at Lord's', and he justified this forecast by scoring 144 and 83 against MCC and Ground, in an innings that included some enormous hits. At The Oval he lifted a ball over the pavilion into the road, the biggest hit ever seen at that ground. Lyons finished second on the averages to Graham but scored more runs, 1605 at 28.66.

Turner again had a big workload and bowled 1148 overs for his 160 wickets at an average cost of 13.76. Trumble continued his development towards greatness with 123 wickets at 16.39, and Giffen in the most valuable contribution of them all took 148 wickets at 17.89 and scored 1280 runs at 23.70. Giffen's complaint was that he was never given a bowl when wickets were easy to take, only when other bowlers had failed.

On their way home the Australians played four matches in America against the odds and two on level terms against Philadelphia. In a shock result Philadelphia defeated Australia by an innings and 77 runs, scoring 525 runs and then bundling Australia out for 190 and 258. *A History of Philadelphia Cricket* commented: 'Any cricketer picked up from the deck of an ocean liner after a long voyage, slipped into a railroad car in New York, rushed into cricket flannels at Belmont, stepping out to play on turf lurching and heaving beneath him will completely exonerate the Australians.' A week later the Australians had recovered their land-legs and they beat Philadelphia by six wickets, Trumble finishing with a match analysis of 13 for 96.

Reporters eager to uncover the reasons for their failures in England and learn the truth about the brawls between team-mates swarmed aboard the *Warrimoo* before it had been tied up at the Sydney dock and most of the Australian side were beseiged in their cabins. Among the first disclosures was that manager Cohen's attempts to learn about what went on during English tours had so angered the players that they had broken into his cabin on the last leg of the voyage home and confiscated his account books.

Cohen had triggered this assault by informing players their tour dividend would amount to between £50 and £80, only a fraction of the sums paid all previous teams. When the players took hold of the books and studied match receipts, Cohen agreed to pay £190 a man. His attempt to retain the major share of the profits for the penniless Australasian Cricket Council had proved a dismal flop.

The players went ashore without any semblance of a welcome

and for the rest of their first day home were shadowed to hotels and bars by inquisitive reporters, the South Australians and Victorians taking refuge aboard the *Adelaide*, which was to take them south. Manager Cohen said some of the team had been repeatedly drunk and that he had been beaten up. Bruce admitted he had threatened to pull Blackham's nose and Blackham said he was ready to do the same. Trott said the manager had been unanimously disliked by the players, and their mistrust had been justified by his action with the tour accounts.

Coningham blamed heavy drinking and Blackham for the team's troubles. 'When a man's full of champagne overnight, he's not fit for much next day,' said Coningham, who described how he found a team-mate asleep on the hotel stairs when he went down for breakfast one morning. Blackham had given Victorians in the team priority and had been unable to shed his inter-colonial jealousies. Bannerman had run the side with similar New South Wales bias when he deputised for Blackham, leaving the South Australians fuming. Newspapers like the *Australasian* reported this in columns that even today make depressing reading.

Jim Phillips, who spent part of each year on the Lord's ground staff and part at the Melbourne Cricket Club, had great success as the umpire for Stoddart's team in Australia. (MCC Library)

Western Australia had ended its isolation from Australian cricket by sending a team to play in the east, while the eighth Australian team were on the way to England. After exhaustive trials and weeks of studying the skills of candidates the selectors picked 13 players for a trip that cost the Western Australian Cricket Association a hefty £30 a man in a period before rail links with Perth were built. The team comprised F.D. North, P.L. Hussey, W.A. Bateman, W. Back, T. Cullinan, E.G. Bishop, H.R. Orr, W.V. Duffy, A.A. Moffatt, H. Wilson, E.A. Randell, F. Bennett and J.W.C. Bird. Bird came from Albany, Bennett from York and Back from Rottnest Island. The rest were from Perth.

The trip proved a triumph for F.D. North, instigator of the venture and manager of the side. The *West Australian* said: 'The team has not been formed without a good deal of criticism, and F.D. North, the first to really take up the project in earnest, may be congratulated on having, by his patience and tact, beaten down a great many obstacles.' The team travelled from Perth to Albany, where they boarded the mail steamer for Adelaide. They had no previous experience on well-prepared turf wickets, then unknown in the west, when they opened their tour with a warm-up one-day match against the Adelaide Club, who made 211. Western Australia replied with 232 but their players clearly had difficulty adjusting to their initial outing on grass.

Western Australia's historic entry into first-class cricket began on 27 March, 1893 on Adelaide Oval against a South Australia XI that included Ernie Jones, Fred Jarvis, brother of the Australian team's reserve wicket-keeper, Clem and Peter Hill, a family that produced six state players, and James Edward Gooden, one of five Goodens who appeared for the Norwood club. South Australians in turn showed great interest in assessing the skills of William Bateman, who in January, 1889, had made 105 not out for Fremantle against a Perth XI, the first century recorded in Western Australia.

Like many who followed them, the Western Australians found Jones too quick for them and he hit their stumps six times in taking 6 for 53 and 3 for 55. Duffy, North and Orr batted well. South Australia lost five wickets cheaply chasing Western Australia's 111, before Alf Edwards (60), Bill Read (50) and Fred Jarvis (69) staged a recovery that took the South Australian total to 236. Western Australia never looked likely to save the match after their openers were both run out.

A grand century from the former miner Jack Harry paved the way to a Victorian victory over the Western Australians the following week in Melbourne. Harry made 114, Percy Lewis, the East Melbourne wicket-keeper, 63, and the coloured right-hander Sam Morris, then groundsman for the Richmond club, 52. North reached 77 in Western Australia's second innings, and he continued this fine form in the next match by scoring 102 against Melbourne Cricket Club. Orr matched that performance by scoring 107 against a Victorian Junior XI. After a good win over Geelong, Western Australia ended their tour with a rain-affected draw against Ballarat.

Although this first venture against other colonies did not yield a win, the efforts of the Western Australian team encouraged councils and politicians in Perth to support their team. On 3 February, 1894, the WACA ground, on reclaimed swampland in East Perth, was used for the first time, and the WACA received permission to borrow £3000 to pay for ground improvements. The gold discoveries at Coolgardie and Kalgoorlie in 1892 and 1893 respectively had brought great prosperity and a dramatic increase in population to Western Australia. New cricket clubs sprang up, including one in Kalgoorlie, and the number of cricketers in the west

The missionary Lefroy, with the Aboriginal team he trained at New Norcia, Western Australia. (Jack Pollard Collection)

doubled overnight. Success of Perth's turf pitch encouraged North to telegraph the Victorian Cricket Association for confirmation of their promised visit to Perth. He had to wait six years for the promise to be fulfilled.

Through the 1890s Aboriginal cricketers flourished. An Aboriginal side from New Norcia Mission, coached and captained by H.B. Lefroy, a white cleric, proved one of the best in Western Australia and did so well on visits to Perth white teams undertook the two-day coach trip to New Norcia to play return matches. In South Australia, Aborigines from a settlement at Poonindie made regular trips to play matches in the Adelaide suburb of Grange, where their skills impressed locals.

Queensland made their debut in inter-colonial cricket a week behind Western Australia when a Queensland XI captained by Walter Bradley played New South Wales on level terms at the Brisbane Exhibition Ground. Queensland won by 14 runs, scoring 100 and 78 against New South Wales' 64 and 100. Off-spinner William Hoare, from the Woolloongabba club, was Queensland's match-winner, taking 6 for 12 in New South Wales' first innings and 3 for 33 in the second. In a bowlers' match Andrew Newell took 6 for 25 and 4 for 27 for New South Wales and rangy Syd Callaway 5 for 25 in the second Queensland innings.

The match was played in the year of Brisbane's worst-ever floods, and heavy rain left the pitch a spinner's delight. Hoare's low

133

trajectory prevented batsmen getting to him on the half-volley and he hardly delivered a ball that was not in line with the stumps.

Queensland's success made headlines in every colony and ensured their cricket wide coverage thereafter. Searching for outstanding performances, capital city papers began to publish some wonderful efforts in schoolboy and bush cricket. A bowler named Gordon Neale made headlines in a minor country match in the 1892–93 season by taking 10 wickets for five runs, including three hat-tricks. Teams from Sofala and Wattle Flat in a New South Wales country match both had innings of 49 and 37, which experts were inclined to call a 'double tie'. In Adelaide, 16-year-old Clem Hill scored 360 retired for Prince Alfred College in the 1893–94 annual match against St Peter's College. Hill made 214 on the first day and a further 146 on the second day, his team scoring 621. Hill's innings surpassed the record of 252 set by Joe Darling for Prince Alfred College in 1885–86 when he batted for six hours.

Joe Darling was the sixth son of the Honourable John Darling, a merchant-farmer and member of the South Australian Legislative Council. John Darling hated the idea of Joe wasting his life playing cricket and banished him to the Roseworthy Agricultural School and then to the management of one of John's properties at Mundoora after his graduation from Prince Alfred's. Joe was out of cricket for two years but returned to Adelaide in 1893–94 to open a sports store and rekindle his Test cricket ambitions.

Darling, who had not played on a turf pitch for five years, made his debut for South Australia against New South Wales at Adelaide Oval on 15 December, 1893. South Australia began with an innings of 106 to which New South Wales replied with 118. On the second and third days Giffen scored 205 in 390 minutes and Lyons hit a whirlwind 82 in South Australia's total of 483. Batting two short because of injuries, New South Wales made only 234, leaving South Australia winners by 237 runs.

With Ernie Jones bowling at alarming pace, South Australia settled into a highly competent, efficiently led outfit, an ideal mixture of gifted youngsters like Darling and Hill and seasoned veterans like Giffen and Lyons. They recovered from a bad start in their first innings against Victoria in Melbourne thanks to a last-wicket stand of 48, Darling contributing 63, Jones 42. Giffen made 103 and South Australia won by 74 runs before a holiday crowd of 24,000. They had bad luck in Sydney, where rain brought about their only defeat of the season. When New South Wales beat

Victoria by 19 runs in a controversial match, the return Victoria versus South Australia match in Adelaide decided the Shield competition.

Blackham claimed Test umpire Jack Tooher treated Victoria unfairly when they needed 85 runs with five wickets in hand at the start of the last day. Tooher ruled the pitch was unfit for play and delayed the start for almost two hours while it dried. Blackham said Victoria were only allowed to bat when the pitch had become a 'sticky', the Australian term for the gluepots that resulted when hot sun hits a wet pitch. Tooher objected to Blackham's accusations and retired. The New South Wales Cricket Association threatened to ban any team under its control from playing against Blackham until he apologised. This in turn jeopardised the Sheffield Shield competition, then in its second year, and virtually made impossible the job of selectors picking a Test team to oppose Stoddart's English visitors in 1894–95. The Australasian Cricket Council had boldly appointed the selectors despite player opposition.

The Sheffield Shield trophy was still being made, Blackham had not apologised to Tooher, and the Australasian Cricket Council's selectors appeared likely to become an unwanted group, when the showdown match between Victoria and South Australia began in Adelaide at the end of February, 1894. Affie Jarvis had a broken finger and South Australia brought in Rowland Hill for his only first-class match as wicket-keeper. Hill injured a hand during the match and 'Dinny' Reedman had to take over until he broke a finger. John Noel went behind the stumps for the rest of the match.

The Hon. F.S. Jackson, later Governor of Bengal, who made his Test debut in 1893 against Blackham's Australian team. He made 91 and 103 in his two Tests. (MCC Library)

Reedman scored 113 and Darling 81 not out on the first day, South Australia reaching 5 for 290. More than 7000 spectators saw South Australia then collapse to be all out for 316 next morning. A tense fight followed, with every run contested, but by stumps on the second day Victoria were 7 for 200. From then on the match swung South Australia's way with Lyons scoring 101 and George Giffen 89 not out in their second innings. Left to make 370 to win, Victoria fought doggedly to make 312, going down by 58 runs. SACA secretary John Creswell was ecstatic, for not only had the crowd averaged more than 5000 per day, but his hiring of a military band to play at the intervals (five shillings per musician, ten shillings for the bandmaster) had been justified. Takings enabled the SACA to pay off debts of £1327 and buy medals for each man in their first winning Shield team.

The Sheffield Shield was officially handed over for the first time on 14 July, 1894, at half-time in the Norwood v. Port Adelaide football match on Adelaide Oval. The official box was draped in Lord Sheffield's colours of purple, gold and crimson for the ceremony, along with a British ensign. Without rooms of its own in which to hang the Shield, the SACA handed it for safe-keeping to Sir Edwin Smith, who had rescued the SACA from insolvency several times. South Australia's triumph not only made cricket in that colony viable but made sure of Adelaide Oval staging one of the five Tests when England next toured Australia, in 1894–95.

Blackham finally issued a statement, following South Australia's Shield win, indicating he had never sought to charge umpire Tooher with dishonesty, but merely wanted to point out that he had made a mistake. Tooher said he would never accept a forced apology but felt the matter should be dropped as the Victorian Cricketers' Association now said it was never intended to imply that he was dishonest or unfair. At this the NSWCA lifted its ban on members playing against Blackham. Harry Moses, NSW captain on the day Blackham condemned Tooher, immediately announced he was retiring.

William Lockwood, who took 6 for 101 in his Test debut against the 1893 Australians and then bowled England to victory with eight wickets in the Second Test, travelled to Australia in 1894–95.
(Jack Pollard Collection)

The thirteenth English team to visit Australia comprised A.E. Stoddart (Captain), A.C. MacLaren, A. Ward, J.T. Brown, W. Brockwell, F.G.J. Ford, R. Peel, L.H. Gay, W. Lockwood, J. Briggs, H. Philipson, W. Humphreys and T. Richardson. Some London critics complained that it was not strong enough to extend Australia's best because it lacked the services of W.G. Grace, Arthur Shrewsbury and Stanley Jackson, but the team was an intriguing blend of youth and experience. Stoddart was an immediate success as captain. One newspaper said: 'His manner contrasts distinctly with the bombastic way in which old W.G. used to swagger about. Stoddy moves among the crowd most unpretentiously as if he was walking upon velvet.'

Johnny Briggs had to struggle to control his weeping wife as the side left but they arrived in Adelaide in fine shape. Stoddart said they brought more professionals than originally planned because he failed to secure enough amateurs of the required standard. The Englishmen continued what one reporter called the 'old obnoxious English tradition' of amateurs staying separately from the professionals in superior hotels.

The Melbourne Cricket Club won admirers by underwriting the

tour despite the collapse of its bank, the City of Melbourne, in June, 1893. At the time the club was overdrawn £233 at the bank. The club's president Frank Grey-Smith used his influence to arrange a £500 overdraft with the only Melbourne bank to survive the crash, the National.

England began the tour on 3 November, 1894, playing a draw against Eighteen of Gawler on asphalt, before moving to Adelaide for their initial first-class match. Johnny Briggs told newcomers to make sure they carefully watched George Giffen, whom he called 'the finest cricketer the world has seen'. Giffen, who had been in training for months – running miles on the road and staying for hours at the nets – took 5 for 174 and 6 for 49, and made 64 and 58 not out, and England lost by four wickets after scoring 476 in their first innings.

The teams reached the Fifth Test at Melbourne, on 1–6 March, 1895, with two wins apiece. The decider, billed as 'the match of the century', attracted world-record crowds. The Saturday audience of 28,000 was the largest to attend a single day's play to that time. Queen Victoria was reported to be among those eager for regular reports of a tremendous struggle.

Chasing 297 to win in the final innings, England were in danger at 2 for 48. Stocky Yorkshireman John Thomas Brown then played one of Test cricket's most majestic innings, reaching 50 in only 28 minutes and his century in 95 minutes. The only mistake he made in an innings of 140 – a miscue through the slips – attracted a rendition of 'Rule Britannia' on a tin whistle from someone in the crowd. Brown's third-wicket partnership of 210 with Albert Ward, 93, took England to victory by six wickets. George Giffen scored 475 runs and took 34 wickets for the losers in a brilliant all-round performance. Giffen took over the Australian captaincy after injuries in the First Test finally drove Jack Blackham from cricket.

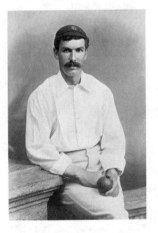

Tom Richardson, another great fast bowler, also made his debut against the 1893 Australians and was chosen for the 1894–95 tour. (MCC Library)

A summer of record-breaking saw the emergence of some gifted Australian youngsters – Victor Trumper, Albert Trott, Monty Noble, Frank Iredale, Ernie Jones, Charlie McLeod (brother of Robert), and Tom McKibbin – with the Australasian Cricket Council adopting a minor role and leaving the administration of England's tour to the Melbourne Cricket Club. There were many controversies, none more discussed than Giffen's action in allowing the Melbourne wicket to be watered and rolled when it started to break up after two days' play. The rolling continued all the Sunday rest day, and cost Australia the match, but George did not want

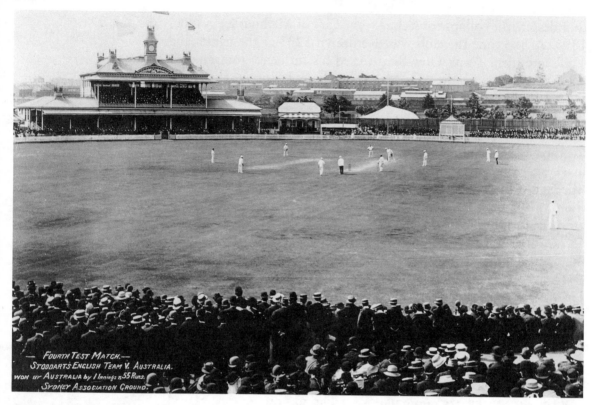

— FOURTH TEST MATCH.—
STODDART'S ENGLISH TEAM V. AUSTRALIA.
WON BY AUSTRALIA BY 1 Innings & 55 Runs.
SYDNEY ASSOCIATION GROUND.

Stoddart's thirteenth English touring team in action during the Fourth Test at Sydney in 1894–95. Harry Graham's 104 in this match helped Australia to victory. (SCG Archives)

an early finish that would have disappointed New Year holiday-makers.

For Arthur Coningham the series against Stoddart's men carried an enduring memory. With the first ball in his only Test that summer, Coningham had the great Archie MacLaren caught in slips. Coningham later set up as a bookmaker and in 1899, still eccentric, conducted his own divorce case, naming Dr Father O'Haran, administrator of St Mary's Cathedral in Sydney, as his wife's lover. The case caused a sensation which almost overshadowed Federation of Australia celebrations. Arthur spoke with silvery eloquence, quoted great poets, and at one stage was ordered by the judge to remove the loaded gun strapped to his waist. He lost the case, but showed once again that he was a big occasion player.

CHAPTER TEN

THE GOLDEN AGE

The successful Australian tours of English teams led by W.G. Grace and Andrew Stoddart in the early 1890s ushered in what became known as cricket's Golden Age. This late Victorian and Edwardian period produced tense, exciting cricket of a very high standard until the First World War. At opposite ends of the world an array of magnificent players produced standards of batsmanship, bowling and fielding in 11 Test rubbers, six in England and five in Australia, that continually boosted the game's prestige.

In England, class distinctions held firm, with county professionals denied their initials in newspapers, forced to accept grubby lodgings, and address their amateur captains as 'Sir'. Watching the cricket, most Englishmen shared Cecil Rhodes's view that the British were the world's leading race, despite appalling rates of infant mortality, drunkenness, poverty and prostitution, and a male life expectancy of 46 years.

In Australia, brilliance on the field contrasted with a turbulent struggle between famous players and newly elected officials who sought to take over the game's finances, team selections, and the appointment of captains and managers. But verbal abuse, common in the committee rooms, never strayed on to the field as English and Australian opponents maintained a standard of ethics and sportsmanship never since equalled. Nor were the birth-pains of Federation ever shown at the inter-colonial cricket as Australians applauded their rivals' triumphs and gracefully accepted their own setbacks.

The dramatic Tests against Stoddart's first touring team in 1894–95, which showed a profit for the Melbourne Cricket Club of £7000 from total receipts of £18,000, brought fascinating comparisons between the Sydney and Melbourne grounds. The

Sydney Cricket Ground Trust announced that it collected £3500 a year in members' fees, whereas the MCG made £6000 a year from its members. The SCG Trust chairman Phillip Sheridan, eager to expand membership, instructed Ned Gregory three weeks before the New South Wales v. Victoria match in 1896 to build a scoreboard to replace the mounted board that showed only the individual scores of the batting side, name of the bowler, and the sides' totals. Gregory had been pestering the Trust for years to improve the board and had his own design ready. In three weeks he erected a board 20 metres wide and three metres high which sat on top of a 28-metre wide refreshment room. Numbers and letters, each half a metre high, were printed on calico and moved into position on brass rollers. It became one of the wonders of the cricket world.

By the time the scoreboard was shown to the public the rebellious eccentric Arthur Coningham had forsaken Queensland and moved to New South Wales, where he joined the South Sydney Cricket Club and took up his bookmaking business. He appeared at Randwick and other big racecourses bearing a large bag with the

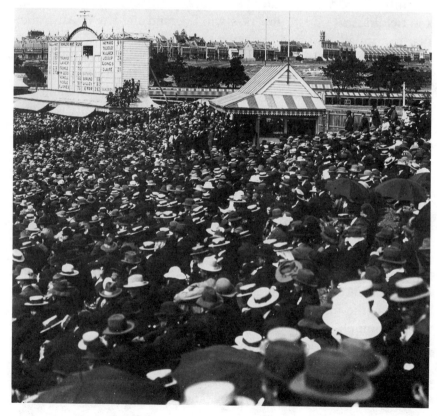

A corner of the Sydney Cricket Ground looking down on Ned Gregory's scoreboard during the 1901–02 England v. Australia series. England won by an innings and 124 runs thanks to 116 from MacLaren. (NSW Government Printer)

words 'Coningham – The Cricketer' inscribed in white paint. Just before he left Brisbane Coningham made 151 out of 262 and 51 out of 272 for Queensland against New South Wales.

Coningham the swashbuckler had rebelled against the way conservative dentist Dr Robbie MacDonald ran the Queensland team and was glad to accept an offer to become South Sydney's ground bowler. Dr MacDonald, a stubborn, unattractive right-hand batsman, played for the Stanley, Oakfield, Brisbane, Valley, South Brisbane and Rockhampton clubs at various times in a career that also saw him bob up each year in the Leicestershire county team in England. He held a number of important posts in cricket administration and had to deal with the problems created for the Queensland Cricket Association by the rival National Cricket Union, a Brisbane body that conducted a strong club competition and catered for those who liked to play on Wednesdays.

The National Cricket Union boasted that there were players in its ranks far superior to most who turned out in the Queensland XI. This was certainly true of three National Union stars: Bill McGlinchy, William Hoare and William ('Farmer') Lewis. McGlinchy had played for New South Wales from 1885–86 to 1892–93, and went to New Zealand with the New South Wales team in 1889–90.

The first Australian team to visit New Zealand after the formation of the New Zealand Cricket Council in 1894 was an official New South Wales side. Test bowler Syd Callaway headed the NSW bowling averages for the tour with 40 wickets at 9.10. He later settled in New Zealand, giving up probable tours of England in the Australian side to coach and play for Canterbury, South Island and New Zealand. The leading NSW batsmen on that trip were the 19-year-olds Leslie Oswald Sheridan Poidevin – later to play for Lancashire and the Gentlemen – and David James Noonan. Poidevin, who first attracted attention when he scored 231 and took 19 wickets in a school match, averaged 40.80, Noonan 35.50. NSW beat Canterbury, Otago and Wellington, drew with Auckland, and lost a tight match against New Zealand.

In Melbourne, Jack Worrall created a sensation in February, 1896, when he made 417 not out, the first score over 400 in Australia, for Carlton, in their world-record total of 922 against Melbourne University. On the same day East Melbourne made 876 against Richmond and Melbourne scored 683 against St Kilda. Hero of the East Melbourne innings was Paddy McShane, who

Jack Worrall, who later was often credited with inventing the word 'Bodyline'. (Jack Pollard Collection)

earlier both umpired a Test and then played in one.

Tom Garrett (NSW), Billy Bruce (Vic.) and George Giffen (SA) picked the 1896 Australian team to tour England and originally named James Kelly, a brawny, heavily moustached member of the crack Paddington side, and Jack Harry, as the team's wicket-keepers. Affie Jarvis had put on too much weight to be considered. The selectors changed their minds shortly after announcing the touring side and substituted Alfred Johns, captain of Melbourne University, for Harry. Harry sued the Australasian Cricket Council for compensation and settled for £160. His omission was attributed to his lack of social graces. He did not drink but was known as 'a rough diamond'. He travelled to England with the Australians, however, and joined the Lord's ground staff, often turning out in 1896 for MCC and Ground. The man who replaced him in the Australian team, Johns, was a master behind the stumps but had brittle hands that made him injury-prone.

The ire the selectors encountered over the Harry farce was mild compared with the furore that greeted their omission of Albert Trott. He had taken 19 wickets and scored 331 runs at an average of 55.1 against Stoddart's team and also proved a match-winner that summer in taking 6 for 77 for Victoria against New South Wales. Deeply hurt by his omission he went to London, qualified for Middlesex, and in a career that made him one of the most valuable players in cricket was only briefly seen again on Australian fields.

A luckier addition to the 1896 team was Clem Hill. He was not among the team originally announced but after he scored 206 not out for South Australia against New South Wales in Sydney was offered a place in the side at special terms of £200, plus expenses. Hill, then only 18, accepted.

The 1896 Australian team elected Harry Trott captain and accepted the Australasian Cricket Council's appointment of show business entrepreneur Harry Musgrove as manager. Musgrove, who had played in the Melbourne Test in 1884 when Murdoch's players went on strike, beat a field of 30 applicants for the manager's job. The team was A.E. Johns, C.J. Eady, J. Darling, H. Donnan, H. Graham, T.R. McKibbin, H. Trumble, E. Jones, G.H.S. Trott, F.A. Iredale, G. Giffen, J.J. Kelly, S.E. Gregory and C. Hill.

The tour opened with a famous match against Lord Sheffield's XI at Sheffield Park in which Ernie Jones hit W.G. Grace on the knee, thigh and ribs with his first three deliveries and then let go a flier that passed through Grace's beard. The legend is that when

Grace asked Jones what he was up to, Ernie said: 'Sorry, doctor, she slipped.' Lord Sheffield paid both teams' hotel bills and told the players he was disappointed the wine bill was so small.

The Australians found that even the best-known of their professional opponents eked out a precarious living, dependent on sustaining good form and remaining injury-free. Lesser-known professionals often had second jobs as gardeners, lace-workers, paper-hangers or bricklayers. All worried about the winter months when their county retainers were reduced to a few pounds a week, and all were treated like second-class citizens by well-paid phoney amateurs like W.G. Grace, A.O. Jones, Read, MacLaren, Jessop, Stoddart and others who had no occupations beyond playing cricket. 'I have heard some English captains speak to their professionals like dogs,' said Joe Darling.

Ric Sissons, in his prize-winning book *The Players*, provides many heart-breaking instances of professionals' earnings in the Golden Age, listing old professionals who died penniless in workhouse infirmaries entirely forgotten by their county committees. These committees were horrified when the professionals struck for more pay but provided lavish gifts and testimonials for their 'amateur' stars. Eric Midwinter's life story of W.G. Grace calculated that he received £120,000 from cricket. According to Sir Home Douglas, Grace used some of his £10,458 payment from two testimonials to pay his gambling debts.

The shame of it was that not enough money was spent on improvements to grounds. Lord's, often criticised for using sheep to cut the outfield grass, looked like a newly tilled paddock for the First Test on 22 June, 1896, and crowd facilities were primitive. A crowd of 30,000 attended the start, many of them forced to pack on to the grass inside the fence where they knelt to get a clear view. Unsettled by Tom Richardson's bowling and by the crowd movement, Australia were beaten by six wickets despite a record second-wicket stand of 221 in 161 minutes by Trott and Syd Gregory. Richardson, who drank a pint of stout for every hour he bowled, took 13 wickets in his 58.3 overs.

Both captain Trott and manager Musgrove approved the inclusion of Kumar Sri Ranjitsinhji, later His Highness Jam Saheb of Nawanagar, before he was named in the England team for the Second Test at Old Trafford in July. The Australians believed it would be heartless to exclude him when India had no place in Test cricket, but this precedent later created immense problems with

Syd Gregory, known as 'little Titch' among team-mates, made eight tours of England and played in 58 Tests. He was born to play big cricket on the present site of Sydney Cricket Ground. (Mitchell Library, Sydney)

Prince Ranjitsinhji, the remarkable Indian batsman whom Australia encountered for the first time in 1896 in England. (MCC Library)

some Test players' bona fides. Lord Harris, for five years governor of Bombay, strongly opposed 'Ranji's' selection despite his brilliant batting for Cambridge University and Sussex.

In England's second innings, 'Ranji' became the first batsman to score a century before lunch in a Test, adding 113 in 150 minutes to his overnight score of 41. His 154 not out left Australia to make 126 in two hours to win. Bowling without a rest, Richardson dismissed six batsmen, but Australia won by three wickets. Giffen made it a Test to remember by becoming the first player to take 100 wickets and score 1000 runs in Test cricket.

By the time of the Third Test at The Oval from 10–12 August 1896 Hugh Trumble had emerged as a magnificent bowler, bounding in to fully exploit his 193-cm height from a full extension of his long right arm. 'That great camel, Hughie Trumble,' 'Plum' Warner said of him. Another English captain, Johnny Douglas, said Trumble's proper place was in the trees in the bush. When Stanley Jackson twice fell to Trumble's subtle variations in the Test, he said: 'You devil, Hughie, but I'll pick that slower one sooner or later.' Despite Trumble's 6 for 59 and 6 for 30, Australia lost the Test by 66 runs when Peel (6 for 23) and Hearne (4 for 19) routed them for 44 on a hopelessly wet pitch. The English professionals Gunn and Lohmann refused to play in the match when their request for a fee of £20 instead of the usual £10 was rejected.

Trott emerged from the tour with a very high rating as a captain. His team won 20 of their 34 first-class matches, and left eight drawn. They were unbeaten by county teams. Apart from his tactical acumen, Trott was one of the best-ever point fieldsmen, sent back all of the great batsmen of his time with his leg-breaks, and scored more than 1000 runs on all his four tours of England. He saw that justice was done when Clem Hill was placed on the same financial terms as his team-mates after scoring 130 against Derbyshire, one of the best of the 18 hundreds made by the Australians, who had only three made against them.

Stoddart took out his resentment of W.G. Grace by preferring to play for Middlesex rather than alongside Grace in international matches against the Australians, but he accepted the captaincy of the fourteenth English team to Australia in 1897–98, which had 'Ranji' as a major attraction.

Australians were puzzled by the absence from this English team of the popular left-arm spinner Bobby Peel, who had often proved a match-winner in his 20 Tests against Australia. The team was

A.C. MacLaren, K.S Ranjitsinhji, T. Hayward, N.F. Druce, G.H. Hirst, A.E. Stoddart, W. Storer, J.R. Mason, E. Wainwright, J. Briggs, J.H. Broad, J.T. Hearne and T. Richardson. It turned out that Peel had been banished from cricket, for urinating on the pitch, by his Yorkshire captain Lord Hawke. Too drunk to know in which direction to bowl, Peel said: 'Lord Hawke put his arm around me and helped me out of the ground – and first-class cricket. What a gentleman!'

Harry Trott took his Australian team home through America and New Zealand for 11 matches, winning two of their three matches against Philadelphia and losing the third. Trott arrived home to find he was no longer an anonymous local postman but a national hero. While the Australians were away former Test captain Percy McDonnell had died of a heart attack in September, 1896, two months short of his thirty-sixth birthday. In Melbourne, the eight leading clubs from the Victoria Cricketers' Association had formed the Victoria Cricket League and taken all the association's assets. The new league in turn supported formation of the Victorian Cricket Association.

Clem Hill frustrated England's bowlers throughout the summer, showing a relish for pace seldom matched at Test level. He began with a dazzling 200 in England's opening match against South Australia, which 'Ranji' saved with an innings of 189 on his first Australian appearance. By the Fourth Test, when England had to win with Australia 2–1 up, Hill was in exhilarating form. Joe Darling's father had just given his son a cheque for £78 to honour a promise of £1 for every run Joe scored over 100 in the previous Test. 'One has to be canny with Joe – he bats better when the silver is up,' said the Hon. John Darling MP, but this time Joe went for 12 and the Australian innings was in disarray at 6 for 58 when Hill arrived.

Hill put on 165 for the seventh wicket with Trumble (46) and a further 60 for the eighth wicket with Kelly (32), repeatedly pulling balls wide of the off-stump to the square-leg boundary. His 188 remains the highest score by a batsman under 21 – Hill was 20 years 317 days old – in England v. Australia Tests, and although Darling scored three centuries in the series it was Hill's leg hitting that demoralised England's bowlers and led to Australia's 4–1 triumph.

England were handicapped by the absence of Stoddart in the first two Tests because he was too griefstricken to play, following the

Archie MacLaren, who took over the England captaincy when Stoddart became griefstricken at the death of his mother, led the fifteenth English team in Australia. (MCC Library)

145

death of his mother. MacLaren and Ranjitsinhji were left to carry the batting following frequent failures of other batsmen against Ernie Jones, Hugh Trumble and Monty Noble. Umpire James Phillips no-balled Jones for throwing twice but there was no denying Ernie's devastating pace in the Fifth Test in Sydney when he took 6 for 82 and 3 for 61, badly bruising all the English batsmen. Umpire Phillips had aroused protests from the Englishmen when he allowed play to proceed in the Fourth Test as smoke from bushfires ringed the MCG. 'If we came off because of patchy light like that, they'd never get half the matches played in England finished,' said Phillips. Ranji's tour came after immigration officials waived the statutory £100 fee normally charged coloured people for entering the colonies.

Although rheumatism troubled him throughout the tour, Richardson ended his Test career with 88 wickets in only 14 matches, including five wickets in an innings 11 times. He was one of the finest sights in cricket in his prime years, tall, black-haired, black-moustached, impressively built, his long-striding run culminating in a high, poised leap on delivery. He continued in the Surrey side until 1904, retiring with a remarkable 2105 wickets at an average cost of 18.4 runs. He died of what the French doctors described as 'congestion of the brain' while on holiday in the south of France in 1912, aged only 41.

Harry Trott also disappeared from Test cricket after leading a fine Australian side to victory, confessing to doctors that he had lost all sight in one eye during the last Test in Sydney. All eight Tests in which he had been Australia's captain had been finished, Australia winning five and losing three. Trott's illness baffled doctors and eventually affected his reason. He recovered after a long spell in an asylum and a public subscription which helped restore his finances. He appeared occasionally for Victoria between 1900–01 and 1907–08 and in 1912 at the age of 46 averaged 37 runs an innings on a New Zealand tour with a South Melbourne club XI. He is not often mentioned in discussion about great Australian captains but Hugh Trumble and Clem Hill both rated Trott the best leader they ever played under. 'An unsurpassed analyst of opponents' weaknesses,' Trumble said.

Australia's success in the Tests and the strong showing of each of the colony teams against the Englishmen encouraged administrators throughout Australia to build their associations into bigger, more active institutions. Our cricketers were like Dame Nellie

Melba's singing – something citizens in all colonies could be proud of, a unifying force in the rush towards Federation.

When Percy Bowden became secretary of the New South Wales Cricket Association at a salary of £1 a week, he beat 13 candidates for the job. By the time New South Wales defeated Stoddart's team, Bowden had pushed his salary up to £100 a year and been given his own telephone. In Perth, the first paid secretary of the Western Australian Cricket Association, Harry Brown, was appointed in the 1896–97 season at £100 a year, beating 21 other applicants. In Sydney, Victor Trumper made amends for early failures in the New South Wales team by scoring 292 not out against the visiting Tasmanian team in 1898. Frank Iredale made 196 and NSW totalled 839. Heavily beaten, Tasmanians took solace in their defeat of Victoria by 365 runs that summer. By then spectators at the Sydney Cricket Ground walked across Moore Park over former swampland looking up at rows of Moreton Bay fig trees. A special Ladies' Stand separated female non-smokers from male smokers.

Trumper joined the Paddington Cricket Club in the spring of 1896 as a fast bowler, but in the 1897–98 season he became the first to score 1000 runs in the Sydney club competition, scoring six centuries in eight innings and averaging 204. In 1898–99, he made 562 in only three innings for Paddington. Monty Noble advocated Trumper's inclusion in the tenth Australian team to England in 1899, but he was not a selector. The team was chosen by Hugh Trumble (Vic.), Joe Darling (SA), and Syd Gregory (NSW) and initially

The 1899 Australian team to England (L to R): back, J.J. Kelly, M.A. Noble, H. Trumble, C.E. McLeod, B.J. Wardill (Manager); centre, E. Jones, F. Laver, J. Darling (Captain), S.E. Gregory, A.E. Johns, W.P. Howell; front, C. Hill, V.T. Trumper, F.A. Iredale. (Jack Pollard Collection)

147

only Gregory agreed with Trumper's selection. Trumble and Darling thought his eagerness to attack every ball showed a lack of patience.

The 1899 team played the customary matches around the colonies to collect money towards their fares to England, with Trumper turning out for the opposition. He made 6 and 46 in Sydney, 46 and 26 in Melbourne, but in Adelaide showed his true ability with a marvellous innings of 75. Darling and Trumble realised as they watched Trumper's brilliant shot-making that they had erred and added Trumper to the touring team as the fourteenth player. He would have to act as an assistant to manager Ben Wardill, helping with laundry and mail and getting autographs for English fans. His tour bonus would be £200, compared with the £700 the other members of the team were to receive. The rest of the team were: J. Darling (Captain), C. Hill, M.A. Noble, J. Worrall, F. Laver, F. Iredale, H. Trumble, S.E. Gregory, J.J. Kelly, E. Jones, C.E. McLeod, W.P. Howell and A.E. Johns.

Darling, nicknamed 'Paddy' because of his resemblance to boxer Paddy Slavin, was widely known as a cricketer who despised any unethical act. He showed his toughness by throwing Ernie Jones in a dressing-room wrestling bout – a sport at which Jones loved to show his superiority – and by the manner in which he debated finer points of cricket law with the hierarchy at Lord's. He was responsible for many changes that benefited cricketers everywhere.

Darling's captaincy was wise and efficient, his readiness to discipline players who misbehaved consistent and fair. He knew how disappointed English officials had been at the behaviour of some previous Australian teams and he did not want it to happen again but he was not prepared for his men to be slighted or unfairly blamed for misdemeanours. His batting had the same stamp of authority and he curbed the left-hander's urge to hit across the line, driving straight and with the full face of the bat whenever possible. He had his team practise on a deliberately flooded Adelaide pitch before they left for England to become accustomed to the wet pitches so common there, but then found they had to endure a long, dry summer.

The Australians incurred one of the three defeats they suffered on a tour of 35 matches in only the second match, when they were caught on a pitch heavy with rain against Essex. Harding Young, a left-arm medium-pacer, splendidly exploited the conditions to take 4 for 42 and 7 for 32, which earned him an unexpected place in the Test team at Leeds and Manchester, where both pitches were damp for a few hours.

Australia's captain in 1899, left-handed batting star Joe Darling, a man of formidable physical strength who helped change several important laws of the game. (MCG Museum)

For the first time in England, five Tests were played, each of three days. Australia outplayed England for most of the First Test at Trent Bridge on 1–3 June, 1899, but England escaped with a draw when Darling badly missed Hayward at short leg with England 4 for 40 in their second innings, needing 290 to win. Shortly afterwards Frank Laver dislodged the bails with an underhand flick with Ranjitsinhji out of his ground. Ranji, who had made 30, started walking towards the pavilion but umpire Dick Barlow recalled him, shouting: 'You're not out.' Ranji returned and in one of his greatest innings went on to 93 not out. Darling reported Barlow to Lord's and Lord Harris promised not to use him again in Tests. England were on 7 for 155 when time ran out.

The Second Test at Lord's saw the sad omission of W.G. Grace from the English side after the great batsman had shown continual discomfort against Jones's pace. He could no longer bend to get his hands to low balls in the field and spectators had begun deriding this once superb fieldsman. 'It's no, use, Jacker, I shan't play again,' he told Sir Stanley Jackson, as he left Trent Bridge.

Hill, 22, and Trumper, 21, both of whom were considered too immature for Tests by some critics, were Australia's batting stars in the Second Test, but the match-winner was Ernie Jones, whose fearsome pace blasted batsmen out early in both England innings. MacLaren won the toss but lost his stumps in the third over of the match, Jones taking 7 for 88 in England's innings of 206. Hill (135) and Trumper (135 not out) gave Australia a 215-run lead before Jones took two wickets for six runs. England struggled to 240 and Australia knocked off the required runs without loss to go one-up in the series.

Victor Trumper, whose brilliant batting earned him a pay rise during the 1899 tour, moving down the pitch to drive. (MCC Library)

The Third Test at Leeds was full of incident until rain forced a draw on the final day after Hearne had performed a hat-trick by dismissing Hill, Gregory and Noble for ducks. Johnny Briggs had an epileptic fit after the first day's play and was sent to Cheadle Asylum. He returned to cricket a year later, had a further breakdown, and died in the asylum.

The Fourth Test caused a change in the laws of cricket, which at that time compelled sides 120 runs in arrears to follow on, and inadvertently penalised the fielding team. England scored 372 on a splendid Old Trafford pitch, thanks to a 113-run stand by Hayward (130) and Lilley (58). Australia managed only 196 in response and followed on 176 behind, which meant England fielded for two days in hot weather. Noble saved the match for Australia by batting for a total of 510 minutes.

After scoring 4 for 435 on the first day of the Fifth Test at The Oval, England lacked the bowlers capable of twice dismissing Australia cheaply and this match, too, fizzled out in a draw, leaving Australia one-up in a closely fought series. Jackson (118), Hayward (137) and Syd Gregory (117) again demonstrated the ascendancy of bat over ball with innings full of lovely strokes. Only Jones, whose 26 wickets in the five Tests cost 25.26, showed distinction as a bowler, sustaining his pace and fire for long periods on wickets that often had too much dew on them to suit him.

Clem Hill missed two of the five Tests because of a growth on his nose but made a big impression on the editor of *Wisden* who, after praising Hill's driving and cutting, said he turned balls to the legside from outside his off stump in a manner 'that had to be seen to be believed'. Hill topped Australia's Test averages with 60.20 but attributed much of his success to Trumper's willingness to take most of the strike against bowlers who worried Hill.

Trumper played the finest innings of the tour when he made 300 not out against Sussex at Hove, the highest score by an Australian in England to that time, surpassing Murdoch's 286 not out on the same ground in 1882. In the dressing-room after he had declared at 4 for 624 Darling told his team that none of them could bat as well as Trumper. They decided then to put Trumper on the same financial terms that they all enjoyed.

The president of the Surrey club, in a speech at a dinner for the Australians, deplored the unwillingness of English batsmen to show the enterprise Trumper, Hill, Darling and other Australians displayed. Darling rose and said brighter cricket would result if hits into the crowd were rewarded with six as they were in Australia. The English practice at the time was to count five for hits over chains into the crowd and six only for blows that completely cleared the ground. Advised to write to Lord's on the issue, Darling had all hits over fence or chains rewarded with six runs, and celebrated by introducing that rule first in South Australia, making the Australian custom legal. Darling also brought a change in the law on substitutes when he objected to W.G. Grace's habit of putting athletic young men in the field for old men like himself who only came out to bat. Darling forced captains to nominate their 12 players before play began and only use the twelfth by permission of the opposing captain.

Alf Johns, a controversial selection as wicket-keeper for the 1896 and 1899 Australian teams to England, had a genius for the job but suffered from soft hands. (Jack Pollard Collection)

CHAPTER ELEVEN

CLEM'S BIG-SCORE TWITCHES

Around the colonies that became states and formed the new nation of Australia from New Year's Day 1901, the unhappiness that a small group of players continued to take all the profits from English tours persisted. Even after the Australasian Cricket Council disappeared in 1900, having held only a few meetings, Joe Darling found himself continually defending players' rights to the cash their skills attracted through the gates.

Most states depended on revenue from well-established capital city grounds like the WACA, SCG and the MCG during finals of district or electorate competitions. International cricket remained firmly in the control of the Melbourne Cricket Club, rapidly becoming the biggest money-maker in cricket and never a supporter of the Council.

Darling's career as Australia's most innovative cricket captain was interrupted soon after he returned from England when his father bought him a 4000-hectare sheep station called 'Stonehenge' in Tasmania. They bought the property, sight unseen, on the recommendation of a Hobart woolbroker's agent, and Joe soon found the condition of 'Stonehenge' had been entirely misrepresented to his father. But he plunged into the development of the property, which was about 34 km east of Oatlands in an isolated Midlands location and heavily over-run by rabbits.

While Darling built nearly fifty kilometres of rabbit-proof boundary fences to help keep his property pest-free and hired permanent hunters and their dogs to eradicate the rabbit – killing more than a hundred rabbits a day each – hundreds of young Australians joined up to fight in the Boer War. The war, which began in October, 1899, had prevented Darling's tenth Australian team touring South Africa on their way home. John Ferris, who had been such a valuable bowler a decade before, died in Durban of enteric fever while serving in the war. Five months later the NSWCA approved the erection of a memorial tablet to Ferris at the SCG at a cost 'not exceeding £10'. The tablet was unveiled in the Members' pavilion in 1904. For years Charlie Turner could occasionally be seen, drink in hand, in front of the tablet. He called it 'having a drink with Jack Ferris'.

The Boer War forced the postponement of an English tour of Australia in 1900–01 and gave the state associations the chance to consolidate club competitions. Joe Darling was occupied with harvesting and shearing in January, 1901, when his home state of South Australia suffered one of the most overwhelming defeats in the history of cricket. New South Wales scored 918, then a first-class record, with Iredale (118), Noble (153), Gregory (168), Duff (119) and Poidevin (140 not out) hitting centuries. South Australia made 157 and 158 and New South Wales won by an innings and 605 runs. Earlier in the season New South Wales had lost to South Australia in Adelaide when Clem Hill scored 365 not out, the highest score in Australian first-class cricket to that time. Hill batted for 8 hours 35 minutes and his score included an eight (four run, four overthrows) and 35 fours.

Hill aged 18, when he topped the Australian first-class averages with 371 runs in seven innings. At 24, he made 365 not out against New South Wales in Adelaide in 1900–01. (Mitchell Library, Sydney)

Hill's innings overshadowed a superb knock of 230 in 275 minutes by Victor Trumper for New South Wales against Victoria. Despite Trumper's innings Victoria won the match by scoring the 344 needed with their last men at the wicket in the final innings. This was the match in which respected umpire Bob Crockett grabbed the headlines by calling Aboriginal fast bowler Jack Marsh 17 times for throwing.

Darling, Trumble and Iredale had agreed in conversations at Lord's with MCC chiefs that some disciplinary measures against chuckers were overdue but the Australians were shocked to find a culprit in their own ranks. Marsh, one of the few Aborigines of genuine Test status, was unlucky to come into big cricket when administrators were preoccupied with the throwing problem that was far more rampant in England. He was a full-blood, born in Yugilbar on the Clarence River, discovered by an official of the Sydney Cricket Club, who was impressed by the remarkable whip in his arm when he saw Marsh throwing boomerangs at La Perouse. He could bowl very fast, with a relaxed, fluent action and the doubts over the legality of his delivery only appeared when he sought a truly terrifying pace.

In a trial match to help selectors pick the 1900–01 New South Wales team, Marsh clean-bowled Trumper, whose stroke was too late. The umpire who witnessed this from square leg came off promising to no-ball Marsh for chucking if he bowled the same way next day. To forestall trouble, the Sydney club secretary arranged for a doctor to encase Marsh's arm in splints and bandages. Marsh arrived at the ground with a medical certificate which said he could not throw the ball with his arm bound up like that. Marsh bowled just as fast with his arm in the splints and at the luncheon interval the umpire said he had been humiliated. Everyone at the ground thought the chucking stigma had been refuted for good by Marsh and his advisors.

Marsh took 24 wickets in four inter-state matches in that season and in March 1902 opened the bowling for New South Wales against Queensland in Brisbane. Alec Henry, another Aboriginal pace bowler, opened for Queensland, and this remains the only match in which Aborigines have been on opposing sides. Henry took 3 for 101, Marsh 5 for 131 and the match was drawn.

The customary flurry of withdrawals complicated selection of the English team to tour Australia in 1901–02. The MCC initially accepted the Melbourne Cricket Club's request to organise the tour but when Wilfred Rhodes and George Hirst would not tour and several county committees refused to release players for the tour, the MCC withdrew. Archie MacLaren was persuaded to take over and he picked a side comprising C. Blythe, S.F. Barnes, G.L. Jessop, A.A. Lilley, T. Hayward, J.R. Gunn, H.G. Garnett, C.P. McGahey, G. Robson, A.O. Jones, L.C. Braund, W.G. Quaife and J.T. Tyldesley, which he captained himself. MacLaren's choice of Barnes, a virtually unknown bowler from the Lancashire League without any first-class experience, was the major shock, but Barnes proved a master of flight and deception, worthy of a place among the greatest of bowlers.

MacLaren was aware that England had to find a bowler to match Ernie Jones, who had returned home after the 1899 tour of England ranked as the fastest bowler Australia had produced. He had given the finest English batsmen a bruising time, and easy singles often went begging when batsmen knew Jones was to bowl the following over. He was also a superb fieldsman with an arm that could rifle returns in with awesome power and he gave 'keeper Joe Kelly as much of a battering from out in the covers as he did batsmen when bowling. Trumble in the slips became a key man as he caught the many snicks Jones induced.

MacLaren's team soon learned what a rare crowd-pleaser Jones had become in the opening match of their tour from 8 to 13 November, 1901, at Adelaide Oval. Jones jumped the fence instead of going through the gate and went out to the middle through a corridor of gawking young faces. If he hit the stumps with the ball or made one of his big hits with the bat, the applause was deafening and when he took a catch the entire arena erupted. When the Prince of Wales asked Jones if he attended St Peter's College, Adelaide, Jones said: 'Yes, I take the dust cart through there regularly.'

England found South Australia far too strong all-round and were easily beaten by 233 runs. At Melbourne in the next match Barnes's subtle variations and pin-point accuracy were too much for a strong Victorian side in a low-scoring affair. England struggled for runs on a wet pitch, Charles McLeod taking 5 for 75 in England's first innings of 166 and 5 for 57 in the second innings of 174, but with more rain before play on the third day Barnes's 12 for 99 gave England a 118-run win, and after only one performance showed him as the bowler Australia had to overcome to win the Tests.

In the Tests, the loss of Barnes through injury early in the third Test upset the balance between the sides. Without their match-winner, England's batting stars wilted and only MacLaren and Hayward made runs consistently. The Australians soon proved that their batting in the First Test – in which they were twice dismissed in under three hours – was an aberration. Hill, with successive innings of 99, 98 and 97 was the batsman who regularly frustrated English hopes.

Clem Hill demonstrates the stance from which he made 45 first-class centuries, including 13 in England. He was also Australia's worst 'nervous nineties' victim with scores of 96, 97, 98, 98 and 99 in Tests. (MCC Library)

Hill's appalling luck in his sequence of nineties was shown in Adelaide when he was caught two short of his century. As Hill walked off, Tyldesley urged him to return to the crease. 'Go back, Clem, I took the catch standing on the cycling track,' said Tyldesley. Hill explained that the captains had agreed the fence and not the bike track should form the boundary. In the second innings Hill chopped down on a ball when three short of a century. He middled it but realised the ball was rolling back towards the stumps. He swung round to stop it and knocked off the leg bail.

Australia did an excellent job to win the Tests 4–1 after losing the first match. Both sides used spinners so often they consistently bowled 25 overs an hour. Standing up to both Noble and Saunders,

Joe Kelly dismissed eight batsmen in the Fourth Test, a Test wicket-keeping record that was not matched until Gil Langley sent back eight Englishmen in 1956.

MacLaren's fifteenth English team won six and lost five of their 11 first-class matches, and won three and drew eight of their matches against the odds. Jessop, Jones and Gunn were notable failures. For Australia, Hill scored more than 500 Test runs without a century, averaging 52.10. The series also saw the start of the famous Duff and Trumper opening pairing and the introduction to Tests of Victorian spinners Warwick Armstrong and Jack Saunders.

A place could not be found in the Australian team for C.J. Eady, the burly Tasmanian solicitor who in March and April, 1902, scored 566 in 477 minutes, a world club-cricket record. Eady took four afternoons to reach that score, hitting 13 fives and 68 fours, and he added 429 for the seventh wicket with W. Abbott (143) for Break-O'Day against Wellington at Hobart. Ill-health had prevented Eady showing his true form in England in 1896.

Hill's great friend and mentor Joe Darling, who shared many long partnerships with him for South Australia and Australia. (MCG Museum)

The arrival of rail travel between the states had taken the hardship out of travelling between capital cities but the English tourists found the long delays at border towns due to differences in track gauges hard to understand. The visitors went home fascinated by the Melbourne Cricket Club's weekly concerts, in stands lit up by the new electric lights, that attracted crowds of up to 5000 people. The concerts produced healthy profits for the club and for the Boer War soldiers' fund. Balloonists made regular flights over Melbourne from the ground and Australian Rules football, rifle shooting, bowls and skittles were offered to members. They also turned up in large numbers to watch the annual Austral Wheel Race between professionals on pennyfarthing bikes who wore satin caps and silk shirts.

Despite the Australian team's triumph the Englishmen found a strong undercurrent of bitterness towards leading players within district cricket clubs. All attempts to form a national cricket control authority had failed. J.C. Davis, editor of the *Referee* and a delegate to the New South Wales Cricket Association, put a motion to the association in November, 1901, urging a national cricket board, but his motion lapsed because he wanted one Sheffield Shield player from each State appointed to the new board. Ernest Edward

Bean of North Melbourne, who was said to be 'almost paranoid' in his hatred of the Melbourne Cricket Club, began correspondence with Sydney officials about Davis's idea but it took a further three years for the board to emerge.

Billy McElhone, son of outspoken politician John McElhone who once brawled with an opposition MP inside the New South Wales parliament, worked tirelessly for formation of a national control body. He said it was essential for the development of all cricket that the control of overseas tour finances be taken away from the players. Neither Bean nor McElhone were ever outstanding players, but Bean did play eight matches for Victoria and included an innings of 103 not out among his 282 runs for the state. Both bitterly resented Joe Darling's speech when the 1899 Australian team arrived home, in which Darling called the Melbourne Cricket Club 'the Marylebone of Australia'.

Apart from Darling, who inherited his father's great skills in public debate, the players had some articulate spokesmen in their struggle for representation on the proposed national control body. George Giffen had served on the Australasian Council, and was widely respected for his honesty and candour. Monty Noble served as a Paddington club delegate to the New South Wales Cricket Association to great effect, showing a talent for straight-talking that was close to magnetism. He was a striking figure as he went out to bat, remindful of the handsomest Roman gladiators. His parents hailed from Egham in Surrey and his mother had wanted him to be a concert soloist, but his rich baritone was lost to the public when he chose dentistry.

The players' closest allies were Ben Wardill, secretary of the Melbourne Cricket Club, and Phil Sheridan, originally appointed to the Sydney Cricket Ground Trust on the recommendation of the New South Wales Cricket Association but a continual critic of Association policies. Through Sheridan, an amiable Irishman of Catholic origin who had a close association with practising Mason and secretary of the NSWCA Richard Driver, the Melbourne Cricket Club always knew in advance of McElhone's moves for a national body.

Sheridan was not a conniving man but he admired all that the players had done in establishing international cricket, and came down solidly on their side rather than that of the free-loading officials so despised by Joe Darling. Ranjitsinhji described Sheridan as a vivacious, active man always full of fun and high spirits.

'One can always tell when Phillip Sheridan is in the room for the amount of talking and laughing that is going on,' Ranji wrote. 'His ready wit is indeed astonishing; he always turns everything into a joke. One cannot sit a few moments by his side without being convulsed with laughter. He is a firm and true friend.'

Darling scoffed at the 'dead heads' among association officials and their guests all his life and said they 'sponged on the game' with their lavish entertaining during big matches. He forced the associations to pay for taxis to the grounds for all participating players, insisted that the players control their own dressing-rooms with a man on the door to prevent unwelcome guests, and on one occasion confiscated a tea urn from an association table to ensure his players had first use of it during the short tea interval.

The players were all keen to enlarge the scope of international cricket without help from Australian associations. At the end of the fifteenth English tour by MacLaren's team England–Australia had played 69 Tests and aroused in other cricket-playing nations a strong desire to join in the Test programme. The Parsees' tours of England in 1886 and 1888 had, despite frequent losses, engendered the hope that India might one day play full internationals against England and Australia. The first West Indian tour of England had been made in 1900, despite the West Indians' loss of their captain H.B. Austin, who had to fight in the Boer War. This followed the tours of the West Indies by three English teams under the captaincy of R.S. Lucas (1894–95), Lord Hawke (1896–97) and Sir Arthur Priestley (1896–97).

Joe Darling's eleventh Australian team of 1902 agreed to play Tests in South Africa on the way home from England, following South African tours by English teams led by C. Aubrey Smith (1888–89), W.W. Read (1891–92) and Lord Hawke (1895–96). Darling was reluctant to leave his wife Alice, by then the mother of four, and the Tasmanian property which he had already made one of the best in the state, free of rabbits, with a Merino herd whose best rams he exhibited at shows and a prize-winning orchard, but eventually agreed to lead the tour.

The team came to be regarded as one of the greatest Australia has ever put into the field. There were virtually no surprises when the 14 players were announced, but all Darling's leadership qualities were required when the side ran into bitterly cold and wet conditions. On soaked pitches, the Australians were forced to drop their leading strike bowler, Ernie Jones, from three Tests but their all-round strength enabled them to overcome this on grounds where Jones lost his footing.

The selectors recognised the rapid advance of Waverley (Sydney) club wicket-keeper Hanson Carter, whose family had migrated from Yorkshire and opened funeral parlours in the eastern suburbs. Carter, born at Halifax in 1878, made his debut for New South Wales in 1897–98 as understudy to Joe Kelly and during Kelly's absence on Test duty had given some brilliant displays for the state side. Kelly was 35 and still kept wicket standing up, straight-backed, both hands in the air as the bowlers approached. Carter, whose father had been Mayor of Waverley, was the first Australian 'keeper to squat on his haunches, a lean cricketer with dramatic little steps as he changed ends. Many believed he was superior to the veteran Kelly but a player who had taken eight catches in a Test could not be left at home, so they both went.

The make-up of the team also meant the end of any hopes Tom McKibbin had of regaining his place in international cricket. He had not been used in Tests after fellow Australian Test bowler Fred Spofforth named him as a chucker in an article for the *Sporting Times*. He was no-balled for throwing in both England and Australia, but never in a first-class match, and repeatedly proved he was one of the most prodigious spinners of the ball known to cricket, three times taking 14 wickets in a match. 'I shall remember for a long time the really ludicrous attempts of Walter Read to dispose of McKibbin's breaks at Kennington Oval,' wrote George Giffen. 'Fully a dozen balls Read received without playing one, and then he was bowled neck and crop.'

Overlooked by selectors for the Test teams that opposed MacLaren's England side in 1901–02, McKibbin was forced to accept the official view that he was a chucker. At the age of 30, he had to watch Victorian Jack Saunders, whose action was decidedly suspect, spin his way into a trip with the 1902 team to England. McKibbin went to Western Australia to play for a spell and returned to his home at Rockley, near Bathurst, NSW, in 1906. He was later spotted humping a bluey around bush towns, earning a few shillings occasionally by repairing shearing machinery.

The complete 1902 touring team was J. Darling (Captain), C. Hill, M.A. Noble, R.A. Duff, V.T. Trumper, W.W. Armstrong, A.J.Y. Hopkins, S.E. Gregory, H. Trumble, J.J. Kelly, E. Jones, H. Carter, W.P. Howell, J.V. Saunders and Major B. Wardill

(Manager). The Australians travelled to England in the same ship as MacLaren's returning English party, the mailboat SS *Omrah*. Monty Noble arranged several concerts during the voyage that gave his baritone solos plenty of scope, but the item that drew most applause was leg-spinner Len Braund's version of 'The Blind Boy'. There was widespread discussion on the *Omrah* over Les Poidevin's decision to concentrate on his medical studies instead of taking his chances as a first-class cricketer. Most members considered Poidevin would have been in the team had he been available. Poidevin was playing for London Counties after taking his medical degree at Edinburgh University and now proposed to qualify for the Lancashire county team.

Dr L.O.S. Poidevin, who played 13 times for New South Wales, 105 times for Lancashire and scored 7022 first-class runs at 32.96 between 1895 and 1908. He also played Davis Cup tennis for Australia.
(Mitchell Library, Sydney)

At practice, before the Australians' first match, a Clem Hill drive broke Hugh Trumble's right thumb. Over the next few weeks five of the fourteen players went to bed with influenza and some of them had to leave their beds to play. English cricket fans saw Australians in green caps for the first time following the adoption of green and gold as the nation's official colours when Federation occurred. A coat of arms still had not been officially promulgated but the players got fairly close to it with a blazer emblem showing a kangaroo and an emu over a map of Australia.

The English teams for this Test series were chosen by a carefully picked panel comprising Lord Hawke, Gregor MacGregor and Herbert Bainbridge, all of them Cambridge University graduates with experience against Australian teams. They co-opted captain Archie MacLaren. Their appointment encouraged English fans to believe that at last Lord's gave priority to Tests over county matches, but brilliant cricket by the Australians repeatedly brought the panel's tactical moves unstuck.

The main culprit was Trumper, who defied the difficult conditions to score 2570 runs, although he often threw his hand away after reaching a century, reasoning that he had enjoyed his share of batting and it was time team-mates had a turn. Trumper's top score was only 128, but his batting lifted the entire Australian team, seven of whom made centuries and scored more than 1000 tour runs. Clem Hill said he owed his survival to Trumper in several important matches. 'If Victor noticed I was having trouble against a certain bowler, he would simply take all the strike against that bowler, hit him out of the attack, and then let me have strike again,' said Hill.

Charles Fry, Test cricketer and author, was captivated by

Trumper's opening partner Reggie Duff, whom he described as having 'a face like a good-looking brown trout, and full of Australian sunshine'. Duff had no doubt about who was the dominant partner in their many fine opening stands. Buckling on his pads for a Test, he said: 'Victor is taking me for a run again.' Both were blessed with an array of unorthodox strokes that bewildered the finest bowlers.

Even against the fastest bowling Trumper only wore a glove on his lower hand, preferring to rely on his skill to protect the bare upper one. His ability to approach all bowling as if he was in a village green match intrigued *Wisden*. 'All bowlers came alike to him,' *Wisden* said. 'They were simply unable to check his wonderful hitting. The way in which he took good length balls and sent them to the boundary had to be seen to be believed. His cutting and off-driving approached perfection and he did everything with such grace and style that his batting was always a delight to the eye.' Trumper had 11 innings over 100 on the tour but never once showed any interest in going on to 200.

The tour involved 39 matches, all 11-a-side, and Australia won 23, drew 14 and lost only two. The first two Tests were drawn after sporadic rain. Australia won the Third Test comfortably at Bramall Lane, Sheffield, where Clem Hill scored the only Test century ever made on that ground – it was also the only Test ever played there! Australia then retained the Ashes by remaining calm in one of Test cricket's most thrilling finishes at Old Trafford, winning by just three runs. The Fifth Test went to England by one wicket when their last pair scored the 15 required to win, mainly in singles. Commentators emphasised that the English teams for the Edgbaston and The Oval Tests were unique because all 11 players had made first-class centuries, which demonstrated the merit of Australia's 2–1 triumph.

Australia's batting twice failed miserably. At Edgbaston in the First Test Australia were dismissed for 36 runs, their lowest score in Tests, in only 85 minutes! Apart from one over from Braund which allowed them to switch ends, George Hirst and Wilfred Rhodes bowled unchanged. Hirst took 3 for 15, Rhodes 7 for 17, in a memorable display of tight, subtle left-arm bowling. Unable to get at Hirst because of his fast-medium pace, the Australians tried to hit Rhodes's slows, with fatal results. Australia followed on but bad light stopped play and only 75 minutes' cricket was possible on the last day, with Australia saving the match.

Wilfred Rhodes, who played Test cricket from 1899 to 1920, took 100 wickets in a season 23 times in England and ended his career with an astonishing 4204 wickets at 16.72 apiece. (Ken Kelly)

Immediately after this narrow escape the Australians faced Hirst and F.S. Jackson on a wet Leeds pitch against the Yorkshire county side. With Trumble recovering from his hand injury and half the team with 'flu, the Australians were out for 23, the lowest-ever score by an Australian XI against a county side. Hirst took 5 for 9, Jackson 5 for 12, and Yorkshire won by five wickets.

The team's injury problems became so bad before the match against Cambridge University that the Australians were forced to call up their indefatigable team traveller, 38-year-old Dr Rowland Pope, to play. Rowley Pope accompanied every Australian team overseas at his own expense and took with him 40 pieces of luggage that contained everything the players might need. Apart from splints, bandages and an array of small scissors, he had items like bicycle pumps and a buttonhook to help Monty Noble fasten his non-laced boots. An essential part of Pope's gear was books on the regions through which the team travelled – very helpful to Darling when composing his captain's speeches. Pope played for New South Wales in 1885 after learning cricket from coach Tom Kendall at Hutchins' School in Hobart, and played in the Melbourne Test against Shrewsbury's English team in that season. He made his debut at Lord's as a substitute in the 1886 Australian team and now managed two not out for the eleventh Australian touring team.

Reggie Duff, who toured England in 1902 and 1905 in teams captained by Darling. A brilliant fieldsman, he opened the batting with Victor Trumper. (Mitchell Library, Sydney)

With warmer weather, injured and 'flu-ridden players recovered. Trumble reappeared to take 14 for 84 against an England XI, Derbyshire were defeated by seven wickets and Yorkshire beaten by 44 runs to avenge the earlier debacle.

Australia won the Third Test at Bramall Lane, Sheffield, because of brilliant batting by Trumper and Hill in the second innings. Trumper made 62 out of 80 in 50 minutes and after Barnes dismissed Darling for a 'pair', Hill and Gregory put on 107 in 65 minutes, of which Hill's share was 77. Hill went on to 119. These innings swung a tense, evenly contested match, conducted under appalling conditions, Australia's way and left England to score 339 to win. Noble's 6 for 52 had England out for 195, giving Australia victory by 143 runs. A dark haze from the smoke stacks of local steel factories reduced visibility throughout the match, and ground staff illegally rolled the pitch before England batted on the last morning. The Australians voted not to make an official protest but Darling withheld the customary tip for the head groundsman.

The Fourth Test at Old Trafford was one of the most exciting ever played, with two outstanding teams fighting tenaciously for supremacy while all England anxiously awaited the outcome. The ground was soaked and Trumper and Duff set a cracking pace, seeking to exploit the bowlers' inability to sustain rhythm on greasy run-ups. After a delayed start, Trumper hit 100 in 108 minutes before lunch, when he was 103, and Australia 1 for 173. Trumper was out to the fifth ball after the resumption for 104. Hill (65) and Darling (51) then put on 71, Darling twice hitting the ball right out of the ground. In deteriorating light on a drying pitch, Lockwood swept through the tail to have Australia out for 299. Lockwood finished with 6 for 48.

England slumped to 5 for 45 against Saunders and Trumble on a spinners' pitch, but next day Jackson and Braund added 141 in two hours of exhilarating batting. Jackson, 77 when Braund was bowled by Noble, received dogged assistance from the tail-enders and was last out, his 128 having taken 255 minutes. Leading by 37 runs, Australia lost 3 for 10, with spectators now hoping for an England win. Fred Tate, preferred to Hirst in a last-minute surprise, then dropped Darling on the square-leg fence. This allowed Darling to make 37 and lift the total to 86.

Left to score 126 to win on a difficult pitch, England put on 44 for the first wicket. At lunch Jackson boasted that England had the game won. Darling refused to concede. 'We've only got to get two or three of you and we'll frighten out the rest,' Darling said.

Back on the pitch two great catches lifted the Australians as they applied relentless pressure. Duff scampered a long way round the outfield to catch MacLaren brilliantly for 38, running at great speed as he clutched the ball. Then Hill ran right round the square-leg boundary to send back Lilley whose reaction was 'What a bloody fluke!' Rain drove the players from the field at 8 for 109 and again at 9 for 123. When they returned, with England one boundary from victory, Saunders's first ball missed Tate's stumps by a hair's breadth. The second delivery knocked back Tate's off stump. Australia had won by three runs and retained the Ashes by taking a 2–0 lead.

Shrewdly guided by Darling and manager Wardill, the Australians enjoyed a tour without the slightest hint of misbehaviour. In London they mingled with princes and maharajahs, prime ministers and presidents, who had gathered for the coronation of King Edward VII. The crowning had to be postponed when

Edward almost died from appendicitis, but there were many spectacular parties to celebrate the final surrender of the Boers in the Transvaal. General Kitchener's victory allowed the Australian cricketers to confirm their tour of South Africa on the way home.

Three uncharacteristic catching lapses cost Australia the Fifth Test. Chasing Australia's first innings of 324, England were struggling on 7 for 137 to pass the follow-on score of 175, when Hill dropped Lockwood. The follow-on was avoided and Australia was forced to bat on a rain-affected pitch. With a first-innings lead of 141, they were out for 121 in their second innings, leaving England to make 263 to win. At 5 for 48, England's chances appeared hopeless but Jessop scored 50 in 43 minutes and 100 in 75 minutes before he was out for 104 in one of the fastest Test centuries ever. The Australians dropped him twice before he reached 20.

England still needed 76 with three wickets left when Jessop was out. Lilley and Lockwood narrowed the gap to 15. Hirst and Lilley decided to get the runs needed in singles. Armstrong got his hands to a catch in slips but dropped it as he over-balanced, and Hirst and Lilley picked off the runs to give England a memorable one-wicket win. Darling was criticised for bowling Trumble unchanged throughout the match, but it was his fieldsmen who let Australia down.

One significant event of the 1902 tour passed almost unnoticed by the tourists. At Lord's between 25 and 27 August B.J.T. Bosanquet introduced a completely new delivery. 'The first time I bowled the googly was against the Australians, late one evening at Lord's in 1902,' said Bosanquet. 'I had Joe Kelly out for a duck and he returned to the pavilion very puzzled. Not one of the Australians tumbled to the fact that it was not an accident.' Kelly, in fact, only attracted laughter from team-mates when he announced: 'There's a bloke out there bowling leg-breaks that turn in from the off.'

B.J.T. Bosanquet, inventor of the bosey or googly, who won a Sydney Test with his new delivery. (MCC Library)

Trumble took the tour bowling honours with 140 wickets at 14.27, and Trumper headed the batting with an average of 48.49 in compiling his 2570 runs. Armstrong surprised by finishing ahead of Noble for the all-rounders' honours, with 1087 runs at 25.51 and 81 wickets and 17.40. Despite a strong challenge from Carter, Kelly held his Test wicket-keeping berth by making 23 catches and 12 stumpings.

Unsettled by their 17-day sea voyage from England and long

train trip to Johannesburg for the First Test against South Africa, the Australians found adjustment to the matting pitch at 1800 metres above sea level on the Wanderers' Ground difficult. South Africa began on 11 October, 1902, with 454, Louis Tancred contributing 97, 'Buck' Llewellyn 90. Trumper, Hill and Duff batted well but Australia were sent back for 296 and forced to follow on. Hill then made 142, the first century by an Australian against South Africa, to revive Australia's prospects. Noble chimed in with 53 not out, Armstrong 59, and Australia declared at 7 for 372. Left to score 215 to win, South Africa were 4 for 101 when time ran out.

After a high-scoring draw against Fifteen of Transvaal, Australia found Llewellyn in grand form in the Second Test at Johannesburg. His 101 lifted South Africa to a first-innings lead of 65 runs after Australia made 175. Armstrong then gave a tremendous display of driving by batting through the second innings for 159 not out. South Africa, chasing 245 to win, were out for 85. Saunders spun the ball off the mat at a height that did not miss the stumps to take 7 for 34.

Howell, who had learned how to bowl effectively on the mat in Penrith district cricket, had 11 for 79 against Fifteen of Natal at Durban, and 17 for 54 against Fifteen of Western Province. He continued in this devastating form in the Third Test at Cape Town, which Australia won by ten wickets. Howell took 4 for 18 and 5 for 81 and in the five South African matches he took 48 wickets at 9.60 each. The Australians were probably the first national team to tour South Africa as the English team that preceded them went through private invitations.

Back home in Sydney the eleventh Australian team completed their programme with a final match against Thirteen of New South Wales. The players each received £800 from their seven-month tour, including £250 from Australia's first visit to South Africa. This payment was not enough to save Syd Gregory from bankruptcy. A manager he employed to run his sports store and barbershop while he was on tour carelessly ran this normally profitable business into big debts that made Syd insolvent. He had to take a job as a clerk for the Water Board to support his wife and children.

Warwick Armstrong continued his wonderful form in inter-state cricket when the first Victorian team visited Queensland in January,

W.D. HOWELL N.S.W.

Penrith beekeeper Bill Howell, who made three tours to England between 1899 and 1905, appearing in 18 Tests and taking 519 first-class wickets. (Jack Pollard Collection)

1903, those stinging drives of his warming Queensland hands as he went to 145. Harry Graham made 101 and Bertie Tuckwell, from the St Kilda club, 93 not out in Victoria's score of 400. Queensland, still 24 years away from Sheffield Shield status, could not master Saunders and Fred Collins in their first innings of 123, and later were overwhelmed by Frank Laver and Armstrong for 40.

By then James Rainey Munro Mackay, better known as 'Sunny Jim' had earned a permanent place in the New South Wales team. Mackay played for the Burwood club, captained by George Pitty Barbour, a headmaster with a talent for cricket administration. At their best there was little to choose between Mackay and Trumper, who in 1902–03 played one of the greatest innings in Sydney club cricket by scoring 335 for Paddington against Redfern on Redfern Oval. Trumper hit 22 fives and 39 fours to make 266 of his runs in boundary hits. He batted for only 180 minutes but scored at a rate of 110-an-hour in an opening partnership of 423 with Dan Gee. Members of the bowling club alongside the ground adjourned play to avoid being hit and watched Trumper in awe. He broke so many nearby windows householders boarded up those that were left. One hit smashed a second-floor window of John Hunter's Boot Factory 150 metres from the crease.

Paddington declared at 9 for 618 and bundled Redfern out for 53 and 122. Noble, a former schoolmate of Trumper's at Cleveland Street Boys' High, took 7 for 27 in Redfern's first innings but did not bowl in the second. Paddington still won by an innings and 443 runs.

The understanding Trumper and Duff had developed on the 1902 English tour showed in two long opening partnerships in Sheffield Shield matches that summer. At Sydney they put on 298 against South Australia, Trumper scoring 178 in 133 minutes with 29 fours, to set up a 10-wicket win for New South Wales. A fortnight later on the same ground they had a stand of 267 for the first wicket against Victoria, Trumper making 130 in 137 minutes with 72 of his runs coming in boundaries. This meant that in two victories that assured New South Wales of the Sheffield Shield Trumper had hit 47 boundaries. In setting up the five-wicket win over Victoria, he treated quality bowling from Armstrong, Saunders and Laver with contempt, swatting good-length deliveries off his stumps.

Lord Hawke was busy in England organising a team for an

18-match tour designed to help develop New Zealand cricket, but just before the side left his mother fell ill and he asked Pelham Warner to take over as captain. The team had one match against Eighteen of Canada on the way out and won all their 18 matches in New Zealand. On the way home, they called in for three matches against Australian teams. Albert Trott, who had been coaching in New Zealand, joined Warner's team for these matches. England lost to Victoria and South Australia and had a draw against New South Wales.

Warner was captivated by the Bulli soil pitches in Sydney that season and wrote in the *Westminster Gazette*: 'This Bulli soil is wonderful in its resistance to wet. You can put a piece in a bucket for a week and at the end of that time it will be almost as hard as when it went in. I have some pieces in my cricket bag and if you do not believe me come to Lord's during a Middlesex match and I'll prove my statement.'

Plum Warner, captain of the sixteenth England team in Australia in 1903–04. (Jack Pollard Collection)

Warner returned to Australia as captain of the English touring team in 1903–04. Archie MacLaren, the Melbourne Cricket Club's original nominee for the job, wanted the tour postponed a year because Barnes and Lockwood were unavailable, so the Melbourne CC turned to Lord's and asked them to arrange the tour. The MCC in turn invited Warner to lead their side, a controversial appointment as he was not then captain of his county, Middlesex. Warner invited five players who had previously toured Australia – T. Hayward, J.T. Tyldesley, G.H. Hirst, L.C. Braund and A.F.A. Lilley, to join his team, plus newcomers E.G. Arnold, R.E. Foster, A.E. Relf, A. Fielder, A.E. Knight, H. Strudwick, B.J.T. Bosanquet and W. Rhodes. He took team spirit seriously and asked that amateurs and professionals in the side be booked in the same hotels, the first time an English team had done this in Australia.

The sixteenth English team to Australia undertook a programme of 20 matches. They won eight, lost two and drew one of their matches on even terms, and won two and drew seven of their matches against the odds. They were a very strong, well-prepared outfit, fully supported by a Lord's hierarchy determined to end England's defeat in four successive Test series with Australia.

Australia had suffered a major blow with the retirement of Ernie Jones after the 1902 tour of England, and had to play the first three Tests in 1903–04 against a powerful batting line-up without a fast bowler. Albert ('Tibby') Cotter emerged as a dangerous pace bowler in the last two Tests but by then England had a 2–1 lead. Even more damaging was the loss of Joe Darling, who decided to concentrate on his Tasmanian property.

Reggie Foster gave England a wonderful start with an innings of 287 in the First Test at Sydney. This remains the highest score by any batsman in his Test debut. England won by 5 wickets.

Captained by Noble, the Australians were far too sceptical about the threat of Bosanquet's revolutionary delivery, the googly, also known as the wrong-un or bosey. Their scepticism was based on the failure of many bowlers over the years with so-called mystery balls. Warner had a splendid bowling line-up in Hirst, Arnold, Braund and Rhodes that allowed him to keep Bosanquet in reserve, seldom inviting him to bowl, until the eighteenth match of the tour, the Fourth Test, when he sprung the trap and gave Bosanquet a 15-over spell in which he took 5 for 12 and clinched the Ashes for England. Any doubts over whether the googly would remain part of the bowlers' repertoire were abandoned then, although Bosanquet admitted he had only limited control of the delivery.

'Tibby' Cotter, outstanding fast bowler, made his debut for Australia in 'Bosanquet's match'. He proved the speedster Australia had been seeking since Ernie Jones' retirement. (Mitchell Library, *Sydney*)

Bosanquet had restricted use of the googly in earlier encounters with Australia's batsmen and had been rested from the Second Test on an unsuitable pitch, but in conditions that suited him, he staged his own cricket revolution. England's 157-run win gave them the Ashes for the first time in nine years. The anti-climactic Fifth Test in Melbourne produced an Australian victory by 218 runs. England won the series 3–2 and Hugh Trumble took a hat-trick in his last Test with his last three balls in Test cricket.

Later it was disclosed that the professionals on this first tour by an English team funded by the Marylebone Cricket Club received £300, plus a bonus if the tour was financially successful. No bonus was forthcoming and after paying all the amateurs' fares and expenses the MCC lost £1500 on the tour. Rhodes headed the bowling for England with 62 wickets at 14.61, 31 of them in Tests. He had the unique honour of opening the batting for England in his final Test series after going in last in his first Tests. Foster topped the English Test batting averages with 486 runs at 60.75. For Australia Cotter headed the Test bowling averages with 11 wickets at 13.63 but his contribution was nowhere near as useful as Trumble's 24 Test wickets at 16.58. Trumper was again the main contributor among Australia's Test batsmen with 574 runs at an average of 63.77 per innings.

CHAPTER TWELVE

BICKERING THAT ENDURED

Years of covert negotiations among supporters of a national cricket control body reached fruition at a conference in the New South Wales Cricket Association's rooms in Elizabeth Street, Sydney, on 9 January, 1905. There, under the guidance of William Perry McElhone, the NSWCA's legal advisor, representatives of the South Australian, Victorian and New South Wales associations drafted a constitution for a body to be known as the Australian Board of Control for International Cricket.

The players were not represented at this meeting but all those present agreed that these three states should have two delegates on the Board and the players two, making up an executive of eight. The suggestion was that Test and Sheffield Shield players should nominate one delegate each. Queensland, Western Australia and Tasmania were not invited to join. The proposed constitution empowered the Board to take control of all tours of Australia by English teams and of all overseas tours by Australian teams. The draft constitution also gave the Board the right to approve a panel of umpires capable of handling first-class matches and to administer all changes in the laws of cricket for member associations.

McElhone and his main conspirator, Ernie Bean, strongman of the Victorian Cricket Association, scheduled the formation of the Board for a meeting at Wesley College in Melbourne on 6 May, 1905, knowing that their chief protagonist, Joe Darling, would be in England, captaining the Australian team whose four months' tour began on 4 May. They intended to use those four months to establish the Board's authority in defiance of Darling's opposition.

While work on the Board's constitution proceeded, the Melbourne Cricket Club sent letters to all Melbourne cricket clubs, explaining why a Board of Control was not needed. Before it was formally founded the Board offered to advance the team money to finance the 1905 tour of England. The players rejected this and borrowed the money they required from the Melbourne Cricket Club.

The Australian team were involved in a match against the Gentlemen of England at Crystal Palace in London when the Australian Board of Control for International Cricket held its first formal meeting in rooms of Wesley College. The meeting was under the chairmanship of Lawrence Arthur Adamson, the rotund, moustached headmaster of the school, renowned for his true-blue amateurism and stern opposition to professionalism in sport. Adamson, born at Douglas on the Isle of Man in 1860, was the 'Mr Chips' of Victorian education, a highly respected citizen noted for his ethical attitude.

Delegates to that first meeting were Frank Iredale, George Barbour, Billy McElhone and A.W. ('Abbie') Green, representing the NSWCA, Ernie Bean, Harry Rush and Adamson, then president of the VCA, with the Melbourne barrister Edward Mitchell representing the Melbourne Cricket Club. G.M. Colledge and J. Allen attended as observers for the Queensland Cricket Association. G. Mostyn Evan and A. Robinson were there without a vote for the South Australian Cricket Association. The South Australians, on Joe Darling's recommendation, had declined an invitation to join the Board until the Board defined what it meant by 'financial control', an attitude McElhone said showed they were pawns of the Melbourne Cricket Club. Western Australia and Tasmania were not represented but unlike Queensland had decided that the cost of sending observers was not justified.

From the start the Board's existence depended on it crushing opposition from the Melbourne Cricket Club, which many Australian cricket lovers wanted to take over administration of the game as the Marylebone Cricket Club had done at Lord's. By electing McElhone its first secretary, the Board engaged in direct conflict with the Melbourne Cricket Club, for it was well known that he shared Bean's hatred of that club.

The players stuck with seasoned tourists in choosing the twelfth Australian team to tour England in 1905, and elected Darling captain for the third successive English tour. He was then 34 and his family had grown from four to six children since he last played Test cricket. When his sons delivered a load of wood to him at

Stonehenge, he chastised them for cutting it into manageable lengths – he liked to cut wood for his daily exercise. Darling travelled to England ahead of the team, via Suez. The main party played five matches in New Zealand and proceeded to England via Fiji, Hawaii and Canada. The team was J. Darling (Captain), M.A. Noble, W.W. Armstrong, C. Hill, V.T. Trumper, A.J. Hopkins, R.A. Duff, S.E. Gregory, D.R.A. Gehrs, C.E. McLeod, J.J. Kelly, A. Cotter, P.M. Newland, F. Laver and W.P. Howell.

Laver, born at Castlemaine, Victoria, was also the team manager and treasurer, a tall, gangling cricketer with consistently impressive results who enjoyed immense popularity among the players. With the bat, he could thrash even classy bowling, frustrating noted wicket-takers through his unorthodoxy, and his high-actioned medium-pacers were ideal for English conditions. He kept neat account books for each player and at the end of the trip handed them all albums containing a photographic record of their matches.

Newland, a South Australian picked as Joe Kelly's deputy wicket-keeper, badly fractured his jaw in a deck cricket match after leaving New Zealand and was in pain for much of the tour. Wives accompanied the team for the first time. Newly-weds Mrs Clem Hill and Mrs Phil Newland went with the team through North America. Mrs Trumper joined Victor in England, where their daughter Anne Louise was born. Another innovation was the appointment of an official scorer for the first time. Bill Ferguson, who was to spend 52 years on the job and score in 208 Tests, got the job while sitting in Noble's dental chair waiting for him to fill a tooth. Ferguson received £2 a week from team funds and paid all his own expenses, including boat fare.

The Australians encountered a serious new approach to winning the Tests by the MCC, which had swept away old problems of match fees and county teams having priority over star players. England's captain, the Hon. F.S. Jackson, had the full support of the MCC, who consulted him over selections, the batting order, and even minor details. Warner and MacLaren were both passed over on Jackson's appointment.

Bosanquet produced a match-winning display by taking 8 for 107 from 32.4 overs in the final innings of the First Test, but the Second and Third Tests were drawn, largely because of rain. Short of top-class bowlers, Darling had to give Armstrong long spells bowling his leg-breaks to packed legside fields, a tactic Hearne had used for years. In the wet Australia's batting lacked its usual steadiness, though they did score 620 against Hampshire. Rotund Harry Baldwin lumbered up to the stumps in his third appearance against touring Australian teams but his 4 for 134 could not prevent Australia winning by an innings and 112 runs.

Jackson, winner of all seven tosses against Australia that summer, foiled Australia's all-out bid for a win in the Fourth Test with a marvellous 113 at Old Trafford. Facing an England total of 446, Australia had to bat twice on a difficult, drying pitch, and England won by an innings and 80 runs to retain the Ashes. At The Oval in the final Test only Duff's 146 allowed Australia to escape with a draw. Of Jackson, his biographer, James P. Coldham, said: 'His Yorkshire grit and Harrow bravado had led England to a famous victory.' Jackson scored 776 runs at 70.54 against Australia that summer, proving the one man in England whom players like MacLaren and Fry could serve without swallowing their pride.

The noted Hampshire off-spinner Harry Baldwin who played against several Australian touring teams. (MCC Library)

Darling's twelfth Australian team won only 15 of their 35 first-class matches, with 17 drawn. Armstrong headed the batting averages and was second in the bowling, with 1902 runs at 50.05 and 122 wickets at 18.20. Trumper and Noble disappointed, and the bowling too often failed against fine batting, although lovable Bill Howell, on his third English tour, had hostile spells when that massive farmer's hand of his got the ball to turn.

In a conference at Lord's before they went home, Darling, Laver and Noble said that in their view the new Board in Australia was not truly representative of Australian cricket and should not be allowed to run England's Australian tours until its membership widened. The last Australian match ended at Hastings on 13 September, 1905. Five days before the Australian Board accepted a Queensland application for membership, promising Queensland a Test match when English teams toured Australia.

True to its promise to the senior Australian players, the MCC declined the Board's invitation to tour Australia in 1906–07 on the grounds that the Board was not genuinely representative of Australian cricket. This was a tribute to the esteem in which Lord's held Darling and clear evidence that cricket's ruling body recognised that Queensland cricket was below Sheffield Shield standard.

Joe Darling quit first-class cricket at the end of this tour, after scoring 10,635 runs at 34.52, 1657 of those runs in 34 Tests at 28.56. Three of his 19 centuries were in Tests, and he had a highest score of 210 in 270 minutes against Queensland in 1898–99. In his 18 Tests as Australian captain he had made that job the most prestigious in Australian sport, and set standards many of his successors found hard to match. From his day on Australian cricket captains enjoyed a status akin to senior Cabinet Ministers.

The Board's attempt to secure recognition at Lord's had a long-term effect on the development of Queensland, which did not get a place in the Sheffield Shield competition until 1926–27 and the right to stage a Test until 1928–29 – 23 years after Bean, McElhone and their associates promised it Test status. Queensland may have enjoyed Board membership ahead of South Australia, but two decades rolled by in which it had to be content with occasional visits from southern states. In those years promising Queensland players left their home state to seek recognition. The dashing all-rounder from Warwick, Alan Marshal, went to Surrey, Toowoomba's Jack Cuffe went to Worcestershire, Bert Ironmonger to Victoria, and Queensland had to continually plug gaps in their state team with imported players, most of whom had failed to win selection for New South Wales and Victoria.

Darling gave the Board a gutsy fight in their attempts to force South Australia to join. He attended Board meetings as a South Australian delegate without voting rights and expressed disgust at the manner in which the meetings were conducted. He proved that the minutes the Board issued on their meetings were false and had clearly been doctored after the meetings broke up. 'Everything on the agenda was privately discussed at a prior meeting of the delegates from Victoria, New South Wales and Queensland,' Darling said. 'Some Board delegates, particularly Bean and McElhone, boasted that they would drive out of the game all the players who supported the Melbourne Cricket Club in its plans to sponsor further English tours.'

Officially, the South Australian Cricket Association persisted with the argument that the players had the right to at least two delegates on the Board, without pushing for the players' rights to match fees.

The twelfth Australian team reassembled in Sydney in January, 1906, to play a match against New South Wales for the benefit of its plucky wicket-keeper Joe Kelly. The match attendance exceeded all forecasts and Kelly received £1300, to go with the £900 he had already been paid by Frank Laver as his player's bonus for the 1905 English trip. Laver had in fact distributed some cheques to 1905 tourists before they left England to frustrate any attempt by the Board to get their hands on tour profits. The team had voted to pay Syd Gregory an advance of £500 when it discovered his wife was so ill she needed two nurses to look after her.

Darling's team defeated New South Wales in a tense finish. Faced with the apparently forlorn prospect of scoring 525 to win, the New South Wales openers Austin Diamond and 'Sunny Jim' Mackay put on 244 for the first wicket, Mackay batting in a marvellously free manner like Trumper in his prime. Mackay made 136, Diamond 97. The brothers Mick and Edgar Waddy joined the run-feast by adding 145 for the fourth wicket, but after the sixth New South Wales wicket fell Cotter's pace proved too much for the tail-enders. Jack O'Connor took 11 wickets for New South Wales with his medium-pacers (6 for 50 and 5 for 138).

'Sunny Jim' Mackay, who migrated to South Africa after missing selection in the 1905 Australian team to England. He lost the sight of an eye in a car crash when he seemed likely to force his way into the South African side to tour England in 1907. (Jack Pollard Collection)

Several years after Darling's 1905 tourists disbanded it was disclosed that the selectors deliberately omitted Victorian Jack Saunders because they feared the Australian-born umpire 'Dimboola Jim' Phillips would no-ball Saunders for throwing. Phillips umpired in four of the five Tests involving the Australians and he had been at the centre of a campaign by the county captains to eliminate chucking. In a conference at Lord's in 1900 each county captain was asked to write down the names of players they believed to throw the ball. The majority of them included Charles Fry's name and this virtually ended his career as a bowler. Phillips had initiated this process by no-balling Fry for throwing at Brighton in what *Wisden* called 'a case of long-delayed justice'. Undoubtedly the absence of Saunders deprived the Australians of a bowler the side sorely needed. He took five wickets in an innings 48 times, in a career that brought him 553 first-class wickets at 21.81, and he was often unplayable on wet pitches such as those the 1905 side encountered in England. Ironically, he was never called for throwing in 14 years of first-class cricket.

Early in 1906 the Melbourne Cricket Club secured written agreements from eleven New South Wales players guaranteeing that they would be available if the Melbourne club brought out a team from England. Cotter, Duff, Noble, Trumper, Carter, Mackay, Hopkins, the Reverend 'Mick' Waddy, Diamond, Duff and 25-year-old George Garnsey all signed up. The deal remained secret for months but when news of it leaked out there was turmoil among the state associations. Ernie Bean stood up at a Victorian Cricket

Association meeting and accused the Melbourne Cricket Club of treachery and in the uproar that followed the VCA chairman Lawrence Adamson resigned.

In Sydney McElhone moved quickly to assert the New South Wales Cricket Association's authority. One by one the eleven players were paraded before the NSWCA's executive committee and questioned about their dealings with the Melbourne club. All were threatened with immediate suspension unless they repudiated their promise to play against an English team sponsored by the Melbourne club. Ten of the eleven players accepted suspension; only the Reverend 'Mick' Waddy escaped with a promise to write to the Melbourne Cricket Club and withdraw from his agreement with them.

'Sunny Jim' Mackay was the first of the rebels called before the NSWCA executive. Mackay refused to renounce his contract. His scoring in the 1905–06 season had been of Bradmanesque proportions, with 203 against Queensland in Brisbane, 90 versus South Australia in Adelaide, 194 versus Victoria in Melbourne, 105 and 102 against South Australia in Sydney and 4 and 136 for New South Wales against an Australian XI, but he preferred to migrate to South Africa rather than dishonour his promise to the Melbourne CC. Two brilliant centuries for Transvaal had South Africans hailing him as 'the best batsman in the world'. Then on 13 May, 1907, he was knocked down by a motor bike near Johannesburg. He lingered near death for days and when he recovered the sight of one eye was permanently impaired. Back in Australia he tried eight times to bat for his old club, Burwood, but balls that he would have hammered in his prime clean-bowled him. Clem Hill said: 'Undoubtedly the best player Australia produced who never reached a Test match was Jim Mackay. If he had gone to England with an Australian side he might in time have proved as marvellous as Victor Trumper.'

At a meeting of the NSWCA on 14 May, 1906, McElhone was noisily cheered when he announced that the Association and not the players would run the sport. Monty Noble stood up and bravely defended the players, arguing that players who had been denied representation on the Australian Board could not be charged with disloyalty to the NSWCA. The Paddington club supported Noble and Trumper and offered to include them in all their fixtures. To save the club embarrassment, Noble and Trumper resigned from the club. In Adelaide, Darling and Hill announced they would not play in Sydney until Noble and Trumper had their suspensions lifted and in Melbourne Frank Laver followed suit.

The affair was unresolved when Trumper made a long tour of Queensland in April and May, 1906, taking a squad of outstanding players to centres that could only be reached by boat. Accompanied by 'Tibby' Cotter, Bert Hopkins and nine others drawn from Sydney clubs, they gave Queensland cricket a major boost. For Trumper, it was a heartwarming venture, with entire townships crowding the wharves to welcome his team before escorting them to the local cricket field. At Charters Towers Victor and Ernie Bubb put on 100 in 30 minutes. At Townsville Syd Redgrave made 168, Tom Foster 155. Invited to give an exhibition before the match against Eighteen of Townsville, Trumper made 75 out of 136 in 25 minutes. At Mount Morgan he hit 179 not out in 80 minutes.

Returning to Sydney Trumper went to work in the sports store operated by Hanson Carter, who found Victor a difficult employee. He let impoverished lads take bats and other gear without paying and delayed attending to paying customers while he studied barefoot boys' grips on the bat handle.

In April, 1906, the Melbourne Cricket Club had resigned from the Victorian Cricket Association and joined Caulfield, Elsternwick and other clubs to form the Victorian Cricket League. Bean claimed the Melbourne club offered financial support to the other rebel clubs to join them. The Melbourne club denied this but could not overcome the major problem in a city conditioned to electorate cricket competitions of not having a district of its own from which it could draw players. Finally the Melbourne club disbanded the Victorian Cricket League in return for a seat on the Australian Board of Control. The VCA agreed that all Test matches and inter-state games would be played on the MCG for as long as the Board existed and that the VCA would pay the Melbourne club reasonable fees for these matches.

The NSWCA lifted its suspension on the ten cricketers in August, 1906, which allowed the ten to play for the state in 1906–07 if chosen. The NSWCA showed spite, however, by insisting that none of the ten should hold office for three years, a petty move aimed at Noble, the only club delegate among the ten. It was an uneasy peace, with Joe Darling continually urging the players to remain firm in letters from his Tasmanian home. Darling fathered nine more children at Stonehenge and family commitments gradually decreased his ability to counter the Board's moves to erode the players' rights.

To prevent further postponement of an English team's Australian tour, the Board amended its constitution to define what was meant by 'control of finance'. The amendment said the Board would provide the necessary funds to send teams away but would not interfere with the players' division of tour profits. The Board also gave the players the right to appoint their own tour manager, provided they submitted the manager's name for approval to the Board.

Although the changes to the constitution still did not give the players representation on the Board, South Australia joined the Board on 20 April, 1907, on the strict condition that Adelaide would be given a Test when English teams visited Australia. Once South Australia joined the Board it had the representation needed to satisfy the MCC at Lord's. Thereafter South Australia was treated as a foundation member although it had not joined the Board until two years after New South Wales and Victoria and 20 months after Queensland. Tasmania gave up her opposition to the Board despite Darling's advice that it should stay out, and joined on 9 August, 1907.

McElhone, Bean and the rest of the Board executive had ended the Melbourne Cricket Club's aspirations to run Australian cricket the way the MCC did in England, but the Board's fight with leading players proved much harder for them to win. England's 1907–08 Australian tour proceeded under Board sponsorship but the Test players' lack of a representative on the Board manifested itself in their outspoken criticism of the way the Board conducted its affairs. Bean, McElhone and their Sydney colleague George Barbour made decisions in private meetings and delegates from the other states found they merely had to rubber-stamp these decisions. There was little scope for discussion.

Newspapers found McElhone a devious man and published as many satirical cartoons of him as they featured on politicians like Billy Hughes. Barbour, captain of the Burwood First XI in which Austin Diamond and 'Sunny Jim' Mackay starred in Sydney – and later headmaster of Toowoomba Grammar School in Queensland – held an opposing view: 'It has never been my lot to be associated with a straighter or more fearless protagonist,' he wrote of McElhone. 'When the position called for straight speaking he never shrank and he could call to his aid an expressive and forceful vocabulary.'

Bean, who worked for the Victorian Government Printing

Dour North Melbourne delegate to the VCA and the Board of Control, Ernest Edward Bean, who formed a formidable alliance with Sydney solicitor Billy McElhone. (Herald, Melbourne)

Service, took over as Board chairman when Adamson left, and he was followed by Barbour, in 1907–08, when Arthur Owen Jones brought the seventeenth English team to Australia. Jones, a graduate of Cambridge, where he had won his Blue in 1893, was an attractive, aggressive batsman, handy leg-break bowler and superb slips fieldsman, who was credited with inventing the gully position. In the summer before he left for Australia he had led Nottinghamshire to the English county championship without a single defeat.

Jones's team included Rhodes, Braund, Barnes, Blythe and Fielder, who had all been to Australia before. The new tourists were Joe Hardstaff, John Berry Hobbs, John Neville Crawford, Kenneth Lotherington Hutchings, Frederick Luther Fane, Ernest George Hayes, Joseph Humphries and Jones's vice-captain Dick Young, a Cambridge Blue who kept wicket in glasses and played soccer for England. George Gunn began the tour as the team's scorer, with the management aware he could fill in for injured players on a 19-match tour spread over almost six months. The English professionals in the team received £300, plus all expenses, and a £2-a-week out-of-pocket allowance. The new Australian Board of Control announced that all the Australians who played in the Tests would receive a £25 'honorarium'!

Jones's team was a long way from the best England could field. Foster, Hayward, Hirst, Tyldesley and Lilley were all invited to tour, but refused, which opened the way for so many newcomers. C.B. Fry was not invited. The tour opened before a record attendance in Perth where the visitors were the first English team to play. Ernie Jones played for Western Australia, but turned out to be a burnt-out shell of a once-great bowler and could not prevent the English opener Frederick Fane – an Irishman – scoring 133 in a 200-minute knock. This set up an English win by an innings and 134 runs. Western Australia acquitted themselves well, and the big disappointment for Perth fans was that Crawford was run out for 43 just as he began to live up to his great reputation as a hitter. Earlier that year he had smashed a ball through the window of the Surrey dressing-room. His 103 in 90 minutes against Kent had included hits that 'soared away like a bird' and made people crowd on the roof of the stand to avoid being hit.

England enjoyed a successful spin around the states, defeating South Australia, New South Wales and Queensland and playing a draw with Victoria. When the Tests began, however, the weaknesses in the team's batting, due to the poor pay offered to

Frederick Luther Fane, the only Irishman to captain England in Australia, which he did while A.O. Jones was recovering from pneumonia in the first three Tests of the 1907–08 series. (Ken Kelly)

quality players, became apparent. Jones missed eight matches after the Queensland game because of illness and Gunn had to be pressed into service. Although not an official member of the side, he made two centuries in the rubber and held his place when Jones recovered.

Australia won the series 4–1, but in the Test which England won in Melbourne Gervys Hazlitt missed a chance to create a historic Test tie. Hazlitt threw wildly, when an accurate throw would have run out one of the last two English batsmen as they scampered for the winning run. Of the Australian newcomers to Tests, Hazlitt, Vernon Ransford, Charlie Macartney, Jack O'Connor, Warren Bardsley and Roger Hartigan all consolidated their status, but tall Peter McAlister completely failed to reproduce his excellent form for Victoria.

Hartigan, a Brisbane auctioneer, had four days' leave from his job to play in the Third Test at Adelaide. At the end of the fourth day he was not out at stumps, after putting on 217 with Clem Hill, lifting Australia from 7 for 180 to 397. That night he cabled his boss for an extension of his leave. Back came the reply: 'Stay as long as you are making runs.' Hartigan went on to 116 on debut.

Undertaker – and wicket-keeper – Hanson Carter, who often drove a hearse to the cricket. (Mitchell Library, Sydney)

Macartney, who had originally won his place in the New South Wales team as a slow left-arm spinner, impressed with his all-round skills, playing several useful innings. Hanson Carter resumed the Test career delayed by Joe Kelly's consistency. Noble captained an Australian side which introduced eight players to Tests with an authority that never allowed them to lose the big advantage they had over England in the field.

Trumper followed two ducks in the Fourth Test with one of his greatest innings in the Fifth. On a drying pitch, Australia were in danger at 2 for 52 in the second innings, after trailing by 144 on the first innings, when Trumper entered. He made 166 in masterly fashion, driving and pulling with a regal zest that had even Sydney Barnes shaking his head, to give Australia an unexpected lead of 278. Rain fell before England batted and with Saunders (5 for 82) turning the ball sharply, England fell 49 runs short of their target.

The Australian Board of Control's parsimony in not offering more attractive terms to the proven English crowd-pleasers was reflected in the record of the seventeenth English team, which won only seven of their 18 matches, played seven draws and lost four of the matches on level terms. Their one match against the odds against Eighteen of Bendigo was drawn, and their failure to entertain often drew jibes from the crowds. The Board distributed the tour's small profit only to the three states that staged Tests – Victoria, South Australia and New South Wales – despite Joe Darling's view that all the states represented on the Board should receive a share. Darling said it was scandalous that Tasmania, which had produced three Test players, George Bailey, Ken Burn and Charles Eady, should not receive a penny.

The 1907–08 Sheffield Shield competition attracted almost as much public interest as the Tests. This was largely due to the presence of talented newcomers in every state, but also to the inclusion in the Victorian side of Frank Tarrant, who was on leave from Middlesex. Tarrant at 27 was at the peak of a career that was to bring him 17,952 runs and 1506 wickets and in the deciding match at Sydney he thwarted New South Wales after Noble had made a century in each innings, 176 and 123. Noble and Syd Gregory put on 315 in a fourth-wicket stand but were on the losing side after Tarrant made a double century. Chasing 593 to win, New South Wales fell 21 runs short on the seventh day. This was Victoria's fifth Sheffield Shield win, compared to nine by New South Wales, and one by South Australia.

Much to the chagrin of Ernie Bean and Bill McElhone, and to the delight of Joe Darling, a Fijian cricket team visited five Australian states towards the end of the 1907–08 summer. Bean and McElhone told a Board meeting early in the summer that a Fijian request to tour could not be approved, as such a tour would conflict with the government's White Australia policy. McElhone, in one of his most eloquent speeches, said no blacks would be allowed to play cricket in Australia, but somebody on the Board wrote to the Fijians and told them to come anyway.

The Fijians arrived in March, 1908, and proved a colourful crowd-pleasing lot, taking the field in single file, wearing calf-length skirts or sulus, sporting vast bushy hairdos and very big bare feet, which seemed impervious to heavy knocks. Their 26-match tour won such wide public support Darling asked at the next Board meeting for minutes of the previous meeting to be read. It was found that these favoured a Fijian tour. Darling said that the minutes had been faked and succeeded in having the Board's original objection to the Fijian tour recorded. The name of the Board member who wrote and told the Fijians to tour was never discovered. Fiji won five, lost five and drew 16 of their 26 matches, and during the tour one of their players,

D. R. GEHRS S. A.

Donald Raeburn Algernon Gehrs, known to team-mates as Algie, set South Australian records for fast scoring but was a failure at Test level. (Jack Pollard Collection)

179

The 1908 Fijian team in Australia played barefooted but remained impervious to heavy knocks. Their star player, Prince Ratu Kadavulevu, is in the middle of the front row with tour organiser and captain, Lieut. Marsden. (Mitchell Library, *Sydney*)

Ratu Kadavulevu, won public admiration by rescuing two men swept out by heavy seas at Newcastle.

The Boad of Control appointed Percy McAlister as treasurer of the thirteenth Australian team to tour England in 1909, after McAlister won selection as a player. The rest of the team refused to accept McAlister's role as book-keeper, which they knew was a thinly veiled attempt to provide the Board with the tour accounts. They elected Frank Laver as manager. Clem Hill refused to tour, having undertaken two long tours in the first three years of his marriage, and said he preferred not to take a risk on the Board honouring its promises on tour payments. Noble insisted on an election for the captaincy although he had already been appointed to the job by the Board. He wanted the players to pick him, not the Board.

Just before the team left, the Board welshed on its promise not to interfere with tourists' terms by demanding five per cent of the first £6000 the tour earned and 12.5 per cent of all profits above that amount. Instead of allowing the players to follow the customary procedure of sharing tour profits evenly, the Board offered the team in which there were nine newcomers to England a lump sum of £400 per man, plus all expenses. Worst of all, the Board rejected pleas from Laver and Noble to pay players with little resources a small advance for additional gear before the side left.

Only a captain of immense dedication could have overcome all these difficulties and mould a winning team as Noble did. 'Plum' Warner was so impressed he rated Noble Australia's best-ever captain and Lord Hawke agreed. C.B. Fry named Noble captain of the Earth XI to play Mars. Noble achieved this honoured status by paying careful attention to the smallest detail. Nobody in his teams ever fell over because of faulty laces and not one opposing captain put on a substitute fieldsman without Noble knowing why. The team comprised: M.A. Noble (Captain), W. Bardsley, W.W. Armstrong, V.S. Ransford, V.T. Trumper, P.A. McAlister, S.E. Gregory, C.G. Macartney, R.J. Hartigan, H. Carter, A.J.Y. Hopkins, J.D.A. O'Connor, F.J. Laver, A. Cotter, W. Carkeek and W.J. Whitty.

Noble studied opposing batsmen with an intensity that newcomers to the Australian side could scarcely believe, and he had no superior in blocking a great player's favourite shots. The English selectors made the 1909 series easier for him by continually changing their minds and only Lilley and MacLaren appeared in all five Tests.

The Noble magic took time to work but he held his nerve after losing three matches, including the First Test by ten wickets, inside a month. His team recovered to win the Second Test by nine wickets and the Third Test by 126 runs. The last two Tests were drawn, to give Australia the rubber 2–1. They suffered their fourth defeat near the end of the tour at Scarborough.

Monty Noble captained the 1909 tourists to England.
(John Fairfax)

With Hanson Carter's co-operation from behind the stumps, Noble's uncanny choice of the right bowler for prevailing conditions lifted the displays of Billy Whitty, Frank Laver, Bert Hopkins, Jack O'Connor and Charlie Macartney, all of whom had match-winning spells. The fielding throughout was magnificent because every man gave the task full concentration – when Macartney began chatting to a girl on the boundary fence, Noble moved him into the slips!

The batting lacked distinction but was efficient enough to match an England team that had declined since 1905. Ransford made a century in his first appearance in a Lord's Test and proved a worthy deputy for Hill and Darling. Macartney was a major surprise as a bowler, winning the Leeds Test with 11 for 85. Bardsley easily topped the batting averages with 2072 runs at 46.04, although Trumper deliberately ran him out at his highest tour score, 219 against Essex, to give team-mates a knock. Bardsley survived this lesson in team spirit to score a century in each innings of the final Test. Armstrong averaged 43.97 with the bat and took 113 wickets for only 16.39

Sydney-born left-arm pace bowler Billy Whitty, who moved to Adelaide to improve his Test prospects, took 65 wickets in 14 Tests. (SACA Archives)

apiece. The Australians defeated Worcestershire despite a six-wicket haul by G.H. Simpson-Hayward, last of the great lob bowlers, who a few months later took 23 South African wickets.

In between his managerial duties Frank Laver, then 39, found time to take 70 wickets with his late swingers, including 8 for 31 in the Manchester Test. On return, McAlister, the Board's tour treasurer, said he had been unable to keep accurate books of account because Laver refused him the information he required. The Board asked Laver to produce the books he kept. Laver refused, explaining that his books contained many private entries about the players' affairs, but he offered to attend a Board meeting to answer any queries about receipts and expenditure.

Not long after the 1909 Australian side arrived home, Noble retired. He was a few weeks off 37 and still a bachelor without family commitments, but he was driven from cricket by the bickering and abusive administration. He had played in 22 Tests, and won eight out of 15 as captain, with five losses and two draws at a time in the Golden Age of Cricket when England fielded teams of the highest quality. He was indeed a champion all-weather man, able to judge how pitches would behave after light showers, deluges, under hot sun or heavy winds. In 248 first-class matches, he made 13,975 runs at 40.74 with 37 centuries, and took 625 wickets at 23.11.

The Australians were followed home by Jack Crawford, who had captained Surrey against them in the absence of Henry ('Shrimp') Leveson-Gower. Crawford had accepted an appointment as a master at St Peter's College, Adelaide, after a bitter row which the Surrey committee tried to keep secret. It emerged that Crawford had strongly objected when Surrey omitted Tom Rushby, Jack Hobbs and other regulars from the return match with Australia, claiming that Surrey insulted the Australians by playing a weak side against them. The Surrey committee, incensed by this challenge to their authority, ordered that Crawford never again be invited to play for them. Thus, at 23, Crawford began a new life in the South Australian Sheffield Shield team.

Neville Cardus wrote that Crawford's break with Surrey was a sad deprivation of fame and pleasure to himself and a grievous loss to English cricket. 'It is as certain as anything in a man's life can be confidently postulated,' wrote Cardus, 'that had he continued to play in English cricket in the rising years to his prime, he would have taken his place among the select company of England's captains.'

*　　*　　*

South Australia began their 1909–10 Shield campaign by defeating Victoria by an innings in a match that demonstrated how valuable Clem Hill would have been had he forgotten his grievances with the Board and gone to England in 1909. Hill (176 run out) and Algie Gehrs (118) put on 253 for the third wicket, lifting the total to 590. Victoria made 284 and 97. Hill continued this great form in the next match against New South Wales by scoring 205 out of South Australia's 397 in response to 184. New South Wales failed by four runs to prevent an innings defeat when Crawford took 6 for 59 in an innings of 209. A slightly built, pale-faced all-rounder named Herbie Collins made his debut for New South Wales in this match, taking 1 for 35 with his left-arm spinners.

From the surfeit of gifted spinners operating in Sydney at the time New South Wales picked the eccentric Syd Emery for the match against Victoria in Melbourne. Emery spun the ball like a top but his length often was wayward. This time he hit the spot often enough to take 7 for 28 and 5 for 85, giving New South Wales victory by 272 runs.

Warwick Armstrong, in the first decade of this century when he was trying to consolidate his place in the Australian XI, was a trim figure. In later years he weighed 22 stone. (Public Library of Victoria)

After Christmas Victoria and South Australia had a great match in Melbourne, before Victoria emerged with an 81-run triumph. This was one of the first matches attended by spectators who had travelled to the MCG by electric trams. Victoria began with a modest 206; Clem Hill, 185, and Crawford, 75, gave South Australia a 154-run lead by pushing South Australia to a total of 360. Victoria then staged a spirited recovery in which Armstrong figured in a 170-run fourth-wicket stand with Dave Smith, a cocky right-hander from the Richmond club. Smith made 146, Armstrong 124. South Australia reached 5 for 195 in their chase for the 305 needed to win, but their last five wickets fell for 28 runs to Jack Saunders's clever spin.

South Australia clinched the Shield by beating New South Wales by seven wickets at the SCG. On a pitch that was soaked at one end, Whitty took 5 for 43 to have New South Wales out for 92. South Australia took a first-innings lead of 115. Charles Kelleway, a tall, handsome all-rounder with plenty of grit but few shots, made 108 in New South Wales' second innings of 289, Crawford taking 7 for 92. He then gave an immaculate display of firm, front-foot driving to reach 73 not out in South Australia's second innings of 3 for 178. Later that summer the dour Kelleway came into consideration for Tests against the South African tourists in 1910–11 by taking seven wickets with a crafty display of swing bowling in an

The Bega women's cricket team in 1910 all wore hats that could be firmly stuck on their heads and always appeared in long skirts. (Mitchell Library, *Sydney*)

Australia versus The Rest match for Charlie Turner's benefit.

The first South African team to tour Australia arrived in October, 1910, for a programme of 22 matches, to find Australian cricket in turmoil. All through the previous winter leading players, supported by the Melbourne Cricket Club, had engaged in what was called 'The Battle of the Pamphlets' with the Board of Control. Both sides issued three lengthy brochures which they handed to the public on street corners.

One of the intriguing facts in the pamphlets was the disclosure that the Australian Board of Control had only agreed to play in the ambitious 1912 Triangular tournament in England, scheduled as a world championship of cricket, on condition that South Africa visit Australia beforehand. Predictably, the South African bowlers found the wickets in Sydney and Melbourne much harder to extract spin from than the matting pitch at Johannesburg. Banking everything on spin, South Africa were heavily handicapped by the lack of one genuine pace bowler. They lost seven of their 22 matches, won 12 and drew three.

They lost the First Test by an innings after Bardsley (132) and Hill (191) hammered their spinners, but in the Second Test at Melbourne reached 506 in their first innings and appeared to have the match won with only 170 needed to win in the last innings. But Whitty bowled his left-arm swing with great hostility to take 6 for 17, supported by Cotter who took 4 for 47, and Australia won by 87 runs. At Adelaide on 7–13 January, 1911, South Africa batted with great determination to win a six-day struggle by 38 runs. John Zulch (105), Sibley Snooke (103) and Aubrey Faulkner (115) made centuries for South Africa which offset a magnificent 214 not out from Trumper.

Australia played South Africa at their own game in the Fourth and Fifth Tests, by including the googly bowler Dr Herbert Vivian ('Ranji') Hordern, who triumphed immediately and his 14 wickets helped Australia to victory in both matches.

Faulkner, with 732 runs at an average of 73.20 in the Tests, and the captain Percy Sherwell, whose 'keeping some critics rated as good as Blackham's, were the big successes for South Africa. In a hot, rainless summer, four Australians scored more than 400 runs in the Tests, Trumper returning to the masterly form he had shown in England in 1902 to head the averages with 662 runs at 94.57. Whitty had a wonderful series with 37 Test wickets at 17.08. The Board of Control earned much-needed cash from excellent attendances at all the South Africans' major matches.

The Sydney dentist Dr Herbert ('Ranji') Hordern, rated by some experts as the best-ever Australian exponent of the googly. He played in only 33 first-class matches, including two Tests v. South Africa and five v. England, but took 217 wickets at 16.79. (SCG Archives)

Surprise of the 1910–11 Australian domestic season was Adelaide Oval's groundsman Alby Wright, who in between preparing wickets for Shield and Test matches, bowled leg-spinners at the nets to the South Australian batsmen. Pressed into service for the state team he had set a world record in the 1905–06 season by scoring six successive ducks, but now he redeemed himself by taking wickets so regularly he lifted his first-class tally to 110. In Sydney, South Australia shocked the New South Wales batsmen by opening their bowling with Whitty at one end and Wright bowling leg-spinners at the other. This unusual attack had New South Wales out for 195. Chasing 647 to win, New South Wales were out for 361 in the final innings, giving South Australia victory by 285 runs. Wright took 5 for 75 and 6 for 103.

McElhone became chairman of the Board of Control in 1911. Soon after, Hugh Trumble, who had succeeded Ben Wardill as Melbourne Cricket Club secretary, nominated as an Australian selector but did not get a single vote. Trumper received four of a possible 11 votes, but failed to make the Board selection panel, which comprised Frank Iredale, Clem Hill and Peter McAlister. The situation between Board and players was becoming explosive.

CHAPTER THIRTEEN
BOARD-ROOM BRAWL

England arrived to tour Australia in spring 1911. Despite the presence of a powerful team led initially by 'Plum' Warner and after Warner collapsed with a duodenal ulcer by Johnny Douglas, so much space was devoted in newspapers to the feud between the Board and the players, cricket fans had difficulty discovering the scores of England's matches. The tour was half over before Australians realised there were only three amateurs, Warner, Douglas and Foster, in the English line-up, the eighteenth to tour Australia. The team was: P.F. Warner, J.W.H.T. Douglas,

Australian grounds could scarcely hold the crowds that wanted to see England play Australia in 1911–12, as this shot of the SCG during the Fifth Test shows. (NSW Government Printer)

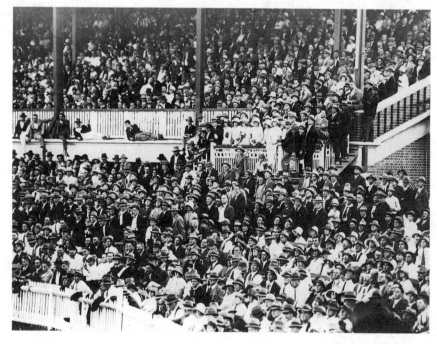

F.R. Foster, J.B. Hobbs, W. Rhodes, F.E. Woolley, S.F. Barnes, J.W. Hearne, G. Gunn, E.J. Smith, C.P. Mead, J.W. Hitch, H. Strudwick, S.P. Kinneir, J. Vine and J. Iremonger.

Australia won the First Test at Sydney, on 15–21 December, 1911 when Hordern took 12 wickets for 175 in a magnificent display of googly bowling against a classy batting team. England recovered to win the Second Test in Melbourne by eight wickets and the Third Test in Adelaide by seven wickets. On 3 February, 1912, Iredale, McAlister and Hill, who had captained Australia in all three Tests, met in the NSWCA Sydney office to pick the team to play England in the Fourth Test at Melbourne. McAlister was immediately critical of Hill's captaincy, and Hill warned McAlister not to keep insulting him or he would pull his nose.'You are the worst captain I've ever seen,' said McAlister, at which point Hill reached across the table and slapped McAlister's face. McAlister rushed around the table and grappled with Hill. Locked together they swayed around the room, with their blood spattering the clothing of Iredale and Board secretary Sydney Smith. All the initial attempts to separate them were futile.

'Whether the first blow was struck with the open or shut fist, it roused McAlister to retaliation, and he rushed around the table and grappled with Hill,' reported the *Australasian*. 'They fought fiercely, and, locked in each other's arms, swayed around the room, crushing against the table and walls. The two spectators, Iredale and Smith, were powerless to interfere, and in spite of their efforts to separate the combatants, the struggle proceeded. At the end of the bout McAlister was on his back on the floor and Hill was standing over him. McAlister got to his feet, and as they struggled dangerously close to the window, Syd Smith leaned forward and grabbed Hill's coat tails and pulled him off, Iredale leaning across and holding McAlister. Between them Iredale and Smith pushed McAlister through the door and barred his re-entry.'

Hill told Smith he would resign and was advised to put it in writing. Hill did so later at his hotel and Smith collected it from him. It was then agreed that Iredale and McAlister should pick the Test team and in the event of a deadlock, Harry Blinman, a South Australian delegate to the Board, would have a vote to break the impasse.

When the train taking McAlister home pulled into Melbourne, he was surrounded by reporters who noted his cut and bruised face. He claimed that Hill had given him no notice of the attack. 'I would not

Two of the three men involved in the infamous punch-up are in this picture. L to R: Edgar Mayne, Frank Iredale and Percy McAlister. Iredale tried to separate McAlister and Clem Hill. (Jack Pollard Collection)

Percy McAlister, whose jibes prompted Hill to act, looked harmless enough at this net practice for the Victorian team. (VCA Archives)

have minded so much had he invited me outside because then I would have known what to expect,' said McAlister. 'You can see that my face is cut in several places. It must have been knocked against the table and walls.'

Iredale was initially reluctant to discuss the fight but in view of what had been printed he realised he could not keep the affair secret. 'They went at it hammer and tongs,' he said. 'Very few blows were struck. It was more like a wrestling match. Smith and I did our best to part them but they were all over the place and when the big table was upset, I was pinned to the floor. I strained my side and can still feel the effects.'

'How long did it last?' said one reporter.

'Well, about twenty minutes, I should think,' Iredale replied. 'They were both very game and determined. We are all very sorry about the whole affair, and I don't think anyone regrets it more than the participants.'

The fight came two weeks after six leading Australian players had sent a letter to the Board respectfully reminding Board members that a decision to send a Board representative to England with the power of manager of the 1912 Australian team for the Triangular tournament was unconstitutional. The letter said that if the players were not allowed to select their own manager, as the Board rules provided, a breach of faith would have been committed. The letter suggested the Board should follow the same procedure that had operated for the 1909 tour, by selecting 14 players who would then pick the manager–player on the same terms as the rest of the team.

The letter said the signatories would be glad to make the trip if this occurred, but added: 'Failing compliance with our request, we have to inform you with much regret that none of us will be available for selection or to play if selected . . . Yours truly, C. Hill, W.W. Armstrong, V.T. Trumper, V.S. Ransford, A. Cotter, H. Carter'.

The Board secretary, Syd Smith, replied that the Board was not abrogating any part of its constitution. Smith's letter, a monumental piece of double-talk, said the Board's agreement for the 1912 tour was with the Marylebone Cricket Club and had nothing to do with its constitution, although the Board was taking all responsibility for the tour. The players would be told the Board's terms when chosen and they would have the chance then to refuse to tour if they were not satisfied. The Board had only expressed the view that one of its representatives should go as manager and if the players did not agree they could still nominate a manager acceptable to the Board. Smith's letter ended: 'While the board is anxious at all times to send the best possible team, at the same time I am sure it will not permit any number of cricketers to dictate terms or conditions on which a visit is to be made or, if a manager is to be appointed, the terms of his appointment.'

A special meeting of the Board on 2 February, 1912, received the players' letter and endorsed the secretary's reply. The players' defence of their promised rights was described as defiance of constituted authority that could not be tolerated. The meeting also decided to inform the players that the manager appointed would be paid £500, plus expenses, which would be charged against the tour. Suggestions of a conference between the players and Board members, to decide if applicants for the manager's job were qualified, were discarded.

Iredale and McAlister picked the team for the Fourth Test against England in Melbourne, and on instructions from the Board also named the first ten players for the tour of England. They were Hill, Trumper, Roy Minnett, Bardsley, Armstrong, Carter, Cotter, Ransford, Carkeek and Hordern. Macartney, whom Hill had strongly supported for inclusion in the Fourth Test team, was missing from both lists.

Hordern withdrew because he could not spare the time away from his dental practice, and the six star players who had written to the Board had their tour invitations cancelled. While cricket buffs were still discussing the selectors' brawl and the prospect of a sub-standard team going to England, the touring English team beat Australia by an innings and 225 runs in Melbourne to regain the Ashes. Clem Hill refused to blame Australia's defeat on the quarrels with the Board and gave credit instead to marvellous bowling by Barnes, Foster and Douglas.

Frank Rowbotham Foster was a notable figure in the English team, a thoughtful, disciplined right-hand middle-order batsman and a fiery fast left-arm bowler whose reputation suffered because of his experiments with leg theory. Bardsley, so effective in the previous series in England, had no answer to Foster's deliveries, which moved quickly across his body from outside the leg-stump. He had his stumps removed four times in eight innings in the rubber, which saw him dropped from Tests for the first time since 1909.

Major Ben Wardill, secretary of the Melbourne Cricket Club, struggled against the Board of Control for almost 30 years. (MCG Library)

Queensland cricket fans celebrated when John William ('Ginger') McLaren, a right-arm fast bowler easily spotted in the field because of his flaming red hair, won selection in Australia's Fifth Test team. He was the first native-born Queenslander to play Test cricket but a few months earlier had thrown his cricket career into jeopardy by acting as a special constable recruited by the government to break a wharf labourers' strike. Australian trade unions threatened to picket the grounds if McLaren played in Tests and for this reason selectors made him twelfth man for the Fourth Test.

McLaren had difficulty with his approach run in the Test and in a match extended to seven days by two days of heavy rain was unimpressive. England won by 70 runs to clinch the series 4–1. Frank Woolley swung the match for England with a lovely innings of 133 not out. Barnes took 34 wickets in the five Tests at 22.88, Foster 32 wickets at 21.62, completely dominating some of the finest batsmen Australia has produced. When Clem Hill went to the crease for his final Test innings – he had announced his decision to retire – the expected applause did not eventuate. Ray Robinson said Hill's lukewarm reception reflected the influence McElhone had on Sydney newspapers. The English team completed their tour with 12 wins, five draws and one loss. 'Plum' Warner, reviewing the tour for *Wisden*, said:

Vernon Ransford ended his Test career when he refused to go to England in 1912 under the Board's conditions. He continued playing for Victoria until 1927. (Ric Smith)

This was a very great performance, but at the present time Australian cricket is honeycombed with an amount of personal feeling and bitterness that is incredible. This must have militated against our opponents showing their true form; but it does not explain away our decisive victories.

Before he left Australia Warner made a strenuous attempt to prevent the 1912 Triangular competition in England becoming a financial flop. He pleaded with the six defectors from the Australian team to change their minds but they remained adamant that they would not tour on the terms offered by the Board. He sought assistance from the Australian Prime Minister, Andrew Fisher, the state governors, and the Governor-General, and three times persuaded the Board of Control to postpone their announcement of the team.

In Melbourne the celebrated Pamphlet War had intensified with the formation of a group supporting the players called the

Citizens Cricket Committee. This included parliamentarians W.L. Baillieu and Agar Wynne, the chairman of the Melbourne Stock Exchange, W.J. Roberts, the chairman of the Board of Works, W.J. Carre Riddell, Test cricketers John Trumble and Billy Bruce, and the Davis Cup tennis hero Norman Brookes. The committee met at the Athenaeum Club in March, 1912, when it was decided to issue a pamphlet setting out the facts leading up to the six players' defection.

The pamphlet said the members of the Board of Control had no cricket experience and had shown no conciliatory spirit in dealing with prominent players, ignoring them in elections for selection panels, and breaking faith with them on promises about tour profits and the appointment of tour captains and managers.

The Victorian Cricket Association promptly issued a rebuttal pamphlet that attacked the Melbourne Cricket Club for retaining tour profits and failing to use these funds for the benefit of other clubs. The VCA pamphlet said that in the ten years prior to the Board's formation in 1905 the Melbourne Cricket Club handed only £1444 to the VCA, which limited the VCA's distribution to the clubs to £450. In the five years of the Board's existence, the VCA had been able to increase this distribution to the clubs to £2380. The VCA pamphlet added that it had balance sheets in its possession which showed that the 1893 Australian team to England had returned with a profit of £16,461, for a split of £830 to each player.

The VCA pamphlet made great play out of the inconsistencies of payments when they were managed by the players. Frank Laver had received £2000 for his work as player–manager from the £15,049 profit of the 1905 tour, but rising young players who won great fame for Australian cricket were paid paltry amounts, one of them £179 and the other £200. These payments apparently referred to Clem Hill and Victor Trumper, both of whom were added to touring teams at the last minute and both of whom had their payments increased following their highly successful tours.

Laver described in the Citizens' Cricket Committee pamphlet how McElhone gave him an advance of only £200 instead of the £500 he requested to get the 1909 tour started. This had forced him into the embarrassing position of having to ask the Board's London representative, Dr Les Poidevin, for £500 to pay some early tour bills.

Laver issued a pamphlet of his own in May, 1912, in which he said he had made every effort to help McAlister keep the 1909 tour accounts and had shown McAlister the team's accounts during the tour. Finally the Melbourne Cricket Club issued a pamphlet which it addressed 'To the Cricketing Public of Australia, and of England', in which the club denied all blame for the six players' defection and pointed out that in the early years Board administrators had been unseen when tour losses occurred but had only rushed in when the tours became profitable.

In Melbourne, Ernie Bean got all the credit for subduing the players. In Sydney, there was no doubt that Billy McElhone was responsible for quashing the rebellion. Attempts to censure the Board at NSWCA and VCA meetings were snuffed out by impassioned speeches from McElhone and Bean. Clem Hill, in a letter to the *Sydney Morning Herald* in March, 1912, said: 'If it is considered desirable that control of Australian cricket should be left in the hands of one man, by all means do it openly, but do not pretend to invest all the Board with this power when you know it is held by an individual.' Hill stuck to his decision to retire from Test cricket. He had made 17,213 runs at 43.57 in first-class cricket, with 45 centuries, and his 6274 runs at 52.28 remained a Sheffield Shield record until Don Bradman came along.

'Tibby' Cotter preferred to defy the Board of Control and miss the 1912 tour of England, rather than accept the Board's manager.
(Illustrated News)

Hill had a great affection for horses and he turned to them to replace the cricket in his life. He worked initially in his family's coach-building business and then took work as a stipendiary steward and handicapper for the South Australian Jockey Club. In 1937, he became the Victorian Amateur Turf Club's handicapper and moved his family to Melbourne, living in Toorak. Every year he set the weights for runners in the Caulfield Cup.

On 29 February, 1912, just before the Australian team left for the Triangular tournament in England, Monty Noble sent a letter to the *Sydney Morning Herald* claiming that the Board of Control had acted unjustly and dishonestly and violated its own constitution. Noble added: 'I am a strong supporter of the Board, and I believe in the principle of Board control, but I am strongly against the present personnel. They have had six years now to bring everybody into line, and to legislate for Australian cricket, and they have absolutely failed. In those six years they have not been credited with one single act of conciliation or forbearance.'

One of the strange developments in the Board's removal of the players' right to appoint a manager was the election of Queenslander George Stanton Crouch to take the 1912 Australian team to England. When South Australian delegates to the Board argued that according to the constitution the players could appoint their own manager, Victorian delegate Harry Rush laughed. 'Oh, we swept that regulation away last night,' Rush said. When voting for the manager's job was taken, McElhone switched his allegiance. Instead of voting for the Victorian candidate, Peter McAlister, as he had promised, McElhone nominated his own candidate, Ernest Hume, who had toured New Zealand with the New South Wales team in 1895–96. Piqued that McElhone would not continue to support McAlister, the Victorians Rush and Bean voted for the remaining candidate, Crouch, who had played in five inter-state matches between 1903 and 1906 but had no managerial experience. Crouch's appointment showed that men able to outwit the cleverest English batsmen and vie with the best English bowlers were no match for bureaucratic backroom boys, said Ray Robinson.

The Board persuaded Syd Gregory, still battling the effects of his bankruptcy, to take over the captaincy of the 1912 team at the age of 42. The team Gregory took to England is widely recognised as the worst Australia has ever sent away, and had only nine wins in 37 matches. They not only had an appalling record in an extremely wet English summer but they misbehaved. Right up to the eve of their departure public meetings in Sydney, Melbourne and Hobart heard stirring speeches urging the last-minute inclusion of the six defectors. Knowing that this would have meant recasting the tour party so that six of them missed a trip, some of the survivors acted like men on borrowed time, drinking and malingering with churlish disregard for the team's reputation.

Back in Australia major companies offered to underwrite the expense of a second Australian team to England that would include the six defectors, plus rising players like Arthur Mailey, Bert Collins, Johnnie Moyes and the giant young New South Wales left-arm pace bowler, Jack Massie. But the Marylebone Cricket Club refused to recognise such a team.

Ten of the 15 players in the Australian side had never been to England before and when the rain came – as it did in most matches – only Bardsley, Macartney (who had eventually been included in the side) and Kelleway tried to adjust so that they could

The Australian team for the 1912 Triangular series in England: back, W. Bardsley, R.E. Mayne, J.W. McLaren, D. Smith, E. Hume (Assistant Manager); front, R.B. Minnett, G.R. Hazlitt, C.G. Macartney, S.E. Gregory, G.S. Crouch (Manager), W. Carkeek, W.J. Whitty. (Mitchell Library, *Sydney)*

score runs. Gregory was long past his best with the bat and in the field and too soft-hearted to discipline players' misbehaviour. The bowlers were all accustomed to hard, dry pitches and were an unpredictable lot on damp pitches. Roy Minnett bowled handy right-arm medium pace, Gervys Hazlitt turned his medium-pace off-breaks appreciably, Syd Emery continually struggled for control with his googlies, Thomas James Matthews appeared to get more topspin than turn on his leg-breaks and only Bill Whitty could be relied on for lengthy accurate spells with left-arm medium pace.

The rest of the team was made up of players considered lucky to get a trip, C.B. Jennings, J.W. McLaren, H.W. Webster, D.B.M. Smith, W. ('Barlow') Carkeek and Edgar Mayne. The wretched weather quickly demonstrated their limitations.

Kelleway had none of the attractive qualities of Macartney and Bardsley, but he alone among the players new to England defied the damp and often treacherous pitches. He was purely and simply a defensive batsman – *Wisden* called him 'a weariness to the flesh' – but he was of great value to his side. He was very difficult to dislodge and was so lacking in strokes most cricket followers agreed with the critic who said: 'One Kelleway in a side is enough. Two or three would be intolerable.'

Nottinghamshire defeated the Australians by six wickets in the first match of their tour, on 6–8 May, 1912, at Trent Bridge. On mostly dry pitches, the Australians then had their best run of the tour by winning six successive matches against moderate opposition, including the First Test at Old Trafford against South Africa.

Australia's victory over South Africa by an innings and 88 runs took only two days and helped spoil the tournament at the box office by convincing the public that the South Africans were not up to international standard. Kelleway, ever the big occasion player, scored 114 and Bardsley 121 to lift Australia's first-innings total to 448. The Australians then dismissed South Africa for 265 and 95, Matthews taking hat-tricks in each innings – an achievement that remains unique in Test history.

At 4 p.m. on the second day South Africa were within 40 runs of preventing the follow-on with three wickets left. Matthews bowled Beaumont and had Pegler and Ward lbw with successive balls to take his first hat-trick. Gregory enforced the follow-on and at 5 for 70 in South Africa's second innings Matthews had his second hat-trick by bowling Taylor and cleverly dismissing both Schwartz and Ward caught and bowled with his slower ball. Ward had a 'king pair' as the third victim in both hat-tricks. The two hat-tricks on the same day were the only wickets Matthews took in the match. In a three-nation competition, in which teams led by Gregory, Charles Fry, and Frank Mitchell

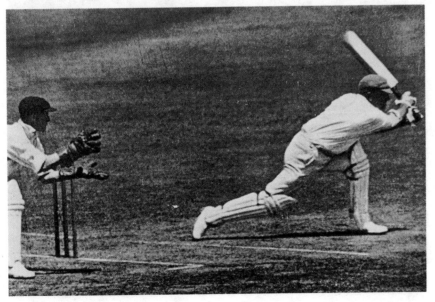

The incomparable Charlie Macartney, who stayed out of the 1912 showdown with the Board of Control, driving through the covers. (NSWCA Archives)

met each other three times, he destroyed interest in six of the nine matches.

Foster (5 for 16 and 3 for 54) and Barnes (5 for 25 and 6 for 85) reproduced the same hostility they had shown in Australia in 1911–12 to give England victory over South Africa by an innings in the second match of the tournament and set up a crucial match against Australia. Unhappily, rain upset all forecasts and brought about a tame draw after brilliant batting by Hobbs (107) and Macartney (99). England and Australia then easily defeated South Africa, before Australia returned to Old Trafford for the second match with England.

At that stage Australia's tour suddenly fell apart and they did not win another match. Rain and poor leadership transformed the second half of the tour into a disaster. Australia were beaten twice by Lancashire, and once each by England, Notts, Surrey, Hampshire, by a Combined Surrey and Middlesex XI and by C.B. Fry's XI.

England sustained their supremacy in the contest by then defeating South Africa and Australia in successive Tests at The Oval. Barnes gave further proof of his mastery by bowling unchanged through both South African innings to take 13 for 57 and give

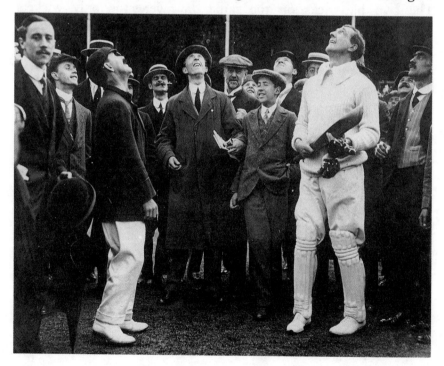

Australian captain Syd Gregory, left, tossing with England captain Charles Fry, before an England v. Australia Test during the Triangular series. (Mitchell Library, *Sydney*)

England a 10-wicket win. Woolley then set up England's triumph over Australia in the final match of the tournament by taking 5 for 29 and 5 for 20 in the Australian innings of 111 and 65. This time Barnes was only needed to soften Australia up in the first innings with 5 for 30. Hazlitt's 7 for 25 in England's second innings could not prevent England winning by 244 runs and did not stop claims that he was a chucker at a time when English cricket prided itself on having purged county teams of this offence.

Final standings in the Triangular tournament had England clear winners with four victories from six matches, with two draws, Australia second with two wins, three draws and one loss, and South Africa last with five losses and one draw. *Wisden* commented:

In the special circumstances, personal considerations should have been put aside and made subordinate to the prime need to send Australia's best team to the Triangular tournament. The Board of Control carried its point, but as regards the prestige of Australian cricket, the victory was dearly won.

The 1912 Australians' record, considering all the triumphs that had come from previous tours to England, remains the worst by an Australian team overseas and proved a financial disaster to English counties who expected big rewards from the competition. The first-class counties received £157 each from the tournament, the second-class counties £24. Total receipts were a disappointing £12,463. Of this Australia received £2986, South Africa £1878.

The tour resulted in a loss to the Australian Board of £1286 after it paid £196 to each of the contracted profit-share players and £400 to the four lucky players who had accepted the lump-sum offers before leaving Australia.

Macartney and Bardsley, whose batting had saved Australia from complete disaster, returned home directly from England, missing the team's six matches in America and Canada. Australia had need of them when they lost a one-day match at Manheim on 27 September, 1912 to the Gentlemen of Philadelphia by two runs. The Philadelphians scored 185 and 74, Australia 122 and 135, in a celebrated victory for American cricket due largely to Barton King, who took 5 for 40 and 4 for 38 in the two Australian innings.

Tour manager Crouch submitted a report on the players' behaviour to the Board of Control in which he said some members of the team behaved so badly the English ostracised them. He urged that future selection of Australian teams to England should be based on factors other than cricket ability. 'From a national point of view it is desirable that you should send men who will realise the responsibilities of their position and be a credit to their country,' Crouch said. *Wisden* said: 'It may be added that some of the players were not at all satisfied with Crouch as manager.'

When Crouch's report was received by the Board in Melbourne, the *Australasian* said that it bore out everything the rejected senior players had predicted. 'The Board should not wonder now that players who for years have been in the forefront of Australian cricket, should have insisted on the right to appoint their own manager, to ensure the team was looked after by a man of experience, and that men who could not appreciate how an Australian team lives in England should not be selected,' the paper said.

Amid reports that when the team was crossing from England to Ireland after completion of the English part of their tour Crouch had been forced to order that no more liquor be sold on board ship, the Board of Control in December, 1912, appointed a committee to investigate Crouch's complaints. Nearly two months later that committee asked four members of the 1912 team to explain incidents on the tour. They were captain Syd Gregory, who had eight trips to England in all, wicket-keeper 'Barlow' Carkeek, spin-bowler T.J. Matthews and batsman Dave Smith. The first three attended but Smith declined on the grounds of ill health. After a two-day hearing the committee refused to comment and said their deliberations were private, but it became known that some players were given 'Never To Tour Again' cards in their official records.

Crouch's report described unsavoury incidents at hotels and dinners for the team. The Board's committee of enquiry heard of foul language persistently used by one player, complaints from other passengers on the *Marama*, which took the team from Auckland to Sydney, that all-night roistering kept them from sleep, and of Edgar Mayne's refusal to share a cabin on the voyage home with one of the heavy drinkers.

When Board secretary Syd Smith announced that the Board would in future assume the right to assess if a player was worthy of representing Australia for reasons other than cricket, it became clear that the days of players' control of overseas tours had gone forever. Of the six rebels, Hill, Trumper, Cotter and Ransford never

Thomas James Matthews, the jockey-sized Melbourne curator, took two hat-tricks in one day for Australia v. South Africa. They were the only wickets he took in the match. (Jack Pollard Collection)

again played Test cricket. Only Armstrong and Carter continued their international cricketing careers. Frank Laver appeared a few times for Victoria but was mainly confined to club and social cricket.

Syd Gregory retired after the 1912 tour, his eighth trip to England and his third through America. His career total of 58 Tests remained the highest by an Australian until Ray Lindwall passed it 44 years later. All but six of Gregory's Tests were against England. He made 15,192 first-class runs at 28.55, with 25 centuries. In Tests he made 2282 runs at 24.53, with four centuries, and in Sheffield Shield matches for New South Wales he scored 3626 runs and eight centuries. He was one of cricket's greatest cover-point fieldsmen and one of Australia's worst captains.

Bean and McElhone did not end their feuding with leading players after the 1912 tour. In fact, Bean renewed his efforts to depose Warwick Armstrong as Victoria's captain. Victorian right-arm fast-medium bowler Jim Kyle disclosed that two VCA executive members had repeatedly urged him to propose somebody to oppose Armstrong as state captain. Kyle said he refused because Armstrong always treated him well as a bowler. 'If this is the sort of thing that goes on in big cricket I don't care if I ever play for Victoria again,' said Kyle.

Armstrong's blustering, autocratic style upset plenty of people but his tactical acumen, all-round skills and the players' admiration kept him on the job. The players still controlled the appointment of the captain. The Melbourne University leg-break bowler, Dr A.E.V. ('German') Hartkopf, however was not allowed to vote for Armstrong when first selected for Victoria in 1911–12 on the grounds that he was twelfth man.

The defectors quickly demonstrated how much they had been missed in the Triangular tournament when the 1912–13 Sheffield Shield matches got underway. At Sydney against South Australia, Trumper made 201 not out for New South Wales, Clem Hill 138 for South Australia, and the four days' play yielded 1570 runs before New South Wales won by 84 runs. Trumper continued this dazzling form by scoring 138 against Victoria, who lost by eight wickets despite Armstrong's 118 not out. South Australia wound up a memorable summer by defeating Victoria for the second time to clinch the Shield. Crawford made 163 and then took 8 for 66 in Victoria's first innings. He was particularly severe on the bowling

Warwick Armstrong, the man sportswriters called 'The Big Ship', hammers a drive to the boundary. He refused to go to England in 1912 under the Board of Control's conditions.
(MCG Library)

of Jack Ryder, who had taken 13 for 155 in the first South Australia v. Victoria match earlier in the season.

Ryder would not be denied, however, and showed just why he was so admired by young would-be cricketers in the Collingwood district with a swashbuckling 71 in Victor Trumper's benefit match in Sydney in February, 1913. The match provided a cricket feast, with Trumper leading the New South Wales side against The Rest of Australia. The Rest batted first and scored 358, thanks to a hard-hitting 76 from 'Johnnie' Moyes. After an emotional welcome to the crease, Trumper made 126 not out and New South Wales reached 389. The Rest managed 265 in their second innings but when time ran out New South Wales were still 89 short of victory with three wickets in hand. Ryder had 8 for 88 in the two New South Wales innings. Trumper received £2950 from the match, the most lucrative testimonial held in Australia to that time.

Trumper's batting continued to dominate Australian cricket and when Edgar Mayne organised a tour of America by an Australian team in 1913 he was quick to secure Trumper's promise that he would tour. Two days before the team boarded the *Niagara* to sail to America Trumper withdrew. He could not afford to go. He had been refused an advance to provide for his family while he was away by the NSWCA-appointed officials who acted as trustees of his testimonial fund. All Trumper's business ventures had failed and he was working as a commercial traveller.

The Board of Control allowed the team to go to America but insisted the tour be labelled 'Unofficial'. The team comprised Austin Diamond, whom the players elected captain, Charlie Macartney, Arthur Mailey, Warren Bardsley, Syd Emery, Les Cody, Percy Arnott, Jack Crawford, Granville ('Jimmy') Down, Gordon Campbell, Herbie Collins and Edgar Mayne.

Mailey, a romantic who normally spent his days up to his knees in mud repairing burst pipes for the Sydney Water Board, was elated to discover that he had been recommended for the tour by his idol Victor Trumper. In a team that lacked a pace bowler, Trumper reasoned that Mailey's googlies and leg-breaks would be what was required to dismiss hundreds of batsmen.

The Australians played 53 matches, for 49 wins, three draws and only one defeat. Percy Arnott's 101 in 45 minutes was the fastest of the 24 centuries scored by the Australians. Macartney topped the list with seven centuries, followed by six from Bardsley, three each from Arnott and Mayne, and one each from Crawford, Collins and

Campbell, the wicket-keeper who had made 23 appearances for South Australia.

Macartney headed both the batting and bowling averages, scoring 2390 runs at 45.92 and taking 189 wickets at 3.81. Crawford took most wickets – 213 at 5.85. Mailey had 183 at 7.26 and Emery 127 at 8.61. Eight of the team made more than 1000 runs, with Macartney's 186 against a combined Canada and United States XI the highest score of the tour. H.A. Furness's 106 not out for the Gentlemen of Philadelphia was the sole century scored against an Australian team which had six bowlers of leg-breaks and googlies.

The Australians romped through the tour, enjoying the luxury hotels and grounds of surprising scenic appeal. Their sole loss came after ten successive wins in Pittsburgh, Bermuda, Rhode Island and New York in the return match against the Germantown club.

The Australians returned home to discover that Mailey's great rival 'Ranji' Hordern had retired, fearing that injuries to his fingers could upset his future in dentistry. He had dismissed five batsmen in an innings 23 times, and taken ten wickets in a match nine times. In all, he took 217 first-class wickets at 16.77, 46 of them in Tests, at a cost of 23.36.

'The comparison between Hordern, Mailey and Clarrie Grimmett is of more than academic interest,' Johnnie Moyes wrote 37 years later. 'Two became world-famous figures in cricket and the third, Hordern, rarely comes into discussion because he played so little. I'm inclined to place Hordern ahead of the others. He was as good as Mailey on hard Australian wickets and better than Grimmett; in England he would have been as outstanding as Grimmett. With his control of length, his disguised deliveries, his ability to flight the ball, and his clever fingers, I don't see how he could have failed.'

The Board of Control blocked a second tour of America in 1914 on the grounds that it interfered with the Board's programme of overseas tours. This dismayed the players whose tour had convinced them that there were wonderful opportunities for cricket in North America. They argued that a return trip to the US could easily be fitted into the northern summer of 1914 without upsetting the Board's plans to visit South Africa in 1914–15. The Board disagreed and eventually the US promoter, R.B. Benjamin, withdrew support.

Throughout the pre-World War I years Dr Les Poidevin represented the Board in England, wining and dining officials at his own expense to safeguard Australian tour matches. When he died in 1931, his son said Dr Poidevin left his family in poverty.

CHAPTER FOURTEEN

SOLDIERS LEAD
THE REVIVAL

Warren Bardsley, who scored more than 2000 runs on three of his four tours of England. (NSWCA Library)

Having survived by winning control of big match gates, the Australian Board of Control for International Cricket remained money-orientated. Reading through minutes of the Board's early meetings, there is very little on how Australia could help expansion of the game, and almost nothing on players' rights or conditions. The Board's priorities led to half a century of shameful neglect of New Zealand cricket, and to a patronising approach to matches against India and South Africa, countries where the Board could see little profit in the early years.

Even when larger ships took the hardship out of trans-Tasman voyages, New Zealand had to be content mainly with visits by Australian club sides. Warwick Armstrong took a Melbourne club team over in 1906–07, Harry Trott led a South Melbourne visit in 1912–13, and J.C. Davis arranged two trips by unofficial NSW sides. These visits inspired a New Zealand team led by Don Reese to play seven matches in Australia in 1913–14.

Reese's side sustained heavy defeats by New South Wales and Victoria, but they beat Northern New South Wales, Queensland and Southern New South Wales, and had the best of drawn matches with South Australia and the Melbourne Cricket Club. Reese made 96 and 130 not out against South Australia and ended the tour with 307 runs at 43.80. The New Zealanders were captivated by the individual brilliance of Clem Hill, Charlie Macartney, Herbie Collins, J.N. Crawford, Warren Bardsley, and other batsmen who appeared in the Golden Age, but it was Victor Trumper's special magic that enslaved them. They agreed with Frank Iredale, who wrote: 'To be near him seemed to me an honour. His was one of those natures which called to you. In his presence, you felt good to be alive.'

Macartney captained New South Wales for the first time against Reese's team instead of Trumper, who was beset with financial problems. The New South Wales batsmen hammered the New Zealand bowling to score 513 runs and set up a win by an innings and 247 runs.

A hard-hitting New South Wales team captained by the Reverend Ernest Frederick ('Mick') Waddy won eight of their nine matches in Ceylon in January, 1914. Their sole defeat was historic, as it was the first time a Ceylon side had ever defeated a visiting first-class team and was not repeated for 50 years until a President's XI beat Pakistan in 1964. The New South Wales tour was organised by Ceylon's leading cricket writer S.P. Foenander. Eager to entertain, Waddy's team hit 29 sixes on the tour, 18 of them coming from the bat of the Waverley club's Norman Ebsworth, while Hazlitt and Minnett were also crowd pleasers.

The team comprised the Reverend E.F. Waddy, G.R. Hazlitt, R.B. Minnett, N. Ebsworth, W. Cameron, P.S. Arnott, G.S. Hall, E.J. Long, P.W. Docker, N.H. Gregg, N.M. Gregg, C.T. Docker and W. Pitt. The Victorian Cricket Association strongly objected to Waddy's team touring, claiming the venture prejudiced the popularity of inter-state cricket. The VCA asked the NSWCA to ban players leaving the state during the cricket season. Waddy said it was absurd to suggest that revenue from inter-state matches would fall because of the tour, but several noted players declined his invitation to join the tour, among them Warren Bardsley.

In the only match with pretensions of first-class status of the tour Waddy's XI defeated Ceylon by two wickets at the Nondescripts Cricket Club's ground at Cinnamon Gardens, Colombo. New South Wales scored 103 and 8 for 74, Ceylon 106 and 70. Waddy said that in C. Horan, who took 31 wickets at 10.02 against the visitors, Ceylon had a left-arm bowler of world-class stature, a bowler the equal of the outstanding New South Welshman Jack Massie (he was the son of Hugh Massie, who toured England with the 1882 Australian team). Waddy scored the only century of the tour, 127 against an All-English Up Country side.

The following month Charlie Macartney, who had missed the Ceylon tour, scored 110 for New South Wales against Tasmania in Sydney, helping to lift his team to a score of 451. Tasmania replied with 163 and 108, to lose by an innings and 180 runs, overwhelmed by Massie's pace.

Harry Hilliard, whose death in 1914 at 88 removed the last cricketer alive in the twentieth century who had played in Hyde Park and Domain matches and the first inter-colonial games. (Mitchell Library, *Sydney*)

Mainland states at that time looked on Tasmanian matches as the ideal apprenticeship for aspiring Sheffield Shield players. For Tasmanian cricket officials, the major problem was the continual drain of players to English universities and to other states. Ted McDonald and Ashley Facy, both Tasmanian-born, played regularly for Victoria from the 1911–12 season, knowing this gave them a better chance of fulfilling Test team aspirations.

The success of Reese's 1913–14 team in Australia inspired Sir Arthur Sims, a widely travelled New Zealand wool-broker who had played for Canterbury and New Zealand, to invite Monty Noble and Frank Laver to assemble an Australian side to visit New Zealand later in 1913–14. The Australian Board of Control was unhappy about this venture and reluctant to risk funds of its own on such a tour, but decided not to intervene. The Australian team was M.A. Noble (Captain), V.T. Trumper, V.S. Ransford, H.L. Collins, J.N. Crawford, W.W. Armstrong, F.J. Laver, A.A. Mailey, W. McGregor, L.A. Cody, E.L. Waddy, Dr C.E. Dolling and C. McKenzie. Trumper, whose son Victor junior was born on 7 October, 1913, joined the team after it had played three matches.

He struck form with a dazzling 94 in 94 minutes at Wanganui and from then on large crowds turned up whenever he was expected to bat. Noble adjusted his batting order to ensure Trumper batted when the largest crowds were present. At Lancaster Park, Christchurch, early in March, 1914, Australia were 7 for 209 in reply to the Canterbury team's 92 when Trumper went in to bat. He was off the mark at once and in a flurry of brilliant glances, late cuts and pull shots moved to 50 in 26 minutes, 100 in 73 minutes and 150 in 92 minutes. Sixes bounced into nearby ponds and off the scorers' box as Trumper swept to 250 in 152 minutes. At 293, after he had put on 433 for the eighth wicket with Sir Arthur Sims, he was out when he skied a ball to point in his first mistake of the innings. Trumper hit 44 fours and three sixes, and at one stage he and Sims added 100 runs in 21 minutes. Australia won the match by an innings and 364 runs.

Trumper again batted at no. 9 at Temuka against Fifteen of South Canterbury, and put on 289 runs in 69 minutes for the eighth wicket with Crawford. They moved the total from 450 to 550 in just 23 minutes. Trumper reached his century in 54 minutes and his 135 runs included 20 fours and one six. Crawford and Noble added 50 in nine minutes after Trumper left. Crawford's stands with Trumper and Noble put on 200 in an hour.

*The most famous
photograph in cricket
history, with Victor
Trumper jumping out to
drive. His death in 1915
pushed war news off the
nation's front pages.*
(George Beldham)

At Eden Park, Auckland, in March, 1914, Trumper went to the
crease when Australia was on 3 for 231 in the main match of the tour
against New Zealand. He scored 81 in an hour, falling lbw when he
missed with his leg glance through his legs. Waddy, Dolling, Armstrong and Crawford made centuries and New Zealand were beaten
by an innings after scoring 269 and 228, Australia declaring at 6 for
610. A leg-spinner named Clarrie Grimmett played in two matches
against Australia without taking a wicket. For Trumper, the New
Zealand tour proved a magnificent last showing of his genius.

Despite the outbreak of war in Europe in August, 1914, the Sheffield
Shield competition went ahead in 1914–15, simply because of the
Board's confidence that the British Empire would quickly defeat
Germany. Dr Ramsay Mailer, believing the war would be brief, had
his motion to postpone the Board's international programme for
a year unanimously accepted. This meant that the Australian team
that was to visit South Africa in 1914–15 would make the tour
instead in 1915–16.

The original team for South Africa was announced as: W.W.
Armstrong (Captain), T.J.E. Andrews, E.P. Barbour, W. Bardsley,
F. Baring, W. Carkeek, G.R. Hazlitt, C. Kelleway, C.G. Macartney,
R.E. Mayne, A.G. Moyes, J. Ryder and W.J. Whitty, with G.C.

Campbell as manager. Hill, Hordern, Massie, Ransford and Trumper were unavailable. Bert Folkard went into the team when Hazlitt dropped out and later Dr R.L. Park replaced Barbour.

Bert Ironmonger virtually won the Sheffield Shield for Victoria in 1914–15 by taking 32 wickets at only 17.15 runs apiece, confirming Hugh Trumble's high opinion of his left-arm slows. Ironmonger, born at Pine Mountain, near Ipswich, in Queensland in 1882, was known as the district bowling champion as a teenager because of his wicket-taking for the Albert Club and made his first-class debut in the Queensland team in 1909–10 against Victoria. Hugh Trumble was so impressed with him he persuaded Bert to go south to further his Test hopes.

Ironmonger had lost the top half of his left index finger in an accident on his father's farm involving a chaff-cutter. Medical help was too far away so his sister dipped the finger in a cup of flour, the only treatment it ever received. Balancing the ball on the top of the stub, Ironmonger could bowl for hours on a good length, just moving the ball enough to beat the bat. He was a lifetime novice with the bat and a clumsy, unbending fieldsman, who had to be shielded by his captains. In 25 seasons of first-class cricket, he managed 30 catches in 96 matches, but when he held one he often made headlines.

British defeats and the failure at Gallipoli in 1915 shattered dreams of early victory in the war. Parliamentarians and patriotic headmasters began to attack cricketers who did not join up. Wesley headmaster and Australian Cricket Board founder L.A. Adamson made an impassioned speech accusing Victorian Sheffield Shield players who had not joined up, as many New South Wales players had done, of cowardice. 'New South Wales has sent nearly all her leading players to the front,' said noted educationist E.H.C. Oliphant. 'Victoria has not provided one of her chief players.'

Ernie Bean replied that 11 Victorian Shield players were serving overseas, but the public were aware that only Dr Roy Park, of the 1914–15 Victorian premiership team, had gone to war. Several Test cricketers received white feathers in the mail, although they would never admit it.

Victor Trumper helped pick the New South Wales team to play South Australia over the 1914 Christmas holidays, but was not well enough to join the side. The specialist treating him for kidney disease, Dr Herbert Bullmore, put him to bed. His condition deteriorated quickly and Dr Bullmore – whose daughter Gretel was to marry media magnate Frank Packer and become mother of Clyde and Kerry – sent Trumper to Sydney's St Vincent's Hospital. Trumper died there on 28 June, 1915, in his wife's arms. Dr Bullmore said death was due to convulsions caused by chronic nephritis, which newspapers called Bright's Disease.

Trumper's death was splashed across the front pages of English and Australian newspapers. Tributes to his unique batting style poured in. His funeral attracted enormous crowds and a procession eight kilometres long behind the coffin borne by pallbearers Monty Noble, 'Tibby' Cotter, Syd Gregory, Hanson Carter, Warren Bardsley and Warwick Armstrong. They took him from his Chatswood home to Milson's Point, by water to near where Sydney's Opera House now stands, and then through the streets to Waverley Cemetery. He was 37.

Dr Herbert Bullmore, Victor Trumper's doctor in his final days, was a former Rugby international and father of Gretel, Frank Packer's first wife and mother of Clyde and Kerry Packer. (Jack Pollard Collection)

Speculation about Trumper's origins have persisted ever since his premature death. For years cricketers talked about him being born out of wedlock in 1877, four years before his parents were married, at a time when illegitimacy was shameful. But in 1985 schoolteacher Peter Sharpham set forth the view that Victor was an orphan adopted by the Trumper family. He bore little resemblance to his brothers and sisters and there was no record of his birth, which even illegitimate children had registered. Frustrated in searches of Australian records for Trumper's origins, experts have turned to New Zealand.

Gervys Hazlitt died at the King's School, Parramatta, on 30 October 1915, aged 27. It had been known for years that he had a weak heart, but few realised that he had defied doctors to play for Australia. Hazlitt's death came one week after Dr W.G. Grace died of a heart attack in England following a Zeppelin raid over London. Just before that Andrew Stoddart and Albert Trott had both shot themselves in the head, and in November 1917, Albert Trott's brother Harry died in a Melbourne asylum. Of the cricketers at the front, on 31 October 1917, 'Tibby' Cotter died in the Australian Light Horse attack on Beersheba, his magnificent torso wrecked by machine-gun fire. No bowler before or since had so frequently broken batsmen's stumps, and he often sent bails on 50-metre flights – his admirers measured the distance from the wicket to where the bails landed.

Despite the cries of cowardice from the Melbourne establishment, a large number of Australia's best cricketers ended up in England where the Armistice was signed on 11 November, 1918. Some of them were recovering from wounds, and others like Jack Massie and Johnnie Moyes were too badly hurt for them to contemplate playing any further first-class cricket. All of them had to take their turn with thousands of other servicemen in Europe waiting for the ships to take them home.

'Plum' Warner staged two successful matches at Lord's between English and Dominion XIs designed to get big cricket re-started. Faced with the problem of keeping thousands of homesick men amused and out of trouble while they waited to be repatriated the service chiefs formed the Australian Imperial Forces (AIF) Sports Board, which soon had competitions against other nations' servicemen going in athletics, tennis, boxing and soccer. The King's Cup for rowers and a similar competition for rugby teams were organised in 1919 and their success led to the idea of an AIF cricket team touring Britain and playing Test matches against England.

At a meeting in Melbourne the Australian Board of Control for International Cricket agreed to the formation of an Australian team comprising players still in the Army and appointed Major Gordon Campbell, the South Australian wicket-keeper who had toured the US with the unofficial Australian team in 1913, as manager. The Board agreed to pay £150 towards the expenses of each selected player and £200 for the AIF team's scorer, Bill Ferguson.

After early trials the AIF team looked certain to become a very powerful outfit, quite capable of extending the best eleven England could put into the field. Then Dr E.P. Barbour, Dr R.L. Park and Dr C.J. Tozer announced their withdrawals because they had to get home to re-establish their medical practices. Injuries to great fast bowler Jack Massie, which he sustained in the trenches in Gallipoli and France, proved too severe for him to resume playing. Charlie Macartney withdrew to return home following the death of his father. Confronted with all these withdrawals by top-class players, the Marylebone Cricket Club decided to withhold their financial support for the AIF team and with it the sanctioning of the matches against England as Tests.

A further blow to the AIF team came when Major Gordon Campbell resigned as manager and selector. The AIF Sports Board's supervisor, Major Syd Middleton, who had played for the first Wallabies in Britain in 1908, immediately replaced Campbell with the 65-year-old Irishman Howard Lacy, a wealthy supporter of the Mitcham Club in Surrey, who had organised several wartime cricket matches for Australian and New Zealand cricketers. Lacy had a big

The massive figure of New South Wales pace bowler Jack Massie shown during Army training. He was badly wounded twice in the war and played no more cricket. (SCG Archives)

influence on the Surrey county club and with their help set about organising an itinerary for the AIF team.

Meanwhile Middleton had Captain Cyril Docker called up from Salisbury Plains to assist in two months of exhaustive trials. Docker circulated news of the trials to every Australian service unit in Europe, seeking players with first-class or first-grade club experience in Australia. A dozen nets were required at Lord's to try out all those who took the chance to dodge the boredom of daily parade-ground drill. The Army's money ran out as the number of trialists multiplied but Australian businessmen in London, the Australian Comforts Fund and the Australian government all came up with funds.

On 14 May 1918, the AIF Sports Board trimmed the number of trialists to 24 and the selectors used this group as the pool from which they selected teams for 12-a-side matches until the fitness of several players was tested. They then reduced the team, knowing they had reserves who could be called on to replace the injured. The team comprised E.A. Bull, H.L. Collins, C.T. Docker, J.M. Gregory, H.F.T. Heath, C. Kelleway, A.W. Lampard, E.J. Long, H.S.B Love, J.T. Murray, C.C. O'Connor, W.A.S. Oldfield, C.E. Pellew, W.S. Stirling, J.M. Taylor, W.L. Trenerry, C.B. Willis and S.C. Winning.

Between 14 May and 10 September, 1919, the AIF team played 28 first-class matches and four others around England and Scotland and helped revive cricket at a first-class level. They developed into an outstanding team and lost only four matches, winning 15 and drawing 13. Cambridge University, MCC and Ground Staff, Yorkshire, Lancashire, Derbyshire, Worcestershire, Warwickshire, Sussex and Essex were among the teams they defeated. A second AIF team toured schools and minor counties while the top team played out its first-class programme and probably did just as important a job in reviving interest in cricket as major schools and universities.

Initially, Charles Kelleway captained the AIF XI after the selectors nominated him for the job without holding the traditional team election. After the sixth match against Surrey at The Oval Field Marshal Birdwood, GOC of the Australian forces in Europe, sent for Herbie Collins and told him he was to take over captaincy of the side. Collins, a lance-corporal, was staggered that he had been asked to replace Kelleway, who held the rank of captain. Birdwood said: 'Kelleway is a good cricketer, but unfortunately he quarrels. I understand that he has already had three arguments, including one

The AIF team which revived cricket in England and around the Australian states immediately after World War I: back, S.C. Winning, E.J. Long, C.T. Docker, J.M. Gregory, C.B. Willis; front, J.M. Taylor, E. Bull, H.L. Collins (Captain), E. Cameron, W.L. Trenerry, W.A.S. Oldfield. (J.C. Davis Collection, Sydney)

with a curator. I'm sending him back on the next ship.'

Kelleway refused to accept the sack, however, and travelled to Brighton with the team for the next match against Sussex. He insisted that he would play despite Collins's pleas for him to step down. Finally the players conferred and told Kelleway they would not join him if he took the field. Kelleway left the team and was on his way home within a few days. He bore Collins no ill-feeling and later played under Collins's captaincy for both New South Wales and Australia.

Under Collins the AIF team ignored all considerations of rank and Captains Ted Long and Bill Trenerry played quite happily with Gunner Johnny Taylor and Corporal Bert Oldfield. They called each other by their first names, borrowed each other's gear and ate together at the same table. The team spirit they quickly found allowed them to give every side they met a tough match. One of their most enjoyable matches was against Surrey, who included Jack Crawford – who had emigrated to Adelaide following a row in 1909 – in their side. This allowed him to play full-time once again for his county and gave him the chance to appear against 'Nip' Pellew, who had been one of Crawford's pupils at St Peter's College, Adelaide.

They learned in newspapers from home that Ernie Bean had told a meeting of the Australian Board of Control people were tired of the Sheffield Shield competition and that it should be replaced by a more suitable contest. Bean said the Victorian Cricket Association's recommendation was that the first side to win the Shield twice should keep it and a new trophy be substituted. But at a Board meeting in October 1919, after the impressive results of the AIF team's matches were received, the Board delegates voted enthusiastically for resumption of the Shield competition.

The AIF team, drawn from the three strongest Shield states, virtually guaranteed an attractive Shield competition once they returned home. South Australians Pellew, Stirling and Murray demonstrated that they would add strength to their state XI. Victorians Willis and Lampard showed form that would be valuable, and all the New South Wales members of the team demonstrated they would be in the forefront of state team contenders.

In John Morrison Gregory, the AIF tour developed a pace bowler of awesome power who could destroy the morale of even top-class batsmen. Gregory was a product of Shore (Sydney Church of England Grammar) School in Sydney, where he had played in the First XI and the rugby XV, as well as winning the school athletic championship. He had joined up at 18 before he had a chance to further the Gregory family's great name in cricket. Army life had seen him mature into a marvellous physical specimen who bounded to the crease with a characteristic 'kangaroo hop' that generated exceptional pace from his tall (193-cm) and solid (90-kg) frame. With the bat, he hit with skill and power, scoring very quickly, thanks to a reach that made half volleys of good length balls.

The South African cricket-lover Sir Abe Bailey and his countrymen were so impressed with the exciting brand of cricket played by the AIF team they arranged for their government to invite the side to spend six weeks in South Africa on their way home. Bailey guaranteed to finance the tour and when the South African Minister for Defence, Senator Pearce, visited London it was quickly arranged. Ernie Cameron, who had been Howard Lacy's assistant manager on the English tour, took over as manager for the eight first-class matches and two social games in South Africa.

The AIF beat Eastern Province, Natal, Western Province, Transvaal, two college fifteens, and twice triumphed against full-strength South African teams. Captain Herbie Collins scored the

Charles Kelleway, who was sacked by his Field Marshal after leading the AIF team in their first few matches. (J.C. Davis Collection)

211

The remarkable reach of AIF star Jack Gregory is shown in this shot of him driving. He batted left-handed, bowled right-handed. (J.C. Davis Collection)

team's sole century in South Africa, with an innings of 235 in the first match against South Africa at Johannesburg. Jack Gregory was the leading wicket-taker in South Africa, with 47 wickets at an average cost of 13.04, including figures of 9 for 32 against Natal at Durban and 7 for 21 against Natal at Maritzburg, and 6 for 46 against South Africa at Johannesburg.

Although they were anxious to return to their families after the years away, the AIF team agreed before they left South Africa to play matches against each of the states when they arrived home. They felt it was their duty to help restore public interest in big cricket. They sailed a fortnight before Christmas 1919, but when they arrived to play South Australia in Adelaide they were amazed to find the South Australian players were in Melbourne. The Board had botched a simple administrative exercise yet again.

The players took the train from Adelaide to Melbourne and had to fill in time practising while the Victoria v. South Australia match was played. They saw an outstanding eighth-wicket partnership of 215 between Armstrong (143) and Dr Roy Park. Park batted for six hours 40 minutes to score 228. Park, Armstrong and the Sydney batsmen Tommy Andrews and Jim Bogle were among the players who immediately showed Australian cricket would recover quickly from the war. Bogle, a doctor who had won Blues in five sports at Sydney University, made 200 that season for New South Wales against South Australia in Adelaide, after making 145 in his first appearance in 1918–19.

Gregory made a dramatic debut in Australian first-class cricket by taking 7 for 22 for the AIF against Victoria, with most of his victims caught in the slips trying to play rising deliveries of frightening pace. Only four Victorians reached double figures. Carl Willis's 111 enabled the AIF to take a first-innings lead of 195 runs and win the match in the last over amid intense spectator enthusiasm by four wickets. At Brisbane the AIF appeared certain to defeat Queensland after an innings of 135 from Collins when rain washed out play; this match had been hurriedly arranged by the Board to replace the proposed AIF v. South Australia fixture.

In the AIF team's final match at Sydney from 31 January to 3 February 1920, Gregory gave another magnificent all-round display. He took eight wickets for 130 runs, held three fine catches in the slips, and made 122 and 102 with the bat. Collins recovered from a first-innings duck to score 129 in the AIF's second innings, his ninth century since the AIF tour began. The AIF team's win by 203 was warmly applauded. They had shown their strength against the winners of the Sheffield Shield that season and provided Australia with seven new Test players.

The AIF team won 25 of their 47 matches in three countries and lost only four. Their bowlers dismissed 648 batsmen, and their batsmen scored 32 centuries. Considering that some of them had returned after years in the trenches, had been badly gassed and carried war injuries, their sparkling cricket was a remarkable achievement. They made a wonderful contribution to cricket and must rank as one of Australia's most significant teams.

Herbie Collins enjoyed telling how Gregory became a specialist slips fieldsman during the ten months of the AIF team's tour. 'He was so ungainly, he spiked his own finger fielding in the outfield in one of our early games,' Collins said. 'I put him in the slips to recover and he held 66 catches for us in that position.' In all, Jack Gregory was to hold 195 catches in the slips in his first-class matches.

Gregory, the post-First World War superstar of Australian cricket, was a natural right-hander and he always bowled with the right arm. He had been kidded into batting left-handed in backyard matches by his brothers Alban and Warwick. One of their neighbours in the Sydney suburb of Strathfield had an orchard of delicious apples just where a left-hander's legside shots landed, and the lads could always get a good feed from Jack's hefty swings. They were the sons of Charles Smith Gregory and cousins of Test batsman Syd Gregory, captain of the unfortunate 1912 Australian side in the Triangular tournament. They had three sisters, Edith, Mena and Claire, whose main role in fielding was to goad Jack to make the hits that would end up with all six Gregorys biting into apples.

Jack Gregory took 198 wickets in his first year of first-class cricket, 131 in 25 matches for the AIF in England, 47 in eight matches on the South African leg of the tour, and 20 from three matches in Australia. He also scored 1727 runs, including three centuries. These astounding figures were achieved by a cricketer who had not progressed beyond North Sydney's third grade when he joined up. He only got the chance to show his worth as an opening bowler because Cyril Docker, the man picked for the job, injured his back. Nobody could be surprised, however, given the special talents of the Gregory family who by the 1919–20 season had seven members who had played for New South Wales and four for Australia.

Apart from supplying seven future Test players, the AIF team made a big contribution to Australian cricket at all levels. Only Cyril Docker, badly concussed during the war, did not play after the AIF tour ended. Gregory and Collins went automatically into the Test team, while Oldfield, Pellew and Taylor later forced their way into Tests, and Kelleway and 'Hammy' Love, who had been involved in the early matches in England, figured prominently in Australian first-class matches for years. Eric Bull played frequently for the Mosman club in Sydney, Ted Long for North Sydney, 'Oke' O'Connor for Waverley, Charlie Winning for Paddington, Carl Willis for Prahran, Bill Trenerry for Paddington and Mosman, Bill Stirling for Adelaide and East Torrens, Jack Murray for East Torrens and Allie Lampard for Richmond and Prahran – and all of them for their respective states.

At Melbourne, in the AIF team's match against Victoria, Jack Gregory met Edgar Arthur ('Ted') McDonald for the first time. Over the next two seasons they were to develop into one of the best opening bowling partnerships Test cricket has known. McDonald had made his first-class debut as a batsman in 1909–10 for Tasmania, but for reasons that have never been disclosed left the island hurriedly. He joined the Victorian team in 1911–12, by which time his bowling talents had emerged. The presence of both these gifted bowlers gave Australia the luxury of opening a Test with a pace bowler at each end, whereas selectors previously had restricted their approach to a Spofforth, Ernie Jones or Tibby Cotter, never using two bowlers of this type.

Australia was undoubtedly better prepared for the resumption of Test cricket than England, who had suffered a far bigger upheaval. *Wisden* carried pages and pages of obituaries of noted cricketers throughout the war years and eight years without Tests had seen the loss of entire generations of emerging public school cricketers.

The Australian Board of Control invited MCC to send out a team to Australia within a few months of hostilities ending, but Lord's declined, preferring to allow their key players to find form in county cricket, which resumed in 1919 after four blank years. This allowed 'Plum' Warner to end his playing days leading Middlesex to a dramatic win in the 1920 county championship.

Reggie Spooner originally accepted an invitation to captain the English team to Australia but later withdrew for domestic reasons. Johnny Douglas was chosen to replace him and given a team comprising P.G.H. Fender, E.R. Wilson, J.B. Hobbs, H. Strudwick, J.W. Hitch, J.W. Hearne, E.H. Hendren, F.E. Woolley, C.H. Parkin, J.W.H. Makepeace, W. Rhodes, A. Dolphin, A. Waddington, H. Howell and C.A.G. Russell. The team left England with English supporters confident about their batting strength but doubtful about the bowling on flint-hard Australian pitches. Only seven of the 16 players – Hobbs, Hearne, Woolley, Rhodes, Strudwick, Hitch and Douglas – had been to Australia before, which showed the extent of the rebuilding forced on the selectors, who took a major risk by including Cecil Parkin after only five county matches. Parkin, known to all by his nickname 'Ciss', was an eccentric who bowled off-breaks at a cleverly varied pace.

Parkin was among the professionals in the English team who once again travelled second-class while their amateur team-mates went first-class. Lord's ducked this golden chance to bring equality and harmony to their Test teams after such a long break. Lord Hawke and Lord Harris, who had both worked to improve professionals' wages and conditions and had insisted on a higher standard of behaviour from the professionals, could not understand the fuss when Australian newspapers reported the difference in travel bookings. 'I know some of our professionals would prefer to travel

Norman Callaway, who died in the trenches in France, left a first-class average of 207 from his sole appearance for New South Wales. (J.C. Davis Collection)

215

second-class than dress every night for dinner,' said Lord Hawke.

The England tour began in Perth in late October 1920 and lasted until mid-March, during which the team played 22 matches, winning nine, losing six and leaving seven unfinished. This result appalled cricket lovers in England, but seemed appropriate for a side that had to spend its first week in Australia in quarantine at Fremantle because a case of typhoid had been discovered on board.

In Victoria the feud between Armstrong and Ernie Bean continued, with Bean and his fellow Victorian selectors trying to convince their team Armstrong was too old at 41 to hold the captaincy. Batting and bowling for hours almost every day in the nets as the Melbourne Cricket Club's ground bowler, Armstrong refused to restrain his gargantuan appetite for food and drink, but by scoring 157 not out and 245 for Victoria against South Australia to become the first man to score a century and a double century in the same match virtually assured himself of the Australian captaincy against the Englishmen.

Armstrong's leadership took Australia to a 5–0 win by margins depressing to every England supporter. Douglas had too many aged, non-athletic fieldsmen to hide in the field to match the fleet-footed, robustly fit Australians, though he had some stars such as 'Patsy' Hendren in the outfield and wicket-keeper Strudwick. The younger Englishmen were bamboozled by Mailey's googly, which they appeared completely unable to detect.

Dr Claude Tozer, a candidate for Australia's cricket captaincy when he was murdered by his deranged lover. (Jack Pollard Collection)

At Adelaide Australia was outplayed for three days but played themselves back into the match by scoring 582 in their second innings, using what historian Irving Rosenwater called a 'batting depth of unparalleled power'. Kelleway (147), Armstrong (121) and Pellew (104) led the Australian fight-back.

Armstrong's popularity with crowds built up at roughly the same rate as his weight and at 140 kg (22 stone) he had strong claims to being Australia's favourite cricket captain. He did some inspired things, such as throwing the ball to Mailey to open the bowling against Hobbs in the Second Test and instructing him to concentrate on his top-spinner. Mailey had Hobbs out lbw. Armstrong had remembered getting Hobbs out himself with a top-spinner.

At Sydney in December 1920 Dr Claude Tozer, whose four knocks that summer for the Gordon Club had produced 110, 211, 131 and 39 and had people talking of him as a future state or even Australian captain – he already had a Shield century to his credit – visited a patient, Mrs Dorothy Mort, on his way home from the First Test. He told her he intended to end their romance and marry another woman. Mrs Mort shot him twice and then tried to shoot herself. Next day, the Australians wore black armbands. Mrs Mort was found not guilty of Dr Tozer's murder on the grounds of insanity.

Despite his wonderful triumph leading the Australian side in 1920–21, Armstrong won the job as captain of the 1921 Australian side to England by only one vote. This was the first time Board members had taken the appointment of a captain out of the players' hands. Bean had worked like a demon to dethrone him but was a vote short when the Board made their decision. Board secretary Syd Smith, normally tight-lipped with Australia's cricket secrets, made an uncharacteristic blunder in disclosing the closeness of the vote, perhaps because his position was unpaid.

Smith, who was originally chosen as secretary of the Board by Billy McElhone, did the job without payment until 1926, with trips as manager of Australian teams his only reward. The Board gave him his first trip by appointing him manager of the 1921 team. Kelleway was unavailable for this fifteenth Australian team to England for business reasons, and although he had headed the bowling averages in the previous rubber against England, with 15 Test wickets at 21 runs apiece, this great Australian team did not miss him. The team comprised: W.W. Armstrong (Captain), H.L. Collins (Vice-captain), T.J.E. Andrews, W. Bardsley, H. Carter, J.M. Gregory, H.S.T.L. Hendry, C.G. Macartney, R.E. Mayne, A.A. Mailey, E.A. McDonald, J. Ryder, J.M. Taylor, W.A.S. Oldfield and C.E. Pellew.

On the voyage to England in the *Osterley* Armstrong told a team meeting the programme they faced had been arranged by a mob of novices. Some of the team were apprehensive about offending the Board and reviving the acrimony of the 1912 row, but the meeting instructed manager Smith to write to all the counties Australia was due to play immediately before a Test asking if they would drop the third day of their matches. Oxford University, Gloucestershire and Warwickshire agreed and this gave the Australians a rest day before the Tests at Nottingham, Lord's and Leeds. Smith made sure in scheduling later tours that the rest day before Tests was obligatory.

The Australians found English cricket still in shock after the 5–0 defeat of Douglas's team in the previous Australian summer. It was a drubbing Englishmen found difficulty comprehending because of the thoroughness of England's triumph when the countries last met in 1911 and 1912. But Gregory and McDonald proceeded to humble the best of England's batting just as Barnes and Foster had done to the Australians in 1911–12. McDonald (138) took more wickets but Gregory (116 victims) was more frightening. Between them they handed out a fearful battering and England used 30 players in a one-sided series. Handicapped by the absence of Hobbs through injury and illness, England succumbed inside three days in the first three Tests. The English selectors were so rattled they used only two players, Douglas and Woolley, in all five Tests. Australia was so strong they could afford to omit Mailey from the Fifth Test, but he still took 134 wickets on tour, Australia winning the series 3–0 with two drawn.

Eleven Australians scored centuries on the tour, with Macartney's 345 in a day against Nottingham the highlight. Macartney went to the crease with the score one for one after Bardsley had been bowled. He was missed in the slips when he had made nine and from then went on to make 47 fours and four sixes. He reached 300 in only 198 minutes, which remains the fastest triple century in first-class cricket, and batted 232 minutes in all. Australia reached 675 and had Notts out for 58 and 100 to win by an innings and 517 runs, Australia's best-ever win.

In the Fourth Test Armstrong bowled two consecutive overs, the first instance of this in Test cricket. Rain on the first day reduced the match to a two-day fixture, and with England on 4 for 341 Lord Lionel Tennyson declared. Hanson Carter, a renowned authority on the rules, told Armstrong the declaration was illegal as there was less than 100 minutes batting available to the fielding side. Armstrong told his players to stay on the field and 25 minutes later England resumed batting, with Carter's point proved. Armstrong bowled before and after the break in the confusion.

Of the 39 matches played that summer, the Australians won 23, drew 14 and lost two right at the end of the tour. Archie MacLaren, who had told friends he could pick a side to beat the Australians, saw his boast come true. His all-amateur England XI scored 43 and 326 to beat Australia, 174 and 167, by 28 runs at Eastbourne, South African Aubrey Faulkner winning the match with 153.

Until Bradman's 1948 team went through a tour of England unbeaten, the performance by Armstrong's team was ranked the best-ever by an Australian team in England. In a gesture that was completely out of character, the Australian Board of Control showed its appreciation of the persistently high gates by granting all 15 players a £200 bonus.

Syd Smith, in his book *With the Fifteenth Australians*, said the takings of the tour amounted to £35,644 8s 4d, so the Board could well afford to spend £3000 on players' bonuses, and give Bill Ferguson £100 for his work as scorer and baggageman.

The Board of Control's bonus was not the only loot Armstrong picked up as a reward for leading Australia to eight successive Test wins. Back in Melbourne Prime Minister Billy Hughes presented him with a cheque for £2500, collected the previous summer to fight Bean's campaign to oust him as Australia's captain. Hughes told the Town Hall audience: 'When Warwick goes into the field, the Englishmen are half beaten; when he takes the ball, they are wholly beaten.'

This kind of idolatory has come to all Australia's winning captains and given the job a special aura in Australian society. Armstrong, usually unequivocal and always gruff, had become the second Australian to play in 50 Tests, scoring 2863 runs at 38, and taking 87 Test wickets at 33, and with that kind of all-round record Australians did not care if team-mates often found him rude and intolerant. Here was a man who could go in and make a century after four stiff whiskies, who condescendingly referred to abstainers in his side as 'my lemonade brigade', but also a man who could take a joke against himself.

After Mailey had taken 3 for 21 in Gloucestershire's first innings on the 1921 tour, Armstrong told his team he was going to bowl himself to 'pick up a few of these cheap wickets'. Barnett and Keigwin proceeded to hit Armstrong all over the field amid increasing laughter from Armstrong's fieldsmen. Finally he handed the ball back to Mailey, who took his famous 10 for 66 to win the match by an innings and give himself the perfect book title.

Armstrong's new-found affluence allowed him to resign the job he had held since 1911 as the Melbourne Cricket Club's £228-a-year pavilion clerk, a job which entailed supervising 20 volunteer ground bowlers and issuing cricket gear to members. Hunter Hendry took his place, moving down from Sydney to get the daily practice such a tall (193 cm) man needed to remain in Test contention. Armstrong became the Victorian agent for Peter Dawson's Scotch whisky distillery, who could scarcely have made a better choice. He became so adept at selling whisky he was appointed Australian

One of the heroes of the 1921 team, Charlie Macartney, pulling a ball to leg with characteristic nonchalance. (Sport & General)

manager for James Buchanan's Scotch whisky in 1935 and when he died at 68 Ray Robinson calculated that the £90,000 he left made him Australia's richest cricket captain, bar one.

Armstrong had had immense difficulty remaining in the physical trim that allowed him to play regularly on the 1921 tour of England. He had had to join Ted McDonald in the boilerroom of the ship shovelling coal to help keep his weight down on the voyage to England, and on hot days in England had continued to wear several sweaters while fielding to ensure he perspired freely. At 140 kg, newspapers called him 'The Big Ship', and it was embarrassing to watch him trying to get up when he fell down in the field. He used his bulk cleverly when batting, but had to take an exceptional number of balls on the legs. The continual pounding on his legs prevented him joining his team for the six matches in South Africa on the way home from England, which included three four-day Tests and he handed over the captaincy to Herbie Collins while he finalised his job arrangements in England.

The Australians won four of their matches in South Africa and left the other two drawn. They defeated Transvaal, Natal and Western Province comfortably enough, but had to wait for the Third Test before they had a win in the Test rubber. The First Test at Durban ended with the South Africans 207 runs in arrears with only three wickets left. The Second Test at Johannesburg was drawn after Herbie Collins scored 203 – the first double-century by an Australian against South Africa in South Africa – and Jack Gregory made a century in 70 minutes on his way to 119, still the fastest hundred in all Test cricket. Gregory faced 67 balls in the 70 minutes. In 1985, Vivian Richards made a century v. England at St John off 56 balls, but took 81 minutes to reach 100.

Jack Ryder's 142 won the Third Test at Cape Town for the Australians. None of the South African batsmen could handle Mailey, who took 35 wickets in the six matches at 22.91 each, or Gregory, whose 30 wickets cost 14.83 each, but South African critics voted Collins the best cricketer on either side, and rated his left-arm spinners as difficult on the mat as Mailey's googlies.

CHAPTER FIFTEEN

NIGHT-OWL HERBIE TAKES OVER

For several years after the 1921 tour Syd Smith had great influence within the Australian Board of Control. Despite the careless itinerary which Armstrong continued to adjust throughout the tour, Smith had provided the Board with its first major success since its stormy formation 16 years earlier, and had come home with funds that assured the Board's future. The Board could look forward to the new arrangement of four-yearly tours to England and the expectation of similar returns.

Smith failed, however, to prevent the return to England of Ted McDonald in 1922 in a deal with the Lancashire county committee that made him the highest-paid professional in England. McDonald, the son of a tinsmith from Launceston, Tasmania, had played in only 11 Tests for Australia, but during that time he established himself as one of the great fast bowlers. Bert Oldfield, who kept wicket to them both, regarded McDonald as a far superior bowler to Jack Gregory. His action was more graceful and rhythmic, and although he seldom bowled with the wind behind him as Gregory did, he matched Gregory for pace, and could turn the ball back from the off with 'none of the superfluous pounding of the earth or waving of the hands' characteristic of Gregory.

Smith would have received strong support from Lord's had he argued that Australians had hardly seen McDonald. *Wisden* strongly opposed his signing and the whole idea of English counties importing Australian players. Under the deal, McDonald played Lancashire League cricket for Nelson while he qualified for Lancashire. Nelson received £500 compensation for bringing him to England and were also given two first-class matches, one in 1925 and one in 1926, from which they received ten per cent of the gate receipts.

McDonald was released to play for Lancashire in 1924, but in the interim Lancashire had the right to call on his services for their matches against Yorkshire at Old Trafford. Finally, McDonald was to be paid £500 a year by Lancashire and given a benefit after only five years instead of the customary ten. When McDonald moved into a house bought specially for him by the Lancashire club, near Old Trafford, he paid rent of only £40 a year and Lancashire even paid for the removalist. He repaid the county generously by taking 205 wickets in his first full season at an average of 18.67.

The signing of McDonald opened the way for a stream of talented Australians to play in the Lancashire League. This became a path particularly appealing to players just below Test status and deprived the Australian public of a chance to watch some wonderful crowd-pleasers. Smith could not be blamed, of course, for the sustained exodus to the Lancashire League, but it certainly left the Board with problems when Lancashire clubs bid for Test stars.

The demands of his family's funeral business in Sydney forced Hanson Carter to join Armstrong and Edgar Mayne in retirement from Tests after the 1921 tour. Carter had toured England three times and upheld the tradition of Australia playing brilliant 'keepers. He was the last to wear open-slatted pads and the first to squat on his haunches, and although he often drove to Australian grounds in a hearse after conducting funerals, had a fine sense of humour. He had only one Christian name, but was so widely known as 'Sammy' and 'Sep', his entry in record books frequently appeared as H.S. Carter. As a batsman he was notorious for his 'shovel shot', a blow in which he clumped bowlers over his front shoulder to the fine-leg fence, and he made two first-class centuries with it.

Carter was good enough to force one of the heroes of the AIF team, Bert Oldfield, to serve a long apprenticeship before Oldfield got the job as Test 'keeper. Both of them took some wonderful legside catches off Gregory, anticipating glances and catching them by moving wide to their left side, but the real test of their skill came in 'keeping to Mailey, the capricious imp who went straight from all-night revelries to the ground in his dinner suit and dodged rebukes by taking a handful of wickets.

The 1921 Australians persistently scored at more than 60 runs an hour, eleven of them had captained their club or state teams, and as a group they had an inspirational effect on young Australians because of their approach to cricket. A schoolboy named Don Bradman was taken by train from the family home at Bowral in the central highlands of New South Wales to watch Charlie Macartney bat. Young Bradman was so captivated by the audacity and confidence in Macartney's innings of 170 that he told his father that night in the train returning home that all he wanted to be was a Test batsman.

Mailey had a similar influence on the career of Fleetwood-Smith, according to Greg Growden's recently published biography, *A Wayward Genius*. 'Mailey's bright demeanour left a deep impression on an enthusiast still uncertain if his fingers and wrist could bowl such a line,' says Growden. Fleetwood-Smith immediately sensed that his own erratic temperament and desire to bowl spin of an innovative style could be accommodated if he adopted Mailey's outwardly carefree approach.'

Having lost eight Tests in a row against Australia, England built up for the 1924–25 series in Australia with a visit to South Africa in 1922–23, where they won 2–1 with two Tests drawn, and a tour by a team skippered by old warhorse Archie MacLaren to New Zealand, also in 1922–23, that included matches in Australia on the way out and on the way home. In this period Hobbs and Sutcliffe developed into a formidable opening pair and they formed the basis of English hopes for the twentieth English team under Gilligan,

The twentieth English team to tour Australia (L to R): back, J.L. Bryan, R. Tyldesley, M. Tate, F.C. Toone (Manager), W.W. Whysall, A.P.F. Chapman, A. Sandham; centre, J.W. Hearne, H. Strudwick, A.E.R. Gilligan (Captain), J.B. Hobbs, F.E. Woolley; front R. Kilner, E.P. Hendren, A.P. Freeman, H. Sutcliffe, H. Howell. (Jack Pollard Collection)

after Reggie Spooner declined the job. The team was: A.E.R. Gilligan, J.L. Bryan, A.P.F. Chapman, J.W.H.T. Douglas, J.B. Hobbs, H. Sutcliffe, E.H. Hendren, A. Sandham, F.E. Woolley, J.W. Hearne, W.W. Whysall, R. Kilner, M.W. Tate, R.K. Tyldesley, A.P. Freeman, H. Strudwick and H. Howell, with F.C. Toone as manager.

Hobbs and Sutcliffe did not disappoint in a hard-fought series that captivated the entire cricket world. Sutcliffe made 734 runs at 81.55 in the Tests, Hobbs 573 at 63.66, but Australia – captained by Herbie Collins – still won the first three Tests and the series 4–1. Australia won despite the loss of Macartney. Some reports blamed his absence from the Tests on a nervous breakdown, but Charlie attributed it to a leg wound suffered on war service. England had appalling luck with injuries, with both Gilligan and Tate breaking down and Freeman unfit to play for a period, leaving only Kilner and Woolley of their regular bowlers.

In a summer which provided eight-ball overs, Australia's batsmen repeatedly recovered from precarious positions to produce big totals. They lost 3 for 47 in the first innings of the Second Test in Melbourne and still managed 600. At Adelaide in the Third Test, they lost 4 for 69 but reached 489. Ponsford, in his debut series, had scores of 110 and 128. Of the bowlers, only Tate, who took 38 wickets at 23 each, prospered until the last Test when Grimmett took 11 for 82 for Australia. A total of 514,084 spectators watched the five Tests, and takings for the tour were £65,784.

Grimmett's 5 for 45 and 6 for 37 in his first Test won him the recognition he had been seeking for ten years. He had migrated from his hometown of Dunedin in New Zealand in 1914 at the age of 23 and played his way from third grade to first grade in his first summer with the Sydney district club. Although his 28 wickets in his first season in 1917 cost only ten runs each he judged that he would have problems beating Mailey, Andrews, Collins or Macartney for a spinner's role in the state side and moved to Melbourne. He received invaluable coaching from Jack Saunders in his time with South Melbourne, but found the Victorian selectors' attitude to spin inconsistent, alternating between the state seconds and the senior side. He moved to the Prahran club when he married and took 228 wickets in four seasons for them without consolidating his state place. In 1923–24, he moved to South Australia after taking 8 for 86 for Victoria against South Australia in a Shield match.

Bowling in a cap so that he did not remind selectors of his bald

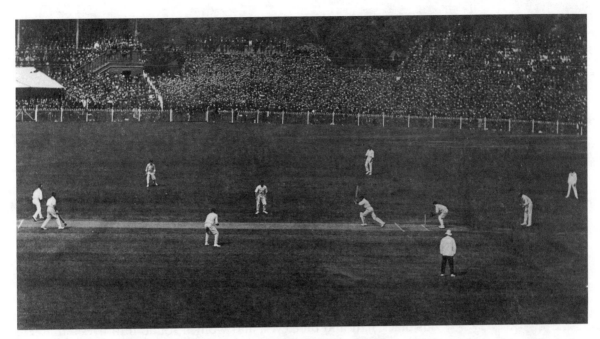

head, he took 668 wickets for South Australia over the next 15 years. He was an astonishing leathery little man, who preferred black tea to alcohol and moved about with a Groucho Marx walk, wheeling in to bowl with a low round-arm action that mixed leg-breaks, googlies and top-spinners with equal accuracy.

Although he did not make his debut for South Australia and Australia until he was 34, Grimmett's bag for that state is 668, 256 wickets ahead of the next best bowler, George Giffen (412), and his 11 years in Tests yielded a further 216 wickets at 24.21, for a career total of 1424 wickets at 22.28. Victorians puzzled about how such a uniquely gifted bowler was lost to their state found the answer when one of the selectors said Ernie Bean did not want him because of Grimmett's New Zealand birth.

Bean had no qualms about the qualifications of Ponsford, who made his debut for Australia in the same series as Grimmett. Ponsford made his debut for St Kilda first grade at 16, but after forcing his way into the state side four years later found it difficult at a time when there was a surfeit of talent to hold a regular state team spot. He had to break the world record for first-class batting by scoring 429 in 477 minutes, in his third match for Victoria in February, 1923, against Tasmania, to consolidate his state spot. In England, Ponsford's feat in passing Archie MacLaren's world record 424 – for Lancashire v. Somerset in 1895 – was belittled

Hobbs and Sutcliffe during their first-wicket partnership of 283 runs in reply to Australia's record total of 600 at the MCG in January, 1925. (Jack Pollard Collection)

by critics who claimed Tasmanian cricket was not of first-class standard.

Overweight and wide-bottomed, Ponsford was a highly deceptive right-hander whose appearance disguised his precise, assured foot-work. He moved down to drive with such certainty he was never out lbw in 48 Tests and only once was out stumped. His belief in his own ability was such that he would ask umpires for a fresh block as each 100 came up. When he mishit a ball on to his own stumps after scoring 352 for Victoria against New South Wales in 1926, he looked round at his broken wicket and said, 'Cripes, I am unlucky.'

Ponsford made his Test debut in the same match as the remarkably versatile South Australian sporting hero Victor York Richardson, who captained his state at Australian Rules football, was in state tennis and golf teams, played first-grade hockey and lacrosse, and won swimming and gymnastic championships. He was tall and straight-backed, with a pencil-thin moustache to go with his black hair and blue eyes, and women found him irresistible. He made a good start to his Test career with 138 in his second Test and 83 in his fourth, and already was bringing off the brilliant saves and catches that were to place him among the greatest of close-in fieldsmen.

These talented new players were cleverly moulded into the Australian team by the sphinx-like captain Herbie Collins, who at the time of the 1924–25 series was a stipendiary steward for the Associated Racing Club at its five Sydney pony-racing courses. One owner he carpeted about his horse's reversal of form explained it this way: 'I saw you get 114 in the Test and next time I watched you bat you got a blob – my horse is like that.' Collins sustained the skill he had perfected in Army two-up schools by winning three Test tosses in succession against Gilligan, who checked to confirm that Collins's coin had a head as well as a tail after losing the Adelaide toss.

Collins was a keen, inscrutable student of his players' skills with a way of taking responsibility for their failures but allowing them to take the credit for their triumphs. He was happiest at the gaming tables of backstreet Sydney clubs, or wherever he found a game of poker. His players knew he would bet on anything but he never joined them in rainy day card games because he got no amusement from beating amateurs. He was absolutely imperturbable in a crisis, and when Ponsford repeatedly played and missed at Tate in his

Noted late-night gambler Herbie Collins in an impromptu game of two-up in Melbourne soon after he became Australia's Test captain. (Mitchell Library, Sydney)

initial Test innings he cleverly took all the strike until Ponsford settled down. They put on 190 for the second wicket.

When Collins was appointed a New South Wales selector at the start of the 1924–25 season, he looked for combinations, rather than individual heroes, players who fitted into the team's overall tactical plans. He had no hesitation dropping Harry Rock after Rock had played four outstanding innings for New South Wales in 1924–25. Rock scored 127 and 27 not out, 235 and 51, and was omitted when Collins, Taylor, Bardsley, Andrews and Kelleway returned from Test duty. Rock, the son of the Cambridge Blue, Warwickshire and Tasmanian player C.W. Rock, was lost to Australian cricket after qualifying as a doctor. In five first-class matches for New South Wales he had made 711 runs at 118.5.

Although he was prepared to discard Rock, Collins certainly was not ready to pass over Alan Kippax, whom he recognised as a right-hand stylist of tremendous personal charm, with a repertoire of shots seldom matched. Kippax made his debut for New South Wales in 1918–19 but had to wait until the last Test of the 1924–25 series to get the call to Test cricket. He made an elegant 42. This followed innings of 127, 122 and 212 not out for New South Wales against Victoria.

Despite the high scoring by Rock and Kippax and the all-round

227

skills of the New South Wales team, Victoria won the 1924–25 Sheffield Shield competition. After several years' absence, Frank Tarrant proved a key performer for Victoria. At Adelaide, where South Australia had a 175-run first-innings lead Tarrant played a major role in Victoria's recovery to win with an innings of 86. Victoria's victory was their tenth Sheffield Shield win, compared to 16 by New South Wales and three by South Australia.

The intensity of the 1924–25 Shield competition began ten vintage years of outstanding Shield cricket. In every state cricketers eager for Test recognition produced displays that attracted the crowds. Grimmett, Ponsford, Richardson, Ryder, Kippax, Ironmonger and a second Richardson named Arthur, were all to star in Shield matches that captivated a generation of cricket buffs. Sadly, they were not joined by the revered left-hand batting prodigy Francis Aloysius O'Keeffe, an outstanding player for Waverley and New South Wales, who followed Ted McDonald to the Lancashire League and played for the Church club while he qualified for Lancashire. He died of peritonitis on 26 March 1924, aged 27, just three months before he qualified for Lancashire.

An aggregate crowd of 89,386 had turned up for the New South Wales v. Victoria match at the MCG in the December–January 1923–24 holiday period and, as new stands were built to accommodate the growing population, record daily crowds attended at Sydney in 1928 (58,598), Adelaide in 1933 (50,962) and Brisbane in 1936 (30,598). The Shield matches were so well patronised that crowds of more than 30,000 regularly attended in the 1920s and 1930s. The numbers of women at the cricket increased and they sat with their families, knitting or even shelling peas for the evening meal.

The spectators at all the main grounds were so well-behaved few policemen were spotted. Nobody ever jumped the fence to shake hands with a century-maker or a bowler completing hat-trick. Slow-handclapping was unknown, although there were plenty of comments shouted from crowds who could quickly spot a show-pony or a malingerer.

From the start of big cricket in Australia, spectators had always believed their admission money entitled them to shout from the stands to the players on the field if they felt the need. 'Plum' Warner questioned this right when he led the English team to Australia in 1903–04 and claimed the barrackers were ill-mannered oafs who

had no right to utter. Ranjitsinhji also allowed Australian crowds to upset him, but he said after he had realised too late that it was hazardous to comment on Australian crowds to English pressmen.

In the 1920–21 series England's vice-captain Rockley Wilson cabled home strong criticisms of spectators who jeered at a lame Jack Hobbs fielding with a strained thigh muscle. When Wilson came out to bat in the second innings, there were cries of 'squealer', 'liar' and 'Wilson the squib', from onlookers who succeeded in unsettling Wilson. He returned to the pavilion looking 'profoundly aggrieved' after being dismissed cheaply.

The most notorious Australian barracker of them all was a large (185-cm, 90-kg) fleshy Sydney rabbit-trader named Stephen Harold Gascoigne (1878–1942), widely known as 'Yabba', who held court in the middle of the Sydney Cricket Ground Hill for thirty years. Yabba, whose father had been a storekeeper at Oxford before

A section of the old Brewongle Stand in Sydney during the 1920–21 England v. Australia Tests. (NSW Government Printer)

229

migrating to Australia, had an ex-soldier's vocabulary which dated back to his service in the Boer War. His voice carried like a bell right across the middle of the SCG so that his witticisms could be clearly heard in the Members' Stand. He had a wonderful sense of timing and although there was a touch of the larrikin in his quips his affection for underdogs made him a celebrity, the major reason for the Hill's worldwide reputation for noisy, knowledgeable barracking.

Yabba seldom missed a match or even a day's play, arriving at the ground in mid-morning after hawking rabbits to housewives in Glebe and Balmain from the back of his hand-drawn cart. He rested his hamper and several bottles of beer half-way down the Hill, looking down the pitch from mid-on. He wore his food seller's white coat until it became too hot, when he removed the coat to reveal his braces.

Many of Yabba's wisecracks have worn thin since he first used them, through repetition by onlookers who lacked his sound knowledge of the game. When a slow batsman scored after several maiden overs he hollered: 'Whoa, there! He's bolted!' After a young tail-ender lost his stumps first ball, Yabba called: 'Don't worry, son, it would have bowled me.' Watching the Nawab of Pataudi fail to score for half an hour, he advised the umpire: 'Put a penny in him, George, he's stopped registering!'

Although he enjoyed cutting down the game's tall poppies, the *Sydney Morning Herald* reported that Yabba refused to join in when spectators criticised women cricketers for coming out late after lunch in a Sydney match. Cries such as 'Shake it up with the powder puff, girls,' and 'Women never are on time,' circled the stands until one spectator called to Yabba to join in. 'Why should I?' Yabba replied. 'The girls are playing all right for me. Leave 'em alone.'

Yabba was particularly generous in his comments about umpires, all of whom he referred to by their first names. After their unimpressive start in international matches, Australian umpires had begun to match standards with the best English umpires by the 1920s. Bob Crockett ('The Chief Justice') had carried on in the tradition of 'Dimboola Jim' Phillips, the man who inspired him to take up umpiring, and had stood in a record 32 Tests when he retired after the 1924–25 England v. Australia series. Crockett was the umpire who refused to signal a boundary when a fieldsman deliberately kicked the ball into the fence to prevent the striker taking three runs and retaining the strike at the end of the over.

Crockett said the kick was contrary to the spirit of the game.

Crockett umpired inter-state matches for two seasons after he quit Test matches declaring that his eyesight was no longer keen enough for international cricket. In 1926, admirers handed him a cheque for £1043 at the tea interval of a Melbourne match as a tribute to his long service to cricket. Crockett thanked them, looked at his watch, and announced it was time to resume, precise, unemotional and lacking in sentiment after 38 years of umpiring.

The new scoreboard at the back of the SCG Hill, where it did not obscure the view of many spectators as the old board had, proved one of the successes of the 1924–25 season. Englishman 'Patsy' Hendren won the affection of the crowd by jumping the fence and picking his way through spectators to the board to congratulate the 20 men who worked inside. They offered Patsy a beer and on his way back down the Hill Patsy shook hands with Yabba.

New South Wales compiled totals of 708, 705, 642, 593 and 554 in the 1925–26 Sheffield Shield competition and 11 of the 13 players used averaged more than 40. Helped by his 271 not out against Victoria, Kippax averaged 112 for the season. New South Wales twice beat Victoria by an innings.

In what historian Harry Altham called 'a domestic blunder difficult to comprehend or to justify', the Australian Board of Control announced the team to tour England in 1926 in two parts. They named 12 'certainties' for the tour in January and a further four players after the last Shield match in March. Selectors' deals to ensure players from their home state were picked meant that out-of-form players toured at the expense of those in match-winning shape.

Monty Noble labelled the exclusion of Alan Kippax in favour of Arthur Richardson 'a crime against the youth of Australia'. Kippax was then at his best, a batsman of silken, artistic quality who was scoring centuries almost every weekend in Shield or club matches. Ray Robinson said his batting should have been weighed in carats, not runs. To discard him for a plodding cricketer like Richardson, 38, was incomprehensible. In the three seasons before this sixteenth Australian team to England was named, Kippax had outscored every Australian batsman, had failed to reach 20 only three times, and had by far the best average. His omission from the 1926 tour deprived him of the chance of touring to England until he was 33.

Bespectacled Arthur Richardson, whose selection ahead of Alan Kippax for the 1926 English tour was called 'A crime against the youth of Australia'. (Jack Pollard Collection)

Former players, selectors and officials chatting with the governor, Lord Foster, at Government House in Sydney in 1923. Monty Noble is on the governor's right with J.J. Kelly. (Mitchell Library, *Sydney*)

The Australian team was: H.L. Collins (Captain), W.M. Woodfull, J. Ryder, C.G. Macartney, W. Bardsley, W.H. Ponsford, T.J.E. Andrews, J.M. Gregory, H.S.T.L. Hendry, A.J. Richardson, J.M. Taylor, J.L. Ellis, W.A.S. Oldfield, S.C. Everett, C.V. Grimmett, A.A. Mailey and S. Smith (manager).

With Gregory ineffective because of his knee injury and McDonald settled in Lancashire, the Australians lacked a penetrating opening bowler. Selectors hoped Sam Everett would fill the role but he flopped. The team had to rely on spin bowling and on unresponsive pitches wins were so rare English critics said spectators who paid to see the normal high standard Australian displays were defrauded. Mailey took 141 tour wickets, Grimmett 116, but they produced only 12 wins in six months.

The first four Tests were played over three days and this was the reason for four draws. Bardsley's customary pessimism made him so glum before the Second Test Collins said: 'Cheer up, Bards, it can't be that bad.' Bardsley went out and batted right through the Australian innings for 193 not out, demonstrating yet again why he made more runs and centuries than any other visitor to England until Bradman arrived.

Collins went to hospital with neuritis before the Third Test and at 44 Bardsley took over as Australia's oldest captain. Macartney made 161 at this Leeds Test after scoring 133 in the Second at Lord's, and when he made 109 at Manchester he became the first

batsman to score three centuries in a Test series in England. Another record went at Manchester when Hobbs became the first professional to captain England since Shrewsbury in 1887–88, when he stood in for Carr.

Neither team had come close to a win when they reached the Fifth Test at The Oval, which meant the match was timeless. England surprised by recalling Wilfred Rhodes at the age of 48 and dropping Frank Woolley after an unbroken run of 52 Tests. An even bigger shock was the appointment of the acrobatic young giant Percy Chapman, then 26, a pillar of English amateurism, as captain, in place of Carr. Arthur Mailey showed his assessment of these events by appearing on the front steps of the Australians' hotel on the first morning of the match in his dinner jacket. Syd Smith was about to deliver a stinging reprimand when Mailey asked him to postpone it until the end of the day.

Mailey dismissed six of the first seven English batsmen, including Hobbs with a high full toss that knocked back his leg stump, and England were out for 280. Mailey escaped Smith's rebuke. 'Five wickets wouldn't have done it,' said Mailey. Next morning Collins and Gregory put on 109 and Australia took a 22-run lead when Oldfield made 67. The match was splendidly poised on the third night with Mailey tucked up early in bed.

Heavy overnight rain forced Collins into the worst miscalculation of his career. Thinking Gregory would slip about on the soaked pitch, he persevered with Richardson for far too long. Hobbs and Sutcliffe later confessed they deliberately tried to make Richardson's bowling look dangerous for fear Collins would bring on Gregory, whom they believed would have been unplayable in the conditions. This was cleverly done by masters of wet-wicket batting, each man dropping his wrists at the last moment when the ball kicked or spat up from the turf. They put on 172, batting with judgement, while Richardson sent down 42 overs of off-breaks.

Hobbs's even 100 and Sutcliffe's 161 took England to 436. When Australia batted after more heavy rain, Larwood removed Woodfull, Macartney and Andrews before Chapman brought on Rhodes with his left-arm spin. On a pitch that was ideal for him, Rhodes disposed of the last four Australians. 'From the moment Rhodes went on, the match was over,' said one London paper. By a margin of 289 runs, England regained the Ashes after 14 years. England did not drop a catch in the match but the game had turned through the confidence trick by Hobbs and Sutcliffe on poker-faced Herbie Collins, the master of detecting such dodges.

Australia had lost a gripping series with a very strong batting team that had a pop-gun attack. Eight players scored 29 centuries, with Bardsley's 1424 runs taking his total on four trips to England to an impressive 7866 at 49 an innings. Woodfull topped the batting averages, however, with 1672 runs at 57.65, which included eight centuries. Woodfull reached 201, the tour's highest score. Macartney again showed his all-round class by taking 49 wickets at 17.81 to go with his 1561 runs at 53.82.

Collins, the legendary lucky cricketer, had the unluckiest few months of his career. Before the 1926 team arrived in England he was disciplined by Syd Smith for agreeing to write a series of articles for the Beaverbrook newspapers in England for the handsome fee of £1000. He was working on the articles with an English journalist when Smith told him publication would breach his tour contract. Collins believed his considered views of the approaching Tests would not cause the Australian Board of Control any embarrassment and would help boost crowds, but he was forced to cancel the Beaverbrook deal. He said later he should have gone ahead with the articles, paid the Board's £50 fine, and charged it to Lord Beaverbrook.

Poor Herbie even missed the thrill of watching Macartney score a century before lunch in the Leeds Test. Collins was propped up in hospital when Macartney, who had been dropped fourth ball, reached his century out of 131 in 103 minutes and scored 112 in 116 minutes before lunch. Told of Macartney's innings, Collins scratched about by his bedside and finally sent a telegram that read: 'God bless you, Macka, you little crackerjack – Bert'. Macartney kept it till he died.

Neither Mailey nor Collins wanted their careers to end with a defeat and English critics were quick to point out in their reviews of the 1926 Tests that both were at the peak of their careers, but back in Australia Collins found himself replaced as captain of Waverley first grade and as captain of New South Wales by tour-discard Alan Kippax. Australia's loss of the Ashes was coupled with Collins's role as chairman of the selection committee – the others were Clem Hill and Jack Ryder – by the officials who brought him down. The Melbourne *Argus* added that Collins's policy in treating matches against county teams simply as practice for the Tests had robbed Australia of her big psychological advantage and dissipated the Australians' winning habits.

Collins retired, giving ill-health as the reason, but everyone close to him said it was because of the lack of support he received when Australia lost the Ashes. Collins scored 9924 runs at 40.01 in first-class cricket, 1352 of them at 45.07 in Tests, a fine record considering he did not play his first Test until he was five weeks short of 32. Australia won five of the 11 Tests while he was captain and sustained only one defeat. He drilled his players to look at him after every ball and by a slight movement of a hand or by bending a finger he would adjust their fielding position without clapping or calling to them. He was always the last player to get dressed at the end of a Test day, sitting silently in a corner with his togs on, going over events, studying lessons that could be used next day. Mailey called him 'Squirrel' and insisted Collins's eyes were brighter at night.

After he retired Collins took out a bookmaker's licence. Other bookies said neither working as a steward or a bookmaker had as much appeal for him as punting. He had some big wins, but there were too many losing days as a bookie and he then became a commission agent.

At 42, just five years after he relinquished the Australian captaincy, Collins was forced to seek assistance from the Cricketers' Fund set up in 1922 by the New South Wales Cricketers' Association to help famous old players down on their luck. He was caring for his invalid mother at the time and often had no money to buy her the medicine she needed. At 51 he married the 24-year-old daughter of a racing steward, Marjorie Paine. The marriage lasted 11 years, during which they produced a son, before Collins won a petition for divorce on the grounds that his wife had left him. He remained dependent on the Cricketers' Fund until just before his death in 1959.

Having lost the Ashes, Herbie Collins had to search for a new job. Here he is shown wearing a bookmaker's bag at a Sydney race meeting. (J.C. Davis Collection)

235

Loss of the Ashes also brought a severe setback to the career of the 1926 team manager, Syd Smith, who was dropped by the Gordon Club as their delegate to the New South Wales Cricket Association on his return home. The Gordon members were still angry over the omission from the 1926 team of local hero Charles Kelleway and they made Smith the scapegoat even though he had had nothing to do with the team selection.

Smith received unexpected help from the New South Wales Junior Cricket Union, which had its delegate to the NSWCA, Jack Durham, stand down. Smith was appointed in his place, and although he lost the secretaryship of the Australian Board of Control, he regained his place on the NSWCA and within a year was elected a vice-president, a position he held unchallenged until his death in 1972, aged 92.

Mailey played one more season of first-class cricket after the 1926 tour but Collins, Bardsley, Kelleway and Gregory all declined to assist their state. Mailey did not play in the historic match in Brisbane, on 26–30 November 1926, in which Queensland made their Sheffield Shield debut against New South Wales. Set 400 to win in the final innings, Queensland made a gallant effort to score the runs, O'Connor playing a superb innings of 196, failing by only eight runs. In the same match Kippax reminded the national

Queensland's first Sheffield Shield team (L to R): back, *H.D. Noyes, E.C. Bensted, N.C. Beeston;* centre, *F.J. Gough, F.M. Brew, H.J.R. Higgins, R.K. Oxenham;* front, *W. Rowe, F.C. Thompson, L.P.D. O'Connor (Captain), A.D.A. Mayes, L.E. Oxenham.* (QCA Archives)

selectors of their error in omitting him from that year's English tour by scoring 127 and 131.

At Sydney in the return match a week later O'Connor scored two centuries, 103 and 143 not out, to help Queensland to a brilliant five-wicket victory over the dominant Shield state. This time Kippax scored 4 and 182, Charlie Macartney 144, Norbert Phillips 144 and a 17-year-old youngster named Archie Jackson, playing in his first season, 100. Queensland's triumph in only their second Shield match made heroes overnight of O'Connor and Ron Oxenham, who took 3 for 29 with the ball and scored 134 not out and 52.

Mailey appeared for New South Wales's following match on the

The scoreboard tells the story in December, 1926, when Victoria reached 1107 and Mailey took 4 for 362.
(Sun-News Pictorial)

MCG against Victoria, who had carried all before them to that stage. Ponsford (352) and Woodfull (133) put on 375 for the first wicket in 223 minutes, Hendry (100) and Ponsford adding a further 219 for the second wicket in 117 minutes. This set Victoria on the way to a world-record total of 1107. Ponsford hit 36 fours. Jack Ryder played the brightest knock in the innings, with 295 in 245 minutes, which included six sixes and 33 fours. Victoria added 449 runs while Ryder was at the crease.

Mailey finished with 4 for 362 off 64 overs, the worst figures of his career, and boasted that he was just finding his length when the last Victorian, Jack Ellis, was run out. 'I would have had better figures had a chap in the fifth row of the crowd not dropped so many catches off my bowling,' said Mailey. New South Wales were dismissed for 221 and 230 and lost by an innings and 656 runs.

Against all the odds, South Australia won the Shield for the fourth time when Victoria failed to win the last match of an enthralling season against Queensland in Brisbane. Following centuries by Ron Oxenham (104) and Eric Knowles (144) for Queensland, Victoria made a bold effort to score the 753 runs needed to win in the last innings. Ponsford and Hendry put on 225 runs for the first wicket, but they could not compensate for deplorable batting in their first innings when they were all out for 86, Ron Oxenham capturing 4 for 18.

Mailey made his final appearance in first-class cricket at the end of the 1926–27 season. By then most of the officials who had provoked the 1912 showdown with the players had disappeared but some of those who were left informed Mailey he had to choose between cricket and daily journalism.

Most people felt he was driven out of big cricket at the age of 41, when he still had plenty of bowling tricks to bamboozle even the greatest batsmen. He took a remarkable 779 wickets in first-class cricket at 24.10 and five wickets in an innings 61 times.

In June 1927 Malaya provided a major upset by defeating a strong Australian side led by Woodfull at Selangor, Kuala Lumpur. Malaya scored 108 and 158, Australia 85 and 142, giving the home side victory by 39 runs. Australia won the return match in Singapore by 136 runs, declaring at 6 for 341. Malaya managed 69 and 136 in reply. The Australian public were unmoved, all their attention focused on a humble country lad whose rise gave Depression victims hope for better days.

CHAPTER SIXTEEN
BOWRAL BOY

As the 1927–28 season got under way, the New South Wales practice nets at the Sydney Cricket Ground were like meetings of a war cabinet. All who attended realised the state's position as Australia's dominant cricket team was in jeopardy. South Australia held the Sheffield Shield, Victoria was mounting a formidable challenge through the batting of Ponsford, Woodfull and Ryder and the bowling of Blackie and Ironmonger, and Queensland had defeated New South Wales in only her second Shield outing.

The New South Wales coach George Garnsey handed out advice on batting and bowling with special intensity. The selectors, Johnnie Moyes, Dick Jones and Harold ('Mudgee') Cranney, all practising cricketers, went into frequent huddles to discuss skills they had just seen in young players, and occasionally took an opinion on tactics from Harry Donnan, Dr Herbert Hordern or Charles Turner.

The selectors were worried about the lack of talented new bowlers and had persuaded the NSWCA to adopt a scheme for the start of the 1926–27 season called 'Coaching For Young Bowlers'. This enabled selectors to go anywhere in the state to invite promising young bowlers to attend the SCG nets for special coaching. One of the bowlers discovered was William Joseph O'Reilly, a student with the Sydney Teachers' College who held an appointment at Wingello. O'Reilly played in the Wingello side against Bowral, who had developed a prolific run-getting youngster named Donald George Bradman. Although they were looking for bowlers somebody at the SCG nets suggested sending Bradman an invitation and on Monday 11 October 1926, the 17-year-old Bradman turned up with his father.

There was a story that Bradman made his first appearance at the

Don Bradman while singing in the church choir and having piano lessons, learned to drive a car to take clients on inspection tours of Bowral properties. At weekends he played in the Bowral cricket team dominated by the Whatman family.
(Mitchell Library, *Sydney*)

Sydney nets wearing dark braces, but Bradman has always denied this jibe at his naivety, although he admits he was an uncoached country lad on his first venture away from concrete pitches. All who watched were impressed by Bradman and Cranney tried to persuade his Sydney club, Central Cumberland, to take on the Bowral boy. Bradman accepted, but before he played a match for Central Cumberland they found they did not have the money to pay his fare from Bowral to Sydney each weekend.

Bradman returned to Bowral and later that month scored 170 before retiring for Bowral against Exeter. This won him an invitation to return to Sydney to play for Southern Districts in the 1926 Country Week competition. Meanwhile Dick Jones continued his efforts to get the St George Club committee to give Bradman a trial and they agreed to do so while he was in Sydney for Country Week. Bradman made 110 in 110 minutes on 27 November for St George against Petersham.

St George thereupon agreed to pay Bradman's fares to and from Bowral to their Sydney matches from the start of the 1927–28 season. Over the following seven seasons Bradman averaged 91.57 for the club. Before he left the bush, however, he played an innings of 320 for Bowral against Moss Vale in the final of the Picard Cup. This improved on the previous Berrima district record of 300, which Bradman had set two seasons earlier. His 320 included 43 fours, one five and six sixes and took him two Saturday afternoons.

He began his first full season with St George with ten weeks of modest scoring, but 130 not out against Paddington and 125 not out for a combined St George–University XI against Riverina proved enough to win him selection in the state team when Jack Gregory and 'Hammy' Love withdrew and Charlie Macartney retired. He joined the New South Wales team on the train that went to Adelaide through Broken Hill and during the trip confessed to champion leg-puller Halford Hooker that he really enjoyed playing the piano, which his sister Lillian had taught him. Hooker kidded Bradman that piano-playing strengthened the back muscles and as soon as the team arrived at their hotel coaxed the youthful spinner Hughie Chilvers on to the dance floor to tap dance, baited by the challenge that he could not dance as fast as Bradman could play. Considering the tough debater and committee-room negotiator he later became, Bradman hammering at the keys while Chilvers danced furiously presents a fascinating picture.

Bradman was originally twelfth man for the NSW side to play

South Australia but went into the team when Archie Jackson developed boils. He scored 118, but English Test star Patsy Hendren who was at the match in his capacity as South Australian coach was more impressed by Bradman's fielding. 'His throw was so fast and so accurate, its speed quite astounding in one so small,' said Hendren. Bradman's innings included a stand of 111 with his captain Alan Kippax, the first of 15 century partnerships they were to share and the first of 164 century stands in Bradman's first-class career.

New South Wales' first innings total of 519 proved insufficient, however, South Australia replying with 481 thanks to a century from Karl Schneider (108) and then dismissing New South Wales for only 150 in their second knock. Grimmett took 8 for 57 to put South Australia back in the match and by clean-bowling Bradman emerged from their first clash with honours even. Left to score 189 to win, South Australia won by one wicket.

Bradman's century in his initial first-class match encouraged cricket writers to dig into his past. They found that he had been born at Cootamundra in the home of the local midwife, Mrs Eliza Ellen Scholtz, known as 'Granny' Scholtz, on 27 August 1908, when Don's mother and father, George and Emily Bradman, lived in a cottage at Yeo Yeo, between Wallendbeen and Stockinbingal. Don's grandfather, Charles Bradman, had migrated from the southern tip of Suffolk in 1852 and after marrying Elizabeth Biffen at Berrima Church, near Bowral, settled in Jindalee in 1873. Don's father George was born at Cootamundra on 29 November 1875. Apart

Bradman's parents, George and Emily Bradman, photographed in the late 1920s. George worked as a carpenter doing form work when the Sydney Cricket Ground concrete bike track was laid down. (National Library of Australia)

from Don, 'Granny' Scholtz delivered three other Bradman children (all except Don's youngest sister Elizabeth May). She lived until she was 93 and every year Don sent her a telegram for her birthday.

When Don was in his second year, his mother's ill-health forced George Bradman to move his family from the house at Yeo Yeo to Bowral, 82 miles south-west of Sydney, where it was felt the invigorating climate of the southern highlands would help Emily Bradman. The Bradmans lived at 52 Shepherd Street until 1924 and there in the backyard Don went through the now famous ritual every afternoon after school, hitting a golf ball with a stump into the stone base of a water tank for hours at a time. When his mother arrived home he put out a kerosene tin for a wicket and persuaded her to bowl at him.

New South Wales were beaten again in Bradman's second Shield match after Ponsford made 202 following a 227 opening stand with Woodfull (99). Bradman scored 31 and 6. Blackie clean-bowled him in New South Wales's second innings of 152 and took 6 for 32 to give Victoria the match by 222 runs.

Bradman's confidence in his own ability was unmistakable, his enthusiasm for the game infectious, and people who saw him and Archie Jackson chasing the ball said they were like playful puppies. In the nets there was a special class in their strokeplay and nobody had any doubt they were watching the emergence of two champions. Even when Bradman was out for a duck in his first appearance for New South Wales on the SCG, clean-bowled by Queensland leg-spinner Frank Gough, the experts' faith in Bradman remained. Jackson encouraged this support for youth by scoring 131 and 122 against South Australia, and Bradman rounded off the season with 134 not out against Victoria in a drawn match that yielded eight centuries.

At the end of that first season in big cricket, Bradman left Bowral to live in Sydney with Frank Cush and his wife at Frederick Street, Rockdale. He became the secretary of the newly opened Sydney office of his Bowral employer, real estate agent Percy Westbrook. The move ended his regular trips to and from Bowral and also removed doubts about his eligibility to play for St George.

'I have always been grateful to Frank Cush and his wife,' Bradman said. 'By taking me into the kind of warm family home that I was used to they gave me a chance to relax. I never felt homesick while I stayed with them.' The NSWCA paid state players £1 a day match expenses at that time, and £1 5s when they were away.

Bradman found himself frequently compared with Archie Jackson, the boy from the Balmain slums whose family were so poor Arthur Mailey, Balmain's captain, chipped in his weekly match fees. Apart from their youth and the British migrant forebears, they had little in common in either their batting technique or temperament. Jackson, born at Rutherglen in Scotland, was a slight figure who always looked in need of a good meal. Dr H.V. Evatt was one of those who helped pay his school fees. Jackson was an unashamed admirer of Alan Kippax and many who watched him bat were reminded of Kippax's graceful, artistic style.

Bradman had the same lovely footwork as Jackson but hit the ball with more control. Jackson's best drives often went to hand whereas Bradman's went through the gaps. Jackson had played on turf wickets from early childhood. Archibald Jackson senior had migrated to Australia at the age of 41 and worked in the shipyard at Cockatoo Island. At night in his cottage 80 metres from Birchgrove cricket ground Archie senior had to tie up the door handles to prevent his son falling victim to his chronic problem of sleepwalking. Young Archie sang in the local church choir alongside another aspiring schoolboy cricketer, Bill Hunt.

Bradman was also a choir boy – at St Jude's Church, Bowral. For two years after leaving school he had agonised over whether he should concentrate on a career as a tennis player rather than play cricket. The cricket talent in his family came from his mother's relatives, the Whatmans. Don had begun as the scorer for the Bowral team, for whom George and Richard Whatman starred, riding to matches seated on a wooden box in the back of a lorry that ran on solid rubber tyres. When work was scarce in Bowral George Bradman did the form work before they poured concrete for the bike track inside the SCG.

Bradman began the 1928–29 season in splendid form, hitting 106 not out for St George against Gordon at Chatswood, but he failed in a special Test trial match on 19–22 October in Melbourne (14 and 5). A week later he made his bid for Test selection with scores of 131 and 133 not out for New South Wales against Queensland in Brisbane. Hal Hooker won this match for New South Wales by taking ten wickets for less than 12 runs each. Hooker was the star again when New South Wales met Victoria over Christmas on the MCG. Chasing Victoria's 376, New South Wales were 9 for 263 when Hooker and Kippax added 307, a world record for the tenth wicket, by batting for five hours.

Archie Jackson, shown here when initially picked for the Balmain first grade side in Sydney, became a close friend of Donald Bradman. (J.C. Davis Collection)

Bradman at the nets when he first got into the New South Wales team. He was never coached and relied solely on his own judgement of pitches and playing conditions. (West Australian, Perth)

With Kippax on 260 not out, Hooker could not resist lifting his head and making a mighty swing at a ball from a'Beckett, lifting a simple catch to Ryder with his own score on 62. Kippax was very disappointed at this indiscretion. 'I had backed you to get a hundred and you would have, too, had you kept your head down,' he told Hooker.

At the age of 20, Bradman made his first appearance against England on the SCG and virtually saved New South Wales from defeat by the 1928–29 tourists. Wally Hammond took the honours with an innings of 225, which, with 140 from Jardine and 167 from Patsy Hendren, lifted the England total to 7 for 734. Bradman batted nervously in his first innings but still managed 87. Following on 385 behind, New South Wales reached 3 for 364 before time ran out. Bradman was on 132 not out, Kippax on 136 not out, after an unbroken stand of 249 that had Yabba and other spectators on The Hill shouting with glee.

Both Bradman and Archie Jackson were in the Australian XI that played England four days later in Sydney, Bradman remaining unbeaten in the first innings with 58, and Jackson chiming in with a similarly impressive knock of 61 in the second innings. But the selectors for the First Test could find a place for only one of them, Bradman. This was the first Test ever played at Brisbane and ended Queensland's 23-year fight for a Test that had been promised when she first joined the Australian Board of Control. Throughout those years the Board had resisted staging a Test in Brisbane because it feared takings would fall well short of those at Sydney and Melbourne. The Queensland delegates to the Board, Jack ('Czar Czar') Hutcheon and Roger Hartigan, had repeatedly pushed Queensland's case and public meetings had been held in Brisbane to protest against the state's exclusion from the Test itinerary, without success.

Failure to find a permanent home for first-class matches had been as harmful to Queensland's cause as southern fears that tropical rainstorms would interrupt Brisbane Tests. Big matches were held at Eagle Farm, Queen's Park, the Albert Ground, Breakfast Creek, Bowen Bridge Road and the Agricultural Society's Exhibition Ground, before the five-acre site at Woolloongabba was dedicated as the Brisbane Cricket Ground. Thousands of tonnes of soil had been deposited at 'The Gabba', pitches levelled and grandstands built, but the Exhibition Ground, a natural amphitheatre, was preferred for Queensland's initial promotion of Test cricket

FIRST TEST MATCH
30·11·28 TO 5·12·28.
PHOTO TAKEN 1·12·28.
ATTENDANCE 24422.
GATE MONEY £2261·0·5.

although doubts existed about its wicket lasting the extra days of a Test.

By the time they got to Brisbane for this historic match, Percy Chapman's twenty-first English team were match-hardened. Their captain had worked them thoroughly in the nets, an expert masseur accompanied the side for the first time, and no illness or malingering escaped their manager Frederick Toone. The team, picked by a special MCC committee, was A.P.F. Chapman, W.R. Hammond, D.R. Jardine, E.H. Hendren, L.E.G. Ames, J.B. Hobbs, H. Sutcliffe, M. Leyland, C.P. Mead, G.E. Tyldesley, H. Larwood, M.W. Tate, G. Geary, J.C. White, G. Duckworth, S.J. Staples and A.P. Freeman. Woolley, Holmes and Hallows, who had strong claims, were all omitted. Ames and Duckworth were the new 'keepers, Tate the only genuine all-rounder, and Chapman compensated for his lack of leadership experience by acting on advice from the wily, alert 46-year-old Hobbs.

Fast bowler George Geary had his nose smashed in the first match of the tour in Perth on 18–20 October 1928. Officials could not find a stretcher and carried Geary off on a kitchen table. He did not play for a month and was unfit for the First Test.

The decision to give Brisbane a Test deprived Sydney of one of the two Tests it normally staged. This led to fierce protests in Sydney and the NSWCA's delegates to the Board of Control were angrily condemned. Queensland not only gained a Test this season but succeeded in having a representative on the Test selection committee for the first time. Selectors were Warren Bardsley (NSW), Ernie Bean (Vic.), Dr Charles Dolling (SA) and Jack Hutcheon (Qld). The team they picked included Bradman, who made his debut three months after his twentieth birthday, and Bert Ironmonger, who claimed he was 41 but was really 46. This made Ironmonger the oldest Australian to appear in Tests, a record that only lasted a

Brisbane's first Test was held at the Exhibition Ground, a natural amphitheatre where Agricultural Society members got in free. Later Tests moved permanently to Woolloongabba. (QCA Archives)

Percy Chapman's English team, the twenty-first to tour Australia, included the great medium-pace bowler Maurice Tate, shown here behind his captain. Tate called Bradman his 'bunny', words he lived to regret. (SCG Archives)

fortnight until Don Blackie made his Test debut at 46 years 253 days.

Bradman had won his place after only nine first-class matches and had never sighted a wet pitch, let alone batted on one. He was lbw to Tate's slower ball for 18 in the first innings, and when he was forced to bat on a 'sticky' in the second innings made only one before he was caught by Chapman off 'Farmer' White, who took 4 for 7. As Bradman walked off, Maurice Tate called to White: 'What do you mean by stealing my bunny?' Bradman's dismissal came from one of four catches Chapman made in the match. Indeed, the brilliance of Chapman's catching had what Harry Altham called a disturbing effect on Australia's morale whenever they faced Larwood or Tate.

Gregory at 33 bowled with exceptional pace and fire, but after 41 overs in England's first innings a recurrence of the cartilage trouble in his left knee forced him to retire. He never played again. Kelleway also disappeared from big cricket – with food poisoning – and after a marvellous show of powerful batting England won by 675 runs.

The Australian Board of Control, shown at a 1927 meeting, remained faceless men, unknown to the public. They were (L to R): back, Dr A. Robertson, C. Campbell, J. Hutcheon, Dr R. Mailey, H.W. Hodgetts, jnr; centre, Clem Hill, S. Smith, H. Gregory, R.A. Oxlade, E.E. Bean, H.C. Smith, W. Bull. (J.C. Davis Collection)

Brisbane escaped criticism of its first Test promotion largely because of the sensational events on the field. Dressing-room facilities were primitive. Pressmen and spectators who did not take their own food along went hungry, and the crowd was contained inside barbed-wire barriers. The prospect of further Tests at the Exhibition Ground disappeared, however, when it was discovered that thousands of spectators had got in free by showing their Agricultural Society membership badges, a loss of revenue that angered all Board members.

Bradman showed he was not unsettled by the disappointment of his Test debut by scoring 131 and 133 against Queensland in Brisbane, but he was made twelfth man for the Second Test. His place went to Otto Nothling, a remarkable all-rounder of German descent who had made 121 for Queensland against New South Wales and taken 5 for 78 against the Englishmen for Queensland. Nothling played rugby for Australia as a fullback against New Zealand, was a superb athlete, 190.5 cm in height, and was an outstanding sprinter. The first time he picked up a javelin he set a new Australian record. He later became president of the Queensland Cricket Association.

England won the Second Test at Sydney by eight wickets thanks

Bradman's amazing scoring brought many requests to meet him from famous players. Here he is shown with Charles Bannerman, Australia's first century-maker, at the Sydney Cricket Ground. (Sydney Morning Herald)

to an innings of 251 by Hammond. Bradman had a close look at it fielding as a substitute for Ponsford, whose left hand had been broken by a ball from Larwood. A record Sydney crowd of 58,446 celebrated Hobbs's forty-sixth birthday by taking up a collection for him. Hobbs was so delighted he insisted on going up onto The Hill to thank spectators and was seen in earnest conversation with Yabba. Nothling failed to take a wicket and was unluckily run out for 44 in the second innings, a display that failed to save his Test place.

Bradman returned for the Third Test at Melbourne and with scores of 79 and 112 confirmed the Test berth that he was to hold for the rest of his spectacular career. He made 40 and 58 run out in the Fourth and 123 and 37 not out in the Fifth Test, in which Australia had their sole win of the series by five wickets. In the Fourth Test at Adelaide Archie Jackson became the youngest player to reach a century in England v. Australia Tests by scoring 164 on his debut at the age of 19 years 152 days.

Australia's selectors helped England to her 4–1 win in this absorbing series by their indecision over the captaincy. They appointed Ryder for the first two Tests although he was a stranger to the job and only told him just before he went out to bat in the

ENGLAND				ENGLAND			V	AUSTRALIA				
1ST INNINGS	334		BOWLERS	WKTS	RUNS	BATSMEN	OUT	B	RUNS	FALL OF WKTS		
2ND INNINGS		1	LARWOOD	9	2	WOODFULL	C 2	1	1	FOR	1	
AUSTRALIA		2	TATE	7	7	HENDRY	C 1	2	2	2	6	
1ST INNINGS		3	WHITE	1	30	KIPPAX	B 3	3	3	3	19	
2ND INNINGS		4	GEARY	3	2	RYDER	LB 3	63	4	145	
WICKETS		5	HAMMOND	3	2	BRADMAN	C 2	40	5	227	
BLACKIE		6	JARDINE			JACKSON	LB 3	164	6	287	
OLDFIELD		7	HENDREN			OXENHAM.R	C 3	15	7	323	
		8	CHAPMAN			A'BECKETT	H 3	36	8	336	
SUNDRIES	6	9	HOBBS			GRIMMETT	B 2	4	9	365	
TOTAL	369	10	SUTCLIFFE						10	

The Adelaide Oval scoreboard, now protected by a National Trust order, showing Archie Jackson's famous 164 on debut. (SACA)

Third Test that he was captain. Woodfull, the popular and highly respected Victorian captain, offered to stand down from that job to give Ryder experience. Throughout the Test series Ryder pleaded with the selectors to give him a pace bowler to replace Gregory. They did not agree to his request until the Fifth Test, when Tim Wall swung the match Australia's way by taking 3 for 123 and 5 for 66.

Bradman scored 1690 runs in first-class cricket in 1928–29, still a record for an Australian season, but his average of 93.88 was to become common as his career advanced. His success had encouraged the selectors to bring Archie Jackson into the Australian side. When they added 82 together in the Adelaide Test, every run was applauded by a nation glued to their radios or assembled in the capital cities outside newspaper offices sporting giant scoreboards. Years afterwards cricket buffs recalled the thrill of Jackson's dazzling cover drive to the first ball after lunch. With his score on 97, Jackson had the 40-minute break to become agitated, but he confidently stepped into Larwood's inswinger and smashed it through the covers to the fence.

The first radio description of cricket anywhere in the world was introduced in Sydney in 1922–23 during a match between teams captained by Herbie Collins and Charlie Macartney for Charles

Among Bradman's team-mates when he began his first-class career in 1927–28, were 'Cassie' Andrews, left, and Wendell Bill, shown going out to open for New South Wales. (NSWCA Library)

Bannerman's benefit. The experiment worked so well it was announced that the first commentaries on Tests would begin during the 1924–25 Australian tour by the English team captained by Arthur Gilligan. The commentators had no difficulty describing play from the stands, though most stations preferred to use end-of-day summaries either by the captains or noted ex-cricketers.

Radio's major difficulty came in describing matches in England for Australian audiences before long-range radio and other forms of instant communication became available. Short-wave transmissions were received occasionally when weather permitted but they were not sufficiently advanced to bounce the signal off the ionosphere with any reliability. So the Australian Broadcasting Commission, under the direction of general manager Charles Moses, developed 'phantom' Test broadcasts from all the English Test grounds. A team of commentators in the ABC Sydney studios took their material from Eric Scholl, an ABC staff man sent to England because of his expertise with codes. Scholl's cables from the 1938 Test grounds, one per over, were handed to a team of decoders who enlarged and deciphered the contents before handing them to a group of experts, Monty Noble, Vic Richardson, Alan McGilvray and Hal Hooker. Using pre-recorded crowd noises, and tapping pencils on tables to simulate the sound of bat hitting ball, the experts re-enacted the match with remarkable efficiency. Moses insisted listeners knew how it was done.

They quickly learned where all the fieldsmen were positioned so they could elaborate on a cable reading 'Hammond sweeps Fleetwood Barnes Four' to 'Hammond sweeps the next ball from Fleetwood-Smith. Barnes races round the boundary but I don't think he can cut it off. No, the ball beats him over the boundary ropes for another four,' at which point the sound effects man would increase the crowd excitement until the ball went over the boundary and became four, accompanied by sustained applause. It was ingenious and kept much of Australia awake until the small hours of the morning.

For the next two decades Bradman was to have a dominant role in Tests, batting with unsurpassed reliability to score a century at an average more than every third time he batted. His batting was so proficient that many of his 16 first-class ducks received more publicity than his centuries. No Australian has scored more centuries or come close to him for consistency. The astonishing deeds in the Bradman legend brought him 17 more lines than Stalin in *Who's Who* by the time the Second World War began, helped build entire grandstands on major Australian grounds, and left Australia with a superior won-and-lost record to any of the cricket nations.

Bradman's success against Chapman's team was especially commendable as midway through the season he lost his job when Percy Westbrook closed his Sydney real estate office. The Sydney sports group, Mick Simmons, offered him a job almost immediately selling sporting goods but settling into a strange new world proved a worrying time for a country boy as the effects of the great Depression swept the country.

Harold Gilligan, brother to England captain Arthur, stopped off in Australia for five matches with an English XI before going on to a lengthy tour of New Zealand. This gave candidates for Australia's 1930 tour of England a chance to press their selection claims. Gilligan's team took a pounding from controversial pace bowler Ron Halcombe before they defeated Western Australia in early November 1929, and a stylish 146 from Frank Woolley gave them victory over South Australia. At Melbourne a Victorian team that included seven Test players beat Gilligan's XI by seven wickets. Don Blackie paved the way for the Victorian win by taking 5 for 82 and 7 for 25.

One of the unlucky players in the New South Wales team when Bradman joined it was Arthur Allsopp, who had a first-class average of 45.90 but missed out on overseas tours. (Allsopp family)

New South Wales gave the Englishmen a hammering, declaring at 8 for 629 in their first innings, with Bradman (157), Kippax (108) and Arthur Allsopp (117) scoring centuries, and Stan McCabe contributing 90. England replied with 469, Woolley compiling 219. Jackson was 168 not out when Kippax declared again at 3 for 305. The match had to be left drawn when Leicestershire captain Edward Dawson played a lengthy innings for 83 not out.

Allsopp's 117 in his first big match won him a place among the top contenders for the 1930 tour of England. He was just as impressive as Bradman, Jackson and McCabe, striking the ball powerfully and confidently from a copybook stance, and he was outstanding in the field. Officials completely misjudged his background, however, thinking he had been guilty of some crime because he worked for Dr Parsonage's home for delinquent boys. Allsopp's mother had died when he was six and he bounced from one relative's home to another until Dr Parsonage gave him a job.

Allsopp's team-mate Stan McCabe received far more sympathetic treatment. McCabe made a duck in his first match for St Joseph's

College in Sydney, a duck in his first match for New South Wales Seconds, and another duck in his initial first-class match in 1928–29, but selectors dismissed these failures because they could see the rich promise in his fluent technique. McCabe played all bowling skilfully but was particularly severe on pace bowlers who drew from him a daring array of cuts, drives and hooks. McCabe, virtually a cripple, almost failed the 1930 team medical. Doctors let McCabe tour knowing that when he stood at ease none of his toes touched the ground.

Bradman dominated the trial by scoring 124 and 225 for Woodfull's side. His team still had to follow on against Ryder's XI, for whom Jackson had made 182 in a total of 663. Bradman opened up in the second innings and was 205 not out by stumps. Thus he had scored 329 on the same day.

A month later he surpassed even this effort, however, by scoring a world record 452 not out for New South Wales against Queensland. This remained the highest score made on a turf pitch anywhere in the world until 1994. After failing in the first innings, he went in to bat at the SCG with New South Wales on 1 for 22 in their second innings. By stumps on Saturday night he was 205 not out. Refreshed after the Sunday rest day, he carried his score to 452 on Monday, passing 300 in 288 minutes and 400 in 377 minutes.

Bradman driving at the old Sydney Cricket Ground no. 2 for a Country XI before he played in a Test, showing plenty of confidence and copybook technique. (John Fairfax)

A savage pull to the square-leg fence took his score past Ponsford's world record of 437. Queenslander players carried him shoulder-high from the field when Kippax declared. He hit 49 fours in 415 minutes batting during which time he made only two mistakes, neither of them a chance, clocking up his runs at 65 an hour and allowing the Queensland bowlers only one maiden over in the 117 they bowled.

That innings changed Bradman's life by placing him ahead of all other batsman, and from that Monday, 6 January 1930, he became a national sporting hero, hounded in a manner no other cricketer has ever been, and privacy became very precious to him. To 1995, only West Indian Brian Lara's 501 not out surpassed Bradman's 452 not out on grass, though Pakistan's Hanif Mohammad was run out on a matting pitch on 499, trying for his five hundredth run.

Rain interrupted the last match of the 1929–30 Australian season between Victoria and New South Wales in Sydney. The selectors, who were due to announce the Australian team for England after the match ended, were asked to finalise their selections during the break in play. Jack Ryder studied the lists presented by fellow selectors Dr Charles Dolling and Dick Jones and went out to bat when the rain cleared knowing he had missed the touring team.

The team was W.M. Woodfull (Captain), D.G. Bradman, A.L. Kippax, W.H. Ponsford, A. Jackson, S.J. McCabe, V.Y. Richardson, A.G. Fairfax, E.L. a'Beckett, W.A.S. Oldfield, P.M. Hornibrook, C.V. Grimmett, A. Hurwood, T.W. Wall and C.W. Walker. Only four of them – Ponsford, Woodfull, Oldfield and Grimmett – had been to England before. From the day the team was announced Ryder never spoke another word to fellow selector Dick Jones and refused to attend functions Jones arranged. In the 37 years until he died in 1967, Jones never gave any explanation of how the incumbent Australian captain, Ryder, missed the 1930 English tour.

Bradman packing for his memorable 1930 tour of England, where he made all his critics humble. (Sydney Morning Herald)

New South Wales cricket fans bitterly resented the omission of Bill O'Reilly, whose leg-break bowling looked as vital to Australia's future as the batting of Bradman, McCabe and Jackson. The truth was that the selectors had no option but to omit O'Reilly because the New South Wales Education Department had exiled O'Reilly to Kandos, an isolated town in the central-west of the state where he had no chance to push his claims. Queenslanders were equally irate over the exclusion of Ron Oxenham and puzzled over how the selectors could have picked Percy Hornibrook and Alex Hurwood ahead of Oxenham from the Queensland side. Charlie Walker's inclusion as deputy 'keeper to Oldfield was attributed to his skill in taking spin – he had made 20 stumpings that summer. Victorians were perplexed by Ironmonger's omission and defended him when it was argued that the missing half of his left index finger created a stub which influenced his action and led to allegations that he was a chucker. But in 96 first-class matches Ironmonger was never no-balled for throwing.

Despite his phenomenal scoring, Bradman's batting received a lot of cricitism from so-called experts, who predicted he would fail in England because of flaws in his technique. They claimed his grip on the bat handle was wrong, that he played too many cross-bat shots, and hit too many defensive shots in the air. Although he had nine first-class centuries to his name by the time he turned 21, the Surrey and England all-rounder Percy Fender forecast that the great luck Bradman had had with his uncontrolled strokes would bring failure on English pitches.

Queenslander Percy Hornibrook, unlikely omission in 1921 and 1926, took 96 wickets at 18.79 on the 1930 English tour, at the age of 31. (Courier-Mail, Brisbane)

Bradman answered this by scoring 236 in 280 minutes against Worcestershire in the first match of the 1930 tour, between 30 April and 2 May. Three weeks later he went in with Australia 1 for 11 against the Surrey side captained by Fender at The Oval. He reached 100 in 145 minutes and then cut loose, flogging the Surrey bowlers to move from 100 to 200 in 80 minutes. Fender was powerless to stop this onslaught and Bradman ended on 252 not out in Australia's 5 for 379.

Melbourne auctioneer Bill Kelly, who managed the team, had been forced to work hard to persuade Woodfull to accept the captaincy. When Kelly telephoned Woodfull at Melbourne High School, where Woodfull worked as a mathematics master, Woodfull was reluctant to allow his name to go into the Australian Board of Control's ballot for the captaincy, even though he had been praised for his leadership of Carlton and a young Australian XI in New Zealand. Woodfull, a clergyman's son, was 32, and when he accepted the captaincy he led his team, in which six players were under 23, with rare modesty but great skill.

England's ageing team included Hobbs, 47, Hendren, 41, White, 39, Geary, 36, and Tate, 35, and they managed to win the First Test by 93 runs because of their greater experience on a wet pitch than Australia's youngsters. Set to score 429 to win, Australia made 335 and would have got closer but for two sensational setbacks. In the first McCabe was brilliantly caught by an unknown player, Sydney Copley, a member of the Notts ground staff fielding as England's thirteenth man. Duleepsinhji, England's nominated twelfth man, was already on the field substituting for Sutcliffe when Larwood had to go off and Copley replaced him. Bradman and McCabe were in full flight, having put on 77 in 70 minutes, when Copley sprinted hard and dived a full three metres to catch McCabe, rolling over and over but still clutching the ball. In the second piece of high drama Bradman's left boot got stuck in his right pad and he could not move his feet at all. A googly from Robins turned in on Bradman's stumps without him offering a shot and flicked the off bail. With Bradman out for 131 Australia had slumped from 3 for 229 to 5 for 267 and they never recovered.

Bradman (254) and Grimmett (8 for 272) continued their dominance in the Second Test, which Australia won by seven wickets. The Third Test at Headingley was drawn after Bradman made 334, 105 of them before lunch, 115 between lunch and tea, and 89 between tea and stumps for a total of 309 on the first day.

Clarrie Grimmett clean
bowls Frank Woolley to
claim his first Test victim
at Sydney in March, 1925.
(Sydney Mail)

Rain forced a draw in the Fourth Test and the teams went to the
Fifth Test at The Oval all square with one win apiece.

This timeless Test extended to the sixth day. England began by
scoring 405 in their first innings, Sutcliffe scoring 161. Australia's
batsmen treated this as a frivolous target, scoring 695 with a
wonderful display of powerful strokeplay. Ponsford and Woodfull
put on 159 for the first wicket, Ponsford reaching 110. Bradman
then batted for 438 minutes and hit 16 fours in his third double
century of the rubber. His 232 took his aggregate in the five Tests
to 974, average 139.14, and remains a world record for any Test
series. England's second innings ended at 251, leaving Australia

Bradman acknowledges the crowd's applause at Leeds in 1930 on his way to a Test record score of 334. He also made scores of 131, 254 and 232 in that series. (Daily Mail, London)

winners by an innings and 29 runs. Australia had recaptured the Ashes on their captain's thirty-third birthday.

Bradman's mastery of the English bowling won all the headlines and the *Daily Mail* suggested that England in future would be wise to offer Australia 100 runs in return for a promise that Bradman would not bat. But the players' praise all went to Woodfull for his captaincy. The author R.C. Robertson-Glasgow said of him: 'He reminded me of a master who gets the whole school to and from a picnic without losing a boy or his reason. He was the most calm-browed cricketer I have ever seen.'

Bradman topped the tour batting averages with 2960 runs at 98.66 but five other Australians all made more than 1000 runs and the side included six century-makers. Grimmett was again a consistent match-winner with 144 wickets on the tour at a very economical 16.84 each and Queenslander Percy Hornibrook's left-arm spinners took 96 wickets at 18.79. All the team fielded splendidly with Bradman at that time one of the greatest fieldsmen seen in England, gathering and throwing with a speed that astonished spectators. The team won 12 of their 34 matches, lost one, had one tie against Gloucestershire, one match was abandoned and they played 19 draws.

Bradman's ten centuries on the 1930 tour took the total of runs he scored from 1 November 1929 to 31 October 1930 to 4546 in first-class matches, the most on record by an Australian in one year. He made a further 2000-odd in minor matches. Almost as remarkable was the quiet manner in which he accepted his success. Naturally withdrawn, he never lingered at the bar or quaffed beer in the dressing-room, preferring a pot of tea. He celebrated his 334 at Leeds playing records alone in his hotel room.

The tour brought record profits for both English and Australian authorities. Australia's share from all matches on the tour was £38,180 sterling, which must have left the Australian Board of Control in an affable mood because they granted permission for Bradman's employers, Mick Simmons, to take him off the *Oronsay* when it reached Adelaide and for him to travel independently the rest of the way home. At Fremantle Bradman refused to ride in a single-seater car and insisted on motoring to a Perth luncheon with team-mates, but he undoubtedly erred in leaving the team at Adelaide, and flying to Melbourne and on to Goulburn in the *Southern Cloud*. This was a misconceived journey in a famous monoplane piloted by T.S. Shortridge. The controls iced up and

Bradman follows his captain Bill Woodfull on to the field at Lord's in 1930, when Australia won by seven wickets after scoring 729. (National Library of Australia)

the aircraft lost its way, arriving two hours late at Essendon airport where a crowd Melbourne newspapers estimated at 10,000 waited to welcome Bradman. He was frozen as he stepped from the unheated *Southern Cloud* and it took a big effort of will for him to go aboard again and resume the flight to Goulburn. There Mick Simmons had a car driven by the champion racing driver Norman ('Wizard') Smith ready to rush him at breakneck speed (112 kph) to Mick Simmons's store in Sydney's Haymarket.

By the time the rest of the Australian team reached Sydney Bradman had completed the biggest promotional binge seen in Australia to that time. Pants, shirts, bats and pads that he endorsed were swooped on by his fans. To his team-mates Bradman usurped the honour that belonged to Woodfull, but to the young country boy with little money in the bank that risky plane trip in *Southern Cloud* meant a chance to make money in grim economic times.

Vic Richardson, Woodfull's vice-captain, said on Adelaide radio as he got home: 'We could have played any team without Bradman, but we could not have played a blind school without Grimmett.' Not long afterwards the Board of Control fined Bradman £50 for selling his life story to the London *Star*. Bradman said he had not breached his contract because nothing in the story referred to the 1930 tour, but the Board took the £50 anyway from his tour allowance. To Australians the Board's action was a niggardly effort by men disdainful of battlers.

CHAPTER SEVENTEEN

A LUCKY DUCK

The adulation aroused by Bradman's feats on the 1930 English tour intensified as Australia fought its way out of the great Depression. This slight, boyish figure became a symbol of hope for people struggling to feed their families, for everything he attempted succeeded.

Grade cricket matches that normally were sparsely attended attracted big crowds when he played. When the St George Club hired the Viceroy Theatre at Kogarah for a welcome-home function for Bradman and Australian team-mate Alan Fairfax, every seat was taken and the overflow stood around the walls. Mick Simmons asked Bradman to make so many public appearances he began to hate them. Officials were delighted when 12,000 spectators turned up to watch him bat for New South Wales against South Australia in the first Sheffield Shield match of the 1930–31 summer. Although he had not picked up a bat since the end of the English tour, Bradman scored 61 and 121 in 142 minutes.

This was the first time Bradman and the other players had appeared in a first-class match with the new larger, higher stumps, and they found that the stumps made no difference to their cricket. The Australian Board of Control had always shown an eagerness to tamper with the rules of the Sheffield Shield competition and it was one of these changes that gave Victoria the 1930–31 competition by a single point. The struggle was keen throughout, with Test places against the West Indies, who toured Australia that season, at stake. Victoria and New South Wales were level when the last Shield match between South Australia and Victoria began in Adelaide. The match was a draw but the point Victoria received as the team that led on the first innings in a drawn game gave her the Shield.

Bradman attended lunches and dinners, wrote newspaper articles and made so many promotional appearances for Mick Simmons it was a relief for him to get out on a cricket field. He was dismissed for 73 and 29 playing in the Jack Ryder testimonial match in Melbourne, falling each time to Arthur Mailey's top-spinner, performances newspapers judged as a failure by normal Bradman standards until a statistician discovered the second innings of 29 took him past 4000 runs in a calendar year, the first time this had been achieved anywhere in the world.

On the morning of the First Test match between Australia and the West Indies in Adelaide on 12 December, 1930, extracts from a book by Geoffrey Tebbutt *On Tour With the 1930 Australians* were splashed across the headlines in Australian newspapers. Tebbutt accused Bradman of being aloof from his team-mates in England and suggested he had been mean in not sharing with team-mates the £1000 an Australian businessman, Arthur Whitelaw, had presented to him for scoring 334.

The allegations of aloofness, the first of many such charges that were to dog Bradman's career, did not unsettle him but he scored only four runs before he was brilliantly caught in the gully by Jackie Grant off a particularly fast ball from Herman Griffiths. Bradman captured his first Test wicket, however, when he had the West Indies' wicket-keeper Ivan Barrow judged lbw for 27 in the West Indies' second innings. This enabled Bradman to return his best-ever Test bowling analysis, 1 for 8 off five overs.

Australia won that historic initial Test against the West Indies by ten wickets thanks to the bowling of Grimmett, who took 11 wickets in the match, 7 for 87 and 4 for 96, and to her great batting strength. Kippax made 146 in Australia's first innings and when Australia was left to score 169 to win in the final innings, openers Ponsford (92 not out) and Jackson (70 not out) made the task look easy.

The West Indies had first played Test cricket in 1928 when they lost all three Tests in England, and as their first Australian tour progressed it became clear that the 16 players they sent lacked the variety in attack to trouble the formidable Australian batting line-up. The West Indian team was G.C. Grant (Captain), L.S. Birkett, C.A. Roach, E.A.C. Hunte, L.M. Constantine, E.L. St Hill, G.A. Headley, F.R. Martin, I. Barrow, O.C. Scott, E.L. Bartlett, J.E.D. Sealy, H.C. Griffith, G.N. Francis, F.I. de Caires and O.S. Wight. Griffith, Constantine and Francis bowled fast and accurately

The thrilling West Indian all-rounder Learie Constantine in the SCG nets during the 1930–31 Australian tour. Australia won the series 4–1. (SCG Archives)

but the rest of the attack provided little quality support.

Some of the West Indian players first met on the ship that brought them to Australia and their captain 'Jackie' Grant, a Cambridge Blue for both cricket and soccer, had little time to develop team spirit or a match-winning plan. The team included two of the finest entertainers in the history of cricket in Constantine and Headley, and the energy and acrobatics of the entire side made them crowd-pleasers in all their 16 matches. But they sustained eight losses and won only five matches, with three draws.

Grimmett maintained his ascendancy over the West Indian batsmen throughout the summer and finished with 33 wickets from the five Tests at an average of 17.96 apiece. Ironmonger took 22 wickets at 14.68, but on firm, hard wickets the West Indies always struggled to get Australia out. They lost the first four Tests, Ponsford making 183 in the Second Test, which Australia won by an innings and 172 runs. In the Third Test Bradman batted for five hours for 223, his highest score to that time in a home Test, Ponsford contributing 109. Australia's total of 558 set up victory by an innings and 217 runs. Bradman got another century (152) in the Fourth Test and with Ironmonger taking 11 for 79, Australia won by an innings and 122 runs.

Four–nil down, the West Indies secured one of cricket's most surprising wins when they caught Australia on a 'sticky' wicket in Sydney in the Fifth Test. An unbeaten knock for 123 by Freddie

Martin and an invigorating exhibition of all-round-the-wicket strokeplay by Headley allowed West Indies to declare at 6 for 350. The St George club-mates Bradman (43) and Fairfax (54) top-scored in Australia's response of 224 on a difficult pitch. The West Indies struggled to 5 for 124 in their second innings before Grant gambled by declaring. This left Australia to score 251 on a pitch bathed in sunshine after continuous rain.

Griffith bowled Bradman for his first Test duck and five Australian wickets were down for 65. McCabe and Fairfax put on 79 in a stand that seemed likely to provide an Australian victory, but Grant took a magnificent catch to dismiss McCabe for 40, and Fairfax was left on 60 not out when Australia were out 31 runs short of their target on 220.

After starting with a century, Bradman scored 695 runs in six Sheffield Shield innings for New South Wales in the 1930–31 season. This included a score of 258 against South Australia in Adelaide when he and Archie Jackson (166) put on 334 for the second wicket, a Shield record. A young left-arm spinner named Bill Hunt, who had grown up in the Balmain district with Jackson, took 28 wickets at 18 runs each for New South Wales.

Victoria's batting depth was very impressive that season, with Ponsford and Woodfull leading the way. Keith Rigg forced his way into the Test team with one of the best of his 14 first-class centuries for Victoria v. the West Indies. Leo O'Brien made 119, his first Shield century, at Sydney in January against New South Wales, and the St Kilda right-hander Hector Oakley made a lot of runs.

The Queensland Sheffield Shield team continued to improve, despite a long-running dispute between the leading players and the official selectors that had led to the retirement of Leo O'Connor. Cec Thompson scored 275 not out, the highest innings for Queensland to that time, in the match against New South Wales in Sydney, Ron Oxenham maintained his splendid all-round form, Alex Hurwood forced his way into the Test team but disappeared after two matches, and Aboriginal pace bowler Eddie Gilbert had a controversial debut.

Gilbert bowled at alarming speed from an approach run of only four or five strides, his arm swinging in a blur that made it difficult to decide if he was throwing. Probably only his faster deliveries, let fly twice an over, were outright throws. The whole situation was complicated by Gilbert's innocence of whether his delivery was fair or illegal. His arms were exceptionally long, hanging below his

The dashing Victorian left-hander Leo O'Brien, who quickly established himself as a contender for Test honours after his debut in 1929–30.

261

Eddie Gilbert, the express bowler who lived in a tent in the backyard of the Queensland Cricket Association's secretary, lets a ball go. Even at the nets his pace was fearsome.
(Mitchell Library, *Sydney*)

knees, and his action was similar to that Aborigines use in launching a spear from a woomera or weapon-thrower. The remarkable feature of his bowling was that he achieved speed that was at times terrifying with a small, wiry frame. He weighed only 57 kilograms and was 173 centimetres tall. His 15 Shield wickets for 502 runs in his first season would have been a lot better had the Queensland fieldsmen held all the catches off the edge that Gilbert provided.

Gilbert was born at Woodford, not far north of Brisbane, in 1908, at a time when there was strong public support for the White Australia policy, a concept designed to protect the jobs of white men at a time of cheap Chinese and Kanaka labour. The Protector of Aborigines in Brisbane would not agree to Gilbert's transfer from the Barambah Aboriginal settlement until he was found a regular job and a suitable place to live. The Queensland Cricket Association got round this by arranging for Eddie to sleep in a tent in their secretary's backyard during first-class matches. He returned to Barambah, where he was a ward of the state and had first attracted attention in country matches, after the cricket finished.

He forced his way into the Queensland side by taking 6 for 29 for Country Colts against Brisbane City Colts, followed by 6 for 82 for Queensland Colts against New South Wales Colts. He had a drama-charged match against the West Indies, taking 5 for 25 and 2 for 26 before retiring hurt. Learie Constantine hit him for six and Gilbert immediately rushed down the pitch to congratulate Constantine. Later Gilbert responded with a six of his own off Constantine.

In the Queensland team Gilbert found himself among players who, dismayed by the incompetence of their own officials, created an unprecedented situation when they rebelled and set up their own selection committee. The Queensland Cricket Association responded by suspending five state players, Frank Gough, Vic Goodwin, Charles Bensted, Gordon Amos, and 'Pud' Thurlow. Others, including Cec Thompson and 'Mo' Biggs, were asked to show cause why they should not also be suspended. The suspensions prevented the players appearing for their clubs as well as for Queensland.

The dispute ended with the vindication of the players and the appointment of a special committee to review the constitution of the Queensland Cricket Association. State selectors were firmly instructed not to betray confidential opinions of players, one of the causes of the players' grievances.

*   *   *

After the first-class cricket ended and the West Indies went home, Bradman went on tour in March and April 1931 with a team captained by Alan Kippax. Their aim was to take cricket to parts of northern Queensland where the game was never seen. By the time they reached Rockhampton, Bradman had scored 651 runs and taken 33 wickets with his right-arm leg-breaks, but in the first few minutes of the Rockhampton match he sprained an ankle so badly he needed hospital treatment over the next 18 months. The injury weakened the ankle and may have contributed to his breakdown at The Oval in 1938. At the time his main disappointment was that he missed an innings of 173 at Gympie in which Stan McCabe hit 18 sixes or 108 runs.

For a long time Bradman had to spend two hours a day on the massage table and he had periods of idleness in which to contemplate his future. At 22 he knew he was not going to get rich on the Australian Board of Control's match fees, which for the series against the West Indies had amounted to £30-a-match, plus rail fares with sleepers to and from matches outside Sydney, and accommodation during Tests. He did not want to spend the rest of his life selling sporting goods or appearing on radio; what he wanted was a career outside cricket in which he could absorb himself and forget big cricket.

This was a major reason why he rejected an offer from the Lancashire League to play for the Accrington Club. Learie Constantine, who had played in the League for Nelson in 1929 and had seen Bradman on the West Indies tour in 1930–31, was the intermediary in early negotiations and reported enthusiastically on Bradman's suitability for League matches. Later Bradman asked his friend, journalist Claude Spencer, to handle negotiations.

Towards the end of August 1931 news of Bradman's interest in the Lancashire League leaked from England. The Accrington chairman, Herbert Crawshaw, confirmed that Bradman had been offered the princely signing-on fee of £1000 sterling a season, a weekly salary, bonuses of £5 for every innings over 50, £5 for taking five wickets, plus newspaper contracts and the customary collections during League matches. The Australian Board of Control had by then inserted a clause in tour contracts binding players to continue in Australian cricket for two years after tours ended, which meant Bradman could not go to the Lancashire League until the northern summer of 1933. He could have gone earlier than that but only at the risk of a life suspension from Australian cricket, a path chosen by Alan Fairfax.

The Victorian women's cricket team in Sydney for the 1931 inter-state match against New South Wales. (SCG Archives)

Bradman wanted to return to England with the Australian team in 1934, but his chances of doing that were problematical if he played in the Lancashire League beforehand. The prospect of losing Bradman horrified some Australians; others upheld his right to exploit his talents. The London *Observer* commented: 'Bradman is an ornament to his own country, and in that capacity is always welcome here, but as a salaried run-getter for an English club he would only be a reminder of how money deranges the natural order of things.' With advice pouring in on him from throughout the cricket world, Bradman spent four days contemplating the Accrington contract before deciding not to sign.

Next day large crowds stormed Mick Simmons to congratulate Bradman, some of them blocking the pavement in front of the store. 'I never wanted to leave home,' he said. 'I am happier today than I have been for a long time and I slept well last night.' His decision meant a big financial sacrifice at a time when he was about to become engaged to be married. Instead of going to Lancashire he signed a two-year contract with three Sydney firms who between them paid him a reported £30 a week. All three agreed to allow him whatever time off he needed to pursue his cricket career.

Under this alternative deal Bradman had to write regular cricket articles for the *Sydney Sun*, broadcast regularly on radio 2UE, and work in F.J. Palmer and Sons men's store, which issued new notepaper headed 'The Home of Don Bradman'. Stan McCabe replaced Bradman on the staff of Mick Simmons. All three employers reported a big increase in business when Bradman joined them.

Meanwhile the Australian Women's Cricket Council was formed on 23 March 1931, with New South Wales, Victoria and Queensland the foundation members. The Council emerged 57 years after the first women's cricket matches were played in Australia at Bendigo, and it immediately staged the first inter-state women's tournament. Plans for South Australia and Western Australia to join were not fulfilled until the 1935–36 season, the year after the women played their first Test match at the Brisbane Exhibition ground against England.

As the dole queues lengthened in the Depression of the early 1930s the New South Wales Cricket Association secretary Harold Heydon reduced his own salary by ten per cent to match the general decline in wages. Heydon's salary was not restored to £600 a year until 1934. The sharemarket had crashed and thousands of people were bankrupted and when leading New South Wales cricketers Roy Levy, 'Cassie' Andrews, Frank Ward and Ernie Laidler arrived in Brisbane looking for work they found the lines of unemployed and the hessian shacks housing the poor just as crowded as they were in Sydney. Laidler and Ward returned to Sydney but Levy and Andrews stayed to play for Queensland.

Back in Sydney Laidler and Ward found that Bradman had been replaced as the talk of Sydney grade cricketers by a big, strapping leg-break and googly bowler named William O'Reilly, who had come to Sydney from his teaching job at Kandos on the central western slopes and joined the North Sydney Club. O'Reilly taught at Kogarah Boys' High in the St George district and had some enjoyable badinage that season with his pupils as he took 54 first-grade wickets at a cost of only 7.88 each and bowled North Sydney to the premiership. North Sydney did not score 200 in an innings in the entire summer but O'Reilly and his colleague Clem Hill, a fellow school-teacher who bowled left-arm medium-pacers but no relation to the great Hill, took the premiership for them, with St George runners-up. O'Reilly also took 25 Shield wickets that season at 21.0 each.

Bill Ponsford, whose record-breaking feats presented Bradman with special targets. Ponsford scored more than 400 twice and was the first to score six centuries in an Australian season. (John Fairfax)

On 3 November 1931, Bradman went to Blackheath in the Blue Mountains west of Sydney to play in a match to celebrate the opening of a new ground and to test a new malthoid wicket. Malthoid was a pavement-like coating that covered concrete pitches and made matting unnecessary. Bradman showed his liking for the new surface by scoring 256, which included 14 sixes and 29 fours. He scored a century in three overs during this innings, starting with an over from off-spinner Bill Black that yielded 6,6,4,2,4,4,6,1. The single at the end of the over gave him the strike for the next over from Horrie Baker, later Town Clerk of Lithgow, whom Bradman hit for 6,4,4,6,6,4,6,4. Wendell Bill hit singles from the first and fifth deliveries of Black's next over, which produced 1,6,6,1,1,4,4,6. Bradman thus scored 100 out of 102 in only 22 balls. Black, who had boasted about getting Bradman out for only 52 a few weeks earlier in Lithgow, was taken off after his two overs cost 62 runs.

Bradman's century was not timed but it has aroused careful study by statisticians ever since. Bradman believed it must have been faster than the 18 minutes Laurie Quinlan took to score 100 for Trinity Cricket Club against Mercantile Cricket Club at Cairns in 1910 in what is generally regarded as the fastest century scored in Australia at any level of cricket.

Quinlan's Trinity CC were out for 71 in their first innings, and Mercantile CC made 222 in reply. With time running out for his side, Quinlan went in to bat at 4.41 p.m. and was not out on 100 when Trinity declared at 4.59 p.m. Left to score 123 in 65 minutes to win outright, Mercantile CC scored 5 for 127 so Quinlan's innings was to no avail and he ended up on the losing side. Quinlan hit eight sixes and eight fours in his innings but must have been slowed down by his five twos, two threes and four singles.

Three days after his Blackheath outing Bradman joined the New South Wales team in Brisbane for the first Sheffield Shield match of the 1931–32 season against Queensland. Just before play began Archie Jackson, coughing blood, was rushed to hospital. Gilbert's opening over for Queensland on a green-top pitch will always be regarded as the fastest ever seen in Australia by those fortunate enough to have watched it. Moving in off that short run, Gilbert let his extended arm swing in a whirl that defied the eye.

His first ball took off at a pace that forced freckle-faced Wendell Bill to top-edge a catch to wicket-keeper Len Waterman away in the distance. Bradman swayed back to dodge the second ball, which hit the peak of his cap and carried the cap back to Waterman's feet. With his cap back on his head, Bradman fell in a heap dodging further head-high bouncers. One ball knocked the bat from his hands and another sailed over the wicket-keeper's head. Bradman tried to hook the sixth ball and edged it into the gloves of Waterman, who was then standing half-way to the boundary.

After seven balls Gilbert had 2 for 0. In the stands, the New South Wales manager Arthur Rose jumped about claiming Gilbert had tried to make an Aunt Sally of Bradman by throwing every ball. When team-mates commiserated with Bradman, he said: 'Luckiest duck I ever made.' The short run Gilbert used clearly shocked the victims of his remarkable pace; from a longer run they would have been more prepared for it. Bradman rated Gilbert's over the fastest he ever faced and added that he found Gilbert's pace on a green-top quite bewildering.

Unfortunately, the New South Wales captain Alan Kippax had been hit on the head playing in a country match not long before. Kippax, one of the best-ever exponents of the hook shot, had lost all confidence in the shot when a ball hit a spike concealed underneath matting and had kicked up into his face. Hit again by Gilbert, Kippax retired hurt. McCabe then played one of his most spectacular knocks for 229 not out, repeatedly hooking the tiring Gilbert off his eyebrows. Fingleton helped wear Gilbert down by batting for more than four hours to score 93 and after the disastrous start New South Wales made 432. Eleven batsmen failed to score in the match, which New South Wales ended up winning by an innings and 238 runs.

The legitimacy of Gilbert's bowling overshadowed South Africa's second tour of Australia under the captaincy of wicket-keeper Horace Brakenridge ('Jock') Cameron. But it was spin, not pace, the South Africans found puzzling. Cameron was rated a superior 'keeper to Bert Oldfield, a man with a touch of class to whom 'stumping was a nonchalant gesture of a smoker flicking cigarette ash', but he was given an attack lacking in quality that was entirely based on pace. This worked wonders on matting wickets in South Africa but on hard Australian turf pitches gave the South Africans many laborious days chasing strokes from Australia's surfeit of batting stars.

Right at the last minute the South African tour was in jeopardy when it was discovered that prevailing exchange rates greatly reduced the value of the Springbok rand compared with Australia's pound. The South African players decided to go ahead with the tour nevertheless, for very little reward and knowing they had to keep a careful watch on costs. The South African team was: H.B. Cameron (Captain), D.P.D. Morkel, X.C. Balaskas, A.J. Bell, L.S Brown, J.A.J. Christy, S.H. Curnow, E.L. Dalton, Q. McMillan, B. Mitchell, N.A. Quinn, S.S.L. Steyn, H.W. Taylor, E.A. Van Der Merwe, K.G. Viljoen, C.L. Vincent and manager J.H. Tandy.

Batsmen Christy, Viljoen and Mitchell did well in matches against the states but in the big matches the South Africans found Australia's well-balanced attack too much for them. Grimmett foreshadowed what was to come when he took 6 for 50 in South Africa's first innings against South Australia. Ironmonger followed with 5 for 87 and 5 for 21 for Victoria v. South Africa.

At Sydney against New South Wales Taylor scored 124 in South Africa's total of 425. South Africa then dismissed New South Wales for 168 and declared their second innings closed at 3 for 190, with the home side needing 448 to win. Fingleton made 117 and Bradman and McCabe carried on scoring so freely New South Wales were 3 for 430 and only 18 runs short of victory when time ran out, Bradman having scored 135, McCabe 79 not out. Gilbert took 4 for 42 in South Africa's second innings against Queensland but selectors resisted the temptation of playing him in an Australian team still short of a genuinely fast bowler.

Bradman continued in tremendous form in the Tests. He scored 226 in the First Test at Brisbane, which Australia won by an innings and 163 runs, 219 in South Africa's return match in Sydney against New South Wales, 112 in the Second Test in Sydney, where Australia won by an innings and 155 runs after Rigg joined Bradman with a century (127), and 167 in the Third Test at Melbourne, which Australia won by 169 runs.

Australia introduced Bill Hunt, Bill O'Reilly and 'Pud' Thurlow for the Fourth Test in Adelaide after Nitschke and 'Perka' Lee had disappointed in the first two Tests. O'Reilly impressed with his accuracy and looked an ideal partner for Grimmett, who took all bowling honours with 7 for 116 and 7 for 83 to give Australia a ten-wicket triumph after another brilliant innings by Bradman, this time for 299. The South Africans' vulnerability to spin showed again in their return match against Victoria when Fleetwood-Smith took 6 for 80 in his third first-class match before rain brought a draw.

The Fifth Test at Melbourne produced a vicious 'sticky' wicket and the smallest aggregate of runs in all Test cricket. Ironmonger was unplayable and had South Africa out for only 36 in 90 minutes. Australia replied with 153 with Bradman absent hurt, but it was enough to win the match by an innings. South Africa managed only 45 at their second attempt. Ironmonger took 6 for 18 to go with his 5 for 6 in the first innings and give him 11 for 24 in the match. Grimmett did not get a bowl after dominating the first four Tests. Bradman made 805 runs in four completed innings with Australia winning the series 5–0. Ironmonger's 31 wickets in the rubber cost only 9.67 each, whereas Grimmett's 33 wickets looked costly at 16.87.

Umpire Andy Barlow ended whatever chance Eddie Gilbert had of playing Test cricket by calling him 13 times in three overs for chucking in Queensland's Melbourne match against Victoria. Gilbert took it in good part and appeared to have slowed down his pace when he appeared against South Australia in Adelaide. Here umpire George Hele carefully watched him but found nothing illegal in his action, and Gilbert completed the season with 21 Shield wickets.

Bradman scored seven centuries that 1931–32 summer in first-class cricket, averaging 116.91. In grade cricket he made a further 785 runs at 112.14 for the St George Club. New South Wales won the Sheffield Shield for the nineteenth time, taking the competition on averages after finishing level with South Australia. McCabe finished the season with the freakish average of 438 after three high innings: 229 not out, 106 and 103 not out.

On 30 April 1932 Bradman married Jessie Menzies, daughter of a Mittagong farmer, at St Paul's Church, Burwood, New South Wales. He had known Jessie since their schooldays together and they had been engaged for five months. The ceremony was conducted by Canon E.S. Hughes, later president of the Victorian Cricket Association, whom Bradman brought to Sydney for the service. One of the guests was Bob Nicholson, who had been one of the bowlers to suffer from Bradman's bat at Blackheath.

The Bradmans had a brief honeymoon in Melbourne in a house offered to them by an admirer before joining the team Arthur Mailey took on an unofficial tour of North America. Mailey knew that the Australian Board of Control had to approve a tour by players under their jurisdiction and was careful to get Board sanction for a 52-match trip that lasted 100 days. He arranged the trip with

Jessie Menzies, now Lady Bradman, was the daughter of a farmer. She worked for a time in a Bowral bank. (National Library of Australia)

the assistance of the Canadian Pacific Railway, American government offices, the Canadian Cricket Board and various shipping lines and invited South Australian captain Vic Richardson to lead it. The Board allowed the tour on condition that Mailey submit detailed accounts of all match receipts, and travel and accommodation expenses. The Board further stipulated that none of the players involved on the tour should receive more than £100 from tour profits and that any profits above that amount be distributed by the Board at its discretion.

The Board lifted its customary ban on wives accompanying touring teams to allow Jessie Bradman to join the tour for 26 days of their trip. Mailey's team comprised V.Y. Richardson (Captain), D.G. Bradman, P.H. Carney, H. Carter, L.O'B. Fleetwood-Smith, W.F. Ives, A.F. Kippax, S.J. McCabe, R.N. Nutt, E.F. Rofe and E.K. Tolhurst, with A.A. Mailey as player-manager and Dr Rowley Pope as medical officer, baggagemaster and scorer. Long before the trip was over Richardson was grateful that Pope took along his normal 40 pieces of luggage, for Richardson was required to make more than 30 speeches on the trip and, like Darling before him, Richardson was able to consult Pope's books which this time covered everything from the American revolution to the histories of Canadian and US cricket. Tourists in need went straight to Pope's cabin, where he dispensed sleeping pills, seasickness tablets, shoe laces, sunburn cream, salves for torn fingers, a range of cricket caps and tips on how to tie a black tie.

Mailey could not include Archie Jackson in his team. Jackson had been committed to Bodington Sanitorium in the Blue Mountains on the advice of the New South Wales Cricket Association's Cricketers' Fund trustees. The NSWCA paid Bodington's fees of three guineas a week from the fund. Jackson became restless at Bodington, however, and after a period in a cottage at Leura, where the NSWCA also paid the bills, moved north to Brisbane, naively thinking the warmer climate would improve his health.

Grimmett was among Mailey's original selections but had to pull out because of his work as a signwriter in Adelaide. Mailey picked Fleetwood-Smith to replace him from a wide range of spinners, reasoning that the huge number of batsmen they had to dismiss would have more trouble with a left-arm bowler of prodigious turn, if somewhat erratic length, than they would with a bowler like Bert Ironmonger whose length was more consistent but who seldom turned the ball very far.

Some of the team paid their own fares for a tour which was only confirmed by several of the American sponsors when it became certain that Bradman would be in the line-up. Jessie Bradman acted as the team's hostess when it entertained, attended all receptions, and helped Richardson compose his speeches.

The tourists suffered from one recurring problem – the certainty that manager Mailey would be missing when they were required to produce their health cards, passports or travel tickets. Mailey, of course, could not resist the opportunity of playing cricket in places with names like Moose Jaw, Medicine Hat, Kicking Horse Flats and Saskatoon, for he had after all bowled his googlies in Piccadilly Circus after midnight in his dinner jacket. He bowled enough to take 240 wickets on the tour at 6.50 apiece and often was on hand to ensure that hospitable hosts were not dismissed for a duck. 'Better call no-ball, umpire,' he would say. 'This chap hasn't scored.' According to Rowley Pope, whose records on the tour were neatly and painstakingly kept, Mailey's team scored more than 10,000 runs on their trip and dismissed more than 1000 batsmen.

Bradman was photographed with the idolised baseballer Babe Ruth in New York at Yankee Stadium and played in the match against famous actor C. Aubrey Smith's Hollywood XI, which fielded Boris Karloff in the slips. This was the same 'Round the Corner' Smith who had captained an English team on a tour of Australia in 1887–88. Jean Harlow was among spectators to whom Douglas Fairbanks explained the game.

All of Mailey's team except Rofe and Carney had appeared in Sheffield Shield matches. Hanson Carter was the oldest player at 54. None of their matches were first-class and around half of them were against the odds. There was very little grass on any of the fields on which they played and the pitches seldom were rolled, but they had a wonderful time.

Rowley Pope's score sheets showed that Bradman played in 49 of the 51 games, scored 3779 runs, made 18 centuries and took more than 100 wickets, a reasonable effort for a player on his honeymoon. His 260 against Western Ontario was the highest score of the tour. Mailey's choice of Fleetwood-Smith proved sound when he took 249 wickets, including two hat-tricks, at nine runs apiece.

Bradman returned to Australia with Mailey's team in the *Monowai* knowing that another tough series against England lay ahead in the southern summer of 1932–33. At Lord's the shock of Australia's

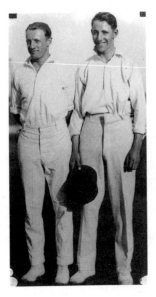

Bradman and Archie Jackson at the start of their careers. (J.C. Davis Collection)

victory in the 1930 series touched off long hours of discussion about the English captaincy. Chapman's left-handed batting coupled with his zest for life off the field had ended his reign as captain at the age of 30.

Initially, Douglas Robert Jardine did not want a second trip to Australia and he turned down the tour captaincy when approached by 'Plum' Warner, one of the English team selectors. Warner sought out Jardine's father, a fellow Oxonian cricket Blue, and told him the MCC wanted his son to run the show in Australia in 1932–33. The elder Jardine had a talk with his son and Douglas changed his mind. From the day he was appointed to lead the tour he brought exceptional energy and enthusiasm to the task.

Jardine and the entire cricket world knew that the chances of the twenty-second English team in Australia regaining the Ashes and the leading position among cricket nations dependend on how effectively they could prevent Bradman repeating his prodigious scoring of 1930. They had to find a way of destroying Bradman's morale and of getting him out cheaply.

Going over the facts of Bradman's unique achievements like Sherlock Holmes searching for a vital clue, Jardine came to the day rain interrupted play in the Fifth Test at The Oval in 1930. When it appeared certain there would be no more play the umpires appeared and said the match would resume at 6.25 p.m. This strange decision meant that there would be only one over before the scheduled time for stumps. Bradman and Jackson came out as the not out batsmen and were hooted for dawdling to the crease. Larwood emulated his Notts team-mate Bill Voce, bumped the ball short, and it reared up viciously from the wet pitch. The Australians survived the over easily enough but in that over Bradman showed unmistakable signs of flinching when the ball was bounced in at his ribs, a reaction Englishmen had never seen before from him.

Jardine invited Larwood, Voce and their county captain Arthur Carr to dine with him in London and Larwood agreed immediately that Bradman had ducked away awkwardly from his bouncers in the over that should never have been bowled at The Oval. Jardine asked Larwood if he could sustain an attack in which the ball persistently bounced up into Bradman's chest and head and when Larwood agreed that he could, the infamous form of attack known as Bodyline was born.

CHAPTER EIGHTEEN
BODYLINE

'I told Mr Jardine I thought Bradman had flinched, and he said he was aware of that,' said Larwood. 'There had been a lot of talk among county cricketers about this, and I had heard it said that Bradman could well have a weakness against fast, rising balls pitched on the leg stump . . . For all I knew Bradman might hit me all over the legside, but it was worth the effort.'

Jardine had not played in the Test at The Oval but he had a very reliable grapevine. Part of the information he pooled to help defuse the Bradman menace came from George Duckworth, who kept wicket at The Oval and insisted that Bradman recoiled and lost his confidence against balls he thought might hit him. Archie Jackson, who had batted at the other end, said Duckworth was the first in the English team to notice Bradman's discomfort.

There was nothing wrong with captains scheming to expose a rival batsman's weaknesses, but Australians have always argued that in devising the tactics to counter Bradman Jardine endangered all the Australian top-order batsmen's good health with an attack that was intended to maim. Jardine took the leg theory that had been used for 50 years in English cricket and by his placement of the field and the use of an exceptional pair of bowlers in Larwood and Voce, created more ill-will than cricket had ever known.

The key factor was the field settings. Batsmen had the right to protect themselves but with the fields Jardine set they could not do so without the certainty of a deflection that would get them out. Fields with seven men on the legside and only one patrolling the offside in front of the crease, gave batsmen little chance of avoiding an edge against a bowler whose deliveries reached a speed of close to 100 mph.

Douglas Jardine, at practice. On hearing of his appointment as MCC captain to Australia in 1930, former Test player Rockley Wilson said: 'We shall win the Ashes – but we may lose an Empire.'(Sport & General)

Bradman and his wife Jessie returning to Australia just before the Bodyline series, unaware of the tactics Jardine planned. (National Library of Australia)

Before his team left England Jardine took advice on leg theory from Percy Fender, his Surrey captain whose anti-Australian views were well known, and Vallance Jupp, who as captain of Northants had tried leg theory against the 1930 Australians. He began to call in regularly at Frank Foster's flat in St James to discuss the field settings Foster had used in Australia in 1911–12. When Duleepsinhji dropped out of the touring party, Jardine had him replaced by a fast bowler, G.O.B. Allen, instead of another batsman.

Jardine, then 32, was a monosyllabic introvert who often ignored hands offered for a handshake, read Chaucer in spare moments, preferred his Harlequin cap to his English one, and ruled his team with an iron hand. He declined a gift of a bottle of Scotch for every man in the team to safeguard their fitness, confiscated Freddie Brown's golf clubs because he believed golf encouraged cross-bat shots and clashed with pressmen in Perth, where he insisted he was in Australia to play Test cricket and not to provide newspapers with stories.

The team he led was strong, but overloaded with pace bowlers. The gifted spinners in the side (Verity and Tom Mitchell) had only a support role in Jardine's plans, and medium-pacer Maurice Tate, a match-winner in Australia in 1928–29, was barely used at all. The English team was D.R. Jardine (Captain), H. Sutcliffe, W.R. Hammond, the Nawab of Pataudi, M. Leyland, E. Paynter, R.E.S.

Wyatt, L.E.G. Ames, G.O.B. Allen, H. Larwood, H. Verity, F.R. Brown, W. Voce, G. Duckworth, W.E. Bowes and T.B. Mitchell. Tate joined the tour late, after several matches.

Jardine went trout-fishing while England played the sixth match of their tour against an Australian XI in Melbourne, leaving his deputy Bob Wyatt to have an experimental run with his Bodyline tactics. When Wyatt rang him after Australia's first innings, Jardine was elated to learn that all the leading Australian batsmen had flinched before England's bouncer-laden attack. Bowes, Larwood, Voce and Allen had all inflicted painful blows on the batsmen, and Larwood had Bradman out cheaply in both innings.

Only outstanding bowling displays by Ron Oxenham and Lisle Nagel prevented a full exposure of England's tactics. Oxenham varied his right-arm off-breaks with rare subtlety to take 5 for 53 and have England out for 282. Nagel, 198 cm tall (6 ft 6 in), used his long arms and exceptional height to achieve swing with his right-arm medium-pacers that befuddled the Englishmen in their second innings and had them out for only 60 runs. Wearing a bandage to protect his bowling arm, injured when cranking his car, Nagel took 8 for 32. Rain ended play with the Australian XI needing 106 to win with eight wickets left, and the performance of the Australian bowlers grabbed the headlines instead of the bruises Bowes, Larwood and Voce had inflicted on opposing batsmen.

Jack Hobbs, in the packed press box, commented on the English bowlers' attempts to hit the batsman's body. 'The bowling looked very dangerous stuff,' Hobbs wrote. 'These were real shock tactics. Bradman, wonderful player though he is, ducked away like anyone else. Most of all, I was impressed with Larwood. I don't think I have ever seen him bowl faster.'

Larwood was rested from the next match against New South Wales, but Voce continued the campaign to break the batsmen's confidence. Jack Fingleton, who made 115 not out for New South Wales, said: 'There was nothing half-hearted about Voce's bowling. He bowled with studied intent to hit the body, the ball pitching at the half-way mark and sometimes shorter; he had four or five short-legs with two men covering the deep. Voce bowled Bradman but for the main purpose the stumps were meant to serve they may as well have been in the pavilion. Most of Voce's deliveries, if they did not meet a rib in transit, cleared the leg stumps, or a space outside the leg stump, by feet. A blow on the ribs would be followed by a precisely similar ball.'

These early matches gave birth to the ill-feeling that prevailed between the players throughout the Test series. For a time the Englishmen apologised to batsmen who were hit but the blows became so frequent apologies appeared hypocritical and off the field opposing players never tried to socialise or share a beer after a day's play. Fingleton said that he had achieved his wildest dream by scoring a century but walked off the field without joy or elation, conscious of the physical pummelling he had taken from Voce, and the way the Englishmen had betrayed the game's highest ideals.

The famous Australian statesman Herbert Evatt, inaugural president of the United Nations, and in 1932–33 a NSWCA executive, said: 'I was revolted by that day's play. It made me feel that I never afterwards wanted to see a single day's play in that series.' Fingleton's mother felt the same and refused to attend another match involving England.

By the time the First Test began in Sydney on 2 December 1932, the English tactics in bowling at Bradman rather than at the stumps had already succeeded and his six innings against the tourists had yielded 3, 10, 36, 13, 18 and 23, or 103 runs. Figures apart, he had shown in those six innings that this type of bowling really upset him and he withdrew, because of illness, from the First Test. Stan McCabe played one of the greatest innings of all time in that match, batting for 242 minutes and hitting 25 fours to reach 187. Australia were still overwhelmed and lost the Test by ten wickets.

Unlike Fingleton's mother, McCabe's mother joined spectators for this match but just before he went in to bat McCabe asked friends to prevent his mother jumping the fence if he was hit. McCabe hooked Larwood and Voce off his bald head and was lucky when these shots landed clear of fieldsmen as he scored 51 of the last 55 runs in Australia's first innings, in only 33 minutes.

McCabe's innings thrilled all cricket lovers and made Australians believe the four pace bowlers in the English plot could be thwarted when Bradman returned. Bradman, declared unfit for the First Test by Board of Control doctors who said he was run down and listless, watched the Test from the stand and then had a fortnight at the seaside recuperating for the Second Test. He had plenty on his mind.

The Board of Control placed no restrictions on players discussing each day's events on the radio when they were invited to the microphone, although the Board banned all comment in newspapers. Bradman wrote to the Board seeking permission to write on his matches, which he said was part of the contract that had kept

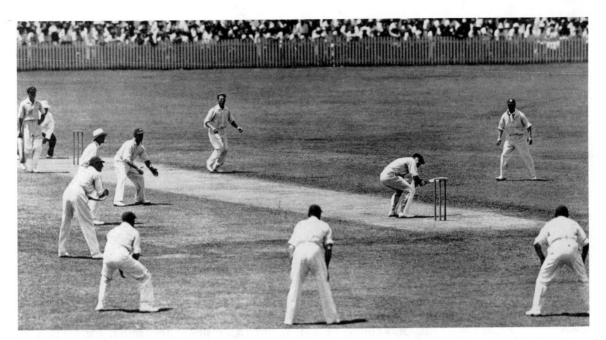

him in Australia. If he could not write for the Sun newspaper group he would have to declare himself unavailable.

For weeks the problem remain unresolved, with Bradman writing and broadcasting on his matches and insisting he had to continue to do so. The Board was in confusion, concerned that their biggest drawcard would not play. Finally Sir Hugh Denison, chairman of the Sun newspapers and part-owner of the radio station for whom he was contracted to broadcast, announced Bradman's release from his contract to ensure he could take his place in the Test team.

Reporters covering the English tour struggled to find a word that would accurately describe Jardine's tactics. They tried 'Shock Body Blows', 'Human Skittles' and 'Balls That Maim', but could not get a condensed word that was appropriate. Larwood thought it was the Sydney *Sun*'s Claude Corbett, but Jardine was more accurate in thinking it was Hugh Buggy, the Melbourne *Herald* cricket writer who coined the term. Jack Worrall spoke of 'half-pitched slingers on the body line', which Buggy read, and Buggy also studied an article by R.E.W. Wilmot in the Melbourne *Argus* that said England's attack was persistently in 'line with the body'. To save money in the days of high telegram costs, Buggy used his own cablese to form the word 'Bodyline' and a young sub-editor named Ray Robinson who handled the cable liked the word and headlined it. Overnight the word became infamous.

Woodfull ducks under a bouncer from Larwood, closely watched by a ring of legside fieldsmen. Only one man patrolled the offside in front of point. (John Fairfax)

A record crowd of 63,993 watched Bradman's return to the Test arena for the Second Test and when he came through the gate with Australia 2 for 67 he was clapped all the way to the crease by a crowd that only hushed as Bowes began his approach, knowing Bradman was in form as he had scored 157 for New South Wales against Victoria only a few days before. Bradman moved slightly away to the offside for Bowes's first ball, swung hard at it, and edged it into his stumps. The 63,993 spectators sat silently in disbelief as Bradman began the long walk back to the pavilion. Jardine, for the only time in the series, lost control and yelled in delight as he lifted both arms above his Harlequin cap.

O'Reilly turned the match for Australia by dismissing ten batsmen for less than 13 runs each. Wall helped (4 for 52) in England's first innings and Ironmonger (4 for 26) completed Australia's dominance. Australia led by 59 on the first innings and on the third day a record crowd of 70,000 saw Bradman score a brilliant 103 not out. Left to score 251 to win in the last innings England found O'Reilly and Ironmonger too much for them and were out for 139, leaving Australia victors by 111 runs.

By now all the Australian batting stars had been hit hard and often and had the impression Larwood was trying to hit them and not the stumps. Vic Richardson, a powerful hooker, told Adelaide newspapers he took guard a foot outside the off stump and Larwood's deliveries still came straight at him. Woodfull, cricket's modest, quiet man, had taken several stunning blows over the heart. English fans reading these allegations at home were more inclined to believe the English players who said the Melbourne pitch had been drugged to suit Australia's spinners and negate England's pace attack.

The Third Test at Adelaide was aptly described in *Wisden* as the most unpleasant ever played. Jardine was so aroused by the ill-feeling towards his players he barred the public from watching his team practise at the Adelaide Oval nets in the days leading up to the Test. On the morning of the match 400 mounted police waited on the no. 2 ground, ready to be called in case of a demonstration. A further 400 foot police ringed the inside of the ground, each man standing just inside the fence. The prevailing atmosphere was a disgrace to cricket.

Even without Bradman's copy, sensation followed sensation. The retired former Test umpire A.C. Jones said he believed Bodyline should be banned under the rule of fair and unfair play and that Larwood or Voce should be no-balled whenever they aimed

deliveries at the body. Then it was disclosed that Sydney-born 'Gubby' Allen had refused to bowl to Bodyline fields and had thrown the ball back to Jardine when Jardine refused to revert to orthodox field placings. Allen wrote many letters to his father during the series, making plain his loathing of Jardine and Bodyline. The Nawab of Pataudi also rebelled against Jardine's tactics in Melbourne when Woodfull took a blow over the heart by refusing Jardine's instructions to move from the offside to the already packed legside. Jardine said: 'I see that His Highness is a conscientious objector.' Pataudi missed selection in the remaining Tests.

The reluctance of English cricket fans to believe the accusations of unfair play on the other side of the world stemmed from the knowledge that their representatives in the Tests were all from institutions proud of their ethical conduct. Warner, England's manager, went to Rugby before he attended Oxford University; his assistant Richard Cameron Palairet, was Repton and Oxford; Jardine was Winchester and Oxford; Freddie Brown, Leys and Cambridge; Allen, Eton and Cambridge; the Nawab of Pataudi, Winchester and Oxford. England could hardly have had a more blue-blooded lot in charge.

England batted first and scored 341. Midway through the second day Australian batsmen wearing pads to cover the ribs and heart, pads over the elbows, reinforced thigh pads and the customary groin protectors, faced the English speedsters before the biggest crowd ever packed into Adelaide Oval – 50,962. The secretary of the

SACA hung pictures of the crowd in his office to convince those who claimed it was impossible. The crush in the stands forced people to stand up for the entire day.

Fingleton was caught behind by Ames off Allen with only one run scored. Larwood, bowling with four slips, then hit Woodfull a tremendous blow over the heart with the last ball of the second over. Thus infuriated spectators who booed and catcalled all around the ground as fieldsmen moved in to sympathise with Woodfull. At this the police inside the ground turned to face the crowd.

Larwood started his approach run for the first ball of his next over, but Jardine clapped his hands to stop him before he reached the crease. Jardine signalled most of his offside fieldsmen into their legside Bodyline positions, leaving one man, Verity, to patrol the entire offside from Wyatt in the gully. Seven men were stationed from deep fine leg to silly mid-on.

The unhappy timing of Jardine's field changes sent the crowd wild and they demonstrated against Jardine's action for several minutes. Jardine calmly waited for the protest to subside. Even in the Members' Enclosure normally quiet-spoken people were shouting their rage and joined in counting the Englishmen out.

In between the shouting, Woodfull was hit repeatedly by balls just short of a length, as he struggled gamely to 22. Jardine took a constant stream of abuse, some of it extremely vulgar, without emotion, even fielding out on the boundary where he was easy prey for the demonstrators. Bradman chose to make himself a moving target, flittering about the crease and swishing a ball from Verity for six, but generally moving towards the legside before Larwood came in. He played a couple of tennis shots at bouncers that sailed high over his head that delighted spectators but only scored eight before Larwood had him caught by Allen. McCabe went the same way for the same score. Ponsford battled on to 85, taking an awful beating that raised bruises all over his torso. When he came off with Vic Richardson at the end of the day, Ponsford lifted his shirt to show team-mates his bruises. 'It'll take another ten for me to get a hundred,' he said.

Woodfull was in the Australian dressing-room receiving treatment for his bruises when 'Plum' Warner entered with Palairet. Woodfull had just showered but the livid mark above the heart stood out.

'We have come to say how sorry we are and to offer our sympathy,' said Warner.

'I don't want to see you, Mr Warner,' Woodfull said. 'There are two sides out there. One is trying to play cricket, the other is not. The game is too good to be spoilt. It is time some people got out of it.'

This interlude and implications of Woodfull's words did not leak out immediately and when they did Woodfull was very upset that what had been a private exchange had become public. He blamed Fingleton for the leak because Fingleton was the only journalist in the Australian team, but Fingleton maintained until he died that Bradman was responsible and accused Bradman of secretly meeting Claude Corbett on the night after the Warner–Woodfull incident. Corbett worked for the Sydney Sun group that employed Bradman, and was frightened by the enormity of the story and decided to share it with colleagues in the press box.

On Adelaide radio Monty Noble strongly condemned Bradman's approach to Bodyline and said Bradman had let Australia down by refusing to bat normally. Noble also castigated Woodfull for not insisting that Bradman played a more disciplined innings. 'Bradman suddenly developed a sensational desire to score off everything, regardless of the safety of his wicket,' Noble said. 'His opponents revelled in his indiscretion and laughed up their sleeves because they knew he was reacting the way they wanted him to.'

On the third morning Ponsford and Oldfield resumed batting and moved quietly along until Oldfield tried to pull a ball, got his feet mixed up, and edged the ball into his skull. Oldfield always blamed himself for this and not the bowler, Larwood. When he was carried off, doctors found that he had a fractured linear bone in the skull, which would have been fatal if it had been an inch lower.

Oldfield's injury occurred at a time when Jardine was using an orthodox field, for contrary to the general belief, Bodyline fields were used in spells and not continuously. But after he hit Oldfield Larwood was hooted every time he bowled. The ugliest sustained demonstration in the history of Australian cricket saw people in the stands joining those in the outer in gusts of booing. They counted

Bert Oldfield, hit on the forehead by a Larwood bouncer, suffered a fractured skull in the incident that caused international uproar and led to an exchange of angry cables between English and Australian administrators.
(Adelaide Advertiser)

Jardine out, they hooted Larwood and shouted insults at him and they kept it up throughout the time it took England to dispose of the last Australian batsmen.

Provoked by the demonstration, the Australian Board of Control held an emergency meeting at the ground and later informed Warner and Palairet that they intended to send a cable protesting at the style of attack England was using to Lord's. Warner asked if he might have the chance of reading the cable before it was sent as he might be able to suggest a useful phrase or word change. Warner was told the following cable had already been sent:

Bodyline assuming such proportions as to menace the best interests of the game, making protection of the body by the batsmen the main consideration. This is causing intensely bitter feeling between the players as well as injury. In our opinion it is unsportsmanlike. Unless stopped at once it is likely to upset the friendly relations between England and Australia.

Apart from Jack Hobbs, there was only one English pressman on the tour, Bruce Harris, of the London *Evening Standard*. Like his Australian counterparts Harris was astonished that the Board should send such a cable without conferring first with Warner and Palairet. Newspapers immediately condemned the tactless wording of the cable, lawyers were sought for opinions on whether the cable was defamatory, and learned judges asked if attacks on a batsman's head and body were an indictable offence.

The cable was drafted by four members of the Board of Control, B.V. Scrymgour, H.W. Hodgetts and R.F. Middleton of South Australia, and W.L. Kelly of Victoria, who acted in anger when Jardine moved fieldsmen into the leg trap when Woodfull was struck on the heart. The cable was read over the telephone to the Board chairman, Dr Allan Robertson, who was in Melbourne and had the final right of approval of the wording.

Eight members of the Board, including the delegates from Tasmania, Victoria, Western Australia and South Australia, approved sending the message. The Queensland and New South Wales delegates argued that the cable should not be sent until Woodfull was consulted.

Jardine was completely unconcerned by the abuse he received on the field but he became very worried that the MCC hierarchy at Lord's might not support him. He called a team meeting to ensure his players remain loyal to him. Allen said that he had carefully read the cable and believed there was no way the MCC would accept the charge of bad sportsmanship. 'Nobody calls an Englishman unsporting and gets away with it,' Allen said, and his judgement proved sound.

Parliamentarians and diplomats in Canberra and Whitehall joined the controversy as the Test was played out. Secretary for the Dominions, J.H. Thomas, summoned MCC chiefs to Downing Street, overshadowing Hitler's dissolution of the Reichstag in London papers. In Adelaide, Australian players labelled squealers felt they were on a war footing.

Jardine batted for four and a quarter hours for 56 in England's second innings and when Bradman clean bowled Hammond for 85 shouts of glee erupted all over Adelaide Oval. Left to score 532 to win, Australia managed 193, Bradman scoring 66. Woodfull batted right through the Australian innings for the second time in his career to finish on 73 not out, with England winning by 338 runs.

On 24 January 1933, the Marylebone Cricket Club sent the following reply to the Australian Board's cable:

We, Marylebone Cricket Club, deplore your cable. We deprecate your opinion that there has been unsportsmanlike play. We have the fullest confidence in our captain, team and managers, and are convinced they would do nothing to either infringe the Laws of Cricket, or the spirit of the game. We have no evidence that our confidence has been misplaced. Much as we regret accidents to Woodfull and Oldfield, we understand that in neither case was the bowler to blame.

If the Australian Board of Control wishes to propose a new law or rule it shall receive our careful consideration in due course. We hope the situation is now not as serious as your cable would seem to indicate, but if it is such as to jeopardise the good relations between English and Australian cricketers and you consider it desirable to cancel the remainder of the programme we would consent but with great reluctance.

The Australian Board of Control considered this MCC cable for a week, during which Allen repeatedly told Jardine Australian officials had helped his cause by using the word 'unsportsmanlike' in their first cable. On 31 January the Board of Control sent a second cable to Lord's reasserting that Bodyline was dangerous to players but not retracting the word 'unsportsmanlike'. At this Warner sought the help of the British Government's Australian representative Ernest Crutchley, who in turn spoke to Australian Prime Minister Joe Lyons.

After a visit to the Prime Minister's office, Board chairman Dr Robertson sent a telegram to Board secretary Bill Jeanes saying the Prime Minister had asked him to have the word 'unsportsmanlike' withdrawn. Robertson's telegram said he had no doubt England's method of attack would be modified if the word was retracted and ended with the words 'Government fears successful conversion endangered'.

This meant that the Australian government was afraid that the conversion loans – old loans from England that were being negotiated to allow for easier repayment – might be endangered and they were of crucial importance to the capital-starved Australian economy during its emergence from the Depression.

The governor of South Australia, Lord Gowrie, was on leave in England but in his absence the acting governor Sir George Murray invited Warner and several cricket-loving businessmen to Government House to discuss the Bodyline affair. Warner condemned what was being done, but insisted Jardine had complete control on the field. Sir George informed Gowrie of the dangers Bodyline presented and Gowrie thought it so important he consulted the Cabinet minister responsible for the Dominions, Jimmy Thomas.

On 8 February 1933, two days before the Fourth Test was due to start in Brisbane, the Board of Control sent a further cable to Lord's which began, 'We do not regard your sportsmanship as being in question . . .'. Jardine rang Lord's to confirm this cable's wording and was satisfied. The tour proceeded and Australia's loans were saved. England regained the Ashes by winning the Fourth Test by six wickets, but none of the high-level diplomacy improved the bitter feeling among the players.

Jardine was refused admission to the Australian dressing-room when he called to confer with Woodfull, who had to go out into a corridor to discover what Jardine wanted. Spectators continued their jibes against him to the end of the tour. Australia's selectors sought to embarrass him by including the left-handers Len Darling, Ernie Bromley and Leo O'Brien, which forced Jardine to swing his eight legside fieldsmen from one side of the pitch to the other when any of the three batted with right-handers. Like slamming the door in his face, none of this worried Jardine, who continued with Bodyline in the Fifth Test although the Ashes were already won.

Lord Gowrie, then governor of South Australia, who was involved in diplomatic manoeuvres to force Australia to withdraw charges of unsportsmanlike behaviour by England. (Mitchell Library, Sydney)

The Australian selectors helped England to finish the series 4–1 up with some strange decisions. They sent Australia into the Fourth Test with only three recognised Test bowlers – Wall, O'Reilly and Ironmonger – and in the Fifth Test let Woodfull experiment with the erratic 'Bull' Alexander. When Alexander asked if he could bowl a few bouncers at the Englishmen Woodfull refused. But the oddest selection of all was in naming South Australian Bert Tobin as twelfth man for the Fourth Test although he had never scored 100 or taken five wickets in a match in his life. Tobin confessed he was amazed at being chosen.

Ironmonger appeared in the last four Tests of this rubber in his fifty-first year. The selectors never bothered to check when he said he was 47 although it was obvious to anyone in the dressing-room that something was amiss. Bill O'Reilly, in his book *Tiger*, described Ironmonger's preparation for a day's bowling in the Brisbane Test:

He was a heavily built man, six-foot high and fifteen and a half stone, and those of us who looked carefully as he prepared for the fray saw that he wore two long pieces of rubber band about six inches wide wrapped firmly around each thigh. Beside this he pulled an elastic knee guard over each knee. On his feet he had two pairs of woollen socks, and he thrust his feet into boots with leather soles an inch thick. On that day in Brisbane when the temperature reached well over 100 degrees Fahrenheit he deserved the Victoria Cross. When he had bowled about ten overs I met him as we were changing ends and I can recall the tortured look in his eyes when he enquired what my reaction was to the pitch.

This was the match in which Stan McCabe suggested to Woodfull that a glass of champagne might revive his bowlers at the end of a hard day in the field. Woodfull, a teetotaller, agreed, and sent dressing-room attendant Sid Redgrave out for a bottle with instructions to charge it to the Board of Control. Redgrave returned empty-handed and said the Queensland Cricket Association president Jack Hutcheon refused permission for alcohol to be served. Woodfull burst angrily through the door and returned himself with a bottle within a few minutes.

On the last day of the Brisbane Test, 16 February 1933, Archie Jackson died of tuberculosis at Ingarfield Private Hospital, aged 23. He had become engaged to his sweetheart Phyllis Thomas only a few days before, after collapsing while playing club cricket for Northern Suburbs, Brisbane. Dr Evatt paid for his parents and lifelong friend Bill Hunt to fly to Brisbane from Sydney in a plane piloted by noted aviator P.G. Taylor. Hunt took Jackson's body back to Sydney in the same train that carried the English and Australian cricketers.

Pallbearers at Archie Jackson's funeral during the 1932–33 Bodyline season. Jackson died during the Brisbane Test and his body was returned to Sydney for burial after a long parade through Sydney streets. (J.C. Davis Collection)

Jackson received one of Sydney's biggest funerals, a mile-long cortege moving from the Jacksons' Balmain cottage to the Field of Mars cemetery in Ryde. Bradman, Woodfull, Vic Richardson, Oldfield, McCabe and Ponsford were chosen as his pallbearers but on the day McCabe became ill and was replaced by Kippax.

A memorable Test series wound up with a memorable catch. Larwood, after proving that he ranked among the finest fast bowlers by taking 33 Test wickets at 19.51 against one of the best-ever Australian batting sides, seemed certain to add to his honours with a Test century. But at 98, in what turned out to be his final Test, Ironmonger held a very difficult catch at mid-on. Larwood hit the ball to Ironmonger's left side, always a problem for the big man because of his injured hand. Ironmonger took it with consummate ease. It was one of only 30 catches Ironmonger held in 90 first-class matches spread over 24 years.

Larwood broke down in this match with a fracture of two small bones in his toes. The injury became so painful Larwood could

Oldfield plays a ball from Larwood through the packed legside field during the Fifth Test in Sydney in 1932–33. (John Fairfax)

barely walk but Jardine insisted he complete the over, bowling by swinging his arm over without an approach run, until Bradman was out for 71. Bradman left the field with Larwood, both aware that Bradman's astonishing run-getting had been dramatically curbed. Bodyline had served its purpose.

England completed their 22-match tour with ten wins, ten draws, one loss and a tie against Victoria. This first tie by an English team in Australia came when Victoria were set to score 178 in two hours to win. They wanted seven from the last over and scored just six of them, finishing on 3 for 177 after innings of 88 by Keith Rigg and 56 not out by Ernie Bromley.

Sutcliffe, with 1318 runs at 73.22, was the only English batsman to score 1000 runs on the tour but Hammond made the highest score, 203 against Victoria at Melbourne. Seven Englishmen made centuries. Larwood was the most effective English bowler, with 49 first-class wickets at 16.67.

Bradman headed the Australian Test batting averages, but with a drastically reduced average of 56.57. O'Reilly was the most impressive Australian bowler with 27 Test wickets at 26.81. Seven Australian batsmen scored centuries against the Englishmen, including 152 by Arthur Chipperfield and 117 by Ray Little, both for Northern Districts in the match at Newcastle.

'My constant dread,' said George Hele, who umpired all five Bodyline Tests, 'was that a batsman would be killed.'

The extent to which Larwood and the Bodyline fields subdued Bradman was demonstrated by Bradman's Sheffield Shield performance that summer. He played in only three Shield matches but scored 600 runs at an average of 150, with a highest score of 238 against Victoria in Sydney. Ponsford also scored 200 in this match, which New South Wales won by nine wickets to ensure their twentieth success in the Shield. At Brisbane in the Shield match against Queensland, Victorian left-handers Leo O'Brien and Len Darling had an Australian record stand of 301 for the fourth wicket to set up a masssive 329-run defeat for Queensland. O'Brien made 145 not out, Darling 185.

The sensation of the 1932–33 Shield competition came in the Sydney match between New South Wales and South Australia when Tim Wall took all ten New South Wales wickets in one innings. Wall's onslaught sent New South Wales back for only 113 in their first innings after New South Wales had reached 2 for 87 by lunch. After the interval Wall dismissed Fingleton, McCabe, Ray Rowe and Frank Cummins without conceding a run. The pitch offered Wall little assistance but a stiff breeze helped him swing the ball a long way. He bowled six of his victims in taking 10 for 36.

Wall was a great favourite with crowds because of the manner in which he ambled back to his mark after each delivery. He always looked exhausted by the effort he put into his bowling, but he could bowl for hours off his 27-stride approach. Spectators heckled him wherever he appeared but nobody enjoyed it more than Wall.

Three years after the formation of the Australian Women's Cricket Council, the first women's Test match was played at Brisbane, from 28 to 31 December, 1934. Big crowds attended the English women's team as they played their way round the southern states and some 3000 spectators watched the Test start at Brisbane's Exhibition Ground. Australia batted first and succumbed to a mixture of nervousness and splendid bowling by England's Myrtle Maclagan, who took 7 for 10 from 17 overs. Kath Smith made 25 for Australia, who were all out for 47 in just under two hours. England had the match under control by stumps with her score at 5 for 116.

About 5000 people watched Australia dismiss England for 154 on the second day and reach 5 for 99 in their second innings by stumps. Essie Shevill was 63 not out when the Australian innings ended at 138, leaving England to score only 31 to win. They accomplished this with the loss of only one wicket to win by nine wickets. Overall attendance for the match was 9000.

England repeated this triumph in the Second Test at Sydney early in January. Australia began with a first innings of 162, Kath Smith contributing 47. England's Myrtle Maclagan then scored 119, the first century in women's Tests, in a record opening stand of 145 with Betty Snowball, which allowed England to declare at 5 for 301. They then dismissed Australia for 148 and hit off the ten runs required for victory for the loss of two wickets. The aggregate attendance for this Test was 12,197.

Australia produced their best display of the series in the final Test at Melbourne. Leg-spinner Peggy Antonio took 6 for 49 and had England out for 162 despite another half-century by Myrtle Maclagan. Australia responded with a first innings of 150 and when England declared her second innings closed at 7 for 153 Australia held out for a draw, finishing on 8 for 104 when time ran out. This gave England the rubber 2–0 and brought the total attendance for the three Tests to 34,197, a highly encouraging response to women's cricket. All the English players paid their own fares and bought their own gear for a 21-match tour that lasted six months. The English girls remained unbeaten, winning 15 matches and drawing five. Their captain, Betty Archdale, later became headmistress of Abbotsleigh, a prominent Sydney girls' school.

Before the 1933–34 Sheffield Shield programme began a conference of all the states adopted an 'anti-Bodyline law' proposed by South Australia, which empowered umpires to no-ball bowlers who tried to intimidate batsmen. Bowlers who repeated the offence were barred from bowling for the rest of the innings. Only New South Wales opposed introduction of a law their delegates called 'a mind-readers' law'. New South Wales were so angry that the smaller states had the new law passed they tried to remove all voting rights from the non-Sheffield States – Tasmania and Western Australia – and have them relegated to associate membership of the Board of Control. The proposal was defeated by ten votes to three.

Aware of the simmering anger created by the Bodyline series, the Board of Control instructed its London representative, Dr Robert McDonald, to secure a promise from the MCC that Bodyline bowling would be outlawed for the Australian tour of England in 1934. The MCC declined but an MCC sub-committee comprising Lord Hawke, Lord Lewisham, Sir Stanley Jackson and MCC secretary William Findlay agreed that bowling which made a direct assault on batsmen was undesirable. When McDonald said that Australia was entitled to know if England's tactics in 1934 would justify bringing four fast bowlers to England, Lord Hawke said: 'Reprisals, by Gad!'

Some members of the Australian Board supported discontinuing Tests against England but secretary Syd Smith strongly supported the tour for fear all Test cricket would disappear. Most of the states wanted a guarantee from England before the tour that there would be no repetition of Bodyline, but without taking a vote the Board cabled Australia's acceptance of the tour invitation.

The deliberations of the Board's special anti-Bodyline committee were a waste of time. The Australian Board of Control chairman, Oxlade, advocated appeasement and was rewarded with the CBE in the 1934 New Year's Honours list, while in London letters on Bodyline in the Dominions Office files were destroyed. In the 1990s, historians searching for the origins of the Australian republican movement claimed it began with Bodyline.

CHAPTER NINETEEN
BRADMAN NEAR DEATH

'My own experience of Australians is that if they cannot win they will not stand to be beaten if they can avoid it. They will go to almost any length to avoid defeat . . . To Australians, cricket is a business pure and simple – a matter of money – and success is all that matters to them . . . The only Australians I would give twopence for are Charlie Macartney and Arthur Mailey.'

These were the words of Arthur William Carr, the Notts captain, whose team included both the Bodyline bowling villains Harold Larwood and Bill Voce. Both were magnificent professionals from humble beginnings and both knew that hanging on to the easier life cricket offered meant doing as they were told.

Carr's intransigence was the main obstacle the Australians encountered on their eighteenth tour of England in 1934. The Australian Board only accepted MCC's invitation to tour by eight votes to five and most of Australia's leading batsmen felt betrayed by the Board's acceptance before securing an agreement that outlawed Bodyline.

The tension eased before the tour began. The MCC took a ready-made excuse to make Larwood the scapegoat for events on the Bodyline tour when he gave a series of interviews to Carr on the voyage home from Australia. Larwood's interviews, featured daily in London newspapers, broke his tour contract but he refused to apologise and was banned from Test selection. He continued in county cricket until 1938, frequently troubled by a leg injury he blamed on hard Australian wickets. Not long afterwards Jardine notified the London *Evening Standard* in an exclusive telegram of his retirement as England's captain. Jardine retired at 34, a cold, authoritarian figure who led England in 15 Tests against

Australia, New Zealand, India and West Indies and suffered only one defeat.

The English selectors removed the third threat to a happy Australian tour by overlooking Voce for the Tests. Voce remained the best fast left-arm bowler in cricket, a tall, powerfully framed man with a lovely loose arm action, but the bouncer-laden attack he favoured had been banned by 17 county captains at a special meeting at Lord's in November 1933.

The Australian team, captained by the instinctively tactful Woodfull and managed by the Tasmanian Harold Bushby, was W.M. Woodfull (Captain), D.G. Bradman (Vice-captain), A.F. Kippax, W.H. Ponsford, W.A. Brown, A.G. Chipperfield, B.A. Barnett, S.J. McCabe, L.S. Darling, W.J. O'Reilly, W.A.S. Oldfield, E.H. Bromley, C.V. Grimmett, H.I. Ebeling, T.W. Wall and L.O'B. Fleetwood-Smith. The omission of Fingleton, whose place went to Chipperfield, was widely criticised. Chipperfield had played only three times for New South Wales and was chosen on the recommendation of former Test skipper Warren Bardsley who rated Chipperfield the finest slips fieldsman he had ever seen. The selection of Fleetwood-Smith gave Woodfull a three-pronged spin attack with O'Reilly and Grimmett, but also meant Ironmonger had missed his last chance for a trip to England, where conditions would have been ideal for his left-arm spin.

Fleetwood-Smith, like Ironmonger, told fibs about his age. He claimed to have been born in 1910 but in fact was born in 1908. The two extra years proved no disadvantage to him either on the field or in the conquest of a long line of girlfriends. His womanising was so successful team-mates soon learned they could improve their social life by following him around and taking over his cast-offs. And what a performer! Fleetwood-Smith's biographer Greg Growden says that on some nights he had no trouble slotting four or five women into his schedule.

Bradman and Fleetwood-Smith became very close because of their mutual enjoyment of piano-playing. They would sit round pianos in the team's hotels for hours at a time. They were an odd pair, completely different in character, Bradman the withdrawn, inhibited loner, Fleetwood-Smith the fun-loving party-goer, but to team-mates they often seemed inseparable. Hanson Carter had predicted long before Fleetwood-Smith joined the Australian team that one day he would win a Test for Australia because he bowled a mixture of left-arm spin rare in Australia.

Fleetwood-Smith's selection was thoroughly deserved but it cost the Sydney leg-spinner Hughie Chilvers a trip many less talented bowlers have enjoyed. From the time he won selection in the New South Wales side in 1929–30 Chilvers was recognised as a world-class spinner, with a top-spinner that beat even champion batsmen. He was destined to take 151 first-class wickets, 11 times capturing five wickets in an innings and three times taking ten wickets in a match, but the master-spinners Grimmett, O'Reilly and Fleetwood-Smith denied him a Test.

Bradman faced his second English tour as vice-captain, a clear indication that the Board of Control wanted him groomed for the Test captaincy. His three-part contract with clothing store F.J. Palmer, the Sydney *Sun* and radio station 2UE had expired in February 1934, before the team left, and after weeks of looking round for a job outside cricket he agreed to join the Adelaide stock-broking firm run by Harry Hodgetts, a South Australian delegate to the Australian Board of Control. Hodgetts promised to train him in broking and to make him captain of South Australia's Shield team.

After informing the NSWCA of his new job, Bradman moved to Adelaide and set up house in Kensington Park with his wife Jessie. He became alarmed at his indifferent health and his lack of energy in matches and although the Board of Control doctors passed him fit to tour England, he went to two Adelaide specialists at his own expense. They said he was simply run down and would recover by the end of the long voyage to England.

Woodfull's fears that his team would not field well were quickly ended by Bradman, Billy Brown, Chipperfield, Ernie Bromley and Len Darling, who drew continuous applause for their brilliance in gathering and throwing. Bromley had an unbelievable throwing arm with which he fired in returns right over the bails like rifle shots. Behind the stumps Oldfield lifted the entire team's displays with his own brand of error-free wicket-keeping. Knowing he had never kept before to a left-arm googly bowler he took Fleetwood-Smith out to a park before they left home for long sessions in which he learned how to detect the googly.

Bradman was slightly groggy before the first match at Worcester on 2 May against Worcestershire but Woodfull persuaded him to play so that his withdrawal would not give England a psychological boost. Bradman made 206 in 208 minutes but was aware of a drain on his resources.

The First Test at Nottingham produced some new faces in Ken Farnes, the tall, rangy Essex pace bowler who took Larwood's place, Cyril Walters who took over the England captaincy when Wyatt dropped out, and Australian batsmen Bill Brown and Arthur Chipperfield. At 5 for 153, with Woodfull, Ponsford, Brown, Bradman and Darling all out, Chipperfield joined McCabe. They moved the score along to stumps when Chipperfield was 17 not out, McCabe 61 not out. Next morning McCabe fell for 65 but Chipperfield added 82 to his overnight score to reach 99 by lunch. Grimmett partnered Chipperfield after the break, but at age 42 Grimmett could not be called for a quick single, so Chipperfield tried to hit Farnes to the boundary off the third ball and edged a catch to Ames. Chipperfield thus became the first man to score 99 on debut.

O'Reilly and Grimmett bowled Australia to victory by 238 runs with only ten minutes to spare on the final day, cleverly exploiting a wearing pitch. O'Reilly took 4 for 75 and 7 for 54, Grimmett 5 for 81 and 3 for 39.

Hedley Verity levelled the series for England in the Second Test at Lord's, where Australia were caught on a wet pitch in their second innings after Brown had made a stylish 105 in Australia's first. Verity began with 7 for 61 and on a spiteful pitch excelled himself in the second innings by taking 8 for 43. England won by

Postmen safely delivered this fan letter to Bradman during his 1934 English tour. (Jack Pollard Collection)

Bradman returns to the pavilion after scoring 304 in the Leeds Test in 1934, his second triple century in successive Tests on that ground. (National Library of Australia)

an innings and 38 runs after Australia had failed by only seven runs to avoid the follow-on.

The Third Test was drawn after 1307 runs were scored in four days at Manchester for the fall of only 20 wickets. The Australians were relieved to escape without a loss as most of the side were handicapped by throat infections and Chipperfield defied doctors by leaving hospital to bat. The Fourth Test also produced a draw, but not until Bradman and Ponsford shared a 388-run stand for the fourth wicket that broke all records. Bradman finished with 304, Ponsford 181. Heavy rain on the fourth night and all the fifth day prevented a result.

England still had a chance of saving the Ashes when the teams moved to The Oval for the Fifth Test, on 18–22 August 1934. Australia batted and lost their first wicket at 21 when Clark bowled Brown. The next wicket did not fall until the score reached 472. Bradman (244) and Ponsford (266) put the issue beyond doubt by stumps when Australia was 2 for 475. Grimmett and O'Reilly, assisted by Hans Ebeling's medium-pacers, wore down England's batting in the final innings and Australia won by 562 runs to take the rubber 2–0.

The only unpleasant incidents on the entire tour occurred in the twenty-sixth match of the tour against Nottinghamshire, who fielded 11 professionals but were without Carr and Larwood. Voce took 8 for 66 to have Australia out for 237 and Notts replied with 183. At the end of the first day Woodfull sent for the Notts secretary and told him the agreement under which Australia were visiting England had been broken. Voce had bowled with five batsmen close in on the legside which gave batsmen little chance of escape when they defended their bodies against his surfeit of bouncers. Woodfull said that if Voce took the field when Australia batted a second time, the Australians would return to London without finishing the match. The Notts committee announced Voce had shin soreness and could not take the field for the second innings but this did not convince spectators, who had seen him score 22 runs in Notts first innings without the slightest hint of soreness. Spectators booed the Australian batsmen but the match petered out in a draw.

This was how English newspaper posters greeted Bradman's batting in the 1934 Test series against England. (Jack Pollard Collection)

Bradman's 304 at Leeds and his 244 at The Oval have been ranked among the great Test innings but Bradman himself believes his 132 v. H.D. Leveson-Gower's XI in the Scarborough Festival match among the best innings he ever played. 'Shrimp' Leveson-Gower broke his promise that the match would be a light-hearted social event and treated it as an extra Test by including four of England's finest bowlers – Bowes, Farnes, Verity and Nichols. Angered by this breach of faith, Bradman launched himself into the attack from the moment he reached the crease, hitting a six and 24 fours in 90 minutes. Bradman reached his century in 82 minutes and added 32 more in eight minutes, scoring 102 of his runs in boundaries. His 132 remains the highest score before lunch in an English first-class game.

The eighteenth Australian team won 15 of their 34 matches, drew 18 and sustained one loss. Chipperfield, Kippax, Bradman, Ponsford and Bromley were all incapacitated at various stages of the tour by influenza or diptheria and Bromley had to be rushed to hospital for an appendicitis operation on the eve of the Fifth Test. Right at the end of the tour Bradman collapsed and was rushed to hospital with a gangrenous appendix. The noted Melbourne surgeon Sir Douglas Shields performed an emergency operation and for several days Bradman was near death, with all visitors banned except manager Bushby. Blood transfusions were given and for days the hospital foyer was filled with reporters. Gloom spread across Australia as the seriousness of Bradman's condition became known.

Jessie Bradman rushed from Australia to be by her husband's bedside, but by the time she arrived he had survived the critical post-surgery period and the threat of peritonitis. He recovered slowly as a guest in R.W.V. Robins's house, followed by time in Switzerland and the French Riviera, and after arrival back home went to his father-in-law's farm at Mittagong for several months' recuperation. Doctors ordered him not to play cricket in the 1934–35 Australian season and he resigned as an Australian selector because he could not travel round to watch the players.

Vic Richardson took Bradman's place as a national selector and following the retirement of Bill Woodfull captained the Australian team that toured South Africa in 1935–36. Richardson had missed the 1934 English tour but knew he had remarkable line-up of batting stars from which to choose even without Bradman and the two Williams, Ponsford and Woodfull, who had retired. Australians had scored 33 centuries in England, and had only 18 scored against them. Bradman had made 2020 runs at 84.16, the best of the six batsmen who made more than 1000 runs. O'Reilly had headed the bowling averages with 109 first-class wickets at 17.04, Fleetwood-Smith had taken 106 wickets at 19.20 and Grimmett 109 at 19.80.

The Australian Board of Control gave Ponsford and Woodfull a joint testimonial in Melbourne, on 16–20 November 1934. They had established themselves as one of Australia's best opening pairs and had shared 23 century partnerships, plus five others that passed 200 runs. Woodfull's retirement at the age of 37 was known before play began in the testimonial but Ponsford's decision to quit only became known after the match began. They delighted the crowd by putting together yet another century stand, this time for 132,

The Sydney Daily Telegraph's front-page report on Bradman's near-fatal illness at the end of the 1934 English tour came from the then revolutionary 'beam wireless' service. (Jack Pollard Collection)

Woodfull scoring 111 in three hours, Ponsford 83 in two and a half hours.

Ponsford's retirement at 34 was premature for a player of such gifts, but he had become tired of run-getting after 14 seasons in which he made 47 centuries and scored 13,819 runs at 65.18, highest score 437. Woodfull had played one season less but his consistency brought him near Ponsford's total. Woodfull made 13,388 runs at 64.99 with 49 centuries. Woodfull, known as 'The Unbowlable' or 'The Worm Killer' through his use of a short backlift, scored 2300 runs in Tests at 46.0, with seven centuries. Ponsford, known only as 'Puddin'', made 2122 Test runs at 48.22.

Some of Ponsford's friends blamed his early retirement on Bradman. They said he was sick of being compared with Bradman and resented the constant assessments of their worth to the Australian side. Bill O'Reilly said he always found Ponsford harder to bowl against than Bradman. 'Bradman gave you some hope and you always felt you had a small chance of getting him out,' said O'Reilly. 'But with Ponsford you had no hope.'

O'Reilly was involved in a delightful prank against Ponsford when he came in to bat in a Shield match for Victoria against New South Wales. By pre-arrangement the New South Welshmen challenged the width of Ponsford's bat, claiming it was wider than the legal limit. The joke was supposed to have ended there with the umpire measuring Ponny's bat, but to everyone's surprise the umpire found that the bat was in fact a trifle too wide, which must have been caused by Ponsford's incessant middling of the ball. Amid laughter, they scraped the edges of Ponsford's bat with beer-bottle tops until it satisfied the umpires.

Ponsford's other great claim to fame was his ability to detect rain. When he had to bat the next day, he spent anxious nights staring out into the dark sniffing the breeze, and he endured many a restless night when rain threatened. On tour, team-mates made a habit of going down to breakfast and asking, 'How did Ponny sleep?' It became a reliable guide that if he had had a bad night rain was imminent.

With Bradman unable to take up his place in the South Australian team, Victoria won the 1934–35 Sheffield Shield competition with a young team that triumphed outright in their first five matches. O'Brien, Darling and Rigg all scored well but Victoria owed most to Fleetwood-Smith, who had returned from England a superb bowler. He took 60 Shield wickets at 18.95 apiece, a record for the competition. His bowling completely compensated for Victoria's loss of the 51-year-olds Blackie and Ironmonger. Blackie retired with 211 first-class wickets at 24.10, 14 of them in three Tests at 31.71, Ironmonger took 464 first-class wickets at 21.50, 74 of them in 14 Tests at 17.97. Both were 'discovered' by Test selectors at an age when most players have long since retired.

Fleetwood-Smith received valuable support from Victoria's right-arm fast bowler Ernie ('Goldie') McCormick, a tall, slim Melbourne jeweller, who bowled off one of the longest approach runs ever used by an Australian. McCormick marked out his 31-stride run as if he needed engineers to help him, beginning with two skips, followed by 20 running paces. He bowled with curiously stiff arms, which hung beside his thighs, and came thundering in like a runaway drill sergeant. When his run-in got him to the stumps on line, his pace off the bat was frightening. He once bounced the ball off the head of his captain at Richmond, Les Keating, and on successive Saturdays broke the jaws of North Melbourne's Roy Waters and Essendon's Ian Leembruggen.

Ernest Harvey Bromley, in 1934 the first Western Australian born player to tour with an Australian team, appeared in only one Test. (Jack Pollard Collection)

McCormick was born at North Carlton and learned to play cricket at Yarra Park School, Punt Road. His father, J.L. McCormick, was one of the founders of La Mascotte Club, parent body of the Collingwood Club. Ernie started as a wicket-keeper but was so fast and fiery when called on for a stint as a bowler in the practice nets, he accepted advice to become a pace bowler. He operated in the years just after Bodyline and when he hit batsmen spectators often hooted him for trying to maim, ignorant of the fact that he had only two short legs.

The brilliant young Tasmanian Cyril Badcock left home for South Australia after considering offers from New South Wales and Victoria and his presence partly compensated for the absence of Bradman. When South Australia compiled their best-ever Shield score of 7 for 644 declared, Badcock was one of four century-makers.

The vigour and the enterprise of the Western Australian and Tasmanian cricket authorities continued unabated as they tried to improve their case for inclusion in the Sheffield Shield programme. Western Australia invited New South Wales to Perth for two matches which were designed to test the calibre of the state side. Fingleton made 124 in the first match and 100 in the second, both matches ending in draws. Tasmania continued her long-running rivalry against Victoria in Melbourne, where the South Hobart spinner Syd Putnam took 7 for 102. Des Fitzmaurice made 102 in Victoria's first innings, Arthur Allsopp 122 in the second, but Tasmania escaped with a draw.

The 1935–36 Shield competition suffered from the absence of Australia's personality cricketers on the first full tour of South Africa and through a tour of India by an Australian team captained by Frank Tarrant and sponsored by the Maharajah of Patiala. Bradman followed his doctors' advice not to join the South African tour but after weeks of long walks and extensive golf took over the captaincy of South Australia from Vic Richardson, who was leading the Australian team in South Africa.

In his Shield debut for his adopted state, Bradman put on 202 for the second wicket with Badcock. Badcock finished with 150, Bradman 117, which lifted South Australia to a total of 575 against New South Wales. Frank Ward, the leg-spinner who had failed to find work in Queensland when he left the St George Club and could not beat O'Reilly and Chilvers for a spot in the New South Wales team, had eventually come to South Australia. He took 6 for 127 and had New South Wales out for 351. New South Wales followed on and lost by an innings and five runs. Bradman followed with 233 that set up another win over Queensland, and 357 against Victoria in Melbourne. He confirmed his complete recovery by making 739 runs at an average of 123.16 in Shield matches and 1173 runs at 130.33 in all first-class matches that summer. Badcock took the headlines from him for a time with an innings of 325 against Victoria in Adelaide.

This was an eventful season in Australia, with Bradman's duck against New South Wales in Sydney giving Alan McGilvray and big Bob Hynes material they dined off for years, Eddie Gilbert taking 19 wickets for Queensland, and a lovely strokemaker named Ray Robinson scoring 613 runs at 61.30 for New South Wales. Robinson – no relation to the cricket author – was stylish, elegant, and made many of his New South Wales team-mates look like hacks.

But all the important action was in South Africa that summer, with the remarkably popular Victor Richardson leading Australia with rare flair. The team Richardson took to South Africa comprised B.A. Barnett, W.A. Brown, A.G. Chipperfield, L.S. Darling, J.H.W. Fingleton, L.O'B. Fleetwood-Smith, C.V. Grimmett, S.J. McCabe, E.L. McCormick, L.P.J. O'Brien, W.A.S. Oldfield,

W.J. O'Reilly, M.W. Sievers and manager S.H.D. Rowe. Nine of the team had toured England in 1934.

The retirements of Woodfull and Ponsford gave Brown and Fingleton an opportunity of establishing themselves as a top-flight opening pair, a task they took to with unconcealed relish. Bradman's absence gave McCabe further chances to show his brilliance and Wall's absence provided McCormick with his opening as a team comedian and a quality fast bowler. But by the time of the First Test at Durban on 14–18 December 1934 the Australian spinners O'Reilly, Grimmett and Fleetwood-Smith had taken such a firm grip on matches that McCormick was moved to say: 'I just take the shine off the ball for those vultures who feed on the bones of fast bowlers, the spinners.'

Australia won the First Test by nine wickets with the spinners taking 18 wickets, the Second Test at Johannesburg was drawn with Australia in sight of victory after the spinners took 11 wickets, and Australia won the Third Test at Cape Town by an innings and 78 runs after the spinners took 19 wickets. Grimmett had 5 for 32 and 5 for 66 in the Third Test. Mayhem by the Australian spinners continued in the Fourth Test at Johannesburg, where the spinners' bag reached 15 wickets. Victory by an innings and six runs followed in the Fifth Test at Durban. Australia's 4–0 success in the Tests was matched in games against the provinces and on the entire tour Australia won 13 of their 16 matches, ten of these wins by an innings.

Chipperfield scored his first Test century (109) in the First Test, Fingleton made three successive centuries (112, 108, 118) in the last three Tests, and Dudley Nourse scored South Africa's highest Test score, 231 in the Second Test. The batting honours of the tour belonged to Stan McCabe, whose 189 not out in the Second Test ranks among the finest innings ever played. McCabe reached his first 50 in 40 minutes. He hit with such power from then until the end of his innings South African captain Herbie Wade appealed to the umpires against the light, claiming his fieldsmen were in danger in the face of such hitting in poor light.

The spirit Richardson extracted from the Australians meant that each tourist showed fine form and Australia virtually routed the South African line-up that had beaten an England XI only three months earlier in England. Australians scored 21 individual centuries on the tour, with Fingleton heading the averages on 1192 runs at 79.16, after hitting six centuries. Brown was the only other

Bradman and his teammate on the 1930 and 1934 tours of England, Clarrie Grimmett, were keen rivals on the tennis court. (National Library of Australia)

Stan McCabe played three of the classic innings in cricket history, one against Bodyline, one in South Africa and the other at Nottingham. All three were produced in adversity.
(SCG Archives)

Australian to exceed 1000 runs, with 1065 at 62.64. O'Reilly took most wickets, 95 at 13.56, but Grimmett was not far behind with 92 victims at 14.80 each.

The Australians agreed to play an additional match for the benefit of 'Jock' Cameron, who had died just before their tour began, but when planning for this match began Transvaal officials said Australia's cricket supremacy was so pronounced a baseball match might draw a larger crowd and more money for Cameron's widow. The Australians agreed, knowing that Len Darling had represented Australia at baseball, Ben Barnett had played second base for Victoria and Ernie McCormick had a big reputation as a first base. Leo O'Brien pitched regularly in Victorian first-grade baseball and Vic Richardson had represented South Australia at baseball.

The Wanderers' Baseball Club supplied gear for the Australians, including manager Harold Rowe, and all 15 took their places in the dugout wearing Wanderers' uniforms and cricket boots. With Australia six runs ahead at 11–5 in the last innings, McCabe took a catch in the outfield and forgot the game was baseball and tossed the ball in the air and kept tossing it. Two runners got home before shouts from team-mates to throw the ball to the catcher reached him. Trailing 7–11, Transvaal had two men on bases when one of their batters made a long soaring hit into the outfield. Grimmett staggered back into the path of the ball, raised one hand, then the other, and eventually caught the ball – in his bare hand instead of the one wearing the mitt – to end the match in Australia's favour.

The Australians completed their tour of South Africa – 'happiest tour I was ever on' said O'Reilly – while Bradman proved his return to fitness back home and a team of colourful Australian veterans toured India. This was the side captained by Jack Ryder, organised by Frank Tarrant, and sponsored by the Maharajah of Patiala, that began life with an invitation to the Australian Board of Control from the Indian Cricket Board to send a team. All expenses were guaranteed but the Australian Board at first rejected the idea because of the clash with the South African tour. There was a big public outcry at this as most of the players the Indians wanted to see were veterans with little hope of playing any further Test cricket.

Melbourne *Truth* said the Australian Board's action in refusing to send a second-string team of deserving players without a penny cost to Australia disgusted all followers of the game. The Board relented under criticism and gave permission for the tour, which proceeded after the fabulously rich Maharajah of Patiala recovered from a serious illness in Paris with thousands of his subjects praying for his recovery. The Australian team comprised J. Ryder (Captain), C.G. Macartney, H.H. Alexander, A.H. Allsopp, O.W. Bill, F.J. Bryant, J.L. Ellis, H.S.T.L. Hendry, H. Ironmonger, T.W. Leather, H.S. Love, F. Mair, R.O.G. Morrisby, L.E. Nagel and R.K. Oxenham. The Australian Board denied Jack Nitschke and Hugh Chilvers places on the Indian tour on the grounds that they might be needed as substitutes for players injured on the official tour of South Africa. Author Ray Robinson called this a petty move and said that in denying Chilvers his sole chance of an overseas trip the Board had shown a shabby spirit.

The Indian tour began in late October 1935, and lasted through 23 matches until the middle of February. The Australians were a highly talented bunch with a distinguished past but eventually the tiring effects of the extreme heat, constant travelling and stomach problems wore them down. They had 11 victories but three of the last seven matches were lost.

There were four representative matches. Australia won the first by nine wickets and the second by eight wickets, but the third brought their first defeat, by 68 runs, and a close struggle in the other big match ended with India winning by 33 runs. The major disaster of the tour was at Secunderabad where Australia lost by an innings and 115 runs, the most emphatic win India had ever had over a visiting overseas team.

Manager Frank Tarrant demonstrated that he was still able to bowl the accurate left-arm spinners that he had first shown the Indians in 1911. When illness affected the team, Tarrant brought in the former Victorian player Frank Warne, who had just qualified for Worcestershire, to make up the Australian side. Ryder proved the highest scoring batsman of the tour, with 1121 runs at 48.74, but the 20-year-old Tasmanian Ron Morrisby was not far behind with 958 runs at 36.85. Ron Oxenham was the best of the Australian bowlers with 101 wickets at 8.19 each. Entire harems watched the matches from colourful tents draped in mosquito nets.

Allsopp, after missing two English tours for which critics said he was a certain selection (1930 and 1934), spent 11 weeks in an Indian hospital and was left with damaged eyesight and stomach ulcers.

The tour was the last hurrah for Frank Tarrant, regarded by many as the outstanding all-rounder of his generation. Tarrant made more than 1000 runs in an English season nine times and achieved the

A.B.C. CERTIFICATE 100,902 DAILY

The Telegraph

NEW NEWS

CITY FORECAST: Mostly Fine With Cloud

LATE CITY EDITION

LIGHTEN THE PEOPLE'S BURDENS !

HOTEL SYDNEY
for
Silver Grills
and
Barbecue Chickens

Vol. 5.—No. 139

SYDNEY, SATURDAY, JULY 27, 1935

Registered at the General Post Office, Sydney for Transmission by Post as a Newspaper

PRICE, 1½d

RUPTURE SUFFERERS

CRICKET BAN AN AFFRONT TO INDIA

Government May Be Asked To Step In

TRADE REACTION IS FEARED

Representations may be made to the Commonwealth Government over the decision of the Cricket Board of Control to prevent seven Australian cricketers joining Mr. Frank Tarrant's team for India.

On two previous occasions—once over the "body-

R. K. Oxenham, the only one of the eight cricketers refused permission to tour India, who appears to have any prospect of defeating the ban, and (right), the Maharajah of Patiala, who invited the team.

Turf Chairman Would Gaol Shop-Bettors

CITY 'GAMBLING DENS'

Taxes And Radio Resented

BRISBANE, Friday. — Imprisonment of starting-price bettors and increased police powers for

The Australian Board of Control's decision to refuse permission for seven players to tour India in 1935 while the Test team was in South Africa attracted this front page spread in the Sydney Telegraph. The Board claimed some of the seven might be required as replacements if any of the South African tourists were hurt. (Jack Pollard Collection)

double eight times by also taking 100 wickets. He made 33 centuries and four double centuries and took 1506 wickets at 17.52 in first-class matches. He held 304 catches and took five wickets in an innings an amazing 133 times. He retained his Australian citizenship while living in London but never played in a Test. Tarrant had to persuade the Maharajah of Patiala to lodge £4500 in an Australian bank, to ensure the Australians got home – a belittling condition for one of the world's richest men.

Bradman entered an absorbing phase of his career in the 1936–37 Australian summer. He took over the South Australian captaincy against strong opposition from fans and officials loyal to Vic Richardson, who had done such a fine job in South Africa with the Australian team. The Australian Board of Control, however, was dominated by businessmen and clearly wanted Bradman as Australia's captain, for they were well aware of his powers in drawing extra fans through the turnstiles.

Bradman's absence from the New South Wales team had hit that state hard financially, leaving the NSWCA treasurer puzzled over why stronger efforts had not been made to retain him. Bradman had not captained New South Wales, and had only brief experience in the job with the St George and North Sydney clubs. On tour in England in 1934, he had received grounding in Australian cricket's

Very little escaped these keen cricket fans at the front of the Sydney Hill in the late 1930s. Even the uncomfortable wooden benches failed to distract their attention from what happened out on the pitch.
(Jack Pollard Collection)

toughest job when he deputised for Woodfull in six matches.

The South Australian Cricket Association knew the Board of Control would not look beyond the state captains in picking a Test captain for the matches with England in 1936–37. But they upset a lot of supporters by appointing Bradman in preference to the long-serving Richardson, who was 41. This anger did not last very long because Bradman's presence immediately attracted improved crowds to Adelaide Oval. As many writers have pointed out, he was a unique captain because he could rely on his own score and even if his team-mates did not score a run, his side's total would still be competitive.

The MCC recognised that a captain of exceptional tact was necessary for England's 1936–37 Australian tour if the damage of the Bodyline fiasco was to be repaired. They selected George Oswald Browning ('Gubby') Allen for the job. The endless post-mortems had disclosed that Allen had refused to co-operate with Jardine by bowling to packed legside fields. Allen gave Phillip Derriman this account of his confrontation with Jardine during the Bodyline tour:

Douglas came to me in the dressing-room and told me he wanted me to bowl a few bouncers and have a stronger legside field. I said, 'No, Douglas, I never bowl like that and I don't think it's the way the game should be played.' When he insisted, I said he should make up his mind if he wanted me to play or not.

305

Bradman's first Test as captain saw him with a team that included several bald heads (L to R): back, A.G. Chipperfield, E.L. McCormick, M.W. Sievers, W.J. O'Reilly, F.A. Ward; front, R.H. Robinson, L.P. O'Brien, S.J. McCabe, D.G. Bradman, J.H. Fingleton, W.A. Oldfield, at Brisbane, 1936, v. England. (National Library of Australia)

Allen took over the English captaincy for the series against India in 1936 and acquitted himself well enough to win the job ahead of Bob Wyatt.

The major surprises in the tourists' team were the inclusion of Bill Voce, whose Bodyline activities should have disqualified him from selection, and the omission of Eddie Paynter, who had performed heroically on the Bodyline tour. It later emerged that MCC had accepted Voce's apology for bowling an excessive quota of bouncers against the 1934 Australians in their match against Nottinghamshire. Allen's twenty-third English team to Australia was: G.O.B. Allen, R.W.V. Robins, R.E.S. Wyatt, K. Farnes, W.R. Hammond, H. Verity, M. Leyland, L.E.G. Ames, W. Voce, C.J. Barnett, J. Hardstaff, T.S. Worthington, W.H. Copson, J.M. Sims, A.E. Fagg, L.B. Fishlock and G. Duckworth, with R. Howard as manager.

Before the first Test the Queensland Cricket Association refused Stan McCabe's wife a ticket in the main stand. 'We told Bradman he would have difficulty finding a quorum to join him in the middle if the ticket was not provided,' said O'Reilly. 'The QCA quickly changed its mind.'

After the customary spin round the states, England went into the First Test at Brisbane, from 4 to 9 December 1936, in indifferent

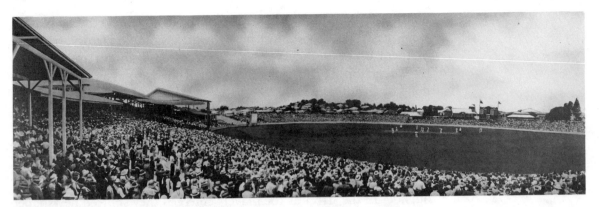

form, but they lifted their standards. McCormick – after dismissing Worthington with the first ball of the match – had to retire with lumbago. Leyland put on 99 with Barnett and went on to a fine 126. Fingleton scored his fourth successive Test century, but was out first ball of the next innings. With McCormick unable to bat, Australia were caught on a soaked pitch and were out for 58 in their second innings, their lowest total at home this century. England pressed home their advantage in the Second Test in Sydney when Hammond made 231 not out and set up victory by an innings and 22 runs, and a 2–0 lead.

Vast crowds continued to turn up for international matches when 'Gubby' Allen brought a 'peace-making' English team to Australia in 1936–37. This was the scene for the First Test in Brisbane. (QCA Archives)

Although the tour playing conditions had seen Australia twice caught on sticky wickets, the successive defeats touched off snide rumours about the players' late-night parties and fondness for the bottle. Even when Australia won the Third Test in Melbourne before crowds that broke all known attendance records the rumours persisted. Australia won by a massive 365 runs after a record six-wicket stand of 346 by Fingleton and Bradman, who batted for 7 hours 38 minutes and scored 270 in his longest Test innings. The aggregate attendance of 350,534 for this match remains the Australian record. Takings were £30,124, with a crowd of 87,798 attending on the third day.

At the end of the match messages were circulated in the Australian dressing-room instructing several players to immediately proceed to the Australian Board of Control rooms nearby. Five players, O'Reilly, McCabe, Darling, O'Brien and Fleetwood-Smith – all of them Catholics – were welcomed by the Board chairman Dr Allan Robertson and other Board members: Aubrey Oxlade, Roger Hartigan and Harry Hodgetts, Bradman's employer.

Dr Robertson read from two foolscap pages a turgid lesson about cricketers who drank too much, neglected physical fitness, kept late hours and did not give their captain their full support. The players were mystified, having just brought off a notable victory, and one of them asked if they were being accused of any of the offences Dr Robertson had just described. Dr Robertson assured them that none of them were being charged.

'In that case this is all tiggy-touchwood and we may as well leave,' said O'Reilly. Cigarettes were handed round and the meeting broke up with the Board members asking the players not to talk to the press about this meeting. One of the players told the Board members the press corps had followed them from the ground and were waiting outside. In the street as the players emerged they spotted newspaper posters that read: 'Board Carpets Five Test Men'.

The purpose of this bizarre interlude has never been disclosed, nor has the name of the instigator. McCabe asked Bradman who was responsible and Bradman said he knew nothing about it. Later Bradman was told the Board did not consult him because it did not want to embarrass him.

Australia went on to a handsome series triumph by winning the Fourth Test in Adelaide by 148 runs, thanks to a ten-wicket coup by Fleetwood-Smith and 212 by Bradman, and an innings and 200-run victory in the Fifth Test at Melbourne. Fleetwood-Smith produced an unplayable delivery to clean-bowl Hammond in Adelaide that made good Hanson Carter's forecast that he would one day win a Test for Australia. The Fifth Test produced the unusual spectacle of two cricketers developed in Tasmania playing for Australia, Badcock and fast bowler Laurie Nash.

The five Tests drew 943,513 spectators, a record attendance until the 1994–95 Ashes series. In his first series as Australia's captain Bradman made 810 runs at an average of 90.0, the best by any captain in a Test rubber. O'Reilly was Australia's leading wicket-taker, with 25 Test victims at 22.20 each.

The Australian Board of Control chairman Dr Robertson summed up the series: 'I doubt if England will ever again produce a team to make an even go with Australian cricketers. In my lifetime they are not going to produce a team to beat us.' It did not take long for Dr Robertson to regret his words bitterly.

CHAPTER TWENTY
BALD HEADS NO GUIDE

Bert Oldfield was typical of the Test cricketers who appeared between the wars, dapper, undemonstrative, immaculately attired on and off the field. He was a wicket-keeper who never fell down or somersaulted but did everything neatly and stylishly, served as a vestryman at St Andrew's Cathedral in Sydney, and attended reunions of the soldiers who had been with him when he was buried in a trench in Polygon Wood during a German bombardment of France in 1917.

Oldfield adhered to the high ethics of cricket in 169 first-class matches, diligently rehearsed his skills, and never appealed unless a batsman was out. Once in a Test match the umpire rejected English 'keeper Bert Strudwick's appeal for a caught behind, but Oldfield walked off because he knew he had hit the ball. Jack Hobbs did the same when Oldfield appealed, although he was unsure if he was out.

After appearing in his fifty-eighth Test against 'Gubby' Allen's English team in 1936–37, Oldfield played one further season of first-class cricket, appearing for New South Wales against Queensland, Victoria and South Australia as he had done since the First World War, graceful, quietly spoken and lacking any flamboyance.

Victoria won the Sheffield Shield in 1936–37, their third success in four seasons and their sixteenth win overall, by avoiding defeat. Keith Rigg, their leading run-getter with 593 runs at 65.88, hit a century in each match against New South Wales, whose stars – McCabe, Fingleton, O'Reilly and Oldfield – were absent on Test duty.

At the end of that southern summer the first Australian women's team toured England under the leadership of Margaret Peden, one of the organisers of the initial England–Australia series in 1934–35. The Australians lost only one match, the Second Test. They won the First Test and drew the Third, leaving honours even. The captaincy of Peden and her English rival Betty Archdale helped establish amicable relations between the countries and assured the future of international women's cricket.

In 1937–38 there were some marvellous performances in the Sheffield Shield competition, which New South Wales won for the first time in five years thanks mainly to the bowling of O'Reilly, who took 33 wickets at only 14.06 runs each. He was strongly supported by Fingleton, who made 494 runs at 54.88, McCabe, who hit two centuries, and Sid Barnes, whose 492 runs at 44.72 were achieved in a highly entertaining style. Barnes at that stage of his career played every stroke known to cricket, including lofted hooks, all the cuts and occasional drives over fieldsmen's heads.

By then Clarrie Grimmett had become a magnificent spin bowler. Although he was in his late forties, he practised every day on his backyard pitch or at the Adelaide Oval. He trained a fox terrier to help him at home, a dog who knew he should not start retrieving until Clarrie had bowled eight balls.

The pleasure of deceiving never left him and as his total of dismissals for South Australia climbed past 500 he kept learning. One day he was coaching at St Peter's College, Adelaide, when a little boy approached him and said: 'I know when you're going to bowl your bosey, Mr Grimmett.' Grimmett could scarcely believe it and asked the lad to make good his boast. 'Well, you start with the ball behind your back – but for other balls you hold the ball by your side.' From then on Grimmett held the ball behind his back at the start of every delivery and developed a longer arm swing that allowed him to hold back all types of deliveries at will.

One of Grimmett's most dangerous deliveries was the flipper, a googly with top-spin, which he let go from the back of his hand. Even batsmen who picked the googly (or bosey) often were beaten by the extra pace the flipper made off the pitch. Grimmett's fingers clicked as the flipper left his right hand, and when he discovered batsmen were detecting it from the clicking noise, he taught himself to click the fingers of his left hand to hoodwink batsmen into thinking they were getting the flipper.

Only three Australian right-hand spinners have bowled the flipper effectively: Grimmett, who taught it to Bruce Dooland, and Richie

Benaud, who learned it from Dooland. George Tribe bowled the left-hander's version of the flipper. Significantly, all four were bowlers who enjoyed long sessions in the nets rehearsing their skills.

Grimmett and Oldfield had amazing powers of observation and shared information about batsmen as well as their love of tea drinking. Grimmett started bowling with his cap on when he heard selectors discussing his advancing age and his bald head. When he bowled Tommy Andrews with a ball that turned sharply, he noticed Andrews signalling how far the ball turned to next batsman Alan Kippax. He made sure the following ball did not turn at all and uprooted Kippax's stumps with a top-spinner. But the consistency with which he confused great batsmen did not, as author Robertson-Glasgow said, prevent Grimmett using his Groucho Marx walk to his place at cover point when the overs ended.

'You could not say that Grimmett was old or young,' Robertson-Glasgow wrote. 'He and the calendar never reached any proper understanding. Just as Mr Pickwick was obviously born in tights and gaiters, so Grimmett surely began in a large-peaked dark green cap with ripe views on the status of the top-spinner.'

Both Oldfield and Grimmett were omitted when the nineteenth Australian team to tour England in 1938 was announced by selectors Bradman, Bill Johnson (Vic.) and 'Chappie' Dwyer (NSW). The team was: D.G. Bradman (Captain), W.A. Brown, A.L. Hassett, S.G. Barnes, C.L. Badcock, J.H.W. Fingleton, S.J. McCabe, B.A. Barnett, A.G. Chipperfield, M.G. Waite, C.W. Walker, E.C.S. White, F.A. Ward, W.J. O'Reilly, L.O'B. Fleetwood-Smith and E.L. McCormick.

Oldfield immediately retired, with 661 dismissals to his credit from 399 catches and 262 stumpings, and six first-class centuries. His 130 Test dismissals from 78 catches and 52 stumpings was a record that endured for half a century. Grimmett elected to continue in Shield cricket for South Australia at the age of 46. The most surprised people over his omission from the English tour were the 30 batsmen he had dismissed that summer, who just could not believe Frank Ward, a spinner who often faltered under pressure, had been given Grimmett's place in the touring team.

Oldfield's retirement left cricket buffs in the southern states arguing over the merits of Charlie Walker and Ben Barnett as the next Australian Test 'keeper. This angered Queenlanders who believed they had a candidate superior to both Walker and Barnett in Don Tallon, who had received a lot of coaching from Oldfield

The formidable spin bowling twosome that took Australia to many victories in the 1930s: top, Bill O'Reilly, balding but shunning a cap, and Clarrie Grimmett, who preferred a cap to keep selectors' thoughts off his age. (Jack Pollard Collection)

and had the same stylish footwork and effective glove work. Bradman later admitted that at the time the 1938 team was picked he did not appreciate Tallon's true ability.

Grimmett had not helped his tour prospects by openly condemning the selectors who dropped him from the 1936–37 series against England. He was very cranky about that and he bowled in the nets against Bradman as if his life depended on it. 'Grimmett's omission was the most biased, ill-considered piece of selection known to Australian cricket and made my own tour of England a litany of frustration,' Grimmett's mate O'Reilly wrote later.

The two big improvers in the Australian team were Arthur Lindsay Hassett and Sidney George Barnes, right-hand batsmen on whom much of Australia's Test future depended. Hassett and Barnes were both versatile all-round games players, quick-footed, nimble-witted and superb fieldsmen in any position. Barnes was a splendid wicket-keeper, Hassett had a fine throwing arm. Both had a highly developed sense of fun that led them to some famous pranks but their backgrounds and temperaments were completely different.

Barnes was born into a family that bred sheep in the Charters Towers district of north-western Queensland. His father died just before Sid was born in 1916, and, unable to care for her family in the outback, Sid's mother brought her brood to Sydney. Young Sid became an urchin accustomed to back-lane brawls and bare-footed schoolmates, among the slum kids of Stanmore. He was a smart-aleck with no instinct for mateship, who left a trail of misdeeds at every cricket club he ever joined.

A youthful Lindsay Hassett going out to bat on the 1938 tour of England, the first of his four tours there. (Daily Mail, London)

Hassett was born in 1913, one of six sons of a Geelong real estate agent. Barnes learned his cricket in back streets, Hassett learned on the playing fields of Geelong College, where he was captain of cricket and football. Hassett was the Victorian Public Schools tennis champion in 1931, a top-grade squash player, and in five years at the College scored 2191 runs in 41 innings, with five centuries. His brother Harry was an inter-state tennis player and his brother Dick played cricket for Victoria as a googly bowler. Hassett had a strong belief in mateship and although he mixed in the highest social circles was never desperate to make money. Barnes could not get enough of the stuff.

Not long before the 1938 team left for England, a lean 18-year-old from Sunshine, Victoria, named Keith Ross Miller, made 181 against Tasmania in his first-class debut. Shortly afterwards

*The Australian team sight-
seeing at Pompeii on their
way to England in 1938.*
(Sydney Morning Herald)

he appeared for Victoria against South Australia in Adelaide and
found Grimmett impossible to 'read'. Miller gave up all attempts
to pick Grimmett's breaks from his hand and simply played off-
breaks when the ball pitched outside the off stump and legbreaks
when it landed outside the leg peg.

Bradman warmed-up for the English tour by scoring 983 runs,
with four centuries, in Sheffield Shield matches, and in all first-
class games passed 1000 runs for the ninth time in nine playing
seasons. He scored 246 and 39 not out against Queensland and in
the return match hit 107 and 113. At Sydney he took over as wicket-
keeper when Charlie Walker broke a finger against New South
Wales, and was responsible for three of the four dismissals that
occurred while he wore the gloves.

The composition of the 1938 Australian team to England
overlooked four impressive Sydney cricketers, J.G. ('Ginty') Lush,
Harold Mudge, Vic Jackson, who had done well for New South
Wales, and Jack Walsh. Lush was particularly frustrated as he had
taken 6 for 43 and 7 for 72 against England in 1936–37 in a display
that led to a New South Wales victory. His 13 wickets included
a spell of three wickets in four balls. Nine days later the selectors
preferred Tasmanian football hero Laurie Nash, who never played

L. O'B. Fleetwood-Smith, who was given to making bird calls on the field. (Age, Melbourne)

Champion footballer Laurie Nash, who won a place in the Australian Test team without ever appearing in Sheffield Shield matches. (Herald, Melbourne)

Shield cricket, for the Fifth Test. Nash had taken 4 for 18 against South Africa back in 1931–32.

Frustrated by their omission from the Australian team all four accepted offers to join Sir Julien Cahn's team in Nottingham. Lush, who had received £1 a day for Shield appearances, went off to England on £600 a year, with all expenses paid. Sir Julien Cahn's XI, drawn from all the cricket-playing nations, played midweek and weekend matches on Sir Julien's private ground. Sir Julien, who had become a multi-millionaire through furniture retailing, captained his side occasionally, wearing pneumatic pads pumped up by his chauffeur. He had his mascot, a wooden fox with an adjustable tail, fastened into the ground in front of the pavilion. When things went badly for Sir Julien's side he had the fox's tail lowered.

On the voyage to England with the 1938 team, Sid Barnes fell on the wet deck when the ship was in Gibraltar. Ships' doctors said his wrist was sprained but when the team arrived in London X-rays showed it was broken. With Barnes unable to play for three months, Bradman asked manager Bill Jeanes to cable the Australian Board of Control for a replacement. He expected either Keith Rigg or Ross Gregory, who had made such an outstanding international debut against England in 1936–37, to join them. To their amazement, the Board refused to send an extra player, a decision that threw additional strain on a team that had more than the usual share of illness and injuries.

Bradman began the tour with his customary double century against Worcestershire at Worcester and his 258 included 33 fours. This was the third time he had started an English tour in this way. Fast bowler Ernie McCormick, reputed to be the fastest bowler Australia had ever sent to England, was not as fortunate. The portly umpire Herbert Baldwin, a former Surrey leg-spinner, no-balled McCormick 17 times in his first two overs. After his first over went to 14 balls and the second to 15, Bradman asked Baldwin if McCormick was 'dragging'. Baldwin replied that McCormick was jumping at least a yard over the line in his delivery stride.

McCormick tried an approach run of 30 yards, cut it down to a few strides, moved his markers about, but still overstepped the crease 19 times in his first three overs. At one stage he tried to solve his problems by bursting down his approach run towards the crowd. 'Shut the gate or he'll be out in the road,' a voice cried. Amid all his adjustments, McCormick lifted one ball high enough to tempt opener Charles Bull to try and hook. The ball flew from the edge of the bat into Bull's face and he retired with one eye completely shut. Despite McCormick's contribution of 35 no-balls, Worcestershire were defeated by an innings and 77 runs, Fleetwood-Smith taking 8 for 98 and 3 for 38.

For the rest of the tour McCormick tried to solve the problems with his approach run, studying slow-motion films, spreading markers out at various stages, and accepting his ordeal in good spirit. 'I'll be right after lunch – the umpire's hoarse,' he said during one match. But he achieved a century of no-balls by the tenth match, including 50 in his first 48 overs. With plenty of time to swing the bat under the old front-foot rule, batsmen scored from 49 of his 100 no-balls.

Bradman risked McCormick in only 17 of the team's 36 matches. Apart from two displays at Lord's, where he took 6 for 58 against Middlesex and broke through the early English batting in both innings of the Test match, he accomplished little that was valuable. He apologised to officials for giving them so much trouble. Playing golf in Ireland, he called to his caddie to ask if he had found a ball lost in long grass and when the caddie indicated the ball had been found, McCormick said: 'Well now you can come and find me.'

McCormick's failure attracted more headlines, but the bowling of Ted White, Fleetwood-Smith and Ward also fell far below expectations, leaving O'Reilly with an enormous burden. O'Reilly sent down 709.4 overs on the tour, compared with 335 by McCormick, 375 from White, 555 from Fleetwood-Smith and 526 from Ward. He was the only bowler to take more than 100 wickets, his 104 victims costing a praiseworthy 16.59 apiece. Chipperfield's tour was ruined by appendicitis and a badly injured finger, and he bowled only 54 overs when normally he would have been expected to have taken some of the work from O'Reilly.

Comparison of the form of the wicket-keepers Barnett and Walker became impossible when Walker twice injured his left hand and was able to play in only nine matches. Barnes could not play until the end of June but on the last few weeks of the tour proved a worthy Australian team representative, batting with confidence rare in newcomers to England, defending stoutly, and showing an eagerness to dispatch bad balls.

The First Test at Nottingham, from 10 to 14 June 1938, saw Barnett and Hassett make their Test debuts for Australia, and Edrich, Reg Sinfield, Doug Wright, Len Hutton and Dennis Compton make their first Test appearances against Australia.

Ernie ('Goldie') McCormick, faster than Lindwall, funnier than Charlie Chaplin, who achieved a century of no balls in ten matches in England in 1938. (MCG Library)

Hammond took over the English captaincy as an amateur although he had played all his previous cricket against Australia as a professional. He was at that time the finest batsman in England and most experts forecast that the duel between Hammond and O'Reilly would decide the Tests.

Hammond, born at Dover in Kent in 1903, had his qualifications to play for Gloucestershire queried by Lord Harris when he entered county cricket in 1920 and could not play in championship matches until 1923. Australians could understand this delay to the start of his career, but found Hammond's adoption of amateur status once he had been paid impossible to comprehend. The change in status may have allowed Hammond to take over the England captaincy – English amateurs would not accept the authority of a professional captain – but in the southern hemisphere at least it was another example of MCC hypocrisy.

The Australians fought hard to protect an Australian Test record on the opening morning at Nottingham when Charlie Barnett gave England an exhilarating start. With the boundaries flowing from Barnett, the Australians realised he might steal a record of which they were proud by scoring a century before lunch on the first day. Only Australians – Trumper, Macartney and Bradman – had achieved the feat, and by chasing every ball to the boundary the Australians frustrated Barnett's attempt to join them, keeping him to 99 not out at the interval. Hutton made 100 in the opening stand with Barnett of 219.

Barnett reached his century from the first ball after lunch and was out for 126 in 175 minutes. O'Reilly removed Edrich and Hammond, but 102 from Compton and 216 from Eddie Paynter saw England reach 8 for 658. Batting on the worn pitch, Australia found Wright's lifting leg-breaks deceptive and at 6 for 194 were in danger of heavy defeat when Stan McCabe produced one of the most spectacular displays of aggressive strokeplay cricket has known. Supported by three left-handed tail-enders, Barnett, O'Reilly and McCormick, he cleverly retained the strike, hooking and driving with devastating power and occasionally moving back to square-cut balls to the fence.

After McCabe reached his century in 140 minutes, fours sped from his bat. Three overs from Wright produced 44 runs and McCabe rushed to his second century in only 84 minutes, the last 50 of it in 24 minutes. Bradman called his team-mates out of the dressing-room to watch. 'Don't miss a ball of this,' he said.

McCabe's timing and shot selection was flawless and his batting was so precisely controlled there was no hint of slogging in it, although he scored 72 of the 77 runs added in 28 minutes for the last wicket. Fleetwood-Smith batted with him in this stand but had so little of the strike there was no chance to improve on his five not out.

Of the last ten overs bowled at the Australians, McCabe managed to take the strike for eight overs, and in that period he hit 16 of his 34 fours, with almost all of England's fieldsmen stationed near the fence. Neville Cardus called it 'moving cricket which swells the heart', one of the greatest innings ever seen anywhere in any period of the game's history. Bradman called it the greatest innings he ever saw or hoped to see. When it ended, with McCabe caught in the covers by Compton, trying to hit Verity out of the ground, McCabe had scored 232 out of the 300 added while he was at the crease.

McCabe was trembling like a thoroughbred racehorse after a classic win when he arrived back in the Australian dressing-room. It was the third majestic innings of his career, comparable with his 187 not out in the First Test of the Bodyline series in 1932–33 at Sydney, and his 189 not out at Johannesburg in the Second Test against South Africa in 1935–36. Australia failed to win any of these matches, despite McCabe's outstanding scores.

McCabe's 232-run contribution at Nottingham took Australia to 411, not enough to avoid the follow-on, and Australia had to bat skilfully on the last day on a worn pitch to save the match. The crowd wanted more of the thrills McCabe had provided and when Brown started the Australian second innings with a subdued, workmanlike stand of 89, spectators hooted his partner Fingleton for stonewalling.

Fingleton responded by removing his batting gloves and sitting on the turf beside the pitch. This only caused the crowd to intensify their booing. Fingleton stayed where he was despite suggestions from umpires Frank Chester and Emett Robinson that he resume. Finally spectators quietened down and he continued batting. There were raucous cheers when he was caught by Hammond off Edrich for 40.

Brown (133) and Bradman (144) batted for most of the day, aware that victory was impossible and Australia's only option was to play for a draw. Bradman annoyed the crowd when he asked Sinfield not to worsen the worn pitch by planting his foot in front of the stumps. Further catcalls followed and Bradman stood clear

King George VI shakes hands with Arthur Chipperfield during the Australians' appearance at Lord's on the 1938 tour.
(Sport & General)

of the crease until the noise subsided. Australia were 6 for 427 when time ran out.

Hammond gave England a fine start in the Second Test at Lord's by scoring 240, including 222 in 182 minutes with Paynter for the fourth wicket. Chasing 494, Australia responded gamely by scoring 422, Brown contributing 206 not out in batting right through the innings. This was Australia's hundredth Test century against England. The match petered out in a draw, with Bradman on 102 not out and Australia 111 short of victory on 6 for 204.

Bradman called his team together after the Lord's Test and told them of his anger over a ruling he had just received from the Australian Board of Control. According to the players' tour contracts their wives were not permitted to join them during the tour. Bradman had asked that his wife Jessie join him in England after the final Test, but the Board said the tour did not end until the team arrived home, and refused his request. Bradman drafted a letter to the Board resigning from all Test cricket, but he was talked out of posting it by the team doctor, Dr Rowley Pope. The Board subsequently relented after receiving a cable from all the other players, and allowed wives to join their husbands after the last match in England.

The Third Test, scheduled for Old Trafford from 8 to 12 July, was abandoned without the captains tossing, a ball being bowled or the captains naming their teams, because of rain. This gave McCormick a week off in which to get his approach run organised but the soft pitch presented for the Fourth Test at Leeds did not suit him. The spin helped O'Reilly and Fleetwood-Smith, however, and they made all the English batting stars fight for runs. England's selectors left out spinner Tom Goddard on a pitch that was ideal for him and relied instead on the pace of Farnes and Bowes.

Bradman and O'Reilly won the match for Australia with admirable displays. O'Reilly took 5 for 66 and 5 for 56, striking vital blows when he bowled Edrich (12), Hammond (76) and Compton (14) in England's first innings and when he sent back Hardstaff and Hammond with successive balls in the second. Bradman's 103 took three hours and was his third Test century in succession at Leeds. Left to score 105 to win in failing light, Australia benefited from England's misfielding, but at 4 for 64 England still had a chance.

Bradman instructed his batsmen not to appeal against the light despite the threatening rainclouds and Hassett, in a gem of an innings, began to drive and pull confidently. He took Australia to within 14 of their target before he was out for 33, and after an interruption for rain when nine were needed, Australia got home by five wickets. Shortly after play ended with Australia retaining the Ashes, rain swamped the ground.

The Australians believed umpire Chester won the game for Australia when he no-balled O'Reilly. This so enraged O'Reilly he bounced up to the crease for the next ball, arms flailing, wrist cocked, face strained in anger, took his characteristic stoop at the moment of delivery by bending his right knee, and knocked back Hardstaff's stumps with a vicious leg-break.

In the final innings O'Reilly walked up and down the Australian dressing-room with his pads on, hoping he would not be needed as they neared the target and the weather closed in. On the other side of the massage table Bradman ate bread and jam to curb his nerves, unable to watch for the first time in his life. Manager Jeanes felt the strain so badly he had to go for a walk outside the ground.

One of the tour's big mysteries was why Badcock continued to fail in Tests while he scored so heavily against county teams. His stroke play was assured and confident, his footwork dazzling in minor matches. At Taunton he made his fourth tour century, 110, during a match-winning stand with Bradman (202) against Somerset but he never did show this brand of skill and confidence in Tests.

McCormick could not play in the Fifth Test because of neuritis but he had done nothing to justify his inclusion in any case, and the Australians had to open their attack with Merv Waite and Stan McCabe. O'Reilly took the first English wicket at 29 when he had Edrich lbw, but the next wicket did not fall until the score reached 411. Hutton gave a remarkable display of concentration and stamina in two and a half days of risk-free batting, although he should have been out at 40. On that score he jumped down the pitch to drive Fleetwood-Smith, missed, and looked back to see Barnett fumble and miss the easy stumping chance.

Hutton continued on, glued to the crease, and taking his runs in deflections, cuts and occasional drives. He was so laborious that when he drove a ball past O'Reilly at the bowler's end O'Reilly called: 'Congratulations – I didn't know you had the strength.' Leyland went for 187 after a 382-run stand with Hutton and six hours' batting.

As a boy of 14, Hutton had watched Bradman hit 334 – the highest individual score in Tests. Now, in his third appearance for England at the age of 22, he left that figure behind by scoring 364 in an innings that extended over 13 hours 20 minutes and included 35 fours, 15 threes, 18 twos and 143 singles. Bradman was the first to congratulate him when he passed Bradman's record England v. Australia score, but as Hutton approached the record Bradman pressured him by pushing fieldsmen in closer to the bat. Hutton completely missed the ball at 331, but went past Bradman's record with a perfect square-cut off Fleetwood-Smith.

Jack Fingleton, left, and Don Bradman running the gauntlet of small boys who waited for hours outside the Australians' hotel just to get a look at some of the 1938 Australian team. (Daily Mail, *London*)

Hutton's 797-minute innings, from half-past eleven on Saturday morning to half-past two on Tuesday afternoon with the Sunday rest day, ended when Hutton lifted a stroke towards cover and Hassett held the catch low down. It was the longest innings ever played in first-class cricket until then. England increased the scoring rate when he was out but kept building on their total, Arthur Wood and Hardstaff sharing a century stand.

Soon after Wood left for 53, Bradman took a spell bowling his leg-spinners, caught his foot in a hole, and fractured the same ankle that had sent him to hospital years before in Rockhampton. He was carried off on the shoulders of team-mates. Bradman's injury influenced Hammond to declare before England reached 1000, on 7 for 903 on the third afternoon. Fingleton was unable to continue because of a pulled muscle and O'Reilly had worn the skin from his finger trying to spin the ball.

O'Reilly's 85 overs had yielded 3 for 178 and included 26 maidens. Infuriated by the practice of doping and over-rolling Test pitches to eliminate every possible imperfection, O'Reilly said: 'Where's the groundsman's hut? If I had a rifle I'd shoot him now.' Fleetwood-Smith had finished with 1 for 298 after bowling 87 overs, the worst analysis in Test history.

321

Bowes dismissed Badcock before a run had been scored when the Australian innings began and McCabe left at 19. Hassett and Barnes batted splendidly, but once they left the batting folded and Australia were all out for 201, Brown narrowly missed batting right through the innings for the second time in the rubber when he was last out for 69. Hutton enlivened proceedings by deliberately kicking a shot from Brown worth a single to the boundary, aiming to give batting bunny Fleetwood-Smith the strike. The umpire gave Brown five for the shot and allowed him to retain the stroke.

Following on the Australians showed they were completely demoralised by surrendering for 123. Ray Robinson later reported that the Australian batsmen were told not to allow the exhausted Australian bowlers to bowl again as the tour still had six matches to run. England's winning margin of an innings and 579 runs remains the biggest in all Test cricket and came just 16 months after the chairman of the Australian Board of Control Dr Robertson predicted that Australia would never lose a match in his lifetime.

Bradman and Fingleton did not bat in either innings for Australia and Verity and Farnes did not get to bat for England. Leyland was the first player to make a century in his first and last Test against Australia. Although Australia batted only nine men in her innings and so robbed England of much of the glory of her win, *Wisden* correctly pointed out that nothing in the condition of the pitch excused the poor resistance of so many Australian Test batsmen.

Apart from the last Test, the nineteenth Australian team to England suffered only one other defeat – by 'Shrimp' Leveson-Gower's side at Scarborough in their last first-class fixture. Sent in for their second innings late on the second afternoon 57 runs behind, Australia opened with Ward and O'Reilly, who refused to run for singles so that each continued to face one bowler. This negative policy, in a traditionally social match marked by big hitting, continued next morning when the Australians were out for 102, their smallest total of the tour. Yorkshiremen Hutton and Sutcliffe scored the 46 needed without being separated, giving Leveson-Gower's XI victory by ten wickets.

The nineteenth Australian team were a high-scoring outfit, which compiled 35 centuries, 13 of them by Bradman, and had 12 scored against them. They retained the Ashes thanks to inspired bowling by O'Reilly at Leeds, but always struggled to get good teams out. They won 20 of their 36 matches, drew 13, lost two and had one abandoned. O'Reilly topped the bowling averages for the second successive tour, which demonstrated the folly of his omission in 1930. Bradman's 2429 runs at 115.66 topped the batting averages, although five other batsmen made more than 1000 runs.

Londoners were rehearsing air-raid drills as the Australians left for home, and the parks were already lined with trenches. Travel agents warned the players against travelling in Europe, and only a few disregarded that advice, moving through cities where people practised gas mask routines and accepted conscription and an all-out war against Hitler as inevitable.

Fresh from his English triumphs, Bradman led South Australia to success in the Sheffield Shield competition with more phenomenal batting, scoring 801 runs in six innings at an average of 160.20. He began with 118 in the Melbourne Cricket Club's centenary match, and followed with 143, 225, 107, 186 and 135 not out, equalling C.B. Fry's feat in 1905 by scoring six successive centuries. Fifteen thousand people turned up at the Adelaide Oval to watch him pass that record with another century but he made only five. Free of Test burdens, Badcock made 271 not out and 100 in consecutive knocks. Grimmett was easily the most effective Shield bowler, with 27 wickets at 20.85.

'Dainty' Ironmonger, Australia's oldest first-class player in the 1930s, shows Bob Menzies and Lindsay Hassett the stub of his left index finger, lost in a childhood accident with a chaff cutter. (MCG Library)

Tallon also showed how badly the 1938 English tour selectors had erred when he equalled two world records. At Sydney v. New South Wales he dismissed six New South Wales batsmen in each innings, his match bag of 12 victims equalling that of Pooley, of Sussex, in 1868. At Brisbane he sent back seven Victorians in an innings for a new Queensland and Australian record.

War began on 3 September 1939, but at the wish of the Federal Government the Australian Board of Control continued the Sheffield Shield competition in 1939–40. Hassett, who had scored 830 runs at 92.22 in the season after his return from England, produced a wonderful double effort in Sydney by scoring 122 in each innings against New South Wales, repeatedly lifting O'Reilly back over his head to the boundary. After one such stroke that was pure vintage Hassett, O'Reilly hollered: 'You little bastard – you wouldn't know the difference between a leg break and a wrong 'un.' Hassett laughed and said: 'With you bowling, Bill, I don't have to.'

Hassett had been blamed for installing a muddied goat in the room O'Reilly shared with McCabe at Grindlefoot in the Derbyshire Peaks during the 1938 tour. O'Reilly towered 22 cm over Hassett but no other batsman could detect his wrong 'un with Hassett's consistency. A Sydney barracker who noticed this used to call, 'Go easy, Bill, or I'll send for Hassett,' when O'Reilly scattered lesser batsmen's stumps.

Despite the punishment he took from Hassett, O'Reilly returned to the 1939–40 Shield competition after a season's rest for a summer of inspired bowling. He took 52 Shield wickets at 13.55, and playing for St George in the Sydney first-grade competition took 86 wickets at 7.74 each. Many of his victims turned up in service uniforms.

The outcome of the Shield competition depended on the New South Wales v. South Australia match in Sydney where Bradman, in superb form, faced O'Reilly. New South Wales won a wonderful match by 237 runs. A newcomer named Mort Cohen helped New South Wales by scoring 74 and 70, which only slightly overshadowed McCabe's 59 and 55, and solid batting right down the order by New South Wales made Grimmett pay heavily for his wickets. He took 6 for 118 and 5 for 111. South Australia lacked batting depth once Bradman and Badcock left. O'Reilly, 6 for 77 and 4 for 62, received grand support from a burly Commando named Cec Pepper, who had 5 for 49, including Bradman's wicket, in South Australia's second innings.

Bradman enlisted initially in the RAAF after a summer in which he scored 1062 Shield runs for eight times out, including 267 v. Victoria. His age, 31, was on the limit for air crew, so he agreed to switch to the Army as a lieutenant to help with their physical fitness training. He had three spells of chronic fibrositis before the Army invalided him out. Rest was the only cure. He went back to Bowral in intense pain, incapable of lifting his right arm. Jessie Bradman had to shave him each day. His Test career appeared over.

The Sheffield Shield competition was suspended in 1940–41 and replaced by ten inter-state matches. At Christmas 1941, a few weeks before his twentieth birthday, Arthur Robert Morris, a left-hander who had been carefully nurtured by the St George club, created a world record by scoring a century in each innings, 148 and 111, in his initial first-class match for New South Wales v. Queensland in Sydney.

State players Ian Johnson, Lindsay Hassett, Ben Barnett, Keith Miller, Ross Gregory and Barrie Scott joined up from Victoria; Cec Pepper, Arthur Morris, Stan Sismey, Bill Hunt, Albert Cheetham, Jim Minter, Ray Lindwall, Bert Oldfield and Jack Pettiford from New South Wales; Ross Stanford, Dick Whitington, Ken and Phil Ridings, Charlie Walker, Graham Williams, Don Bradman and Merv Waite from South Australia; Glen Baker, Frank Sides and Bill Brown from Queensland.

The Melbourne Cricket Ground was taken over by US forces and later by the RAAF, and most capital city cricket venues billeted troops. Sid Barnes was exempted after brief Army service to make chemicals needed for mosquito repellant with golfer Norman von Nida for servicemen in jungle regions!

CHAPTER TWENTY-ONE

ON A VERANDAH
AT LORD'S

Sir Pelham Warner invited Australian Prime Minister John Curtin and Australia's Commander-in-Chief, Field Marshal Sir Thomas Blamey, to Lord's in 1944 to watch a match between the RAAF and a British Services XI. During the match featuring Wally Hammond, Len Hutton, Bill Edrich and Dennis Compton, Warner told his guests how the exuberant cricket played in war-time matches by Keith Carmody, Keith Miller, Stan Sismey, Bob Cristofani and other Australian servicemen had delighted spectators.

Curtin replied: 'You Englishmen will always be able to find plenty of Australians to defend those twenty-two yards of turf out there. Lord's and its traditions belongs just as much to Australia as it does to England, you know.'

Warner believed the Marylebone Cricket Club had made a big mistake in withdrawing the official Test label from matches played by Herbie Collins's Services XI immediately after the First World War. He did not want that error repeated but the Australian Board of Control disagreed. Apart from the splendid cricket played in England by servicemen on leave, Warner knew of excellent matches being played in the Middle East and when he asked if some of the Test stars dotted about the Pacific could be found, Blamey said: 'I dare say we could find some of them for you. Only a few million Japanese to stop us.'

Blamey was intensely loyal to the Army and he determined at once that if there were to be any Victory Tests in England immediately after the war then the teams would include Australian soldiers. He left Warner with the promise that he would do all in his power to get the best Australian Army players like Gunner

Hassett, Captain Albert Cheetham and Sergeant Cecil Pepper to London for the big matches.

The artful Blamey did this by establishing a special unit called the AIF Reception Unit with the particular role of greeting and rehabilitating prisoners-of-war and organising victory ceremonies in Europe. This was how Hassett, Cheetham, Pepper and other noted cricketers found themselves seconded from their wartime units and shipped to Europe aboard the SS *Bloemfontein* as the Pacific war came to an end. Unfortunately, Blamey was not willing to arouse the suspicions of the American supreme commander, General Douglas MacArthur, by including all the famous players in the Pacific, which is why Arthur Morris, Colin McCool and Ray Lindwall were among those who were not in the Reception Unit.

But early in 1945 Hassett and his colleagues found themselves marching down Broadway to New Yorkers' cheering. Shortly afterwards some of them parachuted into German prisoner-of-war camps in Europe to look after the interests of Australian prisoners, but by the time the unit assembled at its headquarters in the Cumberland Hotel, Eastbourne, on England's south coast, they knew their secondary role was to make sure they won as many places in the Victory Test teams as the RAAF.

The RAAF had a big advantage as many of their officers had played regularly in wartime matches at Lord's and other grounds. While Gunner Hassett and his soldier mates were playing in matches in Cairo and other major Army centres in the Middle East, Squadron Leader Carmody and Pilot Officer Miller appeared in matches between missions in southern England. Hassett's AIF side beat a combined South African and New Zealand team at Egypt's El Gezireh Country Club at the same time as Stan Sismey flew missions in Sunderland flying boats in the Mediterranean. By the time Hassett had moved to an anti-aircraft battery in New Guinea, Squadron Leader Ken Ridings had been killed on a Sunderland patrol in the Bay of Biscay.

Carmody had won the respect of all the RAAF players for the enterprising captaincy he had brought to their wartime matches. From his childhood in Bradman's classes, organised by retailer F.J. Palmer to boost sales of 'Don Bradman Cricket Sets', to experience in Mosman Club's first-grade side in Sydney, he had graduated into the New South Wales team in the 1939–40 season as an unusually aggressive opening batsman. He was never afraid to loft the ball, and he used the sweep shot a lot. His fame would endure, however, because of his invention of what became known as the 'Carmody field'. Other captains had used several men in slips but not in the umbrella formation Carmody used to pack his slips area with catchers. Carmody was the big loser in the Board of Control's decision not to give official 'Test' status to the five matches promoted as 'Tests' in Britain.

Hassett arrived in England with the AIF Reception Unit just after Carmody was shot down while attacking four German ships off the Hook of Holland in early 1945. Carmody was scooped from the water by German sailors and sent to several camps for interrogation before being force-marched 250 kilometres to a prison camp near Berlin. Russians freed him when they reached the outskirts of Berlin but held him for weeks of further questioning. Finally he escaped, crossed the River Elbe, and joined the Americans, arriving back in England just as the Australian Services XI was formed.

The RAAF men in the side rated Carmody a hero and considered that he should be captain as he had done the job impressively in the war years. Blamey's staff officers had anticipated an RAAF challenge for Hassett's position as captain but had failed to persuade him to take a higher rank. He had advanced from gunner to lance-bombardier to sergeant and the best he would accept was Warrant Officer II, which his duties with the Reception Unit justified. He refused a commission based on his ability as a cricketer, although Blamey, the AIF staff commander in London Lieutenant-General Ken Smart, Hassett's unit commander Brigadier Eugene Gorman

The Australian Services team at Bombay in 1945. Hassett is in shorts in the middle, with Miller second on his left. (Jack Pollard Collection)

and team-mate Pepper all tried to change his mind.

The RAAF's senior officers in England, including their liaison officer to the War Office, Squadron Leader Rex Rentoul, expressed their annoyance when Hassett was appointed captain of the Services XI for the entire Victory series (the Australian Board of Control had not yet agreed that the series should have Test status). They said Hassett should have the job for the first match only and that the issue should be put to a team vote for the other matches when Carmody would be available.

Hassett remained calm. Forgetting the inter-services friction, he prepared for the Victory 'Tests' by taking service teams to villages near London for one-day matches. His players included John McMahon, a left-arm slow bowler from Balaklava, South Australia, who had served with the AIF in the Middle East before transferring to the RAAF; Cec Pepper, the all-rounder from Forbes, NSW, who had hit seven sixes and eight fours in an innings of 81 for New South Wales v. Queensland in November, 1939; Graham Williams, who had played 17 matches for South Australia and had just returned from teaching blind POWs how to read Braille; Dick Whitington, the Adelaide lawyer who had appeared in 32 matches for South Australia; and Captain Albert Cheetham, the Balmain club all-rounder with 18 matches for New South Wales behind him.

Hassett led his players in some hilarious post-match singing sessions, usually balancing his tiny frame on top of a beer keg while he conducted them through 'Down Came a Blackbird', 'The Desert Song' or 'Champagne Charlie'. Hassett's specialty was his rendition of 'There's a Bridle Hanging on the Wall', which he finished wiping mock tears from his eyes, gazing mournfully at a handkerchief tucked over a clock or pot to represent the bridle. None of the players were paid their daily expenses allowance until they sang a solo.

Keith Miller sensed the Air Force's resentment towards Hassett when he joined the side, but he soon realised Hassett had not sought the captaincy. 'We were all so happy to be alive, we soon forgot it,' said Miller, who not long before had walked away from a Mosquito he had been forced to bellyland when an engine caught fire while returning from a mission over Germany.

None of Hassett's team shared in the gate takings from the Victory 'Tests', which attracted hundreds of thousands of pounds for British charities. Miller received 16s 6d a day as a Flying Officer, Hassett 12s a day as a Warrant Officer. The Mayor of Blackpool called on Hassett for a speech after a match celebrating the end of the war. Hassett looked down from the stand and began: 'Never have I seen so many ugly men at the cricket . . .' And as stray boos arose ' . . . nor so many beautiful women.' He toyed with his audience from then on, their laughter often preventing him from continuing.

Apart from Ken Farnes and Hedley Verity, who both died in the war, England had their pre-war Test team from which to pick their Victory Test teams against Hassett's Services XI. They were so strong England's selectors had difficulty fitting all their Test players into the side and did not bother about flying Dennis Compton home from Burma.

Hassett was the only Test cricketer in the Australian line-up, which included six state players and four who had not progressed beyond grade cricket. While Wally Hammond captained some of the finest players ever to play for England, Hassett led a team of good singers who knew how to approach a beer.

These apparently mismatched teams began the revival of international cricket on 19 May 1945 at Lord's. On the very first day, with England on 4 for 200 and seemingly headed for a big total, Hassett made a major discovery when he gave Keith Miller a bowl. Jogging in from around 12 paces, Miller achieved alarming pace and immediately bowled Edrich. Hassett gave him extra slips and Australia bundled England out for 267.

When the Services XI replied, Miller top-scored with 105, Hassett contributed 77, Stanford 49, Pepper 40, Charles Price 35, and near the end Graham Williams chimed in with 53 to give Services a surprise 188-run lead. England's second innings yielded 294, which left the Services with 107 to win in 70 minutes. Despite two run outs, the Services reached their target right on stumps to win by six wickets, Pepper making certain of the match with a mighty six into the top tier of the grandstand with only a few balls left. Around 17,000 people watched the exciting finish and a further 67,000 paid the one shilling admission, providing the Red Cross with £2000 from the three days' play.

Although he had played an important role in the first 'Test', Flying Officer Ross Stanford insisted on standing down for Squadron Leader Carmody for the Second 'Test' at Bramall Lane, Sheffield, from 23 to 26 June 1945. Pepper bowled splendidly but could not prevent Hammond scoring a match-winning 100, on a ground still showing fire scars from German bombing. Washbrook made 63, Pope 35 and England managed 286.

Carmody's stylish 47 proved the best effort in Australia's first

Two of the biggest hitters in the history of Australian cricket, Cec Pepper, left, and Keith Miller, taking the field for the 1945 Victory 'Test' at Lord's. (SCG Archives)

Hassett and team-mate Cec Pepper in the Bramall Lane dressing-room at Sheffield with Englishman Dick Pollard during the Second Victory 'Test' in 1945. Both teams changed in the same room. (Daily Mirror, London)

innings of 147, which Hammond helped confine with brilliant slips catching. Miller was run out for the second time in three innings. Balding George Pope, who always bowled in a cap, took 5 for 85 for England.

Miller, starting to enjoy his new role as a bowler, sent down one remarkable over as England extended her lead to 330. He rapped Hutton on the left forearm with the first ball and then struck Washbrook a nasty blow on the foot. Washbrook was still limping when a short bumper hit him on the head, and nobody was surprised when he meekly edged the next delivery to Sismey behind the stumps. Australia made a brave start in the chase for victory, with Workman (63) and Whitington (61) putting on 108 for the first wicket, but steady medium-pace bowling by Pope and Pollard brought regular dismissals and England won by 41 runs.

The teams returned to Lord's for the Third 'Test' with the rubber level at one win apiece, and on a good batting strip Bob Cristofani thrilled the audience by taking nine wickets for less than a hundred runs (4 for 43 and 5 for 49). Hutton impressed by scoring 104 and 69, but none of the other English batsmen were comfortable against a Services attack that combined the whirlwind pace of Miller (6 for 87 in the match) and the sharp spin of Pepper and Cristofani. Trailing by 60 on the first innings, the Services bundled England out for 164 in the second and then scored the 225 needed to win for the loss of six wickets.

The Fourth 'Test', also at Lord's, proved memorable for the high standard of batting and because of Jimmy Workman's adventures

Services wicket-keeper Stan Sismey, who frequently left the field to have shrapnel fragments removed from his torso, a legacy of a wartime air battle. (Sismey family)

for the Services XI. Miller (118), Sismey (59) and Pepper (57) helped lift the Australian total to 388. Fishlock (69), Hammond (83) and Washbrook (112) responded with thrilling, lively stroke play that allowed England to declare at 7 for 468, an 80-run lead. Workman had to take over as the Services wicket-keeper when Sismey was hurt but after he had conceded 51 extras Hammond sportingly allowed Carmody to take the gloves. Workman no sooner had been relieved of the 'keeping duties than he dived wide to his right at point and scooped up a wonderful catch to dismiss Hammond.

The match ended in a draw with Australia 4 for 140, just 60 runs ahead. Off the field there was a surprise when Lord's officials expressed their disappointment that the Australian Board of Control had refused to grant the matches full Test status. The Board said the Victory 'Tests' would be accepted as first-class matches but not as full internationals. 'Plum' Warner was particularly annoyed at this because he considered the standard reached in the Victory 'Tests' and the big crowds they attracted merited Test recognition.

The teams finished with two wins apiece when England won the Fifth 'Test' at Old Trafford. England dismissed Australia for 173 and took a 70-run lead with 243 in reply. The 24-year-old Cristofani, after taking 5 for 55 with his brisk, right-arm leg-breaks, lifted Australia's second innings with an outstanding 110 not out. At 8 for 105 the Services XI appeared doomed, but with Williams defending desperately at the other end Cristofani hammered the bowling for 95 minutes, using the square-cut, hook, off-drive and pull shot. The crowd erupted when he hooked Pope for a spectacular six – a carry of over 80 metres – on to the pavilion, and followed with a pull off Wright to reach 101 out of 126 added after Williams joined him. Hammond took the new ball as Cristofani took the score past 200 and W.E. Phillipson quickly sent back Williams and Ellis, leaving Cristofani undefeated on 110. He had hit a six and 13 fours, and batted for 143 minutes, scoring all bar 31 of the 141 added while he was at the crease.

This innings, coupled with his 14 wickets in three 'Tests', brought Cristofani into Test contention, but when he arrived back in Australia he was a consistent failure. St George and New South Wales officials gave him many opportunities but he just could not extract the same spin from hard Australian pitches that he had secured in England, and Australians saw little daring in his batting.

Three days after the Fifth Victory 'Test' Pettiford, Miller, Pepper, Cristofani, Williams and Ellis returned to Lord's to play for The

Dominions, captained by Learie Constantine, the great West Indian all-rounder. New Zealander Martin Donnelly gave The Dominions a fine start with an innings of 133, to which Hammond replied with 121 for England. With only 20 runs separating the teams, Miller then played one of the greatest innings ever seen at Lord's in The Dominions' second innings. Driving commandingly off the front foot, he scored 185 in 165 minutes. All of his seven sixes were dramatic but one, an on-drive off Hollies, set the crowd a-buzz when it lodged in the roof of the broadcasting box above the players' dressing-room. Miller went from his overnight 61 to 185 in 90 minutes, during which he and Constantine put on 117 runs. England required 357 to win in 270 minutes and made a bold bid to get them, but when Hammond was out for his second century of the match (102) the Englishmen finished 45 runs short.

Hassett then took the Services to Scarborough for the traditional match against Leveson-Gower's XI. This time Pepper outshone everyone with an innings of 168 that included six enormous sixes. Miller coasted, with 71, which included three sixes, and Australia scored 506. Pepper took six wickets as the Australians went on to defeat Leveson-Gower's handpicked side by an innings and 108 runs.

Elated by their emergence from such a demanding summer with honours even, the Australians received little recognition for their achievements back in Australia. They were all desperate to get home, some after four years away, but were forced to obey when Field-Marshal Blamey ordered them to play hard matches in India on the way. Blamey was merely reacting to pressure from the Indian government for his cricketers to do for India what they had done for England and get the first-class game re-started.

Hassett's team were surprised by the high standard of their Indian opposition, which Hassett considers has never since been matched. The Indian stars included Vijay Merchant, Vinoo Mankad, Lala Amarnath, Rusi Modi, Gul Mohamed, Madhusudan Rege and Vijay Hazare, all at the peak of their powers. In contrast to the bright, adventurous cricket the Australians had just encountered from a celebrating England, the Indians played dour, risk-free cricket for a defensive captain, Merchant. This, together with the usual sprinkling of frustrating umpires' decision, resulted in an arduous tour.

The first match in front of 30,000 Punjabis at Lahore against North Zone, from 28 to 30 October 1945, involved a rail trip of

44 hours each way from Bombay and 4000 kilometres, on an ancient frontier train whose engine driver constantly blew his whistle to clear beggars, cows and peddlers from the tracks.

Abdul Hafeez made 173, Imtiaz Ahmed 138 not out in North Zone's 410. The Services XI managed 351 in reply, with Pepper 77 and Hassett 71. North Zone were 7 for 103 in their second innings when time ran out. By then more than half the Services team had dysentery and they spent much of the next match, against the Maharajah of Patiala's XI at New Delhi, with an eye on the nearest toilets.

The Services made their highest score of the tour in the first representative match against India at Bombay from 10 to 13 November 1945. Pettiford (124) and Carmody (113) had a second-wicket stand of 177, before Pepper (95) and Workman (76) added valuable runs. India responded to the Services' 531 with 339, not enough to avoid the follow-on. India went ahead with a second innings of 304 but Merchant had little choice but to play for a draw. The second representative match at Calcutta a fortnight later also ended in a draw after centuries by Whitington (155) and Pettiford (101) for the Services and 155 not out from Merchant for India.

After defeating South Zone by six wickets in their only win of the tour, the Australians were outplayed in the third representative match at Madras despite a fine century by Hassett (143) and some exciting hitting by Pepper (87). Modi's brilliant stroke play took him to 203 after Merchant (113) played a long, sound innings that subdued the Services' attack. Leading by 186 on the first innings, India dismissed the Services for 275 and only had to score 89 to win.

By defeating the strong Services side 1–0 in the three-'Test' rubber and conceding them only one win in their ten matches, India proved just as difficult to beat as Hammond's English teams had been. Only in wicket-keeping were the Indians below top standard. Sismey's stylish glovework was a revelation to Indian spectators who were puzzled throughout the tour by his sudden absences from the field. They were unaware that slivers of shrapnel had worked their way to the surface of the skin in his back in their hot climate.

The Services players flew home from Colombo, via the Cocos Islands, in an overloaded RAAF Liberator, sitting on their service kitbags and cricket bags. They were met in Perth by Major Bert Oldfield, who informed them he had been deputed to take them round Australia for matches against each state. They were amazed to learn that Bradman, fully recovered from his fibrositis, would captain South Australia in the second of these matches.

Captain Bert Oldfield, who met the Services team after the final leg of their long tour. (Australian Army Archives)

Miller justified the glowing reports of his powers that had preceded him with a dazzling innings of 80 against Western Australia in Perth over Christmas 1945. Western Australia made 322 to gain a first-innings lead of 21, thanks to a splendid 88 by Doug McKenzie. Williams made 61 of the Services' 301.

The Services team arrived in Adelaide to find that although Bradman's health had recovered, he had suffered a serious setback a few months earlier when his employers, H. W. Hodgetts, collapsed. Bradman was among the creditors Hodgetts could not pay. He had been forced to set himself up as Don Bradman & Co., brokers with a seat on the Adelaide Stock Exchange. The South Australian Cricket Association had elected him to replace Hodgetts as one of their delegates to the Australian Board of Control.

Bradman was 37 and apart from two innings against Queensland (68 and 52 not out), had played so little cricket during the war nobody knew if his health would support regular first-class appearances. The Services rested Miller, but began with an innings of 304, Whitington reaching 77, Pepper 63. Bradman began tentatively when South Australia batted and before he found his timing a top-spinner from Pepper hit him low on the front pad as he played forward.

Pepper and wicket-keeper Sismey were certain the great man was lbw, and when umpire Jack Scott rejected their appeals, Pepper showed his displeasure. 'What do you have to do to get him out?' he shouted at Scott. Bradman went on to 112, and with Reg Craig (141), lifted South Australia to 319. The match petered out to a tame draw, but after play ended umpire Scott lodged a report on Pepper's behaviour with the South Australian Cricket Association, which forwarded it to the Australian Board of Control.

Ian Johnson, the only genuine off-spinner in Australia's immediate post-war teams, spent the war years in the RAAF. He confessed that he 'partied' his way through New Zealand in 1945–46 to celebrate the peace. (Daily Mail, London)

At Melbourne against Victoria only Miller handled Ian Johnson's subtly flighted off-spinners comfortably. Johnson took 10 for 44 (6 for 27 and 4 for 17) to set up Victoria's victory by an innings and 151 runs. This heavy defeat did enormous harm to the Services XI's reputation and made many Australians sceptical about the stories they had read of the players' achievements in England. These doubts were compounded when the Services lost by an innings and eight runs to New South Wales in Sydney.

The Services tour ended with draws against Queensland in Brisbane, where leg-spinner Colin McCool had a match bag of 11 for 174, and against Tasmania in Hobart, where Stanford made 153, his finest knock of the tour, and Malcolm Thomas scored 164, the highest-ever score by a Tasmanian on debut.

The Services team had failed to win a match in Australia and lost the series against India, but they had done a marvellous job by re-establishing first-class cricket so soon after the wars in Europe and the Pacific. Within a few months Hassett and Miller were in action again for Australia in Tests, but none of the other Services players appeared in further international cricket.

Miller's performances for the Services side were compared with those of Jack Gregory for the first AIF team after the First World War. Both were big hitters and match-winning fast bowlers and both went on to distinguished Test careers. Of the other Services players, Cec Pepper proved a sad loss to Australian cricket. Convinced that Jack Scott's report on his Adelaide tantrum would end his hopes of a place in Australian Test teams, Pepper went off to complete his career in the Lancashire League, depriving Australians of a chance to enjoy his massive hitting and classy spin bowling.

Hassett's job in captaining the Services team virtually went unrewarded when Australia sent a team to New Zealand at the end of the 1945–46 season. Hassett got only one vote for the captaincy, which, with Bradman unavailable, went to Bill Brown. The team won all five matches played by wide margins, defeating Auckland, Canterbury, Otago and Wellington, with O'Reilly and Toshack

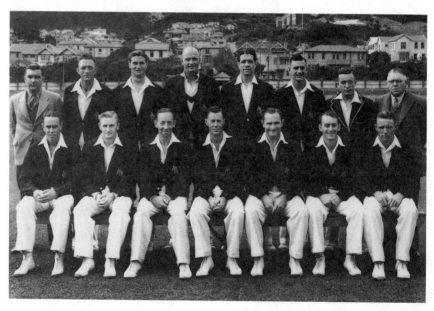

Bill Brown's Australian team that played New Zealand in the first-ever Test between the countries in 1946. Australia won the match, which was not given Test status until 1948, by an innings and 103 runs. (Australian Cricket Board)

both achieving sensational bowling figures and six batsmen compiling centuries.

In the first-ever Test against New Zealand, at Basin Reserve, Wellington, on 29 and 30 March 1946, Australia caught New Zealand twice on a rain-soaked pitch. O'Reilly took 5 for 14 and 3 for 19, Toshack, a deadly accurate left-hand spinner, 4 for 12 and 2 for 6. Australia declared at 8 for 199 despite Cowie's 6 for 40, and won by an innings and 103 runs.

The Australians were paid £1 a day by the Board of Control, but such large crowds attended their matches the New Zealand authorities asked the Board to increase the allowance or pay the 12 players a bonus. The Board refused and the players arrived home out of pocket, with only a blazer to show for their time away from their jobs.

O'Reilly realised when he completed the Test at Wellington that his knee could no longer stand the strain of big cricket. He sat in the Australian dressing-room, slowly removed each boot and then tossed them calmly through an open window. He had taken 774 wickets in first-class cricket at 16.60, and 144 wickets at 22.59 in his 27 Tests, and in his last Test had humbled the New Zealanders so badly the Australian Board of Control denied them another Test for 27 years.

The retirement of O'Reilly, McCabe, Fingleton, Fleetwood-Smith, McCormick, Grimmett, Waite and Oldfield from Australia's pre-war teams and the deaths of Ross Gregory and Charlie Walker on active service left the field wide open to a gifted group of cricketers, ambitions fired by frustrations that the war had cheated them.

Victoria wanted to resume the Sheffield Shield competition in 1945–46, the first summer after the war, but mainly because of New South Wales' opposition the Shield matches did not start again until 1946–47. The season of non-competition matches proved Australia had formidable bowling strength, with players like Miller, Lindwall, Dooland, Toshack, George Tribe, Colin McCool, Fred Freer, Queenslander Len Johnson and the gawky Victorian Bill Johnston taking wickets consistently. The batting did not look anywhere near as strong, with Bill Brown, Lindsay Hassett, Ken Meuleman, Rex Rogers, Ron Hamence and Arthur Morris all outshone by Sid Barnes, who appeared in a class of his own. Clearly, Australia's recovery depended on whether Bradman could continue in Tests. Bradman helped select the team Brown took to New

Zealand, along with Jack Ryder and 'Chappie' Dwyer, but made no forecasts about his own future.

England prepared for her first post-war tour of Australia – and her twenty-fourth overall – with a three-Test series at home against India. After an interval of seven years Test cricket returned to Lord's in June 1946, when England defeated an Indian team captained by the Nawab of Pataudi by ten wickets. Hardstaff batted 315 minutes to set up this victory by scoring 205 not out. This gave the Surrey medium-pacer Alec Bedser scope in his Test debut to take 11 wickets (7 for 49 and 4 for 96). The other two Tests were drawn.

The English team for the Australian tour was W.R. Hammond (Captain), N.W.D. Yardley, P.A. Gibb, A.V. Bedser, D.C.S. Compton, W.J. Edrich, T.G. Evans, L.B. Fishlock, J. Hardstaff, L. Hutton, J.T. Ikin, J. Langridge, R. Pollard, T.P.B. Smith, W. Voce, C. Washbrook and D.V.P. Wright, with Major R. Howard as manager and Bill Ferguson scorer and baggagemaster. Bedser's twin brother Eric travelled with the side, which sailed to Australia in 24 days in the *Stirling Castle*.

Criticism that the team was too old proved correct long before the First Test, with Voce, Hardstaff and Langridge well past their prime and Gibb a fumbling 'keeper who emphasised England's lack of skill in the field.

Matched against the Englishmen was an Australian side that included only three survivors from the team humiliated at The Oval eight years before, Bradman, Hassett and Barnes. The rest were a fit, athletic lot, better for the discipline they had learned in the services. The big question was whether Bradman, who had returned against the advice of doctors at the age of 38, could endure five-day matches. He looked pale and unwell as he went out in the heat of the Woolloongabba ground with Hammond to toss, but from the moment he won that toss everything fell into place for Australia.

Morris was out caught in the slips by Hammond off Bedser with Australia's score on nine. This took Bradman to the crease, and for two or three overs he was so out of touch Barnes had to shield him. Hammond could not believe his luck for it appeared only a matter of time before one of Bradman's snicks or pushes went to hand. At 46, Barnes left and Hassett joined Bradman in what became an historic partnership.

Facing his old rival Bill Voce, Bradman chopped down on a half-volley and the ball flew to Jack Ikin in the gully. The Englishmen

Wally Hammond, who captained the first English team to visit Australia after the Second World War, proved to be past his best, but occasionally produced superb drives such as this.
(Sydney Morning Herald)

believed it was an easy catch but umpire George Borwick and Hassett considered it a bump ball. When Bradman did not depart, the Englishmen made a belated appeal. Borwick ruled not out, but in the press box several English critics took a different view. In the Australian dressing-room Keith Miller, seeing the Englishmen congratulate Ikin, had reached for his bat and gloves and prepared for his Test debut.

Rejection of the English appeal caused little agitation, but when Bradman and Hassett were still together at lunch the visiting English pressmen quizzed their players over the affair. Norman Yardley and Doug Wright, who had been close to Ikin behind the stumps, said they thought Ikin had made a fair catch. After lunch Bradman batted with all his old assurance and added 276 for the third wicket with Hassett, a record for England–Australia Tests. Bradman hit 19 fours on his way to 187 and was not dismissed until the fourth ball of the second day.

Hassett then shared another long stand with Miller before the fourth wicket fell at 428. Hassett scored 128, Miller 79, McCool 95 and Ian Johnson 47, continuing the punishment of the English bowlers until Australia reached 645, their highest score in Australia v. England Tests. Miller bowled Hutton and England ended the third day on 1 for 21.

Back to his best after early fears about his fitness, Bradman takes the field in Sydney against England. He and Barnes each made 234. (Sydney Morning Herald)

Overnight a violent storm gave England a treacherous pitch on which to bat and half the side were out for 56 despite a brave and clever innings by Edrich. A further storm arrived and within half an hour the stumps were afloat, with hailstones as big as golf balls crashing down on the field and stand roof. On the fifth day 15 wickets fell in three and a half hours despite the absence of fast bowler Lindwall, who had chickenpox. Bradman set off a buzz right round the ground when he took Toshack out before play started and showed him where he wanted him to pitch the ball. Toshack took 6 for 82 in England's second innings and finished the match with 9 for 99. Miller took the honours, however, with 9 for 77 (7 for 60 and 2 for 17). Australia's win by an innings and 332 runs was her first in Brisbane over England and her biggest winning margin in Australia, sweet revenge for the humiliation at The Oval in 1938.

Australia's luck held in the Second Test at Sydney when Bradman and Barnes set a world record of 405 runs in 393 minutes. Chasing England's 255, Australia scored 659, Barnes and Bradman both scoring 234. Barnes's innings lasted 642 minutes and many spectators believed he deliberately threw it away when he was on the same score as Bradman. Australia won by an innings and 33 runs.

The Third and Fourth Tests were drawn after further heavy scoring. At Melbourne in the Third Test Lindwall (100) and Tallon (92) added 154 runs in 88 minutes. At Adelaide in the Fourth Test both Morris (122 and 124 not out) and Compton (147 and 103 not out) scored centuries in each innings. Australia took the rubber 3–0 by winning the Fifth Test in Sydney by five wickets after Hutton retired ill for 122 in England's first innings and was unable to take any further part in the match.

Hammond's team had one of the worst records of any English team to visit Australia, winning only four of its 25 matches, with three losses and 18 draws, but they did a splendid job in restoring Test cricket to popularity with Australians who packed grounds for their matches. Hutton (1267 runs at 70.38) and Compton (1432 runs at 65.09) were the best English batsmen and Wright the best bowler (51 wickets at 33.31).

Success of the Australian team had an unfortunate aftermath when some fine cricketers lost hope of making future Test teams and headed for England, including Bill Alley, Jack Pettiford, Ken Grieves, Jock Livingston, Fred Freer, George Tribe, Vic Jackson and Bruce Dooland. Most of them headed for the Lancashire League but some of them ended up in English county teams.

Tribe was a particularly damaging loss as he had taken 33 wickets in helping Victoria win the 1946–47 Sheffield Shield competition and 86 wickets in only 13 first-class matches. He had disappointed in his three Tests against Hammond's team, though, so believed he was not certain of a Test berth.

Victoria won the first Sheffield Shield competition after the Second World War by winning five of their six matches and drawing the other. The batting of Sam Loxton (average 143), Hassett (141.75) and Miller (133.40) provided the foundation for Victoria's success but Tribe's clever bowling also played a major role. Tallon, who had finally gained his Test place, was rated the best 'keeper in the world after the England–Australia series, but Bradman always made sure Tallon practised in the nets with Tribe to ensure Tallon could 'read' Tribe's left-handed googly.

The Board of Control admitted Western Australia to the 1947–48 Sheffield Shield competition on a restricted basis. Western Australia

Ray Lindwall joined Keith Miller as the spearhead of the Australian attack immediately after Test cricket resumed. (Sydney Morning Herald)

played four matches compared with seven by the other states, and the Shield was decided on averages. All the states were committed to send teams to Adelaide and to secure entry into the competition Western Australia had to pay the fares from Adelaide of teams visiting Perth. New South Wales declined to collect the fare subsidy from the WACA for the nine seasons it applied.

The Shield matches were conducted at the same time as an Indian team captained by Lala Amarnath toured Australia. This first official tour by an Indian team was handicapped by the inability of Vijay Merchant and Rusi Modi, who had scored heavily against the Services side two years earlier, to join the tour. Amarnath increased his team's difficulties by refusing an offer from the Australian Board of Control to cover the Test match pitches, apparently reasoning that his bowlers would get more benefit than the Australians from bowling on soaked pitches. Bradman won the toss in four of the five Tests and in two of them India were trapped on wet pitches.

The Indian team was: L. Amarnath, V.S. Hazare, D.G. Phadkar, V. Mankad, G. Kishenchand, H.R. Adhikari, C.T. Sarwate, Gul Mahomed, C.S. Nayudu, M.S. Ranvirsinhji, S.W. Sohoni, J.K. Irani, Amir Elahi, K.M. Rangnekar, P. Sen, Rai Singh and C.R. Rangachari. By sending 17 players for a 14-match tour, India made Amarnath's task in playing all his men into form virtually impossible. Amarnath showed great skill early in the tour with innings of 144, 94 not out and 228 not out, and later hit 172 not out, 171 and 135, but he failed in Tests, scoring only 140 in ten innings. Hazare achieved the individual honours of the tour by scoring a century in each innings (116 and 145) of the Fourth Test.

India won only two of their 14 matches and suffered seven defeats. They were outclassed in the Tests, which Australia won 4–0, and in three Tests Australia only had to bat once. Australia's superiority usually made a win certain by the end of the first day.

One highspot of the tour came when India defeated the strong Australian XI in Sydney. Bradman completed his hundredth first-class century in this match and was involved in a long stand with Miller, who made 86, but India still won the match by 47 runs. The other highlight came from Vinoo Mankad, an all-rounder of the highest class, who made Test history in the Second Test at Sydney by running out Billy Brown where Brown backed up too early and was yards out of his crease before the ball left Mankad's hand. Mankad had previously warned Brown for taking the same liberty when India played the Australian XI and when Brown repeated the offence Mankad ran him out. Mankad gave Brown no warning when he again ran him out in the Test, but ever since the achievement of this kind of dismissal has been referred to as 'a Mankad'.

Toshack did not need Bradman to show him where to pitch the ball when Australia caught India on a vicious sticky wicket in the Brisbane Test. Toshack took 5 for 2 and 6 for 29, to finish with the astonishing match figures of 11 for 31.

Meanwhile Western Australia made a dramatic entry into Sheffield Shield cricket by defeating South Australia in Perth by an innings and 124 runs following a brilliant 198 by captain–coach Keith Carmody. Western Australia followed by beating the previous summer's Shield winners, Victoria, on the first innings. A dazzling 170 in three hours by Miller, who had changed states, ended Western Australia's run in Sydney, where New South Wales won by 98 runs, but they clinched the Shield by beating Queensland in Brisbane by 183 runs.

By then every cricketer in Australia had his mind on the 1948 tour of England, the twentieth by an Australian team, but only the eighth organised by the Australian Board of Control. Australia was at the top of the cricket world, thanks to Bradman's matchless skill, but now in his fortieth year he was to gamble that he could make the tour a memorable farewell.

A star of the immediate postwar period was Petersham's exciting left-hander Bill Alley, who attacked from the first delivery he faced. Alley came from the Hawkesbury River region north of Sydney where he learned to box with famous fighter Vic Patrick. To earn extra money while he played grade cricket Alley had 28 professional bouts, winning them all. He was hailed as a future champion when he was hit in the face by a fierce pull from Jock Livingston at cricket practice. His jaw was so badly smashed he could not fight again.

Forced to concentrate on cricket, Alley played 12 matches for New South Wales, mainly as an opener, but when Arthur Morris returned from army duty selectors gave Morris Alley's spot. This caused Alley's departure for England, where he scored 19,612 runs in 350 matches for Somerset, including 3019 in the 1961 season. He also took 768 first-class wickets. Not bad for a player whose county career did not begin until he was 38, after five seasons in league cricket.

CHAPTER TWENTY-TWO

THE ONLY UNBEATEN TEAM

Don Bradman's 1948 side remains the only Australian team to go through an English tour without defeat. They won all the four Tests completed, won half their 34 matches with an innings to spare, two by ten wickets, one by nine wickets, two by eight wickets, and one by 409 runs, and 11 of their batsmen scored 50 centuries. Seven of their batsmen hit 1000 runs in the five months they were in England. They achieved totals of 350 or more in 24 innings, whereas the highest total scored against them outside of the Tests was Nottinghamshire's 8 for 299. They only failed to reach 200 twice on the entire tour, but managed to dismiss the opposition for less than 200 37 times, and seven times for under 100.

The figures clearly demonstrate the superiority the Australians enjoyed but they do not show the euphoria the team aroused everywhere they travelled. This was an England recovering from a savage war in which food and clothing rationing prevailed, luxuries were short, and steaks a rarity, while many of the grounds the Australians visited still bore traces of wartime bombing raids. Wherever they appeared, flags were hoisted just to celebrate the Australians' presence and that old English tradition, the black tie dinner, had a warmth and bonhomie all later tours lacked.

For a fee of 250 guineas a match the BBC broadcast descriptions of the matches across the world in a hook-up – the first 'live' description – that produced hundreds of all-night parties in Australia and caused power failures in New Zealand. In Britain, people congregated on the platforms of railway stations just to get a glimpse of the Australians when they passed through, and in the streets leading up to the Test grounds vast, snake-like queues six or eight across crammed all available footpath space. For the big matches

Bradman waves his hat to well-wishers who greeted the 1948 Australian team on its arrival in England. Hassett is beside him with Miller's hands on his shoulders, Neil Harvey in front with bat. (Sport & General)

there was always a chance there would be more people locked out than were inside the grounds.

Australia's share of the tour profits, £75,000, more than doubled the Board of Control's previous best cheque from an English tour. The Board paid each of the 17 players in the team £800, £150 of which was kept and handed to each player with a silver cigarette case as a good behaviour bonus when the tour was over.

The team was: D.G. Bradman, A.L. Hassett, A.R. Morris, W.A. Brown, S.G. Barnes, S.J.E. Loxton, R.N. Harvey, K.R. Miller, I.W. Johnson, R.A. Hamence, C.L. McCool, R.R. Lindwall, D. Tallon, R.A. Saggers, D.T.H. Ring, W.A. Johnston and E.R.H. Toshack, with Bill Ferguson as scorer–baggagemaster. The Board of Control's doctors instructed Tallon to have his tonsils removed before the team sailed to England in the *Strathaird*.

The team included only four players who had previously toured England – Bradman, Hassett, Barnes and Brown – although Miller had had valuable experience of English pitches in the Services' matches. Only two of the team, Toshack and Harvey, had not served in the forces, though Barnes's period in uniform had been very brief. The team was chosen to exploit fully the tour condition that a new ball could be taken every 55 overs, which virtually denied spinners a major role in the Tests before a ball was bowled.

From the day they arrived in England manager Keith Johnson had to arrange for each man to undertake daily sessions signing autographs. Bradman had to borrow a secretary from an insurance company to answer fan mail while he was at the cricket and every evening signed letters she had typed that day.

Bradman regarded Ernie Toshack, a tall, swarthy left-hand bush bowler of unusual technique, as a key figure in the team and probably helped Toshack get through his tour medical check-up. Melbourne doctors at first were doubtful that Toshack's knee would stand up to the tour, but a second check on the leg by Sydney doctors passed him as fit to go.

Toshack, known in the team as the 'Black Prince', used a stock left-arm delivery that cut towards a right-hand batsman's legs, but he varied it with finger spin and drifters, and a well-concealed fast one, all delivered over the wicket. Bradman rated him the ideal bowler for English conditions and made a special study of Toshack's fields, usually giving him four men on the off, including a slip, and five men on the legside, but if the pitch was wet he moved in a leg slip and pushed Barnes into short leg.

Barnes was the team's livewire wheeler-dealer, determined to make good the years lost in the war. He filled his cabin with goods in short supply in England that he knew he could sell there at a profit. At the nets he drilled himself to eliminate the shots that were risky and only play high percentage shots that would accumulate runs. Ray Robinson said Barnes sometimes got bricked-up inside his run factory. Everybody who knew the pre-war Barnes regretted the absence of elegant cuts and glances he now judged to be too risky.

Baby of the team was quick-footed Neil Harvey, at 19 the only player under 26, a left-hander impervious to tension, and the fourth son of former coalminer Horace Harvey to play Shield cricket. Neil's brothers, Clarence ('Mick'), Merv and Ray, all won selection in the Victorian team from Melbourne's Fitzroy club.

The team's bowling depended heavily on the charismatic partnership of Raymond Russell Lindwall, ex-Army signalman with a rhythmical approach run who exploded in the delivery stride, and Keith Miller, who had gone to Boston the previous year to bring home an American bride. Batsmen who survived this pair were confronted by a tall, gangling farmer from Ondit in Victoria named Bill Johnston, who swung his left-arm fast-medium deliveries sharply, and when the shine left the ball came on with left-arm spinners. Ian Johnson's looped off-spin, Sam Loxton's medium-pacers, and the leg-spin of Colin McCool and Doug Ring gave Bradman variety he seldom needed to call on.

In the field, they were a magnificent outfit. McCool was widely accepted as the world's finest slips field but was little superior to Miller, who had the knack of making dramatic catches in big matches. Sid Barnes was a remarkably agile short-leg fieldsman who added menace to the bowling of all the pace men but especially to the drifters from Toshack. Harvey was a superlative cover fieldsman and Hassett in the deep was safe and reliable. All the team had powerful throwing arms and every man held his catches. Tallon and his deputy Ron Saggers were fast and proficient stumpers and could hold the most difficult chances without muddying their creams.

Bradman had begun previous tours with a double century against Worcestershire at Worcester, but this time he was content with 107, which with Arthur Morris's 138 was enough to ensure victory by an innings and 17 runs before a record attendance. Miller made 202 not out in the second match against Leicestershire to set up a second-innings victory.

At Bradford in the third match of the tour the Australians came closer to defeat than in any other game. On a wet pitch, Miller lowered his pace to bowl off-breaks and his 6 for 42 had Yorkshire out for 71. Australia struggled to 101 in reply thanks to the

Bradman on his way to a century in the first match of the 1948 tour. He had begun with double centuries on three previous tours. (Ken Kelly)

hostility of Wardle and Smailes on a drying pitch. Johnston (6 for 18) and Miller (3 for 49) then combined to send back Yorkshire for 89, leaving Australia with only 60 to win. They lost six wickets scoring them and only bold hitting by Harvey and Tallon lifted the score from 31 to the target.

That night at the team's hotel Bradman assessed Australia's narrow escape and said: 'That's it, then. Either Sid or I will need to play in every match.' This high valuation of Barnes was endorsed by England's opening bowler Alec Bedser. 'Barnes always had something in reserve,' said Bedser. 'Often you would think you were through his defence only to have him come with a last moment dab or tap that got him out of trouble.'

Barnes and Morris formed such an efficient opening pair, Brown had to be omitted from three Tests although he scored eight centuries and hit 1448 runs at 57.92 on tour. Harvey only got into the Test team when Barnes was injured in the Third Test. McCool, who had taken 18 wickets and scored a century in the previous series against England in 1946–47, did not appear in a Test in 1948.

The Australians won the First Test at Nottingham and the Second at Lord's by wide margins. At Nottingham Bradman (138) scored his twenty-eighth Test century while Hassett (137) made his highest score against England, Australia winning by eight wickets despite Compton's 184. At Lord's Morris (105) and Barnes (141) helped Australia to a 409-run win. Barnes backed himself to get a century at the home of cricket and offered to double his bets about it when he made a duck in the first innings. There were no takers.

Barnes was badly hurt in the Third Test at Old Trafford when he failed to take note of a bowling change and continued to occupy his spot at silly leg two or three metres from the bat. Barnes thought the deadly accurate Toshack was bowling but was flattened when tail-ender Dick Pollard hammered a ball from Ian Johnson into his kidneys. Barnes had to be carried off and that night took some convincing that Johnson and not Toshack had delivered the ball that caused his injury. 'Would have killed an ordinary man,' he said of the hit that flew like a rifle shot into his back. He collapsed next day when he tried to resume batting and took no further part in the match.

Australia's fielding faltered for the only time in this match when the normally reliable Hassett twice dropped Washbrook on the boundary when Washbrook fell for Lindwall's trap and tried to hook fast, rising bouncers. After his second lapse Hassett borrowed

Policemen carrying Sid Barnes from the field after he had been hit in the kidneys fielding close to batsman Dick Pollard in the 1948 Manchester Test. (Associated Press, London)

a helmet from a policeman and held it in an upturned position in front of him, signalling to Lindwall that he was now equipped for such catches. Injuries to Compton, who mishit a ball into his head which required stitching, and to Barnes, intensified a grim struggle that had swung England's way when rain intervened. England at that stage were 316 runs ahead with only three second-innings wickets down, but two days of rain dispelled the possibility of an Australian defeat.

England outplayed Australia for most of the first four days of the Fourth Test at Leeds, but a succession of English blunders and brilliant batting by the Australians turned a wonderful match Australia's way. England had opening partnerships in excess of 100 in both innings and still lost by seven wickets, a result that allowed Australia to retain the Ashes she had held since 1934.

The England selectors erred badly by not including a leg-spinner and when Australia were given 404 to win in 345 minutes on the last day Yardley, the English captain, was forced to try part-time spinners Compton and Hutton. Morris (182) and Bradman (173) slaughtered this inept attack although they were forced to bat in holes worn in the crease by four days of hectic cricket. England's fielding lapses prevented them breaking the Morris–Bradman stand until they had added 301 and by then the match was won. Harvey hit the winning boundary 15 minutes from time. Australia had 66 fours in this amazing run-chase, 33 by Morris and 29 by Bradman.

This was the first time in Test history that a team had scored more than 400 runs in the final innings to achieve victory. The match aggregate of 1723 runs was the highest, with Washbrook (143) and Edrich (111) contributing impressive centuries for the losers, and Harvey reaching 112. Morris's superb batting in his innings of 182 surpassed even his innings against Gloucestershire in which he hit 42 fours on his way to 290, including 100 before lunch.

Australia's discipline in a crisis allowed her to triumph in the Fourth Test although England appeared certain to win several times. With England on 2 for 423 in the opening innings of the match, Australia recovered to have England all out for 496. When Australia batted, Morris, Hassett and Bradman were out with the score on only 68, before Australia fought back with 121 onslaught by Harvey and Miller which Loxton carried on for a further 105 runs. Loxton hit five sixes and nine fours, Harvey 17 fours. With eight wickets down Australia were still 141 runs behind, but the tail-enders made 103 of those to reduce the deficit to only 38. Bill Johnston, acting

The crowd outside the Headingley ground for the England v. Australia Test in 1948. More than 40,000 were inside the ground, an estimated 10,000 waiting in vain outside. (Jack Hickes)

as a runner for the injured Toshack, chose to take up position half-way to the boundary but the hilarious laughter his gawky, bounding strides attracted also helped Lindwall to take his score to 77.

England were on top yet again when their tail backed up fine batting by the top order to take the total to 8 declared for 365. Despite the size of the task they faced to score the 404 runs needed, Bradman told his batsmen to go for the runs from the start, and his confidence that aggression would prevail proved correct.

The Fifth Test at The Oval completed England's humiliation

when Australia had them out for 52 in only 150 minutes batting on the first day. This was England's lowest score in a home Test with Australia and dispelled all theories that England may have been unlucky in the earlier Tests. Lindwall completed England's destruction by taking 6 for 20. Hutton, 30, was the only batsman to reach double figures, in an innings which saw five players fail to score.

Barnes and Morris softened up the English bowling by putting on 117 for the first wicket for Australia and Bradman went to the crease for his last Test innings accompanied by boisterous, emotional applause from the capacity crowd which stood and cheered his every step to the wicket. Yardley shook his hand in congratulations, the English team gave him three cheers and the little man settled over his bat needing just four runs to average more than 100 in his Test career.

The bowler fated to bowl at Bradman was Eric Hollies, the toothy Warwickshire leg-spin and googly bowler, whose father had been a noted lob bowler. Hollies, who in 1946 had taken all ten wickets against Notts at Edgbaston, offered to stand down from the Test when Australia clinched the Ashes because Warwickshire were still in contention for the county championship. Warwickshire officials talked him out of it.

Bradman survived the first ball although he was still deeply touched by the warmth of his reception but he edged the second ball, a googly, on to his stumps just firmly enough to dislodge a bail. His Test career had ended in the cruellest of anti-climaxes. He turned and looked at the undisturbed stumps and walked slowly

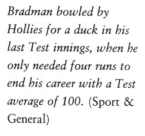

Bradman bowled by Hollies for a duck in his last Test innings, when he only needed four runs to end his career with a Test average of 100. (Sport & General)

from the field before a stunned, silent crowd. Some spectators blamed the tears aroused by the crowd's applause, but Bradman refuted this and praised Hollies, who was good enough to have taken 100 wickets in a season 14 times, for delivering an exceptionally good ball.

Morris stayed at the other end until he made 196, taking Australia to a 337-run lead on the first innings. Batting in appalling light after rain, Hutton (64), Edrich (28) and Compton (39) all found Lindwall hard to pick up in the gloom and after they left the English batting collapsed. Evans clearly did not see the ball that bowled him and after last man Hollies was out with Australia winners by an innings and 149 runs more than 5000 spectators crowded up to the pavilion to give further cheers for Bradman and his team.

Bradman hit 11 centuries on the tour and was the only Australian to score more than 2000 runs. In 31 innings he made 2428 runs at 89.92. He farewelled English cricket by scoring three centuries – 150 v. The Gentlemen at Lord's, 143 v. South of England at Hastings and 153 v. Leveson-Gower's XI at Scarborough – and by bowling the last over of the match at Scarborough.

Bill Johnston was the only Australian bowler to take more than 100 wickets. Watching him from the press box while he captured 102 victims at 16.42 each, Bill O'Reilly said Johnston's weakness was that he never lost his temper. Lindwall finished slightly ahead of Johnston in the bowling averages with 86 wickets at 15.68. Toshack played in only 15 of the 34 matches but did what Bradman wanted of him by taking 11 valuable wickets in his four Tests. Australia's bowling was so good only four batsmen scored centuries against them in a summer of splendid batting conditions.

Johnston the country boy said he could not believe the idolatry by the English of Bradman. Dignitaries queued to shake his hand, hotel managements rolled out red carpets for him, and King George V strolled across the lawns of Balmoral with him. The only unpleasantness on a tour that was as much a celebration as a test of cricket skills was when the Right Honourable Lionel Hallam, the third Baron Tennyson, son of a former Governor-General of Australia, appeared at the Australian dressing-room at Lord's and asked to see Bradman. An attendant advised Bradman not to see Lord Tennyson, who had had a good lunch.

At the end of the Australians' tour when Bradman was knighted Lionel Tennyson said the honour to Bradman belittled knighthoods and claimed Bradman was 'a mannerless little man'. Tennyson's son later apologised to Bradman, who must have considered Tennyson's reaction strange in a man who had inherited his own title from his poet grandfather.

Sid Barnes arrived home with trunks laden with cashmere sweaters, tartan socks and golf shoes, all scarce in Australia, along with rolls of suiting and Harris tweed sports coats, and the latest model cricket bats, pads and batting gloves. He had traded consistently through the seven-month tour to compensate for what he said was the Board of Control's shortfall in player payments. The truth was that like all his team-mates he would have made the tour for nothing had he been compelled to do so.

Barnes's eagerness to extract the latest styles in suiting from Yorkshire mill owners, plus his dealings in autographed bats, upset his normally easy-going room-mate Arthur Morris, who found sleep hard to get with Sid around. 'I remember tradesmen dropping a load of goods into our room,' said Morris. 'Half an hour later another group arrived to carry it away.' Morris finally persuaded Toshack to take his place and move in with Barnes.

During the tour Sid had taken movies of all the Australians' matches, capturing highlights such as the 721 runs they scored in a day against Essex at Southend, and the emotional crowd farewell to Bradman. At Lord's and Balmoral Castle he was careful to ask Lord Gowrie's approval before filming the Royal Family with the Australians. According to Barnes, Lord Gowrie said: 'Go ahead, I'm sure His Majesty would like it.' At Lord's, where film rights had been sold, Barnes ignored an official who tried to prevent him filming.

Barnes called his English tour bonus tram-fare money and scoffed at the 30 shillings a day paid to Sheffield Shield players. He said the £1 a day paid to members of Billy Brown's team for their New Zealand tour was an affront and the tour blazer he received for that trip the worst he had seen. He traded the blazer soon after he arrived home. On the ship going to England for the 1948 tour he paid a small boy to stamp 5000 autographs with a rubber stamp to avoid undertaking the chore himself, and he was the only member of the team whose photograph was omitted from a tobacco company's programme on the tour. The company paid the players £5 each and Barnes wanted £50.

After barnstorming round major cities showing his 1948 tour film to paying audiences, Barnes made himself unavailable for Sheffield Shield matches in the 1948–49 season, arguing that he could not afford it. He played grade cricket regularly but he played in only one first-class match that summer, in the Bradman Testimonial match at Melbourne when he was included in Hassett's XI against Bradman's XI. He scored 32 and 89 in that match, from 3 to 7 December, which raised £10,000 for Bradman, but selectors left him out of the Kippax–Oldfield match from 25 February to 1 March later that summer between teams captained by Hassett and Morris.

Barnes batting with a toy bat in one of his many pranks that displeased the Australian Cricket Board. (Age, Melbourne)

Barnes's omission from this match followed his announcement that he could not go on the tour of South Africa which immediately followed. He said he could not afford to leave his employment for the £450 out-of-pocket expenses the Board of Control paid each touring player. The selectors announced they wanted to use the joint Kippax–Oldfield testimonial match as a trial for would-be tourists and took him at his word and left him out.

Bradman played in his own testimonial match, scoring 123, his one hundred and seventeenth first-class century, and 10. Six weeks later, he appeared in the Sydney match between Hassett's XI and Morris's XI played as a testimonial for A.F. Kippax and W.A. Oldfield. This match raised £3015 for each of the recipients. Bradman appeared for Morris's team and scored 53 before a crowd of 41,575, who gave him a tumultuous welcome. Morris's side won by eight wickets after Jack Moroney had scored 217.

New South Wales took the Shield for the twenty-third time by winning seven matches, four outright, and three on the first innings. This expected triumph was overshadowed by Bradman's decision to make yet another appearance for South Australia in Adelaide, from 4 to 8 March 1949. It was a generous move to help boost the receipts for a match set aside as a benefit for former South Australian all-rounder and Test cricketer, Arthur Richardson.

Bradman played under the captaincy of Phil Ridings and his appearance had the desired effect on the crowd. Bradman scored only 30. He twisted his ankle fielding in Victoria's second innings and could not bat in South Australia's second innings. Bradman's retirement from the match left him with first-class career figures that read:

Innings	Not Outs	Centuries	Runs	Average
338	43	117	28 067	95.14

This meant that Bradman scored a century on average slightly better than every third time he batted, a feat of consistency no other batsman has remotely approached. Over his entire career he maintained a scoring rate of 42 runs an hour. His 452 not out for New South Wales against Queensland in 1929–30 remains the highest first-class innings on turf, and has only been exceeded on matting. He had six innings of more than 300 runs and 37 over 200. He was bowled 78 times (26 per cent of his dismissals), was caught 174 times, hit wicket once, leg-before-wicket 27 times, stumped 11 times and run out four times.

The English county court judge, B.J. Wakley, who devoted an entire book to the statistics of Bradman's career, calculated that 74 of Bradman's first-class centuries were chanceless, and a further 20 were chanceless up to 100, and that Bradman gave his hand away 46 times. He made only 16 ducks, six of them first ball, three second ball, and had only seven ducks in 57 Tests. He was a batsman who always tried to keep the ball down and in his entire career hit only 44 sixes and seven fives, but he hit 2586 fours, which gave him 10,643 of his runs in boundaries.

None of the great bowlers against whom he played can claim to have enjoyed any ascendancy over him. Grimmett dismissed him ten times, but Bradman scored 1709 runs against Grimmett at an average of 62.29. Hedley Verity also got him out ten times, but Bradman managed ten centuries and 2895 runs at an average of 74.23 against Verity. Alec Bedser dismissed him eight times, six of them in succession, but in 19 innings Bradman made 1487 against Bedser, with six centuries, at an average of 92.93. Larwood had Bradman out seven times, but Bradman scored seven centuries and 2009 runs against him at an average of 87.34.

Bradman enjoys an early morning cup of tea with a biscuit during his long career as an Australian Test selector. (Herald & Weekly Times, Melbourne)

Unlike many of his Test-team colleagues Bradman did not retire into obscurity once his first-class career ended, but continued as an administrator and selector. He was one of the selectors – with Jack Ryder and 'Chappie' Dwyer – who picked the following team to tour South Africa in 1949–50: A.L. Hassett (Captain), R.N. Harvey, I.W. Johnson, W.A. Johnston, S.J.E. Loxton, R.R. Lindwall, J. Moroney, A.R. Morris, R.A. Saggers, A.K. Walker, K.A. Archer, D. Tallon, C.L. McCool and G. Noblet, with E.A. Dwyer as manager. Barnes, Bill Brown, New South Wales batsman Bill Donaldson and Toshack were not considered although Toshack had not officially retired.

The omission of Miller caused a furore and in some books and magazines it has been attributed to Bradman's annoyance with

Miller for bowling bouncers at him in the Kippax–Oldfield testimonial match. But when Bill Johnston misread a traffic sign and was hurt early on the South African tour, Miller was flown across to replace him. Miller went straight into the Test team. Gil Langley, who replaced Tallon before the team left, broke a finger after six matches, leaving Ron Saggers to keep wicket in the Tests.

The newcomers in the Australian team included the Sydney left-arm fast bowler Alan Walker, who after a splendid tour of Britain, France and North America with the 1947–48 Wallabies as a rugby centre, had rapidly made his mark in first-class cricket. Walker was an extremely wristy bowler whose action was suspect although he played in all seven matches for the state Shield team captained by Arthur Morris. He proved a worthy ally to Lindwall, and his hostility allowed Morris to rest Miller when his back problems recurred.

Walker clinched his place in the South African touring line-up with a hat-trick against Queensland and in his first season of big cricket headed the Shield bowling averages for all states with 38 wickets at 13.36. Walker was an old boy of Sydney Grammar School, and he developed his cricketing skills at Saturday morning coaching classes conducted by Les Gwynne and George Lowe which attracted boys from all over Sydney to Manly Oval.

Jack Moroney, a right-hand opening batsman with a prolific record for the Petersham–Marrickville club, was another Great Public Schools graduate, developed at St Joseph's College, Hunters Hill. Moroney forced his way into the Australian team by scoring 655 runs at 72.77 in the 1948–49 Shield season, including 122 v. Queensland, 59 and 98 v. South Australia, 100 not out v. Victoria, and 217 in the Kippax–Oldfield testimonial match. He probably would have won international recognition earlier had he not been clumsy in the field.

Room-mates throughout the South African tour were Queenslander Ken Archer and South Australian Geff Noblet, the side's other newcomers. Archer was a Queensland opening batsman, who scored 523 runs in the Shield competition at an average of 43.58. He was rated one of the finest fieldsmen in Australia with a throwing arm that had attracted interest from US baseball clubs, and with Moroney looked the best candidate for Barnes's Test place. Noblet was a highly versatile cricketer who could open the bowling with medium-pacers that swung sharply or bowl off-spinners for long periods. His action started with a hop and ended with a pronounced flick of his hand and attracted accusations that he threw, but in four years with the South Australian side he had never been no-balled for chucking.

Hassett was an impressive captain from the start of the 21-match tour against Natal from 28 to 31 October 1949 at Durban. He fitted comfortably into leadership without losing his sense of fun, though he could be firm in pressing home an advantage. He was determined that as the first Australian team to visit South Africa since Vic Richardson's side in 1935–36 his men should play entertaining cricket and enjoy themselves.

They had five wins and three draws before the First Test at Johannesburg at the end of December, when both openers Morris and Moroney went for ducks and the third Australian wicket fell at 71. From then on Australia gained the upper hand and centuries from Hassett (112) and Loxton (101) lifted the score to 413. Loxton hit 14 fours in scoring his first Test century in 120 minutes. South Africa followed on after collapsing for 137, Miller taking 5 for 40 in only his second tour appearance. Johnston had 6 for 44 in a total of 191 when South Africa batted again, leaving Australia winners by an innings and 85 runs.

The Second Test at Cape Town followed a similar pattern. All hope South Africa had was dispelled by the end of the first day with Australia 4 for 312 at stumps. Harvey made 178, Moroney 87, Miller 58, Hassett 57. Next day Australia went on to 7 for 526 declared. Only Eric Rowan (67) and Dudley Nourse (65) could handle McCool's leg-breaks in South Africa's innings of 278. McCool had 5 for 41. Lindwall was the destroyer when South Africa followed on, taking 5 for 32 in an innings of 333, but it was McCool who dismissed the Springbok's top-scorer, Nourse, for 114. An eight-wicket win gave Australia a firm grip on the series.

Hassett's clever captaincy allowed Australia to retain that grip in a dramatic Third Test South Africa appeared sure to win. Indeed Hassett's scheming in this match, from 20 to 24 January 1950 at Durban, ranks as a classic in cricket captaincy and gives Hassett a place among the very best who have held the job for Australia.

Eric Rowan played a long, defiant hand for 143 and Nourse supported him with a stubborn 66 to lift South Africa to 311 on the first day. Overnight rain provided Australia with a perilous batting surface which Tayfield exploited to have them out for 75. Tayfield had 7 for 23 from only 8.4 overs, remarkable figures for a bowler in his first Test series. Nourse had all the Sunday rest day to decide if he should enforce the follow-on but with further rain forecast chose to bat again.

Here Hassett instructed his bowlers deliberately to prolong the South African innings once they got Nourse for only 27. Miller knew the pitch provided prodigious turn from his first delivery but with fieldsmen out near the fence to reduce the number of boundaries thereafter only tried to bowl straight. At 6 for 90 the Australians lengthened their approach runs and made sure every single took a long time as the pitch dried out. The South Africans scored only nine runs while they were losing their last four wickets.

South Africa were all out for 99. Left to score 336 to win, Australia struggled to 3 for 80 by stumps. The last day began with Australia still requiring 256 to win with seven wickets left. Neil Harvey varied his normal free-flowing style to one of dogged defence and gradually the pitch improved. Helped first by Loxton (59) and later by McCool (39 not out) Harvey batted for five hours 30 minutes in a flawless knock for 151 not out, which saw Australia home by 5 wickets with 25 minutes to spare. Harvey put on 145 for the fifth wicket with Loxton and 106 unfinished with McCool, and Australia lost only two wickets in the entire day.

Colin McCool, brilliant all-rounder, who opted to complete his career in England after successful tours with Australian teams. (Daily Telegraph, Sydney)

Having made sure of the rubber, Australia played a draw in the Fourth Test back at Johannesburg, where Moroney (118) and Morris (111) made centuries after an opening stand of 214. South Africa replied to Australia's 8 for 465 declared with 352, which made a result impossible. Moroney hit another century (101 not out) to become the first Australian to complete separate hundreds against South Africa, and Harvey, too, completed a century (100) before time ran out.

Australia finished the rubber 4–0 up with a mighty batting display in the Fifth Test at Port Elizabeth, where Morris, 157, Harvey, 116, and Hassett, 167, hit centuries in a total of 7 for 549 declared. South Africa managed only 158 and 132 to be beaten by an innings and 259 runs. This took South Africa's sequence of matches without a win to 28 since their last Test success in 1935.

Australia completed the tour with 14 wins and seven draws from their 21 first-class matches, with Harvey easily the most successful batsman and Johnston the best bowler. Harvey made 1526 runs at 76.30, including eight centuries. Johnston took 56 wickets at 13.75. The Australians scored 33 centuries between them, and had only three centuries scored against them. South Africa's batsmen lacked confidence against Australia's pace attack and their fielding was always inferior to Australia's.

New South Wales retained the Sheffield Shield while their Test players were absent in South Africa in 1949–50. Paddington all-rounder Ronnie James took over the state captaincy when Miller was called to South Africa and headed his team's batting averages with 341 runs at an average of 49.0.

The only setback in New South Wales' Shield triumph was the loss to Victoria in Melbourne over Christmas when two NSW 19-year-olds, Jimmy Burke and Richie Benaud, shared a 138-run stand in 135 minutes. Burke continued for six hours to reach 162 not out after Benaud departed for 68. Victoria got to within seven runs of New South Wales' first-innings total of 360 before unorthodox spinner Jack Iverson, 34, a former Ninth Division sergeant, helped dismiss New South Wales for only 123 in their second innings. Iverson took 46 wickets in the season at 16.60.

Iverson's special delivery was a ball he let go with the middle finger of his left hand tucked in behind the ball. He had perfected this bent fingergrip flicking tennis balls at fellow servicemen in New Guinea and later found that because of his exceptionally long fingers he could manage it on a full-length cricket pitch.

The Victorians lost their chance of winning the Shield when they were defeated in the return match against New South Wales in Sydney, where a big, burly left-hander named Alan Davidson took 5 for 28 in Victoria's first innings of 123. Iverson bowled with commendable accuracy and again puzzled batsmen with his bent finger delivery to take 6 for 30, but Victoria's batsmen were powerless against the excellent New South Wales bowling.

Davidson and Iverson both won selection in the team of 14 players that made a 14–match tour of New Zealand at the end of the 1949–50 Australian summer. The team was W.A. Brown (Captain), P.L. Ridings, J.W. Burke, A.K. Davidson, W.G. Driver, L.D. Duldig, R. Howard, J.B. Iverson, L.J. Johnson, K.D. Meuleman, C.W. Puckett, D.T. Ring, S.G. Sismey and D. Tallon. They were unbeaten and won eight of their ten victories by an innings.

The tour was mainly aimed at developing young New Zealand players and no Tests were played, but probably did more to build the confidence of aspiring Australians for the matches against the visiting Englishmen the following summer.

Roy Howard, the attractive Victorian right-hand batsman who toured New Zealand with the 1949–50 Australian team. He was forced to concentrate on his job for his family's sake after scoring three first-class centuries. (Roy Howard)

CHAPTER TWENTY-THREE

END OF A WINNING STREAK

Sid Barnes continued to bedevil the Australian Board of Control through the 1950s, sniping away about poor pay for Test and Shield players, official bungling, selectors' mistakes, umpires' decisions, and anything worth a newspaper quote. He enjoyed himself at the expense of Freddie Brown's English team in 1950–51 when they turned out one of the clumsiest fielding sides to tour Australia.

The Australian Board of Control ignored Barnes. Bill Jeanes, Board secretary from 1927 until 1954, and Harold Heydon, secretary of the New South Wales Cricket Association from 1926 to 1950, barely acknowledged Barnes's existence, and never commented on issues Barnes raised, however important. They tried to lift international cricket above controversy and in the years before advertising discovered the game and there was no television their dignified approach worked.

The Board relied on the schools to keep supplying district clubs with talented youngsters and did not have to find money for vast junior coaching schemes. They were not involved in superannuation schemes or provident funds for players, and revenue through the turnstiles was high enough to eliminate the need for corporate sponsorships.

Brown's English team played its way through 25 matches in a friendly atmosphere and in the Tests faced an Australian team a long way below the competence of the 1948 side. The loss of Bradman, Barnes and Toshack, and to a lesser extent McCool, had weakened the team and Tallon's decline coincided with the slump of the pace bowlers, who were not as threatening.

Australians found Brown a jovial John Bull type with a face like a Toby jug, a Cambridge graduate who had spent three years in a prisoner-of-war camp after being captured by Rommel's Afrika Korps. He had been forgotten by England's selectors after touring Australia with Jardine's Bodyline team in 1932–33, but was recalled to big cricket in 1949 after an absence of 16 years. When the Marylebone Cricket Club could not persuade Norman Yardley or George Mann, captain of the Middlesex county side, to take the twenty-fifth English team to Australia, they fell back on this gutsy antique.

Brown and Hassett had known each other since they played in wartime matches together in the Middle East, but the English team included seven players under 26 so many of the newcomers were completely unknown to Australians. Brown's team was: L. Hutton, C. Washbrook, R.T. Simpson, D.C.S. Compton, W.G.A. Parkhouse, J.G. Dewes, A.J.W. McIntyre, T.G. Evans, T.E. Bailey, A.V. Bedser, D.V.P. Wright, D.B. Close, W.E. Hollies, D.S. Sheppard, J.J. Warr and R. Berry.

Compton's place in the team was in doubt until just before they sailed because of a knee injury, aggravated in matches on the wing for Arsenal soccer club. Washbrook declined the original invitation to tour but was allowed to fly out and join the side after they arrived. By the end of the Third Test Brown had to telephone Lord's and ask for bowlers to replace the injured Wright (groin muscle) and Bailey (broken thumb). J.B. Statham and R. Tattersall were flown out to play in a country match just before the Fourth Test. Tattersall's omission from the original party had been strongly criticised, but Bill Edrich's omission was just as puzzling.

From the start Brown played every match belligerently and showed plenty of pluck in his own endeavours with bat and ball. England went into the First Test at Brisbane, from 1 to 5 December 1950, with an unbeaten record from their 10 warm-up matches in Australia, having defeated WA Colts and South Australia, and escaped with a rainy draw from a hammering against New South Wales when Morris (168) and Miller (214) lifted the state's score to 3 for 509 declared.

In the Test Hutton began the excitement that lasted throughout the series when he caught Moroney for a duck off the fourth ball of the match. By the end of the first day Australia had been bundled out for 228 by Bailey and Bedser. An overnight storm washed out the second day and when play resumed after the Sunday rest day it was clear England faced a major task avoiding the follow-on on a wretched pitch.

The M.A. Noble stand in Sydney midway through its construction. Funds attracted to the game by Bradman helped finance this venture. (Mitchell Library, *Sydney*)

From 0 for 28, England collapsed to 7 for 68, which was enough to avoid the follow-on enforceable when teams are 200 behind, but Brown chose instead to declare in an effort to get Australia in on the still treacherous pitch. Although they were 160 runs in the lead, Australia began disastrously when Moroney was again out for a duck. His 'spectacles' had critics searching the record books while the fun continued in the middle. Morris and Loxton were out before a run had been scored and, after Harvey had top-scored with 12 runs in a total of 7 for 32, Hassett retaliated by declaring.

Brown watched Hassett go on to the field and clap his hands with a perplexed air. When he enquired what was going on, Hassett simply said: 'It's your move, old chap.' England had to score 193 to win with 70 minutes remaining that day, plus all of the last day. With further rain unlikely, they had a great chance to win if they could survive the day with most of their batting intact.

Lindwall scattered Simpson's stumps with a fierce yorker, the first ball of the England innings. Washbrook and Dewes defended gamely for half an hour before Lindwall removed Washbrook and Miller bowled Dewes. Panic set in then. Reserve wicket-keeper Arthur McIntyre, selected as a batsman, was run out trying for an absurd fourth run, and three wickets fell in two overs by batsmen chasing runs instead of stonewalling.

England required 163 with four wickets left when the last day began and Hassett immediately pushed all his fieldsmen in close to hide the truth that all spite had left the pitch. Evans popped up

Neil Harvey, who was at the peak of his powers in the early 1950s and hailed as a forthcoming Australian captain, but had to concede the job to his friend Richie Benaud. (Ern McQuillan)

a catch, Compton did the same off the next ball, both anticipating lift that was not there. Hutton continued to bat cleverly with the pitch drying out, helping Brown to take the score to 8 for 77 before Brown misread Iverson and was caught. Wright and Hutton then put on 45 for the last wicket before Wright went trying to hook the last ball before lunch off Iverson. England's score of 122, 62 of them from Hutton, gave Australia victory by 70 runs.

At Melbourne in the Second Test, in conditions ideal for seam bowling, England enjoyed another wonderful opening day by dismissing Australia for 194. Bedser took 4 for 37, Bailey 4 for 40, and only inaccurate bowling from Wright that allowed Hassett to reach 52 extended the Australian innings. A tremendous tussle followed as England's batsmen tried to give their side the advantage but Miller, Lindwall and Johnston combined with the remarkable Iverson (4 for 38 off 18 overs) to confine England to 197, a lead of only three runs. Brown's pugnacious 62 kept English hopes alive.

Two rest days followed, a Sunday and Christmas Day, during which a fierce sun beat down on the pitch and opened up large cracks and kept the ball low. Wright sent back Morris but disappointed on a surface ideal for his leg-spinners. Brown bowled much more accurately to take 4 for 26, destroying the middle order, and Australia lost their last nine wickets for 99 to be all out for 181.

Left to score 179 to win, England faced 25 minutes of Lindwall bowling at a ferocious pace, but it was Iverson and Johnson who began the slump in England's batting by removing Washbrook and Bailey before stumps. Lindwall found Simpson playing too late early next morning and now at a time when aggression was needed, the English batsmen closed up shop. Only Hutton played sensibly but when he went for 40 all hope disappeared for England and Australia won by 28 runs. For the first time since 1896, neither side had reached 200 in any of the four innings. *Wisden* said the lack of nerve and experience in a crisis allowed Australia to go two-up.

Australia clinched the rubber by winning the Third Test in Sydney by an innings and 13 runs. Hutton made 62 in his normal opening spot before Miller dismissed him and Compton in three balls. On the second morning Brown played a spirited innings of 79, which included nine fours, but England had to be satisfied with a total of 290. Steady batting by all the Australians except Morris, whom Bedser bowled for a duck, took Australia to 426 in reply.

Iverson then played the crucial role in the entire series by taking 6 for 27 to have England out for 123 and give Australia the match by an innings and 13 runs. Iverson's spin was sharp, he made the ball lift and gather speed, and he kept a consistent length.

Morris made amends with a fine knock for 206 in the Fourth Test at Adelaide, where Jimmy Burke made 101 not out in his Test debut. Len Hutton again starred for England with 156 not out, but the Australian bowling and fielding was too much for his teammates. Leading by 99 on the first innings, Australia tightened their grip on the match by scoring 8 for 403 declared in the second, Miller contributing 99. Freddie Brown, injured in a car accident, did not bat in England's second innings, realising it was futile to try and prevent England's defeat. This was Australia's twenty-fifth Test without defeat in a record that stretched back to 1938, a sequence of 20 wins and five draws.

Arthur Morris, who forged strong partnerships with Barnes and Miller. (Ern McQuillan)

Reg Simpson set up a surprise England win in the Fifth Test at Melbourne by scoring 156 not out in a wonderful display of shot-making, but it was the old warhorse Alec Bedser who clinched it by taking 5 for 46 and 5 for 59 and restricting Australia to 217 and 197. Hutton did his part with 79 and 60 not out in the second innings and fittingly hit the winning run.

Bedser's ten-wicket haul in the Fifth Test gave him 30 wickets for the rubber at an average of 16.06, but England's 4–1 defeat left him upset with the tour selectors. 'If we had had some of the old hands instead of kids like Dewes, Sheppard, Close and Berry we'd have won easily,' Bedser said. Australia had badly missed Barnes, who was highly paid to cover the series for newspapers. None of the opening combinations that were tried compensated for his loss.

Burke's introduction to the Test team brought mixed reactions from spectators, for although still only 20 he was known as an iron-willed person who could sustain his refusal to play strokes through long, laborious innings, but he was also a popular figure with a very large green cap who laughed easily. After one strokeless hour in Sydney a spectator yelled from The Hill: 'Burke, I wish you were a statue and I was a pigeon.'

With the Australian side clearly in decline, England's modest attempts to end her long stranglehold on the Ashes attracted far smaller crowds than the previous series in Australia in 1946–47. The tour profit was only £3842, a tenth of that for Hammond's Ashes challenge.

Although Iverson proved an enormous success in the Tests he did not enjoy the same success against New South Wales batsmen as

Sam Loxton, one of the great characters in Australia's Test team immediately after the Second World War.
(John Fairfax & Sons)

he had against England. Miller was angry when his turn came to bat in the nets before the First Test and Hassett ordered Iverson to stop bowling. Hassett did not want Miller or Morris to bat against Iverson when he knew Victoria's Shield chances might be hurt if New South Wales players had practice reading his unorthodox range of deliveries.

Morris and Miller conferred and decided to make a concerted attack on Iverson when Victoria met New South Wales in Sydney and to upset Iverson's normal accuracy by taking guard half a metre outside the leg stump. Hassett's Victorian side had triumphed in Melbourne, when Hassett, swaying inside and under kicking deliveries from Miller, Lindwall and Walker, scored a splendid 179. The return in Sydney, where Morris and Miller attacked Iverson, produced a New South Wales win. Morris made 182, Miller 83 and Iverson's 20 overs cost 108 runs, which a normal spinner would have accepted as a setback not worth worrying about. But Iverson decided cricket was a cruel game, and although he later took his magic to India with a Commonwealth XI, he faded from the game after one season of glory with figures of 21 wickets at 15.24 apiece for 1950–51.

He continued in the 1951–52 season for one match in Melbourne between Victoria and Queensland, but was freely hit by batsmen in both innings, finishing with 3 for 90 and 2 for 124. He helped save Victoria from defeat by playing a dead bat for the last 25 minutes. Next season he played twice, then quit. 'I've lost it,' he said. 'They're playing me too easily. I'm going out to graze for a bit.'

On 23 October 1973, unorthodox spin bowler Jack Iverson shot himself in the head at his home in Brighton, Victoria. He was 58 and apparently successful in real estate. He joined a strange list of Australian cricketers who have suicided that includes Dick Wardill, Billy Bruce, Albert Trott, Jack Cuffe (Queensland, New South Wales and Worcestershire), Tom Wills, Bruce Suche (Queensland), Barry Fisher (Queensland), Sid Barnes and Jimmy Burke.

More resilient than Iverson were two West Indian spin bowlers, Sonny Ramadhin and Alf Valentine, who had shaken English cricket supporters in 1950. They had taken 59 wickets in the four-Test series, performances that enabled the West Indies to beat England at home for the first time by a margin of 3–1. Valentine took 33 Test wickets, bowling left-arm finger spinners, and Ramadhin had 26 wickets bowling right-arm off-breaks.

Neither Valentine nor Ramadhin had played regular first-class cricket when they arrived in England at the age of 20. They were regarded as fill-ins on a tour designed to 'blood' them for higher honours later on, but so marked was their supremacy over the best English batsmen, the West Indies won 19 of their 38 matches, lost three and drew 16.

Ramadhin furthered his claims to be rated a world-class bowler by taking 79 wickets at 19.65 for the Commonwealth XI which toured India at the same time as Brown's team visited Australia. Three outstanding Australian cricketers, George Tribe, Bruce Dooland and Ken Grieves, played in the Commonwealth side which was unbeaten in 27 matches, winning 13 and settling for draws in 14. They confirmed the high ranking of Ramadhin and advised Australians they were going to watch spin bowling of the highest quality when Ramadhin and Valentine toured Australia in 1951–52 in a series many saw as a virtual world championship.

The Australian Board of Control put the itinerary together quickly once the West Indies accepted their invitation to tour. Apart from Ramadhin and Valentine, the West Indies team included dashing batsmen known as the 'Three Ws' – Walcott, Weekes and Worrell. Their tour was insured against any losses that might be caused by interruptions to the programme by the war in Korea, where Australia was among the 15 nations fighting alongside the US.

Sid Barnes went to the chairman of the Australian Board of Control, Aubrey Oxlade, before the West Indies arrived and asked if there were any official grudges that would prevent his selection in the Australian team if he got into peak physical shape and returned to big cricket. Oxlade assured him the Board had no grievance against him and Test selection depended on the runs Barnes scored. Barnes began running in a sweat suit each morning and night around Lindfield Oval and when grade cricket began showed splendid form for the Gordon club. With the Australian team weaker than at any time since the war, Barnes's Test selection appeared likely.

The West Indians' Australian programme discarded the normal practice of starting in Perth, travelling around the southern states and on up the east coast to the First Test in Brisbane. The reasons for the change were not known but Hassett had one look at the fixture list and immediately criticised the notion of giving the West Indies only one first-class match before the First Test. 'The West Indies have suffered from sheer stupidity in the organisation of their tour,' said Hassett.

The West Indies team in Australia in 1951–52 (L to R): S. Ramadhin, K.R. Rickards, D.St E. Atkinson, S.C. Guillen, J. Trim, W. Ferguson; centre, C.A. Merry (Manager), A.F. Rae, A.L. Valentine, C.L. Walcott, P.E. Jones, R.E. Marshall, W. Ferguson (Scorer); front, R.J. Christiani, F.M. Worrell, G.E. Gomez, J.D. Goddard (Captain), J.B. Stollmeyer, E.de C. Weekes. (NSWCA Library)

The West Indian team that began their tour with a one-day benefit in Sydney for scorer Bill Ferguson was: J.D.C. Goddard (Captain), F.M.M. Worrell, C.L. Walcott, E.de C. Weekes, R.E. Marshall, J.B. Stollmeyer, R.J. Christiani, K. Rickards, D.St E. Atkinson, S. Ramadhin, A.L. Valentine, J. Trim, P.E. Jones, A.F. Rae, G.E. Gomez, S.C. Guillen and W. Ferguson, with Cyril Merry as manager.

After their one-day outing in Sydney, the West Indians went to Canberra for a match against the Prime Minister's XI, played New South Wales Country in Newcastle, and Queensland Country in Townsville, before their initial first-class match against Queensland at the Gabba. They left Ramadhin and Valentine out of this game and paid the penalty. McCool took 6 for 83 to swing the match Queensland's way. Chasing 198, Queensland reached 455, Aub Carrigan contributing 169, 'Mick' Harvey 90 and 'Slasher' Mackay 79, against an attack in which only Gomez and Goddard commanded respect. Gomez made 97 not out in West Indies' second innings of 282 and they were beaten by ten wickets.

After their disastrous start, the West Indies made a tense fight of the First Test in Brisbane. Australia fed their batsmen a mixture of pace and short-pitched deliveries that whistled round their ears and only Goddard appeared untroubled by it. Worrell, Weekes, Christiani and Marshall began well but failed to unveil the shots that had made the team famous. The Australians in turn were unimpressive against Ramadhin and Valentine, struggling for runs until Miller used his long reach to get down the pitch to Ramadhin. Valentine's 5 for 99 restricted Australia to 226 and a 10-run lead.

Five catches were dropped off Valentine in 30 minutes.

Weekes gave the match the distinction it had lacked with a glorious 70 in the West Indian second innings. Gomez held out gamely for 55. Umpire Andy Barlow warned Miller for intimidation when he let loose a succession of waist-high deliveries at Marshall, but leg-spinner Doug Ring's flight and variation produced the best figures (6 for 80) in a total of 245. Australia only wanted 236 to win and were in danger at 5 for 149, but a sixth-wicket stand of 54 by Lindwall and young Hole made certain of the victory.

Barnes marked his return to international cricket with a duck for New South Wales v. West Indies in Sydney, where a sporting declaration by Morris set the visitors 380 to win. A magnificent 114 by Marshall, 65 by Worrell, 59 by Rickards and 54 from Walcott took the West Indies to within 24 runs of a win but several superb catches turned the match to New South Wales.

Barnes was in superlative form in the nets and while the Second Test was on in Sydney went south as captain of the New South Wales team. Officials and spectators gave him a warm welcome. In Adelaide he made 57 and 28 against South Australia. Then, after Australia had gone two-up by defeating the West Indies by seven wickets in the Second Test, he paired up again in Melbourne with his old partner Morris, their stand yielding 210 runs. Barnes made 107, Morris 210, and New South Wales reached 533, enough for an innings win. Two of the three Test selectors, Jack Ryder and 'Chappie' Dwyer, went to the dressing-room to congratulate Barnes on his batting.

There was clearly a need for Barnes in the Test team as Australia's opening stands in the two Tests had disappointed, following similar failures in South Africa the previous summer. Reporters waited in vain for the Third Test team, only to be told the Board of Control had rejected the side named by Ryder, Dwyer and Bradman, and referred it back to them for reconsideration. Board chairman Oxlade said that under its constitution the Board could reject a player from a national team for reasons other than cricket. He did not specifically name Barnes but everyone knew Barnes was the cause of the Board's objections.

The Sydney *Daily Mirror* called the Board's action 'a gratuitous insult to the intelligence of its selectors' and said it was also an insult to the New South Wales Cricket Association which had approved Barnes's return to big cricket. The *Sydney Morning Herald* deplored the Board's action in not making the complaint against Barnes known.

The Third Test went ahead without Barnes with the Board attracting flak right up until the first ball was bowled. Hassett had to drop out with a muscle pulled at practice and selectors named Phil Ridings, who was present at Adelaide Oval, to replace him. But the Board refused to let Ridings play and Hassett had to act as twelfth man. Morris took over the captaincy. Twenty wickets fell for 207 runs on the first day because of a damp pitch. The West Indies made 105 in reply to Australia's 82, and after three days Australia sustained only her second defeat in 29 post-war matches. This just added heat to the Barnes affair.

Hassett returned for the Fourth Test at Melbourne, where the opening pair – Morris and Moroney – again failed, adding only 17 and 27. This time a 38-run stand for the last wicket saved Australia, and gave them a one-wicket win that clinched the series. Earlier in the match Worrell (108) and Hassett (102) had scored centuries but when Australia's last pair, Johnston and Ring, came together defeat seemed inevitable for Australia. Goddard moved his fieldsmen in for the kill, but Ring outsmarted him by lifting his shots over close-in fieldsmen positioned for catches. Amid great excitement the score edged closer to the target until Johnston, who had defended while Ring did all the hitting, opened up himself and made the winning hit.

In the dressing-room Hassett asked Johnston if he was nervous as he and Ring gathered the runs required. Johnston said: 'Nervous? Don't be silly. How could I be nervous when I knew we had no hope?' It transpired that Johnston and Ring had done the same thing several times for the Richmond club in district cricket.

Johnston was in the limelight again in the Fifth Test at Sydney, where he and Miller routed the West Indies for 78, their lowest-ever total against Australia. Miller took 5 for 26, Johnston 3 for 25 – this on a perfect pitch on the first day, when Australia, batting first, had already collapsed for 116, and 19 wickets fell. The Australians again unsettled the West Indian side with a barrage of bouncers and Lindwall was allowed to bowl 15 bouncers at Weekes in 40 deliveries. The West Indies had no pace bowler with whom they could retaliate and right to the end their fielding failed to match Australia's, who wrapped up the series 4–1 with a 202-run triumph.

Strangely enough, umpires were not as reluctant to warn bowlers for excessive use of the bouncer in that summer's Shield matches. Umpire Herb Elphinston warned Alan Walker for intimidatory bowling for New South Wales against South Australia when Walker

Ken Meuleman, Victorian-born right-hander, was one of Australia's highest scoring batsmen in the 1950s, but was denied a Test place by the brilliance of Morris and Barnes. (VCA Archives)

hit Bruce Bowley on the head. In Sydney, when Victorian batsmen showed resentment against the fiery New South Wales attack, umpire H. McKinnon warned some bowlers.

The over-use of the bouncer led to frank discussions at a NSWCA meeting, which decided to ask the Board of Control to change the laws relating to intimidatory bowling so that umpires at the bowler's end could no-ball offenders. The move petered out as so many did at Board level.

For weeks rumour-mongers had had a free rein while newspapers dug deep to find reasons for Barnes being blacklisted by the Board. He was known to have lampooned Board members in the commentary that accompanied his movie of the 1948 tour. But had he disobeyed firm instructions from team manager Keith Johnson not to film the Royal Family? Had he been drunk on tour? Had he stolen from other players' pockets in the dressing-room? One prominent doctor alleged Barnes had stolen a car on the 1948 tour, sold it, and forced the Board to reimburse the owner. Barnes wrote to Bradman about the car-stealing charge. Bradman said he knew nothing about it.

The Board's autocrats appeared to have won the day when a Mr Jacob L. Raith wrote a letter to the Sydney *Daily Mirror* which said: 'The Board would not have excluded Mr Barnes from the Australian XI capriciously, but only for a matter of sufficiently serious nature. In declining his request to publish reasons, the Board may be acting kindly towards him.' Barnes immediately sued Raith, whom he had never met, for libel.

Raith defended the case on the grounds of truth and public benefit but after his counsel, Mr J. Smyth, QC, had cross-examined members of the Board – secretary Bill Jeanes, chairman Aubrey Oxlade, selector Edmund Dwyer and Keith Johnson – Raith withdrew. A very poor picture of Australian cricket administration was presented to the court as one by one these influential Board members were quizzed. Oxlade agreed that Barnes's action in jumping a Melbourne turnstile was not a cardinal sin. Johnson admitted a verbal report he gave the Board on Barnes's behaviour on the 1948 tour was different from his written report.

Smyth, in his summing-up to the jury, said: 'You can see now why the Board was so reluctant to help us, why the Board was so anxious that none of its records should be available to the court.' Smyth added: 'We hear it said solemnly by the Board of so-called responsible citizens that six years ago Barnes jumped over a stile. Then he does the dreadful thing of taking his cap off and bowing to the crowd, to the great embarrassment of the Board . . . Did you ever hear such tommy rot? . . . My client foolishly, as it turns out, believed that this Board was an impartial body of cricket administrators. You can well imagine what Mr Raith thinks of them now.'

Barnes received no damages. He had never sought any. Raith paid his costs and Barnes's counsel Jack Shand commended Raith for his courage in withdrawing and clearing Barnes's name. Barnes had won a handsome victory and he immediately set to work training to get himself fit for Australia's 1953 tour of England, rejecting offers to write on that tour for newspapers. For weeks he went to daily practice at Chatswood Oval, knowing he had to first get into Australia's team for the 1952–53 matches against the visiting South Africans.

Barnes opened with Morris in the first match of the season late in October 1952, but made only 18 in the Brisbane match against Queensland and 15 when the teams moved to Sydney. The next match, between Victoria and New South Wales in Melbourne from 21 to 25 November, was virtually a Test trial, and Barnes took command of the Victorian attack in a wonderful innings of 152. He punished Test bowlers Johnston, Ring and Johnson in a vintage knock that set up New South Wales' victory by an innings and 35 runs.

He was not picked in the Australian team for the First Test v. South Africa in Brisbane early in December, and he said then that the Board had had its revenge for the humiliation he had caused it in his court case. At 36, he gave up the struggle to regain his Test place and when the New South Wales team went on to Adelaide he suggested he drop out and give one of the up-and-coming youngsters their chance. The selectors should not have agreed if they wanted to field their best team. They blundered again when they co-operated with Barnes's plan to make a joke of his twelfth man's role.

Barnes went out on to Adelaide Oval at the drinks break in a lounge suit, sporting a red carnation in the buttonhole, carrying iced towels, a scent spray, a mirror to help players straighten their hair and a portable radio. The farce was prolonged because he had so much gear he forgot to take out enough drinks and an attendant had to be sent for more. The New South Wales manager Cyril Jago helped him take out the radio.

Ray Lindwall had to replace Barnes as the New South Wales opening batsman and although he made 70 South Australia won by three wickets. The New South Wales batsmen struggled on a damp pitch while the player with most experience on such a pitch carried the drinks. Les Favell, who had switched from the St George club in Sydney, won the match for South Australia with 105 in the second innings. Like Barnes, Favell was a marvellous exponent of the hook and cut shots.

Barnes stopped going to the nets and in his last first-class match made 18 at no. 9 for New South Wales against the South Africans, sharing a useful stand with 17-year-old Ian Craig, who made 213 not out. After a career in which his formidable talents were never really fulfilled, he retired with 8333 first-class runs to his credit at an average of 54.11, and 57 wickets at 32.21. His Test average was higher, with 1072 runs at 63.06. He made 26 centuries.

For fees far higher than the Board of Control paid him for playing, Barnes moved into the press box, leaving Board members convinced that his Adelaide antics as twelfth man proved he was unfit for the Test team.

Ron Archer, hailed as a future Australian Test captain, until injury prematurely ended his career. (West Australian)

Australian spectators quickly learned that the captaincy of Jack Cheetham had transformed the South Africans into one of the finest fielding sides of all time and a force all the cricket nations should respect. However, the Board of Control, convinced of the superiority of Australia's team, had the South African Board of Control lodge a guarantee against losses before the Springbok visit proceeded.

Under Cheetham the South Africans had broken their run of 28 Tests without a win by defeating England by 71 runs at Trent Bridge in 1951. To prepare for their Australian tour, they went through a programme of callisthenics advised by the famous Springbok rugby player Dr Danie Craven.

The South African team was J.E. Cheetham (Captain), R.A. McLean, D.J. McGlew, W.R. Endean, H.J. Keith, K.J. Funston, G.A.S. Innes, A.R.A. Murray, J.H.B. Waite, J.C. Watkins, P.N.F. Mansell, E.B. Norton, H.J. Tayfield, M.G. Melle and E.R.H. Fuller, with Ken Viljoen as manager. Eric Rowan was informed by letter in October 1951 that following incidents in England earlier that year he would not be considered for the Australian tour. Clive van Ryneveld declined to tour and Cuan McCarthy, studying at Cambridge University, was available but not selected.

The South Africans spent up to four hours a day practising their

371

fielding before their first tour match in Perth. Their programme reverted to the established pattern of starting in Perth and playing each of the southern states in turn, moving on up the east coast to the First Test in Brisbane. These early matches demonstrated the big advances made by their off-spinner Hugh Tayfield, who took a hat-trick in Melbourne against Victoria and quickly became a crowd favourite.

Australia won the First Test at the Gabba from 5 to 10 December 1952 by 96 runs, but for four days the South Africans made such a fight of it experts immediately revised assessments of their status. Backed by inspired fielding their bowlers gave Australia's batsmen a tough fight for runs. South Africa's batsmen handled Australia's pace bowling comfortably but had trouble with Ring's leg-spin. In the end a fighting 109 from Harvey and fiery bowling on the fifth day by a reinvigorated Lindwall proved the difference between the sides.

South Africa had their first win over Australia in 42 years in the Second Test at Melbourne, with a display that had critics comparing them with the greatest fielding sides. To secure this victory, they overcame a miserable start. At 3 for 27 and then 7 for 126 in their first innings, their prospects looked grim, but a stubborn 51 from Murray lifted the total to 227. The fielding when Australia batted was spectacular. Morris drove powerfully and the ball bounced off Cheetham at silly mid-off. Tayfield spun round, made several strides back, and scooped up the catch with a full-length dive. Cheetham and McGlew took breathtaking catches and Endean ran round the boundary fence to intercept a shot from Miller that was within inches of becoming a six. This was the best of 26 catches Endean took on the tour.

With Australia leading by only 16 runs on the first innings, Endean then defied determined Australian bowling for seven and a half hours without offering a chance. His 162 not out swung the game, taking South Africa to 388. Miller completed the double of 100 wickets and 1000 runs in Tests when he had Waite caught by Hole in this innings. Chasing 373 to win, Australia had trouble scoring against Tayfield, who had one spell of nine overs without conceding a run, during which he dismissed Miller, Langley and Hole. His 13 wickets in the match for 165 runs resulted from his persistent accuracy and brilliance in dislodging batsmen who made good starts. Australia were all out for 290 to give South Africa victory by 82 runs.

Australia resisted the temptation of including Ian Craig after his superb 213 not out for New South Wales against South Africa, going into the Third Test at Sydney with the side unchanged from that beaten in Melbourne. This time Lindwall and Harvey gave Australia a match-winning advantage in the first two days. Lindwall swept through the South African batting with a memorable show of controlled pace and late swing, taking 8 for 112 in the match. Harvey's 190 consolidated Australia's strong position and took the total to 443, which won them the Test by an innings and 38 runs.

The Fourth Test at Adelaide was drawn following further heavy scoring by Australia, McDonald contributing 154, Hassett 163, Harvey 84 and Hole 59. South Africa saved the follow-on by seven runs and held on to save the match, with Miller and Lindwall unfit to bowl in the final innings.

With the forthcoming tour of England in mind, the selectors rested Miller and Lindwall from the Fifth Test in Melbourne, bringing in the burly Queensland rugby star Ron Archer (to bowl right-arm fast-medium pacers) and Craig, at 17 years 239 days the youngest Australian to appear in Test cricket.

By scoring 520 in their first innings, thanks to a brilliant 205 by Harvey, Australia got off to a good start. Harvey batted for almost five hours but at times was overshadowed by Craig, who made 53 in a surprisingly confident and stylish manner. Waite, 64, Watkins, 92, McLean, 81, Cheetham, 66, and Mansell, 52, all batted with great pluck to lift South Africa to 435 in reply. In Australia's second innings of 209 Craig top-scored with 47, which gave him 100 runs for the match. At the start of the last day South Africa wanted 201 to win with nine wickets intact. Steady risk-free batting pushed the score along steadily until McLean completed the task for South Africa with a brisk 76 not out that included 14 fours.

South Africa's six-wicket victory enabled them to share a rubber against Australia for the first time, with two wins apiece. By scoring his eighth century against South Africa, Harvey took his run aggregate for the series to 834, the highest by a batsman from either country in all Australia–South Africa matches. Tayfield's 30 wickets in the rubber was the highest by a South African on any overseas tour. South Africa won seven matches in all on the tour, drew 11 and lost three, and in their greatest triumph had shown that the wonderful Australian side Bradman had moulded in 1948 was disintegrating.

Bill Alley performed prodigious feats in England as the Australian Test team declined. Selectors failed to call on him, as they did in the 1990s with Alderman and Moody. (Sydney Daily Telegraph)

CHAPTER TWENTY-FOUR
THE ASHES SURRENDERED

"And here comes Craig, the baby of the team."
—Sprod in the News Chronicle.

A cartoon in the London News Chronicle *which greeted Ian Craig's arrival in the twenty-first Australian team in 1953, aged 18. His selection was a flop, with 14 of Craig's 16 team-mates averaging more with the bat.*
(Jack Pollard Collection)

Hassett's twenty-first Australian team to tour England no longer had the edge over their English opponents that Australia had enjoyed in the 15 post-war Tests. The seasoned Test players who were the nucleus of the side were still splendid entertainers, but age eroded their superiority, and the youngsters were slow in advancing to Test class. The entire team suffered from the new Australian habit of covering pitches against rain, a procedure that denied them practice on damp pitches similar to those regularly encountered in England.

The team was chosen by Bill Brown, Phil Ridings and Jack Ryder. Bradman withdrew from the selection panel because of his commitments to cover the tour for the London *Daily Mail*. The veteran Sydney Test selector Edmund Alfred ('Chappie') Dwyer, who had served on the selection panel since 1931, was sacked, although at the age of 59 he was still agile and alert, a well-liked figure who kept his secrets to himself. His dismissal left Australia's strongest cricket state, New South Wales, without a voice on the national selection panel, and was blamed on the favourable evidence he had given for Sid Barnes in the celebrated court case the previous year.

The Board initially decided to take 16 players but when it was realised they would be away for eight months Ian Craig was added to the party as seventeenth man. They lost only one of their 35 matches, but that defeat cost Australia the Ashes they had held for 19 years, the longest period on record. On that score they go down as a failure but they will always be remembered for the sustained entertainment they provided.

They set a number of landmarks. It was the first tour to have the matches televised, an oddity that made the whole of Britain stop work to watch the screen when the Tests were on, and they broke

374

all records for crowds and gate-takings. A total of 1,494,979 people paid £226,000 sterling to watch the 80 days' play on the tour. Aggregate attendance at the five Tests was 270,650. The Australian Board of Control received £A134,898 from the tour, more than double the profit from the 1948 tour by Bradman's unbeaten side.

The team was A.L. Hassett (Captain), A.R. Morris, R.G. Archer, R. Benaud, I.D. Craig, A.K. Davidson, J.H. de Courcy, R.N. Harvey, J.C. Hill, G.B. Hole, W.A. Johnston, G.R.A. Langley, R.R. Lindwall, C.C. McDonald, K.R. Miller, D.T. Ring and D. Tallon.

The major surprise was the inclusion of the Victorian Jack Hill, who bowled his top-spinners at a brisk pace, but seldom turned them from the leg as his grip suggested. He made the ball bounce awkwardly and had been a useful member of the Victorian team since 1945–46. In 1952–53 his 21 wickets at 18.33 in Shield matches included a bag of 7 for 51 against South Australia in Melbourne, which encouraged selectors to believe he would do well in England. Hill was an outstanding Australian Rules footballer who captained St Kilda before that career was cut short by a fractured skull.

Colin McCool, a wonderful slips fieldsman with extensive honours in batting and bowling, chose to miss the tour and play instead for East Lancashire while he qualified for an English county, Somerset. His absence and the retirement of Jack Iverson provided a golden opportunity for a leg-spinner, which selectors hoped Richie Benaud would accept. Benaud was the 22-year-old son of a school-teacher named Louis Benaud, a descendant of a family that had

The English team that regained the Ashes in 1953 (L to R): back, T.E. Bailey, P.B.H. May, T.W. Graveney, J.C. Laker, G.A.R. Lock, J.H. Wardle, F.S. Trueman; front, W.J. Edrich, A.V. Bedser, L. Hutton (Captain), D.C.S. Compton, T.G. Evans.

migrated to Australia from La Rochelle in France. Lou, a veteran first-grader for Parramatta, was one of the few cricketers to have taken all 20 wickets in a match.

The Tests see-sawed throughout the summer, with each side enjoying periods of ascendancy. In the First Test at Trent Bridge Bedser gave England a fine start by uprooting Graeme Hole's middle stump with the first ball of his second over. Morris, 67, and Hassett, 115, took Australia's score to 124 in an admirable fight-back which Miller continued with a gritty 55 but, from 3 for 237, the last seven batsmen fell for only 12 runs and Australia were all out for 249. Bedser bowled five of his victims in taking 7 for 55.

Lindwall matched Bedser's peformance by taking 5 for 5, three of his victims falling with the score on 17, and with belligerent support Davidson and Hill had England out for 144. Davidson, 23, had the thrill of dismissing Hutton, Australia's main problem, in his Test debut. Bedser carried on in the second innings with his late swing and nip from the pitch, carving through Australia's batting. His 7 for 44 gave him match figures of 14 for 99, and with two days left England wanted 187 to win with nine wickets left, but rain prevented play until late on the final afternoon and the match fizzled out in a draw.

This was the match in which Tallon misinterpreted Hassett's instructions to 'Go for the light'. Tallon thought Hassett wanted him to hit out and did not appeal against the fading light. Similar incidents later on the tour led to Tallon acquiring the nickname 'Deafy', when he did not hear snicks that team-mates regarded as catches.

John Rutherford, left, and Ken Mackay, arrive on the field late after becoming lost leaving the Australian dressing-room in corridors within the Lord's pavilion. (Sport & General)

The Second Test at Lord's produced a world-record gate for a cricket match of £57,716 sterling and one of cricket's classic rearguard actions. Australia seemed to have the Test won when Lindwall's 32 runs from boundaries in an innings of 50 increased their lead to 342 going into the last innings. Three England wickets fell before stumps and with a day to play England were 3 for 12. Just before stumps Willie Watson, the fair-haired Yorkshire left-hander, gave a catch to short leg which was dropped. The pitch was crumbling and taking spin.

On the final morning only Compton was dismissed by lunch. The Australians sauntered about the field in a lethargic mood which Sid Barnes later attributed to a late-night celebration that began watching *Guys and Dolls* and ended with a session at the Café de

Paris nightclub. Trevor Bailey joined Watson on Compton's departure and for the next five hours and 40 minutes they hit the ball right in the middle of their dead bats. Forced to persevere with his fast bowlers in case spinners Benaud and Ring should give away quick runs and allow England a chance to reach their target, Hassett stuck with his heroes in so many matches, Lindwall, Miller and Johnston. Only when time for a result had run out did Ring get a long bowl, and had Watson taken edging a googly into slips. Watson's 109 had saved England. Bailey departed minutes later for 71 after batting for four hours 17 minutes. Freddie Brown completed the England rescue effort with a pugnacious 28 and a great match ended in a draw.

The Third Test at Old Trafford produced another draw although the rain created a sensational climax. Harvey's 122 gave Australia a first-innings lead of 42, but on a pitch taking spin because of the rain Australia collapsed in their second to 8 for 35 when the time ran out. Davidson alone among the Australians appeared comfortable against the spinning ball. Australia were on top throughout the Fourth Test at Leeds because of excellent fast bowling by Lindwall and Miller, but another brave effort by Bailey, who batted for 262 minutes on the last day, saved England.

This took the teams to The Oval for the Fifth Test with the outcome of the rubber still in doubt. Hassett objected to famous umpire Frank Chester standing in this match following some strange decisions earlier on the tour by Chester, and Frank Lee and Dai Davies umpired the match, in which fiery Freddie Trueman, the former Yorkshire miner, made his debut against Australia. All-night queues for seats recorded on television frightened away many would-be spectators on the first day, but there were still 26,300 present when play began.

England led by 31 on the first innings and when hot sun fell on a pitch that had received intermittent rain Laker and Lock became match-winners. At 6 for 85, with the spinners in command, Archer and Davidson hit magnificent sixes, adding 50 so quickly both Laker and Lock changed their fields. Laker bowled down the leg side with only three men on the off and Lock outside the off stump with three on the leg side. This slowed the scoring and had Australia out for 162. Left to score 132 to win, England scored them for the loss of only two wickets. With nine runs needed, Hassett went on to bowl with Morris and when Compton hit the winning runs by clubbing Morris to the boundary, hordes of happy, laughing

Tony Lock, Surrey and England left-arm bowler, whose delivery attracted a shout from Hassett of 'Strike One', so convinced was the Australian captain that Lock threw. (Sport & General)

377

English fans invaded the ground. Both captains addressed the huge crowd in front of the pavilion.

Australia had paid dearly for the lack of a reliable opening pair, which Barnes would have remedied if he had toured. Hassett showed his concern over this problem by opening himself and when McDonald faltered he also tried Hole in the position.

The Australians appeared to tighten up during the Tests and were far more relaxed and adventurous in other matches. Free of tension, they gave some magnificent hitting performances, culminating in the last big match at Scarborough, where Benaud hit 11 sixes in an innings of 135 out of 209 in 110 minutes. Altogether 34 sixes were hit in this match, Australia defeating Tom Pearce's XI by two wickets and achieving their target of 320 in 220 minutes.

Australia's strength was obvious in their record of scoring 30 centuries in first-class matches while only seven were scored against them. Most of the team considered Lock threw the ball occasionally but none of them went public about it on a happy, ethical tour both teams enjoyed.

Freddie Trueman grounded his right foot well short of the crease to compensate for his extended drag, presenting big problems for Australian batsmen. (Ken Kelly)

Harvey headed the Australian batting averages by scoring ten centuries in a total of 2040 runs at 65.80. Miller (51.17) was the only other Australian to average over 50 for the tour, although seven players scored more than 1000 runs. The statistical hero of the tour, however, was big Bill Johnston, once out in scoring 102 runs, which remained his batting average. The prospect of such a batting dunce topping the averages caused Hassett to jump the fence and remind players Johnston had to remain not out in the festival matches at the end of the tour.

Hassett retired at the end of the 1953 English tour after captaining Australia 24 times, for 14 wins, four losses and six draws. He played in 43 Tests altogether, scoring 3073 runs at 46.56. After his retirement he conceded that he probably would have more runs had he not curbed his stroke play after the war and he urged Norm O'Neill and other natural shot-makers not to make the same mistake. Hassett played in 216 first-class matches, made 59 centuries, 23 of them for Victoria, and a total of 16,890 runs at 58.24. He also held 170 catches. Few cricketers have done so much to boost Australia's prestige.

Hassett's retirement started discussion among Australian sports fans over his successor as captain. Most cricket buffs wanted Keith Miller to take over because Miller embodied the aggressive spirit they believed would restore the fortunes of a declining Test team. He had led New South Wales with distinction since the state selectors sacked Arthur Morris – while Morris was away playing cricket in Hong Kong – and as Australia's most talented player appeared to the uninitiated ideal for the leader's role.

The Australian Board of Control had other ideas and appointed Victorian captain Ian Johnson, who had been dropped from the Australian team that toured England in 1953. Hassett stirred Johnson into regaining peak fitness at a New Year's Eve party in Melbourne, by chastising Johnson for his lack of effort. Johnson was annoyed at first and denied his effort was lacking. Hassett replied; 'You know you're not getting stuck into it. You're just coasting. If you've got any brains at all you'll get stuck into it and you'll be captain of Australia. There's no one else who can do the job.'

Lindsay Hassett, who led a declining, unlucky side, received an MBE from the Queen at Buckingham Palace midway through the 1953 tour. (United Press International)

Hassett's words irked Johnson but they had the desired effect. Johnson made 1953–54 his most successful season, taking 37 wickets at 16.37, and began to think he might get back into the Australian side. Through the winter he undertook a tough programme of callisthenics and by the start of the 1954–55 season he was in better shape than at any time since he flew Beaufighters during the war.

Bill Jeanes quit as secretary of the Australian Board of Control early in 1954 after 25 years in the job, and later that year Jack Ledward, a tactful, hard-working former Victorian Sheffield Shield player, took over. Ledward had appeared in 21 first-class matches for Victoria between 1934 and 1938 and scored two first-class hundreds. He had been secretary of the Victorian Cricket Association since 1951. His appointment put the daily administration of Australian cricket firmly in Victorian hands.

The sports pages debated the claims of Miller and Morris for the Test captaincy and only mentioned Johnson as a long shot. Among the cricketers who keenly followed the debate were the group of youngsters Miller captained in the New South Wales side, each with his own story to tell about the great man's unorthodoxy. Bob Simpson for example told how he went on the field as New South Wales' twelfth man while Miller was captain. When he asked Miller where he wanted him to field, Miller appeared surprised for a moment and then said: 'Go there,' and pointed to the slips. This was at a time when it was considered unethical to position a twelfth man in a catching position. Simpson went into the slips, took outstanding catches to dismiss Neil Harvey and Harry Lambert, and remained in the slips for the rest of his career.

Len Hutton retained the captaincy of the English team to tour Australia in 1954–55 but Hutton knew the bluebloods of amateurism at Lord's opposed his appointment. He was a very wary leader, knowing that one false step would incur the wrath of the traditionalists. The MCC had, in fact, considered Peter May for the job but decided May at 24 was not ready and appointed him vice-captain. As captain of the twenty-sixth English team to visit Australia, Hutton, 38, was the first professional to take a team to Australia since the MCC became responsible for foreign tours in 1903–04.

The English team was L. Hutton (Captain), P.B.H. May, R.T. Simpson, W.J. Edrich, T.E. Bailey, M.C. Cowdrey, D.C.S. Compton, A.V. Bedser, T.G. Evans, J.H. Wardle, J.B. Statham, T.W. Graveney, R. Appleyard, J.E. McConnon, P.J. Loader, F.H. Tyson, K.V. Andrew and J.V. Wilson, with former Test 'keeper George Duckworth scorer and baggagemaster.

The Board of Control named Ian Johnson, nearing 36, to captain Australia against Hutton's team, ending all discussion about Morris or Miller taking the job. Johnson, son of a North Melbourne wine

The Australian team for the Third Test, (L to R): back, L. Favell, J. Burke, R. Archer, J. Ledward (Manager), G. Hole, L. Maddocks; front, R. Benaud, W. Johnston, A. Morris, I. Johnson (Captain), K. Miller, R. Lindwall, N. Harvey.

and spirit merchant who also was a Test selector, flighted his off-breaks more than any bowler of his generation, reasoning that on Australia's hard pitches he had more chance beating batsmen in the air than off the pitch. Some opponents called him 'The Grunter' because of the grunt he combined with energetic efforts to loop the ball up at the right height and still spin the ball.

Johnson's major problem as Test captain was to keep performing well enough to justify his place in the side. His success with his off-spinners and middle-order batting was so elusive Sid Barnes called him the 'non-playing captain', a cruel jibe at a whole-hearted cricketer noted for his public relations acumen. Johnson was the first Victorian captain to invite pressmen into the dressing-room at the end of a day's play to clear up any uncertainties.

Hutton approached every match grimly determined not to make a mistake that would encourage the anti-professional lobby. His negative approach irked Australian batsmen trying to push the scoring rate along. 'Blame The Yawns On Hutton', was the headline for one newspaper story by Arthur Morris.

Eleven dropped catches by English fieldsmen helped Australia to a total of 8 for 601 declared in the First Test at Brisbane and led to Australia's only win of the series, by an innings. Bedser, who had seven catches dropped off his bowling in Brisbane, learned he had been dropped from the Second Test in Sydney by reading a team sheet pinned on the hotel board. 'Funny bloke, Hutton,' said Bedser, who dismissed 236 batsmen in his 51-Test career. 'When I was sick on the tour, he was in the next room but he never once popped in to see how I was.'

Neither Johnson nor Miller could play in Sydney because of injury and with Frank Tyson generating a fearsome pace England drew level with a 38-run win. The Australian team, held up by Hutton's frequent conferences, could not achieve any flow of runs against an English attack that bowled at the disgraceful rate of 85 balls an hour. Tyson took 4 for 45 and 6 for 85 and was particularly impressive when Australia was chasing 223 to win. Tyson finished the match with a huge lump on his head, the result of having been knocked out by a Lindwall bouncer he turned his back on in England's first innings.

With the teams apparently evenly matched on one win apiece, Tyson swung the rubber England's way with a memorable display of pace bowling in the Third Test at Melbourne. This time he bundled Australia out for 111 when they required 240 to win. Tyson

Frank Tyson showing the speed that devastated Australia in 1954–55, starting his delivery stride well before he reached the stumps. (Ken Kelly)

finished with 7 for 27, Australia lost their last eight wickets for only 34 runs and England won by 128 runs.

Bushfires ringed Melbourne during this match and on the centre of the Melbourne ground temperatures were calculated at 41°C (106°F). By the end of play on Saturday the heat caused large cracks to appear in the pitch. On the Sunday rest day the ground staff illegally watered the pitch, afraid that the cracks would widen and prevent the match being completed. The captains agreed to continue when the illegal watering was discovered.

Tyson continued his dominance over Australia's top-order batsmen in the Fourth Test at Adelaide, and after another hard-fought match England emerged winners by five wickets. This gave them the series 3–1 and made Hutton's side the first since 1932–33 to win a rubber in Australia. The Fifth Test, upset by rain, was drawn.

Other bowlers have taken more than Tyson's 28 wickets in

this series, but nobody has ever so thoroughly demoralised Australia's batsmen. The sight of him knocking back the stumps with batsmen only beginning their strokes thrilled huge audiences. England's 23 matches in Australia attracted 1,108,923 spectators who paid £A185,203 to watch them. They lost only two matches, scored 17 centuries, and had only four scored against them. Compton led batting averages with 799 first-class runs at 57.07. Tyson's 51 first-class wickets cost 19.92 each. Most people who attended the series were annoyed by England's slow over-rate and Hutton's time-wasting policy – he frequently held three discussions in an over with his bowlers about their fields – but the man who drove people from the grounds swearing never to go again was Trevor Bailey.

Arthur Morris summed up the universal detestation for Bailey: 'If there were 22 Trevor Baileys in a match, who would ever go and watch it? There would never be any tours if the money had to come from such matches.'

By playing Sheffield Shield matches at the same time as the Tests in 1954–55, the Board of Control forced the states to promote promising youngsters to replace Test players. The high standard of the Shield competition demonstrated yet again the strength of the Australian district club system, with the path open to young men to play their way up through lower grades to the firsts and then make the big step to the state team. Peter Burge (Queensland), Peter Philpott and Pat Crawford (New South Wales) and John Drennan (South Australia) were among those who made that big jump by 1954–55.

Keith Miller's captaincy of New South Wales in their victory over England, and his leadership in the state's fifth Shield win in nine post-war seasons, earned him the vice-captaincy of the first-ever Australian team to tour the West Indies, in early 1955, ahead of Morris but it should have brought him the captaincy. Miller's original club, South Melbourne, proud of their record in producing six Australian captains (Blackham, Harry Trott, Armstrong, Woodfull, Hassett and Johnson), reserved space for him on the wall where they hang their Test leaders' portraits, but he did not make it.

The Australians set off for the Caribbean aware that they had to rehabilitate themselves after the severe drubbing by England. Their captain, Ian Johnson, faced the biggest test of all, with just nine first-class matches, including five Tests, in which to prove himself worthy of the job.

The Australians found in their three months of island-hopping that black and coloured men had largely replaced whites in teams that were supported by fervent, noisy crowds who regarded cricket as a second religion. Bottle-throwing spectators, disputes over umpiring decisions, policemen with batons charging spectators to keep them away from players and steel bands in the front seats had all become part of cricket in the islands.

The Australian team, chosen by Bradman, Ryder and Dudley Seddon, was: I.W. Johnson (Captain), K.R. Miller, R.G. Archer, R. Benaud, P.J.P. Burge, A.K. Davidson, L.E. Favell, R.N. Harvey, J.C. Hill, W.A. Johnston, G.R.A. Langley, R.R. Lindwall, C.C. McDonald, L.V. Maddocks, A.R. Morris and W.J. Watson, with Burge's father, T.J. Burge, an official with long experience in dealing with cricketers in Queensland, as manager.

After a briefing from the Australian Department of Foreign Affairs, Johnson did a splendid public relations job on this tour. When the team arrived he broke away from a welcoming group of English reporters to join a posse of West Indian journalists. The West Indians conveyed this friendliness to their readers and told them to forget about the White Australia policy and look only for bright cricket from Johnson's men. After Australia won the First Test at Sabina Park, Jamaica, by nine wickets with a day to spare, Johnson picked up a tiny barefoot brown boy and carried him off the field in his arms, talking about the game with him. The crowd loved it and Jamaicans pressed in close, trying to eavesdrop.

Big Clyde Walcott scored a century in each innings of the drawn Second Test at Port of Spain, Trinidad, in April 1955. The audience of 28,000 was the biggest to watch a Test in the West Indies to that time, with every seat in the stand and every tree full. Walcott made 126 and 110 but Weekes was not overshadowed with 139 and 87 not out. The Australians forced the draw when McDonald, 110, Morris, 111, and Harvey, 133, made centuries that helped boost Australia's first-innings total to 600.

Johnson had the satisfaction of clinching the series at the Bourda ground at Georgetown, British Guiana, with a crafty bowling display that yielded 7 for 44 from 22.2 overs in West Indies' final innings. This was the outstanding bowling feat on the ground to that time and gave Australia a 2–0 lead with two Tests to play.

The Australians tightened their grip on the rubber by scoring 668 in the first innings of the Fourth Test at Bridgetown, Barbados, but the West Indies escaped defeat. Miller, 137, and Lindwall, 118, led the run feast for Australia, and when Miller dismissed Weekes and Collie Smith in one over to take the West Indies to 6 for 146 in their first innings an Australian win looked certain.

Inexplicably, Johnson took Miller off in what can only be regarded as one of the worst-ever bowling changes, and Atkinson, 219, and Depeiza, 122, put on a Test record of 347 for the seventh wicket. Lindwall refused when Johnson offered him a bowl at one point in this stand. Johnson tried to insist on his captain's right to decide on who bowled and Miller had to intervene when the exchange became heated. 'He shouldn't have to bowl if he doesn't want to,' said Miller.

George Tribe, left-arm spinner, who performed outstanding feats for Northants in the 1950s at a time when Australia was desperately short of bowlers of his quality. He took five wickets in an innings 93 times and scored seven centuries. (Camera Press)

In the dressing-room, with the Australians' frustration brimming over, Miller told Johnson he could not captain a team of schoolboys. Johnson objected to being rebuked in front of his players and offered to settle the issue outside with his fists. Other players stepped between them and after tempers cooled Johnson and Miller rode back to the team's hotel in the same cab.

When Australia batted a second time, their lead cut to 158, Holt at third slip dropped McDonald and Lindwall off Dewdney, and Archer off Worrell, all before they had scored. Holt needed police protection from angry spectators as the players left the field. Test cricketer Leslie Hylton was about to be hanged for the murder of his wife in a widely publicised case. Next day at the ground a poster appeared: 'Hang Holt. Save Hylton.' West Indies were 6 for 234, chasing 408 to win, when time ran out.

Walcott raised West Indian hopes with another magnificent century in the first innings of the Fifth Test at Kingston, Jamaica, but his 155 proved insignificant in the face of an unprecedented Australian onslaught. Five Australians scored centuries after Australia started with 2 for 7. McDonald, 127, and Harvey, 204, put on 295 for the third wicket. Miller, 109, Archer, 128, and Benaud, 121, then flogged the weary bowlers. Johnson declared at 8 for 758 when Benaud was out after hitting two sixes and 15 fours, taking only 78 minutes to reach 100. Australia's total remains the second highest in international cricket after England's 7 for 903 in 1938 at The Oval v. Australia.

Walcott scored his second century of the match, 110, but to no avail and Australia ran out winners by an innings and 82 runs. Miller

385

Collie Smith, who scored a brilliant century in his Test debut at Kingston against Australia, but lost his life in a car accident a few years later. (Ken Kelly)

added 8 wickets for 165 runs to his century. The Australians made 15 centuries on the tour, Miller and Harvey contributing three each in the Tests. They had 13 scored against them, including five by Walcott, and two each from Collie Smith and Weekes. Harvey had a Test average of 108.33, Walcott 82.70.

The first-ever West Indian tour by Australia was a triumph for Ian Johnson, who apart from leading an unbeaten team set new procedures for captains. He took his players out to meet the locals and at receptions and lunches his bonhomie was reminiscent of Hassett at his peak. On the field he averaged 47.75 with the bat in Tests and took 14 wickets at 29.14, including that match-winning display in the Third Test.

In Australia, Sid Barnes remained scathing in his assessment of Johnson as a player. Johnson took it all without complaint, knowing that having Barnes as your critic probably was helpful among the true power-brokers of Australian cricket.

The return home brought sad news for Arthur Morris, one of Johnson's co-selectors in the West Indies. While he was away he discovered that his wife of less than a year had been diagnosed as suffering from cancer. She had not told him for fear of upsetting his cricket, but on hearing how advanced the cancer was Morris quit big cricket. In 46 Tests he had opened for Australia in 77 of his 79 innings, scoring 3533 runs at 46.48. He ranks among the best of the small band of left-handed batsmen who have performed great deeds for Australian cricket, with 46 first-class centuries to his credit, 12 of them in Tests. In all first-class matches he made 12,614 runs at 53.67, figures he undoubtedly would have improved on had it not been for the tragedy that forced his retirement at 33, although he returned for one Cavaliers' tour in 1963.

Under Miller's captaincy New South Wales won the Sheffield Shield for the third successive year in 1955–56. At Sydney in the match against South Australia from 18 to 21 November he threw the ball to Davidson to open the bowling after New South Wales declared at 8 for 215. The breeze from the Randwick end, which Miller enjoyed, was missing. Just before Davidson delivered his first ball Miller felt his hair lift in the wind and called for the ball. He took 7 for 12, the best ever Shield bowling analysis, and had South Australia out for 27, the lowest total in an inter-state match for 72 years, and the lowest ever in Shield competition. Three of the four batsmen Miller bowled – Favell, Hole and Langley – were Test players. Davidson ended up not getting a bowl.

The testimonial match in Sydney in mid-January 1956 for Arthur Mailey and Johnny Taylor, between teams captained by Ian Johnson and Ray Lindwall, was an official trial for the 1956 tour of England. John Rutherford made the long journey from Western Australia for the match. On the way to Perth airport he was injured in a car accident and he spent most of the 3000-mile flight treating his cuts and bruises. He made 113, the most significant of his six first-class centuries and this earned him the honour of becoming the first Western Australian player to be chosen for an Australian touring team. Mailey and Taylor both received £A3590 from the match during which Mailey, in a lounge suit, went out on to the field in a lunch break and clean-bowled Taylor with his only delivery. 'I should have always bowled with a coat on,' said Mailey.

The twenty-second Australian team to tour England was away from 1 April to 8 November 1956, played 31 first-class matches in England and four on the way home in India and Pakistan. Morris accompanied the team as a commentator, using the fees to pay his wife's medical bills. Miller hesitated for weeks about going because of a back injury but finally decided to go. Pat Crawford had to

Peter May, who led England to a 2–1 victory over Australia in the 1956 Ashes series in England. (Sport & General)

get out of an agreement to play Lancashire League cricket to join the side.

The team was I.W. Johnson (Captain), K.R. Miller (Vice-captain), R.G. Archer, R. Benaud, P.J.P. Burge, G.R.A. Langley, R.R. Lindwall, C.C. McDonald, J.W. Burke, I.D. Craig, W.P.A. Crawford, A.K. Davidson, R.N. Harvey, K.D. Mackay, L.V. Maddocks, J.W. Rutherford and J.W. Wilson, with Bill Dowling as manager. They faced an English team captained by Peter May, an amateur who had gone to the right schools. Hutton had retired at the age of 39 with 129 first-class centuries to his name, but in some English newspapers he never did qualify to have his initials printed with his surname, and as a professional he was never honoured with the captaincy of Yorkshire, though he led England 23 times.

Johnson landed in England unsure of the Test line-up. Five of his side were on their first tour. From the start he used some matches simply for practice and did not go all out to beat county teams, trying instead to give all his 17 players a chance to find form. At Leicester Miller made 281 not out, batting for six and a half hours with no sign of a declaration from Johnson.

Surrey defeated the Australians at The Oval between 16 and 18 May 1956 when Jim Laker took all ten wickets for 88 runs in Australia's first innings of 259. This was the first time an English county team had beaten Australia for 44 years and the first time a bowler had taken all ten wickets against Australia since 1878 when another Surrey player, Edward Barratt, did it for The Players. Surrey made 347 in their first innings with Johnson's looped off-spinners comparatively ineffective. Australia collapsed for 107 in their second innings, with Lock taking 7 for 49 and digging the ball in, and Surrey only had to make 20 runs for a famous victory.

This proved a forerunner to the important tour matches, most of which were played on pitches that suited spinners and did not help an Australian attack based on pace. It was also apparent that the tremendous fighting spirit customary in Australian teams was missing, with too many big names ageing and unable or unwilling to support their captain. The English youngsters May, Cowdrey and Sheppard had all made significant advances whereas Australia's youthful crop – Craig, Burge, Crawford and Rutherford – were disappointing. Most English critics believed Craig had had such a disastrous tour of England in 1953 he was lucky to get a second trip.

After rain forced a draw in the First Test at Nottingham, Australia had their first win in England since 1948 by winning the

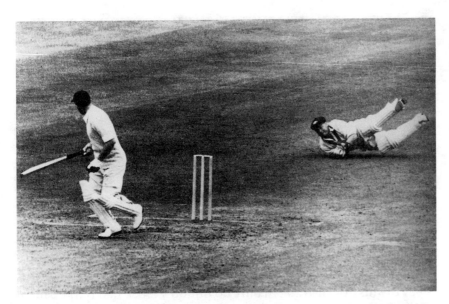

Gil Langley dives wide to catch Johnny Wardle in the Second Test at Lord's in 1956. (Sport & General)

Second Test at Lord's by 185 runs. McDonald and Burke laid the foundations with an opening stand of 137 on the first day, wicket-keeper Langley set a world record by dismissing nine batsmen in the match and Miller took ten wickets in a Test for the first time in his career. Benaud, showing the benefit of long hours in the nets, bowled well, and took one of the greatest catches seen at Lord's when he reached above his head as he fell in the gully and caught Cowdrey's powerfully hit cut in one hand. However Benaud's 97 proved his only outstanding innings of the tour.

Four days before the Third Test at Leeds the pitch was under water and this proved of immense assistance to the English spinners Lock and Laker, who took 18 wickets between them. England scored 325 after May, 101, and Washbrook, 98, put on 187 for the fourth wicket but by the time Australia batted, worn patches appeared in the pitch and May quickly brought on Laker and Lock to exploit them. Six wickets fell for 69 runs before Miller and Benaud took the score to 142. The last four wickets put on only two runs. Following on 182 runs in arrears, Australia managed only 140, losing by an innings and 42 runs.

The Old Trafford pitch for the Fourth Test was a disgrace. When the groundsman swept it at lunchtime on the first day clouds of dust obscured his assistants. It was a spinner's paradise but Johnson's 41 overs cost 151 runs, which made his four wickets expensive. England finished with 459 thanks to centuries by Peter Richardson (104) and the Reverend David Sheppard (113). Lock

389

Groundsmen preparing the pitch at Old Trafford, Manchester, for Australia's first innings raised clouds of dust with ordinary brooms from a surface that had not been watered, ideal for spinners. (Sport & General)

and Laker were in action 18 minutes after Australia began batting. They dismissed Australia in only 80 minutes. Lock had Burke caught in the gully by Cowdrey but the other wickets all fell to Laker, whose 9 for 37 came from 16.4 overs. Laker clearly had a psychological edge over the Australians following his ten wickets in an innings for Surrey.

Australia followed on and Laker finished with 10 for 53 and 19 for 90 in the match. All Laker's wickets fell at the same end. By winning at Manchester by an innings and 170 runs, England retained the Ashes and brought the dominance Australia had enjoyed since 1938 to an emphatic conclusion. Laker, who had not been able to find a place in the previous English team in Australia, completed the rubber with a record 46 wickets at an amazing average cost of 9.60. Australia went through a Test series for the first time without one batsman scoring a century.

Australia won only nine of their 31 matches in England, losing three, and leaving 19 unfinished. Most of the players holidayed on the Continent for a month before they assembled at Rome airport for brief visits to Pakistan and India. They had three days' practice in Karachi, insufficient preparation for a Test match to be played on matting. They knew when they began the First Test against Pakistan on 11 October 1956 that right-arm fast-medium bowler Fazal Mahmood was their danger man. Fazal had taken 12 wickets against England two years earlier at The Oval to inspire a Test win that shocked the cricket world.

The two teams combined to score only 95 runs on the first day, with Fazal taking 6 for 34 to have Australia out for 80. Miller top-scored with 21. Pakistan completed their first innings with 199 before Fazal got to work again and took a further 7 for 80 for a match analysis of 13 for 114 which included three wickets in four balls in the second innings. Pakistan scored the 69 runs needed to win for the loss of one wicket.

Miller bowled 12 overs without taking a wicket in Pakistan's second innings before his knee gave out and ended his Test career. He was a crowd-pleaser without a rival who could arouse spectators with every switch of his mane of black hair, aggressive but casual and able to swing a match in a few overs whether batting, bowling or catching. He made 14,183 runs at 48.90 in first-class matches, 2958 of them in 55 Tests at 36.96, and took a total of 497 first-wickets at 22.30, 170 of them in Tests at 22.97. He also held 136 catches, some of them among the most remarkable seen in cricket.

Two days after their defeat by Pakistan Australia took the field for the first of three Tests against India. They emerged from this mini-series 2–0 winners, with the other Test a draw. Lindwall set up the first win in Madras by taking 7 for 43 in India's second innings, and solid batting led to a win by an innings and five runs. At Brabourne Stadium in Bombay neither side made any headway against some efficient batting, Burke (160) and Harvey (140) both making centuries. Then in the last match of a long, arduous tour Benaud took 6 for 52 and 5 for 53 to give Australia victory by 94 runs at Eden Park Gardens in Calcutta.

All the Australians suffered from stomach troubles and Lindwall labelled his only experience as Australian captain in Bombay as a Test match without bowlers. More than 1000 runs were scored in the match but the bowlers could not average five wickets a day.

Ian Johnson departed from Test cricket with seven wins, five draws and five losses from his 17 Tests as Australia's captain. He completed the double, 109 wickets at 29.19 and 1000 runs at 18.51, to join an exclusive group, in his very last Test. Not long after he arrived home he took over as secretary of the Melbourne Cricket Club, beating 44 other applicants for the job previously held by Vernon Ransford, Hugh Trumble and Ben Wardill.

Jim Laker, whose 19 wickets for 90 runs in 1956 at Old Trafford all came from one end and remains the most wickets in a first-class match. His 10 for 53 in Australia's second innings was the second time he took all ten wickets in an innings against Ian Johnson's side. (Ken Kelly)

CHAPTER TWENTY-FIVE

THE BENAUD ERA

Bill Dowling, in his manager's report on the 1956 Australian tour, praised Ron Archer's intelligent application and paid tribute to the manner in which Ian Craig fought his way back into the Test side. The leadership potential of both players impressed him. Dowling took over as Australian Board of Control chairman in 1957 and was at the centre of discussions on the appointment of a new Test captain.

The Board sought a captain who would bring a fresh approach to the revival of the Test side. Archer lost all chance when he broke down in Pakistan, Lindwall at 36 had reached the veteran category after 55 Tests, and Harvey had not shown any leadership qualities in his 48 Tests. Benaud was best left to improve his spin bowling, and might infect the team with his own lack of aggression if he ran the show.

Thus by arrangement with the Board New South Wales replaced Miller as state captain with Craig, who was 21 years and 164 days old, and had already twice toured England. From the start he impressed, handling the organisational and social aspects of the job splendidly. A good mixer, he got on well with his players who all knew he had not sought the captaincy.

In his fourth match as state captain Craig was confined to bed in the team's Melbourne hotel with a bout of tonsillitis, when news arrived that his team was in trouble at St Kilda. Chasing 161 to win on a drying pitch, New South Wales were 7 for 70 following hostile spells by Ian Meckiff and Lindsay Kline. Craig jumped out of bed and took a taxi to the ground, where he joined Richie Benaud at the crease and put on 75 runs. When Craig went for 24, Burke, who had retired hurt with a broken finger, returned with his hand heavily bandaged. With the scores level, Burke was caught behind.

This was the first tie in the 100-year history of inter-colony and -state cricket and the first in the 65-year history of the Sheffield Shield. Throughout their match-saving stand Craig had been unable to call loud enough for Benaud to hear.

A dogged fourth-wicket partnership by Sid Carroll and Craig saved New South Wales from outright defeat in the return match against Victoria in Sydney. The point saved enabled New South Wales to win the Sheffield Shield for the fourth successive season.

Continuing Craig's grooming, the Board appointed him captain of one of the youngest combinations to represent Australia, for 12 matches in New Zealand between February and April 1957. Harvey was the oldest member of the team at 28, Norman O'Neill the youngest at 19 and most of the side were in their early twenties. The team was I.D. Craig (Captain), R.N. Harvey, P.J.P. Burge, R. Benaud, N.C. O'Neill, R.B. Simpson, L.E. Favell, J.W. Martin, J. Drennan, R.A. Gaunt, B.N. Jarman, L.F. Kline, W.J. Watson and I. Meckiff.

Most of the players in that team date Australia's climb back to international honours from the New Zealand matches. The Australians took time to adjust to the slow pace of wet New Zealand pitches, but gained confidence as the matches progressed and completed the tour unbeaten. Both the first two representative matches – they were not classed as Tests – were drawn. Australia won the third by ten wickets. Of the seven first-class matches, Australia won five. Australia's batsmen and bowlers mostly did well and only wicket-keeper Jarman did not fulfil expectations. Despite the side's youth, team harmony was better than for several years.

After completing a three-year pharmacy course at Sydney University, Craig received Board of Control approval to go to England for six months' training by the Boots chain of chemist shops. He flew from England to join the 14 players flown to South Africa from Australia for the 22-match 1957–58 tour. Archer was in the original party chosen for this trip but withdrew because of the thigh injury sustained in Pakistan and was replaced by fellow Queenslander Ken Mackay. For Mackay, this was a chance to redeem himself, following his failures in England. Craig was particularly impressive amid the confusion at the start of the tour when the designated manager, South Australian Jack Jantke, had a heart attack and remained at home with the agreed daily schedules. A South African, C.J.R. Howard of Bulawayo, looked after the Australians temporarily

Australian cricketers (L to R) Les Favell, Ken Mackay, Neil Harvey, Bob Simpson and Alan Davidson with a toy kangaroo presented to them by an airline official before they flew to South Africa in 1957–58. (Qantas Airlines)

while replacement manager Jack Norton was flown out from Sydney.

The team selected by Bradman, Jack Ryder and Dudley Seddon was I.D. Craig (Captain), R.N. Harvey (Vice-captain), R. Benaud, P.J.P. Burge, J.W. Burke, A.K. Davidson, J. Drennan, L.E. Favell, A.T.W. Grout, B.N. Jarman, L.F. Kline, K.D. Mackay, C.C. McDonald, I. Meckiff and R.B. Simpson. The surprises were the preference for Meckiff ahead of Lindwall and the choice of Simpson instead of Norman O'Neill. Simpson had shown consistent all-round skill for Western Australia. He was the son of a former soccer professional with Stenhousemuir in the Scottish League, and had played first-grade cricket in Sydney at the age of 15. Lindwall was judged to be past his best and when Meckiff and Drennan were injured Ray Gaunt was flown over as a reinforcement.

Splendidly captained by Craig, Australia won an absorbing series 3–0. Australia's batting was attractive and productive throughout and the South Africans could not master the pace and swing of Davidson nor the leg-spin of Benaud. Grout kept wicket superbly and clearly established his superiority to Jarman. Craig developed Australia into such a powerful side they were rarely extended and had 11 wins and nine draws in an unbeaten tour.

South Africa began the First Test at Johannesburg from 23 to 28 December 1957 with a record opening stand of 176 by Jackie McGlew, 108, and Trevor Goddard, 90. John Waite made 115 that lifted South Africa to 9 declared for 470. Helped by a fine 122 from Benaud, Australia fought back strongly and honours finished even. Grout in his first Test set a then world record of six catches in an innings.

Australia won the Second Test at Cape Town by an innings and 141 runs. Colin McDonald, 99, and Jimmy Burke, 189, put on 190 for the first wicket and pushed Australia to a total of 449. South Africa were forced to follow on when they managed only 209 in reply. Kline ended the match with a hat-trick and match figures of 6 for 47, but Benaud was the match-winner with 9 for 144, including 5 for 49 in the second innings. The South Africans played themselves into a strong position in the Third Test at Durban, where McGlew made his second century (105) of the series, but slow, unimaginative batting cost South Africa all chance of a win, after Adcock took 6 for 43 in Australia's first innings.

Australia won the Fourth Test at Johannesburg by ten wickets to go two up after Benaud, 100, and Mackay, 83 not out, pushed the first innings score to 401. Benaud took 4 for 70 and 5 for 84 in another fine display of leg-break bowling. Australia prevailed again in the Fifth Test at Port Elizabeth to take the rubber 3–0. The margin this time was eight wickets. Davidson had 4 for 44 and 5 for 38, Benaud 5 for 82 in the second innings. Benaud's 106 wickets in first-class matches at 19.40 and his four centuries in compiling 817 runs at 51.06 were the major reason Australia completed a South African tour for the fifth time without defeat.

South Africa failed under Clive van Ryneveld's captaincy to achieve the team spirit and excellence in the field they showed under Cheetham four years earlier. Tayfield was completely frustrated by Mackay and all the Springbok bowlers took heavy punishment from an Australian team that scored 23 centuries and had only eight compiled against them. Burke was the only Australian to top 1000 runs, with 1041 at 65.06.

Back home in Australia Craig had a severe bout of hepatitis and tried to return to cricket before he was fully recovered. He scored ducks in his first two big matches on his return before retiring for the rest of the 1958–59 season on doctors' advice. The selectors handed the captaincy to Harvey for an Australian XI match against Peter May's touring English team but apparently were not impressed when England won by 345 runs. A week before the First Test they bypassed Harvey to appoint Benaud captain with England looking such a formidable outfit. Sir Donald Bradman told them:

Betty Wilson shows the technique that enabled her to take 7 for 7 and score a century for Australia v. England in 1958.
(Central Press)

'I only hope we can give you a good game.'

England, in fact, had had major problems finalising their touring party. Laker declared himself unavailable and then changed his mind. Yorkshire left-arm spinner Johnny Wardle was named in the original side but wrote a series of articles for the *Daily Mail* criticising the administration of the Yorkshire club. His criticism appeared justified as Yorkshire had allowed top-class players Willie Watson, Bob Appleyard and Frank Lowson to leave the club, but the thin-skinned Yorkshire officials declared that Wardle had broken his contract with the county by writing the articles and struck him from their playing staff. The MCC then withdrew Wardle's tour invitation and he joined reporters covering the tour.

Sixteen players left England for Australia without Wardle's replacement being named. On the voyage Willie Watson, then captain of Leicestershire, injured a knee, and required an operation. There was plenty of time to fly out replacements before the tour began but MCC hesitated until Raman Subba Row fractured his wrist just before the First Test. They then reinforced the side by flying out Ted Dexter and John Mortimore. The enlarged England team, the twenty-seventh to tour Australia, thus comprised: P.B.H. May (Captain), M.C. Cowdrey, T.E. Bailey, E.R. Dexter, T.G. Evans, T.W. Graveney, J.C. Laker, P.J. Loader, G.A.R. Lock, C.A. Milton, J.B. Mortimore, P.E. Richardson, J.B. Statham, R. Swetman, R. Subba Row, F.S. Trueman, F.H. Tyson and W. Watson, with F.R. Brown as manager and George Duckworth scorer and baggagemaster. Bill Ferguson, scorer and baggagemaster on 43 international tours, had died at Bath in 1957.

Norman O'Neill, omitted from the previous summer's South African tour, had since shown such superb form the Australian selectors rushed him to Perth for the second match of England's tour against a Combined XI. O'Neill gave a thrilling display to score 104, which was every bit as accomplished as Peter May's 113 for England in a drawn match. Statham and Laker fully tested O'Neill, who batted for 280 minutes in taking a long look at the bowling. He hit 10 fours.

Benaud's reign as Australian captain began with an eight-wicket win over England in the First Test at the Gabba from 5 to 10 December 1958. Basing his attack on Davidson's left-arm pace over the wicket that moved across right-hand batsmen, he found England's batsmen vulnerable and with the help of remarkable catches immediately destroyed any psychological advantage England held.

Benaud was one of the most dedicated cricketers in the practice nets, regularly devoting hours to eradicating faults and improving skills. Here he is preparing for a batting session. (Ern McQuillan)

Davidson, who developed on a hillside pitch at Lisarow, near Gosford, New South Wales, was a fascinating bowler. He had come into big cricket as a tearaway who wanted to bowl fast enough to scare batsmen out, but a leg injury had forced him to slow down and with the reduced pace he found he could swing the ball more and swing it late. He had even great players like May and Cowdrey playing down the wrong line in Brisbane.

The large contingent of English pressmen covering the tour took exception to the action of Ian Meckiff, and by the time they reached Melbourne for the Second Test the tour was in disarray. Australians claimed England played negative cricket that would drive spectators from the game, there was mounting controversy over umpiring and pace bowlers' dragging, and finally the allegation that Meckiff was a chucker.

Watching Meckiff from behind the fence it was impossible to decide on the legality of his action. He had an extremely whippy left arm, which had a bend in it that could not be straightened, and he let the ball go from a bent elbow wind-up, achieving his pace from double-jointed shoulders. His wrists were half as wide as the average bowler's. The whole thing came together in the bowling stride in a blur the naked eye could not decipher and there were never any pictures which showed one way or another if he was a chucker.

Ian Meckiff demonstrates the wristy left-arm action that upset the English players under Peter May in 1958–59 and led to his dismissal from big cricket after the 1963–64 Brisbane Test v. South Africa. (SCG Archives)

Australia repeated their tactics in the Second Test at Melbourne, with the left-arm pace moving across right-handers. Only May, who made 113 in England's first innings, coped with it. Statham bowled bravely to restrict Australia to a first-innings lead of 49, taking 7 for 57. Brilliant catching and the Englishmen's failure to pick up Meckiff's late swing tumbled England out for 87 in their second innings, their lowest score in Australia since 1903–04. Australia lost two wickets scoring the 39 required to win.

The Third Test at Sydney was drawn after Cowdrey took 6 hours 2 minutes to reach 100 not out, the slowest century on record in England v. Australia matches. Knowing he had to win to keep the series alive, May sent Australia in to bat when he won the toss in the Fourth Test at Adelaide and the fate of the Ashes was virtually decided when McDonald and Burke put on 171 for Australia before they were parted. Burke appeared to be caught off his glove in the first half-hour but umpire McInnes gave him not out. Thereafter McInnes took heavy criticism from English reporters. McInnes gave Mackay not out to an appeal for a catch but Mackay walked out.

Gordon Rorke in the midst of his famous slide. With his giant frame balanced on the toe of his right foot, he could cover alarming distances up the pitch towards batsmen. (John Fairfax & Sons)

Later McDonald gave his wicket away after scoring 170 when Burke, his runner, appeared to be run out but was not seen by McInnes, who allowed Burke to get behind him.

Gordon Rorke, who had replaced the injured Meckiff for this match, had an amazing action in which he took the weight of his entire body on the outside edge of his front foot, sliding metres up the pitch. This unique delivery stride took him closer to the batsman than any other bowler. The Englishmen joked about feeling his hot breath on them when they faced him. Brian Chapman called Rorke 'a honey of a chucker' in the London *Daily Express*, but in fact Rorke's drag caused more problems than his arm action. Bowling in extreme heat for 52 overs he dismissed Cowdrey, May, Graveney, Watson and Lock for 101 runs and with Benaud mesmerising the tail-enders Australia won by ten wickets.

Meckiff returned for the Fifth Test in Melbourne, giving Benaud the luxury of four fast bowlers. Opener Bailey was out first ball he faced to a lifter from the veteran Lindwall and England were never in the match after that. McDonald had several narrow escapes for Australia, including being given not out when a bail was dislodged as he glanced Trueman for four, before he settled down to an innings of 133. This helped Australia to a 146-run first-innings lead. The Australian pace attack made all the English batsmen struggle for survival and Australia were left with only 69 runs to score to win and wrap up the series 4–0. The failure of Tyson to achieve anywhere near the pace he generated four years earlier proved critical for an England team dogged by injuries.

Unhappily, the controversies over chuckers and dragging overshadowed a marvellous performance by Australia in regaining the Ashes, and a miserable effort by England in winning only four of their 17 first-class matches virtually escaped criticism in England. Lindwall took the record he had been seeking by passing Grimmett's total of 216 Test wickets, Grout equalled Tallon's record of 20 dismissals in a Test series against England, and Bailey ended his Test career for England with a pair.

Despite his success in his first series as Australia's captain, Benaud found himself involved in a problem that increased in intensity as the English tour progressed and the witch-hunt against chucking and dragging gained impetus. The Australian Cricket Board initially tried to duck the problem by arguing that not a single bowler had been called in what became a rather sordid series as the accusations of cheating multiplied. Australians were far from happy about

Lock's action and deplored the spectacle of Laker and Lock rubbing the new ball on the pitch without any reprimand from umpires. Time-wasting was so bad that England managed only 51 overs in a day during the Adelaide Test and crowds had to endure days when only 150 runs were scored.

The chucking row continued as experts all around the cricket world tried to improve on the law on throwing. Bradman favoured the *Oxford Dictionary* definition: 'To deliver the ball with a sudden straightening of the arm,' and insisted the problem was best left to umpires. John Arlott said the issue was best left to barristers, not cricket writers or officials. London sportswriter Jim Manning compared the problem with defining the action of a trotter.

New South Wales continued their domination of the Sheffield Shield while the English tour was in progress by winning the Shield for the sixth successive season but for the first time since Bob McLean in 1949–50 a South Australian-born batsman, Gavin Stevens, headed the Shield batting averages. Stevens made 859 runs at 85.90, including 259 not out against New South Wales in Sydney. Other impressive newcomers were South Australian John Lill, Victorian Bill Lawry and the Western Australian Barry Shepherd.

Undeterred by the allegations of chucking and dragging Rorke produced an inspired spell for New South Wales against Queensland in Sydney when he took six wickets for eight runs and performed the hat-trick. Rorke's team-mate Jimmy Burke retired at 28 after 24 Tests, taking accusations that he was the worst of all chuckers into his weekly appearances in grade cricket. Burke scored 7563 first-class runs at 45.01 and made eight first-class centuries, three of them in Tests. Burke also took 101 first-class wickets at 29.12.

The appointment of Benaud as captain saw the introduction of players hugging and embracing bowlers and catchers and emotional scenes oldtimers found repugnant. Author Ray Robinson commented that from a practical point of view the only issue was whether the caresses encouraged bowlers and catchers to do better and he was sure they did.

Benaud was rewarded for regaining the Ashes from England with the captaincy of the Australian team that toured India and Pakistan between November 1959 and January 1960. In three busy months the Australians played eight Tests and three other first-class matches. The team was R. Benaud (Captain), P.J.P. Burge, A.K. Davidson, L.E. Favell, A.T.W. Grout, R.N. Harvey, B.N. Jarman, L.F. Kline,

*Benaud the batsman was
aggressive, alert and
steadily improved his
average as he matured,
scoring 11,719 first-class
runs at 36.50.*
(John Fairfax & Sons)

R.R. Lindwall, C.C. McDonald, K.D. Mackay, I. Meckiff, N.C. O'Neill, G.F. Rorke and G.B. Stevens. Maddocks was originally chosen as the reserve wicket-keeper but Jarman replaced him when he withdrew. Dr Ian McDonald, brother of Colin McDonald, accompanied the team as the official team doctor.

Australia won the First Test at Dacca against Pakistan by eight wickets. Benaud, wary of groundsmen who could vary the tension of the mat, sent Kline to the ground two hours before play began with strict instructions that the mat had to be kept tight when Australia batted. The Australians arrived at the ground to hear Kline yelling: 'Pull, you bastards!' to the Dacca ground staff.

Hanif Mohammad, 66, figured in useful stands after Pakistan lost their first wicket with only three runs on the board, and at 3 for 145 Pakistan appeared set for a big score. But they were all out for 200, Benaud taking 4 for 69, Davidson 4 for 42. Harvey batted splendidly for Australia but after he was bowled by Fazal Mahmood, the batting was disappointing, and only Grout's bold 66 not out gave Australia the lead. Fazal continued his outstanding form against Australia with 5 for 71 from 35.5 overs.

From 2 for 57, Pakistan slumped to 5 for 81 in their second innings, and never recovered. Mackay bowled off-spinners at medium-pace to a perfect length to finish with 6 for 42, with 27 maidens in his 45 overs. Benaud gave him handy support with 4 for 42. Pakistan's 134 meant Australia needed only 110 to win and they ran out winners by eight wickets.

Australia won the Second Test at Lahore by seven wickets to become the first visiting country to win a series in Pakistan. They dismissed Pakistan for 146 and 366 on a grass pitch. The pace and swing of Davidson and Meckiff followed by the spin of Benaud and Kline had wickets falling regularly and only Saeed Ahmed, who took six hours to make 166 in Pakistan's second innings, held up the Australian attack. Norman O'Neill's hard-hitting 134, which included 19 fours, produced an Australian first-innings total of 391. Left to score 122 to win in even time, Australia made them with 12 minutes to spare.

The Third Test at Karachi was drawn. Pakistan made a fine start on the mat, reaching 1 for 124, but was all out for 287. Australia struggled after losing 2 for 33, but a last-wicket partnership of 50 by Davidson and Lindwall kept the deficit down to 30. Hanif made 101 not out in the Pakistani second innings of 8 declared for 194, part of which was watched by President Eisenhower, the first US

Norman O'Neill, who averaged 45.56 per innings in his 42 Tests, lets fly with his favourite sweep shot. For 12 years he had the appeal of a matinee idol for cricket fans. (Ern McQuillan)

president to watch Test cricket. Australia were left 120 minutes in which to score 225 to win, a task they never seriously attempted.

After his memorable display of stamina and skill against Pakistan, Benaud took 3 for 0 and 5 for 76 in a match-winning performance against India from 12 to 16 December in New Delhi. Davidson began India's collapse by taking two of the first three wickets for 32 runs before Benaud completed the rout and had them out for 135. Australia responded with 468, Harvey top-scoring with 144, followed by 78 from Mackay and some useful hitting by tail-enders Grout, 42, and Meckiff, 45 not out. India made a splendid start to their second innings but after Kline and Benaud took the ball wickets tumbled. From 1 for 121, India were all out for 206, Australia winning by an innings and 127 runs.

Benaud's wonderful run of success faltered in the Second Test at Kanpur, where off-spinner Patel took 14 wickets for 124 runs to give India a surprising win by 119 runs on a newly laid turf wicket. Davidson took 12 for 124 for Australia. Left to score 225 for victory in the final innings, Australia managed only 105, with Rorke absent ill.

Rorke was rushed to hospital with gastroenteritis on Christmas Eve and after losing eight kilograms in weight was flown home to Australia. He took almost two years to recover and never played

401

Considered lucky to get the job, Benaud lost only four of his 27 matches as Australia's captain. Here a young fan seeks an autograph after another Australian triumph.
(NSWCA Library)

Test cricket again. He remains one of the most controversial bowlers of all time, a giant with a freakish delivery slide that caused changes in the law on dragging, although no other pace bowlers could match his sleight of foot. His four Tests brought only ten wickets at 20.30, astounding figures for a player who so disturbed the law-makers.

After a draw in the Third Test at Bombay, where Contractor (108), Harvey (102) and O'Neill (163) hit centuries, Australia went to a 2–1 lead by winning the Fourth Test at Madras by an innings and 55 runs. Favell's 101 and Mackay's 89 helped lift Australia's first-innings total to 342. India then collapsed for 149 and 138, Benaud taking 5 for 43 and 3 for 43, and changing the bowling cleverly to sustain the pressure.

The Fifth Test was drawn, O'Neill scoring another century (113) and Benaud taking a further seven wickets. By defeating both Pakistan and India comfortably Australia had confirmed its ranking as the world's no. 1 cricket team.

Stevens was in hospital for the Australians' last two tour matches and was later found to have a rare form of hepatitis. He was flown home seriously ill and played no more first-class cricket. Kline was found to have a chronic sinus infection before the last Test and flew home early. All the team suffered from severe bouts of dysentery.

The Australians arrived home in time for the concluding matches in the Sheffield Shield competition. Benaud took over as New South Wales captain from Craig and ensured they retained the Shield with a nine-wicket win over Western Australia. Simpson had given Western Australia victory over New South Wales in their first clash in Perth with an innings of 236 not out, but in the return match in Sydney his team-mates could not handle Benaud, who took 6 for 74 in both innings. Simpson played two splendid innings, 98 and 161, to no avail. Simpson, who was on the field for all bar 20 minutes of the Sydney match, scored 902 runs in six Shield innings at an average of 300.06.

At the end of the season an Australian Second XI toured New Zealand for six first-class matches under the captaincy of Ian Craig. Simpson further enhanced his reputation by heading the batting averages with 518 runs at 74.0. He proved a masterly slips field, a useful change bowler with his leg-spinners, and was a model opening batsman, repeatedly giving his side good starts.

Craig was a major disappointment and averaged only 28.44 in his nine first-class innings. His captaincy was also criticised, particularly in the last representative match when he did not enforce the follow-on that appeared certain to give Australia victory. The pace bowler Frank Misson improved as the tour progressed. Australia finished with only two wins from six first-class matches, with four left drawn.

All over the cricket world prominent umpires confessed they were apprehensive about calling bowlers for chucking without official assurances that their futures would not be jeopardised. Meckiff announced that he was modifying his action, but in the English summer of 1960 the spotlight moved from him to the South African Geoff Griffin, who was no-balled eight times for throwing. Griffin left the South African team for special instruction with Alf Gover, which failed to eliminate his problems. He was called six times for throwing in South Africa's match against Hampshire and at Lord's in the Second Test was called 11 times by umpire Frank Lee.

The no-balling of Griffin was on the front page of English newspapers when Sir Donald Bradman and Board chairman Bill Dowling arrived. Australia considered that a meeting of the Imperial Cricket Conference with chucking on the agenda was so important they sent their senior administrators rather than follow normal procedure and have their London representative attend. By the time of the London conference 14 bowlers had been branded chuckers by umpires around the cricket world.

Bradman confessed that defining a throw was the most difficult problem he had encountered in cricket and called for goodwill in solving a problem that was so involved two men of equal sincerity could take opposite views. He got the goodwill he sought when the West Indian team captained by Frank Worrell arrived for the 1960–61 series against Australia. Worrell, the first black captain of the West Indies on tour, went to extraordinary lengths to revive spectator support for cricket in Australia, insisting that his side play bright, enterprising cricket and only bowl bouncers intelligently.

By the time of the First Test in Brisbane, the West Indies had already suffered two defeats but they were also established as one of the most entertaining teams to visit Australia. Requiring 233 runs to win in 310 minutes on the final day, Australia lost their last wicket to a run-out off the seventh ball of the last over with the scores level. The first tie in Test history came after some brilliant cricket, including a magnificent knock of 132 by Sobers, 100 runs and ten wickets in the match by Davidson and 181 by O'Neill.

This historic match ushered in a captivating series that aroused

One of the great moments in cricket history, with West Indian players leaping high in jubilation as Joe Solomon's throw hits the stumps to create the first tied Test in 1960–61 at the Gabba. (Ron Lovitt, Age, *Melbourne)*

the entire cricket world and delighted Australian households. Australia went one-up in the Second Test at Melbourne, because of more superb bowling by Davidson, whose 6 for 53 restricted the West Indies' first innings to 181. Hall thrilled spectators by bowling at a fearsome pace for 4 for 51 and 2 for 32, before Australia won by seven wickets. The West Indies levelled the series in the Third Test at Sydney, winning by 222 runs after spinners Gibbs and Valentine bamboozled Australia's gifted batting line-up. Sobers' 168 in this match was one of the finest centuries ever seen on the SCG.

The Fourth Test at Adelaide produced some superb batting by Rohan Kanhai, who made 117 and 115. He began proceedings one morning by hitting Benaud's first ball for six. The match reached a dramatic climax after a hat-trick by Lance Gibbs when Ken Mackay and Lindsay Kline survived the last 100 minutes against the full fury of the West Indian pace bowlers to give Australia a draw.

Kline went straight from the practice wickets to join 'Slasher' Mackay, as last man in, with no chance of victory and the words of a woman spectator who had watched his pathetic efforts in the nets ringing in his ears. The woman had seen the embarrassment of Norm O'Neill and Johnnie Martin as they got Kline out every second ball in his 20-minute warm-up. 'Waste of time sending him in,' she shouted. In the dressing-room the other Australians started to pack their bags. After Kline and Mackay batted out time, with the nation listening to the broadcast of every ball, Kline went looking for the woman but could not find her.

Lindsay Kline surrounded by West Indian fieldsmen during his epic last wicket stand that saved the series and the Adelaide Test for Australia in 1960–61. Kline had looked hopeless in the nets. (Adelaide News)

This draw took the teams to the Fifth Test in Melbourne with one win each. The second day's play attracted 90,800 spectators, then a world record for a cricket match. Sobers bowled unchanged for the last 41 eight-ball overs in Australia's first innings during which Davidson scored his thousandth Test run, having already taken 100 Test wickets.

The final innings began with Australia needing 258 runs to win. Simpson gave Australia a defiant start by scoring 18 off the first over and 24 from the first ten balls he faced, batting brilliantly against sharply turning deliveries until he was bowled for 92. With four runs wanted and three wickets left Grout back-cut Valentine towards the fence. The off bail was then spotted on the ground, but when wicket-keeper Gerry Alexander appealed umpires Col Egar and Col Hoy conferred. Unable to decide how the bail fell, they gave Grout not out. Thousands of spectators invaded the field when Mackay, beaten by a ball that spun but missed the stumps, ran through for a bye that settled the match. Australia had won the most exciting series in her history by two wickets and a margin of two Tests to one.

The West Indian tour of 22 matches was watched by 956,015 people who paid £A213,530 for the joy of it. Two days after play ended the West Indians were paraded through Melbourne in open cars and given a tickertape send-off. 'I can't tell you how overwhelmed the boys were,' wrote Worrell. 'The tears came easily on that extraordinary procession and I couldn't be bothered wiping them away. It was incredible.'

*   *   *

Frank Worrell polishes the trophy that bears his name and has become the symbol of supremacy between Australian and West Indian teams. A happy shot taken at the end of the remarkable 1960–61 series. (Herald & Weekly Times, Melbourne)

Shortly afterwards the twenty-third Australian team to tour England in 1961 was named, and included only one player new to touring, Bill Lawry, although Booth, Misson and Quick only had experience from their brief tour of New Zealand. Grout was lucky to pass the medical for the tour as he had a history of blackouts, some of them at Queensland net practices. The team was: R. Benaud (Captain), B.C. Booth, P.J.P. Burge, A.K. Davidson, W.M. Lawry, K.D. Mackay, C.C. McDonald, G.D. McKenzie, R.A. Gaunt, A.T.W. Grout, R.N. Harvey, B.N. Jarman, L.F. Kline, F.M. Misson, N.C. O'Neill, I.W. Quick and R.B. Simpson, with Syd Webb, QC, as manager.

The tour began under an agreement between the MCC and the Australian Board of Control for a truce against chuckers for the first five weeks. Both countries agreed that any player guilty of chucking could be reported to the MCC without umpires no-balling them, but without Burke, Slater, Meckiff or Rorke in their side the Australians had little to worry about. The only bowler reported was Harold Rhodes of Derbyshire for his bowling at Lord's for MCC against Australia. Australia sustained a grievous blow when Benaud suffered a shoulder injury in the first match against Worcestershire. He was never properly fit for the rest of the tour. England took

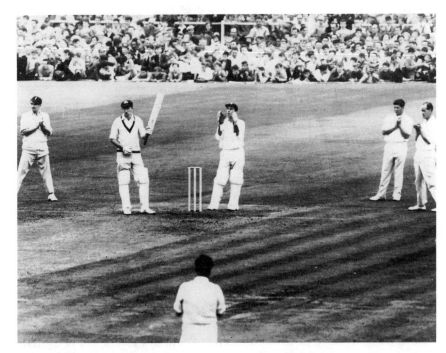

Bill Lawry acknowledges the crowd's applause after reaching his century in Australia's second innings at Old Trafford in 1961. (Sport & General)

a similar blow when May failed to recover from groin strain in time for the First Test and Cowdrey had to take over the captaincy.

Two evenly matched teams prepared to go for victory rather than safety played out a memorable rubber. After a draw in the First Test at Edgbaston, Australia won the Second Test at Lord's by five wickets thanks to a notable display by Graham McKenzie, who took 5 for 37 in England's second innings on his Test debut. England levelled by winning the Third Test at Leeds by eight wickets when Trueman took 5 for 0 in a spell of 24 balls bowling off-cutters.

Australia won the series and retained the Ashes when she won a thrilling Fourth Test at Manchester in which the advantage swung back and forth for four and a half days. On the final morning Australia appeared in a hopeless position with a lead of only 158 when their last pair, Davidson and McKenzie, came together. Davidson hit out in spectacular style while McKenzie defended and they added 98 for the last wicket, Davidson finishing on 77 not out. Set to score 256 at 67 runs an hour England had the task well in hand when Dexter made a marvellous 76 in 84 minutes.

Benaud decided Australia could not save the game without bowling England out and after dismissing Dexter bowled May round his leg by pitching in footmarks allegedly left by Trueman. Brilliant catching by Simpson helped Australia's cause and the last

One of Australia's great opponents in the Benaud years, England's Ted Dexter, on his way to a glorious 180 in the Edgbaston Test of the 1961 series won by Australia. (Ken Kelly)

English wicket fell 54 runs short with 20 minutes left. Benaud, an inspiration to his side while fielding in the gully, took 6 for 70. England could still have drawn the series by winning the Fifth Test at The Oval but fine centuries by O'Neill, 117, and Burge, 181, put Australia out of danger.

Lawry was the surprise success of the tour, heading both the Test and first-class batting averages. He made 2019 runs at 61.18 on the tour, 420 of them at 52.50 in Tests, silencing those who considered him lucky to beat Ian Craig for a place in the team. The real hero in England in 1961 however was Richie Benaud, who kept his promise to provide entertaining cricket, pushing his luck but bringing it off with an incredible spell of 5 for 12 in 25 balls at Manchester. Harold Rhodes' reaction was: 'If you put your head in a bucket of slops, Benordy, you'd come up with a mouthful of diamonds.'

In Australia the thrills of the 1960–61 Tests with the West Indies rubbed off on the 1961–62 season when 363,360 spectators, the best aggregate since 1927–28, attended Shield matches. The Shield was exciting in the 1960s because no overseas teams visited in four of the ten summers. New South Wales continued their winning sequence with a side that included seven players from the 1961 team to England, but the presence of Wes Hall (Queensland), Garfield Sobers (South Australia) and Rohan Kanhai (Western Australia) boosted crowds.

England mounted a blooded challenge for the Ashes in the following 1962–63 Australian season by sending a team managed by the Duke of Norfolk, England's premier duke, and captained by 'Lord Ted' Dexter. The team was E.R. Dexter (Captain), M.C. Cowdrey, D.A. Allen, B.R. Knight, K.F. Barrington, L.J. Coldwell, T.W. Graveney, R. Illingworth, G. Pullar, J.D.F. Larter, A.C. Smith, F.J. Titmus, J.T. Murray, P.H. Parfitt, J.B. Statham, F.S. Trueman and the Reverend D.S. Sheppard. Just before the team left the Advisory County Cricket Committee announced that henceforth all English cricketers would enjoy equal privileges and the terms 'amateur' and 'professional' would be discarded.

Benaud was six weeks past his thirty-second birthday when the twenty-eighth English team began its challenge for the Ashes in Brisbane on 30 November 1962. Benaud had never properly recovered from the shoulder injury sustained at Worcester. He could still drop his leg-breaks on an accurate length but the bite and sharpness had gone out of the spin. His batsmen were a consistent, often brilliant lot, and his team outclassed England in the field but too often it was left to just Benaud and Davidson to get England out. England had similar problems because Statham and Trueman were past their fiery best. Three of the five Tests were drawn and each team had one win, leaving Australia with the Ashes at the end of a disappointing rubber. England's win came in the Second Test in Melbourne when Trueman took 5 for 62 in Australia's second innings, following a 175-run stand by Dexter (93) and Cowdrey (113). Australia's success was in Sydney in the Third Test when Davidson (5 for 25) and McKenzie (3 for 26) routed England for 104.

More interesting than the Tests were the Shield matches, in which Victoria broke New South Wales' nine-year supremacy. Captained by Lawry, Victoria benefited from the contributions of left-hander Bob Cowper, son of a former rugby international, who scored 813 runs at an average of 101.62, and the South Melbourne right-hander Ian Redpath, who made 637 runs at 63.70, and from the bowling of Alan Connolly, who took 36 wickets at 27.72.

Ian Meckiff's attempt to modify his bowling action so that it would satisfy umpires received setbacks when he was no-balled for throwing in Victoria's match v. South Australia in Adelaide and in Victoria's match against Queensland in Brisbane. Surprisingly, Meckiff was picked in the Australian team the next season for the First Test against the touring South Africans in Brisbane from 6 to 11 December, 1963. The South African team was T.L. Goddard (Captain), E.J. Barlow, K.C. Bland, R.G. Pollock, A.J. Pithey, D.T. Lindsay, J.H.B. Waite, P.R. Carlstein, P.L. van der Merwe, W.S. Farrer, D.B. Pithey, P.M. Pollock, C.G. Halse, Dr M.A. Seymour and J.T. Partridge, with Ken Viljoen as manager.

Benaud handed Meckiff the ball after Davidson had bowled the first over of the Test but umpire Col Egar no-balled him for throwing his second, third, fifth and ninth deliveries. By the time Meckiff delivered the twelfth ball to complete the over, everyone knew his career was over. Benaud did not give him another bowl.

The match ended in a draw and when it was over the injured Benaud relinquished the Australian captaincy. He played under Bob Simpson in three of the four Tests that followed in that series and then retired. Benaud had lost only four of his 28 Tests as Australia's captain and earned himself a place among the great Australian captains.

CHAPTER TWENTY-SIX

CRUELTY TO CHUCKERS

Bob Simpson's cricket philosophy had no place for exhibitionism. He believed that with a disciplined approach players could drill themselves into winning habits. Winners were always neatly attired, never made public appearances in jump suits or thongs, and kept their temper. In his 29 Tests as Australia's captain, between January 1964 and January 1968, he did his best to curb the joyful fieldsmen's embraces Richie Benaud's team had started. For Bob, a handshake was reward enough for an important dismissal.

Through the last four Tests against Trevor Goddard's South Africans in 1963–64, and campaigns against England in 1964, India and Pakistan in 1964–65, the West Indies in 1964–65, England in 1965–66, South Africa in 1966–67 and India in 1967–68, he discouraged hugging and shows of elation, but still tried to build team spirit.

Simpson first played for Australia while he lived in Western Australia, but by the time he took over the captaincy he had moved back to Sydney, his birthplace. Bobby went to Tempe Boys High School, where he captained the First XI at the age of 12. To amuse schoolmates he caught house flies in mid-air with either right or left hand and later these amazing reflexes made him the greatest of all slips fieldsmen. He polished his natural talent with regular practice and at every net session had a batsman hit balls at him from a few metres away. 'Harder – hit it harder,' he would yell.

South Africa shared the 1963–64 rubber against Australia 1–1, with Simpson proving a dour, unsmiling leader in the last four Tests, lacking Benaud's warmth but proving just as hard to beat. The South African team, the fourth to tour Australia, included two sets of brothers, A.J. and D.B. Pithey and R.G. and P.M. Pollock. They had a brilliant fieldsman in Colin Bland but overall did not field as well as Cheetham's 1952–53 side.

They found that in Simpson and Lawry Australia had developed an outstanding opening pair, who made it very difficult to dismiss their team for low totals. Lawry was a plumber who raced pigeons as a hobby and when he took up his left-handed stance and looked down the pitch his large nose seemed to sniff defiance at the bowler. An unkind Indian critic dubbed him a cricket Pinocchio. He and the right-handed Simpson were masters of the short run, picking up singles that forced fieldsmen to change sides and broke up their concentration.

The South Africans' matches, all hard-fought, attracted 500,000 spectators, more than any previous South African touring team, but costs were so high the tour made only £3000 profit. They visited more country towns than most tourists, with 14 of their matches not rated first-class. They won five, lost three and drew six of their 14 first-class matches.

After the draw in the First Test, Australia introduced Victorian right-hand batsman Ian Redpath for the injured O'Neill in the Second Test at Melbourne. On the advice of his father Redpath made his Test debut as an amateur, refusing the £85 match fee, which included £15 expenses. His father feared that if Ian failed to succeed as a cricketer he would disqualify himself as a rover for the Geelong Amateurs Australian Rules team. This had happened to St Kilda all-rounder Bill Pearson after he played 14 matches for Victoria in 1936–37. Pearson was allowed back into amateur football on condition he return the money he had received by playing as a 'professional' in the Sheffield Shield team. Redpath junior went two seasons, including two Tests, without accepting match fees.

Ian Redpath, Victorian antiques expert who played his first two seasons in big cricket without pay rather than jeopardise his future as an amateur footballer. (VCA Archives)

He made 97 in his Test debut, putting on 219 for the first wicket with Lawry, who made 157, a stand that was largely responsible for Australia's eight-wicket win. Despite this promising start, Redpath was dropped for the rest of the series when O'Neill returned. The Third Test in Sydney was drawn, and South Africa levelled the rubber in the Fourth Test in Adelaide, where Eddie Barlow, 201, had a 341-run stand with Graeme Pollock, 175, the highest in all Tests by South Africans. The Fifth Test in Sydney was drawn, following centuries by Burge (102) and Bland (126).

Barlow, a bespectacled right-hander built like Billy Bunter, made six of the 19 centuries the South Africans hit on tour, and Graeme Pollock, then only 19, scored five first-class hundreds. None of the

Ian Meckiff survived 18 Test appearances before he was railroaded out of big cricket, with 269 first-class wickets to his name. (Ern McQuillan)

Australians took more than McKenzie's 16 wickets (at 43.06) in the Tests, but Peter Pollock (average 28.40) and seamer Joe Partridge (33.32) both took 25 wickets for South Africa. Only Lawry (Test average 88.50) and Booth (55.11) lived up to their reputations among the Australian batsmen.

South Australia won the Sheffield Shield in 1963–64 for the first time since 1952–53 by defeating the holders, Victoria, by an innings in the South Australians' last match of the summer. Les Favell captained them with flair, and was immeasurably helped by Gary Sobers's all-round brilliance and the consistency of batsmen John Lill and Ian McLachlan. Ian Chappell, a youngster from Glenelg club, showed outstanding all-round skills and leg-spinner Rex Sellers took 46 wickets at 26.63. In a season of high scoring, Bob Simpson made 1524 runs, which included 359 for New South Wales against Queensland in Brisbane. In the same match Peter Burge made 283, the highest score by a Queenslander in first-class cricket.

Australian cricket was controlled at that time by Allan Barnes, from the Board of Control's Sydney office. Barnes, who had taken over from Jack Ledward in 1960, acted on the instructions of consecutive Board chairmen Sir Donald Bradman, Tim Caldwell and Bob Parish until 1980. The Board saw the introduction of the front-foot rule for bowlers in 1963–64, mainly because of the dragging exploits of Gordon Rorke. The rule replaced the law that compelled bowlers to keep their back legs behind the level of the stumps.

Selectors Bradman, Ryder and Seddon picked the twenty-fourth team to tour England and had the difficult task of replacing Benaud, Harvey and Davidson, all outstanding Test players who had retired. The team was R.B. Simpson (Captain), B.C. Booth, P.J.P. Burge, A.N. Connolly, G.E. Corling, R.M. Cowper, A.T.W. Grout, N.J.N. Hawke, B.N. Jarman, W.M. Lawry, G.D. McKenzie, J.W. Martin, N.C. O'Neill, J. Potter, I.R. Redpath, R.H.D. Sellers and T.R. Veivers, with Ray Steele as manager. Ian Chappell was very unlucky to miss selection and the choice of Potter ahead of McLachlan was unjustified.

Corling was a surprise selection as one of the team's four fast-medium bowlers and he was the youngest in the team at 22, three weeks younger than McKenzie. Sellers, a tall, loose-limbed leg-spinner born at Bulsar in India, received a letter from Prime Minister

Bob Menzies granting him Australian citizenship just before the team sailed in the *Orcades*. Soon after the players arrived in England he had to have a cyst removed from his spinning finger and missed most of the tour.

Rain interrupted play on four days of the First Test at Trent Bridge from 4 to 9 June, 1964, forcing a draw. At Lord's, nine days later, rain prevented any chance of a result by washing out the first two days and returning after lunch on the final day. Burge won the rubber for Australia with an innings of 160 at Leeds in the Third Test, Australia winning by seven wickets. The Fourth Test at Manchester and the Fifth at The Oval were also drawn, leaving Australia winners of the Ashes 1–0.

Simpson batted for 762 minutes for 311 in the Fourth Test. This was his maiden Test century, in his fifty-second Test innings. He started with an opening partnership of 201 with Lawry. Australia declared at 8 for 656. England reached 611 in reply, with Barrington scoring 256 and Dexter 174. This is the only instance on record of both teams scoring more than 600 in the same Test. Veivers, originally told he would have just one over, bowled an Australian record 571 balls in England's innings, including a spell of 51 overs unchanged. He finished with 3 for 155. Trueman became the first bowler to take 300 Test wickets when he had Neil Hawke caught by Cowdrey in the Fifth Test. McKenzie's 29 wickets equalled the record for an Australian bowler in England held by Grimmett.

The Australians achieved their main task in retaining the Ashes but had such obvious limitations in bowling they were fortunate to bring home £30,000 profit from the English part of their tour. The five Tests were watched by 354,436 people. They scored 25 centuries and had 19 scored against them. Veivers, likened to a koala asleep in a gum tree by an English writer, bowled a prodigious 754.3 overs, 226 of them maidens, and his 52 wickets cost 36.17. McKenzie took most wickets, 88 at 22.45.

Simpson's team suffered a sensational defeat by The Netherlands in a one-day match at The Hague on 29 August, 1964. Australia made 197 in their innings, O'Neill top-scoring with 87. The Netherlands hit 7 for 201 in reply. London columnist Jim Manning claimed it was the most staggering sporting result since America beat England at soccer in 1954. Jack Potter had his skull fractured during this match and had to fly home without accompanying the team to India and Pakistan. Potter's injury forced Anglican parish councillor Brian Booth to deny scriptural tenets and make himself

Neil Hawke, South Australian born, also played for Western Australia and Tasmania in a career that took him on five overseas tours with Australian teams. He took 91 wickets in his 27 Tests. (John Fairfax & Sons)

available for matches in India and Pakistan that involved Sunday play.

On the last leg of a tour lasting seven months, Simpson rallied his team to defeat India by 139 runs at Madras, with McKenzie taking 10 for 91 in the match. India reversed this result at Bombay by winning only their second match in 15 Tests against Australia by two wickets. O'Neill was named in the Australian team but took no part in it because of stomach trouble. The Third Test against India was drawn after prolonged rain. In the final tour match Simpson bowled 50 overs of leg-spin against Pakistan in the Karachi Test and also made a century in each innings, 153 and 115.

Pakistan's ambition to match it with the best cricket nations was further demonstrated on a short visit to Australia in the three weeks before Christmas 1964. They played four matches without taking risks. After a draw against Queensland in Brisbane Pakistan went to Melbourne for the first Test in Australia between the countries. Hanif Mohammad, most gifted of four famous brothers, kept wicket as substitute 'keeper after Abdul Kadir was injured batting and captained Pakistan. Ian Chappell made his Test debut in this match. He scored 11 runs and did not take a wicket.

Hanif, the man who had lifted Bradman's world record from 452 to 499, made 104 and 93, and became the first Pakistani batsman to score 3000 Test runs. Honours were even, Pakistan scoring 287 and 326, Australia 448 and 2 for 88. McKenzie's match bag of 7 for 140 gave him 71 wickets in 14 Tests during 1964. Simpson totalled 1381 runs from 14 Tests in four countries in 1964, a record for a calendar year that surpassed Denis Compton's 1159 runs in nine Tests in three countries in 1947. All this time he was picking up catches in the slips with his unequalled reliability. He had solved the problem of taking catches in the stomach area, where slips fieldsmen have difficulty cupping their hands properly, by perfecting a technique in which he let the ball hit his chest as he clasped it.

For Australia's leading batsmen the 1964–65 Shield competition provided chances to force their way into the Australian team to tour the West Indies in 1965. Doug Walters, an all-rounder who learned his cricket on an antbed pitch in the country town of Dungog, partnered Lyn Marks in a record stand of 378 in 307 minutes for New South Wales against South Australia in Adelaide. Walters made 253, which included a six and 23 fours, Marks 185 with 20 fours. They beat the previous best third-wicket partnership for New South Wales by Bradman and Archie Jackson in 1930–31 by 44 runs. Walters followed his brilliant batting by taking 7 for 63 with the ball.

New South Wales then flew on to Perth to play Western Australia, aware that outright victory could win them the Shield. A tense struggle ensued with Walters again at the centre of events. Led by Tony Lock, former England and Surrey star, Western Australia scored 184 and 273, with Walters taking 2 for 44 and 5 for 92. Walters, 57, and Marks, 75, took New South Wales to 9 for 302 declared in their first innings and Walters was on 34 not out when New South Wales reached 5 for 156 to win by five wickets and take the Shield.

Western Australia's vastly improved displays brought sighs of relief from state association treasurers in eastern states. Not only had crowds and ground membership grown at the WACA but the Western Australian team was attracting more spectators on their eastern trips.

Three Western Australians were included in the Australian team for the ten-match tour of the West Indies in 1965. The West Indies at that time had never won a series against Australia but their team now included the frightening pace bowler Charlie Griffith, who in 1962 at Barbados had knocked down Indian captain Nari Contractor, fracturing his skull so badly Contractor hovered near death for several days. The Australians knew that the West Indian umpire Cortez Jordan had called Griffith for throwing in 1962 and that several respected English critics regarded Griffith as a chucker. But relief from umpires was unlikely and Australia's 1965 series against West Indies appeared to depend on Simpson's batsmen's clashes with the Hall–Griffith pace combination.

The Australian team was R.B. Simpson (Captain), B.C. Booth, P.J. Allan, R.M. Cowper, A.T.W. Grout, N.J.N. Hawke, W.M Lawry, B.N. Jarman, G.D. McKenzie, L.C. Mayne, N.C. O'Neill, P.I. Philpott, B.K. Shepherd, D.J. Sincock, G. Thomas and S.C. Trimble. McKenzie, Mayne and Shepherd were Western Australians. Most commentators believed Trimble was lucky to be selected ahead of the gregarious Ian Chappell, a compulsive hooker who would have tackled the West Indian bowlers, on an unhappy tour which saw Australians repeatedly hit by bouncers. Trimble was only half-way through his career in the Queensland team but was destined never to win Test selection.

Charlie Griffith, who was allowed to continue in Test cricket for the West Indies, had an action that umpires finally agreed was illegal, largely because officials could not define a 'throw'. (Jack Pollard Collection)

Arguments over the legality of Griffith's bowling overshadowed everything in a series labelled as the unofficial world championship. Pictures taken by Richie Benaud certainly suggested Griffith threw occasional deliveries. Among the Australians, there was a strong conviction that Griffith threw his faster deliveries. There were no official complaints from Australian team manager Bob Parish, but protests would have been justified in the first two Tests, at Kingston and Port-of-Spain. Curiously, the controversy over Griffith's short-pitched deliveries distracted experts from his most dangerous delivery, the yorker.

Sobers had an outstanding series in his debut as West Indian captain, following Sir Frank Worrell. His versatility at international level was astonishing, for he could bowl fast-medium swingers, often using the new ball, and he had two types of spin, turning the ball both with the fingers and the wrist. He was also an inspiration to his players wherever he fielded. His batting in the Tests disappointed, with 69 his top score, but in the Australians' match against Barbados at Bridgetown he produced a dazzling 183 not out. His captaincy was assured and tactically sound.

Hall won the First Test at Kingston for West Indies with a sustained display of fast, straight bowling that gave him 5 for 60 and 4 for 45 on a pitch of unpredictable bounce. The sight of big Wes tearing in to bowl with his St Christopher medal swinging freely on a chain inside his open-neck shirt provided an absorbing spectacle, and Brian Booth's 56 in Australia's second innings was the only Australian score of any significance against him.

Centuries by Cowper (143) and Booth (117) took Australia to an 87-run first-innings lead in the Second Test at Port-of-Spain, where Griffith unleashed a torrid attack. Dropped catches denied Australia a winning chance after they had brilliantly run out both Basil Butcher (117) and Sobers (69) to end a classic exhibition of stroke play.

A dispute between rival island umpiring associations threatened the staging of the Third Test at Georgetown for a time, but the match went ahead when Gerry Gomez, the former Test all-rounder, agreed to umpire. Gomez, at the forefront of moves to lift the standards of umpiring in the West Indies, ordered the creases to be re-marked before play began. Australia were left to score 357 to win after thrilling batting by Kanhai, 89, in West Indies' first innings. Australia appeared to have a chance at 1 for 80 at tea, but Gibbs took four wickets in 15 minutes after the interval to clinch victory. Gibbs's 6 for 29 from 22.2 overs on a pitch that took only a little spin was the result of ill-disciplined batting.

Two–nil down and apparently outclassed, Australia dominated the drawn Fourth Test at Bridgetown, when Lawry and Simpson batted through the first day and on the second day became the first openers in history each to score double centuries. Their stand of 382 was only 31 short of a world record, set by Mankad and Roy for India v. New Zealand. Umpire Kippin cautioned Griffith for excessive use of the bouncer to add to the West Indies' discomfort and Cowper made a century with almost effortless ease. Chasing 6 declared for 650, the West Indies made 573. Kanhai managed 129, Nurse 201, but only a vigorous 54 by Griffith enabled West Indies to avoid the follow-on. The West Indian revival continued in their second innings when they finished only 11 runs short of scoring 253 in 270 minutes to win. The draw gave the West Indies the rubber.

Australia won the Fifth Test by ten wickets with three days to spare, Hawke breaking through in both West Indian innings and McKenzie finishing them with three wickets in four balls. Australia finished with only three victories and two losses from ten first-class matches, with five matches drawn. O'Neill, who topped Australia's tour batting averages with 617 runs at 68.55, brought the bitterness of the series to the surface by angrily attacking Griffith and the West Indians' reliance on bouncers in a series of articles at the end of the tour for the London *Daily Mail*. The West Indian Board of Control officially protested over the articles and the Australian Board of Control fined O'Neill, rejecting his argument that the tour had ended, and that he was free of tour commitments.

Two years later in England umpire Arthur Fagg, a former Test batsman, no-balled Griffith for throwing and eight times for over-stepping and this cast a shadow over Griffith's Test career. He finished with 94 Test wickets at 28.54, six short of the coveted 100 wickets that appeared his to command. As with Meckiff, the tragedy was that he was allowed to pass through the various levels of cricket to Shell Shield and Tests without any official attempt to correct his action and on retirement was forced to live out his days branded a cheat.

Like Meckiff, Griffith found himself a social oddity, a man pointed at as he entered a room by people who whispered he was a rebel. Meckiff's son was nicknamed 'Chucker' by his schoolmates,

Doug Walters, shown at practice early in the first-class career he began in 1962–63, had his career interrupted by compulsory Army service after scoring centuries in his first two Tests. (Ern McQuillan)

his wife and relatives were pestered in supermarkets. When Meckiff hit his ball into a bunker on a round of golf, players in another group called that he should 'chuck it out'. The wisecracks of work-mates who called him 'Chucker' caught on in pubs and cricket clubs and at one stage he felt constrained to become a recluse.

Peter Allan developed so well on the West Indian tour he won a place in the Australian team to play England in the First Test at Brisbane in 1965–66. The boy from Dungog, Doug Walters, who was still only 19, made his debut in the same Test. Walters, whose mother bowled to him on their backyard pitch in between milking 150 cows a day, forced his way into Tests with two vigorous centuries and two eighties for New South Wales.

The English team, captained by former Oxford University and Leicestershire right-hand batsman Mike Smith, arrived with the declared intention of playing bright cricket, but a viral infection prevented several players finding early tour form. This was the first English team to escape the long sea voyage to Australia, thought to be so helpful in building spirit among touring players, and travel by air. The team was M.J.K. Smith (Captain), M.C. Cowdrey, K.F. Barrington, F.J. Titmus, J.M. Parks, W.E. Russell, B.R. Knight, R.W. Barber, J.H. Edrich, G. Boycott, J.T. Murray, D.A. Allen, P.H. Parfitt, D.J. Brown, K. Higgs, I.J. Jones and J.D.F. Larter, with Billy Griffith as manager.

Griffith said he had been instructed by the MCC to ensure the team played attractive cricket that would help the game's crowd appeal in Australia. He promised he would make a careful study of batsmen's scoring rates and the times taken by bowlers to get through their overs. The policy succeeded so well that even players like Boycott and Barrington, noted for their stodgy cricket, showed some dash. Barry Knight was not in the original party but was flown out as a reinforcement when injuries sidelined Larter and Brown.

Smith was a very impressive captain for the first half of the tour but when his wife and children joined him just before Christmas his leadership fell away and he lost form. This caused widespread discussion among the large contingent of cricket writers covering the tour and most considered that caring for a family in a strange country interfered with Smith's already onerous job.

Bob Barber became the major crowd-pleaser in the English team by attacking from the first ball he received. While he was at the crease playing strokes, England scored at a rate that troubled

Australia. Australia's big success was Doug Walters, who began his international career with 129 against England for New South Wales in Sydney and followed with a delightful innings of 155 in the First Test at the Gabba between 10 and 15 December, 1965. Walters was the ninth Australian to score a century in his Test debut, emulating the feat of Charles Bannerman, Harry Graham, Reg Duff, Roger Hartigan, Herbie Collins, Bill Ponsford, Archie Jackson and Jim Burke. Only Neil Harvey and Jackson were younger than Walters's 19 years 357 days when they scored Test hundreds.

In Simpson's absence with a broken wrist, Brian Booth became captain. Booth, son of a market gardener from Perthville six miles out of Bathurst, NSW, stretched his innate sense of fair play to the limit when he allowed Boycott to paw a Philpott spinner away from his stumps. Most commentators believed the dour Simpson would never have been so kind, but that was typical of a Test in which both sides behaved like choir boys. Grout at one point apologised to Boycott for appealing for a catch when he realised Boycott had hit the ground, not the ball. England escaped with a draw despite Lawry's 166, Walters's 155 and Philpott's 5 for 90 in England's first innings.

On the way to the Second Test in Melbourne England had a lucky win over South Australia in Adelaide where Les Favell twice declared to boost spectators' enjoyment. In the first innings, Alan Shiell was on 202 not out when the declaration came at 7 for 459 and in the second innings Ian Chappell was 113 not out when Favell waved his batsmen in at 4 for 253. England won the match by six wickets.

The Second Test appeared within England's grasp when their makeshift 'keeper Parks missed a simple offside chance to stump Burge off Barber. Burge survived until he and Walters had made the match safe for Australia. Walters, just 20, scored his third successive century against England, Burge 120. Fifteen of the 22 players had a bowl.

Simpson had to miss the Third Test in Sydney because of chickenpox. In his absence, none of the Australian bowlers nor the tactics of stand-in captain Booth could contain Boycott, 84, Barber, 185, and Edrich, 103, and England's first innings of 488 proved too high for Australia, who responded with 221 and 174 to lose by an innings and 93 runs.

Simpson showed how much his absence had meant to Australia by scoring 225 in the Fourth Test at Adelaide, where he and Lawry had an opening stand of 244. Australia never lost the advantage

*Keith Slater, no-balled
twice for throwing between
1957–58 and 1964–65,
had a high knee-action
approach, taking off in a
kangaroo hop with his
right wrist cocked.*
(John Fairfax & Sons)

this scoring provided and won by an innings and nine runs to level
the series. It ended all square when the Fifth Test at Melbourne
was drawn, following a 727-minute innings by Cowper which
produced 307 runs, including 20 fours. It was the longest first-class
innings in Australia and the longest ever played against an English
team overseas. Cowper apologised to spectators. 'That must have
been boring to watch,' he said.

This was the last of Grout's 51 Tests. He quit at the end of the
season after 20 summers in the Queensland side and 183 first-class
matches. A happy, cheerful soul of infectious enthusiasm, he
dismissed 587 batsmen, taking 473 catches and making 114
stumpings. His resemblance to Don Tallon was uncanny, for even
their footwork was similar, and they had the same air of inevitability
in holding catches. Grout went out of Tests at 39 and died two
years later. Team-mates had had no inkling of his heart problems.

Grout collected his Provident Fund payment from the Australian
Board of Control but Brian Booth, who also disappeared from Tests
after that series against England, was not as lucky. Booth finished
on 29 Tests, one short of the Provident Fund qualifying mark. The
26 first-class centuries and 11,265 runs he scored at 45.42 by the
time he retired, with 92 appearances for New South Wales – which
won the Sheffield Shield again that year – did not help.

After scoring 1332 runs in first-class cricket at an average of 70.11
and making a dramatic introduction to Tests, Doug Walters had
the misfortune to be called-up for compulsory Army service. He won
many friends by the manner in which he accepted his two years in
the Army without complaint. Graeme Watson, who was able to
have his Army service deferred because of his studies in architecture,
replaced Walters in the Australian team that visited South Africa
in the summer of 1966–67 under Simpson's captaincy.

South Africa had soundly defeated England on their 1965 tour of
England but they were unable to try their strength against the West
Indies because of their government's apartheid policies. For this
reason they were keen to beat Australia to claim world cricket
leadership. The Australian team was R.B. Simpson (Captain),
W.M. Lawry, G.C. Becker, I.M. Chappell, R.M. Cowper, N.J.N.
Hawke, J.M. Hubble, G.D. McKenzie, J.W. Martin, I.R. Redpath,
D.A. Renneberg, K.R. Stackpole, H.B. Taber, G. Thomas, T.R.
Veivers and G.D. Watson, with Bill Jacobs, long-time Fitzroy first-
grader, as manager.

The Australian Board of Control were assured before the tour began that the South Africans had no objections to the inclusion in the Australian team of Grahame Thomas, who had American Indian blood and was a coloured person under their laws. Thomas was shown every courtesy, but suffered badly from homesickness throughout the tour. Neil Hawke broke his collarbone playing Australian Rules football before the team left and had to have the injury pinned before he was allowed to tour.

Simpson was a major figure on the tour, regularly seen encouraging his players at the nets and putting them through routines of callisthenics and fielding drills, but his weakness in complaining too often about umpiring decisions did Australia a disservice. He had made subtle changes in his batting technique since he first came into top-class cricket, changing from long-handled to short-handled bats to restrict his backswing and opening up his formerly side-on stance, so that more of his broken nose faced bowlers.

Transvaal beat Australia by 76 runs in the third match of the tour in a tension-packed finish. This was Australia's first ever defeat in South Africa in 64 years. Ali Bacher, the 24-year-old Transvaal captain, swung the match for his side by scoring 235 in the second innings. A century by Lance (107) gave Australia the enormous task of scoring 490 in 400 minutes to win. At 6 for 379 they had a chance but the loss of three quick wickets left the last pair, Hawke and Hubble, to save the game by playing out time. They defended grimly until eight minutes from stumps when Tillim bowled Hawke with his googly.

This early show of South Africa's strength was borne out in the Tests. South Africa took the series 3–1 with wins in the First, Third and Fifth Tests. Australia won the Second Test and the Fourth was drawn. The Australian bowling was the weakest ever sent to South Africa, with Graham McKenzie forced to do most of the hard work. Australia's early batting was outstanding but they could not always carry a six- or seven-man tail.

Graeme Pollock, established as the greatest batsman in South Africa's history, made a masterly 90 to help his side to a 233-run win in the First Test at Johannesburg, where Dennis Lindsay made 182. Pollock followed with an innings of 209 in the Second Test at Cape Town, virtually carrying South Africa for six hours after Simpson (153) and Stackpole (134) had lifted Australia to 542. Pollock's 350-minute innings proved insufficient to prevent an Australian win, however, by six wickets with 24 minutes to spare.

McKenzie played a big part in this victory with 5 for 65 and 3 for 67 and was by far the best of the eight bowlers Simpson tried.

Australia started the Third Test at Durban dramatically when McKenzie caught and bowled Barlow with his first ball. From there South Africa gradually got on top, Lindsay contributing another century (137). South Africa went on to an eight-wicket win after dismissing Australia for 147 in their first innings. The Fourth Test at Johannesburg was drawn when rain fell on the final day, following Lindsay's third century of the series. His 131 included four sixes and broke the record for a wicket-keeper in a Test series, an aggregate he lifted to 606 runs by the end of the rubber.

Graeme Pollock celebrated his twenty-third birthday by scoring 105 in the first innings of the Fifth Test at Port Elizabeth, which South Africa won by seven wickets to clinch their first series win over Australia. Peter Pollock, Graeme's brother, became the fourth South African to take 100 wickets in Tests when he dismissed Redpath in the second innings. Goddard was the Springbok bowling star, however, with 26 wickets in the five Tests at 16.23. Simpson headed Australia's Test batting averages, but his figures, 483 runs at 48.30, compared unfavourably with those of Lindsay (606 at 86.57) and Graeme Pollock (537 at 76.71).

The tour made a $75,000 profit, but left Australia with a lot of rebuilding to do. Of the 17 first-class matches Australia played, only seven were won, with five losses and five draws. The Australian catching was often shoddy, and only Taber, of the five players introduced to Australia's Test team, justified his selection.

Jimmy Higgs, who joined the exclusive club of 22 Australians who have been no-balled for throwing, says he was unaware that he had been called.
(VCA Library)

While Australia's senior players toured South Africa, a bowler of match-winning potential emerged on a tour of New Zealand by an Australian Second XI. This was John William Gleeson, a telephone linesman from Tamworth in north-eastern New South Wales, who propelled the ball off a bent middle finger in the style of Jack Iverson. Gleeson preferred pitches with pace in them and the damp, soggy strips in New Zealand did not suit him, but he still kept producing deliveries which fooled even the most experienced batsmen.

Gleeson's selection in the team for New Zealand captained by Les Favell came after only five first-class matches in which he took 23 wickets at 18.22, taking him to the top of the 1966–67 Sheffield Shield averages. Gleeson had begun his cricket as a wicket-keeper and had twice toured the world with the Australian Emus team, an outfit made up of country cricketers who paid their own expenses for the trip. He was inspired to begin experiments with his unorthodox spin after seeing photographs of Iverson's grip. He started with table tennis balls and later bowled old cricket balls at gum trees. He had more variety than Iverson, using the leg-break more, and mixing off-breaks with straight deliveries that bounced high.

The Australian team in New Zealand was L.E. Favell (Captain), B.C. Booth, P.J.P. Burge, N.C. O'Neill, P.I. Philpott, K.G. Cunningham, B.N. Jarman, A.N. Connolly, J.W. Gleeson, A.R. Frost, R.C. Bitmead, E.W. Freeman, A.P. Sheahan and G.R. Davies. They played ten matches, all rated first-class, and apart from four unofficial 'Tests' had one match against each of the provincial teams who competed in New Zealand's Plunket Shield competition. Canterbury defeated them by four wickets at Christchurch, and New Zealand beat them by 159 runs in the First 'Test' at New Plymouth. The performance of New Zealand's leading players in restricting Australia to two wins, six draws and the two losses was highly gratifying to their officials, who had struggled for years to demonstrate their improved standards to Australians. To win a 'Test' and hold Australia to draws in the other three was a surprise to New Zealand's most ardent fans.

Two of the young stars of that Australian tour, Gleeson and the elegant Victorian right-hand batsman Paul Sheahan, made their debuts for Australia against India in the summer of 1967–68. This was a particularly important test for Gleeson as the Indians were regarded as experts against spin bowling. The Indian team: the Nawab of Pataudi (Captain), R.F. Surti, Abid Ali, F.M. Engineer, A.L. Wadekar, V. Subramanya, C.G. Borde, E.A.S. Prasanna, R.G. Nadkarni, D.N. Sardesai, B.S. Bedi, U.N. Kulkarni and B.S. Chandrasekar. M.L. Jaisimha arrived after seven matches had been played, and with only a few days' practice scored 74 and 101, India's only century in the Tests.

India failed to win a first-class match and were beaten in all four Tests. Pataudi batted with surprising skill for a man who had lost an eye the previous year in a car accident at Oxford. He could not move down the pitch and had to play mostly from the back foot, but he hit loose balls hard and sometimes lofted bowlers into the outfield. He was a charismatic captain, pulling his cap down to shade his lost eye and generally batting with his side in trouble.

Surti proved an enthusiastic cricketer whose all-round skills were enough to secure him a subsequent job as coach with the Queensland Cricket Association and he played for Queensland in the Sheffield Shield competition for several seasons, a versatile left-arm bowler who could begin at medium-pace and come on later with leg-spin. Prasanna lived up to his reputation as a master off-spinner, taking 25 wickets in the Tests against Australia at 27.44.

Cowper and Simpson both scored two Test centuries for Australia and Lawry and Ian Chappell one each. Walters secured leave from the Army in time to play in two Tests and head the Australian Test averages with 254 runs at 127.0, followed by Cowper's 485 runs at 69.28 and Simpson's 294 runs at 58.80. Lawry, who took over the Australian captaincy from Simpson for the last two Tests, was the only other Australian batsman to average over fifty against a poor quality Indian attack, making 369 runs at 52.71.

Simpson, who had announced his retirement, played in the last Test under Lawry's captaincy. Before he retired Simpson gave one final showing of his glorious ability to break up a fielding team's concentration with his running between wickets, repeatedly scampering through for quick singles in a 191-stand for the first wicket with Lawry in the Melbourne Test. Simpson retired after a successful 52-Test career, at the age of 31, with no thought of ever returning to international cricket. He continued to play grade cricket for the Western Suburbs club in Sydney and was involved for one season in a Double Wicket Cricket promotion that flopped.

In 1965 he had been served with a writ from Ian Meckiff who alleged Simpson libelled him in his book *Captain's Story*. This was the first case of an Australian cricketer suing a team-mate. After five years the case was settled out of court, with Simpson apologising and the payment of an amount said to be $10,000 to Meckiff. Simpson was 37 when he gave his pads to Peter Toohey and his bat to Phil Kolleard, team-mates in Western Suburbs first-grade.

CHAPTER TWENTY-SEVEN
SACK FOR THE PHANTOM

A shy man who, when he was first selected for Australia, refused to come down from thirteenth floor of a new Melbourne hospital where he was working as a plumber to meet reporters, William Morris Lawry proved a tough, gutsy captain. He refused to allow a substitute runner for the injured Chandu Borde in his first Test as Australian captain until he knew the extent of Borde's injury, and quickly showed the Australian fieldsmen he expected them to remain alert for his signals.

Although he had played under two Australian captains who were spinners, Lawry showed little understanding of any form of spin bowling. His spinners knew that if they were hit for fours, they would be taken off. Lou Rowan, who umpired in many of Lawry's Tests, said in *The Umpire's Story* that Lawry stifled his bowlers and that his disgusted comments whenever a batsman scored runs were nothing short of demoralising to bowlers.

William Morris Lawry, one-time Melbourne plumber, known to team-mates as 'The Phantom' because of his addiction to the comic-strip character of that name, during his 25-Test run as Australia's captain. (Ern McQuillan)

Lawry was happier with pace than spin but was quite content for his Victorian team-mates Alan Connolly and Bob Cowper to bowl short of a length or outside the stumps and make scoring difficult. To bring on Gleeson or Ashley Mallett and increase the chances of taking a wicket often appeared not to occur to him.

In the Brisbane Test against India – Lawry's first as captain – he neglected Gleeson so long in favour of Victorians Connolly and Cowper a barracker shouted: 'Hey Lawry, give Gleeson a bowl – his grandmother lives in Geelong.'

Gleeson was a tough proposition for any captain, a bowler without any precedents to follow in setting fields. In 24 Tests, which included all except two of Lawry's span as Australian captain, Gleeson's requests for fieldsmen to be put into precise positions were repeatedly denied. Lawry usually put men in orthodox positions but declined to try variations that might intercept a batsman's favourite shot. Gleeson accepted Lawry's ignorance of his needs but Mallett was capable of long dissertations on his low opinion of Lawry as a skipper.

A New Zealand team had made a brief tour of Australia at the start of the 1967–68 season, to prepare for India's visit to New Zealand at the end of India's Australian tour. This was only the second official New Zealand visit to Australia, the first being in 1925–26, although New Zealand sides had popped into Australia on their way to and from England and South Africa.

The New Zealanders were denied a Test and had to be satisfied with matches against South Australia, Victoria, New South Wales and Queensland, after playing country games as a warm-up. They did not win a match but in the initial first-class fixture against South Australia provided some of the most exhilarating batting ever seen on Adelaide Oval when big Dick Motz, in a desperate bid to snatch victory, hit six sixes and ten fours in an innings of 94. South Australia won by only 24 runs. Later against Victorian Country Motz hit 70 runs in 46 minutes and in one over clubbed 36 runs from four sixes and three fours.

A tame draw against Victoria followed, with Cowper drawing yawns for his 78 runs in 210 minutes before Sheahan made a fine 161. The New Zealanders' only century on the tour came from the bat of Vic Pollard at the Gabba against Queensland. Pollard's 125 and opener Bruce Murray's 98 had New Zealand in a sound position when rain curtailed play. New South Wales beat the New Zealanders by 131 runs in Sydney in their final first-class match, thanks to a chanceless 137 not out by Simpson, batting down the order.

The major surprise of the 1967–68 Australian summer was Western Australia's win in the Sheffield Shield under captain Tony Lock. This was Western Australa's first win in the Shield since 1947–48 when they had a modified programme of four matches, and the first victory since Western Australia was given a full programme of eight matches. The win was achieved through a ten-wicket triumph over Victoria in what was virtually the final, and was a wonderful tribute to the hard work Lock had put into improving Western Australia's cricket. He was not only his team's most effective bowler, with 42 wickets at 17.21, but he played several

valuable hard-hitting tail-ender's innings, and repeatedly took superb catches. On the eve of the match against Victoria in Perth in which his side completed the job, he received an emergency call to join the English team in the West Indies.

Lawry made the mistake of putting Western Australia in to bat after winning the toss on a perfect batting pitch. Western Australia's new opener, R.D Bowe, made 86 and John Inverarity, in yet another display of sustained concentration, scored 173 after batting for five hours to reach 142 on the first day. Connolly's 7 for 101 was a fine effort but he could not prevent Western Australia reaching 405. Well supported by Lock (4 for 58), Laurie Mayne had Victoria out for 196 by taking 5 for 56. Lock enforced the follow-on and his bowlers pressed on to a notable success, despite a fighting 103 by Lawry.

Inverarity and McKenzie won places in the Australian team that toured England in 1968, but the selectors preferred South Australian Eric Freeman to Mayne. Freeman had advanced his claims by taking 11 for 97 against New Zealand earlier in the season, including 8 for 47 in the New Zealanders' second innings. Similarly, Sheahan had pressed his tour claims with an innings of 161 against New Zealand in Melbourne. Sheahan also finished on top of the first-class batting averages with 973 runs at 64.87.

England's hopes of beating Australia received a boost when they defeated the West Indies 1–0 in a torrid series in the Caribbean, which saw demonstrations involving bottle-throwing and an all-out bouncer war between the teams. John Snow and strapping Welshman Jeff Jones retaliated when Hall and Griffith bowled bouncers in the Bridgetown Test, peppering the batsmen for more than an hour and leaving Rohan Kanhai bruised and sore all over his chest. England's victory in the Port-of-Spain Test clinched the series and set the stage for an eventful rubber against Australia. England's team included Basil D'Oliveira, the coloured batsman who had been barred from playing in his native Cape Town and had made his way into Test cricket via the Lancashire League and the Worcestershire county team.

Australia's twenty-fifth white tour of England began exactly 100 years after the English tour by the all-Aboriginal side. The Australian team was W.M Lawry (Captain), B.N. Jarman (Vice-captain), I.M. Chappell, A.N. Connolly, R.M. Cowper, E.W. Freeman, J.W. Gleeson, N.J.N. Hawke, R.J. Inverarity, L.R. Joslin, G.D. McKenzie, A.A. Mallett, I.R. Redpath, D.A. Renneberg, A.P.Sheahan, H.B. Taber and K.D. Walters, with Bob Parish as manager. The team was chosen by Sir Donald Bradman, Neil Harvey and Jack Ryder, who was then 79 years old and peered at the players on whom he passed judgement through powerful binoculars. Ryder remained a selector until he was 84, and even in his eighties was seen bowling a few down to Test batsmen.

Australia made a great start to the series in the First Test at Manchester when Lawry, 81, Walters, 81, Sheahan, 88, and Chappell, 73, combined to produce a first-innings total of 357. McKenzie (3 for 33) and Cowper (4 for 48) then set Australia on the path to victory by dismissing England for 165. Walters's 86 in Australia's second innings gave him his most productive match in England and lifted Australia's lead to 412. All the Australian bowlers impressed the crowd as they worked their way through the England batting line-up to win by 159 runs. Lawry allowed Gleeson only 6.3 overs in the first innings but gave him 30 overs in the second, Gleeson returning 3 for 44.

The Second Test at Lord's, the two-hundredth match between England and Australia, attracted advance bookings of £73,000, or £14,000 more than the takings for any other cricket match in England. The captains used a gold sovereign presented for the occasion by Australian Prime Minister Bob Menzies. But rain on each of the five days reduced the playing time by more than 15 hours and despite all the efforts of the ground staff the spectators had to be satisfied with a thrilling 83 by Colin Milburn who hit two sixes and 12 fours before Walters caught him on the boundary and the match finished in a draw. Australia's 78, in reply to England's 351, was their lowest total in England since 1912.

The Third Test at Birmingham was also drawn after Cowdrey celebrated becoming the first cricketer to play 100 Tests by scoring 104. Lawry retired with a fractured finger when Snow hit him in the first over of Australia's innings. McKenzie deputised as captain in that match but in the Fourth Test at Headingley Jarman took over as captain and wicket-keeper. Graveney captained England in the absence of Cowdrey. Another draw meant that Australia retained the Ashes, as the best England could do was to share the series by winning the Fifth Test.

Glamorgan made history by defeating Australia for the second time on successive tours, at Swansea from 3 to 5 August, 1968. Glamorgan won because of their magnificent catching. Sheahan's superb 137, on the final day when Australia was chasing 365 to win, only served to reduce the winning margin to 79 runs.

Basil D'Oliveira was never afraid to move forward to drive. (Ken Kelly)

England duly won the Fifth Test to square the series at one win apiece because of centuries by Edrich (164) and D'Oliveira (158). Lawry returned to score 135 in Australia's first innings but it was not enough to prevent defeat by 226 runs. England won after volunteers from the crowd helped groundstaff clear The Oval of water that flooded the outfield in a freak storm. Australia appeared to have saved the match until D'Oliveira bowled Jarman with 36 minutes left. Cowdrey then brought on Derek Underwood, who had a splendid series, and he sent back Mallett and McKenzie inside six balls. Underwood bowled Gleeson and had Inverarity lbw to give England their fifth wicket in half an hour and seal victory.

D'Oliveira was picked in the England team for the coming tour of South Africa when Tom Cartwright withdrew, because of his admirable form with bat and ball against Australia. Prime Minister Vorster refused to accept the English team if it included D'Oliveira but the MCC refused to omit him and preferred to cancel the tour.

Largely because of ineffectual leadership, the twenty-fifth Australian team was among the most disappointing to tour England. They won only eight of their 25 first-class matches, lost three and had 14 draws. Prevented from playing on wet pitches at home, where all wickets were covered, the Australians lacked the experience to succeed in an English summer when 100 hours were lost to rain. Lawry concentrated on avoiding defeat. One London critic summed up Lawry's contribution to a dismal series as: 'A corpse with pads on.'

Ian Chappell made a highly impressive debut in England, heading the Australian team's first-class batting averages with 1261 runs at 48.50, at the same time as his younger brother Greg was enjoying a successful first season with Somerset. The only other Australian batsman to score more than 1000 runs was Ian Redpath, with 1474 at 43.35. Redpath scored four of the 13 centuries Australians made on the tour, Chappell three.

English cricket suffered a grievous blow when Ken Barrington collapsed from a heart attack in October 1968, before the Australian first-class season began. Playing in an Australian Double Wicket competition with $20,000 prizemoney, Barrington partnered Colin Milburn. Gary Sobers and Wes Hall won the competition from Graeme and Peter Pollock.

Two overseas teams toured Australia in the 1968–69 summer, a powerful West Indian party of 17 players captained by Garfield Sobers, and a 16-strong British women's team captained by Rachael Heyhoe. The men's team dominated the sports pages but the women enjoyed a hard-fought tour.

The West Indian team was G.S. Sobers (Captain), R.B. Kanhai, M.C. Carew, B.F. Butcher, C.H. Lloyd, S.M. Nurse, R.C. Frederiks, D.A.J. Holford, J.L. Hendriks, G.S. Camacho, T.M. Findlay, L.A. King, C.C. Griffith, R.M. Edwards, W.W. Hall, L.R. Gibbs and C.A. Davis. The British women's team comprised R. Heyhoe (Captain), E. Barker, E. Bakewell, H. Dewdney, A. Disbury, C. Evans, S. Hodges, J. Moorhouse, S. Plant, L. Thomas, J. Clark, L. Clifford, J. Cruwys, M. Pilling, A. Sanders and C. Watmough. The women's team was assisted by a British government grant of £2000 sterling towards the return fares to Australia, and by securing the help of more than 50 firms and women's cricket bodies, the amount each player had personally to contribute was reduced to £200.

The English women played 14 matches in Australia, won eight and drew six. They won nine of the 11 matches in New Zealand and drew two. Their big disappointment was that although they emerged undefeated after four months of effort in 25 matches, all three Tests in Australia failed to produce a result. They did manage to produce, however, a woman cricketer of the highest calibre in Enid Bakewell, who achieved the double with 1031 runs at 39.65

and 118 wickets at 9.7. She scored 113 in her first Test appearance against Australia and scored successive centuries in the Second Test against New Zealand, 124 and 114.

On her return home Mrs Bakewell, a left-arm spin bowler, was given a civic reception by the Mayor of Nottingham to celebrate her tour achievements, and she became the first woman ever granted a special feature in *Wisden's Cricket Almanack*, which ended with the words: 'Enid's 1968–69 achievements will remain a challenge to women cricketers wherever they may play. They will remain unforgotten not only by her fellow tourists but by her opponents in Australia and New Zealand for a very long time to come.'

Australia's male cricketers had only a month's rest after their English tour before they began the 1968–69 Sheffield Shield competition and prepared to take on the fourth West Indian touring team to Australia. All of Australia's younger players struck form immediately and by the time of the First Test in Brisbane they had already inflicted defeat on an ill-disciplined touring side whose captain, Sobers, absented himself from the team for long periods. Ian Chappell made a wonderful 188 not out and Paul Sheahan 111 not out in an unbeaten fourth wicket stand to give a Combined XI victory over the West Indies in Perth. At Adelaide South Australia beat the West Indies by ten wickets after Ian Chappell scored 125 and Kevin McCarthy, a pace bowler, made 127.

In the First Test the pitch at the Gabba broke up as play progressed, and by winning the toss the West Indies secured a match-winning advantage. They won by 125 runs despite attractive centuries by Lawry, 105, and Ian Chappell, 117. Clive Lloyd's 129 in his debut against Australia proved the innings that swung the match. Only Ian Chappell, Sheahan and McKenzie resisted for long against the swing of Sobers and spin of Gibbs when Australia were set to score 366 to win.

Thereafter Australia took the great West Indian team of the 1960s apart, outplaying them in every department of the game to win the series 3–1. Hall and Griffith could no longer blast through opposition batting at will. Kanhai, Nurse and Butcher lacked their old consistency and the youthful newcomers Lloyd, Comacho, Fredericks and Davis were slow in advancing to Test class. Temperamentally, the West Indians appeared unable to regroup and they were a forlorn lot long before the tour ended.

Lawry, known to team-mates as 'The Phantom' because of his

Fast-medium pace bowlers Graham McKenzie, top, and Alan Connolly, who were bowlers more to Lawry's liking than spinners.

(Jack Pollard Collection)

addiction to the comic strip, enjoyed his best series as Australian captain, showing much more flexibility than he normally did and using his bowlers cleverly. The batting of Walters, Chappell and Lawry gave Australia a succession of high totals. After injury kept him out of the First Test, Walters scored 699 runs and his lowest score was 50. Chappell became one of the finest batsmen of his generation and Lawry's steady, effective scoring could not be curbed. Among the bowlers, McKenzie and Connolly were consistently penetrative and Gleeson's 26 wickets played a major part in Australia's triumph. Australia looked a better side in the field when Taber took over behind the stumps from Jarman after the Fourth Test.

Australia won the Second Test in Melbourne by an innings and 30 runs largely because of Lawry's 205 and Chappell's 165. Walters could not get his timing right but still made 76 and shared a 123-run stand with Lawry. Australia led by 283 after each side batted in the Third Test at Sydney and only Butcher's 101 held them up. Their ten-wicket win gave them a 2–1 advantage that should have been increased in the Fourth Test at Adelaide. With an hour to play Australia wanted 62 to take the match off 120 balls with only three batsmen out. Then Chappell fell lbw to Griffith, and in the next 14 minutes Walters, Freeman and Jarman were run out, with Sheahan partially at fault at the other end. McKenzie and Gleeson went cheaply, leaving the final pair, Sheahan and Connolly, to handle the last 26 balls. They survived some erratic bowling by Sobers and the match ended in a draw with Australia still 21 runs short of the target.

Australia lost 3 for 51 at the start of the Fifth Test in Sydney before Lawry and Walters added 336 in 405 minutes for the fourth wicket to put victory beyond the West Indies. Lawry made 151, Walters 242 and Australia reached 619. Five catches by Taber helped restrict the West Indies' first innings to 279. Lawry declined to enforce the follow-on, allowing his batsmen to tighten Australia's grip on the match. Redpath made 132 and Walters, by scoring 103, became the first batsman to score a double century and a century in the same Test. Centuries by Sobers, 113, and Nurse, 137, failed to save West Indies from an enormous (382-run) defeat.

The 26 catches the usually brilliant West Indians dropped had a big effect on the outcome of this disappointing series and gave a false impression of the Australians' status. By allowing opposing batsmen to score 21 centuries against them on the tour, the West

Indian bowlers looked second-rate, but their catching was so bad that author Ray Robinson estimated that in the Tests alone Australia were allowed 1000 additional runs.

Spectators enjoyed some spectacular events in that season's Sheffield Shield matches. These included Western Australian Colin Milburn's famous opening assault on Queensland's bowlers in the Shield match at the Gabba. Milburn, a pot-bellied 108-kilogram opener whose training included sinking schooners of beer, put on 382 for the first wicket with team-mate Derek Chadwick. Milburn was so overweight he found running between the wickets trying, so he hit the ball over or into the fence instead. Milburn made 243 with 38 fours and four sixes, including 181 between lunch and tea. Some of his sixes bounced into the streets outside the ground. Chadwick made 91, and then Inverarity, 108, and Becker, 112, took the score to 5 declared for 615.

This brand of explosive hitting was typical of Milburn, who later lost an eye in a car crash, which virtually ended his first-class career but he took it in good spirit. When a hospital nurse produced a selection of glass eyes for him to try, he said: 'I'd better get a bloodshot one for the mornings.' After his discharge from hospital he once laughed so boisterously over a joke, his glass eye fell out, whereupon half the press corps forgot the match and got down on their hands and knees to search for Ollie's eye.

Milburn's hitting helped lift Western Australia to the lead in the Shield competition with one match to play. The west's hopes foundered in Sydney when South Australia dismissed New South Wales for 110 to make certain of first-innings points, before sweeping on to outright victory, thanks to a dazzling 102 from Greg Chappell. This gave South Australia a ninth Sheffield Shield win and their third since Hitler's war.

The Australian Board of Control originally arranged a tour of India and Pakistan in 1969–70, but when Pakistan pulled out, the Board generously agreed to complete the tour with 12 weeks in South Africa, whose cricketers had undergone three years of isolation as a result of their government's refusal to accept D'Oliveira. This turned out to be one of the toughest assignments ever undertaken by an Australian cricket team, because the two months the Australians spent in Ceylon and India before they got to South Africa brought daily disturbances such as disputes with umpires and stone-throwing, and exposed Lawry's deficiencies as a leader.

The Australian team was the last selected by Bradman, who had been picking touring teams since 1938. With the help of Neil Harvey and Phil Ridings, Bradman chose W.M. Lawry (Captain), I.M. Chappell (Vice-captain), A.N. Connolly, E.W. Freeman, J.W. Gleeson, J.T. Irvine, R.C. Jordon, G.D. McKenzie, A.A. Mallett, L.C. Mayne, I.R. Redpath, A.P. Sheahan, K.R. Stackpole, H.B. Taber and K.D. Walters, with Fred Bennett as manager. Twelve members of the team flew to Colombo from Australia, but Mayne, McKenzie and Connolly flew from England and were delayed in Calcutta, unable to get a connecting flight for three days. The team played three one-day matches in Ceylon and had a draw in their sole three-day fixture against Ceylon, but saw enough to realise Ceylon were improving rapidly.

After a first-class match at Poona, the Australians began the First Test at the giant Brabourne Stadium in Bombay on 4 November 1969. Their opposition was undecided until the last moment. There was such a public outcry over the omission of Venkataraghavan that one of the selected Indian players, Subrato Guha, agreed to stand down and let Venkat take his place in the Indian side.

Venkat was given out caught behind by Taber off Connolly in India's second innings. Spectators heard a radio announcer question the decision and immediately went on the rampage, but as stones, oranges and soft-drink bottles rained on to the ground and hessian screens and awnings were set alight Lawry refused to stop play. The scorers complained they could not do their job because of the smoke from small fires around the ground but Mallett bowled Prasanna before stumps. Helmeted police escorted the Australians from the field but could not prevent Gleeson being hit behind the right ear by a flying bottle or Lawry being struck by two rattan chairs. Next day the Australians celebrated an eight-wicket win.

The ruckus in Bombay set the pattern for the entire tour, with Lawry's players taunted and harassed wherever they played. The Second Test at Kanpur was drawn after splendid centuries by Viswanath (137) and Sheahan (114) went almost unnoticed. India drew level by winning the Third Test at Delhi by seven wickets despite a fine 138 from Ian Chappell, with conditions deteriorating. Political and trade-union tensions mounted and the Australians were compelled to practise for the Fourth Test at Eden Gardens, Calcutta, in front of 10,000 baying fans. Outside the ground posters accused Doug Walters of having fought in Vietnam, when in fact Walters had never left Australia during his Army service.

Australian manager Fred Bennett appealed to Indian cricket officials to ensure his players were protected around the clock. Senior police and Army officers met to discuss security and special units of the Eastern Frontier Rifles were summoned, but before the start of the fourth day's play six people were killed and 30 of the hundreds injured were admitted to hospital after a pitched battle between police and people frustrated in their attempts to buy seats. Only 8000 six-rupee tickets were offered in a stadium that held 60,000, and all those who missed out chose to do battle.

Mike Coward, in his book *Cricket Beyond the Bazaar*, said: 'The Australians were deeply shocked by the death of six people and manager Bennett composed a message of sympathy as the government ordered an inquiry into the tragedy.' In reaction to the riot the crowd grew restless when Lawry and Stackpole set out to score the 39 runs Australia needed to win. Spectators on the upper deck of the Ranji section dropped bottles and other missiles on those below, forcing the occupants to seek refuge on the field. In the period it took to restore order Lawry clashed with a newspaper photographer and was accused of striking the man, Miran Adhikary of the Bengali daily, *Basmali*.

Stackpole insisted that Lawry only prodded Adhikary with his bat, but Adhikary stumbled and hurt himself when he fell on his photographic equipment. A damning photograph of the incident appeared around the world. Lawry and Stackpole provided an escort for the Nawab of Pataudi, centre of the crowd's anger, as they hurried off, and Australia were victors by ten wickets with more than a day to spare and a precious 2–1 lead in the series.

Frustrated by the absence of Australian reporters who could put his team's point of view, Lawry had to endure allegations in Indian newspapers that he deliberately struck the press cameraman. That night at the Australians' hotel, McKenzie and Redpath, calmest of men, were alleged to have assaulted pressmen who refused to leave the team's celebration dinner. The pressmen retired to the hotel's liquor permit room and later tried to enter rooms occupied by the players, who ejected them. On the way to Calcutta airport to play the next match at Bangalore, the Australians were stoned by a mob who concealed themselves in a ricefield until the players' bus came by. Windows and seats sustained the worst of the hail of rocks but one huge stone crashed into a seat only inches from John Gleeson.

At the airport, the police chief who had removed the escort that normally guarded the players shook his head in disbelief when he saw the battered bus. In the face of this provocation Lawry resorted to rude finger signs on the field. This only encouraged hecklers to single him out and during the Fifth Test at Madras from 24 to 28 December 1969 spectators' shouting, whistling and drum-beating forced him to protest to the umpires, who said they were powerless to reduce the din. Mallett won the match for Australia by taking 10 for 144, and finished the five Tests with 28 wickets at 19.10 each.

The Australians arrived in South Africa following their 3–1 defeat of India full of optimism. The Australians were on a winning streak after their victory over the West Indies the previous summer at home and now India. They had their best batsman, Ian Chappell, in dominant form, they had discovered an inspirational 'keeper in Taber who completed 16 dismissals in India, and they had all their spinners in wicket-taking mood.

South Africa defeated them 4–0, inflicting on what looked a very strong side one of the worst drubbings ever suffered by an Australian team. Their superiority was so marked Lawry's morale disintegrated. He upset colleagues and spectators with more vulgar hand signals, seldom mixed with opponents at the end of a day's play, and virtually became a prisoner in his team's hotels. The Victorians in the team felt obliged to support him but players from other states had no such loyalty and did not hide their disappointment in him. The team became a disoriented rabble, unable to hold a catch. They dropped 70 catches in their 12 matches, almost 30 of them in the four Tests, according to South African writer Geoffrey Chettle.

To give batsmen of the calibre of Graeme Pollock, Barry Richards and Eddie Barlow two or three reprieves proved fatal. Four South Africans averaged more than fifty in the Tests, Graeme Pollock, 73.85, Richards, 72.57, Barlow, 51.42, and Irvine, 50.42. The Australians hit seven centuries and had twelve scored against them, with Redpath heading their Test averages at 47.16. Connolly and Gleeson were the only Australian bowlers to reach international standard. Connolly took 39 wickets in his nine matches and Gleeson 59 wickets in nine matches on pitches that rarely helped his spin.

South Africa beat Australia for the first time at Newlands, Cape Town, by winning the First Test by 170 runs. South Africa won the Second Test at Durban by an innings and 129 runs, thanks to 274 from Graeme Pollock and 140 from Barry Richards, which lifted their first innings total to 622 for 9 declared, a record South African Test score. The South African humbling of Australia continued in the Third Test at Johannesburg and the Fourth Test at Port Elizabeth. South Africa's clean sweep was the first in her history but did not prevent her excommunication from international cricket at the end of the Australian tour. Australia won only four of the 12 first-class matches on the tour, losing four and leaving four drawn.

In the final match Ian Chappell took over the captaincy. Ian Redpath's 152 included six sixes and 19 fours and he made his last 52 runs in 12 minutes, including 32 runs off a six-ball over from Rosendorff, to lead the Australian charge to victory by an innings and 185 runs.

Ian Chappell soon after he took over as Australia's Test captain. He proved a tenacious leader who inspired loyalty.
(Patrick Eagar)

The South African part of Australia's tour made $250,000 profit but the Australian Board of Control rejected manager Bennett's recommendation to pay the players a bonus of $500. South Africa wanted a fifth Test and at Ian Chappell's suggestion all the Australians asked for $500 to play. The Australian Board, despite the fact that all its costs were guaranteed by the Wanderer's Club, meanly refused to play the extra match. The Australian team arrived home with the magnificent spirit so carefully built by Benaud and Simpson in tatters.

A 13-man New Zealand team toured Australia while the Test side was in South Africa. The New Zealanders played a draw with Tasmania in Hobart, a draw in Melbourne with Victoria and a draw with New South Wales in Sydney, before winning a limited-over competition by defeating Victoria in the final in Melbourne by six wickets. Victoria had a successful season, though, winning the Shield.

An Australian 'B' team returned this visit by playing eight matches in New Zealand in February and March 1970, under the captaincy of Sam Trimble. The Australian team was S.C. Trimble, G.S. Chappell, G.R. Davies, A. Turner, R.J. Inverarity, G.D. Watson, J.A. Steele, J.A. MacLean, D. Chadwick, T.J. Jenner, D.A. Renneberg, A.L. Thomson, D.K. Lillee and K.J. O'Keeffe.

The Australians won two matches and left the other six drawn. They defeated Otago by an innings and 50 runs at Dunedin, mainly because of a splendid all-round contribution by Inverarity, who made 108 and then took 5 for 28 with his drifting left-arm slows. At Napier they had their other win against a New Zealand Under-23 side, whom they beat by an innings and 20 runs. Lillee took

6 for 40 and 3 for 26. The three representative matches produced heavy scoring but no results.

Bad light and rain contributed to an unsatisfactory tour, Lillee's first overseas venture, which lost $11,000. This represented a heavy blow for New Zealand cricket as the earlier visit to Australia had lost $3500. Lillee at that time bowled at a furious pace, but lacked control. Greg Chappell was the best player on the tour, scoring 519 runs at 57.66, although Trimble's 213 in the third representative match gave him a higher aggregate, 555 at 55.50.

Important changes in the administration of cricket were underway in England, where a Labour government had set up a Sports Council to assist in the administration of all sports. After 65 years of sponsoring English tours overseas, the Marylebone Cricket Club handed the responsibility to a new organisation called the National Cricket Council. This council, soon after its formation, applied to the Sports Council for compensation for following government advice to cancel the 1970 South African tour because South Africa would not accept D'Oliveira. The Sports Council handed over £75,000 when the Cricket Council expected £200,000.

The National Cricket Council's selectors, A.V. Bedser, D. Kenyon, C. Washbrook and A.C. Smith, picked the English team that toured Australia in 1970–71. England prepared for the visit to Australia with matches at home against The Rest of the World, which had to replace the proposed South African tour of England. After watching all the prospective tourists, the selectors settled on this team for Australia: R. Illingworth (Captain), M.C. Cowdrey, G. Boycott, J.H. Edrich, B.W. Luckhurst, B.L. D'Oliveira, A.P.E. Knott, J.H. Hampshire, K.W.R. Fletcher, J.A. Snow, R.W. Taylor, P. Lever, R.G.D. Willis, D. Wilson, K. Shuttleworth, A. Ward and D.L. Underwood. Willis replaced the injured Ward.

The Englishmen originally faced a programme that included six Tests, with one in Perth for the first time. The scheduled Third Test in Melbourne, from 1 to 5 January 1971, was abandoned without a ball being bowled, but some statisticians have argued ever since that because the toss was held and won by England it ranks as a match, even though the players did not take the field. The Board of Control concurred with this, for it paid the Australian players' match fees and attributed the Test to their Provident Fund records. An extra Test was added, which the Board chose to call the Seventh Test.

The First Test provided a major shock when Brian Taber was omitted from the Australian team after handling the wicket-keeper's role with distinction for 16 Tests. Taber's 60 Test dismissals included four stumpings. He had not fulfilled his promise as a batsman, scoring only 353 runs at 16.05 an innings, but his work behind the stumps had lived up to the highest traditions of Australian wicket-keeping. His replacement, Rodney Marsh, a lumpy, slow-moving Western Australian with billiard-table legs, drew guffaws and cries of 'Iron Gloves' all round the Gabba when he made his debut in the First Test. Some old-timers could not believe such a cumbersome man would survive a match in international cricket.

Australia had a lucky start when Stackpole was given not out on 18 when he was clearly run out, and he went on to make 207. Walters made a classy 112, but from 2 for 372, eight Australian wickets fell for 61 runs and they were all out for 433. England gave a commendable display of team batting to take a 31-run lead but a draw always seemed likely with neither side's bowlers able to break through.

Test cricket began in Perth on 11 December, 1970, when Lawry won his second successive toss and sent England in. The move misfired as the WACA pitch proved ideal for batting. Luckhurst made 131, after a first-wicket stand of 171 with Boycott, 70. Australia appeared hopelessly placed at 5 for 107 in reply to England's 397 but Greg Chappell in his Test debut joined Redpath in a match-saving stand of 219. Chappell's 108 was full of lovely drives, regal cuts and clever on-side dabs and was applauded for several minutes. Redpath's 171 was a far more cautious innings but he kept going for eight hours despite his uncertainty against Snow. A draw was a fair result to a match that attracted 85,000 people over five days, twice as many as the Brisbane Test.

Greg Chappell, who scored a century against Illingworth's team in his Test debut at the WACA in 1970–71, playing a typically graceful legside shot. (Patrick Eagar)

Already the coolness under pressure of the English captain Ray Illingworth had made a deep impression and it was obvious he commanded greater support from his players than Lawry enjoyed from the Australians. Snow, the son of a Sussex vicar, showed marked hostility whenever he took the ball, lifting the ball into the rib cage and over good players' heads despite his low arm action.

A conference between members of the Australian Board of Control led by Sir Donald Bradman, the English team manager D.G. Clark, and visiting MCC chiefs, Sir Cyril Hawker and 'Gubby' Allen decided as rain washed away the Third Test to replace it with

John Snow, son of clergyman, made the ball lift alarmingly despite a low arm action for Illingworth's thirtieth English team in Australia.
(Ken Kelly)

a Seventh Test. This decision placed a big strain on Illingworth, already harassed by a high injury toll, but the ultimate absurdity was to credit umpires Tom Brooks and Lou Rowan with an extra Test to their career records when they never went through the gates.

All the negative aspects of Test cricket, dreary batting and the lack of full-blooded stroke-play, bowling aimed at intimidating rather than taking wickets, were on view in the Fourth Test at Sydney when England achieved their biggest win by a run margin over Australia since 1936–37. This was a match that could not have been better contrived to drive spectators away. England scored only 267 on the first day for the loss of seven wickets, and after Australia replied to England's 332 with 236, Boycott was allowed to bat on for 6 hours 50 minutes during which time he seldom offered an aggressive stroke. He left the scene unbeaten on 142 not out but Test cricket was infinitely poorer for an innings where he rarely hit the ball in the middle of the bat.

England won by 299 runs after five days, with Lawry batting through the Australian second innings for 60 not out, but by then most spectators had left for the beach and Sydney Cricket Ground members were threatening not to renew their subscriptions.

The Fifth Test at Melbourne and the Sixth at Adelaide were drawn. Ian Chappell, 111, Luckhurst, 109, and D'Oliveira, 117, made hundreds in Melbourne and Edrich, 130, Boycott, 119 not out, Ian Chappell, 104, and Stackpole, 136, scored centuries in Adelaide, where Dennis Lillee took 5 for 84 in his Test debut. This left the rubber up for decision in the Seventh Test at Sydney, with England one-up but Australia able to draw level by winning.

Just before the finish of the Sixth Test Bill Lawry became the first Australian captain to be sacked before a series ended. The selectors, Bradman, Harvey and Loxton, decided the Test team required a more adventurous leader and Board of Control members, aware of Lawry's misdemeanours in India and South Africa, favoured dismissing a captain who had not had a win in nine Tests. They appointed Ian Chappell to what everybody hoped would be a bright new era in Australian cricket. Chappell's reign was to bring a few surprises. Although elated at his appointment, Chappell felt only disgust for the manner of Lawry's sacking. He was well aware of Lawry's petulance under pressure in India and South Africa, but vowed that the Board would never get the chance to treat him so shabbily.

CHAPTER TWENTY-EIGHT

THE SHOP STEWARD
TAKES OVER

Ian Michael Chappell ran the Australian cricket team like a trade-union shop steward, and fought for his players' rights in the same fashion. He expected all his players to contribute to the team's benefit, provide loyalty, and shed sweat on the field without complaint, and in return he fought the bosses for them.

He had a Test captain's pedigree. His father, Martin Chappell, had headed the Adelaide district club's batting averages. His mother was the daughter of Vic Richardson, who captained Australia on a South African tour and in five Tests, and both his brothers, Greg and Trevor, followed him into Test cricket.

He achieved most of the goals in his life but too often on the way a boisterous streak prevented him enjoying success. Somehow on the trip from backyard games to matches for Prince Alfred's College and on the grade cricket with Glenelg and Shield cricket with South Australia he not only failed to acquire any polish but developed an objection to it. Sophistication deserted him.

Chappell's bravery, superfine technique and ability to deliver on big occasions fell victim to his language and ethical blindspots. He did not invent sledging in cricket but he intensified it. The great New Zealand batsman, Glenn Turner, whose coloured wife received a mention or two in Ian's on-the-field commentaries, said that sharing a dressing-room with Chappell was similar to a stint in Vietnam.

Even former team-mates like Len Pascoe rebelled over Ian's abuse, their complaints serving only to endorse English assessments of him as one of cricket's barbarians. With such a make-up, it is impossible to give credence to Chappell's comment that in taking over the Australian team he was determined he would not receive the treatment the Board of Control handed out to Bill Lawry.

Ken Eastwood, the inexperienced Victorian opener selectors gave Ian Chappell to replace Lawry. (Age, Melbourne)

Ian took over the Test captaincy at a time when Australian tours overseas and visits to Australia by four of the five cricket-playing nations had dramatically increased. The Australian captain was asked for his view so often on big issues he seemed to be cricket's spokesman, a role that rightly belonged to the chairman of the Board of Control.

Chappell had no time to learn the job. He took over the captaincy for a match Australia had to win, to share the series, against the thirtieth England team at Sydney in 1971, and held the job through 30 Tests without a break. Bradman was chairman of the Board when Ian became Test captain and neither he nor his successor Tim Caldwell were given to controversial public statements. Their style was to put out press releases that were noted for their understatement. The result was that Ian Chappell sometimes sounded like the voice of Australian cricket. His dressing-room conferences with a dozen or more media reporters at the end of each day's play were thoughtful, painstaking commentaries cricket writers had not enjoyed since the days before the Board of Control gagged Richie Benaud and insisted all comment come from bumbling old Syd Webb.

The selectors gave him a team for his debut as Test skipper that never had a chance against the seasoned outfit Ray Illingworth led. To deprive Chappell of an opener of Lawry's experience and replace him with Victorian Ken Eastwood, a 35-year-old of obvious limitations, was indefensible. The gamble of bringing in big Tony Dell to do what Mckenzie, Thomson and Duncan had failed to do was just as reprehensible and Ian had to use eight bowlers before an eventful match was over.

Chappell showed he was his own man by inviting England to bat after winning the toss in his first Test as captain. The spin of Jenner (3 for 42) and O'Keeffe (3 for 48) had England out for 184, but after tea on the second day, crowd disturbances prompted Illingworth churlishly to lead England from the field. The crowd objected to Snow's barrage of bouncers, culminating when he flattened Jenner. The bouncer row that had been simmering for four months erupted as Jenner went down, and the hooting of the Englishmen intensified as Jenner was led away, blood oozing from his head.

Before John Snow bowled to the next batsman, Dennis Lillee, umpire Lou Rowan called to Snow, who ignored him. 'Just a minute, John,' said Rowan. 'I'm not impressed with your

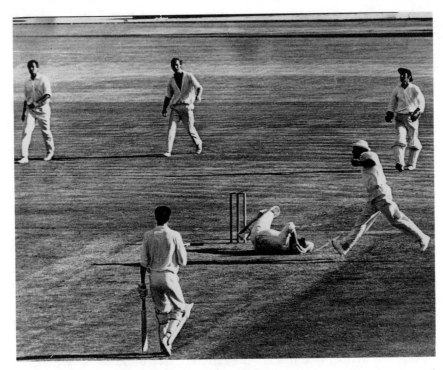

The incident that led to England's walk-off from the Sydney ground in 1970–71, with Terry Jenner flattened by a John Snow bouncer.
(News Limited)

performance and I am giving you a first warning.' Rowan turned and signalled to his fellow umpire Tom Brooks at square leg with one finger raised. Snow whirled around and shouted, 'That's the first bouncer I've bowled this over! Your blokes have been bowling seven an over.' Illingworth rushed to the bowler's end to support Snow, the surly undertones of the exchange clear to the crowd.

Rowan repeated his warning and Snow objected in terms that were clearly unbecoming to a vicar's son. A great roar of passionate booing followed Snow as he moved in and delivered the last ball of his over to Lillee. The booing continued as the English players sat on the grass to take drinks. Empty beer cans, oranges, and half-empty soft drink cans bounced on to the field. Attendants began clearing the cans as the drinks break ended and Snow insisted on fielding at the north-east corner of the field where the booing was still noisy. Illingworth tried to persuade him to change position but Snow insisted on standing out on the fence at backward square leg. He was greeted with taunts to which he responded with unmistakable gestures. Boys reached out to shake his hand but one drunk in an orange shirt grabbed Snow's shirt and hauled him against the fence.

Snow shook himself free and moved to a spot about ten metres

After being warned by umpire Rowan following the Jenner incident, Snow went to the boundary fence where a demonstrating spectator accosted him.
(Herald & Weekly Times)

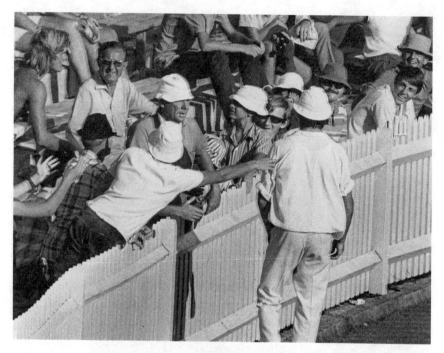

inside the fence, but more cans landed all around him. Watching the tins landing at Snow's feet, Illingworth ran to him to protest. Snow refused to be pulled away. More cans landed at Snow's feet and Illingworth waved his team from the field.

Experts in the crowd believed England forfeited the match by walking off. Sacked captain Bill Lawry immediately claimed he had won a bet he had had with Richie Benaud on Australia winning. Some of the English players were clearly concerned about forfeiting because they remained.

Rowan went to the dressing-room and warned Illingworth that his team would forfeit the match unless they immediately returned to the field, where policemen were busy herding spectators back to their seats. John Edrich blamed the walk-off on drinking. 'Don't tell me your bowlers have been drinking!' said Rowan.

With Australia chasing 223 to win in the final innings, Snow broke his hand on the boundary fence attempting to catch Stackpole, but Stackpole was the only Australian batsman to stay for very long and when he was out for 67 England completed a notable victory by 62 runs to win the series 2–0. Not one lbw decision was given against an Australian batsmen in the entire rubber.

Chappell had to pick up the pieces left from the series in which Australia had been comprehensively outplayed. England had lost

Greg Chappell dives full length to catch Basil D'Oliveira off Ashley Mallett in what proved D'Oliveira's last Test. (Patrick Eagar)

only one of their 14 first-class matches and her batsmen scored 22 centuries while her bowlers allowed only 14 to be scored against them. Boycott led the English Test batting averages on 93.85, but Australia's most successful batsman, Stackpole, averaged 52.25.

Disappointed in the Tests, Chappell had the satisfaction of winning the Sheffield Shield in his first season after taking over the state captaincy from Les Favell. Supported by the great South African Barry Richards, his brother Greg Chappell, opener Ashley Woodcock, and the pace bowlers Jeff Hammond and Kevin McCarthy, Chappell gave South Australia enterprising leadership and was particularly impressive in his handling of the spinners Jenner and Mallett. Richards scored 1538 runs in the first-class season at an average of 109.86, including an innings of 365 in 372 minutes against Western Australia in Perth.

The 1970–71 Australian summer also saw striking improvements in public support for one-day cricket, with an England v. Australia match in Melbourne attracting 46,000 spectators and a six-state 40-over competition attracting large, enthusiastic audiences.

Basil D'Oliveira appeared in all six Tests for England and his 707 runs on the English tour included four centuries that boosted his average to 50.50. A knee injury prevented him bowling regularly but he stood up to an arduous tour well. English critics found him far more impressive than he had been on his initial tour with England in the West Indies.

During the Australian winter of 1971 a tour of Australia by the fifth South African rugby team was accompanied by such violent demonstrations by Australians opposed to the South African government's apartheid policies, the Australian Cricket Board appointed a special committee to report on whether South Africa's Australian cricket tour in 1971–72 should proceed. The committee, comprising Sir Donald Bradman, Syd Webb and Bob Parish, decided cricket could not risk repetition of the ugly scenes in which police had to use smoke bombs and hospitals overflowed with battered and bleeding protesters and a full meeting of the Board withdrew South Africa's invitation to tour.

Ian Chappell hooks a six against The Rest of the World in the 1971–72 Australian season. He was a compulsive but skilful hooker, always ready to accept the gamble of making the shot. (News Limited)

The Board secretary Allan Barnes moved quickly to replace the South African tour with a tour by a World XI involving two limited-over matches and 12 first-class games, including five five-day fixtures against Australia, and matches against each of the states. The World XI included players from six countries: G.StA. Sobers (Captain), Intikhab Alam, H.M. Ackerman, Asif Masood, B.S. Bedi, R.S. Cunis, F.M. Engineer, S.M. Gavaskar, N. Gifford, A.W. Greig, R.A. Hutton, R.B. Kanhai, C.H. Lloyd, R.W. Taylor and Zaheer Abbas, with Bill Jacobs, the noted Melbourne commentator, as manager.

Assembling this team at short notice was a splendid achievement by Barnes, who was confronted by a major obstacle early on the tour when Kanhai and Lloyd were injured in the match against South Australia, Lloyd so badly that his entire career was in jeopardy for a time. Late in December the Pollock brothers, Graeme and Peter, were flown in as replacements.

The multi-national World XI suffered so many injuries it was often difficult to negotiate a path into the team's dressing-room. Doctors, masseurs and X-ray machines barred the way on a tour on which Bill Jacobs calculated there were 35 injuries. The visit proved invaluable to Australian cricket in demonstrating the promise of Dennis Lillee, the young Perth pace bowler, and Bob Massie's ability to swing the ball.

446

Lillee had just returned from a season with Haslingden in the Lancashire League, where he broke one batsman's leg so badly he could not move from the crease. Lillee developed a virus and asked to be taken off after taking the wickets of Gavaskar and Engineer in the World XI's first innings against Australia in Perth. Ian Chappell persuaded him to continue and he bowled Australia to victory by an innings and 11 runs, taking 8 for 29 and 4 for 63. Long before the end of the series, in which Lillee took 24 wickets in four matches at 20.08, it was clear Australia had found the fast bowler they had been looking for since Alan Davidson retired.

In the Sydney match against the World XI Massie took 7 for 76. The World XI won two of the five representative matches, Australia one and there were two draws. Ian Chappell was at his best, scoring four centuries and featuring in some splendid stands with Doug Walters and brother Greg, but the outstanding innings of the summer was Garfield Sobers's 254 against Australia in Melbourne. Sobers batted for 6 hours 16 minutes and hit two sixes and 35 fours. Sir Donald Bradman hailed Sobers's batting in these words: 'I believe Sobers's innings was probably the best ever seen in Australia. The people who saw Sobers enjoyed one of the historic events of cricket; they were privileged to have such an experience.'

There was a near-tragedy in this match when Australian opening batsman Graeme Watson was hit twice. In the first innings he took a blow behind the ear from Pollock and in the second innings a bouncer from Greig fractured his nose and cheekbone. He was rushed to St Vincent's Hospital, where doctors decided to operate. Watson haemorrhaged and was on the danger list until heart massage and transfusions of 40 pints of blood saved him.

The World XI's Australian tour was a major triumph for the Board of Control. More than 458,000 people watched the tour matches, turning up in numbers that averaged 10,000 more per match than for the last South African tour in 1963–64. Although restricted by injuries, all the major drawcards succeeded. Sobers was masterly, Kanhai only slightly inferior in topping the tour batting averages with 525 runs at 65.62. Tony Greig emerged as a world-class cricketer and led the World XI bowling averages with 26 wickets at 28.53. Greg Chappell (425 runs at 106.25), Ian Chappell (634 runs at 79.25) and Stackpole (490 runs at 54.44) showed they would be a formidable threesome in England in 1972.

With all of Australia's leading players available and pressing their claims for the English tour, the 1971–72 Sheffield Shield competition produced brilliant cricket. Western Australia won the Shield for the third time by one point from South Australia, under a new bonus points system that eliminated points for first-innings wins. Crowds at the decisive match between Western Australia and South Australia in Perth created a record for the WACA of 25,000. Western Australia's win was a triumph for their coaching panel who had produced a squad with all-round depth where every team berth was keenly contested.

Ross Edwards led the state's batting averages with four centuries in six matches, scoring 586 runs at 58.60, followed by Inverarity (641 at 53.41). New-ball bowlers McKenzie (22 wickets at 22.31), Massie (25 at 24.28) and Lillee (24 at 18.75) accounted for 71 of the 128 batsmen Western Australia dismissed in the competition. It was no surprise when Western Australia won six places in the 1972 Australian side to tour England.

The continued omission of Lawry was disgraceful, for he was still a great opener, whatever his deficiencies as a captain. Forced to shop around for a partner to open with Stackpole the selectors opted for Bruce Francis, the Sydney right-hand batsman who had had experience with Accrington in the Lancashire League in 1970 and with Essex in 1971 in English county cricket. The team was I.M. Chappell (Captain), D.J. Colley, K.R. Stackpole, G.S. Chappell, R. Edwards, B.C. Francis, J.W. Gleeson, J.R. Hammond, R.J. Inverarity, D.K. Lillee, A.A. Mallett, R.W. Marsh, R.A.L. Massie, A.P. Sheahan, H.B. Taber, K.D. Walters and G.D. Watson, with Ray Steele as manager.

From the time they took off from Sydney to fly to London via San Francisco, the team disappointed traditionalists with their standards of dress. Ian Chappell set the pace in a team of shaggy maned players with droopy moustaches by wearing a mauve safari suit, and appalled collar-and-tie stalwarts by appearing on the balcony at Lord's in a purple jump suit.

The Australian dressing-room featured some colourful language and incessant cribbage matches in which Douggie Walters indulged his fondness for pranks and rock stars could be found downing Australian beer at the end of the day. One of Walters's favourite tricks was to spread banknotes carelessly about the room. When someone bent to pick up the notes Walters reeled them in on a fishing line that operated from a button in his pocket. Ian Chappell encouraged all his players to linger in the dressing-room for a couple of hours after each day's play. The cameraderie this developed helped mould the Australians into a better team. To English critics they represented cricket's jeans generation, freewheeling types who worshipped their bluntly spoken captain.

Ray Steele wrote, in a foreword for Chappell's book *Tiger Among The Lions*, that the twenty-sixth Australian team under Chappell was less concerned with averages than any team he had ever toured with. Ian taught his men how to recover from seemingly hopeless positions and their desire to succeed became so strong that when Bob Massie failed to make the Test side he was seen in the nets coaching the bowler who replaced him.

Chappell was unlucky when he started his first campaign in England, losing the toss on rival captain Illingworth's fortieth birthday on a seamer's pitch at Old Trafford. His batsmen had so little experience of such a wicket that by just after lunch on the fifth day England won the first Test of a home series against Australia for the first time since 1930. Tony Greig top-scored in both innings of his first official Test, England winning by 89 runs.

Robert Arnold Lockyer Massie gave an amazing performance at Lord's to win the Second Test for Australia in his Test debut. Massie's analysis, 16 for 137, remains a record for any bowler at Lord's. Only Jim Laker and S.F. Barnes have taken more wickets in a Test. Massie swung the ball so sharply and so consistently through both England innings the batsmen kept inspecting the balls used, apparently thinking they had lost their shape or that Massie was using hair oil or some illegal substance to retain the shine. Only two years earlier Massie had been denied a contract by Northamptonshire after a trial with their second XI. He took 8 for 84 and 8 for 53 in the Test.

The Third Test at Trent Bridge ended in a draw despite centuries by Stackpole, 114, and Edwards, 170 not out, for Australia. England retained the Ashes by winning the Fourth Test on a shocker of a pitch at Headingly by nine wickets. The pitch took spin from the first hour and rain and a fungus infection prevented the use of a heavy roller. By the third morning the Australians found Underwood virtually unplayable and he finished the match with 4 for 37 and 6 for 45.

The Australians went to The Oval for the Fifth Test frustrated by the conditions in two Tests which had prevented them showing their true ability. Lillee took 5 for 58 and 5 for 123 to complete the rubber with 31 wickets, a record for Australia in England that

The members' pavilion at Lord's rises to applaud Greg Chappell for his superb 131 in 1972 which set up his team's victory. (Patrick Eagar)

lasted until 1981. Marsh also set a record with 23 dismissals behind the stumps. Chappell's team attracted more than 13 million calls to the English telephone scores service during the game. The match was only the second six-day Test in England and the first Test involving an Australian team that did not include a New South Wales player.

The Australians won 11 of their 26 matches, but even in the five they lost they remained bold and aggressive. They closed at 2 for 262 against Sussex, for example, and gave the county the chance to become the first Sussex side since 1888 to defeat Australia by scoring 261 in 180 minutes. Sussex got the runs, with Greig hitting three sixes in an over and 36 runs from 18 balls in the first innings.

A record 383,345 people paid £261,283 to watch the Tests, but the feature of the tour was the introduction for the first time of three limited-over international matches to replace a sixth Test. The Prudential Insurance group provided £30,000 sponsorship, £4000 of which was allocated to prize money. They drew a total attendance of 55,000 over the English Bank Holiday weekend. England won two £1000 cheques for winning two matches, two £200 Man of the Match awards, and Amiss received £200 as the Man of the Series. The matches were played over 55 overs and the overall result was in doubt until the last over of the final game in Birmingham, which England won by two wickets.

The arrival of sponsorship for big cricket spread quickly round the world, with England setting the pattern. English television and radio paid £100,000 for rights to broadcast the five Tests and the three one-day matches in 1972. A further £230,000 came from the Benson and Hedges and Gillette companies. In all, sponsorships meant MCC ended the season with £600,000 of the big firms' money. Each of the 17 counties received £25,000 as their share of the kitty.

Ian Chappell took a keen interest in these promotions and from the time he returned home began lobbying Board of Control officials for higher pay for Test players. He was giving cricket a new image and he wanted to make sure his team benefited from the changes that were on the way. He was well aware that Ross Edwards had lost his job with a Perth accountancy firm by touring in 1972, and that the bank balance of almost every player in his team suffered through going on a five-month tour for which the Australian Board of Control paid them $2000 each. Team manager Ray Steele could not have failed to hear the players' persistent claims for financial help, but back in Australia far too many Board members still regarded the honour of playing for your country as a reward beyond price.

The Board's share of profits from the 1972 English tour amounted to $62,536, compared with $85,000 in 1968 and $87,000 in 1964; they remained highly conservative in their attitude to commercial television. They blindly continued with the ball-by-ball coverage on ABC radio and limited time on ABC television. In the process the Board made Alan McGilvray a national figure of unprecedented popularity. He was a dull broadcaster when he began, and John Arlott was openly critical of his work, but by careful application he became a commentator of unmatched skill, widely loved.

The Board at this time was the despair of advertising agencies who could see profits from the huge market cricket commanded slipping away. The use of a space satellite to broadcast the Fifth Test in 1972 from England had opened up vast opportunities for television networks, offering clear pictures of major sporting events from virtually anywhere in the world. The success of limited-over cricket, which guaranteed a result within a few hours, further heightened these marketing opportunities. Bradman described television as the most powerful medium ever invented but nobody on the Board realised that fees from television were the solution to their player-payment problems. The long-promised Players' Provident Fund, under which fees for each big match appearance were put away until the end of the players' careers, remained on hold while young players faced increasing strains on their normal family lives.

The leading players' financial concerns were partly due to the packed international programme the Board undertook in the 1970s. Most of the team that toured England in 1972 arrived home in mid-September and by 20 October the first Sheffield Shield matches began, followed on 15 November by the first match on Pakistan's 1972–73 Australian schedule. With a hard tour of the West Indies to follow from February to April, 1973, time with their wives and children was restricted, let alone any chance to seek advancement in their jobs.

The Pakistan team which visited Australia in 1972–73 included several highly experienced cricketers with impressive backgrounds in county and international matches. They were captained by a shrewd performer in Intikhab Alam, whose leg-spin bowling for the World XI had earned him many admirers. The team was Intikhab Alam, Asif Iqbal, Saeed Ahmed, Nasim-ul-Ghani, Majid Khan, Mushtaq Mohammad, Pervez Sajjad, Mohammad Ilyas, Salim Altaf, Wasim Bari, Asif Masood, Sarfraz Nawaz, Sadiq Mohamad, Talat Ali, Majid Usman and Masood Iqbal, with Wing-Commander M.E.Z. Ghazali as manager. Pakistan had never won a Test in Australia and had only one win at home against Australia, at Karachi in 1956, to encourage them.

The Pakistanis had a disastrous lead-up to the three-Test series, losing to Western Australia, Victoria and Northern New South Wales at Newcastle, but the spirit Ian Chappell worked so hard to build was badly needed by the Australians in the Tests. In two of the three Tests Pakistan were in a winning position but Australia escaped by holding their nerve in the crisis and fighting their way out of trouble.

The experiments in trying Bruce Francis and Graeme Watson as opening partners for Stackpole in England had not worked. Now Ian Redpath, shrugging off his disappointment at missing the English tour, made a strong bid for the second opener's spot. New-ball bowlers, Max ('Tangles') Walker, a 190–cm tall man who pushed the wrong foot forward in his delivery stride, and a heavily muscled former javelin thrower and soccer star, Jeff Thomson, were thrown into the Second Test at Melbourne after Australia over-whelmed Pakistan in the First Test. This uncharacteristic gamble with untried talent paid off handsomely and both Walker and Thomson enjoyed long, fruitful careers.

Despite the one-sided nature of the contest more than 115,721 spectators attended the Melbourne Test and takings reached $91,450. The Pakistanis were a popular side, sprinkled with polished professionals, but they were given a hopeless itinerary by officials afraid their venture would fail. Limiting the Test rubber to three matches played over three weeks exhausted both teams, but Australia at least could call on fresh players.

The Third Test featured two highly contrasting bowling displays from Australian bowlers. With Australia only 158 runs ahead, Pakistan reached 2 for 83 and appeared to have the match won. The huge, lumbering frame of Walker then took control, and in 30 deliveries he conceded only three runs in taking five wickets, giving Australia victory by 52 runs. His 6 for 15 underlined his place in the third Australian team to tour the West Indies. Walker's spell was in stark contrast to that by leg-spinner John Watkins earlier in the match when Watkins had six overs of long hops, full tosses and deliveries so wide batsmen could not reach them. Watkins had trouble landing on the pitch used for the match and his poor display was attributed to nervousness.

Both Walker and Watkins were included in the Australian team for the West Indies, Watkins in preference to the accomplished

Max Walker, an integral member of the Ian Chappell teams, resting on his bat. He was a tireless bowler of accurate swing. (VCA Archives)

Gleeson. Paul Sheahan declared himself unavailable for the tour, opting to devote himself instead to a schoolmaster's career. The Australian team was I.M. Chappell (Captain), K.R. Stackpole (Vice-captain), J. Benaud, G.S. Chappell, R. Edwards, J.R. Hammond, T.J. Jenner, D.K. Lillee, R.W. Marsh, R.A.L. Massie, K.J. O'Keeffe, I.R. Redpath, M.H.N. Walker, K.D. Walters and J.R. Watkins, with Bill Jacobs as manager.

The Australians had matured into a resourceful, quick-thinking outfit. They found the West Indians at the end of an era, with Sobers unable to continue his captaincy because of damaged knee cartilages. His successor, Rohan Kanhai, was probably the only West Indian certain of his place in a team that had to be almost completely rebuilt.

The First Test at Kingston, Jamaica, soon showed that Dennis Lillee was badly handicapped by a back injury. Chappell gave him a tough 26-over trial but he failed to generate any of the pace or fire he had shown in England. After he had conceded 132 runs without taking a wicket, Walker and Hammond took over as the main pace bowlers. Neither extracted enough life from an unresponsive pitch to force a result.

Selectors asked Sobers for a doctor's certificate to prove his fitness when he offered his services for the Second Test at Bridgetown, Barbados. Sobers was indignant at this request and refused, whereupon he was ruled out for the rest of the series. The issue dominated sports pages for the remainder of Australia's visit, with most West Indians agreeing with the politician who argued that Sobers on one leg was preferable to most players on two.

Leg-spinner Kerry O'Keeffe found Ian Chappell a supporter of slow bowlers, keen to give them a go when pace bowling failed. (Ken Kelly)

Lillee's back did not improve as he made the rounds of a variety of doctors. He was diagnosed variously as suffering from muscle trouble or hairline fractures to the vertebrae, and forbidden from playing any further cricket. He made only five appearances, one more than Watkins, whose nervousness refused to depart and restricted him to only four matches. Australia's woes multiplied when Massie completely lost his ability to swing the ball and in his struggle to get it back sent down a succession of long hops and full tosses.

Walker and Hammond had to do all of the early bowling, with Jenner, O'Keeffe and Ian Chappell providing spin, and Walters and Greg Chappell some makeshift medium-pace. Both Walker and Hammond sustained their accuracy for long periods on the hottest days, in exceptional displays of stamina.

Two long partnerships failed to provide a result in the Second

Test. At 2 for 14 on the first morning the Chappell brothers, Ian and Greg, put on 129 before Ian was tragically run out for 72. Greg continued to 126. Marsh, who had made four centuries in the Australian season – including an innings of 238 against Pakistan – clubbed his way to 78 to take Australia to 324. West Indies were 5 for 179 in reply when Kanhai (105) and David Murray (90) put on 165, Kanhai realising that on such a low pitch a draw was inevitable.

Ian Chappell sprained his ankle playing tennis two days before the Third Test at Port-of-Spain, from 23 to 28 March 1973, and should not have played. He fielded throughout in the slips and although he could not move down the pitch to half volleys was one of Australia's heroes in a memorable win. Walters set it up for Australia by scoring a century between lunch and tea on the first day. This lifted Australia to a total of 332, with Walters unrecognisable as the batsman who had been dropped from the Test side in England the previous year after averaging only 7.7 runs an innings in four Tests. The Australians' task was made easier when Lance Rowe tore ligaments in his ankle and took no further part in the match.

Leading by 52 on the first innings, Australian hopes were boosted by a fine 97 from Ian Chappell, who found handy partners in Redpath (44) and Walters (32). After Chappell was eighth out, the tail-enders added an invaluable 50 runs, including 33 for the last wicket by Walker and Hammond. Set to make 334, West Indies reached 4 for 268 by lunch on the last day when Ian Chappell gave his side a colourful, abusive pep talk. Shocked by this outburst, the Australians went out and took the last five wickets for only 21 runs to win by 44 runs.

The Australians needed all their fighting qualities to win the Fourth Test at Georgetown, Guyana, after Clive Lloyd played a superb innings of 178 that lifted the West Indies' first innings score to 366. Steady batting by the Chappell brothers, Ian for 109, Greg for 51, followed by another wonderful showing of smart footwork against quality spin by Walters (81), took Australia to within 21 runs of this total. The pitch had badly deteriorated when West Indies batted but they foolishly threw their wickets away and were out for 109, their worst score at home for 38 years. They offered little resistance as Stackpole and Redpath hit off the 135 needed to win by ten wickets and give Australia an outstanding 2–0 series win as the final Test was drawn.

Walker, on his first overseas tour, was the remarkable success in a team of Australian heroes, taking 41 first-class wickets at 20.48, 26 of them in the Tests. Greg Chappell made most runs, 1110 at 69.37, but Walters finished ahead in the first-class averages with 69.50. Ian Chappell topped the Australian Test batting averages with 77.42 compared with Walters' 77.0. Four Australians made a total of 12 tour centuries and the team had nine centuries scored against them.

For Australia to go through a 12-match tour of the West Indies unbeaten without any contribution from Lillee and Massie, who had played such a commanding part in the previous rubber against England, was one of the biggest achievements in Ian Chappell's reign of 30 Tests as Australian captain. He was repeatedly forced to take over the role of opening batsman as in only three of those 30 Tests did his openers put on 100 runs and in 29 innings managed less than 20 runs.

The Board of Control refused a request for a reinforcement for Lillee in the West Indies. Lillee returned home to spend months in plaster, and those familiar with stress fractures in the back said his career was finished.

Jeff Thomson bowling at Lord's in 1975 when his partnership with Dennis Lillee shocked English cricket fans. (Patrick Eagar)

Lillee did not play in the six Tests against New Zealand in the summer of 1973–74, three in Australia in 1973–74 and three in March 1974 in New Zealand. Tony Dell, Gary Gilmour, Alan Hurst and Geoff Dymock were all tried as partners for Max Walker in these matches. They brought to an end Australia's neglect of New Zealand, dating back to 1878 when the first white Australian team stopped off there on their way to England. Australia finished the six-Test sequence with three wins, two draws and one loss. New Zealand's success at Christchurch in March by a margin of five wickets was her first-ever against Australia and only her eighth win in 113 official Tests.

His reputation established, Ian Chappell lessened the strain of Test captaincy by handing over to his brother Greg in lesser matches in New Zealand. Greg had switched from South Australia to play for Queensland in 1973, and soon after taking over the Queensland captaincy from Jack McLean he recommended that Queensland acquire Jeff Thomson, the Sydney fast bowler who terrorised batsmen in the grade competition. Thomson had made the mistake of appearing in his Test debut against Pakistan with a broken bone in his foot but returned to the New South Wales team with his injury mended for the last match of the season and bowled at terrifying speed against Queensland in Sydney.

On this sole viewing the Queensland selectors Ken Mackay and Peter Burge accepted Greg Chappell's advice about Thomson and lured him to play in Brisbane. By the time Mike Denness's thirty-first English team toured Australia in 1974–75 Lillee's injured back had mended by following a long programme of callisthenics in Perth and he joined Thomson in opening the bowling for Australia. Maverick Thomson was under a life suspension from soccer for flattening a referee in a Sydney church match.

Almost every Englishman carried nasty bruises by the time the six-Test series ended with Australia 4–1 winners and the other Test drawn. The English team comprised: M.H. Denness (Captain), J.H. Edrich (Vice-captain), A.W. Greig, A.P.E. Knott, K.W.R. Fletcher, D. Lloyd, D.L. Amiss, F.J. Titmus, C.M. Old, R.G.D. Willis, B.W. Luckhurst, D.L. Underwood, P. Lever, M. Hendrick, R.W. Taylor and G.G. Arnold, with Alec Bedser as manager. Cowdrey was flown out as reinforcement when Amiss and Edrich both broke bones in their hands.

Lillee and Thomson took 13 wickets between them in the First Test, 11 wickets in the Second Test, 12 in the Third, 10 in the Fourth and 11 in the Fifth Test. Thomson tore ligaments in his shoulder playing tennis during the Fifth Test and had to withdraw from the Sixth. Lillee was injured after bowling only 6 overs and took just one wicket; England had her only win of the series.

Lillee in his delivery stride was a frightening sight for batsmen, accurate, argumentative and extremely fast. (Patrick Eagar)

This overwhelming series victory virtually assured Ian Chappell of the captaincy of the twenty-seventh Australia side to tour England in 1975. The four-Test rubber between two evenly matched teams was played immediately after the inaugural World Cup limited-over competition in which the West Indies defeated Australia in the final. After defeating Pakistan and England in preliminary rounds, Australia lost all chance in the final when five batsmen were run out.

The Test rubber was marred by the actions of vandals in the Third Test at Leeds when Australia was leading 1–0 and required 225 to win with seven wickets in hand. The other two Tests in the series were drawn. The Australian team was: I.M. Chappell (Captain), G.S. Chappell (Vice-captain), R. Edwards, G.J. Gilmour, A.G. Hurst, B.M. Laird, D.K. Lillee, R.B. McCosker, A.A. Mallett, R.W. Marsh, R.D. Robinson, J.R. Thomson, A. Turner,

M.H.N. Walker, K.D. Walters and J.D. Higgs. Robinson and Higgs were not in the World Cup side, which was limited to 14 players.

Lillee and Thomson took 12 wickets to help Australia to an innings and 85-run win in the First Test at Birmingham, the Second Test at Lord's was drawn after they took a further eight wickets and Lillee made 73 not out, his career highest score, and in the Third Test McCosker was on 95 not out and within sight of his initial Test 100 when play had to be abandoned. Vandals campaigning for the release of a prisoner badly damaged the pitch with knives and oil, sneaking into the Leeds ground during the night. Rain which fell from 4 p.m. on the afternoon play was abandoned might have made a result impossible anyway. McCosker got his elusive century in the drawn Fourth Test in which he shared a 277-run stand with Ian Chappell.

Ian gave brother Greg the Australian captaincy in six of the 15 matches in England, with Ian thrice playing under Greg's captaincy. Greg had also had 11 wins in 21 matches as Queensland's captain to that stage – although without a Sheffield Shield, Western Australia having won in 1972–73, Victoria the following year, and Western Australia again in 1974–75 – so when Australia's selectors named Greg Chappell Test captain at the age of 27, he brought plenty of experience to the job.

Greg became the first player to score two centuries in his first match as Test captain when he made 123 and 109 not out against Clive Lloyd's West Indian touring team at Brisbane in 1975–76. Australia won by eight wickets, but suffered a reverse in the Second Test at Perth when Roy Fredericks scored 169 off 145 balls and Lloyd made 149. Ian Chappell's 156 could not save his brother's team from defeat by an innings and 87 runs. Australia then won four Tests in succession in a golden four weeks to give Greg's Australians a 5–1 triumph in the series. Australia won because they were more disciplined under pressure than a team that played as if they were involved in limited-overs matches instead of Tests.

Unfortunately the West Indian leaders, Clive Lloyd and Vivian Richards, attributed their humiliating defeat to the domination of the Australian pace bowlers, who took 87 of the 98 wickets that fell in the series and liberally sprinkled their overs with bouncers. This shaped West Indian tactics for the next two decades.

CHAPTER TWENTY-NINE

THE PACKER YEARS

Kerry Francis Bullmore Packer caused the biggest upheaval in the history of Australian cricket when he bought the exclusive services of 66 of the world's best cricketers for two seasons in 1977–79, but he almost put his money into tennis instead of cricket. Packer worked on a deal for months with Lawn Tennis Association president Wayne Reid and secretary Garry Daly in which the LTAA agreed to build new courts for Packer at Sydney's White City and bring all the top-ranked tennis stars to Australia.

In February 1976 Packer asked the Board of Control for an appointment so that he could bid for exclusive rights to televise Test and Sheffield Shield cricket and exploit satellite communications. The Board kept him waiting for months during which they completed a deal with the Australian Broadcasting Commission for $207,000 for television rights to big cricket for three years. When Packer finally met Board officials in Melbourne in May 1976 he offered them $2.5 million for a five-year contract, but was told the Board had already signed with the ABC.

Frustrated by the Board's conservatism, Packer was about to sign the tennis deal when in through his office door came Perth journalist John Cornell, manager of comedian Paul Hogan. Cornell informed Packer that there was enormous discontent among Australian Test cricketers over the Board's match payments and the Board's refusal to increase them. Dennis Lillee calculated that he made $150 a Test, or $30 a day, after tax and deductions for expenses. Ian Chappell had gone on record in his book *Chappelli* that he received $470 from his Sheffield Shield appearances in 1975–76 and this coupled with his Test appearance payments for the matches against the West Indies earned him $4800. Chappell called it 'fish and chips money'.

Kerry Packer batting in a journalists' match at Harrogate, England, in 1977, when the revolt he inspired against cricket's establishment had just begun. (Patrick Eagar)

459

The players appointed former Test batsman Bob Cowper, then a Melbourne stockbroker, as their representative. The Board refused to accept Cowper's submissions on match fees, tour programmes or sponsorships, which he collected after talks with the five Sheffield Shield captains. Packer gave Cowper a long hearing, and after Cornell's Perth journalistic colleague Austin Robertson junior, joined the discussions, Packer decided to spend millions of dollars on big cricket, starting with the 1977–78 season.

Working under instructon from Ian Chappell and Cowper, Robertson signed the players wanted for the company that became known as World Series Cricket. Each player received an initial payment when he signed the WSC contract. Christopher Forsyth, publicity director of Packer's Nine network in Melbourne, became WSC publicity chief and Richie Benaud and his second wife Daphne were hired as consultants to advise Packer on strategy when the advent of WSC became public. From the outset, all of those involved were amazed by Packer's willingness to spend money. When they suggested Shield players who might join WSC for small fees, Packer said: 'Why not do the thing properly? Let's get the best to play Australia's best.'

While Packer was preparing his secret strategy, the Australian Cricket Board introduced a reshaped Provident Fund for the leading players and most state associations followed suit. But the funds received little publicity because the Board did not want to embarrass players in their relations with the taxation department. The funds rewarded players for long service at both the Test and Shield level, with the Board or state body putting set sums away for the players for each appearance. The money was invested for the players at bank interest and was payable to them two years after their retirement at the discretion of the Board or association.

Despite this thinly disguised attempt to make players behave themselves, sledging, swearing and outbursts against umpiring decisions increased. Umpires had to intervene several times after confrontations between players and displays of bat-throwing. Ian Chappell captained South Australia to win the 1975–76 Sheffield Shield with a brand of combative cricket *Wisden* said had probably never been seen before in Australian cricket.

Greg Chappell was again Test captain when Pakistan arrived in December 1976 for a five-match tour that included three Tests. Before they agreed to tour the Pakistani professionals threatened not to come unless their pay was increased. The first team chosen met with such a hostile reception it was immediately scrapped and another group of selectors was appointed to choose the team that comprised Mushtaq Mohammad (Captain), Asif Iqbal, Zaheer Abbas, Majid Khan, Javed Miandad, Imran Khan, Sadiq Mohammad, Sarfraz Nawaz, Salim Altaf, Wasim Bari, Iqbal Qasim, Mudassar Nazar, Sikander Bakht, Asif Masood, Wasim Raja, Taslim Arif, Intikhab Alam and Haroon Rashid.

After a draw in the First Test at Adelaide when Australia refused to try and score 56 runs in 15 overs to win, Australia won the Second Test at Melbourne by 348 runs. Greg Chappell, 121, Gary Cosier, 168, and Rick McCosker, 105, scored well for Australia, but Lillee's 6 for 82 and 4 for 53 swung the match.

The Chappell family, Trevor, Greg and Ian, with their parents Martin and Jeanne at a Melbourne match. (Ken Piesse)

Pakistan won their first Test in Australia when Imran Khan took 6 for 102 and 6 for 63 in the Third Test at Sydney. Imran's match figures of 12 for 165 remain the best by a Pakistani in Australia. Asif Iqbal made 120 in Pakistan's first innings of 360 and they only wanted 32 to win in the final innings to record an historic win.

Shaken by this setback, Greg Chappell introduced early morning callisthenics and jogging when Australia toured New Zealand for six matches, including two Tests, at the end of the summer. Doug Walters appeared at the exercise sessions under protest but managed an innings of 250 in the First Test at Christchurch. He put on 217 in a thrilling display for the seventh wicket with Gilmour. Walters's 250 was his best score in Tests and took 394 minutes. He hit two sixes and 30 fours and Gilmour 101. The match was drawn.

The Australian team for this month-long tour was G.S. Chappell (Captain), R.W. Marsh (Vice-captain), R.J. Bright, G.J. Cosier, I.C. Davis, G.J. Gilmour, K.J. Hughes, A.G. Hurst, D.K. Lillee, R.B. McCosker, K.J. O'Keeffe, A. Turner, M.H.N. Walker and K.D. Walters, with Roger Wootton as manager.

The team was close to full strength with Thomson the only major absentee following the retirement of Ian Chappell, Ian Redpath, Ashley Mallett, Ross Edwards and Terry Jenner. Thomson missed all but the first Test against Pakistan with a dislocated shoulder. The gifted Western Australian Kimberley John Hughes was on his first overseas trip as a result of several brilliant innings, including 137 not out for Western Australia v Pakistan.

During the Second Test at Auckland Austin Robertson took Doug Walters under a grandstand and secured his signature on a WSC contract that guaranteed Walters $25,000 a year for three years.

461

Greg Chappell also agreed to join World Series Cricket during the Auckland Test, for a signing-on fee of $11,666 plus a salary of $35,000 a year for five years and a $5000 consultancy and commentator's fee. This made Greg Chappell the highest paid player on the WSC books.

WSC were moving quickly, with Robertson handing out deposit cheques once the contracts were ratified by Packer's legal staff. Lillee signed for $35,000 a year for three years, Ian Redpath for one year at $16,500, and Mick Malone for $19,000 a year for three years with a five-year option.

Australia won the Second Test at Eden Park, Auckland, from 25 February to 1 March 1977 by ten wickets. Lillee took 5 for 51 and 6 for 72, for a match bag of 11 for 123, this feat taking him past 150 Test wickets. Australia led by 148 on the first innings after sending New Zealand back for 229. Richard Hadlee's 81 forced Australia to bat a second time but they scored the 28 runs needed without loss.

In February 1977 Packer offered the English County Cricket Board $118,00 for television rights to the five Tests to be played from June to August that year in England between England and Australia. His offer easily topped that from the ABC but the TCCB referred it to the Australian Board of Control before they accepted. The Board said a decision was the prerogative of the TCCB but added that it hoped the support the ABC had given to cricket over the years would not be forgotten. The Board said a joint arrangement should be possible under which the ABC would not be totally excluded from television coverage. Packer was outraged at this and like a card player whose tactics go awry immediately doubled his original offer to $236,000, which won him the sole rights from the TCCB.

Each of the Australian players received $2430 for the month they spent in New Zealand. The presence of Austin Robertson and John Cornell at the Australians' matches made reporters suspicious but Cornell satisfied them by saying he had gone to New Zealand to sign Lillee for Packer's television show 'A Current Affair'. The Australians lost their two limited-over matches but were undefeated in three-day matches and the tour made a profit of $35,000 for the New Zealand hosts.

The players returned home for the Centenary Test in Melbourne from 12 to 17 March to find all Australia talking about this

Hans Ebeling, the former Test player who conceived the idea of staging the Centenary Test in Melbourne. He was rewarded for months of preparation by a wonderful reunion of old players. (Age, Melbourne)

promotion. Staged to commemorate the hundredth anniversary of the first of all Tests in Australia, the match was the idea of Hans Ebeling, who had played one Test for Australia in 1934 and had served a term as chairman of the Melbourne Cricket Club. His idea of inviting every player surviving from the century of England v. Australia matches worked superbly. Airlines co-operated and 244 former Test players went to Melbourne. A further 26 informed the Melbourne Club they were too old for the trip, which became the biggest reunion in cricket history.

Former Test captain Jack Ryder was the oldest Australian player present at the age of 87, and he died a month later. Percy Fender, 84, was the oldest Englishman, blind, but able to follow events through descriptions passed on by his grandson. The hotel where the old players stayed provided a feast of cricket nostalgia. Most of the old cricketers had to be introduced to rivals they did not recognise after 50 years, but over lunch and dinner as past triumphs and failures were relived the pleasure they got from it was moving, emotional stuff.

The match eventually lived up to the occasion but by half-way through the second day England was in such awful trouble there was talk of staging limited-over matches to retain the spectators until the Queen arrived on the fifth day. England, captained by Tony Greig, had dismissed Australia for 138 on the first day and Willis broke Rick McCosker's jaw. Greg Chappell, 40, and Rod Marsh, 28, were the only Australians to justify selection.

Then the match turned on the second day: Lillee and Walker were at the peak of their considerable powers as they tumbled England out for 95. Lillee took 6 for 26, Walker 4 for 54, with four acrobatic catches by Marsh completing the rout and taking him past Wally Grout's record for an Australian wicket-keeper of 187 dismissals. The crowd were determined to enjoy themselves and kept up a chant of 'Lilleeee' throughout his 13.3-over stint.

Marsh's popularity with the crowd swelled as he shook hands with Bradman at the parade of the game's guests, and he repaid this hero-worship by reaching 95 not out by stumps on the third day. Overnight there was much discussion on whether Marsh would become the first Australian 'keeper to make a century in Tests. There was plenty to talk about as David Hookes, 22, a left-hander from West Torrens club in Adelaide, had hit Tony Greig for five successive fours with sweet cover drives that did not lift the ball a centimetre off the turf, Ian Davis had charmed with a knock

David Hookes, a team-mate of Ian Chappell in the South Australian side, several years after his Centenary Test triumph in which he hit Tony Greig for five successive fours. (Herald & Weekly Times)

Rick McCosker, right, going out to bat in the Centenary Test with a broken jaw. Packer contracts were exchanged in the dressing-room during this match. (News Limited)

of 68 and Doug Walters joined in the scoring spree with some delightful scoring strokes.

On the third evening, as Marsh neared his century, there was a buzz all round the vast ground as Rick McCosker went to the crease with his shattered jaw heavily strapped. Batting at no. 10, he had a thrilling partnership with Marsh of 54 runs, which allowed Greg Chappell to declare at 9 for 419 and leave England to score 463 in 11 hours to win, Marsh remaining unbeaten on 110. The English bowling had been completely subdued by the enterprising stroke play but the English fielders had remained tireless and nimble. Randall often drew applause with dazzling saves at deep mid-on.

At stumps on the fourth day Randall was 87 not out, England 2 for 191. The match looked evenly poised. On the final day Lillee knocked Randall down with a bouncer but Randall captivated spectators by bouncing straight up. He batted in a restless, jaunty style, mixing clever dabs with audacious pulls and heavy drives. Another Lillee bouncer had him weaving away and doffing his cap as he bowed to Lillee. Yet another bouncer drew a wonderful tennis shot from him which he smashed away to the square-leg fence.

This was a superb duel, with Lillee requiring all his remarkable stamina to keep Randall guessing. Marsh responded to the big occasion when umpire Tom Brooks gave Randall out, rushing forward to consult with Brooks and inform him the ball had bounced before he caught it. Randall resumed amid noisy cheers for Marsh and added 13 more runs before he was brilliantly caught close in on the legside by Cosier off an O'Keeffe spinner. Randall's 174 had taken 446 minutes and included 21 fours and won him the Man of the Match.

England remained defiant, with Greig (41) and Knott (42) pushing the score closer to the target before Greig miscued to another O'Keeffe spinner. Lillee then dismissed Old and O'Keeffe trapped Lever leg before, then Lillee had Knott lbw for the final wicket. Australia had won by 45 runs, miraculously the same margin as a hundred years earlier.

Austin Robertson moved cautiously among the Board members and old players who thronged the dressing-rooms to hand out their congratulations. He had $75,000 in signing-on cheques from WSC in his briefcase, each in an individually addressed envelope, and in full view of Board executives he passed them over to the players. Guests from the Marylebone Cricket Club at Lord's saw him complete his duties, saying to each player 'Here are your theatre tickets.' Next day Ross Edwards signed with WSC for a $8333 deposit on a two-year contract for $25,000 to complete the recruitment of the 28 Australian players Ian Chappell had selected.

Robertson then turned his attention to the 18 West Indians and 22 players from the rest of the world the WSC brains trust wanted. One of these was Tony Greig, who went to Sydney the day after the Centenary Test ended to keep an appointment with Packer to arrange for him to join Channel Nine as a cricket commentator. Greig has since been wrongly accused of suggesting the idea of WSC cricket to Packer and becoming its recruitment officer, but he was a comparative latecomer and the notion that he abused his position as England's captain is wrong.

Greig, in fact, agonised over what he should do once he had heard Packer's exciting proposals. Austin Robertson did most of the signing Greig was alleged to have done, though Greig was so thrilled with Packer's concepts he advised anybody hesitating about joining not to delay. Derek Underwood and Alan Knott were among those Greig inspired with the whole idea of WSC.

Robertson had some luck when Greig joined him at the Trinidad Hilton to chase signatures. The West Indies were in the midst of a Test series against Pakistan and much to everybody's surprise Mushtaq Mohammad, from a family steeped in cricket tradition, signed for $25,000 a year for three years and brought Imran Khan with him at the same terms. One by one the others on Robertson's list joined, Asif Iqbal at $25,000 a year, Clive Lloyd at $30,000 a year, Viv Richards at $25,000 a year, Andy Roberts at $25,000 a year and Michael Holding at $25,000 a year, all for a three-year period.

Robertson and Greig then turned their efforts to signing South Africans Clive Rice, Barry Richards, Garth Le Roux, Eddie Barlow and Mike Proctor, all of them isolated by a lack of big cricket since the D'Oliveira affair, and impressed by the WSC concept. The signings continued until the twenty-eighth Australian touring team went to England for a tour involving five Tests and 22 first-class matches.

Len Pascoe, fiery New South Wales and Australian pace bowler who became one of the 68 players to sign up with Packer's World Series Cricket. (Ken Kelly)

The Australian Board of Control's euphoria over the promotion of the Centenary Test lasted until the third match of the 1977 tour when Australia played Greig's county, Sussex, at Hove. When rain caused abandonment of the match, Greig invited the tourists and the media to a party at his home. There, in a convivial atmosphere, reporters aware that big moves were afoot had their suspicions confirmed, and within a few hours the Packer signings and his plans for WSC were flashed around the world. Because of the venue of the leak Greig was considered a ringleader in the players' revolt; he was not until then, but he quickly became one.

Austin Robertson had completed the signing of 66 players, 28 of them Australians, 18 West Indians, and 20 from the rest of the world, only a few days before the Australian team left for England. All the Board of Control team signed tour contracts before they left home and 13 of the Board's team also had Packer contracts in their luggage.

Cricket was never the same again after the formation of World Series Cricket was disclosed. Lifelong friendships were broken, the players' lack of loyalty was condemned, and after they overcame their original astonishment Board officials began to examine possible reprisals. For weeks the players were unable to put any effort into their practice sessions, and the four players with Board contracts who had not signed for Packer – Cosier, Dymock, Hughes and Sergeant – joked among themselves over who might be the next Australian captain.

The Australian team was without Lillee, who was unavailable because of the recurrence of his back problems. McCosker's jaw was checked before he was allowed to tour, and specialists also examined

The Pakistani team on a training run during their 1978–79 Australian tour, with captain Mushtaq Mohammad fourth from the front. (Ern McQuillan)

the shoulder injury Thomson had sustained in a collision with Alan Turner in the Adelaide Test against Pakistan. The team was: G.S. Chappell (Captain), R.W. Marsh (Vice-captain), R.J. Bright, G.J. Cosier, I.C. Davis, K.J. O'Keeffe, L.S. Pascoe, R.D. Robinson, G. Dymock, D.W. Hookes, K.J. Hughes, R.B. McCosker, M.F. Malone, C.S. Sergeant, J.R. Thomson, M.H.N. Walker and K.D. Walters, with former Test 'keeper Len Maddocks as manager.

Administrators and critics in England, India, Pakistan and the West Indies called the WSC revolt an Australian problem, but the reality was that with players from so many nations involved it was a world problem. One side-effect was that the West Indies only agreed to free their players for WSC matches on condition white cricketers resident in South Africa were not used. Packer, at a conference with the Prime Minister of Jamaica, Michael Manley, recognised that West Indians regarded the fight against apartheid as 'a sacred responsibility' and he later cancelled Graeme Pollock's WSC contract. Pollock's compensation was never revealed.

In England, the first Test series televised to Australia was played out by players more interested in their futures with Packer than in the outcome of the Tests. Manager Len Maddocks carpeted Greg Chappell, accusing him of disloyalty to the Board, and the tour proceeded against a background of nasty reprisals against WSC signatories. Chappell tried to rally his players at special team meetings but as if aware of the heresy they had committed in the name of financial security the Australians allowed the series to be dominated by Geoffrey Boycott. No more deadening influence could be bestowed on any Test series. England won 3–0 and even Thomson's feat in taking his hundredth Test wicket in the final match could not uplift a rubber that had endured two Boycott centuries, 191 at Headingley and 107 at Trent Bridge.

One of Ian Chappell's great assets in his years as Australia's captain was wicket-keeper Rod Marsh, in his prime a wonderful hitter. Here he clubs a boundary on his way to 42 in 1977 in the Prudential Cup match v. England at Old Trafford. (Ken Kelly)

Back in Australia the establishment tried to prevent the successful launching of WSC cricket by restricting Packer's choice of venues. He was initially denied use of major grounds such as the MCG and SCG when the associations claimed priority over the use of these grounds. This was to cause Packer heavy losses in the first season of WSC – estimated at $4 million – but he proved too powerful a manipulator behind the scenes for the ground bans to last.

At the end of what ranks as the unhappiest of all tours involving Australians, Packer launched an action in the London High Court seeking an injunction and damages from the International Cricket Conference for banning its players from all matches under his

Packer and the sacked England captain Tony Greig leaving the London High Court where they won a resounding victory that cost cricket's hierarchy an estimated $500,000. (Patrick Eagar)

control. The hearing lasted 31 days and the judgment of 221 pages took five and a half hours to read. It ruled that any attempt to prevent players appearing for Packer by changing ICC rules was an unreasonable restraint of trade. Costs amounting to £200,000 sterling were awarded against the ICC and the Test and County Cricket Board, whose solace was that they had received £150,000 from Packer for the television rights to the dreary 1977 Tests.

Greg Chappell announced his retirement as Australian captain at the end of a tour on which his team won only five of their 22 first-class matches, losing four, and leaving 13 drawn. They were beaten by Greg Chappell's former county, Somerset, for the first time and Minor Counties scored at a rate of 80 runs an hour to beat them at Sunderland by six wickets.

The Board of Control lost little time in naming Bob Simpson as Chappell's successor, seeking to install a leader with the drive and purpose so lacking in the 1977 side in England. Simpson had been out of Test cricket for ten years and was 41, but knew that he would not be facing bowlers of express pace when India toured Australia in 1977–78. Simpson had endeared himself to officials the previous year by negotiating a sponsorship deal with the brewer Tooheys, who agreed to put up $15,000 in incentive payments for the New South Wales team. He took over a national team keen to win as much as possible of the $245,000 a cigarette company offered players over a 15-month period but both deals had come too late to forestall Packer.

The WSC players found their lives had changed. Ian Chappell, who had come out of retirement to captain the Australian rebels, now insisted they wore slacks and blazers off the field instead of track suits. Socially, they were outcasts. Ray Bright was barred from playing club cricket and had to appear for Footscray Technical College. Richie Robinson had to play on malthoid as coach of North Alphington to get some cricket. North Melbourne sacked Ian Chappell as their captain-coach and Melbourne Cricket Club refused Max Walker a place in their team. Wayne Prior lost the driver's job the SACA had found for him and Bruce Laird, Rodney Marsh, Dennis Lillee, Ross Edwards, Mick Malone, Robbie Langer and Graham McKenzie were all barred from WACA club cricket.

Richie Benaud became a prime target for traditionalists and attacks on his alleged disloyalty intensified when Christopher Forsyth disclosed in his book *The Great Cricket Hijack* that Packer paid Benaud $30,000. It was Benaud who roused the rebels to show pride and determination in their cricket in a speech he made to them at a players' meeting just before WSC matches began.

'I want you to think about what it means to be called "a disapproved person", said Benaud. 'That's how the cricket establishment see us. If you are a disapproved person on a racecourse, you are a person who is warned off. What right have they – because we accept a retainer from a client – to call us disapproved people?'

The public soon realised that WSC matches – managed in the first year by Andrew Caro – were not the exhibition matches VCA president Ray Steele had in mind when he said he hoped nobody would watch WSC cricket. WSC proved an innovative and resolute rival to Test cricket. Coloured clothing for players and umpires upset traditionalists but spectators loved it. New rules for limited-over cricket that forced fieldsmen inside circles for the first 15 overs proved popular, as did the use of microphones in the pitch. But the intensity of the competition was their most impressive feature, for the teams played to a very high standard and were never afraid of battering each other with bouncers. The helmets that had crept into the game with the increase in bouncers were absolutely essential in WSC matches. Often their dressing-rooms were like casualty wards.

With 66 players from which to choose, only the best remained for the major WSC promotions. The rest were relegated to the suburbs to run schoolboy coaching classes devised by Benaud as an adjunct to WSC. Doug Walters found himself out in the sticks for most of the first year. Ian Redpath ruptured his achilles tendon jumping in the air in elation after bowling Clive Lloyd in a warm-up match. Packer paid him in full.

Given the high standard of the cricket, Packer and his WSC staff were very disappointed in the attendances at his first summer's matches. Packer's losses were offset by the high ratings WSC matches won on television, and on Chris Forsyth's estimate of $4364 an hour cricket was far cheaper television than first-run American dramas, which got $5000 an hour, or the $28,000 an hour Packer paid for an Australian-produced drama like 'The Sullivans'. The high public appeal in nine hours of televised cricket a day for 51 days of the year was not lost on advertising agencies.

Absence of the WSC stars weakened the Australian team to something approaching the level of the touring Indian team and a tense, even struggle drew larger crowds than on any previous Indian tour. Simpson scored a marvellous 89 in the Australian second innings to help Australia to a 16-run win in the First Test at the Gabba. Australia fielded a patched-up side because of the defections to WSC but were helped by the emergence of talented youngsters in almost every state. Six players made their debut in the First Test and by the end of the series 12 players had been introduced to Test cricket. With the rubber level at two Tests all, India made a thrilling attempt to score 493 to win the Fifth Test but failed by only 47 runs.

Simpson's 89 in the First Test, 176 in the Second Test and 100 in the Fifth represented a remarkable comeback and assured him of the captaincy of the Australian team to visit the West Indies early in 1978. He headed the Test averages with 539 runs at 53.90, the best figures on either side, although Gavaskar made three Test centuries. The Australian public had great pleasure in watching an Indian Test attack based entirely on spin, with Bishen Bedi taking 31 wickets at 23.87 with his left-arm slows and Bhagwat Chandrasekhar taking 28 Test wickets at 25.14 with right-arm leg-breaks.

Nineteen new Sheffield Shield players had to be found in a season conducted in an emotional atmosphere, in which supporters of both WSC and traditional cricket sniped at each other. Establishment cricket was the loser for there was a steep increase in the abuse of umpires, excessive appeals, deliberate slow play and post-match criticism of opponents by state captains. All Shield players received higher match fees and Test appearance fees were also increased, which the Board attributed to higher income from sponsors.

The Board's claim of higher income was hard to rationalise in a year which saw the introduction of Tasmania to the Shield competition and a surfeit of Shield cricket. Shield crowds were well down on previous years. In Perth attendances fell by 34 per cent although Western Australia retained the Shield. Bearded Queenslander David Ogilvie set a record by scoring six Shield centuries, a feat even Bradman, McCabe, Ponsford and Kippax did not match.

Tasmania joined the Shield competition 126 years after staging Australia's initial first-class match, with a restricted programme of five matches. The Lancashire all-rounder Jack Simmons captained Tasmania, whose team included Yorkshireman John Hampshire and Denis Baker, a fast bowler who had played regularly for Western Australia. Wicket-keeper Roger Woolley became the first Tasmanian to score a Shield century for Tasmania by scoring 103 in Launceston v. Queensland.

The first international match staged in Australia since 1905

Western Australian Bruce Laird who played some brave, exciting innings for World Series Australian teams, swings a ball to the boundary, watched by Steve Rixon and Rick McCosker. (News Limited)

outside the control of the Australian Cricket Board was played at VFL Park in the Melbourne suburb of Waverley on 16 November 1977, when a side led by Ian Chappell defeated R.D. Robinson's XI by two runs in a limited-over game. From then on WSC featured three teams, an Australian XI captained by Ian Chappell, a World XI led by Tony Greig, and a West Indian XI captained by Clive Lloyd. After six preliminary matches selectors for each team settled on their sides for six 'Super Tests' in the capital cities, to be played on pitches that were a wonder of modern groundsmanship. The pitches began in hot-houses and when sufficient growth had been obtained were moved around from ground to ground in giant trays that were slipped into place when there was no time to prepare conventional wickets. Packer hired the former Woolloongabba curator John Maley especially to supervise this and despite sceptics the pitches were a wonderful success.

Australia's women cricketers shocked the experts by winning the four-nation World Cup in India early in 1978. Sharon Tredrea, whom English Test umpire Dickie Bird rated as fast as most men, was the star bowler of the competition and also scored more runs than any other Australian. She achieved cut and swing in a fashion unusual in women's cricket, collected her runs quickly and was by far the biggest hitter in teams from England, New Zealand, India and Australia.

Sharon Tredrea, Australia's outstanding woman cricketer in the 1980s, an all-rounder who combined lively right-arm fast bowling with forceful batting. She led Australia's successful World Cup defence in 1982 when her team won 12 of its 13 matches. (Jack Pollard Collection)

Although the loss of so many key players to WSC seriously weakened Australia's official team, the Board of Control proceeded with the West Indian tour of 1978. None of the WSC players were considered when Phil Ridings, Sam Loxton and Neil Harvey picked the following side: R.B. Simpson (Captain), J.R. Thomson (Vice-captain), I.W. Callen, W.B. Clark, G.J. Cosier, W.M. Darling, J.D. Higgs, K.J. Hughes, T. Laughlin, S.J. Rixon, C.S. Sergeant, P.M. Toohey, G.M. Wood, G.N. Yallop, B. Yardley and A.D. Ogilvie.

The West Indies had no thought about excluding their WSC rebels and they gave the West Indies victory inside three days in both the First Test at Port-of-Spain, Trinidad, and the Second Test at Bridgetown, Barbados. Roberts took 12 wickets in these two matches, Garner 13. A dispute between the WSC players and the West Indian Board ended with the WSC players withdrawing from the remaining three Tests and that evened up the contest. The last three Tests were tense and eventful with Australia producing a splendid batting effort to make 7 for 362 in the last innings to win

In the second year of the Packer revolt Bob Simpson led an establishment team on tour in the West Indies, where they encountered riots and demonstrations. Here Jamaican police fire tear gas to stop bottle-throwing while players watch. (Ron McKenzie)

the Third Test, and the West Indies giving an equally praiseworthy display to win the Fourth and retain the Frank Worrell trophy. The series ended with police wielding truncheons, vainly trying to clear the Queen's Park ground of demonstrators. The West Indian Board offered to extend the match to make up for the time lost but one umpire, and the stand-by, refused to co-operate. Without the WSC players for the last three Tests against a second-rate Australian side the West Indian Board lost $100,000 on the tour.

On his return from this unsuccessful West Indian tour, Simpson asked the Australian Board for a guarantee that he would be picked to play against England in the 1978–79 summer. The Board refused and Simpson retired after adding ten Tests to his record in his comeback. Brearley's thirty-third English touring team beat Australia 5–1 but had only one player, Ian Botham, who matched the excitement created by a string of players in Packer's WSC troup.

The Australian captain Graham Yallop later published a book on the series called *Lambs to the Slaughter*, an apt description of a half-strength Australian team. Rodney Hogg won the headlines by taking 41 wickets in his initial Test series, bowling very fast and straight, and sustaining his hostility for long periods surprising in a player who admitted he was asthmatic. Hogg, a big, curly haired blond, walked off the field when he chose and continually altered his field without consulting Yallop. Hogg suggested they survey the back of Adelaide Oval when Yallop challenged him for going off – 'and I don't think he had a tennis match in mind,' wrote Yallop.

The English team, splendidly led by the University lecturer credited with introducing the helmet to modern cricket, was: J.M. Brearley (Captain), R.G.D. Willis, R.W. Tolchard, D.W. Randall, D.I. Gower, G. Boycott, G. Miller, I.T. Botham, G.A. Gooch, R.W. Taylor, P.H. Edmonds, C.M. Old, C.T. Radley, J.E. Emburey, J.K. Lever and M. Hendrick. They began their tour in Adelaide where they found the WSC theme song 'C'mon Aussies, C'mon' a great popular hit.

Packer had pulled off a masterstroke during the winter when he won permission to stage WSC matches at the Gabba and the SCG. The New South Wales government sacked the trust that ran the SCG, and appointed a new trust that allowed Packer to build the lights needed for night cricket. On 28 November 1978, when the lights went on for the first time, more than 50,000 people attended the SCG. The surge of people eager to get in was so great Packer told the gatemen not to worry about collecting entrance money but to throw the gates open. The cricket matched the air of a big occasion that flooded the ground. This was the night Packer's WSC was accepted and his dominance of the future of Australian cricket made secure.

Wisden said that WSC matches attracted 730,000 through the gates in the 1978–79 season compared with the 580,000 who watched traditional cricket. The Australian Cricket Board lost $445,000 that summer, while Packer's JP Sports and Television Corporation Ltd reported a 26 per cent increase in profits. When the Australian season ended he sent his players off to the Caribbean for five 'Super Tests' which provided more fiercely contested cricket and rescued the West Indian Board's finances. Back in Australia, while the world's best players were slugging it out, Pakistan played out an acrimonious two-Test series which ended with each side on one win apiece, and Victoria took the Sheffield Shield.

Two years of WSC had brought horrendous losses to traditional cricket and by April 1979 both sides wanted a settlement. There was great relief around the entire cricket world when Packer agreed to disband WSC from 31 January 1980 in return for the exclusive television rights he had always sought. The Australian Cricket Board retained the right to select teams and deal with sponsors, but Packer's outfit, PBL Sports, became responsible for the promotion

Rodney Hogg, who got his big chance to play international cricket when Lillee and Pascoe signed for WSC, took 41 wickets in the 1978–79 series v. England. (Herald & Weekly Times)

of all first-class cricket. Packer also won the right to play night cricket with players wearing coloured clothing, but one important point he did not win was for the players' performances in WSC matches to be included in their career statistics. Greg Chappell is thus deprived of 1578 runs at 58.44 and five centuries, Lillee 79 wickets at 23.91 and Marsh 54 dismissals, for 16 matches played in first-class conditions.

The state cricket associations lost more than $1 million in the Packer dispute. The NSWCA sold Cricket House, its home since 1931, at an unfavourable price. Twenty Shield matches in 1978–79 drew only 137,000 fans. Profit from England's Ashes tour dipped to $126,000, compared to $501,000 from the previous tour. The amateur game was bleeding to death when Ray Steele and Bob Parish negotiated the peace.

Since the settlement the fees Packer has paid the Australian Cricket Board has allowed the Board to distribute more than $30 million to the states, who in turn make annual payments to clubs that would have been beyond their wildest dreams a few years before. Packer's televised cricket opened the floodgates to sponsors and every state's Shield team now enjoys hefty financial support. All the capital city grounds have had millions spent on improvements. Banks, oil companies, brewers, wool boards, insurance companies and clothing makers have joined the tobacco company that spent $8 million a year on cricket.

Australia's last venture before the Packer agreement took effect was an 11-match tour of India in September and October 1979. The ACB erred in scheduling a tour at a time when the heat was still oppressive and pitches certain to be affected by rain. Captain Kim Hughes and senior players Allan Border and Graeme Yallop did a superb job, to allow Australia to escape with three losses, but India won the Tests 2–0.

The West Indies and England both visited Australia in 1979–80, each playing three Tests against the hosts as well as a series of one-day internationals. Australia – strengthened by the return of the Packer rebels and with Greg Chappell back as captain – won 3–0 against England but lost to West Indies 2–0. Immediately after, Australia toured Pakistan for a three-Test rubber. Pakistan won the First Test at Karachi by 7 wickets, and the other Tests were drawn. Highlights were Greg Chappell's 235 and Graeme Yallop's 172 in the Second Test at Faisalabad, and Allan Border's magnificent double innings of 150 not out and 153 in the Third Test at Lahore.

CHAPTER THIRTY

BORDER THREATENS TO QUIT

Australians played their international cricket at a hectic pace in the 1980s. Between the Centenary Test against England at Lord's in September 1980, and the Fifth Test against India at the WACA in February 1992, Australians figured in 104 Tests spread over 30 series. Don Bradman played in 38 Tests in the 12 years between his Test debut in 1928 and the 1939–40 season. Allan Border, in a similar period to the end of the 1991–92 summer, had 96 Tests. Both missed one Test through ill-health or injury and Bradman missed the entire tour of South Africa in 1935–36 through illness, but the difference is striking.

The frenetic upsurge in Australian players' involvement in big cricket was a direct result of Kerry Packer's programmers scheduling 600 hours of televised cricket each Australian summer. To sustain high ratings for such a large cricket content, the Australian Cricket Board had to bring two overseas countries to tour every season. And for every visiting team Australia had to reciprocate.

The programme made the players' claims for higher pay easy to attain and once the money from the Packer telecasts started to roll in the Board introduced a scheme under which the 30 leading players received annual salaries of at least $30,000. This created a pool of wealthy young cricketers who received regular pay packets from the Board, fees for sponsoring bats, pads and other equipment, limited over ($1250) and Test ($3750) appearance fees, Shield ($1300) appearance fees, bonuses for outstanding displays from sponsors, and payments from the Board and state associations into their Provident Fund accounts. A few also were paid to speak at sportsmen's dinners, to open fetes and launch products ranging from books to sportswear.

Ian Chappell was reprimanded for this prank when he moved the stumps to a spot where he believed Doug Walters's wide deliveries had more chance of hitting them. (News Limited)

The affluence the Packer years brought to Australian cricket also confirmed the Australian cricket captain as the most prestigious figure in Australian sport. The Board paid the captain a special allowance per Test for handling the media, a demanding job which often began with phone calls at six a.m. and included running daily end-of-play interviews in the Australian dressing-room.

The Provident Funds run by both the ACB and the state associations were an interesting replacement for the old idea of giving long-serving players benefit matches. Dates for these matches were always hard to fit into the annual schedule of first-class matches and public support often disappointed both administrators and recipients. The Board staged about 30 benefit matches between the first in 1905–06 for Joe Kelly and the last in 1956–57 for Bill O'Reilly and Stan McCabe, receipts ranging from the £9432 paid to Bradman in 1948–49 to the £331 paid C.T.B. Turner in 1909–10.

In the benefit for Vic Richardson and Clarrie Grimmett in 1937–38, the crowd was just beginning to arrive in large numbers when Grimmett scattered Bradman's stumps with a huge leg-break just before lunch. 'There y'are, I told Don I could still bowl the leg-break and he didn't believe me,' said Grimmett as Bradman departed. 'Maybe, Grum, but you've cost us a couple of thousand quid each with that leg-break,' said Richardson. O'Reilly sent back Badcock, Morrisby and Ray Robinson in seven runs during the Bardsley–Jack Gregory testimonial in Sydney in 1936. Vic Richardson took O'Reilly off as Bradman came in and O'Reilly complained he did not get a bowl at Bradman until he was 80. Bradman went on to 212.

All the Australian Provident Funds stipulate that amounts due to players be paid two years after they retire, at the discretion of the Board of Control or the state associations. The scheme is under regular revision but for the 1991–92 season the following scale of payments applied: on a qualifying mark of 1 to 20 Tests, $300 per match; 21 to 30 Tests, $500; 31 to 40 Tests, $700; 41 to 50 Tests, $800; 51 to 60 Tests, $900; 61 to 70 Tests, $1000; 71 to 80 Tests, $1100; 81 Tests and over, $1200. Thus Allan Border, who had played in 125 Tests at the start of the 1991–92 season, has built up an entitlement of more than $150,000. He would also have a large sum due to him from the QCA Provident Fund for his state team matches. The Board has already paid out large sums to Rodney Marsh (97 Tests), Greg Chappell (88 Tests), Dennis Lillee (70 Tests) and Bob Simpson (61 Tests). The unlucky ones are the players who played a lot of Tests before the Board's scheme began in 1974.

The top players earn every cent on offer. They have only a short rest between tours each year, have to attend pre-season training sessions for their states and continue to perform consistently enough to remain on the Board's payroll and retain their Test places. The competition for places is tough and persistent failure can create intense pressure.

Kim Hughes was probably the most notable Australian casualty to pressure. He demonstrated in the 1980 Centenary Test against England at Lord's that there were few more spectacular hitters in cricket, peppering the stands with big hits before rain washed out play. Once again all surviving English and Australian Test players were flown in from around the world, but the gods appeared displeased at the switch of the match from The Oval where the first Test was played in England in 1880 and deluged Lord's on the second and third days, forcing a draw. Graeme Wood made 112, Kim Hughes 117, in Australia's first innings of 5 for 385 declared, and Pascoe (5 for 59) and Lillee (4 for 43) gave Australia a 180-run lead.

Apart from its packed Test schedule of the last decade, Australia appeared in a heavy programme of limited-over cricket, including the World Cup in England in 1983, won by India, the 1987 World Cup in India which Australia won, and a tournament in Melbourne in 1984–85 involving seven nations to celebrate the one hundred and fiftieth anniversary of the founding of the state of Victoria. There were several Australian tours to Sharjah for limited-over tournaments and the Young Australian team also toured Zimbabwe. All states have played in limited-over competitions since the 1969–70 season and the national teams that have come to Australia each summer for Tests have also been required to play one-day competitions in coloured clothing under lights.

Night cricket became an unfailing public attraction of enormous proportions, attracting an audience new to cricket who cheered raucously, joshed the players and brought with them painted banners. Many of them were family groups, with parents bringing their kids. English critics, seeking to belittle Packer's success, said the night cricket audiences behaved like Beatles' concertgoers. They were certainly different to normal cricket galleries, urging the players on to exciting finishes which invariably came with only a few balls to spare. The lights had the effect of bringing the players closer to spectators and even from 100 metres away sweat pouring down batsmen's faces was easy to see. Most matches provided a clear-cut result, which fans appreciated.

One of the most controversial limited-over matches came in the 1980–81 Australian season when Trevor Chappell bowled the last ball underarm, on the instructions of his brother Greg, to deprive New Zealand of any chance of winning a 50-over match against Australia in Melbourne. New Zealand needed six to win from the last ball, a seemingly impossible task, but Trevor Chappell made sure last man Brian McKechnie, a rugby All-Black, had no chance to lift the ball into the crowd by rolling it along the ground. The stunned New Zealander blocked it and threw his bat and gloves down in disgust.

In the uproar that followed New Zealand Prime Minister Muldoon called the underarm ball an act of cowardice. Richie Benaud said on television, 'It was the most gutless thing I have ever seen on a cricket field.' One state wanted the Australian victory annulled and the match replayed, but underarm bowling was allowed in the rules to that time and the Australians went on to win the $35,000 first prize by taking the best-of-five finals series.

Kim Hughes, one of the leading players who remained loyal to the Australian Cricket Board during the Packer signings. (News Limited)

Only a few months later in England Trevor Chappell made history by becoming the third member of his family to play Test cricket for Australia. Watched by his parents, Martin and Jeanne Chappell, Trevor made his Test debut against England at Nottingham at the age of 28. Ian was 21 when he played his first Test, Greg 22. Ten sets of brothers had played in Tests in Australia before Trevor took the record for the Chappells by becoming the third brother to achieve that feat.

The twenty-ninth Australian team to England in 1981 was captained by Kim Hughes. When Greg Chappell declared himself unavailable for the tour most experts believed the furore created by the underarm ball influenced his decision. The team was K.J. Hughes (Captain), R.W. Marsh, T.M. Alderman, M.F. Kent, G.R. Beard, G.F. Lawson, A.R. Border, R.J. Bright, J. Dyson, T.M. Chappell, R.M. Hogg, D.K. Lillee, S.J. Rixon, D.M. Wellham, G.M. Wood, G.N. Yallop and for the first time included a coach, Peter Philpott.

Despite the absence of Greg Chappell and Doug Walters, who was overlooked following four disappointing English tours, Australia outplayed England for most of an extraordinary series and

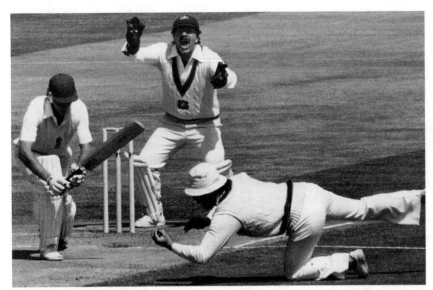

One-day cricket popularised by Packer's troupe dramatically improved fielding, as Allan Border shows in snapping up this catch to dismiss David Gower off Ray Bright at Birmingham in 1981. (Ken Kelly)

could easily have led 3–0, but in the end Australia collapsed in the second innings of the Third Test at Headingley, after a devastating display of hitting by Ian Botham rescued England. At 7 for 135, England was still 92 behind in their second innings and bookmakers had England at 500–1 to win. Lillee and Marsh invested £4 each at those odds. Then Botham hit an astonishing 149 not out. Despite this epic display which saw Botham add 106 in the session between tea and stumps, Australia still only had to make 130 to win on the last day. At 1 for 56 Marsh and Lillee appeared to have lost their money but Australia's last nine wickets fell for 55 runs, with Bob Willis taking 8 for 43. This was only the second time in history that a team won a Test after following on, with England emerging victor by 18 runs.

Australia never recovered the ascendancy in a series where Rodney Marsh became the most accomplished wicket-keeper in history by passing Alan Knott's record of 263 dismissals for England. At Birmingham in the Fourth Test England performed the same kind of long-odds recovery, winning by 29 runs, and in the Fifth Test at Old Trafford England won by 103 runs to take the Ashes, Botham striking again with 118 in 123 minutes that included 13 fours and six sixes.

Michael Whitney, a 22-year-old surfer with an Afro hairdo, made an unexpected Test debut in the Fifth Test when he was called up to help Australia just as he was preparing to take the field for Gloucestershire against Hampshire at Cheltenham. Whitney had been called into the Gloucestershire side from the Fleetwood league team. The Australian team management were forced to use him when Lawson and Hogg were unfit. He took 2 for 50 and 2 for 74 with his left-arm fast deliveries and held his place in the drawn Sixth Test at The Oval.

Back in Australia, the New South Wales Cricket Association, in a move unprecedented in its 123-year history, had given idolised all-rounder Doug Walters a benefit season in 1980–81. Now, after watching the Australian team he had graced in 74 Tests go down in defeat, Walters announced his retirement. He had scored 16,180 runs in first-class cricket at 43.84 and taken 190 wickets at 35.69. His laconic acceptance of success or failure won him an enormous following and he remains one of the most naturally talented cricketers Australia has seen. He often went into bat after dropping his cards in the middle of a game of cribbage, and team-mates told of him warming-up by throwing a dart into the dressing-room dartboard. When the craze for banners began in Australia, Walters was the first player fans granted his own stand. He made four of his 15 Test centuries against England, all of them at home.

Kim Hughes's batting failures in England in 1981 allowed Greg Chappell to regain the Australian captaincy for the 1981–82 series in Australia v. Pakistan. The series began with a sensational clash between Dennis Lillee and Javed Miandad. Following comments from Miandad, Lillee deliberately impeded and then kicked Miandad, the Pakistan captain, as Miandad completed a run. Umpire Crafter stepped between them as Miandad swung round and was about to club Lillee with his bat.

Lillee's team-mates fined him $200 but when the umpires complained that this was too lenient, ACB adjudicator Bob Merriman suspended him from two one-day matches. By taking five wickets in an innings for the twentieth time, Lillee helped Australia to a 286-run win. Miandad made no apology for his part in an incident which was the culmination of years of shameful behaviour on Australian fields. Lillee improved his cricket record even further by taking his three hundredth Test wicket in the Second Test against Pakistan in Brisbane. His match bag of 9 for 132 helped Australia to a 10-wicket win and clinched the three-Test rubber. Greg Chappell made 201 in this match, his fourth double-century in Tests. Only Bradman, Hammond and Javed Miandad have made more.

Against all the odds, Pakistan bounced back to win the Third

Test at Melbourne by an innings and 82 runs. Both captains made formal complaints about the pitch but Pakistan made 500 runs on it in their first innings, and then forced Australia to follow on. Australia's second innings of 125 was her lowest ever at home against Pakistan. Border was run out in both innings.

A fortnight later on the same MCG Australia ended a West Indian sequence of 15 Tests without defeat. Lillee became the world record holder by inducing an edge from Larry Gomez which Greg Chappell snapped up in the slips, giving the bowler his three hundred and tenth Test victim. The new record was made on the same ground where off-spinner Lance Gibbs had set the previous mark almost six years earlier. Lillee's 7 for 83 and 3 for 44 gave Australia victory by 58 runs after Kim Hughes returned to form with an even 100 not out.

This was Dennis Lillee at the peak of his powers, a great bowler with a flair for theatre, galloping in to bowl with his lucky charm swinging across his hairy chest, aware of where the cameras were positioned. He bowled an impeccable length, made the ball kick and rear, and his line on or near the off stump was as steady as his glares at batsmen's mistakes. He had a wide range of stances for appeals but the one I liked was when he swung round on the umpire, crouched low and lifted both index fingers as he hollered 'Howzat!'. He could make flicking a bead of perspiration from his forehead dramatic and played with the gallery's emotions as he began his approach for each new ball.

Allan Border plays the classic left-hander's cover drive during a stint with Essex in the 1980s, at a time when he virtually carried Australian Test hopes. (Ken Kelly)

Vic Marks, the Somerset and Oxford University all-rounder, had a word on Lillee's technique when he was asked to define an off-cutter: 'Deliveries batsmen play at and miss when Richie Benaud is commentating,' said Marks. Benaud, of course, was the anchor-man for the group of television commentators handsomely paid by Packer that included the deposed English captain, Tony Greig, Ian Chappell, Max Walker and Bill Lawry.

The second Australia v. West Indies Test of 1981–82 provided a tense struggle between two outstanding teams for SCG fans. Gomez batted for 444 minutes to score 126 in the West Indies' first innings of 384. In the final innings, with Australia chasing 373 to win, Dyson batted for 377 minutes for 127 not out. Yardley took 10 for 185 in a drawn match, including 7 for 37 off his last 77 deliveries.

The battle for supremacy reached fever-pitch in the Third Test at Adelaide where the West Indian pacemen gave the Australians

Dennis Lillee and Javed Miandad confront one another in Perth; umpire Tony Crafter tries to separate them. (West Australian Newspapers)

a severe battering. For most of the match Australia fielded substitutes for Hughes (bruised instep and fractured toe), Greg Chappell (fractured finger) and Lillee (strained groin). Marsh retired with the score on 172 after a Croft bouncer hit him over the left eye and resumed 34 runs later. Gomez (124 not out) swung the match West Indies' way with a record 82-run stand for the eighth wicket in the first innings. Despite 126 by Border, the West Indies needed only 236 in 195 minutes and 20 overs to win and they got them for the loss of five wickets, to share a wonderful series and retain the Frank Worrell trophy.

Greg Chappell faced fans who were still irate over the underarm ball incident when he took an Australian team on a five-match tour of New Zealand at the end of the 1981–82 Australian season in which South Australia regained the Shield from Western Australia. Chappell did a splendid public relations job and succeeded in restoring good relations between the players and New Zealand public, despite several intimidating incidents. When he took the Australians on to the field for the first match at Auckland somebody bowled an ebonite wood ball used in lawn bowls on to the field. More than 42,000 attended this match – 12,000 more than the previous New Zealand record – and takings reached £NZ75,860. Chappell was accidentally knocked over when he left the crease after making 108, but New Zealand won by 46 runs. At the Christchurch Test he had his cap snatched from his head but did not complain.

New Zealanders won £NZ14,000 and the Australians £NZ12,000 of the most substantial prizemoney ever offered in New Zealand. Hadlee also won a £5000 car as Man of the Series. The Australian team was G.S. Chappell (Captain), R.W. Marsh, G.M. Wood, R.J. Bright, B.M. Laird, J. Dyson, K.J. Hughes, A.R. Border, J.R. Thomson, B. Yardley, D.K. Lillee, L.S. Pascoe and T.M. Alderman. Lillee was seldom fit and Thomson did most of the pace bowling.

The three-Test rubber ended 1–1. The First Test at Wellington was drawn, New Zealand won the Second at Auckland by five wickets thanks to Brian Edgar's 161, the highest score by a New Zealander against Australia and superb bowling by Richard Hadlee. Australia won the Third Test at Christchurch by eight wickets, after a brilliant 176 by Greg Chappell, who hit two sixes and 23 fours. Yardley (13 at 23.92) was Australia's best bowler.

There was criticism of Greg Chappell for picking and choosing his tours when he stepped aside to allow Kim Hughes to take an Australian team on a six-week tour of Pakistan in September–October, 1982. Dennis Lillee and fellow pace-bowler Len Pascoe also withdrew, and Rod Marsh arrived late due to his son's illness, and the Australians never really settled down. They did not win one of their nine matches and were comprehensively defeated in all three Tests. Some of the Australian players were patronising in their attitude to the tour, treating it as a nuisance that did not really count in the world cricket scene.

Pakistan retained their unbeaten record over Australia at Karachi by winning the First Test by nine wickets. Moshin Khan became the third batsman given out 'handled the ball' in Tests when he played defensively to a ball from Thomson in Pakistan's first innings. The ball trickled towards the stumps and he knocked it away with his hand. The Australians left the field twice on the third day because of crowd demonstrations. Abdul Qadir's 5 for 76 in Australia's second innings proved the turning point and the Australians had no answer to his spinners throughout a series in which he took 22 wickets. Pakistan won the Second Test at Faisalabad by an innings and three runs after centuries by Mansoor Akhtar and Javed Miandad, and the Third Test at Lahore by nine wickets, thanks to centuries by Moshin Khan and the redoutable Miandad.

The Australian team, lacking in heroes, was splendidly served by Geoff Lawson, who bowled with a pace and bounce that put him ahead of Thomson and Alderman as the main strike bowler, and by the consistency of John Dyson with the bat. Kim Hughes and Border failed to provide the successful partnerships expected from such experienced batsmen. The Australian team was K.J. Hughes (Captain), A.R. Border, G.M. Ritchie, J. Dyson, W.B. Phillips, G.M. Wood, B.M. Laird, G.F. Lawson, B. Yardley, J.R. Thomson, R.W. Marsh, R.J. Bright, P.R. Sleep, T.M. Alderman and I.W. Callen.

A month later Greg Chappell was back in charge of the Australian XI for the five Tests against the thirty-fifth English team to Australia, captained by Bob Willis. England did not consider players who had opposed the British government's anti-apartheid ban by touring South Africa in 1982. This eliminated Graham Gooch, who was sadly missed on a bizarre tour of 23 matches, 11 of them first-class and 12 restricted to one day. The English team was R.G. Willis (Captain), D.W. Randall, D.I. Gower, A.J. Lamb, G. Fowler, E.E. Hemmings, I.T. Botham, D.R. Pringle, C.J. Tavare, G. Miller, R.W. Taylor, N.G. Cowans, V.J. Marks, and G. Cook, with Doug Insole manager and Bernard Thomas masseur on his eleventh successive tour. All England's first-class matches were held before the start of the limited-over competition in which New Zealand joined.

The First Test at the WACA was marred on the second day by an invasion of the playing area by about 20 spectators celebrating England reaching the 400-mark. One of them struck Terry Alderman across the back of the head. Alderman chased the man and in trying to apprehend him pitched forward on to his shoulder as he and the culprit crashed to the turf. Lillee and Border rushed to Alderman's assistance and held the offender until police handcuffed him and led him away. Alderman's dislocated shoulder was quickly put back into place but he could not bowl for the rest of the season.

Brawls between English and Australian supporters continued in the crowd for the rest of the day and police were kept on their toes separating fighting fans. Chappell took the Australians from the field for 14 minutes after the Alderman affair but they returned to finish off the England innings for 411. Twenty-six arrests were made. Botham scored his three thousandth run and took his two hundred and fiftieth wicket to reach a unique Test double, but the match ended in a draw.

Terry Alderman winces with pain from his shoulder as Border comforts him and police lead away the bare-chested man Alderman tried to tackle. The man had cuffed Alderman on the head. (West Australian)

Kepler Wessels, first South African-born player to represent Australia in Tests, became the thirteenth batsman to score a century in his first Test for Australia when Australia defeated England by seven wickets in the Second Test at the Gabba from 26 November to 1 December 1982. Marsh also excelled, setting an England v. Australia record by holding nine catches in a match, equalling Gil Langley's record of dismissing ten batsmen in a match, and achieving the record total of 300 Test catches. Wessels's first innings of 162 gave Australia a seven-wicket win.

Australia took a 2–0 lead by winning the Third Test in Adelaide by eight wickets. Greg Chappell's 115 gave Australia a first-innings lead of 222 and made him the third Australian behind Clem Hill and Don Bradman to score 2500 Test runs against England. Pacemen Thomson and Lawson swung the match for Australia, despite Gower's 114 in the follow-on. England extended the struggle for the Ashes to the Fifth Test at Sydney with a thrilling three-run win in the Fourth Test at Melbourne. Needing 292 to win in the fourth innings, Australia appeared beaten when their ninth wicket fell at 218. Then Border and Thomson united in a stand that took Australia to within 37 runs of victory, with a day to play. Although one delivery could have ended the drama 18,000 took advantage of the offer of free admission on the last day. The score edged towards the target until a boundary was needed.

Thomson, who had been allowing everything not in line with the stumps to pass, attempted to hit a wide delivery but only got an edge. The ball flew to Tavare at second slip but before he got his hands up, it him on the shoulder, bouncing over his head to Miller, who took the catch near his knees. The final 34 runs on that last morning had taken 18 overs. The result repeated Australia's winning margin over England in 1902 at Old Trafford. The only closer results were the two tied Tests, between Australia and the West Indies and Australia and India.

Australia regained the Ashes lost to England in 1977 by holding England to a draw in the Fifth Test in Sydney. Umpire Mal Johnson gave Dyson not out before a run had been scored but film of the incident showed that Dyson was clearly out. Lawson took 34 wickets in the five Tests at 20.20, Thomson 22 at 18.68, providing Marsh with a record 28 catches. After performing so dramatically in the previous series in England, Botham failed to have any influence on any of the Tests, with Lawson and Thomson repeatedly finding the edge of his bat.

Attendances totalled 554,142 for the Tests but on no single day did the crowds go anywhere near the 84,153 and 71,393 who watched limited-over matches straight after the Tests ended. In a three-cornered contest, England were eliminated before the finals in which Australia won $100,000 prize money by beating New Zealand.

The 1982–83 Sheffield Shield competition was decided for the first time by a final involving the two leading teams after the six states had met twice. New South Wales surprised by taking the Shield for the first time in 17 seasons, defeating hot favourites Western Australia in the final at Perth. New South Wales won by 54 runs, with Trevor Chappell dominating the match with an outstanding all-round display.

The season saw another significant move with the introduction of an under-25 tour of Zimbabwe by a side labelled Young Australia. Dirk Wellham captained the initial Young Australian XI and in 1983 Mike Veletta skippered a Young Australia team that included Craig McDermott, Tony Dodemaide and Ian Healy, who all later appeared in Tests. By 1991, 273 players who began in the inter-state schoolboys' carnivals had gone on to the first-class level.

The Australian Cricket Board's efforts to stimulate schoolboy cricket came amid increasingly gloomy reports that schoolmasters all round the nation were giving up the previously obligatory practice of coaching a cricket team. More and more schoolboys were turning to surfing or tennis as their summer sports, with teachers' unions banning compulsory sports tuition by its members.

To help prepare Sri Lanka for the 1983 World Cup in England Greg Chappell took an Australian side to Sri Lanka for six matches, including a Test, in April 1983. Australia overwhelmed the Sri Lankans in the inaugural Test between the countries, declaring at 4 for 514 in their only innings. This was enough to win by an innings and 38 runs. Kepler Wessels and David Hookes made centuries, Hookes recording his in a session, in what proved Greg Chappell's forty-eighth and last Test as Australia's captain. Chappell withdrew from the Australian side for the 1983 World Cup in England because of a neck injury, handing over to Kim Hughes. Australia won only two of their six matches in the competition topped by India. Eight nations took part and they all had at least one win in matches played over 60 overs, but Australia never recovered from a first-round defeat by Zimbabwe.

Pakistan's 11-match tour of Australia in 1983–84 brought the end of the Chappell era in Australian cricket and the retirement of Dennis Lillee and Rodney Marsh, who had helped make the period so successful. A competent but dispirited Pakistani side played their way through the tour with their captain, Imran Khan, out of action with shin soreness, a deputy, Zaheer Abbas, who appeared to have lost his nerve against pace, and a main strike bowler, Abdul Qadir, who had no answer when Australia played up to six left-handers against him.

With Greg Chappell playing under Kim Hughes's captaincy, Australia reached the Fifth Test in Sydney 1–0 up after winning the First Test in Perth. Having decided that this would be his last appearance for Australia, Greg Chappell deliberately invited all his relatives to fly in for the occasion, reasoning that he always played better under pressure. His unforgettable final innings of 182 runs in 530 minutes saw him pass Bradman's Australian record of 6996 Test runs and become only the sixth player to score more than 7000. As well, he took two catches in the match, which took him past Colin Cowdrey's world record of 120 Test catches.

Lillee also retired after this match, which Australia won by 10 wickets, having taken eight wickets and lifting his career total to

355 Test dismissals at 23.92. Marsh announced his retirement a few days later, disappearing from the Test scene with the same number of dismissals as Lillee, 355, 343 of them sent back with those wonderful acrobatic catches, 12 by stumpings. All had set world records, Marsh by taking 95 Test catches off Lillee's bowling.

Between 1966 and 1983 Greg Chappell scored 74 first-class centuries, compiled 24,535 runs at 52.50, and held 371 catches in first-class cricket. He captained Australia in 48 of his 88 Tests for 21 wins, 14 draws and 13 losses, cleverly prepared for Test captaincy by his brother Ian who stood in the slips in nine Tests while Greg ran the team, three of those Tests after the Packer settlement. Greg also took 291 first-class wickets with slow-medium deliveries at 29.76. Sir Donald said: 'Greg's runs were made with an aesthetic and imperious quality few others have emulated.'

Lillee took 861 first-class wickets at 23.13 and scored 2257 runs at 13.93, and if he had a weakness it was that he did not get the runs his batting deserved because of his heavy workload. Marsh had three Test centuries and four scores in the nineties in his 3633 Test runs, and would have averaged far higher than 26.52 but for an end-of-career slump when he made 50 only twice in his last 48 Test knocks. In all, he scored 11,607 first-class runs at 31.17 and dismissed 870 batsmen, 805 caught and 65 stumped.

Greg Chappell's farewell century atoned for his underarm ball gaff, which for a few hours had Board delegates eager to sack him.

Kim Hughes took the fifth Australian team to the West Indies in 1983–84, knowing the retirement of Chappell, Lillee and Marsh badly weakened his team. Australia's results were even worse than expected. They were overwhelmed in the last three Tests after hanging on desperately for draws in the first two, and lost the limited-over matches 3–1. They also lost a large number of friends by challenging umpires' decisions, behaviour that could not be excused by their high injury toll.

The Australian team was K.J. Hughes (Captain), A.R. Border, T.M. Alderman, T.G. Hogan, R.M. Hogg, D.W. Hookes, D.M. Jones, G.F. Lawson, J.N. Maguire, G.R.J. Matthews, W.B. Phillips, C.G. Rackemann, G.M. Ritchie, S.B. Smith, K.C. Wessels and R.D. Woolley, with G.M. Wood a reinforcement. Woolley was Marsh's successor as wicket-keeper, the first Tasmanian to play for Australia since Tasmania joined the Sheffield Shield competition.

Woolley appeared in only six of the ten first-class matches on

Terry Alderman, a keen competitor for Australia throughout the 1980s.
(Ken Kelly)

the tour and in one Test, and when he broke his finger at George-town against Guyana Hughes called it a blessing in disguise, a remark that displeased Woolley, who said his tour was a waste of time. Opening batsman Wayne Phillips kept wicket in four Tests and returned home established as the side's number one 'keeper.

Rain curtailed play in the First Test at Georgetown; Border saved Australia with two courageous knocks in the Second Test at Port-of-Spain, but thereafter the West Indian pace bowlers gained a dominance the Australians could not break, Garner, Marshall and Holding proving too fast and too talented. The West Indies won by ten wickets in the Third Test at Bridgetown, by an innings and 36 runs in the Fourth Test at St John's, and by ten wickets in the Fifth Test at Kingston.

In September and October 1984 Australia played five one-day matches against India to help the Indians celebrate the Golden Jubilee of the Ranji Trophy. Hughes had his players' support throughout and the Australians won all three of the matches completed, with rain preventing a result in the other two. On their way home from India several of the Australians were contacted by representatives of the South African Cricket Union. Their secret discussions presented the Australian Cricket Board with another major crisis when it was disclosed that some Australians proposed to join a rebel tour of South Africa. The South Africans followed up this initial contact by approaching Australians on their way home from a four-nation competition in Sharjah.

When news of the rebels' plans to tour South Africa leaked, the Australian Cricket Board decided it could do nothing about the players that it did not have under contract – Alderman, Hohns, McCurdy, Rixon, Shipperd and Michael Taylor – but decided to sue all the players with whom it had contracts who went to South Africa. The South Africans' plan had been to keep the rebel tours secret until the thirtieth Australian tour of England in 1985 was over, but the early leaks upset that planning.

The West Indians continued their winning sequence the following month, November 1984, by defeating Australia by an innings and 112 runs in Perth and an eight-wicket win in Brisbane.

Five successive defeats by big margins against West Indies was too much for Kim Hughes, who had become only a shadow of the batsman who had scored 24 first-class centuries. Before a packed media conference in Brisbane he announced his resignation as Australian captain, petulantly blaming the sniping of critics instead of sheeting it home to the 19 players who had failed Australia in those five Tests. Hughes, reading from a prepared statement, said the constant criticism from former players over four or five seasons had taken their toll and he believed it was in the interests of the Australian team to stand down. He broke down towards the end of the statement and quit the room in tears, leaving manager Bob Merriman to finish the reading. Hughes had led Australia in 28 Tests, for 13 losses, four wins, and 11 draws, and at no stage of his reign had he appeared captaincy material. 'Cry Baby, Kim' was the cruel headline that greeted his departure.

Allan Border took over the Australian captaincy for the Third Test at Adelaide against the West Indies from 7 to 11 December 1984 and at the end of the 1991–92 Australian season was still leading the side. His team lost by 191 runs in his first match in the big job, but managed to draw the Fourth Test in Melbourne and finished the season with a morale-boosting victory by an innings and 55 runs in Sydney when spinners Bob Holland and Murray Bennett took 15 of the 20 West Indian wickets. The crowd of 25,000 gave Clive Lloyd a standing ovation in his final Test.

Sir Donald Bradman rated the West Indian team that defeated Australia in six successive Tests as deserving comparison with the

1902, 1921 and 1948 Australian teams and probably superior to any of these great Australian sides in the field. Bradman said the sole criticism of the West Indians was their slow over-rate.

After confusion due to the South African overtures, the following team went to England in 1985: A.R. Border (Captain), D.M. Wellham, D.C. Boon, G.M. Ritchie, W.B. Phillips, S.P. O'Donnell, K.C. Wessels, G.M. Wood, A.M.J. Hilditch, R.B. Phillips, G.R.J. Matthews, C.J. McDermott, J.R. Thomson, M.J. Bennett, G.F. Lawson, D.R. Gilbert and R.G. Holland. The Federal Minister for Sport, John Brown, wanted the ACB to take punitive action against players who went to South Africa, but Bruce Francis, the South African Cricket Union's Australian agent, called this the most obnoxious request ever put to a sporting organisation. The ACB believed they had a good case but finally accepted a settlement whereby the South Africans paid the costs the Board had incurred for legal advice.

The 16 players who finally went to South Africa for what proved to be two tours were: K.J. Hughes (Captain), J. Dyson, S.B. Smith, G.N. Yallop, M.D. Haysman, M.D. Taylor, T.V. Hohns, S.J. Rixon, R.J. McCurdy, T.M. Alderman, C.G. Rackemann, J.N. Maguire, G. Shipperd, R.M. Hogg, T.G. Hogan and P.I. Faulkner. What a fine team could have come from the best of the two sides.

Long before Kim Hughes's rebels had completed their first South African tour, the Australian public had lost interest in the team. Match attendances fell below expectations, the cricket failed to inspire, and even disclosures towards the end of the tour that the South African government was paying most of the bills aroused little public comment in Australia.

Carl Rackemann said in an article in the English *Wisden Cricket Monthly* that he joined the rebels solely for the financial security it would bring. He claimed South African authorities were only interested in cricket, not politics, and that the rebel tours were an attempt to prevent cricket dying in South Africa.

According to the Cape Town newspaper *Business Day* the Australian players were paid for under a complicated business deal between the two major sponsors, the National Panasonic television company, and Yellow Pages telephone directory, under which they would pay only ten per cent of their sponsorship bills. The remaining 90 per cent of the money would come from rebates from the South African government. The two tours of South Africa were expected

An historic moment as the lights go on for the first time at the Melbourne Cricket Ground during the 1984–85 VCA Centenary celebrations. (News Limited)

to cost $5 million, with some players receiving up to $300,000 each.

The Australian public treated the news with the lack of interest reserved for most of the big-money deals in professional sport, but supported the Australian players' right to make the choice, regardless of whether they were political pawns giving moral backing to apartheid or were just looking for a trip to somewhere new. Australia's defeat in the third international by 61 runs, which gave South Africa the first series 1–0 after two earlier draws, barely rated a mention in the Australian sports pages.

Border's team, restricted by the absence of rebel bowlers Hogg, Rackemann, Alderman and Maguire, lost the First Test at Headingley by five wickets, but did well to win the Second Test at Lord's by four wickets when leg-spinner Bob Holland had a match-winning 5 for 68 in England's second innings. Needing one win to retain the Ashes, the Australians faltered badly and suffered two crushing defeats that left England's superiority indisputable. Border scored centuries in the first four tour matches and his eight hundreds on the tour included two in Tests, but he lacked support from his batsmen in the important matches.

Border was shocked by his team's inability to recover when in

Craig McDermott traps England opener Graham Gooch leg before wicket in the First Test at Headingley in 1985. (Patrick Eagar)

trouble, a habit that continued in the series that followed at home against New Zealand when Richard Hadlee took 33 wickets in three Tests to give his team their first series win over Australia. New Zealand won the First and Third Tests, Australia the Second, with the emergence of Greg Matthews as a crowd-pleasing all-rounder Australia's only solace. Matthews, after disappointing tours of the West Indies and England, blossomed suddenly to score 115 in the First Test, discarding his ponytail hairdo and jewel in the ear lobe.

When the fifth Indian team arrived to tour Australia towards the end of the 1985 Kepler Wessels had disqualified himself from selection for Australia by refusing to accept a cut in pay. The Board felt justified because of Wessels's alleged role in recruiting players for the rebel tours to South Africa. He played out the rest of his contract with Queensland and then joined the rebel tour of South Africa in 1986–87. Forced to introduce new players the selectors brought in Western Australian farmer Geoff Marsh, string-bean left-arm pace bowler Bruce Reid, Victorian fast bowler Merv Hughes and all-rounder Steve Waugh, one of the gifted Sydney cricket family.

Sunil Gavaskar again delighted Australians with his attractive stroke play. His driving off the front foot on both sides of the wicket was superb, but other Indian batsmen were often too slow and the team suffered badly from the loss of form of youthful leg-spinner Laxman Sivaramakrishnan. The Indian team was Kapil Dev (Captain), S.M. Gavaskar, Chetan Sharma, M. Amarnath, K. Srikkanth, M. Azharuddin, D.B. Vengsarkar, N.S. Yadav, R.J. Shastri, R.M.H. Binny, S.M.H. Kirmani, L. Sivaramakrishnan, R.S. Ghai, R.R. Kulkarni, K.S. More and A. Malhotra.

Despite an ill-considered preparation India drew all three Tests in a series that produced some attractive batting. Gavaskar made 166 not out in Adelaide and 172 in Sydney, Boon 123 in Adelaide and 131 in Sydney. Border made 163 and Matthews 100 not out, his second Test century, in Melbourne. Amarnath, 138, and Srikkanth, 116, also hit centuries in Sydney, where India reached 600 for the first time on foreign soil.

Border reached a low point in his time as Australian captain when New Zealand beat Australia 1–0 in a three-Test series in New Zealand in February–March, 1986. Upset by a trail of capitulations in the previous year, Border took Australia's eight-wicket defeat at Auckland as the ultimate insult and said he would resign unless Australia won the one-day series against New Zealand that followed.

'I've said everything I can to that bunch – if they don't know now how I feel, they never will. The guys should be hurting pretty bad because Test careers are on the line. You can only stick with blokes for so long. I'm basically leaving it to the players. They are going to show me whether they really want to play for Australia and whether they really want to play under me. It's reached a point where if we continue to lose, you've got to let someone else come in and see if they can do something different . . . The fellas are not responding to me. The enjoyment level has gone out of it.'

To the relief of Australia's cricket hierarchy, Border withdrew his resignation threat even though the Australians could only draw the one-day series with New Zealand 2–2. The Australian team, obviously still unsettled by the losses to the South African rebel tour, was: A.R. Border (Captain), D.C. Boon, G.R. Marsh, G.M. Ritchie, G.R.J. Matthews, W.B. Phillips, B.A. Reid, T.J. Zoehrer, S.R. Waugh, R.J. Bright, C.J. McDermott, D.R. Gilbert and S.P. Davis.

Matthews made his third Test century, 130, in the First Test at Wellington, Border made 140 and 114 not out in the Second Test at Christchurch, the second time he had made two centuries in a Test, and in the Third Test at Auckland Marsh made 118 and Boon batted right through the Australian second innings for 58 not out.

In Sydney while the Test players were away, New South Wales won the Sheffield Shield for the thirty-ninth time in a thrilling final against Queensland. For the second successive year, Queensland were foiled by tail-enders in a match they had to win. They built up early supremacy when Kerr and Wessels put on 107 for the second wicket of their first innings, Wessels going on to 166 in his last match for Queensland. Sam Trimble's son Glenn carried on this heavy scoring by adding 112, his first Shield century, and only a spirited effort by Whitney, 6 for 65, restricted Queensland to 9 declared for 436.

Thomson, who was also playing his final match for Queensland, gave Queensland the advantage by bundling New South Wales out for 294, helped by Harry Frei and Dirk Tazelaar. Queensland declared for the second time at 7 for 133 after Peter Taylor took 4 for 31, leaving New South Wales to score 275 to win. Queensland appeared to have the Shield won when the eighth New South Wales wicket fell at 254. Queensland threw everything into capturing the last two wickets but Bennett and Holland denied them for nine overs. They only added four runs in that spell but they saved the match and won the Shield for their side, showing some of the spirit Border was desperately searching for in the Australian team.

Jeff Thomson received a standing ovation as he left the SCG, cursing his inability to shift Holland and Bennett. He had dipped deep into his enormous physical reserves but had been frustrated by a dead, unresponsive pitch. He was 36 and no longer a shock bowler able to spread pain and alarm among his opponents, but the crowd showed they still admired this dynamic, uncomplicated cricketer. He retired with 675 first-class wickets to his credit at an average cost of 26.58, 200 of them in Tests at a cost of 28.00, one of the great fast bowlers of all time who brought the ball up from behind his body, giving batsman a late sight of it as he went through a slinging action that he had used throwing javelins as a youth. No other bowler ever kept an English dressing-room so busy, with masseurs carrying ice packs for bruises and handing out special pads for forearms, rib cages and chests. Jimmy Burke once said that after batting for an hour against Thommo your batting gloves felt like pretzels.

Geoff Lawson, a longtime servant of Australian and New South Wales cricket. (Sport & General)

CHAPTER THIRTY-ONE

THE ASHES REGAINED

Only six months after expressing his disgust over team-mates' displays, Allan Border got the show of mental toughness he craved in the stifling heat of the M.A. Chidambaram Stadium in the Madras suburb of Chepauk, as the four and a half million people of Madras waited uneasily for the onset of the north-east monsoon. Their clothes clinging to perspiring bodies and with drinking water severely rationed, his Australian players engaged in one of cricket's historic matches.

The Australians had won only one Test away from Sydney in almost three years and had only three wins in their previous 25 Tests. Their Indian opponents had just crushed England 2–0 in a three-Test series in England. The heat was so intense coach Bob Simpson agreed with Border there was little point in practising on the eve of the match and instead they took the team for a swim in the Bay of Bengal.

Border had just come from a successful season in England with Essex which he had treated as a holiday for his family. The players he joined had been honing their skills in intensive workouts with Simpson since the last week in August, but some of them still had to confirm their worth when Border went out to toss for the first of three five-day Tests on 18 September 1986.

Boon and Marsh opened the match for Australia but with the score on 48 Marsh was out and Dean Jones went in, promoted to Border's no. 3 spot. Boon proved his quality by scoring 122 and at stumps Australia were 2 for 211. On the second day Jones, having completed his first half-century in Test cricket in 162 minutes during which he faced 146 deliveries, began to strike the ball with exciting freedom, using his feet cleverly to thwart the spinners and driving with a new-found authority. At 87, he vomited beside the pitch, but quickly resumed and took his score to 97 when Ray Bright, sent in as nightwatchman when Boon was dismissed, was out after contributing 30 runs in a 76-run stand. Bright was so distressed by the heat a doctor had to be sent to him.

Border was at the other end when Jones reached his century, and together they put on 178 runs. At lunch the Australian masseur Erroll Alcott put Jones in a bath and tried to hydrate him with fruit juice and lift his potassium level with a banana. As he moved past 150, he began to lose control of his bodily functions, urinating inside his flannels and pitching forward as he disgorged the fluids and mineral substitutes Alcott and twelfth man Dave Gilbert brought to him. Sunil Gavaskar suggested a lime-based solution but Jones could not keep it down.

Dean Jones hammers away a boundary for Victoria at the MCG. His heroic innings at Madras will be long remembered. (Herald & Weekly Times)

Mike Coward, describing this in his book *Cricket Beyond the Bazaar*, said that when Jones was not vomiting he was racked with pain as his body dehydrated, but his batting did not suffer. 'The more pain and discomfort Jones experienced, the harder he struck the ball and the more precisely he placed it,' said Coward. 'He batted like a man possessed.'

At 174 Jones confided to Border that he could not go on. His stomach was in his mouth, and he had pins and needles in his hands. Border opted to goad him. 'Okay, I'll get someone tough out here,' said Border. Jones responded as Border hoped and carried on, angry and aggressive. He became the first Australian to score a double century against India after batting for seven hours 15 minutes. His second century had come from 99 balls in 164 minutes, and included 13 fours and two sixes.

At the tea interval team-mates undressed him and held him in the shower. Border, Simpson and team manager Alan Crompton conferred on whether Jones's health might be seriously affected if he resumed but when they put it to Jones, he insisted on going out again. He lasted another 14 minutes before being bowled by a ball he could not focus on for a total score of 210, which included two sixes and 27 fours, and took eight hours and 24 minutes to achieve. Border had only been able to contribute 64 runs while Jones made 114 in their partnership.

Jones's innings was only one of the remarkable events in the match. Border reached his nineteenth Test century, before declaring with Australia on 7 for 574. Bowling in a cap, as Grimmett had done half a century earlier, Matthews took 5 for 103 to have India out for 397. By then the heat had taken its toll and players were yelling insults at each other. Angry players milled together in packs disputing calls when umpires rejected their appeals.

Border declared for the second time in the match with Australia on 5 for 170 in their second innings, leaving India to score 348 to win. The Indians' quiet opening stand of 55 suggested they had opted for a draw but a century stand from Gavaskar – playing in his hundredth consecutive Test – and Amarnath took India to 2 for 190 at tea. With 20 overs left, India had reduced their target to 118 runs with seven wickets in hand. Then Bright, ill throughout the match, sent back Gavaskar for 90 and two runs later caught Kapil Dev off Matthews. Azharuddin was out charging wildly at Bright.

With 30 balls left, India wanted only 18 runs. The match appeared India's until Chetan Sharma and More went in one over from Bright.

Umpire Dotiwalla, who clashed repeatedly with the Australians, complained to Border that the Australians were taking too long to bowl their overs. Yadav struck Matthews for six, but with India needing only four to win was bowled off his pads next ball trying to repeat the shot. Turbaned Maninder Singh played out the rest of Bright's over, leaving Shastri to face the last over with nine men out.

Shastri mishit the first ball with a shot he believed would win the Test and collected two instead of four. He then made an enormous tactical error by taking a single to bring the scores level but exposed Maninder to Matthews. The 30,000 spectators sat silently as Matthews strutted in. Half the Australian team appealed when the delivery hit Maninder on the pad but umpire Vikramraju shook his head. Matthews's fifth delivery was more on line and this time Vikramraju gave Maninder out lbw as the ball thudded into the pad.

The Australians were stunned to have taken part in only the second tie in Test history, 26 years after they participated in the first tie in Brisbane against the West Indies. To have secured an lbw decision from an Indian umpire with only one ball to go was even more amazing. Matthews had taken five wickets in each innings to finish with 10 for 249 and, despite the heat, had bowled 68.1 overs.

Australian coach Bob Simpson, the only man involved in both tied Tests, said: 'I think there was more drama somehow in the Madras tie. The weather was so much tougher there and the players had to endure considerable discomfort for five consecutive days.

There was confusion in Brisbane with players asking each other who had won, but there was no confusion about the result in Madras. I doubt if any cricketer ever had to push himself as hard as Dean Jones did in Madras. He dehydrated to such an extent he could not keep any fluid down, and when he was out we had to rush him to hospital and get liquid into him intravenously. It was a fantastic innings and I am not sure he had fully recovered by the end of the tour.'

The Madras tie proved the biggest morale-boost for the Australians since Border became captain, achieved in heat of 40°C. Although they lost the one-day internationals 2–3, the Australians were unbeaten in their seven first-class matches and for the first time prevented the great Kapil Dev from taking a single wicket in a Test series. Altogether, India tried 18 umpires in the Tests and one-day matches, but Border admitted at the end of the tour that Australia's misgivings over the standards of Indian umpiring were groundless.

Despite their continued high profits from cricket telecasts, Packer's network remained selective in the matches it showed viewers. Despite the tensions and disturbances of the 1986 Indian tour, Channel Nine did not cover it and there was no ball-by-ball coverage of the rebel tours of South Africa. A large contingent of Australian reporters went to South Africa when the rebel matches began but once they realised forecast demonstrations would not occur the pressmen returned home and left the rebels largely unreported. Public lack of interest was blamed.

Players' performances in the years of South Africa's exile were initially accepted as first-class, although later denied. The impressive feats in World Series Cricket matches during the Packer revolt have never been granted even temporary recognition.

Australia's selectors had always supported their Test 'keepers, picking the man they regarded as the best for the job and allowing him to remain in the Test team while results were acceptable. They adopted a completely different policy after Marsh's retirement, trying Roger Woolley, Wayne Phillips, Tim Zoehrer and Greg Dyer in quick succession, apparently blaming wicket-keeping blunders for Australia's failures.

The 1986–87 series in Australia against England began with Tim Zoehrer the first choice, but when Zoehrer was hurt after two Tests, economics graduate Greg Dyer took over for one Test until Zoehrer recovered. Packer's influence prevented the Englishmen appearing

Tasmania's most prolific batsman David Boon, glancing to leg at the WACA. Batting or fielding, he has been an invaluable Test player. (Sunday Times, *Perth*)

in Sydney until the thirteenth week of the tour, which involved three trips to Perth and back. Advertising buffs explained that this stemmed from larger returns from televising matches into Sydney and Melbourne with their high populations than from playing in those cities.

The other major change in England's itinerary compared with pre-Packer years was in the high number of limited-over matches. England faced Australia five times in Tests, but seven times in one-day games. The tour included only 11 first-class matches, compared with 19 non-first-class matches. *Wisden*'s John Thicknesse commented: 'Since the alliance with Packer in 1979, the pursuit of money through a saturation of one-day cricket, sapping players' stamina and leading to bad habits in technique, has too often seemed the Australian Board's main objective, if not the only one. A wiser course might be the pursuit of excellence by giving greater encouragement to the Sheffield Shield.'

England arrived in Australia after eight defeats in 11 Tests without a single win, and three lost series in succession. But in Mike Gatting they had a pugnacious, determined skipper, strongly supported by managers Peter Lush and Micky Stewart, and between them they extracted from their team three performances that swung the series. The English team was M.W. Gatting (Captain), D.I. Gower, I.T. Botham, N.A. Foster, B.C. Broad, B.N. French, A.J. Lamb, J.J. Whitaker, C.W.J. Athey, C.J. Richards, J.E. Emburey, W.N. Slack, P.A. DeFreitas, G.R. Dilley, G.C. Small and P.H. Edmonds.

England began disastrously, losing their initial first-class match to Queensland at the Gabba by five wickets and turning in a woeful display against Western Australia in Perth before escaping with a draw. The Australian selectors attributed England's Perth failure to the bowling of new-ball bowlers Bruce Reid and Chris Matthews, and three days later they were in Australia's team that faced England in the First Test at the Gabba. Australia seemed set to take a commanding position when Border won the toss and sent England in, with the conditions highly favourable to pace bowling.

Australia lost her chance for dominance in the first hour of play, with Reid, Merv Hughes and Matthews bowling like novices, although Reid did get one ball to move away and dismiss Broad. Hughes, who had been called an imposter on his debut against India the previous year, seldom got a delivery on line and his lack of skill was the despair of 'keeper Zoehrer. Big Chris Matthews completely succumbed to nerves and seldom bowled a ball on the stumps.

Botham exploited England's good luck encountering such an amateurish attack with an accomplished innings of 138. Border at one stage had eight men on the boundary trying to deprive Botham of the strike but a 92-run stand by Botham and DeFreitas assured Botham of his century and England of a big total. Botham hit four sixes, all straight drives, and 13 fours, before Hughes sprinted hard to catch him at long leg. Australia had to follow on when Dilley took 5 for 68, his first five-wicket bag in Tests. Marsh batted for 392 minutes to score 110 in Australia's second innings but England only had to score 75 to win in their second innings.

The Second Test at Perth produced another poor display by Australia's pace bowlers, Hughes, Lawson and Matthews, and faded out to a draw after Australia spilt vital catches. Only twenty wickets fell for 1209 runs in the Third Test at Adelaide, where four batsmen made centuries and a further draw always appeared certain. At Melbourne a dour 112 from Chris Broad, his third century in successive matches, combined with splendid bowling from Gladstone Small (5 for 48) and Ian Botham (5 for 41), paved the way to England's Fourth Test win by an innings and 14 runs, a triumph that wrapped up the series.

To that stage the cricket from both sides had seemed spiritless, but for the Fifth Test in Sydney the Australian selectors enlivened the entire rubber by picking a ginger-haired 30-year-old off-spinner named Peter Taylor. Most of the experienced reporters on the tour were convinced a mistake had been made when Taylor's name was read out. 'Peter Who?' became the catchcry, with the cognoscenti believing the wrong Taylor had been named in a team that lacked an opening partner for Geoff Marsh. Surely Mark Taylor, who had been making runs in impressive fashion for New South Wales, was the man the selectors intended to play? Peter Taylor had had only six first-class matches, whereas Mark Taylor had hit 186 at his previous outing on the SCG.

Peter Taylor turned out wonderful television material, a gutsy fighter who let his off-breaks go at the top of a kangaroo-style hop, and a left-hand batsman who gave the ball a big thump. 'My main trauma was wondering if I'd make an idiot of myself,' he said. 'I could see myself becoming a laughing stock. It was just a matter of getting the ball on the batsman's side of the pitch.' In a rags-to-riches tale, he took 6 for 78 and 2 for 76, scored 11 and 42 in a Man-of-the-Match debut, had Allan Lamb caught in his third

The batsman's view of lanky Bruce Reid, the Perth pace man who has overcome severe back problems to win Test stardom. (Sunday Times, Perth)

over and dismissed Botham twice, including first ball in the second innings.

The Australians completed their first Test win in more than a year, Dean Jones contributing 184 not out in Australia's first innings and leg-spinner Peter Sleep taking 5 for 72 on the last day. Attendance at the ground was only 93,429 for the five days, but there was barely a television set in the nation that did not follow the final moments as Sleep bowled Emburey, who had had 18 of the 30 hours' play on the field.

With new-ball bowlers Rackemann, Alderman, Hogg and McCurdy absent in South Africa, Craig McDermott and Geoff Lawson out of form, and Chris Matthews, Merv Hughes and Bruce Reid too immature for the job, the mystery of this entire England v. Australia series was why selectors did not give Mike Whitney a Test after he took 7 for 70 when New South Wales defeated England at Newcastle.

England's once strong opposition to wearing coloured clothing was no longer a worry to her players. Three times they enjoyed audiences in excess of 50,000 for limited-over night matches in Melbourne. The popularity of night cricket continued to rise in a season that saw the Australian Board stage two series with huge prize money: a four-nation tournament in Perth, which formed part of the America's Cup celebrations, and the customary WSC series in which England defeated Australia 2–0 after the West Indies had been eliminated. Losses on the Sheffield Shield – won by Western Australia that year – exceeded $1 million, with Channel Nine showing no wish to promote Shield matches or even screen controversial Shield disputes.

However, when Channel Nine's agreement for exclusive rights to televise Australian cricket expired in 1987, there was no opposition to extending Kerry Packer's rights for a further five years. The scepticism that the Australian Cricket Board's negotiators Ray Steele and Bob Parish had sold out cheaply had disappeared. The annual distribution to the states of $2 million or more and the continued interest of major firms in sponsoring cricket silenced all critics of the deal, while Channel Nine had proved it could sell everything from spanners to dishwashers through its cricket broadcasts.

The English team's visit had firmly established wild-eyed Merv Hughes, a muscular giant from Euroa in Victoria where Bodyline-era pace bowler 'Bull' Alexander had ruled for more than 50 years,

as a crowd-puller. Big Merv bowled very fast, trying to blast batsmen out, but had little deviation or subtlety with which to fool Test-class batsmen. When his captains signalled that they required him to bowl soon, he went through a routine of callisthenics which spectators imitated behind his back. Small boys spent hours making their Merv Hughes banners before they went to the MCG and his huge, bushy moustache became as well known as John Newcombe's. His dad said he was just a big pup, always carrying on.

Hughes bowled with admirable verve and was just as fast an hour before stumps as he was at the start of a day's play, but he had a curious soft shoe stretch in the middle of his run-up and a front-on delivery that detracted from his penetration. Team-mates called him 'Fruitfly', rating him a pest with his dressing-room by-play.

At the end of the 1986–87 season in Australia, the Australian Cricket Board's media manager Ian McDonald managed a team that played in the four-nation Sharjah Cup in the United Arab Emirates. This unique event had begun in 1984 on the whim of an Arab businessman, Abdul Rahman Bukhatir, who had become addicted to cricket as a student in Pakistan. He spent more than £5 million to get the project started, digging a hole in the desert which he filled with black soil brought in by hundreds of lorries. Over the top he laid grass and had a splendid turf wicket put down, which he surrounded with a stadium that sits on the outskirts of Sharjah. Australia has been sending teams to Sharjah's limited-over competitions since 1985, Sheik Bukhatir paying all expenses.

The 1987 Australian team did not win a match, but David Boon won the Player of the Series award by scoring 71 v. Pakistan, 62 v. India, 87 v. New Zealand, and 73 v. England. Unfortunately, Greg Matthews misbehaved and the initial reaction of the Australian management was that Matthews should be sent straight home. Finally, McDonald, Simpson and captain Border agreed to sleep on it and decide on Matthews's penalty in the morning.

Matthews received a $1000 fine under the Players' Code of Behaviour, the highest fine incurred since the scheme began, and a penalty that threw his immediate international future into doubt. He was not included in the team Australia sent to the fourth World Cup in India in October and November, 1987, and thereafter often lost the Test off-spinner's spot to Peter Taylor despite his heroism in the Madras tie.

Australia went to the fourth World Cup, a limited-over competition, in India and Pakistan during October and November, 1987, as one of the underdogs. Coach Bob Simpson refused to listen to the forecasts and drilled his players in the basic skills despite the stultifying heat and their frequent stomach problems. Manager Alan Crompton and captain Border matched Simpson's enthusiasm, building up a confidence that prevailed in a series of tense finishes. The Australian team comprised A.R. Border (Captain), G.R. Marsh, D.C. Boon, T.M. Moody, G.C. Dyer, P.L. Taylor, B.A. Reid, C.J. McDermott, S.R. Waugh, S.P. O'Donnell, D.M. Jones, T.B.A. May, M.R.J. Veletta and A.K. Zesers.

Australia beat the World Cup holders India by one run in the very first match in Madras, after Marsh made 110 to help lift the Australian total to 270. At Indore they beat New Zealand by three runs in a match reduced to 30 overs, thanks to Boon's 87. They easily overcame Zimbabwe by 96 runs, lost the return to India by 56 runs, won their second match against New Zealand by 17 runs, and the second match with Zimbabwe by 70 runs. This took them into the semi-finals in which they accounted for Pakistan by 18 runs, with the entire top order contributing solid, sensible innings.

Batting first in the final Australia managed 253 before 70,000 spectators in Calcutta from England's 50 overs. This was after Boon and Marsh sent them off to a fine start by scoring 52 from the first

The team that won the 1987 World Cup: back (L to R), E.A. Alcott (Physiotherapist), M.R. Veletta, S.R. Waugh, T.B.A. May, B.A. Reid, T.M. Moody, A.K. Zesers, D.M. Jones, R.B. Simpson (Coach); front, G.C. Dyer, S.P. O'Donnell, D.C. Boon, A.R. Border (Captain), A.B. Crompton (Manager), G.R. Marsh, C.J. McDermott, P.L. Taylor.

ten overs. Following Boon's dismissal for 75, Border and Veletta added 73 in ten overs. England's last six overs cost 65 runs, including 11 in the last over from DeFreitas.

England were in a great position at 2 for 135 from 31 overs and the heat appeared to be worrying the Australians. Gatting then played a reverse sweep, which flew off his shoulders into Dyer's gloves. England were always struggling from then on. Steve Waugh ran out Athey with a brilliant throw and then bowled Lamb. In the forty-ninth over Waugh dismissed DeFreitas, conceding only two runs. England had to score 17 from the last over and McDermott restricted them to ten.

Australia's World Cup victory stemmed from their openers Boon and Marsh, who made more than 800 runs in the team's eight matches, Boon 446 at 55.75, Marsh 428 at 61.14. Veletta played three knocks over 40, including a valuable 45 in the final, and lifted the entire team's display with his brilliance in the field. McDermott was the outstanding bowler of the competition with 18 wickets at 19.0.

Only a few days after Australia's World Cup triumph, all-rounder Simon O'Donnell, only 24, was told he had cancer. He had been Australia's hero in the World Cup win over England by conceding only 35 runs in his ten overs. The applause had barely faded when he discovered that a lump on his rib cage was cancerous.

O'Donnell withdrew from big cricket, had the affected rib removed, and began a long period of chemotherapy. Often the treatment was so exhausting he wondered if he could continue, but his friends kept him going. Despite embarrassment over losing his hair during the treatment, he tried to visit his Victorian team-mates in the MCG dressing-room as often as he could. He found the dressing-room interludes took his mind off his problems, especially the day they brought in a light bulb and stuck it in his mouth. He knew he was on the way to recovery when his team-mates invited him to hit up with them in the nets.

On their return home Australia missed O'Donnell's non-stop aggression. Craig McDermott lost form and Merv Hughes was discarded after a wild, uncontrolled display against New Zealand in the First Test at Brisbane in the 1987–88 series. Richard Hadlee, who had taken 15 wickets at the Gabba two years earlier, found the Australian batsmen a more determined, technically sounder lot this time and took only three wickets. Boon's 143 was full of those lovely deflections, square cuts and hefty drives that come so fluently from him when he is in form.

New Zealand bounced back by scoring 9 declared for 485 in their first innings of the Second Test in Adelaide, Andrew Jones and Martin Crowe both scoring centuries. Australia topped this by 11 runs because of a ten-hour innings from Border, who survived an appeal for a catch by Jeff Crowe at wide mid-on when he was 66. With bowler Patel and team-mates leaping about, Crowe sportingly signalled 'no catch' and Border proceeded to 205. On the way he passed the Test aggregates of Sir Leonard Hutton (6971) and Sir Donald Bradman (6996), and overtook Greg Chappell's 7110 run record by an Australian Test batsman. His 205 was his career-best score.

The match fizzled out in a draw after Australia had taken 11-run first-innings lead but not before Richard Hadlee had taken five wickets or more for the thirtieth time in a Test by dismissing Bruce Reid. Only 26 wickets fell in the five days, showing up weaknesses in the Australian attack which selectors hoped to correct by bringing in Anthony Ian Christopher Dodemaide, an all-rounder of French ancestry, for the deciding Third Test in Melbourne.

'Dodders', as team-mates called him, proved a superb subject for television, sporting generous black eyebrows, luxuriant moustache and a thick mop of shining black hair. He impressed immediately with the subtlety of his right-arm swingers, taking 1 for 48 in the first innings, and 6 for 58 in the second, with an enterprising knock of 50 in between.

But Dodders was upstaged, despite this dream start, by a dogged display from tail-enders Michael Whitney and Craig McDermott right at the end of the Test. Hadlee had then taken ten wickets in a Test for a record eighth time and drawn level with Ian Botham's all-time Test record of 373 Test wickets. With nine Australians out, Hadlee required just the final wicket to become the unchallenged world record holder, but the Australians frustrated him, holding out for 4.5 overs, a monumental performance given their past record with the bat.

Queensland failed once again in 1987–88 to win the Sheffield Shield after finding big money to include Botham in their team. He pulled large crowds into the Gabba, but could not find the swing in clear conditions that came easily to him in the murky and overcast conditions in England. He bowled so many bad balls it seems unfair to all the other great bowlers who preceded him that he should hold the world record for Test dismissals, even briefly. But he could take breathtaking catches, make runs, and helped rising youngsters, and Queensland had a good buy in Botham until he boarded the plane to Perth for a crucial match against Western Australia. On that flight Botham was alleged to have put a headlock on a passenger who asked for some quiet. In Tasmania in a post-match celebration with Lillee, they did enough damage to attract demands for compensation.

The Queensland Cricket Association terminated Botham's contract and the Queensland team's main sponsor questioned the entire administration of cricket in Queensland. Botham failed to make a century, and never took more than three wickets in an innings, but with 29 wickets and 646 runs would have survived to play out his three-year contract but for his misbehaviour off the field. In winning their eleventh Sheffield Shield, Western Australia proved invincible in Perth, where they won four matches, drew against Victoria, then won the final.

From 29 January to 2 February 1988 the New South Wales Cricket Association staged a match on the Sydney Cricket Ground for the ACB as part of Australia's Bicentenary celebrations. Months of planning went into the match, with all surviving English and

Michael Whitney shows his delight in taking another wicket. He has had to overcome crippling knee injuries to regain his Test spot. (News Limited)

Australian Test players invited to attend at the ACB's expense. The Melbourne replay of the first-ever Test had worked very well, but this time there were dozens of polite refusals from famous players unwilling to submit themselves to the long flight and ten days of non-stop parties. There were parades in horse-drawn open carriages, displays of famous photographs, lavish dinners, and for the first time the MCC allowed the famous Ashes trophy to leave Lord's and travel under special escort to Sydney. A dinner-dance held inside a giant marquee at North Sydney Oval at a cost of $175-a-head sold out quickly.

Before a ball was hit the organisers, deluded perhaps by the success of all the preliminaries, announced the match was a sell-out and informed journalists that tickets were unobtainable. Thousands stayed away, believing the quest for tickets was a waste of time and only 103,831 spectators attended, at least 100,000 short of NSWCA hopes.

England helped kill interest in the match by dawdling to 2 for 221 on the first day. The only fireworks came from Chris Broad, who after boring the crowd into a comatose state by batting for seven hours in which he seldom offered an aggressive stroke, petulantly smashed down his stumps when he played on to Steve Waugh on 139. Broad clearly found it difficult to accept his dismissal. Team manager Micky Stewart fined Broad £500, or $A1200, and the English camp excused the leniency of the punishment by arguing that all teams were doing it.

Australia made 214 in reply to England's 425, having to follow on by 12 runs. Boon's 184 not out in Australia's second innings was the best thing in the match and made a draw inevitable. The crowd showed as much interest in a computerised match conducted on the giant electronic scoreboard between English and Australian 'Living Legends'. Great roars arose as past heroes' scores lit up the board and when Australia was given as the winner by 37 runs, the entire audience burst into cheers. Two days later Australia won a special limited-over match in Melbourne by 22 runs in front of 52,159 spectators, more than half as many as had attended any of the five days of the Sydney yawn.

The television cameras moved to Perth in February 1988 for Sri Lanka's first Test in Australia. Yet again the visitors' pre-Test programme handicapped their Test display. The Sri Lankans went into the Test from a limited-over tournament in which they played so poorly only the first session of play was televised each day. The four days the Test lasted attracted a total of only 10,607 spectators, the lowest attendance at a Test in Australia since 1887–88, and the fourth smallest on record.

The Sri Lankan team was R.S. Madugalle (Captain), A.P. Gurusinha, J.R. Ratnayeke, A. Ranatunga, R.S. Mahanama, P.A. de Silva, R.G. de Alwis, D.S.B.P. Kuruppu, G.F. Labrooy, S.M.S. Kaluperuma, C.P.H. Ramanayake, K.N. Amalean, S. Jeganathan and M.A.R. Samarasekera. The captain, Ranjan Madugalle, had played in 19 Tests, but of the Sri Lankans' most experienced Test players, Duleep Mendis, with 23 Tests behind him, was left at home and Wettimuny had retired.

Boon and Marsh, rapidly becoming one of Australia's most successful opening pairs, put on 120 for the first wicket. When they left, Dean Jones and Border added 156 runs in 151 minutes for the third wicket. Jones reached his century from a shot when he was 98: he was dropped at mid-wicket and ran two. Border had no such luck and was out for 88. Australia's 455 total was enough to provide victory by an innings and 108 runs when the Australian bowlers ran through the Sri Lankans for 194 and 153, Hughes with 5 for 67, his first five-wicket Test bag.

Greg Dyer kept wicket for Australia in this Test against Sri Lanka but when the Australian team to tour Pakistan for three Tests and five one-day matches in 1988 was announced his place was taken by Queenslander Ian Healy. Dyer had been out of favour since the Melbourne Test with New Zealand in December, 1987, when he claimed a catch against Andrew Jones which television replays clearly showed had bounced. But Healy had played in only six first-class matches. Selectors had been watching him since his days in teenaged Australian teams. He beat a talented group of 'keepers – Dyer, Zoehrer and Victorian Michael Dimattina – for the job in Pakistan, apparently because of his skill in taking spin. The Australian team was A.R. Border (Captain), G.R. Marsh, P.L. Taylor, G.M. Wood, P.R. Sleep, M.R.J. Veletta, J.D. Siddons, D.C. Boon, I.A. Healy, D.M. Jones, S.R. Waugh, A.I.C. Dodemaide, T.B.A. May, B.A. Reid and C.J. McDermott.

The tour developed into one of the most controversial in which Australia has been involved, an unhappy exercise in cricket diplomacy undertaken with Pakistan on the brink of civil war following the death in a plane crash of General Zia ul Haq, president of Pakistan. Ethnic violence was at a peak and caused cancellation of two one-day matches, and the first of the international matches had to be called off because of floods.

The Australians had been bemused the previous year by reports of clashes between England captain Mike Gatting and Pakistan umpires, but found themselves struggling against the same problem. The First Test at Karachi from 15 to 20 September 1988 ended in victory for Pakistan by an innings and 188 runs, but left the Australians so incensed over the umpiring of Mahboob Shah there were reports that the players wanted to return home in protest without completing the tour. Happily, tour manager Col Egar squashed that idea but opinion was that Pakistani officials erred by not replacing Mahboob Shah for the Second Test.

Javed Miandad reached 211 in the First Test by surviving a series of highly confident lbw appeals and Pakistan's first innings went into the third day. Then on a worn pitch the Australians floundered against the spin of Iqbal Qasim and Abdul Qadir, who took 14 wickets between them and set up the Pakistan triumph. In the Second Test at Faisalabad the Australians again found it impossible to get an lbw decision against Miandad, who made 43 and 107. Ijaz Ahmed increased the Australians' problems by scoring 122 three days after his twentieth birthday, but a typically resolute innings of 133 not out from Border allowed Australia to emerge with a draw.

Australia went close to squaring the series in the Third Test at Lahore, Pakistan hanging on grimly through the final overs to get a draw. Border set Pakistan 269 to win in 300 minutes but the Pakistanis refused the challenge. They dithered along defensively until Taylor took three wickets in 14 balls to leave them at 7 for 131 with 16 overs remaining. The hero of the tour was Bruce Reid, who was unable to bowl on the final day of this Test after taking 20 wickets at 20.35. The fractures in his back later sidelined him for months while doctors implanted a metal frame to support his spine.

Australia's adventures on a tour that yielded only a solitary win – in Hong Kong – five draws and a loss in first-class matches, and daily complaints about pitches and umpires, led to increased discussion over the need for neutral umpires on all international tours. In the series that followed between Australia and the touring West Indians, television replays repeatedly disclosed mistakes by Australian umpires. This caused Sir Donald Bradman to announce that he favoured the use of a third umpire off the field who would have the benefit of watching immediate replays and could signal the result to colleagues on the field.

The West Indians visited in 1988–89, led by Vivian Richards, who announced it would be his last Australian visit. His team was I.V.A. Richards (Captain), C.G. Greenidge, D.L. Haynes, R.B. Richardson, A.L. Logie, R.A. Harper, W.K.M. Benjamin, C.L. Hooper, P.J.L. Dujon, K.L.T. Arthurton, C.E.L. Ambrose, C.A. Walsh, M.D. Marshall, I.R. Bishop, B.P. Patterson and D. Williams, with Clive Lloyd as manager.

The conduct of Clive Lloyd on this tour of 11 first-class and 11 one-day matches disappointed his many Australian fans. Lloyd objected to criticism before the tour began about low over-rates and their ruinous effect on attendances. He supported his players whenever they disputed an umpire's decision, and he made no effort to correct the problem of no balls in a series in which his bowlers were called nearly 250 times for over-stepping the front crease.

Boredom drove the public away when the West Indies were in the field and none of the Tests was well attended. Despite the brilliance of their fielding and catching, they took so long to bowl their overs many fans were only prepared to catch the highlights on television news rather than sit through interminable overs with bowlers retreating almost to the sightboards in their approach runs. Intimidatory bowling and the frequency with which batsmen were hit became a small issue compared with the slow over-rates and the West Indians had $22,000 docked from their winnings for not reaching the agreed 90 overs a day, or 15 overs an hour. Richards belittled the offence by saying winning was more important to his team than money.

For three Tests the West Indies' tactics of kicking the ball up into the rib cage or forcing batsmen to absorb frequent blows in among the sprinkling of bouncers paid off. They won the First Test in Brisbane by nine wickets, the Second Test at Perth by 169 runs and the Third Test in Melbourne by 285 runs and retained the Frank Worrell Trophy. Courtney Walsh took an unusual hat-trick in the first Test by dismissing Dodemaide to end Australia's first innings and then dismissing Veletta and Wood with his first two deliveries in the second innings. At Perth, where he took 13 for 217 and won the Man of the Match award, Merv Hughes completed a hat-trick in three separate overs, taking wickets with the last ball of his 36th over and the first ball of his 37th over, which ended the West Indian first innings, and then taking a wicket with the first ball of the second innings.

Australia were a revitalised side in the last two Tests, both played on slower, grassless pitches. They won the Fourth Test in Sydney by seven wickets, inflicting a rare defeat on the West Indies as they had done in 1984–85 with an attack based on spin. Border's 7 for 46 with his left-arm spin gave Australia an advantage they never lost in the West Indies' first innings. At Adelaide in the Fifth Test Australia made 515 in their first innings, and a wonderful 7 for 89 by Mike Whitney gave them command. Only a fighting 104 by Gordon Greenidge, his first century in 32 Test innings in Australia, saved the West Indies from defeat.

In marked contrast to the Tests, the 15 one-day matches that followed, with Pakistan joining in, were watched by almost half a million people, an average of 33,300 a day. The 24 days of Test cricket drew 325,000 spectators at an average daily rate of 13,541.

Mark Taylor, one of the outstanding successes of Australia's 1989 English tour, on his way to 136, his first Test century, at Leeds. (Patrick Eagar)

The Australian public's distaste for lethargic Test cricket soon showed. Two disastrous series defeats in the mid-'80s, and players who were the despair of their captain, had Test gates falling. Some critics argued that Test cricket was doomed. The ACB reacted by setting up a Cricket Academy for aspiring youngsters, organising spin-bowling clinics around the States, increasing expenditure for Kanga cricket in school playgrounds, offering fast bowlers help through Pace Australia and by paying Test men more.

The Australian Cricket Academy was founded in 1988, to help talented players between the ages of 17 and 21 make the jump from outstanding club performers to first-class representatives, and quickly became the envy of the cricket world. The Academy began under the direction of former Australian batsman Jack Potter, with 16 scholarship winners, most of them picked on their form in the 1988 World Youth Cup. They were accommodated at St Mark's College in Adelaide, within walking distance of Adelaide Oval where extensions were made beneath the John Creswell Stand to give them indoor pitches and their own offices.

Students at the Academy spent up to five hours a day on cricket, with at least 15 hours a week devoted to examination studies or trade training. The scheme cost more than half a million dollars a year and was jointly funded by the Commonwealth Bank, the Federal government, the South Australian Sports Institute and the

South Australian Cricket Association. It has gone from strength to strength.

Special electronic equipment at the Academy analyses players' technique and the boys put it all together in matches around the Australian States and against touring teams. Rodney Marsh, a tough, outspoken but invariably shrewd judge of cricketers, with 96 Tests behind him, took over from Potter in 1991 and has since produced a flood of Test candidates. Marsh moved his family from Perth and the Academy to the beachside suburb of Glenelg, and his main worry has been to find spots for his graduates in six State teams. The 'fast-tracking' of Australian Cricket Academy graduates into Sheffield Shield teams seems certain to improve the standards of that competition and, officials hope, bring crowds back to Australia's most important domestic tournament. The standard of scholars from the Academy has proved so high many of them are pencilled in as prospective Test players.

Intensive coaching from their mid-teens, overseas tours for Under-19-year-olds, annual tournaments for State schoolboy teams, and the final polish at the Australian Cricket Academy has given Australia's rising players crowd-pleasing skills. Their athleticism gives Australian teams a huge advantage over creaky-jointed opponents.

Entry to the Academy is keenly sought after, for at a time of high unemployment, becoming a Test cricketer is something to aim at. It guarantees big financial rewards, frequent overseas travel, and constant media exposure, with the promise of endorsements that can set up a good player for life.

CHAPTER THIRTY-TWO

THE PUSH FOR TOP SPOT

Allan Border knew the urgent need for remedial action when he took the thirty-first Australian team to England in 1989. His task was to transform the team he had once threatened to quit because of their gutless displays into a side that would bring crowds back to big cricket. He decided on a tougher, less friendly approach and imposed increased discipline on the team, keeping them focused and cutting down their social engagements.

Very quickly the team became aware they belonged to a highly-motivated outfit, destined for gruelling training routines. The spirit Border inspired was shown in every important innings he played on that tour. He would go to the crease with jaw firmly set, ready to take heavy knocks to survive and keep the runs flowing, pleasantries discarded.

The team Border led comprised G.R. Marsh, S.R. Waugh, M.A. Taylor, D.M. Jones, T.V. Hohns, G.F. Lawson, M.G. Hughes, T.M. Alderman, G.D. Campbell, I.A. Healy, M.R.J. Veletta, T.M. Moody, T.B.A. May, C.G. Rackemann, T.J. Zoehrer, and D.C. Boon. They were experienced, tough, talented and gave Border the confidence to attack from the first ball of the first Test early in June at Headingley. Five days later Australia emerged handsome winners by 210 runs. Continuing the Australian revival that had started in the last two Tests of the 1988–89 series in Australia against the West Indies, they declared at 7 for 601 in their first innings after a magnificent display of batting and an equally exhilarating show of running between wickets. Coach Bob Simpson's tireless efforts had at last got them to copy the art of running for which he was famous.

This restoration of Australia's prestige through its batsmen was much appreciated by their bowlers, three of whom emerged over the following decade as match winners. The big totals gave them a chance to triumph. Terry Alderman, Craig McDermott and, later on, Shane Warne won deserved comparison with the great Australian bowlers of the past, helped by Merv Hughes, Tim May, Steve Waugh, Geoff Lawson, Bruce Reid, Tony Dodemaide and Greg Matthews, all of whom made important contributions.

Border's value to the team was not restricted to his batting and captaincy. He was a superb fieldsman, catching and throwing to end threatening stands, saving runs and uplifting team-mates with his marvellous reflexes. He took over Australia's captaincy at a time of increased media pressure and handled hundreds of interviews at all hours of the day. All the top-order batsmen shared in Australia's success in 1989. The team lacked bowling resources such as Bradman enjoyed in 1948 but Terry Alderman prevented that hurting, thanks to shrewd, innovative Border field placements.

Alderman's 41 Test wickets at a cost of only 17.36 runs each were taken against a technically unsound English batting line-up that probed and fidgeted with angled bats against the swing. Only Allan Lamb with 125 in the First Test, David Gower with 106 in the Second Test, and Robin Smith with 143 in the Fourth Test and 101 in the Fifth held up Australia's inexorable move towards a series triumph. Alderman took 19 of his wickets lbw, while Merv Hughes's 19 Test wickets cost 32.36 apiece and his big heart only barely compensated for his lack of deviation. Alderman took most wickets on the tour with 70 at 15.64, followed by Geoff Lawson with 69 at 20.97, including 29 Test wickets at 27.27.

Trevor Hohns looked a valuable member of the Test side and it was easy to understand why he had been such a useful player in the two rebel tours of South Africa in 1985 and 1986. He was very smart in the field, bowled several spells of cleverly mixed leg-breaks and googlies, with some classy batsmen among his 11 Test victims, and proved a stumbling block for England's bowlers with his left-handed batting.

The find of the 1989 tour, Mark Anthony Taylor – born at Leeton, NSW, on 27 October 1964, and built like his bulky bank officer father – spent his early years in Wagga where he developed skill as an Australian Rules footballer. He showed outstanding form as a left-handed batsman in the Lindfield Shires competition in Sydney while he was at Chatswood Boys High School, and at 15 State selector Neil Marks persuaded him to join the Northern

Team-mates congratulate Steve Waugh after he had K.J. Barnett caught behind in the Third Test at Edgbaston, in one of his few appearances at the bowling crease on Australia's 1989 English tour. (Patrick Eagar)

Districts club. Taylor played rugby league at the University of New South Wales and represented Combined Universities in Brisbane as a full-back. He plays golf and writes right-handed, though.

Taylor proved temperamentally ideal for the testing opening batsman role, allowing Boon to bat at number 3. Taylor was always a great cutter, but as his confidence grew became more positive hooking and pulling and more selective in his driving. His slips fielding was impressive, his judgement of a run faultless, never more so than when he and Geoff Marsh batted all day in the Fifth Test at Trent Bridge to finish unbeaten on 301. Next day they went on to 329, the highest Australian opening stand against England.

Taylor made his debut for New South Wales in 1985–86 and began his Test career in 1988–89, a wonderful season in which he scored 1241 runs at an average of 49.64, with three centuries and a top score of 159. He opened for Australia with Geoff Marsh in the Fourth and Fifth Tests against the West Indies, contributing 36 in an opening stand of 98 with Marsh in the Fifth Test before he was run out. His consistency earned him the trip to England in 1989 and from then on he was the instigator of most of Australia's big totals.

On his first English tour he established himself as one of the world's best left-handed batsmen and one of Australia's finest openers. His 839 runs in six Tests has only been exceeded by Bradman and Hammond, and in the Trent Bridge Test, after Marsh went for 138, Taylor continued to 219, and Australia to 602 for 6 declared.

But even Taylor's Test average of 83.90 took second place on that tour to Steve Waugh's 126.50. Steven Rodger Waugh, born in the Sydney suburb of Canterbury on 2 June 1965, was rushed into Tests one season after his debut for New South Wales, unlike his twin brother, Mark Edward Waugh, who had to wait until he played 100 first-class games before he was chosen for Australia v. England in 1990–91. Steve always batted with a touch of class, but did not confirm his Test status until that 1989 English tour, when thousands of English cricket buffs savoured his driving and cutting, that was remindful of Stan McCabe in the 1930s.

Dean Jones, who made a thrilling 122 in the Sixth Test at Lord's, also captured spectators' adulation with electrifying running between wickets and established a big reputation in limited-over cricket with his habit of rushing the scoring along. All the top-order batsmen shared in Australia's 4–0 series win, which made Border's

Australians the first since Woodfull's 1934 team to regain the Ashes in England.

The euphoria of the 1989 English tour, which ended with ticker-tape parades through Sydney and Melbourne, carried on into seasons crammed with international cricket. Australia made a five-match trip to India in October 1989, to compete in the Nehru Cup, a limited-over event. They returned to host visits by New Zealand, Sri Lanka and Pakistan. Perth saw the most absorbing match of the summer against New Zealand, when David Boon's 200 and Dean Jones's 99 – lbw to Danny Morrison – made Australia safe from defeat on 9 declared for 521. New Zealand followed-on after scoring 231 but were rescued by a grand innings from Mark Greatbatch, who batted almost 11 hours for 146, a rebuff for Australian bowlers who had humbled England a few months earlier.

The Sri Lankans played 27 matches on a tour which lasted three months. They drew the First Test in Brisbane after leading by 51 runs on the first innings, Tom Moody (106), Mark Taylor (164) and Avarinda de Silva (167) scoring centuries. The Second Test at Bellerive Oval was the first ever held in Tasmania on a ground the Tasmanian Cricket Council spent $1.7 million developing. Australia won by 173 runs after Tasmanian Greg Campbell, bothered by a shoulder injury in England in 1989, delighted locals by opening the bowling with Alderman. Sri Lankan captain Ranatunga complained of racial abuse in this Test but the Australians said the words he complained about were just ordinary cricket banter.

Pakistan's chance to show Australians the skills that had become the talk of the cricket world was badly handicapped when match-winning spinner Abdul Qadir opted to return home before the First Test at the MCG. Qadir said he had a damaged finger but team-mates blamed his departure on his dislike of hard, fast Australian pitches. Mushtaq Ahmed was flown out to replace Qadir in a team comprising Imran Khan (Captain), Javed Miandad, Wasim Akram, Ijaz Ahmed, Saleem Yousuf, Saeed Anwar, Shoaib Mohammad, Tauseef Ahmed, Aamer Malik, Waqar Younis, Nadeem Ghauri, Rameez Raja and Aaqib Javed.

Wasim Akram gave a spectacular demonstration of his all-round talents in the first two Tests and won the Man-of-the-Series award despite Mark Taylor's splendid batting. Wasim took 6 for 62 in the First Test at Brisbane to restrict Australia to 223. That proved enough to give Australia a 116-run lead, however, with none of the Pakistanis scoring 20. Mark Taylor then put Australia in a winning position with 101. Ijaz Ahmed batted for seven and a half hours to try and save the match but when he was out to a magnificent catch by Geoff Marsh, Pakistan collapsed and Australia won by 92 runs.

Don Bradman, looking in superb health at 82, opened the stand named after him before the Second Test in Adelaide, where Pakistan were saved from a defeat by a sixth-wicket stand of 191 by Imran Khan and Wasim Akram in the second innings. Wasim had made 52 to lift Pakistan to 257 in their first innings, and then took five Australian wickets. Javed Miandad stayed for three hours before Imran, 136, and Wasim, 123, came together. Wasim hit 18 fours and a six in his initial Test century. Time ran out before a result could be achieved but not before Dean Jones (116 and 121 not out) became the first Australian to score centuries in each innings of an Adelaide Test since A.R. Morris in 1946–47.

The Pakistanis were all fired up for the Third Test in Sydney by a curious incident in the previous match against Victoria. Umpire Robin Bailhache instructed the acting Pakistan captain, Rameez Raja, to take Mushtaq Ahmad out of the attack for continually running down the pitch after delivering the ball. Bailhache had previously given Mushtaq several warnings to stop this habit. The Pakistani players refused to accept Bailhache's instructions and were supported by their manager, Intikhab Alam, who came on to the field and led his players off. After dressing-room discussions Ahmed was allowed to continue bowling, but the Pakistanis were clearly upset when they lost by 59 runs.

The Sydney Test, in the event, was rained off, but not before Mark Taylor (101 not out) scored his sixth century for Australia in nine months. This gave Taylor the Bradman-like average of 97.50 for the three-Test series. Wasim's 17 wickets in the three games cost only 18.70 apiece.

The following month Australia sent a full-strength team to New Zealand to play in a three-way limited-over competition with India and New Zealand, followed by a single Test at Wellington. The Australians carried off a major share of the limited-over prizemoney, largely because of Dean Jones, who won three Man-of-the-Match awards. Australia were unbeaten in this series, beating India twice and New Zealand three times, with Jones turning singles into twos and outfield hits into threes, making six runs an over easy.

Caught on a sodden Test pitch at Wellington on which Border

batted after winning the toss, on the expectation that it would not improve, Australia were bundled out for 110 in the first innings. On such a pitch they were no match for the wiles of Richard Hadlee who seamed every ball about. New Zealand replied with 202 before John Bracewell turned in a match-winning 6 for 65, turning his off-spinners sharply on the drying pitch. New Zealand captain John Wright then put a home win beyond doubt with a savage attack on Peter Taylor, who carried Australia's hopes. Wright hit 17 fours and a six, his second 50 off only 74 balls, finishing on 117 not out, with his team winning by nine wickets.

Four days later Peter Taylor lost his place in the New South Wales team for the Sheffield Shield final against Queensland in Sydney, selectors preferring leg-spinner Adrian Tucker. Geoff Lawson dropped out on the morning of the match and Mark Taylor took over the New South Wales captaincy ahead of Steve Waugh, the popular favourite for Border's job when Border surrendered the Test captaincy. The final was all over by stumps on the second day when Queensland, chasing 360, were 8 for 91. Centuries in both innings by Mark Taylor (107 and 100) increased Queensland's woes and they eventually were thrashed by 345 runs.

Australia did not play to their potential in the 1990–91 series against the 37th England team, captained by Graham Gooch, but the Englishmen were so disappointing they did not have to do so. Australia won three of the five Tests and had the better of the two that were drawn. The Australian batting was dogged without showing brilliance, with Border, Boon, Marsh, Healy and Greg Matthews all hanging in to build innings totals. The Australian bowling, that had lost penetration after the 1989 tour of England, gained a more impressive look when Craig McDermott and Bruce Reid returned to their best after injury. Reid's lift and awkward bounce unsettled all the Englishmen and McDermott's pace and late swing were well rewarded.

Gooch's team was G.A. Gooch (Captain), D.I. Gower, A.J. Lamb, W. Larkins, R.A. Smith, A.J. Stewart, R.C. Russell, C.C. Lewis, G.C. Small, E.E. Hemmings, M.P. Bicknell, A.R.C. Fraser, M.A. Atherton, D.E. Malcolm, J.E. Morris, and P.C.R. Tufnell. P.A.J. DeFreitas and P.J. Newport were used to relieve a heavy injury toll, with England's need for a quality all-rounder to replace Ian Botham more obvious as the tour progressed. Gooch was unable to play for a long period because of a finger infection and when

One of the most successful Australian batsmen in the early 1990s, Tom Moody. Despite a succession of brilliant innings in English county cricket he found Test selection difficult to secure. (Sunday Times, Perth)

he returned for the Second Test Australia succeeded in an all-out effort to contain him. He played some lovely strokes but winning matches while leading such a spiritless side proved beyond him.

Australia's main problem was to find places for Tom Moody and Mark Waugh, who had shown their value with a string of centuries in English county cricket. England could not sustain the initiative they held briefly in all five Tests. England collapses became a regular part of the series, and they won only one of their 11 first-class matches on the tour.

The revival by Bruce Reid, the 203 cm (6 ft 8 in) Perth fast bowler, and McDermott, the lion-hearted Queensland red-head, was timely in a series in which Mark Taylor, Dean Jones and Steve Waugh, all striking successes in England in 1989, managed only 458 runs between them in 21 innings. Waugh was dropped in favour of his brother Mark for the Fourth Test in Adelaide, with Steve breaking the news to his twin at their parents' home. When Steve congratulated Mark on being chosen, Mark said: 'Whose place am I taking?' and Steve said, 'Mine'. Few doubted that Steve would be back after his unbroken run of 42 Tests.

Australia won the First Test by ten wickets after Reid's bounce and Alderman's swing converted England's second innings into a procession. England were all out for 114. By then 30 wickets had fallen in 14 hours play, but Taylor and Marsh made nonsense of the notion that there were major problems with the pitch by scoring the 157 needed to win before stumps on the third day. Reid did the damage in the Second Test at Melbourne by taking 6 for 97 and 7 for 51, to set up Australia's comfortable eight-wicket victory, England wasting a lovely century by Gower. At Sydney in the drawn Third Test Gower hit another century (123) and shared a 139-run stand with Mike Atherton (105).

Mark Waugh, by four minutes the younger of the 25-year-old twins, produced a majestic 138 on his debut in the Fourth Test at Adelaide. Set to make 472 to win, England reached 203 in the final innings before Reid dismissed Gooch (117) and Atherton (87) and the match fizzled out with England defending on 5 for 335. McDermott's eleven wickets (8 for 79 and 3 for 60) allowed Australia to reassert herself and win the Fifth Test at Perth by nine wickets to take the rubber three-nil.

Strengthened by the inclusion of regal shotmaker Mark Waugh, Australia toured the West Indies between February and May 1991, confident of a series win over the virtual world champions. The tour proved a major disappointment with the West Indies indulging in their usual time-wasting, slow overs, and bouncing whatever they could get away with at the batsmen's body. Rain spoiled two Tests and virtually converted the series into a three-Test contest, but for once Packer's Channel Nine cameras took Australian cricket buffs overseas. What magnificent pictures they sent back!

Here were Caribbean cricket celebrants hanging from high trees, men playing saxophones and trumpets in the crowds while women sashayed in any available space, eccentrics who changed their suits five times a day and after each change reclaimed a front-row seat. Steel bands belted away amid groups who offered a few samba steps when an Australian wicket fell. One character swung out over the field behind a piano strung up on grandstand ropes. Packed galleries who put up half their month's pay to get in for a day made every session into a party.

The series deteriorated into a succession of fiery, niggling duels, with verbal altercations in mid-pitch highlighted by the cameras. Umpires warned Courtney Walsh for intimidatory bowling in the match against Jamaica just before the First Test when Walsh hit Mark Waugh on the ear and forced his temporary retirement, dismissed Healy with a steepling bouncer, and inflicted a cut above McDermott's right eye that required nine stitches. Waugh returned to make 108 and Australia won the game easily. The West Indians' lack of sympathy for the wounded and the gleeful reaction of spectators as McDermott was led away accounted for all the abusive language that accompanied every match from then on. The tour ended with administrators from both countries at loggerheads, each blaming the other for the acrimony.

There was courage from both teams, but Australia were simply outgunned in cricket liberally sprinkled with bouncers. The West Indian battery of Patterson, Ambrose, Marshall and Walsh were superior to an Australian attack handicapped by the absence of Bruce Reid, whose heavily metalled back brought pain that restricted him to two Tests. McDermott was left to match the opposition fusillade on his own, with big Merv Hughes lacking the accuracy to consistently trouble batsmen of the quality of Richie Richardson, Desmond Haynes, Gordon Greenidge, Vivian Richards, Gus Logie and Jeffrey Dujon. Alderman was picked for only one Test and one wondered why he had been taken to the Caribbean at all.

The Australian team was A.R. Border (Captain), G.R. Marsh, M.A. Taylor, D.C. Boon, M.E. Waugh, S.R. Waugh, M.R.J. Veletta,

Mark Waugh waves to fans in the stands after reaching a century on the first day of his first Test in 1991 v. England in Adelaide.
(Patrick Eagar)

P.L. Taylor, M.G. Hughes, M.R. Whitney, T.M. Alderman, C.J. McDermott, G.R.J. Matthews, I.A. Healy, D.M. Jones, and B.A. Reid, with coach Bob Simpson to attend to team drills, net practice, discipline and rule disputes – roles that kept him extremely busy and by the end of the tour drew a taunt from West Indian captain Vivian Richards: 'I'm not a great admirer of Bob Simpson,' said Richards. 'I've lost respect for him after seeing the way he operates.'

Richards' players showed exceptional spirit in recovering from dangerous positions in the Tests after losing a limited-over series at home for the first time, Australia winning 4–1. Haynes (damaged left toe), Greenidge (right collarbone) and Logie (cut right eye) all needed medical treatment and x-rays. After taking a blow in the face while hooking, Logie lifted the West Indies from 6 for 75 with a brave knock of 77 not out in the First Test at Kingston, but rain on the fourth and fifth days prevented a result. Boon was hit flush on the jaw by a Patrick Patterson bouncer but refused even to rub it, strutting off unbeaten on 109, his tenth Test century.

Dazzling hundreds full of fine shots, by Haynes (111) and Richardson (182), who together put on 297 for the second wicket set the West Indies on the path to a ten-wicket win in the Second Test at Georgetown, Guyana. By the Third Test at Queen's Park Oval, Port-of-Spain, Trinidad, it was clear the West Indian pace bowlers also had the ability to score vital runs while depriving Australia's tail of the same luxury. Dujon and Ambrose shared a stand of 87 before rain brought the draw.

Australia wilted badly in their first innings of the Fourth Test at Bridgetown, Barbados, after taking a winning position by dismissing the West Indies for 149. All ten wickets fell to the pace men in Australia's sad reply of 134. This West Indian recovery set the stage for a magnificent innings of 226 from Gordon Greenidge that swung the entire rubber. In danger of losing his Test berth at the end of a distinguished career, Greenidge batted like a millionaire for 11 hours 26 minutes, striking drives and cuts that live in memory. His fourth double century in Tests was also the highest score ever by a West Indian against Australia. Faced with batting for 153 overs or scoring 552 to save the match, Australia surrendered for 208, the last six wickets falling for 18 runs to superlative fast bowling.

Amid all the niggling, time-wasting, swearing and body-bruising, Desmond Haynes took it upon himself to break all the rules by coaching the umpires. Haynes got his comeuppance when Merv

Hughes accidentally ran him out in the Fifth Test at St John's, Antigua. The ball ricocheted off Hughes's hand as he tried to field a Greenidge drive and hit the stumps at the bowler's end with Haynes out of his ground. Hughes taunted Haynes, whose reply was both colourful and vehement. 'On the first day of the series Haynes retired hurt with a damaged toe; on the last day he withdrew with a damaged reputation,' wrote Mike Coward in his book *Caribbean Odyssey*. Mark Waugh's 139, including a breezy, entertaining fifth-wicket stand with Dean Jones (81) gave Australia victory by 157 runs. This was the West Indies' first defeat on the ground and Australia's first win in the Caribbean since 1978.

At the presentation ceremony at the end of this match series the West Indian Board president Sir Clyde Walcott regretted the soured relations between the countries and the absence of the Frank Worrell Trophy, which could not be found. In fact, the trophy had been lost since the 1984–85 West Indies tour of Australia. Sir Clyde chastised both teams for the manner in which they had played the series. Commentators added that it was appropriate that a trophy named after a staunch advocate of sportsmanship and fair play should not be on view after such a miserable series.

By the time Australia played India at home in a five-Test series in 1991–92 the International Cricket Council had moved to prevent such obnoxious player behaviour by introducing international referees for all Tests, and establishing a players' Code of Conduct. The Indian team for their first full tour since 1977–78 was M. Azharuddin (Captain), R.J. Shastri, S.R. Tendulkar, K.S. More, M.M. Prabhakar, S.V. Manjrekar, N.S. Sidhur, Kapil Dev, D.B. Vengsarkar, K. Srikkanth, J. Srinath, S. L. Venkatapathy Raju, C.S. Pandit and S.T. Banerjee. The five Tests the team played were historic as the first to be played under the international Code of Conduct, which compelled each side to bowl 90 overs in a day or risk fines, the first to restrict bowlers to two bouncers an over, and the first controlled by neutral referees. A fortnight before the Indian tour began Greg Matthews was fined $500 for disputing an umpire's decision in a Western Australia v. New South Wales Shield match in Perth.

Former England captain Mike Smith's presence as the neutral referee nominated by the ICC cost the Australian Board around $60,000, but players' conduct had become so bad all members of the ICC agreed to pay similar bills to bring in superior discipline. Australian Test batsman Peter Burge was appointed to the panel

Big Merv Hughes, the pie-eating crowd-pleaser from the Victorian country town of Euroa, presents a frightening view for batsmen as he lets go another bomb, moustache flaring. (Herald & Weekly Times)

Sachin Tendulkar, who at 18 years 256 days became the youngest player ever to score a Test century in Australia. (John Fairfax & Sons)

of international referees, with the England v. New Zealand series in England his first assignment.

The referees had the power to impose heavy fines for infringements on the spirit of the game, particularly abuse of umpires who retained all decisions on the field. Most Australian critics said the appointment was long overdue and praised the ICC for showing some authority at last. Neither referee in the India–Australia series – Peter May and Mike Smith – reported a player for misbehaviour, but Indian dissatisfaction with the disparity of lbw decisions in Australia's favour could have been justified. 'There must have been changes in the lbw law we don't know about', said Abbas Ali Baig, the Indian manager, and television replays showed he may have been entitled to complain.

An eventful, emotional Test series produced intense discussion over umpires' mistakes, with Australia's 4–0 margin tarnished by several of the 14 lbw decisions in their favour. Ian Healy became the fourth Australian wicket-keeper to complete 100 Test dismissals (after Rod Marsh, Wally Grout and Bert Oldfield), Bruce Reid took his 100th Test wicket, Sachin Tendulkar at 18 years 256 days became the youngest Test century maker in Australia, Kapil Dev followed Richard Hadlee as the second bowler to take 400 Test wickets, and by taking 31 wickets Craig McDermott beat the Australian record of 29 wickets in a rubber against India, held jointly by Richie Benaud and Alan Davidson.

Australia won the First Test at Brisbane by ten wickets, McDermott taking nine wickets and Hughes seven, against batsmen demoralised in the previous game against New South Wales by Whitney (9 for 82), Holdsworth (5 for 61). Bruce Reid replaced Whitney in the Second Test in Melbourne and with six wickets in each innings (12 for 126) took Australia to a second win inside four days. A virtually unknown leg-spinner named Shane Warne made his debut in the Third Test in Sydney, but his 45 overs produced only Shastri's wicket for 150 runs after Shastri carted him all over the SCG on his way to 206. Loss of overs to bad light and rain cost India any chance of a win after batting and bowling better than Australia and dramatically improving their fielding.

Eight Indian batsmen departed lbw in the Fourth Test at Adelaide, but only two of their appeals against Australians were upheld, with 21 wickets falling in the first two days. David Boon stopped the rot with 135 run out, sharing a 221-run stand with Mark Taylor (100). This proved the difference, with India, requiring

372 to win, falling 38 short. India only got so close through dropped catches and a splendid 106 from Azharuddin. Tom Moody made a triumphant return to Tests with innings of 50 and 101 in the Fifth Test at Perth, where Boon got his third century of the series and Whitney had his career-best 7 for 27, most of them taken in the slips cordon.

Unhappily, the Perth game saw the end of Geoff Marsh's Test career, selectors preferring specialist opener Wayne Phillips, long-time Victorian Shield batsman. Border openly expressed his disgust over the omission of Marsh, who for six years had taken all that the world's fastest bowlers thundered down at him and had been an integral part of Australia's revival, figuring in some memorable opening stands with Boon and Taylor. Marsh often anchored Australia's innings while shotmakers attacked. His replacement, Phillips, making his debut with Paul Reiffel, was a balding, grinding force in Victoria's batting, but managed only 22 runs in two Test knocks. All chance of Marsh continuing in the Test XI disappeared, though, with the emergence over the next few seasons of gifted Academy graduates Michael Slater, Matthew Hayden, Justin Langer, Greg Blewett, Damien Martyn, Michael Bevan, Michael Divenuto and Ricky Ponting.

Ravi Shastri during the big hitting innings in which he threatened to knock Shane Warne out of big cricket before he began his remarkable career. (News Limited)

The fifth World Cup in 1992 produced a further sprinkling of umpires' blunders for television to analyse, and exposed the farcical rules that apply in abbreviated cricket when rain interrupts play. English newspapers blamed the umpiring errors on Australians, blissfully ignorant of the use of umpires from all nine competing nations. South Africa were shamefully dismissed from the Cup when umpires refused to let her have a crack at scoring 22 off 13 balls in the semi-finals. The players went off for rain but when it eased organisers refused the brief extension of time required for the 13 deliveries and instead announced that South Africa needed 22 runs off seven balls to win as one over had been lost. Amid chaos, officials conferred and revised this ruling, subtracting another over from the equation, and giving South Africa a target of 22 runs from one ball. The match ended with winners, England, being booed, and the losers doing a lap of honour!

Overall it was a mesmerising month of hectic travelling, close finishes and some brilliant cricket, much of it in unexpected places, from the 126 competing players, with snarls, vulgar hand signs, and baseball slides into floodlit boundaries, culminating in a dramatic 22-run win by Pakistan in the final. Melbourne's new Southern

Former chief executive of the Australian Cricket Board, David Richards, who took over as the ICC's first permanent chief administrator in 1993. (Age, Melbourne)

Stand, which cost $144 million and seats 30,000 (more than the entire population of Richie Richardson's birthplace, Antigua), a memorable sight at sundown, was full for the first time. The crowd of 87,182 paid $2 million to be present, while an estimated one billion people watched it in 29 countries on television. Many of these first-time viewers must have been captivated by the use of miniature cameras inside the stumps which conveyed wicket-keepers' encouragement of their bowlers, but, by careful adjustment, none of the blasphemy. Australia lost four of her eight matches and did not deserve a semi-final berth.

The 100th staging of the Sheffield Shield competition in 1992–93 ended with New South Wales again the winners. They had won the Shield 41 times, Victoria 25, Western Australia 13, South Australia 12. Queensland had made 61 attempts to win the Shield without a win, Tasmania 15 attempts. Earlier, in the ninety-ninth Shield competition, Victoria revived to take the trophy after finishing last the previous season, thanks to dynamic leadership from Simon O'Donnell, fully recovered from the cancer which had upset his international career in 1987. He offended Victorian officials early in the summer by labelling their administration inept, but returned to favour when he led Victoria to win the Shield final over hot favourites New South Wales.

Queensland's continued failure to win the Shield had become frequent fare for comedians, and the source of debates among cricket buffs through the Queensland Cricket Association's policy of importing famous players to help her to her first win. It failed to work in 1987–88 with Ian Botham and again in 1990–91 with Graeme Hick.

By the mid-1990s most States based their hopes for Shield points on Academy old boys because their Test players were too heavily committed to the busy international programme to make regular contributions. Rodney Marsh said that intensive coaching from experts like Terry Jenner, Ashley Mallett, Ian Healy, Dennis Lillee and the Chappell brothers advanced Academy students' careers by two or three years, and by the end of the century Marsh believed Australian teams will be dominated by Academy products.

To increase the crowd appeal of Shield cricket, the ACB introduced penalties for teams that failed to bowl 16 overs in an hour. They also doubled the penalty for bowling no-balls, which meant scoring eight runs from a single delivery was possible, and initiated appointment of three umpires for Shield matches, to allow one to take an occasional rest and lessen the strain that brings poor decisions.

The West Indies toured Australia in 1992–93 with a new captain, Richie Richardson, who was on his first full series, and without champions like Vivian Richards, Gordon Greenidge, wicket-keeper–batsman Jeffrey Dujon and their highest wicket-taker Malcolm Marshall, who had all retired. Australia were narrowly denied victory in the First Test at Brisbane when umpires incurred the wrath of Australian captain Border by refusing several lbw appeals. The West Indies were 8 for 133, chasing 231 to win when play ended. Match referee Raman Subba Row fined Border $2000 and Merv Hughes $400 for dissent. Australia then won the Second Test at Melbourne by 139 runs when Shane Warne, in his fifth Test, took 7 for 52 in the final innings. In the Third Test at Sydney, Border (74) passed 10,000 Test runs, and Australia ran up a score of 503 for 9 wickets declared.

Australia appeared to have established a clear-cut ascendancy, with a series win in sight and the end of the West Indies run as world's number one. Then a remarkable innings of 277 by 21-year-old Brian Lara completely changed the match and the series. Lara hit 38 fours off 372 balls in seven hours 54 minutes and gave only one chance, a low catch to Steve Waugh in the gully at 172. The West Indies forced a draw and thereafter won every match on their itinerary, including the final two Tests and four limited-over matches. They levelled the rubber with a one-run win in Adelaide, Test cricket's lowest margin, and overwhelmed Australia in the Fifth Test in Perth to take the series 2–1.

Lara rescued the series for the West Indies with his unforgettable innings, but from then on the irresistible bowling of big Curtly Ambrose dominated proceedings. He sent back Australia's two most reliable batsmen, David Boon and Allan Border, for a single run when Australia wanted 186 to win in Adelaide and at Perth settled the series with a spell of 7 for 1 off 32 balls after lunch on the first day. His 33 wickets equalled the record for a West Indies v. Australia rubber, jointly held by Clarrie Grimmett and Alan Davidson, and his 19 wickets in the last two Tests cost less than 11 runs each. This was Australia's eighth successive defeat in a series against the West Indies and the seventh in which Border played.

The West Indian team was R.B. Richardson (Captain), D.L. Haynes, B.C. Lara, K.L.T. Arthurton, J.C. Adams, P.V. Simmons,

J.R. Murray, C.L. Hooper, I.R. Bishop, C.E.L. Ambrose, C.A. Walsh, D. Williams, K.C.G. Benjamin, A.C. Cummins, B.P. Patterson and A.L. Logie. The acrimony that had marred the previous series between the teams was missing and relations remained amicable despite the tensions of a hard-fought series in which Australia's hopes were shattered once again by the breakdown of Bruce Reid after the First Test. Merv Hughes did not falter and his 20 wickets at 21.60 were a fitting reward for a brave effort.

The series showed that Shane Warne, a blond from East Sandringham Juniors, sporting a gold bracelet and earstud, was learning fast. He had come into Test cricket the previous summer against India when Trevor Hohns could not be enticed to rejoin the Test XI. Ravi Shastri had given Warne a belting in Sydney, but shortly after Warne helped win a Test against Sri Lanka in Colombo at a crucial stage when Sri Lanka appeared likely to win. His 7 for 52 in Melbourne against the West Indies sent him off to New Zealand in the Australian team with growing confidence. His 17 wickets in the three Tests of a drawn series (one win apiece) drew high praise from New Zealand captain Martin Crowe, who described Warne as the best leg-spinner in the world and predicted an outstanding English tour for Warne later that year.

New Zealand captain Martin Crowe, whose high rating of Shane Warne's bowling was ignored by English critics. (Patrick Eagar)

Crowe's forecast was scoffed at by English cricket fans, many of whom had never seen a class leg-spinner, but it turned out to be almost an understatement when Border let Warne loose. Border told him to bowl mainly leg breaks and withhold all his tricks before the Tests and from the moment he clean bowled Mike Gatting with a spectacular first ball in the First Test at Old Trafford Warne became the star of the tour. His bowling enthralled spectators and created a world-wide revival in leg-spin bowling. He took 75 wickets on the tour at 22.64, 34 of them in the six Tests, and his overs cost only two runs each.

Australia's team for this 32nd tour of England was A.R. Border (Captain), I.A. Healy, D.C. Boon, M.E. Waugh, D.R. Martyn, S.R. Waugh, M.L. Hayden, M.J. Slater, M.A. Taylor, M.G. Hughes, B.P. Julien, P.R. Reiffel, S.K. Warne, T.J. Zoehrer, C.J. McDermott, T.B.A. May and W.J. Holdsworth. The team scored 32 centuries and had 10 scored against them. They won the Test series 4–1, won the one-day internationals by three matches to nil and had only two losses in their 21 matches.

This English tour enhanced the reputations of several Australians and introduced a marvellous new talent in opening batsman Michael

Jonathon Slater, born in Wagga Wagga on 21 February 1970. He played only two games in 1991–92, his first-class debut season, but in 1992–93 forced his way into the touring team through sheer weight of runs, scoring 1019 for New South Wales at 59.94 with three centuries. In England tour selectors preferred Matthew Hayden as Mark Taylor's partner for the early one-day games but Slater won selection for the First Test with some outstanding knocks.

He proved one of the most exciting stroke makers in cricket with a breezy first wicket stand of 128 with Taylor, who went on to 124. This helped Australia to a first innings lead of 79 and allowed them to take control of the match in the second innings through a 180-run stand by Steve Waugh (78 not out) and Ian Healy (102 not out). Healy's century was his first in Tests and his first in first-class matches. Australia won by 170 runs after Gooch was out handled the ball for 133.

The Second Test at Lord's produced a 260-run opening stand by Taylor (111) and Slater (152), Boon (164 not out) rushing the score on to 4 for 632 before Border declared. Robin Smith became the first batsman in Ashes history to be given out by the third umpire after television replays in this match. Warne took four wickets in each innings as England crumpled for 205 and 365 to give Australia victory by an innings and 62 runs.

Slater followed with a century before lunch (111) against Combined Universities at Oxford. The Third Test at Trent Bridge was drawn but the Fourth Test at Headingley produced another massive Australian win after Slater and Taylor had begun with a stand of 86. Slater was out for 67 setting an example in aggressive shot-play which Boon (107), Border (200 not out) and Steve Waugh (157 not out) carried on until Australia declared at 4 for 653, including an unbeaten 332-run stand by Border and Waugh. England were out for 200 and 305, Australia winning by an innings and 148 runs. Reiffel took eight wickets in the match and May 4 for 65 in England's second innings.

With the Ashes won, Australia continued her domination in the Fifth Test at Edgbaston, Mark Waugh scoring a stylish 137, sharing a brisk 153-run stand with his brother Steve (59), Reiffel taking 6 for 71 in England's first innings, May 5 for 89 and Warne 5 for 82 in the second. The talking point of a match Australia won by eight wickets was the leg-break with which Warne bowled Gooch for 48 in his second knock. The ball pitched in footmarks outside the leg stump and spun right round Gooch's outstretched leg.

Devon Malcolm broke through the Australian top-order batting in each innings of the Sixth Test at the Oval and Angus Fraser cut through the middle order for England to secure a surprise victory by 161 runs. A draw seemed certain until Australia's batting collapsed on the final day. This was Mike Atherton's first success as England's captain following Gooch's resignation after the Fourth Test. Australia's Ashes triumph was not greeted at home with the euphoria that had accompanied the team's 1989 victories and it was generally agreed the team was not as well balanced, with McDermott out of form and forced to fly home early through illness.

Boon led Australia's batting averages with 1437 runs at 75.83, including nine centuries. Mark Waugh (1361 at 71.63), Matthew Hayden (1150 at 57.50) and Michael Slater (1275 at 52.73) all scored more than 1000 runs on a tour which saw Healy stress his value with 499 runs at 38.38 and 53 dismissals (42 catches, 11 stumpings). Healy's combination with Warne, the sensation of the tour, earned him comparisons with the great Australian 'keepers Oldfield, Tallon and Grout.

The Australians returned for a three-Test series against New Zealand with the opening partnership between Slater and Taylor well established. They put on 198 in the drawn First Test in Perth, Slater falling at 98 and Taylor going on to 142. They scored 65 in the Second Test at Hobart before Taylor left for 27 and this time Slater went on to 168. Boon (106) and Mark Waugh (111) also scored centuriees before Border declared at 6 for 544. On a pitch that did not unduly help spinners, May (5 for 65 and 2 for 45) and Warne (3 for 36 and 6 for 31) then bowled Australia to one of her biggest wins over New Zealand, by an innings and 222 runs.

Warne's meteoric rise continued in this series, his confidence high after the great success in England, and he finished with 18 wickets from the three Tests, seldom bowling a loose ball. His range of deliveries confounded batsmen facing sharp spin for the first time. Backed by a ring of brilliant close-in fieldsmen and a menacing 'keeper in Healy, he provided a wonderful spectacle as he helped himself to eight more wickets in the Third Test at Brisbane. This time Australia's winning margin was an innings and 96 runs. Border (105) and Steve Waugh (147) batted splendidly but it was the new glamour boy Shane Keith Warne, whom team-mates called 'Hollywood', who aroused applause with his 74 not out.

CHAPTER THIRTY-THREE

THE WARNE PHENOMENON

Three weeks after the New Zealand rubber ended in December, 1993, Australia began a six-Test programme against South Africa. Six Test wins during 1993 had erased the memory of Australia's collapses against the West Indies and in one Test against England, and created an inflated rating of the Australian side which the South Africans soon corrected. Australia were certainly a powerful unit at their best, but prone to bouts of the vapours in a crisis. The Springboks took two Tests to expose it.

Rain restricted the First Test in Melbourne to just under 16 hours' play and eliminated any chance of a result before most Australians realised Kepler Wessels's team were dangerous, highly motivated opponents fired by an eagerness to celebrate their return after 30 years' absence from Australia. The team was K.C. Wessels (Captain), W.J. Cronje, B.M. McMillan, J.N. Rhodes, D.J. Callaghan, E.L.R. Stewart, P.L. Symcox, R.P. Snell, D.B. Rundle, C.R. Matthews, A.A. Donald, P.S. de Villiers, D.J. Cullinan and D.J. Richardson. The half-brothers Gary and Peter Kirsten were flown in as replacements when injuries inhibited the team.

South Africa were 1 for 91 on the first day of the Second Test before Warne wove his magic again to take 7 for 56, three of them with 'flippers', the googly that gains pace off the pitch. Chasing a paltry 169, Australia were confined to a 123-run lead by lack of aggression against tidy, but never hostile bowling. Warne took another five wickets in South Africa's second innings to leave Australia with 117 to win.

At 1 for 51, Australia appeared set for an easy victory, but Fanie de Villiers took four wickets, three in five balls, to have Australia at 4 for 63 at the start of the last day. Here Australia's nerve failed.

Steve Waugh shows elation after taking a wicket in the Third Test at Edgbaston in 1993. He seems to reserve his best for English spectators. (Philip Brown)

Batsmen bereft of strokes prodded apprehensively at splendid bowling by de Villiers and Donald. Damien Martyn managed only six singles from 59 balls. Cronje ran out Warne to increase the pressure on Australia, and only a bold 29 not out from McDermott took the score past 100. South Africa won by five runs. There were eight maidens in de Villiers's 23.3 overs and he emerged South Africa's hero with 6 for 43.

Wessels had to fly home with a badly broken finger immediately after this historic South African triumph. Hansie Cronje took over the South African captaincy and immediately showed there was no lack of resolve in his team, with a spirited revival in the seven limited-over games before the Third Test. South Africa won the first of the three one-day finals, Australia the last two, with Allan Border bowling the last over in his last appearance as Australian captain on the SCG.

Steve Waugh, who had been replaced by Martyn in the First and Second Tests, returned from injury for the Third Test with an innings of 164 full of flashing cuts and drives. Border (84) helped him put on 208 for the fifth wicket. Steve Waugh then took 4 for 26 to underline his all-round value and give Australia a first innings lead of 196. After narrowly avoiding the follow-on South Africa were set 321 to win but McDermott and Warne finished them off with four wickets each. This took the teams to South Africa for the second half of their programme with a win apiece.

Steve Waugh's rebuff to selectors who had had the temerity to drop him continued in a tense, eventful tour in which Australia had to come from behind in both the Tests and limited-over matches. Steve headed both the batting and bowling averages. Matthew Hayden, given a Test chance when Mark Taylor became ill, failed in both innings, and the flood of runs that had been a feature of Hayden's Sheffield Shield batting (seven centuries and 1136 runs at 126.22 in six matches) completely dried up.

The Australian tour created unprecedented interest among both black and white South Africans, who paid 10 million rand to watch Australia's matches, 3.5 million rand ($A1.3 million) of which went to developing cricket in black areas. More than a thousand black South Africans from Soweto, scene of many deaths during apartheid protests, cheered Hansie Cronje all the way to his match-winning 122 in the First Test at the Wanderers' ground in Johannesburg.

South Africa recovered in this match from nervous, unsound batting against pace to their best performance since the apartheid ban was lifted. Australia surrendered a winning position when Mark Waugh and Allan Border were run out on the second day. On the third day the match referee fined Warne and Merv Hughes 1000 rand each for abusing batsmen they had just dismissed and making vulgar gestures towards the dressing room. Hughes was also fined $2000 for a nasty exchange with a spectator whose comments upset him as he left the field. The Australian Cricket Board added $4000 to the fines mindful, no doubt, that Warne had left the Academy in 1991 for disciplinary reasons.

Warne recovered his composure to take four wickets in South Africa's second innings, but even rain on the last day could not save Australia from a miserable 197-run defeat against a lively, accurate medium and fast attack. The contest between Warne and the leading South African batsmen continued to ebb and flow but on unresponsive wickets he still ended up with 15 victims from the three Tests. He helped Steve Waugh (5 for 28) complete the destruction of South Africa's batting in the Second Test at Cape Town with three wickets, his 30 overs costing only 38 runs. Trailing by 74 on the first innings, South Africa's second innings of 164 gave Australia an easy nine-wicket win.

South Africa bowled out Australia for a modest 269 in the first innings of the Third Test at Durban but then frittered away their advantage with slow, unenterprising batting, taking nearly 14 hours (832 minutes) to reach 422. Slater (95) and Mark Waugh (113 not out) restored Australia's batting prestige in the dying hours of a highly disappointing match which left the teams all square on two wins each after their extended summer.

Not long after the Australians returned home Allan Border retired from Test cricket in unhappy circumstances following a mix-up with ACB executives over the disclosure of his decision to end 15 years in international cricket, in which he played more Tests (156) and scored more runs than any player in the world. Statistics can never convey Australian cricket's debt to this plucky little bloke. His Test average seldom deviated from the low 50s in a career that yielded 11,174 Test runs, with 27 centuries. He hit 28 sixes and 1162 fours and averaged 50.63. Border used a small range of strokes – short-arm jabs, full-blooded drives and occasional lusty pulls – scoring 41 runs off every hundred balls he faced. In 265 Test innings, he made only 11 ducks. When he left the Test arena, he continued playing first-class cricket for Queensland, aiming to help his adopted state to their first Sheffield Shield win. At Melbourne in 1995 he twice batted with a chipped elbow to steer Queensland to a win over Victoria.

Border's successor, Mark Taylor, took Australia to Pakistan in late 1994 as the first captain since Ian Craig in 1957 to begin his reign offshore. The Australian team was M.A. Taylor (Captain), I.A. Healy, J. Angel, D.C. Boon, M.G. Bevan, D.W. Fleming, J.L. Langer, T.B.A. May, C.J. McDermott, G.D. McGrath, G. Robertson, M.J. Slater, S.K. Warne, M.E. Waugh and S.R. Waugh. The Australian Cricket Board offered massive bonuses of $75,000 to the players for every series they could win against Pakistan, England and the West Indies, knowing that over nine months Australia faced 13 Tests and almost 30 limited over matches.

The Pakistan tour ended with Australia failing to win any of the three Tests, after dropping 13 catches and forfeiting winning positions in all of them. But the Australians gave a bold showing and held the team ranked second only to the West Indies in world cricket to the narrowest of winning margins. Pakistan won the First Test by one wicket when Inzamamul Haq and Mushtaq Ahmed added 57 runs for the last wicket to save Pakistan's 39-year undefeated run in Karachi. England's 'Dickie' Bird said it was the best match he ever umpired.

Ian Healy believed he cost Australia victory when he missed a stumping off the last ball. He lost sight of a low, skidding Shane Warne leg-break, with Inzamamul out of his crease. Umpire Bird signalled four leg-byes which gave Pakistan the match, as Pakistan had needed three to win or two to tie. Television replays later showed the ball had not come off Inzamamul's leg as Bird signalled, but had missed everything.

At Rawalpindi in the second Test Warne dropped Aamer Sohail in the deep early in Pakistan's second innings after Pakistan followed on 261 runs behind. Sohail made 72. But the worst blunder came when Taylor dropped Saleem Malik when he was on 20. Malik went on to 237. Damien Fleming, in his Test debut, enlivened play when he became the eighth Australian to take a Test hat-trick after Malik saved the game. Fleming dismissed Aamer Malik, Inzamamul Haq and Saleem Malik with successive balls. Fleming had had three previous hat-tricks: two in Melbourne club cricket and one for an Australian Youth team in the West Indies.

Healy took five catches in Pakistan's innings of 537 but he also broke his thumb and he went home early with Steve Waugh (shoulder damage). Phil Emery flew in to replace Healy in the Third Test at Lahore. Emery dismissed five batsmen in Pakistan's second innings but also dropped Saleem Malik 38 runs before Malik reached 142. The draw gave Pakistan the series 1–0. Australia's sloppy catching in the Tests robbed them of victory over a Pakistan XI badly weakened by the strange withdrawal of Wasim Akram and Waqar Younis from the Third Test. For the sixth series in 18 months Warne was Australia's leading wicket-taker, matching Richie Benaud's record of 18 victims in three Tests in 1959–60. Michael Bevan proved an excellent replacement for Allan Border at number 5, but Michael Slater was Australia's top scorer, with 244 runs at 48.80.

All of this proved secondary, however, when the *Sydney Morning Herald* disclosed two months later that gamblers tried to bribe Australian players during the Pakistan tour. Shane Warne and Tim May were initially named 'as the players the racketeers asked to 'throw' matches, but a few days later Mark Waugh also was named. Wilkins said Warne and May were offered $70,000 each, Waugh $134,000. The players immediately rejected the approaches. Manager Col Egar confirmed he knew of the bribe offers, which were being investigated by the Australian Cricket Board.

In India, centre of cricket bookmaking on the sub-Continent, newspapers cited examples of Test players whose lifestyles had dramatically improved. In Pakistan, Test team manager Intikhab Alam said that after Australia's tour he asked his players to swear on the Koran that they would not get involved in gambling before they started a tour of Zimbabwe. In England, the International Cricket Council announced it was enquiring into all reported instances of cricket gambling.

Warne's enthusiasm despite a heavy workload shows in this appeal. Some fans worry that he will be 'burnt-out' by overwork.
(News Limited)

Warne's ascendancy over batsmen uneasy and hesitant against leg spin continued throughout the five-Test series against Mike Atherton's England team in 1994–95. Nine of the 16 players in England's party visited Australia for the first time. To help them selectors sent veterans Graeme Gooch and Mike Gatting, who were really too old for this kind of cricket. The move was a dismal failure, although Gatting made a Test century, and for much of the tour the English team played like a leaderless legion, morale low, mercilessly hammered by Fleet Street reporters, their ranks continually depleted by injuries.

Atherton had attracted unwelcome headlines during England's

Craig McDermott bowling in England demonstrates the fiercely competitive outlook that has taken him to second place behind Dennis Lillee among Australia's Test wicket-takers. (Ken Kelly)

1994 series against South Africa when television closeups showed him removing dirt from his trouser pocket to rub on the ball at Lord's, but at The Oval soon after in the final Test Devon Malcolm sent back nine batsmen in a display that had boosted English hopes of success in Australia. The team Atherton brought comprised M.A. Atherton (Captain), A.J. Stewart, J.E. Benjamin, J.P. Crawley, P.A.J. DeFreitas, M.W. Gatting, G.A. Gooch, D. Gough, G.A. Hick, D.E. Malcolm, M.J. McCague, S.J. Rhodes, G.P. Thorpe, P.C.R. Tufnell, S.D. Udal, and C. White. Numerous injuries forced England to use A.R.C. Fraser, C.C. Lewis, R.C. Russell, N.H. Fairbrother and M.R. Ramprakash as reinforcements at various stages, so that England fielded 21 players on the tour.

England's optimism that Malcolm's pace would destroy Australia's batting went awry when he missed the First Test through chickenpox. In his absence Warne turned in the finest figures of his career, 8 for 71, to win the First Test in Brisbane for Australia. English batsmen to that stage had averaged 1.7 runs an over against him in seven Tests, and nobody since Bradman had had a more profound influence on Australian cricket. With his habit of wearing his cap backwards, his blond hair, diamond ear stud, thick gold neck chain and bracelet he was a striking sight, but it was Warne's exceptional wrist strength and armoury of spinning deliveries that had England rattled.

Australia's 184-run victory stemmed from a combination of Warne's bowling (11 for 110), heavy scoring by Slater (176 and 45), Taylor (59 and 58) and Mark Waugh (140), and McDermott's return to form (6 for 53 and 2 for 90), backed by superb catching and fielding. England's threadbare attack without Malcolm – who watched the match on television from his hotel bed – looked forlornly dispirited, totally lacking support from fieldsmen who refused to chase the ball to the boundary, missed their captain's signals and conceded dozens of runs through sheer lack of concentration. By the time England reached Melbourne for the Second Test Fleet Street were describing them as the worst touring side in memory, with captain and coach out of their depth, and called for the dismissal of the English selectors.

Atherton misjudged the deliberately moist Melbourne pitch when he won the toss and sent Australia in, consigning his batsmen to last use of a wicket bound to help Warne. Australia made only 279, thanks to lively bowling from Gough and tidy work from DeFreitas and Tufnell, but England succumbed again to Warne whose 6 for

64 left them trailing by 67 in the first innings. Boon then chimed in with 131 which allowed Taylor to declare at 7 for 320, a lead of 387. McDermott bowled superbly to take 5 for 42 before Warne performed his first Test hat-trick to bundle England out for 92 and give Australia victory by a massive 295 runs.

After trapping DeFreitas lbw and Gough caught behind, Warne sought advice from fellow Victorian Damien Fleming, who had taken a hat-trick only a few months earlier against Pakistan. 'Well, I'd close my eyes and try not to think about bowling the perfect ball,' said Fleming. 'That's what I think I'll do too,' said Warne, and then bowled an over-spun leg-break that bounced off Devon Malcolm's gloves. David Boon leapt metres to his right to clutch under the ball a few centimetres from the turf. Warne did not wait for the umpire's decision but rushed up the pitch to thank Boon for a superfine catch. Alec Stewart, who had 11 painkillers in his broken hand during the game, was left destitute on 8 not out by team-mates who failed to match his guts.

Gough's flair emerged again in the Third Test at Sydney. First he took England's first innings score from 7 for 197 to a competitive 309 with a defiant half century. Then he ripped through the Australian batting by taking 6 for 49, lifting his wickets in three Tests to 20, showing spirit missing in his colleagues that roused SCG spectators to prolonged applause. Only three Australians made double figures in a first innings total of 116.

Gough's performance gave England an edge which Atherton squandered by delaying his declaration too long. He finally declared at 2 for 255 mid-afternoon the fourth day, with Graeme Hick on 98 not out, and Australia set off to score 449 to win. More than 25,000 people attended the last day, with the promise of a thrilling finish after Slater and Taylor had put on 208 for the first wicket in yet another outstanding opening partnership. Australia were mounting a chase for the runs with Taylor (113) and Slater (103) still together at lunch but a two-hour delay for rain forced Taylor to abandon the chase. From then Australia were in trouble, losing 5 for 27 at one stage, as Angus Fraser extracted nip and swerve from the pitch, and were 7 for 292 when Shane Warne and Tim May came together and batted out the last 19 overs.

Apart from his ultra-cautious declaration, Atherton erred with defensive field placements, opting to save runs rather than chase wickets and this familiar English fear of losing allowed Australia to escape. Atherton appeared to forget that Australia merely had

Shane Warne in action during the Third Test against England in Sydney in 1995. (Patrick Eagar)

to draw the game to retain The Ashes and forfeited a victory that was there for the taking.

Atherton's timidity was underlined when his team won the Fourth Test in Adelaide, where a wonderful show of aggression with the bat by Phil DeFreitas gave England's bowlers the runs needed to produce an unlikely victory. DeFreitas made 88 in even time. Devon Malcolm had worked his way back to peak fitness and bowled at frightening speed, upsetting all the Australian top order, DeFreitas moved the ball about a lot, Fraser pinned batsmen down with steady line and length, and Chris Lewis contributed some splendid bursts with leg-cutters. Gough had broken down before he bowled a ball in a World Series match and had to return to England, after a praiseworthy first tour.

Even an impressive century from Greg Blewett (118) in his Test debut, aged 23, could not save Australia. England won by 106 runs, scoring 353 and 328. Australia made 419 in the first innings, apparently enough to avoid defeat. Then England came storming back for only her second win in four series against Australia by dismissing the home side for 156.

The teams moved to Perth for the Fifth Test with Mike Atherton desperate for a victory that would allow England to square the rubber at two Tests each, but the gap between the countries widened again in the face of high quality bowling by McDermott and Warne. England's chances disappeared in a further string of dropped catches. Malcolm bowled at express speed and repeatedly found the edges of Australian bats, only to have his fieldsmen put down simple catches or simply not get their hands to them at all. To increase England's woes he dropped a caught and bowled chance and a high, edged sweep to the fine leg boundary. Australia made 420 and 8 declared for 329, England 295 and 123, to give Australia her fourteenth win in 22 matches, with six draws.

Despite England's displays in the Sydney and Adelaide Tests, Australia's 3–1 triumph had some critics doubting the entire future of Ashes series. 'Time to Burn The Urn', said the *Bulletin* headline on Ian Chappell's tour review. Australia's performance was not vintage either, the bowling lacked depth and variety, with only McDermott and Warne of consistent Test quality, and the batting remained subject to breakdowns despite the record of scoring more than 500 12 times and more than 600 five times in 62 Tests from 1989 to 1995.

Australian cricket had clearly been jolted out of its lethargy, judging by crowd support for the Test team in 1994–95, but how long that support can continue for Ashes matches when England shows such a clear lack of basic principles remains a worry for all purists. Brisbane, Sydney and Melbourne crowds were the largest for an Ashes series since 1982–83, the Adelaide aggregate was the best since 1974–75, and Perth the highest since the inaugural Test in 1970–71. More than one million attended the Tests of 1994–95, the first time that had been achieved. The $1.7 million gate takings for the Sydney Test was the highest ever for a Test in Australia, but given the strength of the West Indies and Pakistan, England v. Australia matches will be lucky to retain such popular support.

'In their hour of need, England's officials have dithered and dallied and done a lot of window-dressing while achieving little,' wrote Ian Chappell. 'Australian administrators set about improving the situation while their English counterparts did little . . . The days of Guy Fawkes are past, but if they're not careful someone will put a bomb under them.'

Australia's team were certainly not over-confident when they set off for their fourth tour of the West Indies between March and May 1995. They expected to take a battering from the West Indian pace men whom they felt certain would target bowlers McDermott, Warne, Fleming, May and Reiffel, but they believed the West Indies could be beaten by a policy of non-stop aggression. The Australian team was M.A. Taylor (Captain), I.A. Healy, D.C. Boon, G.S. Blewett, S.K. Warne, S.R. Waugh, M.E. Waugh, C.J. McDermott, T.B.A. May, G.D. McGrath, R.T. Ponting, P.R. Reiffel, M.J. Slater, D.W. Fleming and J.L. Langer. Only Ricky Ponting, 20, had no Test experience. McDermott (sprained ankle) and Fleming (torn shoulder) broke down and had to be replaced by Brendon Julian and Carl Rackemann, but only Julian arrived in time to be considered for the First Test.

Deprived of proven strike bowlers, Australia looked vulnerable. They had a history of collapsing under pressure. Batsmen were suspect against bouncers. Shane Warne was showing signs of wear: after an unprecedented workload in 1993 and 1994, bowling 2600 overs in 80 matches, his shoulder and fingers seemed to be rebelling. Yet the team had only one bad day on a difficult tour involving seven first-class matches and five limited-over internationals.

News of Queensland's first Sheffield Shield win after 63 attempts and defeats in six finals reached the Australians just before the First

Test. Trevor Barsby (151), Matthew Love (146) and Allan Border (98) lifted Queensland to a first-innings total of 664. Watched by an emotional 'Gabba crowd, Queensland dismissed South Australia for 214 and 349, exploiting opposition weaknesses picked up on coach John Buchanan's computer to win by an innings and 101 runs.

In the Caribbean years of hard work were rewarded by a 2–1 victory in a Test series that confirmed the decline of a once-great West Indies side. Success stemmed from Taylor's captaincy, Steve Waugh's batting (average 107.25) against bouncer-laden pace, Healy's wicket-keeping and Reiffel and McGrath's dominance over West Indian batting stars.

The Australians overcame injuries, a 4–1 defeat in the one-day series, hospitalisation of coach Bob Simpson, loss of all four Test tosses and their own batting failures. Even players whose overall form disappointed contributed to this success: Blewett flopped in three Tests but hit a handsome 69 in the Fourth; Healy's batting disappointed but his 74 not out assured victory in the opening Test; Shane Warne's expected harassment of top-order batsmen did not eventuate, yet he consistently mopped up the tail to finish with 15 Test victims for a career total of 176 wickets at 24.09.

From the First Test in Barbados, which the Australians won by ten wickets, their fielding prevented long partnerships blossoming. After a draw in the Second Test in Antigua, the West Indies drew level with a nine-wicket win at Port-of-Spain although they did not bat well. Here Australia had their one bad day, batting poorly on a beast of a pitch. The Fourth Test in Jamaica produced two West Indian batting failures, and far too many short-pitched balls against gutsy batting by the Waughs, who put on 231 runs in under 240 minutes. Steve's 200 was a majestic effort that gave Australia her thirty-second win in 81 Tests against the West Indies.

Failure of the umpires to prevent the bowling of more than two bouncers an over marred a dramatic series in which the highest West Indian total was only 265, despite the presence of world record-holder Brian Lara. The tour was a great triumph for Taylor's captaincy, and the all-round skills of Steve Waugh, but all the Australians deserved the acclaim that greeted them on their return.

AUSTRALIAN CRICKET STATISTICS
Sheffield Shield Results and Test Match Scorecards 1876-1995

Charlie Wat

It should be noted that the Third Test in 1890 between England and Australia, to be played at Old Trafford, Manchester, and the Third Test in 1938, also between England and Australia at Old Trafford, were both abandoned before the teams were announced. These tests therefore do not appear in the scorecards that follow.

SHEFFIELD SHIELD WINNERS FROM 1892–93 TO 1994–95

1892–93 Victoria	1927–28 Victoria	1964–65 New South Wales
1893–94 South Australia	1928–29 New South Wales	1965–66 New South Wales
1894–95 Victoria	1929–30 Victoria	1966–67 Victoria
1895–96 New South Wales	1930–31 Victoria	1967–68 Western Australia
1896–97 New South Wales	1931–32 New South Wales	1968–69 South Australia
1897–98 Victoria	1932–33 New South Wales	1969–70 Victoria
1898–99 Victoria	1933–34 Victoria	1970–71 South Australia
1899–00 New South Wales	1934–35 Victoria	1971–72 Western Australia
1900–01 Victoria	1935–36 South Australia	1972–73 Western Australia
1901–02 New South Wales	1936–37 Victoria	1973–74 Victoria
1902–03 New South Wales	1937–38 New South Wales	1974–75 Western Australia
1903–04 New South Wales	1938–39 South Australia	1975–76 South Australia
1904–05 New South Wales	1939–40 New South Wales	1976–77 Western Australia
1905–06 New South Wales	1940–46 No Competition	1977–78 Western Australia
1906–07 New South Wales	1946–47 Victoria	1978–79 Victoria
1907–08 Victoria	1947–48 Western Australia	1979–80 Victoria
1908–09 New South Wales	1948–49 New South Wales	1980–81 Western Australia
1909–10 South Australia	1949–50 New South Wales	1981–82 South Australia
1910–11 New South Wales	1950–51 Victoria	1982–83* New South Wales
1911–12 New South Wales	1951–52 New South Wales	1983–84* Western Australia
1912–13 South Australia	1952–53 South Australia	1984–85* New South Wales
1913–14 New South Wales	1953–54 New South Wales	1985–86* New South Wales
1914–15 Victoria	1954–55 New South Wales	1986–87* Western Australia
1915–19 No Competition	1955–56 New South Wales	1987–88* Western Australia
1919–20 New South Wales	1956–57 New South Wales	1988–89* Western Australia
1920–21 New South Wales	1957–58 New South Wales	1989–90* New South Wales
1921–22 Victoria	1958–59 New South Wales	1990–91* Victoria
1922–23 New South Wales	1959–60 New South Wales	1991–92* Western Australia
1923–24 Victoria	1960–61 New South Wales	1992–93* New South Wales
1924–25 Victoria	1961–62 New South Wales	1993–94* New South Wales
1925–26 New South Wales	1962–63 Victoria	1994–95* Queensland
1926–27 South Australia	1963–64 South Australia	

* The winner of the Sheffield Shield since 1982–83 season has been decided by the 2 top teams at the end of the competition playing a final at the Top of the Table's home ground.

THE WINNERS (TO 1994–95)

State	First Season	Played	Won	Lost	Drawn	Ties	Abandoned
New South Wales	1892–93	619	277	161	180	1	—
Victoria	1892–93	651	230	173	204	1	3
South Australia	1892–93	650	174	268	166	1	—
Queensland	1926–27	498	121	183	190	1	3
Western Australia	1947–48	383	128	109	146	—	—
Tasmania	1977–78	158	19	55	82	—	—
Total		1438					

SHEFFIELD SHIELD PLACINGS (TO 1994–95)

State	1st	2nd	3rd	4th	5th	6th	Seasons
New South Wales	42	23	16	8	4	—	93
Victoria	25	25	25	8	4	6	93
South Australia	12	25	27	8	20	1	93
Queensland	1	14	14	22	11	1	63
Western Australia	13	5	9	14	7	—	48
Tasmania	—	1	2	3	2	10	18
Total	93	93	93	63	48	18	

AUSTRALIA'S CRICKET TESTS
Men (1877–1995)

Opponent	Played	Won	Lost	Drawn	Tied
England	285	111	90	84	—
West Indies	81	32	27	21	1
South Africa	59	31	13	15	—
India	50	24	8	17	1
Pakistan	37	12	10	15	—
New Zealand	32	13	7	12	—
Sri Lanka	7	4	0	3	—
Total	551	227	155	167	2

Women (1934–1995)

	Played	Won	Lost	Drawn
England	33	7	6	20
New Zealand	12	4	1	7
West Indies	2	0	0	2
India	10	3	0	7
Total	57	14	7	36

AUSTRALIA v ENGLAND 1876-77 (First Test)

At Melbourne Cricket Ground, 15, 16, 17, 19 March

Result: Australia won by 45 runs

Australia

Batsman	First Innings	R		Second Innings	R
C.Bannerman	retired hurt	165		b Ulyett	4
N.F.D.Thomson	b Hill	1		c Emmett b Shaw	7
T.P.Horan	c Hill b Shaw	12		c Selby b Hill	20
D.W.Gregory*	run out	3	(9)	b Shaw	3
B.B.Cooper	b Southerton	15		b Shaw	3
W.E.Midwinter	c Ulyett b Southerton	5		c Southerton b Ulyett	17
E.J.Gregory	c Greenwood b Lillywhite	0		c Emmett b Ulyett	11
J.M.Blackham†	b Southerton	17		lbw b Shaw	6
T.W.Garrett	not out	18		c Emmett b Shaw	0
T.K.Kendall	c Southerton b Shaw	17	(4)	not out	17
J.R.Hodges	b Shaw	0		b Lillywhite	8
Extras	(B 4, LB 2, W 2)	8		(B 5, LB 3)	8
		245			**104**

1/2 2/40 3/41 4/118 5/142 6/143 7/197 8/243 9/245

1/7 2/27 3/31 4/31 4/35 6/58 7/71 8/75 9/75

Bowling: First Innings—Shaw 55.3-34-51-3; Hill 23-10-42-1; Ulyett 25-12-36-0; Southerton 37-17-61-3; Armitage 3-0-15-0; Lillywhite 14-5-19-1; Emmett 12-7-13-0. Second Innings—Shaw 34-16-38-5; Ulyett 19-7-39-3; Hill 14-6-18-1; Lillywhite 1-0-1-1.

England

Batsman	First Innings	R		Second Innings	R
H.Jupp	lbw b Garrett	63	(3)	lbw b Midwinter	4
J.Selby†	c Cooper b Hodges	7	(5)	c Horan b Hodges	38
H.R.J.Charlwood	c Blackham b Midwinter	36	(4)	b Kendall	13
G.Ulyett	lbw b Thompson	10	(6)	b Kendall	24
A.Greenwood	c E.J.Gregory b Midwinter	1	(2)	c Midwinter b Kendall	5
T.Armitage	c Blackham b Midwinter	9	(8)	c Blackham b Kendall	3
A.Shaw	b Midwinter	10		st Blackham b Kendall	2
T.Emmett	b Midwinter	8	(9)	b Kendall	9
A.Hill	not out	35		c Thompson b Kendall	0
J.Lillywhite*	c and b Kendall	10	(1)	b Hodges	4
J.Southerton	c Cooper b Garrett	6		not out	1
Extras	(LB 1)	1		(B 4, LB 1)	5
		196			**108**

1/23 2/79 3/98 4/109 5/121 6/135 7/145 8/145 9/168

1/0 2/7 3/20 4/22 5/62 6/68 7/92 8/93 9/100

Bowling: First Innings—Hodges 9-0-27-1; Garrett 18.1-10-22-2; Kendall 38-16-54-1; Midwinter 54-23-78-5; Thompson 17-10-14-1. Second Innings—Kendall 33.1-12-55-7; Midwinter 19-7-23-1; D.W.Gregory 5-1-9-0; Garrett 2-0-9-0; Hodges 7-5-7-2.

Umpires: C.A.Reid and R.B.Terry

AUSTRALIA v ENGLAND 1876-77 (Second Test)

At Melbourne Cricket Ground, 31 March, 2, 3, 4 April

Result: England won by four wickets

Australia

Batsman	First Innings	R		Second Innings	R
N.F.D.Thomson	lbw b Hill	18		b Lillywhite	41
C.Bannerman	b Hill	10	(3)	c Jupp b Ulyett	30
J.M.Blackham†	c Lillywhite b Hill	5	(10)	lbw b Southerton	26
T.W.Garrett	b Hill	12	(7)	c Jupp b Lillywhite	18
T.J.D.Kelly	b Ulyett	19	(4)	b Southerton	35
W.E.Midwinter	c Emmett b Lillywhite	31		c Greenwood b Lillywhite	12
F.R.Spofforth	b Ulyett	0	(8)	b Hill	17
W.L.Murdoch	run out	3	(5)	c Shaw b Southerton	8
T.K.Kendall	b Lillywhite	7		c Southerton	12
D.W.Gregory*	not out	43	(2)	c Ulyett b Lillywhite	43
J.R.Hodges	run out	2		not out	0
Extras	(B 8, LB 5, W 1)	14		(B 10, LB 7)	17
		122			**259**

1/29 2/30 3/50 4/60 5/96 6/104 7/108 8/114 9/119

1/88 2/112 3/135 4/164 5/169 6/196 7/203 8/221 9/259

Bowling: First Innings—Shaw 42-27-30-0; Lillywhite 29-17-36-2; Hill 27-12-27-4; Ulyett 14.1-6-15-2. Second Innings—Hill 21-9-43-1; Ulyett 19-9-33-1; Lillywhite 41-15-70-4; Shaw 32-19-27-0; Emmett 13-6-23-0; Southerton 28.3-13-46-4.

England

Batsman	First Innings	R		Second Innings	R
H.Jupp	b Kendall	1	(8)	b Kendall	1
A.Shaw	st Blackham b Spofforth	0		not out	0
A.Greenwood	b Hodges	22		c Murdoch b Hodges	22
H.R.J.Charlwood	c Kelly b Kendall	14		b Kendall	0
J.Selby†	b Kendall	0	(2)	b Spofforth	2
G.Ulyett	b Spofforth	52	(5)	c Spofforth b Hodges	63
T.Emmett	c Kendall b Spofforth	48	(6)	b Midwinter	8
A.Hill	run out	49	(7)	not out	17
T.Armitage	c Thompson b Midwinter	21			
J.Lillywhite*	not out	2			
J.Southerton	c Thompson b Kendall	0			
Extras	(B 5, LB 12, NB 1)	18		(B 8, LB 1)	9
		261		(6 wkts)	**122**

1/0 2/4 3/55 4/72 5/88 6/162 7/196 8/255 9/259

1/2 2/8 3/9 4/54 5/76 6/112

Bowling: First Innings—Kendall 52.2-21-82-4; Spofforth 29-6-67-3; Midwinter 21-8-30-1; Hodges 12-2-37-1; Garrett 5-2-10-0; Thompson 11-6-17-0. Second Innings—Kendall 17-7-24-2; Spofforth 15-3-44-1; Garrett 1-0-7-0; Hodges 6-2-13-2; Midwinter 13.1-6-25-1.

Umpires: S.Cosstick and R.B.Terry

AUSTRALIA v ENGLAND 1878-79 (Only Test)

At Melbourne Cricket Ground, 2, 3, 4 January

Result: Australia won by 10 wickets

England

Batsman	First Innings		Second Innings	
G.Ulyett	b Spofforth	0	b Spofforth	14
A.P.Lucas	b Allan	6	c Boyle b Allan	13
A.J.Webbe	b Allan	4	lbw b Allan	0
A.N.Hornby	b Spofforth	2	b Spofforth	4
Lord Harris*	b Garrett	33	c Horan b Spofforth	36
V.P.F.A.Royle	b Spofforth	3	c Spofforth b Boyle	18
F.A.MacKinnon	b Spofforth	0	b Spofforth	5
T.Emmett	c Horan b Spofforth	0	(9) not out	24
C.A.Absolom	c A.C.Bannerman b Boyle	52	(8) c and b Spofforth	6
L.Hone†	c Blackham b Spofforth	7	b Spofforth	6
S.S.Schultz	not out	0	c and b Spofforth	20
Extras	(B 4, LB 2)	6	(B 10, LB 4)	14
		113		160

1/0 2/7 3/10 4/14 5/26 6/26 7/26 8/89 9/113
1/26 2/28 3/28 4/34 5/78 6/103 7/103 8/118 9/128

Bowling: *First Innings*—Spofforth 25-9-48-6; Allan 17-4-30-2; Garrett 5-0-18-1; Boyle 7-1-11-1. *Second Innings*—Spofforth 35-16-62-7; Allan 28-11-50-0; Garrett 10-6-18-0; Boyle 10-4-16-1.

Australia

Batsman	First Innings		Second Innings	
C.Bannerman	b Emmett	15	not out	15
W.L.Murdoch	c Webbe b Ulyett	4	not out	4
T.P.Horan	c Hone b Emmett	10		
A.C.Bannerman	b Schultz	73		
F.R.Spofforth	c Royle b Emmett	39		
T.W.Garrett	c Hone b Emmett	26		
F.E.Allan	b Hornby	5		
H.F.Boyle	c Royle b Emmett	28		
J.M.Blackham†	b Emmett	6		
T.J.D.Kelly	c Webbe b Emmett	10		
D.W.Gregory*	not out	12		
Extras	(B 19, LB 2, W 7)	28		
		256	(0 wkts)	19

1/16 2/30 3/37 4/101 5/131 6/158 7/215 8/224 9/234

Bowling: *First Innings*—Emmett 59-31-68-7; Ulyett 62-24-93-1; Lucas 18-6-31-0; Schultz 6.3-3-16-1; Hornby 7-7-0-1; Royle 4-1-6-0; Harris 3-0-14-0. *Second Innings*—Schultz 1.3-0-10-0; Ulyett 1-0-9-0.

Umpires: P.Coady and G.Coulthard

ENGLAND v AUSTRALIA 1880 (Only Test)

At Kennington Oval, London, 6, 7, 8 September

Result: England won by 5 wickets

England

Batsman	First Innings		Second Innings	
E.M.Grace	c Alexander b Bannerman	36	(6) b Boyle	0
W.G.Grace	b Palmer	152	(7) not out	9
A.P.Lucas	b Bannerman	55	c Blackham b Palmer	2
W.Barnes	b Alexander	28	(5) c Moule b Boyle	5
Lord Harris*	c Bonnor b Alexander	52		
F.Penn	b Bannerman	23	(4) not out	27
A.G.Steel	c Boyle b Moule	42		
Hon.A.Lyttelton†	not out	11	(1) b Palmer	13
G.F.Grace	c Bannerman b Moule	0	(2) b Palmer	0
A.Shaw	b Moule	0		
F.Morley	run out	2		
Extras	(B 8, LB 11)	19	(NB 1)	1
		420	(5 wkts)	57

1/91 2/211 3/269 4/281 5/322 6/404 7/410 8/410 9/413
1/2 2/10 3/22 4/31 5/31

Bowling: *First Innings*—Boyle 44-17-71-0; Palmer 70-27-116-1; Alexander 32-10-69-2; Bannerman 50-12-111-3; McDonnell 2-0-11-0; Moule 12.3-4-23-3. *Second Innings*—Boyle 17-7-21-2; Palmer 16.3-5-35-3.

Australia

Batsman	First Innings		Second Innings	
A.C.Bannerman	b Morley	32	(3) c Lucas b Shaw	8
W.L.Murdoch*	c Barnes b Steel	0	not out	153
T.U.Groube	b Steel	11	(4) c Shaw b Morley	0
P.S.McDonnell	c Barnes b Morley	27	(5) lbw b W.G.Grace	43
J.Slight	c G.F.Grace b Morley	11	(6) c Harris b W.G.Grace	0
J.M.Blackham†	c and Morley	0	(7) c E.M.Grace b Morley	19
G.J.Bonnor	c G.F.Grace b Shaw	2	(8) b Steel	16
H.F.Boyle	not out	36	(2) run out	3
G.E.Palmer	b Morley	6	c and b Steel	4
G.Alexander	c W.G.Grace b Steel	6	c Shaw b Morley	33
W.H.Moule	c Morley b W.G.Grace	6	b Barnes	34
Extras	(B 9, LB 3)	12	(B 7, LB 7)	14
		149		327

1/28 2/39 3/59 4/84 5/84 6/89 7/97 8/113 9/126
1/8 2/13 3/14 4/97 5/101 6/143 7/181 8/187 9/239

Bowling: *First Innings*—Morley 32-9-56-5; Steel 29-9-58-3; Shaw 13-5-21-1; W.G.Grace 1.1-0-2-1. *Second Innings*—Morley 61-30-90-3; Steel 31-6-73-2; Shaw 33-18-42-1; W.G.Grace 28-10-66-2; Barnes 8.3-3-17-1; Lucas 12-7-23-0; Penn 3-1-2-0.

Umpires: H.H.Stephenson and R.Thoms

AUSTRALIA v ENGLAND 1881-82 (First Test)
At Melbourne Cricket Ground, 31 December, 2, 3, 4 January
Result: Match Drawn

England

G.Ulyett c McDonnell b Cooper	87		st Blackham b Cooper	23
R.G.Barlow c Bannerman b Palmer	0		st Blackham b Palmer	33
J.Selby run out	55		c Boyle b Cooper	70
W.Bates c Giffen b Boyle	58		c Bannerman b Cooper	47
A.Shrewsbury c Blackham b Evans	11		b Cooper	16
W.E.Midwinter b Evans	36		c Massie b Cooper	4
T.Emmett b Evans	5		b Cooper	6
W.H.Scotton run out	21		not out	50
A.Shaw* c Boyle b Cooper	5		c Cooper b Boyle	40
R.Pilling† c Giffen b Cooper	5		b Palmer	3
E.Peate not out	4		run out	2
Extras (LB 6, NB 1)	7		(B 7, LB 2, NB 5)	14
	294			**308**

1/5 2/142 3/151 4/187 5/227 / 1/37 2/96 3/179 4/183 5/188
6/232 7/277 8/284 9/289 / 6/197 7/217 8/300 9/304

Bowling: *First Innings*—Palmer 36-9-73-1; Evans 71-35-81-3; Cooper 32.2-8-80-3; Boyle 18-9-18-1; Giffen 3-0-12-0; Bannerman 10-3-23-0. *Second Innings*—Palmer 77-19-77-2; Evans 73-45-63-0; Cooper 61-19-120-6; Boyle 14.3-6-19-1; McDonnell 4-1-15-0.

Australia

H.H.Massie st Pilling b Midwinter	2			
A.C.Bannerman b Ulyett	38	(4)	b Ulyett	8
W.L.Murdoch*† b Ulyett	39		not out	22
P.S.McDonnell b Midwinter	19	(5)	not out	33
T.P.Horan run out	124	(3)	c Emmett b Bates	26
G.Giffen b Emmett	30			
J.M.Blackham† b Emmett	2	(1)	b Bates	25
G.E.Palmer c Pilling b Bates	34			
E.Evans b Bates	3			
H.F.Boyle not out	4			
W.H.Cooper st Pilling b Peate	7			
Extras (B 4, LB 11, W 3)	18		(B 9, LB 3, W 1)	13
	320			**127** (3 wkts)

1/9 2/82 3/97 4/113 5/220 / 1/35 2/70 3/72
6/226 7/305 8/309 9/309

Bowling: *First Innings*—Peate 59-24-64-1; Midwinter 39-21-50-2; Bates 41-20-43-2; Emmett 35-12-61-2; Ulyett 20-5-41-2; Barlow 23-13-22-0; Shaw 20-11-21-0. *Second Innings*—Ulyett 15-3-30-1; Emmett 16-11-19-0; Bates 13-2-43-2; Peate 11-5-22-0.

Umpires: J.Lillywhite and J.Swift

AUSTRALIA v ENGLAND 1881-82 (Second Test)
At Sydney Cricket Ground, 17, 18, 20, 21 February
Result: Australia won by five wickets

England

G.Ulyett c Murdoch b Evans	25	(2)	lbw b Palmer	67
R.G.Barlow b Palmer	31	(1)	c Boyle b Garrett	62
J.Selby c and b Evans	6		c Blackham b Palmer	2
W.Bates c Murdoch b Palmer	4		b Palmer	5
A.Shrewsbury b Palmer	7		c McDonnell b Garrett	22
W.E.Midwinter c Blackham b Palmer	4		b Palmer	8
W.H.Scotton b Palmer	30		lbw b Garrett	12
T.Emmett b Evans	10		c McDonnell b Garrett	9
A.Shaw* c Massie b Palmer	11		b Evans	30
R.Pilling† b Palmer	1		b Jones	9
E.Peate not out	1		not out	1
Extras (LB 1)	1		(B 3, LB 2)	5
	133			**232**

1/39 2/47 3/64 4/73 5/77 / 1/122 2/124 3/130 4/156
6/90 7/115 8/123 9/132 / 5/165 6/175 7/183 8/204 9/230

Bowling: *First Innings*—Palmer 58-36-68-7; Evans 57-32-64-3. *Second Innings*—Palmer 66-29-97-4; Garrett 36-12-62-4; Evans 40.1-19-49-1; Jones 11-4-19-1.

Australia

H.H.Massie c Shrewsbury b Bates	49	(2)	b Ulyett	22
J.M.Blackham c Shaw b Midwinter	40	(1)	c and b Bates	4
E.Evans run out	11			
W.L.Murdoch*† c Emmett b Bates	10	(3)	c Barlow b Midwinter	49
T.P.Horan run out	4	(4)	b Ulyett	21
P.S.McDonnell b Bates	14	(5)	b Shaw	25
S.P.Jones c Emmett b Ulyett	37	(6)	not out	13
T.W.Garrett c Shrewsbury b Peate	4	(7)	not out	31
G.E.Palmer b Bates	16			
H.F.Boyle c Shrewsbury b Ulyett	0			
G.Coulthard not out	6			
Extras (B 1, LB 2, NB 1, W 2)	6		(B 3, LB 1)	4
	197			**169** (5 wkts)

1/78 2/102 3/103 4/111 5/132 / 1/10 2/28 3/67 4/113
6/133 7/140 8/167 9/168 / 5/127

Bowling: *First Innings*—Peate 52-28-53-1; Midwinter 34-16-43-1; Emmett 6-2-24-0; Ulyett 22.2-16-11-2; Bates 72-43-52-4; Barlow 8-4-8-0. *Second Innings*—Bates 24-11-37-1; Ulyett 15-4-48-2; Peate 20-12-22-0; Emmett 6-3-17-0; Midwinter 18-8-23-1; Shaw 20.1-15-12-1; Barlow 4-1-6-0.

Umpires: J.Lillywhite and J.Swift

AUSTRALIA v ENGLAND 1881-82 (Third Test)
At Sydney Cricket Ground, 3, 4, 6, 7 March
Result: Australia won by 6 wickets

England

G.Ulyett b Palmer	0	(2) b Garrett	23
R.G.Barlow c Blackham b Garrett	4	(1) c and b Garrett	8
J.Selby c Massie b Palmer	13	b Palmer	1
W.Bates c and b Palmer	1	c Bannerman b Garrett	2
A.Shrewsbury c and b Boyle	82	c Boyle b Garrett	47
W.E.Midwinter b Palmer	12	b Palmer	10
W.H.Scotton c Jones b Garrett	18	b Palmer	1
T.Emmett b Garrett	4	b Garrett	2
A.Shaw* b Boyle	3	b Garrett	6
R.Pilling† b Palmer	12	b Palmer	23
E.Peate not out	11	not out	8
Extras (B 22, LB 6)	28	(B 2, NB 1)	3
	188		134

1/2 2/8 3/17 4/35 5/56 1/28 2/29 3/33 4/42 5/60
6/148 7/154 8/159 9/164 6/70 7/73 8/79 9/113

Bowling: *First Innings*—Palmer 45.2-23-46-5; Garrett 60-24-85-3; Jones 8-5-11-0; Boyle 27-18-18-2 *Second Innings*—Palmer 40-19-44-4; Garrett 36.1-10-78-6; Boyle 4-1-9-0.

Australia

A.C.Bannerman c Midwinter b Midwinter	70	(2) c Pilling b Peate	14
H.H.Massie b Bates	0	(1) c Midwinter b Peate	9
W.L.Murdoch* c Ulyett b Bates	6	c Midwinter b Bates	4
T.P.Horan c and b Bates	1	not out	16
P.S.McDonnell c Midwinter b Peate	147	c Emmett b Peate	9
G.Giffen c Pilling b Peate	2		
J.M.Blackham† b Peate	4		
S.P.Jones not out	7	(6) not out	6
T.W.Garrett b Peate	0		
G.E.Palmer b Midwinter	6		
H.F.Boyle c Pilling b Peate	3		
Extras (B 6, LB 8, W 2)	16	(B 2, LB 3, W 1)	6
	262	(4 wkts)	64

1/0 2/10 3/16 4/215 5/228 1/14 2/21 3/39 4/49
6/235 7/244 8/245 9/252

Bowling: *First Innings*—Peate 45-24-43-5; Bates 38-17-67-3; Ulyett 3-1-10-0; Midwinter 62-25-75-2; Shaw 8-4-14-0; Emmett 16-6-37-0. *Second Innings*—Peate 25-18-15-3; Bates 24.3-13-43-1.

Umpires: J.Lillywhite and J.Swift

AUSTRALIA v ENGLAND 1881-82 (Fourth Test)
At Melbourne Cricket Ground, 10, 11, 13, 14 (no play) March
Result: Match drawn

England

G.Ulyett c Blackham b Garrett	149	c Palmer b Boyle	64
R.G.Barlow c Blackham b Garrett	16	run out	56
J.Selby b Spofforth	7	not out	48
W.Bates st Blackham b Garrett	23	not out	52
A.Shrewsbury lbw b Palmer	1		
W.E.Midwinter c Palmer b Boyle	21		
W.H.Scotton st Blackham b Giffen	26		
T.Emmett b Giffen	27		
A.Shaw* c Murdoch b Garrett	3		
R.Pilling† not out	6		
E.Peate c and b Garrett	13		
Extras (B 10, LB 7)	17	(B 12, LB 2)	14
	309	(2 wkts)	234

1/32 2/49 3/98 4/109 5/177 1/98 2/152
6/239 7/281 8/284 9/288

Bowling: *First Innings*—Spofforth 51-14-92-1; Garrett 54.2-23-80-5; Palmer 23-5-70-1; Boyle 18-4-33-1. *Second Innings*—Palmer 20-5-47-0; Garrett 27-6-62-0; Boyle 25-9-38-1; Spofforth 15-3-36-0; Giffen 8.3-1-25-0; Bannerman 2-0-12-0.

Australia

W.L.Murdoch* b Midwinter	85
A.C.Bannerman c and b Midwinter	37
T.P.Horan c and b Midwinter	20
P.S.McDonnell c Barlow b Ulyett	52
H.H.Massie c Emmett b Shaw	19
G.Giffen c Scotton b Peate	14
J.M.Blackham† c Pilling b Midwinter	6
T.W.Garrett c Ulyett b Bates	10
G.E.Palmer c Ulyett b Bates	32
H.F.Boyle c Shrewsbury b Bates	6
F.R.Spofforth not out	3
Extras (B 2, LB 7, NB 1, W 6)	16
	300

1/110 2/149 3/153 4/189 5/228
6/247 7/247 8/280 9/297

Bowling: Bates 28.1-14-49-3; Peate 20-6-38-1; Emmett 19-14-22-0; Ulyett 24-8-40-1; Midwinter 41-9-81-4; Barlow 15-6-25-0; Shaw 16-6-29-1.

Umpires: G.Coulthard and J.Lillywhite

ENGLAND v AUSTRALIA 1882 (Only Test)

At Kennington Oval, London, 28, 29 August

Result: Australia won by 7 runs

Australia

Batsman	First Innings			Second Innings	
A.C.Bannerman	c Studd b Barnes	9		c Studd b Barnes	13
H.H.Massie	b Ulyett	1		b Steel	55
W.L.Murdoch*	b Peate	13	(4)	run out	29
G.J.Bonnor	b Barlow	1	(3)	b Ulyett	2
T.P.Horan	b Barlow	3		c Grace b Peate	2
G.Giffen	b Peate	2		c Grace b Peate	0
J.M.Blackham†	c Grace b Barlow	17		c Lyttelton b Peate	7
T.W.Garrett	c Read b Peate	10	(10)	not out	2
H.F.Boyle	b Barlow	2	(11)	b Steel	0
S.P.Jones	c Barnes b Barlow	0	(8)	run out	6
F.R.Spofforth	not out	4	(9)	b Peate	0
Extras	(B 1)	1		(B 6)	6
		63			**122**

1/6 2/21 3/22 4/26 5/30 6/30 7/48 8/53 9/59
1/66 2/70 3/70 4/79 5/79 6/99 7/114 8/117 9/122

Bowling: *First Innings*—Peate 38-24-31-4; Ulyett 9-5-11-1; Barlow 31-22-19-5; Steel 2-1-1-0. *Second Innings*—Peate 21-9-40-4; Ulyett 6-2-10-1; Barlow 13-5-27-0; Steel 7-0-15-2; Barnes 12-5-15-1; Studd 4-1-9-0.

England

Batsman	First Innings			Second Innings	
R.G.Barlow	c Bannerman b Spofforth	11	(3)	b Spofforth	0
W.G.Grace	b Spofforth	4	(1)	c Bannerman b Boyle	32
G.Ulyett	st Blackham b Spofforth	26	(4)	c Blackham b Spofforth	11
A.P.Lucas	c Blackham b Boyle	9	(5)	b Spofforth	5
Hon.A.Lyttelton†	c Blackham b Spofforth	2	(6)	b Spofforth	12
C.T.Studd	b Spofforth	0	(10)	not out	0
J.M.Read	not out	19	(8)	b Spofforth	0
W.Barnes	b Boyle	5	(9)	c Murdoch b Boyle	2
A.G.Steel	b Garrett	14	(7)	c and b Spofforth	0
A.N.Hornby*	b Spofforth	2	(2)	b Spofforth	9
E.Peate	c Boyle b Spofforth	0		b Boyle	2
Extras	(B 6, LB 2, NB 1)	9		(B 3, LB 1)	4
		101			**77**

1/13 2/18 3/57 4/59 5/60 6/63 7/70 8/96 9/101
1/15 2/15 3/51 4/53 5/66 6/70 7/70 8/75 9/75

Bowling: *First Innings*—Spofforth 36.3-18-46-7; Garrett 16-7-22-1; Boyle 19-7-24-2. *Second Innings*—Spofforth 28-15-44-7; Garrett 7-2-10-0; Boyle 20-11-19-3.

Umpires: L.Greenwood and R.Thoms

AUSTRALIA v ENGLAND 1882-83 (First Test)

At Melbourne Cricket Ground, 30 December, 1, 2 January

Result: Australia won by 9 wickets

Australia

Batsman	First Innings		Second Innings	
A.C.Bannerman	st Tylecote b Leslie	30	not out	25
H.H.Massie	c and b C.T.Studd	4	c and b Barnes	0
W.L.Murdoch*	b Leslie	48	not out	33
T.P.Horan	c Barlow b Leslie	0		
P.S.McDonnell	b Bates	43		
G.Giffen	st Tylecote b Steel	36		
G.J.Bonnor	c Barlow b Barnes	85		
J.M.Blackham†	c Tylecote b C.T.Studd	25		
F.R.Spofforth	c Steel b Barnes	9		
T.W.Garrett	c C.T.Studd b Steel	0		
G.E.Palmer	not out	0		
Extras	(B 4, LB 2, NB 3, W 2)	11		
		291		**(1 wkt) 58**

1/5 2/81 3/81 4/96 5/162 6/190 7/251 8/287 9/287
1/0

Bowling: *First Innings*—C.T.Studd 46-30-35-2; Barnes 30-11-51-2; Steel 33-16-68-2; Barlow 20-6-37-0; Read 8-2-27-0; Bates 21-7-31-1; Leslie 11-1-31-3. *Second Innings*—C.T.Studd 14-11-7-0; Barnes 13-8-6-1; Steel 9-4-17-0; Bates 13.1-7-22-0; Barlow 4-2-6-0.

England

Batsman	First Innings			Second Innings	
R.G.Barlow	st Blackham b Palmer	10		b Spofforth	28
Hon.I.F.W.Bligh*	b Palmer	0	(5)	b Spofforth	3
C.F.H.Leslie	c Garrett b Palmer	4	(7)	b Giffen	4
C.T.Studd	b Spofforth	0	(3)	b Palmer	21
A.G.Steel	b Palmer	27	(4)	lbw b Giffen	29
W.W.Read	b Palmer	19		b Giffen	29
W.Bates	c Bannerman b Garrett	28	(8)	c Massie b Palmer	11
E.F.S.Tylecote†	b Palmer	33	(2)	b Spofforth	38
G.B.Studd	run out	7		c Palmer b Giffen	0
W.Barnes	b Palmer	26		not out	0
G.F.Vernon	not out	11		lbw b Palmer	3
Extras	(B 8, LB 1, NB 3)	12		(LB 1)	1
		177			**169**

1/2 2/7 3/8 4/36 5/45 6/96 7/100 8/117 9/156
1/64 2/75 3/105 4/108 5/132 6/150 7/164 8/164 9/164

Bowling: *First Innings*—Spofforth 28-11-56-1; Palmer 52.2-25-65-7; Garrett 27-6-44-1. *Second Innings*—Palmer 36.1-11-61-3; Garrett 2-1-4-0; Spofforth 41-15-65-3; Giffen 20-7-38-4.

Umpires: E.H.Elliott and J.Swift

AUSTRALIA v ENGLAND 1882-83 (Second Test)

At Melbourne Cricket Ground, 19, 20, 22 January

Result: England won by an innings and 27 runs

England

R.G.Barlow	b Palmer	14
C.T.Studd	b Palmer	14
C.F.H.Leslie	run out	54
A.G.Steel	c McDonnell b Giffen	39
W.W.Read	c and b Palmer	75
W.Barnes	b Giffen	32
E.F.S.Tylecote†	c b Giffen	0
Hon.I.F.W.Bligh*	b Giffen	0
W.Bates	c Horan b Palmer	55
G.B.Studd	b Palmer	1
F.Morley	not out	0
Extras	(B 3, LB 3, NB 4)	10
		294

1/28 2/35 3/106 4/131 5/195
6/199 7/199 8/287 9/293

Bowling: Spofforth 34-11-57-0; Palmer 66.3-25-103-5; Giffen 49-13-89-4; Garrett 34-16-35-0.

Australia

H.H.Massie	b Barlow	43	(7) c C.T.Studd b Barlow		10
A.C.Bannerman	b Bates	14	(1) c Bligh b Bates		14
W.L.Murdoch*	not out	19	(2) b Bates		17
T.P.Horan	c and b Barnes	3	(5) c Morley b Bates		15
P.S.McDonnell	b Barnes	3	(6) b Bates		13
G.Giffen	c and b Bates	0	(8) c Bligh b Bates		19
G.J.Bonnor	c Read b Bates	0	(4) c Morley b Barlow		34
J.M.Blackham†	b Barnes	5	(3) b Barlow		6
T.W.Garrett	b Bates	10	c Barnes b Bates		6
G.E.Palmer	b Bates	7	c G.B.Studd b Bates		4
F.R.Spofforth	b Bates	0	not out		14
Extras	(B 6, LB 3, NB 1)	10	(B 1)		1
		114			153

1/56 2/72 3/75 4/78 5/78   1/21 2/28 3/66 4/72 5/93
6/78 7/85 8/104 9/114   6/104 7/113 8/132 9/139

Bowling: First Innings—C.T.Studd 4-1-22-0; Morley 23-16-13-0; Barnes 23-7-32-2; Barlow 22-18-9-1; Bates 26.2-14-28-7. Second Innings—Bates 33-14-74-7; Barlow 31-6-67-3; Barnes 3-1-4-0; Morley 2-0-7-0.

Umpires: E.H.Elliott and J.Swift

AUSTRALIA v ENGLAND 1882-83 (Third Test)

At Sydney Cricket Ground, 26, 27, 29, 30 January

Result: England won by 69 runs

England

R.G.Barlow	c Murdoch b Spofforth	28	(3) c Palmer b Horan		24
C.T.Studd	c Blackham b Garrett	21	(1) b Spofforth		25
C.F.H.Leslie	lbw b Spofforth	0	(2) b Spofforth		8
A.G.Steel	b Garrett	17	lbw b Spofforth		6
W.W.Read	c Massie b Bannerman	66	b Horan		21
W.Barnes	b Spofforth	2	lbw b Spofforth		3
E.F.S.Tylecote†	run out	66	c Bonnor b Spofforth		0
W.Bates	c McDonnell b Spofforth	17	c Murdoch b Horan		4
G.B.Studd	b Palmer	3	(10) c Garrett b Spofforth		8
Hon.I.F.W.Bligh*	b Palmer	13	(9) not out		17
F.Morley	not out	2	b Spofforth		0
Extras	(B 8, LB 3, NB 1)	12	(B 5, LB 2)		7
		247			123

1/41 2/44 3/67 4/69 5/76   1/13 2/45 3/55 4/87 5/94
6/191 7/223 8/224 9/244   6/94 7/97 8/98 9/115

Bowling: First Innings—Giffen 12-3-37-0; Palmer 38-21-38-2; Spofforth 51-19-73-4; Garrett 27-8-54-2; Bannerman 11-2-17-1; McDonnell 4-0-16-0. Second Innings—Spofforth 41.1-23-44-7; Garrett 13-3-31-0; Palmer 9-3-19-0; Horan 17-10-22-3.

Australia

G.Giffen	st Tylecote b Bates	41	b Barlow		7
A.C.Bannerman	c Bates b Morley	94	c Bligh b Barlow		5
W.L.Murdoch*	lbw b Steel	19	c G.B.Studd b Morley		0
P.S.McDonnell	b Steel	0	(5) c Bligh b Morley		0
T.P.Horan	c Steel b Morley	19	(4) run out		8
H.H.Massie	c Bligh b Steel	1	c C.T.Studd b Barlow		11
G.J.Bonnor	c G.B.Studd b Morley	0	b Barlow		8
J.M.Blackham†	b Barnes	27	b Barlow		26
T.W.Garrett	c Barlow b Morley	0	(11) b Barlow		0
G.E.Palmer	c G.B.Studd b Barnes	7	not out		2
F.R.Spofforth	not out	0	(9) c Steel b Barlow		7
Extras	(B 6, LB 2, NB 1, W 1)	10	(B 6, LB 2, W 1)		9
		218			83

1/76 2/140 3/140 4/176 5/177   1/11 2/12 3/18 4/18 5/30
6/178 7/196 8/196 9/218   6/33 7/56 8/72 9/80

Bowling: First Innings—Bates 45-20-55-1; Morley 34-16-47-4; Steel 26-14-27-3; Barlow 47.1-31-52-1; Barnes 13-6-22-1; C.T.Studd 14-11-5-0. Second Innings—Morley 35-19-34-2; Barlow 34.2-20-40-7.

Umpires: E.H.Elliott and J.Swift

AUSTRALIA v ENGLAND 1882-83 (Fourth Test)

At Sydney Cricket Ground, 17, 19, 20, 21 February
Result: Australia won by 4 wickets

England

Batsman	1st innings		2nd innings	
R.G.Barlow	c Murdoch b Midwinter	2	c Bonnor b Midwinter	20
C.T.Studd	run out	48	c Murdoch b Midwinter	31
C.F.H.Leslie	c Bonnor b Boyle	17	b Horan	19
A.G.Steel	not out	135	b Spofforth	21
W.W.Read	c Bonnor b Boyle	11	b Spofforth	7
E.F.S.Tylecote†	b Boyle	5	b Palmer	0
W.Barnes	b Spofforth	2	(9) c and b Boyle	2
W.Bates	c Bonnor b Midwinter	9	(7) not out	20
Hon.I.F.W.Bligh*	b Palmer	19	(8) c Murdoch b Horan	48
G.B.Studd	run out	3	c Murdoch b Boyle	10
F.Morley	b Palmer	0	c Bannerman b Palmer	9
Extras	(B 4, LB 7, NB 1)	12	(B 8, LB 1, NB 1)	10
		263		197

1/13 2/37 3/110 4/150 5/156 6/159 7/199 8/236 9/263
1/54 2/55 3/77 4/99 5/100 6/112 7/137 8/178 9/192

Bowling: *First Innings*—Palmer 24-9-52-2; Midwinter 47-24-50-2; Spofforth 21-8-56-1; Boyle 40-19-52-3; Horan 12-4-26-0; Evans 11-3-15-0. *Second Innings*—Spofforth 28-6-57-2; Boyle 23-6-35-2; Palmer 43.3-19-59-2; Midwinter 23-13-21-2; Horan 9-2-15-2.

Australia

Batsman	1st innings		2nd innings	
A.C.Bannerman	c Barlow b Morley	10	(3) c Bligh b C.T.Studd	63
G.J.Bonnor	c Barlow b Steel	87	c G.B.Studd b Steel	3
W.L.Murdoch*	b Barlow	0	(2) c Barlow b Bates	17
T.P.Horan	c G.B.Studd b Morley	4	c and b Bates	0
G.Giffen	c G.B.Studd b Leslie	27	st Tylecote b Steel	32
W.E.Midwinter	b Barlow	10	(8) not out	8
J.M.Blackham†	b Bates	57	(6) not out	58
G.E.Palmer	c Bligh b Steel	0		
E.Evans	not out	22	(7) c Leslie b Steel	0
F.R.Spofforth	c Bates b Steel	1		
H.F.Boyle	c G.B.Studd b Barlow	29		
Extras	(B 10, LB 3, W 2)	15	(B 10, LB 4, W 4)	18
		262	(6 wkts)	199

1/31 2/34 3/39 4/113 5/128 6/160 7/164 8/220 9/221
1/44 2/51 3/51 4/107 5/162 6/164

Bowling: *First Innings*—Barlow 48-21-88-3; Morley 44-25-45-2; Barnes 10-2-33-0; Bates 15-6-24-1; Leslie 5-2-11-1; Steel 18-6-34-3; C.T.Studd 6-2-12-0. *Second Innings*—Bates 39-19-52-2; Barlow 37.1-20-44-0; Morley 12-9-4-0; Leslie 8-7-2-0; Steel 43-9-49-3; C.T.Studd 8-4-8-1; Barnes 16-5-22-0.

Umpires: E.H.Elliott and J.Swift

ENGLAND v AUSTRALIA 1884 (First Test)

At Old Trafford, Manchester, 10 (no play), 11, 12 July
Result: Match drawn

England

Batsman	1st innings		2nd innings	
W.G.Grace	c Palmer b Boyle	8	b Palmer	31
A.N.Hornby*	st Blackham b Boyle	0	(9) st Blackham b Palmer	4
G.Ulyett	b Spofforth	5	c Bannerman b Boyle	1
A.Shrewsbury	b Boyle	43	b Palmer	25
A.G.Steel	c Midwinter b Spofforth	15	c Blackham b Bonnor	18
A.P.Lucas	not out	15	(2) b Giffen	24
W.Barnes	c and b Boyle	0	(6) b Palmer	8
T.C.O'Brien	b Spofforth	0	c Bannerman b Spofforth	20
R.G.Barlow	c Bonnor b Boyle	6	(7) not out	14
R.Pilling†	c Scott b Boyle	0	b Spofforth	3
E.Peate	b Spofforth	2	not out	8
Extras	(LB 1)	1	(B 18, LB 5, NB 1)	24
		95	(9 wkts)	180

1/6 2/13 3/13 4/45 5/83 6/83 7/84 8/93 9/93
1/41 2/44 3/70 4/106 5/108 6/114 7/139 8/145 9/154

Bowling: *First Innings*—Spofforth 32-10-42-4; Boyle 25-9-42-6; Palmer 6-2-10-0. *Second Innings*—Spofforth 41-17-52-2; Boyle 20-8-27-1; Palmer 36-17-47-4; Giffen 29-15-25-1; Bonnor 4-1-5-1.

Australia

P.S.McDonnell	c Pilling b Steel	36
A.C.Bannerman	lbw b Ulyett	6
W.L.Murdoch*	c Grace b Peate	28
G.Giffen	c and b Barnes	16
W.E.Midwinter	c Grace b Ulyett	37
G.J.Bonnor	hit wkt b Peate	6
J.M.Blackham†	lbw b Steel	8
H.J.H.Scott	b Grace	12
G.E.Palmer	not out	14
F.R.Spofforth	c Shrewsbury b Peate	13
H.F.Boyle	b Ulyett	4
Extras	(LB 2)	2
		182

1/10 2/56 3/86 4/90 5/97 6/118 7/141 8/157 9/172

Bowling: Peate 49-25-62-3; Ulyett 30-17-41-3; Barlow 8-3-18-0; Steel 13-5-32-2; Barnes 19-10-25-1; Grace 11-10-2-1.

Umpires: C.K.Pullin and J.Rowbotham

ENGLAND v AUSTRALIA 1884 (Second Test)

At Lord's, London, 21, 22, 23 July
Result: England won by an innings and 5 runs

Australia

Batsman	1st innings		2nd innings	
P.S.McDonnell	b Peate	0	b Steel	20
A.C.Bannerman	b Peate	12	c and b Ulyett	27
W.L.Murdoch*	lbw b Peate	10	c Shrewsbury b Ulyett	17
G.Giffen	b Peate	63	c Peate b Barnes	5
W.E.Midwinter	b Peate	3	(7) b Ulyett	6
G.J.Bonnor	c Grace b Christopherson	25	(5) c and b Ulyett	4
J.M.Blackham†	run out	0	(8) retired hurt	0
H.J.H.Scott	c sub (W.L.Murdoch) b Steel	75	(6) not out	31
G.E.Palmer	c Grace b Peate	7	b Ulyett	13
F.R.Spofforth	c Barlow b Grace	0	c Shrewsbury b Barlow	11
H.F.Boyle	not out	26	b Ulyett	10
Extras	(B 5, LB 3)	8	(B 1)	1
		229		**145**

1/0 2/25 3/32 4/46 5/88 6/93 7/132 8/155 9/160
1/33 2/60 3/65 4/73 5/84 6/90 7/118 8/133 9/145

Bowling: *First Innings*—Peate 40-14-85-6; Barlow 20-6-44-0; Ulyett 11-3-21-0; Christopherson 26-10-52-1; Grace 7-4-13-1; Steel 1.2-0-6-1. *Second Innings*—Peate 16-4-34-0; Barlow 21-8-31-1; Ulyett 39.1-23-36-7; Christopherson 8-3-17-0; Steel 10-2-26-1.

England

W.G.Grace	c Bonnor b Palmer	14
A.P.Lucas	c Bonnor b Palmer	28
A.Shrewsbury	st Blackham b Giffen	27
G.Ulyett	b Palmer	32
A.G.Steel	b Palmer	148
Lord Harris*	b Spofforth	4
R.G.Barlow	c Palmer b Bonnor	38
W.W.Read	b Palmer	12
Hon.A.Lyttelton†	b Palmer	31
E.Peate	not out	8
S.Christopherson	c Bonnor b Spofforth	17
Extras	(B 15, LB 5)	20
		379

1/37 2/56 3/90 4/120 5/135 6/233 7/272 8/348 9/351

Bowling: Spofforth 55.1-19-112-2; Palmer 75-26-111-6; Giffen 22-4-68-1; Boyle 11-3-16-0; Bonnor 8-1-23-1; Midwinter 13-2-29-0.

Umpires: F.H.Farrands and C.K.Pullin

ENGLAND v AUSTRALIA 1884 (Third Test)

At Kennington Oval, London, 11, 12, 13 August
Result: Match drawn

Australia

A.C.Bannerman	c Read b Peate	4
P.S.McDonnell	c Ulyett b Peate	103
W.L.Murdoch*	c Peate b Barnes	211
H.J.H.Scott	c Lyttelton b Barnes	102
G.Giffen	c Steel b Ulyett	32
G.J.Bonnor	c Read b Grace	8
W.E.Midwinter	c Grace b Lyttelton	30
J.M.Blackham†	lbw b Lyttelton	31
G.E.Palmer	not out	8
F.R.Spofforth	b Lyttelton	4
H.F.Boyle	c Harris b Lyttelton	1
Extras	(B 7, LB 10)	17
		551

1/15 2/158 3/365 4/432 5/454 6/494 7/532 8/545 9/549

Bowling: Peate 63-25-99-2; Ulyett 56-24-96-1; Steel 34-7-71-0; Barnes 52-25-81-2; Barlow 50-22-72-0; Grace 24-14-23-1; Read 7-0-36-0; Scotton 5-1-20-0; Harris 5-1-15-0; Lyttelton 12-5-19-4; Shrewsbury 3-2-2-0.

England

Batsman	1st innings		2nd innings	
W.G.Grace	run out	19		
W.H.Scotton	c Scott b Giffen	90		
W.Barnes	c Midwinter b Spofforth	19		
A.Shrewsbury	c Blackham b Midwinter	10	(3) c Scott b Giffen	37
A.G.Steel	lbw b Palmer	31		
G.Ulyett	c Bannerman b Palmer	10		
R.G.Barlow	c Murdoch b Palmer	0	(1) not out	21
Lord Harris*	lbw b Palmer	14	(4) not out	6
Hon.A.Lyttelton†	b Spofforth	8	(2) b Boyle	17
W.W.Read	b Boyle	117		
E.Peate	not out	4		
Extras	(B 8, LB 7, NB 3, W 6)	24	(B 3, LB 1)	4
		346	(2 wkts)	**85**

1/32 2/60 3/75 4/120 5/136 6/136 7/160 8/181 9/332
1/85 2/73

Bowling: *First Innings*—Bonnor 13-4-33-0; Palmer 54-19-90-4; Spofforth 58-31-81-2; Boyle 13-7-24-1; Midwinter 31-16-41-1; Giffen 26-13-36-1; Scott 3-0-17-0. *Second Innings*—Palmer 2-1-2-0; Spofforth 6-2-14-0; Boyle 8-1-32-1; Midwinter 3-0-15-0; Giffen 7-1-18-1.

Umpires: F.H.Farrands and C.K.Pullin

AUSTRALIA v ENGLAND 1884-85 (First Test)

At Adelaide Oval, 12, 13, 15, 16 December
Result: England won by 8 wickets

Australia

Batsman	First innings		Second innings	
A.C.Bannerman	lbw b Peel	2	(2) c Scott b Boyle	2
P.S.McDonnell	b Attewell	124	run out	83
W.L.Murdoch*	c Hunter b Peel	5	(3) not out	26
H.J.H.Scott	b Peel	19	(5) lbw b Peel	
J.M.Blackham†	c Attewell b Bates	66	(1) b Peel	
G.Giffen	b Bates	4	(4) c Shrewsbury b Peel	
G.J.Bonnor	c Read b Bates	4	b Barnes	28
G.E.Palmer	c Shrewsbury b Bates	6	not out	
H.F.Boyle	c Hunter b Bates	1	(10)	
G.Alexander	run out	3	(9) st Hunter b Peel	
W.H.Cooper	not out	0	(6) c Shrewsbury b Barnes	
Extras	(B 7, W 2)	9	(B 4)	4
		243		191

1/28 2/47 3/95 4/190 5/224 6/227 7/233 8/239 9/242
1/28 2/56 3/125 4/139 5/160 6/160 7/171 8/182 9/191

Bowling: *First Innings*—Attewell 50-23-48-1; Peel 41-15-68-3; Ulyett 10-3-23-0; Flowers 10-1-27-0; Barnes 14-2-37-0; Bates 24.1-10-31-5. *Second Innings*—Peel 40.1-15-51-5; Bates 9-3-26-0; Barnes 31-10-51-3; Attewell 18-10-26-0; Flowers 16-4-27-0; Ulyett 2-1-3-0.

England

Batsman	First innings		Second innings	
W.H.Scotton	st Blackham b Giffen	82	(2) c Scott b Boyle	2
A.Shrewsbury*	b Boyle	0	(3) not out	26
G.Ulyett	c Alexander b Boyle	68		
W.Barnes	b Palmer	134	not out	28
W.Bates	c Giffen b Palmer	18		
W.Flowers	b Palmer	15	(1) c Scott b Palmer	7
J.M.Read	c and b Giffen	14		
J.Briggs	c Blackham b Palmer	1		
W.Attewell	not out	12		
R.Peel	b Palmer	4		
J.Hunter†	run out	1		
Extras	(B 18, LB 1, NB 1)	20	(B 4)	4
		369	(2 wkts)	67

1/11 2/107 3/282 4/306 5/325 6/344 7/349 8/349 9/361
1/8 2/14

Bowling: *First Innings*—Boyle 63-25-95-2; Giffen 56.2-26-80-2; Bonnor 16-10-23-0; Palmer 73-37-81-5; McDonnell 3-0-11-0; Scott 4-1-9-0; Alexander 10-3-24-0. *Second Innings*—Palmer 16-5-23-1; Boyle 9-3-21-1; Giffen 6-0-19-0.

Umpires: N.Cole and I.A.Fisher

AUSTRALIA v ENGLAND 1884-85 (Second Test)

At Melbourne Cricket Ground, 1, 2, 3, 5 January
Result: England won by 10 wickets

England

Batsman	First innings		Second innings	
W.H.Scotton	b Bruce	13	not out	7
A.Shrewsbury*	c Worrall b Morris	72	not out	0
W.Barnes	b Morris	58		
W.Bates	b Bruce	35		
W.Flowers	c Worrall b Bruce	5		
J.M.Read	b Jones	3		
J.Briggs	c Horan b Jones	121		
G.Ulyett	b Jones	0		
W.Attewell	c Jones b Worrall	30		
R.Peel	b Jones	5		
J.Hunter†	not out	39		
Extras	(B 7, LB 12, NB 1)	20		
		401	(0 wkts)	7

1/28 2/144 3/161 4/191 5/194 6/204 7/204 8/254 9/303

Bowling: *First Innings*—Bruce 55-22-88-3; Worrall 56-28-97-1; Marr 11-6-11-0; Trumble 23-9-41-0; Robertson 11-3-24-0; Morris 34-14-73-2; Jones 25.2-9-47-4; Horan 1-1-0-0; Bruce 0.1-0-4-0. *Second Innings*—Marr 1-0-3-0.

Australia

Batsman	First innings		Second innings	
S.P.Jones	lbw b Peel	19	b Ulyett	9
S.Morris	lbw b Attewell	4	(10) not out	10
T.P.Horan*	c Shrewsbury b Peel	63	c Hunter b Barnes	16
J.W.Trumble	c and b Barnes	59	c and b Barnes	11
A.H.Jarvis†	c Briggs b Flowers	82	lbw b Peel	10
R.J.Pope	c Flowers b Attewell	0	b Peel	3
A.P.Marr	b Barnes	0	c and b Barnes	5
H.A.Musgrove	c Read b Barnes	4	c Bates b Peel	9
J.Worrall	b Flowers	34	c and b Barnes	6
W.Bruce	not out	3	(2) c Hunter b Barnes	45
W.R.Robertson	c Barnes b Peel	0	b Barnes	2
Extras	(B 3, LB 4, NB 2, W 2)	11		
		279		126

1/4 2/46 3/124 4/190 5/193 6/193 7/203 8/276 9/278
1/29 2/66 3/80 4/83 5/86 6/95 7/99 8/108 9/116

Bowling: *First Innings*—Peel 102.1-56-78-3; Attewell 61-35-54-2; Barnes 50-27-50-3; Flowers 29-12-46-2; Ulyett 15-7-23-0; Bates 17-11-17-0. *Second Innings*—Flowers 11-6-11-0; Peel 44-26-45-3; Ulyett 8-3-19-1; Briggs 8-3-13-0; Barnes 38.3-26-31-6.

Umpires: E.H.Elliott and J.Lillywhite

AUSTRALIA v ENGLAND 1884-85 (Third Test)

At Sydney Cricket Ground, 20, 21, 23, 24 February
Result: Australia won by 6 runs

Australia

A.C.Bannerman c Peel b Flowers	13		c Shrewsbury b Ulyett	16
S.P.Jones st Hunter b Flowers	28	(4)	b Attewell	22
T.P.Horan c Hunter b Attewell	7		b Bates	36
H.J.H.Scott c Ulyett b Attewell	5	(5)	c Barnes b Attewell	4
G.J.Bonnor c Barnes b Flowers	18	(2)	b Ulyett	29
J.W.Trumble c Read b Attewell	13		c Ulyett b Bates	32
H.H.Massie* c Scotton b Flowers	2		b Bates	21
A.H.Jarvis† b Attewell	0		c and b Peel	2
F.R.Spofforth st Hunter b Flowers	3	(11)	c Attewell b Bates	0
T.W.Garrett not out	51		not out	0
E.Evans c Hunter b Ulyett	33	(9)	b Bates	1
Extras (B 3, LB 5)	8		(B 1, LB 1)	2
	181			**165**

1/45 2/46 3/56 4/73 5/77   1/37 2/56 3/91 4/95 5/119
6/83 7/83 8/92 9/101   6/151 7/161 8/165 9/165

Bowling: *First Innings*—Peel 32-13-51-0; Attewell 71-47-53-4; Ulyett 12.2-8-17-1; Flowers 46-24-46-5; Bates 6-2-6-0. *Second Innings*—Ulyett 39-25-42-2; Peel 20-10-24-1; Attewell 58-36-54-2; Flowers 20-14-19-0; Bates 20-10-24-5.

England

W.H.Scotton c Jarvis b Horan	22		b Spofforth	2
A.Shrewsbury* c and b Spofforth	18		b Spofforth	24
G.Ulyett b Spofforth	2		run out	4
W.Barnes st Jarvis b Spofforth	0		c Jarvis b Trumble	5
W.Bates c Evans b Horan	12		c Jarvis b Spofforth	31
J.Briggs c Scott b Horan	3		b Spofforth	1
W.Flowers c Jarvis b Spofforth	24		c Evans b Spofforth	56
J.M.Read c Evans b Horan	4		b Spofforth	56
W.Attewell b Horan	14		run out	0
R.Peel not out	8		c Jarvis b Trumble	3
J.Hunter† b Horan	13		not out	5
Extras (B 8, LB 3, NB 2)	13		(B 7, LB 9, NB 1, W 3)	20
	133			**207**

1/31 2/33 3/33 4/46 5/56   1/14 2/18 3/29 4/59 5/61
6/70 7/82 8/111 9/111   6/92 7/194 8/194 9/199

Bowling: *First Innings*—Spofforth 48-23-54-4; Garrett 6-2-17-0; Horan 37.1-22-40-6; Evans 4-1-9-0. *Second Innings*—Spofforth 48.1-22-90-6; Garrett 21-8-31-0; Trumble 26-13-26-2; Horan 9-4-23-0; Evans 4-1-8-0; Jones 3-0-9-0.

Umpires: E.H.Elliott and J.W.Payne (J.Bryant deputised)

AUSTRALIA v ENGLAND 1884-85 (Fourth Test)

At Sydney Cricket Ground, 14, 16, 17 March
Result: Australia won by 8 wickets

England

A.Shrewsbury* b Giffen	40	(2)	c Bonnor b Spofforth	16
G.Ulyett b Giffen	10	(1)	c Garrett b Palmer	2
W.H.Scotton c Blackham b Giffen	4		c Jones b Spofforth	0
W.Barnes b Giffen	50		c Bannerman b Spofforth	20
W.Bates c and b Jones	64		c Blackham b Palmer	1
J.M.Read b Giffen	47		c Bannerman b Spofforth	6
W.Flowers b Giffen	14		c Jones b Palmer	7
J.Briggs c Palmer b Spofforth	3		run out	5
W.Attewell b Giffen	1		not out	1
R.Peel not out	17		c and b Spofforth	0
J.Hunter† b Spofforth	13		b Palmer	4
Extras (B 5, LB 1)	6		(B 14, NB 1)	15
	269			**77**

1/52 2/52 3/76 4/159 5/186   1/3 2/16 3/19 4/20 5/27
6/219 7/222 8/229 9/252   6/42 7/66 8/69 9/69

Bowling: *First Innings*—Giffen 52-14-117-7; Palmer 16-5-35-0; Spofforth 29-10-61-2; Garrett 2-1-5-0; Trumble 12-5-16-0; Horan 5-2-12-0; Jones 10-5-17-1. *Second Innings*—Spofforth 20-8-30-5; Palmer 19.1-7-32-4.

Australia

G.E.Palmer b Ulyett	0	(1)	c Ulyett b Peel	3
T.W.Garrett b Barnes	32	(2)	b Barnes	8
J.W.Trumble b Peel	5			
P.S.McDonnell c Attewell b Ulyett	20			
A.C.Bannerman c Shrewsbury b Flowers	51			
G.Giffen c Attewell b Barnes	1			
T.P.Horan c Barnes b Ulyett	9	(3)	not out	12
G.J.Bonnor c Bates b Barnes	128			
S.P.Jones run out	40	(4)	not out	15
J.M.Blackham*† not out	11			
F.R.Spofforth c Read b Barnes	1			
Extras (B 5, LB 1, NB 3, W 2)	11			
	309		(2 wkts)	**38**

1/0 2/15 3/40 4/98 5/108   1/7 2/16
6/119 7/134 8/288 9/308

Bowling: *First Innings*—Ulyett 54-25-91-3; Peel 31-12-53-1; Attewell 18-13-22-0; Bates 17-5-44-0; Barnes 35.3-17-61-4; Flowers 14-5-27-1. *Second Innings*—Barnes 9-3-15-1; Peel 9-4-16-1; Attewell 3-1-4-0; Flowers 3.3-2-3-0.

Umpires: E.H.Elliott and P.G.McShane (H.H.Massie deputised)

ENGLAND v AUSTRALIA 1886 (First Test)

At Old Trafford, Manchester, 5, 6, 7 July
Result: England won by 4 wickets

Australia

Batsman	First innings	Runs	Second innings	Runs
S.P.Jones	lbw b Grace	87	c Ulyett b Steel	12
H.J.H.Scott*	c Barlow b Ulyett	21	b Barlow	47
G.Giffen	b Steel	3	c Shrewsbury b Barlow	1
A.H.Jarvis†	c Scotton b Ulyett	45	c Lohmann b Barlow	4
G.J.Bonnor	c Lohmann b Barlow	4	b Barlow b Peate	2
J.W.Trumble	c Scotton b Steel	24	c Ulyett b Barlow	4
W.Bruce	run out	5	(8) c Grace b Barlow	0
T.W.Garrett	c Pilling b Lohmann	5	(9) c Grace b Ulyett	22
J.M.Blackham	not out	7	(7) lbw b Barlow	8
G.E.Palmer	c Lohmann b Ulyett	4	c Pilling b Barlow	8
F.R.Spofforth	c Barlow b Ulyett	2	not out	20
Extras	(W 1)	1	(B 3)	3
Total		**205**		**123**

1/58 2/71 3/134 4/141 5/181 6/187 7/188 8/192 9/201
1/37 2/42 3/44 4/55 5/68 6/70 7/70 8/73 9/103

Bowling: *First Innings*—Peate 19-7-30-0; Lohmann 23-9-41-1; Steel 27-5-47-2; Ulyett 36.1-20-46-4; Barlow 23-15-19-1; Grace 9-3-21-1. *Second Innings*—Peate 46-25-45-1; Lohmann 5-3-14-0; Steel 8-3-9-1; Ulyett 6.3-3-7-1; Barlow 52-34-44-7; Grace 1-0-1-0.

England

Batsman	First innings	Runs	Second innings	Runs
W.H.Scotton	c Trumble b Garrett	21	b Palmer	20
W.G.Grace	c Bonnor b Spofforth	8	c Palmer b Giffen	4
A.Shrewsbury	b Spofforth	31	c and b Giffen	4
W.W.Read	c Scott b Garrett	51	c Jones b Spofforth	9
A.G.Steel*	c Jarvis b Palmer	12	(6) not out	19
R.G.Barlow	not out	38	(5) c Palmer b Spofforth	30
G.Ulyett	b Spofforth	17	c Scott b Garrett	8
J.Briggs	c Garrett b Spofforth	1	not out	2
G.A.Lohmann	b Giffen	32		
E.Peate	st Jarvis b Palmer	6		
R.Pilling†	c Bruce b Palmer	2		
Extras	(B 2, LB 2)	4	(B 10, LB 1)	11
Total		**223**	**(6 wkts)**	**107**

1/9 2/51 3/80 4/109 5/131 6/156 7/160 8/206 9/219
1/7 2/15 3/24 4/62 5/90 6/105

Bowling: *First Innings*—Spofforth 53-22-82-4; Giffen 32-15-44-1; Garrett 45-23-43-2; Bruce 10-7-9-0; Palmer 17.2-4-41-3. *Second Innings*—Spofforth 29.2-13-40-2; Giffen 24-9-31-2; Garrett 17-9-14-1; Palmer 7-3-11-1.

Umpires: C.K.Pullin and J.West

AUSTRALIA v ENGLAND 1884-85 (Fifth Test)

At Melbourne Cricket Ground, 21, 23, 24, 25 March
Result: England won by an innings and 98 runs

Australia

Batsman	First innings	Runs	Second innings	Runs
A.C.Bannerman	c Peel b Ulyett	5	c sub (G.F.Vernon) b Ulyett	2
W.Bruce	c Briggs b Peel	15	(6) c Bates b Attewell	35
G.Giffen	b Ulyett	13	c Peel b Ulyett	12
T.P.Horan*	lbw b Ulyett	0	(5) b Attewell	20
S.P.Jones	lbw b Peel	0	(4) b Peel	17
F.H.Walters	b Ulyett	7	(8) c Attewell b Flowers	5
A.H.Jarvis†	c Hunter b Peel	15	(7) lbw b Attewell	10
J.W.Trumble	not out	34	not out	15
P.G.McShane	c Hunter b Barnes	9	(11) lbw b Attewell	9
T.W.Garrett	c Briggs b Barnes	6	(2) b Ulyett	6
F.R.Spofforth	b Attewell	50	(10) c sub (A.H.Jarvis) b Flowers	1
Extras	(B 5, LB 1, NB 3)	9	(B 5)	5
Total		**163**		**125**

1/21 2/21 3/21 4/34 5/34 6/45 7/67 8/89 9/99
1/4 2/17 3/26 4/60 5/60 6/91 7/100 8/106 9/108

Bowling: *First Innings*—Peel 41-26-28-3; Ulyett 23-7-52-4; Barnes 28-12-47-2; Flowers 9-6-9-0; Attewell 5-1-18-1. *Second Innings*—Ulyett 15-7-25-3; Peel 30-16-37-1; Attewell 36.1-22-24-3; Flowers 21-7-34-3.

England

Batsman	How out	Runs
W.Barnes	c Horan b Bruce	74
W.H.Scotton	b Bruce	27
J.M.Read	b Giffen	13
G.Ulyett	b Spofforth	1
A.Shrewsbury*	not out	105
W.Bates	c Walters b Bruce	61
W.Flowers	b Spofforth	16
J.Briggs	c Walters b Trumble	43
W.Attewell	c Bannerman b Trumble	0
R.Peel	b Trumble	0
J.Hunter†	b Giffen	18
Extras	(B 10, LB 14, NB 4)	28
Total		**386**

1/61 2/96 3/97 4/141 5/256 6/324 7/324 8/335 9/337

Bowling: Giffen 74.3-31-132-2; Bruce 51-13-99-3; Spofforth 49-21-71-2; Trumble 28-14-29-3; Garrett 8-6-12-0; McShane 3-2-3-0; Jones 5-2-7-0; Horan 3-0-5-0.

Umpires: J.H.Hodges and J.Phillips (J.C.Allen, T.W.Garrett and J.Lillywhite deputised)

ENGLAND v AUSTRALIA 1886 (Second Test)

At Lord's, London, 19, 20, 21 July

Result: England won by an innings and 106 runs

England

W.G.Grace c Jarvis b Palmer		18
W.H.Scotton b Garrett		19
A.Shrewsbury c Bonnor b Trumble		164
W.W.Read c Spofforth b Giffen		22
A.G.Steel* lbw b Spofforth		5
W.Barnes c Palmer b Garrett		58
R.G.Barlow c Palmer b Spofforth		12
G.Ulyett b Spofforth		19
E.F.S.Tylecote† b Spofforth		0
J.Briggs c Jones b Trumble		0
G.A.Lohmann not out		7
Extras (B 24, LB 4, NB 1)		29
		‾‾‾
		353

1/27 2/77 3/112 4/119 5/280
6/303 7/333 8/333 9/340

Bowling: Garrett 72-40-77-2; Evans 36-20-37-0; Palmer 38-15-45-1; Spofforth 56-26-73-4; Trumble 14-4-27-2; Giffen 40-18-63-1; Jones 3-1-2-0.

Australia

S.P.Jones c Grace b Briggs	25	(4)	b Briggs	17
H.J.H.Scott* lbw b Briggs	30	(5)	b Briggs	2
G.Giffen b Steel	3	(6)	b Barlow	1
A.H.Jarvis† b Briggs	3	(7)	not out	13
G.J.Bonnor c Grace b Steel	0	(8)	b Briggs	3
J.W.Trumble c Tylecote b Briggs	0	(3)	c Tylecote b Barnes	20
G.E.Palmer c Shrewsbury b Barnes	20	(1)	c Lohmann b Barlow	48
J.M.Blackham b Briggs	23	(9)	b Briggs	5
T.W.Garrett not out	7	(2)	b Briggs	4
F.R.Spofforth b Barnes	5	(11)	c and b Briggs	0
E.Evans c Ulyett b Barnes	0	(10)	run out	0
Extras (B 4, LB 1)	5		(B 13)	13
	‾‾‾			‾‾‾
	121			126

1/45 2/52 3/59 4/60 5/62   1/6 2/56 3/91 4/95 5/98
6/67 7/99 8/109 9/121   6/105 7/120 8/126 9/126

Bowling: First Innings—Barnes 14.3-7-25-3; Lohmann 7-3-21-0; Briggs 34-22-29-5; Steel 21-8-34-2; Barlow 6-3-7-0. Second Innings—Barnes 10-5-18-1; Lohmann 14-9-11-0; Briggs 38.1-17-45-6; Steel 16-9-14-0; Barlow 25-20-12-2; Ulyett 8-3-13-0.

Umpires: F.H.Farrands and C.K.Pullin

ENGLAND v AUSTRALIA 1886 (Third Test)

At Kennington Oval, London, 12, 13, 14 August

Result: England won by an innings and 217 runs

England

W.G.Grace c Blackham b Spofforth		170
W.H.Scotton b Garrett		34
A.Shrewsbury c Bonnor b Trumble		44
W.W.Read c Jones b Spofforth		94
W.Barnes c Evans b Trumble		3
A.G.Steel* st Blackham b Trumble		9
R.G.Barlow c Trumble b Garrett		3
G.Ulyett c McIlwraith b Garrett		0
J.Briggs c Trumble b Spofforth		53
E.F.S.Tylecote† not out		10
G.A.Lohmann b Spofforth		7
Extras (B 3, LB 2, NB 2)		7
		‾‾‾
		434

1/170 2/216 3/287 4/293 5/305
6/314 7/320 8/410 9/418

Bowling: Giffen 62-32-96-0; Garrett 99-55-88-3; Palmer 47-21-80-0; Spofforth 30.1-12-65-4; Evans 13-10-6-0; Trumble 47-14-83-3.

Australia

S.P.Jones c Grace b Lohmann	2	(3)	c Read b Lohmann	2
G.E.Palmer c Barlow b Briggs	15	(6)	st Tylecote b Steel	35
G.Giffen c Shrewsbury b Briggs	5	(4)	c and b Lohmann	47
H.J.H.Scott* c Tylecote b Lohmann	6	(5)	c Grace b Lohmann	4
J.W.Trumble c Read b Lohmann	13	(7)	c Read b Briggs	18
J.McIlwraith b Lohmann	2	(1)	c Tylecote b Briggs	7
J.M.Blackham† c and b Briggs	0	(8)	c Grace b Briggs	5
T.W.Garrett c Grace b Lohmann	9	(10)	c Shrewsbury b Lohmann	4
W.Bruce c Ulyett b Lohmann	9		b Lohmann	11
E.Evans not out	1	(2)	run out	3
F.R.Spofforth b Lohmann	4		not out	5
Extras (B 4)	4		(B 7, LB 1)	8
	‾‾‾			‾‾‾
	68			149

1/2 2/11 3/22 4/34 5/35   1/11 2/14 3/26 4/30 5/84
6/35 7/44 8/49 9/67   6/120 7/129 8/131 9/137

Bowling: First Innings—Lohmann 30.2-17-36-7; Briggs 30-17-28-3. Second Innings—Lohmann 37-14-68-5; Briggs 32-19-30-3; Barlow 14-8-13-0; Barnes 7-4-10-0; Steel 7-1-20-1.

Umpires: R.P.Carpenter and F.H.Farrands

AUSTRALIA v ENGLAND 1886-87 (First Test)

At Sydney Cricket Ground, 28, 29, 31 January

Result: England won by 13 runs

England

W.Bates c Midwinter b Ferris	8		b Ferris	24
A.Shrewsbury* c McShane b Ferris	2		b Ferris	29
W.Barnes c Spofforth b Turner	0		c Moses b Garrett	32
R.G.Barlow b Turner	2		c Jones b Ferris	4
J.M.Read c Spofforth b Ferris	5		b Ferris	0
W.Gunn b Turner	0		b Turner	4
W.H.Scotton c Jones b Turner	1	(9)	c Spofforth b Garrett	6
J.Briggs c Midwinter b Turner	5		b Spofforth	33
G.A.Lohmann c Garrett b Ferris	17	(7)	lbw b Ferris	3
W.Flowers b Turner	2		c McDonnell b Turner	14
M.Sherwin† not out	0		not out	21
Extras (B 2, LB 1)	3		(B 7, LB 7)	14
	45			**184**

1/11 2/11 3/13 4/13 5/13
6/17 7/21 8/29 9/41

1/31 2/80 3/92 4/92 5/98
6/99 7/103 8/128 9/153

Bowling: *First Innings*—Turner 18-11-15-6; Ferris 17.3-7-27-4. *Second Innings*—Turner 44.2-22-53-2; Ferris 61-30-76-5; Spofforth 12-3-17-1; Midwinter 4-1-10-0; Garrett 12-7-8-2; McShane 3-0-6-0.

Australia

P.S.McDonnell* b Barnes	14	(2)	lbw b Barnes	0
J.M.Blackham† c Sherwin b Lohmann	4	(1)	b Barnes	5
H.Moses b Barlow	31		c Shrewsbury b Barnes	24
S.P.Jones c Shrewsbury b Bates	31		c Read b Barnes	18
C.T.B.Turner b Barlow	31		c and b Barnes	7
A.C.Bannerman not out	15		b Lohmann	4
P.G.McShane lbw b Briggs	5		b Briggs	0
W.E.Midwinter c Shrewsbury b Barlow	0		lbw b Barnes	10
T.W.Garrett b Lohmann	12		c Gunn b Lohmann	10
F.R.Spofforth b Lohmann	2		b Lohmann	5
J.J.Ferris c Barlow b Barnes	1		not out	0
Extras (B 1)	1		(B 12, LB 2)	14
	119			**97**

1/8 2/18 3/64 4/67 5/86
6/95 7/96 8/116 9/118

1/4 2/5 3/29 4/38 5/58
6/61 7/80 8/83 9/95

Bowling: *First Innings*—Barnes 22.1-16-19-2; Lohmann 21-12-30-3; Briggs 14-5-25-1; Barlow 35-23-25-3; Bates 21-9-19-1. *Second Innings*—Barlow 13-6-20-0; Barnes 46-29-28-6; Bates 17-11-8-0; Lohmann 24-11-20-3; Briggs 7-5-7-1.

Umpires: C.Bannerman and H.Rawlinson

AUSTRALIA v ENGLAND 1886-87 (Second Test)

At Sydney Cricket Ground, 25, 26, 28 February, 1 March

Result: England won by 71 runs

England

W.Bates c Ferris b Turner	8		b Turner	30
A.Shrewsbury* b Turner	9		b Turner	6
J.M.Read b Turner	11	(4)	st Burton b Ferris	2
W.Gunn b Turner	9	(5)	c Cottam b Ferris	10
R.G.Barlow c Allen b Ferris	34	(3)	not out	42
G.A.Lohmann b Ferris	2		b Ferris	6
W.H.Scotton b Turner	0		b Ferris	2
J.Briggs b Ferris	17		b Garrett	16
W.Flowers c Allen b Ferris	37		b Turner	18
R.Wood lbw b Ferris	6		b Midwinter	0
M.Sherwin† not out	4		b Turner	5
Extras (B 9, LB 3, NB 2)	14		(B 12, LB 5)	17
	151			**154**

1/14 2/19 3/35 4/38 5/43
6/50 7/73 8/130 9/145

1/21 2/42 3/47 4/59 5/73
6/77 7/98 8/136 9/137

Bowling: *First Innings*—Ferris 45-16-71-5; Turner 53-29-41-5; Midwinter 3-1-2-0; Lyons 2-0-11-0. *Second Innings*—Turner 64.1-33-52-4; Garrett 10-6-7-1; Midwinter 6-3-9-1.

Australia

J.J.Lyons b Lohmann	11	(4)	c Gunn b Bates	0
W.F.Giffen b Lohmann	2	(6)	b Briggs	0
R.C.Allen b Lohmann	14		c sub (C.T.B.Turner) b Bates	30
H.Moses b Flowers	28	(2)	st Sherwin b Bates	33
P.S.McDonnell* c Gunn b Lohmann	10	(1)	c Gunn b Lohmann	35
W.E.Midwinter b Lohmann	1	(7)	c Sherwin b Lohmann	4
J.T.Cottam b Lohmann	1	(5)	st Sherwin b Briggs	3
C.T.B.Turner c and b Flowers	9		c Briggs b Bates	9
T.W.Garrett b Lohmann	1		c Sherwin b Briggs	20
J.J.Ferris b Lohmann	1		run out	2
F.J.Burton† not out	0		not out	2
Extras (B 5, LB 1)	7		(B 9, LB 3)	12
	84			**150**

1/12 2/15 3/40 4/56 5/59
6/65 7/82 8/83 9/83

1/51 2/86 3/86 4/95 5/95
6/106 7/121 8/129 9/135

Bowling: *First Innings*—Briggs 20-6-34-0; Lohmann 27.1-12-35-8; Flowers 8-3-9-2. *Second Innings*—Lohmann 40-16-52-2; Briggs 22-9-31-3; Flowers 13-5-17-0; Barlow 9-2-12-0; Bates 26-13-26-4.

Umpires: C.Bannerman and J.Swift (W.Gunn deputised)

AUSTRALIA v ENGLAND 1887-88 (Only Test)

At Sydney Cricket Ground, 10, 11 (no play), 13 (no play), 14, 15 February
Result: England won by 126 runs

England

	1st		2nd
A.Shrewsbury c Turner b Ferris	44	b Ferris	1
A.E.Stoddart c McShane b Turner	16	c Blackham b Turner	17
G.Ulyett c Burton b Turner	5	b Ferris	5
W.W.Read* b Turner	10	b Turner	8
J.M.Read c and b Turner	0	c Bannerman b Turner	39
R.Peel hit wkt b Ferris	3	st Blackham b Turner	9
W.Newham c Worrall b Ferris	9	lbw b Turner	17
G.A.Lohmann c Jones b Ferris	12	(8) c Blackham b Turner	12
J.Briggs b Turner	0	(7) c Worrall b McShane	0
W.Attewell not out	7	not out	14
R.Pilling† run out	3	b Turner	5
Extras (B 4)	4	(B 7, LB 5)	12
	113		**137**

1/27 2/36 4/54 5/57
6/86 7/102 8/103 9/103

1/9 2/15 3/27 4/54 5/82
6/82 7/84 8/111 9/131

Bowling: *First Innings*—Turner 50-27-44-5; Ferris 47-25-60-4; Garrett 3-1-5-0. *Second Innings*—Turner 38-23-43-7; Ferris 16-4-43-2; McShane 21-7-39-1.

Australia

	1st		2nd
A.C.Bannerman c Ulyett b Lohmann	2	c Attewell b Lohmann	2
S.P.Jones b Shrewsbury b Peel	0	(4) c Shrewsbury b Lohmann	0
H.Moses c W.W.Read b Turner	3	c Briggs b Lohmann	3
F.J.Burton c Stoddart b Lohmann	1	(5) c Pilling b Peel	1
J.Worrall st Pilling b Peel	6	(10) b Lohmann	0
F.G.McShane c Shrewsbury b Peel	0	(9) b Peel	0
P.S.McDonnell* b Lohmann	3	(2) b Peel	6
J.M.Blackham† c Shrewsbury b Peel	2	not out	25
T.W.Garrett c Pilling b Lohmann	10	(7) c Shrewsbury b Peel	1
C.T.B.Turner not out	8	(6) lbw b Attewell	12
J.J.Ferris c W.W.Read b Peel	0	c Shrewsbury b Attewell	5
Extras (B 6, W 1)	7	(B 2, LB 1)	3
	42		**82**

1/2 2/3 3/10 4/16 5/18
6/21 7/23 8/26 9/37

1/8 2/8 3/20 4/21 5/44
6/47 7/53 8/60 9/61

Bowling: *First Innings*—Lohmann 19-13-17-5; Peel 18.3-9-18-5. *Second Innings*—Lohmann 32-18-35-4; Peel 33-14-40-4; Attewell 4.2-2-4-2.

Umpires: C.Bannerman and J.Phillips

ENGLAND v AUSTRALIA 1888 (First Test)

At Lord's, London, 16, 17 July
Result: Australia won by 61 runs

Australia

	1st		2nd
A.C.Bannerman c Grace b Lohmann	0	b Peel	0
P.S.McDonnell* c O'Brien b Peel	22	b Lohmann	1
G.H.S.Trott c Lohmann b Peel	0	b Lohmann	3
G.J.Bonnor b Lohmann	6	c Lohmann b Peel	8
J.M.Blackham† b Briggs	22	run out	1
S.M.J.Woods c Gunn b Briggs	18	c Grace b Peel	3
C.T.B.Turner c Lohmann b Peel	21	c Grace b Briggs	12
J.D.Edwards not out	0	c Sherwin b Lohmann	0
A.H.Jarvis c Lohmann b Peel	3	(11) c Barnes b Peel	4
J.Worrall c Abel b Briggs	2	b Lohmann	4
J.J.Ferris c Sherwin b Steel	14	(9) not out	20
Extras (B 5)	5	(B 3, LB 1)	4
	116		**60**

1/0 2/3 3/28 4/32 5/65
6/76 7/76 8/79 9/82

1/1 2/1 3/13 4/15 5/18
6/18 7/18 8/42 9/49

Bowling: *First Innings*—Lohmann 20-9-28-2; Peel 21-7-36-4; Briggs 21-8-26-3; Barnes 6-0-17-0; Steel 3.2-2-4-1. *Second Innings*—Lohmann 14-4-33-4; Peel 10.2-3-14-4; Briggs 4-1-9-1; Steel 1-1-0-0.

England

	1st		2nd
W.G.Grace c Woods b Ferris	10	c Bannerman b Ferris	24
R.Abel b Ferris	3	c Bonnor b Ferris	8
W.Barnes c Jarvis b Turner	3	(9) st Blackham b Ferris	1
G.A.Lohmann lbw b Turner	2	(10) st Blackham b Ferris	0
W.W.Read st Blackham b Turner	4	(4) b Turner	3
T.C.O'Brien b Turner	0	(5) b Turner	4
R.Peel run out	8	(3) b Turner	4
A.G.Steel* st Blackham b Turner	3	(6) not out	10
W.Gunn c Blackham b Ferris	2	(7) b Ferris	8
J.Briggs b Woods	17	(8) b Turner	0
M.Sherwin† not out	0	c Ferris b Turner	0
Extras (LB 1)	1		
	53		**62**

1/5 2/14 3/18 4/22 5/22
6/22 7/26 8/35 9/49

1/29 2/34 3/38 4/39 5/44
6/55 7/56 8/57 9/57

Bowling: *First Innings*—Turner 25-9-27-5; Ferris 21-13-19-3; Woods 4-2-6-1. *Second Innings*—Turner 24-8-36-5; Ferris 23-11-26-5.

Umpires: F.H.Farrands and C.K.Pullin

ENGLAND v AUSTRALIA 1888 (Second Test)

At Kennington Oval, London, 13, 14 August

Result: England won by an innings and 137 runs

Australia

Batsman	First Innings		Second Innings	
A.C.Bannerman	c Lohmann b Barnes	13	b Barnes	5
P.S.McDonnell*	c Lohmann b Peel	0	b Peel	32
G.H.S.Trott	b Briggs	13	st Wood b Peel	4
G.J.Bonnor	b Briggs	0	c Wood b Barnes	5
J.D.Edwards	b Lohmann	26	c Read b Barnes	0
A.H.Jarvis	b Briggs	5	(9) b Peel	8
S.M.J.Woods	run out	0	c Abel b Barnes	7
C.T.B.Turner	b Briggs	0	b Peel	18
J.M.Blackham†	b Briggs	0	(10) c Lohmann b Barnes	4
J.Worrall	c Grace b Barnes	8	(11) not out	0
J.J.Ferris	not out	13	(6) run out	16
Extras	(B 1, LB 1)	2	(LB 1)	1
		80		100

1/0 2/22 3/22 4/40 5/49 6/49 7/50 8/50 9/63
1/34 2/38 3/43 4/45 5/62 6/62 7/72 8/89 9/98

Bowling: *First Innings*—Lohmann 29.3-21-21-1; Peel 8-4-14-1; Briggs 37-24-25-5; Barnes 16-9-18-2. *Second Innings*—Lohmann 6-4-11-0; Peel 28.2-13-49-4; Briggs 6-3-7-0; Barnes 29-16-32-5.

England

W.G.Grace*	c Edwards b Turner	1
J.Shuter	b Turner	28
G.Ulyett	c Blackham b Turner	0
W.W.Read	b Turner	18
R.Abel	run out	70
W.Barnes	c Worrall b Turner	62
F.H.Sugg	b Turner	31
R.Peel	b Woods	25
J.Briggs	b Woods	0
G.A.Lohmann	not out	62
H.Wood†	c Bannerman b Ferris	8
Extras	(B 6, LB 4, W 2)	12
		317

1/2 2/6 3/46 4/53 5/165 6/191 7/241 8/242 9/259

Bowling: Turner 60-24-112-6; Ferris 32.5-15-73-1; Trott 7-2-25-0; Woods 32-10-80-2; Worrall 4-1-15-0.

Umpires: R.P.Carpenter and F.H.Farrands

ENGLAND v AUSTRALIA 1888 (Third Test)

At Old Trafford, Manchester, 30, 31 August

Result: England won by an innings and 21 runs

England

W.G.Grace*	c Bonnor b Turner	38
R.Abel	b Turner	0
G.Ulyett	b Turner	0
W.W.Read	b Turner	19
W.Barnes	b Ferris	24
F.H.Sugg	b Woods	24
W.Gunn	lbw b Turner	15
R.Peel	lbw b Ferris	11
J.Briggs	not out	22
G.A.Lohmann	run out	0
R.Pilling†	c Bonnor b Woods	17
Extras	(B 2)	2
		172

1/0 2/6 3/58 4/59 5/96 6/115 7/127 8/135 9/136

Bowling: Ferris 40-20-49-2; Turner 55-21-86-5; Woods 18.1-6-35-2.

Australia

Batsman	First Innings		Second Innings	
P.S.McDonnell*	c Grace b Peel	15	b Lohmann	0
A.C.Bannerman	b Peel	1	c Grace b Peel	0
G.H.S.Trott	st Pilling b Peel	17	run out	0
G.J.Bonnor	run out	5	c Grace b Peel	0
J.D.Edwards	b Peel	0	(9) c Grace b Peel	1
C.T.B.Turner	b Peel	0	(8) b Briggs	26
S.M.J.Woods	c Read b Briggs	4	b Lohmann	0
J.M.Blackham†	c Read b Lohmann	15	(5) b Lohmann	5
J.J.Lyons	c Lohmann b Peel	22	(6) b Briggs	32
J.Worrall	b Peel	0	(11) not out	0
J.J.Ferris	not out	0	(10) c Abel b Peel	3
Extras	(B 2)	2	(B 2, LB 1)	3
		81		70

1/16 2/32 3/35 4/39 5/39 6/43 7/45 8/81 9/81
1/0 2/0 3/1 4/7 5/7 6/7 7/55 8/56 9/70

Bowling: *First Innings*—Peel 26.2-17-31-7; Lohmann 17-9-31-1; Briggs 9-4-17-1. *Second Innings*—Peel 16-4-37-4; Lohmann 8-3-20-3; Briggs 7.1-2-10-2.

Umpires: F.H.Farrands and C.K.Pullin

ENGLAND v AUSTRALIA 1890 (First Test)

At Lord's, London, 21, 22, 23 July
Result: England won by 7 wickets

Australia

J.J.Lyons b Barnes	55	(4)	c Attewell b Peel	33
C.T.B.Turner c Attewell	24		lbw b Peel	2
W.L.Murdoch* c and b Attewell	9	(5)	b Lohmann	19
J.E.Barrett c Grace b Ulyett	9	(1)	not out	67
G.H.S.Trott run out	12	(3)	b Peel	0
S.E.Gregory b Attewell	0		c Lohmann b Barnes	9
P.C.Charlton st MacGregor b Peel	6		lbw b Grace	2
J.M.Blackham† b Peel	5		c Barnes b Grace	10
J.J.Ferris b Attewell	8		lbw b Lohmann	8
E.J.K.Burn st MacGregor b Peel	0	(11)	c MacGregor b Attewell	19
H.Trumble not out	1	(10)	c Barnes b Lohmann	5
Extras (LB 3)	3		(LB 2)	2
	132			**176**

1/66 2/82 3/93 4/109 5/111   1/6 2/8 3/48 4/84 5/106
6/113 7/120 8/131 9/131   6/109 7/119 8/136 9/142

Bowling: *First Innings*—Lohmann 21-10-43-0; Peel 24-11-28-3; Attewell 32-15-42-4; Barnes 6-2-16-1; Ulyett 3-3-0-1. *Second Innings*—Lohmann 29-19-28-3; Peel 43-23-59-3; Attewell 42.2-22-54-1; Barnes 6-3-10-1; Ulyett 6-2-11-0; Grace 14-10-12-2.

England

W.G.Grace* c and b Turner	0		not out	75
A.Shrewsbury st Blackham b Ferris	4		lbw b Ferris	13
W.Gunn run out	14		c and b Ferris	34
W.W.Read c and b Ferris	1		b Trumble	13
J.M.Read b Lyons	34		not out	2
G.Ulyett b Lyons	74			
R.Peel c and b Trumble	16			
W.Barnes b Lyons	9			
G.A.Lohmann c and b Lyons	19			
G.MacGregor† b Lyons	0			
W.Attewell not out	0			
Extras (LB 2)	2			
	173		(3 wkts)	**137**

1/0 2/14 3/20 4/20 5/92   1/27 2/101 3/135
6/133 7/147 8/162 9/166

Bowling: *First Innings*—Turner 35-17-53-1; Ferris 40-17-55-2; Trott 3-0-16-0; Lyons 20.1-7-30-5; Trumble 12-7-17-1. *Second Innings*—Turner 22-12-31-0; Ferris 25-11-42-2; Lyons 20-6-43-0; Trumble 8-1-21-1.

Umpires: A.Hill and C.K.Pullin

ENGLAND v AUSTRALIA 1890 (Second Test)

At Kennington Oval, London, 11, 12 August
Result: England won by 2 wickets

Australia

J.J.Lyons c W.W.Read b Martin	14	(4)	b Martin	21
C.T.B.Turner c Sharpe b Lohmann	12	(7)	b Martin	0
W.L.Murdoch* b Martin	2	(5)	b Lohmann	6
J.E.Barrett c Lohmann b Martin	2	(1)	b Martin	4
G.H.S.Trott c MacGregor b Martin	39	(6)	c Cranston b Martin	25
E.J.K.Burn c MacGregor b Lohmann	7	(2)	b Martin	15
J.M.Blackham† b Martin	1	(8)	b Lohmann	1
J.J.Ferris c Lohmann b Sharpe	6	(3)	lbw b Lohmann	1
P.C.Charlton b Martin	10		b Sharpe	11
S.E.Gregory b Lohmann	2	(11)	not out	4
H.Trumble not out	0	(10)	b Martin	6
Extras			(B 7, LB 1)	8
	92			**102**

1/16 2/27 3/27 4/32 5/39   1/4 2/5 3/36 4/43 5/49
6/46 7/70 8/85 9/92   6/53 7/54 8/90 9/92

Bowling: *First Innings*—Martin 27-9-50-6; Lohmann 32.2-19-34-3; Sharpe 6-3-8-1. *Second Innings*—Martin 30.2-12-52-6; Lohmann 21-8-32-3; Sharpe 9-5-10-1.

England

A.Shrewsbury c Trott b Turner	4		lbw b Ferris	9
W.G.Grace* c Trumble b Ferris	0		c Trumble b Ferris	16
W.Gunn b Ferris	32		st Blackham b Ferris	1
W.W.Read b Turner	1		b Turner	6
J.Cranston run out	16	(6)	c Trumble b Turner	15
J.M.Read c Murdoch b Charlton	19	(5)	c Barrett b Turner	35
W.Barnes c Murdoch b Charlton	5	(8)	lbw b Ferris	5
G.A.Lohmann c Gregory b Ferris	3	(7)	c Blackham b Ferris	2
G.MacGregor† c Turner b Ferris	1		not out	2
J.W.Sharpe not out	5		not out	2
F.Martin c Turner b Charlton	1			
Extras (B 9, LB 3, NB 1)	13		(LB 1, NB 1)	2
	100		(8 wkts)	**95**

1/0 2/10 3/16 4/55 5/79   1/24 2/25 3/28 4/32
6/90 7/91 8/93 9/94   5/83 6/83 7/86 9/93

Bowling: *First Innings*—Turner 22-12-37-2; Ferris 25-14-25-4; Trumble 2-0-7-0; Charlton 6-0-18-3. *Second Innings*—Turner 25-9-38-3; Ferris 23-8-49-5; Charlton 3-1-6-0.

Umpires: C.K.Pullin and J.Street

AUSTRALIA v ENGLAND 1891-92 (First Test)

At Melbourne Cricket Ground, 1, 2, 4, 5, 6 January

Result: Australia won by 54 runs

Australia

A.C.Bannerman c Read b Sharpe	45	c Grace b Sharpe	41
J.J.Lyons c Grace b Peel	19	c Abel b Briggs	51
G.Giffen lbw b Peel	57	b Attewell	
W.Bruce b Sharpe	57	c Lohmann b Sharpe	40
H.Donnan b Sharpe	9	(9) c and b Lohmann	2
H.Moses c Lohmann b Sharpe	23	run out	15
G.H.S.Trott c MacGregor b Sharpe	6	lbw b Attewell	23
R.W.McLeod b Sharpe	14	b Peel	31
S.T.Callaway b Attewell	21	(10) not out	13
C.T.B.Turner b Peel	29	(5) c Peel b Lohmann	19
J.M.Blackham*† not out	4	c MacGregor b Peel	0
Extras (B 5, LB 6)	11		
	240		**236**

1/32 2/36 3/123 4/136 5/136
6/148 7/168 8/191 9/232

1/66 2/67 3/120 4/152 5/152
6/182 7/197 8/210 9/236

Bowling: *First Innings*—Sharpe 51-20-84-6; Peel 43-23-54-3; Attewell 21.1-11-28-1; Lohmann 28-14-40-0; Briggs 3-1-13-0; Stoddart 5-2-10-0. *Second Innings*—Sharpe 54-25-81-2; Peel 16.5-7-25-2; Lohmann 39-15-53-2; Attewell 61-32-51-2; Briggs 21-9-26-1.

England

W.G.Grace* b McLeod	50	(5) c Bannerman b Turner	25
R.Abel b McLeod	32	c Blackham b Turner	28
G.Bean c Bruce b Giffen	50	c McLeod b Trott	3
A.E.Stoddart c Giffen b McLeod	0	(2) b Callaway	35
J.M.Read c and b Giffen	36	(4) b Trott	11
R.Peel b McLeod	19	b Turner	6
G.A.Lohmann lbw b Giffen	3	c Bannerman b Turner	0
J.Briggs c Bruce b Turner	41	c Trott b McLeod	4
W.Attewell c Bannerman b Turner	8	(10) c Donnan b Turner	24
G.MacGregor† not out	9	(9) c sub (S.E.Gregory) b Trott	16
J.W.Sharpe c Blackham b McLeod	2	not out	5
Extras (B 9, LB 2, NB 3)	14	(LB 1)	1
	264		**158**

1/84 2/85 3/85 4/171 5/179
6/187 7/232 8/249 9/256

1/60 2/60 3/71 4/75 5/93
6/93 7/98 8/125 9/139

Bowling: *First Innings*—Trott 10-2-25-0; Giffen 20-3-75-3; Turner 16-3-40-2; McLeod 28.4-12-53-5; Callaway 14-2-39-0; Bruce 3-0-18-0. *Second Innings*—McLeod 23-8-39-1; Turner 33.2-14-51-5; Trott 19-2-52-3; Callaway 4-1-7-1; Giffen 3-0-8-0.

Umpires: T.Flynn and J.Phillips

AUSTRALIA v ENGLAND 1891-92 (Second Test)

At Sydney Cricket Ground, 29, 30, January 1, 2, 3 February

Result: Australia won by 72 runs

Australia

A.C.Bannerman c Abel b Lohmann	12	c Grace b Briggs	91
J.J.Lyons c Grace b Lohmann	41	(3) c Grace b Lohmann	134
G.Giffen c Abel b Lohmann	6	(4) lbw b Attewell	49
H.Moses c Grace b Lohmann	29	absent hurt	
C.T.B.Turner c MacGregor b Lohmann	15	(7) not out	14
W.Bruce c Bean b Attewell	15	(5) c Briggs b Sharpe	72
G.H.S.Trott b Lohmann	15	(2) c Sharpe b Lohmann	1
R.W.McLeod c Attewell b Lohmann	13	(6) c Read b Peel	18
W.F.Giffen c and b Lohmann	1	(8) b Briggs	3
S.T.Callaway run out	1	c Grace b Briggs	0
J.M.Blackham*† not out	3	(9) lbw b Briggs	0
Extras (B 3, LB 3)	6	(B 6, LB 2, W 1)	9
	144		**391**

1/31 2/57 3/62 4/90 5/117
6/123 7/126 8/132 9/141

1/1 2/175 3/254 4/347 5/364
6/376 7/391 8/391 9/391

Bowling: *First Innings*—Briggs 10-2-24-0; Sharpe 10-1-31-0; Lohmann 43.2-18-58-8; Attewell 31-20-25-1. *Second Innings*—Lohmann 51-14-84-2; Briggs 32.4-8-69-4; Attewell 46-24-43-1; Sharpe 35-7-91-1; Peel 35-13-49-1; Grace 16-2-34-0; Stoddart 4-1-12-0.

England

W.G.Grace* b Turner	26	c Blackham b Turner	5
R.Abel not out	132	c W.F.Giffen b G.Giffen	1
G.Bean b G.Giffen	19	c Lyons b Turner	4
A.E.Stoddart c Blackham b McLeod	27	b Turner	69
J.M.Read c Turner b G.Giffen	3	c and b G.Giffen	22
R.Peel c G.Giffen b Turner	20	st Blackham b G.Giffen	6
G.A.Lohmann c G.Giffen b Turner	10	c Bruce b G.Giffen	15
G.MacGregor† lbw b McLeod	3	c and b G.Giffen	12
J.Briggs lbw b Trott	28	c Trott b Turner	12
W.Attewell b Trott	0	c and b G.Giffen	0
J.W.Sharpe c Bannerman b G.Giffen	26	not out	4
Extras (B 10, LB 2, W 1)	13	(B 4, LB 2)	6
	307		**156**

1/50 2/79 3/123 4/127 5/152
6/167 7/178 8/235 9/235

1/2 2/6 3/11 4/64 5/83
6/116 7/134 8/140 9/140

Bowling: *First Innings*—Turner 37-11-90-2; McLeod 18-6-55-2; G.Giffen 28.2-5-88-4; Trott 14-3-42-2; Callaway 17-10-19-0. *Second Innings*—Turner 23.2-7-46-4; G.Giffen 28-10-72-6; Trott 5-0-11-0; Callaway 10-6-21-0.

Umpires: T.Flynn and J.A.Tooher

AUSTRALIA v ENGLAND 1891-92 (Third Test)

At Adelaide Oval, 24, 25, 26, 28 March
Result: England won by an innings and 230 runs

England

R.Abel st Blackham b Trott	24	
W.G.Grace* b McLeod	58	
A.E.Stoddart lbw b G.Giffen	134	
J.M.Read c Gregory b Turner	57	
G.Bean c McLeod b Lyons	16	
R.Peel c G.Giffen b Turner	83	
G.A.Lohmann lbw b G.Giffen	0	
J.Briggs b Turner	39	
H.Philipson c Blackham b McLeod	1	
G.MacGregor† run out	31	
A.W.Attewell not out	43	
Extras (B 5, LB 7, W 1)	13	
	499	

1/47 2/121 3/218 4/272 5/327
6/333 7/412 8/425 9/425

Bowling: G.Giffen 51.1-17-154-2; McLeod 41-11-78-2; Turner 46-17-111-3; Donnan 9-2-22-0; Lyons 5-0-22-1; Bruce 9-3-19-0.

Australia

J.J.Lyons c Peel b Briggs	23	c Stoddart b Briggs	19
A.C.Bannerman c Bean b Lohmann	12	b Briggs	1
G.Giffen run out	5	c Bean b Attewell	27
W.Bruce lbw b Lohmann	5	lbw b Attewell	37
C.T.B.Turner c Lohmann b Briggs	10	c Grace b Briggs	5
S.E.Gregory c Abel b Briggs	3	c Peel b Briggs	7
R.W.McLeod b Briggs	20	c Grace b Lohmann	30
G.H.S.Trott b Briggs	0	st Philipson b Briggs	16
W.F.Giffen b Lohmann	3	c Peel b Briggs	2
H.Donnan c Bean b Briggs	7	not out	11
J.M.Blackham*† not out	7	b Attewell	9
Extras (B 5)	5	(B 3, LB 2)	5
	100		**169**

1/30 2/38 3/48 4/48 5/51   1/1 2/42 3/51 4/85 5/91
6/66 7/66 8/73 9/90   6/99 7/120 8/124 9/157

Bowling: First Innings—Briggs 21.5-4-49-6; Lohmann 21-8-46-3; Attewell 34-10-69-3; Lohmann 6-2-8-1. Second Innings—Briggs 28-7-87-6; Attewell 11-3-41-0; Flowers 11-3-21-1.

Umpires: G.E.Downs and W.O.Whitridge

ENGLAND v AUSTRALIA 1893 (First Test)

At Lord's, London, 17, 18, 19 July
Result: Match drawn

England

A.Shrewsbury c Blackham b Turner	106	b Giffen	81
A.E.Stoddart* b Turner	24	b Turner	13
W.Gunn c Lyons b Turner	2	c Graham b Giffen	77
F.S.Jackson c Blackham b Turner	91	c Bruce b Giffen	5
J.M.Read b Bruce	6	c McLeod b Bruce	1
R.Peel c Bruce b Trumble	12	(9) not out	0
W.Flowers b McLeod	35	(6) b Turner	4
E.Wainwright c Giffen b Turner	1	b Giffen	26
W.H.Lockwood b Bruce	22	(7) b Giffen	0
G.MacGregor† not out	5		
A.W.Mold b Turner	0		
Extras (B 19, LB 9, NB 2)	30	(B 16, LB 9, NB 1, W 1)	27
	334	1/27 2/179 3/195 (8 wkts dec.)	**234**

1/29 2/31 3/168 4/189 5/213   4/198 5/198 6/198 7/234 8/234
6/293 7/298 8/313 9/333

Bowling: First Innings—Turner 36-16-67-6; Bruce 22-4-58-2; Trumble 19-7-42-1; Trott 9-2-38-0; McLeod 21-6-51-1; Giffen 18-3-48-0. Second Innings—Turner 32-15-64-2; Bruce 20-10-34-1; Trumble 11-2-33-0; Trott 2-0-5-0; McLeod 25-11-28-0; Giffen 26.4-6-43-5.

Australia

J.J.Lyons b Lockwood	7
A.C.Bannerman c Shrewsbury b Lockwood	17
G.Giffen b Lockwood	0
G.H.S.Trott c MacGregor b Lockwood	33
R.W.McLeod b Lockwood	5
S.E.Gregory c MacGregor b Lockwood	57
H.Graham c MacGregor b Mold	107
W.Bruce c Peel b Mold	23
C.T.B.Turner b Flowers	0
H.Trumble not out	2
J.M.Blackham*† lbw b Mold	2
Extras (B 15, LB 1)	16
	269

1/7 2/7 3/50 4/60 5/75
6/217 7/264 8/265 9/265

Bowling: Peel 22-12-36-0; Lockwood 45-11-101-6; Mold 20.1-7-44-3; Wainwright 11-3-41-0; Flowers 11-3-21-1.

Umpires: W.Hearn and J.Phillips

ENGLAND v AUSTRALIA 1893 (Second Test)

At Kennington Oval, London, 14, 15, 16 August
Result: England won by an innings and 43 runs

England

W.G.Grace*	c Giffen b Trumble	68
A.E.Stoddart	b Turner	83
A.Shrewsbury	c Graham b Giffen	66
W.Gunn	b Giffen	16
A.Ward	c and b Giffen	55
W.W.Read	b Giffen	52
F.S.Jackson	run out	103
J.Briggs	b Giffen	0
W.H.Lockwood	c and b Giffen	10
G.MacGregor†	lbw b Giffen	5
A.W.Mold	not out	0
Extras	(B 19, LB 4, W 2)	25
		483

1/151 2/151 3/200 4/303 5/311
6/442 7/442 8/456 9/478

Bowling: Turner 47-18-94-1; Trumble 47-16-101-1; McLeod 23-6-57-0; Giffen 54-17-128-7; Trott 6-1-33-0; Bruce 3-0-19-0; Lyons 7-1-26-0.

Australia

A.C.Bannerman	c MacGregor b Lockwood	10	c Read b Lockwood	55
J.J.Lyons	b Briggs	19	(7) c Grace b Lockwood	31
G.H.S.Trott	b Lockwood	0	(4) c Read b Lockwood	92
S.E.Gregory	lbw b Briggs	9	(5) c Shrewsbury b Briggs	6
H.Graham	c MacGregor b Lockwood	0	(6) b Briggs	42
G.Giffen	c MacGregor b Lockwood	4	(3) b Lockwood	53
W.Bruce	not out	10	(2) c Jackson b Mold	22
H.Trumble	b Briggs	5	b Briggs	8
R.W.McLeod	c Lockwood b Briggs	2	c Jackson b Briggs	5
C.T.B.Turner	b Briggs	7	b Briggs	0
J.M.Blackham*†	run out	17	not out	2
Extras	(B 5, LB 3)	8	(B 18, LB 15)	33
		91		349

1/30 2/31 3/32 4/32 5/40
6/48 7/57 8/59 9/69

1/54 2/126 3/165 4/189 5/295
6/311 7/340 8/342 9/342

Bowling: First Innings—Lockwood 19-9-37-4; Mold 4-0-12-0; Briggs 14.3-5-34-5. Second Innings—Lockwood 29-7-96-4; Mold 23-8-73-1; Briggs 35-6-114-5; Jackson 11-3-33-0.

Umpires: H.Draper and C.K.Pullin

ENGLAND v AUSTRALIA 1893 (Third Test)

At Old Trafford, Manchester, 24, 25, 26 August
Result: Match drawn

Australia

A.C.Bannerman	c MacGregor b Briggs	19	b Richardson	60
J.J.Lyons	c MacGregor b Briggs	27	b Mold	33
G.Giffen	b Richardson	17	c Brockwell b Richardson	17
G.H.S.Trott	c Grace b Richardson	9	b Mold	12
W.Bruce	c Read b Richardson	68	c Shrewsbury b Richardson	36
H.Graham	lbw b Mold	18	(6) st MacGregor b Briggs	3
S.E.Gregory	b Briggs	0	(7) lbw b Richardson	3
H.Trumble	b Richardson	35	(9) run out	8
R.W.McLeod	b Briggs	2	(8) c Read b Richardson	6
C.T.B.Turner	b Richardson	0	(5) c Mold b Briggs	27
J.M.Blackham*†	not out	0	not out	23
Extras	(B 5, LB 4)	9	(B 4, LB 4)	8
		204		236

1/32 2/59 3/69 4/73 5/129
6/130 7/194 8/198 9/201

1/56 2/79 3/92 4/99 5/153
6/170 7/173 8/182 9/200

Bowling: First Innings—Mold 28-11-48-1; Richardson 23.4-5-49-5; Briggs 42-18-81-4; Brockwell 3-0-17-0. Second Innings—Mold 23-6-57-2; Richardson 44-15-107-5; Briggs 28.3-11-64-2.

England

A.E.Stoddart	run out	0	c Gregory b Trumble	42
W.G.Grace*	b Bruce	40	c Trott b McLeod	45
A.Shrewsbury	c Bruce b Giffen	12	not out	19
W.Gunn	not out	102	b Trumble	11
A.Ward	c Blackham b Turner	13	b Trumble	0
W.W.Read	b Giffen	12	not out	0
W.Brockwell	c Gregory b Giffen	11		
J.Briggs	b Giffen	2		
G.MacGregor†	st Blackham b Turner	12		
T.Richardson	b Bruce	16		
A.W.Mold	b Trumble	0		
Extras	(B 17, LB 6)	23	(B 1)	1
		243	(4 wkts)	118

1/4 2/43 3/73 4/93 5/112
6/136 7/165 8/196 9/238

1/78 2/100 3/117
4/117

Bowling: First Innings—Giffen 67-30-113-4; Turner 53-22-72-2; Bruce 17-5-26-2; Trumble 3.2-1-9-1. Second Innings—Giffen 6-3-8-0; Turner 7-1-18-0; Bruce 9-4-19-0; Trumble 25-4-49-3; McLeod 16-7-21-1.

Umpires: C.Clements and J.Phillips

AUSTRALIA v ENGLAND 1894-95 (First Test)

At Sydney Cricket Ground, 14, 15, 17, 18, 19, 20 December

Result: England won by 10 runs

Australia

J.J.Lyons	b Richardson	1		b Richardson	25
G.H.S.Trott	b Richardson	12		c Gay b Peel	8
G.Giffen	c Ford b Brockwell	161		lbw b Briggs	41
J.Darling	b Richardson	0		c Brockwell b Peel	53
F.A.Iredale	c Stoddart b Ford	81	(6)	c and b Briggs	5
S.E.Gregory	c Peel b Stoddart	201	(5)	c Gay b Peel	16
J.C.Reedman	c Ford b Peel	17		st Gay b Peel	4
C.E.McLeod	b Richardson	15		not out	2
C.T.B.Turner	c Gay b Peel	1		c Briggs b Peel	2
J.M.Blackham*†	b Richardson	74	(11)	c and b Peel	2
E.Jones	not out	11	(10)	c MacLaren b Briggs	1
Extras	(B 8, LB 3, W 1)	12		(B 2, LB 1, NB 4)	7
		586			**166**

1/10 2/21 3/21 4/192 5/331   1/26 2/45 3/130 4/135 5/147
6/379 7/400 8/409 9/563   6/158 7/159 8/161 9/162

Bowling: *First Innings*—Richardson 55.3-13-181-5; Peel 53-14-140-2; Briggs 25-4-96-0; Brockwell 22-7-78-1; Ford 11-2-47-1; Stoddart 3-0-31-1; Lockwood 3-2-1-0. *Second Innings*—Richardson 11-3-27-1; Peel 30-9-67-6; Lockwood 16-3-40-0; Briggs 11-2-25-3.

England

A.C.MacLaren	c Reedman b Turner	4	b Giffen	20
A.Ward	c Iredale b Turner	75	b Giffen	117
A.E.Stoddart*	c Jones b Giffen	12	c Giffen b Turner	36
J.T.Brown	run out	22	c Jones b Giffen	53
W.Brockwell	c Blackham b Jones	49	b Jones	37
R.Peel	c Gregory b Giffen	4	b Giffen	17
F.G.J.Ford	st Blackham b Giffen	30	c and b McLeod	48
J.Briggs	b Giffen	57	c and b McLeod	42
W.H.Lockwood	c Giffen b Trott	18	b Trott	29
L.H.Gay†	c Gregory b Reedman	33	b Trott	4
T.Richardson	not out	0	not out	12
Extras	(B 17, LB 3, W 1)	21	(B 14, LB 8)	22
		325		**437**

1/14 2/43 3/78 4/149 5/155   1/44 2/115 3/217 4/245 5/290
6/211 7/211 8/252 9/325   6/296 7/385 8/398 9/420

Bowling: *First Innings*—Jones 19-7-44-1; Turner 44-16-89-2; Giffen 43-17-75-4; Trott 15-4-59-1; McLeod 14-2-25-0; Reedman 3.3-1-12-1; Lyons 2-2-0-0. *Second Innings*—Jones 19-0-57-1; Turner 35-14-78-1; Giffen 75-25-164-4; Trott 12.4-2-22-2; McLeod 30-7-67-2; Reedman 6-1-12-0; Lyons 2-0-12-0; Iredale 2-1-3-0.

Umpires: C.Bannerman and J.Phillips

AUSTRALIA v ENGLAND 1894-95 (Second Test)

At Melbourne Cricket Ground, 29, 31 December, 1, 2, 3 January

Result: England won by 94 runs

England

A.C.MacLaren	c Trott b Coningham	0		b Turner	15
A.Ward	c Darling b Trumble	30		b Turner	41
A.E.Stoddart*	b Turner	10		b Giffen	173
J.T.Brown	c Trumble b Turner	0		c Jarvis b Bruce	37
W.Brockwell	c Iredale b Coningham	0		b Turner	21
R.Peel	c Trumble b Turner	6		st Jarvis b Giffen	53
F.G.J.Ford	c Giffen b Trumble	9		c Trott b Giffen	24
W.H.Lockwood	not out	3	(9)	not out	33
J.Briggs	c Bruce b Turner	5	(8)	lbw b Giffen	31
H.Philipson†	c Darling b Turner	1		b Giffen	30
T.Richardson	c Iredale b Trumble	0		c Gregory b Giffen	11
Extras	(LB 9, NB 2)	11		(B 1, LB 2, NB 3)	6
		75			**475**

1/0 2/19 3/23 4/26 5/44   1/24 2/101 3/191 4/222 5/320
6/58 7/60 8/70 9/71   6/362 7/383 8/402 9/455

Bowling: *First Innings*—Coningham 11-5-17-2; Turner 20-9-32-5; Trumble 9.1-4-15-3. *Second Innings*—Coningham 20-4-59-0; Giffen 78.2-21-155-6; Turner 55-21-99-3; Trott 17-0-60-0; Trumble 26-6-72-0; Bruce 4-0-21-1; Lyons 2-1-3-0.

Australia

J.J.Lyons	b Richardson	14	(7)	b Peel	2
W.Bruce	c Ford b Peel	54	(1)	c Stoddart b Peel	4
G.Giffen*	c Philipson b Briggs	43		c Brown b Brockwell	32
S.E.Gregory	c Ward b Richardson	12		b Richardson	2
J.Darling	b Lockwood	5		b Brockwell	2
F.A.Iredale	b Richardson	68		b Peel	10
G.H.S.Trott	run out	95	(2)	c and b Brockwell	16
A.Coningham	c Philipson b Richardson	3	(9)	b Peel	10
H.Trumble	b Richardson	2	(10)	run out	1
A.H.Jarvis†	c Brown b Briggs	4	(8)	b Richardson	11
C.T.B.Turner	not out	26		not out	1
Extras	(B 5, LB 1, NB 1)	7		(W 2)	2
		333			**123**

1/98 2/191 3/206 4/214 5/216   1/4 2/12 3/15 4/53 5/80
6/241 7/254 8/263 9/268   6/86 7/108 8/110 9/116

Bowling: *First Innings*—Richardson 23-6-57-5; Peel 14-4-21-1; Lockwood 5-0-17-1; Briggs 13.5-2-26-2. *Second Innings*—Richardson 40-10-100-2; Peel 40.1-9-77-4; Lockwood 25-5-60-0; Briggs 12-0-49-0; Ford 5-2-7-0; Brockwell 14-3-33-3.

Umpires: T.Flynn and J.Phillips

AUSTRALIA v ENGLAND 1894-95 (Third Test)

At Adelaide Oval, 11, 12, 14, 15 January
Result: Australia won by 382 runs

Australia

W.Bruce b Richardson	11	(2)	c Brockwell b Briggs	80
G.H.S.Trott run out	48	(1)	b Peel	0
G.Giffen* c Lockwood b Brockwell	58		c Ford b Peel	24
F.A.Iredale b Richardson	7		c and b Peel	140
J.Darling c Philipson b Briggs	10		c Philipson b Lockwood	3
S.E.Gregory c Brown b Richardson	6		b Richardson	20
J.Harry b Richardson	2		b Richardson	6
J.Worrall run out	0		c Peel b Briggs	11
A.H.Jarvis† c and b Lockwood	13		c Brown b Peel	29
A.E.Trott not out	38		not out	72
S.T.Callaway b Richardson	41		b Richardson	11
Extras (B 2, NB 1, W 1)	4		(B 7, LB 7, NB 1)	15
	238			**411**

1/31 2/69 3/84 4/103 5/120   1/0 2/44 3/142 4/145 5/197
6/124 7/137 8/157 9/157   6/215 7/238 8/283 9/347

Bowling: *First Innings*—Richardson 21.1-4-75-5; Peel 16-1-43-0; Brockwell 20-13-30-1; Ford 8-2-19-0; Briggs 8-2-34-1; Lockwood 8-2-33-1. *Second Innings*—Peel 34-6-96-4; Richardson 31.2-8-89-3; Lockwood 15-2-70-1; Brockwell 10-1-50-0; Briggs 19-3-58-2; Ford 6-0-33-0.

England

A.C.MacLaren b Callaway	25		c Iredale b A.E.Trott	35
J.Briggs b Callaway	12	(9)	b A.E.Trott	0
W.Brockwell c Harry b Callaway	5	(6)	c and b A.E.Trott	24
A.Ward c Bruce b Giffen	5	(2)	b A.E.Trott	13
A.E.Stoddart* b Giffen	1	(3)	not out	34
J.T.Brown not out	39	(5)	b A.E.Trott	2
R.Peel b Callaway	0		c and b A.E.Trott	0
F.G.J.Ford c Worrall b Giffen	21		c G.H.S.Trott b A.E.Trott	14
W.H.Lockwood c Worrall b Giffen	7	(10)	c Iredale b A.E.Trott	1
H.Philipson† c Gregory b Giffen	0	(4)	b Giffen	1
T.Richardson c Worrall b Callaway	0		c A.E.Trott b Giffen	12
Extras (B 2)	2		(B 5, LB 2)	7
	124			**143**

1/14 2/30 3/49 4/50 5/56   1/52 2/52 3/53 4/64 5/102
6/64 7/111 8/111 9/124   6/102 7/128 8/128 9/130

Bowling: *First Innings*—A.E.Trott 3-1-9-0; Giffen 28-11-76-5; Callaway 26.3-13-37-5. *Second Innings*—Callaway 7-1-19-0; Giffen 33.1-12-74-2; A.E.Trott 27-10-43-8.

Umpires: J.Phillips and G.H.G.Searcy

AUSTRALIA v ENGLAND 1894-95 (Fourth Test)

At Sydney Cricket Ground, 1, 2 (no play), 4 February
Result: Australia won by an innings and 147 runs

Australia

G.H.S.Trott c Brown b Peel	1
W.Bruce c Brockwell b Peel	15
G.Giffen* b Peel	8
H.Moses b Richardson	1
H.Graham st Philipson b Briggs	105
S.E.Gregory st Philipson b Briggs	5
F.A.Iredale c and b Briggs	0
J.Darling b Richardson	31
A.E.Trott not out	85
A.H.Jarvis† c Philipson b Briggs	5
C.T.B.Turner c Richardson b Lockwood	22
Extras (B 3, LB 1, NB 1, W 1)	6
	284

1/2 2/20 3/26 4/26 5/51
6/51 7/119 8/231 9/239

Bowling: Peel 24-5-74-3; Richardson 22-5-78-2; Briggs 22-4-65-4; Ford 2-0-14-0; Lockwood 8.5-3-22-1.

England

A.C.MacLaren st Jarvis b G.H.S.Trott	1	(4)	c Bruce b Giffen	0
A.Ward c and b Turner	7		c Darling b Giffen	6
J.Briggs b G.H.S.Trott	11	(8)	c Bruce b Giffen	6
A.E.Stoddart* st Jarvis b G.H.S.Trott	7	(3)	c Iredale b Turner	0
J.T.Brown not out	20	(1)	b Giffen	0
W.Brockwell c Darling b Turner	0	(5)	c Bruce b Turner	17
F.G.J.Ford c G.H.S.Trott b Giffen	0		c Darling b Giffen	11
R.Peel st Jarvis b Turner	0	(6)	st Jarvis b Turner	0
H.Philipson† c Graham b Giffen	4		c and b Turner	9
T.Richardson c and b Giffen	2		not out	10
W.H.Lockwood absent hurt	-		absent hurt	-
Extras (B 7, LB 3, NB 2)	12		(B 5, LB 7, NB 1)	13
	65			**72**

1/2 2/20 3/24 4/31 5/40   1/0 2/5 3/5 4/12 5/14
6/43 7/56 8/63 9/65   6/29 7/47 8/52 9/72

Bowling: *First Innings*—G.H.S.Trott 14-5-21-3; Turner 19-10-18-3; Giffen 5.5-1-14-3. *Second Innings*—Giffen 15-7-26-5; Turner 14.1-6-33-4.

Umpires: C.Bannerman and J.Phillips

AUSTRALIA v ENGLAND 1894-95 (Fifth Test)

At Melbourne Cricket Ground, 1, 2, 4, 5, 6 March

Result: England won by 6 wickets

Australia

Batsman		1st		2nd
G.H.S.Trott b Briggs		42	b Peel	42
W.Bruce c MacLaren b Peel		22	c and b Peel	11
G.Giffen* b Peel		57	b Richardson	51
F.A.Iredale b Richardson		8	b Richardson	18
S.E.Gregory c Philipson b Richardson		70	b Richardson	30
J.Darling c Ford b Peel		74	b Peel	50
J.J.Lyons c Philipson b Lockwood		55	b Briggs	15
H.Graham b Richardson		6	lbw b Richardson	10
A.E.Trott c Lockwood b Peel		10	b Richardson	0
A.H.Jarvis† not out		34	not out	14
T.R.McKibbin c Peel b Briggs		23	c Philipson b Richardson	13
Extras (B 3, LB 10)		13	(B 5, LB 6, NB 2)	13
		414		257

1/40 2/101 3/126 4/142 5/284 6/286 7/304 8/335 9/367

1/32 2/75 3/125 4/148 5/179 6/200 7/219 8/219 9/248

Bowling: *First Innings*—Richardson 42-7-138-3; Peel 48-13-114-4; Lockwood 27-7-72-1; Briggs 23.4-5-46-2; Brockwell 6-1-22-0; Ford 2-0-9-0. *Second Innings*—Richardson 45.2-7-104-6; Peel 46-16-89-3; Lockwood 16-7-24-0; Briggs 16-3-37-1.

England

Batsman		1st		2nd
A.Ward b McKibbin		32	(2) b G.H.S.Trott	93
W.Brockwell st Jarvis b G.H.S.Trott		5	(1) c and b Giffen	5
A.E.Stoddart* st Jarvis b G.H.S.Trott		68	lbw b G.H.S.Trott	11
J.T.Brown b A.E.Trott		30	c Giffen b McKibbin	140
A.C.MacLaren hit wkt b G.H.S.Trott		120	not out	20
R.Peel c Gregory b Giffen		73	not out	15
W.H.Lockwood c G.H.S.Trott b Giffen		5		
F.G.J.Ford c A.E.Trott b Giffen		11		
J.Briggs c G.H.S.Trott b Giffen		0		
H.Philipson† not out		10		
T.Richardson lbw b G.H.S.Trott		11		
Extras (B 8, LB 8, W 4)		20	(B 6, LB 5, NB 1, W 2)	14
		385	(4 wkts)	298

1/6 2/110 3/112 4/166 5/328 6/342 7/364 8/364 9/366

1/5 2/28 3/238 4/278

Bowling: *First Innings*—Giffen 45-13-130-4; G.H.S.Trott 24-5-71-4; A.E.Trott 30-4-84-1; McKibbin 29-6-73-1; Bruce 5-1-7-0. *Second Innings*—G.H.S.Trott 20.1-1-63-2; Giffen 31-4-106-1; A.E.Trott 19-2-56-0; McKibbin 14-2-47-1; Bruce 3-1-10-0; Lyons 1-0-2-0.

Umpires: T.Flynn and J.Phillips

ENGLAND v AUSTRALIA 1896 (First Test)

At Lord's, London, 22, 23, 24 June

Result: England won by 6 wickets

Australia

Batsman		1st		2nd
H.Donnan run out		1	(11) b Hearne	8
J.Darling b Richardson		22	b Richardson	0
G.Giffen c Lilley b Lohmann		0	b Richardson	32
G.H.S.Trott* b Richardson		0	c Hayward b Richardson	143
S.E.Gregory c Philipson b Richardson		14	c Lohmann b Hearne	103
H.Graham b Richardson		0	b Richardson	10
C.Hill b Lohmann		1	b Hearne	5
C.J.Eady not out		10	(1) c Lilley b Richardson	2
H.Trumble b Richardson		0	(8) c Lilley b Hearne	24
J.J.Kelly† b Lilley b Lohmann		0	(9) not out	24
E.Jones c Jackson b Richardson		4	(10) c Jackson b Hearne	4
Extras (B 1)		1	(B 7, LB 4, W 1)	12
		53		347

1/3 2/3 3/4 4/26 5/26 6/31 7/41 8/45 9/46

1/0 2/3 3/62 4/283 5/289 6/300 7/304 8/308 9/318

Bowling: *First Innings*—Richardson 11.3-3-39-6; Lohmann 11-6-13-3. *Second Innings*—Richardson 47-15-134-5; Lohmann 22-6-39-0; Hayward 11-3-44-0; Hearne 36-14-76-5; Jackson 11-5-28-0; Grace 6-1-14-0.

England

Batsman		1st		2nd
W.G.Grace* c Trumble b Giffen		66	(5) c Hill b Trumble	7
A.E.Stoddart b Eady		17	not out	30
R.Abel b Eady		94	(2) c sub (F.A.Iredale) b Jones	4
J.T.Brown b Jones		9	c Kelly b Eady	36
W.Gunn c Kelly b Trumble		25	(6) not out	13
F.S.Jackson c Darling b Giffen		44		
T.W.Hayward not out		12	(3) b Jones	13
A.F.A.Lilley† b Eady		0		
G.A.Lohmann c sub (F.A.Iredale) b Giffen		1		
J.T.Hearne c Giffen b Trott		1		
T.Richardson c Hill b Trott		6		
Extras (B 5, LB 2)		7	(B 3, LB 4, W 1)	8
		292	(4 wkts)	111

1/38 2/143 3/152 4/197 5/256 6/266 7/266 8/267 9/286

1/16 2/20 3/42 4/82

Bowling: *First Innings*—Jones 26-6-64-1; Giffen 26-5-95-3; Eady 29-12-58-3; Trott 7.4-2-13-2; Trumble 19-3-55-1. *Second Innings*—Jones 23-10-42-2; Giffen 1-0-9-0; Eady 3-0-11-1; Trumble 20-10-37-1; Trott 0.1-0-4-0.

Umpires: J.Phillips and W.A.J.West

ENGLAND v AUSTRALIA 1896 (Second Test)

At Old Trafford, Manchester, 16, 17, 18 July

Result: Australia won by 3 wickets

Australia

Batsman	1st innings	Runs	2nd innings	Runs
F.A.Iredale	b Briggs	108	b Richardson	11
J.Darling	c Lilley b Richardson	27	c Lilley b Richardson	16
G.Giffen	c and b Lilley	80	c Ranjitsinhji b Richardson	6
G.H.S.Trott*	c Brown b Lilley	53	c Lilley b Richardson	2
S.E.Gregory	c Stoddart b Briggs	25	c Ranjitsinhji b Briggs	33
H.Donnan	b Richardson	12	c Jackson b Richardson	15
C.Hill	c Jackson b Richardson	9	c Lilley b Richardson	14
H.Trumble	b Richardson	24	not out	17
J.J.Kelly†	c Lilley b Richardson	27	not out	8
T.R.McKibbin	not out	28		
E.Jones	b Richardson	4		
Extras	(B 6, LB 8, W 1)	15	(LB 3)	3
		412	(7 wkts)	125

1/41 2/172 3/242 4/294 5/294
6/314 7/325 8/352 9/403

1/20 2/26 3/28 4/45
5/79 6/95 7/100

Bowling: *First Innings*—Richardson 68-23-168-7; Briggs 40-18-99—2; Jackson 16-6-34-0; Hearne 28-11-53-0; Grace 7-3-11-0; Stoddart 6-2-9-0; Lilley 5-1-23-1. *Second Innings*—Richardson 42.3-16-76; Briggs 18-8-24-1; Hearne 24-13-22-0.

England

Batsman	1st innings	Runs	2nd innings	Runs
A.E.Stoddart	st Kelly b Trott	15	b McKibbin	41
W.G.Grace*	st Kelly b Trott	2	c Trott b Jones	11
K.S.Ranjitsinhji	c Trott b McKibbin	62	not out	154
R.Abel	c Trumble b McKibbin	26	c McKibbin b Giffen	13
F.S.Jackson	run out	18	c McKibbin b Giffen	1
J.T.Brown	c Kelly b Trumble	22	c Iredale b Jones	19
A.C.MacLaren	c Trumble b McKibbin	0	c Jones b Trumble	15
A.F.A.Lilley†	not out	65	c Trott b Giffen	19
J.Briggs	b Trumble	0	st Kelly b McKibbin	16
J.T.Hearne	c Trumble b Giffen	18	c Kelly b McKibbin	9
T.Richardson	run out	2	c Jones b Trumble	1
Extras	(B 1)	1	(B 2, LB 3, W 1)	6
		231		305

1/2 2/23 3/104 4/111 5/140
6/140 7/154 8/166 9/219

1/33 2/76 3/97 4/109 5/132
6/179 7/232 8/268 9/304

Bowling: *First Innings*—Jones 5-2-11-0; Trott 10-0-46-2; Giffen 19-3-48-1; Trumble 37-14-80-2; McKibbin 19-8-45-3. *Second Innings*—Jones 17-0-78-2; Trott 7-1-17-0; Giffen 16-1-65-3; Trumble 29.1-12-78-2; McKibbin 21-4-61-3.

Umpires: A.Chester and J.Phillips

ENGLAND v AUSTRALIA 1896 (Third Test)

At Kennington Oval, London, 10, 11, 12 August

Result: England won by 66 runs

England

Batsman	1st innings	Runs	2nd innings	Runs
W.G.Grace*	c Trott b Giffen	24	b Trumble	9
F.S.Jackson	c McKibbin b Trumble	45	b Trumble	2
K.S.Ranjitsinhji	b Giffen	8	st Kelly b McKibbin	11
R.Abel	c and b Trumble	26	c Giffen b Trumble	21
A.C.MacLaren	b Trumble	20	b Jones	6
T.W.Hayward	b Trumble	0	c Trott b Trumble	13
E.G.Wynyard	c Darling b McKibbin	10	c Kelly b McKibbin	3
R.Peel	b Trumble	0	b Trumble	0
A.F.A.Lilley†	c Iredale b Trumble	2	c McKibbin b Trumble	6
J.T.Hearne	b McKibbin	8	b McKibbin	1
T.Richardson	not out	1	not out	10
Extras	(LB 1)	1	(LB 2)	2
		145		84

1/54 2/78 3/78 4/114 5/114
6/131 7/132 8/135 9/138

1/11 2/12 3/24 4/50 5/56
6/67 7/67 8/67 9/68

Bowling: *First Innings*—Giffen 32-12-64-2; Trumble 40-10-59-6; McKibbin 9.3-0-21-2. *Second Innings*—Giffen 1-0-4-0; Trumble 25-9-30-6; McKibbin 20-8-35-3; Jones 3-0-13-1.

Australia

Batsman	1st innings	Runs	2nd innings	Runs
J.Darling	c MacLaren b Hearne	47	b Hearne	0
F.A.Iredale	run out	30	c Jackson b Hearne	3
G.Giffen	b Hearne	0	(4) b Hearne	1
G.H.S.Trott*	b Peel	5	(3) c sub (W.Brockwell) b Peel	3
S.E.Gregory	b Hearne	1	c Richardson b Peel	6
C.Hill	run out	1	b Peel	0
H.Donnan	b Hearne	10	c Hayward b Peel	0
J.J.Kelly†	not out	10	lbw b Peel	3
H.Trumble	b Hearne	3	not out	7
E.Jones	c MacLaren b Peel	3	b Peel	3
T.R.McKibbin	b Hearne	0	c Abel b Hearne	16
Extras	(B 8, LB 1)	9	(B 2)	2
		119		44

1/75 2/77 3/82 4/83 5/84
6/85 7/112 8/116 9/119

1/0 2/3 3/7 4/7 5/11
6/11 7/14 8/19 9/25

Bowling: *First Innings*—Peel 20-9-30-2; Hearne 26.1-10-41-6; Richardson 5-0-22-0; Hayward 2-0-17-0. *Second Innings*—Peel 12-5-23-6; Hearne 13-8-19-4; Richardson 1-1-0-0.

Umpires: W.Hearn and J.Phillips

AUSTRALIA v ENGLAND 1897-98 (First Test)

At Sydney Cricket Ground, 13, 14, 15, 16, 17 December
Result: England won by 9 wickets

England

J.R.Mason b Jones	6	(2) b McKibbin	32
A.C.MacLaren* c Kelly b McLeod	109	(1) not out	50
T.W.Hayward c Trott b Trumble	72		
W.Storer† c and b Trott	43		
N.F.Druce c Gregory b McLeod	20		
G.H.Hirst b Jones	62		
K.S.Ranjitsinhji c Gregory b McKibbin	175	(3) not out	8
E.Wainwright b Jones	10		
J.T.Hearne c and b McLeod	17		
J.Briggs run out	1		
T.Richardson not out	24		
Extras (LB 11, W 1)	12	(B 5, NB 1)	6
	551	(1 wkt)	80

1/26 2/162 3/224 4/256 5/258   1/80
6/382 7/422 8/471 9/477

Bowling: *First Innings*—McKibbin 34-5-113-1; Jones 50-8-130-3; McLeod 28-12-80-3; Trumble 40-7-138-1; Trott 23-2-78-1. *Second Innings*—Jones 9-1-28-0; Trumble 14-4-40-0; McKibbin 5-1-22-1.

Australia

J.Darling c Druce b Richardson	7	(2) c Druce b Briggs	101
J.J.Lyons b Richardson	3	(7) c Hayward b Hearne	25
F.A.Iredale c Druce b Hearne	25	(1) b Briggs	18
C.Hill b Hearne	19	b Hearne	96
S.E.Gregory c Mason b Hearne	46	run out	31
G.H.S.Trott* b Briggs	10	run out	27
J.J.Kelly† b Richardson	1	(8) b Richardson	46
H.Trumble c Storer b Mason	70	(9) not out	2
C.E.McLeod not out	50	(6) c Druce b Hearne	26
T.R.McKibbin b Hearne	0	(11) b Hearne	6
E.Jones c Richardson b Hearne	0	(10) lbw b Richardson	3
Extras (B 1, LB 1, NB 4)	6	(B 12, LB 1, NB 10, W 4)	27
	237		408

1/8 2/24 3/56 4/57 5/86   1/37 2/135 3/191 4/269 5/271
6/87 7/138 8/228 9/237   6/318 7/321 8/382 9/390

Bowling: *First Innings*—Richardson 27-8-71-3; Hirst 28-7-57-0; Hearne 20.1-7-42-5; Briggs 20-7-42-1; Hayward 3-1-11-0; Mason 2-1-8-1. *Second Innings*—Richardson 41-9-121-2; Hearne 38-8-99-4; Briggs 22-3-86-2; Hayward 5-1-16-0; Hirst 13-3-49-0; Mason 2-0-10-0.

Umpires: C.Bannerman and J.Phillips

AUSTRALIA v ENGLAND 1897-98 (Second Test)

At Melbourne Cricket Ground, 1, 3, 4, 5 January
Result: Australia won by an innings and 55 runs

Australia

C.E.McLeod b Storer	112
J.Darling c Hirst b Briggs	36
C.Hill c Storer b Hayward	58
S.E.Gregory b Briggs	71
F.A.Iredale c Ranjitsinhji b Hirst	89
G.H.S.Trott* c Wainwright b Briggs	79
M.A.Noble b Richardson	17
H.Trumble c Hirst b Mason	14
J.J.Kelly† c Richardson b Hearne	19
E.Jones run out	7
T.R.McKibbin not out	2
Extras (B 14, NB 1, W 1)	16
	520

1/43 2/167 3/244 4/310 5/434
6/453 7/478 8/509 9/515

Bowling: Richardson 48-12-114-1; Hirst 25-1-89-1; Briggs 40-10-96-3; Mason 11-1-33-1; Hayward 9-4-23-1; Storer 16-4-55-1.

England

A.C.MacLaren* c Trumble b McKibbin	35	c Trott b Trumble	38
J.R.Mason b McKibbin	3	b Trumble	3
E.Wainwright c Jones b Noble	21	(8) b Noble	11
K.S.Ranjitsinhji b Trumble	71	(3) b Noble	27
T.W.Hayward c Jones b Trott	23	(4) c Trumble b Noble	33
W.Storer† c Kelly b Trumble	51	(5) c Trumble b Noble	1
G.H.Hirst b Jones	0	(6) lbw b Trumble	3
N.F.Druce lbw b Trumble	44	(7) c McLeod b Noble	15
J.T.Hearne b Jones	1	(10) c Jones b Noble	0
J.Briggs not out	46	(9) c Trott b Trumble	12
T.Richardson b Trumble	3	not out	2
Extras (B 10, LB 3, NB 4)	17	(B 3, LB 1, W 1)	5
	315		150

1/10 2/60 3/74 4/133 5/203   1/10 2/65 3/71 4/75 5/80
6/208 7/223 8/224 9/311   6/115 7/128 8/144 9/148

Bowling: *First Innings*—McKibbin 28-7-66-2; Trumble 26.5-5-54-4; Jones 22-5-54-2; Trott 17-3-49-1; Noble 12-3-31-1; McLeod 14-2-44-0. *Second Innings*—Trumble 30.4-12-53-4; McLeod 7-2-13-0; McKibbin 4-0-13-0; Trott 7-0-17-0; Noble 17-1-49-6.

Umpires: C.Bannerman and J.Phillips

AUSTRALIA v ENGLAND 1897-98 (Third Test)

At Adelaide Oval, 14, 15, 17, 18, 19 January
Result: Australia won by an innings and 13 runs

Australia

C.E.McLeod b Briggs	31
J.Darling c Storer b Richardson	178
C.Hill c Storer b Richardson	81
S.E.Gregory c Storer b Hirst	52
F.A.Iredale b Richardson	84
G.H.S.Trott* b Hearne	3
M.A.Noble b Richardson	39
H.Trumble not out	37
J.J.Kelly† b Stoddart	22
E.Jones run out	8
W.P.Howell b Hearne	16
Extras (B 16, LB 5, NB 1)	22
	573

1/97 2/245 3/310 4/374 5/389
6/474 7/493 8/537 9/552

Bowling: Richardson 56-11-164-4; Briggs 63-27-128-1; Hearne 44.1-15-94-2; Hirst 24.1-6-62-1; Hayward 9-1-36-0; Mason 11-2-41-0; Storer 3-0-16-0; Stoddart 4-1-10-1.

England

A.C.MacLaren b Howell	14	c Kelly b Noble	14
J.R.Mason b Jones	11	c Jones b Noble	11
K.S.Ranjitsinhji c Noble b Trumble	6	c Trumble b McLeod	6
T.W.Hayward b Jones	70	c and b McLeod	1
W.Storer† b Howell	4	c Hill b McLeod	6
N.F.Druce c Darling b Noble	24	b Noble	27
G.H.Hirst c Trumble b Noble	85	lbw b McLeod	6
A.E.Stoddart* c Jones b Howell	15	c Jones b McLeod	24
J.Briggs c Kelly b Noble	14	not out	0
J.T.Hearne b Howell	0	c and b Noble	4
T.Richardson not out	25	c Jones b Noble	0
Extras (B 2, LB 6, W 2)	10	(B 2, LB 6, NB 2, W 3)	13
	278		282

1/24 2/30 3/34 4/42 5/106   1/10 2/152 3/154 4/160 5/212 282
6/172 7/206 8/223 9/224   6/235 7/262 8/278 9/282

Bowling: First Innings—Howell 54-23-70-4; Jones 27-3-67-2; Trumble 17-3-39-1; Noble 24.5-5-78-3; Trott 4-0-14-0. Second Innings—Howell 40-18-60-0; Noble 33-7-84-5; Trumble 16-5-37-0; McLeod 48-24-65-5; Trott 6-0-18-0; Jones 1-0-5-0.

Umpires: C.Bannerman and J.Phillips

AUSTRALIA v ENGLAND 1897-98 (Fourth Test)

At Melbourne Cricket Ground, 29, 31 January, 1, 2 February
Result: Australia won by 8 wickets

Australia

C.E.McLeod b Hearne	1	not out	64
J.Darling c Hearne b Richardson	12	c Druce b Hayward	29
C.Hill c Storer b Hearne	188	lbw b Hayward	0
S.E.Gregory c Storer b Richardson	0		
F.A.Iredale c Storer b Hearne	0		
M.A.Noble c and b Hearne	4		
G.H.S.Trott* c Storer b Hearne	7		
H.Trumble c Mason b Storer	46		
J.J.Kelly† c Storer b Briggs	32		
E.Jones c Hayward b Hearne	20		
W.P.Howell not out	9	not out	21
Extras (B 3, W 1)	4	(NB 1)	1
	323	(2 wkts)	115

1/1 2/25 3/25 4/26 5/32   1/50 2/56
6/58 7/223 8/283 9/303

Bowling: First Innings—Richardson 26-2-102-2; Hearne 35.4-13-98-6; Hayward 10-4-24-0; Briggs 17-4-38-1; Stoddart 6-1-22-0; Storer 4-0-24-1; Wainwright 3-1-11-0. Second Innings—Hearne 7-3-19-0; Briggs 6-1-31-0; Hayward 10-4-24-2; Wainwright 9-2-21-0; Mason 4-1-10-0; Ranjitsinhji 3.4-1-9-0.

England

A.C.MacLaren b Howell	8	(3) c Iredale b Trumble	45
E.Wainwright c Howell b Trott	6	(1) c McLeod b Jones	2
K.S.Ranjitsinhji c Iredale b Trumble	24	(4) b Noble	55
T.W.Hayward c Gregory b Noble	22	(5) c and b Trumble	25
N.F.Druce lbw b Jones	24	(7) c Howell b Trott	16
W.Storer† c and b Trumble	2	(9) c Darling b McLeod	26
J.R.Mason b Jones	30	(8) b Howell	26
A.E.Stoddart* c Darling b Jones	17	(6) b Jones	25
J.Briggs not out	21	(2) c Darling b Howell	23
J.T.Hearne c Trott b Jones	0	not out	4
T.Richardson b Trott	20	c Trumble b McLeod	2
Extras		(B 1, LB 11, NB 1, W 1)	14
	174		263

1/14 2/16 3/60 4/60 5/67   1/7 2/63 3/91 4/147 5/157
6/103 7/121 8/148 9/148   6/192 7/209 8/257 9/257

Bowling: First Innings—Howell 16-7-34-1; Trott 11.1-1-33-2; Noble 7-1-21-1; Trumble 15-4-30-2; Jones 12-2-56-4. Second Innings—Howell 30-12-58-2; Jones 25-7-70-2; Trott 12-2-39-1; Trumble 23-6-40-2; Noble 6-6-31-1; McLeod 8.2-4-11-2.

Umpires: C.Bannerman and J.Phillips

AUSTRALIA v ENGLAND 1897-98 (Fifth Test)
At Sydney Cricket Ground, 26, 28 February, 1, 2 March
Result: Australia won by 6 wickets

England

A.C.MacLaren* b Trott	65	c Darling b Jones	0
E.Wainwright c Hill b Trumble	49	b Noble	6
K.S.Ranjitsinhji c Gregory b Trott	2	lbw b Jones	12
T.W.Hayward b Jones	47	c Worrall b Trumble	43
W.Storer† b Jones	44	c Gregory b Trumble	31
N.F.Druce lbw b Noble	64	c Howell b Trumble	18
G.H.Hirst b Jones	44	c Trott b Jones	7
J.R.Mason c Howell b Jones	7	b Trumble	11
J.Briggs b Jones	0	b Howell	29
J.T.Hearne not out	2	not out	0
T.Richardson b Jones	1	b Howell	6
Extras (B 2, LB 5, NB 1, W 2)	10	(LB 12)	12
	335		**178**

1/111 2/117 3/119 4/197 5/230
6/308 7/318 8/324 9/334

1/0 2/16 3/30 4/99 5/104
6/121 7/137 8/148 9/172

Bowling: *First Innings*—Noble 26-6-57-1; Howell 17-6-40-0; Trumble 26-4-67-1; Jones 26.2-3-82-6; Trott 23-6-56-2; McLeod 11-4-23-0. *Second Innings*—Jones 26-3-61-3; Noble 15-4-34-1; Howell 6.1-0-22-2; Trott 7-1-12-0; Trumble 24-7-37-4.

Australia

C.E.McLeod b Richardson	64	b Hearne	
J.Darling c Mason b Briggs	14	c Wainwright b Richardson	160
C.Hill b Richardson	8	b Richardson	0
J.Worrall c Ranjitsinhji b Richardson	26	c Hirst b Hayward	62
S.E.Gregory c Storer b Richardson	21	not out	22
M.A.Noble c Storer b Richardson	31	not out	15
G.H.S.Trott* c Ranjitsinhji b Hearne	18		
H.Trumble b Richardson	12		
J.J.Kelly† not out	27		
W.P.Howell c MacLaren b Richardson	10		
E.Jones c Storer b Richardson	1		
Extras (B 5, NB 1, W 1)	7	(B 6, NB 4, W 1)	11
	239	(4 wkts)	**276**

1/36 2/45 3/99 4/132 5/137
6/188 7/188 8/221 9/232

1/23 2/40 3/233 4/252

Bowling: *First Innings*—Richardson 36.1-7-94-8; Briggs 17-4-39-1; Hearne 21-9-40-1; Storer 5-1-13-0; Mason 13-7-20-0; Hayward 4-0-12-0; Hirst 4-1-14-0. *Second Innings*—Richardson 21.4-1-110-2; Hearne 15-5-52-1; Hirst 7-0-33-0; Briggs 5-1-25-0; Mason 11-1-27-0; Hayward 3-0-18-1.

Umpires: C.Bannerman and J.Phillips

ENGLAND v AUSTRALIA 1899 (First Test)
At Trent Bridge, Nottingham, 1, 2, 3 June
Result: Match drawn

Australia

J.Darling* b Hearne	47		b Rhodes	14
F.A.Iredale c Hayward b Hearne	6	(4)	run out	20
M.A.Noble b Rhodes	41	(2)	lbw b Rhodes	45
S.E.Gregory b Hirst	48			
C.Hill run out	52	(3)	c Grace b Jackson	80
V.T.Trumper b Hearne	0	(5)	b Jackson	11
J.J.Kelly† c Hirst b Hearne	26	(9)	not out	11
F.J.Laver b Rhodes	3	(7)	b Jackson	3
W.P.Howell c Hayward b Rhodes	3	(10)	not out	4
H.Trumble not out	16	(8)	c Ranjitsinhji b Rhodes	38
E.Jones c Fry b Rhodes	4	(6)	c Ranjitsinhji b Hearne	3
Extras (B 8, LB 1)	9		(LB 1)	1
	252		(8 wkts dec.)	**230**

1/14 2/85 3/109 4/166 5/167
6/229 7/229 8/229 9/248

1/18 2/111 3/151 4/170 5/173 6/177 7/180 8/226

Bowling: *First Innings*—Rhodes 35.2-13-58-4; Hearne 59-28-71-4; Grace 20-8-31-0; Hirst 24-9-42-1; Jackson 11-3-27-0; Hayward 3-0-14-0. *Second Innings*—Rhodes 20-3-60-3; Hearne 29-10-70-1; Grace 2-0-6-0; Hirst 11-4-20-0; Jackson 26-8-57-3; Hayward 6-2-16-0.

England

W.G.Grace* c Kelly b Noble	28	b Howell	1
C.B.Fry b Jones	50	c Jones b Trumble	9
F.S.Jackson c Darling b Noble	8	b Howell	0
W.Gunn b Jones	14	b Jones	3
K.S.Ranjitsinhji b Jones	42	not out	93
T.W.Hayward run out	0	b Trumble	28
J.T.Tyldesley c Laver b Howell	22	c Kelly b Trumble	10
W.Storer† b Jones	4	lbw b Jones	3
G.H.Hirst b Howell	6		
W.Rhodes c Kelly b Jones	6		
J.T.Hearne not out	4		
Extras (LB 3, NB 6)	9	(B 5, NB 2, W 1)	8
	193	(7 wkts)	**155**

1/75 2/91 3/93 4/116 5/117
6/172 7/176 8/178 9/185

1/1 2/1 3/10 4/19 5/82 6/140 7/155

Bowling: *First Innings*—Jones 33-6-88-5; Howell 28.4-12-43-2; Trumble 13-7-17-0; Noble 16-4-36-2. *Second Innings*—Jones 22-9-31-2; Howell 37-18-54-2; Trumble 29-16-39-3; Noble 11-5-23-0.

Umpires: R.G.Barlow and V.A.Titchmarsh

ENGLAND v AUSTRALIA 1899 (Second Test)

At Lord's, London, 15, 16, 17 June
Result: Australia won by 10 wickets

England

A.C.MacLaren* b Jones	4	(6)	not out	88
C.B.Fry c Trumble b Jones	13		b Jones	4
K.S.Ranjitsinhji c and b Jones	8		c Noble b Howell	0
C.L.Townsend st Kelly b Howell	5		b Jones	8
F.S.Jackson b Jones	73		c and b Trumble	37
T.W.Hayward b Noble	1	(1)	c Trumble b Laver	77
J.T.Tyldesley c Darling b Jones	14		c Gregory b Laver	4
G.L.Jessop c Trumper b Trumble	51		c Trumble b Laver	4
A.F.A.Lilley† not out	19		b Jones	12
W.Mead b Jones	7	(11)	lbw b Noble	0
W.Rhodes b Jones	2	(10)	c and b Noble	2
Extras (B 2, LB 6, W 1)	9		(B 2, LB 2)	4
	206			**240**

1/4 2/14 3/20 4/44 4/45
6/66 7/161 8/184 9/194

1/5 2/6 3/23 4/94 5/160
6/166 7/170 8/212 9/240

Bowling: *First Innings*—Jones 36.1-11-88-7; Howell 14-4-43-1; Noble 15-7-39-1; Trumble 15-9-27-1. *Second Innings*—Jones 36-15-76-3; Howell 31-12-67-1; Noble 19.4-8-37-2; Trumble 15-6-20-1; Laver 16-4-36-3.

Australia

J.Worrall c Hayward b Rhodes	18	not out	11
J.Darling* c Ranjitsinhji b Rhodes	9	not out	17
C.Hill c Fry b Townsend	135		
S.E.Gregory c Lilley b Jessop	15		
M.A.Noble c Lilley b Rhodes	54		
V.T.Trumper not out	135		
J.J.Kelly† c Lilley b Mead	9		
H.Trumble c Lilley b Jessop	24		
F.J.Laver b Townsend	0		
E.Jones c Mead b Townsend	17		
W.P.Howell b Jessop	0		
Extras (LB 4, NB 1)	5		
	421	(0 wkts)	**28**

1/27 2/28 3/59 4/189 5/271
6/306 7/386 8/387 9/421

Bowling: *First Innings*—Jessop 37.1-10-105-3; Mead 53-24 91-1; Rhodes 39-10-108-3; Jackson 18-6-31-0; Townsend 15-1-50-3; Ranjitsinhji 2-0-6-0; Hayward 6-0-25-0. *Second Innings*—Jessop 6-0-19-0; Rhodes 5-1-9-0.

Umpires: T.Mycroft and W.A.J.West

ENGLAND v AUSTRALIA 1899 (Third Test)

At Headingley, Leeds, 29, 30 June, 1 (no play) July
Result: Match drawn

Australia

J.Worrall run out	76		c sub (J.T.Tyldesley) b Young	16
J.J.Kelly† c Fry b Briggs	0	(7)	c Lilley b Hayward	33
M.A.Noble run out	0	(5)	c Ranjitsinhji b Hearne	0
S.E.Gregory c Lilley b Hearne	0	(4)	c MacLaren b Hearne	0
C.Hill c Lilley b Young	34	(3)	b Hearne	0
J.Darling* c Young b Briggs	9	(2)	c Fry b Young	16
V.T.Trumper b Young	12	(6)	c Ranjitsinhji b Jackson	32
H.Trumble not out	20		run out	56
F.J.Laver st Lilley b Briggs	7		c Lilley b Hearne	45
E.Jones b Young	5		c Brown b Hayward	2
W.P.Howell c Ranjitsinhji b Young	7		not out	2
Extras (B 2)	2		(B 17, LB 3, NB 1, W 1)	22
	172			**224**

1/8 2/17 3/24 4/95 5/114
6/131 7/132 8/151 9/164

1/34 2/34 3/34 4/34 5/39
6/97 7/140 8/213 9/215

Bowling: *First Innings*—Hearne 23-5-69-1; Briggs 30-11-53-3; Young 19.1-11-30-4; Jackson 5-1-18-0. *Second Innings*—Hearne 31.3-12-50-4; Young 26-5-72-2; Jackson 11-6-13-1; Brown 7-0-22-0; Hayward 10-1-45-2.

England

J.T.Brown c Trumble b Noble	27		not out	14
A.C.MacLaren* c and b Trumble	9			
K.S.Ranjitsinhji c Worrall b Noble	11			
W.G.Quaife b Jones	20	(2)	not out	1
F.S.Jackson b Trumble	9			
C.B.Fry b Noble	38			
T.W.Hayward not out	40			
A.F.A.Lilley† c Hill b Trumble	55			
J.T.Hearne b Trumble	3			
H.I.Young c Kelly b Trumble	0			
J.Briggs absent ill	-			
Extras (B 3, LB 5)	8		(LB 4)	4
	220		(0 wkts)	**19**

1/27 2/38 3/53 4/69 5/119
6/119 7/212 8/220 9/220

Bowling: *First Innings*—Trumble 39.3-16-60-5; Noble 42-17-82-3; Howell 13-3-29-0; Jones 21-9-34-1; Laver 3-1-7-0. *Second Innings*—Jones 4-2-7-0; Noble 3-1-8-0.

Umpires: W.Hearn and M.Sherwin

ENGLAND v AUSTRALIA 1899 (Fourth Test)

At Old Trafford, Manchester, 17, 18, 19, July

Result: Match drawn

England

W.G.Quaife c Darling b Noble	8	c Iredale b Jones	15
C.B.Fry b Jones	9	c Iredale b Trumble	4
K.S.Ranjitsinhji c Worrall b Jones	21	not out	49
A.C.MacLaren* b Noble	8	c Iredale b Trumble	6
F.S.Jackson c Trumble b Jones	44	not out	14
T.W.Hayward c Jones b Howell	130		
W.Brockwell c Worrall b Noble	20		
A.F.A.Lilley† lbw b Laver	58		
H.I.Young b Howell	43		
J.T.Hearne c Iredale b Trumble	1		
W.M.Bradley not out	23		
Extras (B 3, LB 3, W 1)	7	(B 4, NB 2)	6
	372	(3 wkts)	94

1/14 2/18 3/47 4/47 5/107 6/154 7/267 8/324 9/337

1/12 2/39 3/54

Bowling: *First Innings*—Jones 42-9-85-3; Noble 38-19-85-3; Trumble 29-10-72-1; Howell 19.1-7-45-2; Laver 13-2-27-1. *Second Innings*—Jones 8-0-33-1; Trumble 13-3-33-2; Howell 6-2-22-0.

Australia

F.J.Laver c Lilley b Bradley	0	(9) not out	14
J.J.Kelly† b Young	9	(8) c Lilley b Ranjitsinhji	26
W.P.Howell b Bradley	0		
J.Worrall b Bradley	14	(1) c Brockwell b Young	53
M.A.Noble not out	60	(2) c and b Hearne	89
S.E.Gregory lbw b Young	5	(5) c Ranjitsinhji b Hearne	1
V.T.Trumper b Young	14	(4) b Hearne	63
J.Darling* b Young	4	(6) c sub (W.Rhodes) b Young	39
H.Trumble c MacLaren b Bradley	44	(3) c Ranjitsinhji b Bradley	39
F.A.Iredale c Lilley b Bradley	31	(7) not out	36
E.Jones b Jackson	0		
Extras (B 14, W 1)	15	(B 14, LB 2, NB 1, W 1)	18
	196	(7 wkts dec.)	346

1/1 2/6 3/14 4/26 5/35 6/53 7/57 8/139 9/195

1/93 2/117 3/205 4/213 5/255 6/278 7/319

Bowling: *First Innings*—Young 29-10-79-4; Bradley 33-13-67-5; Brockwell 6-2-18-0; Hearne 10-6-7-0; Jackson 3.3-1-9-1; Ranjitsinhji 1-0-1-0. *Second Innings*—Young 37-12-81-2; Bradley 46-16-82-1; Brockwell 15-3-36-0; Hearne 47-26-54-3; Jackson 18-8-36-0; Ranjitsinhji 12-5-23-1; Hayward 3-1-10-0; Quaife 3-1-6-0.

Umpires: A.B.Hide and J.Lillywhite

ENGLAND v AUSTRALIA 1899 (Fifth Test)

At Kennington Oval, London, 14, 15, 16 August

Result: Match drawn

England

F.S.Jackson b Jones	118
T.W.Hayward c Iredale b McLeod	137
K.S.Ranjitsinhji c Howell b Jones	54
C.B.Fry c Worrall b Jones	60
A.C.MacLaren* c Trumper b Trumble	49
C.L.Townsend b Jones	38
W.M.Bradley run out	0
W.H.Lockwood b Trumble	24
A.O.Jones b Noble	31
A.F.A.Lilley† c Iredale b Noble	37
W.Rhodes not out	8
Extras (B 9, LB 6, NB 1, W 4)	20
	576

1/185 2/316 3/318 4/428 5/436 6/436 7/479 8/511 9/551

Bowling: Jones 53-12-164-4; Noble 35.4-12-96-2; Trumble 39-11-107-2; McLeod 48-15-131-1; Howell 15-3-43-0; Worrall 3-0-15-0.

Australia

J.Worrall c Hayward b Lockwood	55	c Lilley b Hayward	75
H.Trumble c and b Jones	24	(7) not out	3
V.T.Trumper c Lilley b Jones	6	(4) c and b Rhodes	69
M.A.Noble b Lockwood	9	(3) not out	69
J.Darling* c Fry b Lockwood	71	(6) run out	6
S.E.Gregory c Jones b Lockwood	117	(5) b Rhodes	2
F.A.Iredale b Lockwood	9		
J.J.Kelly† lbw b Jones	4	(2) b Rhodes	77
C.E.McLeod not out	31		
E.Jones b Lockwood	4		
W.P.Howell b Lockwood	22		
Extras (B 5, LB 10, NB 6, W 1)	22	(B 7, NB 4, W 4)	15
	352	(5 wkts)	254

1/38 2/44 3/85 4/120 5/220 6/242 7/257 8/340 9/340

1/116 2/208 3/224 4/228 5/243

Bowling: *First Innings*—Bradley 29-12-52-0; Rhodes 25-2-79-0; Lockwood 40.3-17-71-7; Jones 30-12-73-3; Townsend 5-0-16-0; Jackson 14-7-39-0. *Second Innings*—Bradley 17-8-32-0; Rhodes 22-8-27-3; Lockwood 15-7-33-0; Jones 12-2-43-0; Townsend 8-4-9-0; Jackson 13-2-54-0; Hayward 11-3-38-1; Fry 2-1-3-0.

Umpires: W.Richards and A.A.White

AUSTRALIA v ENGLAND 1901-02 (First Test)

At Sydney Cricket Ground, 13, 14, 16 December
Result: England won by an innings and 124 runs

England

A.C.MacLaren*	lbw b McLeod	116
T.W.Hayward	c Hill b Trumble	69
J.T.Tyldesley	c McLeod b Laver	1
W.Quaife	b Howell	21
G.L.Jessop	b McLeod	24
A.O.Jones	c Kelly b Noble	9
A.F.A.Lilley†	c Laver b McLeod	84
L.C.Braund	c Jones b McLeod	58
J.R.Gunn	c and b Jones	21
S.F.Barnes	not out	26
C.Blythe	c Trumble b Laver	20
Extras	(B 6, LB 7, NB 1, W 1)	15
		464

1/154 2/163 3/193 4/220 5/236
6/272 7/396 8/405 9/425

Bowling: Jones 36-8-98-1; Noble 33-17-91-1; Howell 21-8-52-1; Laver 17-6-39-2; Trumper 1-1-0-0. Trumble 34-12-85-1; McLeod 44-17-84-4.

Australia

S.E.Gregory	c Braund b Blythe	48	(5)	c MacLaren b Braund	43
V.T.Trumper	c and b Barnes	2		c Lilley b Blythe	34
C.Hill	b Barnes	46		b Braund	0
M.A.Noble	st Lilley b Braund	2		c Lilley b Blythe	14
W.P.Howell	c Braund b Blythe	9	(10)	not out	31
C.E.McLeod	b Barnes	0		b Blythe	0
J.J.Kelly†	b Blythe	0		c Barnes b Blythe	12
J.Darling*	c Quaife b Barnes	39	(1)	c Jessop b Braund	3
F.J.Laver	c Quaife b Braund	6		st Lilley b Braund	0
H.Trumble	not out	5	(8)	c Lilley b Barnes	26
E.Jones	c Jessop b Barnes	5		c Jones b Braund	7
Extras	(B 1, LB 3, NB 2)	6		(B 5, LB 2)	7
		168			172

1/3 2/89 3/97 4/112 5/112   1/12 2/12 3/52 4/59 5/59
6/112 7/112 8/142 9/163   6/89 7/129 8/136 9/147

Bowling: First Innings—Barnes 35.1-9-65-5; Braund 15-4-40-2; Gunn 5-0-27-0; Blythe 16-8-26-3; Jessop 1-0-4-0. Second Innings—Barnes 16-2-74-1; Braund 28.4-8-61-5; Blythe 13-5-30-4.

Umpires: R.Callaway and R.M.Crockett

AUSTRALIA v ENGLAND 1901-02 (Second Test)

At Melbourne Cricket Ground, 1, 2, 3, 4 January
Result: Australia won by 229 runs

Australia

V.T.Trumper	c Tyldesley b Barnes	0	(8)	c Lilley b Barnes	16
J.Darling*	c Lilley b Blythe	19		c Tyldesley b Barnes	23
C.Hill	b Barnes	15	(7)	c Jones b Barnes	99
H.Trumble	c Braund b Blythe	16	(1)	c Braund b Barnes	16
M.A.Noble	c Lilley b Blythe	16	(9)	lbw b Blythe	16
S.E.Gregory	st Lilley b Blythe	0	(5)	c Jones b Barnes	17
R.A.Duff	c Braund b Barnes	32	(10)	b Braund	104
J.J.Kelly†	c Quaife b Barnes	5	(3)	run out	3
W.W.Armstrong	not out	4	(11)	not out	45
W.P.Howell	b Barnes	1	(4)	c Hayward b Barnes	0
E.Jones	c MacLaren b Barnes	14	(6)	c MacLaren b Barnes	5
Extras	(B 6)	6		(B 7, LB 1, NB 1)	9
		112			353

1/0 2/32 3/34 4/34 5/38   1/32 2/42 3/42 4/42 5/48
6/81 7/85 8/90 9/94   6/98 7/128 8/167 9/233

Bowling: First Innings—Barnes 16.1-5-42-6; Blythe 16-2-64-4. Second Innings—Barnes 64-17-121-7; Blythe 31-7-85-1; Braund 53.2-17-114-1; Jessop 1-0-9-0; Gunn 6-1-13-0; Jones 1-0-2-0.

England

A.C.MacLaren*	c Jones b Trumble	13	(2)	c Trumble b Noble	1
T.W.Hayward	c Darling b Trumble	0	(1)	st Kelly b Trumble	12
J.T.Tyldesley	c Gregory b Trumble	2		c Trumble b Noble	66
W.Quaife	b Noble	0		b Noble	25
G.L.Jessop	st Kelly b Noble	27		c Gregory b Noble	32
J.R.Gunn	st Kelly b Noble	0	(9)	c Jones b Trumble	2
A.F.A.Lilley†	c Trumper b Noble	6	(6)	c Darling b Noble	0
A.O.Jones	c Kelly b Noble	0		c Darling b Trumble	6
L.C.Braund	not out	2	(7)	c Darling b Noble	25
S.F.Barnes	c and b Noble	1		not out	0
C.Blythe	c Trumper b Noble	4		c and b Trumble	6
Extras	(B 6)	6		(B 1, LB 1, NB 4)	6
		61			175

1/5 2/16 3/16 4/24 5/36   1/2 2/29 3/80 4/123 5/123
6/51 7/51 8/56 9/57   6/156 7/173 8/175 9/175

Bowling: First Innings—Trumble 8-1-38-3; Noble 7.4-2-17-7. Second Innings—Jones 12-2-33-0; Noble 26-5-60-6; Trumble 22.5-10-49-4; Howell 15-6-23-0; Armstrong 2-1-3-0; Trumper 2-1-1-0.

Umpires: R.Callaway and R.M.Crockett

AUSTRALIA v ENGLAND 1901-02 (Third Test)

At Adelaide Oval, 17, 18, 20, 21, 22, 23 January

Result: Australia won by 4 wickets

England

A.C.MacLaren* run out	67		b Trumble	44
T.W.Hayward run out	90		b Trumble	47
J.T.Tyldesley c and b Trumble	0		run out	25
G.L.Jessop c Trumper b Trumble	1	(5)	b Trumble	16
A.F.A.Lilley† lbw b Trumble	10	(7)	b McLeod	21
W.Quaife c Kelly b Howell	68	(4)	lbw b Trumble	44
L.C.Braund not out	103	(6)	b Howell	17
A.O.Jones run out	5		c and b Trumble	11
J.R.Gunn b Noble	24		lbw b Trumble	5
S.F.Barnes c Hill b Noble	5		absent hurt	
C.Blythe c Hill b Noble	2	(10)	not out	10
Extras (B 9, NB 3, W 1)	13		(B 6, W 1)	7
	388			**247**

1/149 2/160 3/164 4/171 5/186
6/294 7/302 8/371 9/384

1/80 2/113 3/126 4/144 5/165 247
6/204 7/218 8/224 9/247

Bowling: *First Innings*—Trumble 65-23-124-3; Noble 26-10-58-3; Howell 36-10-82-1; Armstrong 18-5-45-0; Trumper 6-3-17-0; McLeod 19-5-49-0. *Second Innings*—Noble 21-7-72-0; Howell 27-9-54-1; Trumble 44-18-74-6; Armstrong 5-0-9-0; McLeod 14-3-31-1.

Australia

J.Darling* c MacLaren b Blythe	1	(5)	c Hayward b Jessop	69
V.T.Trumper run out	65		b Gunn	25
C.Hill c Tyldesley b Braund	98		b Jessop	97
R.A.Duff lbw b Braund	43	(1)	hit wkt b Gunn	4
S.E.Gregory c Blythe b Braund	55	(4)	c Braund b Gunn	23
W.W.Armstrong c and b Gunn	9	(8)	not out	9
H.Trumble b Gunn	13	(6)	not out	62
W.P.Howell c Braund b Gunn	3			
M.A.Noble b Gunn	14	(7)	run out	13
J.J.Kelly† not out	5			
C.E.McLeod b Gunn	7			
Extras (B 2, LB 6)	8		(B 9, LB 3, NB 1)	13
	321		(6 wkts)	**315**

1/1 2/138 3/197 4/229 5/260
6/288 7/289 8/302 9/309

1/5 2/50 3/98 4/194
5/255 6/287

Bowling: *First Innings*—Braund 46-9-143-3; Blythe 11-3-54-1; Barnes 7-0-21-0; Gunn 42-14-76-5; Jessop 7-0-19-0. *Second Innings*—Gunn 38-14-88-3; Braund 25-5-79-0; Blythe 41-16-66-0; Hayward 7-0-28-0; Jessop 23-9-41-2.

Umpires: P.Argall and R.M.Crockett

AUSTRALIA v ENGLAND 1901-02 (Fourth Test)

At Sydney Cricket Ground, 14, 15, 17, 18 February

Result: Australia won by 7 wickets

England

A.C.MacLaren* c Duff b Saunders	92		c Kelly b Noble	5
T.W.Hayward b Saunders	41		b Noble	12
J.T.Tyldesley c Kelly b Noble	79		c Trumble b Saunders	10
W.Quaife c Kelly b Saunders	4		lbw b Noble	15
G.L.Jessop c Noble b Saunders	0		b Saunders	15
L.C.Braund lbw b Trumble	17		b Saunders	0
C.P.McGahey b Trumble	18		c Kelly b Saunders	13
A.F.A.Lilley† c Kelly b Noble	40		c Trumble b Noble	13
A.O.Jones c Kelly b Trumble	15		c Kelly b Noble	6
J.R.Gunn not out	0		not out	13
C.Blythe b Noble	4		c Kelly b Saunders	8
Extras (B 5, NB 2)	7		(LB 2)	2
	317			**99**

1/73 2/179 3/188 4/188 5/225
6/245 7/267 8/312 9/312

1/5 2/24 3/36 4/57 5/57
6/57 7/60 8/78 9/88

Bowling: *First Innings*—Noble 33.2-12-78-3; Saunders 43-11-119-4; Howell 22-10-40-0; Trumble 38-18-65-3; Armstrong 2-1-8-0. *Second Innings*—Saunders 24.1-8-43-5; Noble 24-7-54-5.

Australia

H.Trumble* c MacLaren b Jessop	6	(1)	lbw b Blythe	25
V.T.Trumper c Braund b Jessop	7		c Lilley b Gunn	30
C.Hill c Jones b Jessop	21			
S.E.Gregory c Braund b Jessop	5	(5)	not out	12
M.A.Noble lbw b Braund	56			
R.A.Duff c Lilley b Blythe	39	(2)	not out	51
W.W.Armstrong b Braund	55			
A.J.Y.Hopkins c Lilley b Braund	43			
J.J.Kelly† not out	24			
W.P.Howell c MacLaren b Gunn	35	(4)	c sub (H.G.Garnett) b Gunn	0
J.V.Saunders b Braund	0			
Extras (B 7, NB 1)	8		(LB 1, NB 2)	3
	299		(3 wkts)	**121**

1/7 2/18 3/30 4/48 5/119
6/160 7/205 8/252 9/288

1/50 2/105 3/105

Bowling: *First Innings*—Braund 60-25-118-4; Jessop 26-5-68-4; Gunn 16-5-48-1; Blythe 37-17-57-1. *Second Innings*—Jessop 7-0-23-0; Braund 15-2-55-0; Blythe 6-0-23-1; Gunn 8.3-1-17-2.

Umpires: C.Bannerman and R.Callaway

AUSTRALIA v ENGLAND 1901-02 (Fifth Test)

At Melbourne Cricket Ground, 28 February, 1, 3, 4 March
Result: Australia won by 32 runs

Australia

V.T.Trumper b Blythe	27		c McGahey b Braund	18
R.A.Duff b Braund	10		c and b Braund	28
C.Hill c Jones b Gunn	28		c Lilley b Hayward	87
S.E.Gregory c Jones b Gunn	25		b Gunn	41
M.A.Noble lbw b Hayward	7		c MacLaren b Gunn	16
H.Trumble* c Quaife b Hayward	3	(7)	b Blythe	22
W.W.Armstrong not out	17	(6)	lbw b Braund	20
A.J.Y.Hopkins c Lilley b Hayward	4	(9)	c MacLaren b Blythe	0
J.J.Kelly† c Gunn b Hayward	0	(8)	not out	11
C.J.Eady b Gunn	5		c Gunn b Braund	3
J.P.F.Travers c Braund b Gunn	9		c and b Braund	1
Extras (B 7, NB 1, W 1)	9		(B 3, LB 1, NB 4)	8
	144			255

1/16 2/54 3/81 4/98 5/104
6/108 7/112 8/112 9/125

1/30 2/52 3/131 4/149 5/208
6/224 7/249 8/249 9/252

Bowling: *First Innings*—Jessop 1-0-13-0; Braund 10-2-33-1; Blythe 9-2-29-1; Hayward 16-9-22-4; Gunn 17-6-38-4. *Second Innings*—Hayward 22-4-63-1; Braund 26.1-4-95-5; Gunn 28-11-53-2; Blythe 13-3-36-2.

England

A.C.MacLaren* c and b Trumble	25		run out	25	(4)
G.L.Jessop c Hopkins b Trumble	35		c Trumper b Trumble	16
W.Quaife c Trumble b Noble	3		lbw b Noble	4
J.T.Tyldesley c Kelly b Eady	13		c Eady b Trumble	36	(5)
T.W.Hayward c Trumper b Travers	19		c Travers b Trumble	15	(2)
L.C.Braund c Hopkins b Trumble	32		c Hill b Noble	2
A.F.A.Lilley† c Eady b Trumble	41		c Duff b Noble	9
C.P.McGahey b Trumble	0		c Hill b Noble	7
A.O.Jones c Kelly b Eady	10		c and b Noble	28
J.R.Gunn lbw b Eady	8		c Hill b Noble	0
C.Blythe not out	0		not out	5
Extras (B 1, LB 2)	3		(LB 2, NB 1)	3
	189			178

1/50 2/62 3/64 4/91 5/96
6/164 7/168 8/173 9/186

1/40 2/64 3/87 4/87 5/93
6/104 7/120 8/157 9/161

Bowling: *First Innings*—Noble 26-4-80-1; Trumble 25-4-62-5; Travers 8-2-14-1; Eady 8.3-2-30-3. *Second Innings*—Noble 33-4-98-6; Trumble 30.3-7-64-3; Eady 2-0-13-0.

Umpires: C.Bannerman and R.M.Crockett

ENGLAND v AUSTRALIA 1902 (First Test)

At Edgbaston, Birmingham, 29, 30, 31 May
Result: Match Drawn

England

A.C.MacLaren* run out	9
C.B.Fry c Kelly b Jones	0
K.S.Ranjitsinhji b Armstrong	13
Hon.F.S.Jackson b Jones	53
J.T.Tyldesley lbw b Howell	138
A.F.A.Lilley† c Jones b Noble	2
G.H.Hirst c Armstrong b Trumper	48
G.L.Jessop c Hopkins b Trumper	6
L.C.Braund b Jones	14
W.H.Lockwood not out	52
W.Rhodes not out	38
Extras (LB 3)	3
(9 wkts dec.)	376

1/5 2/13 3/35 4/112 5/121
6/212 7/230 8/264 9/295

Bowling: Jones 28-9-76-3; Noble 44-15-112-1; Trumper 13-5-35-2; Armstrong 25-6-64-1; Howell 26-8-58-1; Hopkins 6-2-28-0.

Australia

V.T.Trumper b Hirst	18		c Braund b Rhodes	14
R.A.Duff c Jessop b Rhodes	2		c Fry b Braund	15
C.Hill c Braund b Hirst	1		not out	10
S.E.Gregory lbw b Hirst	0		not out	1
J.Darling* c Jessop b Rhodes	3		
M.A.Noble st Lilley b Rhodes	0		
W.W.Armstrong c Lilley b Rhodes	5		
A.J.Y.Hopkins c Lilley b Rhodes	0		
J.J.Kelly† not out	1		
E.Jones c Jackson b Rhodes	0		
W.P.Howell c Fry b Rhodes	5		
Extras (B 3)	3		(LB 4, NB 1, W 1)	6
	36		(2 wkts)	46

1/9 2/10 3/14 4/17 5/25
6/25 7/31 8/35 9/35

1/16 2/41

Bowling: *First Innings*—Hirst 11-4-15-3; Rhodes 11-3-17-7; Braund 1-0-1-0. *Second Innings*—Hirst 9-6-10-0; Rhodes 10-5-9-1; Braund 5-0-14-1; Jackson 4-2-7-0.

Umpires: W.Hearn and J.Phillips

ENGLAND v AUSTRALIA 1902 (Second Test)

At Lord's, London, 12, 13 (no play), 14 (no play) June

Result: Match Drawn

England

A.C.MacLaren* not out	47
C.B.Fry c Hill b Hopkins	0
K.S.Ranjitsinhji b Hopkins	0
Hon.F.S.Jackson not out	55
J.T.Tyldesley	
A.F.A.Lilley†	
G.H.Hirst	
G.L.Jessop	
L.C.Braund	
W.H.Lockwood	
W.Rhodes	
Extras	0
	(2 wkts) 102

1/0 2/0

Bowling: Jones 11-4-31-0; Hopkins 9-3-18-2; Saunders 3-0-15-0; Trumper 8-1-33-0; Armstrong 5-0-5-0; Noble 2-2-0-0.

Australia

V.T.Trumper
R.A.Duff
A.J.Y.Hopkins
C.Hill
S.E.Gregory
J.Darling*
M.A.Noble
W.W.Armstrong
J.J.Kelly†
E.Jones
J.V.Saunders

Umpires: C.E.Richardson and V.A.Titchmarsh

ENGLAND v AUSTRALIA 1902 (Third Test)

At Bramall Lane, Sheffield, 3, 4, 5 July

Result: Australia won by 143 runs

Australia

V.T.Trumper b Braund	1	c Lilley b Jackson	62
R.A.Duff c Lilley b Barnes	25	c Hirst b Rhodes	1
C.Hill c Rhodes b Barnes	18	c MacLaren b Jackson	119
J.Darling* c Braund b Barnes	0	c Braund b Barnes	0
S.E.Gregory c Abel b Barnes	11	run out	29
M.A.Noble c Braund b Rhodes	47	b Jackson	8
A.J.Y.Hopkins c Braund b Barnes	27	not out	40
W.W.Armstrong c and b Braund	25	b Rhodes	26
J.J.Kelly† b Barnes	0	c Hirst b Rhodes	0
H.Trumble c and b Jackson	32	b Rhodes	0
J.V.Saunders not out	0	b Rhodes	1
Extras (B 3, LB 5)	8	(LB 3)	3
	194		289

1/3 2/39 3/39 4/52 5/73 6/127 7/137 8/137 9/194

1/20 2/80 3/80 4/187 5/214 6/225 7/277 8/287 9/287

Bowling: *First Innings*—Hirst 15-1-59-0; Braund 13-4-34-2; Barnes 20-9-49-6; Jackson 5.1-1-11-1; Rhodes 13-3-33-1. *Second Innings*—Hirst 10-1-40-0; Braund 12-0-58-0; Barnes 12-4-50-1; Jackson 17-2-60-3; Rhodes 17-3-63-5; Jessop 4-0-15-0.

England

A.C.MacLaren* b Noble	31	(4) c Trumper b Noble	63
R.Abel b Noble	38	c Hill b Noble	8
J.T.Tyldesley c Armstrong b Noble	22	b Trumble	14
Hon.F.S.Jackson c Gregory b Saunders	3	(6) b Noble	14
C.B.Fry st Kelly b Saunders	1	lbw b Trumble	4
A.F.A.Lilley† b Noble	8	(7) b Noble	9
L.C.Braund st Kelly b Saunders	0	(8) c Armstrong b Noble	9
G.H.Hirst c Trumble b Saunders	8	(8) b Noble	0
G.L.Jessop c Saunders b Noble	12	(9) lbw b Trumble	55
W.Rhodes not out	7	not out	7
S.F.Barnes c Darling b Saunders	7	(1) b Trumble	5
Extras (B 4, LB 3, NB 1)	8	(B 4, LB 1, NB 1, W 1)	7
	145		195

1/61 2/86 3/101 4/101 5/102 6/106 7/110 8/130 9/131

1/14 2/75 3/84 4/98 5/162 6/165 7/174 8/174 9/186

Bowling: *First Innings*—Trumble 18-10-21-0; Saunders 15.3-4-50-5; Trumper 4-1-8-0; Noble 19-6-51-5; Armstrong 5-2-7-0. *Second Innings*—Trumble 21.5-3-49-4; Saunders 12-0-68-0; Trumper 6-0-19-0; Noble 21-4-52-6.

Umpires: J.Phillips and W.Richards

ENGLAND v AUSTRALIA 1902 (Fourth Test)

At Old Trafford, Manchester, 24, 25, 26 July

Result: Australia won by 3 runs

Australia

V.T.Trumper c Lilley b Rhodes		104	c Braund b Lockwood	4
R.A.Duff c Lilley b Lockwood		54	b Lockwood	3
C.Hill c Rhodes b Lockwood		65	b Lockwood	0
M.A.Noble c and b Rhodes		2	(6) c Lilley b Lockwood	4
S.E.Gregory c Lilley Rhodes		3	lbw b Tate	24
J.Darling* c MacLaren b Rhodes		51	(4) c Palairet b Rhodes	37
A.J.Y.Hopkins c Palairet b Lockwood		0	c Tate b Lockwood	2
W.W.Armstrong b Lockwood		5	b Rhodes	3
J.J.Kelly† not out		4	not out	2
H.Trumble c Tate b Lockwood		0	lbw b Tate	4
J.V.Saunders b Lockwood		3	c Tyldesley b Rhodes	0
Extras (B 5, LB 2, W 1)		8	(B 1, LB 1, NB 1)	3
		299		86

1/135 2/175 3/179 4/183 5/256
6/256 7/288 8/292 9/292

1/7 2/9 3/10 4/64 5/74
6/76 7/77 8/79 9/85

Bowling: *First Innings*—Rhodes 25-3-104-4; Jackson 11-0-58-0; Tate 11-1-44-0; Braund 9-0-37-0; Lockwood 20.1-5-48-6. *Second Innings*—Rhodes 14.4-5-26-3; Tate 5-3-7-2; Braund 11-3-22-0; Lockwood 17-5-28-5.

England

L.C.H.Palairet c Noble b Saunders		6	b Saunders	17
R.Abel c Armstrong b Saunders		6	(5) b Trumble	21
J.T.Tyldesley c Hopkins b Saunders		22	(2) c Armstrong b Saunders	16
A.C.MacLaren* b Trumble		1	c Duff b Trumble	35
K.S.Ranjitsinhji lbw b Trumble		2	(4) lbw b Trumble	4
Hon.F.S.Jackson c Duff b Trumble		128	c Gregory b Saunders	7
L.C.Braund b Noble		65	st Kelly b Trumble	3
A.F.A.Lilley† b Noble		7	c Hill b Trumble	4
W.H.Lockwood run out		7	b Trumble	0
W.Rhodes c and b Trumble		5	not out	4
F.W.Tate not out		5	b Saunders	4
Extras (B 6, LB 2)		8	(B 5)	5
		262		120

1/12 2/13 3/14 4/30 5/44
6/185 7/203 8/214 9/235

1/44 2/68 3/72 4/92 5/97
6/107 7/109 8/109 9/116

Bowling: *First Innings*—Trumble 43-16-75-4; Saunders 34-5-104-3; Noble 24-8-47-2; Trumper 6-4-6-0; Armstrong 5-2-19-0; Hopkins 2-0-3-0. *Second Innings*—Trumble 25-9-53-6; Saunders 19.4-4-52-4; Noble 5-3-10-0.

Umpires: J.Moss and T.Mycroft

ENGLAND v AUSTRALIA 1902 (Fifth Test)

At Kennington Oval, London, 11, 12, 13 August

Result: England won by 1 wicket

Australia

V.T.Trumper b Hirst		42	run out	2
R.A.Duff c Lilley b Hirst		23	b Lockwood	6
C.Hill b Hirst		11	c MacLaren b Hirst	34
J.Darling* c Lilley b Hirst		3	c MacLaren b Lockwood	15
M.A.Noble c and b Jackson		52	b Braund	13
S.E.Gregory b Hirst		23	b Braund	9
W.W.Armstrong b Jackson		17	b Lockwood	21
A.J.Y.Hopkins c MacLaren b Lockwood		40	c Lilley b Lockwood	3
H.Trumble not out		64	(10) not out	7
J.J.Kelly† c Rhodes b Braund		39	(11) lbw b Lockwood	2
J.V.Saunders lbw b Braund		0	(9) c Tyldesley b Rhodes	2
Extras (B 5, LB 3, NB 2)		10	(B 7, LB 2)	9
		324		121

1/47 2/63 3/69 4/82 5/126
6/174 7/175 8/256 9/324

1/6 2/9 3/31 4/71 5/75
6/91 7/99 8/114 9/115

Bowling: *First Innings*—Lockwood 24-2-85-1; Rhodes 28-9-46-0; Hirst 29-5-77-5; Braund 16.5-5-29-2; Jackson 20-4-66-2; Jessop 6-2-11-0. *Second Innings*—Lockwood 20-6-45-5; Rhodes 22-7-38-1; Hirst 5-1-7-1; Braund 9-1-15-2; Jackson 4-3-7-0.

England

A.C.MacLaren* c Armstrong b Trumble		10	b Saunders	2
L.C.H.Palairet b Trumble		20	b Saunders	6
J.T.Tyldesley b Trumble		33	b Saunders	0
T.W.Hayward b Trumble		0	c Kelly b Saunders	7
Hon.F.S.Jackson c Armstrong b Saunders		2	c and b Trumble	49
L.C.Braund c Hill b Trumble		22	c Kelly b Trumble	2
G.L.Jessop b Trumble		13	c Noble b Armstrong	104
G.H.Hirst c and b Trumble		43	not out	58
W.H.Lockwood c Noble b Saunders		25	lbw b Trumble	0
A.F.A.Lilley† c Trumper b Trumble		0	c Darling b Trumble	6
W.Rhodes not out		0	not out	6
Extras (B 13, LB 2)		15	(B 5, LB 6)	11
		183		263 (9 wkts)

1/31 2/36 3/62 4/67 5/67
6/83 7/137 8/179 9/183

1/5 2/5 3/10 4/31 5/48 (9 wkts)
6/157 7/187 8/214 9/248

Bowling: *First Innings*—Trumble 31-13-65-8; Saunders 23-7-79-2; Noble 7-3-24-0. *Second Innings*—Trumble 33.5-4-108-4; Saunders 24-3-105-4; Noble 5-0-11-0; Armstrong 4-0-28-1.

Umpires: C.E.Richardson and A.A.White

SOUTH AFRICA v AUSTRALIA 1902-03 (First Test)

At Old Wanderers, Johannesburg, 11, 13, 14 October
Result: Match drawn

South Africa

W.A.Shalders c and b Jones	19		c Kelly b Jones		0
L.J.Tancred c Duff b Trumper	97		b Armstrong		24
C.B.Llewellyn b Trumper	90	(6)	not out		4
J.H.Sinclair c and b Hopkins	44		b Armstrong		19
C.M.H.Hathorn c Gregory b Jones	45	(3)	c Armstrong b Noble		31
C.J.E.Smith b Hopkins	13	(5)	not out		16
H.M.Taberer*† b Hopkins	1				
A.W.Nourse c Hopkins b Noble	72				
E.A.Halliwell† c Darling b Jones	57				
P.G.Thornton not out	1				
G.A.Rowe c Jones b Noble	4				
Extras (B 5, LB 4, NB 1)	10		(B 4, LB 3)		7
	454		(4 wkts)		**101**

1/31 2/204 3/223 4/296 5/304 / 6/306 7/325 8/449 9/449
1/5 2/44 3/74 4/90

Bowling: *First Innings*—Jones 21-5-78-3; Armstrong 13-3-88-0; Trumble 23-1-103-0; Trumper 12-0-62-2; Hopkins 12-1-59-3; Noble 14-2-54-2. *Second Innings*—Jones 7-3-22-1; Armstrong 7-2-24-2; Trumble 11-3-24-0; Hopkins 2-0-17-0; Noble 5-1-7-1.

Australia

V.T.Trumper c Rowe b Llewellyn	63		b Taberer		37
W.W.Armstrong b Sinclair	11	(4)	c Halliwell b Thornton		59
C.Hill c Nourse b Sinclair	76		c and b Sinclair		142
R.A.Duff not out	82	(2)	c Halliwell b Rowe		15
M.A.Noble b Sinclair	0	(6)	not out		53
J.Darling* st Halliwell b Sinclair	0	(5)	b Llewellyn		14
S.E.Gregory lbw b Llewellyn	0		b Llewellyn		4
A.J.Y.Hopkins c Tancred b Llewellyn	1		lbw b Llewellyn		30
H.Trumble c Thornton b Llewellyn	13		not out		0
J.J.Kelly† c Halliwell b Llewellyn	25				
E.Jones c Sinclair b Llewellyn	0				
Extras (B 22, LB 2)	24		(B 13, LB 5)		18
	296		(7 wkts dec.)		**372**

1/60 2/106 3/195 4/196 5/196 / 6/199 7/217 8/242 9/296
1/42 2/67 3/231 / 4/277 5/281 6/297 7/354

Bowling: *First Innings*—Rowe 5-1-28-0; Taberer 4-1-23-0; Llewellyn 22-3-92-6; Sinclair 20-1-129-4. *Second Innings*—Rowe 11-1-55-1; Taberer 6-1-25-1; Llewellyn 26-3-124-3; Sinclair 23-2-115-1; Nourse 8-2-15-0; Thornton 4-0-20-1.

Umpires: F.Hearne and A.Soames

SOUTH AFRICA v AUSTRALIA 1902-03 (Second Test)

At Old Wanderers, Johannesburg, 18, 20, 21 October
Result: Australia won by 159 runs

Australia

V.T.Trumper b Kotze	18	(3)	c Shalders b Sinclair		13
R.A.Duff b Middleton	43	(4)	b Sinclair		44
C.Hill st Halliwell b Kotze	6	(8)	c Kotze b Llewellyn		12
W.W.Armstrong run out	49	(1)	not out		159
M.A.Noble c Kotze b Llewellyn	5		lbw b Llewellyn		24
J.Darling* c Anderson b Llewellyn	6		b Llewellyn		4
S.E.Gregory b Kotze	1	(2)	c Llewellyn b Kotze		13
A.J.Y.Hopkins c Nourse b Llewellyn	20	(9)	c Llewellyn b Nourse		8
J.J.Kelly† c Halliwell b Llewellyn	16	(10)	c Hathorn b Llewellyn		9
W.P.Howell c Nourse b Llewellyn	0	(11)	b Llewellyn		9
J.V.Saunders not out	0	(7)	b Sinclair		1
Extras (B 10, W 1)	11		(B 8, LB 5)		13
	175				**309**

1/29 2/35 3/125 4/125 5/138 / 6/138 7/140 8/172 9/172
1/40 2/87 3/143 4/180 5/188 / 6/201 7/238 8/263 9/290

Bowling: *First Innings*—Kotze 20-2-64-3; Middleton 13-3-27-1; Llewellyn 18.1-3-43-5; Sinclair 4-0-30-0. *Second Innings*—Kotze 17-2-71-1; Middleton 4-0-15-0; Llewellyn 31.4-9-73-5; Sinclair 26-0-118-3; Nourse 3-0-19-1.

South Africa

L.J.Tancred lbw b Noble	19	(3)	c Kelly b Howell		29
W.A.Shalders b Howell	42	(4)	b Saunders		3
C.M.H.Hathorn c Armstrong b Noble	12	(2)	b Saunders		1
J.H.Sinclair b Howell	101		b Howell		18
C.J.E.Smith c Kelly b Trumper	12	(6)	b Howell		4
C.B.Llewellyn c and b Trumper	10	(5)	b Saunders		0
A.W.Nourse c and b Trumper	5	(8)	not out		18
E.A.Halliwell*† c Kelly b Noble	4	(9)	b Saunders		0
J.H.Anderson* c Howell b Saunders	32	(7)	c Darling b Saunders		11
J.J.Kotze b Saunders	0	(11)	st Kelly b Saunders		0
J.Middleton not out	0	(10)	b Saunders		0
Extras (B 3)	3		(LB 1)		1
	240				**85**

1/58 2/66 3/91 4/136 5/154 / 6/170 7/179 8/231 9/240
1/4 2/20 3/46 4/51 5/51 / 6/66 7/66 8/77 9/77

Bowling: *First Innings*—Trumper 12-1-60-3; Saunders 9-1-32-2; Howell 13-1-52-2; Noble 15-2-75-3; Armstrong 2-0-16-0; Hopkins 2-1-2-0. *Second Innings*—Trumper 3-0-27-0; Saunders 11-2-34-7; Howell 8-3-23.

Umpires: F.Hearne and F.E.Smith

SOUTH AFRICA v AUSTRALIA 1902-03 (Third Test)

At Newlands, Cape Town, 8, 10, 11 November

Result: Australia won by 10 wickets

Australia

R.A.Duff c Tancred b Kotze	34	not out ... 20
V.T.Trumper b Llewellyn	70	not out ... 38
C.Hill not out	91	
W.W.Armstrong b Llewellyn	3	
M.A.Noble c Smith b Sinclair	9	
A.J.Y.Hopkins b Llewellyn	16	
S.E.Gregory c Smith b Llewellyn	11	
J.Darling* b Llewellyn	1	
J.J.Kelly† b Kotze	1	
W.P.Howell b Llewellyn	2	
J.V.Saunders run out	4	
Extras (B 6, LB 4)	10	(NB 1) ... 1
	252	**(0 wkts) 59**

1/100 2/121 3/129 4/142 5/179
6/223 7/226 8/227 9/230

Bowling: First Innings—Llewellyn 30.5-4-97-6; Kotze 17-1-49-2; Sinclair 12-0-55-1; Middleton 8-1-28-0; Nourse 3-0-13-0. Second Innings—Llewellyn 4-1-19-0; Kotze 2.5-1-16-0; Sinclair 2-0-22-0; Middleton 1-0-1-0.

South Africa

L.J.Tancred b Howell	0	c and b Howell ... 2
W.A.Shalders c Darling b Saunders	11	c Darling b Hopkins ... 40
C.J.E.Smith b Saunders	16	c and b Trumper ... 45
J.H.Sinclair b Howell	0	st Kelly b Saunders ... 104
P.S.Twentyman-Jones b Howell	0	b Hopkins ... 0
C.B.Llewellyn b Howell	1	st Kelly b Howell ... 8
C.M.H.Hathorn run out	19	st Kelly b Saunders ... 18
A.W.Nourse b Saunders	15	b Howell ... 5
E.A.Halliwell*† run out	13	b Howell ... 0
J.J.Kotze b Saunders	2	b Howell ... 0
J.Middleton not out	1	not out ... 0
Extras (B 4, LB 3)	7	(LB 1, NB 1) ... 2
	85	**225**

1/12 2/12 3/12 4/12 5/14
6/36 7/60 9/83

1/2 2/81 3/115 4/115 5/134
6/216 7/221 8/225 9/225

Bowling: First Innings—Howell 17-6-18-4; Saunders 12.2-2-37-4; Noble 4-0-23-0. Second Innings—Howell 26-6-81-5; Saunders 17.1-3-73-2; Noble 6-3-6-0; Trumper 6-1-26-1; Hopkins 8-0-37-2.

Umpires: W.H.Creese and F.Hearne

AUSTRALIA v ENGLAND 1903-04 (First Test)

At Sydney Cricket Ground, 11, 12, 14, 15, 16, 17 December

Result: England won by 5 wickets

Australia

R.A.Duff c Lilley b Arnold	3	(3) c Relf b Rhodes ... 84
V.T.Trumper c Foster b Arnold	1	(5) not out ... 185
C.Hill c Lilley b Hirst	5	(4) run out ... 51
M.A.Noble* c Foster b Arnold	133	(6) st Lilley b Bosanquet ... 22
W.W.Armstrong b Bosanquet	48	(7) c Bosanquet b Rhodes ... 27
A.J.Y.Hopkins b Hirst	39	(8) c Arnold b Rhodes ... 20
W.P.Howell c Relf b Arnold	5	(10) c Lilley Arnold ... 4
S.E.Gregory c Smith b Bosanquet	23	(1) c Lilley b Rhodes ... 43
F.J.Laver lbw b Rhodes	4	c Relf b Rhodes ... 6
J.J.Kelly† c Braund b Rhodes	10	(2) b Arnold ... 13
J.V.Saunders not out	11	run out ... 2
Extras (NB 3)	3	(B 10, LB 15, NB 1, W 2) ... 28
	285	**485**

1/2 2/9 3/12 4/118 5/200
6/207 7/259 8/263 9/271

1/36 2/108 3/191 4/254 5/334
6/393 7/441 8/468 9/473

Bowling: First Innings—Hirst 24-8-47-2; Arnold 32-7-76-4; Braund 26-9-39-0; Bosanquet 13-0-52-2; Rhodes 17.2-3-41-2; Relf 6-1-27-0. Second Innings—Hirst 29-1-79-0; Arnold 28-2-93-2; Rhodes 40.2-10-94-5; Bosanquet 23-1-100-1; Braund 12-2-56-0; Relf 13-5-35-0.

England

T.W.Hayward b Howell	15	st Kelly b Saunders ... 91
P.F.Warner* c Kelly b Laver	0	b Howell ... 8
J.T.Tyldesley b Noble	53	c Noble b Saunders ... 9
E.G.Arnold c Laver b Armstrong	27	
R.E.Foster c Noble b Saunders	287	(4) st Kelly b Armstrong ... 19
L.C.Braund b Howell	102	(5) c Noble b Howell ... 0
G.H.Hirst b Howell	0	(6) not out ... 60
B.J.T.Bosanquet c Howell b Noble	2	(7) not out ... 1
A.F.A.Lilley† c Hill b Noble	24	
A.E.Relf c Armstrong b Saunders	31	
W.Rhodes not out	40	
Extras (B 6, LB 7, NB 2, W 1)	16	(B 3, LB 1, W 2) ... 6
	577	**(5 wkts) 194**

1/0 2/49 3/73 4/117 5/309
6/311 7/318 8/332 9/447

1/21 2/39 3/81 4/82
5/181

Bowling: First Innings—Saunders 36.2-8-125-2; Laver 37-12-119-1; Howell 31-7-111-3; Noble 34-8-99-3; Armstrong 23-3-47-1; Hopkins 11-1-40-0; Trumper 7-2-12-0; Gregory 2-0-8-0. Second Innings—Noble 12-2-37-0; Howell 31-18-35-2; Saunders 18.5-3-51-2; Laver 16-4-37-0; Armstrong 18-6-28-1.

Umpires: R.M.Crockett and A.C.Jones

AUSTRALIA v ENGLAND 1903-04 (Second Test)
At Melbourne Cricket Ground, 1, 2, 4, 5 January
Result: England won by 185 runs

England

P.F.Warner*	c Duff b Trumble	68	c Trumper b Saunders	3
T.W.Hayward	c Gregory b Hopkins	58	c Trumper b Trumble	0
J.T.Tyldesley	c Trumble b Howell	97	c Trumble b Howell	62
R.E.Foster	retired ill	49	absent ill	—
L.C.Braund	c Howell b Trumble	20	(4) b Saunders	3
A.E.Knight	b Howell	2	(7) lbw b Trumble	0
G.H.Hirst	c Noble b Howell	7	(5) c Gregory b Howell	4
W.Rhodes	lbw b Trumble	2	(6) lbw b Trumble	9
A.F.A.Lilley†	c Howell b Trumble	4	(8) st Kelly b Trumble	0
A.E.Relf	not out	3	(9) not out	10
A.Fielder	b Howell	1	(10) c Hill b Trumble	4
Extras	(LB 3, W 1)	4	(B 7, LB 1)	8
		315		**103**

1/122 2/132 3/277 4/279 5/297   1/3 2/7 3/27 4/40 5/74
6/306 7/306 8/314 9/315   6/74 7/74 8/90 9/103

Bowling: *First Innings*—Trumble 50-10-107-4; Noble 6-3-4-0; Saunders 16-3-60-0; Howell 34.5-14-43-4; Armstrong 25-6-43-0; Hopkins 20-2-50-1; Trumper 1-0-4-0. *Second Innings*—Trumble 10.5-2-34-5; Saunders 8-0-33-2; Howell 8-3-25-2; Hopkins 2-1-3-0.

Australia

R.A.Duff	st Lilley b Rhodes	10	c Braund b Rhodes	8
V.T.Trumper	c Tyldesley b Rhodes	74	c Relf b Rhodes	35
C.Hill	c Rhodes b Hirst	5	c Relf b Rhodes	20
M.A.Noble*	c sub (H.Strudwick) b Rhodes	0	not out	31
S.E.Gregory	c Hirst b Rhodes	0	c Rhodes b Hirst	13
A.J.Y.Hopkins	c sub (H.Strudwick) Relf	18	c and b Rhodes	7
H.Trumble	c sub (H.Strudwick) b Rhodes	2	c Braund b Rhodes	0
W.W.Armstrong	c Braund b Rhodes	1	c Hayward b Rhodes	0
J.J.Kelly†	run out	8	c Lilley b Rhodes	7
W.P.Howell	c Fielder b Rhodes	0	c Hirst b Rhodes	3
J.V.Saunders	not out	2	c Fielder b Hirst	0
Extras	(LB 1)	1	(B 1)	1
		122		**111**

1/14 2/23 3/33 4/33 5/67   1/14 2/59 3/73 4/77 5/86
6/73 7/97 8/105 9/116   6/90 7/90 8/102 9/105

Bowling: *First Innings*—Rhodes 15.2-3-56-7; Hirst 8-1-33-1; Relf 2-0-12-1; Braund 5-0-20-0. *Second Innings*—Rhodes 15-0-68-8; Hirst 13.4-4-38-2; Relf 1-0-5-0.

Umpires: P.Argall and R.M.Crockett

AUSTRALIA v ENGLAND 1903-04 (Third Test)
At Adelaide Oval, 15, 16, 18, 19, 20 January
Result: Australia won by 216 runs

Australia

R.A.Duff	b Hirst	79	c Braund b Hirst	14
V.T.Trumper	b Hirst	113	lbw b Rhodes	59
C.Hill	c Lilley b Arnold	88	b Fielder	16
M.A.Noble*	st Lilley b Arnold	59	c Bosanquet b Braund	65
S.E.Gregory	c Tyldesley b Arnold	8	c Rhodes b Braund	112
A.J.Y.Hopkins	b Bosanquet	0	(7) run out	7
W.W.Armstrong	lbw b Rhodes	10	(6) c Hirst b Bosanquet	39
H.Trumble	b Bosanquet	4	c and b Bosanquet	9
C.E.McLeod	run out	8	b Bosanquet	2
J.J.Kelly†	lbw b Bosanquet	1	st Lilley b Bosanquet	13
W.P.Howell	not out	3	not out	1
Extras	(B 7, LB 5, W 3)	15	(B 8, LB 2, NB 1, W 3)	14
		388		**351**

1/129 2/272 3/296 4/308 5/310   1/48 2/81 3/101 4/263 5/289
6/343 7/360 8/384 9/384   6/320 7/324 8/326 9/350

Bowling: *First Innings*—Fielder 7-0-33-0; Arnold 27-4-93-3; Rhodes 14-3-45-1; Bosanquet 30.1-4-95-3; Braund 13-1-49-0; Hirst 15-1-58-2. *Second Innings*—Hirst 13-1-36-1; Arnold 19-3-74-0; Bosanquet 15.5-0-73-4; Rhodes 21-4-46-1; Fielder 25-11-51-1; Braund 21-6-57-2.

England

T.W.Hayward	b Howell	67	(2) lbw b Hopkins	20
P.F.Warner*	c McLeod b Trumble	79	(1) c and b Trumble	48
J.T.Tyldesley	c Kelly b Hopkins	0	(4) c Noble b Hopkins	0
R.E.Foster	c Howell b Noble	16	(5) b McLeod	21
L.C.Braund	c Duff b Hopkins	25	(6) b Howell	13
G.H.Hirst	c Trumper b Trumble	44	(7) b Trumble	58
B.J.T.Bosanquet	c Duff b Hopkins	10	(9) c Trumper b Hopkins	10
W.Rhodes	c Armstrong b McLeod	9	(10) run out	8
E.G.Arnold	not out	23	(3) b Hopkins	9
A.F.A.Lilley†	run out	0	(8) c and b Howell	28
A.Fielder	b Trumble	14	not out	6
Extras	(B 4, LB 1, W 4)	9	(LB 2, W 2)	4
		245		**278**

1/47 2/48 3/88 4/99 5/116   1/148 2/150 3/160 4/160 5/195
6/146 7/173 8/199 9/234   6/231 7/231 8/256 9/256

Bowling: *First Innings*—McLeod 24-6-56-1; Trumble 28-9-49-3; Howell 13-4-28-1; Hopkins 24-5-68-3; Armstrong 10-3-25-0; Noble 3-0-10-1. *Second Innings*—Howell 20-5-52-2; McLeod 25-4-46-1; Trumble 33-8-73-2; Hopkins 28.1-9-81-4; Armstrong 7-2-15-0; Trumper 4-0-7-0.

Umpires: P.Argall and R.M.Crockett

AUSTRALIA v ENGLAND 1903-04 (Fourth Test)

At Sydney Cricket Ground, 26, 27, 29 (no play), February 1, 2, 3 March

Result: England won by 157 runs

England

T.W.Hayward c McAlister b Trumble	18		lbw b Trumble	52
P.F.Warner* b Noble	0	(9)	not out	31
J.T.Tyldesley c Gregory b Noble	16	(4)	b Cotter	5
R.E.Foster c McAlister b Noble	19	(2)	c Noble b Hopkins	27
A.E.Knight not out	70		c McAlister b Cotter	9
L.C.Braund c Trumble b Noble	39		c McLeod b Hopkins	19
G.H.Hirst b Noble	25		c Kelly b McLeod	18
B.J.T.Bosanquet b Hopkins	12		c Hill b McLeod	7
E.G.Arnold lbw b Noble	0	(3)	c Kelly b Noble	0
A.F.A.Lilley† c Hopkins b Trumble	24		b McLeod	6
W.Rhodes st Kelly b Noble	10		c Cotter b Cotter	29
Extras (B 6, LB 7, NB 1, W 2)	16		(B 1, LB 6)	7
	249			210

1/4 2/34 3/42 4/66 5/155
6/185 7/207 8/208 9/237

1/49 2/50 3/57 4/73 5/106
6/120 7/138 8/141 9/155

Bowling: *First Innings*—Cotter 14-1-44-0; Noble 41.1-10-100-7; Trumble 43-20-58-2; Hopkins 8-3-22-1; McLeod 8-5-9-0. *Second Innings*—Trumble 28-10-49-1; Noble 19-8-40-1; McLeod 20-5-42-3; Hopkins 14-5-31-2; Cotter 18.3-3-41-3.

Australia

R.A.Duff b Arnold	47		b Arnold	19
V.T.Trumper b Braund	7	(4)	lbw b Arnold	12
C.Hill c Braund b Arnold	33		st Lilley b Bosanquet	26
P.A.McAlister c Arnold b Rhodes	2	(2)	b Hirst	1
A.J.Y.Hopkins b Braund	9	(7)	st Lilley b Bosanquet	0
C.E.McLeod b Rhodes	18	(8)	c Lilley b Bosanquet	6
J.J.Kelly† c Foster b Arnold	5	(10)	c Foster b Arnold	10
M.A.Noble* not out	6	(5)	not out	53
S.E.Gregory c Foster b Rhodes	6	(6)	lbw Bosanquet	0
H.Trumble c Lilley b Rhodes	0	(9)	st Lilley b Bosanquet	0
A.Cotter c Tyldesley b Arnold	0		b Hirst	34
Extras (B 1, W 1)	2		(B 10)	10
	131			171

1/28 2/61 3/72 4/97 5/101
6/116 7/124 8/126 9/130

1/7 2/35 3/59 4/76 5/76
6/76 7/86 8/90 9/114

Bowling: *First Innings*—Hirst 13-1-36-0; Braund 11-2-27-2; Rhodes 11-3-33-4; Arnold 14.3-5-28-4; Bosanquet 2-1-5-0. *Second Innings*—Hirst 18.5-2-32-2; Braund 16-3-24-0; Arnold 12-3-42-2; Rhodes 11-7-12-0; Bosanquet 15-1-51-6.

Umpires: P.Argall and R.M.Crockett

AUSTRALIA v ENGLAND 1903-04 (Fifth Test)

At Melbourne Cricket Ground, 5, 7, 8 March

Result: Australia won by 218 runs

Australia

R.A.Duff b Braund	9	(7)	c Warner b Rhodes	31
V.T.Trumper c and b Braund	88	(5)	b Hirst	0
C.Hill c Braund b Rhodes	16	(6)	c Warner b Hirst	16
M.A.Noble* c Foster b Arnold	29	(8)	st Lilley b Rhodes	19
P.A.McAlister st Lilley b Braund	36	(1)	c Foster b Arnold	9
D.R.A.Gehrs c and b Braund	19	(10)	c and b Hirst	5
A.J.Y.Hopkins c Knight b Braund	32	(9)	not out	25
C.E.McLeod c Rhodes b Braund	8	(2)	c Bosanquet b Braund	0
H.Trumble c Foster b Braund	6	(11)	c Arnold b Hirst	0
J.J.Kelly† not out	6	(3)	c and Arnold	24
A.Cotter b Braund	8	(4)	b Hirst	0
Extras (B 4, LB 4)	8		(B 1, LB 3)	4
	247			133

1/13 2/67 3/142 4/144 5/159
6/218 7/221 8/231 9/235

1/9 2/9 3/13 4/13 5/43
6/49 7/92 8/115 9/133

Bowling: *First Innings*—Hirst 19-6-44-0; Braund 29.1-6-81-8; Rhodes 12-1-41-1; Arnold 18-4-46-1; Bosanquet 4-0-27-0. *Second Innings*—Rhodes 15-2-52-2; Arnold 8-3-23-2; Braund 4-1-6-1; Hirst 16.5-4-48-5.

England

T.W.Hayward b Noble	0		absent ill	-
W.Rhodes c Gehrs b Cotter	3	(8)	not out	16
E.G.Arnold c Kelly b Noble	0	(10)	c Duff b Trumble	19
P.F.Warner* c McAlister b Cotter	0	(5)	c and b Trumble	11
J.T.Tyldesley c Gehrs b Noble	10	(3)	c Hopkins b Cotter	15
R.E.Foster b Cotter	18	(2)	c Trumper b Trumble	30
G.H.Hirst c Trumper b Cotter	0	(6)	c McAlister b Trumble	1
L.C.Braund c Hopkins b Noble	5	(1)	c McAlister b Cotter	0
A.E.Knight b Cotter	0	(4)	c Kelly b Trumble	0
B.J.T.Bosanquet c Noble b Cotter	16	(7)	c Gehrs b Trumble	4
A.F.A.Lilley† not out	6	(9)	lbw b Trumble	0
Extras (B 1, NB 1)	2		(B 1, LB 4)	5
	61			101

1/0 2/0 3/4 4/5 5/23
6/26 7/36 8/36 9/48

1/0 2/24 3/38 4/47 5/54
6/61 7/61 8/61 9/101

Bowling: *First Innings*—Noble 15-8-19-4; Cotter 15.2-2-40-6; McLeod 1-1-0-0. *Second Innings*—Cotter 5-0-25-2; Noble 6-2-19-0; Trumble 6.5-0-28-7; McLeod 5-0-24-0.

Umpires: P.Argall and R.M.Crockett

ENGLAND v AUSTRALIA 1905 (First Test)

At Trent Bridge, Nottingham, 29, 30, 31 May

Result: England won by 213 runs

England

T.W.Hayward b Cotter	5		c Darling b Armstrong	47
A.O.Jones b Cotter	4	(4)	b Duff	30
J.T.Tyldesley c Duff b Laver	56		c and b Duff	61
A.C.MacLaren c Kelly b Hopkins	0	(2)	c Duff b Laver	140
Hon.F.S.Jackson* b Cotter	27		not out	82
B.J.T.Bosanquet b Laver	8		b Cotter	6
J.R.Gunn b Cotter	0			
G.L.Jessop b Laver	0			
A.F.A.Lilley† c and b Laver	37			
W.Rhodes c Noble b Laver	29	(7)	not out	39
E.G.Arnold not out	2			
Extras (B 21, LB 5)	26		(B 11, LB 9, W 1)	21
	196		(5 wkts dec.)	426

1/6 2/24 3/40 4/49 5/98   1/145 2/222
6/119 7/119 8/139 9/187   3/276 4/301 5/313

Bowling: *First Innings*—Cotter 23-2-64-3; Laver 31.3-14-64-7; McLeod 8-2-19-0; Armstrong 6-3-4-0; Noble 3-0-19-0. *Second Innings*—Cotter 17-1-59-1; Laver 34-7-121-1; McLeod 28-9-84-0; Armstrong 52-24-67-1; Noble 7-1-31-0; Duff 15-2-43-2.

Australia

R.A.Duff c Hayward b Gunn	1		c and b Bosanquet	25
V.T.Trumper retired hurt	13		absent hurt	
C.Hill b Jackson	54	(5)	c and b Bosanquet	8
M.A.Noble c Lilley b Jackson	50	(3)	st Lilley b Bosanquet	7
W.W.Armstrong st Lilley b Rhodes	27	(4)	c Jackson b Bosanquet	6
J.Darling* c Bosanquet b Jackson	0	(2)	b Bosanquet	40
A.Cotter c and b Jessop	45		b Rhodes	18
S.E.Gregory c Jones b Jackson	2	(6)	c Arnold b Bosanquet	51
C.E.McLeod b Arnold	4		lbw b Bosanquet	13
F.J.Laver c Jones b Jackson	5	(8)	st Lilley b Bosanquet	5
J.J.Kelly† not out	1	(10)	not out	6
Extras (B 16, LB 2, W 1)	19		(B 4, LB 3, W 2)	8
	221			188

1/1 2/129 3/130 4/130 5/200   1/62 2/75 3/82 4/93 5/100
6/204 7/209 8/216 9/221   6/139 7/144 8/175 9/188

Bowling: *First Innings*—Arnold 11-2-39-1; Gunn 6-2-27-1; Jessop 7-2-18-1; Bosanquet 7-0-29-0; Rhodes 18-6-37-1; Jackson 14.5-2-52-5. *Second Innings*—Arnold 4-2-7-0; Jessop 1-0-1-0; Bosanquet 32.4-2-107-8; Rhodes 30-8-58-1; Jackson 5-3-6-0.

Umpires: J.Carlin and J.Phillips

ENGLAND v AUSTRALIA 1905 (Second Test)

At Lord's, London, 15, 16, 17 (no play) June

Result: Match drawn

England

A.C.MacLaren b Hopkins	56	b Armstrong	79
T.W.Hayward lbw b Duff	16	c Laver b McLeod	8
J.T.Tyldesley c Laver b Armstrong	43	b Noble	12
C.B.Fry c Kelly b Hopkins	73	not out	36
Hon.F.S.Jackson* c Armstrong b Laver	29	b Armstrong	0
A.O.Jones b Laver	1	c Trumper b Armstrong	5
B.J.T.Bosanquet c and b Armstrong	6	not out	4
W.Rhodes b Hopkins	15		
A.F.A.Lilley† lbw b McLeod	0		
S.Haigh b Laver	14		
E.G.Arnold not out	7		
Extras (B 20, LB 2)	22	(B 2, LB 4, NB 1)	7
	282	(5 wkts)	151

1/59 2/97 3/149 4/208 5/210   1/18 2/63 3/136
6/227 7/257 8/258 9/258   4/136 5/146

Bowling: *First Innings*—McLeod 20-7-40-1; Laver 34-8-64-3; Armstrong 30-11-41-2; Noble 34-13-61-0; Duff 7-4-14-1; Hopkins 15-4-40-3. *Second Innings*—McLeod 15-5-33-1; Laver 10-4-39-0; Armstrong 10-2-30-3; Noble 13-2-31-1; Hopkins 2-0-11-0.

Australia

V.T.Trumper b Jackson	31
R.A.Duff c Lilley b Rhodes	27
C.Hill c Bosanquet b Jackson	7
M.A.Noble c Fry b Jackson	7
W.W.Armstrong lbw b Jackson	33
J.Darling* c Haigh b Arnold	41
S.E.Gregory c Jones b Rhodes	5
A.J.Y.Hopkins b Haigh	16
C.E.McLeod b Haigh	0
F.J.Laver not out	4
J.J.Kelly† lbw b Rhodes	2
Extras (B 3, LB 5)	8
	181

1/57 2/73 3/73 4/95 5/131   6/138 7/171 8/175 9/175

Bowling: Haigh 12-3-40-2; Rhodes 16.1-1-70-3; Jackson 15-0-50-4; Arnold 7-3-13-1.

Umpires: J.Phillips and W.Richards

ENGLAND v AUSTRALIA 1905 (Third Test)

At Headingley, Leeds, 3, 4, 5 July

Result: Match drawn

England

T.W.Hayward b McLeod	26	c Hopkins b Armstrong	60
C.B.Fry c Noble b McLeod	32	c Kelly b Armstrong	30
J.T.Tyldesley b Laver	0	st Kelly b Armstrong	100
D.Denton c Duff b McLeod	0	c Hill b Armstrong	12
Hon.F.S.Jackson* not out	144	c Duff b Armstrong	17
G.H.Hirst c Trumper b Laver	35	not out	40
B.J.T.Bosanquet b Duff	20	not out	22
A.F.A.Lilley† b Noble	11		
S.Haigh c Noble b Armstrong	11		
A.Warren run out	7		
C.Blythe b Armstrong	0		
Extras (B 10, LB 1, NB 2, W 2)	15	(B 1, LB 6, NB 1, W 6)	14
	301	(5 wkts dec.)	**295**

1/51 2/54 3/57 4/64 5/133
6/201 7/232 8/282 9/301

1/80 2/126 3/170
4/202 5/258

Bowling: *First Innings*—Armstrong 26.3-6-44-2; Noble 23-6-59-1; Laver 29-10-61-2; McLeod 37-13-88-3; Hopkins 9-4-21-0; Duff 4-1-13-1. *Second Innings*—Armstrong 51-14-122-5; Noble 20-3-68-0; Laver 10-4-29-0; McLeod 23-6-62-0.

Australia

V.T.Trumper b Warren	8	c Hirst b Warren	0
R.A.Duff c Lilley b Blythe	48	b Hirst	17
C.Hill c and b Hirst	7	c Warren b Haigh	33
M.A.Noble c Hayward b Warren	2	st Lilley b Bosanquet	62
W.W.Armstrong c Hayward b Warren	66	lbw b Blythe	32
J.Darling* c Bosanquet b Warren	5	b Blythe	2
A.J.Y.Hopkins c Lilley b Jackson	36	b Blythe	17
S.E.Gregory run out	4	not out	0
C.E.McLeod c Lilley b Haigh	8	not out	10
J.J.Kelly† not out	1		
F.J.Laver b Warren	3		
Extras (B 4, LB 1, W 2)	7	(B 11, NB 2, W 6)	19
	195	(7 wkts)	**224**

1/26 2/33 3/36 4/96 5/105
6/161 7/166 8/191 9/191

1/0 2/36 3/64 4/117
5/121 6/152 7/199

Bowling: *First Innings*—Hirst 7-1-37-1; Warren 19.2-5-57-5; Blythe 8-0-36-1; Jackson 4-0-10-1; Haigh 11-5-19-1; Bosanquet 4-0-29-0. *Second Innings*—Hirst 10-2-26-1; Warren 20-4-56-1; Blythe 24-11-41-3; Jackson 8-2-10-0; Haigh 14-4-36-1; Bosanquet 15-1-36-1.

Umpires: J.Phillips and V.A.Titchmarsh

ENGLAND v AUSTRALIA 1905 (Fourth Test)

At Old Trafford, Manchester, 24, 25, 26 July

Result: England won by an innings and 80 runs

England

A.C.MacLaren c Hill b McLeod	14
T.W.Hayward c Gehrs b McLeod	82
J.T.Tyldesley b Laver	24
C.B.Fry b Armstrong	17
Hon.F.S.Jackson* c Cotter b McLeod	113
R.H.Spooner c and b McLeod	52
G.H.Hirst c Laver b McLeod	25
E.G.Arnold run out	25
W.Rhodes not out	27
A.F.A.Lilley† lbw b Noble	28
W.Brearley c Darling b Noble	0
Extras (B 17, LB 20, NB 1, W 1)	39
	446

1/24 2/77 3/136 4/176 5/301
6/347 7/382 8/387 9/446

Bowling: Cotter 26-4-83-0; McLeod 47-8-125-5; Armstrong 48-14-93-1; Laver 21-5-73-1; Noble 15-5-33-2.

Australia

M.A.Noble b Brearley	7	(4)	c Rhodes b Brearley	10
V.T.Trumper c Rhodes b Brearley	11		lbw b Rhodes	30
C.Hill c Fry b Arnold	11		c sub (A.O.Jones) b Arnold	27
W.W.Armstrong b Rhodes	29	(5)	b Brearley	9
R.A.Duff c MacLaren b Brearley	11	(1)	c Spooner b Brearley	60
J.Darling* c Tyldesley b Jackson	73		c Rhodes b Brearley	0
D.R.A.Gehrs b Arnold	0	(8)	c and b Rhodes	11
C.E.McLeod b Brearley	6	(9)	c Arnold b Rhodes	6
A.Cotter c Fry b Jackson	11	(10)	run out	0
F.J.Laver b Rhodes	24	(11)	not out	6
J.J.Kelly† not out	16	(7)	c Rhodes b Arnold	5
Extras (B 9)	9		(B 4, NB 1)	5
	197			**169**

1/20 2/21 3/27 4/41 5/88
6/93 7/146 8/146 9/166

1/55 2/121 3/122 4/133 5/133
6/146 7/146 8/158 9/158

Bowling: *First Innings*—Hirst 2-0-12-0; Brearley 17-3-72-4; Arnold 14-2-53-2; Rhodes 5.5-1-25-2; Jackson 7-0-25-2. *Second Innings*—Hirst 7-2-19-0; Brearley 14-3-54-4; Arnold 15-5-35-2; Rhodes 11.3-3-36-3; Jackson 5-0-20-0.

Umpires: J.Carlin and J.E.West

ENGLAND v AUSTRALIA 1905 (Fifth Test)

At Kennington Oval, London, 14, 15, 16 August
Result: Match drawn

England

A.C.MacLaren c Kelly b Armstrong	6	(3)	c Kelly b Armstrong	6
T.W.Hayward hit wkt b Hopkins	59		lbw b Armstrong	2
J.T.Tyldesley b Cotter	16	(4)	not out	112
C.B.Fry b Cotter	144	(5)	c Armstrong b Noble	16
Hon.F.S.Jackson* c Armstrong b Laver	76	(6)	b Cotter	31
R.H.Spooner b Cotter	0	(7)	c sub (D.R.A.Gehrs) b Noble	79
G.H.Hirst c Noble b Laver	5			
E.G.Arnold c Trumper b Cotter	40	(1)	b Cotter	0
W.Rhodes b Cotter	36			
A.F.A.Lilley† b Cotter	17			
W.Brearley not out	11			
Extras (B 11, LB 1, NB 7, W 1)	20		(B 4, LB 5, NB 5, W 1)	15
	430		**(6 wkts dec.)**	**261**

1/12 2/32 3/132 4/283 5/291 1/0 2/8 3/13 4/48
6/306 7/322 8/394 9/418 5/103 6/261

Bowling: *First Innings*—Cotter 40-4-148-7; Noble 18-6-51-0; Armstrong 27-7-76-0; McLeod 13-2-47-0; Laver 17-3-41-2; Hopkins 11-2-32-1; Duff 4-1-15-0. *Second Innings*—Cotter 21-2-73-2; Noble 14.3-3-56-2; Armstrong 30-13-61-2; McLeod 11-2-27-0; Laver 3-0-18-0; 17-3-41-2; Hopkins 1-0-11-0.

Australia

V.T.Trumper b Brearley	4		c Spooner b Brearley	28
R.A.Duff c and b Rhodes	146			
C.Hill c Rhodes b Brearley	18		b Arnold	34
M.A.Noble c MacLaren b Jackson	25		b Hirst	3
W.W.Armstrong c sub (A.O.Jones) b Hirst	18		not out	32
J.Darling* b Hirst	57		not out	12
A.J.Y.Hopkins b Brearley	1	(2)	run out	10
C.E.McLeod b Brearley	0			
J.J.Kelly† run out	42			
A.Cotter c Fry b Brearley	6			
F.J.Laver not out	15			
Extras (B 17, LB 9, NB 4, W 1)	31		(B 4, LB 1)	5
	363		**(4 wkts)**	**124**

1/5 2/44 3/159 4/214 5/237 1/27 2/49 3/58 4/92
6/247 7/265 8/293 9/304

Bowling: *First Innings*—Hirst 23-6-86-3; Brearley 31.1-8-110-5; Arnold 9-0-50-0; Rhodes 21-2-59-0; Jackson 9-1-27-1. *Second Innings*—Hirst 9-2-32-1; Brearley 11-2-41-1; Arnold 9-2-17-1; Rhodes 8-0-29-0.

Umpires: J.Phillips and W.A.J.West

AUSTRALIA v ENGLAND 1907-08 (First Test)

At Sydney Cricket Ground, 13, 14, 16, 17, 18 (no play), 19 December
Result: Australia won by 2 wickets

England

R.A.Young† c Carter b Cotter	13	(7)	b Noble	3
F.L.Fane* c Trumper b Cotter	2		c Noble b Saunders	33
G.Gunn c Hazlitt b Cotter	119		c Noble b Cotter	74
K.L.Hutchings c and b Armstrong	42		c Armstrong b Saunders	17
L.C.Braund b Cotter	30	(6)	not out	32
J.Hardstaff, sr b Armstrong	12	(5)	b Noble	63
W.Rhodes run out	1	(1)	c McAlister b Macartney	29
J.N.Crawford b Armstrong	31		c Hazlitt b Cotter	5
S.F.Barnes b Cotter	1		b Saunders	11
C.Blythe b Cotter	5		c Noble b Saunders	15
A.Fielder not out	16		lbw b Armstrong	6
Extras (B 7, LB 6, NB 2, W 1)	16		(B 2, NB 7, W 3)	12
	273			**300**

1/11 2/18 3/91 4/208 5/221 1/56 2/82 3/105 4/218 5/223
6/223 7/246 8/253 9/271 6/227 7/241 8/262 9/293

Bowling: *First Innings*—Cotter 21.5-0-101-6; Hazlitt 9-2-32-0; Armstrong 26-10-42-0; Saunders 11-0-42-0; Macartney 3-0-5-0; Noble 6-1-14-0. *Second Innings*—Cotter 26-1-101-2; Saunders 23-6-68-4; Armstrong 27-14-33-1; Macartney 14-2-39-1; Hazlitt 4-2-24-0; Noble 15-5-23-2.

Australia

V.T.Trumper b Fielder	43	(7)	b Barnes	3
P.A.McAlister c Hutchings b Barnes	3		b Crawford	41
C.Hill c Gunn b Fielder	87		b Fielder	1
M.A.Noble* c Braund b Fielder	37		b Barnes	27
W.W.Armstrong c Braund b Fielder	7		b Crawford	44
V.S.Ransford c Braund b Rhodes	24		c and b Blythe	13
C.G.Macartney c Young b Fielder	35	(2)	c Crawford b Fielder	9
H.Carter† b Braund	25		c Young b Fielder	61
G.R.Hazlitt not out	18	(10)	not out	34
A.Cotter b Braund	2	(9)	not out	33
J.V.Saunders c Braund b Fielder	10			
Extras (B 4, LB 2, NB 2, W 2)	10		(B 6, LB 3)	9
	300		**(8 wkts)**	**275**

1/4 2/72 3/164 4/177 5/184 1/7 2/12 3/27 4/75
6/222 7/253 8/277 9/281 5/95 6/124 7/185 8/219

Bowling: *First Innings*—Fielder 30.2-4-82-6; Barnes 22-3-74-1; Blythe 12-1-33-0; Braund 17-2-74-2; Crawford 5-1-14-0; Rhodes 5-2-13-1. *Second Innings*—Fielder 27.3-4-88-3; Barnes 30-7-63-2; Blythe 19-5-55-1; Crawford 8-2-33-2; Rhodes 7-3-13-0; Braund 7-2-14-0.

Umpires: R.M.Crockett and W.Hannah

AUSTRALIA v ENGLAND 1907-08 (Second Test)

At Melbourne Cricket Ground, 1, 2, 3, 4, 6, 7 January

Result: England won by 1 wicket

Australia

Batsman	1st innings		2nd innings	
V.T.Trumper	c Humphries b Crawford	49	(2) lbw b Crawford	4
C.G.Macartney	b Crawford	37	(6) c Humphries b Barnes	15
C.Hill	b Fielder	16	b Fielder	75
M.A.Noble*	c Hutchings b Crawford	61	(1) b Crawford	64
W.W.Armstrong	c Humphries b Crawford	31	b Barnes	77
P.A.McAlister	run out	10	(4) run out	15
V.S.Ransford	run out	27	c Hutchings b Barnes	18
A.Cotter	b Crawford	17	(9) lbw b Crawford	27
H.Carter†	not out	15	(8) c Fane b Barnes	53
G.R.Hazlitt	b Crawford	1	b Barnes	3
J.V.Saunders	b Fielder	0	not out	0
Extras	(LB 1, W 1)	2	(B 12, LB 8)	20
Total		**266**		**397**

1/84 2/93 3/111 4/168 5/197 6/214 7/240 8/261 9/265

1/126 2/131 3/135 4/162 5/268 6/303 7/312 8/361 9/392

Bowling: *First Innings*—Fielder 27.5-4-77-2; Barnes 17-7-30-0; Rhodes 11-0-37-1; Braund 16-5-41-0; Crawford 29-1-79-5. *Second Innings*—Fielder 27-6-74-1; Crawford 33-6-125-3; Barnes 27.4-4-72-5; Braund 18-2-68-0; Rhodes 16-6-38-0.

England

Batsman	1st innings		2nd innings	
F.L.Fane*	b Armstrong	13	(2) b Armstrong	50
J.B.Hobbs	b Cotter	83	(1) b Noble	28
G.Gunn	lbw b Cotter	15	lbw b Noble	0
K.L.Hutchings	b Cotter	126	c Cotter b Macartney	39
L.C.Braund	b Cotter	49	b Armstrong	30
J.Hardstaff, sr	b Saunders	12	c Ransford b Cotter	19
W.Rhodes	b Saunders	32	run out	15
J.N.Crawford	c Ransford b Saunders	16	c Armstrong b Saunders	10
S.F.Barnes	c Hill b Armstrong	14	not out	38
J.Humphries†	b Cotter	6	lbw b Armstrong	16
A.Fielder	not out	6	not out	18
Extras	(B 3, LB 3, NB 3, W 1)	10	(B 9, LB 7, NB 2, W 1)	19
Total		**382**	(9 wkts)	**282**

1/27 2/61 3/160 4/268 5/287 6/325 7/353 8/360 9/369

1/54 2/54 3/121 4/131 5/162 6/196 7/198 8/209 9/243

Bowling: *First Innings*—Cotter 33-4-142-5; Saunders 34-7-100-3; Noble 9-3-26-0; Armstrong 34.2-15-36-2; Hazlitt 13-1-34-0; Macartney 12-2-34-0. *Second Innings*—Cotter 28-3-82-1; Saunders 30-9-58-1; Armstrong 30.4-10-53-3; Noble 22-7-41-2; Hazlitt 2-1-8-0; Macartney 9-3-21-1.

Umpires: P.Argall and R.M.Crockett

AUSTRALIA v ENGLAND 1907-08 (Third Test)

At Adelaide Oval, 10, 11, 13, 14, 15, 16 January

Result: Australia won by 245 runs

Australia

Batsman	1st innings		2nd innings	
V.T.Trumper	c Fielder	4	b Barnes	0
M.A.Noble*	c Hutchings b Barnes	15	c Gunn b Fielder	65
C.G.Macartney	lbw b Braund	75	b Barnes	9
P.A.McAlister	c Hutchings b Crawford	28	c Hutchings b Crawford	17
W.W.Armstrong	c Humphries b Fielder	17	c Hutchings b Braund	34
V.S.Ransford	b Barnes	44	(7) c Rhodes b Braund	25
C.Hill	c Humphries b Barnes	5	(9) c Gunn b Crawford	160
R.J.Hartigan†	lbw b Barnes	48	c sub (R.A.Young) b Barnes	116
H.Carter†	lbw b Hutchings	24	(10) not out	31
J.D.A.O'Connor	not out	10	(6) b Crawford	20
J.V.Saunders	b Fielder	1	run out	0
Extras	(B 3, LB 5, NB 3, W 3)	14	(B 20, LB 7, W 2)	29
Total		**285**		**506**

1/11 2/35 3/114 4/140 5/160 6/191 7/215 8/273 9/275

1/7 2/35 3/71 4/127 5/135 6/179 7/180 8/423 9/501

Bowling: *First Innings*—Fielder 27.5-5-80-4; Barnes 27-8-60-3; Rhodes 15-5-35-0; Crawford 14-0-65-1; Braund 9-1-26-1; Hutchings 2-1-5-1. *Second Innings*—Fielder 23-3-81-1; Barnes 42-9-83-3; Crawford 45.5-4-113-3; Braund 23-3-85-2; Rhodes 27-9-81-0; Hutchings 7-0-34-0.

England

Batsman	1st innings		2nd innings	
J.B.Hobbs	c Carter b Saunders	26	not out	23
F.L.Fane*	run out	48	b Saunders	0
G.Gunn	b O'Connor	65	c Trumper b O'Connor	11
K.L.Hutchings	c and b Macartney	23	b O'Connor	0
L.C.Braund	b Macartney	0	c Hartigan b O'Connor	47
J.Hardstaff, sr	b O'Connor	61	c Macartney b Saunders	72
W.Rhodes	c Carter b O'Connor	38	c Armstrong b O'Connor	9
J.N.Crawford	b Armstrong	62	c and b Saunders	7
S.F.Barnes	c and b Armstrong	12	c McAlister b Saunders	8
J.Humphries†	run out	7	b O'Connor	1
A.Fielder	not out	0	c Ransford b Saunders	1
Extras	(B 12, LB 2, NB 5, W 2)	21	(B 3, NB 1)	4
Total		**363**		**183**

1/58 2/98 3/138 4/138 5/194 6/277 7/282 8/320 9/363

1/8 2/9 3/15 4/128 5/138 6/146 7/162 8/177 9/182

Bowling: *First Innings*—O'Connor 40-8-110-3; Saunders 36-6-83-1; Noble 18-4-38-0; Armstrong 18-4-55-2; Macartney 18-3-49-2; Hartigan 2-0-7-0. *Second Innings*—O'Connor 21-6-40-5; Saunders 21.4-4-65-5; Armstrong 10-1-43-0; Macartney 4-1-17-0; Noble 7-1-14-0.

Umpires: R.M.Crockett and J.Laing

AUSTRALIA v ENGLAND 1907-08 (Fourth Test)

At Melbourne Cricket Ground, 7, 8, 10, 11 February

Result: Australia won by 308 runs

Australia

M.A.Noble* b Crawford	48	b Crawford	10
V.T.Trumper c Crawford b Fielder	0	b Crawford	0
C.Hill b Barnes	7	run out	25
P.A.McAlister c Jones b Fielder	37	c Humphries b Fielder	4
S.E.Gregory c Fielder b Crawford	10	lbw b Fielder	29
W.W.Armstrong b Crawford	32	not out	133
V.S.Ransford c Braund b Fielder	51	c Humphries b Rhodes	54
C.G.Macartney c Hardstaff b Fielder	12	c Gunn b Crawford	29
H.Carter† c and b Crawford	2	c Braund b Fielder	66
J.D.A.O'Connor c Fielder b Crawford	2	c Humphries b Barnes	18
J.V.Saunders not out	1	c Jones b Fielder	2
Extras (B 1, LB 10, NB 1)	12	(B 7, LB 2, NB 6)	15
	214		385

1/14 2/14 3/89 4/103 5/105
6/196 7/196 8/198 9/212

1/4 2/21 3/28 4/65 5/77
6/162 7/217 8/329 9/374

Bowling: *First Innings*—Fielder 22-3-54-4; Barnes 23-11-37-1; Braund 12-3-42-0; Crawford 23.5-3-48-5; Rhodes 5-0-21-0. *Second Innings*—Barnes 35-13-69-1; Crawford 25-5-72-3; Fielder 31-2-91-4; Rhodes 24-5-66-1; Braund 7-0-48-0; Hutchings 2-0-24-0.

England

J.B.Hobbs b Noble	57	c and b Saunders	0
G.Gunn c and b Saunders	13	b Saunders	43
J.Hardstaff, sr c Carter b O'Connor	8	c Carter b Saunders	39
K.L.Hutchings b Saunders	8	b Noble	3
L.C.Braund run out	4	b Macartney	10
W.Rhodes c McAlister b Saunders	0	c Carter b O'Connor	2
J.N.Crawford b Saunders	1	c Carter b O'Connor	1
A.O.Jones* b Noble	3	c Saunders b O'Connor	31
S.F.Barnes c O'Connor b Noble	3	not out	22
J.Humphries† not out	1	c Carter b Saunders	11
A.Fielder st Carter b Saunders	4	b Armstrong	20
Extras (B 1, LB 2, NB 1)	4	(LB 4, NB 1)	5
	105		186

1/58 2/69 3/88 4/90 5/90
6/92 7/96 8/100 9/103

1/0 2/61 3/64 4/79 5/88
6/88 7/128 8/132 9/146

Bowling: *First Innings*—O'Connor 6-1-40-1; Armstrong 1-0-4-0; Macartney 6-1-18-0; Saunders 15.2-8-28-5; Noble 6-0-11-3. *Second Innings*—Saunders 26-2-76-4; O'Connor 21-3-58-3; Noble 12-6-14-1; Armstrong 3.1-0-18-1; Macartney 6-1-15-1.

Umpires: P.Argall and R.M.Crockett

AUSTRALIA v ENGLAND 1907-08 (Fifth Test)

At Sydney Cricket Ground, 21, 22, 24, 25, 26, 27 February

Result: Australia won by 49 runs

Australia

M.A.Noble* b Barnes	35		lbw b Rhodes	34
C.G.Macartney c Crawford b Barnes	9	(5)	c Jones b Crawford	12
J.D.A.O'Connor c Young b Crawford	9	(2)	b Barnes	6
S.E.Gregory c and b Barnes	44		b Crawford	56
C.Hill c Hutchings b Barnes	12	(6)	c Young b Crawford	44
W.W.Armstrong c and b Crawford	3	(7)	c Gunn b Crawford	32
V.T.Trumper c Braund b Barnes	10	(3)	c Gunn b Rhodes	166
V.S.Ransford c Gunn b Barnes	11		not out	21
R.J.Hartigan c and b Crawford	1		b Crawford	5
H.Carter† not out	1		c Hobbs b Rhodes	22
J.V.Saunders c Young b Barnes	0		c Young b Rhodes	0
Extras (B 9, LB 1)	10		(B 21, LB 3)	24
	137			422

1/10 2/46 3/46 4/64 5/73
6/94 7/124 8/129 9/137

1/25 2/52 3/166 4/192 5/300
6/342 7/373 8/387 9/422

Bowling: *First Innings*—Rhodes 10-5-15-0; Barnes 22.4-6-60-7; Crawford 18-4-52-3. *Second Innings*—Barnes 27-6-78-1; Crawford 36-10-141-5; Rhodes 37.4-7-102-4; Braund 20-3-64-0; Hobbs 7-3-13-0.

England

J.B.Hobbs b Saunders	72		c Gregory b Saunders	13
F.L.Fane b Noble	0		b Noble	46
G.Gunn not out	122		b Macartney	0
K.L.Hutchings run out	13		b Macartney	2
J.Hardstaff, sr c O'Connor b Saunders	17		b Saunders	8
J.N.Crawford c Hill b Saunders	6	(10)	not out	24
L.C.Braund st Carter b Macartney	31	(6)	c Noble b Saunders	0
W.Rhodes c Noble b Armstrong	10	(7)	b Noble	69
R.A.Young† st Carter b Macartney	0	(8)	c O'Connor b Saunders	11
A.O.Jones* b Macartney	1	(9)	b Armstrong	34
S.F.Barnes run out	9		b Saunders	11
Extras (B 6, LB 3)	9		(B 5, LB 6)	11
	281			229

1/1 2/135 3/168 4/189 5/197
6/245 7/264 8/271 9/271

1/21 2/26 3/30 4/51 5/57
6/87 7/123 8/176 9/198

Bowling: *First Innings*—Noble 28-9-62-1; Saunders 35-5-114-3; O'Connor 6-0-23-0; Macartney 15.1-3-44-3; Armstrong 12-2-29-1. *Second Innings*—Noble 24-6-56-2; Saunders 35.1-9-82-5; Macartney 15-5-24-2; Armstrong 18-7-27-1; O'Connor 13-3-29-0.

Umpires: W.Hannah and A.C.Jones

ENGLAND v AUSTRALIA 1909 (First Test)

At Edgbaston, Birmingham, 27, 28, 29 May

Result: England won by 10 wickets

Australia

Batsman	1st Innings	R	2nd Innings	R
A.Cotter	c Hirst b Blythe	2	(9) c Tyldesley b Hirst	15
W.Bardsley	c MacLaren b Hirst	2	(6) c Thompson b Blythe	6
W.W.Armstrong	b Hirst	24	(7) c Jessop b Blythe	0
V.T.Trumper	c Hirst b Blythe	10	(5) c Rhodes b Hirst	1
M.A.Noble*	c Jessop b Blythe	15	(1) c Jones b Hirst	11
S.E.Gregory	c Rhodes b Blythe	0	(3) c Thompson b Blythe	43
V.S.Ransford	b Hirst	1	(4) b Blythe	43
C.G.Macartney	c MacLaren b Blythe	10	lbw b Blythe	1
H.Carter†	lbw b Hirst	0	(8) c Hobbs b Hirst	1
J.D.A.O'Connor	lbw b Blythe	8	c Lilley b Hirst	13
W.J.Whitty	not out	0	not out	9
Extras	(LB 1, NB 1)	2	(B 7, LB 1)	8
Total		**74**		**151**

1/5 2/7 3/30 4/46 5/47 6/52 7/58 8/59 9/71

1/4 2/16 3/97 4/99 5/103 6/103 7/106 8/123 9/125

Bowling: *First Innings*—Hirst 23-8-28-4; Blythe 23-6-44-6. *Second Innings*—Hirst 23.5-4-58-5; Blythe 24-3-58-5; Thompson 4-0-19-0; Rhodes 1-0-8-0.

England

Batsman	1st Innings	R	2nd Innings	R
A.C.MacLaren*	b Macartney	5	(1) not out	62
J.B.Hobbs	lbw b Macartney	0	(2) not out	35
J.T.Tyldesley	b O'Connor	24		
C.B.Fry	b Macartney	0		
A.O.Jones	c Carter b Armstrong	28		
G.H.Hirst	lbw b Armstrong	15		
G.L.Jessop	b Armstrong	22		
W.Rhodes	not out	15		
A.F.A.Lilley†	c Ransford b Armstrong	0		
G.J.Thompson	run out	6		
C.Blythe	c Macartney b Armstrong	1		
Extras	(B 4, LB 1)	5	(B 5, LB 3)	8
Total		**121**	**(0 wkts)**	**105**

1/0 2/13 3/13 4/61 5/61 6/90 7/103 8/107 9/116

Bowling: *First Innings*—Whitty 17-5-43-0; Macartney 17-5-21-3; Noble 1-0-2-0; O'Connor 5-2-23-1; Armstrong 15.3-7-27-5. *Second Innings*—Whitty 5-1-18-0; Macartney 11-2-35-0; O'Connor 3.2-1-17-0; Armstrong 13-5-27-0.

Umpires: J.Carlin and F.Parris

ENGLAND v AUSTRALIA 1909 (Second Test)

At Lord's, London, 14, 15, 16 June

Result: Australia won by 9 wickets

England

Batsman	1st Innings	R	2nd Innings	R
T.W.Hayward	st Carter b Laver	16	run out	6
J.B.Hobbs	c Carter b Laver	19	c and b Armstrong	9
J.T.Tyldesley	lbw b Laver	46	st Carter b Armstrong	3
G.Gunn	lbw b Cotter	1	b Armstrong	0
J.H.King	c Macartney b Cotter	60	b Armstrong	4
A.C.MacLaren*	c Armstrong b Noble	7	(8) b Noble	24
G.H.Hirst	b Cotter	31	b Armstrong	1
A.O.Jones	b Cotter	8	(6) lbw b Laver	26
A.E.Relf	c Armstrong b Noble	17	(10) b Armstrong	3
A.F.A.Lilley†	c Bardsley b Noble	47	(9) run out	25
S.Haigh	not out	1	run out	5
Extras	(B 8, LB 3, NB 2, W 3)	16	(B 2, LB 3, NB 10)	15
Total		**269**		**121**

1/23 2/41 3/44 4/123 5/149 6/175 7/199 8/205 9/258

1/16 2/22 3/22 4/23 5/34 6/41 7/82 8/90 9/101

Bowling: *First Innings*—Laver 32-9-75-3; Macartney 8-3-10-0; Cotter 23-1-80-4; Noble 24.2-9-42-3; Armstrong 20-6-46-0. *Second Innings*—Laver 13-4-24-1; Cotter 18-3-35-0; Noble 5-1-12-1; Armstrong 24.5-11-35-6.

Australia

Batsman	1st Innings	R	2nd Innings	R
P.A.McAlister	lbw b King	22	not out	19
F.J.Laver	b Hirst	14		
W.Bardsley	b Relf	46	(2) c Lilley b Relf	0
W.W.Armstrong	c Lilley b Relf	12		
V.S.Ransford	not out	143		
V.T.Trumper	c MacLaren b Relf	28		
M.A.Noble*	c Lilley b Relf	32		
S.E.Gregory	c Lilley b Relf	14	(3) not out	18
A.Cotter	run out	0		
C.G.Macartney	b Hirst	5		
H.Carter†	b Hirst	7		
Extras	(B 16, LB 8, NB 2, W 1)	27	(B 4)	4
Total		**350**	**(1 wkt)**	**41**

1/18 2/84 3/90 4/119 5/198 6/269 7/317 8/317 9/342

1/4

Bowling: *First Innings*—Hirst 26.5-2-83-3; King 27-5-99-1; Relf 45-14-85-5; Haigh 19-5-41-0; Jones 2-0-15-0. *Second Innings*—Hirst 8-1-28-0; Relf 7.4-4-9-1.

Umpires: C.E.Dench and J.Moss

ENGLAND v AUSTRALIA 1909 (Third Test)

At Headingley Leeds, 1, 2, 3 July
Result: Australia won 126 runs

Australia

Batsman	First innings		Second innings	
P.A.McAlister	lbw b Hirst	3	c Sharp b Barnes	21
S.E.Gregory	b Barnes	46	b Hirst	0
V.S.Ransford	run out	45	lbw b Barnes	24
M.A.Noble*	b Hirst	3	(5) c Rhodes b Barnes	31
W.Bardsley	hit wkt b Rhodes	30	(7) c Lilley b Barnes	2
W.W.Armstrong	c Lilley b Brearley	21	(4) b Rhodes	45
V.T.Trumper	not out	27	(6) b Barnes	2
C.G.Macartney	c Fry b Rhodes	4	b Brearley	18
A.Cotter	b Rhodes	2	c MacLaren b Rhodes	3
H.Carter	lbw b Barnes	1	c Lilley b Barnes	30
F.J.Laver	c Lilley b Brearley	0	not out	13
Extras	(LB 4, NB 1, W 1)	6	(B 15, LB 2, NB 1)	18
Total		**188**		**207**

1/6 2/86 3/100 4/104 5/140 6/154 7/167 8/169 9/171

1/0 2/14 3/52 4/118 5/122 6/126 7/127 8/150 9/183

Bowling: *First Innings*—Hirst 26-6-65-2; Barnes 25-12-37-2; Brearley 14.1-1-42-2; Rhodes 8-2-38-3. *Second Innings*—Hirst 17-3-39-1; Barnes 35-16-63-6; Brearley 24.1-6-36-1; Rhodes 19-3-44-2; Sharp 1-0-7-0.

England

Batsman	First innings		Second innings	
C.B.Fry	lbw b Cotter	1	b Cotter	7
J.B.Hobbs	b Macartney	12	b Cotter	30
J.T.Tyldesley	c Armstrong b Macartney	55	c and b Macartney	7
J.Sharp	st Carter b Macartney	61	b Cotter	11
A.C.MacLaren*	b Macartney	17	c Cotter b Macartney	1
W.Rhodes	c Carter b Laver	12	c Armstrong b Macartney	16
G.H.Hirst	b Macartney	4	(8) b Cotter	0
A.F.A.Lilley†	not out	4	(7) lbw b Cotter	2
S.F.Barnes	b Macartney	1	b Macartney	1
W.Brearley	b Macartney	6	not out	4
G.L.Jessop	absent hurt	–	absent hurt	–
Extras	(B 1, LB 4, NB 4)	9	(B 1, LB 1, NB 5, W 1)	8
Total		**182**		**87**

1/8 2/31 3/137 4/146 5/157 6/169 7/171 8/174 9/182

1/17 2/26 3/60 4/61 5/61 6/82 7/82 8/82 9/87

Bowling: *First Innings*—Cotter 17-1-45-1; Macartney 25.3-6-58-7; Armstrong 16-5-33-0; Laver 13-4-15-1; Noble 13-5-22-0. *Second Innings*—Cotter 16-2-38-5; Macartney 16.5-5-27-4; Armstrong 3-1-8-0; Laver 2-0-6-0.

Umpires: W.Richards and W.A.J.West

ENGLAND v AUSTRALIA 1909 (Fourth Test)

At Old Trafford, Manchester, 26, 27, 28 July
Result: Match drawn

Australia

Batsman	First innings		Second innings	
S.E.Gregory	b Blythe	21	b Hirst	5
W.Bardsley	b Barnes	9	c MacLaren b Blythe	35
V.S.Ransford	lbw b Barnes	4	(7) not out	54
M.A.Noble*	b Blythe	17	b Blythe	13
V.T.Trumper	c Hutchings b Barnes	2	(6) c Tyldesley b Rhodes	48
W.W.Armstrong	not out	32	(5) lbw b Rhodes	30
A.J.Y.Hopkins	b Blythe	3	(8) c Barnes b Rhodes	9
C.G.Macartney	b Barnes	5	c Barnes b Blythe	51
A.Cotter	c Tyldesley b Blythe	17	(3) c MacLaren b Rhodes	4
H.Carter	lbw b Barnes	13	lbw b Barnes	12
F.J.Laver	b Blythe	11		
Extras	(B 6, LB 7)	13	(B 9, LB 8, NB 1)	18
Total		**147**	(9 wkts dec.)	**279**

1/13 2/21 3/45 4/48 5/58 6/66 7/86 8/110 9/128

1/16 2/77 3/106 4/126 5/148 6/237 7/256 8/262 9/279

Bowling: *First Innings*—Hirst 7-0-15-0; Barnes 27-9-56-5; Blythe 20.3-5-63-5. *Second Innings*—Hirst 12-3-32-1; Barnes 22.3-5-66-1; Blythe 24-5-77-3; Sharp 1-0-3-0; Rhodes 25-0-83-4.

England

Batsman	First innings		Second innings	
P.F.Warner	b Macartney	9	b Hopkins	25
R.H.Spooner	c and b Cotter	25	b Laver	58
J.T.Tyldesley	c Armstrong b Laver	15	b Hopkins	11
J.Sharp	c Armstrong b Laver	3	not out	8
W.Rhodes	c Carter b Laver	5	not out	0
K.L.Hutchings	b Laver	9		
A.C.MacLaren*	lbw b Laver	16		
A.F.A.Lilley†	not out	26		
G.H.Hirst	c Hopkins b Laver	1		
S.F.Barnes	b Laver	0		
C.Blythe	b Laver	1		
Extras	(B 2, LB 3, NB 4)	9	(B 2, LB 4)	6
Total		**119**	(3 wkts)	**108**

1/24 2/39 3/44 4/50 5/63 6/72 7/99 8/103 9/103

1/78 2/90 3/102

Bowling: *First Innings*—Noble 8-2-11-0; Macartney 18-6-31-1; Laver 18.2-7-31-8; Cotter 8-1-37-1. *Second Innings*—Macartney 7-2-16-0; Laver 21-12-25-1; Cotter 5-0-14-0; Armstrong 10-6-16-0; Hopkins 12-4-31-2.

Umpires: W.Richards and W.A.J.West

ENGLAND v AUSTRALIA 1909 (Fifth Test)

At Kennington Oval, London, 9, 10, 11 August

Result: Match drawn

Australia

Batsman	1st innings		2nd innings	
S.E.Gregory b Carr	1	run out		74
W.Bardsley b Sharp	136	lbw b Barnes		130
M.A.Noble* lbw b Carr	2	c MacLaren b Barnes		55
W.W.Armstrong lbw b Carr	15	c Woolley b Carr		10
V.S.Ransford b Barnes	3	not out		36
V.T.Trumper c Rhodes b Barnes	73	st Lilley b Carr		20
C.G.Macartney c Rhodes b Sharp	50	not out		4
A.J.Y.Hopkins c Rhodes b Sharp	21			
A.Cotter b Carr	7			
H.Carter† lbw b Carr	4			
F.J.Laver not out	8			
Extras (B 1, LB 3, NB 1)	5	(B 4, LB 3, NB 2, W 1)		10
	325		(5 wkts dec.)	**339**

1/9 2/27 3/55 4/58 5/176   1/180 2/267 3/268
6/259 7/289 8/300 9/304   4/294 5/335

Bowling: *First Innings*—Carr 34-2-146-5; Barnes 19-3-57-2; Sharp 16.3-3-67-3; Woolley 4-1-6-0; Hayes 4-0-10-0; Rhodes 12-3-34-0. *Second Innings*—Carr 35-1-136-2; Barnes 27-7-61-2; Sharp 12-0-34-0; Woolley 6-0-31-0; Hayes 2-0-14-0; Rhodes 14-1-35-0; Hutchings 4-0-18-0.

England

Batsman	1st innings		2nd innings	
R.H.Spooner b Cotter	13	c and b Macartney		3
A.C.MacLaren* lbw b Cotter	15			
W.Rhodes c Carter b Cotter	66	(2) st Carter b Armstrong		54
C.B.Fry run out	62	not out		35
J.Sharp c Gregory b Hopkins	105			
F.E.Woolley c Cotter	8	not out		0
E.G.Hayes lbw b Armstrong	4	(3) c sub (R.J.Hartigan) b Armstrong		9
K.L.Hutchings c Macartney b Cotter	59			
A.F.A.Lilley† not out	2			
S.F.Barnes c Carter b Hopkins	0			
D.W.Carr b Whitty	0			
Extras (B 8, LB 4, NB 6)	18	(LB 2, NB 1)		3
	352		(3 wkts)	**104**

1/15 2/36 3/140 4/187 5/201   1/14 2/27 3/88
6/206 7/348 8/348 9/351

Bowling: *First Innings*—Cotter 27.4-1-95-6; Armstrong 31-7-93-1; Laver 8-1-13-0; Macartney 16-2-49-0; Hopkins Noble 8-1-29-0; Gregory 1-0-4-0. *Second Innings*—Cotter 8-1-21-0; Armstrong 7-4-8-2; Macartney 8-2-11-1; Hopkins 8-0-40-0; Gregory 2-0-21-0.

Umpires: J.Moss and W.Richards

AUSTRALIA v SOUTH AFRICA 1910-11 (First Test)

At Sydney Cricket Ground, 9, 10, 12 (no play), 13, 14 December

Result: Australia won by an innings and 114 runs

Australia

V.T.Trumper run out	27
W.Bardsley b Pearse	132
C.Hill* b Pearse	191
D.R.A.Gehrs b Pearse	67
W.W.Armstrong b Schwarz	48
V.S.Ransford b Schwarz	11
C.G.Macartney b Schwarz	1
C.Kelleway not out	14
H.Carter† st Sherwell b Schwarz	5
A.Cotter st Sherwell b Schwarz	0
W.J.Whitty c Snooke b Sinclair	15
Extras (B 12, LB 4, NB 1)	17
	528

1/52 2/276 3/420 4/427 5/445
6/453 7/499 8/511 9/511

Bowling: Llewellyn 14-0-54-0; Sinclair 19.4-0-80-1; Schwarz 25-6-102-5; Vogler 15-0-87-0; Faulkner 12-0-71-0; Nourse 12-0-61-0; Pearse 12-0-56-3.

South Africa

Batsman	1st innings		2nd innings	
L.A.Stricker b Cotter	2	(7) lbw b Whitty		4
J.W.Zulch b Cotter	4	(4) run out		1
C.O.C.Pearse c Trumper b Cotter	16	(10) run out		31
A.W.Nourse c Kelleway b Cotter	5	(6) not out		64
G.A.Faulkner c Kelleway b Whitty	62	c Bardsley b Whitty		43
C.B.Llewellyn b Cotter	0	(8) c Macartney b Whitty		19
S.J.Snooke b Whitty	3	(3) b Cotter		4
J.H.Sinclair b Cotter	1	(2) b Cotter		6
R.O.Schwarz c Trumper b Whitty	61	c Carter b Whitty		0
P.W.Sherwell*† not out	8	(1) c Whitty b Kelleway		60
A.E.E.Vogler b Whitty	0	b Kelleway		0
Extras (LB 6, NB 6)	12	(LB 1, NB 7)		8
	174			**240**

1/5 2/10 3/29 4/38 5/38   1/24 2/38 3/44 4/98 5/124
6/44 7/49 8/149 9/174   6/144 7/183 8/183 9/237

Bowling: *First Innings*—Cotter 20-2-69-6; Whitty 24-11-33-4; Armstrong 8-3-16-0; Kelleway 9-1-33-0; Macartney 7-4-11-0. *Second Innings*—Whitty 21-4-75-4; Macartney 5-1-12-0; Cotter 17-2-73-2; Armstrong 9-1-35-0; Kelleway 15.1-4-37-2.

Umpires: R.M.Crockett and W.G.Curran

AUSTRALIA v SOUTH AFRICA 1910-11 (Second Test)

At Melbourne Cricket Ground, 31 December, 2, 3, 4 January

Result: Australia won by 89 runs

Australia

```
V.T.Trumper      b Pegler ................. 34    b Faulkner ................ 159
W.Bardsley       c Snooke b Sinclair ...... 85    st Sherwell b Schwarz ...... 14
C.Hill*          b Llewellyn .............. 39    b Schwarz .................... 0
D.R.A.Gehrs      b Llewellyn ............... 4    st Sherwell b Schwarz ....... 22
C.G.Macartney    run out ................... 7    c Snooke b Llewellyn ......... 5
V.S.Ransford     run out .................. 58    c Sinclair b Schwarz ........ 23
W.W.Armstrong    c Sherwell b Faulkner .... 75 (8) b Llewellyn .............. 29
C.Kelleway       c Faulkner b Stricker .... 18 (7) c Sherwell b Llewellyn ... 48
H.Carter†        not out .................. 15    b Pegler ..................... 0
A.Cotter         c Stricker b Schwarz ...... 3    c Sherwell b Llewellyn ...... 15
W.J.Whitty       c Nourse b Faulkner ....... 6    csub (J.M.M.Commaille) b Llewellyn 15
                                                  not out ...................... 5
Extras           (LB 3, NB 1) .............. 4    (LB 6, NB 1) ................. 7
                                            ―――                              ―――
                                            348                              327
```

1/59 2/160 3/164 4/164 5/184 1/35 2/35 3/89 4/94 5/176
6/262 7/309 8/337 9/340 6/237 7/279 8/279 9/305

Bowling: *First Innings*—Nourse 8-3-24-0; Snooke 5-1-19-0; Pegler 10-0-43-1; Schwarz 13-0-66-1; Llewellyn 10-0-69-2; Sinclair 13-1-53-1; Faulkner 10.4-0-34-2. *Second Innings*—Nourse 5-1-18-0; Snooke 8-1-24-0; Schwarz 22-2-76-4; Llewellyn 16-0-81-4; Pegler 6.3-1-24-1; Sinclair 8-0-32-0; Faulkner 12-1-55-1; Stricker 2-1-10-0.

South Africa

```
J.W.Zulch           b Cotter ................ 42 (8) not out ................... 6
P.W.Sherwell*†      c Carter b Cotter ....... 24 (1) b Whitty ................ 16
G.A.Faulkner        c Armstrong b Whitty ... 204    c Kelleway b Whitty ....... 8
A.W.Nourse          b Kelleway .............. 33    lbw b Cotter .............. 2
L.A.Stricker        b Armstrong ............. 26 (2) lbw b Cotter ............. 0
C.B.Llewellyn       b Armstrong .............. 5    b Cotter ................. 17
S.J.Snooke          ........................ 77    c Armstrong b Whitty ...... 9
J.H.Sinclair        not out ................. 58 (5) lbw b Whitty ............. 3
R.O.Schwarz         b Whitty ................. 0    c Kelleway b Cotter ....... 7
C.O.C.Pearse        b Armstrong .............. 6    c Kelleway b Whitty ....... 0
S.J.Pegler          lbw b Armstrong .......... 8    lbw b Whitty .............. 0
Extras              (B 2, LB 10, NB 9, W 2) . 23    (B 6, LB 3, NB 3) ........ 12
                                             ―――                             ―――
                                             506                             80
```

1/34 2/141 3/251 4/298 5/312 1/1 2/28 3/31 4/34 5/46
6/402 7/469 8/469 9/482 6/66 7/69 8/77 9/80

Bowling: *First Innings*—Cotter 43-5-158-2; Whitty 29-6-81-3; Kelleway 17-3-67-1; Armstrong 48-9-134-4; Macartney 16-5-43-0. *Second Innings*—Cotter 15-3-47-4; Whitty 16-7-17-6; Armstrong 1-0-4-0.

Umpires: R.M.Crockett and W.Hannah

AUSTRALIA v SOUTH AFRICA 1910-11 (Third Test)

At Adelaide Oval, 7, 9, 10, 11, 12, 13 January

Result: South Africa won by 38 runs

South Africa

```
P.W.Sherwell*†      lbw b Armstrong ......... 11    lbw b Whitty ............... 1
J.W.Zulch           c Macartney b Whitty ... 105    c Carter b Whitty ........ 14
G.A.Faulkner        c Hill b Armstrong ...... 56    c Armstrong b Whitty .... 115
A.W.Nourse          b Cotter ................ 10    c Armstrong b Kelleway ... 39
C.M.H.Hathorn       b Whitty ................. 9 (10) b Whitty ................. 2
C.B.Llewellyn       run out ................. 43    b Whitty ................. 80
S.J.Snooke          c Kelleway b Cotter .... 103 (8) run out ................ 25
J.H.Sinclair        c Armstrong b Kelleway .. 20 (9) c Hill b Whitty ........ 29
L.A.Stricker        c Kelleway b Armstrong .. 48 (5) b Macartney ............. 6
R.O.Schwarz         b Armstrong ............. 15 (11) not out ................ 11
S.J.Pegler          not out ................. 24 (7) c Cotter b Kelleway .... 26
Extras              (B 6, LB 10, NB 18, W 4)  38    (B 4, LB 2, NB 5, W 1) .. 12
                                             ―――                             ―――
                                             482                             360
```

1/31 2/166 3/189 4/191 5/205 1/10 2/29 3/106 4/119 5/228
6/302 7/338 8/400 9/429 6/273 7/317 8/319 9/327

Bowling: *First Innings*—Cotter 38-4-100-2; Whitty 34-7-114-2; Armstrong 42.4-9-103-4; Kelleway 24-6-72-1; Macartney 27-9-51-0; Gehrs 1-0-4-0. *Second Innings*—Whitty 39.2-5-104-6; Cotter 23-3-64-0; Armstrong 33-3-90-0; Kelleway 23-4-64-2; Macartney 12-3-26-1.

Australia

```
C.G.Macartney       b Llewellyn .............. 2 (9) lbw b Schwarz ............ 0
C.Kelleway          c Sherwell b Llewellyn .. 47 (4) c Sherwell b Sinclair .. 65
V.S.Ransford        b Llewellyn ............. 50 (5) c Llewellyn b Schwarz ... 0
W.Bardsley          lbw b Nourse ............ 54 (2) c and b Faulkner ....... 58
V.T.Trumper         not out ................ 214 (1) b Llewellyn ............ 28
D.R.A.Gehrs         c Schwarz b Faulkner .... 20 (8) c Sherwell b Schwarz ... 22
C.Hill*             c Snooke b Schwarz ...... 16 (3) c Schwarz b Sinclair ... 55
W.W.Armstrong       b Sinclair .............. 30 (7) b Schwarz .............. 48
H.Carter†           lbw b Schwarz ........... 17 (6) c Llewellyn b Faulkner . 11
A.Cotter            c Snooke b Llewellyn ..... 8    not out ................. 36
W.J.Whitty          c Sherwell b Sinclair .... 1    c Schwarz b Pegler ...... 11
Extras              (B 4, LB 2) .............. 6    (LB 5) ................... 5
                                             ―――                             ―――
                                             465                             339
```

1/7 2/94 3/111 4/227 5/276 1/63 2/122 3/170 4/171 5/187
6/319 7/384 8/430 9/458 6/263 7/285 8/285 9/292

Bowling: *First Innings*—Llewellyn 31-4-107-4; Pegler 20-2-92-0; Schwarz 19-2-68-2; Faulkner 11-0-59-1; Stricker 1-0-4-0; Sinclair 25.5-3-86-2; Nourse 12-2-43-1. *Second Innings*—Snooke 5-0-21-0; Nourse 5-0-31-0; Llewellyn 12-0-48-1; Pegler 0.4-0-58-1; Schwarz 15-3-48-4; Faulkner 15-3-56-2; Sinclair 21-2-72-2.

Umpires: R.M.Crockett and G.A.Watson

AUSTRALIA v SOUTH AFRICA 1910-11 (Fourth Test)

At Melbourne Cricket Ground, 17, 18, 20, 21 February

Result: Australia won by 530 runs

Australia

V.T.Trumper b Faulkner	7	(6)	c Sherwell b Vogler	87
W.Bardsley c Schwarz b Pegler	82	(3)	run out	15
C.Hill* b Llewellyn	11	(5)	st Sherwell b Pegler	100
W.W.Armstrong run out	48		c Sherwell b Vogler	132
D.R.A.Gehrs st Sherwell b Vogler	9	(2)	c Snooke b Faulkner	58
C.Kelleway run out	59	(1)	run out	18
V.S.Ransford lbw b Schwarz	75		b Faulkner	95
A.Cotter b Pegler	10		c sub (C.O.C.Pearse) b Vogler	0
H.V.Hordern c Vogler b Pegler	7		c sub (C.O.C.Pearse) b Schwarz	24
H.Carter† run out	5		c Snooke b Faulkner	2
W.J.Whitty not out	5		not out	39
Extras (B 7, LB 7, W 1)	15		(B 4, LB 3, NB 1)	8
	328			**578**

1/9 2/24 3/126 4/146 5/182
6/289 7/310 8/317 9/328

1/48 2/88 3/106 4/260 5/403
6/418 7/420 8/491 9/496

Bowling: *First Innings*—Llewellyn 15-1-65-1; Faulkner 18-2-82-1; Schwarz 15-2-34-1; Vogler 8-2-30-1; Sinclair 14-2-40-0; Pegler 17.4-3-40-3; Stricker 5-1-18-0; Nourse 2-0-4-0. *Second Innings*—Sinclair 13-1-71-0; Schwarz 38-4-168-1; Pegler 17-1-88-1; Faulkner 28.2-5-101-3; Zulch 3-0-26-0; Nourse 7-0-31-0; Stricker 3-0-14-0; Vogler 15-3-59-3.

South Africa

J.W.Zulch run out	2		c Trumper b Cotter	15
L.A.Stricker b Hordern	4		c Carter b Cotter	0
G.A.Faulkner c Gehrs b Hordern	20		b Whitty	80
A.W.Nourse not out	92		c and b Hordern	28
S.J.Snooke b Whitty	1		b Hordern	7
J.H.Sinclair b Hordern	0		lbw b Hordern	19
R.O.Schwarz b Whitty	18		c Carter b Whitty	1
P.W.Sherwell*† csub(T.J.Matthews)b Whitty	41		c Kelleway b Hordern	0
C.B.Llewellyn b Whitty	7		absent hurt	
S.J.Pegler c Hill b Cotter	15	(9)	c Gehrs b Hordern	8
A.E.E.Vogler b Cotter	0	(10)	not out	2
Extras (B 4, LB 1)	5		(B 7, LB 1, NB 1, W 2)	11
	205			**171**

1/7 2/23 3/36 4/37 5/38
6/65 7/156 8/171 9/205

1/2 2/25 3/88 4/108 5/151
6/158 7/161 8/165 9/171

Bowling: *First Innings*—Cotter 6.5-0-16-2; Whitty 22-5-78-4; Hordern 15-1-39-3; Armstrong 8-2-25-0; Kelleway 11-1-42-0. *Second Innings*—Cotter 6-1-22-2; Whitty 9-2-32-2; Kelleway 8-0-25-0; Hordern 14.2-2-66-5; Armstrong 3-0-15-0.

Umpires: R.M.Crockett and W.Hannah

AUSTRALIA v SOUTH AFRICA 1910-11 (Fifth Test)

At Sydney Cricket Ground, 3, 4, 6, 7 March

Result: Australia won by 7 wickets

Australia

C.Kelleway c Snooke b Llewellyn	2	(5)	not out	24
C.G.Macartney lbw b Schwarz	137		c Nourse b Schwarz	56
H.V.Hordern lbw b Sinclair	50			
W.Bardsley c and b Sinclair	94	(1)	b Nourse	39
W.J.Whitty c Nourse b Llewellyn	13			
V.T.Trumper b Schwarz	31	(3)	not out	74
C.Hill* st Sherwell b Schwarz	13			
W.W.Armstrong c Pearse b Schwarz	0			
V.S.Ransford st Sherwell b Schwarz	6	(4)	b Nourse	0
A.Cotter st Sherwell b Schwarz	8			
H.Carter† not out	1			
Extras (B 7, LB 2)	9		(B 1, LB 3, W 1)	5
	364			**(3 wkts) 198**

1/2 2/126 3/271 4/296 5/317
6/346 7/346 8/351 9/361

1/74 2/134 3/134

Bowling: *First Innings*—Llewellyn 25-0-92-2; Faulkner 12-2-38-0; Sinclair 27-6-83-2; Pegler 6-1-31-0; Schwarz 11.4-0-47-6; Nourse 5-1-26-0; Pearse 9-0-36-0; Zulch 1-0-2-0. *Second Innings*—Pearse 3-0-14-0; Llewellyn 8-1-43-0; Schwarz 9-0-42-1; Sinclair 6-1-22-0; Pegler 4-0-22-0; Faulkner 5-0-18-0; Nourse 8.1-0-32-2.

South Africa

J.W.Zulch st Carter b Hordern	150	(2)	b Ransford	15
C.O.C.Pearse b Whitty	0	(11)	lbw b Hordern	0
G.A.Faulkner b Armstrong	52	(4)	b Cotter	92
A.W.Nourse b Armstrong	3	(5)	c Cotter b Whitty	28
L.A.Stricker c Macartney b Hordern	19	(6)	b Cotter	42
J.H.Sinclair c Ransford b Hordern	1	(8)	c and b Whitty	12
S.J.Snooke b Hordern	18		c Carter b Whitty	12
C.B.Llewellyn c Carter b Kelleway	24	(9)	b Whitty	3
R.O.Schwarz run out	13	(10)	not out	6
P.W.Sherwell*† c Bardsley b Whitty	5	(1)	b Armstrong	14
S.J.Pegler not out	0	(3)	c Cotter b Hordern	26
Extras (B 1, LB 8, NB 1)	10		(B 3, LB 4, NB 5, W 2)	14
	160			**401**

1/4 2/47 3/70 4/81 5/87
6/115 7/128 8/144 9/160

1/19 2/64 3/207 4/278 5/357
6/368 7/385 8/392 9/398

Bowling: *First Innings*—Cotter 8-2-24-0; Whitty 11.1-3-32-2; Hordern 21-3-73-4; Kelleway 4-1-4-1; Armstrong 6-1-17-2. *Second Innings*—Cotter 18-1-60-2; Armstrong 26-4-68-1; Hordern 30.1-1-117-2; Whitty 27-5-66-4; Kelleway 7-1-46-0; Macartney 10-0-21-0; Ransford 4-2-9-1.

Umpires: R.M.Crockett and A.C.Jones

AUSTRALIA v ENGLAND 1911-12 (First Test)

At Sydney Cricket Ground, 15, 16, 18, 19, 20, 21 December

Result: Australia won by 146 runs

Australia

Batsman		Runs		Runs
W.Bardsley	c Strudwick b Douglas	30	b Foster	12
C.Kelleway	c and b Woolley	20	b Douglas	70
C.Hill*	run out	46	b Foster	65
W.W.Armstrong	st Strudwick b Hearne	60	b Foster	28
V.T.Trumper	c Hobbs b Woolley	113	c and b Douglas	14
V.S.Ransford	c Hearne b Barnes	26	c Rhodes b Barnes	34
R.B.Minnett	c Foster b Barnes	90	(8) b Douglas	17
H.V.Hordern	not out	17	(7) b Foster	18
A.Cotter	c and b Barnes	6	lbw b Douglas	2
H.Carter†	b Foster	13	c Gunn b Foster	15
W.J.Whitty	b Foster	0	not out	9
Extras	(B 9, LB 15, NB 2)	26	(B 16, LB 7, NB 1)	24
		447		**308**

1/44 2/77 3/121 4/198 5/278   1/29 2/150 3/169 4/191 5/218
6/387 7/420 8/426 9/447   6/246 7/268 8/274 9/283

Bowling: *First Innings*—Foster 29-6-105-2; Douglas 24-5-62-1; Barnes 35-5-107-3; Hearne 10-0-44-1; Woolley 21-2-77-2; Rhodes 8-0-26-0. *Second Innings*—Foster 31.3-5-92-5; Douglas 21-3-50-4; Barnes 30-8-72-1; Woolley 6-1-15-0; Hearne 13-2-51-0; Rhodes 3-1-4-0.

England

Batsman		Runs		Runs
J.B.Hobbs	c Hill b Whitty	63	c Carter b Cotter	22
S.Kinneir	b Kelleway	22	c Trumper b Hordern	30
G.Gunn	b Cotter	4	c Whitty b Hordern	62
W.Rhodes	c Hill b Hordern	41	(5) c Trumper b Hordern	0
C.P.Mead	c and b Hordern	0	(4) run out	25
J.W.Hearne	c Trumper b Kelleway	76	(7) b Hordern	43
F.R.Foster	b Hordern	56	(6) c Ransford b Hordern	21
F.E.Woolley	b Hordern	39	c Armstrong b Cotter	7
J.W.H.T.Douglas*	c Trumper b Hordern	0	b Hordern	32
S.F.Barnes	b Hordern	9	b Hordern	14
H.Strudwick†	not out	0	not out	12
Extras	(B 3, LB 3, NB 1, W 1)	8	(B 14, LB 8, NB 1)	23
		318		**291**

1/45 2/53 3/115 4/129 5/142   1/29 2/69 3/141 4/141 5/148
6/231 7/293 8/293 9/310   6/167 7/177 8/263 9/276

Bowling: *First Innings*—Cotter 19-0-88-1; Whitty 28-13-60-1; Kelleway 16.5-3-46-3; Hordern 27-5-85-5; Armstrong 9-3-28-0; Minnett 2-1-3-0. *Second Innings*—Whitty 20-8-41-0; Cotter 27-3-71-2; Hordern 42.2-11-90-7; Kelleway 19-6-27-0; Armstrong 15-3-39-0.

Umpires: R.M.Crockett and W.G.Curran

AUSTRALIA v ENGLAND 1911-12 (Second Test)

At Melbourne Cricket Ground, 30 December, 1, 2, 3 January

Result: England won by 8 wickets

Australia

Batsman		Runs		Runs
W.Bardsley	c Strudwick b Barnes	2	c Gunn b Foster	13
C.Kelleway	lbw b Barnes	0	run out	16
C.Hill*	b Barnes	4	c Gunn b Barnes	0
W.W.Armstrong	c Smith b Barnes	4	b Foster	90
V.T.Trumper	b Foster	13	b Barnes	2
V.S.Ransford	c Smith b Hitch	43	c Smith b Foster	32
R.B.Minnett	c Hobbs b Barnes	2	b Foster	34
H.V.Hordern	not out	49	(8) c Mead b Foster	31
A.Cotter	run out	14	(7) c Hobbs b Foster	41
H.Carter†	c Smith b Douglas	29	b Barnes	16
W.J.Whitty	b Woolley	14	not out	0
Extras	(B 5, LB 4, NB 1)	10	(B 14, LB 7, NB 2, W 1)	24
		184		**299**

1/0 2/5 3/8 4/11 5/33   1/28 2/34 3/34 4/38 5/135
6/38 7/80 8/97 9/140   6/168 7/232 8/235 9/298

Bowling: *First Innings*—Foster 16-2-52-1; Barnes 23-9-44-5; Hitch 7-0-37-1; Douglas 15-4-33-1; Hearne 1-0-8-0; Woolley 0.1-0-1-0. *Second Innings*—Foster 38-9-91-6; Barnes 32.1-7-96-3; Douglas 10-0-38-0; Hearne 1-0-5-0; Woolley 3-0-21-0; Hitch 5-0-21-0; Rhodes 2-1-3-0.

England

Batsman		Runs		Runs
W.Rhodes	c Trumper b Cotter	61	c Carter b Cotter	28
J.B.Hobbs	c Carter b Cotter	6	not out	126
J.W.Hearne	c Carter b Cotter	114	(4) not out	12
G.Gunn	lbw b Armstrong	10	(3) c Carter b Whitty	43
C.P.Mead	c Armstrong b Whitty	11		
F.R.Foster	c Hill b Cotter	9		
J.W.H.T.Douglas*	b Hordern	9		
F.E.Woolley	c Ransford b Hordern	23		
E.J.Smith†	b Hordern	5		
S.F.Barnes	lbw b Hordern	1		
J.W.Hitch	not out	0		
Extras	(B 2, LB 10, NB 4)	16	(B 5, LB 5)	10
		265		**(2 wkts) 219**

1/10 2/137 3/174 4/213 5/224   1/57 2/169
6/227 7/258 8/260 9/262

Bowling: *First Innings*—Cotter 21-2-73-4; Whitty 19-2-47-1; Hordern 23.1-1-66-4; Kelleway 15-7-27-0; Armstrong 15-4-20-1; Minnett 5-0-16-0. *Second Innings*—Cotter 14-5-45-1; Whitty 18-3-37-1; Hordern 17-0-66-0; Armstrong 8-1-22-0; Kelleway 7-0-15-0; Minnett 2-0-13-0; Ransford 1.1-0-11-0.

Umpires: R.M.Crockett and D.A.Elder

AUSTRALIA v ENGLAND 1911-12 (Third Test)

At Adelaide Oval, 12, 13, 15, 16, 17 January
Result: England won by 7 wickets

Australia

W.Bardsley c Smith b Barnes	5		b Foster	63
C.Kelleway b Foster	1		b Douglas	37
H.V.Hordern c Rhodes b Foster	25	(7)	c and b Barnes	5
V.S.Ransford not out	8	(8)	b Hitch	38
W.W.Armstrong b Foster	33		b Douglas	25
V.T.Trumper b Hitch	26	(11)	not out	1
C.Hill* st Smith b Foster	0	(4)	c Hitch b Barnes	98
R.B.Minnett b Foster	0	(6)	c Hobbs b Barnes	38
T.J.Matthews c Mead b Barnes	5		b Barnes	53
A.Cotter b Barnes	11		b Barnes	15
H.Carter† c Gunn b Douglas	8	(3)	c Smith b Woolley	72
Extras (B 3, LB 6, NB 2)	11		(B 26, LB 3, NB 2)	31
	133			**476**

1/6 2/6 3/65 4/84 5/88
6/88 7/97 8/113 9/123

1/86 2/122 3/279 4/303 5/342 476
6/360 7/363 8/447 9/475

Bowling: *First Innings*—Foster 26-9-36-5; Barnes 23-4-71-3; Douglas 7-2-7-1; Hearne 2-0-6-0; Hitch 2-1-2-1. *Second Innings*—Foster 49-15-103-1; Barnes 46.4-7-105-5; Douglas 29-10-71-2; Hearne 10-0-61-0; Hitch 11-0-69-1; Woolley 7-1-30-1; Rhodes 1-0-6-0.

England

J.B.Hobbs c Hordern b Minnett	187	lbw b Hordern	3
W.Rhodes lbw b Cotter	59	not out	57
G.Gunn c Hill b Cotter	29	c Cotter b Kelleway	45
J.W.Hearne c Hill b Kelleway	12	c Kelleway b Matthews	2
C.P.Mead c and b Hordern	46	not out	2
F.R.Foster b Armstrong	71		
J.W.H.T.Douglas* b Minnett	35		
F.E.Woolley b Cotter	20		
E.J.Smith† c sub (J.Vine) b Cotter	22		
S.F.Barnes not out	2		
J.W.Hitch c sub (C.G.Macartney) b Hordern	0		
Extras (B 7, LB 8, NB 3)	18	(B 1, LB.1, NB 1)	3
	501	(3 wkts)	**112**

1/147 2/206 3/260 4/323 5/350
6/435 7/455 8/492 9/501

1/5 2/102 3/105

Bowling: *First Innings*—Cotter 43-11-125-4; Hordern 47.1-4-143-2; Kelleway 23-3-46-1; Matthews 33-8-72-0; Minnett 17-3-54-2; Armstrong 14-0-43-1. *Second Innings*—Cotter 5-0-21-0; Hordern 11-3-32-1; Armstrong 6-1-12-0; Minnett 4-1-12-0; Matthews 9.2-3-24-1; Kelleway 7-3-8-1.

Umpires: R.M.Crockett and G.A.Watson

AUSTRALIA v ENGLAND 1911-12 (Fourth Test)

At Melbourne Cricket Ground, 9, 10, 12, 13 February
Result: England won by an innings and 225 runs

Australia

H.V.Hordern b Barnes	19	(11)	c Foster b Douglas	5
C.Kelleway c Hearne b Woolley	29	(1)	c Smith b Barnes	5
W.Bardsley b Foster	0		b Foster	3
V.T.Trumper b Foster	17		b Barnes	28
C.Hill* c Hearne b Barnes	22		b Douglas	11
W.W.Armstrong b Barnes	7		b Douglas	11
R.B.Minnett c Rhodes b Foster	56		b Douglas	7
V.S.Ransford c Rhodes b Foster	4		not out	29
T.J.Matthews c Gunn b Barnes	3	(10)	b Foster	10
A.Cotter b Barnes	15	(9)	c Mead b Foster	8
H.Carter† not out	6	(2)	c Hearne b Douglas	38
Extras (B 1, LB 5, NB 7)	13		(B 9, LB 2, NB 7)	18
	191			**173**

1/53 2/53 3/69 4/74 5/83
6/124 7/152 8/165 9/170

1/12 2/20 3/76 4/86 5/101 173
6/112 7/117 8/127 9/156

Bowling: *First Innings*—Foster 22-2-77-4; Barnes 29.1-4-74-5; Woolley 11-3-22-1; Rhodes 2-1-1-0; Hearne 1-0-4-0. *Second Innings*—Foster 19-3-38-3; Barnes 20-6-47-2; Douglas 17.5-6-46-5; Hearne 3-0-17-0; Woolley 2-0-7-0.

England

J.B.Hobbs c Carter b Hordern	178
W.Rhodes c Carter b Minnett	179
G.Gunn c Hill b Armstrong	75
J.W.Hearne c Armstrong b Minnett	0
F.R.Foster c Hordern b Armstrong	50
J.W.H.T.Douglas* c Bardsley b Armstrong	0
F.E.Woolley c Kelleway b Minnett	56
C.P.Mead b Hordern	21
J.Vine not out	4
E.J.Smith† c Matthews b Kelleway	7
S.F.Barnes c Hill b Hordern	0
Extras (B 2, LB 4, NB 9, W 4)	19
	589

1/323 2/425 3/425 4/486 5/486
6/513 7/565 8/579 9/589

Bowling: Cotter 37-5-125-0; Kelleway 26-2-80-1; Armstrong 36-12-93-3; Matthews 22-1-68-0; Hordern 47.5-5-137-3; Minnett 20-5-59-3; Ransford 2-1-8-0.

Umpires: R.M.Crockett and W.A.Young

AUSTRALIA v ENGLAND 1911-12 (Fifth Test)

At Sydney Cricket Ground, 23, 24, 26 (no play), 27, 28, 29 (no play) February, 1 March

Result: England won by 70 runs

England

J.B.Hobbs c Ransford b Hordern	32	c Hazlitt b Hordern	45
W.Rhodes b Macartney	8	lbw b Armstrong	30
G.Gunn st Carter b Hordern	52	b Hordern	61
J.W.Hearne c Macartney b Armstrong	4	b Hordern	18
F.R.Foster st Carter b Hazlitt	15	b McLaren	4
J.W.H.T.Douglas* c Ransford b Hordern	18	b Armstrong	8
F.E.Woolley not out	133	c Armstrong b Hazlitt	11
J.Vine b Hordern	36	not out	6
E.J.Smith† b Hordern	0	b Hordern	13
S.F.Barnes c Hordern b Hazlitt	5	c Ransford b Armstrong	4
J.W.Hitch b Hazlitt	4		
Extras (B 10, LB 4, NB 2, W 1)	17	(B 8, NB 2)	10
	324		214

1/15 2/69 3/83 4/114 5/125   1/76 2/76 3/105 4/110 5/146
6/162 7/305 8/305 9/312   6/178 7/185 8/201 9/209

Bowling: *First Innings*—McLaren 16-2-47-0; Macartney 12-3-26-1; Hordern 37-8-95-5; Hazlitt 31-6-75-3; Armstrong 25-8-42-1; Minnett 8-1-22-0. *Second Innings*—Macartney 7-0-28-0; Hazlitt 12-2-52-1; Armstrong 17.3-7-35-3; Hordern 25-5-66-5; McLaren 8-1-23-1; Minnett 1-1-0-0.

Australia

V.T.Trumper c Woolley b Barnes	5		c Woolley b Barnes	50
S.E.Gregory c Gunn b Douglas	32		c Smith b Barnes	40
C.Hill* c Smith b Hitch	20		b Foster	8
W.W.Armstrong lbw b Barnes	33		b Barnes	33
R.B.Minnett c Douglas b Hitch	0		c Woolley b Barnes	61
V.S.Ransford c Hitch b Foster	29		b Woolley	9
H.Carter† c sub (C.P.Mead) b Barnes	11	(8)	c Woolley b Foster	23
C.G.Macartney c and b Woolley	26	(7)	c Woolley b Foster	27
H.V.Hordern run out	1		run out	4
G.R.Hazlitt run out	0		c Rhodes b Foster	4
J.W.McLaren not out	0		not out	0
Extras (B 14, LB 2, NB 1, W 2)	19		(B 22, LB 8, NB 2, W 1)	33
	176			292

1/17 2/59 3/81 4/82 5/133   1/88 2/101 3/117 4/209 5/220
6/133 7/171 8/175 9/176   6/231 7/278 8/287 9/287

Bowling: *First Innings*—Foster 16-0-55-1; Barnes 19-2-56-3; Hitch 9-0-31-2; Douglas 7-0-14-1; Woolley 2-1-1-2. *Second Innings*—Foster 30.1-7-43-4; Barnes 39-12-106-4; Douglas 9-0-34-0; Hitch 6-1-23-0; Woolley 16-5-36-1; Rhodes 2-0-17-0.

Umpires: R.M.Crockett and A.C.Jones

AUSTRALIA v SOUTH AFRICA 1912 (First Test)

At Old Trafford, Manchester, 27, 28 May

Result: Australia won by an innings and 88 runs

Australia

C.B.Jennings c Schwarz b Pegler	32
C.Kelleway c Ward b Pegler	114
C.G.Macartney b Pegler	21
W.Bardsley c and b White	121
S.E.Gregory* st Ward b Pegler	37
R.B.Minnett c and b Schwarz	12
T.J.Matthews not out	49
S.H.Emery b Schwarz	1
G.R.Hazlitt lbw b Schwarz	0
W.Carkeek† b Pegler	4
W.J.Whitty st Ward b Pegler	33
Extras (B 14, LB 9, W 1)	24
	448

1/62 2/92 3/294 4/314 5/328
6/375 7/376 8/376 9/385

Bowling: Faulkner 16-2-55-0; Nourse 14-1-62-0; Pegler 45.3-9-105-6; Schwarz 32-0-142-3; Hartigan 9-0-31-0; White 6-1-29-1.

South Africa

G.P.D.Hartigan c Carkeek b Emery	25		b Kelleway	4
H.W.Taylor c Carkeek b Whitty	0	(5)	b Matthews	21
A.W.Nourse b Whitty	17		c Bardsley b Whitty	18
S.J.Snooke b Whitty	7		b Whitty	9
G.A.Faulkner not out	122	(2)	b Kelleway	0
G.C.White lbw b Whitty	22		c Carkeek b Kelleway	9
F.Mitchell* b Whitty	11		b Kelleway	0
R.O.Schwarz b Hazlitt	19		c and b Matthews	0
R.Beaumont b Matthews	31	(10)	b Kelleway	17
S.J.Pegler lbw b Matthews	0	(11)	not out	8
T.A.Ward† lbw b Matthews	0	(9)	c and b Matthews	0
Extras (B 2, LB 5, NB 3, W 1)	11		(B 5, LB 1, NB 3)	9
	265			95

1/4 2/30 3/42 4/54 5/143   1/1 2/22 3/43 4/43 5/70
6/167 7/200 8/265 9/265   6/70 7/70 8/70 9/78

Bowling: *First Innings*—Hazlitt 16-4-46-1; Whitty 34-12-55-5; Emery 37-10-94-1; Kelleway 11-3-27-0; Matthews 12-3-16-3; Minnett 6-2-16-0. *Second Innings*—Whitty 6-3-15-2; Kelleway 14.2-4-33-5; Matthews 8-1-38-3.

Umpires: G.Webb and A.A.White

ENGLAND v AUSTRALIA 1912 (First Test)

At Lord's, London, 24, 25, 26 June
Result: Match drawn

England

J.B.Hobbs b Emery		107
W.Rhodes c Carkeek b Kelleway		59
R.H.Spooner c Bardsley b Kelleway		1
C.B.Fry* run out		42
P.F.Warner b Emery		4
F.E.Woolley c Kelleway b Hazlitt		20
F.R.Foster c Macartney b Whitty		20
J.W.Hearne not out		21
E.J.Smith† not out		14
S.F.Barnes		
H.Dean		
Extras (B 16, LB 4, NB 2)		22
	(7 wkts dec.)	310

1/112 2/123 3/197 4/211 5/246
6/255 7/285

Bowling: Whitty 12-2-69-1; Hazlitt 25-6-68-1; Matthews 13-4-26-0; Kelleway 21-5-66-2; Emery 12-1-46-2; Macartney 7-1-13-0.

Australia

C.B.Jennings c Smith b Foster		21
C.Kelleway b Rhodes		61
C.G.Macartney c Smith b Foster		99
W.Bardsley lbw b Rhodes		21
S.E.Gregory* c Foster b Dean		10
D.B.M.Smith not out		24
T.J.Matthews b Dean		0
G.R.Hazlitt b Rhodes		19
S.H.Emery		
W.J.Whitty		
W.Carkeek†		
Extras (B 17, LB 5, NB 4, W 1)		27
	(7 wkts)	282

1/27 2/173 3/226 4/233 5/243
6/243 7/282

Bowling: Foster 36-18-42-2; Barnes 31-10-74-0; Dean 29-10-49-2; Hearne 12-1-31-0; Rhodes 19.2-5-59-3.

Umpires: J.Moss and A.E.Street

AUSTRALIA v SOUTH AFRICA 1912 (Second Test)

At Lord's, London, 15, 16, 17 July
Result: Australia won by 10 wickets

South Africa

G.A.Faulkner b Whitty	5	(6)	c and b Matthews	6
L.J.Tancred lbw b Matthews	31		c Bardsley b Hazlitt	19
G.C.White c Carkeek b Minnett	0		b Matthews	18
C.B.Llewellyn c Jennings b Minnett	8		b Macartney	59
A.W.Nourse b Hazlitt	11		lbw b Kelleway	10
H.W.Taylor c Kelleway b Hazlitt	93	(7)	not out	10
L.A.Stricker lbw b Kelleway	48	(1)	b Hazlitt	13
F.Mitchell* b Whitty	12		b Matthews	3
R.O.Schwarz b Whitty	0		c Macartney b Matthews	1
S.J.Pegler c Bardsley b Whitty	25		c Kelleway b Macartney	14
T.A.Ward† not out	1		b Macartney	7
Extras (B 12, LB 14, NB 2, W 1)	29		(B 9, NB 4)	13
	263			173

1/24 2/25 3/35 4/56 5/74   1/28 2/54 3/62 4/102 5/134
6/171 7/203 8/213 9/250   6/136 7/142 8/146 9/163

Bowling: First Innings—Minnett 15-6-49-2; Whitty 31-9-68-4; Hazlitt 19-9-47-2; Matthews 13-5-32-1; Kelleway 11-3-38-1. Second Innings—Whitty 9-0-41-0; Hazlitt 13-1-39-2; Matthews 13-2-29-4; Kelleway 8-1-22-1; Macartney 14.1-5-29-3.

Australia

C.B.Jennings b Nourse	0		not out	22
C.Kelleway lbw b Faulkner	102			
C.G.Macartney b Nourse	9			
W.Bardsley lbw b Llewellyn	164			
S.E.Gregory* b Llewellyn	5			
R.E.Mayne st Ward b Pegler	23	(2)	not out	25
R.B.Minnett b Pegler	39			
T.J.Matthews c Faulkner b Pegler	9			
G.R.Hazlitt b Nourse	0			
W.Carkeek† not out	6			
W.J.Whitty lbw b Pegler	3			
Extras (B 24, LB 3, NB 1, W 2)	30		(B 1)	1
	390		(0 wkts)	48

1/0 2/14 3/256 4/277 5/316
6/353 7/375 8/379 9/381

Bowling: First Innings—Nourse 36-12-60-3; Pegler 29.5-7-79-4; Schwarz 11-1-44-0; Faulkner 28-3-86-1; Llewellyn 19-2-71-2; Taylor 2-0-12-0; Stricker 3-1-8-0. Second Innings—Nourse 6.1-2-22-0; Pegler 4-1-45-0; Faulkner 2-0-10-0.

Umpires: J.Moss and A.E.Street

ENGLAND v AUSTRALIA 1912 (Second Test)

At Old Trafford, Manchester, 29, 30, 31 (no play) July

Result: Match drawn

England

J.B.Hobbs b Whitty	19
W.Rhodes b Whitty	92
R.H.Spooner b Whitty	1
C.B.Fry* c sub (J.W.McLaren) b Matthews	19
J.W.Hearne b Hazlitt	9
F.E.Woolley c Kelleway b Whitty	13
F.R.Foster c and b Matthews	13
E.J.Smith† c Emery b Hazlitt	4
S.Haigh c Kelleway b Hazlitt	9
S.F.Barnes not out	1
J.W.Hitch b Hazlitt	4
Extras (B 9, LB 9, NB 1)	19
	203

1/37 2/39 3/83 4/140 5/155
6/181 7/185 8/189 9/199

Bowling: Hazlitt 40.5-12-77-4; Whitty 27-15-43-4; Kelleway 6-1-19-0; Matthews 12-4-23-2; Emery 7-1-22-0.

Australia

C.B.Jennings not out	9
C.Kelleway not out	3
W.Bardsley	
S.E.Gregory*	
C.G.Macartney	
R.E.Mayne	
T.J.Matthews	
S.H.Emery	
W.J.Whitty	
G.R.Hazlitt	
W.Carkeek†	
Extras (B 2)	2
	(0 wkts) 14

Bowling: Foster 1-0-3-0; Haigh 6-4-3-0; Woolley 6-3-6-0.

Umpires: G.Webb and W.A.J.West

AUSTRALIA v SOUTH AFRICA 1912 (Third Test)

At Trent Bridge, Nottingham, 5, 6, 7 (no play) August

Result: Match drawn

South Africa

L.J.Tancred* c Kelleway b Matthews	30
H.W.Taylor b Whitty	2
A.W.Nourse b Whitty	64
G.A.Faulkner c Kelleway b Emery	15
C.B.Llewellyn b Emery	12
L.A.Stricker lbw b Macartney	37
S.J.Snooke b Kelleway	20
G.C.White not out	59
R.Beaumont b Hazlitt	26
S.J.Pegler b Hazlitt	24
T.A.Ward† c Emery b Matthews	2
Extras (B 30, LB 7, NB 1)	38
	329

1/2 2/79 3/116 4/140 5/154
6/196 7/225 8/232 9/282

Bowling: Whitty 30-10-64-2; Minnett 8-3-12-0; Hazlitt 28-10-48-2; Matthews 20.5-7-27-2; Emery 21-1-87-2; Kelleway 8-2-18-1; Macartney 13-2-35-1.

Australia

C.B.Jennings run out	9
C.Kelleway c Faulkner b Pegler	37
C.G.Macartney c Faulkner b Llewellyn	34
W.Bardsley run out	56
S.E.Gregory* b Pegler	18
R.B.Minnett c Nourse b Faulkner	31
T.J.Matthews b Pegler	21
S.H.Emery b Faulkner	5
G.R.Hazlitt not out	2
W.J.Whitty b Pegler	0
W.Carkeek† st Ward b Faulkner	1
Extras (B 2, LB 3)	5
	219

1/19 2/61 3/101 4/127 5/171
6/199 7/212 8/216 9/216

Bowling: Pegler 36-6-80-4; Faulkner 20.1-2-43-3; Taylor 12-5-19-0; Llewellyn 22-3-60-1; Nourse 4-1-12-0.

Umpires: G.Webb and W.A.J.West

ENGLAND v AUSTRALIA 1912 (Third Test)

At Kennington Oval, London, 19, 20, 21, 22 August

Result: England won by 244 runs

England

Batsman	1st innings	R		2nd innings	R
J.B.Hobbs	c Carkeek b Macartney	66		c Matthews b Whitty	32
W.Rhodes	b Minnett	49		b Whitty	0
R.H.Spooner	c Hazlitt b Macartney	1		c Jennings b Whitty	0
C.B.Fry*	c Kelleway b Whitty	5		c Jennings b Hazlitt	79
F.E.Woolley	lbw b Minnett	62		b Hazlitt	4
J.W.Hearne	c Jennings b Whitty	1		c Matthews b Hazlitt	14
J.W.H.T.Douglas	lbw b Whitty	18		lbw b Hazlitt	24
F.R.Foster	b Minnett	19		not out	3
E.J.Smith†	b Whitty	4		b Hazlitt	0
S.F.Barnes	c Jennings b Minnett	7		c Whitty b Hazlitt	0
H.Dean	not out	0		b Hazlitt	0
Extras	(B 2, LB 10, NB 1)	13		(B 14, LB 1)	15
		245			**175**

1/107 2/109 3/127 4/131 5/144
6/180 7/216 8/233 9/239

1/7 2/7 3/51 4/56 5/91
6/170 7/171 8/171 9/175

Bowling: First Innings—Whitty 38-12-69-4; Matthews 14-5-43-0; Hazlitt 26-10-48-0; Macartney 19-6-22-2; Minnett 10.1-3-34-4; Kelleway 7-2-16-0. Second Innings—Whitty 33-13-71-3; Matthews 10-3-21-0; Hazlitt 21.4-8-25-7; Macartney 22-5-43-0.

Australia

Batsman	1st innings	R	Order	2nd innings	R
S.E.Gregory*	c Rhodes b Barnes	1	(5)	c Douglas b Dean	1
C.Kelleway	lbw b Woolley	43		c Douglas b Dean	0
C.G.Macartney	b Barnes	4		b Dean	30
W.Bardsley	b Barnes	30		run out	0
C.B.Jennings	c and b Woolley	0	(1)	c Fry b Woolley	14
R.B.Minnett	c Rhodes b Woolley	0		lbw b Woolley	4
D.B.M.Smith	c Smith b Woolley	6		c Douglas b Dean	0
T.J.Matthews	c Fry b Barnes	2		c and b Woolley	1
W.J.Whitty	c Foster b Barnes	0		b Woolley	3
G.R.Hazlitt	not out	2		c Dean b Woolley	5
W.Carkeek†	c Barnes b Woolley	5		not out	0
Extras	(B 12, LB 6)	18		(B 1, LB 5, W 1)	7
		111			**65**

1/9 2/19 3/90 4/90 5/92
6/96 7/104 8/104 9/104

1/0 2/46 3/46 4/47 5/51
6/51 7/51 8/54 9/65

Bowling: First Innings—Barnes 27-15-30-5; Dean 16-7-29-0; Foster 2-0-5-0; Woolley 9.4-3-29-5. Second Innings—Barnes 4-1-18-0; Dean 9-2-19-4; Woolley 7.4-1-20-5; Rhodes 2-1-1-0.

Umpires: J.Moss and A.E.Street

AUSTRALIA v ENGLAND 1920-21 (First Test)

At Sydney Cricket Ground, 17, 18, 20, 21, 22 December

Result: Australia won by 377 runs

Australia

Batsman	1st innings	R	Order	2nd innings	R
C.G.Macartney	b Waddington	19	(3)	b Douglas	69
H.L.Collins	run out	70	(1)	c Waddington b Douglas	104
W.Bardsley	c Strudwick b Hearne	22	(2)	b Hearne	57
C.Kelleway	run out	33	(6)	c Russell b Woolley	78
W.W.Armstrong*	st Strudwick b Woolley	12	(7)	b Parkin	158
J.M.Gregory	c Strudwick b Woolley	8	(9)	run out	0
J.M.Taylor	lbw b Hearne	34	(5)	lbw b Woolley	51
C.E.Pellew	c Hendren b Hearne	36	(4)	c Woolley b Parkin	16
J.Ryder	run out	5	(8)	run out	6
W.A.S.Oldfield†	c Hobbs b Parkin	7		c Strudwick b Parkin	16
A.A.Mailey	not out	10		not out	0
Extras	(B 4, LB 6, NB 1)	11		(B 17, LB 7, NB 2)	26
		267			**581**

1/40 2/80 3/140 4/162 5/173
6/176 7/244 8/249 9/250

1/123 2/234 3/241 4/282 5/332 581
6/519 7/536 8/540 9/578

Bowling: First Innings—Hitch 10-0-37-0; Waddington 18-3-35-1; Parkin 26.5-5-58-1; Hearne 34-8-77-3; Woolley 23-7-35-2; Douglas 3-0-14-0. Second Innings—Hitch 8-0-40-0; Waddington 23-4-53-0; Parkin 35.3-5-102-3; Hearne 42-7-124-1; Douglas 26-3-79-2; Woolley 36-11-90-2; Rhodes 22-2-67-0.

England

Batsman	1st innings	R	Order	2nd innings	R
C.A.G.Russell	b Kelleway	0		c Oldfield b Gregory	5
J.B.Hobbs	b Gregory	49		lbw b Armstrong	59
J.W.Hearne	c Gregory b Mailey	14		b Gregory	57
E.H.Hendren	c Gregory b Ryder	28		b Kelleway	56
F.E.Woolley	c Mailey b Ryder	52		st Oldfield b Mailey	16
J.W.H.T.Douglas*	st Oldfield b Mailey	21		c Armstrong b Mailey	45
W.Rhodes	c Gregory b Mailey	3		c Ryder b Mailey	19
J.W.Hitch	c Kelleway b Gregory	7		c Taylor b Gregory	3
A.Waddington	run out	7		b Kelleway	4
C.H.Parkin	not out	0		b Kelleway	7
H.Strudwick†	lbw b Gregory	2		not out	1
Extras	(B 3, LB 4)	7		(B 6, LB 3)	9
		190			**281**

1/0 2/50 3/70 4/144 5/145
6/158 7/165 8/180 9/188

1/5 2/105 3/149 4/170 5/178
6/231 7/264 8/271 9/279

Bowling: First Innings—Kelleway 6-2-10-1; Gregory 23.1-3-56-3; Mailey 23-4-95-3; Ryder 6-1-20-2; Armstrong 1-0-2-0. Second Innings—Kelleway 5.5-3-45-3; Gregory 33-6-70-3; Macartney 3-0-7-0; Mailey 24-2-105-3; Ryder 17-6-24-0; Armstrong 10-0-21-1.

Umpires: R.M.Crockett and A.C.Jones

AUSTRALIA v ENGLAND 1920-21 (Third Test)

At Adelaide Oval, 14, 15, 17, 18, 19, 20 January
Result: Australia won by 119 runs

Australia

H.L.Collins c Rhodes b Parkin	162	c Hendren b Parkin	24
W.Bardsley st Strudwick b Woolley	14	b Howell	16
C.Kelleway c Fender b Parkin	4	b Howell	147
J.M.Taylor run out	5	c Strudwick b Fender (6)	38
W.W.Armstrong* c Strudwick b Douglas	11	b Howell	121
C.E.Pellew run out	35	c Strudwick b Parkin (7)	104
J.M.Gregory c Strudwick b Fender	10	not out (8)	78
J.Ryder c Douglas b Parkin	44	c Woolley b Howell (4)	3
W.A.S.Oldfield† lbw b Parkin	50	b Rhodes	10
E.A.McDonald b Parkin	2	b Rhodes	4
A.A.Mailey not out	3	b Rhodes	13
Extras (B 6, LB 8)	14	(B 5, LB 10, NB 5, W 4)	24
	354		582

1/32 2/45 3/55 4/96 5/176
6/209 7/285 8/347 9/349

1/34 2/63 3/71 4/265 5/328
6/454 7/477 8/511 9/570

Bowling: *First Innings*—Howell 26-1-89-0; Douglas 24-6-69-2; Parkin 20-2-60-5; Woolley 21-6-47-0; Fender 12-0-52-1; Rhodes 5-1-23-0. *Second Innings*—Howell 34-6-115-4; Douglas 19-2-61-0; Woolley 38-4-91-0; Parkin 40-8-109-2; Fender 22-0-105-1; Rhodes 25.5-8-61-3; Hobbs 7-2-16-0.

England

J.B.Hobbs c and b Mailey	18	b Gregory	123
W.Rhodes run out	16	lbw b McDonald	4
J.W.H.Makepeace c Gregory b Armstrong	60	c and b McDonald	30
E.H.Hendren b Gregory	36	b Mailey	51
F.E.Woolley c Kelleway b Gregory	79	b Gregory	0
C.A.G.Russell not out	135	b Mailey	59
J.W.H.T.Douglas* lbw b Mailey	60	c Armstrong b Gregory	32
P.G.H.Fender b McDonald	2	c Ryder b Mailey	42
C.H.Parkin st Oldfield b Mailey	12	st Oldfield b Mailey	17
H.Strudwick† c Pellew b Mailey	9	c Armstrong b Mailey	1
H.Howell c Gregory b Mailey	18	not out	4
Extras (B 8, LB 5, NB 5)	18	(LB 3, NB 4)	7
	447		370

1/25 2/49 3/111 4/161 5/250
6/374 7/391 8/416 9/437

1/20 2/125 3/183 4/185 5/243
6/292 7/308 8/321 9/341

Bowling: *First Innings*—McDonald 24-1-78-1; Gregory 36-5-108-2; Mailey 32.1-3-160-5; Armstrong 23-10-29-1; Ryder 6-0-29-0. *Second Innings*—McDonald 24-0-95-2; Kelleway 8-2-16-0; Mailey 29.2-3-142-5; Armstrong 16-1-41-0; Ryder 9-2-19-0; Gregory 20-2-50-3.

Umpires: R.M.Crockett and D.A.Elder

AUSTRALIA v ENGLAND 1920-21 (Second Test)

At Melbourne Cricket Ground, 31 December, 1, 3, 4 January
Result: Australia won by an innings and 91 runs

Australia

H.L.Collins c Hearne b Howell	64
W.Bardsley c Strudwick b Woolley	51
R.L.Park b Howell	0
J.M.Taylor c Woolley b Parkin	68
W.W.Armstrong* lbw b Douglas	39
C.Kelleway c Strudwick b Howell	9
C.E.Pellew b Parkin	116
J.Ryder c Woolley b Douglas	13
J.M.Gregory c Russell b Woolley	100
W.A.S.Oldfield† c and b Rhodes	24
A.A.Mailey not out	8
Extras (B 1, LB 3, NB 2, W 1)	7
	499

1/116 2/116 3/118 4/194 5/220
6/251 7/282 8/455 9/469

Bowling: Howell 37-5-142-3; Douglas 24-1-83-2; Parkin 27-0-116-2; Hearne 14-0-38-0; Woolley 27-8-87-2; Rhodes 8.3-1-26-1.

England

J.B.Hobbs c Ryder b Gregory	122	b Kelleway	20
W.Rhodes b Gregory	7	c Collins b Armstrong	28
J.W.H.Makepeace lbw b Armstrong	4	c Gregory b Armstrong	4
E.H.Hendren c Taylor b Gregory	67	c and b Collins	1
C.A.G.Russell c Collins b Gregory	0	c Armstrong b Collins	5
F.E.Woolley b Gregory	5	b Ryder	50
J.W.H.T.Douglas* lbw b Gregory	15	b Gregory	9
C.H.Parkin c Mailey b Gregory	4	c Taylor b Armstrong	9
H.Strudwick† not out	21	c Oldfield b Armstrong	24
H.Howell st Oldfield b Armstrong	5	not out	0
J.W.Hearne absent ill	-	absent ill	-
Extras (NB 1)	1	(B 3, LB 3, NB 1)	7
	251		157

1/20 2/32 3/174 4/185 5/201
6/208 7/213 8/232 9/251

1/36 2/53 3/54 4/58 5/70
6/104 7/141 8/151 9/157

Bowling: *First Innings*—Kelleway 19-1-54-0; Gregory 20-1-69-7; Armstrong 24.3-8-50-2; Ryder 14-2-31-0; Park 1-0-9-0; Collins 9-0-37-0. *Second Innings*—Kelleway 12-1-25-1; Gregory 12-0-32-1; Armstrong 15.2-5-26-4; Collins 17-5-47-2; Ryder 10-2-17-1; Pellew 1-0-3-0.

Umpires: R.M.Crockett and D.A.Elder

AUSTRALIA v ENGLAND 1920-21 (Fourth Test)

At Melbourne Cricket Ground, 11, 12, 14, 15, 16 February
Result: Australia won by 8 wickets

England

J.B.Hobbs c Carter b McDonald	27		lbw b Mailey	13
W.Rhodes c Carter b Gregory	11		c Gregory b Mailey	73
J.W.H.Makepeace c Collins b Mailey	117		lbw b Mailey	54
E.H.Hendren c Carter b Mailey	30		b Kelleway	32
F.E.Woolley lbw b Kelleway	29		st Carter b Mailey	0
J.W.H.T.Douglas* c and b Mailey	50		st Carter b Mailey	60
A.Waddington b Mailey	0	(8)	c and b Mailey	6
P.G.H.Fender c Gregory b Kelleway	3	(7)	c Collins b Mailey	59
A.Dolphin† b Kelleway	1		c Gregory b Mailey	0
C.H.Parkin run out	10		c Bardsley b Mailey	4
H.Howell not out	0		not out	0
Extras (B 1, LB 5)	6		(B 5, LB 5, NB 3, W 1)	14
	284			315

1/18 2/61 3/104 4/164 5/270   1/32 2/145 3/152 4/152 5/201
6/270 7/271 8/274 9/275   6/305 7/307 8/307 9/315

Bowling: *First Innings*—McDonald 19-2-46-1; Gregory 18-1-61-1; Mailey 29.2-1-115-4; Ryder 10-5-10-0; Armstrong 5-1-9-0; Kelleway 18-2-37-3. *Second Innings*—Gregory 14-4-31-0; McDonald 23-2-77-0; Mailey 47-8-121-9; Kelleway 23-8-47-1; Ryder 10-3-25-0.

Australia

H.L.Collins c Rhodes b Woolley	59		c Rhodes b Parkin	32
W.Bardsley b Fender	56		run out	38
J.Ryder lbw b Woolley	7		not out	52
J.M.Taylor hit wkt b Fender	2			
J.M.Gregory c Dolphin b Parkin	77	(4)	not out	76
C.E.Pellew b Fender	12			
W.W.Armstrong* not out	123			
C.Kelleway b Fender	27			
H.Carter† b Fender	0			
A.A.Mailey run out	13			
E.A.McDonald b Woolley	0			
Extras (B 1, LB 6, NB 5, W 1)	13		(B 5, LB 5, NB 1, W 2)	13
	389		(2 wkts)	211

1/117 2/123 3/128 4/133 5/153   1/71 2/81
6/298 7/335 8/335 9/376

Bowling: *First Innings*—Howell 17-2-86-0; Douglas 4-0-17-0; Waddington 5-0-31-0; Parkin 22-5-64-1; Fender 32-5-122-5; Woolley 32.1-14-56-3. *Second Innings*—Howell 10-1-36-0; Douglas 5-1-13-0; Woolley 14-4-39-0; Parkin 12-2-46-1; Fender 13.2-2-39-0; Rhodes 10-2-25-0.

Umpires: R.M.Crockett and D.A.Elder

AUSTRALIA v ENGLAND 1920-21 (Fifth Test)

At Sydney Cricket Ground, 25, 26, 28 February, 1 March
Result: Australia won by 9 wickets

England

J.B.Hobbs lbw b Gregory	40	(5)	c Taylor b Mailey	34
W.Rhodes c Carter b Kelleway	26		run out	25
J.W.H.Makepeace c Gregory b Mailey	3		c Gregory b Kelleway	7
E.H.Hendren c Carter b Gregory	5	(6)	st Carter b Mailey	13
F.E.Woolley b McDonald	53	(1)	c and b Kelleway	
C.A.G.Russell c Gregory b Mailey	19	(8)	c Gregory b Armstrong	35
J.W.H.T.Douglas* not out	32		c and b Mailey	68
P.G.H.Fender c Gregory b Kelleway	2	(9)	c Kelleway b McDonald	40
E.R.Wilson c Carter b Kelleway	5	(4)	st Carter b Mailey	5
C.H.Parkin c Taylor b Kelleway	9		c Gregory b Mailey	36
H.Strudwick† b Gregory	2		not out	5
Extras (B 3, LB 2, NB 2, W 1)	8		(B 3, LB 5, NB 3)	11
	204			280

1/54 2/70 3/74 4/76 5/125   1/1 2/14 3/29 4/75 5/82
6/161 7/164 8/172 9/201   6/91 7/160 8/224 9/251

Bowling: *First Innings*—Gregory 16.1-4-42-3; McDonald 11-2-38-1; Kelleway 20-6-27-4; Mailey 23-1-89-2. *Second Innings*—McDonald 25-3-58-1; Kelleway 14-3-29-2; Mailey 36.2-5-119-5; Gregory 16-3-37-0; Ryder 2-2-0-0; Armstrong 8-1-26-1.

Australia

H.L.Collins c Fender b Parkin	5		c Strudwick b Wilson	37
W.Bardsley c Fender b Douglas	7		not out	50
C.G.Macartney c Hobbs b Fender	170			
J.M.Taylor c Hendren b Douglas	32			
J.M.Gregory c Strudwick b Fender	93		not out	2
W.W.Armstrong* c Woolley b Fender	0			
J.Ryder b Fender	2			
C.Kelleway c Strudwick b Wilson	32			
H.Carter† c Woolley b Fender	17			
A.A.Mailey b Wilson	5			
E.A.McDonald not out	3			
Extras (B 18, LB 6, NB 2)	26		(B 3, NB 1)	4
	392		(1 wkt)	93

1/16 2/22 3/89 4/287 5/287   1/91
6/313 7/356 8/384 9/384

Bowling: *First Innings*—Douglas 16-0-84-2; Parkin 19-1-83-1; Woolley 15-1-58-0; Wilson 14.3-4-28-2; Fender 20-1-90-5; Rhodes 7-0-23-0. *Second Innings*—Parkin 9-1-32-0; Woolley 11-3-27-0; Fender 1-0-2-0; Rhodes 7.2-1-20-0; Wilson 6-1-8-1.

Umpires: R.M.Crockett and D.A.Elder

ENGLAND v AUSTRALIA 1921 (First Test)

At Trent Bridge, Nottingham, 28, 30 May

Result: Australia won by 10 wickets

England

Batsman	First Innings		Second Innings	
D.J.Knight	c Carter b Gregory	8	run out	38
P.Holmes	b McDonald	30	c Taylor b McDonald	8
G.E.Tyldesley	b Gregory	0	b Gregory	7
E.H.Hendren	b Gregory	0	b McDonald	7
J.W.H.T.Douglas*	c Hendry b McDonald	11	c Hendry b McDonald	13
F.E.Woolley	c Hendry b McDonald	20	c Carter b Hendry	34
V.W.C.Jupp	c Armstrong b McDonald	8	c Pellew b Gregory	10
W.Rhodes	c Carter b Gregory	19	c Carter b McDonald	10
H.Strudwick†	c Collins b Gregory	0	b Hendry	0
H.Howell	not out	0	not out	2
T.L.Richmond	c and b Gregory	4	b McDonald	9
Extras	(B 6, LB 6)	12	(B 4, LB 3, NB 2)	9
Total		**112**		**147**

1/18 2/18 3/18 4/43 5/77 6/77 7/101 8/107 9/108

1/23 2/41 3/60 4/63 5/76 6/110 7/138 8/138 9/140

Bowling: First Innings—Gregory 19-5-58-6; McDonald 15-5-42-4; Armstrong 3-3-0-0. *Second Innings*—Gregory 22-8-45-2; McDonald 22.4-10-32-5; Armstrong 27-10-33-0; Macartney 5-2-10-0; Hendry 9-1-18-2.

Australia

Batsman	First Innings		Second Innings	
W.Bardsley	lbw b Woolley	66	not out	8
H.L.Collins	lbw b Richmond	17		
C.G.Macartney	lbw b Douglas	20	(2) not out	22
J.M.Taylor	c Jupp b Douglas	4		
W.W.Armstrong*	b Jupp	11		
J.M.Gregory	lbw b Richmond	14		
C.E.Pellew	c and b Rhodes	25		
H.Carter†	b Woolley	12		
T.J.E.Andrews	c and b Rhodes	6		
H.S.T.L.Hendry	not out	12		
E.A.McDonald	c Knight b Woolley	10		
Extras	(B 8, LB 5, NB 1)	14		
Total		**232**	**(0 wkts)**	**30**

1/49 2/86 3/98 4/126 5/138 6/152 7/183 8/202 9/212

Bowling: First Innings—Howell 9-3-22-0; Douglas 13-2-34-2; Richmond 16-3-69-2; Woolley 22-8-46-3; Jupp 5-0-14-1; Rhodes 13-3-13-2. *Second Innings*—Jupp 3.1-0-13-0; Richmond 3-0-17-0.

Umpires: H.R.Butt and J.Moss

ENGLAND v AUSTRALIA 1921 (Second Test)

At Lord's, London, 11, 13, 14 June

Result: Australia won by 8 wickets

England

Batsman	First Innings		Second Innings	
D.J.Knight	c Gregory b Armstrong	7	c Carter b Gregory	1
A.E.Dipper	b McDonald	11	b McDonald	40
F.E.Woolley	st Carter b Mailey	95	c Hendry b Mailey	93
E.H.Hendren	b Gregory	0	c Gregory b Mailey	10
J.W.H.T.Douglas*	b McDonald	34	b Gregory	14
A.J.Evans	b McDonald	4	lbw b McDonald	14
Hon.L.H.Tennyson	st Carter b Mailey	5	not out	74
N.E.Haig	c Carter b Gregory	3	b McDonald	0
C.H.Parkin	b Mailey	0	c Pellew b McDonald	11
H.Strudwick†	c McDonald b Mailey	8	b Gregory	12
F.J.Durston	not out	6	b Gregory	2
Extras	(B 1, LB 11, NB 1, W 1)	14	(B 4, LB 3, NB 5)	12
Total		**187**		**283**

1/20 2/24 3/25 4/108 5/120 6/145 7/156 8/157 9/170

1/3 2/97 3/124 4/165 5/165 6/198 7/202 8/235 9/263

Bowling: First Innings—Gregory 16-1-51-2; McDonald 20-2-58-3; Armstrong 18-12-9-1; Mailey 14.2-1-55-4. *Second Innings*—Gregory 26.2-4-76-4; McDonald 23-3-89-4; Mailey 25-4-72-2; Armstrong 12-6-19-0; Hendry 4-0-15-0.

Australia

Batsman	First Innings		Second Innings	
W.Bardsley	c Woolley b Douglas	88	not out	63
T.J.E.Andrews	c Strudwick b Durston	9	lbw b Parkin	49
C.G.Macartney	c Strudwick b Durston	31	b Durston	8
C.E.Pellew	b Haig	43	not out	5
J.M.Taylor	lbw b Douglas	36		
W.W.Armstrong*	b Durston	0		
J.M.Gregory	c and b Parkin	52		
H.S.T.L.Hendry	b Haig	5		
H.Carter†	b Durston	46		
A.A.Mailey	c and b Parkin	5		
E.A.McDonald	not out	17		
Extras	(B 2, LB 5, NB 3)	10	(B 3, LB 2, NB 1)	6
Total		**342**	**(2 wkts)**	**131**

1/19 2/73 3/145 4/191 5/192 6/230 7/263 8/277 9/289

1/103 2/114

Bowling: First Innings—Durston 24.1-2-102-4; Douglas 9-1-53-2; Parkin 20-5-72-2; Haig 20-4-61-2; Woolley 11-2-44-0. *Second Innings*—Durston 9.3-0-34-1; Douglas 6-0-23-0; Parkin 9-0-31-0; Haig 3-0-27-0; Woolley 3-0-10-0.

Umpires: J.Moss and W.Phillips

ENGLAND v AUSTRALIA 1921 (Fourth Test)

At Old Trafford, Manchester, 23 (no play), 25, 26 July

Result: Match drawn

England

C.A.G.Russell b Gregory	101		
G.Brown† c Gregory b Armstrong	31		
F.E.Woolley c Pellew b Armstrong	41		
C.P.Mead c Andrews b Hendry	47		
G.E.Tyldesley not out	78		
P.G.H.Fender not out	44		
C.Hallows		(1) not out	16
C.H.Parkin		(2) c Collins b Andrews	23
C.W.L.Parker		(3) not out	3
Hon.L.H.Tennyson*			
J.W.H.T.Douglas			
Extras (B 12, LB 5, NB 3)	20	(LB 2)	2
1/65 2/145 3/217 4/260	(4 wkts dec.) 362	1/36	(1 wkt) 44

Bowling: *First Innings*—Gregory 23-5-79-1; McDonald 31-1-112-0; Macartney 8-2-20-0; Hendry 2.5-5-74-1; Armstrong 33-13-57-2. *Second Innings*—Hendry 4-1-12-0; Andrews 5-0-21-1; Pellew 3-0-6-0; Taylor 1-0-1-0.

Australia

W.Bardsley b Parkin	3
H.L.Collins lbw b Parkin	40
C.G.Macartney b Parker	13
T.J.E.Andrews c Tennyson b Fender	6
J.M.Taylor b Fender	4
C.E.Pellew c Tyldesley b Parker	17
W.W.Armstrong* b Douglas	17
J.M.Gregory b Parkin	29
H.Carter† b Parkin	0
H.S.T.L.Hendry c Russell b Parkin	4
E.A.McDonald not out	8
Extras (B 22, LB 5, NB 7)	34
1/9 2/33 3/44 4/48 5/78	175
6/125 7/161 8/161 9/166	

Bowling: Parkin 29.4-12-38-5; Woolley 39-22-38-0; Parker 28-16-32-2; Fender 15-6-30-2; Douglas 5-2-3-1.

Umpires: J.Moss and A.E.Street

ENGLAND v AUSTRALIA 1921 (Third Test)

At Headingley, Leeds, 2, 4, 5 July

Result: Australia won by 219 runs

Australia

W.Bardsley c Woolley b Douglas	6	b Jupp	25
T.J.E.Andrews c Woolley b Douglas	19	b Jupp	92
C.G.Macartney lbw b Parkin	115	c and b Woolley	30
C.E.Pellew c Hearne b Woolley	52	(5) c Ducat b White	16
J.M.Taylor c Douglas b Jupp	50	(6) c Tennyson b White	4
J.M.Gregory b Parkin	7	(8) c Jupp b White	3
W.W.Armstrong* c Brown b Douglas	77	not out	28
H.S.T.L.Hendry b Parkin	0	(9) not out	11
H.Carter† b Jupp	34	(4) lbw b Parkin	47
E.A.McDonald not out	21		
A.A.Mailey c and b Parkin	6		
Extras (B 16, LB 7, NB 3)	26	(B 10, LB 4, NB 3)	17
1/22 2/45 3/146 4/255 5/256	407	1/71 2/139 3/193 (7 wkts dec.)	273
6/271 7/271 8/333 9/388		4/223 5/227 6/227 7/230	

Bowling: *First Innings*—Douglas 20-3-80-3; White 25-4-70-0; Parkin 20.1-0-106-4; Hearne 5-0-21-0; Jupp 18-2-70-2; Woolley 5-0-34-1. *Second Innings*—Douglas 11-0-38-0; White 11-3-37-3; Parkin 20-0-91-1; Jupp 13-2-45-2; Woolley 18-4-45-1.

England

F.E.Woolley b Gregory	0	(4) b Mailey	37
H.T.W.Hardinge lbw b Armstrong	25	c Gregory b McDonald	5
J.W.Hearne b McDonald	7	c Taylor b McDonald	27
A.Ducat c Gregory b McDonald	3	(6) st Carter b Mailey	2
J.W.H.T.Douglas b Armstrong	75	b Gregory	8
V.W.C.Jupp c Carter b Gregory	14	(7) c Carter b Armstrong	28
G.Brown† c Armstrong b Mailey	57	(1) lbw b Gregory	46
J.C.White b McDonald	1	(9) not out	6
Hon.L.H.Tennyson* c Gregory b McDonald	63	(8) b Armstrong	36
C.H.Parkin not out	5	b Mailey	4
J.B.Hobbs absent ill		absent ill	
Extras (LB 3, NB 6)	9	(B 3)	3
1/0 2/13 3/30 4/47 5/67	259	1/15 2/57 3/98 4/124 5/126	202
6/164 7/165 8/253 9/259		6/128 7/190 8/197 9/202	

Bowling: *First Innings*—Gregory 21-6-47-2; McDonald 26.1-0-105-4; Armstrong 19-4-44-2; Mailey 17-4-38-1; Hendry 10-4-1-0. *Second Innings*—Gregory 14-1-55-2; McDonald 15-2-67-2; Armstrong 3-0-6-0; Mailey 20.3-71-3.

Umpires: H.R.Butt and A.Millward

ENGLAND v AUSTRALIA 1921 (Fifth Test)

At Kennington Oval, London, 13, 15, 16 August

Result: Match drawn

England

C.A.G.Russell c Oldfield b McDonald	13	not out	102
G.Brown† b Mailey	32	c Mailey b Taylor	84
G.E.Tyldesley c Macartney b Gregory	39		
F.E.Woolley run out	23		
C.P.Mead not out	182		
A.Sandham b McDonald	21		
Hon.L.H.Tennyson* b McDonald	51		
P.G.H.Fender c Armstrong b McDonald	0	(3) c Armstrong b Mailey	6
J.W.Hitch b McDonald	18	(4) not out	51
J.W.H.T.Douglas not out	21		
C.H.Parkin			
Extras (LB 3)	3	(B 1)	1
1/27 2/54 3/84 4/121 5/191 (8 wkts dec.) 403		1/158 2/173 (2 wkts) 244	
6/312 7/312 8/339			

Bowling: First Innings—Gregory 38-5-128-1; McDonald 47-9-143-5; Mailey 30-4-85-1; Armstrong 12-2-44-0. Second Innings—Gregory 3-0-13-0; McDonald 6-0-20-0; Mailey 18-2-77-1; Pellew 9-3-25-0; Andrews 8-0-44-0; Taylor 7-1-25-1; Collins 7-0-39-0.

Australia

H.L.Collins hit wkt b Hitch	14
W.Bardsley b Hitch	22
C.G.Macartney b Douglas	61
T.J.E.Andrews lbw b Parkin	94
J.M.Taylor c Woolley b Douglas	75
C.E.Pellew c Woolley b Parkin	1
W.W.Armstrong* c Brown b Douglas	19
J.M.Gregory st Brown b Parkin	27
W.A.S.Oldfield† not out	28
E.A.McDonald st Brown b Woolley	36
A.A.Mailey b Woolley	0
Extras (B 6, LB 3, NB 1, W 2)	12
1/33 2/54 3/162 4/233 5/239 389	
6/288 7/311 8/338 9/389	

Bowling: Hitch 19-3-65-2; Douglas 30-2-117-3; Fender 19-3-82-0; Parkin 23-4-82-3; Woolley 11-2-31-2.

Umpires: J.Moss and W.Phillips

SOUTH AFRICA v AUSTRALIA 1921-22 (First Test)

At Lord's, Durban, 5, 7, 8, 9 November

Result: Match drawn

Australia

H.L.Collins* b Carter	31	c Chapman b Nourse	47
J.M.Gregory b Blanckenberg	51	(4) b Blanckenberg	6
C.G.Macartney c Nourse b Nupen	59	c Ward b Marx	116
W.Bardsley b Blanckenberg	5	(2) lbw b Carter	23
T.J.E.Andrews b Blanckenberg	3	(6) not out	35
J.Ryder not out	78	(5) b Blanckenberg	58
J.M.Taylor b Carter	18	b Carter	11
H.S.T.L.Hendry c Nourse b Chapman	23	b Carter	13
H.Carter† c Nourse b Blanckenberg	9	not out	1
E.A.McDonald b Carter	2		
A.A.Mailey b Blanckenberg	18		
Extras (B 16, LB 2)	18	(B 12, LB 1, NB 1)	14
1/85 2/95 3/116 4/128 5/175 299		1/44 2/118 3/144 (7 wkts dec.) 324	
6/214 7/276 8/291 9/296		4/250 5/270 6/283 7/314	

Bowling: First Innings—Marx 3-0-6-0; Nourse 11-1-36-0; Nupen 15-2-42-1; Chapman 11-0-51-1; Blanckenberg 24.4-6-78-5; Carter 20-1-68-3. Second Innings—Marx 6-0-20-0; Nourse 8-1-32-0; Nupen 16-3-59-1; Chapman 6-1-33-0; Blanckenberg 30-3-100-2; Carter 21-3-66-3.

South Africa

H.W.Taylor* c Hendry b Gregory	1	(4) c and b McDonald	29
J.W.Zulch c Gregory b Macartney	80	(5) c Taylor b McDonald	17
C.N.Frank c Gregory b McDonald	1	(6) c Gregory b Mailey	38
A.W.Nourse c Hendry b Gregory	32	(1) not out	31
W.V.S.Ling b Gregory	33	(7) c Gregory b McDonald	28
W.F.E.Marx c Macartney b Gregory	0	(3) c Carter b Mailey	28
H.W.Chapman c Gregory b Hendry	4	(8) b Gregory	2
E.P.Nupen c and b Hendry	6	(9) not out	0
T.A.Ward† not out	22	(2) b Gregory	0
J.M.Blanckenberg c Ryder b Gregory	28		
C.P.Carter c Mailey b Gregory	14		
Extras (B 4, LB 3, NB 4)	11	(LB 8, NB 3)	11
1/2 2/9 3/62 4/136 5/136 232		1/1 2/43 3/82 4/112 (7 wkts) 184	
6/154 7/154 8/163 9/214		5/131 6/179 7/182	

Bowling: First Innings—Gregory 25.1-4-77-6; McDonald 20-5-55-1; Mailey 17-2-55-0; Macartney 11-6-13-1; Hendry 7-0-21-2. Second Innings—Gregory 19-7-28-2; McDonald 34-17-64-3; Mailey 31-10-54-2; Hendry 4-0-20-0; Ryder 8-3-7-0.

Umpires: F.W.Grey and A.G.Laver

SOUTH AFRICA v AUSTRALIA 1921-22 (Third Test)

At Newlands, Cape Town, 26, 28, 29 November
Result: Australia won by 10 wickets

South Africa

Batsman	1st innings	Runs	2nd innings	Runs
C.N.Frank	b Ryder	21	b Macartney	23
J.W.Zulch	c Ryder b Macartney	50	c and b Macartney	40
P.A.M.Hands	c Gregory b Ryder	0	(3) c Ryder b Macartney	19
H.W.Taylor*	c Andrews b McDonald	26	(6) c Andrews b Macartney	17
A.W.Nourse	c Mayne b Mailey	11	run out	31
W.V.S.Ling	b McDonald	0	(7) b Macartney	35
W.F.E.Marx	st Carter b Mailey	11	run out	16
J.M.Blanckenberg	st Carter b Mailey	25	(9) c Carter b Mailey	20
T.A.Ward†	b McDonald	2	(2) b McDonald	4
C.P.Carter	not out	19	not out	1
N.Reid	c Mayne b Mailey	11	b Macartney	6
Extras	(LB 2, NB 2)	4	(B 1, LB 2, NB 1)	4
Total		**180**		**216**

1/50 2/54 3/82 4/106 5/107 6/110 7/143 8/146 9/151
1/10 2/58 3/84 4/92 5/122 6/162 7/182 8/203 9/209

Bowling: *First Innings*—Gregory 15-9-11-0; McDonald 19-3-53-3; Macartney 24-10-47-1; Ryder 16-7-25-2; Mailey 14-1-40-4. *Second Innings*—Gregory 9-1-29-0; McDonald 13-2-35-1; Macartney 24.3-10-44-5; Ryder 7-0-15-0; Mailey 26-0-89-2; Collins 1-1-0-0.

Australia

Batsman	1st innings	Runs	2nd innings	Runs
H.L.Collins*	b Blanckenberg	54	not out	0
W.Bardsley	lbw b Blanckenberg	30		
C.G.Macartney	c Nourse b Blanckenberg	44	not out	1
J.Ryder	c Taylor b Carter	142		
J.M.Gregory	c Hands b Blanckenberg	29		
R.E.Mayne	lbw b Reid	15		
T.J.E.Andrews	c Hands b Carter	10		
C.E.Pellew	c Nourse b Reid	6		
H.Carter†	not out	31		
E.A.McDonald	c Ward b Carter	4		
A.A.Mailey	c Taylor b Nourse	14		
Extras	(B 9, LB 5, NB 3)	17		
Total		**396**	**(0 wkts)**	**1**

1/71 2/108 3/153 4/201 5/242 6/281 7/320 8/358 9/361

Bowling: *First Innings*—Marx 7-1-29-0; Nourse 30-5-89-1; Blanckenberg 31-5-82-4; Carter 26-5-104-3; Reid 21-3-63-2; Taylor 5-2-12-0. *Second Innings*—Hands 0.1-0-1-0.

Umpires: H.V.Adams and A.G.Laver

SOUTH AFRICA v AUSTRALIA 1921-22 (Second Test)

At Old Wanderers, Johannesburg, 12, 14, 15, 16 November
Result: Match drawn

Australia

Batsman	1st innings	Runs	2nd innings	Runs
H.L.Collins*	c Lindsay b Carter	203	not out	5
W.Bardsley	b Marx	8	not out	2
J.Ryder	b Blanckenberg	56		
J.M.Gregory	st Ward b Carter	119		
T.J.E.Andrews	st Ward b Carter	3		
J.M.Taylor	c Nupen b Marx	11		
R.E.Mayne	b Carter	1		
H.S.T.L.Hendry	b Carter	15		
W.A.S.Oldfield†	b Marx	2		
E.A.McDonald	not out	4		
A.A.Mailey	st Ward b Carter	4		
Extras	(B 3, LB 15, NB 1)	19		
Total		**450**	**(0 wkts)**	**7**

1/15 2/128 3/337 4/347 5/382 6/383 7/407 8/422 9/446

Bowling: *First Innings*—Marx 16-0-86-0; Nupen 16-2-105-1; Carter 29.5-4-91-6; Blanckenberg 21-2-105-1; Nourse 7-1-44-0, Ling 3-0-20-0. *Second Innings*—Marx 1-0-4-0; Nupen 0.4-0-3-0.

South Africa

Batsman	1st innings	Runs	2nd innings	Runs
J.W.Zulch	hit wkt b McDonald	4	b Gregory	2
C.N.Frank	run out	1	c Collins b Mailey	152
N.V.Lindsay	hit wkt b Gregory	6	b Gregory	29
H.W.Taylor*	c Mailey b Gregory	47	c Hendry b Gregory	80
A.W.Nourse	c sub (C.E.Pellew) b McDonald	64	c Gregory b Ryder	111
W.V.S.Ling	c Hendry b Gregory	36	st Oldfield b Ryder	19
W.F.E.Marx	c Collins b Mailey	7	(8) c Bardsley b Mailey	34
T.A.Ward†	c Taylor b Collins	45	(9) not out	7
J.M.Blanckenberg	b Gregory	22	(7) c Andrews b Mailey	4
E.P.Nupen	b Mailey	0	not out	13
C.P.Carter	not out	0		
Extras	(B 4, LB 4, NB 3)	11	(B 10, LB 5, NB 4)	19
Total		**243**	**(8 wkts dec.)**	**472**

1/6 2/6 3/16 4/95 5/109 6/135 7/164 8/189 9/243
1/6 2/44 3/149 4/355 5/387 6/393 7/446 8/450

Bowling: *First Innings*—Gregory 19.3-1-71-4; McDonald 19-7-43-2; Mailey 22-4-72-2; Hendry 12-2-37-0; Collins 6-2-9-1. *Second Innings*—Gregory 28-7-68-3; McDonald 44-14-121-0; Mailey 43-8-113-3; Hendry 23-6-58-0; Collins 15-12-7-0; Taylor 11-4-19-0; Mayne 1-0-1-0; Ryder 30-9-66-2.

Umpires: S.L.Harris and A.G.Laver

AUSTRALIA v ENGLAND 1924-25 (First Test)

At Sydney Cricket Ground, 19, 20, 22, 23, 24, 26, 27 December
Result: Australia won by 193 runs

Australia

H.L.Collins* c Hendren b Tate	114	(4)	c Chapman b Tate	60
W.Bardsley c Woolley b Freeman	21	(1)	b Tate	22
W.H.Ponsford b Gilligan	110	(5)	c Woolley b Freeman	27
A.J.Richardson b Hearne	22	(2)	c and b Freeman	98
J.M.Taylor c Strudwick b Tate	43	(8)	b Tate	108
V.Y.Richardson b Freeman	42		c Hendren b Tate	18
C.Kelleway c Woolley b Tate	17	(3)	b Gilligan	23
H.S.T.L.Hendry c Strudwick b Tate	3	(7)	c Strudwick b Tate	22
J.M.Gregory c Strudwick b Tate	0		c Woolley b Freeman	2
W.A.S.Oldfield† not out	39		c Strudwick b Gilligan	18
A.A.Mailey b Tate	21		not out	46
Extras (B 10, LB 8)	18		(B 2, LB 5, W 1)	8
	450			**452**

1/46 2/236 3/275 4/286 5/364   1/40 2/115 3/168 4/210 5/241
6/374 7/387 8/387 9/388   6/260 7/281 8/286 9/325

Bowling: *First Innings*—Tate 55.1-11-130-6; Gilligan 23-0-92-1; Freeman 49-11-124-2; Hearne 12.1-3-28-1; Woolley 9-0-35-0; Hobbs 2-0-13-0; Chapman 2-0-10-0. *Second Innings*—Gilligan 27-6-114-2; Tate 33.7-8-98-5; Freeman 37-4-134-3; Hearne 25-2-88-0; Chapman 3-1-10-0.

England

J.B.Hobbs c Kelleway b Gregory	115		c Hendry b Mailey	57
H.Sutcliffe c V.Y.Richardson b Mailey	59		c Gregory b Mailey	115
J.W.Hearne c sub (T.J.E.Andrews) b Mailey	7		b Gregory	0
F.E.Woolley b Gregory	0	(6)	c Mailey b Gregory	123
E.H.Hendren not out	74		c Gregory b Hendry	9
A.Sandham b Mailey	7	(7)	c Oldfield b Mailey	2
A.P.F.Chapman run out	13	(4)	c Oldfield b Hendry	44
M.W.Tate c sub (T.J.E.Andrews) b Mailey	7		c Ponsford b Kelleway	0
A.E.R.Gilligan* b Gregory	1		b Kelleway	1
A.P.Freeman b Gregory	0		not out	50
H.Strudwick† lbw b Gregory	6		c Oldfield b Hendry	2
Extras (B 1, LB 5, NB 3)	9		(B 4, LB 3, NB 1)	8
	298			**411**

1/157 2/171 3/172 4/202 5/235   1/110 2/127 3/195 4/212 5/263
6/254 7/272 8/274 9/274   6/269 7/270 8/276 9/404

Bowling: *First Innings*—Gregory 28.7-2-111-5; Kelleway 14-3-44-0; Mailey 31-3-129-4; Hendry 5-1-5-0; A.J.Richardson 1-1-0-0. *Second Innings*—Gregory 28-2-115-2; Kelleway 21-5-60-2; Mailey 32-0-179-3; A.J.Richardson 5-0-13-0; Hendry 10.7-2-36-3.

Umpires: A.C.Jones and A.P.Williams

AUSTRALIA v ENGLAND 1924-25 (Second Test)

At Melbourne Cricket Ground, 1, 2, 3, 5, 6, 7, 8 January
Result: Australia won by 81 runs

Australia

H.L.Collins* c Strudwick b Tate	9		b Hearne	30
W.Bardsley c Strudwick b Gilligan	19		lbw b Tate	2
A.J.Richardson run out	14		b Tate	9
W.H.Ponsford b Tate	128		b Tate	4
J.M.Taylor c Strudwick b Tate	72		b Tate	90
V.Y.Richardson run out	138		c Strudwick b Hearne	8
C.Kelleway c Strudwick b Gilligan	32		c and b Hearne	17
A.E.V.Hartkopf c Chapman b Gilligan	80		lbw b Tate	0
J.M.Gregory c Gilligan b Tate	44		not out	36
W.A.S.Oldfield† not out	39		lbw b Tate	39
A.A.Mailey lbw b Douglas	1		b Tate	3
Extras (B 18, LB 5, NB 1)	24		(B 11, LB 1)	12
	600			**250**

1/22 2/47 3/47 4/208 5/301   1/3 2/13 3/27 4/106 5/126
6/424 7/439 8/499 9/599   6/166 7/168 8/168 9/239

Bowling: *First Innings*—Tate 45-10-142-3; Douglas 19.5-0-95-1; Tyldesley 35-3-130-0; Gilligan 26-1-114-3; Hearne 13-1-69-0; Woolley 11-3-26-0. *Second Innings*—Tate 33.3-8-99-6; Gilligan 11-2-40-0; Tyldesley 2-0-6-0; Hearne 29-5-84-4; Douglas 4-0-9-0.

England

J.B.Hobbs b Mailey	154		lbw b Mailey	22
H.Sutcliffe b Kelleway	176		c Gregory b Mailey	127
F.E.Woolley b Gregory	0	(5)	lbw b A.J.Richardson	50
J.W.Hearne b Mailey	9		lbw b Gregory	23
E.H.Hendren c Oldfield b Kelleway	32	(6)	b Gregory	18
A.P.F.Chapman c Oldfield b Gregory	28	(9)	not out	4
J.W.H.T.Douglas c Collins b A.J.Richardson	8	(8)	b Mailey	14
R.K.Tyldesley c Collins b Gregory	5	(7)	c Ponsford b Mailey	0
M.W.Tate b A.J.Richardson	34	(11)	b Gregory	0
A.E.R.Gilligan* not out	17		c and b Mailey	0
H.Strudwick† b Hartkopf	4	(3)	lbw b Gregory	22
Extras (B 4, LB 4, NB 4)	12		(B 6, LB 2, NB 2)	10
	479			**290**

1/283 2/284 3/305 4/373 5/404   1/36 2/75 3/121 4/211 5/254
6/412 7/418 8/453 9/458   6/255 7/280 8/289 9/289

Bowling: *First Innings*—Gregory 34-4-124-3; Mailey 30-10-62-2; Hartkopf 26-1-120-1; A.J.Richardson 14-6-20-2. *Second Innings*—Gregory 27.3-6-87-4; Mailey 24-2-92-5; Hartkopf 4-1-14-0; A.J.Richardson 22-7-35-1; Kelleway 18-4-42-0; Collins 11-3-10-0.

Umpires: R.M.Crockett and C.Garing

AUSTRALIA v ENGLAND 1924-25 (Third Test)

At Adelaide Oval, 16, 17, 19, 20, 21, 22, 23 January

Result: Australia won by 11 runs

Australia

H.L.Collins*	b Tate	3		b Freeman	26
A.J.Richardson	b Kilner	69		c Kilner b Woolley	14
J.M.Gregory	b Freeman	6	(9)	c Hendren b Woolley	2
J.M.Taylor	lbw b Tate	0		b Freeman	34
W.H.Ponsford	c Strudwick b Gilligan	31		b Hendren b Kilner	43
V.Y.Richardson	c Whysall b Kilner	4	(7)	c Tate b Woolley	0
J.Ryder	not out	201	(3)	c and b Woolley	88
T.J.E.Andrews	b Kilner	72	(6)	c Whysall b Kilner	1
C.Kelleway	c Strudwick b Woolley	16	(8)	not out	22
W.A.S.Oldfield†	lbw b Kilner	47		b Kilner	4
A.A.Mailey	st Strudwick b Hendren	27		c Sutcliffe b Kilner	5
Extras	(LB 9, NB 4)	13		(B 4, LB 4, NB 3)	11
		489			250

1/10 2/19 3/22 4/114 5/118   1/36 2/63 3/126 4/215 5/216
6/119 7/253 8/308 8/416 9/489   6/217 7/217 8/220 9/242

Bowling: *First Innings*—Tate 18-1-43-2; Gilligan 7.7-1-17-1; Freeman 18-0-107-1; Woolley 43-5-135-1; Kilner 56-7-127-4; Hobbs 3-0-11-0; Hendren 5.1-0-27-1; Whysall 2-0-9-0. *Second Innings*—Tate 10-4-17-0; Kilner 22.1-7-51-4; Freeman 17-1-94-2; Woolley 19-1-77-4.

England

W.W.Whysall	b Gregory	9	(5)	c and b Gregory	75
M.W.Tate	c Andrews b Mailey	27	(8)	b Mailey	21
H.Strudwick†	c Gregory b Kelleway	1	(11)	not out	2
A.P.F.Chapman	b Gregory	26	(6)	c Ryder b Kelleway	58
J.B.Hobbs	c Gregory b Mailey	119	(1)	c Collins b A.J.Richardson	27
H.Sutcliffe	c Oldfield b Ryder	33	(2)	c Ponsford b Mailey	59
F.E.Woolley	c Andrews b Mailey	16	(3)	b Kelleway	21
E.H.Hendren	c Taylor b Gregory	92	(4)	lbw b Kelleway	4
R.Kilner	lbw b A.J.Richardson	6	(9)	c V.Y.Richardson b A.J.Richardson	24
A.E.R.Gilligan*	c Collins b A.J.Richardson	9	(9)	c V.Y.Richardson b Gregory	31
A.P.Freeman	not out	6	(10)	c Oldfield b Mailey	24
Extras	(B 8, LB 10, NB 3)	21		(B 5, LB 5, NB 6, W 1)	17
		365			363

1/15 2/18 3/67 4/69 5/159   1/63 2/92 3/96 4/155 5/244
6/180 7/297 8/316 9/326   6/254 7/279 8/312 9/357

Bowling: *First Innings*—Gregory 26.2-0-111-3; Kelleway 15-6-24-1; Mailey 44-5-133-3; A.J.Richardson 21-7-42-2; Ryder 6-2-15-1; Collins 5-1-19-0. *Second Innings*—Gregory 23-6-71-2; Collins 9-4-19-0; Kelleway 22-4-57-3; Ryder 2-0-11-0; A.J.Richardson 25-5-62-2; Mailey 30.2-4-126-3.

Umpires: R.M.Crockett and D.A.Elder

AUSTRALIA v ENGLAND 1924-25 (Fourth Test)

At Melbourne Cricket Ground, 13, 14, 16, 17, 18 February

Result: England won by an innings and 29 runs

England

J.B.Hobbs	st Oldfield b Ryder	66
H.Sutcliffe	lbw b Mailey	143
J.W.Hearne	c Bardsley b Richardson	44
F.E.Woolley	st Oldfield b Mailey	40
E.H.Hendren	b Ryder	65
A.P.F.Chapman	st Oldfield b Mailey	12
W.W.Whysall	st Oldfield b Kelleway	76
R.Kilner	lbw b Kelleway	74
A.E.R.Gilligan*	c Oldfield b Kelleway	0
M.W.Tate	c Taylor b Mailey	8
H.Strudwick†	not out	7
Extras	(B 6, LB 2, NB 2, W 3)	13
		548

1/126 2/232 3/284 4/307 5/346
6/394 7/527 8/527 9/529

Bowling: Gregory 22-1-102-0; Kelleway 29-5-70-3; Mailey 43.6-2-186-4; Ryder 25-3-83-2; Richardson 26-8-76-1; Collins 6-1-18-0.

Australia

H.L.Collins*	c Kilner b Tate	22	(9)	c Whysall b Kilner	1
A.J.Richardson	b Hearne	19	(9)	lbw b Hearne	3
J.Ryder	b Tate	0	(5)	lbw b Woolley	38
W.Bardsley	run out	24	(2)	b Tate	0
W.H.Ponsford	c Strudwick b Hearne	21	(8)	b Tate	19
J.M.Taylor	c Hendren b Woolley	86	(4)	c Woolley b Gilligan	68
T.J.E.Andrews	c Hearne b Kilner	35	(6)	c Strudwick b Tate	3
C.Kelleway	lbw b Kilner	1	(7)	c Strudwick b Tate	42
J.M.Gregory	c Woolley b Hearne	38	(3)	c Sutcliffe b Kilner	45
W.A.S.Oldfield†	c Chapman b Kilner	3		b Tate	8
A.A.Mailey	not out	4		not out	8
Extras	(B 13, LB 2, NB 1)	16		(B 15)	15
		269			250

1/38 2/38 3/64 4/74 5/109   1/5 2/5 3/64 4/133 5/190
6/170 7/172 8/244 9/257   6/195 7/225 8/234 9/238

Bowling: *First Innings*—Tate 16-2-70-2; Gilligan 6-1-24-0; Hearne 19.3-1-77-3; Kilner 13-1-29-3; Woolley 9-1-53-1. *Second Innings*—Tate 25.5-6-75-5; Kilner 16-3-41-2; Hearne 20-0-76-1; Woolley 6-0-17-1; Gilligan 7-0-26-1.

Umpires: R.M.Crockett and D.A.Elder

AUSTRALIA v ENGLAND 1924-25 (Fifth Test)

At Sydney Cricket Ground, 27, 28, February 2, 3, 4 March

Result: Australia won by 307 runs

Australia

H.L.Collins* c Strudwick b Gilligan	1	(7)	lbw b Tate	28
J.Ryder b Kilner	29		b Gilligan	7
J.M.Gregory run out	29	(1)	lbw b Hearne	22
T.J.E.Andrews c Whysall b Kilner	26	(3)	c Woolley b Hearne	80
J.M.Taylor c Whysall b Tate	15	(4)	st Strudwick b Tate	25
W.H.Ponsford c Woolley b Kilner	80	(5)	run out	5
A.F.Kippax b Kilner	42	(6)	c Whysall b Woolley	8
C.Kelleway lbw b Tate	9		c Whysall b Tate	73
W.A.S.Oldfield† c Strudwick b Tate	29		not out	65
A.A.Mailey b Tate	14		b Tate	0
C.V.Grimmett not out	12		b Tate	0
Extras (B 2, LB 5, NB 2)	9		(B 6, LB 4, NB 1, W 1)	12
	295			**325**

1/3 2/55 3/64 4/99 5/103   1/7 2/43 3/110 4/130 5/152
6/208 7/239 8/239 9/264   6/156 7/209 8/325 9/325

Bowling: *First Innings*—Tate 39.5-6-92-4; Gilligan 13-1-46-1; Kilner 38-4-97-4; Hearne 7-0-33-0; Woolley 5-0-18-0. *Second Innings*—Tate 39.3-6-115-5; Gilligan 15-2-46-1; Kilner 34-13-54-0; Hearne 22-0-84-2; Woolley 8-1-14-1.

England

J.B.Hobbs c Oldfield b Gregory	0		st Oldfield b Grimmett	13
H.Sutcliffe c Mailey b Kelleway	22		b Gregory	0
A.Sandham run out	4		lbw b Grimmett	15
F.E.Woolley b Grimmett	47		c Andrews b Kelleway	28
E.H.Hendren c Ponsford b Gregory	10		c Oldfield b Grimmett	10
J.W.Hearne lbw b Grimmett	16		lbw b Grimmett	24
W.W.Whysall lbw b Grimmett	8		st Oldfield b Grimmett	18
R.Kilner st Oldfield b Grimmett	24		c Ponsford b Collins	1
M.W.Tate b Ryder	25		c Mailey b Kelleway	33
A.E.R.Gilligan* st Oldfield b Grimmett	5		not out	0
H.Strudwick† not out	1		c Mailey b Grimmett	0
Extras (LB 4, NB 1)	5		(B 1, LB 3)	4
	167			**146**

1/0 2/15 3/28 4/58 5/96   1/3 2/31 3/32 4/60 5/84
6/109 7/122 8/157 9/163   6/99 7/100 8/146 9/146

Bowling: *First Innings*—Gregory 9-1-42-2; Kelleway 15-1-38-1; Mailey 5-0-13-0; Ryder 7-0-24-1; Grimmett 11.7-2-45-5. *Second Innings*—Gregory 10-0-53-1; Kelleway 7-1-16-2; Grimmett 19.4-3-37-6; Collins 8-2-36-1.

Umpires: R.M.Crockett and D.A.Elder

ENGLAND v AUSTRALIA 1926 (First Test)

At Trent Bridge, Nottingham, 12, 14 (no play), 15 (no play) June

Result: Match drawn

England

J.B.Hobbs not out	19
H.Sutcliffe not out	13
F.E.Woolley	
J.W.Hearne	
E.H.Hendren	
A.P.F.Chapman	
R.Kilner	
A.W.Carr*	
M.W.Tate	
C.F.Root	
H.Strudwick†	
Extras	
(0 wkts)	32

Bowling: Gregory 8-1-18-0; Macartney 8.2-2-14-0; Richardson 1-1-0-0.

Australia

H.L.Collins*
W.Bardsley
C.G.Macartney
J.M.Taylor
T.J.E.Andrews
W.M.Woodfull
J.Ryder
J.M.Gregory
A.J.Richardson
W.A.S.Oldfield†
A.A.Mailey

Umpires: R.D.Burrows and F.Chester

ENGLAND v AUSTRALIA 1926 (Second Test)

At Lord's, London, 26, 28, 29 June
Result: Match drawn

Australia

H.L.Collins* b Root	1	c Sutcliffe b Larwood	24
W.Bardsley not out	193	not out	
C.G.Macartney c Sutcliffe b Larwood	39	(6) c Root b Woolley	0
W.M.Woodfull c Strudwick b Root	13	(4) b Root	9
T.J.E.Andrews c and b Kilner	10	(2) c Sutcliffe b Root	0
J.M.Gregory b Larwood	7		
J.M.Taylor c Carr b Tate	9		
A.J.Richardson b Kilner	35		
J.Ryder c Strudwick b Tate	28	(7) not out	0
W.A.S.Oldfield† c Sutcliffe b Kilner	19	(5) c Sutcliffe b Tate	11
A.A.Mailey b Kilner	1		
Extras (B 12, LB 16)	28	(B 5, LB 12)	17
	383	**(5 wkts)**	**194**

1/11 2/84 3/127 4/158 5/187
6/208 7/282 8/338 9/379

1/2 2/125 3/163
4/187 5/194

Bowling: *First Innings*—Tate 50-12-111-2; Root 36-11-70-2; Kilner 34.5-11-70-4; Larwood 32-2-99-2; Woolley 2-0-5-0. *Second Innings*—Tate 25-11-38-1; Root 19-9-40-2; Kilner 22-2-49-0; Larwood 15-3-37-1; Woolley 7-1-13-1.

England

J.B.Hobbs c Richardson b Macartney	119
H.Sutcliffe b Richardson	82
F.E.Woolley lbw b Ryder	87
E.H.Hendren not out	127
A.P.F.Chapman not out	50
A.W.Carr*	
R.Kilner	
M.W.Tate	
H.Larwood	
C.F.Root	
H.Strudwick†	
Extras (B 4, LB 4, NB 1, W 1)	10
(3 wkts dec.)	**475**

1/182 2/219 3/359

Bowling: Gregory 30-3-125-0; Macartney 33-8-90-1; Mailey 30-6-96-0; Richardson 48-18-73-1; J.Ryder 25-3-70-1; Collins 2-0-11-0.

Umpires: L.C.Braund and A.E.Street

ENGLAND v AUSTRALIA 1926 (Third Test)

At Headingley, Leeds, 10, 12, 13 July
Result: Match drawn

Australia

W.Bardsley* c Sutcliffe b Tate	0
W.M.Woodfull b Tate	141
C.G.Macartney c Hendren b Macaulay	151
T.J.E.Andrews lbw b Kilner	4
A.J.Richardson run out	100
J.M.Taylor c Strudwick b Geary	4
J.M.Gregory c Geary b Kilner	26
J.Ryder b Tate	42
W.A.S.Oldfield† lbw b Tate	14
C.V.Grimmett c Sutcliffe b Geary	1
A.A.Mailey not out	1
Extras (B 2, LB 4, NB 4)	10
	494

1/0 2/235 3/249 4/378 5/385
6/423 7/452 8/485 9/492

Bowling: Tate 51-13-99-4; Macaulay 32-8-123-1; Kilner 37-6-106-2; Geary 41-5-130-2; Woolley 4-0-26-0.

England

J.B.Hobbs c Andrews b Mailey	49	b Grimmett	84
H.Sutcliffe c and b Grimmett	26	c Richardson	94
F.E.Woolley run out	27	c Macartney b Grimmett	20
E.H.Hendren c Andrews b Mailey	0	not out	4
A.W.Carr* lbw b Macartney	13		
A.P.F.Chapman b Macartney	15	(5) not out	42
R.Kilner c Ryder b Grimmett	36		
M.W.Tate st Oldfield b Grimmett	5		
G.Geary not out	35		
C.G.Macaulay c and b Grimmett	76		
H.Strudwick† c Gregory b Grimmett	1		
Extras (B 4, LB 6, NB 1)	11	(B 5, LB 1)	8
	294	**(3 wkts)**	**254**

1/59 2/104 3/108 4/110 5/131
6/140 7/175 8/182 9/290

1/156 2/208 3/210

Bowling: *First Innings*—Gregory 17-5-37-0; Macartney 31-13-51-2; Grimmett 39-11-88-5; Richardson 20-5-44-0; Mailey 21-4-63-2. *Second Innings*—Gregory 6-2-12-0; Macartney 4-1-13-0; Grimmett 29-10-59-2; Richardson 16-7-22-1; Mailey 18-2-80-0; Ryder 9-2-26-0; Andrews 4-0-36-0.

Umpires: H.R.Butt and W.Reeves

ENGLAND v AUSTRALIA 1926 (Fourth Test)

At Old Trafford, Manchester, 24, 26, 27 July

Result: Match drawn

Australia

W.M.Woodfull c Hendren b Root	117
W.Bardsley* c Tyldesley b Stevens	15
C.G.Macartney b Root	109
T.J.E.Andrews c sub (A.P.F.Chapman) b Stevens	8
W.H.Ponsford c and b Kilner	23
A.J.Richardson c Woolley b Stevens	0
J.Ryder c Strudwick b Root	3
J.M.Gregory c Kilner b Root	34
W.A.S.Oldfield† not out	12
C.V.Grimmett c Stevens b Tate	6
A.A.Mailey b Tate	1
Extras (B 2, LB 1, NB 3, W 1)	7
	335

1/29 2/221 3/252 4/256 5/257 6/266 7/300 8/317 9/329

Bowling: Tate 36.2-7-88-2; Root 52-27-84-4; Kilner 28-12-51-1; Stevens 32-3-86-3; Woolley 2-0-19-0.

England

J.B.Hobbs c Ryder b Grimmett	74
H.Sutcliffe c Oldfield b Mailey	20
G.E.Tyldesley c Oldfield b Macartney	81
F.E.Woolley c Ryder b Mailey	58
E.H.Hendren not out	32
G.T.S.Stevens c Bardsley b Mailey	24
R.Kilner not out	9
A.W.Carr*	
M.W.Tate	
C.F.Root	
H.Strudwick†	
Extras (B 4, LB 3)	7
(5 wkts)	305

1/58 2/135 3/225 4/253 5/272

Bowling: Gregory 11-4-17-0; Grimmett 38-9-85-1; Mailey 27-4-87-3; Ryder 15-3-46-0; Richardson 17-3-43-0; Macartney 8-5-7-1; Andrews 9-5-13-0.

Umpires: H.Chidgey and H.I.Young

ENGLAND v AUSTRALIA 1926 (Fifth Test)

At Kennington Oval, London, 14, 16, 17, 18 August

Result: England won by 289 runs

England

J.B.Hobbs b Mailey	37	b Gregory	100
H.Sutcliffe b Mailey	76	b Mailey	161
F.E.Woolley b Mailey	18	lbw b Richardson	27
E.H.Hendren b Gregory	8	c Oldfield b Grimmett	15
A.P.F.Chapman* st Oldfield b Mailey	49	b Richardson	19
G.T.S.Stevens c Andrews b Mailey	17	c Mailey b Grimmett	22
W.Rhodes c Oldfield b Mailey	28	lbw b Grimmett	14
G.Geary run out	9	c Oldfield b Gregory	1
M.W.Tate b Grimmett	23	not out	33
H.Larwood c Andrews b Grimmett	0	b Mailey	5
H.Strudwick† not out	4	c Andrews b Mailey	2
Extras (B 6, LB 5)	11	(B 19, LB 18)	37
	280		436

1/53 2/91 3/108 4/189 5/213 6/214 7/231 8/266 9/266

1/172 2/220 3/277 4/316 5/373 6/375 7/382 8/425 9/430

Bowling: First Innings—Gregory 15-4-31-1; Grimmett 33-12-74-2; Mailey 33.5-3-138-6; Macartney 7-4-16-0; Richardson 7-2-10-0. Second Innings—Gregory 18-1-58-2; Grimmett 55-17-108-3; Mailey 42.5-6-128-3; Macartney 26-16-24-0; Richardson 41-12-81-2.

Australia

W.M.Woodfull b Rhodes	35		c Geary b Larwood	0
W.Bardsley c Strudwick b Larwood	2	(4)	c Woolley b Rhodes	21
C.G.Macartney b Stevens	25		c Geary b Larwood	16
W.H.Ponsford run out	2	(2)	c Larwood b Rhodes	12
T.J.E.Andrews b Larwood	3	(6)	c Tate b Larwood	15
H.L.Collins* c Stevens b Larwood	61	(5)	c Woolley b Rhodes	4
A.J.Richardson c Geary b Rhodes	16	(8)	b Rhodes	4
J.M.Gregory c Stevens b Tate	73	(7)	c Sutcliffe b Tate	9
W.A.S.Oldfield† not out	33		b Stevens	23
C.V.Grimmett b Tate	35		not out	8
A.A.Mailey c Strudwick b Tate	0		b Geary	6
Extras (B 5, LB 12)	17		(LB 7)	7
	302			125

1/9 2/44 3/51 4/59 5/90 6/122 7/229 8/231 9/298

1/1 2/31 3/31 4/35 5/63 6/83 7/83 8/87 9/114

Bowling: First Innings—Tate 37.1-17-40-3; Larwood 34-11-82-3; Geary 27-8-43-0; Stevens 29-3-85-1; Rhodes 25-15-35-2. Second Innings—Tate 9-4-12-1; Larwood 14-3-34-3; Geary 6.3-2-15-1; Stevens 3-1-13-1; Rhodes 20-9-44-4.

Umpires: F.Chester and H.I.Young

AUSTRALIA v ENGLAND 1928-29 (First Test)
At Exhibition Ground, Brisbane, 30 November, 1, 3, 4, 5 December
Result: England won by 675 runs

England

J.B.Hobbs	run out	49	(2) not out	30
H.Sutcliffe	c Ponsford b Gregory	38	(1) c Duckworth b Larwood	2
C.P.Mead	lbw b Grimmett	8	c and b Larwood	15
W.R.Hammond	c Woodfull b Gregory	44	c Larwood b White	6
D.R.Jardine	c Woodfull b Ironmonger	35	absent ill	-
E.H.Hendren	c Ponsford b Ironmonger	169	(5) c Larwood b Tate	33
A.P.F.Chapman*	c Kelleway b Gregory	50	(6) c Chapman b White	18
M.W.Tate	c Ryder b Grimmett	26	(7) c Larwood b Tate	2
H.Larwood	lbw b Hendry	70	(8) c Chapman b White	7
J.C.White	lbw b Grimmett	14	(9) c Chapman b White	0
G.Duckworth†	not out	5	absent hurt	-
Extras	(LB 10, NB 3)	13	(NB 1)	2
		521		**122**

1/85 2/95 3/108 4/161 5/217 | 1/0 2/7 3/24 4/40 5/71
6/291 7/319 8/443 9/495 | 6/101 7/105 8/116 9/122

Bowling: *First Innings*—Gregory 41-3-142-3; Kelleway 34-9-77-0; Grimmett 40-2-167-3; Ironmonger 44.3-18-79-2; Ryder 6-2-23-0; Hendry 10-1-20-1. *Second Innings*—Hendry 27-6-79-0; Grimmett 44.1-9-131-6; Ironmonger 50-20-85-2; Ryder 14-3-43-0.

Australia

W.M.Woodfull	c Chapman b Larwood	0	lbw b Grimmett	11
W.H.Ponsford	b Larwood	2	c sub (R.K.Oxenham) b Ironmonger	32
A.F.Kippax	c and b Tate	16	lbw b Grimmett	73
H.S.T.L.Hendry	lbw b Larwood	30	c sub (F.C.Thompson) b Ironmonger	28
C.Kelleway	b Larwood	8	not out	65
J.Ryder*	c Jardine b Larwood	33	c Ponsford b Grimmett	45
D.G.Bradman	lbw b Tate	18	c Oldfield b Grimmett	27
W.A.S.Oldfield†	lbw b Tate	2	c Bradman b Grimmett	20
C.V.Grimmett	not out	7	c Ponsford b Grimmett	37
H.Ironmonger	b Larwood	4		
J.M.Gregory	absent hurt	-		
Extras	(B 1, LB 1)	2	(LB 3, NB 1)	4
		122	(8 wkts dec.)	**342**

1/6 2/33 3/46 4/47 5/49 | 1/25 2/69 3/117 4/165 5/228 6/263 7/285 8/342
6/62 7/66 8/66 |

Bowling: *First Innings*—Larwood 14.4-4-32-6; Tate 21-6-50-3; Hammond 15-5-38-0. *Second Innings*—Larwood 7-0-30-2; Tate 11-3-26-2; Hammond 1-0-2-0; White 6.3-2-7-4.

Umpires: D.A.Elder and G.A.Hele

AUSTRALIA v ENGLAND 1928-29 (Second Test)
At Sydney Cricket Ground, 14, 15, 17, 18, 19, 20 December
Result: England won by 8 wickets

Australia

W.M.Woodfull	lbw b Geary	68	run out	111
V.Y.Richardson	b Larwood	27	c Hendren b Tate	0
A.F.Kippax	b Geary	9	(4) lbw b Tate	10
W.H.Ponsford	retired hurt	5	absent hurt	-
H.S.T.L.Hendry	b Geary	37	(3) lbw b Tate	112
J.Ryder*	lbw b Geary	25	(5) c Chapman b Larwood	79
O.E.Nothling	b Larwood	8	(6) run out	44
W.A.S.Oldfield†	not out	41	(7) lbw b Tate	0
C.V.Grimmett	run out	9	(8) c Chapman b Geary	18
D.D.Blackie	b Geary	8	(9) not out	11
H.Ironmonger	c Duckworth b Larwood	1	(10) b Geary	0
Extras	(B 4, LB 9, W 2)	15	(B 5, LB 6, W 1)	12
		253		**397**

1/51 2/65 3/152 4/153 5/171 | 1/0 2/215 3/234 4/246 5/347
6/192 7/222 8/251 9/253 | 6/348 7/370 8/397 9/397

Bowling: *First Innings*—Larwood 26.2-4-77-3; Tate 21-9-29-0; White 38-10-79-0; Geary 18-5-35-5; Hammond 5-0-18-0. *Second Innings*—Larwood 35-5-105-1; Tate 46-14-99-4; Geary 31.4-11-55-2; White 30-5-83-0; Hammond 9-0-43-0.

England

J.B.Hobbs	c Oldfield b Grimmett	40	(1) b Hendry	8
H.Sutcliffe	c Hendry b Ironmonger	11	(2) c sub (D.G.Bradman) b Hendry	4
W.R.Hammond	b Ironmonger	251	(3) not out	2
D.R.Jardine	run out	28	(4) not out	2
E.H.Hendren	c Richardson b Blackie	74		
A.P.F.Chapman*	c Ryder b Blackie	20		
H.Larwood	c Ryder b Grimmett	43		
G.Geary	lbw b Blackie	66		
M.W.Tate	lbw b Blackie	25		
G.Duckworth†	not out	39		
J.C.White	st Oldfield b Hendry	29		
Extras	(B 2, LB 3, NB 1, W 4)	10		
		636	(2 wkts)	**16**

1/37 2/65 3/148 4/293 5/341 | 1/8 2/13
6/432 7/496 8/523 9/592 |

Bowling: *First Innings*—Nothling 42-15-60-0; Grimmett 64-14-191-2; Ironmonger 68-21-142-2; Blackie 59-10-148-4; Hendry 23.1-4-52-1; Ryder 11-3-22-0; Kippax 5-3-11-0. *Second Innings*—Nothling 4-0-12-0; Hendry 3-2-4-2.

Umpires: D.A.Elder and G.A.Hele

AUSTRALIA v ENGLAND 1928-29 (Third Test)
At Melbourne Cricket Ground, 29, 31 December, 1, 2, 3, 4, 5 January
Result: England won by 3 wickets

Australia

W.M.Woodfull c Jardine b Tate	7	c Duckworth b Tate	107
V.Y.Richardson c Duckworth b Larwood	3	b Larwood	5
H.S.T.L.Hendry c Jardine b Larwood	23	st Duckworth b White	12
A.F.Kippax c Jardine b Larwood	100	b Tate	41
J.Ryder* c Hendren b Tate	112	b Geary	5
D.G.Bradman b Hammond	79	c Duckworth b Geary	112
W.A.S.Oldfield† b Geary	3	b White	7
E.L.a'Beckett c Duckworth b White	41	b White	6
R.K.Oxenham b Geary	15	b White	39
C.V.Grimmett c Duckworth b Geary	5	not out	4
D.D.Blackie not out	2	b White	0
Extras (B 4, LB 3)	7	(B 6, LB 7)	13
	397		351

1/5 2/15 3/57 4/218 5/282 6/287 7/373 8/383 9/394
1/7 2/60 3/138 4/143 5/201 6/226 7/252 8/345 9/351

Bowling: *First Innings*—Larwood 37-3-127-3; Tate 46-17-87-2; Geary 31.5-4-83-3; Hammond 8-4-19-1; White 57-30-64-1; Jardine 1-0-10-0. *Second Innings*—Larwood 16-3-37-1; Tate 47-15-70-2; White 56.5-20-107-5; Geary 30-4-94-2; Hammond 16-6-30-0.

England

J.B.Hobbs c Oldfield b a'Beckett	20	lbw b Blackie	49
H.Sutcliffe b Blackie	58	lbw b Grimmett	135
W.R.Hammond c a'Beckett b Blackie	200	run out (4)	32
A.P.F.Chapman* b Blackie	24	c Woodfull b Ryder (6)	5
E.H.Hendren c a'Beckett b Hendry	19	b Oxenham	45
D.R.Jardine c and b Blackie	62	b Grimmett (3)	33
H.Larwood c and b Blackie	0		
G.Geary lbw b Grimmett	1	not out	4
M.W.Tate c Kippax b Grimmett	21	run out (7)	0
G.Duckworth† b Blackie	3	not out (9)	0
J.C.White not out	8		
Extras (B 1)	1	(B 15, LB 14)	29
	417	(7 wkts)	332

1/28 2/161 3/201 4/238 5/364 6/364 7/381 8/385 9/391
1/105 2/199 3/257 4/318 5/326 6/328 7/328

Bowling: *First Innings*—a'Beckett 37-7-92-1; Hendry 20-8-35-1; Grimmett 55-14-114-2; Oxenham 35-11-67-0; Blackie 44-13-94-6; Ryder 4-0-14-0. *Second Innings*—a'Beckett 22-5-39-0; Hendry 23-5-33-0; Blackie 39-11-75-1; Oxenham 28-10-44-1; Grimmett 42-12-96-2; Ryder 5.5-1-16-1.

Umpires: D.A.Elder and G.A.Hele

AUSTRALIA v ENGLAND 1928-29 (Fourth Test)
At Adelaide Oval, 1, 2, 4, 5, 6, 7, 8 February
Result: England won by 12 runs

England

J.B.Hobbs c Ryder b Hendry	74	c Oldfield b Hendry	1
H.Sutcliffe st Oldfield b Grimmett	64	c Oldfield b a'Beckett	17
W.R.Hammond not out	119	and b Ryder	177
D.R.Jardine lbw b Grimmett	1	c Woodfull b Oxenham	98
E.H.Hendren b Blackie	13	c Bradman b Blackie	11
A.P.F.Chapman* c a'Beckett b Ryder	39	c Woodfull b Blackie	0
G.Duckworth† c a'Beckett b Ryder	5	lbw b Oxenham (11)	1
H.Larwood b Hendry	3	lbw b Oxenham (7)	5
G.Geary run out	3	c and b Grimmett (8)	6
M.W.Tate b Grimmett	2	lbw b Oxenham (9)	47
J.C.White c Ryder b Grimmett	0	not out (10)	4
Extras (B 3, LB 7, W 1)	11	(B 6, LB 10)	16
	334		383

1/143 2/143 3/149 4/179 5/246 6/263 7/270 8/308 9/312
1/1 2/21 3/283 4/296 5/297 6/302 7/327 8/337 9/381

Bowling: *First Innings*—a'Beckett 31-8-44-0; Hendry 31-14-49-2; Grimmett 52.1-12-102-5; Oxenham 35-14-51-0; Blackie 29-6-57-1; Ryder 5-1-20-1. *Second Innings*—a'Beckett 27-9-41-1; Hendry 28-11-56-1; Oxenham 47.4-21-67-4; Blackie 39-11-70-2; Grimmett 52-15-117-1; Ryder 5-1-13-1; Kippax 2-0-3-0.

Australia

W.M.Woodfull c Duckworth b Tate	1	c Geary b White	30
A.Jackson lbw b White	164	c Duckworth b Geary	36
H.S.T.L.Hendry c Duckworth b Larwood	2	c Tate b White	5
A.F.Kippax b White	3	c Hendren b White	51
J.Ryder* lbw b White	63	c and b White	87
D.G.Bradman c Larwood b Tate	40	run out	58
E.L.a'Beckett hit wkt b White	36	c Hammond b White	21
R.K.Oxenham c Chapman b White	15	c Chapman b White	12
W.A.S.Oldfield† b Tate	32	not out	15
C.V.Grimmett b Tate	4	c Tate b White	9
D.D.Blackie not out	3	c Larwood b White	0
Extras (LB 5, W 1)	6	(B 9, LB 3)	12
	369		336

1/1 2/6 3/19 4/145 5/227 6/287 7/323 8/336 9/365
1/65 2/71 3/74 4/211 5/224 6/258 7/308 8/320 9/336

Bowling: *First Innings*—Larwood 37-6-92-1; Tate 42-10-77-4; White 60-16-130-5; Geary 12-3-32-0; Hammond 9-1-32-0. *Second Innings*—Larwood 20-4-60-0; Tate 37-9-75-0; White 64.5-21-126-8; Hammond 14-3-21-0; Geary 16-2-42-1.

Umpires: D.A.Elder and G.A.Hele

AUSTRALIA v ENGLAND 1928-29 (Fifth Test)

At Melbourne Cricket Ground, 8, 9, 11, 12, 13, 14, 15, 16 March

Result: Australia won by 5 wickets

England

J.B.Hobbs lbw b Ryder	142		c Fairfax b Grimmett	65
D.R.Jardine c Oldfield b Wall	19		c Oldfield b Wall	0
W.R.Hammond c Fairfax b Wall	38	(4)	c Ryder b Fairfax	16
G.E.Tyldesley c Hornibrook b Ryder	31	(5)	c Oldfield b Wall	21
G.Duckworth† c Fairfax b Hornibrook	12	(11)	lbw b Oxenham	9
E.H.Hendren c Hornibrook b Fairfax	95		b Grimmett	1
M.Leyland c Fairfax b Oxenham	137		not out	53
H.Larwood b Wall	4	(3)	b Wall	11
G.Geary b Hornibrook	4		b Wall	3
M.W.Tate c sub (E.L.a'Beckett) b Hornibrook	15	(8)	c Fairfax b Hornibrook	54
J.C.White* not out	9	(10)	c Oxenham b Wall	4
Extras (B 4, LB 6, NB 2, W 1)	13		(B 19, LB 1)	20
	519			**257**

1/64 2/146 3/235 4/240 5/261 6/401 7/409 8/428 9/470

1/1 2/19 3/75 4/119 5/123 6/131 7/212 8/217 9/231

Bowling: *First Innings*—Wall 49-8-123-3; Hornibrook 48-8-142-3; Grimmett 2.5-11-40-0; Fairfax 27-4-84-1; Ryder 18-5-29-2; Kippax 3-1-2-0. *Second Innings*—Wall 26-5-66-5; Hornibrook 19-5-51-1; Fairfax 7-0-20-1; Grimmett 24-7-66-2; Oxenham 10.3-1-34-1.

Australia

W.M.Woodfull c Geary b Larwood	102	(3)	b Hammond	35
A.Jackson run out	30	(4)	b Geary	46
A.F.Kippax c Duckworth b White	38	(5)	run out	28
J.Ryder* c Tate b Hammond	30	(6)	not out	57
D.G.Bradman c Tate b Geary	123	(7)	not out	37
A.G.Fairfax lbw b Geary	65			
R.K.Oxenham c Duckworth b Geary	6	(1)	b Hammond	48
W.A.S.Oldfield† c and b Geary	38			
C.V.Grimmett not out	9			
T.W.Wall c Duckworth b White	26	(2)	b Hammond	18
P.M.Hornibrook lbw b White	0			
Extras (B 6, LB 9, W 2)	17		(B 12, LB 6)	18
	491		(5 wkts)	**287**

1/54 2/143 3/203 4/203 5/386 6/399 7/409 8/420 9/432

1/51 2/80 3/129 4/158 5/204

Bowling: *First Innings*—Larwood 34-7-83-1; Tate 62-26-108-0; Geary 81-36-105-5; White 75.3-22-136-2; Hammond 16-3-31-1; Leyland 3-0-11-0. *Second Innings*—Larwood 32.1-5-81-0; Tate 38-13-76-0; White 18-8-28-0; Geary 20-5-31-1; Hammond 26-8-53-3.

Umpires: G.A.Hele and A.C.Jones

ENGLAND v AUSTRALIA 1930 (First Test)

At Trent Bridge, Nottingham, 13, 14, 16, 17 June

Result: England won by 93 runs

England

J.B.Hobbs c Richardson b McCabe	78		st Oldfield b Grimmett	74
H.Sutcliffe c Hornibrook b Fairfax	29		retired hurt	58
W.R.Hammond lbw b Grimmett	8		lbw b Grimmett	4
F.E.Woolley st Oldfield b Grimmett	0		b Wall	5
E.H.Hendren b Grimmett	5		c Richardson b Wall	72
A.P.F.Chapman* c Ponsford b Hornibrook	52		b Wall	29
H.Leyland b Grimmett	18	(9)	b Grimmett	7
R.W.V.Robins not out	50		b McCabe	4
M.W.Tate b Grimmett	13	(7)	c Kippax b Grimmett	24
R.K.Tyldesley c Fairfax b Wall	1		b Grimmett	5
G.Duckworth† lbw b Fairfax	4		not out	14
Extras (B 4, LB 7, NB 1)	12		(B 5, LB 1)	6
	270			**302**

1/53 2/63 3/63 4/71 5/153 6/188 7/218 8/241 9/242

1/125 2/137 3/147 4/211 5/250 6/260 7/283 8/283 9/302

Bowling: *First Innings*—Wall 17-4-47-1; Fairfax 21.4-5-51-2; Grimmett 32-6-107-5; Hornibrook 12-3-30-1; McCabe 7-3-23-1. *Second Innings*—Wall 26-4-67-3; Fairfax 15-4-58-0; Grimmett 30-4-94-5; Hornibrook 11-4-35-0; McCabe 14-3-42-1.

Australia

W.M.Woodfull* c Chapman b Tate	2		c Chapman b Larwood	4
W.H.Ponsford b Tate	3		b Tate	39
A.G.Fairfax c Hobbs b Robins	14	(7)	c Robins b Tate	14
D.G.Bradman b Tate	8	(3)	b Robins	131
A.F.Kippax not out	64	(4)	c Hammond b Robins	23
S.J.McCabe c Hammond b Robins	4	(5)	c sub (S.H.Copley) b Tate	49
V.Y.Richardson b Tyldesley	37	(6)	lbw b Tyldesley	29
W.A.S.Oldfield† c and b Robins	4		c Hammond b Tyldesley	11
C.V.Grimmett st Oldfield b Robins	0		c Hammond b Tyldesley	5
P.M.Hornibrook lbw b Larwood	0		c Duckworth b Robins	5
T.W.Wall b Tyldesley	0		not out	8
Extras (B 4, LB 4)	8		(B 17, LB 5)	22
	144			**335**

1/4 2/6 3/16 4/57 5/61 6/105 7/134 8/140 9/141

1/12 2/93 3/152 4/229 5/267 6/296 7/316 8/322 9/324

Bowling: *First Innings*—Larwood 15-8-12-1; Tate 19-8-20-3; Tyldesley 21-8-53-2; Robins 17-4-51-4. *Second Innings*—Larwood 5-1-9-1; Tate 50-20-69-3; Tyldesley 35-10-77-3; Robins 17.2-1-81-3; Hammond 29-5-74-0; Woolley 3-1-3-0.

Umpires: J.Hardstaff, sr and W.R.Parry

ENGLAND v AUSTRALIA 1930 (Second Test)

At Lord's, London, 27, 28, 30 June, 1 July
Result: Australia won by 7 wickets

England

Batsman	First Innings		Second Innings	
J.B.Hobbs	c Oldfield b Fairfax	1	b Grimmett	19
F.E.Woolley	c Wall b Fairfax	41	hit wkt b Grimmett	28
W.R.Hammond	b Grimmett	38	c Fairfax b Grimmett	32
K.S.Duleepsinhji	c Bradman b Grimmett	173	c Oldfield b Hornibrook	48
E.H.Hendren	c McCabe b Fairfax	48	c Richardson b Grimmett	9
A.P.F.Chapman*	c Oldfield b Wall	11	c Oldfield b Fairfax	121
G.O.B.Allen	b Fairfax	3	lbw b Grimmett	57
M.W.Tate	c McCabe b Wall	54	c Ponsford b Grimmett	10
R.W.V.Robins	c Oldfield b Hornibrook	5	not out	11
J.C.White	not out	23	run out	10
G.Duckworth†	c Oldfield b Wall	18	lbw b Fairfax	0
Extras	(B 2, LB 7, NB 1)	10	(B 16, LB 13, W 1)	30
		425		375

1/13 2/53 3/105 4/209 5/236
6/239 7/337 8/363 9/387

1/45 2/58 3/129 4/141 5/147
6/272 7/329 8/354 9/372

Bowling: *First Innings*—Wall 29.4-2-118-3; Fairfax 31-6-101-4; Grimmett 33-4-105-2; Hornibrook 26-6-62-1; McCabe 9-1-29-0. *Second Innings*—Wall 25-2-80-0; Fairfax 12.4-2-37-2; Grimmett 53-13-167-6; Hornibrook 22-6-49-1; McCabe 3-1-11-0; Bradman 1-0-1-0.

Australia

Batsman	First Innings		Second Innings	
W.M.Woodfull*	st Duckworth b Robins	155	not out	26
W.H.Ponsford	c Hammond b White	81	b Robins	14
D.G.Bradman	c Chapman b White	254	c Chapman b Tate	1
A.F.Kippax	b White	83	c Duckworth b Robins	3
S.J.McCabe	c Woolley b Hammond	44	not out	25
V.Y.Richardson	c Hobbs b Tate	30		
W.A.S.Oldfield†	not out	43		
A.G.Fairfax	not out	20		
C.V.Grimmett				
P.M.Hornibrook				
T.W.Wall				
Extras	(B 6, LB 8, W 5)	19	(B 1, LB 2)	3
	(6 wkts dec.)	729	(3 wkts)	72

1/162 2/393 3/585 4/588
5/643 6/672

1/16 2/17 3/22

Bowling: *First Innings*—Allen 34-7-115-0; Tate 64-16-148-1; White 51-7-158-3; Robins 42-1-172-1; Hammond 35-8-82-1; Woolley 6-0-35-0. *Second Innings*—Tate 13-6-21-1; White 2-0-8-0; Robins 9-1-34-2; Hammond 4.2-1-6-0.

Umpires: F.Chester and T.W.Oates

ENGLAND v AUSTRALIA 1930 (Third Test)

At Headingley, Leeds, 11, 12, 14, 15 July
Result: Match drawn

Australia

W.M.Woodfull*	b Hammond	50
A.Jackson	c Larwood b Tate	1
D.G.Bradman	c Duckworth b Tate	334
A.F.Kippax	c Chapman b Tate	77
S.J.McCabe	b Larwood	30
V.Y.Richardson	c Larwood b Tate	1
E.L.a'Beckett	c Chapman b Geary	29
W.A.S.Oldfield†	c Hobbs b Tate	2
C.V.Grimmett	c Duckworth b Tyldesley	24
T.W.Wall	b Tyldesley	3
P.M.Hornibrook	not out	1
Extras	(B 5, LB 8, W 1)	14
		566

1/2 2/194 3/423 4/486 5/491
6/508 7/519 8/544 9/565

Bowling: Larwood 33-5-139-1; Tate 39-9-124-5; Geary 35-10-95-1; Tyldesley 33-5-104-2; Hammond 17-3-46-1; Leyland 11-0-44-0.

England

Batsman	First Innings		Second Innings	
J.B.Hobbs	c a'Beckett b Grimmett	29	run out	13
H.Sutcliffe	c Hornibrook b Grimmett	32	not out	28
W.R.Hammond	c Oldfield b McCabe	113	c Oldfield b Grimmett	35
K.S.Duleepsinhji	b Hornibrook	35	c Grimmett b Hornibrook	10
M.Leyland	c Kippax b Wall	44	not out	1
G.Geary	run out	0		
G.Duckworth†	c Oldfield b a'Beckett	33		
A.P.F.Chapman*	b Grimmett	45		
M.W.Tate	c Jackson b Grimmett	22		
H.Larwood	not out	10		
R.K.Tyldesley	c Hornibrook b Grimmett	6		
Extras	(B 9, LB 10, NB 3)	22	(LB 8)	8
		391	(3 wkts)	95

1/53 2/64 3/123 4/206 5/206
6/289 7/319 8/370 9/375

1/24 2/72 3/74

Bowling: *First Innings*—Wall 40-12-70-1; a'Beckett 28-8-47-1; Grimmett 56.2-16-135-5; Hornibrook 41-7-94-1; McCabe 10-4-23-1. *Second Innings*—Wall 10-3-20-0; a'Beckett 11-4-19-0; Grimmett 17-3-33-1; Hornibrook 11.5-5-14-1; McCabe 2-1-1-0.

Umpires: W.Bestwick and T.W.Oates

ENGLAND v AUSTRALIA 1930 (Fourth Test)

At Old Trafford, Manchester, 25, 26, 28, 29 (no play) July
Result: Match drawn

Australia

W.M.Woodfull*	c Duckworth b Tate	54
W.H.Ponsford	b Hammond	83
D.G.Bradman	c Duleepsinhji b Peebles	14
A.F.Kippax	c Chapman b Nichols	51
S.J.McCabe	lbw b Peebles	4
V.Y.Richardson	b Hammond	1
A.G.Fairfax	lbw b Goddard	49
W.A.S.Oldfield†	b Nichols	2
C.V.Grimmett	c Sutcliffe b Peebles	50
P.M.Hornibrook	c Duleepsinhji b Goddard	3
T.W.Wall	not out	1
Extras	(B 23, LB 3, NB 7)	33
		345

1/106 2/138 3/184 4/189 5/190
6/239 7/243 8/330 9/338

Bowling: Nichols 21-5-33-2; Tate 30-11-39-1; Goddard 32.1-14-49-2; Peebles 55-9-150-3; Leyland 8-2-17-0; Hammond 21-6-24-2.

England

J.B.Hobbs	c Oldfield b Wall	31
H.Sutcliffe	c Bradman b Wall	74
W.R.Hammond	b Wall	3
K.S.Duleepsinhji	c Hornibrook b McCabe	54
M.Leyland	b McCabe	35
A.P.F.Chapman*	c Grimmett b Hornibrook	1
M.W.Tate	c Ponsford b McCabe	15
M.S.Nichols	not out	7
I.A.R.Peebles	c Richardson b McCabe	6
G.Duckworth†	not out	0
T.W.J.Goddard		
Extras	(B 13, LB 12)	25
		(8 wkts) 251

1/108 2/115 3/119 4/192 5/199
6/222 7/237 8/247

Bowling: Wall 33-9-70-3; Fairfax 13-5-15-0; Grimmett 19-2-59-0; Hornibrook 26-9-41-1; McCabe 17-3-41-4.

Umpires: F.Chester and J.Hardstaff, sr

ENGLAND v AUSTRALIA 1930 (Fifth Test)

At Kennington Oval, London, 16, 18, 19, 20, 21 (no play), 22 August
Result: Australia won by an innings and 39 runs

England

J.B.Hobbs	c Kippax b Wall	47	b Fairfax	9
H.Sutcliffe	c Oldfield b Fairfax	161	c Fairfax b Hornibrook	54
W.W.Whysall	lbw b Wall	13	c Hornibrook b Grimmett	10
K.S.Duleepsinhji	c Fairfax b Grimmett	50	c Kippax b Hornibrook	46
W.R.Hammond	b McCabe	13	c Fairfax b Hornibrook	60
M.Leyland	b Grimmett	3	b Hornibrook	20
R.E.S.Wyatt*	c Oldfield b Fairfax	64	b Hornibrook	7
M.W.Tate	st Oldfield b Grimmett	10	run out	0
H.Larwood	lbw b Grimmett	19	c McCabe b Hornibrook	9
G.Duckworth†	b Fairfax	3	b Hornibrook	15
I.A.R.Peebles	not out	3	not out	0
Extras	(LB 17, NB 2)	19	(B 16, LB 3, NB 2)	21
		405		**251**

1/68 2/97 3/162 4/190 5/197
6/367 7/379 8/379 9/391

1/17 2/37 3/118 4/135 5/189
6/207 7/208 8/220 9/248

Bowling: *First Innings*—Wall 37-6-96-2; Fairfax 31-9-52-3; Grimmett 66.2-18-135-4; McCabe 22-4-49-1; Hornibrook 15-1-54-0. *Second Innings*—Wall 12-2-5-0; Fairfax 10-3-21-1; Grimmett 43-12-90-1; McCabe 3-1-2-0; Hornibrook 31.2-9-92-7.

Australia

W.M.Woodfull*	c Duckworth b Peebles	54
W.H.Ponsford	b Peebles	110
D.G.Bradman	c Duckworth b Larwood	232
A.F.Kippax	c Wyatt b Peebles	28
A.Jackson	c Sutcliffe Wyatt	73
S.J.McCabe	c Duckworth b Hammond	54
A.G.Fairfax	not out	53
W.A.S.Oldfield†	c Larwood b Peebles	34
C.V.Grimmett	lbw b Peebles	6
T.W.Wall	lbw b Peebles	0
P.M.Hornibrook	c Duckworth b Tate	7
Extras	(B 22, LB 18, NB 4)	44
		695

1/159 2/190 3/263 4/506 5/570
6/594 7/670 8/684 9/684

Bowling: Larwood 48-6-132-1; Tate 65.1-12-153-1; Peebles 71-8-204-6; Wyatt 14-1-58-1; Hammond 42-12-70-1; Leyland 16-7-34-0

Umpires: J.Hardstaff, sr and W.R.Parry

AUSTRALIA v WEST INDIES 1930-31 (First Test)

At Adelaide Oval, 12, 13, 15, 16 December
Result: Australia won by 10 wickets

West Indies

C.A.Roach	st Oldfield b Hurwood	56	b Hurwood	9
L.S.Birkett	c and b Grimmett	27	st Oldfield b Grimmett	64
G.A.Headley	c Wall b Grimmett	0	st Oldfield b Grimmett	11
F.R.Martin	b Grimmett	39	run out	3
L.N.Constantine	c Wall b Grimmett	1	b Grimmett	14
G.C.Grant*	not out	53	not out	71
E.L.Bartlett	lbw b Grimmett	84	c Grimmett b Hurwood	11
I.Barrow†	c Bradman b Grimmett	12	lbw b Bradman	27
G.N.Francis	lbw b Hurwood	5	b Hurwood	3
O.C.Scott	c Fairfax b Grimmett	3	c Kippax b Hurwood	8
H.C.Griffith	b Hurwood	1	st Oldfield b Grimmett	10
Extras	(B 6, LB 8, NB 1)	15	(B 16, LB 2)	18
		296		249

1/58 2/58 3/118 4/123 5/131
6/245 7/269 8/290 9/295

1/15 2/47 3/52 4/74 5/115
6/138 7/203 8/208 9/220

Bowling: First Innings—Wall 16-0-64-0; Fairfax 11-1-36-0; Grimmett 48-19-87-7; Hurwood 36.1-14-55-3; McCabe 12-3-32-0; Bradman 4-0-7-0. Second Innings—Wall 10-1-20-0; Hurwood 34-11-86-4; Grimmett 38-7-96-4; McCabe 8-2-15-0; Bradman 5-1-8-1; Fairfax 3-2-6-0.

Australia

W.H.Ponsford	c Birkett b Francis	24	not out	92
A.Jackson	c Barrow b Francis	31	not out	70
D.G.Bradman	c Grant b Griffith	4		
A.F.Kippax	c Barrow b Griffith	146		
S.J.McCabe	c and b Constantine	90		
W.M.Woodfull*	run out	6		
A.G.Fairfax	not out	41		
W.A.S.Oldfield†	c Francis b Scott	15		
C.V.Grimmett	c Barrow b Scott	0		
A.Hurwood	c Martin b Scott	0		
T.W.Wall	lbw b Scott	0		
Extras	(B 2, LB 10, NB 7)	19	(B 8, NB 1, W 1)	10
		376	(0 wkts)	172

1/56 2/59 3/64 4/246 5/269
6/341 7/374 8/374 9/374

Bowling: First Innings—Francis 18-7-43-2; Constantine 22-0-89-1; Griffith 28-4-69-2; Martin 29-3-73-0; Scott 20.5-2-83-4. Second Innings—Francis 10-1-30-0; Griffith 10-1-20-0; Martin 11-0-28-0; Constantine 9.3-3-27-0; Scott 13-0-55-0; Birkett 2-0-2-0.

Umpires: G.A.Hele and A.G.Jenkins

AUSTRALIA v WEST INDIES 1930-31 (Second Test)

At Sydney Cricket Ground, 1, 2 (no play), 3, 5 January
Result: Australia won by an innings and 172 runs

Australia

W.H.Ponsford	b Scott	183
A.Jackson	c Francis b Griffith	8
D.G.Bradman	c Barrow b Francis	25
A.F.Kippax	c Bartlett b Griffith	10
S.J.McCabe	lbw b Scott	31
W.M.Woodfull*	c Barrow b Constantine	58
A.G.Fairfax	c Constantine b Francis	15
W.A.S.Oldfield†	run out	0
C.V.Grimmett	b Scott	12
A.Hurwood	c Martin b Scott	5
H.Ironmonger	not out	3
Extras	(B 6, LB 5, NB 3, W 5)	19
		369

1/12 2/52 3/69 4/140 5/323
6/341 7/344 8/361 9/364

Bowling: Francis 27-3-70-2; Constantine 18-2-56-1; Griffith 28-4-57-2; Martin 18-1-60-0; Scott 15.4-0-66-4; Birkett 10-1-41-0.

West Indies

C.A.Roach	run out	7	c Kippax b McCabe	25
L.S.Birkett	c Hurwood b Fairfax	3	c McCabe b Hurwood	8
G.A.Headley	b Fairfax	14	c Jackson b Hurwood	2
F.R.Martin	lbw b Grimmett	10	c McCabe b Hurwood	0
G.C.Grant*	c Hurwood b Ironmonger	6	not out	15
L.N.Constantine	c Bradman b Grimmett	12	b Hurwood	8
I.Barrow†	c Jackson b Fairfax	17	c McCabe b Ironmonger	10
G.N.Francis	b Grimmett	8	c Oldfield b Ironmonger	0
O.C.Scott	not out	15	c Woodfull b Ironmonger	17
H.C.Griffith	c Kippax b Grimmett	8	lbw b Grimmett	0
E.L.Bartlett	absent hurt	-	absent hurt	-
Extras	(B 6, NB 1)	7	(B 1, LB 2, NB 1, W 1)	5
		107		90

1/3 2/26 3/36 4/36 5/57
6/63 7/80 8/88 9/107

1/26 2/32 3/32 4/42 5/53
6/67 7/67 8/90 9/90

Bowling: First Innings—Fairfax 13-4-19-3; Hurwood 5-1-7-0; Grimmett 19.1-3-54-4; Ironmonger 13-3-20-1. Second Innings—Fairfax 5-1-21-0; Hurwood 11-2-22-4; McCabe 7-0-20-1; Ironmonger 4-1-13-3; Grimmett 3.3-1-9-1.

Umpires: E.G.Borwick and W.G.French

AUSTRALIA v WEST INDIES 1930-31 (Third Test)

At Exhibition Ground, Brisbane, 16, 17, 19, 20 January
Result: Australia won by an innings and 217 runs

Australia

Batsman		Runs
W.H.Ponsford	c Birkett b Francis	109
A.Jackson	lbw b Francis	0
D.G.Bradman	c Grant b Constantine	223
A.F.Kippax	b Birkett	84
S.J.McCabe	c Constantine b Griffith	8
W.M.Woodfull*	c Barrow b Griffith	17
A.G.Fairfax	c Sealy b Scott	9
R.K.Oxenham	lbw b Griffith	48
W.A.S.Oldfield†	not out	38
C.V.Grimmett	c Constantine b Francis	4
H.Ironmonger	c Roach b Griffith	2
Extras	(B 2, LB 7, NB 7)	16
		558

1/1 2/230 3/423 4/431 5/441 6/462 7/468 8/543 9/551

Bowling: Francis 26-4-76-3; Constantine 26-2-74-1; Griffith 33-4-133-4; Scott 24-0-125-1; Martin 27-3-85-0; Sealy 3-0-32-0; Birkett 7-0-16-1; Grant 1-0-1-0.

West Indies

Batsman	First Innings	R	Second Innings	R
C.A.Roach	lbw b Oxenham	4	b McCabe	1
F.R.Martin	lbw b Grimmett	21	lbw b Oxenham	11
G.A.Headley	not out	102	c Oldfield b Ironmonger	28
J.E.D.Sealy	c McCabe b Ironmonger	3	(9) not out	16
G.C.Grant*	c McCabe b Grimmett	8	(4) run out	10
L.N.Constantine	c Fairfax b Ironmonger	9	(5) lbw b Oxenham	7
L.S.Birkett	lbw b Oxenham	8	(6) b Grimmett	13
I.Barrow†	st Oldfield b Grimmett	19	(7) st Oldfield b Grimmett	17
O.C.Scott	lbw b Grimmett	0	(8) lbw b Grimmett	15
G.N.Francis	b Oxenham	8	c Oldfield b Grimmett	7
H.C.Griffith	lbw b Grimmett	8	c Bradman b Grimmett	12
Extras	(B 1, LB 2)	3	(B 5, LB 4, NB 2)	11
		193		**148**

1/5 2/36 3/41 4/60 5/94
6/116 7/159 8/162 9/182

1/13 2/29 3/47 4/58 5/72
6/82 7/94 8/112 9/128

Bowling: *First Innings*—Fairfax 7-2-13-0; Oxenham 30-15-39-4; Ironmonger 26-15-43-2; Grimmett 41.3-9-95-4. *Second Innings*—Fairfax 6-2-6-0; McCabe 7-1-16-1; Oxenham 18-5-37-2; Ironmonger 15-8-29-1; Grimmett 14.3-4-49-5.

Umpires: J.P.Orr and A.E.Wyeth

AUSTRALIA v WEST INDIES 1930-31 (Fourth Test)

At Melbourne Cricket Ground, 13, 14 February
Result: Australia won by an innings and 122 runs

West Indies

Batsman	First Innings	R	Second Innings	R
C.A.Roach	c Kippax b Grimmett	20	lbw b Fairfax	7
F.R.Martin	lbw b Ironmonger	17	(6) c Oldfield b Fairfax	10
G.A.Headley	c Jackson b Ironmonger	33	c Fairfax b Ironmonger	11
L.S.Birkett	c McCabe b Ironmonger	9	c Jackson b Ironmonger	13
E.L.Bartlett	st Oldfield b Ironmonger	0	(7) b Fairfax	6
G.C.Grant*	c Oldfield b Ironmonger	0	(5) c McCabe b Ironmonger	3
L.N.Constantine	c Jackson b Grimmett	7	(2) c Kippax b Fairfax	10
I.Barrow†	c Fairfax b Ironmonger	11	c Oxenham b Ironmonger	13
O.C.Scott	run out	0	not out	20
G.N.Francis	not out	0	(11) c Jackson b Grimmett	0
H.C.Griffith	c Fairfax b Ironmonger	0	(10) b Grimmett	4
Extras	(NB 2)	2	(B 3, LB 6, NB 1)	10
		99		**107**

1/32 2/51 3/53 4/81 5/81
6/88 7/88 8/88 9/99

1/8 2/32 3/36 4/49 5/60
6/60 7/67 8/92 9/97

Bowling: *First Innings*—Fairfax 5-0-14-0; Oxenham 6-1-14-0; Ironmonger 20-7-23-7; Grimmett 19-7-46-2. *Second Innings*—Fairfax 14-2-31-4; Ironmonger 17-4-56-4; Grimmett 4.4-0-10-2.

Australia

Batsman		Runs
W.M.Woodfull*	run out	83
W.H.Ponsford	st Barrow b Constantine	24
D.G.Bradman	c Roach b Martin	152
A.Jackson	c Birkett b Constantine	15
S.J.McCabe	run out	2
A.G.Fairfax	c Birkett b Martin	16
A.F.Kippax	b Martin	24
R.K.Oxenham	c Constantine b Griffith	0
W.A.S.Oldfield†	not out	1
C.V.Grimmett		
H.Ironmonger		
Extras	(B 7, LB 3, NB 1)	11
	(8 wkts dec.)	**328**

1/50 2/206 3/265 4/275 5/286
6/325 7/326 8/328

Bowling: Francis 13-0-51-0; Griffith 8-1-33-1; Scott 11-0-47-0; Constantine 25-4-83-2; Martin 30.2-3-91-3; Birkett 2-0-12-0.

Umpires: A.N.Barlow and J.Richards

AUSTRALIA v WEST INDIES 1930-31 (Fifth Test)

At Sydney Cricket Ground, 27, 28 February, 2, 3 (no play), 4 March
Result: West Indies won by 30 runs

West Indies

Batsman	1st Innings		Runs	2nd Innings		Runs
F.R.Martin	not out		123	(2) c McCabe b Grimmett		20
C.A.Roach	lbw b Grimmett		31	(1) c Oldfield b Ironmonger		34
G.A.Headley	lbw b McCabe		105	b Oxenham		30
G.C.Grant*	c McCabe b Ironmonger		62	not out		27
J.E.D.Sealy	c Kippax b Grimmett		4	run out		7
L.N.Constantine	c McCabe b Ironmonger		0	c Bradman b Ironmonger		4
E.L.Bartlett	b Grimmett		1	not out		0
I.Barrow†	not out		7			
O.C.Scott						
G.N.Francis						
H.C.Griffith			2			
Extras	(B 6, LB 5, NB 6, W 1)		18	(B 1, LB 1)		2
			350			124

1/70 2/222 3/332 4/337 5/338 (6 wkts dec.) 350
6/341

1/46 2/66 3/103 (5 wkts dec.) 124
4/113 5/124

Bowling: *First Innings*—Fairfax 21-2-60-0; Oxenham 24-10-51-0; Ironmonger 42-16-95-2; Grimmett 33-7-100-3; McCabe 15-5-26-1. *Second Innings*—McCabe 7-2-17-0; Oxenham 10-4-14-1; Grimmett 18-4-47-1; Ironmonger 16-7-44-2.

Australia

Batsman	1st Innings		Runs	2nd Innings		Runs
W.M.Woodfull*	c Constantine b Martin		22	c Constantine b Martin		18
W.H.Ponsford	c Bartlett b Francis		7	c Constantine b Martin		28
D.G.Bradman	c Francis b Martin		43	b Griffith		0
A.F.Kippax	c Sealy b Constantine		3	c Roach b Constantine		10
K.E.Rigg	c Barrow b Francis		14	c Grant b Martin		16
S.J.McCabe	c Headley b Francis		21	(6) c Grant b Constantine		44
A.G.Fairfax	st Barrow b Scott		54	(8) not out		60
R.K.Oxenham	c Barrow b Francis		0	(9) lbw b Scott		14
W.A.S.Oldfield†	run out		36	(5) lbw b Griffith		0
C.V.Grimmett	not out		15	c Constantine b Griffith		12
H.Ironmonger	b Griffith		0	run out		4
Extras	(B 1, LB 7)		8	(B 3, LB 7, NB 2, W 2)		14
			224			220

1/7 2/66 3/69 4/89 5/89
6/130 7/134 8/196 9/215

1/49 2/49 3/53 4/53 5/65
6/76 7/155 8/180 9/214

Bowling: *First Innings*—Francis 19-6-48-4; Griffith 13.2-3-31-1; Martin 27-3-67-2; Constantine 10-2-28-1; Scott 10-1-42-1. *Second Innings*—Francis 16-2-32-0; Constantine 17-2-50-2; Martin 18-4-44-2; Griffith 13.3-3-50-4; Scott 11-0-30-1.

Umpires: H.J.Armstrong and W.G.French

AUSTRALIA v SOUTH AFRICA 1931-32 (First Test)

At Woolloongabba, Brisbane, 27, 28, 30 (no play) November, 1 (no play), 2, 3 December
Result: Australia won by an innings and 163 runs

Australia

Batsman	Dismissal	Runs
W.M.Woodfull*	lbw b Vincent	76
W.H.Ponsford	c Mitchell b Bell	19
D.G.Bradman	lbw b Vincent	226
A.F.Kippax	c Cameron b Vincent	1
S.J.McCabe	c Vincent b Morkel	27
H.C.Nitschke	c Cameron b Bell	6
R.K.Oxenham	b Bell	1
W.A.S.Oldfield†	not out	56
C.V.Grimmett	b Bell	14
T.W.Wall	lbw b Quinn	14
H.Ironmonger	b Quinn	2
Extras	(B 5, LB 1, NB 1, W 1)	8
		450

1/32 2/195 3/211 4/292 5/316
6/320 7/380 8/407 9/446

Bowling: Bell 42-5-120-4; Morkel 13-1-57-1; Quinn 38.3-6-113-2; Vincent 34-0-100-3; McMillan 10-0-52-0.

South Africa

Batsman	1st Innings	Runs	2nd Innings		Runs
J.A.J.Christy	b Wall	24	c McCabe b Ironmonger		15
S.H.Curnow	b Ironmonger	11	b Grimmett		8
B.Mitchell	run out	58	b Wall		0
H.B.Cameron*†	st Oldfield b Grimmett	4	b Ironmonger		21
H.W.Taylor	b Wall	41	c Oxenham b Ironmonger		47
E.L.Dalton	c and b Ironmonger	11	b Wall		6
Q.McMillan	c McCabe b Ironmonger	0	c Nitschke b Wall	(8)	0
D.P.B.Morkel	c McCabe b Ironmonger	3	b Wall	(7)	5
C.L.Vincent	c Nitschke b Grimmett	10	c sub (K.E.Rigg) b Wall		1
N.A.Quinn	c sub (K.E.Rigg) b Ironmonger	1	c McCabe b Ironmonger		0
A.J.Bell	not out	1	not out		0
Extras	(B 2, LB 4)	6	(B 6, LB 5, NB 3)		14
		170			117

1/25 2/44 3/49 4/129 5/140
6/140 7/152 8/157 9/168

1/16 2/29 3/34 4/78 5/97
6/111 7/111 8/117 9/117

Bowling: *First Innings*—Wall 28-14-39-2; McCabe 11-4-16-0; Grimmett 41.1-21-49-2; Ironmonger 47-29-42-5; Oxenham 11-5-18-0. *Second Innings*—Wall 15.1-7-14-5; Ironmonger 30-16-44-4; Grimmett 15-3-45-1.

Umpires: E.G.Borwick and G.A.Hele

AUSTRALIA v SOUTH AFRICA 1931-32 (Second Test)

At Sydney Cricket Ground, 18, 19, 21 December
Result: Australia won by an innings and 155 runs

South Africa

J.A.J.Christy c Nitschke b Grimmett	14	c Woodfull b Ironmonger	41
B.Mitchell b McCabe	1	c Oldfield b Wall	24
D.P.B.Morkel st Oldfield b Grimmett	20	lbw b Grimmett	17
H.B.Cameron*† b Wall	11	b Wall	0
H.W.Taylor c Lee b Grimmett	7	c Grimmett b Ironmonger	6
K.G.Viljoen b Ironmonger	37	b Grimmett	0
E.L.Dalton b Grimmett	21	c Bradman b Ironmonger	14
C.L.Vincent not out	31	c Ponsford b Grimmett	35
L.S.Brown b McCabe	2	c Wall b Lee	8
N.A.Quinn lbw b McCabe	5	st Oldfield b Grimmett	1
A.J.Bell b McCabe	0	not out	1
Extras (LB 3, W 1)	4	(B 5, LB 8, NB 1)	14
	153		**161**

1/6 2/31 3/36 4/54 5/62
6/91 7/136 8/143 9/153

1/70 2/89 3/89 4/100 5/135
6/100 7/122 8/144 9/160

Bowling: *First Innings*—Wall 18-4-46-1; McCabe 12-5-13-4; Grimmett 24-12-28-4; Ironmonger 12-1-38-1; Lee 7-1-24-0. *Second Innings*—Wall 18-5-31-2; McCabe 3-0-25-0; Grimmett 20.3-7-44-4; Ironmonger 19-10-22-3; Lee 13-4-25-1.

Australia

W.M.Woodfull* c Mitchell b Vincent	58
W.H.Ponsford b Quinn	5
K.E.Rigg b Bell	127
D.G.Bradman c Viljoen b Morkel	112
S.J.McCabe c Christy b Vincent	79
H.C.Nitschke b Bell	47
P.K.Lee c Cameron b Brown	0
W.A.S.Oldfield† c Cameron b Bell	8
C.V.Grimmett not out	9
T.W.Wall c Morkel b Bell	6
H.Ironmonger c Cameron b Bell	0
Extras (B 5, LB 12, W 1)	18
	469

1/6 2/143 3/254 4/347 5/432
6/433 7/444 8/457 9/469

Bowling: Bell 46.5-6-140-5; Quinn 42-10-95-1; Brown 29-3-100-1; Vincent 24-5-75-2; Morkel 12-2-33-1; Mitchell 1-0-8-0.

Umpires: E.G.Borwick and G.A.Hele

AUSTRALIA v SOUTH AFRICA 1931-32 (Third Test)

At Melbourne Cricket Ground, 31 December, 1, 2, 4, 5, 6 January
Result: Australia won by 169 runs

Australia

W.M.Woodfull* c Cameron b Bell	7	c Mitchell b McMillan	161
W.H.Ponsford b Bell	7	c Mitchell b Bell	34
D.G.Bradman c Cameron b Quinn	2	lbw b Vincent	167
A.F.Kippax c Bell b Quinn	52	c Curnow b McMillan	67
S.J.McCabe c Morkel b Bell	22	c Mitchell b McMillan	71
K.E.Rigg c Mitchell b Bell	68	c Mitchell b Vincent	1
E.L.a'Beckett c Mitchell b Quinn	6	b Vincent	4
W.A.S.Oldfield† c Vincent b Quinn	0	lbw b McMillan	0
C.V.Grimmett c Morkel b Bell	9	not out	16
T.W.Wall not out	6	b Vincent	12
H.Ironmonger run out	12	b Quinn	0
Extras (B 1, LB 4, NB 1, W 1)	7	(B 17, LB 3, NB 1)	21
	198		**554**

1/11 2/16 3/25 4/74 5/135
6/143 7/143 8/173 9/179

1/54 2/328 3/408 4/519 5/521 554
6/521 7/524 8/530 9/550

Bowling: *First Innings*—Bell 26.1-9-69-5; Quinn 31-13-42-4; Morkel 3-0-12-0; Vincent 12-1-32-0; McMillan 2-0-22-0; Christy 3-0-14-0. *Second Innings*—Bell 36-6-101-1; Quinn 36.4-6-113-1; Vincent 55-16-154-4; McMillan 33-3-150-4; Morkel 4-0-15-0.

South Africa

B.Mitchell c McCabe b Wall	17	c and b Grimmett	46
S.H.Curnow b Grimmett	47	b Grimmett	9
J.A.J.Christy c McCabe b Ironmonger	16	c Oldfield b Ironmonger	63
H.W.Taylor lbw b Grimmett	11	b Grimmett	38
D.P.B.Morkel lbw b Ironmonger	33	b Ironmonger	4
H.B.Cameron*† st Oldfield b Ironmonger	39	lbw b Ironmonger	13
K.G.Viljoen c Wall b McCabe	111	b Ironmonger	2
C.L.Vincent c Oldfield b Wall	16	c Ponsford b Grimmett	34
Q.McMillan c Oldfield b Wall	29	c Wall b Grimmett	1
N.A.Quinn b McCabe	11	not out	0
A.J.Bell not out	10	b Grimmett	0
Extras (B 3, LB 13, NB 2)	18	(B 8, LB 6, NB 1)	15
	358		**225**

1/39 2/79 3/89 4/108 5/163
6/183 7/225 8/329 9/336

1/18 2/120 3/133 4/138 5/178 225
6/186 7/188 8/208 9/225

Bowling: *First Innings*—Wall 37-5-98-3; a'Beckett 18-5-29-0; Grimmett 63-23-100-2; Ironmonger 49-26-72-3; McCabe 21.3-4-41-2. *Second Innings*—Wall 13-3-35-0; a'Beckett 3-1-6-0; Grimmett 46-14-92-6; Ironmonger 42-18-54-4; McCabe 10-1-21-0; Bradman 1-0-2-0.

Umpires: E.G.Borwick and G.A.Hele

AUSTRALIA v SOUTH AFRICA 1931-32 (Fourth Test)

At Adelaide Oval, 29, 30 January, 1, 2 February
Result: Australia won by 10 wickets

South Africa

S.H.Curnow c Ponsford b Grimmett	20		b McCabe	3
B.Mitchell c and b McCabe	75		c O'Reilly b Grimmett	95
J.A.J.Christy b O'Reilly	7		b Grimmett	51
H.W.Taylor c Rigg b Grimmett	78		b O'Reilly	84
K.G.Viljoen c and b Grimmett	52		b O'Reilly	4
H.B.Cameron*†	0	(8)	b Grimmett	15
D.P.B.Morkel c and b Grimmett	0		b Grimmett	1
C.L.Vincent not out	48	(6)	b Grimmett	5
Q.McMillan b Grimmett	19		c Hunt b Grimmett	3
N.A.Quinn c Ponsford b Grimmett	1		b Grimmett	0
A.J.Bell lbw b O'Reilly	2		not out	0
Extras (LB 2, NB 4)	6		(B 4, LB 3, NB 5)	12
	308			**274**

1/27 2/45 3/165 4/202 5/204 6/204 7/243 8/286 9/300
1/22 2/103 3/224 4/232 5/240 6/246 7/262 8/268 9/274

Bowling: *First Innings*—Thurlow 27-6-53-0; McCabe 17-6-34-1; O'Reilly 39.4-10-74-2; Grimmett 47-11-116-7; Hunt 10-1-25-0. *Second Innings*—Thurlow 12-1-33-0; McCabe 14-1-51-1; O'Reilly 42-13-81-2; Grimmett 49.2-17-83-7; Hunt 6-1-14-0.

Australia

W.M.Woodfull* c Morkel b Bell	82	not out	37
W.H.Ponsford b Quinn	5	not out	27
D.G.Bradman not out	299		
A.F.Kippax run out	0		
S.J.McCabe c Vincent b Bell	2		
K.E.Rigg c Taylor b Bell	35		
W.A.S.Oldfield† lbw b Vincent	23		
C.V.Grimmett b Bell	21		
W.A.Hunt c Vincent b Quinn	0		
W.J.O'Reilly b Bell	23		
H.M.Thurlow run out	0		
Extras (B 18, LB 3, NB 1, W 1)	23	(B 4, LB 5)	9
	513	(0 wkts)	**73**

1/9 2/185 3/191 4/194 5/308 6/357 7/418 8/421 9/499

Bowling: *First Innings*—Bell 40-2-142-5; Quinn 37-5-114-2; Vincent 34-5-110-1; McMillan 9-0-53-0; Morkel 18-1-71-0. *Second Innings*—Quinn 3-0-5-0; Morkel 2-0-5-0; McMillan 7.2-0-23-0; Vincent 7-0-31-0.

Umpires: E.G.Borwick and G.A.Hele

AUSTRALIA v SOUTH AFRICA 1931-32 (Fifth Test)

At Melbourne Cricket Ground, 12, 13 (no play), 15 February
Result: Australia won by an innings and 72 runs

South Africa

B.Mitchell c Rigg b McCabe	2	(4)	c Oldfield b Ironmonger	4
S.H.Curnow c Oldfield b Nash	3		c Fingleton b Ironmonger	16
J.A.J.Christy c Grimmett b Nash	4	(1)	c and b Nash	0
H.W.Taylor c Kippax b Nash	0	(6)	c Bradman b Ironmonger	2
K.G.Viljoen c sub (L.S.Darling) b Ironmonger	1	(8)	c Oldfield b O'Reilly	0
H.B.Cameron*† c McCabe b Nash	11	(5)	c McCabe b O'Reilly	0
D.P.B.Morkel c Nash b Ironmonger	1		c Rigg b Ironmonger	0
C.L.Vincent c Nash b Ironmonger	1	(9)	not out	8
Q.McMillan st Oldfield b Ironmonger	0	(10)	c Oldfield b Ironmonger	0
N.A.Quinn not out	5	(11)	c Fingleton b Ironmonger	5
A.J.Bell st Oldfield b Ironmonger	0	(3)	c McCabe b O'Reilly	6
Extras (B 2, LB 3, NB 3)	8		(B 3, LB 1)	4
	36			**45**

1/7 2/16 3/16 4/17 5/19 6/25 7/31 8/31 9/33
1/0 2/12 3/25 4/30 5/30 6/30 7/32 8/32 9/33

Bowling: *First Innings*—Nash 12-6-18-4; McCabe 4-1-4-1; Ironmonger 7.2-5-6-5. *Second Innings*—Nash 7-4-4-1; Ironmonger 15.3-7-18-6; O'Reilly 9-5-19-3.

Australia

W.M.Woodfull* b Bell	0
J.H.W.Fingleton c Vincent b Bell	40
K.E.Rigg c Vincent b Quinn	22
A.F.Kippax c Curnow b McMillan	42
S.J.McCabe c Cameron b Bell	0
L.J.Nash b Quinn	13
W.A.S.Oldfield† c Curnow b McMillan	11
C.V.Grimmett c Cameron b Quinn	9
W.J.O'Reilly c Curnow b McMillan	13
H.Ironmonger not out	0
D.G.Bradman absent hurt	-
Extras (LB 3)	3
	153

1/0 2/51 3/75 4/75 5/112 6/125 7/131 8/148 9/153

Bowling: Bell 16-0-52-3; Quinn 19.3-4-29-3; Vincent 11-2-40-0; McMillan 8-0-29-3.

Umpires: E.G.Borwick and G.A.Hele

AUSTRALIA v ENGLAND 1932-33 (First Test)

At Sydney Cricket Ground, 2, 3, 5, 6, 7 December

Result: England won by 10 wickets

Australia

W.M.Woodfull* c Ames b Voce	7	b Larwood	0
W.H.Ponsford b Larwood	32	b Voce	2
J.H.W.Fingleton c Allen b Larwood	26	c Voce b Larwood	40
A.F.Kippax lbw b Larwood	8	(6) b Larwood	19
S.J.McCabe not out	187	(4) lbw b Hammond	32
V.Y.Richardson c Hammond b Voce	49	(5) c Voce b Hammond	0
W.A.S.Oldfield† c Ames b Larwood	19	c Leyland b Hammond	1
C.V.Grimmett c Ames b Voce	0	c Allen b Larwood	5
L.E.Nagel b Larwood	0	not out	21
W.J.O'Reilly b Voce	4	(11) b Voce	7
T.W.Wall c Allen b Hammond	4	(10) c Ames b Allen	20
Extras (B 12, LB 4, NB 4)	20	(B 12, LB 2, NB 2, W 1)	17
	360		**164**

1/22 2/65 3/82 4/87 5/216   1/2 2/10 3/61 4/61 5/100
6/231 7/299 8/300 9/305   6/104 7/105 8/113 9/151

Bowling: *First Innings*—Larwood 31-5-96-5; Voce 29-4-110-4; Allen 15-1-65-0; Hammond 14.2-0-34-1; Verity 13-4-35-0. *Second Innings*—Larwood 18-4-28-5; Voce 17.3-5-54-2; Allen 9-5-13-1; Hammond 15-6-37-2; Verity 4-1-15-0.

England

H.Sutcliffe lbw b Wall	194	not out	1
R.E.S.Wyatt lbw b Grimmett	38	not out	0
Nawab of Pataudi‡ b Nagel	112		
M.Leyland c Oldfield b Wall	0		
D.R.Jardine* c Oldfield b McCabe	27		
H.Verity lbw b Wall	2		
G.O.B.Allen c and b O'Reilly	19		
L.E.G.Ames† c McCabe b O'Reilly	0		
H.Larwood lbw b O'Reilly	0		
W.Voce not out	0		
Extras (B 7, LB 17, NB 6)	30		
	524	**(0 wkts)**	**1**

1/112 2/300 3/423 4/423 5/470
6/479 7/518 8/522 9/522

Bowling: *First Innings*—Wall 38-4-104-3; Nagel 43.4-9-110-2; O'Reilly 67-32-117-3; Grimmett 64-22-118-1; McCabe 15-2-42-1; Kippax 2-1-3-0. *Second Innings*—McCabe 0.1-0-1-0.

Umpires: E.G.Borwick and G.A.Hele

AUSTRALIA v ENGLAND 1932-33 (Second Test)

At Melbourne Cricket Ground, 30, 31 December, 2, 3 January

Result: Australia won by 111 runs

Australia

J.H.W.Fingleton b Allen	83	c Ames b Allen	1
W.M.Woodfull* b Allen	10	c Allen b Larwood	26
L.P.J.O'Brien run out	10	b Larwood	11
D.G.Bradman b Bowes	0	not out	103
S.J.McCabe c Jardine b Voce	32	b Allen	0
V.Y.Richardson c Hammond b Voce	34	lbw b Hammond	32
W.A.S.Oldfield† not out	27	b Voce	6
C.V.Grimmett c Sutcliffe b Voce	2	b Voce	0
T.W.Wall run out	1	lbw b Hammond	3
W.J.O'Reilly b Larwood	15	c Ames b Hammond	0
H.Ironmonger b Larwood	4	run out	0
Extras (B 5, LB 1, NB 2, W 2)	10	(B 3, LB 1, NB 1, W 4)	9
	228		**191**

1/29 2/67 3/67 4/131 5/156   1/1 2/27 3/78 4/81 5/135
6/188 7/194 8/200 9/222   6/150 7/156 8/184 9/186

Bowling: *First Innings*—Larwood 20.3-2-52-2; Voce 20-3-54-3; Allen 17-3-41-2; Hammond 10-3-21-0; Bowes 19-2-50-1. *Second Innings*—Larwood 15-2-50-2; Allen 12-1-44-2; Bowes 4-0-20-0; Voce 15-2-47-2; Hammond 10.5-2-21-3.

England

H.Sutcliffe c Richardson b Wall	52	b O'Reilly	33
R.E.S.Wyatt lbw b O'Reilly	13	(7) lbw b O'Reilly	25
W.R.Hammond b Wall	8	(4) c O'Brien b O'Reilly	23
Nawab of Pataudi‡ sr b O'Reilly	15	(3) c Fingleton b Ironmonger	5
M.Leyland b O'Reilly	22	(2) b Wall	19
D.R.Jardine* c Oldfield b Wall	1	(5) c McCabe b Ironmonger	0
L.E.G.Ames† b Wall	4	(6) c Fingleton b O'Reilly	2
G.O.B.Allen c Richardson b O'Reilly	30	st Oldfield b O'Reilly	23
H.Larwood b O'Reilly	9	c Wall b Ironmonger	4
W.Voce c McCabe b Grimmett	6	c O'Brien b O'Reilly	0
W.E.Bowes not out	4	not out	0
Extras (B 1, LB 2, NB 2)	5	(LB 4, NB 1)	5
	169		**139**

1/30 2/43 3/83 4/98 5/104   1/53 2/53 3/70 4/70 5/77
6/110 7/122 8/138 9/161   6/85 7/135 8/137 9/138

Bowling: *First Innings*—Wall 21-4-52-4; O'Reilly 34.3-17-63-5; Grimmett 16-4-21-1; Ironmonger 14-4-28-0. *Second Innings*—Wall 8-2-23-1; O'Reilly 24-5-66-5; Ironmonger 19.1-8-26-4; Grimmett 4-0-19-0.

Umpires: E.G.Borwick and G.A.Hele

AUSTRALIA v ENGLAND 1932-33 (Third Test)

At Adelaide Oval, 13, 14, 16, 17, 18, 19 January

Result: England won by 338 runs

England

Batsman	First Innings	Runs	Second Innings	Runs
H.Sutcliffe	c Wall b O'Reilly	9	c sub (L.P.J.O'Brien) b Wall	7
D.R.Jardine*	b Wall	3	lbw b Ironmonger	56
W.R.Hammond	c Oldfield b Wall	2	(5) b Bradman	85
L.E.G.Ames†	b Ironmonger	3	(7) b O'Reilly	69
M.Leyland	b O'Reilly	83	(6) c Wall b Ironmonger	42
R.E.S.Wyatt	c Richardson b Grimmett	78	(3) c Wall b O'Reilly	49
E.Paynter	c Fingleton b Wall	77	(10) not out	1
G.O.B.Allen	lbw b Grimmett	15	(4) lbw b Grimmett	15
H.Verity	c Richardson b Wall	45	(8) lbw b O'Reilly	40
W.Voce	b Wall	8	(11) b O'Reilly	8
H.Larwood	not out	3	(9) c Bradman b Ironmonger	8
Extras	(B 1, LB 7, NB 7)	15	(B 17, LB 11, NB 4)	32
		341		412

1/4 2/16 3/16 4/30 5/186 6/196 7/228 8/324 9/336

1/7 2/91 3/123 4/154 5/245 6/296 7/394 8/395 9/403

Bowling: *First Innings*—Wall 34.1-10-72-5; O'Reilly 50-19-82-2; Ironmonger 20-6-50-1; Grimmett 28-6-94-2; McCabe 14-3-28-0. *Second Innings*—Wall 29-6-75-1; O'Reilly 50.3-21-79-4; Ironmonger 57-21-87-3; Grimmett 35-9-74-1; McCabe 16-0-42-0; Bradman 4-0-23-1.

Australia

Batsman	First Innings	Runs	Second Innings	Runs
J.H.W.Fingleton	c Ames b Allen	0	b Larwood	0
W.M.Woodfull*	b Allen	22	not out	73
D.G.Bradman	c Allen b Larwood	8	(4) c and b Verity	66
S.J.McCabe	c Jardine b Larwood	8	(5) c Leyland b Allen	7
W.H.Ponsford	b Voce	85	(3) c Jardine b Larwood	3
V.Y.Richardson	c Allen b Allen	28	c Allen b Larwood	21
W.A.S.Oldfield†	retired hurt	41	absent hurt	-
C.V.Grimmett	c Voce b Allen	10	(7) b Allen	6
T.W.Wall	b Hammond	6	(8) b Allen	0
W.J.O'Reilly	b Larwood	0	(9) b Larwood	5
H.Ironmonger	not out	0	(10) b Allen	0
Extras	(B 2, LB 11, NB 1)	14	(B 4, LB 2, NB 5, W 1)	12
		222		193

1/1 2/18 3/34 4/51 5/131 6/194 7/212 8/222 9/222

1/3 2/12 3/100 4/116 5/171 6/183 7/183 8/192 9/193

Bowling: *First Innings*—Larwood 25-6-55-3; Allen 23-4-71-4; Hammond 17.4-4-30-1; Voce 14-5-21-1; Verity 16-7-31-0. *Second Innings*—Larwood 19-3-71-4; Allen 17.2-5-50-4; Voce 4-1-7-0; Hammond 9-3-27-0; Verity 20-12-26-1.

Umpires: E.G.Borwick and G.A.Hele

AUSTRALIA v ENGLAND 1932-33 (Fourth Test)

At Woolloongabba, Brisbane, 10, 11, 13, 14, 15, 16 February

Result: England won by 6 wickets

Australia

Batsman	First Innings	Runs	Second Innings	Runs
V.Y.Richardson	st Ames b Hammond	83	c Jardine b Verity	32
W.M.Woodfull*	b Mitchell	67	c Hammond b Mitchell	19
D.G.Bradman	b Larwood	76	c Mitchell b Larwood	24
S.J.McCabe	c Jardine b Allen	20	(5) b Verity	22
W.H.Ponsford	b Larwood	19	(4) c Larwood b Allen	0
L.S.Darling	c Ames b Allen	17	run out	39
E.H.Bromley	c Verity b Larwood	26	c Hammond b Allen	7
H.S.B.Love†	lbw b Mitchell	5	lbw b Larwood	3
T.W.Wall	not out	6	c Jardine b Allen	2
W.J.O'Reilly	c Hammond b Larwood	6	b Larwood	4
H.Ironmonger	st Ames b Hammond	8	not out	0
Extras	(B 5, LB 1, NB 1)	7	(B 13, LB 9, NB 1)	23
		340		175

1/133 2/200 3/233 4/264 5/267 6/292 7/315 8/317 9/329

1/46 2/79 3/81 4/91 5/136 6/163 7/169 8/169 9/171

Bowling: *First Innings*—Larwood 31-7-101-4; Allen 24-4-83-2; Hammond 23-5-61-2; Mitchell 16-5-49-2; Verity 27-12-39-0. *Second Innings*—Larwood 17.3-3-49-3; Allen 17-3-44-3; Hammond 10-4-18-0; Verity 19-6-30-2; Mitchell 5-0-11-1.

England

Batsman	First Innings	Runs	Second Innings	Runs
D.R.Jardine*	c Love b O'Reilly	46	lbw b Ironmonger	24
H.Sutcliffe	lbw b O'Reilly	86	c Darling b Wall	2
W.R.Hammond	b McCabe	20	(4) c Bromley b Ironmonger	14
R.E.S.Wyatt	c Love b Ironmonger	12		
M.Leyland	c Bradman b O'Reilly	12	(3) c McCabe b O'Reilly	86
L.E.G.Ames†	c Darling b Ironmonger	17	(5) not out	14
G.O.B.Allen	c Love b Wall	13		
E.Paynter	c Richardson b Ironmonger	83	(6) not out	14
H.Larwood	b McCabe	23		
H.Verity	not out	23		
T.B.Mitchell	lbw b O'Reilly	0		
Extras	(B 6, LB 12, NB 3)	21	(B 2, LB 4, NB 2)	8
		356		162 (4 wkts)

1/114 2/157 3/165 4/188 5/198 6/216 7/225 8/264 9/356

1/5 2/78 3/118 4/138

Bowling: *First Innings*—Wall 33-6-66-1; O'Reilly 67.4-27-120-4; Ironmonger 43-19-69-3; McCabe 23-7-40-2; Bromley 10-4-19-0; Bradman 7-1-17-0; Darling 2-0-4-0. *Second Innings*—Wall 7-1-17-1; O'Reilly 30-11-65-1; Ironmonger 35-13-47-2; McCabe 7.4-2-25-0.

Umpires: E.G.Borwick and G.A.Hele

AUSTRALIA v ENGLAND 1932-33 (Fifth Test)

At Sydney Cricket Ground, 23, 24, 25, 27, 28 February
Result: England won by 8 wickets

Australia

Batsman	Dismissal (1st)	R	Dismissal (2nd)	R
V.Y.Richardson	c Jardine b Larwood	0	c Allen b Larwood	0
W.M.Woodfull*	b Larwood	14	b Allen	67
D.G.Bradman	b Larwood	48	b Verity	71
L.P.J.O'Brien	c Larwood Voce	61	c Verity b Voce	5
S.J.McCabe	c Hammond b Verity	73	c Jardine b Voce	4
L.S.Darling	b Verity	85	c Wyatt b Verity	7
W.A.S.Oldfield†	run out	52	c Wyatt b Verity	5
P.K.Lee	c Jardine b Verity	42	b Allen	15
H.H.Alexander	not out	17	lbw b Verity	0
W.J.O'Reilly	b Allen	19	b Verity	1
H.Ironmonger	b Larwood	1	not out	0
Extras	(B 13, LB 9, W 1)	23	(B 4, NB 3)	7
		435		182

1/0 2/59 3/64 4/163 5/244 6/328 7/385 8/414 9/430
1/0 2/115 3/135 4/139 5/148 6/161 7/177 8/178 9/178

Bowling: *First Innings*—Larwood 32.2-10-98-4; Voce 24-4-80-1; Allen 25-1-128-1; Hammond 8-0-32-0; Verity 17-3-62-3; Wyatt 2-0-12-0. *Second Innings*—Larwood 11-0-44-1; Allen 11.4-2-54-2; Hammond 3-0-10-0; Voce 10-0-34-2; Verity 19-9-33-5.

England

Batsman	Dismissal (1st)	R	Dismissal (2nd)	R
D.R.Jardine*	c Oldfield b O'Reilly	18	c Richardson b Ironmonger	24
H.Sutcliffe	c Richardson b O'Reilly	56		
W.R.Hammond	lbw b Lee	101	(4) not out	75
H.Larwood	c Ironmonger b Lee	98		
M.Leyland	run out	42	(3) b Ironmonger	0
R.E.S.Wyatt	c Ironmonger b O'Reilly	51	(2) not out	61
L.E.G.Ames†	run out	4		
E.Paynter	b Lee	9		
G.O.B.Allen	c Bradman b Lee	48		
H.Verity	c Oldfield b Alexander	7		
W.Voce	not out	7		
Extras	(B 7, LB 7, NB 2)	16	(B 6, LB 1, NB 1)	8
		454	(2 wkts)	168

1/31 2/153 3/245 4/310 5/330 6/349 7/374 8/418 9/434
1/43 2/43

Bowling: *First Innings*—Alexander 35-1-129-1; McCabe 12-1-27-0; O'Reilly 45-7-100-3; Ironmonger 31-13-64-0; Lee 40.2-11-111-4; Darling 7-5-3-0; Bradman 1-0-4-0. *Second Innings*—Alexander 11-2-25-0; O'Reilly 15-5-32-0; Ironmonger 26-12-34-2; Lee 12.2-3-52-0; McCabe 5-2-10-0; Darling 2-0-7-0.

Umpires: E.G.Borwick and G.A.Hele

ENGLAND v AUSTRALIA 1934 (First Test)

At Trent Bridge, Nottingham, 8, 9, 11, 12 June
Result: Australia won by 238 runs

Australia

Batsman	Dismissal (1st)	R	Dismissal (2nd)	R
W.M.Woodfull*	c Verity b Farnes	26	b Farnes	2
W.H.Ponsford	c Ames b Farnes	53	b Hammond	5
W.A.Brown	lbw b Geary	29	c Ames b Verity	73
D.G.Bradman	c Hammond b Geary	29	c Ames b Farnes	25
S.J.McCabe	c Leyland b Farnes	65	c Hammond b Farnes	88
L.S.Darling	b Verity	7	c Hammond b Farnes	14
A.G.Chipperfield	c Ames b Farnes	99	c Hammond b Farnes	4
W.A.S.Oldfield†	c Hammond b Mitchell	20	not out	10
C.V.Grimmett	b Geary	39	(10) not out	3
W.J.O'Reilly	b Farnes	7	(9) c Verity b Geary	18
T.W.Wall	not out	0		
Extras	(B 4, LB 5, NB 1)	10	(B 22, LB 9)	31
		374	(8 wkts dec.)	273

1/77 2/88 3/125 4/146 5/143 6/234 7/281 8/355 9/374
1/2 2/32 3/69 4/181 5/219 6/231 7/244 8/267

Bowling: *First Innings*—Farnes 40.2-10.102-5; Geary 43-8-101-3; Hammond 13-4-29-0; Verity 34-9-65-1; Mitchell 21-4-62-1; Leyland 1-0-5-0. *Second Innings*—Farnes 25-3-77-5; Geary 23-5-46-1; Hammond 12-5-25-1; Verity 17-8-48-1; Mitchell 13-2-46-0.

England

Batsman	Dismissal (1st)	R	Dismissal (2nd)	R
C.F.Walters*	lbw b Grimmett	17	b O'Reilly	46
H.Sutcliffe	c Chipperfield b Grimmett	62	c Chipperfield b O'Reilly	24
W.R.Hammond	c McCabe b O'Reilly	25	st Oldfield b Grimmett	16
Nawab of Pataudi, sr	c McCabe Wall.	12	c Ponsford b Grimmett	10
M.Leyland	c and b Grimmett	6	(6) c Oldfield b O'Reilly	18
E.H.Hendren	b O'Reilly	79	(5) c Chipperfield b O'Reilly	3
L.E.G.Ames†	c Wall b O'Reilly	7	b O'Reilly	12
G.Geary	st Oldfield b Grimmett	53	c Chipperfield b Grimmett	0
H.Verity	b O'Reilly	0	not out	0
K.Farnes	b Grimmett	1	c Oldfield b O'Reilly	0
T.B.Mitchell	not out	1	lbw b O'Reilly	4
Extras	(B 5)	5	(B 4, LB 3, NB 1)	8
		268		141

1/45 2/102 3/106 4/114 4/145 6/165 7/266 8/266 9/266
1/51 2/83 3/91 4/103 5/110 6/134 7/135 8/137 9/137

Bowling: *First Innings*—Wall 33-7-82-1; Grimmett 58.3-24-81-3; O'Reilly 37-16-75-4; Chipperfield 3-0-18-0. *Second Innings*—Wall 13-2-27-0; McCabe 2-0-7-0; Grimmett 47-28-39-3; O'Reilly 41.4-24-54-7; Chipperfield 4-1-6-0.

Umpires: F.Chester and A.Dolphin

ENGLAND v AUSTRALIA 1934 (Second Test)

At Lord's, London, 22, 23, 25 June
Result: England won by an innings and 38 runs

England

C.F.Walters c Bromley b O'Reilly	82
H.Sutcliffe lbw Chipperfield	20
W.R.Hammond c and b Chipperfield	2
E.H.Hendren c McCabe b Wall	13
R.E.S.Wyatt* c Oldfield Chipperfield	33
M.Leyland b Wall	109
L.E.G.Ames† c Oldfield b McCabe	120
G.Geary c Chipperfield b Wall	9
H.Verity st Oldfield b Grimmett	29
K.Farnes b Wall	1
W.E.Bowes not out	10
Extras (LB 12)	12
	440

1/70 2/78 3/99 4/130 5/182
6/311 7/359 8/409 9/410

Bowling: Wall 49-7-108-4; McCabe 18-3-38-1; Grimmett 53.3-13-102-1; O'Reilly 38-15-70-1; Chipperfield 34-10-91-3; Darling 6-2-19-0.

Australia

	First Innings		Second Innings	
W.M.Woodfull*	b Bowes	22	c Hammond b Verity	43
W.A.Brown	c Ames b Bowes	105	c Walters b Bowes	2
D.G.Bradman	c and b Verity	36	c Ames b Verity	13
S.J.McCabe	c Hammond b Verity	34	(4) c Hendren b Verity	19
L.S.Darling	c Sutcliffe b Verity	0	(3) b Hammond	10
A.G.Chipperfield	not out	37	c Geary b Verity	14
E.H.Bromley	c Geary b Verity	4	c and b Verity	1
W.A.S.Oldfield†	c Sutcliffe b Verity	23	lbw b Verity	0
C.V.Grimmett	b Bowes	9	c Hammond b Verity	0
W.J.O'Reilly	b Verity	4	not out	8
T.W.Wall	lbw b Verity	0	c Hendren b Verity	1
Extras	(B 1, LB 9)	10	(B 6, NB 1)	7
		284		**118**

1/68 2/141 3/203 4/204 5/205   284
6/311 7/359 8/409 9/410
1/10 2/43 3/57 4/94 5/94   118
6/95 7/95 8/95 9/112

Bowling: First Innings—Farnes 12-3-43-0; Bowes 31-5-98-3; Geary 22-4-56-0; Verity 36-15-61-7; Hammond 4-1-6-0; Leyland 4-1-10-0. Second Innings—Farnes 4-2-6-0; Bowes 14-4-24-1; Verity 22.3-43-8; Hammond 13-0-38-1.

Umpires: F.Chester and J.Hardstaff, sr

ENGLAND v AUSTRALIA 1934 (Third Test)

At Old Trafford, Manchester, 6, 7, 9, 10 July
Result: Match drawn

England

	First Innings		Second Innings	
C.F.Walters	c Darling b O'Reilly	52	not out	50
H.Sutcliffe	c Chipperfield b O'Reilly	63	not out	69
R.E.S.Wyatt*	b O'Reilly	0		
W.R.Hammond	b O'Reilly	4		
E.H.Hendren	c and b O'Reilly	132		
M.Leyland	c sub (B.A.Barnett) b O'Reilly	153		
L.E.G.Ames†	c Ponsford b Grimmett	72		
J.L.Hopwood	b O'Reilly	2		
G.O.B.Allen	b McCabe	61		
H.Verity	not out	60		
E.W.Clark	not out	2		
Extras	(B 6, LB 18, W 2)	26	(B 2, LB 1, W 1)	4
	(9 wkts dec.)	**627**	(0 wkts dec.)	**123**

1/68 2/68 3/72 4/149 5/340
6/482 7/492 8/510 9/605

Bowling: First Innings—Wall 36-3-98-1; McCabe 32-3-98-1; O'Reilly 59-9-189-7; Chipperfield 7-0-29-0; Darling 10-0-32-0. Second Innings—Wall 9-0-31-0; McCabe 13-4-35-0; Grimmett 17-5-28-0; O'Reilly 13-4-25-0.

Australia

	First Innings		Second Innings	
W.A.Brown	c Walters b Clark	72	c Hammond b Allen	0
W.H.Ponsford	c Hendren b Hammond	12		
S.J.McCabe	c Verity b Hammond	137		
W.M.Woodfull*	run out	73	not out	30
L.S.Darling	b Verity	37	not out	33
D.G.Bradman	c Ames b Hammond	30		
W.A.S.Oldfield†	c Wyatt b Verity	13		
A.G.Chipperfield	c Walters b Verity	26		
C.V.Grimmett	b Verity	30		
W.J.O'Reilly	not out	18		
T.W.Wall	run out	43		
Extras	(B 20, LB 13, NB 6, W 4)	43	(B 1, LB 2)	3
		491	(1 wkt)	**66**

1/34 2/230 3/242 4/320 5/378
6/409 7/411 8/419 9/454

1/1

Bowling: First Innings—Clark 40-9-100-1; Allen 31-3-113-0; Hammond 28.3-6-111-3; Verity 53-24-78-4; Hopwood 38-20-46-0. Second Innings—Clark 4-1-16-0; Allen 6-0-23-1; Hammond 2-1-2-0; Verity 5-4-2-0; Hopwood 9-5-16-0; Hendren 1-0-4-0.

Umpires: J.Hardstaff, sr and F.I.Walden

ENGLAND v AUSTRALIA 1934 (Fourth Test)

At Headingley, Leeds, 20, 21, 23, 24 July
Result: Match drawn

England

C.F.Walters	c and b Chipperfield	44
W.W.Keeton	c Oldfield b O'Reilly	25
W.R.Hammond	b Wall	37
E.H.Hendren	b Chipperfield	29
R.E.S.Wyatt*	st Oldfield b Grimmett	19
M.Leyland	lbw b O'Reilly	16
L.E.G.Ames†	c Oldfield b Grimmett	9
J.L.Hopwood	lbw b O'Reilly	8
H.Verity	not out	2
T.B.Mitchell	st Oldfield b Grimmett	9
W.E.Bowes	c Ponsford b Grimmett	0
Extras	(LB 2)	2
		200

1/43 2/85 3/135 4/135 5/168
6/170 7/189 8/189 9/200

1/28 2/70 3/87 4/152 (6 wkts) 229
5/190 6/213

Bowling: *First Innings*—Wall 18-1-57-1; McCabe 4-2-3-0; Grimmett 30.4-11-57-4; O'Reilly 35-16-46-3; Chipperfield 18-6-35-2. *Second Innings*—Wall 14-5-36-0; McCabe 5-4-5-0; Grimmett 56.5-24-72-3; O'Reilly 54-25-88-2; Chipperfield 9-2-21-0.

Australia

W.A.Brown	b Bowes	15
W.H.Ponsford	hit wkt b Verity	181
W.A.S.Oldfield†	c Ames b Bowes	0
W.M.Woodfull*	b Bowes	0
D.G.Bradman	b Bowes	304
S.J.McCabe	b Bowes	27
L.S.Darling	b Bowes	12
A.G.Chipperfield	c Wyatt b Verity	1
C.V.Grimmett	run out	15
W.J.O'Reilly	not out	11
T.W.Wall	lbw b Verity	1
Extras	(B 8, LB 9)	17
		584

1/37 2/39 3/39 4/427 5/417
6/550 7/551 8/557 9/574

Bowling: Bowes 50-13-142-6; Hammond 29-5-82-0; Mitchell 23-1-117-0; Verity 46.5-15-113-3; Hopwood 30-7-93-0; Leyland 5-0-20-0.

Umpires: A.Dolphin and J.Hardstaff, sr

ENGLAND v AUSTRALIA 1934 (Fifth Test)

At Kennington Oval, London, 18, 20, 21, 22 August
Result: Australia won by 562 runs

Australia

W.A.Brown	b Clark	10	c Allen b Clark	1
W.H.Ponsford	hit wkt b Allen	266	c Hammond b Clark	22
D.G.Bradman	c Ames b Bowes	244	b Bowes	77
S.J.McCabe	b Allen	10	c Walters b Clark	70
W.M.Woodfull*	b Bowes	49	b Bowes	13
A.F.Kippax	lbw b Bowes	28	c Walters b Clark	8
A.G.Chipperfield	b Bowes	3	c Woolley b Clark	16
W.A.S.Oldfield†	not out	42	c Hammond b Bowes	0
C.V.Grimmett	c Ames b Allen	7	c Hammond b Bowes	14
H.I.Ebeling	b Allen	7	c Allen b Bowes	41
W.J.O'Reilly	b Clark	33	not out	15
Extras	(B 4, LB 14, NB 13, W 2)	33	(B 37, LB 8, NB 4, W 1)	50
		701		**327**

1/21 2/472 3/488 4/574 5/626   1/13 2/42 3/192 4/213 5/224
6/631 7/638 8/676 9/682   6/236 7/236 8/256 9/272

Bowling: *First Innings*—Bowes 38-2-164-4; Allen 34-5-170-4; Clark 37.2-4-110-2; Hammond 12-0-53-0; Verity 43-7-123-0; Wyatt 4-0-28-0; Leyland 3-0-20-0. *Second Innings*—Bowes 11.3-55-5; Allen 16-2-63-0; Clark 20-1-98-5; Hammond 7-1-18-0; Verity 14-3-43-0.

England

C.F.Walters	c Kippax b O'Reilly	64	b McCabe	1
H.Sutcliffe	c Oldfield b Grimmett	38	c McCabe b Grimmett	28
F.E.Woolley	c McCabe b O'Reilly	4	c Ponsford b McCabe	0
W.R.Hammond	c Oldfield b Ebeling	15	c and b O'Reilly	43
R.E.S.Wyatt*	b Grimmett	17	(6) c Ponsford b Grimmett	22
M.Leyland	b Grimmett	110	(5) c Brown b Grimmett	17
L.E.G.Ames†	retired hurt	33	absent hurt	-
G.O.B.Allen	b Ebeling	19	(7) st Oldfield b Grimmett	26
H.Verity	b Ebeling	11	(8) c McCabe b Grimmett	2
E.W.Clark	not out	2	not out	2
W.E.Bowes	absent ill	-	(9) c Bradman b O'Reilly	3
Extras	(B 4, LB 3, NB 1)	8	(LB 1, NB 2)	3
		321		**145**

1/104 2/108 3/111 4/136 5/142   1/1 2/3 3/67 4/89 5/109
6/263 7/311 8/321   6/122 7/138 8/141 9/145

Bowling: *First Innings*—Ebeling 21-4-74-3; McCabe 6-1-21-0; Grimmett 49.3-13-103-3; O'Reilly 37-10-93-2; Chipperfield 4-0-22-0. *Second Innings*—Ebeling 10-5-15-0; McCabe 5-3-5-2; Grimmett 26.3-10-64-5; O'Reilly 22-9-58-2.

Umpires: F.Chester and F.I.Walden

SOUTH AFRICA v AUSTRALIA 1935-36 (First Test)

At Kingsmead, Durban, 14, 16, 17, 18 December
Result: Australia won by 9 wickets

South Africa

Batsman	First Innings		Second Innings	
B.Mitchell	b Fleetwood-Smith	19	run out	19
I.J.Siedle	lbw b O'Reilly	31	b Grimmett	59
E.A.B.Rowan	c and b Grimmett	66	c and b Grimmett	49
K.G.Viljoen	b Fleetwood-Smith	4	b Fleetwood-Smith	1
A.D.Nourse	b McCormick	30	c Fingleton b Grimmett	91
H.F.Wade*	b O'Reilly	31	lbw b O'Reilly	11
E.L.Dalton	st Oldfield b Fleetwood-Smith	4	c Darling b Grimmett	5
A.B.C.Langton	b Grimmett	0	not out	12
F.Nicholson†	not out	16	b O'Reilly	0
R.J.Crisp	b Fleetwood-Smith	35	b O'Reilly	16
J.B.Robertson	b O'Reilly	9	c Richardson b O'Reilly	9
Extras	(B 1, LB 2)	3	(B 8, LB 1, NB 1)	10
		248		282

1/45 2/59 3/71 4/108 5/168
6/185 7/186 8/187 9/234

1/65 2/86 3/89 4/207 5/233
6/242 7/242 8/242 9/263

Bowling: *First Innings*—McCormick 15-4-50-1; McCabe 10-1-28-0; Grimmett 28-10-48-2; O'Reilly 33.2-17-55-3; Fleetwood-Smith 28-6-64-4. *Second Innings*—McCormick 6-0-26-0; McCabe 2-0-5-0; Grimmett 52-20-83-3; O'Reilly 17-5-49-5; Fleetwood-Smith 37-7-101-1; Chipperfield 1-0-8-0.

Australia

Batsman	First Innings		Second Innings	
W.A.Brown	c Langton b Robertson	66	c Crisp b Dalton	55
J.H.W.Fingleton	c Nicholson b Crisp	2	not out	36
S.J.McCabe	c Rowan b Langton	149	not out	7
L.S.Darling	c Viljoen b Crisp	60		
V.Y.Richardson*	b Langton	2		
A.G.Chipperfield	b Crisp	109		
W.A.S.Oldfield†	lbw b Langton	0		
W.J.O'Reilly	c Rowan b Robertson	11		
C.V.Grimmett	c Nicholson b Robertson	15		
E.L.McCormick	not out	2		
L.O.Fleetwood-Smith	b Langton	1		
Extras	(B 5, LB 2, NB 4, W 1)	12	(B 3, LB 1)	4
		429	(1 wkt)	102

1/12 2/173 3/269 4/277 5/299
6/299 7/329 8/412 9/428

1/93

Bowling: *First Innings*—Crisp 36-7-87-3; Langton 48.2-10-113-4; Robertson 55-11-143-3; Dalton 6-0-25-0; Mitchell 17-2-49-0. *Second Innings*—Crisp 6-1-10-0; Langton 9-0-29-0; Robertson 13-4-24-0; Dalton 1.3-0-12-1; Mitchell 7-0-23-0.

Umpires: J.C.Collings and W.J.Routledge

SOUTH AFRICA v AUSTRALIA 1935-36 (Second Test)

At Old Wanderers, Johannesburg, 24, 26, 27, 28 December
Result: Match drawn

South Africa

Batsman	First Innings		Second Innings	
B.Mitchell	c Oldfield b McCormick	8	(4) c Oldfield b McCabe	45
I.J.Siedle	c Chipperfield b McCormick	22	b Grimmett	34
E.A.B.Rowan	lbw b Grimmett	38	lbw b Grimmett	13
A.D.Nourse	b McCormick	0	(5) c McCormick b McCabe	231
A.W.Briscoe	b O'Reilly	15	(6) lbw b Grimmett	16
H.F.Wade*	b O'Reilly	0	(1) lbw b Grimmett	30
A.B.C.Langton	c Fingleton b O'Reilly	7	(8) b McCormick	16
F.Nicholson†	st Oldfield b Grimmett	27	(7) lbw b Fleetwood-Smith	29
R.J.Crisp	b Grimmett	8	b O'Reilly	35
J.B.Robertson	b O'Reilly	17	b McCormick	3
E.G.Bock	not out	9	not out	2
Extras	(LB 6)	6	(B 13, LB 19, NB 5)	37
		157		491

1/11 2/46 3/50 4/68 5/70
6/78 7/112 8/126 9/139

1/50 2/89 3/90 4/219 5/291
6/397 7/440 8/454 9/466

Bowling: *First Innings*—McCormick 16-5-36-3; O'Reilly 20.2-9-54-4; Grimmett 15-5-29-3; McCabe 6-2-11-0; Fleetwood-Smith 6-2-21-0. *Second Innings*—McCormick 26-3-129-3; O'Reilly 35.3-15-91-1; Grimmett 58-28-111-3; McCabe 9-1-30-2; Fleetwood-Smith 21-5-93-1.

Australia

Batsman	First Innings		Second Innings	
J.H.W.Fingleton	c and b Langton	62	b Mitchell	40
W.A.Brown	c Crisp b Robertson	51	c Nicholson b Crisp	6
S.J.McCabe	c Robertson b Langton	34	not out	189
L.S.Darling	run out	42	not out	37
V.Y.Richardson*	b Langton	2		
A.G.Chipperfield	c Rowan b Langton	0		
W.A.S.Oldfield†	c Briscoe b Mitchell	40		
C.V.Grimmett	b Mitchell	7		
W.J.O'Reilly	b Mitchell	0		
E.L.McCormick	b Mitchell	4		
L.O.Fleetwood-Smith	not out	5		
Extras	(LB 3)	3	(LB 2)	2
		250	(2 wkts)	274

1/105 2/127 3/168 4/170 5/174
6/209 7/241 8/241 9/242

1/17 2/194

Bowling: *First Innings*—Crisp 15-1-49-0; Langton 32-6-85-4; Mitchell 7.3-0-26-4; Bock 14-2-49-0; Robertson 55-11-143-3. *Second Innings*—Crisp 17-3-62-1; Langton 22-6-54-0; Mitchell 15.1-73-1; Bock 9-0-42-0; Robertson 13-3-41-0.

Umpires: R.G.A.Ashman and J.C.Collings

SOUTH AFRICA v AUSTRALIA 1935-36 (Third Test)

At Newlands, Cape Town, 1 (no play), 2, 3, 4 January
Result: Australia won by an innings and 78 runs

Australia

W.A.Brown c and b Robertson	121
J.H.W.Fingleton c Wade b Balaskas	112
S.J.McCabe c and b Balaskas	0
L.S.Darling lbw b Balaskas	12
V.Y.Richardson* lbw b Crisp	14
A.G.Chipperfield b Langton	30
W.A.S.Oldfield† b Robertson	8
C.V.Grimmett not out	30
W.J.O'Reilly b Balaskas	17
E.L.McCormick not out	0
L.O.Fleetwood-Smith	
Extras (B 14, LB 4)	18
Total (8 wkts dec.)	**362**

1/233 2/235 3/251 4/259 5/299
6/313 7/313 8/361

Bowling: Crisp 14-2-30-1; Langton 30-2-94-1; Robertson 29-8-75-2; Balaskas 38-1-126-4; Mitchell 4-0-19-0.

South Africa

I.J.Siedle lbw b Grimmett	1		b Grimmett	59
H.F.Wade* c and b McCabe	0		lbw b Fleetwood-Smith	31
E.A.B.Rowan b Grimmett	12		c Richardson b O'Reilly	19
B.Mitchell c Fingleton b O'Reilly	14	(5)	b Grimmett	0
K.G.Viljoen st Oldfield b Fleetwood-Smith	14	(6)	c O'Reilly b Grimmett	23
A.D.Nourse not out	44	(4)	c and b Grimmett	25
F.Nicholson† b Fleetwood-Smith	0		c and b O'Reilly	4
A.B.C.Langton b Grimmett	3		b O'Reilly	4
R.J.Crisp b Grimmett	0		c Richardson b O'Reilly	0
X.C.Balaskas b Grimmett	0	(11)	b Grimmett	2
J.B.Robertson run out	1	(10)	not out	12
Extras (LB 13)	13		(B 1, LB 2)	3
Total	**102**			**182**

1/0 2/12 3/21 4/29 5/86   1/87 2/97 3/137 4/137 5/139
6/88 7/95 8/95 9/95   6/146 7/156 8/156 9/174

Bowling: First Innings—McCormick 2-1-3-0; McCabe 2-1-9-1; O'Reilly 11-4-24-1; Grimmett 17-4-32-5; Fleetwood-Smith 6.2-0-21-2. Second Innings—McCormick 2-0-8-0; O'Reilly 25-15-35-4; Grimmett 36.4-17-56-5; Fleetwood-Smith 24-4-80-1.

Umpires: R.G.A.Ashman and J.C.Collings

SOUTH AFRICA v AUSTRALIA 1935-36 (Fourth Test)

At Old Wanderers, Johannesburg, 15, 17 February
Result: Australia won by an innings and 184 runs

South Africa

I.J.Siedle lbw b Grimmett	44		b McCormick	0
H.F.Wade* b McCormick	39		b McCormick	2
A.D.Nourse c Oldfield b McCormick	3	(5)	b McCormick	3
K.G.Viljoen b O'Reilly	33	(3)	st Oldfield b Grimmett	7
R.L.Harvey b O'Reilly	5	(6)	c Darling b Grimmett	17
B.Mitchell st Oldfield b Grimmett	16	(4)	not out	48
A.B.C.Langton lbw b O'Reilly	7	(8)	lbw b Grimmett	9
F.Nicholson† b Grimmett	0	(7)	b Grimmett	0
E.P.Nupen b O'Reilly	1		b Grimmett	6
X.C.Balaskas lbw b O'Reilly	0		c O'Brien b Grimmett	0
E.Q.Davies not out	0		c Oldfield b Grimmett	3
Extras (LB 5, W 4)	9		(LB 3)	3
Total	**157**			**98**

1/81 2/91 3/96 4/128 5/137   1/0 2/5 3/21 4/24 5/49
6/153 7/154 8/155 9/157   6/50 7/76 8/82 9/82

Bowling: First Innings—McCormick 11-0-37-2; McCabe 5-2-21-0; Grimmett 26.4-70-3; O'Reilly 21-11-20-5. Second Innings—McCormick 12-2-28-3; McCabe 2-1-0; Grimmett 19.5-9-40-7; O'Reilly 10-3-26-0.

Australia

J.H.W.Fingleton c Langton b Davies	108
W.A.Brown lbw b Langton	34
S.J.McCabe b Davies	40
L.P.J.O'Brien b Balaskas	59
W.A.S.Oldfield† c Balaskas b Nupen	44
L.S.Darling c Wade b Balaskas	16
A.G.Chipperfield lbw b Balaskas	39
V.Y.Richardson* b Davies	21
C.V.Grimmett lbw b Balaskas	4
W.J.O'Reilly not out	56
E.L.McCormick c Mitchell b Davies	13
Extras (B 1, LB 4)	5
Total	**439**

1/99 2/179 3/184 4/260 5/282
6/333 7/352 8/368 9/370

Bowling: Davies 24.4-4-75-4; Langton 30-5-88-1; Balaskas 44-4-165-4; Nupen 14-1-53-1; Mitchell 14-1-53-0.

Umpires: R.G.A.Ashman and J.C.Collings

SOUTH AFRICA v AUSTRALIA 1935-36 (Fifth Test)

At Kingsmead, Durban, 28, 29 February, 2, 3 March
Result: Australia won by an innings and 6 runs

South Africa

I.J.Siedle c Brown b Grimmett	36	c Brown b Grimmett	46
H.F.Wade* c Richardson b Grimmett	26	b O'Reilly	25
B.Mitchell c and b Grimmett	10	not out	72
A.D.Nourse lbw b Grimmett	50	b O'Reilly	41
K.G.Viljoen c Chipperfield b McCormick	56	lbw b Grimmett	25
R.L.Harvey c Oldfield b McCormick	28	c Richardson b Grimmett	1
A.B.C.Langton st Oldfield b Grimmett	1	b Grimmett	3
X.C.Balaskas st Oldfield b Grimmett	2	c Richardson b Grimmett	0
R.J.Crisp b Grimmett	0	(11) c Richardson b O'Reilly	0
E.A.van der Merwe† not out	7	(9) c Richardson b Grimmett	0
E.Q.Davies b McCormick	0	(10) c Richardson b O'Reilly	2
Extras (B 1, LB 5)	6	(B 5, LB 7)	12
	222		**227**

1/44 2/57 3/124 4/125 5/178 6/183 7/199 8/199 9/220

1/63 2/73 3/146 4/196 5/206 6/212 7/220 8/220 9/227

Bowling: *First Innings*—McCormick 20.1-8-37-3; McCabe 7-0-20-0; Grimmett 45.4-8-100-7; O'Reilly 37-15-59-0. *Second Innings*—McCormick 15-1-64-0; McCabe 2-0-11-0; Grimmett 48-23-73-6; O'Reilly 40.1-18-47-4; Chipperfield 8-1-20-0.

Australia

J.H.W.Fingleton b Crisp	118
W.A.Brown c Langton b Mitchell	84
S.J.McCabe c and b Mitchell	1
L.P.J.O'Brien c Van der Merwe b Balaskas	48
L.S.Darling lbw b Mitchell	62
A.G.Chipperfield c Balaskas b Mitchell	18
V.Y.Richardson* b Crisp	45
W.A.S.Oldfield† c Crisp b Langton	29
C.V.Grimmett c Siedle b Mitchell	14
W.J.O'Reilly c Siedle b Langton	13
E.L.McCormick not out	0
Extras (B 19, LB 3, NB 1)	23
	455

1/162 2/164 3/240 4/316 5/333 6/361 7/423 8/433 9/451

Bowling: Davies 18-0-54-0; Crisp 19-2-65-2; Langton 33-9-69-2; Balaskas 51-4-157-1; Mitchell 25.5-2-87-5.

Umpires: J.C.Collings and W.J.Routledge.

AUSTRALIA v ENGLAND 1936-37 (First Test)

At Woolloongabba, Brisbane, 4, 5, 7, 8, 9 December
Result: England won by 322 runs

England

T.S.Worthington c Oldfield b McCormick	0	st Oldfield b McCabe	8
C.J.Barnett c Oldfield b O'Reilly	69	c Badcock b Ward	26
A.E.Fagg c Oldfield b McCormick	4	st Oldfield b Ward	27
W.R.Hammond c Robinson b McCormick	0	hit wkt b Ward	25
M.Leyland b Ward	126	c Bradman b Ward	33
L.E.G.Ames† c Chipperfield b Ward	24	b Sievers	9
J.Hardstaff, jr c McCabe b O'Reilly	43	(8) st Oldfield b Ward	20
R.W.V.Robins c sub (W.A.Brown) b O'Reilly	38	(9) c Chipperfield b Ward	0
G.O.B.Allen* c McCabe b O'Reilly	35	(7) c Fingleton b Sievers	68
H.Verity c Sievers b O'Reilly	7	lbw b Sievers	19
W.Voce not out	4	not out	2
Extras (B 1, LB 3, NB 4)	8	(B 14, LB 4, NB 1)	19
	358		**256**

1/0 2/20 3/20 4/119 5/162 6/252 7/311 8/311 9/343

1/17 2/50 3/82 4/105 5/122 6/144 7/205 8/205 9/247

Bowling: *First Innings*—McCormick 8-1-26-3; Sievers 16-5-42-0; O'Reilly 40.6-13-102-5; Ward 36-2-138-2; Chipperfield 11-3-32-0; McCabe 2-0-10-0. *Second Innings*—Sievers 19.6-9-29-3; McCabe 6-1-14-1; Ward 46-16-102-6; O'Reilly 35-15-59-0; Chipperfield 10-2-33-0.

Australia

J.H.W.Fingleton b Verity	100	b Voce	0
C.L.Badcock b Allen	8	c Fagg b Allen	0
D.G.Bradman* c Worthington b Voce	38	(5) c Fagg b Allen	0
S.J.McCabe c Barnett b Voce	51	(6) c Leyland b Allen	7
R.H.Robinson c Hammond b Voce	2	(7) c Hammond b Voce	3
A.G.Chipperfield c Ames b Voce	7	not out	26
M.W.Sievers b Allen	8	(3) c Voce b Allen	5
W.A.S.Oldfield† c Ames b Voce	6	(4) b Voce	10
W.J.O'Reilly c Leyland b Voce	3	b Allen	0
F.A.Ward c Hardstaff b Allen	0	b Voce	1
E.L.McCormick not out	1	absent ill	–
Extras (B 4, LB 1, NB 5)	10	(NB 6)	6
	234		**58**

1/13 2/89 3/166 4/176 5/202 6/220 7/229 8/231 9/231

1/0 2/3 3/7 4/7 5/16 6/20 7/35 8/41 9/58

Bowling: *First Innings*—Allen 16-2-71-3; Voce 20.6-5-41-6; Hammond 4-0-12-0; Verity 28-11-52-1; Robins 17-0-48-0. *Second Innings*—Voce 6.3-0-16-4; Allen 6-0-36-5.

Umpires: E.G.Borwick and J.D.Scott.

AUSTRALIA v ENGLAND 1936-37 (Second Test)

At Sydney Cricket Ground, 18, 19, 21, 22 December
Result: England won by an innings and 22 runs

England

A.E.Fagg c Sievers b McCormick	11	
C.J.Barnett b Ward	57	
W.R.Hammond not out	231	
M.Leyland lbw b McCabe	42	
L.E.G.Ames† c sub (R.H.Robinson) b Ward	29	
G.O.B.Allen* lbw b O'Reilly	9	
J.Hardstaff, jr b McCormick	26	
H.Verity not out	0	
R.W.V.Robins		
J.M.Sims		
W.Voce		
Extras (B 8, LB 8, NB 4, W 1)	21	

(6 wkts dec.) 426
1/27 2/118 3/247 4/351 5/368 6/424

Bowling: McCormick 20-1-79-2; Sievers 16.2-4-30-0; Ward 42-8-132-2; O'Reilly 41-17-86-1; Chipperfield 13-2-47-0; McCabe 9-1-31-1.

Australia

J.H.W.Fingleton c Verity b Voce	12	(2) b Sims	0
L.P.J.O'Brien c Sims b Voce	0	(1) c Allen b Hammond	17
D.G.Bradman* c Allen b Voce	0	b Verity	82
S.J.McCabe c Sims b Voce	0	lbw b Voce	93
A.G.Chipperfield c Sims b Allen	13	b Voce	21
M.W.Sievers c Voce b Verity	4	(7) run out	24
W.A.S.Oldfield† not out	1	(8) c Ames b Voce	1
W.J.O'Reilly not out	37	(9) b Hammond	3
E.L.McCormick b Allen	10	(10) lbw b Hammond	0
F.A.Ward b Allen	0	not out	1
C.L.Badcock absent ill	-	(6) lbw b Allen	2
Extras (B 1, LB 1, NB 1)	3	(LB 3, NB 4)	7
	80		324

1/1 2/1 3/1 4/16 5/28 6/30 7/31 8/80 9/80
1/38 2/162 3/186 4/220 5/226 6/318 7/319 8/323 9/323

Bowling: First Innings—Voce 8-1-10-4; Allen 5.7-1-19-3; Verity 3-0-17-2; Hammond 4-0-6-0; Sims 2-0-20-0; Robins 1-0-5-0. Second Innings—Voce 19-4-66-3; Allen 19-4-61-1; Hammond 15.7-3-29-3; Sims 17-0-80-1; Verity 19-7-55-1; Robins 7-0-26-0.

Umpires: E.G.Borwick and J.D.Scott

AUSTRALIA v ENGLAND 1936-37 (Third Test)

At Melbourne Cricket Ground, 1, 2, 4, 5, 6, 7 January
Result: Australia won by 365 runs

Australia

J.H.W.Fingleton c Sims b Robins	38	(6) c Ames b Sims	136
W.A.Brown c Ames b Voce	1	(5) c Barnett b Voce	20
D.G.Bradman* c Robins b Verity	13	(7) c Allen b Verity	270
K.E.Rigg c Verity b Allen	16	lbw b Sims	47
S.J.McCabe c Worthington b Voce	63	(8) lbw b Allen	22
L.S.Darling c Allen b Verity	20	(9) b Allen	0
M.W.Sievers st Ames b Robins	1	(10) not out	25
W.A.S.Oldfield† not out	27	(11) lbw b Verity	7
W.J.O'Reilly c Sims b Hammond	4	(1) c and b Voce	0
F.A.Ward st Ames b Hammond	7	(3) c Hardstaff b Verity	18
L.O.Fleetwood-Smith	0	(2) c Verity b Voce	0
Extras (B 2, LB 6, NB 2)	10	(B 6, LB 2, NB 10, W 1)	19
(9 wkts dec.)	200		564

1/7 2/33 3/69 4/79 5/122 6/130 7/183 8/190 9/200
1/0 2/3 3/38 4/74 5/97 6/443 7/511 8/511 9/549

Bowling: First Innings—Voce 18-3-49-2; Allen 12-2-35-1; Sims 9-1-35-0; Verity 14-4-24-2; Robins 7-0-31-2; Hammond 5.3-0-16-2. Second Innings—Voce 29-2-120-3; Hammond 22-3-89-0; Allen 23-2-84-2; Verity 37.7-9-79-3; Robins 11-2-46-0; Sims 23-1-109-2; Worthington 4-0-18-0.

England

T.S.Worthington c Bradman b McCabe	0	c Sievers b Ward	16
C.J.Barnett c Darling b Sievers	11	lbw b O'Reilly	23
W.R.Hammond c Darling b Sievers	32	b Sievers	51
M.Leyland c Darling b O'Reilly	17	not out	111
J.M.Sims c Brown b Sievers	3	(10) lbw b Fleetwood-Smith	0
L.E.G.Ames† b Sievers	3	(5) b Fleetwood-Smith	19
R.W.V.Robins c O'Reilly b Sievers	3	(8) b O'Reilly	61
J.Hardstaff, jr b O'Reilly	3	(6) c Ward b Fleetwood-Smith	17
G.O.B.Allen* not out	0	(7) c Sievers b Fleetwood-Smith	11
H.Verity c Brown b O'Reilly	0	(9) c McCabe b O'Reilly	11
W.Voce not out	7	c Bradman b Fleetwood-Smith	0
Extras (B 5, LB 1, NB 1)	7	(LB 3)	3
(9 wkts dec.)	76		323

1/0 2/14 3/56 4/68 5/71 6/71 7/76 8/76 9/76
1/29 2/65 3/117 4/155 5/179 6/195 7/306 8/322 9/323

Bowling: First Innings—McCabe 2-1-7-1; Sievers 11.2-5-21-5; O'Reilly 12-5-28-3; Fleetwood-Smith 3-1-13-0. Second Innings—Sievers 12-2-39-1; McCabe 8-0-32-0; O'Reilly 21-6-65-3; Fleetwood-Smith 25.6-2-124-5; Ward 12-1-60-1.

Umpires: E.G.Borwick and J.D.Scott

AUSTRALIA v ENGLAND 1936-37 (Fourth Test)

At Adelaide Oval, 29, 30 January, 1, 2, 4 February
Result: Australia won by 148 runs

Australia

J.H.W.Fingleton run out	10	lbw b Hammond	12
W.A.Brown c Allen b Farnes	42	c Ames b Voce	32
K.E.Rigg c Ames b Farnes	20	(5) c Hammond b Farnes	7
D.G.Bradman* b Allen	26	(3) c and b Hammond	212
S.J.McCabe c Allen b Robins	88	(4) c Wyatt b Robins	55
R.G.Gregory lbw b Hammond	23	run out	50
A.G.Chipperfield not out	57	c Ames b Hammond	31
W.A.S.Oldfield† run out	5	c Ames b Hammond	1
W.J.O'Reilly c Leyland b Allen	7	c Hammond b Farnes	1
E.L.McCormick c Ames b Hammond	4	b Hammond	1
L.O.Fleetwood-Smith b Farnes	1	not out	4
Extras (LB 2, NB 3)	5	(B 10, LB 15, NB 1, W 1)	27
	288		433

1/26 2/72 3/73 4/136 5/206
6/226 7/249 8/271 9/283

1/21 2/88 3/197 4/237 5/372
6/422 7/426 8/427 9/429

Bowling: *First Innings*—Voce 12-0-49-0; Allen 16-0-60-2; Farnes 20.6-1-71-3; Hammond 6-0-30-2; Verity 16-4-47-0; Robins 7-1-26-1. *Second Innings*—Farnes 24-2-89-2; Hammond 15.2-1-57-5; Allen 14-1-61-0; Voce 20-2-86-1; Verity 37-17-54-0; Robins 6-0-38-1; Barnett 5-1-15-0; Leyland 2-0-6-0.

England

C.J.Barnett lbw b Fleetwood-Smith	129	(2) c Chipperfield b Fleetwood-Smith	21
H.Verity c Bradman b O'Reilly	19	(1) b Fleetwood-Smith	17
W.R.Hammond c McCormick b O'Reilly	20	(4) b Fleetwood-Smith	39
M.Leyland c Chipperfield b Fleetwood-Smith	45	(5) c Chipperfield b Fleetwood-Smith	32
R.E.S.Wyatt c Fingleton b O'Reilly	7	(6) c Oldfield b McCabe	50
L.E.G.Ames† b McCormick	52	(7) lbw b Fleetwood-Smith	0
J.Hardstaff, jr c and b McCormick	20	(3) b O'Reilly	43
G.O.B.Allen* lbw b Fleetwood-Smith	11	c Gregory b McCormick	9
R.W.V.Robins c Oldfield b b O'Reilly	10	b McCormick	4
W.Voce c Rigg b Fleetwood-Smith	8	b Fleetwood-Smith	1
K.Farnes not out	0	not out	7
Extras (B 6, LB 2, NB 4, W 1)	13	(B 12, LB 2, NB 6)	20
	330		243

1/52 2/108 3/190 4/195 5/259
6/299 7/304 8/318 9/322

1/45 2/50 3/120 4/149 5/190
6/190 7/225 8/231 9/235

Bowling: *First Innings*—McCormick 21-2-81-2; McCabe 9-2-18-0; Fleetwood-Smith 41.4-10-129-4; O'Reilly 30-12-51-4; Chipperfield 9-1-24-0; Gregory 3-0-14-0. *Second Innings*—McCormick 13-1-43-2; McCabe 5-0-15-1; Fleetwood-Smith 30-1-110-6; O'Reilly 26-8-55-1.

Umpires: E.G.Borwick and J.D.Scott

AUSTRALIA v ENGLAND 1936-37 (Fifth Test)

At Melbourne Cricket Ground, 26, 27 February, 1, 2, 3 March
Result: Australia won by an innings and 200 runs

Australia

J.H.W.Fingleton c Voce b Farnes	17
K.E.Rigg c Ames b Farnes	28
D.G.Bradman* b Farnes	169
S.J.McCabe c Farnes b Verity	112
C.L.Badcock c Worthington b Voce	118
R.G.Gregory c Verity b Farnes	80
W.A.S.Oldfield† c Ames b Voce	21
L.J.Nash c Ames b Farnes	17
W.J.O'Reilly b Voce	1
E.L.McCormick not out	17
L.O.Fleetwood-Smith b Farnes	13
Extras (B 1, LB 5, NB 4, W 1)	11
	604

1/42 2/54 3/303 4/346 5/507
6/544 7/563 8/571 9/576

Bowling: Allen 17-0-99-0; Farnes 28.5-5-96-6; Voce 29-3-123-3; Verity 41-5-127-1; Worthington 6-0-60-0; Leyland 3-0-26-0.

England

C.J.Barnett c Oldfield b Nash	18	lbw b O'Reilly	41
T.S.Worthington hit wkt b Fleetwood-Smith	44	c Bradman b McCormick	6
J.Hardstaff, jr c McCormick b O'Reilly	83	b Nash	1
W.R.Hammond c Nash b O'Reilly	14	c Bradman b O'Reilly	56
M.Leyland b O'Reilly	7	c McCormick b F-Smith	28
R.E.S.Wyatt c Bradman b O'Reilly	38	run out	9
L.E.G.Ames† b Nash	19	c McCabe b McCormick	11
G.O.B.Allen* c Oldfield b Nash	0	c Nash b O'Reilly	7
H.Verity c Rigg b Nash	0	not out	2
W.Voce st Oldfield b O'Reilly	3	c Badcock b Fleetwood-Smith	1
K.Farnes not out	0	c Nash b Fleetwood-Smith	0
Extras (LB 12, NB 1)	13	(LB 3)	3
	239		165

1/33 2/96 3/130 4/140 5/202
6/236 7/236 8/236 9/239

1/9 2/10 3/70 4/121 5/142
6/142 7/153 8/162 9/165

Bowling: *First Innings*—McCormick 13-1-54-0; Nash 17.5-1-70-4; O'Reilly 23-7-51-5; Fleetwood-Smith 18-3-51-1. *Second Innings*—McCormick 9-0-33-2; Nash 7-1-34-1; O'Reilly 19-6-58-3; McCabe 1-0-1-0; Fleetwood-Smith 13.2-3-36-3.

Umpires: E.G.Borwick and J.D.Scott

ENGLAND v AUSTRALIA 1938 (First Test)

At Trent Bridge, Nottingham, 10, 11, 13, 14 June
Result: Match drawn

England

C.J.Barnett c McCormick	.....	126
L.Hutton lbw b Fleetwood-Smith	.....	100
W.J.Edrich b O'Reilly	.....	5
W.R.Hammond* b O'Reilly	.....	26
E.Paynter not out	.....	216
D.C.S.Compton c Badcock b Fleetwood-Smith	.....	102
L.E.G.Ames† b Fleetwood-Smith	.....	46
H.Verity b Fleetwood-Smith	.....	3
R.A.Sinfield lbw b O'Reilly	.....	6
D.V.P.Wright not out	.....	1
K.Farnes		
Extras (B 1, LB 22, NB 4)	.....	27

1/219 2/240 3/244 4/281 5/487 (8 wkts dec.) 658
6/577 7/597 8/626

Bowling: McCormick 32-4-108-1; O'Reilly 56-11-164-3; McCabe 21-5-64-0; Fleetwood-Smith 49-9-153-4; Ward 30-2-142-0.

Australia

J.H.W.Fingleton b Wright	9		(8) c Hammond b Edrich	40
W.A.Brown c Ames b Farnes	48		c Paynter b Verity	133
D.G.Bradman* c Ames b Sinfield	51		not out	144
S.J.McCabe c Compton b Verity	232		c Hammond b Verity	39
F.A.Ward b Farnes	2		not out	7
A.L.Hassett c Hammond b Wright	1		(5) c Compton b Verity	2
C.L.Badcock b Wright	9		(6) b Wright	5
B.A.Barnett† c Wright b Farnes	22		(7) lbw b Sinfield	31
W.J.O'Reilly c Paynter b Farnes	9			
E.L.McCormick b Wright	2			
L.O.Fleetwood-Smith not out	5			
Extras (B 10, LB 10, W 1)	21		(B 5, LB 16, NB 5)	26

1/34 2/111 3/134 4/144 5/151 411
6/194 7/263 8/319 9/334

1/89 2/259 3/331 (6 wkts dec.) 427
4/337 5/369 6/417

Bowling: First Innings—Farnes 37-11-106-4; Hammond 19-7-44-0; Sinfield 28-8-51-1; Wright 39-6-153-4; Verity 7.3-0-36-1. Second Innings—Farnes 24-2-78-0; Hammond 12-6-15-0; Sinfield 35-8-72-1; Wright 37-8-85-1; Verity 62-27-102-3; Edrich 13-2-39-1; Barnett 1-0-10-0.

Umpires: F.Chester and E.Robinson

ENGLAND v AUSTRALIA 1938 (Second Test)

At Lord's, London, 24, 25, 27, 28 June
Result: Match drawn

England

C.J.Barnett c Brown b McCormick	18		c McCabe b McCormick	12
L.Hutton c Brown b McCormick	4		c McCormick b O'Reilly	5
W.J.Edrich b McCormick	0	(4)	c McCabe b McCormick	10
W.R.Hammond* b McCormick	240	(6)	c sub (M.G.Waite) b McCabe	2
E.Paynter lbw b O'Reilly	99		run out	43
D.C.S.Compton lbw b O'Reilly	6	(7)	not out	76
L.E.G.Ames† c McCormick b Fleetwood-Smith	83	(8)	c McCabe b O'Reilly	6
H.Verity b O'Reilly	5	(3)	b McCormick	11
A.W.Wellard c McCormick b O'Reilly	4		b McCabe	38
D.V.P.Wright b Fleetwood-Smith	6		not out	10
K.Farnes not out	5			
Extras (B 1, LB 12, NB 10, W 1)	24		(B 12, LB 12, NB 4, W 1)	29

1/12 2/20 3/31 4/253 5/271 494
6/457 7/472 8/476 9/483

1/25 2/28 3/43 (8 wkts dec.) 242
4/64 5/76 6/128 7/142 8/216

Bowling: First Innings—.McCormick 27-1-101-4; McCabe 31-4-86-0; Fleetwood-Smith 33.5-2-139-2; O'Reilly 37-6-93-4; Chipperfield 8.4-0-51-0. Second Innings—McCormick 24-5-72-3; McCabe 12-1-58-2; Fleetwood-Smith 7-1-30-0; O'Reilly 29-10-53-2.

Australia

J.H.W.Fingleton c Hammond b Wright	31	c Hammond b Wellard	4
W.A.Brown not out	206	b Verity	10
D.G.Bradman* b Verity	18	not out	102
S.J.McCabe c Verity b Farnes	38	c Hutton b Verity	21
A.L.Hassett lbw b Wellard	56	b Wright	42
C.L.Badcock b Wellard	0	c Wright b Edrich	0
B.A.Barnett† c Compton b Verity	8	c Paynter b Edrich	14
A.G.Chipperfield lbw b Verity	1		
W.J.O'Reilly b Farnes	42		
E.L.McCormick c Barnett b Farnes	0		
L.O.Fleetwood-Smith c Barnett b Verity	7		
Extras (B 1, LB 8, NB 6)	15	(B 5, LB 3, NB 1, W 2)	11

1/69 2/101 3/152 4/276 5/276 422
6/307 7/308 8/393 9/393

1/8 2/71 3/111 4/175 (6 wkts) 204
5/180 6/204

Bowling: First Innings—Farnes 43-6-135-3; Wellard 23-2-96-2; Wright 16-2-68-1; Verity 35.4-9-103-4; Edrich 4-2-5-0. Second Innings—Farnes 13-3-51-0; Wellard 9-1-30-1; Wright 8-0-56-1; Verity 13-5-29-2; Edrich 5.2-0-27-2.

Umpires: E.J.Smith and F.I.Walden

ENGLAND v AUSTRALIA 1938 (Fourth Test)

At Headingley, Leeds, 22, 23, 25 July
Result: Australia won by 5 wickets

England

W.J.Edrich b O'Reilly	12	
C.J.Barnett c Barnett b McCormick	30	
J.Hardstaff, jr run out	4	
W.R.Hammond* b O'Reilly	76	
E.Paynter st Barnett b Fleetwood-Smith	28	
D.C.S.Compton b O'Reilly	14	
W.F.F.Price† c McCabe b O'Reilly	0	
H.Verity not out	25	
D.V.P.Wright c Fingleton b Fleetwood-Smith	22	
K.Farnes c Fingleton b Fleetwood-Smith	2	
W.E.Bowes b O'Reilly	3	
Extras (LB 4, NB 3)	7	
		223

1/29 2/34 3/88 4/142 5/171
6/171 7/172 8/213 9/215

Bowling: *First Innings*—McCormick 20-6-46-1; Waite 18-7-31-0; O'Reilly 34.1-17-66-5; Fleetwood-Smith 25-7-73-3; McCabe 1-1-0-0. *Second Innings*—McCormick 11-4-18-1; Waite 2-0-9-0; O'Reilly 21.5-8-56-5; Fleetwood-Smith 16-4-34-4.

Australia

J.H.W.Fingleton b Verity	30		lbw b Verity		9
W.A.Brown b Wright	22		lbw b Farnes		9
B.A.Barnett† c Price b Farnes	57	(7)	not out		15
D.G.Bradman* b Bowes	103	(3)	c Verity b Wright		16
S.J.McCabe b Farnes	1	(4)	c Barnett b Wright		15
C.L.Badcock b Bowes	4		not out		5
A.L.Hassett c Hammond b Wright	13	(5)	c Edrich b Wright		33
M.G.Waite c Price b Farnes	3				
W.J.O'Reilly c Hammond b Farnes	2				
E.L.McCormick b Bowes	0				
L.O.Fleetwood-Smith not out	2				
Extras (B 2, LB 3)	5		(B 4, NB 1)		5
	242		5/91	(5 wkts)	107

1/28 2/87 3/128 4/136 5/145
6/195 7/232 8/240 9/240

1/17 2/32 3/50 4/61
5/91

Bowling: *First Innings*—Farnes 26-3-77-4; Bowes 35.4-6-79-3; Wright 15-4-38-2; Verity 1-6-30-1; Edrich 3-0-13-0. *Second Innings*—Farnes 11.3-4-17-1; Bowes 11-0-35-0; Wright 5-0-26-3; Verity 5-2-24-1.

Umpires: F.Chester and E.J.Smith

ENGLAND v AUSTRALIA 1938 (Fifth Test)

At Kennington Oval, London, 20, 22, 23, 24 August
Result: Australia won by an innings and 579 runs

England

L.Hutton c Hassett b O'Reilly	364	
W.J.Edrich lbw b O'Reilly	12	
M.Leyland run out	187	
W.R.Hammond* lbw b Fleetwood-Smith	59	
E.Paynter lbw b O'Reilly	0	
D.C.S.Compton b Waite	1	
J.Hardstaff, jr not out	169	
H.Verity not out	8	
K.Farnes		
W.E.Bowes		
Extras (B 22, LB 19, NB 8, W 1)	50	
	(7 wkts dec.)	903

1/29 2/411 3/546 4/547 5/555
6/770 7/876

Bowling: Waite 72-16-150-1; McCabe 38-8-85-0; O'Reilly 85-26-178-3; Fleetwood-Smith 87-11-298-1; Barnes 38-3-84-1; Hassett 13-2-52-0; Bradman 2.2-1-6-0.

Australia

W.A.Brown c Hammond b Leyland	69	c Edrich b Farnes	15
C.L.Badcock c Hardstaff b Bowes	0	b Bowes	9
S.J.McCabe c Edrich b Farnes	14	c Wood b Farnes	2
A.L.Hassett c Compton b Edrich	42	lbw b Bowes	10
S.G.Barnes b Farnes	41	lbw b Verity	33
B.A.Barnett† c Wood b Bowes	2	b Farnes	46
M.G.Waite b Bowes	8	c Edrich b Verity	0
W.J.O'Reilly c Wood b Bowes	0	not out	7
L.O.Fleetwood-Smith not out	16	c Leyland b Farnes	0
D.G.Bradman* absent hurt	-	absent hurt	-
J.H.W.Fingleton absent hurt	-	absent hurt	-
Extras (B 4, LB 2, NB 3)	9	(B 1)	1
	201		123

1/0 2/19 3/70 4/145 5/147
6/160 7/160 8/201

1/15 2/18 3/35 4/41 5/115
6/115 7/117 8/123

Bowling: *First Innings*—Farnes 13-2-54-1; Bowes 19-3-49-5; Edrich 10-2-55-1; Verity 5-1-15-0; Leyland 3.1-0-11-1; Hammond 2-0-8-0. *Second Innings*—Farnes 12.1-1-63-4; Bowes 10-3-25-2; Verity 7-3-15-2; Leyland 5-0-19-0.

Umpires: F.Chester and F.I.Walden

NEW ZEALAND v AUSTRALIA 1945-46 (Only Test)

At Basin Reserve, Wellington, 29, 30 March

Result: Australia won by an innings and 103 runs

New Zealand

W.A.Hadlee*	c Miller b Toshack	6	b Miller ... 3
W.M.Anderson	b Lindwall	4	b Lindwall ... 1
V.J.Scott	c Barnes b O'Reilly	14	c Tallon b Miller ... 4
W.M.Wallace	c Barnes b Toshack	10	run out ... 14
E.W.T.Tindill†	b Toshack	1	lbw b Toshack ... 13
C.G.Rowe	b O'Reilly	0	b O'Reilly ... 0
L.A.Butterfield	b O'Reilly	0	lbw b O'Reilly ... 0
D.A.N.McRae	c Hassett b O'Reilly	0	(9) c Meuleman b McCool ... 8
C.Burke	lbw b Toshack	1	(8) b Toshack ... 3
J.Cowie	st Tallon b O'Reilly	2	c Toshack b O'Reilly ... 0
D.C.Cleverley	not out	1	not out ... 1
Extras	(B 3)	3	(B 5, NB 2) ... 7
		42	54

1/7 2/15 3/37 4/37 5/37
6/37 7/37 8/39 9/40

1/3 2/5 3/12 4/36 5/37
6/37 7/39 8/41 9/42

Bowling: *First Innings*—Lindwall 8-1-13-1; Toshack 19-13-12-4; O'Reilly 12-5-14-5. *Second Innings*—Lindwall 9-3-16-1; Toshack 10-5-6-2; O'Reilly 7-1-19-3; Miller 6-2-6-2; McCool 0.2-0-0-1.

Australia

W.A.Brown*	c Rowe b Burke	67
K.D.Meuleman	b Cowie	0
S.G.Barnes	c Cowie	54
K.R.Miller	c Hadlee b Burke	30
A.L.Hassett	c Tindill b Cowie	19
C.L.McCool	c Hadlee b Cowie	7
I.W.Johnson	not out	7
D.Tallon†	c Scott b Cowie	5
R.R.Lindwall	c Anderson b Cowie	0
W.J.O'Reilly		
E.R.H.Toshack		
Extras	(B 5, LB 3, NB 2)	10
	(8 wkts dec.)	199

1/9 2/118 3/142 4/174 5/186
6/186 7/196 8/199

Bowling: McRae 14-3-44-0; Cowie 21-8-40-6; Cleverley 15-1-51-0; Butterfield 13-6-24-0; Burke 11-2-30-2.

Umpires: H.W.Gourlay and M.F.Pengelly

AUSTRALIA v ENGLAND 1946-47 (First Test)

At Woolloongabba, Brisbane, 29, 30 November, 2, 3, 4 December

Result: Australia won by an innings and 332 runs

Australia

S.G.Barnes	c Bedser b Wright	31
A.R.Morris	c Hammond b Bedser	2
D.G.Bradman*	b Edrich	187
A.L.Hassett	c Yardley b Bedser	128
K.R.Miller	lbw b Wright	79
C.L.McCool	lbw b Wright	95
I.W.Johnson	lbw b Wright	47
D.Tallon†	lbw b Edrich	14
R.R.Lindwall	c Voce b Wright	31
G.E.Tribe	c Gibb b Edrich	1
E.R.H.Toshack	not out	1
Extras	(B 5, LB 11, NB 11, W 2)	29
		645

1/9 2/46 3/322 4/428 5/465
6/596 7/599 8/629 9/643

Bowling: Voce 28-9-92-0; Bedser 41-5-159-2; Wright 43.6-4-467-5; Edrich 25-2-107-3; Yardley 13-1-47-0; Ikin 2-0-24-0; Compton 6-0-20-0.

England

L.Hutton	b Miller	7	c Barnes b Miller ... 0
C.Washbrook	c Barnes b Miller	6	c Barnes b Miller ... 13
W.J.Edrich	c McCool b Miller	16	lbw b Toshack ... 7
D.C.S.Compton	lbw b Miller	17	c Barnes b Toshack ... 15
W.R.Hammond*	lbw b Toshack	32	b Toshack ... 23
J.T.Ikin	c Tallon b Miller	0	b Tribe ... 32
N.W.D.Yardley	c Tallon b Toshack	29	c Hassett b Toshack ... 0
P.A.Gibb†	b Miller	13	lbw b Toshack ... 11
W.Voce	not out	1	c Hassett b Tribe ... 18
A.V.Bedser	lbw b Miller	1	c and b Toshack ... 18
D.V.P.Wright	c Tallon b Toshack	4	not out ... 10
Extras	(B 8, LB 3, NB 3, W 2)	16	(B 15, LB 7, NB 2, W 1) ... 25
		141	172

1/10 2/25 3/49 4/56 5/56
6/121 7/134 8/136 9/136

1/0 2/13 3/33 4/62 5/65
6/65 7/112 8/114 9/143

Bowling: *First Innings*—Lindwall 12-4-23-0; Miller 22-4-60-7; Toshack 16.5-11-17-3; Tribe 9-2-19-0; McCool 1-0-5-0; Barnes 1-0-1-0. *Second Innings*—Miller 11-3-17-2; Toshack 20.7-2-82-6; Tribe 12-2-48-2.

Umpires: E.G.Borwick and J.D.Scott

AUSTRALIA v ENGLAND 1946-47 (Second Test)

At Sydney Cricket Ground, 13, 14, 16, 17, 18, 19 December

Result: Australia won by an innings and 33 runs

England

L.Hutton	c Tallon b Johnson	39	hit wkt b Miller	37
C.Washbrook	b Freer	1	c McCool b Johnson	41
W.J.Edrich	lbw b McCool	71	b McCool	119
D.C.S.Compton	c Tallon b McCool	5	c Bradman b Freer	54
W.R.Hammond*	c Tallon b McCool	1	c Toshack b McCool	37
J.T.Ikin	c Hassett b Johnson	60	b Freer	17
N.W.D.Yardley	c Tallon b Johnson	25	b McCool	35
T.P.B.Smith	lbw b Johnson	4	c Hassett b Johnson	2
T.G.Evans†	b Johnson	5	st Tallon b McCool	9
A.V.Bedser	b Johnson	14	not out	3
D.V.P.Wright	not out	15	c Tallon b McCool	0
Extras	(B 4, LB 11)	15	(B 8, LB 6, NB 2, W 1)	17
		255		**371**

1/10 2/88 3/97 4/99 5/148
6/187 7/197 8/205 9/234

1/49 2/118 3/220 4/280 5/309
6/327 7/346 8/366 9/369

Bowling: *First Innings*—Miller 9-2-24-0; Freer 7-1-25-1; Toshack 7-2-6-0; Tribe 20-3-70-0; Johnson 30.1-12-42-6; McCool 23-2-73-3. *Second Innings*—Miller 11-3-37-1; Freer 13-2-49-2; Toshack 6-1-16-0; Tribe 12-0-40-0; Johnson 29-7-92-2; McCool 32.4-4-109-5; Barnes 3-0-11-0.

Australia

S.G.Barnes	c Ikin b Bedser	234
A.R.Morris	b Edrich	5
I.W.Johnson	c Washbrook b Edrich	7
A.L.Hassett	c Compton b Edrich	34
K.R.Miller	c Evans b Smith	40
D.G.Bradman*	lbw b Yardley	234
C.L.McCool	c Hammond b Smith	12
D.Tallon†	c and b Wright	30
F.W.Freer	not out	28
G.E.Tribe	not out	25
E.R.H.Toshack		
Extras	(LB 7, NB 2, W 1)	10
	(8 wkts dec.)	**659**

1/24 2/37 3/96 4/159 5/564
6/564 7/595 8/617

Bowling: Bedser 46-7-153-1; Edrich 26-3-79-3; Wright 46-8-169-1; Smith 37-1-172-2; Ikin 3-0-15-0; Compton 6-0-38-0; Yardley 9-0-23-1.

Umpires: E.G.Borwick and J.D.Scott

AUSTRALIA v ENGLAND 1946-47 (Third Test)

At Melbourne Cricket Ground, 1, 2, 3, 4, 6, 7 January

Result: Match drawn

England

L.Hutton	c McCool b Lindwall	2		c Bradman b Toshack	40
C.Washbrook	c Tallon b Dooland	62		b Dooland	112
W.J.Edrich	lbw b Lindwall	89		lbw b McCool	13
D.C.S.Compton	lbw b Toshack	11		run out	14
W.R.Hammond*	c and b Dooland	9		b Lindwall	26
J.T.Ikin	c Miller b Dooland	48		c Hassett b Miller	5
N.W.D.Yardley	b McCool	61		not out	53
T.G.Evans†	b McCool	17	(9)	not out	0
W.Voce	lbw b Dooland	0			
A.V.Bedser	not out	27	(8)	lbw b Miller	25
D.V.P.Wright	b Johnson	10			
Extras	(B 1, LB 12, NB 2)	15		(B 15, LB 6, W 1)	22
		351		(7 wkts)	**310**

1/8 2/155 3/167 4/176 5/179
6/292 7/298 8/298 9/324

1/138 2/163 3/186
4/197 5/221 6/249 7/294

Bowling: *First Innings*—Lindwall 20-1-64-2; Miller 10-0-34-0; Toshack 26-5-88-1; McCool 19-3-53-2; Dooland 27-5-69-4; Johnson 6.5-1-28-1. *Second Innings*—Lindwall 16-2-59-1; Miller 11-0-41-2; Toshack 16-5-39-1; McCool 24-9-41-1; Dooland 21-1-84-1; Johnson 12-4-24-0.

Australia

S.G.Barnes	lbw b Bedser	45		c Evans b Yardley	32
A.R.Morris	lbw b Bedser	21		b Bedser	155
D.G.Bradman*	b Yardley	79		c and b Yardley	49
A.L.Hassett	c Hammond b Wright	12		b Wright	9
K.R.Miller	c Evans b Wright	33		c Hammond b Yardley	34
I.W.Johnson	lbw b Yardley	0	(7)	run out	0
C.L.McCool	not out	104	(6)	c Evans b Bedser	43
D.Tallon†	c Evans b Edrich	35		c and b Wright	92
R.R.Lindwall	b Bedser	9		c Washbrook b Bedser	100
B.Dooland	c Hammond b Edrich	19		c Compton b Wright	1
E.R.H.Toshack	c Hutton b Edrich	6		not out	2
Extras	(NB 2)	2		(B 14, LB 2, NB 3)	19
		365			**536**

1/32 2/108 3/143 4/188 5/188
6/192 7/255 8/272 9/355

1/68 2/159 3/177 4/242 5/333
6/335 7/341 8/495 9/511

Bowling: *First Innings*—Voce 10-2-40-0; Bedser 31-4-99-3; Wright 26-2-124-2; Yardley 20-4-50-2; Edrich 10.3-2-50-3. *Second Innings*—Voce 6-1-29-0; Bedser 34.3-4-176-3; Wright 32-3-131-3; Yardley 20-0-67-3; Edrich 18-1-86-0; Hutton 3-0-28-0.

Umpires: E.G.Borwick and J.D.Scott

AUSTRALIA v ENGLAND 1946-47 (Fourth Test)

At Adelaide Oval, 31 January, 1, 3, 4, 5, 6 February

Result: Match drawn

England

Batsman	First innings		Second innings	
L.Hutton	lbw b McCool	94	b Johnson	76
C.Washbrook	c Tallon b Dooland	65	c Tallon b Lindwall	39
W.J.Edrich	c and b Dooland	17	c Bradman b Toshack	46
W.R.Hammond*	b Toshack	18	c Lindwall b Toshack	22
D.C.S.Compton	c and b Lindwall	147	not out	103
J.Hardstaff, jr	b Miller	67	b Toshack	9
J.T.Ikin	c Toshack b Dooland	21	lbw b Toshack	1
N.W.D.Yardley	not out	18	c Tallon b Lindwall	18
A.V.Bedser	b Lindwall	2	c Tallon b Miller	3
T.G.Evans†	b Lindwall	0	not out	10
D.V.P.Wright	b Lindwall	0		
Extras	(B 4, LB 5, W 2)	11	(B 5, LB 3, NB 3, W 2)	13
		460	(8 wkts dec.)	340

1/137 2/173 3/196 4/202 5/320 6/381 7/455 8/460 9/460

1/100 2/137 3/178 4/188 5/207 6/215 7/250 8/255

Bowling: First Innings—Lindwall 23-5-52-4; Miller 16-0-45-1; Toshack 30-13-59-1; McCool 29-1-91-1; Johnson 22-3-69-0; Dooland 33-1-133-3. Second Innings—Lindwall 17.1-4-60-2; Miller 11-0-34-1; Toshack 36-6-76-4; McCool 19-3-41-0; Johnson 25-8-51-1; Dooland 17-2-65-0.

Australia

Batsman	First innings		Second innings	
M.R.Harvey	b Bedser	12	b Yardley	31
A.R.Morris	c Evans b Bedser	122	not out	124
D.G.Bradman*	b Bedser	0	not out	56
A.L.Hassett	c Hammond b Wright	78		
K.R.Miller	not out	141		
I.W.Johnson	lbw b Wright	52		
C.L.McCool	c Bedser b Yardley	2		
D.Tallon†	b Wright	3		
R.R.Lindwall	c Evans b Yardley	20		
B.Dooland	c Bedser b Yardley	29		
E.R.H.Toshack	run out	0		
Extras	(B 16, LB 6, NB 4, W 2)	28	(LB 2, NB 2)	4
		487	(1 wkt)	215

1/18 2/18 3/207 4/222 5/372 6/389 7/398 8/423 9/486

1/116

Bowling: First Innings—Bedser 30-6-97-3; Edrich 20-3-88-0; Wright 32.4-1-152-3; Yardley 31-7-101-3; Ikin 2-0-9-0; Compton 3-0-12-0. Second Innings—Bedser 15-1-68-0; Edrich 7-2-25-0; Wright 9-0-49-0; Yardley 13-0-69-1.

Umpires: E.G.Borwick and J.D.Scott

AUSTRALIA v ENGLAND 1946-47 (Fifth Test)

At Sydney Cricket Ground, 28 February, 1 (no play), 3, 4, 5 March

Result: Australia won by five wickets

England

Batsman	First innings		Second innings	
L.Hutton	retired ill	122	absent ill	—
C.Washbrook	b Lindwall	0	b McCool	24
W.J.Edrich	c Tallon b Lindwall	60	st Tallon b McCool	24
L.B.Fishlock	b McCool	14	(1) lbw b Lindwall	0
D.C.S.Compton	hit wkt b Lindwall	17	(4) c Miller b Toshack	76
N.W.D.Yardley*	c Miller b Lindwall	2	b McCool	11
J.T.Ikin	b Lindwall	0	(5) st Tallon b McCool	0
T.G.Evans†	b Lindwall	29	(7) b Miller	20
T.P.B.Smith	b Lindwall	2	(8) c Tallon b Lindwall	24
A.V.Bedser	not out	10	(9) st Tallon b McCool	4
D.V.P.Wright	c Tallon b Miller	7	(10) not out	1
Extras	(B 7, LB 8, NB 1, W 1)	17	(B 1, LB 1)	2
		280		186

1/1 2/151 3/188 4/215 5/225 6/225 7/244 8/269 9/280

1/0 2/42 3/65 4/65 5/85 6/120 7/157 8/184 9/186

Bowling: First Innings—Lindwall 22-3-63-7; Miller 15.3-2-31-1; Tribe 28-2-95-0; Toshack 16-4-40-0; McCool 13-0-34-1. Second Innings—Lindwall 12-1-46-2; Miller 6-1-11-1; Tribe 14-0-58-0; Toshack 4-1-14-1; McCool 21.4-5-44-5, Barnes 3-0-11-0.

Australia

Batsman	First innings		Second innings	
S.G.Barnes	c Evans b Bedser	71	c Evans b Bedser	30
A.R.Morris	lbw b Bedser	57	run out	17
D.G.Bradman*	b Wright	12	c Compton b Bedser	63
A.L.Hassett	c Ikin b Wright	24	c Ikin b Wright	47
K.R.Miller	c Ikin b Wright	23	not out	34
R.A.Hamence	not out	30	c Edrich b Wright	1
C.L.McCool	c Yardley b Wright	3	not out	13
D.Tallon†	c Compton b Wright	0		
R.R.Lindwall	c Smith b Wright	0		
G.E.Tribe	c Fishlock b Wright	9		
E.R.H.Toshack	run out	5		
Extras	(B 7, LB 6, NB 6)	19	(B 4, LB 1, NB 4)	9
		253	(5 wkts)	214

1/126 2/146 3/146 4/187 5/218 6/230 7/230 8/233 9/245

1/45 2/51 3/149 4/173 5/180

Bowling: First Innings—Bedser 27-7-49-2; Edrich 7-0-34-0; Smith 8-0-38-0; Wright 29-4-105-7; Yardley 5-2-8-0. Second Innings—Bedser 22-4-75-2; Edrich 2-0-14-0; Smith 2-0-8-0; Wright 22-1-93-2; Yardley 3-1-7-0; Compton 1.2-0-8-0.

Umpires: E.G.Borwick and J.D.Scott

AUSTRALIA v INDIA 1947-48 (First Test)

At Woolloongabba, Brisbane, 28, 29 November, 1, 2, 3 (no play), 4 December

Result: Australia won by an innings and 226 runs

Australia

Batsman		Runs
W.A.Brown c Irani b Amarnath		11
A.R.Morris hit wkt b Sarwate		47
D.G.Bradman* hit wkt b Amarnath		185
A.L.Hassett c Gul Mahomed b Mankad		48
K.R.Miller c Mankad b Amarnath		58
C.L.McCool c Sohoni b Amarnath		10
R.R.Lindwall st Irani b Mankad		7
D.Tallon† not out		3
I.W.Johnson c Rangnekar b Mankad		6
E.R.H.Toshack not out		0
W.A.Johnston		
Extras (B 5, LB 1, W 1)		7
Total (8 wkts dec.)		**382**

1/38 2/97 3/198 4/318 5/344
6/373 7/373 8/380

Bowling: Sohoni 23-4-81-0; Amarnath 39-10-84-4; Mankad 34-3-113-3; Sarwate 5-1-16-1; Hazare 11-1-63-0; Nayudu 3-0-18-0

India

Batsman	1st Innings		2nd Innings	
M.H.Mankad	c Tallon b Lindwall	0	b Lindwall	7
C.T.Sarwate	c Johnston b Miller	12	b Johnston	26
Gul Mahomed	b Lindwall	0	b Toshack	13
H.R.Adhikari	c McCool b Johnston	8	lbw b Toshack	2
G.Kishenchand	c Tallon b Johnston	1	c Bradman b Toshack	13
V.S.Hazare	c Brown b Toshack	10	c Morris b Toshack	0
L.Amarnath*	c Bradman b Toshack	22	b Toshack	18
K.M.Rangnekar	c Miller b Toshack	1	c Hassett b Toshack	5
S.W.Sohoni	c Miller b Toshack	2	c Brown b Miller	0
C.S.Nayudu	not out	0	c Hassett b Lindwall	4
J.K.Irani†	c Hassett b Toshack	2	not out	6
Extras	(B 1, LB 1)	2	(B 3, NB 1)	4
Total		**58**		**98**

1/0 2/0 3/19 4/23 5/23
6/53 7/56 8/58 9/58

1/14 2/27 3/41 4/41 5/72
6/80 7/80 8/89 9/94

Bowling: First Innings—Lindwall 5-2-11-2; Johnston 8-4-17-2; Miller 6-1-26-1; Toshack 2.3-1-2-5. Second Innings—Lindwall 10.7-1-19-2; Johnston 9-6-11-1; Miller 10-2-30-1; Toshack 17-6-29-6; Johnson 3-1-5-0.

Umpires: A.N.Barlow and E.G.Borwick

AUSTRALIA v INDIA 1947-48 (Second Test)

At Sydney Cricket Ground, 12, 13, 15 (no play), 16 (no play), 17, 18 (no play) December

Result: Match drawn

India

Batsman	1st Innings		2nd Innings	
M.H.Mankad	b Lindwall	5	b Lindwall	5
C.T.Sarwate	b Johnston	0	(3) c Johnson b Johnston	3
Gul Mahomed	c Brown b Miller	29	(4) c Bradman b Johnson	5
V.S.Hazare	b Miller	16	(5) not out	13
L.Amarnath*	b Johnson	25	(7) c Morris b Johnson	14
G.Kishenchand	b Johnson	44	(8) c McCool b Johnston	0
H.R.Adhikari	lbw b Johnston	0	(9) not out	0
D.G.Phadkar	c Miller b McCool	51	(6) c Tallon b Miller	2
C.S.Nayudu	c and b McCool	6		
Amir Elahi	c Miller b McCool	4		
J.K.Irani†	not out	1	(2) c Miller b Johnston	13
Extras	(B 5, LB 2)	7	(B 3, LB 3)	6
Total		**188**	**(7 wkts)**	**61**

1/2 2/16 3/52 4/57 5/94
6/95 7/165 8/174 9/182

1/17 2/19 3/26 4/29
5/34 6/53 7/55

Bowling: First Innings—Lindwall 12-3-30-1; Johnston 17-4-33-2; McCool 18-2-71-3; Johnson 14-3-22-2. Second Innings—Lindwall 5-1-13-1; Johnston 13-5-15-3; Miller 6-2-5-1; Johnson 13-7-22-2.

Australia

Batsman		Runs
W.A.Brown run out		18
A.R.Morris lbw b Amarnath		10
D.G.Bradman* b Hazare		13
A.L.Hassett c Adhikari b Hazare		6
K.R.Miller lbw b Phadkar		17
R.A.Hamence c Adhikari b Mankad		25
I.W.Johnson lbw b Phadkar		1
C.L.McCool b Phadkar		9
R.R.Lindwall b Hazare		0
D.Tallon† c Irani b Hazare		6
W.A.Johnston not out		0
Extras (B 1, LB 1)		2
Total		**107**

1/25 2/30 3/43 4/48 5/86
6/92 7/92 8/97 9/105

Bowling: Phadkar 10-2-14-3; Amarnath 14-4-31-1; Mankad 9-0-31-1; Hazare 13.2-1-29-4.

Umpires: A.N.Barlow and E.G.Borwick

AUSTRALIA v INDIA 1947-48 (Third Test)

At Melbourne Cricket Ground, 1, 2, 3, 5 January
Result: Australia won by 233 runs

Australia

S.G.Barnes	b Mankad	12	(4) c Sen b Amarnath	15
A.R.Morris	b Amarnath	45	(5) not out	100
D.G.Bradman*	lbw b Phadkar	132	(6) not out	127
A.L.Hassett	lbw b Mankad	80		
K.R.Miller	lbw b Mankad	29		
R.A.Hamence	st Sen b Amarnath	25		
R.R.Lindwall	b Amarnath	26		
D.Tallon†	c Mankad b Amarnath	2		
B.Dooland	not out	21	(2) lbw b Phadkar	6
I.W.Johnson	lbw b Mankad	16	(1) c Hazare b Amarnath	0
W.A.Johnston	run out	5	(3) lbw b Amarnath	3
Extras	(B 1)	1	(B 3, NB 1)	4
		394	(4 wkts dec.)	255

1/29 2/99 3/268 4/289 5/302
6/339 7/341 8/352 9/387

1/1 2/11 3/13
4/32

Bowling: First Innings—Phadkar 15-1-80-1; Amarnath 21-3-78-4; Hazare 16.1-0-62-0; Mankad 37-4-135-4; Sarwate 3-0-16-0; Nayudu 2-0-22-0. Second Innings—Phadkar 10-1-28-1; Amarnath 20-3-52-3; Hazare 11-1-55-0; Mankad 18-4-74-0; Sarwate 5-0-41-0; Gul Mahomed 1-0-1-0.

India

M.H.Mankad	c Tallon b Johnston	116	b Johnston	13
C.T.Sarwate	c Tallon b Johnston	36	b Johnston	1
Gul Mahomed	c and b Dooland	12	c Morris b Johnson	28
V.S.Hazare	c Tallon b Barnes	17	c Barnes b Miller	10
L.Amarnath*	lbw b Barnes	0	b Lindwall	8
D.G.Phadkar	not out	55	c Barnes b Johnston	13
H.R.Adhikari	st Tallon b Johnson	26	c Lindwall b Johnson	1
K.Rai Singh	c Barnes b Johnson	2	c Tallon b Johnston	24
K.M.Rangnekar	c and b Johnson	6	c Hamence b Johnson	18
P.Sen†	b Johnson	4	c Hassett b Johnson	2
C.S.Nayudu	not out	4	not out	0
Extras	(B 9, LB 3, NB 1)	13	(B 6, LB 1)	7
	(9 wkts dec.)	291		125

1/124 2/145 3/188 4/188 5/198
6/260 7/264 8/280 9/284

1/10 2/27 3/44 4/60 5/60
6/69 7/100 8/107 9/125

Bowling: First Innings—Lindwall 12-0-47-0; Miller 13-2-46-0; Johnston 12-0-33-2; Johnson 14-1-59-4; Dooland 12-0-68-1; Barnes 6-1-25-2. Second Innings—Lindwall 3-0-10-1; Miller 7-0-29-1; Johnston 10-1-44-4; Johnson 5.7-0-35-4.

Umpires: A.N.Barlow and H.Elphinston

AUSTRALIA v INDIA 1947-48 (Fourth Test)

At Adelaide Oval, 23, 24, 26, 27, 28 January
Result: Australia won by an innings and 16 runs

Australia

S.G.Barnes	lbw b Mankad	112
A.R.Morris	b Phadkar	7
D.G.Bradman*	b Hazare	201
A.L.Hassett	not out	198
K.R.Miller	b Rangachari	67
R.N.Harvey	lbw b Rangachari	13
C.L.McCool	b Phadkar	27
I.W.Johnson	b Rangachari	22
R.R.Lindwall	b Rangachari	2
D.Tallon†	lbw b Mankad	1
E.R.H.Toshack	lbw b Hazare	8
Extras	(B 8, LB 6, NB 2)	16
		674

1/20 2/256 3/361 4/503 5/523
6/576 7/634 8/640 9/641

Bowling: Phadkar 15-0-74-2; Amarnath 9-0-42-0; Rangachari 41-5-141-4; Mankad 43-8-170-2; Sarwate 22-1-121-0; Hazare 21.3-1-110-2.

India

M.H.Mankad	b McCool	0	c Tallon b Lindwall	49
C.T.Sarwate	b Miller	11	b Toshack	1
P.Sen†	b Miller	0	(10) not out	0
L.Amarnath*	c Bradman b Johnson	46	(3) b Lindwall	46
V.S.Hazare	lbw b Johnson	116	(4) b Lindwall	145
Gul Mahomed	st Tallon b Johnson	4	(5) b Barnes	34
D.G.Phadkar	lbw Toshack	123	(6) lbw b Lindwall	14
G.Kishenchand	b Lindwall	10	(7) b Lindwall	0
H.R.Adhikari	run out	2	(8) lbw b Miller	51
K.M.Rangnekar	st Tallon b Johnson	8	(9) b Lindwall	0
C.R.Rangachari	not out	0	c McCool b Lindwall	0
Extras	(B 11, LB 8, NB 3)	22	(B 18, LB 3, NB 1)	22
		381		277

1/6 2/6 3/69 4/124 5/133
6/321 7/353 8/359 9/375

1/0 2/0 3/33 4/99 5/139
6/139 7/271 8/273 9/273

Bowling: First Innings—Lindwall 21-6-61-1; Miller 9-1-39-2; McCool 28-2-102-1; Johnson 23.1-5-64-4; Toshack 18-2-66-1; Barnes 9-0-23-0; Bradman 1-0-4-0. Second Innings—Lindwall 16.5-4-38-7; Miller 9-3-13-1; McCool 4-0-26-0; Johnson 20-4-54-0; Toshack 25-8-73-1; Barnes 18-4-51-1.

Umpires: E.G.Borwick and R.Wright

AUSTRALIA v INDIA 1947-48 (Fifth Test)

At Melbourne Cricket Ground, 6, 7, 9, 10 February
Result: Australia won by an innings and 177 runs

Australia

S.G.Barnes	run out	33
W.A.Brown	run out	99
D.G.Bradman*	retired hurt	57
K.R.Miller	c Sen b Phadkar	14
R.N.Harvey	c Sen b Mankad	153
S.J.E.Loxton	c Sen b Amarnath	80
R.R.Lindwall	c Phadkar b Mankad	35
D.Tallon†	c Sen b Sarwate	37
L.J.Johnson	not out	25
D.T.Ring	c Kishenchand b Hazare	11
W.A.Johnston	not out	23
Extras	(B 4, LB 4)	8

1/48 2/183 3/219 4/378 5/457 (8 wkts dec.) 575
6/497 7/527 8/544

Bowling: Phadkar 9-0-58-1; Amarnath 23-1-79-1; Rangachari 17-1-97-0; Hazare 14-1-63-1; Mankad 33-2-107-2; Sarwate 18-1-82-1; Nayudu 13-0-77-0; Adhikari 1-0-4-0.

India

M.H.Mankad	c Tallon b Loxton	111	c Tallon b Lindwall	0
C.T.Sarwate	b Lindwall	0	lbw b Johnston	10
H.R.Adhikari	c Tallon b Loxton	38	c Bradman b Loxton	17
V.S.Hazare	lbw b Lindwall	74	c and b Johnson	10
L.Amarnath*	c Barnes b Ring	12	(6) c Johnson b Ring	8
D.G.Phadkar	not out	56	(5) lbw b Johnston	0
Gul Mahomed	c Lindwall b Johnson	1	c Barnes b Ring	4
G.Kishenchand	b Ring	14	c Barnes b Johnson	0
C.S.Nayudu	c Bradman b Ring	2	c Brown b Ring	0
P.Sen†	b Johnson	13	b Johnson	10
C.R.Rangachari	b Johnson	0	not out	0
Extras	(B 6, LB 2, NB 2)	10	(B 6, LB 1, NB 1)	8

1/3 2/127 3/206 4/231 5/257 331
6/260 7/284 8/286 9/331

1/0 2/22 3/28 4/35 5/51 67
6/51 7/56 9/66

Bowling: First Innings—Lindwall 25-5-66-2; Johnson 30-8-66-3; Loxton 19-1-61-2; Johnston 8-4-14-0; Ring 36-8-103-3; Miller 3-0-10-0; Barnes 2-1-1-0. Second Innings—Lindwall 3-0-9-1; Johnson 5.2-2-8-3; Loxton 4-1-10-1; Johnston 7-0-15-2; Ring 5-1-17-3.

Umpires: A.N.Barlow and G.C.Cooper

ENGLAND v AUSTRALIA 1948 (First Test)

At Trent Bridge, Nottingham, 10, 11, 12, 14, 15 June
Result: Australia won by 8 wickets

England

L.Hutton	b Miller	3	b Miller	74
C.Washbrook	c Brown b Lindwall	6	c Tallon b Miller	1
W.J.Edrich	b Johnston	18	c Tallon b Johnson	13
D.C.S.Compton	b Miller	19	hit wkt b Miller	184
J.Hardstaff, jr	c Miller b Johnston	0	c Hassett b Toshack	43
C.J.Barnett	b Johnston	8	c Miller b Johnston	6
N.W.D.Yardley*	lbw b Toshack	3	c and b Johnston	22
T.G.Evans†	c Morris b Johnston	12	c Tallon b Johnston	50
J.C.Laker	c Tallon b Miller	63	b Miller	4
A.V.Bedser	c Brown b Johnston	22	not out	3
J.A.Young	not out	1	b Johnston	9
Extras	(B 5, LB 5)	10	(B 12, LB 17, NB 3)	32

1/9 2/15 3/46 4/46 5/48 165
6/60 7/74 8/74 9/163

1/5 2/39 3/150 4/243 5/264 441
6/321 7/405 8/413 9/423

Bowling: First Innings—Lindwall 13-5-30-1; Miller 19-8-38-3; Johnston 25-11-36-5; Toshack 14-8-28-1; Johnson 5-1-19-0; Morris 3-1-4-0. Second Innings—Miller 44-10-125-4; Johnston 59-12-147-4; Toshack 33-14-60-1; Johnson 42-15-66-1; Barnes 5-2-11-0.

Australia

S.G.Barnes	c Evans b Laker	62	not out	64
A.R.Morris	b Laker	31	b Bedser	9
D.G.Bradman*	c Hutton b Bedser	138	c Hutton b Bedser	0
K.R.Miller	c Edrich b Laker	0		
W.A.Brown	lbw b Yardley	17		
A.L.Hassett	b Bedser	137		
I.W.Johnson	b Laker	21	(4) not out	21
D.Tallon†	c and b Young	10		
R.R.Lindwall	c Evans b Yardley	42		
W.A.Johnston	not out	17		
E.R.H.Toshack	lbw b Bedser	19		
Extras	(B 9, LB 4, NB 1, W 1)	15	(LB 2, NB 1, W 1)	4

1/73 2/121 3/121 4/185 5/305 509
6/338 7/365 8/472 9/476

1/38 2/48 (2 wkts) 98

Bowling: First Innings—Edrich 18-1-72-0; Bedser 44.2-12-113-3; Barnett 17-5-36-0; Young 60-28-79-1; Laker 55-14-138-4; Compton 5-0-24-0; Yardley 17-6-32-2. Second Innings—Bedser 14.3-4-46-2; Edrich 4-0-20-0; Young 10-3-28-0.

Umpires: F.Chester and E.Cooke

ENGLAND v AUSTRALIA 1948 (Second Test)

At Lord's, London, 24, 25, 26, 28, 29 June
Result: Australia won by 409 runs

Australia

S.G.Barnes c Hutton b Coxon	0	c Washbrook b Yardley	141
A.R.Morris c Hutton b Coxon	105	b Wright	62
D.G.Bradman* c Hutton b Bedser	38	c Edrich b Bedser	89
A.L.Hassett b Yardley	47	b Yardley	0
K.R.Miller lbw b Bedser	4	c Bedser b Laker	74
W.A.Brown lbw b Yardley	24	c Evans b Coxon	32
I.W.Johnson c Evans b Edrich	4	(8) not out	9
D.Tallon† c Yardley b Bedser	53		
R.R.Lindwall b Bedser	15	(7) st Evans b Laker	25
W.A.Johnston st Evans b Wright	29		
E.R.H.Toshack not out	20		
Extras (B 3, LB 7, NB 1)	11	(B 22, LB 5, NB 1)	28
	350	(7 wkts dec.)	460

1/3 2/87 3/166 4/173 5/216   1/122 2/296 3/296
6/225 7/246 8/275 9/320   4/329 5/416 6/445 7/460

Bowling: *First Innings*—Bedser 43-14-100-4; Coxon 35-10-90-2; Edrich 8-0-43-1; Wright 21.3-8-54-1; Laker 7-3-17-0; Yardley 15-4-35-2. *Second Innings*—Bedser 34-6-112-1; Coxon 28-3-82-1; Edrich 2-0-11-0; Wright 19-4-69-1; Laker 31.2-6-111-2; Yardley 13-4-36-2; Compton 3-0-11-0.

England

L.Hutton b Johnson	20	c Johnson b Lindwall	13
C.Washbrook c Tallon b Lindwall	8	c Tallon b Toshack	37
W.J.Edrich b Lindwall	5	c Miller b Toshack	2
D.C.S.Compton c Miller b Johnston	53	c Miller b Johnston	29
H.E.Dollery b Lindwall	0	b Lindwall	37
N.W.D.Yardley* b Lindwall	44	b Toshack	11
A.Coxon c and b Johnson	19	lbw b Toshack	0
T.G.Evans† c Miller b Johnston	9	not out	24
J.C.Laker c Tallon b Johnson	28	b Lindwall	0
A.V.Bedser b Lindwall	9	c Hassett b Johnston	9
D.V.P.Wright not out	13	c Lindwall b Toshack	4
Extras (LB 3, NB 4)	7	(B 16, LB 4)	20
	215		186

1/17 2/32 3/46 4/46 5/133   1/42 2/52 3/65 4/106 5/133
6/134 7/145 8/186 9/197   6/133 7/141 8/141 9/158

Bowling: *First Innings*—Lindwall 27.4-7-70-5; Johnston 22-4-43-2; Johnson 35-13-72-3; Toshack 18-11-23-0. *Second Innings*—Lindwall 23-9-61-3; Johnston 33-15-62-2; Toshack 20.1-6-40-5; Johnson 2-1-3-0.

Umpires: D.Davies and C.N.Woolley

ENGLAND v AUSTRALIA 1948 (Third Test)

At Old Trafford, Manchester, 8, 9, 10, 12 (no play), 13 July
Result: Match drawn

England

C.Washbrook b Johnston	11	c Tallon b Lindwall	85
G.M.Emmett c Barnes b Lindwall	10	c Tallon b Lindwall	0
W.J.Edrich c Tallon b Lindwall	32	run out	53
D.C.S.Compton not out	145	c Miller b Toshack	0
J.F.Crapp lbw b Lindwall	37	not out	19
H.E.Dollery b Johnston	1		
N.W.D.Yardley* c Johnston b Toshack	22		
T.G.Evans† c Johnston b Lindwall	34		
A.V.Bedser run out	37		
R.Pollard b Toshack	3		
J.A.Young c Bradman b Johnston	4		
Extras (B 7, LB 17, NB 3)	27	(B 9, LB 7, W 1)	17
	363	(3 wkts dec.)	174

1/22 2/28 3/96 4/97 5/119   1/1 2/125 3/129
6/141 7/216 8/337 9/352

Bowling: *First Innings*—Lindwall 40-8-99-4; Johnston 45.5-13-67-3; Toshack 41-20-75-2; Johnson 38-16-77-0. *Second Innings*—Lindwall 14-4-37-1; Johnston 14-3-34-0; Loxton 8-2-29-0; Toshack 12-5-26-1; Johnson 7-3-16-0; Miller 14-7-15-0.

Australia

A.R.Morris c Compton b Bedser	51	not out	54
I.W.Johnson c Evans b Bedser	1	c Crapp b Young	6
D.G.Bradman* lbw b Pollard	7	not out	30
A.L.Hassett c Washbrook b Young	38		
K.R.Miller lbw b Pollard	31		
S.G.Barnes retired hurt	1		
S.J.E.Loxton b Pollard	36		
D.Tallon† c Evans b Edrich	18		
R.R.Lindwall c Washbrook b Bedser	23		
W.A.Johnston c Crapp b Bedser	3		
E.R.H.Toshack not out	0		
Extras (B 5, LB 4, NB 3)	12	(NB 2)	2
	221	(1 wkt)	92

1/3 2/13 3/82 4/135 5/139   1/10
6/172 7/208 8/219 9/221

Bowling: *First Innings*—Bedser 36-12-81-4; Pollard 32-9-53-3; Edrich 7-3-27-1; Yardley 4-0-12-0; Young 14-5-36-1. *Second Innings*—Bedser 19-12-27-0; Pollard 10-8-6-0; Edrich 2-0-8-0; Young 21-12-31-1; Compton 9-3-18-0.

Umpires: F.Chester and D.Davies

ENGLAND v AUSTRALIA 1948 (Fourth Test)

At Headingley, Leeds, 22, 23, 24, 26, 27 July
Result: Australia won by 7 wickets

England

L.Hutton b Lindwall	81		c Bradman b Johnson	57
C.Washbrook c Lindwall b Johnston	143		c Harvey b Johnston	65
W.J.Edrich c Morris b Johnson	111		lbw b Lindwall	54
A.V.Bedser c and b Johnson	79	(9)	c Hassett b Miller	17
D.C.S.Compton c Saggers b Lindwall	23	(4)	c Miller b Johnston	66
J.F.Crapp b Toshack	5	(5)	b Lindwall	18
N.W.D.Yardley* b Miller	25	(6)	c Harvey b Johnston	7
K.Cranston b Loxton	10	(7)	c Saggers b Johnston	0
T.G.Evans† c Hassett b Loxton	3	(8)	not out	47
J.C.Laker c Saggers b Loxton	4		not out	15
R.Pollard not out	0			
Extras (B 2, LB 8, NB 1, W 1)	12		(B 4, LB 12, NB 3)	19
	496		(8 wkts dec.)	365

1/168 2/268 3/423 4/426 5/447   1/129 2/129 3/232 4/260 5/277
6/473 7/486 8/490 9/496   6/278 7/293 8/330

Bowling: *First Innings*—Lindwall 38-10-79-2; Miller 17.1-2-43-1; Johnston 38-12-86-1; Toshack 35-6-112-1; Loxton 26-4-55-3; Johnson 33-9-89-2; Morris 5-0-20-0. *Second Innings*—Lindwall 26-6-84-0; Miller 21-5-53-1; Johnston 29-5-95-4; Loxton 10-2-29-0; Johnson 21-2-85-1.

Australia

A.R.Morris c Cranston b Bedser	6	c Pollard b Yardley ... 182
A.L.Hassett c Crapp b Pollard	13	c and b Compton ... 17
D.G.Bradman* b Pollard	33	not out ... 173
K.R.Miller c Edrich b Yardley	58	lbw b Cranston ... 12
R.N.Harvey b Laker	112	not out ... 4
S.J.E.Loxton b Yardley	93	
I.W.Johnson c Cranston b Laker	10	
R.R.Lindwall b Crapp b Bedser	77	
R.A.Saggers† st Evans b Laker	5	
W.A.Johnston c Edrich b Bedser	13	
E.R.H.Toshack not out	12	
Extras (B 9, LB 14, NB 3)	26	(B 6, LB 9, NB 1) ... 16
	458	(3 wkts) 404

1/13 2/65 3/68 4/189 5/294   1/57 2/358 3/396
6/329 7/344 8/355 9/403

Bowling: *First Innings*—Bedser 31.2-4-92-3; Pollard 38-6-104-2; Cranston 14-1-51-0; Edrich 3-0-19-0; Laker 30-8-113-3; Yardley 17-6-38-2; Compton 3-0-15-0. *Second Innings*—Bedser 21-2-56-0; Pollard 22-6-55-0; Cranston 7.1-0-28-1; Laker 32-11-93-0; Yardley 13-1-44-1; Compton 15-3-82-1; Hutton 4-1-30-0.

Umpires: H.G.Baldwin and F.Chester

ENGLAND v AUSTRALIA 1948 (Fifth Test)

At Kennington Oval, London, 14, 16, 17, 18 August
Result: Australia won by an innings and 149 runs

England

L.Hutton c Tallon b Lindwall	30	c Tallon b Miller	64
J.G.Dewes b Miller	1	b Lindwall	10
W.J.Edrich c Hassett b Johnston	3	b Lindwall	28
D.C.S.Compton c Morris b Lindwall	4	c Lindwall b Johnston	39
J.F.Crapp c Tallon b Miller	0	b Miller	9
N.W.D.Yardley* b Lindwall	7	c Miller b Johnston	9
A.J.Watkins lbw b Johnston	0	c Hassett b Ring	2
T.G.Evans† b Lindwall	1	b Lindwall	8
A.V.Bedser b Lindwall	0	b Johnston	0
J.A.Young b Lindwall	0	not out	3
W.E.Hollies not out	0	c Morris b Johnston	0
Extras (B 6)	6	(B 9, LB 4, NB 3)	16
	52		188

1/2 2/10 3/17 4/23 5/35   1/20 2/64 3/125 4/153 5/164
6/42 7/45 8/45 9/47   6/167 7/178 8/181 9/188

Bowling: *First Innings*—Lindwall 16.1-5-20-6; Miller 8-5-5-2; Johnston 16-4-20-2; Loxton 2-1-1-0. *Second Innings*—Lindwall 25-3-50-3; Miller 15-6-22-2; Johnston 27.3-12-40-4; Loxton 10-2-16-0; Ring 28-13-44-1.

Australia

S.G.Barnes c Evans b Hollies	61
A.R.Morris run out	196
D.G.Bradman* b Hollies	0
A.L.Hassett lbw b Young	37
K.R.Miller st Evans b Hollies	5
R.N.Harvey c Young b Hollies	17
S.J.E.Loxton c Evans b Edrich	15
R.R.Lindwall c Edrich b Young	9
D.Tallon† c Crapp b Hollies	31
D.T.Ring c Crapp b Bedser	9
W.A.Johnston not out	0
Extras (B 4, LB 2, NB 3)	9
	389

1/117 2/117 3/226 4/243 5/265
6/304 7/332 8/359 9/389

Bowling: Bedser 31.2-9-61-1; Watkins 4-1-19-0; Young 51-16-118-2; Hollies 56-14-131-5; Compton 2-0-6-0; Edrich 9-1-38-1; Yardley 5-1-7-0.

Umpires: H.G.Baldwin and D.Davies

SOUTH AFRICA v AUSTRALIA 1949-50 (First Test)

At Ellis Park, Johannesburg, 24, 26, 27, 28 December
Result: Australia won by an innings and 85 runs

Australia

Batsman		Runs
A.R.Morris	c Tayfield b McCarthy	0
J.Moroney	run out	0
K.R.Miller	b Mann	21
A.L.Hassett*	b Watkins	112
R.N.Harvey	b Watkins	34
S.J.E.Loxton	st Wade b Tayfield	101
C.L.McCool	b Tayfield	31
I.W.Johnson	c Cheetham b Mann	66
R.A.Saggers†	lbw b McCarthy	14
R.R.Lindwall	c Nel b Tayfield	21
W.A.Johnston	not out	1
Extras	(B 5, LB 5, W 2)	12
Total		**413**

1/0 2/0 3/71 4/163 5/200 6/283 7/320 8/372 9/408

Bowling: McCarthy 25-2-90-2; Watkins 19-3-56-2; Smith 13-0-70-0; Tayfield 28-3-93-3; Mann 28.4-4-92-2.

South Africa

Batsman	First Innings	Runs	Second Innings	Runs
E.A.B.Rowan	b Miller	60	lbw b McCool	32
O.E.Wynne	lbw b Johnston	3	c Saggers b Johnston	33
J.D.Nel	b Johnson	4	c Saggers b Johnston	14
A.D.Nourse*	c Hassett b Johnston	0	c Saggers b Johnson	36
W.W.Wade†	b Miller	2	b Johnston	11
J.E.Cheetham	lbw b Johnston	10	c Hassett b Johnston	35
J.C.Watkins	c Hassett b Miller	36	c Miller b Johnson	0
H.J.Tayfield	lbw b Miller	6	c Miller b Johnson	0
N.B.F.Mann	b Miller	0	lbw b Johnston	13
V.I.Smith	not out	1	c McCool b Johnston	1
C.N.McCarthy	b Johnston	0	not out	0
Extras	(LB 14, NB 1)	15	(B 9, LB 3, NB 2, W 1)	15
Total		**137**		**191**

1/14 2/32 3/40 4/47 5/82 6/112 7/122 9/133
1/50 2/81 3/113 4/133 5/141 6/142 7/142 8/184 9/186

Bowling: First Innings—Lindwall 10-1-22-0; Johnston 12-4-21-2; Miller 15-3-40-5; Johnson 18.2-6-37-3; Loxton 1-0-2-0. Second Innings—Lindwall 8-1-25-0; Johnston 20.1-5-44-6; Miller 11-1-27-0; Johnson 14-0-54-3; McCool 9-3-15-1.

Umpires: R.G.A.Ashman and D.Collins

SOUTH AFRICA v AUSTRALIA 1949-50 (Second Test)

At Newlands, Cape Town, 31 December, 2, 3, 4 January
Result: Australia won by 8 wickets

Australia

Batsman	First Innings	Runs	Second Innings	Runs
A.R.Morris	c Watkins b Tayfield	42	c and b Mann	24
J.Moroney	c Cheetham b Mann	87	lbw b Mann	19
K.R.Miller	b Watkins	58	(4) not out	16
A.L.Hassett*	c and b Mann	57		
R.N.Harvey	c Wade b Mann	178	(3) not out	23
S.J.E.Loxton	b Tayfield	35		
C.L.McCool	not out	49		
I.W.Johnson	c Watkins b Mann	0		
R.R.Lindwall†	not out	8		
R.A.Saggers				
W.A.Johnston				
Extras	(B 8, LB 4)	12	(B 5)	5
Total	(7 wkts dec.)	**526**	(2 wkts)	**87**

1/68 2/172 3/215 4/276 5/416 6/502 7/502
1/37 2/44

Bowling: First Innings—McCarthy 24-2-98-0; Watkins 12-2-59-1; Mann 28-3-105-4; Tayfield 37-4-141-2; Smith 25-0-111-0. Second Innings—McCarthy 4-1-18-0; Watkins 2-0-10-0; Mann 8-1-23-2; Tayfield 6-1-31-0.

South Africa

Batsman	First Innings	Runs	Second Innings	Runs
E.A.B.Rowan	lbw b McCool	67	c Harvey b Johnston	3
O.E.Wynne	c Johnson b Miller	13	c Saggers b Johnston	10
J.D.Nel	lbw b Johnson	38	c McCool b Johnson	19
A.D.Nourse*	c Johnston b Miller	65	lbw b McCool	114
W.W.Wade†	c Saggers b Loxton	4	b McCool	11
J.E.Cheetham	c McCool b Miller	3	b Johnston	11
J.C.Watkins	st Saggers b McCool	35	c Saggers b Lindwall	27
H.J.Tayfield	st Saggers b McCool	15	c Saggers b Lindwall	9
N.B.F.Mann	b McCool	16	b Lindwall	75
V.I.Smith	not out	11	b Lindwall	46
C.N.McCarthy	st Saggers b McCool	0	lbw b Lindwall	4
			not out	0
Extras	(B 2, LB 8, W 1)	11	(B 3, LB 10, NB 2)	15
Total		**278**		**333**

1/33 2/92 3/154 4/169 5/194 6/203 7/241 8/250 9/278
1/5 2/16 3/61 4/80 5/141 6/159 7/225 8/327 9/332

Bowling: First Innings—Lindwall 12-2-33-0; Johnston 17-3-53-0; Johnson 12-1-61-1; Miller 17-3-54-3; McCool 11.4-1-41-5; Loxton 6-0-28-1. Second Innings—Lindwall 15.4-2-32-5; Johnston 24-2-70-3; Johnson 24-5-91-1; Miller 11-1-43-0; McCool 21-3-71-1; Loxton 4-1-6-0; Harvey 3-1-5-0.

Umpires: R.G.A.Ashman and D.Collins

SOUTH AFRICA v AUSTRALIA 1949-50 (Third Test)

At Kingsmead, Durban, 20, 21, 23, 24 January

Result: Australia won by 5 wickets

South Africa

E.A.B.Rowan c Johnston b Miller	143	c Saggers b Lindwall	4
O.E.Wynne b Johnston	18	b Johnson	29
J.D.Nel c and b Johnson	14	lbw b Johnston	20
A.D.Nourse* c Saggers b Johnston	66	c McCool b Johnson	27
W.W.Wade† b Lindwall	24	b Johnston	0
N.B.F.Mann b Johnston	9	(9) lbw b Johnston	0
J.E.Cheetham c Hassett b Johnston	4	(6) c Hassett b Johnson	1
J.C.Watkins b Lindwall	5	(7) st Saggers b Johnson	2
H.J.Tayfield run out	15	(8) b Johnston	2
V.I.Smith b Lindwall	1	b Johnston	4
C.N.McCarthy not out	0	not out	2
Extras (B 3, LB 7, NB 2)	12	(B 5, LB 1, NB 1)	7

1/32 2/75 3/242 4/264 5/283   311   1/9 2/51 3/85 4/85 5/88   99
6/289 7/293 8/304 9/308   6/90 7/93 8/93 9/93

Bowling: *First Innings*—Lindwall 19-3-47-3; Miller 24-5-73-1; McCool 13-3-35-0; Johnston 31.2-5-74-5; Loxton 6-1-31-0; Johnson 16-5-38-1. *Second Innings*—Lindwall 4-1-7-1; Miller 7-0-12-0; Johnston 18.2-6-39-4; Johnson 17-2-34-5.

Australia

A.R.Morris c Smith b Tayfield	25	hit wkt b Tayfield	44
J.Moroney b Tayfield	10	lbw b Tayfield	10
I.W.Johnson lbw b Tayfield	2		
K.R.Miller b Tayfield	2	(3) lbw b Mann	10
A.L.Hassett* lbw b Tayfield	2	(4) lbw b Mann	11
R.A.Saggers† c Cheetham b Mann	2		
C.L.McCool lbw b Mann	1	not out	39
R.R.Lindwall b Mann	7		
R.N.Harvey c and b Tayfield	2	(5) not out	151
S.J.E.Loxton c Cheetham b Tayfield	16	(6) b Mann	54
W.A.Johnston not out	2		
Extras (B 3, LB 1)	4	(B 7, LB 9, NB 1)	17

1/31 2/35 3/37 4/39 5/42   75   1/14 2/33 3/59 4/95 (5 wkts) 336
6/45 7/46 8/53 9/63   5/230

Bowling: *First Innings*—McCarthy 6-2-8-0; Watkins 4-1-9-0; Mann 10-1-31-3; Tayfield 8.4-1-23-7. *Second Innings*—McCarthy 12-3-32-0; Watkins 6-2-10-0; Mann 51.6-13-101-3; Tayfield 49-5-144-2; Smith 5-0-32-0.

Umpires: J.V.Hart-Davis and B.V.Malan

SOUTH AFRICA v AUSTRALIA 1949-50 (Fourth Test)

At Ellis Park, Johannesburg, 10, 11, 13, 14 February

Result: Match drawn

Australia

A.R.Morris c Fullerton b McCarthy	111	c Mann b McCarthy	19
J.Moroney c Fullerton b Melle	118	not out	101
K.R.Miller c Fullerton b Melle	84	(4) not out	33
R.R.Lindwall b Melle	5		
A.L.Hassett* b McCarthy	53		
R.N.Harvey not out	56	(3) b Melle	100
S.J.E.Loxton b Melle	6		
C.L.McCool st Fullerton b Tayfield	8		
I.W.Johnson c sub (J.B.Roothman) b Melle	3		
R.A.Saggers† not out	5		
W.A.Johnston			
Extras (B 8, LB 7, NB 1)	16	(B 5, LB 1)	6

1/214 2/265 3/273 4/382 5/392 (8 wkts dec.) 465   1/28 2/198 (2 wkts) 259
6/418 7/437 8/440

Bowling: *First Innings*—McCarthy 31-4-113-2; Melle 33-3-113-2; Mann 2.5-2-85-0; Begbie 7-0-35-0. *Second Innings*—McCarthy 13-1-56-1; Melle 12-0-58-1; Tayfield 14-2-88-0; Mann 8-1-32-0; Begbie 3-0-19-0; Rowan 1-1-0-0; Nourse 1-1-0-0.

South Africa

E.A.B.Rowan b Lindwall	55
J.D.Nel run out	25
R.G.Draper c Saggers b Johnston	15
A.D.Nourse* c Saggers b Lindwall	5
D.W.Begbie c McCool b Miller	24
P.L.Winslow c and b Miller	19
G.M.Fullerton† c Hassett b McCool	88
H.J.Tayfield c Johnson b Miller	40
N.B.F.Mann b Lindwall	52
M.G.Melle lbw b McCool	14
C.N.McCarthy not out	2
Extras (B 7, LB 5, NB 1)	13

1/84 2/86 3/96 4/115 5/145   352
6/148 7/213 8/307 9/345

Bowling: Lindwall 26-3-82-3; Johnston 29-5-68-1; Miller 28-3-75-3; Loxton 10-2-22-0; Johnson 18-4-52-0; McCool 7-0-29-0; Hassett 1-0-5-0; Harvey 3-0-6-0.

Umpires: D.Collins and D.T.Drew

SOUTH AFRICA v AUSTRALIA 1949-50 (Fifth Test)

At St George's Park, Port Elizabeth, 3, 4, 6 March
Result: Australia won by an innings and 259 runs

Australia

A.R.Morris c Winslow b Melle		157
J.Moroney c Nourse b Melle		7
K.R.Miller c Nourse b Tayfield		22
R.N.Harvey b Begbie		116
A.L.Hassett* c McCarthy b Mann		167
S.J.E.Loxton c Rowan b Mann		43
C.L.McCool c Fullerton b Tayfield		6
I.W.Johnson not out		26
R.A.Saggers† not out		4
G.Noblet		
W.A.Johnston		
Extras (B 1)		1
	(7 wkts dec.)	549

1/16 2/49 3/236 4/350 5/449
6/485 7/545

Bowling: McCarthy 29-3-121-0; Melle 23-2-132-2; Tayfield 25-1-103-2; Mann 36-4-154-2; Begbie 4-0-38-1.

South Africa

E.A.B.Rowan b Johnson		40	c McCool b Miller	0
J.D.Nel b Miller		0	lbw b Johnston	5
R.G.Draper c Johnston b Miller		7	b Johnston	3
A.D.Nourse* c McCool b Miller		37	b Johnston	55
D.W.Begbie c Saggers b Noblet		1	b Johnston	5
P.L.Winslow lbw b Noblet	(7)	0	st Saggers b Johnson	11
G.M.Fullerton† st Saggers b McCool	(6)	18	c Saggers b Loxton	24
H.J.Tayfield st Saggers b McCool		6	st Saggers b McCool	7
M.G.Melle b Miller	(10)	1	lbw b Johnson	6
N.B.F.Mann b Noblet	(9)	41	lbw b Johnson	6
C.N.McCarthy not out		1	not out	4
Extras (B 5, NB 1)		6	(B 3, LB 3)	6
		158		132

1/3 2/19 3/71 4/84 5/84   1/0 2/8 3/12 4/24 5/63
6/95 7/104 8/113 9/117   6/88 7/113 8/115 9/126

Bowling: First Innings— Miller 14-3-42-4; Johnston 11-3-21-3; McCool 5-1-29-2. Second Innings— Miller 8-0-24-1; Johnston 6-1-10-3; Noblet 9-2-16-0; Johnson 7-1-21-3; McCool 14.2-2-48-2; Loxton 4-2-7-1.

Umpires: D.Collins and B.V.Malan

AUSTRALIA v ENGLAND 1950-51 (First Test)

At Woolloongabba, Brisbane 1, 2 (no play), 4, 5 December
Result: Australia won by 70 runs

Australia

J.Moroney c Hutton b Bailey		0	b Bailey	0
A.R.Morris lbw b Bedser		25	c Bailey b Bedser	0
R.N.Harvey c Evans b Bedser		74	(6) c Simpson b Bedser	12
K.R.Miller c McIntyre b Wright		15	(7) c Simpson b Bailey	8
A.L.Hassett* b Bedser		8	lbw b Bailey	3
S.J.E.Loxton c Evans b Brown		24	(4) c Bailey b Bedser	0
R.R.Lindwall c Bedser b Bailey		41	(8) not out	0
D.Tallon† c Simpson b Brown		5		
I.W.Johnson c Simpson b Bailey		23	(3) lbw b Bailey	8
W.A.Johnston c Hutton b Bedser		1		
J.B.Iverson not out		1		
Extras (B 5, LB 3, NB 3)		11	(NB 1)	1
		228	(7 wkts dec.)	32

1/0 2/69 3/116 4/118 5/129   1/0 2/0 3/0 4/12
6/156 7/172 8/219 9/226   5/19 6/31 7/32

Bowling: First Innings—Bailey 12-4-28-3; Bedser 16.5-4-45-4; Wright 16-0-81-1; Brown 11-0-63-2. Second Innings—Bailey 7-2-22-4; Bedser 6.5-2-9-3.

England

R.T.Simpson b Johnston	12	b Lindwall	0
C.Washbrook c Hassett b Johnston	19	c Loxton b Lindwall	6
T.G.Evans† c Iverson b Johnston	16	(6) c Loxton b Johnston	5
D.C.S.Compton c Lindwall b Johnston	5	(9) c Loxton b Johnston	0
J.G.Dewes c Loxton b Miller	1	(3) b Miller	9
L.Hutton not out	8	(8) not out	62
A.J.W.McIntyre b Johnston	1	run out	7
F.R.Brown* c Tallon b Miller	4	(10) c Loxton b Iverson	17
T.E.Bailey not out	1	(4) c Johnston b Iverson	7
A.V.Bedser		(5) c Harvey b Iverson	0
D.V.P.Wright		c Lindwall b Iverson	2
Extras (LB 2, NB 1)	3	(B 6, NB 1)	7
(7 wkts dec.)	68		122

1/28 2/49 3/52 4/52 5/56   1/0 2/16 3/22 4/23 5/23
6/57 7/67   6/30 7/46 8/46 9/77

Bowling: First Innings—Lindwall 1-0-1-0; Johnston 11-2-35-5; Miller 10-1-29-2. Second Innings—Lindwall 7-3-21-2; Johnston 11-2-30-2; Miller 7-3-21-1; Iverson 13-3-43-4.

Umpires: A.N.Barlow and H.Elphinston

AUSTRALIA v ENGLAND 1950-51 (Second Test)
At Melbourne Cricket Ground, 22, 23, 26, 27 December
Result: Australia won by 28 runs

Australia

Batsman	First innings	Runs	Second innings	Runs
K.A.Archer	c Bedser b Bailey	26	c Bailey b Bedser	
A.R.Morris	c Hutton b Bedser	2	lbw b Wright	18
R.N.Harvey	c Evans b Bedser	42	run out	
K.R.Miller	lbw b Brown	18	b Bailey	14
A.L.Hassett*	b Bailey	52	c Bailey b Brown	19
S.J.E.Loxton	c Evans b Close	32	c Evans b Brown	2
R.R.Lindwall	lbw b Bailey	8	c Evans b Brown	7
D.Tallon†	not out	7	lbw b Brown	0
I.W.Johnson	c Parkhouse b Bedser	0	c Close b Bedser	23
W.A.Johnston	c Hutton b Bedser	0	b Bailey	6
J.B.Iverson	b Bailey	1	not out	0
Extras	(B 4, LB 2)	6	(B 10, LB 5)	15
Total		**194**		**181**

1/6 2/67 3/89 4/93 5/177 6/177 7/192 8/193 9/193
1/43 2/99 3/100 4/126 5/131 6/151 7/151 8/156 9/181

Bowling: First Innings—Bailey 17.1-5-40-4; Bedser 19-3-37-4; Wright 8-0-63-0; Brown 9-0-28-1; Close 6-1-20-1. Second Innings—Bailey 15-3-47-2; Bedser 16.3-2-43-2; Wright 9-0-42-1; Brown 12-2-26-4; Close 1-0-8-0.

England

Batsman	First innings	Runs	Second innings	Runs
R.T.Simpson	c Johnson b Miller	4	b Lindwall	23
C.Washbrook	lbw b Lindwall	21	b Lindwall	8
J.G.Dewes	c Miller b Johnston	8	(5) c Harvey b Iverson	5
L.Hutton	c Tallon b Iverson	12	c Lindwall b Johnston	40
W.G.A.Parkhouse	c Hassett b Miller	9	(6) lbw b Johnston	28
D.B.Close	c Loxton b Iverson	1	(7) lbw b Johnston	1
F.R.Brown*	c Johnson b Iverson	62	(8) b Lindwall	8
T.E.Bailey	b Lindwall	12	(3) b Johnson	0
T.G.Evans†	c Johnson b Iverson	49	b Iverson	2
A.V.Bedser	not out	4	not out	14
D.V.P.Wright	lbw b Johnston	2	lbw b Johnston	2
Extras	(B 8, LB 6)	14	(B 17, LB 2)	19
Total		**197**		**150**

1/11 2/33 3/37 4/54 5/54 6/61 7/126 8/153 9/194
1/21 2/22 3/52 4/82 5/92 6/95 7/122 8/124 9/134

Bowling: First Innings—Lindwall 13-2-46-2; Miller 13-0-39-2; Johnston 9-1-28-2; Iverson 18-3-37-4; Johnson 5-1-19-0; Loxton 4-1-14-0. Second Innings—Lindwall 12-1-29-3; Miller 5-2-16-0; Johnston 13.7-1-26-4; Iverson 20-4-36-2; Johnson 13-3-24-1.

Umpires: G.C.Cooper and R.Wright

AUSTRALIA v ENGLAND 1950-51 (Third Test)
At Sydney Cricket Ground, 5, 6, 8, 9 January
Result: Australia won by an innings and 13 runs

England

Batsman	First innings	Runs	Second innings	Runs
L.Hutton	lbw b Miller	62	c Tallon b Iverson	9
C.Washbrook	c Miller b Johnson	18	b Iverson	34
R.T.Simpson	c Loxton b Miller	49	c Tallon b Iverson	0
D.C.S.Compton	b Miller	0	c Johnson b Johnston	23
W.G.A.Parkhouse	c Morris b Johnson	25	run out	15
F.R.Brown*	b Lindwall	79	b Iverson	18
T.E.Bailey	c Tallon b Johnson	15	not out	0
T.G.Evans†	run out	23	(8) b Johnson	14
A.V.Bedser	b Lindwall	3	(7) b Iverson	4
J.J.Warr	b Miller	4	b Iverson	0
D.V.P.Wright	run out	0	absent hurt	-
Extras	(LB 10, NB 2)	12	(B 1, LB 5)	6
Total		**290**		**123**

1/34 2/128 3/128 4/137 5/187 6/258 7/267 8/281 9/286
1/32 2/40 3/45 4/74 5/91 6/119 7/119 8/123 9/123

Bowling: First Innings—Lindwall 16-0-60-2; Miller 15.7-4-37-4; Johnson 31-8-94-3; Johnston 21-5-50-0; Iverson 10-1-25-0; Loxton 5-0-12-0. Second Innings—Lindwall 4-1-12-0; Miller 6-2-15-0; Johnston 10-2-32-1; Iverson 19.4-8-27-6.

Australia

Batsman	First innings	Runs
K.A.Archer	c Evans b Bedser	48
A.R.Morris	b Bedser	0
R.N.Harvey	c Bedser b Brown	70
K.R.Miller	b Bedser	39
A.L.Hassett*	not out	145
S.J.E.Loxton	c Bedser b Brown	17
R.R.Lindwall	lbw b Bedser	18
D.Tallon†	b Brown	77
I.W.Johnson	lbw b Brown	0
W.A.Johnston	run out	0
J.B.Iverson	run out	1
Extras	(B 3, LB 7)	10
Total		**426**

1/1 2/122 3/122 4/190 5/223 6/252 7/402 8/406 9/418

Bowling: Bedser 43-4-107-4; Warr 36-4-142-0; Brown 44-4-153-4; Compton 6-1-14-0.

Umpires: A.N.Barlow and H.Elphinston

AUSTRALIA v ENGLAND 1950-51 (Fourth Test)

At Adelaide Oval, 2, 3, 5, 6, 7, 8 February
Result: Australia won by 274 runs

Australia

Batsman	First Innings		Second Innings	
K.A.Archer	c Compton b Bedser	0	c Bedser b Tattersall	32
A.R.Morris	b Tattersall	206	run out	16
A.L.Hassett*	c Evans b Wright	43	lbw b Wright	31
R.N.Harvey	b Bedser	43	b Brown	68
K.R.Miller	c Brown b Wright	44	b Wright	99
J.W.Burke	b Tattersall	12	not out	101
I.W.Johnson	c Evans b Bedser	16	c Evans b Warr	3
R.R.Lindwall	lbw b Wright	1	run out	31
D.Tallon†	b Tattersall	1	c Hutton b Compton	5
W.A.Johnston	c Hutton b Wright	0	not out	9
J.B.Iverson	not out	0		
Extras	(B 2, LB 1, NB 1, W 1)	5	(B 7, LB 1)	8
		371	(8 wkts dec.)	**403**

1/0 2/95 3/205 4/281 5/310 6/357 7/363 8/366 9/367

1/26 2/79 3/95 4/194 5/281 6/297 7/367 8/378

Bowling: *First Innings*—Bedser 26-4-74-3; Warr 16-2-63-0; Wright 25-1-99-4; Tattersall 25.5-5-95-3; Brown 3-0-24-0; Compton 1-0-11-0. *Second Innings*—Bedser 25-6-62-0; Warr 21-0-76-1; Wright 21-2-109-2; Tattersall 27-2-116-1; Brown 3-1-14-1; Compton 4.6-1-18-1.

England

Batsman	First Innings		Second Innings	
L.Hutton	not out	156	c sub (S.J.E.Loxton) b Johnston	45
C.Washbrook	c Iverson b Lindwall	2	lbw b Johnston	31
R.T.Simpson	b Johnston	29	c Burke b Johnston	61
D.C.S.Compton	c Tallon b Lindwall	5	c sub (S.J.E.Loxton) b Johnston	0
D.S.Sheppard	b Iverson	9	lbw b Miller	41
F.R.Brown*	b Miller	16	absent hurt	–
T.G.Evans†	c Burke b Johnston	13	(6) c Johnson b Miller	21
A.V.Bedser	lbw b Iverson	7	(7) b Morris b Miller	0
R.Tattersall	c Harvey b Iverson	0	(8) b Morris b Johnson	6
J.J.Warr	b Johnston	0	(9) b Johnson	0
D.V.P.Wright	lbw b Lindwall	14	(10) not out	0
Extras	(B 15, LB 5, NB 1)	21	(B 15, LB 3, NB 3, W 2)	23
		272		**228**

1/7 2/80 3/96 4/132 5/161 6/195 7/206 8/214 9/219

1/74 2/90 3/90 4/181 5/221 6/221 7/228 8/228 9/228

Bowling: *First Innings*—Lindwall 13.3-0-51-3; Miller 13-2-36-1; Johnson 15-2-38-0; Iverson 26-4-68-3; Johnston 25-4-58-3. *Second Innings*—Lindwall 10-2-35-0; Miller 13-4-27-3; Johnson 25.6-6-63-2; Johnston 27-4-73-4; Burke 3-1-7-0.

Umpires: A.N.Barlow and A.F.Cocks

AUSTRALIA v ENGLAND 1950-51 (Fifth Test)

At Melbourne Cricket Ground, 23, 24 (no play), 26, 27, 28 February
Result: England won by 8 wickets

Australia

Batsman	First Innings		Second Innings	
J.W.Burke	c Tattersall b Bedser	11	c Hutton b Bedser	1
A.R.Morris	lbw b Brown	50	lbw b Bedser	4
A.L.Hassett*	c Hutton b Brown	92	b Wright	48
R.N.Harvey	c Evans b Brown	1	lbw b Wright	52
K.R.Miller	c and b Brown	7	c and b Brown	0
G.B.Hole	b Bedser	18	b Bailey	63
I.W.Johnson	lbw b Bedser	1	c Brown b Wright	0
R.R.Lindwall	c Compton b Bedser	21	b Bedser	14
D.Tallon†	c Hutton b Bedser	1	not out	2
W.A.Johnston	not out	12	b Bedser	1
J.B.Iverson	c Washbrook b Brown	0	c Compton b Bedser	0
Extras	(B 2, LB 1)	3	(B 2, LB 8, NB 1, W 1)	12
		217		**197**

1/23 2/111 3/115 4/123 5/156 6/166 7/184 8/187 9/216

1/5 2/6 3/87 4/89 5/142 6/142 7/192 8/196 9/197

Bowling: *First Innings*—Bedser 22-5-46-5; Bailey 9-1-29-0; Brown 18-4-49-5; Wright 9-1-50-0; Tattersall 11-3-40-0. *Second Innings*—Bedser 20.3-4-59-5; Bailey 15-3-32-1; Brown 9-1-32-1; Wright 15-2-56-3; Tattersall 5-2-6-0.

England

Batsman	First Innings		Second Innings	
L.Hutton	b Hole	79	not out	60
C.Washbrook	c Tallon b Miller	27	c Lindwall b Johnston	7
R.T.Simpson	not out	156	run out	15
D.C.S.Compton	c Miller b Lindwall	11	not out	11
D.S.Sheppard	c Tallon b Miller	1		
F.R.Brown*	b Lindwall	6		
T.G.Evans†	b Miller	1		
A.V.Bedser	b Lindwall	11		
T.E.Bailey	c Johnson b Iverson	5		
D.V.P.Wright	lbw b Iverson	3		
R.Tattersall	b Miller	10		
Extras	(B 9, LB 1)	10	(LB 2)	2
		320	(2 wkts)	**95**

1/40 2/171 3/204 4/205 5/212 6/213 7/228 8/236 9/246

1/32 2/62

Bowling: *First Innings*—Lindwall 21-1-77-3; Miller 21.7-5-76-4; Johnston 12-1-55-0; Iverson 20-4-52-2; Johnson 11-1-40-0; Hole 5-0-10-1. *Second Innings*—Lindwall 2-0-12-0; Miller 2-0-5-0; Johnston 11-3-36-1; Iverson 12-2-32-0; Johnson 1-0-1-0; Hole 1-0-3-0; Hassett 0.6-0-4-0.

Umpires: A.N.Barlow and H.Elphinston

AUSTRALIA v WEST INDIES 1951-52 (First Test)

At Woolloongabba, Brisbane, 9, 10, 12, 13 November
Result: Australia won by 3 wickets

West Indies

A.F.Rae	b Lindwall	0	lbw b Johnson	25
J.B.Stollmeyer	c Langley b Johnston	8	st Langley b Johnson	10
F.M.M.Worrell	b Johnston	37	st Langley b Ring	20
E.D.Weekes	c Langley b Ring	35	c Hole b Johnston	70
R.J.Christiani	c Ring b Lindwall	22	(6) b Ring	6
C.L.Walcott†	lbw b Lindwall	0	(8) st Langley b Ring	4
R.E.Marshall	b Johnson	28	(7) c Hassett b Miller	30
G.E.Gomez	c Langley b Lindwall	22	(5) c Harvey b Ring	55
J.D.C.Goddard*	b Miller	45	c and b Ring	0
S.Ramadhin	not out	16	not out	2
A.L.Valentine	st Langley b Ring	2	c Morris b Ring	13
Extras	(LB 1)	1	(B 8, LB 2)	10
		216		245

1/0 2/18 3/63 4/92 5/95   1/23 2/50 3/88 4/88 5/96
6/112 7/150 8/170 9/207   6/153 7/184 8/229 9/230

Bowling: *First Innings*—Lindwall 20-4-62-4; Miller 14-3-40-1; Johnston 17-2-49-2; Ring 14-2-52-2; Johnson 5-1-12-1. *Second Innings*—Lindwall 10-0-36-0; Miller 8-2-19-1; Johnston 16-4-41-1; Ring 16-2-80-6; Johnson 18-1-56-2; Hole 1-0-3-0.

Australia

K.A.Archer	c Goddard b Valentine	20	b Gomez	4
A.R.Morris	c Rae b Valentine	33	c Gomez b Ramadhin	48
A.L.Hassett*	b Ramadhin	6	lbw b Ramadhin	35
R.N.Harvey	lbw b Valentine	18	b Ramadhin	42
K.R.Miller	c and b Valentine	46	b Valentine	4
G.B.Hole	lbw b Valentine	20	not out	45
R.R.Lindwall	b Gomez	61	b Ramadhin	29
I.W.Johnson	not out	16	b Ramadhin	8
D.T.Ring	c Walcott b Gomez	0	not out	6
G.R.A.Langley†	lbw b Worrell	0		
W.A.Johnston	run out	2		
Extras	(B 4)	4	(B 3, LB 11, NB 1)	15
		226	(7 wkts)	236

1/30 2/53 3/80 4/85 5/129   1/8 2/69 3/126 4/143
6/188 7/215 8/215 9/216   5/149 6/203 7/225

Bowling: *First Innings*—Worrell 8-0-38-1; Gomez 7.5-2-10-2; Valentine 25-4-99-5; Ramadhin 24-5-75-1. *Second Innings*—Worrell 2-1-2-0; Gomez 3-0-12-1; Valentine 40.7-6-117-1; Ramadhin 40-9-90-5.

Umpires: A.N.Barlow and H.Elphinston

AUSTRALIA v WEST INDIES 1951-52 (Second Test)

At Sydney Cricket Ground, 30 November, 1, 3, 4, 5 December
Result: Australia won by 7 wickets

West Indies

A.F.Rae	c Johnson b Johnston	17	c Ring b Miller	9
J.B.Stollmeyer	c Johnson b Lindwall	36	b Johnson	35
F.M.M.Worrell	b Johnson	64	c Langley b Lindwall	20
E.D.Weekes	b Lindwall	5	b Johnson	56
C.L.Walcott†	c Langley b Ring	60	st Langley b Johnson	10
R.J.Christiani	b Hole	76	c Hassett b Miller	30
G.E.Gomez	lbw b Johnston	54	c Miller b Lindwall	41
J.D.C.Goddard*	c Johnson b Johnston	33	not out	57
P.E.Jones	lbw b Lindwall	1	c Miller b Johnston	7
S.Ramadhin	b Lindwall	0	b Johnston	3
A.L.Valentine	not out	0	b Miller	1
Extras	(B 12, LB 3, NB 1)	16	(B 9, LB 12)	21
		362		290

1/33 2/84 3/99 4/139 5/218   1/19 2/52 3/102 4/130 5/141
6/286 7/359 8/360 9/360   6/210 7/230 8/246 9/268

Bowling: *First Innings*—Lindwall 26-2-66-4; Johnston 25.4-2-80-3; Johnson 14-3-48-1; Miller 21-3-72-0; Ring 17-71-1; Hole 4-1-9-1. *Second Innings*—Lindwall 17-3-59-2; Johnston 24-5-61-2; Johnson 23-2-78-3; Miller 13.2-2-50-3; Ring 7-0-21-0.

Australia

K.A.Archer	c Weekes b Gomez	11	lbw b Worrell	47
A.R.Morris	c Walcott b Jones	11	st Walcott b Ramadhin	30
A.L.Hassett*	c Christiani b Jones	132	not out	46
R.N.Harvey	c Gomez b Goddard	39	lbw b Worrell	1
K.R.Miller	b Valentine	129	not out	6
G.B.Hole	b Valentine	1		
R.R.Lindwall	run out	48		
I.W.Johnson	c Walcott b Jones	5		
D.T.Ring	c Ramadhin b Valentine	65		
G.R.A.Langley†	not out	15		
W.A.Johnston	b Valentine	28		
Extras	(B 12, LB 18, NB 3)	33	(B 6, LB 1)	7
		517	(3 wkts)	137

1/19 2/27 3/106 4/341 5/345   1/49 2/123 3/125
6/348 7/372 8/457 9/485

Bowling: *First Innings*—Jones 27-5-68-3; Gomez 18-2-47-1; Worrell 11-0-60-0; Valentine 30.5-3-111-4; Ramadhin 41-7-143-0; Goddard 24-6-55-1. *Second Innings*—Jones 5-1-16-0; Gomez 5-1-9-0; Worrell 2-0-7-2; Valentine 10-0-45-0; Ramadhin 12.3-1-53-1.

Umpires: A.N.Barlow and H.Elphinston

AUSTRALIA v WEST INDIES 1951-52 (Third Test)

At Adelaide Oval, 22, 24, 25 December
Result: West Indies won by 6 wickets

Australia

Batsman	First Innings	R		Second Innings	R
J.W.Burke	c Stollmeyer b Worrell	3	(9)	b Valentine	15
A.R.Morris*	b Worrell	1	(5)	b Valentine	45
R.N.Harvey	c Guillen b Gomez	10	(6)	c Guillen b Ramadhin	9
K.R.Miller	c Ramadhin b Worrell	4	(7)	lbw b Gomez	35
G.B.Hole	c Worrell b Goddard	23	(8)	c Weekes b Gomez	25
R.R.Lindwall	b Worrell	2	(10)	not out	8
I.W.Johnson	c Stollmeyer b Worrell	11	(1)	c Marshall b Valentine	16
D.T.Ring	c Christiani b Goddard	5	(4)	run out	67
G.R.A.Langley†	b Worrell	5	(2)	b Valentine	23
G.Noblet	b Goddard	8	(3)	c Weekes b Valentine	0
W.A.Johnston	not out	7		lbw b Valentine	0
Extras	(LB 3)	3		(B 8, LB 4)	12
Total		**82**			**255**

1/4 2/5 3/15 4/39 5/41
6/43 7/58 8/62 9/72

1/16 2/20 3/81 4/148 5/162
6/172 7/227 8/240 9/255

Bowling: First Innings—Gomez 5-3-5-1; Worrell 12.7-3-38-6; Goddard 8-1-36-3. Second Innings—Gomez 7-2-17-2; Worrell 9-2-29-0; Goddard 1-0-7-0; Valentine 27.5-6-102-6; Ramadhin 25-4-76-1; Marshall 5-1-12-0.

West Indies

Batsman	First Innings	R		Second Innings	R
R.E.Marshall	c Burke b Johnston	14		c Langley b Ring	29
J.B.Stollmeyer	b Johnston	17		c Miller b Ring	47
J.D.C.Goddard*	c Langley b Lindwall	0			
F.M.M.Worrell	b Miller	6	(3)	c Noblet b Johnston	28
E.D.Weekes	b Johnston	26	(4)	c and b Ring	29
G.E.Gomez	c Langley b Johnston	4	(5)	not out	46
R.J.Christiani	c Miller b Johnston	4	(6)	not out	42
S.C.Guillen†	b Noblet	9			
D.S.Atkinson	c Burke b Johnston	15			
S.Ramadhin	not out	0			
A.L.Valentine	b Noblet	5			
Extras	(LB 5)	5		(B 6, LB 5, W 1)	12
Total		**105**		**(4 wkts)**	**233**

1/25 2/26 3/34 4/44 5/51
6/55 7/85 8/87 9/101

1/72 2/85 3/141 4/141

Bowling: First Innings—Lindwall 4-0-18-1; Johnston 12-0-62-6; Miller 5-1-13-1; Noblet 3.5-0-7-2. Second Innings—Lindwall 13-1-40-0; Johnston 19-4-50-1; Miller 5-0-12-0; Noblet 13-1-30-0; Ring 16.5-3-62-3; Johnson 7-1-27-0.

Umpires: M.J.McInnes and R.Wright

AUSTRALIA v WEST INDIES 1951-52 (Fourth Test)

At Melbourne Cricket Ground, 31 December, 1, 2, 3 January
Result: Australia won by 1 wicket

West Indies

Batsman	First Innings	R		Second Innings	R
K.R.Rickards	b Miller	15	(4)	lbw b Johnston	22
J.B.Stollmeyer	c Langley b Miller	7		lbw b Miller	54
F.M.M.Worrell	b Lindwall	108	(8)	b Johnston	30
E.D.Weekes	c Johnson b Johnston	1	(5)	lbw b Johnston	2
G.E.Gomez	c Langley b Miller	37	(7)	b Johnston	52
R.J.Christiani	run out	37		b Miller	33
J.D.C.Goddard*	b Miller	21	(3)	lbw b Lindwall	0
S.C.Guillen†	not out	22	(1)	c Johnston b Lindwall	0
J.Trim	run out	0		run out	0
S.Ramadhin	c Langley b Johnston	1		run out	0
A.L.Valentine	c Lindwall b Miller	14		not out	1
Extras	(B 2, LB 6, W 1)	9		(B 4, LB 5)	9
Total		**272**			**203**

1/16 2/29 3/30 4/102 5/194
6/221 7/237 8/242 9/248

1/0 2/0 3/53 4/60 5/97
6/128 7/190 8/194 9/184

Bowling: First Innings—Lindwall 18-2-72-1; Miller 19.3-1-60-5; Johnston 20-1-59-2; Ring 9-0-43-0; Johnson 7-0-23-0; Hole 2-0-6-0. Second Innings—Lindwall 17-2-59-2; Miller 16-1-49-2; Johnston 14.3-2-51-3; Ring 7-1-17-0; Johnson 5-0-18-1.

Australia

Batsman	First Innings	R	Second Innings	R
J.Moroney	lbw b Ramadhin	26	lbw b Ramadhin	5
A.R.Morris	b Trim	6	lbw b Valentine	12
A.L.Hassett*	run out	15	lbw b Valentine	102
R.N.Harvey	c and b Ramadhin	83	b Valentine	33
K.R.Miller	b Trim	47	hit wkt b Valentine	2
G.B.Hole	b Valentine	2	c Gomez b Worrell	13
R.R.Lindwall	lbw b Trim	13	c Guillen b Ramadhin	29
I.W.Johnson	c Guillen b Trim	1	c Guillen b Ramadhin	6
D.T.Ring	b Trim	6	not out	32
G.R.A.Langley†	not out	1	lbw b Valentine	1
W.A.Johnston	b Gomez	1	not out	7
Extras	(B 12, LB 4)	16	(B 14, LB 4)	18
Total		**216**	**(9 wkts)**	**260**

1/17 2/48 3/49 4/176 5/176
6/208 7/209 8/210 9/215

1/27 2/93 3/106 4/109 (9 wkts) 260
5/147 6/192 7/218 8/218 9/222

Bowling: First Innings—Trim 12-2-34-5; Gomez 13.3-7-25-1; Valentine 23-8-50-1; Ramadhin 17-4-63-2; Goddard 8-0-28-0. Second Innings—Trim 10-3-25-0; Gomez 9-1-18-0; Valentine 30-9-88-5; Ramadhin 39-15-93-3; Worrell 9-1-18-1.

Umpires: M.J.McInnes and R.Wright

AUSTRALIA v WEST INDIES 1951-52 (Fifth Test)

At Sydney Cricket Ground, 25, 26, 28, 29 January
Result: Australia won by 202 runs

Australia

Batsman	First Innings	R	Second Innings	R
C.C.McDonald	c Worrell b Gomez	32	b Ramadhin	62
G.R.Thoms	b Gomez	16	hit wkt b Worrell	28
A.L.Hassett*	c Guillen b Gomez	18	c Worrell b Valentine	64
R.N.Harvey	b Gomez	20	c Guillen b Worrell	8
K.R.Miller	c Rae b Worrell	1	c Weekes b Valentine	69
G.B.Hole	c Guillen b Worrell	3	b Worrell	62
R.Benaud	c Stollmeyer b Gomez	0	c sub (K.R.Richards) b Worrell	19
R.R.Lindwall	c Worrell b Gomez	4	c Walcott b Gomez	21
D.T.Ring	c Atkinson b Gomez	6	b Gomez	12
G.R.A.Langley†	c Weekes b Worrell	13	b Gomez	8
W.A.Johnston	not out	1	not out	6
Extras	(LB 1)	1	(B 10, LB 8)	18
Total		116		377

1/39 2/49 3/54 4/77 5/78 6/91 7/91 8/97 9/99
1/55 2/138 3/152 4/216 5/287 6/326 7/347 8/353 9/370

Bowling: First Innings—Worrell 12.2-1-42-3; Gomez 18-3-55-7; Atkinson 6-2-18-0. Second Innings—Worrell 23-2-95-4; Gomez 18.2-3-58-3; Atkinson 8-0-25-0; Ramadhin 34-8-102-1; Valentine 30-6-79-2.

West Indies

Batsman	First Innings	R	Second Innings	R
A.F.Rae	c Langley b Johnston	11	c Harvey b Ring	25
J.B.Stollmeyer*	lbw b Johnston	10	lbw b Lindwall	104
C.L.Walcott	b Lindwall	1	c Langley b Miller	12
E.D.Weekes	c Langley b Lindwall	0	c Langley b Lindwall	21
R.J.Christiani	c and b Miller	7	c Johnston b Lindwall (6)	4
F.M.M.Worrell	b Miller	6	run out (5)	18
G.E.Gomez	b Miller	11	b Miller	2
D.S.Atkinson	c Miller	6	hit wkt b Lindwall	2
S.C.Guillen†	not out	13	b Lindwall	6
S.Ramadhin	b Johnston	0	not out	3
A.L.Valentine	c Langley b Miller	6	b Benaud	0
Extras	(B 3, LB 3, W 1)	7	(B 4, LB 11, W 1)	16
Total		78		213

1/17 2/18 3/18 4/34 5/34 6/51 7/56 8/59 9/60
1/48 2/83 3/147 4/191 5/192 6/194 7/200 8/205 9/212

Bowling: First Innings—Lindwall 8-1-20-2; Johnston 7.6-1-26-5. Second Innings—Lindwall 21.2-72-6; Miller 7.6-2-21-1; Ring 13-1-44-1; Benaud 4.3-0-14-1.

Umpires: H.Elphinston and M.J.McInnes

AUSTRALIA v SOUTH AFRICA 1952-53 (First Test)

At Woolloongabba, Brisbane, 5, 6, 8, 9, 10 December
Result: Australia won by 96 runs

Australia

Batsman	First Innings	R	Second Innings	R
C.C.McDonald	c and b Watkins	27	st Waite b Tayfield	17
A.R.Morris	lbw b Watkins	29	c Melle b Tayfield	58
R.N.Harvey	c sub (G.A.R.Innes) b Melle	109	run out (4)	52
A.L.Hassett*	c Waite b Watkins	55	c McGlew b Melle (3)	17
K.R.Miller	b Watkins	3	lbw b Tayfield	3
G.B.Hole	c Tayfield b Melle	8	lbw b Melle	42
R.R.Lindwall	lbw b Melle	5	not out	38
G.R.A.Langley†	c Tayfield b Melle	17	b Watkins	27
D.T.Ring	c Mansell b Melle	13	b Melle	4
I.W.Johnson	lbw b Melle	7	lbw b Watkins	13
W.A.Johnston	not out	1	c McGlew b Tayfield	0
Extras	(B 1, LB 3, NB 2)	6	(B 2, LB 4)	6
Total		280		277

1/55 2/56 3/211 4/216 5/231 6/237 7/252 8/272 9/273
1/48 2/75 3/115 4/123 5/160 6/198 7/246 8/251 9/276

Bowling: First Innings—Melle 20.5-0-71-6; Watkins 24-8-41-4; Tayfield 15-3-59-0; Mansell 8-0-40-0. Second Innings—Melle 26-2-95-3; Watkins 26-13-47-2; Murray 13-7-13-0; Tayfield 33.3-5-116-4.

South Africa

Batsman	First Innings	R	Second Innings	R
D.J.McGlew	c Johnson b Miller	9	lbw b Lindwall	69
J.H.B.Waite†	lbw b Ring	39	st Langley b Johnson	14
W.R.Endean	c Langley b Ring	14	lbw b Lindwall	12
K.J.Funston	b Ring	33	c Langley b Johnson	65
R.A.McLean	c Miller b Johnson	13	b Lindwall	38
J.E.Cheetham*	c Langley b Lindwall	26	b Lindwall	18
J.C.Watkins	c Miller b Ring	25	hit wkt b Johnson	1
P.N.F.Mansell	c Lindwall b Ring	31	b Lindwall	4
A.R.A.Murray	lbw b Johnson	18	not out	11
H.J.Tayfield	lbw b Ring	3	c Langley b Johnson	1
M.G.Melle	not out	7	b Lindwall	4
Extras	(B 3)	3	(B 2, NB 1)	3
Total		221		240

1/13 2/39 3/88 4/103 5/113 6/153 7/177 8/195 9/211
1/20 2/57 3/153 4/170 5/209 6/210 7/215 8/226 9/227

Bowling: First Innings—Lindwall 120-0-48-1; Miller 10-0-46-1; Johnston 7.6-2-21-1; Ring 21.2-72-6; Johnson 12-3-31-1. Second Innings—Lindwall 30-8-60-5; Johnston 26-5-62-2; Ring 17-3-58-0; Johnson 30-7-52-3; Hole 3-0-5-0; Harvey 1-1-0-0.

Umpires: H.Elphinston and R.Wright

AUSTRALIA v SOUTH AFRICA 1952-53 (Third Test)

At Sydney Cricket Ground, 9, 10, 12, 13 January
Result: Australia won by an innings and 38 runs

South Africa

D.J.McGlew run out	24		c Langley b Lindwall	9
J.H.B.Waite† c Morris b Johnston	32		c Hole b Lindwall	0
W.R.Endean b Lindwall	18		lbw b Miller	71
K.J.Funston b Ring	56		c Hole b Miller	16
R.A.McLean b Lindwall	0	(6)	c Benaud b Lindwall	65
J.E.Cheetham* c Johnston b Miller	5	(5)	c Morris b Lindwall	5
A.R.A.Murray c sub (J.H.de Courcy) b Miller	4		c Hole b Benaud	17
J.C.Watkins c sub (J.H.de Courcy) b Miller	17		c Miller b Johnston	48
P.N.F.Mansell b Lindwall	8		c Hole b Benaud	0
H.J.Tayfield not out	3		absent hurt	–
M.G.Melle c Langley b Lindwall	5	(10)	not out	0
Extras (B 1, LB 3, W 1)	5		(LB 1)	1
	173			232

1/54 2/65 3/83 4/83 5/115
6/142 7/144 8/156 9/172
1/9 2/10 3/60 4/68 5/167
6/167 7/232 8/232 9/232

Bowling: *First Innings*—Lindwall 14.2-1-40-4; Miller 17-1-48-3; Johnston 18-5-46-1; Ring 12-4-23-1; Hole 2-0-11-0. *Second Innings*—Lindwall 20-3-72-4; Miller 18-6-33-2; Johnston 14.6-0-51-1; Ring 12-1-54-0; Benaud 5-1-21-2.

Australia

C.C.McDonald c Endean b Tayfield	67
A.R.Morris b Watkins	18
A.L.Hassett* c Funston b Murray	2
R.N.Harvey c Watkins b Murray	190
K.R.Miller lbw b Tayfield	55
G.B.Hole run out	5
R.Benaud lbw b Melle	0
D.T.Ring b Tayfield	58
R.R.Lindwall b Murray	1
G.R.A.Langley† c Mansell b Murray	20
W.A.Johnston not out	7
Extras (B 3, LB 12, NB 4, W 1)	20
	443

1/40 2/49 3/162 4/330 5/344
6/350 7/374 8/379 9/425

Bowling: Melle 23-3-98-1; Watkins 12-5-16-1; Murray 15.2-11-169-4; Tayfield 38-9-94-3; Mansell 7-0-46-0.

Umpires: H.Elphinston and M.J.McInnes

AUSTRALIA v SOUTH AFRICA 1952-53 (Second Test)

At Melbourne Cricket Ground, 24, 26, 27, 29, 30 December
Result: South Africa won by 82 runs

South Africa

D.J.McGlew b Lindwall	46		st Langley b Ring	13
J.H.B.Waite† c Lindwall b Miller	0		c Hole b Miller	62
W.R.Endean c Benaud b Lindwall	2		not out	162
K.J.Funston c Ring b Miller	9		run out	26
R.A.McLean c Lindwall b Ring	27		lbw b Miller	42
J.E.Cheetham* c Johnston b Miller	15		lbw b Johnston	6
J.C.Watkins c Langley b Benaud	19		b Johnston	3
P.N.F.Mansell b Lindwall	24		b Miller	18
A.R.A.Murray c Johnston b Benaud	51		st Langley b Ring	23
H.J.Tayfield c Langley b Miller	23		lbw b Lindwall	22
M.G.Melle not out	4		b Lindwall	0
Extras (B 4, LB 3)	7		(B 1, LB 5, NB 1, W 4)	11
	227			388

1/2 2/9 3/27 4/63 5/93
6/112 7/126 8/156 9/207
1/23 2/134 3/196 4/261 5/284
6/290 7/317 8/353 9/388

Bowling: *First Innings*—Lindwall 14-2-29-3; Miller 21-3-62-4; Johnston 12-2-37-0; Ring 18-1-72-1; Benaud 6.6-1-20-2. *Second Innings*—Lindwall 31.5-4-87-2; Miller 22-5-51-3; Johnston 31-9-77-2; Ring 31-5-115-2; Benaud 6-0-23-0; Hole 7-0-24-0.

Australia

C.C.McDonald c sub (E.R.H.Fuller) b Mansell	82		c Mansell b Murray	23
A.R.Morris c and b Tayfield	43		c Watkins b Melle	1
R.N.Harvey c Cheetham b Tayfield	11	(4)	c Watkins b Tayfield	60
A.L.Hassett* c Melle b Mansell	18	(3)	lbw b Tayfield	21
K.R.Miller c Endean b Tayfield	52		b Tayfield	31
G.B.Hole c Waite b Mansell	13	(7)	b Tayfield	25
R.Benaud b Tayfield	5	(8)	c Melle b Tayfield	45
R.R.Lindwall run out	1	(9)	b Melle	19
D.T.Ring c McGlew b Tayfield	14	(10)	c Melle b Tayfield	53
G.R.A.Langley† not out	0	(6)	b Tayfield	4
W.A.Johnston lbw b Tayfield	2		not out	0
Extras (NB 2)	2		(B 1, LB 6, NB 1)	8
	243			290

1/84 2/98 3/155 4/158 5/188
6/211 7/219 8/239 9/243
1/3 2/34 3/76 4/131 5/139
6/148 7/181 8/216 9/277

Bowling: *First Innings*—Melle 14-0-73-0; Watkins 6-1-15-0; Murray 3-1-11-0; Tayfield 29.4-9-84-6; Mansell 19-3-58-3. *Second Innings*—Melle 11-2-39-2; Watkins 10-2-34-0; Murray 23-7-59-1; Tayfield 37.1-13-81-7; Mansell 14-2-69-0.

Umpires: H.Elphinston and M.J.McInnes

AUSTRALIA v SOUTH AFRICA 1952-53 (Fourth Test)

At Adelaide Oval, 24, 26, 27, 28, 29 January

Result: Match drawn

Australia

Batsman	First Innings	Runs	Second Innings	Runs
C.C.McDonald	st Waite b Tayfield	154	b Mansell	15
A.R.Morris	c Endean b Fuller	1	c Endean b Melle	77
A.L.Hassett*	c McGlew b Mansell	163		
R.N.Harvey	c Tayfield b Fuller	84	(3) c Endean b Watkins	116
K.R.Miller	c Waite b Tayfield	9		
G.B.Hole	c and b Mansell	59	(4) not out	6
R.Benaud	b Melle	6	(5) not out	18
D.T.Ring	c McLean b Tayfield	28		
R.R.Lindwall	lbw b Tayfield	5		
G.R.A.Langley†	not out	2		
W.A.Johnston	run out	11		
Extras	(B 1, LB 7)	8	(B 1)	1
		530	(3 wkts dec.)	233

1/2 2/277 3/356 4/387 5/439
6/448 7/494 8/505 9/517

1/42 2/199 3/209

Bowling: *First Innings*—Melle 26-1-105-1; Fuller 25-2-119-2; Tayfield 44-6-142-4; Mansell 32-1-113-2; McGlew 2-0-9-0; Watkins 6-1-34-0. *Second Innings*—Melle 10-1-50-1; Fuller 3-0-12-0; Tayfield 14-1-65-0; Mansell 7-0-40-1; McGlew 1-0-7-0; Watkins 12-1-58-1.

South Africa

Batsman	First Innings	Runs	Second Innings	Runs
D.J.McGlew	c Hole b Johnston	26	c Langley b Johnston	54
W.R.Endean	c Langley b Benaud	56	(4) b Harvey	17
R.A.McLean	c Hassett b Ring	11	c Hole b Benaud	17
J.H.B.Waite†	c Hole b Benaud	44	(2) b Hole	20
K.J.Funston	c and b Benaud	92	lbw b Johnston	17
J.C.Watkins	b Benaud	76	b Morris	21
J.E.Cheetham*	b Johnston	6	not out	6
P.N.F.Mansell	c Hole b Johnston	33	not out	2
E.R.H.Fuller	b Johnston	16		
H.J.Tayfield	c and b Johnston	0		
M.G.Melle	not out	9		
Extras	(B 12, LB 4, NB 2)	18	(B 16)	16
		387	(6 wkts)	177

1/62 2/79 3/100 4/208 5/270
6/296 7/350 8/374 9/378

1/81 2/95 3/109 4/127
5/156 6/166

Bowling: *First Innings*—Lindwall 13-0-47-0; Johnston 49.3-17-110-5; Miller 2.1-1-1-0; Ring 30-8-88-1; Benaud 44-9-118-4; Hole 3-1-5-0. *Second Innings*—Johnston 24-4-67-2; Hole 9.4-17-1; Benaud 14-5-28-1; Harvey 7-2-9-1; Ring 11-3-25-0; Morris 5-0-11-1; Hassett 1-0-1-0; McDonald 1-0-3-0.

Umpires: M.J.McInnes and R.Wright

AUSTRALIA v SOUTH AFRICA 1952-53 (Fifth Test)

At Melbourne Cricket Ground, 6, 7, 9, 10, 11, 12 February

Result: South Africa won by 6 wickets

Australia

Batsman	First Innings	Runs	Second Innings	Runs
C.C.McDonald	c McLean b Mansell	41	c Watkins b Fuller	11
A.R.Morris	run out	99	lbw b Tayfield	44
R.N.Harvey	c Cheetham b Fuller	205	b Fuller	7
A.L.Hassett*	run out	40	c Endean b Mansell	30
I.D.Craig	c Keith b Fuller	53	c Endean b Tayfield	47
R.G.Archer	c Waite b Fuller	18	c Watkins b Tayfield	0
R.Benaud	c and b Tayfield	20	c Watkins b Fuller	30
D.T.Ring	b Tayfield	14	Endean b Mansell	0
G.R.A.Langley†	b Murray	2	not out	26
W.A.Johnston	c Endean b Tayfield	12	c Cheetham b Fuller	5
G.Noblet	not out	13	b Fuller	1
Extras	(LB 3)	3	(B 7, LB 1)	8
		520		209

1/122 2/166 3/269 4/417 5/450
6/459 7/490 8/493 9/495

1/36 2/44 3/70 4/128 5/129
6/152 7/152 8/187 9/193

Bowling: *First Innings*—Fuller 19-4-74-3; Watkins 23-3-72-0; Tayfield 35.4-4-129-3; Murray 2.5-3-84-1; Mansell 22-0-114-1; Keith 9-0-44-0. *Second Innings*—Fuller 30.2-4-66-5; Watkins 14-4-33-0; Tayfield 32-8-73-3; Mansell 8-3-29-2.

South Africa

Batsman	First Innings	Runs	Second Innings	Runs
W.R.Endean	c Langley b Johnston	16	b Johnston	70
J.H.B.Waite†	run out	64	c Archer b Noblet	18
J.C.Watkins	b Archer	92	b Ring	50
K.J.Funston	lbw b Johnston	16	b Benaud	35
H.J.Keith	b Johnston	10	not out	40
R.A.McLean	lbw b Noblet	81	not out	76
J.E.Cheetham*	c McDonald b Johnston	66		
P.N.F.Mansell	lbw b Johnston	52		
A.R.A.Murray	c and b Johnston	17		
H.J.Tayfield	c Benaud b Ring	17		
E.R.H.Fuller	not out	0		
Extras	(B 1, LB 3)	4	(B 2, LB 6)	8
		435	(4 wkts)	297

1/31 2/129 3/189 4/189 5/239
6/290 7/401 8/402 9/435

1/42 2/124 3/174
4/191

Bowling: *First Innings*—Noblet 30-6-65-1; Archer 33-4-97-1; Johnston 46-8-152-6; Ring 19.1-1-62-1; Benaud 15-3-55-0. *Second Innings*—Noblet 24-9-44-1; Archer 5-0-23-0; Johnston 38-7-114-1; Ring 13-2-55-1; Benaud 15-4-41-1; Hassett 0.5-0-12-0.

Umpires: M.J.McInnes and R.Wright

ENGLAND v AUSTRALIA 1953 (First Test)

At Trent Bridge, Nottingham, 11, 12, 13, 15 (no play), 16 June

Result: Match drawn

Australia

G.B.Hole b Bedser	0	b Bedser	5
A.R.Morris lbw b Bedser	67	b Tattersall	60
A.L.Hassett* b Bedser	115	c Hutton b Bedser	5
R.N.Harvey c Compton b Bedser	0	c Graveney b Bedser	2
K.R.Miller c Bailey b Wardle	55	c Kenyon b Bedser	5
R.Benaud c Evans b Bailey	3	b Bedser	0
A.K.Davidson b Bedser	4	c Graveney b Tattersall	6
D.Tallon† b Bedser	0	c Simpson b Tattersall	15
R.R.Lindwall c Evans b Bailey	0	c Tattersall b Bedser	12
J.C.Hill b Bedser	0	c Tattersall b Bedser	4
W.A.Johnston not out	0	not out	4
Extras (B 2, LB 2, NB 1)	5	(LB 5)	5
	249		123

1/2 2/124 3/128 4/237 5/244
6/244 7/246 8/247 9/248

1/28 2/44 3/50 4/64 5/68
6/81 7/92 8/102 9/115

Bowling: *First Innings*—Bedser 38.3-16-55-7; Bailey 44-14-75-2; Wardle 35-16-55-1; Tattersall 23-5-59-0. *Second Innings*—Bedser 17.2-7-44-7; Bailey 5-1-28-0; Wardle 12-3-24-0; Tattersall 5-0-22-3.

England

L.Hutton* c Benaud b Davidson	43	not out	60
D.Kenyon c Hill b Lindwall	8	c Hassett b Hill	16
R.T.Simpson lbw b Lindwall	0	not out	28
D.C.S.Compton c Morris b Lindwall	0		
T.W.Graveney c Benaud b Hill	22		
P.B.H.May c Tallon b Hill	9		
T.E.Bailey lbw b Hill	13		
T.G.Evans† c Tallon b Davidson	8		
J.H.Wardle not out	29		
A.V.Bedser lbw b Lindwall	2		
R.Tattersall b Lindwall	2		
Extras (B 5, LB 3)	8	(B 8, LB 4, NB 2, W 2)	16
	144	(1 wkt)	120

1/17 2/17 3/17 4/76 5/82
6/92 7/107 8/121 9/136

1/26

Bowling: *First Innings*—Lindwall 20.4-2-57-5; Johnston 18-7-22-0; Hill 19-8-35-3; Davidson 15-7-22-2. *Second Innings*—Lindwall 16-4-37-0; Johnston 18-9-14-0; Hill 12-3-26-1; Davidson 5-1-7-0; Benaud 5-0-15-0; Morris 2-0-5-0.

Umpires: D.Davies and H.Elliott

ENGLAND v AUSTRALIA 1953 (Second Test)

At Lord's, London, 25, 26, 27, 29, 30 June

Result: Match drawn

Australia

A.L.Hassett* c Bailey b Bedser	104	c Evans b Statham	3
A.R.Morris st Evans b Bedser	30	c Statham b Compton	89
R.N.Harvey lbw b Bedser	59	(4) b Bedser	21
K.R.Miller b Wardle	25	(3) b Wardle	109
G.B.Hole c Compton b Wardle	13	lbw b Brown	47
R.Benaud lbw b Wardle	0	c Graveney b Bedser	5
A.K.Davidson c Statham b Bedser	76	c and b Brown	15
D.T.Ring lbw b Wardle	18	lbw b Brown	7
R.R.Lindwall b Statham	9	b Bedser	50
G.R.A.Langley† c Watson b Bedser	1	b Brown	9
W.A.Johnston not out	3	not out	0
Extras (B 4, LB 4)	8	(B 8, LB 5)	13
	346		368

1/65 2/190 3/225 4/229 5/240
6/280 7/291 8/330 9/331

1/3 2/168 3/227 4/235 5/248
6/296 7/305 8/308 9/362

Bowling: *First Innings*—Bedser 42.4-8-105-5; Statham 28-7-48-1; Brown 25-7-53-0; Bailey 16-2-55-0; Wardle 29-8-77-4. *Second Innings*—Bedser 31.5-8-77-3; Statham 15-3-40-1; Brown 27-4-82-4; Bailey 10-4-24-0; Wardle 46-18-111-1; Compton 3-0-21-1.

England

L.Hutton* c Hole b Johnston	145	c Hole b Lindwall	5
D.Kenyon c Davidson b Lindwall	3	c Hassett b Lindwall	2
T.W.Graveney c Hole b Benaud	78	c Langley b Johnston	2
D.C.S.Compton c Hole b Benaud	57	lbw b Johnston	33
W.Watson st Langley b Johnston	4	c Hole b Ring	109
T.E.Bailey c and b Miller	2	c Benaud b Ring	71
F.R.Brown c Langley b Lindwall	22	c Hole b Benaud	28
T.G.Evans† b Lindwall	0	not out	11
J.H.Wardle b Davidson	23	not out	0
A.V.Bedser b Lindwall	1		
J.B.Statham not out	17		
Extras (B 11, LB 1, NB 7, W 1)	20	(B 7, LB 6, NB 6, W 2)	21
	372	(7 wkts)	282

1/9 2/177 3/279 4/291 5/301
6/328 7/328 8/332 9/341

1/6 2/10 3/12 4/73 5/236
6/246 7/282

Bowling: *First Innings*—Lindwall 23-4-66-5; Miller 25-6-57-1; Johnston 35-11-91-2; Ring 14-2-43-0; Benaud 19-4-70-1; Davidson 10.5-2-25-1. *Second Innings*—Lindwall 19-3-26-2; Miller 17-8-17-0; Johnston 29-10-70-2; Ring 29-5-84-2; Benaud 17-6-51-1; Davidson 14-5-13-0; Hole 1-1-0-0.

Umpires: H.G.Baldwin and F.S.Lee

ENGLAND v AUSTRALIA 1953 (Third Test)

At Old Trafford, Manchester, 9, 10, 11, 13 (no play), 14 July

Result: Match drawn

Australia

Batsman	1st innings		2nd innings	
A.L.Hassett*	b Bailey	26	c Bailey b Bedser	8
A.R.Morris	b Bedser	1	c Hutton b Laker	0
K.R.Miller	b Bedser	17	st Evans b Laker	6
R.N.Harvey	c Evans b Bedser	122	(7) b Wardle	0
G.B.Hole	c Evans b Bedser	66	(4) c Evans b Bedser	2
J.H.de Courcy	lbw b Wardle	41	(5) st Evans b Wardle	8
A.K.Davidson	st Evans b Laker	15	(6) not out	4
R.G.Archer	c Compton b Bedser	5	lbw b Wardle	0
R.R.Lindwall	c Edrich b Wardle	1	b Wardle	4
J.C.Hill	not out	8	not out	0
G.R.A.Langley†	c Edrich b Wardle	8		
Extras	(B 6, LB 1, NB 1)	8	(LB 3)	3
		318	(8 wkts)	35

1/15 2/48 3/48 4/221 5/256 6/285 7/290 8/291 9/302
1/8 2/12 3/18 4/18 5/31(8 wkts) 6/31 7/31 8/35.

Bowling: First Innings—Bedser 45-10-115-5; Bailey 26-4-83-1; Wardle 28.3-10-70-3; Laker 17-3-42-1. Second Innings—Bedser 4-1-14-2; Laker 9-5-11-2; Wardle 5-2-7-4.

England

L.Hutton*	lbw b Lindwall	66
W.J.Edrich	c Hole b Hill	6
T.W.Graveney	c de Courcy b Miller	5
D.C.S.Compton	c Langley b Archer	45
J.H.Wardle	b Lindwall	5
W.Watson	b Davidson	16
R.T.Simpson	c Langley b Davidson	31
T.E.Bailey	c Hole b Hill	27
T.G.Evans†	not out	44
J.C.Laker	lbw b Hill	5
A.V.Bedser	b Morris	10
Extras	(B 8, LB 8)	16
		276

1/19 2/32 3/126 4/126 5/149 6/149 7/209 8/231 9/243

Bowling: Lindwall 20-8-30-2; Archer 15-8-12-1; Hill 33-7-97-3; Miller 24-11-38-1; Davidson 20-4-60-2; Harvey 3-2-2-0; Hole 2-0-16-0; Morris 1-0-5-1.

Umpires: D.Davies and H.Elliott

ENGLAND v AUSTRALIA 1953 (Fourth Test)

At Headingley, Leeds, 23, 24, 25, 27, 28 July

Result: Match drawn

England

Batsman	1st innings		2nd innings	
L.Hutton*	b Lindwall	0	c Langley b Archer	25
W.J.Edrich	lbw b Miller	10	c de Courcy b Lindwall	64
T.W.Graveney	c Benaud b Miller	55	b Lindwall	3
D.C.S.Compton	c Davidson b Lindwall	0	lbw b Lindwall	61
W.Watson	b Lindwall	24	c Davidson b Miller	15
R.T.Simpson	c Langley b Lindwall	15	de Courcy b Miller	0
T.E.Bailey	run out	7	c Hole b Davidson	38
T.G.Evans†	lbw b Lindwall	25	c Lindwall b Miller	1
J.C.Laker	c Lindwall b Archer	10	c Benaud b Davidson	48
G.A.R.Lock	b Davidson	9	c Morris b Miller	8
A.V.Bedser	not out	0	not out	3
Extras	(B 8, LB 4)	12	(B 1, LB 8)	9
		167		275

1/0 2/33 3/36 4/98 5/108 6/110 7/133 8/149 9/167
1/57 2/62 3/139 4/167 5/171 6/182 7/239 8/244 9/258

Bowling: First Innings—Lindwall 35-10-54-5; Miller 28-13-39-2; Davidson 20.4-7-23-1; Archer 18-4-27-1; Benaud 8-1-12-0. Second Innings—Lindwall 54-19-104-3; Miller 47-19-63-4; Davidson 29.3-15-36-2; Archer 25-12-31-1; Benaud 19-8-26-0; Hole 3-1-6-0.

Australia

Batsman	1st innings		2nd innings	
A.L.Hassett*	c Lock b Bedser	37	b Lock	4
A.R.Morris	c Lock b Bedser	10	st Evans b Laker	38
R.N.Harvey	lbw b Bailey	71	(4) lbw b Bedser	34
K.R.Miller	c Edrich b Bailey	5		
G.B.Hole	c Lock b Bedser	53	(3) c Graveney b Bailey	33
J.H.de Courcy	lbw b Lock	10	not out	13
R.Benaud	b Bailey	7		
A.K.Davidson	c Evans b Bedser	2	(5) not out	17
R.G.Archer	not out	31		
R.R.Lindwall	b Bedser	9		
G.R.A.Langley†	c Hutton b Bedser	17		
Extras	(B 4, LB 8, W 2)	14	(B 3, LB 4, W 1)	8
		266	(4 wkts)	147

1/27 2/70 3/84 4/168 5/183 6/203 7/203 8/208 9/218
1/27 2/54 3/111 4/117(4 wkts)

Bowling: First Innings—Bedser 28.5-2-95-6; Bailey 22-4-91-3; Lock 23-9-53-1; Laker 9-1-33-0. Second Innings—Bedser 17-1-65-1; Bailey 6-1-9-1; Lock 8-1-48-1; Laker 2-0-17-1.

Umpires: F.Chester and F.S.Lee

ENGLAND v AUSTRALIA 1953 (Fifth Test)

At Kennington Oval, London, 15, 17, 18, 19 August

Result: England won by 8 wickets

Australia

A.L.Hassett* c Evans b Bedser	53	lbw b Laker	10
A.R.Morris lbw b Bedser	16	lbw b Lock	26
K.R.Miller lbw b Bailey	1	(5) c Trueman b Laker	0
R.N.Harvey c Hutton b Trueman	36	b Lock	1
G.B.Hole c Evans b Trueman	37	(3) lbw b Laker	17
J.H.de Courcy c Evans b Trueman	5	run out	4
R.G.Archer c and b Bedser	10	c Edrich b Lock	49
A.K.Davidson c Edrich b Laker	22	b Lock	21
R.R.Lindwall c Evans b Trueman	62	c Compton b Laker	12
G.R.A.Langley† c Edrich b Lock	18	b Lock	2
W.A.Johnston not out	9	not out	6
Extras (B 4, NB 2)	6	(B 11, LB 3)	14
	275		**162**

1/38 2/41 3/107 4/107 5/118
6/160 7/160 8/207 9/245

1/23 2/59 3/60 4/61 5/61
6/85 7/135 8/140 9/144

Bowling: *First Innings*—Bedser 29-3-88-3; Trueman 24.3-3-86-4; Bailey 14-3-42-1; Lock 9-2-19-1; Laker 5-0-34-1. *Second Innings*—Bedser 11-2-24-0; Trueman 2-1-4-0; Lock 21-9-45-5; Laker 16.5-2-75-4.

England

L.Hutton* b Johnston	82	run out	17
W.J.Edrich lbw b Lindwall	21	not out	55
P.B.H.May c Archer b Johnston	39	c Davidson b Miller	37
D.C.S.Compton c Langley b Lindwall	16	not out	22
T.W.Graveney c Miller b Lindwall	4		
T.E.Bailey b Archer	64		
T.G.Evans† run out	28		
J.C.Laker c Langley b Miller	1		
G.A.R.Lock c Davidson b Lindwall	4		
A.V.Bedser b Johnston	10		
F.S.Trueman not out	22		
Extras (B 9, LB 5, W 1)	15	(LB 1)	1
	306	(2 wkts)	**88**

1/37 2/137 3/154 4/167 5/170
6/210 7/225 8/239 9/262

1/24 2/88

Bowling: *First Innings*—Lindwall 32-7-70-4; Miller 34-12-65-1; Johnston 45-16-94-3; Davidson 10-1-26-0; Archer 10.3-2-25-1; Hole 11-6-11-0. *Second Innings*—Lindwall 21-5-46-0; Miller 11-3-24-1; Johnston 29-14-52-0; Archer 1-1-0-0; Hassett 1-1-0-0; Morris 0.5-0-5-0.

Umpires: D.Davies and F.S.Lee

AUSTRALIA v ENGLAND 1954-55 (First Test)

At Woolloongabba, Brisbane, 26, 27, 29, 30 November, 1 December

Result: Australia won by an innings and 154 runs

Australia

L.E.Favell c Cowdrey b Statham	23
A.R.Morris c Cowdrey b Bailey	153
K.R.Miller b Bailey	49
R.N.Harvey c Bailey b Bedser	162
G.B.Hole run out	57
R.Benaud c May b Tyson	34
R.G.Archer c Bedser b Statham	0
R.R.Lindwall not out	64
G.R.A.Langley† b Bailey	16
I.W.Johnson* not out	24
W.A.Johnston	
Extras (B 11, LB 7, NB 1)	19
(8 wkts dec.)	**601**

1/51 2/123 3/325 4/456 5/463
6/464 7/545 8/572

Bowling: Bedser 37-4-131-1; Statham 34-2-123-2; Tyson 29-1-160-1; Bailey 26-1-140-3; Edrich 3-0-28-0.

England

L.Hutton* c Langley b Lindwall	4	lbw b Miller	13
R.T.Simpson b Miller	2	run out	9
W.J.Edrich c Langley b Archer	15	b Johnston	88
P.B.H.May b Lindwall	1	lbw b Lindwall	44
M.C.Cowdrey c Hole b Johnston	40	b Benaud	10
T.E.Bailey b Johnston	88	c Langley b Lindwall	23
F.H.Tyson b Johnston	7	not out	37
A.V.Bedser b Johnston	5	c Archer b Johnson	5
K.V.Andrew† b Lindwall	6	b Johnson	5
J.B.Statham b Johnston	11	(11) c Harvey b Benaud	14
D.C.S.Compton not out	2	(10) c Langley b Benaud	0
Extras (B 3, LB 6)	9	(B 7, LB 2)	9
	190		**257**

1/4 2/10 3/11 4/25 5/107
6/132 7/141 8/156 9/181

1/22 2/23 3/147 4/163 5/181
6/220 7/231 8/242 9/243

Bowling: *First Innings*—Lindwall 14-4-27-3; Miller 11-5-19-1; Archer 4-1-14-1; Johnson 19-5-46-3; Benaud 12-5-28-0; Johnston 16.1-5-47-2. *Second Innings*—Lindwall 17-3-50-2; Miller 12-2-30-1; Archer 15-4-28-0; Johnson 17-5-38-2; Benaud 8.1-1-43-3; Johnston 21-8-59-1.

Umpires: C.Hoy and M.J.McInnes

AUSTRALIA v ENGLAND 1954-55 (Second Test)

At Sydney Cricket Ground, 17, 18, 20, 21, 22 December

Result: England won by 38 runs

England

L.Hutton* c Davidson b Johnston	30	c Benaud b Johnston	28
T.E.Bailey b Lindwall	0	c Langley b Archer	6
P.B.H.May c Johnston b Archer	5	b Lindwall	104
T.W.Graveney c Favell b Johnston	21	c Langley b Johnston	0
M.C.Cowdrey c Langley b Davidson	23	c Archer b Benaud	54
W.J.Edrich c Benaud b Archer	10	b Archer	29
F.H.Tyson b Lindwall	0	b Lindwall	9
T.G.Evans† c Langley b Archer	3	c Lindwall b Archer	4
J.H.Wardle c Burke b Johnston	35	lbw b Lindwall	8
R.Appleyard c Hole b Davidson	8	not out	19
J.B.Statham not out	14	c Langley b Johnston	25
Extras (LB 5)	5	(LB 6, NB 4)	10
	154		**296**

1/14 2/19 3/58 4/63 5/84   1/18 2/55 3/55 4/171 5/222
6/85 7/88 8/99 9/111   6/232 7/239 8/249 9/250

Bowling: First Innings—Lindwall 17-3-47-2; Archer 12-7-12-3; Davidson 12-3-34-2; Johnston 13.3-1-56-3. Second Innings—Lindwall 31-10-69-3; Archer 22-9-53-3; Davidson 13-2-52-0; Johnston 19.3-2-70-3; Benaud 19-3-42-1.

Australia

L.E.Favell c Graveney b Bailey	26	c Edrich b Tyson	16
A.R.Morris* c Hutton b Bailey	12	lbw b Statham	10
J.W.Burke c Graveney b Bailey	44	b Tyson	14
R.N.Harvey c Cowdrey b Tyson	12	not out	92
G.B.Hole b Tyson	12	b Tyson	0
R.Benaud lbw b Statham	20	c Tyson b Appleyard	12
R.G.Archer c Hutton b Tyson	49	b Tyson	6
A.K.Davidson b Statham	20	c Evans b Statham	5
R.R.Lindwall c Evans b Tyson	19	b Tyson	8
G.R.A.Langley† b Bailey	5	b Statham	0
W.A.Johnston not out	0	c Evans b Tyson	11
Extras (B 5, LB 2, NB 2)	9	(LB 7, NB 3)	10
	228		**184**

1/18 2/65 3/100 4/104 5/122   1/27 2/34 3/77 4/77 5/102
6/141 7/193 8/213 9/224   6/122 7/127 8/136 9/145

Bowling: First Innings—Statham 18-1-83-2; Bailey 17.4-3-59-4; Tyson 13-2-45-4; Appleyard 7-1-32-0. Second Innings—Statham 19-6-45-3; Bailey 6-0-21-0; Tyson 18.4-1-85-6; Appleyard 6-1-12-1; Wardle 4-2-11-0.

Umpires: M.J.McInnes and R.Wright

AUSTRALIA v ENGLAND 1954-55 (Third Test)

At Melbourne Cricket Ground, 31 December, 1, 3, 4, 5 January

Result: England won by 128 runs

England

L.Hutton* c Hole b Miller	12	lbw b Archer	42
W.J.Edrich c Lindwall b Miller	4	b Johnston	13
P.B.H.May c Benaud b Lindwall	0	b Johnston	91
M.C.Cowdrey b Johnston	102	b Benaud	7
D.C.S.Compton c Harvey b Miller	4	c Maddocks b Archer	23
T.E.Bailey c Maddocks b Johnston	30	not out	24
T.G.Evans† lbw b Archer	20	c Maddocks b Miller	22
J.H.Wardle b Archer	0	b Johnson	38
F.H.Tyson b Archer	6	c Harvey b Johnston	6
J.B.Statham b Archer	3	c Favell b Johnston	0
R.Appleyard not out	1	b Johnston	6
Extras (B 9)	9	(B 2, LB 4, W 1)	7
	191		**279**

1/14 2/21 3/29 4/41 5/115   1/40 2/96 3/128 4/173 5/185
6/169 7/181 8/181 9/190   6/211 7/257 8/273 9/273

Bowling: First Innings—Lindwall 13-0-59-1; Miller 11-8-14-3; Archer 13.6-4-33-4; Benaud 7-0-30-0; Johnston 12-6-26-1; Johnson 11-3-20-1. Second Innings—Lindwall 18-3-52-0; Miller 18-6-35-1; Archer 24.5-2-85-5; Johnston 8-2-25-1.

Australia

L.E.Favell lbw b Statham	25		b Appleyard	30
A.R.Morris lbw b Tyson	3		c Cowdrey b Tyson	4
K.R.Miller c Evans b Statham	7	(5)	c Edrich b Tyson	6
R.N.Harvey b Appleyard	31		c Evans b Tyson	11
G.B.Hole b Tyson	11	(6)	c Evans b Statham	5
R.Benaud c sub (J.V.Wilson) b Appleyard	15	(3)	b Tyson	22
R.G.Archer b Wardle	23		b Statham	15
L.V.Maddocks† c Evans b Statham	47		b Tyson	0
R.R.Lindwall b Statham	13		lbw b Tyson	0
I.W.Johnson* not out	33		not out	4
W.A.Johnston b Statham	11		c Evans b Tyson	0
Extras (B 7, LB 3, NB 2)	12		(B 1, LB 13)	14
	231			**111**

1/15 2/38 3/43 4/65 5/92   1/23 2/57 3/77 4/86 5/87
6/115 7/134 8/151 9/205   6/97 7/98 8/98 9/110

Bowling: First Innings—Tyson 21-2-68-2; Statham 16.3-0-60-5; Bailey 9-1-33-0; Appleyard 11-3-38-2; Wardle 6-0-20-1. Second Innings—Tyson 12.3-1-27-7; Statham 11-1-38-2; Bailey 3-0-14-0; Appleyard 4-1-17-0; Wardle 1-0-1-0.

Umpires: C.Hoy and M.J.McInnes

AUSTRALIA v ENGLAND 1954-55 (Fourth Test)

At Adelaide Oval, 28, 29, 31 January, 1, 2 February

Result: England won by 5 wickets

Australia

Batsman	First Innings		Second Innings	
C.C.McDonald	c May b Appleyard	48	b Statham	29
A.R.Morris	c Evans b Tyson	25	c and b Appleyard	16
J.W.Burke	c May b Tyson	18	b Appleyard	5
R.N.Harvey	c Edrich b Bailey	25	b Appleyard	7
K.R.Miller	c Bailey b Appleyard	44	b Statham	14
R.Benaud	c May b Appleyard	15	(7) lbw b Tyson	1
L.V.Maddocks†	run out	69	(6) lbw b Statham	2
R.G.Archer	c May b Tyson	21	c Evans b Tyson	3
A.K.Davidson	c Evans b Bailey	5	lbw b Wardle	23
I.W.Johnson*	c Statham b Bailey	41	(11) not out	3
W.A.Johnston	not out	0	(10) c Appleyard b Tyson	3
Extras	(B 3, LB 7, NB 2)	12	(B 4, LB 1)	5
Total		**323**		**111**

1/59 2/86 3/115 4/129 5/175
6/182 7/212 8/229 9/321

1/24 2/40 3/54 4/69 5/76
6/77 7/79 8/83 9/101

Bowling: First Innings—Tyson 26.1-4-85-3; Statham 19-4-70-0; Bailey 12-3-39-3; Appleyard 23-7-58-3; Wardle 19-5-59-0. Second Innings—Tyson 15-2-47-3; Statham 12-1-38-3; Appleyard 12-7-13-3; Wardle 4.2-1-8-1.

England

Batsman	First Innings		Second Innings	
L.Hutton*	c Davidson b Johnston	80	c Davidson b Johnston	5
W.J.Edrich	b Johnson	21	b Miller	0
P.B.H.May	c Archer b Benaud	1	c Miller b Johnston	26
M.C.Cowdrey	c Maddocks b Davidson	79	c Archer b Miller	4
D.C.S.Compton	lbw b Miller	44	not out	34
T.E.Bailey	c Davidson b Johnston	38	lbw b Johnston	15
T.G.Evans†	c Maddocks b Benaud	37	not out	6
J.H.Wardle	c and b Johnson	23		
F.H.Tyson	c Burke b Benaud	1		
R.Appleyard	not out	10		
J.B.Statham	c Maddocks b Benaud	0		
Extras	(B 1, LB 2, NB 4)	7	(B 3, LB 4)	7
Total		**341**	**(5 wkts)**	**97**

1/60 2/63 3/162 4/232 5/232
6/283 7/321 8/323 9/336

1/3 2/10 3/18 4/49 5/90

Bowling: First Innings—Miller 11-4-34-1; Archer 3-0-12-0; Johnson 27-11-60-2; Benaud 36.6-6-120-4; Burke 2-0-7-0. Second Innings—Miller 10.4-2-40-3; Archer 4-0-13-0; Davidson 2-0-7-0; Johnston 8-2-20-2; Benaud 6-2-10-0.

Umpires: M.J.McInnes and R.Wright

AUSTRALIA v ENGLAND 1954-55 (Fifth Test)

At Sydney Cricket Ground, 25 (no play), 26 (no play), 28 (no play) February, 1, 2, 3 March

Result: Match drawn

England

Batsman	First Innings	
L.Hutton*	c Burge b Lindwall	6
T.W.Graveney	c and b Johnson	111
P.B.H.May	c Davidson b Benaud	79
M.C.Cowdrey	c Maddocks b Johnson	0
D.C.S.Compton	c and b Johnson	84
T.E.Bailey	b Lindwall	72
T.G.Evans†	c McDonald b Lindwall	10
J.H.Wardle	not out	5
F.H.Tyson		
R.Appleyard		
J.B.Statham		
Extras	(B 1, LB 3)	4
Total	**(7 wkts dec.)**	**371**

1/6 2/188 3/188 4/196 5/330
6/359 7/371

Bowling: Lindwall 20.6-5-77-3; Miller 15-1-71-0; Davidson 19-3-72-0; Johnson 20-5-68-3; Benaud 20-4-79-1.

Australia

Batsman	First Innings		Second Innings	
W.J.Watson	b Wardle	18	c Graveney b Statham	3
C.C.McDonald	c May b Appleyard	72	c Evans b Graveney	37
L.E.Favell	b Tyson	1	c Graveney b Wardle	9
R.N.Harvey	c and b Tyson	13	c and b Wardle	1
K.R.Miller	run out	19	b Wardle	28
P.J.P.Burge	c Appleyard b Wardle	17	not out	18
R.Benaud	b Wardle	7	b Hutton	22
L.V.Maddocks†	c Appleyard b Wardle	32		
A.K.Davidson	c Evans b Wardle	18		
I.W.Johnson*	run out	11		
R.R.Lindwall	not out	11		
Extras	(B 10, LB 1)	11		
Total		**221**	**(6 wkts)**	**118**

1/52 2/53 3/85 4/129 5/138
6/147 7/157 8/202 9/217

1/14 2/27 3/29 4/67
5/87 6/118

Bowling: First Innings—Tyson 11-1-46-2; Statham 9-1-31-0; Appleyard 16-2-54-1; Wardle 24.4-6-79-5. Second Innings—Tyson 5-2-20-0; Statham 5-0-11-1; Wardle 12-1-51-3; Graveney 6-0-34-1; Hutton 0.6-0-2-1.

Umpires: M.J.McInnes and R.Wright

WEST INDIES v AUSTRALIA 1954-55 (First Test)

At Sabina Park, Kingston, Jamaica, 26, 28, 29, 30, 31 March

Result: Australia won by 9 wickets

Australia

Batsman	First Innings		Second Innings	
C.C.McDonald st Binns b Valentine	50	(3) not out		7
A.R.Morris lbw b Valentine	65	c Gibbs b Weekes		1
R.N.Harvey b Walcott	133			
K.R.Miller lbw b Walcott	147			
R.R.Lindwall lbw b Ramadhin	10			
P.J.P.Burge c and b Atkinson	14			
L.V.Maddocks† b Valentine	1	(1) not out		12
R.Benaud b Walcott	46			
R.G.Archer c Walcott b Holt	24			
I.W.Johnson* not out	18			
W.A.Johnston not out	0			
Extras (B 3, LB 3, W 1)	7			

1/102 2/137 3/361 4/391 5/417 (9 wkts dec.) 515   1/6 (1 wkt) 20
6/430 7/435 8/475 9/506

Bowling: *First Innings*—King 28-7-122-0; Worrell 7-2-13-0; Atkinson 23-9-46-1; Ramadhin 46-12-112-1; Valentine 54-20-113-3; Smith 11-0-27-0; Walcott 26-9-50-3; Gibbs 3-1-5-0; Holt 3-0-20-1. *Second Innings*—King 2-0-10-0; Weekes 2.2-0-8-1; Gibbs 1-0-2-0.

West Indies

Batsman	First Innings		Second Innings	
J.K.Holt c Benaud b Lindwall	31	c Maddocks b Benaud		60
G.L.Gibbs lbw b Archer	12	b Johnston		0
A.P.Binns† c Burge b Archer	0	(7) lbw b Miller		0
E.D.Weekes run out	19	c and b Benaud		1
C.L.Walcott c Benaud b Miller	108	c Archer b Lindwall		39
F.M.M.Worrell b Johnston	9	(8) b Archer		9
O.G.Smith lbw b Lindwall	44	(3) c Harvey b Miller		104
D.S.Atkinson* c Harvey b Miller	1	(6) c Benaud b Miller		30
F.M.King c Maddocks b Lindwall	4	b Lindwall		21
S.Ramadhin not out	12	c Lindwall b Archer		3
A.L.Valentine b Lindwall	0	not out		2
Extras (B 14, LB 2, NB 3)	19	(B 5, NB 1)		6

1/27 2/27 3/56 4/75 5/101 259   1/20 2/122 3/132 4/209 5/213 275
6/239 7/240 8/243 9/253   6/213 7/239 8/253 9/270

Bowling: *First Innings*—Lindwall 24-6-61-4; Archer 19-8-39-2; Johnston 23-4-75-1; Benaud 19-7-29-0; Miller 16-5-36-2. *Second Innings*—Lindwall 16.1-3-63-2; Archer 12-3-44-2; Johnston 16-3-54-1; Benaud 23-7-44-2; Miller 28-9-62-3; Harvey 1-0-2-0.

Umpires: P.Burke and T.A.Ewart

WEST INDIES v AUSTRALIA 1954-55 (Second Test)

At Queen's Park Oval, Port-of-Spain, Trinidad, 11, 12, 13, 14, 15, 16 April

Result: Match drawn

West Indies

Batsman	Runs
J.K.Holt c Johnston b Lindwall	25
J.B.Stollmeyer* b Lindwall	14
C.L.Walcott st Langley b Benaud	126
E.D.Weekes c Johnson b Benaud	139
O.G.Smith b Benaud	0
G.S.Sobers c Langley b Lindwall	47
C.A.McWatt† c Benaud b Miller	4
F.M.King b Lindwall	2
S.Ramadhin b Lindwall	0
L.S.Butler c Johnson b Lindwall	16
A.L.Valentine not out	5
Extras (B 1, LB 3, NB 1)	5

1/39 2/40 3/282 4/282 5/323 382
6/355 7/360 8/360 9/361

Bowling: *First Innings*—Lindwall 24.5-3-95-6; Miller 28-8-96-1; Archer 9-0-42-0; Johnston 7-2-29-0; Johnson 19-5-72-0; Benaud 17-3-43-3. *Second Innings*—Lindwall 17-0-70-0; Miller 11-0-52-0; Archer 8-1-37-3; Johnson 7-0-31-0; Johnston 7-2-26-1; Benaud 12-2-52-0.

Australia

Batsman	First Innings		Second Innings	
C.C.McDonald c Walcott b Valentine	110	lbw b Archer		21
A.R.Morris c King b Butler	111	b Johnson		42
R.N.Harvey lbw b King	133	c Watson b Archer		110
W.J.Watson lbw b Ramadhin	27	not out		87
R.Benaud c Walcott b Ramadhin	5	c Langley b Archer		0
K.R.Miller run out	3	not out		8
R.G.Archer c McWatt b Valentine	84			
I.W.Johnson* c McWatt b Butler	66			
R.R.Lindwall not out	9			
G.R.A.Langley† c King b Walcott	37			
W.A.Johnston not out	1			
Extras (B 5, LB 6, NB 2, W 1)	14	(LB 3, NB 2)		5

1/191 2/259 3/328 4/336 5/345 (9 wkts dec.) 600   1/40 2/103 3/230 (4 wkts) 273
6/439 7/529 8/570 9/594   4/236

Bowling: Butler 40-7-151-2; King 37-7-98-1; Holt 1-1-0-0; Ramadhin 32-8-90-2; Valentine 49-12-133-2; Walcott 19-5-45-1; Sobers 3-1-10-0; Smith 15-1-48-0; Stollmeyer 5-0-11-0.

Umpires: H.B.D.Jordan and E.N.Lee Kow

WEST INDIES v AUSTRALIA 1954-55 (Third Test)

At Bourda, Georgetown, British Guiana, 26, 27, 28, 29 April
Result: Australia won by 8 wickets

West Indies

J.K.Holt	c and b Miller	12	c Langley b Miller	6
J.B.Stollmeyer*	c Archer b Miller	16	c and b Johnson	17
C.L.Walcott	c and b Archer	8	hit wkt b Lindwall	73
E.D.Weekes	c Archer b Benaud	81	c Langley b Johnson	0
F.M.M.Worrell	c Johnson b Archer	9	hit wkt b Benaud	56
G.S.Sobers	c Watson b Johnson	12	(8) b Johnson	11
D.S.Atkinson	b Lindwall	13	st Langley b Johnson	16
C.C.Depeiza†	not out	16	(6) st Langley b Johnson	13
N.E.Marshall	b Benaud	0	c sub (L.E.Favell) b Johnson	8
S.Ramadhin	c Archer b Benaud	0	st Langley b Johnson	2
F.M.King	c Langley b Benaud	13	not out	1
Extras	(B 1, LB 1)	2	(B 1, LB 2, NB 2)	5
		182		**207**

1/23 2/30 3/42 4/52 5/83   1/25 2/25 3/25 4/150 5/162
6/124 7/156 8/156 9/160   6/175 7/186 8/204 9/204

Bowling: First Innings—Lindwall 12-0-44-1; Miller 9-1-33-2; Archer 10-0-46-2; Johnson 9-1-42-1; Benaud 3.5-1-15-4. *Second Innings*—Lindwall 18-1-54-1; Miller 9-3-18-1; Archer 12-3-43-0; Johnson 22.2-10-44-7; Benaud 14-3-43-1.

Australia

C.C.McDonald	b Atkinson	61	b Atkinson	31
A.R.Morris	c Sobers b Atkinson	44	c Walcott b Marshall	38
R.N.Harvey	c Holt b Ramadhin	38	not out	41
W.J.Watson	c and b Ramadhin	6	not out	22
K.R.Miller	c Depeiza b Sobers	33		
R.Benaud	c sub (O.G.Smith) b Marshall	68		
R.G.Archer	st Depeiza b Sobers	2		
I.W.Johnson*	c Stollmeyer b Sobers	0		
R.R.Lindwall	b Atkinson	2		
G.R.A.Langley†	not out	1		
W.A.Johnston	absent hurt	–		
Extras	(LB 2)	2	(NB 1)	1
		257		**(2 wkts) 133**

1/71 2/135 3/147 4/161 5/215   1/70 2/70
6/231 7/231 8/238 9/257

Bowling: First Innings—King 12-1-37-0; Worrell 9-2-17-0; Ramadhin 26-9-55-2; Atkinson 37-13-85-3; Marshall 33.3-16-40-1; Stollmeyer 1-0-1-0; Sobers 16-10-20-3. *Second Innings*—King 3-0-10-0; Worrell 7-2-20-0; Ramadhin 9-1-29-0; Atkinson 15.5-5-32-1; Marshall 13-6-22-1; Sobers 11-4-19-0.

Umpires: E.S.Gillette and E.N.Lee Kow

WEST INDIES v AUSTRALIA 1954-55 (Fourth Test)

At Kensington Oval, Bridgetown, Barbados, 14, 16, 17, 18, 19, 20 May
Result: Match drawn

Australia

C.C.McDonald	run out	46	b Smith	17
L.E.Favell	c Weekes b Atkinson	72	run out	53
R.N.Harvey	c Smith b Worrell	74	c Valentine b Smith	27
W.J.Watson	c Depeiza b Dewdney	30	b Atkinson	0
K.R.Miller	c Depeiza b Dewdney	137	lbw b Atkinson	10
R.Benaud	c Walcott b Dewdney	1	b Sobers	5
R.G.Archer	b Worrell	98	lbw b Atkinson	28
R.R.Lindwall	c Valentine b Atkinson	118	(9) b Atkinson	10
I.W.Johnson*	b Dewdney	23	(8) c Holt b Smith	57
G.R.A.Langley†	b Sobers	53	not out	28
J.C.Hill	not out	8	c Weekes b Atkinson	1
Extras	(B 1, LB 2, NB 1, W 4)	8	(B 9, LB 4)	13
		668		**249**

1/108 2/126 3/226 4/226 5/233   1/71 2/72 3/73 4/87 5/107
6/439 7/483 8/562 9/623   6/119 7/151 8/177 9/241

Bowling: First Innings—Worrell 40-7-120-2; Dewdney 33-5-125-4; Walcott 26-10-57-0; Valentine 31-9-87-0; Ramadhin 24-3-84-0; Atkinson 48-14-108-2; Smith 22-8-49-0; Sobers 11.5-6-30-1. *Second Innings*—Worrell 7-0-25-0; Dewdney 10-4-23-0; Valentine 6-1-16-0; Ramadhin 2-0-10-0; Atkinson 36.2-12-56-5; Smith 34-12-71-3; Sobers 14-3-35-1.

West Indies

J.K.Holt	b Lindwall	22	lbw b Hill	49
G.S.Sobers	c Hill b Johnson	43	lbw b Archer	11
C.L.Walcott	c Langley b Benaud	15	b Benaud	83
E.D.Weekes	c Langley b Miller	44	run out	6
F.M.M.Worrell	run out	16	c Archer b Miller	34
O.G.Smith	c Langley b Miller	2	b Lindwall	11
D.S.Atkinson*	c Archer b Johnson	219	not out	20
C.C.Depeiza†	b Benaud	122	not out	11
S.Ramadhin	c and b Benaud	10		
D.T.Dewdney	b Johnson	0		
A.L.Valentine	not out	2		
Extras	(B 5, LB 4, NB 4, W 2)	15	(B 6, LB 2, W 1)	9
		510		**(6 wkts) 234**

1/52 2/69 3/105 4/142 5/143   1/38 2/67 3/81 4/154 (6 wkts) 234
6/147 7/494 8/504 9/504   5/193 6/207

Bowling: First Innings—Lindwall 25-3-96-1; Miller 22-2-113-2; Archer 15-4-44-0; Johnson 35-13-77-3; Hill 24-9-71-0; Benaud 31.1-6-73-3; Harvey 4-0-16-0; Watson 1-0-5-0. *Second Innings*—Lindwall 8-1-39-1; Miller 21-3-66-1; Archer 7-1-11-1; Johnson 14-4-30-0; Hill 11-2-44-1; Benaud 11-3-35-1.

Umpires: H.B.D.Jordan and E.N.Lee Kow

WEST INDIES v AUSTRALIA 1954-55 (Fifth Test)

At Sabina Park, Kingston, Jamaica, 11, 13, 14, 15, 16, 17 June
Result: Australia won by an innings and 82 runs

West Indies

J.K.Holt	c Langley b Miller	4	c Langley b Benaud	21
H.A.Furlonge	c Benaud b Lindwall	4	c sub (A.K.Davidson) b Miller	28
C.L.Walcott	c Langley b Miller	155	(4) c Langley b Lindwall	110
E.D.Weekes	b Benaud	56	(9) not out	36
F.M.M.Worrell	c Langley b Lindwall	61	(7) b Johnson	12
O.G.Smith	c Langley b Miller	29	c and b Benaud	16
G.S.Sobers	not out	35	(5) c Favell b Lindwall	64
D.S.Atkinson*	run out	8	c Langley b Archer	4
C.C.Depeiza†	c Langley b Miller	0	(3) b Miller	7
F.M.King	b Miller	0	c Archer b Johnson	6
D.T.Dewdney	b Miller	2	lbw b Benaud	0
Extras	(LB 2, W 1)	3	(B 8, LB 6, W 1)	15
		357		319

1/5 2/13 3/95 4/204 5/268
6/327 7/341 8/347 9/347

1/47 2/60 3/65 4/244 5/244
6/268 7/273 8/283 9/289

Bowling: *First Innings*—Lindwall 12-2-64-2; Miller 25.2-3-107-6; Archer 11-1-39-0; Benaud 24-5-75-1; Johnson 22-7-69-0. *Second Innings*—Lindwall 19-6-51-2; Miller 19-3-58-2; Archer 27-6-73-1; Benaud 29.5-10-76-3; Johnson 23-10-46-2.

Australia

C.C.McDonald	b Worrell	127
L.E.Favell	c Weekes b King	0
A.R.Morris	lbw b Dewdney	7
R.N.Harvey	c Atkinson b Smith	204
K.R.Miller	c Worrell b Atkinson	109
R.G.Archer	c Depeiza b Sobers	128
R.R.Lindwall	c Depeiza b King	12
R.Benaud	c Worrell b Smith	121
I.W.Johnson*	not out	27
G.R.A.Langley†		
W.A.Johnston		
Extras	(B 8, LB 7, NB 1, W 9)	25
	(8 wkts dec.)	758

1/0 2/7 3/302 4/373 5/593
6/597 7/621 8/758

Bowling: Dewdney 24-4-115-1; King 31-1-126-2; Atkinson 55-20-132-1; Smith 52.4-17-145-2; Worrell 45-10-116-1; Sobers 38-12-99-1.

Umpires: P.Burke and T.A.Ewart

ENGLAND v AUSTRALIA 1956 (First Test)

At Trent Bridge, Nottingham, 7, 8 (no play), 9, 11, 12 June
Result: Match drawn

England

P.E.Richardson	c Langley b Miller	81	c Langley b Archer	73
M.C.Cowdrey	c Miller b Davidson	25	c Langley b Miller	81
T.W.Graveney	c Archer b Johnson	8	(4) not out	10
P.B.H.May*	c Langley b Miller	73		
W.Watson	lbw b Archer	0	(3) c Langley b Miller	8
T.E.Bailey	c Miller b Archer	14		
T.G.Evans†	c Langley b Miller	0	(5) not out	8
J.C.Laker	not out	9		
G.A.R.Lock	lbw b Miller	0		
R.Appleyard	not out	1		
A.E.Moss				
Extras	(B 5, LB 1)	6	(B 4, LB 1, NB 1, W 2)	8
	(8 wkts dec.)	217	(3 wkts dec.)	188

1/53 2/72 3/180 4/181 5/201
6/203 7/213 8/214

1/151 2/163 3/178

Bowling: *First Innings*—Lindwall 15-4-43-0; Miller 33-5-69-4; Davidson 9.4-1-22-1; Archer 31-10-51-2; Johnson 14-7-26-1; Burke 1-1-0-0. *Second Innings*—Miller 19-2-58-2; Archer 9-0-46-1; Johnson 12-2-29-0; Burke 3-1-6-0; Benaud 18-4-41-0.

Australia

C.C.McDonald	lbw b Lock	1	c Lock b Laker	6
J.W.Burke	c Lock b Laker	11	not out	58
R.N.Harvey	lbw b Lock	64	b Lock	3
P.J.P.Burge	c sub (J.M.Parks) b Lock	7	(5) not out	35
K.R.Miller	lbw b Laker	0		
R.G.Archer	c Lock b Appleyard	33		
R.Benaud	b Appleyard	17		
I.W.Johnson*	c Bailey b Laker	12	(4) lbw b Laker	4
R.R.Lindwall	c Bailey b Laker	0		
G.R.A.Langley†	not out	0		
A.K.Davidson	absent hurt	-		
Extras	(LB 3)	3	(B 10, LB 3, NB 1)	14
		148	(3 wkts)	120

1/10 2/12 3/33 4/36 5/90
6/110 7/148 8/148 9/148

1/13 2/18 3/41

Bowling: *First Innings*—Moss 4-3-1-0; Bailey 3-1-8-0; Laker 29.1-11-58-4; Lock 36-16-61-3; Appleyard 11-4-17-2. *Second Innings*—Bailey 9-3-16-0; Appleyard 19-6-32-0; Laker 30-19-29-2; Lock 22-11-23-1; Graveney 6-3-6-0.

Umpires: T.J.Bartley and J.S.Buller

ENGLAND v AUSTRALIA 1956 (Second Test)

At Lord's, London, 21, 22, 23, 25, 26 June
Result: Australia won by 185 runs

Australia

Batsman	First Innings		Second Innings	
C.C.McDonald	c Trueman b Bailey	78	c Cowdrey b Bailey	26
J.W.Burke	st Evans b Laker	65	c Graveney b Trueman	16
R.N.Harvey	c Evans b Bailey	0	c Bailey b Trueman	10
P.J.P.Burge	b Statham	21	b Trueman	14
K.R.Miller	b Trueman	28	(7) c Evans b Trueman	30
K.D.Mackay	c Bailey b Laker	38	(5) c Evans b Statham	31
R.G.Archer	b Wardle	28	(6) c Evans b Bailey	1
R.Benaud	b Statham	5	c Evans b Trueman	97
I.W.Johnson*	c Evans b Trueman	6	lbw b Bailey	17
G.R.A.Langley†	c Bailey b Laker	14	not out	7
W.P.A.Crawford	not out	0	lbw b Bailey	0
Extras	(LB 2)	2	(B 2, LB 2, NB 4)	8
		285		257

1/137 2/137 3/151 4/185 5/196
6/249 7/255 8/265 9/285

1/36 2/47 3/69 4/70 5/79
6/112 7/229 8/243 9/257

Bowling: First Innings—Statham 35-9-70-2; Trueman 28-6-54-2; Bailey 34-12-72-2; Laker 29.1-10-47-3; Wardle 20-7-40-1. Second Innings—Statham 26-5-59-1; Trueman 28-2-90-5; Bailey 24.5-8-64-4; Laker 7-3-17-0; Wardle 7-2-19-0.

England

Batsman	First Innings		Second Innings	
P.E.Richardson	c Langley b Miller	9	c Langley b Archer	21
M.C.Cowdrey	c Benaud b Mackay	23	lbw b Benaud	27
T.W.Graveney	b Miller	5	c Langley b Miller	18
P.B.H.May*	b Benaud	63	(5) c Langley b Miller	53
W.Watson	c Benaud b Miller	6	(4) b Miller	18
T.E.Bailey	b Miller	32	c Harvey b Archer	18
T.G.Evans†	st Langley b Benaud	0	c Langley b Miller	20
J.C.Laker	b Archer	12	c Langley b Archer	4
J.H.Wardle	c Langley b Archer	0	b Miller	2
F.S.Trueman	c Langley b Miller	7	b Archer	0
J.B.Statham	not out	0	not out	0
Extras	(LB 14)	14	(LB 5)	5
		171		186

1/22 2/32 3/60 4/87 5/128
6/128 7/161 8/161 9/170

1/35 2/59 3/89 4/91 5/142
6/175 7/180 8/184 9/184

Bowling: First Innings—Miller 34.1-9-72-5; Crawford 4.5-2-4-0; Archer 23-9-47-2; Mackay 11-3-15-1; Benaud 9-2-19-2. Second Innings—Miller 36-12-80-5; Archer 31.2-8-71-4; Benaud 28-14-27-1; Johnson 4-2-3-0.

Umpires: D.Davies and F.S.Lee

ENGLAND v AUSTRALIA 1956 (Third Test)

At Headingley, Leeds, 12, 13, 14 (no play), 16, 17 July
Result: England won by an innings and 42 runs

England

Batsman		Runs
P.E.Richardson	c Maddocks b Archer	5
M.C.Cowdrey	c Maddocks b Archer	0
A.S.M.Oakman	b Archer	4
P.B.H.May*	c Lindwall b Johnson	101
C.Washbrook	lbw b Benaud	98
G.A.R.Lock	c Miller b Benaud	21
D.J.Insole	c Mackay b Benaud	5
T.E.Bailey	not out	33
T.G.Evans†	b Lindwall	40
J.C.Laker	b Lindwall	5
F.S.Trueman	c and b Lindwall	0
Extras	(B 4, LB 9)	13
		325

1/2 2/8 3/17 4/204 5/226
6/243 7/248 8/301 9/321

Bowling: Lindwall 33.4-11-67-3; Archer 50-24-68-3; Mackay 13-3-29-0; Benaud 42-9-89-3; Johnson 29-8-59-1.

Australia

Batsman	First Innings		Second Innings	
C.C.McDonald	c Evans b Trueman	2	b Trueman	6
J.W.Burke	lbw b Lock	41	b Laker	16
R.N.Harvey	c Trueman b Lock	11	c and b Lock	69
P.J.P.Burge	lbw b Laker	2	(5) lbw b Lock	5
K.D.Mackay	c Bailey b Laker	2	(8) b Laker	2
K.R.Miller	b Laker	41	(4) c Trueman b Laker	26
R.G.Archer	b Laker	4	(9) c Washbrook b Lock	1
R.Benaud	c Oakman b Laker	30	(6) b Laker	0
L.V.Maddocks†	c Trueman b Lock	0	(10) lbw b Lock	0
I.W.Johnson*	c Richardson b Lock	0	(7) c Oakman b Laker	3
R.R.Lindwall	not out	0	not out	0
Extras	(B 4, LB 6)	10	(B 7, LB 4)	11
		143		140

1/2 2/40 3/59 4/59 5/63
6/69 7/142 8/143 9/143

1/10 2/45 3/108 4/120 5/128
6/136 7/138 8/140 9/140

Bowling: First Innings—Trueman 8-2-19-1; Bailey 7-2-15-0; Laker 29-10-58-5; Lock 27.1-11-41-4. Second Innings—Trueman 11-3-21-1; Bailey 7-2-13-0; Laker 41.3-21-55-6; Lock 40-23-40-3.

Umpires: J.S.Buller and D.Davies

ENGLAND v AUSTRALIA 1956 (Fourth Test)

At Old Trafford, Manchester, 26, 27, 28, 30, 31 July
Result: England won by an innings and 170 runs

England

P.E.Richardson c Maddocks b Benaud	104
M.C.Cowdrey c Maddocks b Lindwall	80
Rev.D.S.Sheppard b Archer	113
P.B.H.May* c Archer b Benaud	43
T.E.Bailey b Johnson	20
C.Washbrook lbw b Johnson	6
A.S.M.Oakman c Archer b Johnson	10
T.G.Evans† st Maddocks b Johnson	47
J.C.Laker run out	3
G.A.R.Lock not out	25
J.B.Statham c Maddocks b Lindwall	0
Extras (B 2, LB 5, W 1)	8
	459

1/174 2/195 3/288 4/321 5/327
6/339 7/401 8/417 9/458

Bowling: Lindwall 21.3-6-63-2; Miller 21-6-41-0; Archer 22-6-73-1; Johnson 47-10-151-4; Benaud 47-17-123-2.

Australia

C.C.McDonald c Oakman b Laker	32	c Oakman b Laker	89
J.W.Burke c Lock b Laker	22	c Lock b Laker	33
R.N.Harvey c Cowdrey b Lock	0	c Cowdrey b Laker	0
I.D.Craig lbw b Laker	8	lbw b Laker	38
K.R.Miller c Oakman b Laker	6	(6) b Laker	0
K.D.Mackay c Oakman b Laker	0	(5) c Oakman b Laker	0
R.G.Archer st Evans b Laker	6	c Oakman b Laker	0
R.Benaud c Statham b Laker	0	b Laker	18
R.R.Lindwall not out	6	c Lock b Laker	8
L.V.Maddocks† b Laker	4	(11) lbw b Laker	2
I.W.Johnson* b Laker	0	(10) not out	1
Extras		(B 12, LB 4)	16
	84		205

1/48 2/48 3/62 4/62 5/62   1/28 2/55 3/114 4/124 5/130
6/73 7/73 8/78 9/84   6/130 7/181 8/198 9/203

Bowling: First Innings—Statham 6-3-6-0; Bailey 4-3-4-0; Laker 16.4-4-37-9; Lock 14-3-37-1. Second Innings—Statham 16-10-15-0; Bailey 20-8-31-0; Laker 51.2-23-53-10; Lock 55-30-69-0; Oakman 8-3-21-0.

Umpires: D.E.Davies and F.S.Lee

ENGLAND v AUSTRALIA 1956 (Fifth Test)

At Kennington Oval, London, 23, 24, 25, 27 (no play), 28 August
Result: Match drawn

England

P.E.Richardson c Langley b Miller	37	c Langley b Lindwall	34
M.C.Cowdrey c Maddocks b Lindwall	0	c Benaud b Davidson	8
Rev.D.S.Sheppard c Archer b Miller	24	c Archer b Miller	62
P.B.H.May* not out	83	not out	37
D.C.S.Compton c Davidson b Archer	94	not out	35
G.A.R.Lock c Langley b Archer	0		
C.Washbrook lbw b Archer	0		
T.G.Evans† lbw b Miller	0		
J.C.Laker c Archer b Miller	4		
F.H.Tyson c Davidson b Archer	3		
J.B.Statham b Archer	0		
Extras (W 2)	2	(B 3, LB 3)	6
	247	(3 wkts dec.)	182

1/1 2/53 3/66 4/222 5/222   1/17 2/100 3/108
6/222 7/223 8/231 9/243

Bowling: First Innings—Lindwall 18-5-36-1; Miller 40-7-91-4; Davidson 5-1-16-0; Archer 28.2-7-53-5; Johnson 9-2-28-0; Benaud 9-2-21-0. Second Innings—Lindwall 12-3-29-1; Miller 22-3-56-1; Davidson 5-0-18-1; Archer 13-3-42-0; Johnson 4-1-7-0; Benaud 1-0-10-0; Burke 4-2-14-0.

Australia

C.C.McDonald c Lock b Tyson	3	lbw b Statham	0
J.W.Burke c Lock b Laker	8	lbw b Laker	1
R.N.Harvey c May b Lock	39	c May b Lock	1
I.D.Craig c Statham b Lock	2	c Lock b Laker	7
I.W.Johnson* b Laker	12	(6) c Lock b Laker	10
A.K.Davidson c May b Laker	8		
K.R.Miller c Washbrook b Statham	61	(5) not out	7
R.G.Archer c Tyson b Laker	9		
R.Benaud b Statham	32	(7) not out	0
R.R.Lindwall not out	22		
G.R.A.Langley† lbw b Statham	0	(B 1)	1
Extras (B 6)	6		
	202	(5 wkts)	27

1/3 2/17 3/20 4/35 5/47   1/0 2/1 3/5 4/10 5/27
6/90 7/111 8/154 9/202

Bowling: First Innings—Statham 21-8-33-3; Tyson 14-5-34-1; Laker 32-12-80-4; Lock 25-10-49-2. Second Innings—Statham 2-1-1-1; Laker 18-4-8-3; Lock 18.1-11-17-1.

Umpires: T.J.Bartley and D.Davies

PAKISTAN v AUSTRALIA 1956-57 (Only Test)

At National Stadium, Karachi, 11, 12, 13, 15, 17 October

Result: Pakistan won by 9 wickets

Australia

Batsman	First Innings	Runs	Second Innings	Runs
C.C.McDonald	c Imtiaz Ahmed b Fazal	17	b Fazal	3
J.W.Burke	c Mathias b Fazal	4	c Mathias b Fazal	10
R.N.Harvey	lbw b Fazal	2	b Fazal	4
I.D.Craig	c Imtiaz Ahmed b Fazal	0	lbw b Fazal	18
K.R.Miller	c Wazir b Fazal	21	b Khan	11
R.G.Archer	c Imtiaz Ahmed b Khan	10	c Fazal b Khan	27
R.Benaud	c Waqar Hassan b Fazal	4	b Fazal	56
A.K.Davidson	c Kardar b Khan	3	c Imtiaz Ahmed b Khan	37
R.R.Lindwall	c Mathias b Khan	2	lbw b Fazal	0
I.W.Johnson*	not out	13	b Fazal	0
G.R.A.Langley†	c Waqar Hassan b Khan	1	not out	13
Extras	(LB 2, NB 1)	3	(LB 2, NB 6)	8
		80		**187**

1/19 2/23 3/24 4/43 5/47
6/52 7/56 8/65 9/76

1/6 2/10 3/23 4/46 5/47
6/111 7/141 8/141 9/143

Bowling: *First Innings*—Fazal Mahmood 27-11-34-6; Khan Mohammad 26.1-9-43-4. *Second Innings*—Fazal Mahmood 48-17-80-7; Khan Mohammad 40.5-13-69-3; Zulfiqar Ahmed 9-1-18-0; Kardar 12-5-12-0.

Pakistan

Batsman	First Innings	Runs	Second Innings	Runs
Hanif Mohammad	c Langley b Miller	0	c Harvey b Davidson	5
Alimuddin	c Lindwall b Archer	10	not out	34
Gul Mahomed	b Davidson	12	not out	27
Imtiaz Ahmed†	c McDonald b Benaud	15		
Waqar Hassan	c Langley b Miller	6		
Wazir Mohammad	c and b Johnson	67		
A.H.Kardar*	lbw b Johnson	69		
W.Mathias	b Johnson	0		
Fazal Mahmood	not out	10		
Zulfiqar Ahmed	c Langley b Lindwall	0		
Khan Mohammad	b Johnson	3		
Extras	(B 5, LB 2)	7	(LB 1, NB 2)	3
		199	(1 wkt)	**69**

1/3 2/15 3/25 4/35 5/70
6/174 7/174 8/189 9/190

1/7

Bowling: *First Innings*—Lindwall 27-8-42-1; Miller 17-5-40-2; Archer 4-0-18-1; Davidson 6-4-6-1; Benaud 17-5-36-1; Johnson 20.3-3-50-4. *Second Innings*—Lindwall 16-8-22-0; Miller 12-4-18-0; Archer 3.5-3-1-0; Davidson 9-5-9-1; Johnson 7.5-2-16-0.

Umpires: Daud Khan and Idris Beg

INDIA v AUSTRALIA 1956-57 (First Test)

At Corporation Stadium, Madras, 19, 20, 22, 23 October

Result: Australia won by an innings and 5 runs

India

Batsman	First Innings	Runs	Second Innings	Runs
M.H.Mankad	c McDonald b Benaud	27	c Langley b Lindwall	11
Pankaj Roy	c Harvey b Benaud	13	c Harvey b Lindwall	9
P.R.Umrigar*	c Craig b Benaud	31	c Langley b Lindwall	25
V.L.Manjrekar	lbw b Benaud	41	b Crawford	16
G.S.Ramchand	c Crawford	5	(5) lbw b Johnson	28
H.R.Adhikari	c Burke b Crawford	5	(6) lbw b Lindwall	0
A.G.Kripal Singh	c Harvey b Crawford	13	(7) not out	20
N.S.Tamhane†	not out	9	(8) c Crawford b Benaud	5
J.M.Patel	c Johnson b Benaud	3	(4) b Lindwall	0
Ghulam Ahmed	c Harvey b Benaud	11	c Burge b Lindwall	13
S.P.Gupte	c McDonald b Benaud	4	b Lindwall	8
Extras	(LB 4)	4	(B 10, LB 5, NB 3)	18
		161		**153**

1/41 2/44 4/98 5/106
6/134 7/134 8/137 9/151

1/18 2/22 3/39 4/63 5/99
6/100 7/113 8/119 9/143

Bowling: *First Innings*—Lindwall 9-1-15-0; Crawford 26-8-32-3; Benaud 29.3-10-72-7; Mackay 20-9-25-0; Johnson 15-10-13-0. *Second Innings*—Lindwall 22.5-9-43-7; Crawford 12-6-18-1; Benaud 20-5-59-1; Johnson 9-5-15-1.

Australia

Batsman	Dismissal	Runs
C.C.McDonald	st Tamhane b Gupte	29
J.W.Burke	c Tamhane b Gupte	10
R.N.Harvey	b Mankad	37
I.D.Craig	c Ramchand b Mankad	40
P.J.P.Burge	lbw b Patel	35
K.D.Mackay	c Tamhane b Ghulam Ahmed	29
R.Benaud	b Ghulam Ahmed	6
R.R.Lindwall	c Adhikari b Gupte	8
I.W.Johnson*	c Roy b Gupte	73
W.P.A.Crawford	st Tamhane b Mankad	34
G.R.A.Langley†	not out	10
Extras	(B 5, LB 3)	8
		319

1/12 2/58 3/97 4/152 5/186
6/186 7/198 8/200 9/287

Bowling: Ramchand 5-1-12-0; Umrigar 4-0-17-0; Gupte 28.3-6-89-3; Ghulam Ahmed 37-17-67-2; Mankad 45-15-90-4; Patel 14-3-36-1.

Umpires: D.D.Desai and M.G.Vijayasarathi

INDIA v AUSTRALIA 1956-57 (Second Test)

At Brabourne Stadium, Bombay, 26, 27, 29, 30, 31 October

Result: Match drawn

India

Batsman	First Innings	R	Second Innings	R
M.H.Mankad	c Burge b Lindwall	0	c Burke b Benaud	16
Pankaj Roy	c Burge b Crawford	31	c Maddocks b Benaud	79
P.R.Umrigar*	b Crawford	8	c and b Lindwall	78
V.L.Manjrekar	c Harvey b Benaud	55	b Rutherford	30
J.M.Ghorpade	b Crawford	0		
G.S.Ramchand	c sub (C.C.McDonald) b Mackay	109	c Maddocks b Wilson	16
D.G.Phadkar	c Maddocks b Benaud	1	not out	3
H.R.Adhikari	c Davidson b Mackay	33	(5) not out	22
N.S.Tamhane†	c Harvey b Davidson	5		
J.M.Patel	c Maddocks b Mackay	6		
S.P.Gupte	not out	0		
Extras	(LB 1, NB 2)	3	(B 1, LB 1, NB 4)	6
Total		251	(5 wkts)	250

1/0 2/18 3/74 4/74 5/130 6/140 7/235 8/240 9/251

1/31 2/131 3/191 4/217 5/242

Bowling: First Innings—Lindwall 22-7-60-1; Crawford 12-3-28-3; Davidson 9-1-24-1; Benaud 25-6-54-2; Mackay 14.2-5-27-3; Wilson 15-6-39-0; Burke 2-0-12-0; Rutherford 1-0-4-0. Second Innings—Lindwall 23-9-40-1; Crawford 13-4-24-0; Davidson 14-9-18-0; Benaud 42-15-98-2; Mackay 17-6-22-0; Wilson 21-11-25-1; Burke 2-0-6-0; Rutherford 5-2-11-1.

Australia

Batsman		R
J.W.Rutherford	c Umrigar b Mankad	161
J.W.Burke	c Tamhane b Gupte	30
R.N.Harvey	c sub (R.G.Nadkarni) b Patel	140
P.J.P.Burge	c Patel b Gupte	83
K.D.Mackay	c Roy b Patel	26
A.K.Davidson	lbw b Ramchand	16
R.Benaud	c sub (R.G.Nadkarni) b Gupte	48
R.R.Lindwall*	not out	8
L.V.Maddocks†	not out	2
W.P.A.Crawford		
J.W.Wilson		
Extras	(B 2, LB 4, NB 3)	9
Total	(7 wkts dec.)	523

1/57 2/261 3/398 4/432 5/459 6/462 7/470

Bowling: Phadkar 39-9-92-0; Ramchand 18-2-78-1; Patel 39-10-111-2; Gupte 38-13-115-3; Mankad 46-9-118-1.

Umpires: A.R.Joshi and B.J.Mohoni

INDIA v AUSTRALIA 1956-57 (Third Test)

At Eden Gardens, Calcutta, 2, 3, 5, 6 November

Result: Australia won by 94 runs

Australia

Batsman	First Innings	R	Second Innings	R
C.C.McDonald	b Ghulam Ahmed	3	lbw b Ramchand	0
J.W.Burke	c Manjrekar b Ghulam Ahmed	10	c Contractor b Ghulam Ahmed	2
R.N.Harvey	c Tamhane b Ghulam Ahmed	7	c Umrigar b Mankad	69
I.D.Craig	c Tamhane b Gupte	36	b Ghulam Ahmed	6
P.J.P.Burge	c Ramchand b Ghulam Ahmed	58	c Ramchand b Ghulam Ahmed	22
K.D.Mackay	lbw b Mankad	5	hit wkt b Mankad	27
R.Benaud	b Mankad	24	b Gupte	21
R.R.Lindwall	b Ghulam Ahmed	8	c Tamhane b Mankad	28
I.W.Johnson*	c Ghulam Ahmed	1	st Tamhane b Mankad	5
W.P.A.Crawford	c Contractor b Ghulam Ahmed	18	not out	1
G.R.A.Langley†	not out	1		
Extras	(B 6)	6	(B 6, LB 2)	8
Total		177	(9 wkts dec.)	189

1/6 2/22 3/25 4/93 5/106 6/141 7/152 8/157 9/163

1/0 2/9 3/27 4/59 5/122 6/149 7/159 8/188 9/189

Bowling: First Innings—Ramchand 2-1-1-0; Umrigar 16-3-30-0; Ghulam Ahmed 20.3-6-49-7; Gupte 23-11-35-1; Mankad 25-4-56-2. Second Innings—Ramchand 2-1-6-1; Umrigar 20-9-21-0; Ghulam Ahmed 29-5-81-3; Gupte 7-1-24-1; Mankad 9.4-1-49-4.

India

Batsman	First Innings	R	Second Innings	R
Pankaj Roy	b Lindwall	13	b Burke	24
N.J.Contractor	lbw b Benaud	22	b Johnson	20
P.R.Umrigar*	c Burge b Johnson	5	c Burke b Benaud	28
V.L.Manjrekar	c Harvey b Benaud	33	c Harvey b Benaud	22
M.H.Mankad	lbw b Benaud	4	c Harvey b Benaud	24
G.S.Ramchand	st Langley b Benaud	2	b Burke	3
A.G.Kripal Singh	c Mackay b Benaud	14	b Benaud	0
P.Bhandari	lbw b Lindwall	17	c Harvey b Burke	2
N.S.Tamhane†	b Benaud	5	b Benaud	0
Ghulam Ahmed	c Mackay b Lindwall	10	b Burke	0
S.P.Gupte	not out	1	not out	0
Extras	(B 7, LB 1, NB 2)	10	(B 5, LB 5, NB 3)	13
Total		136		136

1/15 2/20 3/76 4/80 5/82 6/98 7/99 8/115 9/135

1/44 2/50 3/94 4/99 5/102 6/121 7/134 8/136 9/136

Bowling: First Innings—Lindwall 25.2-12-32-3; Crawford 3-3-0-0; Johnson 12-2-27-1; Benaud 29-10-52-6; Harvey 1-1-0-0; Burke 8-3-15-0. Second Innings—Lindwall 12-7-9-0; Crawford 2-1-1-0; Johnson 14-5-23-1; Benaud 24.2-6-53-5; Burke 17-4-37-4.

Umpires: G.Ayling and B.J.Mohoni

SOUTH AFRICA v AUSTRALIA 1957-58 (Second Test)

At Newlands, Cape Town, 31 December, 1, 2, 3 January

Result: Australia won by an innings and 141 runs

Australia

C.C.McDonald c Waite b Fuller	99		
J.W.Burke b Tayfield	189		
R.N.Harvey c Goddard b Adcock	15		
I.D.Craig* b Goddard	0		
K.D.Mackay lbw b Tayfield	63		
R.Benaud c McGlew b Tayfield	33		
A.K.Davidson c and b Tayfield	21		
R.B.Simpson c Funston b Tayfield	3		
A.T.W.Grout run out	0		
I.Meckiff not out	11		
L.F.Kline lbw b Fuller	5		
Extras (B 1, LB 6, NB 3)	10		
	449		

1/190 2/215 3/220 4/350 5/399
6/408 7/412 8/12 9/434

Bowling: Adcock 27-5-80-1; Goddard 29-9-57-1; Fuller 34.2-3-125-2; Tayfield 51-18-120-5; Westcott 4-0-22-0; van Ryneveld 7-0-35-0.

South Africa

D.J.McGlew c Mackay b Davidson	30	c McDonald b Davidson	0
T.L.Goddard lbw b Benaud	29	not out	56
R.J.Westcott c Simpson b Davidson	0	c Davidson b Benaud	18
J.H.B.Waite† c Simpson b Kline	7	c Benaud b Davidson	8
R.A.McLean c Harvey b Kline	38	c Burke b Benaud	2
W.R.Endean c Davidson b Burke	21	b Benaud	5
K.J.Funston c and b Benaud	2	b Benaud	8
C.B.van Ryneveld* b Benaud	43	c Burke b Benaud	1
E.R.H.Fuller c Harvey b Benaud	5	c Benaud b Kline	0
H.J.Tayfield c Benaud b Kline	21	lbw b Kline	0
N.A.T.Adcock not out	13	c Simpson b Kline	0
Extras (B 6, LB 5, NB 1, W 1)	13	(LB 1)	1
	209		99

1/61 2/61 3/70 4/103 5/118   1/0 2/56 3/69 4/74 5/80
6/121 7/146 8/164 9/209   6/88 7/98 8/99 9/99

Bowling: First Innings—Meckiff 5.4-1-18-0; Davidson 18-5-31-2; Benaud 35-6-95-4; Kline 19.1-5-29-3; Burke 9-2-23-1. Second Innings—Davidson 15-6-18-2; Mackay 5-3-6-0; Benaud 21-6-49-5; Kline 10.4-2-18-3; Burke 6-4-7-0.

Umpires: D.Collins and V.Costello

SOUTH AFRICA v AUSTRALIA 1957-58 (First Test)

At New Wanderers, Johannesburg, 23, 24, 26, 27, 28 December

Result: Match drawn

South Africa

D.J.McGlew* c Simpson b Meckiff	108	c Simpson b Meckiff	6
T.L.Goddard b Meckiff	90	c Grout b Davidson	5
J.D.Nel b Meckiff	4	c Grout b Davidson	7
J.H.B.Waite† c Burge b Benaud	115	c Grout b Meckiff	59
W.R.Endean lbw b Meckiff	50	(6) c Meckiff b Davidson	0
R.A.McLean b Meckiff	50	(5) c Grout b Davidson	77
K.J.Funston lbw b Mackay	2	b Meckiff	27
H.J.Tayfield b Davidson	18	c Grout b Meckiff	3
P.S.Heine b Mackay	7	c Grout b Davidson	2
V.I.Smith not out	2	not out	1
N.A.T.Adcock		c Simpson b Davidson	0
Extras (B 8, LB 4, NB 1, W 1)	14	(B 5, LB 7, NB 1, W 1)	14
	470		201

1/176 2/182 3/237 4/341 5/412 (9 wkts dec.) 1/6 2/19 3/19 4/19 5/148
6/436 7/461 8/465 9/471   6/193 7/196 8/199 9/199

Bowling: First Innings—Davidson 32-4-115-1; Meckiff 31-3-125-5; Mackay 20.6-3-54-2; Benaud 27-7-115-1; Kline 20-6-47-0. Second Innings—Davidson 17.4-4-34-6; Meckiff 26-3-52-3; Mackay 11-1-29-0; Benaud 2-0-15-0; Kline 8-2-18-0; Burke 14-3-39-1.

Australia

C.C.McDonald c Tayfield b Smith	75	st Waite b Smith	25
J.W.Burke c Waite b Heine	16	retired hurt	10
K.D.Mackay c Waite b Heine	3	not out	65
I.D.Craig* b Heine	14	b Tayfield	17
P.J.P.Burge c Waite b Heine	0	b Tayfield	14
R.B.Simpson lbw b Tayfield	60	not out	23
R.Benaud c Heine b Adcock	122		
A.K.Davidson c sub (E.R.H.Fuller) b Heine	24		
A.T.W.Grout† c Endean b Tayfield	21		
I.Meckiff c Smith b Heine	11		
L.F.Kline not out	6		
Extras (B 4, LB 11, NB1)	16	(B 6, LB 2)	8
	368	(3 wkts)	162

1/34 2/40 3/56 4/62 5/151   1/44 2/85 3/118
6/177 7/244 8/313 9/355

Bowling: First Innings—Heine 14.2-3-58-6; Adcock 23-3-106-1; Goddard 16-5-57-0; Tayfield 29-9-101-2; Smith 9-2-30-1. Second Innings—Heine 8-2-17-0; Adcock 3-0-11-0; Goddard 12-6-24-0; Tayfield 33-12-70-2; Smith 16-8-25-1; McGlew 1-0-7-0.

Umpires: A.Birkett and J.H.McMenamin

SOUTH AFRICA v AUSTRALIA 1957-58 (Third Test)

At Kingsmead, Durban, 24, 25, 27, 28, 29 January

Result: Match drawn

Australia

C.C.McDonald c Goddard b Adcock	28		lbw b Tayfield	33
J.W.Burke c Waite b Adcock	2		b Goddard	83
R.N.Harvey c Waite b Adcock	6		b Adcock	68
I.D.Craig* b Goddard	52		c Goddard b Tayfield	0
R.B.Simpson b Goddard	17	(8)	c Tayfield b van Ryneveld	4
K.D.Mackay hit wkt b Adcock	32		not out	52
R.Benaud lbw b Adcock	5	(6)	b van Ryneveld	20
A.K.Davidson c Waite b Heine	12	(7)	c McGlew b Tayfield	4
A.T.W.Grout† b Heine	2		not out	3
L.F.Kline c Goddard b Adcock	0			
R.A.Gaunt not out	0			
Extras (NB 7)	7		(B 19, LB 5, NB 1)	25
	163		**(7 wkts)**	**292**

1/13 2/19 3/54 4/87 5/131
6/142 7/161 8/163 9/163

1/92 2/170 3/179
4/221 5/261 6/274 7/289

Bowling: *First Innings*—Heine 17.4-4-30-2; Adcock 18-2-43-6; Goddard 23-12-25-2; Tayfield 21-7-41-0; van Ryneveld 3-0-17-0. *Second Innings*—Heine 14-1-40-0; Adcock 15-1-34-1; Goddard 42-18-62-1; Tayfield 59-24-94-3; van Ryneveld 17-1-37-2.

South Africa

D.J.McGlew c Grout b Gaunt	105
R.J.Westcott b Gaunt	0
W.R.Endean c Simpson b Benaud	15
J.H.B.Waite† b Davidson	134
T.L.Goddard lbw b Davidson	45
K.J.Funston c Grout b Mackay	27
C.B.van Ryneveld* not out	32
R.A.McLean c Grout b Benaud	11
H.J.Tayfield st Grout b Benaud	0
P.S.Heine c Burke b Benaud	7
N.A.T.Adcock c Grout b Benaud	0
Extras (B 2, LB 5, NB 1)	8
	384

1/6 2/28 3/259 4/259 5/313
6/356 7/371 8/371 9/383

Bowling: Davidson 34-8-62-2; Gaunt 27-2-87-2; Mackay 35-5-77-1; Benaud 50.7-13-114-5; Kline 17-6-36-0.

Umpires: V.Costello and W.Marias

SOUTH AFRICA v AUSTRALIA 1957-58 (Fourth Test)

At New Wanderers, Johannesburg, 7, 8, 10, 11, 12 February

Result: Australia won by 10 wickets

Australia

C.C.McDonald lbw b Tayfield	26	not out	1
J.W.Burke c Waite b Heine	81	not out	0
R.N.Harvey c Waite b Goddard	5		
R.Benaud c Endean b Heine	100		
I.D.Craig* b Heine	3		
A.T.W.Grout† lbw b Adcock	7		
K.D.Mackay not out	83		
R.B.Simpson c Waite b Adcock	6		
A.K.Davidson c Burger b Heine	62		
I.Meckiff c Endean b Heine	26		
L.F.Kline c Waite b Heine	1		
Extras (LB 1)	1		
	401	**(0 wkts)**	**1**

1/43 2/52 3/210 4/213 5/222
6/222 7/234 8/315 9/393

Bowling: *First Innings*—Heine 37.5-6-96-6; Adcock 17-3-37-2; Goddard 43-10-136-1; Tayfield 49-17-107-1; van Ryneveld 3-0-24-0. *Second Innings*—McLean 0.4-0-1-0.

South Africa

D.J.McGlew c Grout b Meckiff	1		c Simpson b Benaud	70
W.R.Endean lbw b Davidson	22		c Simpson b Benaud	38
H.J.Tayfield lbw b Benaud	27	(9)	st Grout b Kline	0
T.L.Goddard c and b Meckiff	9	(3)	c Simpson b Benaud	0
K.J.Funston c Craig b Kline	70		not out	64
R.A.McLean c Grout b Davidson	9	(5)	c Grout b Davidson	0
C.G.D.Burger st Grout b Kline	21		c McDonald b Kline	1
J.H.B.Waite† lbw b Benaud	12	(6)	c Grout b Benaud	10
P.S.Heine c and b Benaud	24	(10)	c Meckiff b Benaud	1
N.A.T.Adcock b Benaud	0	(11)	run out	3
C.B.van Ryneveld* not out	0	(8)	lbw b Kline	0
Extras (B 3, NB 3, W 2)	8		(LB 8, NB 1, W 2)	11
	203			**198**

1/17 2/27 3/46 4/104 5/115
6/166 7/166 8/186 9/194

1/78 2/78 3/147 4/148 5/161
6/180 7/180 8/182 9/183

Bowling: *First Innings*—Meckiff 21-3-38-2; Davidson 19-2-39-2; Kline 9-1-37-2. *Second Innings*—Meckiff 13-2-24-0; Davidson 20-4-44-1; Benaud 20.2-0-70-4; Kline 16-6-27-3; Burke 15-10-8-0.

Umpires: A.Birkett and J.H.McMenamin

SOUTH AFRICA v AUSTRALIA 1957-58 (Fifth Test)

At St George's Park, Port Elizabeth, 28 February, 1, 3, 4 March
Result: Australia won by 8 wickets

South Africa

D.J.McGlew c Simpson b Davidson	14	(7) b Benaud	20
T.L.Goddard c Harvey b Meckiff	17	lbw b Benaud	33
W.R.Endean c McDonald b Davidson	2	(1) c Simpson b Davidson	23
J.H.B.Waite† c Harvey b Davidson	17	(3) b Davidson	0
K.J.Funston c Grout b Davidson	20	(4) c Simpson b Davidson	4
C.B.van Ryneveld* c Burke b Kline	26	b Davidson	5
C.G.D.Burger lbw b Kline	3	(8) not out	37
P.R.Carlstein c and b Kline	32	(9) lbw b Benaud	1
H.J.Tayfield c Burke b Kline	66	(5) c Grout b Davidson	2
P.S.Heine lbw b Benaud	3	lbw b Benaud	15
N.A.T.Adcock not out	3	b Davidson	0
Extras (B 4, LB 5, NB 2)	11	(B 2, LB 2)	4
	214		144

1/1 2/30 3/36 4/57 5/86
6/96 7/105 8/191 9/198

1/55 2/55 3/63 4/63 5/70
6/70 7/97 8/99 9/131

Bowling: *First Innings*—Davidson 20-6-44-4; Meckiff 18-4-76-1; Benaud 12-2-34-1; Mackay 11-3-16-0; Kline 13.6-3-33-4. *Second Innings*—Davidson 26.1-8-38-5; Meckiff 16-8-20-0; Benaud 33-14-82-5.

Australia

C.C.McDonald c Waite b Adcock	58	c Tayfield b Adcock	4
J.W.Burke c Endean b Adcock	8	c and b Tayfield	22
R.N.Harvey lbw b Heine	15		
I.D.Craig* c Endean b Tayfield	17		
R.Benaud c and b Goddard	43	(4) not out	6
R.B.Simpson c Carlstein b Tayfield	23		
K.D.Mackay not out	77		
A.K.Davidson lbw b Heine	4		
A.T.W.Grout† c Endean b Goddard	25	(2) not out	35
I.Meckiff c Waite b Heine	8		
L.F.Kline c Goddard b Tayfield	0		
Extras (B 2, LB 4, NB 7)	13	(B 1)	1
	291	(2 wkts)	68

1/13 2/37 3/124 4/145 5/194
6/199 7/239 8/265 9/278

1/4 2/53

Bowling: *First Innings*—Heine 30-3-68-3; Adcock 24-1-81-2; Goddard 23-9-48-2; Tayfield 30.3-12-81-3. *Second Innings*—Heine 3-0-12-0; Adcock 4-0-18-1; Goddard 1-0-8-0; Tayfield 4-1-25-1; van Ryneveld 0.4-0-4-0.

Umpires: V.Costello and W.Marias

AUSTRALIA v ENGLAND 1958-59 (First Test)

At Woolloongabba, Brisbane, 5, 6, 8, 9, 10 December
Result: Australia won by 8 wickets

England

P.E.Richardson c Mackay b Davidson	11	c and b Benaud	8
C.A.Milton b Meckiff	5	c Grout b Davidson	17
T.W.Graveney c Grout b Davidson	19	(4) run out	36
P.B.H.May* c Grout b Meckiff	26	(5) b Benaud	4
M.C.Cowdrey c Kline b Meckiff	13	(6) c Kline b Meckiff	28
T.E.Bailey st Grout b Benaud	27	b Mackay	68
T.G.Evans† c Burge b Davidson	4	(3) lbw b Davidson	4
G.A.R.Lock c Davidson b Benaud	5	b Meckiff	1
J.C.Laker c Burke b Benaud	13	b Benaud	15
J.B.Statham c Grout b Mackay	2	c McDonald b Benaud	3
P.J.Loader not out	6	not out	0
Extras (LB 1, NB 1, W 1)	3	(B 10, LB 4)	14
	134		198

1/16 2/16 3/62 4/75 5/79
6/83 7/92 8/112 9/116

1/28 2/34 3/96 4/102 5/153
6/161 7/169 8/190 9/198

Bowling: *First Innings*—Davidson 16-4-36-3; Meckiff 17-5-33-3; Mackay 8-1-16-1; Benaud 18.4-9-46-3. *Second Innings*—Davidson 28-12-30-2; Meckiff 19-7-30-2; Mackay 9-6-7-1; Benaud 39.2-10-66-4; Kline 14-4-34-0; Burke 10-5-17-0.

Australia

C.C.McDonald c Graveney b Bailey	42	c Statham b Laker	15
J.W.Burke c Evans b Loader	20	not out	28
R.N.Harvey lbw b Loader	14	c Milton b Lock	23
N.C.O'Neill c Graveney b Bailey	34	not out	71
P.J.P.Burge c Cowdrey b Bailey	2		
K.D.Mackay c Evans b Laker	16		
R.Benaud* lbw b Loader	16		
A.K.Davidson lbw b Laker	25		
A.T.W.Grout† b Statham	2		
I.Meckiff b Loader	5		
L.F.Kline not out	4		
Extras (B 4, LB 1, NB 1)	6	(B 2, LB 3, NB 5)	10
	186	(2 wkts)	147

1/55 2/65 3/88 4/94 5/122
6/136 7/162 8/165 9/178

1/20 2/58

Bowling: *First Innings*—Statham 20-2-57-1; Loader 19-4-56-4; Bailey 13-2-35-3; Laker 10.1-3-15-2; Lock 10-4-17-0. *Second Innings*—Statham 6-1-13-0; Loader 9-1-27-0; Laker 17-3-39-1; Lock 14.7-5-37-1.

Umpires: C.Hoy and M.J.McInnes

AUSTRALIA v ENGLAND 1958-59 (Second Test)

At Melbourne Cricket Ground, 31 December, 1, 2, 3, 5 January

Result: Australia won by 8 wickets

England

	First Innings		Second Innings	
P.E.Richardson	c Grout b Davidson	3	c Harvey b Meckiff	2
T.E.Bailey	c Benaud b Meckiff	48	b Meckiff	14
W.Watson	b Davidson	0	b Davidson	7
T.W.Graveney	lbw b Davidson	0	c Davidson b Meckiff	3
P.B.H.May*	b Meckiff	113	b Meckiff	17
M.C.Cowdrey	c Grout b Davidson	44	c Grout b Meckiff	12
T.G.Evans†	c Davidson b Meckiff	4	run out	11
G.A.R.Lock	st Grout b Benaud	5	c and b Davidson	6
J.C.Laker	not out	22	c Harvey b Davidson	3
J.B.Statham	b Davidson	13	not out	8
P.J.Loader	b Davidson	1	b Meckiff	0
Extras	(B 1, LB 2, W 3)	6	(B 1, LB 1, NB 2)	4
		259		87

1/7 2/7 3/7 4/92 5/210 6/218 7/218 8/233 9/253

1/3 2/14 3/21 4/27 5/44 6/57 7/71 8/75 9/80

Bowling: *First Innings*—Davidson 25.5-7-64-6; Meckiff 24-4-69-3; Mackay 9-2-16-0; Benaud 29-7-61-1; Kline 11-2-43-0. *Second Innings*—Davidson 15-2-41-3; Meckiff 15.2-3-38-6; Benaud 1-0-4-0.

Australia

	First Innings		Second Innings	
C.C.McDonald	c Graveney b Statham	47	lbw b Statham	5
J.W.Burke	b Statham	3	not out	18
R.N.Harvey	b Loader	167	(4) not out	7
N.C.O'Neill	c Evans b Statham	37		
K.D.Mackay	c Evans b Statham	18		
R.B.Simpson	lbw b Loader	0		
R.Benaud*	lbw b Statham	0		
A.K.Davidson	b Statham	24		
A.T.W.Grout†	c May b Loader	8	(3) st Evans b Laker	12
I.Meckiff	b Statham	0		
L.F.Kline	not out	1		
Extras	(LB 3)	3		
		308		(2 wkts) 42

1/11 2/137 3/255 4/257 5/264 6/261 7/295 8/300 9/300

1/6 2/26

Bowling: *First Innings*—Statham 28-6-57-7; Loader 27.2-4-97-3; Bailey 16-0-50-0; Laker 12-1-47-0; Lock 17-2-54-0. *Second Innings*—Statham 5-1-13-0; Laker 4-1-7-1; Lock 3.1-1-11-0.

Umpires: M.J.McInnes and R.Wright

AUSTRALIA v ENGLAND 1958-59 (Third Test)

At Sydney Cricket Ground, 9, 10, 12, 13, 14, 15 January

Result: Match drawn

England

	First Innings		Second Innings	
T.E.Bailey	lbw b Meckiff	8	c sub (R.B.Simpson) b Benaud	25
C.A.Milton	c Meckiff b Davidson	8	c Davidson b Benaud	8
T.W.Graveney	c Harvey b Benaud	33	lbw b Davidson	22
P.B.H.May*	c Mackay b Slater	42	b Burke	92
M.C.Cowdrey	c Harvey b Benaud	34	not out	100
E.R.Dexter	lbw b Slater		c Grout b Benaud	11
R.Swetman†	c Mackay b Benaud	41	lbw b Burke	5
G.A.R.Lock	lbw b Mackay	21	(9) not out	11
F.S.Trueman	c Burke b Benaud	18	(8) st Grout b Benaud	0
J.C.Laker	c Harvey b Benaud	2		
J.B.Statham	not out	11		
Extras	(B 4, LB 5, W 2)	11	(B 11, LB 1, W 1)	13
		219		(7 wkts dec.) 287

1/19 2/23 3/91 4/97 5/98 6/155 7/194 8/200 9/202

1/30 2/37 3/64 4/246 5/262 6/269 7/270

Bowling: *First Innings*—Davidson 12-3-21-1; Meckiff 15-2-45-1; Benaud 33.4-10-83-5; Slater 14-4-40-2; Mackay 8-3-19-1. *Second Innings*—Davidson 33-11-65-1; Meckiff 3-1-7-0; Benaud 33-7-94-4; Slater 18-5-61-0; Mackay 11-2-21-0; Burke 11-3-26-2.

Australia

	First Innings		Second Innings	
C.C.McDonald	c Graveney b Lock	40	b Laker	16
J.W.Burke	c Lock b Laker	12	b Laker	7
R.N.Harvey	b Laker	7	not out	18
N.C.O'Neill	s Swetman b Laker	77	not out	7
L.E.Favell	c Cowdrey b Lock	54		
K.D.Mackay	b Trueman	57		
R.Benaud*	b Laker	6		
A.K.Davidson	lbw b Lock	71		
A.T.W.Grout†	c Statham b Laker	14		
K.N.Slater	not out	1		
I.Meckiff	b Lock	2		
Extras	(B 5, LB 10, NB 1)	16	(B 6)	6
		357		(2 wkts) 54

1/26 2/52 3/87 4/197 5/199 6/208 7/323 8/353 9/355

1/22 2/33

Bowling: *First Innings*—Statham 16-2-48-0; Trueman 18-3-37-1; Lock 43.2-9-130-4; Laker 46-9-107-5; Bailey 5-0-19-0. *Second Innings*—Statham 2-06-0; Trueman 4-1-9-0; Lock 11-4-23-0; Laker 8-3-10-2.

Umpires: C.Hoy and M.J.McInnes

AUSTRALIA v ENGLAND 1958-59 (Fourth Test)
At Adelaide Oval, 30, 31 December, 2, 3, 4, 5 January
Result: Australia won by 10 wickets

Australia

Batsman	First innings	R	Second innings	R
C.C.McDonald	b Trueman	170		
J.W.Burke	c Cowdrey b Bailey	66	not out	16
R.N.Harvey	run out	41		
N.C.O'Neill	b Statham	56		
L.E.Favell	b Statham	4	(1) not out	15
K.D.Mackay	c Evans b Statham	4		
R.Benaud*	b Trueman	46		
A.K.Davidson	c Bailey b Tyson	43		
A.T.W.Grout†	lbw b Trueman	9		
R.R.Lindwall	b Trueman	19		
G.F.Rorke	not out	2		
Extras	(B 2, LB 8, NB 2, W 4)	16	(B 4, LB 1)	5
		476	(0 wkts)	36

1/171 2/276 3/286 4/294 5/369
6/388 7/407 8/445 9/473

Bowling: *First Innings*—Statham 23-0-83-3; Trueman 30.1-6-90-4; Tyson 28-1-100-1; Bailey 22-2-91-1; Lock 25-0-96-0. *Second Innings*—Statham 4-0-11-0; Trueman 3-1-3-0; Lock 2-0-8-0; Cowdrey 1.3-0-9-0.

England

Batsman	First innings	R	Second innings	R
P.E.Richardson	lbw b Lindwall	4	(6) lbw b Benaud	43
T.E.Bailey	b Davidson	4	c Grout b Lindwall	6
P.B.H.May*	b Benaud	37	lbw b Rorke	59
M.C.Cowdrey	b Rorke	84	b Lindwall	8
T.W.Graveney	c Benaud b Rorke	41	not out	53
W.Watson	b Rorke	25	(2) c Favell b Benaud	40
F.S.Trueman	c Grout b Benaud	0	c Grout b Davidson	0
G.A.R.Lock	c Grout b Benaud	2	b Rorke	9
F.H.Tyson	c and b Benaud	0	c Grout b Benaud	33
T.G.Evans†	c Burke b Benaud	4	(11) c Benaud b Davidson	0
J.B.Statham	not out	36	(10) c O'Neill b Benaud	2
Extras	(LB 2, NB 1)	3	(B 5, LB 5, NB 4, W 3)	17
		240		270

1/7 2/11 3/74 4/170 5/173 — 1/89 2/110 3/125 4/177 5/198 270
6/180 7/184 8/184 9/188 — 6/199 7/222 8/268 9/270

Bowling: *First Innings*—Davidson 12-0-49-1; Lindwall 15-0-66-1; Rorke 18.1-7-23-3; Benaud 27-6-91-5; O'Neill 2-1-8-0. *Second Innings*—Davidson 8.3-3-17-2; Lindwall 26-6-70-2; Rorke 34-7-78-2; Benaud 29-10-82-4; Burke 4-2-6-0.

Umpires: M.J.McInnes and R.Wright

AUSTRALIA v ENGLAND 1958-59 (Fifth Test)
At Melbourne Cricket Ground, 13, 14, 16, 17, 18 February
Result: Australia won by 9 wickets

England

Batsman	First innings	R	Second innings	R
P.E.Richardson	c and b Benaud	68	lbw b Benaud	23
T.E.Bailey	c Davidson b Lindwall	0	b Lindwall	0
P.B.H.May*	c Benaud b Meckiff	11	c Harvey b Lindwall	4
M.C.Cowdrey	c Lindwall b Davidson	22	run out	46
T.W.Graveney	c McDonald b Benaud	19	c Harvey b Davidson	54
E.R.Dexter	c Lindwall b Meckiff	0	c Grout b Davidson	6
R.Swetman†	c Grout b Davidson	1	lbw b Lindwall	9
J.B.Mortimore	not out	44	b Rorke	11
F.S.Trueman	c and b Benaud	21	b Rorke	36
F.H.Tyson	c Grout b Benaud	9	c Grout b Rorke	6
J.C.Laker	c Harvey b Davidson	2	not out	5
Extras	(B 4, W 4)	8	(B 9, LB 3, W 2)	14
		205		214

1/0 2/13 3/61 4/109 5/112 — 1/0 2/12 3/78 4/105 5/131
6/124 7/128 8/191 9/203 — 6/142 7/158 8/172 9/182

Bowling: *First Innings*—Davidson 12.5-2-38-3; Lindwall 14-2-36-1; Meckiff 15-2-57-2; Rorke 6-1-23-0; Benaud 17-5-43-4. *Second Innings*—Davidson 21-1-85-2; Lindwall 11-2-37-3; Meckiff 4-0-13-0; Rorke 12.4-2-41-3; Benaud 6-1-14-1.

Australia

Batsman	First innings	R	Second innings	R
C.C.McDonald	c Cowdrey b Laker	133	not out	51
J.W.Burke	c Trueman b Tyson	16	lbw b Tyson	13
R.N.Harvey	c Swetman b Trueman	13	not out	1
N.C.O'Neill	c Cowdrey b Trueman	0		
K.D.Mackay	c Graveney b Laker	23		
A.K.Davidson	b Mortimore	17		
R.Benaud*	c Swetman b Laker	64		
A.T.W.Grout†	c Trueman b Laker	74		
R.R.Lindwall	c Cowdrey b Trueman	0		
I.Meckiff	c and b Trueman	2		
G.F.Rorke	not out	0		
Extras	(B 5, LB 4)	9	(LB 4)	4
		351	(1 wkt)	69

1/41 2/83 3/83 4/154 5/207 — 1/66
6/209 7/324 8/327 9/329

Bowling: *First Innings*—Trueman 25-0-92-4; Tyson 20-1-73-1; Bailey 14-2-43-0; Laker 30.5-4-93-4; Mortimore 11-1-41-1. *Second Innings*—Trueman 6.7-0-45-0; Tyson 6-0-20-1.

Umpires: L.Townsend and R.Wright

PAKISTAN v AUSTRALIA 1959-60 (First Test)

At Dacca Stadium, 13, 14, 15, 17, 18 November
Result: Australia won by 8 wickets

Pakistan

Batsman	First Innings		Second Innings	
Hanif Mohammad	b Mackay	66	b Benaud	19
Ijaz Butt	c Grout b Davidson	0	b Mackay	20
Saeed Ahmed	c Harvey b Davidson	37	b Mackay	15
W.Mathias	c and b Benaud	4	lbw b Mackay	1
D.A.Sharpe	run out	56	lbw b Mackay	35
Wazir Mohammad	c Meckiff b Benaud	13	lbw b Benaud	5
Imtiaz Ahmed†	b Davidson	7	b Mackay	4
Israr Ali	st Grout b Benaud	2	(9) b Benaud	1
Shujauddin	not out	1	(8) c and b Mackay	0
Fazal Mahmood*	b Benaud	1	not out	16
Nasim-ul-Ghani	b Davidson	5	c McDonald b Benaud	14
Extras	(B 5, LB 1, NB 3)	9	(B 7, LB 5, NB 2)	14
Total		200		134

1/3 2/75 3/82 4/145 5/146 6/170 7/184 8/191 9/193
1/32 2/57 3/62 4/68 5/81 6/94 7/117 8/128 9/133

Bowling: First Innings—Davidson 23.5-7-42-4; Meckiff 19-12-16-1; Lindwall 15-1-31-0; Benaud 38-10-69-4; Mackay 19-12-16-1. *Second Innings*—Davidson 11-3-23-0; Meckiff 3-1-8-0; Lindwall 2-0-5-0; Benaud 39.3-26-42-4; Mackay 45-27-42-6.

Australia

Batsman	First Innings		Second Innings	
C.C.McDonald	lbw b Fazal Mahmood	19	not out	44
L.E.Favell	b Israr Ali	0	c and b Israr Ali	4
R.N.Harvey	b Fazal Mahmood	96	b Fazal Mahmood	30
N.C.O'Neill	c Imtiaz Ahmed b Nasim-ul-Ghani	2	not out	26
P.J.P.Burge	c Imtiaz Ahmed b Nasim-ul-Ghani	16		
R.Benaud*	lbw b Nasim-ul-Ghani	7		
K.D.Mackay	b Fazal Mahmood	4		
A.K.Davidson	lbw b Israr Ali	4		
A.T.W.Grout†	not out	66		
R.R.Lindwall	lbw b Fazal Mahmood	2		
I.Meckiff	b Fazal Mahmood	9		
Extras	(LB 9)	9	(B 3, LB 3, NB 2)	8
Total		225	(2 wkts)	112

1/0 2/51 3/53 4/53 5/112 6/134 7/143 8/151 9/189
1/12 2/65

Bowling: First Innings—Fazal Mahmood 35.5-11-71-5; Israr Ali 23-5-85-2; Nasim-ul-Ghani 17-4-51-3; Shujauddin 3-0-9-0. *Second Innings*—Fazal Mahmood 20.1-4-52-1; Israr Ali 9-0-20-1; Nasim-ul-Ghani 10-2-16-0; Shujauddin 8-4-12-0; Saeed Ahmed 1-0-4-0.

Umpires: Khwaja Saeed Ahmed and A.A.Qureshi

PAKISTAN v AUSTRALIA 1959-60 (Second Test)

At Gaddafi Stadium, Lahore, 21, 22, 23, 25, 26 November
Result: Australia won by 7 wickets

Pakistan

Batsman	First Innings		Second Innings	
Hanif Mohammad	c Grout b Meckiff	49	(5) b Kline	18
Imtiaz Ahmed*†	b Davidson	18	c O'Neill b Kline	54
Saeed Ahmed	c Grout b Meckiff	17	st Grout b Kline	166
Alimuddin	b Meckiff	8	(1) b Kline	7
D.A.Sharpe	c Grout b Kline	12	(6) st Grout b Kline	1
Waqar Hassan	c Grout b Davidson	12	(7) b Kline	4
Shujauddin	b Benaud	17	(4) lbw b O'Neill	45
Israr Ali	lbw b Benaud	0	(10) not out	0
Nasim-ul-Ghani	c Stevens b Davidson	6	(8) b Benaud	15
Mohammad Munaf	c Grout b Davidson	5	(9) c Davidson b Kline	19
Haseeb Ahsan	not out	0	c Grout b Benaud	4
Extras	(B 1, LB 1)	2	(B 31, LB 2)	33
Total		146		366

1/39 2/56 3/92 4/109 5/115 6/120 7/121 8/126 9/142
1/45 2/87 3/256 4/312 5/319 6/324 7/325 8/362 9/362

Bowling: First Innings—Davidson 19-2-48-4; Meckiff 19-7-45-3; Benaud 16-6-36-2; Kline 12-6-15-1. *Second Innings*—Davidson 35-9-56-0; Meckiff 22-4-44-0; Benaud 54.4-22-92-2; Kline 44-21-75-7; O'Neill 13-5-37-1; Mackay 6-1-21-0; Harvey 5-2-8-0.

Australia

Batsman	First Innings		Second Innings	
C.C.McDonald	c Imtiaz Ahmed b Haseeb Ahsan	42	c Alimuddin b Munaf	8
G.B.Stevens	c Imtiaz Ahmed b Munaf	9	b Munaf	37
R.N.Harvey	lbw b Munaf	43	not out	43
N.C.O'Neill	st Imtiaz Ahmed b Shujauddin	134	(1) b Israr Ali	4
L.E.Favell	b Israr Ali	32		
A.T.W.Grout†	lbw b Nasim-ul-Ghani	12		
R.Benaud*	b Nasim-ul-Ghani	29	(5) not out	21
A.K.Davidson	c Imtiaz Ahmed b Israr Ali	47		
K.D.Mackay	c Imtiaz Ahmed b Haseeb Ahsan	26		
L.F.Kline	not out	0		
I.Meckiff				
Extras	(B 5, LB 5, NB 7)	17	(B 6, LB 4)	10
Total	(9 wkts dec.)	391	(3 wkts)	123

1/27 2/83 3/114 4/213 5/247 6/310 7/311 8/391 9/391
1/13 2/15 3/77

Bowling: First Innings—Mohammad Munaf 31-8-100-2; Israr Ali 13-5-29-2; Nasim-ul-Ghani 21-3-72-1; Shujauddin 20-2-58-1; Haseeb Ahsan 33.3-8-115-3. *Second Innings*—Mohammad Munaf 10-2-38-2; Israr Ali 5-1-20-1; Nasim-ul-Ghani 3.3-0-18-0; Shujauddin 3-0-16-0; Haseeb Ahsan 4-0-21-0.

Umpires: Khwaja Saeed Ahmed and A.A.Qureshi

PAKISTAN v AUSTRALIA 1959-60 (Third Test)

At National Stadium, Karachi, 4, 5, 6, 8, 9 December
Result: Match drawn

Pakistan

Hanif Mohammad lbw b Lindwall	51	(4) not out	101
Imtiaz Ahmed† b Davidson	18	c Harvey b Davidson	9
Saeed Ahmed c Harvey b Lindwall	91	c Harvey b Davidson	8
Shujauddin c O'Neill b Benaud	5	(6) c Favell b Mackay	4
D.A.Sharpe c Burge b Benaud	4	c Mackay b Lindwall	26
Ijaz Butt c Grout b Benaud	58	(1) run out	8
W.Mathias c Favell b Mackay	43	c Davidson b Benaud	13
Intikhab Alam run out	0	c Burge b Mackay	7
Fazal Mahmood* c Harvey b Benaud	7	c Benaud b Davidson	6
Mohammad Munaf not out	4	c Benaud b Davidson	11
Munir Malik st Grout b Benaud	0	not out	4
Extras (LB 3, NB 3)	6	(LB 2, NB 2)	4
	287	(8 wkts dec.)	194

1/36 2/124 3/143 4/149 5/181
6/265 7/267 8/276 9/287
1/11 2/25 3/25 (8 wkts dec.) 194
4/78 5/91 6/124 7/159 8/179

Bowling: *First Innings*—Davidson 26-5-59-1; Lindwall 25-6-72-2; Benaud 49.5-17-93-5; Mackay 27-8-53-1; O'Neill 4-1-4-0. *Second Innings*—Davidson 34-8-70-3; Lindwall 17-10-14-1; Benaud 26-13-48-1; Mackay 32.4-11-58-2.

Australia

C.C.McDonald b Intikhab Alam	19	lbw b Munir Malik	30
G.B.Stevens c Mathias b Fazal Mahmood	13	c Imtiaz Ahmed b Intikhab Alam	28
A.T.W.Grout† c and b Intikhab Alam	20		
K.D.Mackay c Ijaz Butt b Fazal Mahmood	40		
R.N.Harvey c Imtiaz Ahmed b Fazal Mahmood	54	(3) not out	13
N.C.O'Neill b Munir Malik	6	(4) not out	7
L.E.Favell c Sharpe b Fazal Mahmood	10		
P.J.P.Burge c Sharpe b Mohammad Munaf	12		
R.Benaud* c Imtiaz Ahmed b Munir Malik	18		
A.K.Davidson not out	39		
R.R.Lindwall c Imtiaz Ahmed b Fazal Mahmood	23		
Extras (LB 1, NB 2)	3	(LB 3, NB 2)	5
	257	(2 wkts)	83

1/29 2/33 3/82 4/106 5/122
6/145 7/174 8/184 9/207
1/54 2/76

Bowling: *First Innings*—Fazal Mahmood 30.2-12-74-5; Mohammad Munaf 8-0-42-1; Intikhab Alam 19-4-49-2; Munir Malik 22-5-76-2; Shujauddin 3-0-13-0. *Second Innings*—Fazal Mahmood 10-5-16-0; Mohammad Munaf 3-0-10-0; Intikhab Alam 6-1-13-1; Munir Malik 9-1-24-0; Shujauddin 2-1-9-0; Saeed Ahmed 3-0-6-0.

Umpires: Khwaja Saeed Ahmed and Munawar Hussain

INDIA v AUSTRALIA 1959-60 (First Test)

At Feroz Shah Kotla, Delhi, 12, 13, 14, 16 December
Result: Australia won by an innings and 127 runs

India

Pankaj Roy c Grout b Davidson	0	c Benaud b Kline	99
N.J.Contractor b Davidson	41	c Favell b Benaud	34
P.R.Umrigar c Grout b Davidson	9	(5) c Favell b Kline	32
A.A.Baig b Rorke	9	(3) run out	5
C.G.Borde c Grout b Meckiff	14	(4) c Davidson b Benaud	0
G.S.Ramchand* c Grout b Kline	20	c Davidson b Kline	6
R.G.Nadkarni b Rorke	1	lbw b Benaud	6
P.G.Joshi† b Benaud	15	c Davidson b Kline	8
Surendranath not out	24	c Davidson b Benaud	0
V.M.Muddiah lbw b Benaud	0	not out	0
R.B.Desai c O'Neill b Benaud	0	c Meckiff b Benaud	0
Extras (B 6, LB 2, NB 3)	11	(B 8, LB 5, NB 2)	15
	135		206

1/4 2/8 3/32 4/66 5/69
6/70 7/100 8/131 9/135
1/121 2/132 3/132 4/175
5/187 6/192 7/202 8/206 9/206

Bowling: *First Innings*—Davidson 14-9-22-3; Meckiff 17-4-52-1; Rorke 14-5-30-2; Kline 9-3-15-1; Benaud 3.4-3-0-3; Mackay 1-0-1-0; O'Neill 1-0-4-0. *Second Innings*—Davidson 14-5-16-0; Meckiff 14-3-33-0; Rorke 7-3-5-0; Benaud 46-18-76-5; Kline 24-12-42-4; Harvey 1-1-0-0; O'Neill 5-0-19-0.

Australia

C.C.McDonald b Surendranath	20
L.E.Favell b Surendranath	39
R.N.Harvey lbw b Nadkarni	114
N.C.O'Neill run out	39
K.D.Mackay c Joshi b Umrigar	78
A.K.Davidson c Baig b Desai	25
R.Benaud* c Borde b Umrigar	20
A.T.W.Grout b Umrigar	42
L.F.Kline c and b Ramchand	14
I.Meckiff not out	45
G.F.Rorke c sub (B.K.Kunderan) b Umrigar	7
Extras (B 11, LB 13, NB 1)	25
	468

1/52 2/64 3/143 4/275 5/318
6/353 7/398 8/402 9/443

Bowling: Desai 34.3-3-123-1; Surendranath 38-8-101-2; Borde 15-3-49-0; Muddiah 13-4-32-0; Nadkarni 20-6-62-1; Ramchand 7-1-27-1; Umrigar 15.3-1-49-4.

Umpires: S.K.Ganguli and Mahomed Yunus

INDIA v AUSTRALIA 1959-60 (Second Test)

At Green Park, Kanpur, 19, 20, 21, 23, 24 December
Result: India won by 119 runs

India

Batsman	1st innings		2nd innings	
Pankaj Roy	c Harvey b Benaud	17	c Benaud b Davidson	8
N.J.Contractor	c Jarman b Benaud	24	c Harvey b Davidson	74
P.R.Umrigar	c Davidson b Kline	6	c Rorke b Davidson	14
A.A.Baig	b Davidson	19	c Harvey b Benaud	36
C.G.Borde	c Kline b Davidson	20	c O'Neill b Meckiff	44
G.S.Ramchand*	c Mackay b Benaud	24	c Harvey	5
R.B.Kenny	b Davidson	0	c Jarman b Davidson	51
R.G.Nadkarni	c Harvey b Davidson	25	lbw b Davidson	46
N.S.Tamhane†	b Benaud	1	c Harvey b Davidson	0
J.M.Patel	c Kline b Davidson	4	(11) b Davidson	0
Surendranath	not out	8	(10) not out	4
Extras	(LB 2, NB 2)	4	(B 7, LB 2)	9
Total		152		291

1/38 2/47 3/51 4/77 5/112   1/32 2/72 3/121 4/147 5/153
6/112 7/126 8/128 9/141   6/214 7/286 8/286 9/291

Bowling: *First Innings*—Davidson 20.1-7-31-5; Meckiff 8-2-15-0; Benaud 25-8-63-4; Rorke 2-1-3-0; Kline 15-7-36-1. *Second Innings*—Davidson 57.3-23-93-7; Meckiff 18-4-37-1; Mackay 10-5-14-0; Benaud 38-15-81-1; Kline 7-3-14-0; O'Neill 2-0-12-0.

Australia

Batsman	1st innings		2nd innings	
C.C.McDonald	b Patel	53	st Tamhane b Patel	34
G.B.Stevens	c and b Patel	25	c Kenny b Patel	7
R.N.Harvey	b Patel	51	c Nadkarni b Umrigar	25
N.C.O'Neill	b Borde	16	c Nadkarni b Umrigar	5
K.D.Mackay	lbw b Patel	0	lbw b Umrigar	0
A.K.Davidson	b Patel	41	b Patel	8
R.Benaud*	b Patel	7	c Ramchand b Patel	0
B.N.Jarman†	lbw b Patel	1	b Umrigar	0
L.F.Kline	b Patel	9	b Patel	0
I.Meckiff	not out	1	not out	14
G.F.Rorke	c Baig b Patel	0	absent ill	–
Extras	(B 9, LB 2, NB 4)	15	(B 5, LB 7)	12
Total		219		105

1/71 2/128 3/149 4/159 5/159   1/12 2/49 3/59 4/61 5/78
6/174 7/186 8/216 9/219   6/78 7/79 8/84 9/105

Bowling: *First Innings*—Surendranath 4-0-13-0; Ramchand 6-3-14-0; Patel 35.5-16-69-9; Umrigar 15-1-40-0; Borde 15-1-61-1; Nadkarni 2-0-7-0. *Second Innings*—Surendranath 4-2-4-0; Ramchand 3-0-7-0; Patel 25.4-7-55-5; Umrigar 25-11-27-4.

Umpires: S.K.Ganguli and A.R.Joshi

INDIA v AUSTRALIA 1959-60 (Third Test)

At Brabourne Stadium, Bombay, 1, 2, 3, 5, 6 January
Result: Match drawn

India

Batsman	1st innings		2nd innings	
Pankaj Roy	b Davidson	6	b Meckiff	57
N.J.Contractor	c Benaud b Meckiff	108	b Lindwall	43
P.R.Umrigar	c Harvey b Davidson	0		
A.A.Baig	c Grout b Davidson	50	(4) c Mackay b Lindwall	58
C.G.Borde	b Meckiff	26	(5) b Meckiff	1
G.S.Ramchand*	lbw b Meckiff	0		
R.B.Kenny	b Meckiff	20	(6) not out	55
B.K.Kunderan†	lbw b Lindwall	19	(3) hit wkt b Meckiff	2
R.G.Nadkarni	not out	18	(7) not out	1
S.A.Durani	c Stevens b Benaud	18		
G.M.Guard	c Benaud b Davidson	7		
Extras	(B 9, LB 4, NB 4)	17	(LB 9)	9
Total		289	(5 wkts dec.)	226

1/21 2/154 3/154 4/199 5/199   1/95 2/99 3/111
6/203 7/229 8/246 9/272   4/112 5/221

Bowling: *First Innings*—Davidson 34.5-9-62-4; Lindwall 23-7-56-1; Meckiff 38-12-79-4; Benaud 42-24-64-1. *Second Innings*—Davidson 14-4-25-0; Meckiff 28-8-67-3; Benaud 24-10-36-0; Lindwall 23-7-56-2; O'Neill 3-1-16-0; Harvey 3-1-11-0; Mackay 6-4-6-0.

Australia

Batsman	1st innings		2nd innings	
C.C.McDonald	b Nadkarni	36		
G.B.Stevens	b Nadkarni	22		
R.N.Harvey	b Nadkarni	102		
N.C.O'Neill	c sub (M.M.Sood) b Borde	163		
L.E.Favell	b Nadkarni	1		
A.T.W.Grout†	b Nadkarni	31	(1) not out	22
R.Benaud*	lbw b Nadkarni	14	(3) not out	12
A.K.Davidson	not out	9		
K.D.Mackay	b Borde	0		
R.R.Lindwall	not out	1		
I.Meckiff			(2) b Roy	0
Extras	(B 4, LB 3)	7		
Total	(8 wkts dec.)	387	(1 wkt)	34

1/60 2/63 3/270 4/282 5/358   1/4
6/376 7/379 8/380

Bowling: *First Innings*—Guard 33-7-93-0; Ramchand 35-13-85-0; Umrigar 8-2-19-0; Nadkarni 51-11-105-6; Borde 13-1-78-2. *Second Innings*—Guard 1-0-1-0; Roy 2-0-6-1; Contractor 2-1-5-0; Baig 2-0-13-0; Durani 1-0-9-0.

Umpires: H.E.Choudhury and N.D.Nagarwalla

INDIA v AUSTRALIA 1959-60 (Fifth Test)

At Eden Gardens, Calcutta, 23, 24, 25, 27, 28 January
Result: Match drawn

India

Batsman		Score				Score
B.K.Kunderan† b Mackay		12	b Davidson			0
N.J.Contractor b Benaud		36	c Davidson b Benaud			30
Pankaj Roy c Grout b Davidson		33	lbw b Benaud			39
R.G.Nadkarni c Burge b Lindwall		2	c Grout b Lindwall	(6)		29
R.B.Kenny c Grout b Lindwall		7	c Grout b Mackay	(8)		62
C.D.Gopinath b Benaud		39	c Grout b Benaud	(5)		50
C.G.Borde b Benaud		6	b Meckiff			50
G.S.Ramchand* b Davidson		12	b Benaud	(9)		9
M.L.Jaisimha not out		20	b Mackay	(4)		74
R.B.Desai c Grout b Davidson		17	not out			17
J.M.Patel run out		0	c Benaud b Davidson			12
Extras (B 5, LB 1, NB 3, W 1)		10	(B 11, LB 4, NB 2)			17
		194				**339**

1/30 2/59 3/71 4/83 5/112
6/131 7/142 8/158 9/194
1/0 2/67 3/78 4/78 5/123
6/206 7/289 8/294 9/316

Bowling: First Innings—Davidson 16-2-37-3; Meckiff 17-5-28-0; Mackay 11-5-16-1; Lindwall 16-6-44-2; Benaud 29.3-12-59-3. *Second Innings*—Davidson 36.2-13-76-2; Lindwall 20-3-66-1; Meckiff 21-2-41-2; Benaud 48-23-103-4; Mackay 21-7-36-2.

Australia

Batsman		Score			Score
L.E.Favell b Desai		26	not out		62
A.T.W.Grout† b Patel		50			
R.N.Harvey c Jaisimha b Patel		17	c and b Contractor		36
N.C.O'Neill c Kunderan b Desai		113			
P.J.P.Burge b Desai		60			
C.C.McDonald lbw b Borde		27	run out	(2)	6
K.D.Mackay b Patel		18			
R.R.Lindwall c Kunderan b Desai		10			
A.K.Davidson not out		4			
R.Benaud* c and b Borde		3	not out	(4)	10
I.Meckiff not out		0			
Extras (LB 3)		3	(B 1, LB 5, NB 1)		7
		331	(2 wkts)		**121**

1/76 2/76 3/116 4/266 5/273
6/206 7/289 8/294 9/316
1/20 2/104

Bowling: First Innings—Desai 36-4-111-4; Ramchand 10-1-37-0; Patel 26-2-104-3; Nadkarni 22-10-36-0; Borde 13.1-4-23-3; Jaisimha 4-0-17-0. *Second Innings*—Desai 11-4-18-0; Ramchand 3-2-4-0; Patel 7-1-15-0; Borde 13-1-45-0; Nadkarni 7-4-10-0; Jaisimha 6-2-13-0; Contractor 5-1-9-1.

Umpires: S.K.Ganguli and N.D.Sane

INDIA v AUSTRALIA 1959-60 (Fourth Test)

At Corporation Stadium, Madras, 13, 14, 15, 17 January
Result: Australia won by an innings and 55 runs

Australia

Batsman	Score
C.C.McDonald b Patel	16
L.E.Favell st Kunderan b Nadkarni	101
R.N.Harvey b Desai	11
N.C.O'Neill b Desai	40
P.J.P.Burge b Desai	35
K.D.Mackay st Kunderan b Patel	89
A.K.Davidson lbw b Nadkarni	6
A.T.W.Grout† c Milka Singh b Nadkarni	2
R.Benaud* b Borde	25
I.Meckiff c Roy b Desai	8
L.F.Kline not out	0
Extras (B 3, LB 5, NB 1)	9
	342

1/58 2/77 3/147 4/197 5/216
6/239 7/249 8/308 9/329

Bowling: Desai 41-10-93-4; Ramchand 15-6-26-0; Nadkarni 44-15-75-3; Patel 37-12-84-2; Borde 16-1-55-1.

India

Batsman		Score				Score
Pankaj Roy c Grout b Davidson		1	c O'Neill b Meckiff			3
B.K.Kunderan† b Benaud		71	b Benaud	(4)		33
R.B.Kenny b Mackay		33	c Grout b Meckiff			1
N.J.Contractor c Kline b Benaud		7	c Meckiff b Kline	(2)		41
C.G.Borde c Grout b Kline		3	c Davidson b Benaud			1
G.S.Ramchand* c Harvey b Benaud		13	st Grout b Benaud	(8)		22
A.G.Milka Singh b Davidson		16	b Harvey	(6)		9
R.G.Nadkarni c Kline b Benaud		3	run out	(7)		18
M.M.Sood st Grout b Davidson		0	b Davidson			3
R.B.Desai c McDonald b Benaud		0	not out			0
J.M.Patel not out		2	c Kline b Davidson			7
Extras (B 1, NB 1)		2	(B 4, LB 2, NB 1)			7
		149				**138**

1/20 2/95 3/111 4/114 5/130
6/130 7/145 8/148 9/149
1/7 2/11 3/54 4/62 5/78
6/100 7/127 8/138 9/138

Bowling: First Innings—Davidson 19-6-36-3; Meckiff 7-4-21-0; Benaud 32.1-14-43-5; Kline 15-8-21-1; Harvey 1-0-9-0; Mackay 3-0-17-1. *Second Innings*—Davidson 19-7-33-2; Meckiff 22-10-33-2; Mackay 4-3-1-0; Benaud 35-19-43-3; Kline 12-5-13-1; Harvey 13-7-8-1.

Umpires: N.D.Sane and M.G.Vijayasarathi

AUSTRALIA v WEST INDIES 1960-61 (First Test)

At Woolloongabba, Brisbane, 9, 10, 12, 13, 14 December
Result: Match tied

West Indies

Batsman	1st innings		2nd innings	
C.C.Hunte	c Benaud b Davidson	24	c Simpson b Mackay	39
C.W.Smith	c Grout b Davidson	7	c O'Neill b Davidson	6
R.B.Kanhai	c Grout b Davidson	15	c Grout b Davidson	54
G.S.Sobers	c Kline b Meckiff	132	b Davidson	14
F.M.M.Worrell*	c Grout b Davidson	65	c Grout b Davidson	65
J.S.Solomon	hit wkt b Simpson	65	lbw b Simpson	47
P.D.Lashley	c Grout b Kline	19	b Davidson	0
F.C.M.Alexander†	c Davidson b Kline	60	b Benaud	5
S.Ramadhin	c Harvey b Davidson	12	c Harvey b Simpson	6
W.W.Hall	st Grout b Kline	50	b Davidson	18
A.L.Valentine	not out	0	not out	7
Extras	(LB 3, W 1)	4	(B 14, LB 7, W 2)	23
		453		**284**

1/23 2/42 3/65 4/239 5/210
6/283 7/347 8/366 9/452

1/13 2/88 3/114 4/127 5/210
6/210 7/241 8/250 9/253

Bowling: *First Innings*—Davidson 30-2-135-5; Meckiff 18-0-129-1; Mackay 3-0-15-0; Benaud 24-3-93-0; Simpson 8-0-25-1; Kline 17.6-6-52-3. *Second Innings*—Davidson 24.6-4-87-6; Meckiff 4-1-19-0; Benaud 31-6-69-1; Mackay 21-7-52-1; Kline 4-0-14-0; Simpson 7-2-18-2; O'Neill 1-0-2-0.

Australia

Batsman	1st innings		2nd innings	
C.C.McDonald	c Hunte b Sobers	57	b Worrell	16
R.B.Simpson	b Ramadhin	92	c sub (L.R.Gibbs) b Hall	0
R.N.Harvey	b Valentine	15	c Sobers b Hall	5
N.C.O'Neill	c Valentine b Hall	181	c Alexander b Hall	26
L.E.Favell	run out	45	c Solomon b Hall	7
K.D.Mackay	b Sobers	35	b Ramadhin	28
A.K.Davidson	c Alexander b Hall	44	run out	80
R.Benaud*	lbw b Hall	10	c Alexander b Hall	52
A.T.W.Grout	lbw b Hall	4	run out	2
I.Meckiff	run out	4	run out	2
L.F.Kline	not out	3	not out	0
Extras	(B 2, LB 8, NB 4, W 1)	15	(B 2, LB 9, NB 3)	14
		505		**232**

1/84 2/138 3/194 4/278 5/381
6/469 7/484 8/489 9/496

1/1 2/7 3/49 4/49 5/57
6/92 7/226 8/228 9/232

Bowling: *First Innings*—Hall 29.3-1-140-4; Worrell 30-0-93-0; Sobers 32-0-115-2; Valentine 24-6-82-1; Ramadhin 15-1-60-1. *Second Innings*—Hall 17.7-3-63-5; Worrell 16-3-41-1; Sobers 8-0-30-0; Valentine 10-4-27-0; Ramadhin 17-3-57-1.

Umpires: C.J.Egar and C.Hoy

AUSTRALIA v WEST INDIES 1960-61 (Second Test)

At Melbourne Cricket Ground, 30, 31 December, 2, 3 January
Result: Australia won by 7 wickets

Australia

Batsman	1st innings		2nd innings	
C.C.McDonald	c Watson b Hall	15	c Sobers b Hall	13
R.B.Simpson	c Alexander b Hall	49	not out	27
R.N.Harvey	c Sobers b Worrell	12	c Alexander b Hall	0
N.C.O'Neill	c Sobers b Worrell	40	lbw b Watson	0
L.E.Favell	c Nurse b Sobers	51	not out	24
K.D.Mackay	b Ramadhin	74		
A.K.Davidson	b Hall	35		
R.Benaud*	b Hall	2		
A.T.W.Grout	b Watson	5		
J.W.Martin	b Valentine	55		
F.M.Misson	not out	0		
Extras	(LB 7, NB 2, W 1)	10	(B 4, LB 1, NB 1)	6
		348		(3 wkts) **70**

1/35 2/60 3/105 4/155 5/189
6/242 7/244 8/251 9/348

1/27 2/27 3/30

Bowling: *First Innings*—Hall 12-2-51-4; Watson 12-1-73-1; Sobers 17-1-88-1; Worrell 9-0-50-2; Valentine 11-1-55-1; Ramadhin 5-0-21-1. *Second Innings*—Hall 9.4-0-32-2; Watson 9-1-32-1.

West Indies

Batsman	1st innings		2nd innings	
C.C.Hunte	c Simpson b Misson	1	c Grout b O'Neill	110
J.S.Solomon	c Grout b Davidson	0	hit wkt b Benaud	4
S.M.Nurse	c Grout b Davidson	70	run out	3
R.B.Kanhai	c Harvey b Davidson	84	c Misson b Martin	25
G.S.Sobers	c Simpson b Benaud	9	c Simpson b Martin	0
F.M.M.Worrell*	b Misson	0	c Simpson b Benaud	0
F.C.M.Alexander†	c Favell b Davidson	5	c Grout b Davidson	72
S.Ramadhin	b Davidson	0	st Grout b Benaud	3
W.W.Hall	b Davidson	5	b Davidson	4
C.D.Watson	c McDonald b Benaud	4	run out	5
A.L.Valentine	not out	1	not out	0
Extras	(NB 2)	2	(B 2, LB 2, NB 2, W 1)	7
		181		**233**

1/1 2/1 3/124 4/139 5/142
6/160 7/160 8/166 9/177

1/40 2/51 3/97 4/99 5/99
6/186 7/193 8/206 9/222

Bowling: *First Innings*—Davidson 22-4-53-6; Misson 11-0-36-2; Benaud 27.2-10-58-2; Martin 8-1-32-0; Simpson 1-1-0-0. *Second Innings*—Davidson 15.4-2-51-2; Misson 12-3-36-0; Benaud 20-3-56-3; Martin 20-3-49-2; O'Neill 5-1-10-1.

Umpires: C.J.Egar and C.Hoy

AUSTRALIA v WEST INDIES 1960-61 (Fourth Test)

At Adelaide Oval, 27, 28, 30, 31 January, 1, 2 February

Result: Match drawn

West Indies

Batsman	First Innings	Runs	Second Innings	Runs
C.C.Hunte	lbw b Hoare	6	run out	79
C.W.Smith	c and b Benaud	28	c Hoare b Mackay	46
R.B.Kanhai	c Simpson b Benaud	117	lbw b Benaud	115
G.S.Sobers	b Benaud	1	run out	20
F.M.M.Worrell*	c Misson b Hoare	71	c Burge b Mackay	53
S.M.Nurse	c and b Misson	49	c Simpson b Benaud	5
J.S.Solomon	c and b Benaud	22	(8) not out	16
F.C.M.Alexander†	not out	63	(7) not out	87
L.R.Gibbs	b Misson	18		
W.W.Hall	c Hoare b Benaud	5		
A.L.Valentine	lbw b Misson	0		
Extras	(B 3, LB 3, NB 2, W 5)	13	(B 2, LB 6, NB 1, W 2)	11
Total		393	(6 wkts dec.)	432

1/12 2/83 3/91 4/198 5/271 6/288 7/316 8/375 9/392

1/66 2/229 3/263 4/270 5/275 6/388

Bowling: *First Innings*—Hoare 16-0-68-2; Misson 17.5-2-79-3; Kline 21-3-109-0; Simpson 5-0-17-0. *Second Innings*—Hoare 13-0-88-0; Misson 28-3-106-0; Benaud 27-3-107-2; Kline 12-2-48-0.

Australia

Batsman	First Innings	Runs	Second Innings	Runs
C.C.McDonald	c Hunte b Gibbs	71	run out	2
L.E.Favell	c Alexander b Worrell	1	c Alexander b Hall	4
N.C.O'Neill	c Alexander b Sobers	11	c and b Sobers	65
R.B.Simpson	c Alexander b Hall	85	c Alexander b Hall	3
P.J.P.Burge	b Sobers	45	c Alexander b Valentine	49
R.Benaud*	c Solomon b Gibbs	77	c and b Sobers	17
K.D.Mackay	lbw b Gibbs	29	not out	62
A.T.W.Grout†	c Sobers b Gibbs	0	lbw b Worrell	42
F.M.Misson	b Gibbs	0	c Solomon b Worrell	1
D.E.Hoare	b Sobers	35	b Worrell	0
L.F.Kline	not out	0	not out	15
Extras	(B 2, LB 3, NB 7)	12	(B 9, LB 1, NB 3)	13
Total		366	(9 wkts)	273

1/9 2/45 3/119 4/213 5/221 6/281 7/281 8/281 9/366

1/6 2/7 3/31 4/113 5/129 6/144 7/203 8/207 9/207

Bowling: *First Innings*—Hall 22-3-85-1; Worrell 7-0-34-1; Sobers 24-3-64-3; Gibbs 35.6-4-97-5; Valentine 24.4-7-4-0. *Second Innings*—Hall 13-4-61-2; Worrell 17-9-27-3; Sobers 39-11-87-2; Gibbs 28-13-44-0; Valentine 20-7-40-1; Solomon 3-2-1-0.

Umpires: C.J.Egar and C.Hoy

AUSTRALIA v WEST INDIES 1960-61 (Third Test)

At Sydney Cricket Ground, 13, 14, 16, 17, 18 January

Result: West Indies won by 222 runs

West Indies

Batsman	First Innings	Runs	Second Innings	Runs
C.C.Hunte	c Simpson b Meckiff	34	c O'Neill b Davidson	1
C.W.Smith	c Simpson b Davidson	16	c Simpson b Benaud	55
R.B.Kanhai	c Grout b Davidson	21	b Davidson	3
G.S.Sobers	c and b Davidson	168	c Grout b Davidson	1
F.M.M.Worrell*	c Davidson b Benaud	22	lbw b Benaud	82
S.M.Nurse	c Simpson b Benaud	43	c and b Mackay	11
J.S.Solomon	c Simpson b Benaud	14	c Harvey b Benaud	11
F.C.M.Alexander†	c Harvey b Benaud	0	lbw b Mackay	108
L.R.Gibbs	c Grout b Benaud	0	st Grout b Benaud	18
W.W.Hall	c Grout b Davidson	10	b Mackay	24
A.L.Valentine	not out	0	not out	10
Extras	(B 6, LB 4, W 1)	11	(B 4, LB 7, W 1)	12
Total		339		326

1/48 2/68 3/89 4/152 5/280 6/329 7/329 8/329 9/329

1/10 2/20 3/22 4/123 5/144 6/159 7/166 8/240 9/309

Bowling: *First Innings*—Davidson 21.6-4-80-5; Meckiff 13-1-74-1; Mackay 14-1-40-0; Benaud 23-3-86-4; Martin 8-1-37-0; Simpson 2-0-11-0. *Second Innings*—Davidson 8-1-33-3; Meckiff 5-2-12-0; Mackay 31.4-5-75-3; Benaud 44-14-113-4; Martin 10-0-65-0; Simpson 4-0-16-0.

Australia

Batsman	First Innings	Runs	Second Innings	Runs
C.C.McDonald	b Valentine	34	c Alexander b Valentine	27
R.B.Simpson	c Kanhai b Hall	10	b Sobers	12
R.N.Harvey	c Sobers b Hall	9	c Sobers b Gibbs	85
N.C.O'Neill		71	c Sobers b Gibbs	70
L.E.Favell	c Worrell b Valentine	16	b Gibbs	2
K.D.Mackay	c Solomon b Gibbs	39	c Nurse b Gibbs	0
A.K.Davidson	c Worrell b Valentine	16	(10) b Valentine	1
R.Benaud*	c and b Valentine	3	(7) c and b Valentine	24
J.W.Martin	c Solomon b Gibbs	0	(9) b Valentine	5
A.T.W.Grout†	c Hunte b Gibbs	0	b Gibbs	0
I.Meckiff	not out	0	not out	6
Extras	(B 1, LB 2, NB 1)	4	(B 3, LB 6)	9
Total		202		241

1/17 2/40 3/65 4/105 5/155 6/194 7/200 8/200 9/202

1/27 2/83 3/191 4/197 5/197 6/202 7/209 8/220 9/234

Bowling: *First Innings*—Hall 13-0-53-2; Worrell 9-4-18-0; Gibbs 23-6-46-3; Valentine 24.2-6-67-4; Sobers 5-2-14-1. *Second Innings*—Hall 8-0-35-0; Worrell 4-0-7-0; Gibbs 26-5-66-5; Valentine 25.2-7-86-4; Sobers 9-1-38-1.

Umpires: C.J.Egar and C.Hoy

AUSTRALIA v WEST INDIES 1960-61 (Fifth Test)

At Melbourne Cricket Ground, 10, 11, 13, 14, 15 February
Result: Australia won by 2 wickets

West Indies

Batsman	1st innings	R	2nd innings	R
C.W.Smith	c O'Neill b Misson	11	lbw b Davidson	37
C.C.Hunte	c Simpson b Davidson	31	c Grout b Davidson	52
R.B.Kanhai	c Harvey b Benaud	38	c Misson b Benaud	31
G.S.Sobers	c Grout b Simpson	64	(5) c Grout b Simpson	21
F.M.M.Worrell*	c Grout b Martin	10	(7) c Grout b Davidson	7
P.D.Lashley	c Misson b Benaud	41	(8) lbw b Martin	18
F.C.M.Alexander†	c McDonald b Misson	11	(6) c Mackay b Davidson	73
J.S.Solomon	run out	45	(4) run out	36
L.R.Gibbs	c Burge b Misson	11	c O'Neill b Simpson	8
W.W.Hall	b Misson	21	c Grout b Davidson	21
A.L.Valentine	not out	0	not out	3
Extras	(B 4, LB 4, W 1)	9	(B 5, LB 8, W 1)	14
Total		292		321

1/18 2/75 3/81 4/107 5/200 6/204 7/221 8/235 9/290
1/54 2/103 3/135 4/173 5/201 6/218 7/262 8/295 9/304

Bowling: *First Innings*—Davidson 27-4-89-1; Misson 14-3-58-4; Mackay 14-3-51-1; Simpson 18-3-51-1. *Second Innings*—Davidson 24.7-4-84-5; Misson 10-1-58-0; Mackay 10-2-21-0; Benaud 23-4-53-1; Martin 10-1-36-1; Simpson 18-4-55-2.

Australia

Batsman	1st innings	R	2nd innings	R
R.B.Simpson	c Gibbs b Sobers	75	b Gibbs	92
C.C.McDonald	lbw b Sobers	91	c Smith b Gibbs	11
N.C.O'Neill	b Gibbs	10	(4) c Alexander b Worrell	48
P.J.P.Burge	c Sobers b Gibbs	68	(5) b Valentine	53
K.D.Mackay	c Alexander b Hall	19	(8) not out	3
R.N.Harvey	c Alexander b Sobers	5	c Smith b Worrell	12
A.K.Davidson	c Alexander b Sobers	24	c Sobers b Worrell	12
R.Benaud*	b Gibbs	3	(3) b Valentine	6
J.W.Martin	c Kanhai b Sobers	15	(10) not out	1
F.M.Misson	not out	12		
A.T.W.Grout†	c Hunte b Gibbs	14	(9) c Smith b Valentine	5
Extras	(B 4, LB 8, NB 8)	20	(B 3, LB 9, NB 3)	15
Total		356	(8 wkts)	258

1/146 2/181 3/181 4/244 5/260 6/309 7/309 8/319 9/355
1/50 2/75 3/144 4/176 5/200 6/236 7/248 8/256

Bowling: *First Innings*—Hall 15-1-56-1; Worrell 11-2-44-0; Sobers 44-7-120-5; Gibbs 38.4-7-74-4; Valentine 13-3-42-0. *Second Innings*—Hall 5-0-40-0; Worrell 31-16-43-3; Sobers 13-2-32-0; Gibbs 41-19-68-2; Valentine 21.7-4-60-3.

Umpires: C.J.Egar and C.Hoy

ENGLAND v AUSTRALIA 1961 (First Test)

At Edgbaston, Birmingham, 8, 9, 10, 12, 13 June
Result: Match drawn

England

Batsman	1st innings	R	2nd innings	R
G.Pullar	b Davidson	17	c Grout b Misson	28
R.Subba Row	c Simpson b Mackay	59	b Misson	112
E.R.Dexter	c Davidson b Mackay	10	st Grout b Simpson	180
M.C.Cowdrey*	b Misson	13	b Mackay	14
K.F.Barrington	c Misson b Mackay	21	not out	48
M.J.K.Smith	c Lawry b Mackay	0	not out	1
R.Illingworth	c Grout b Benaud	15		
J.T.Murray†	c Davidson b Benaud	16		
D.A.Allen	run out	11		
F.S.Trueman	c Burge b Benaud	20		
J.B.Statham	not out	7		
Extras	(B 3, LB 3)	6	(LB 18)	18
Total		195	(4 wkts)	401

1/36 2/53 3/88 4/121 5/121 6/122 7/153 8/156 9/181
1/93 2/202 3/239 4/400

Bowling: *First Innings*—Davidson 26-6-70-1; Misson 15-6-47-1; Mackay 29-10-57-4; Benaud 14.3-8-15-3. *Second Innings*—Davidson 31-10-60-0; Misson 28-6-82-2; Simpson 34-12-87-1; Mackay 41-13-87-1; Benaud 20-4-67-0.

Australia

Batsman	Dismissal	R
W.M.Lawry	c Murray b Illingworth	57
C.C.McDonald	c Illingworth b Statham	22
R.N.Harvey	lbw b Allen	114
N.C.O'Neill	b Statham	82
P.J.P.Burge	lbw b Allen	25
R.B.Simpson	c and b Trueman	76
A.K.Davidson	c and b Illingworth	22
K.D.Mackay	c Barrington b Statham	64
R.Benaud*	not out	36
A.T.W.Grout†	c Dexter b Trueman	5
F.M.Misson		
Extras	(B 8, LB 4, NB 1)	13
Total	(9 wkts dec.)	516

1/47 2/106 3/252 4/299 5/322 6/381 7/469 8/501 9/516

Bowling: Trueman 36.5-1-136-2; Statham 43-6-147-3; Illingworth 44-12-110-2; Allen 24-4-88-2; Dexter 5-1-22-0.

Umpires: J.S.Buller and F.S.Lee

ENGLAND v AUSTRALIA 1961 (Second Test)

At Lord's, London, 22, 23, 24, 26 June
Result: Australia won by 5 wickets

England

G.Pullar b Davidson	11	c Grout b Misson	42
R.Subba Row lbw b Mackay	48	c Grout b Davidson	8
E.R.Dexter c McKenzie b Misson	27	b McKenzie	17
M.C.Cowdrey* c Grout b McKenzie	16	c Mackay b Misson	7
P.B.H.May c Grout b Davidson	17	c Grout b McKenzie	22
K.F.Barrington c Mackay b Davidson	4	lbw b Davidson	66
R.Illingworth b Misson	13	c Harvey b Simpson	0
J.T.Murray† lbw b Mackay	18	c Grout b McKenzie	25
G.A.R.Lock c Grout b Davidson	5	b McKenzie	1
F.S.Trueman b Davidson	25	c Grout b McKenzie	0
J.B.Statham not out	11	not out	2
Extras (LB 9, W 2)	11	(B 1, LB 10, W 1)	12
	206		**202**

1/26 2/87 3/87 4/111 5/115
6/127 7/156 8/164 9/167

1/33 2/63 3/67 4/80 5/127
6/144 7/191 8/199 9/199

Bowling: *First Innings*—Davidson 24.3-6-42-5; McKenzie 26-7-81-1; Misson 16-4-48-2; Mackay 12-3-24-2. *Second Innings*—Davidson 24-8-50-2; McKenzie 29-13-37-5; Misson 17-2-66-2; Mackay 8-6-5-0; Simpson 19-10-32-1.

Australia

W.M.Lawry c Murray b Dexter	130	c Murray b Statham	1
C.C.McDonald b Statham	4	c Illingworth b Trueman	14
R.B.Simpson c Illingworth b Trueman	0	(6) c Illingworth b Statham	15
R.N.Harvey* c Barrington b Trueman	27	c Murray b Trueman	4
N.C.O'Neill b Dexter	1	(4) b Statham	0
P.J.P.Burge c Murray b Statham	46	not out	37
A.K.Davidson lbw b Trueman	6	(5) not out	0
K.D.Mackay c Barrington b Illingworth	54		
A.T.W.Grout† lbw b Dexter	0		
G.D.McKenzie b Trueman	34		
F.M.Misson not out	25		
Extras (B 1, LB 12)	13		
	340	(5 wkts)	**71**

1/5 2/6 3/81 4/88 5/183
6/194 7/238 8/238 9/291

1/15 2/15 3/19 4/19
5/58

Bowling: *First Innings*—Statham 44-10-89-2; Trueman 34-3-118-4; Dexter 24-7-56-3; Lock 26-13-48-0; Illingworth 11.3-5-16-1. *Second Innings*—Statham 10.5-3-31-3; Trueman 10-0-40-2.

Umpires: C.S.Elliott and W.E.Phillipson

ENGLAND v AUSTRALIA 1961 (Third Test)

At Headingley, Leeds, 6, 7, 8 July
Result: England won by 8 wickets

Australia

C.C.McDonald st Murray b Lock	54	b Jackson	1
W.M.Lawry lbw b Lock	28	c Murray b Allen	28
R.N.Harvey c Lock b Trueman	73	c Dexter b Trueman	53
N.C.O'Neill c Cowdrey b Trueman	27	c Cowdrey b Trueman	19
P.J.P.Burge c Cowdrey b Jackson	5	lbw b Allen	0
K.D.Mackay lbw b Jackson	6	(9) c Murray b Trueman	0
R.B.Simpson lbw b Trueman	2	(6) b Trueman	3
A.K.Davidson not out	22	(7) c Cowdrey b Trueman	7
R.Benaud* b Trueman	0	b Trueman	0
A.T.W.Grout† c Murray b Trueman	3	(8) c and b Jackson	7
G.D.McKenzie b Allen	8	not out	0
Extras (B 7, LB 2)	9	(LB 2)	2
	237		**120**

1/62 2/113 3/187 4/192 5/196
6/203 7/203 8/204 9/208

1/4 2/49 3/99 4/102 5/102
6/105 7/109 8/109 9/120

Bowling: *First Innings*—Trueman 22-5-58-5; Jackson 31-11-57-2; Allen 28-12-45-1; Lock 2-5-68-2. *Second Innings*—Trueman 15.5-5-30-6; Jackson 13-5-26-2; Lock 10-1-32-0; Allen 14-6-30-2.

England

G.Pullar b Benaud	53	not out	26
R.Subba Row lbw b Davidson	35	b Davidson	6
M.C.Cowdrey c Grout b McKenzie	93	c Grout b Benaud	22
P.B.H.May* c and b Davidson	26	not out	8
E.R.Dexter b Davidson	28		
K.F.Barrington c Simpson b Davidson	6		
J.T.Murray† b McKenzie	6		
F.S.Trueman c Burge b Davidson	4		
G.A.R.Lock lbw b McKenzie	30		
D.A.Allen not out	5		
H.L.Jackson run out	8		
Extras (LB 5)	5		
	299	(2 wkts)	**62**

1/59 2/145 3/190 4/223 5/239
6/248 7/252 8/286 9/291

1/14 2/45

Bowling: *First Innings*—Davidson 47-23-63-5; McKenzie 27-4-64-3; Mackay 22-4-34-0; Benaud 39-15-86-1; Simpson 14-5-47-0. *Second Innings*—Davidson 11-6-17-1; McKenzie 5-0-15-0; Mackay 1-0-8-0; Benaud 6-1-22-1.

Umpires: J.S.Buller and J.G.Langridge

ENGLAND v AUSTRALIA 1961 (Fourth Test)

At Old Trafford, Manchester, 27, 28, 29, 31 July, 1 August

Result: Australia won by 54 runs

Australia

Batsman	1st Innings		2nd Innings	
W.M.Lawry lbw b Statham	74	c Trueman b Allen	102
R.B.Simpson c Murray b Statham	4	c Murray b Flavell	51
R.N.Harvey c Subba Row b Statham	19	c Murray b Dexter	35
N.C.O'Neill hit wkt b Trueman	11	c Murray b Statham	67
P.J.P.Burge b Flavell	15	c Murray b Dexter	23
B.C.Booth c Close b Statham	46	lbw b Dexter	9
K.D.Mackay c Murray b Statham	11	c Close b Allen	18
A.K.Davidson c Barrington b Dexter	0	not out	77
R.Benaud* b Dexter	2	lbw b Allen	1
A.T.W.Grout† c Murray b Dexter	2	c Statham b Allen	0
G.D.McKenzie not out	1	b Flavell	32
Extras (B 4, LB 1)	5	(B 6, LB 9, W 2)	17
	190		**432**

1/8 2/51 3/89 4/106 5/150
6/174 7/185 8/185 9/189

1/113 2/175 3/210 4/274
5/290 6/296 7/332 8/334 9/334

Bowling: *First Innings*—Trueman 14-1-55-1; Statham 21-3-53-5; Flavell 22-8-61-1; Dexter 6.4-2-16-3. *Second Innings*—Statham 44-9-106-1; Trueman 32-6-92-0; Flavell 29.4-4-65-2; Allen 38-25-58-4; Dexter 20-4-61-3; Close 8-1-33-0.

England

Batsman	1st Innings		2nd Innings	
G.Pullar b Davidson	63	c O'Neill b Davidson	26
R.Subba Row c Simpson b Davidson	2	b Benaud	49
E.R.Dexter c Davidson b McKenzie	16	c Grout b Benaud	76
P.B.H.May* c Simpson b Davidson	95	b Benaud	8
D.B.Close lbw b McKenzie	33	c O'Neill b Benaud	8
K.F.Barrington c O'Neill b Simpson	78	lbw b Mackay	5
J.T.Murray† c Grout b Mackay	24	c Simpson b Benaud	4
D.A.Allen c Booth b Simpson	42	c Simpson b Benaud	10
F.S.Trueman c Harvey b Simpson	3	c Benaud b Simpson	8
J.B.Statham c Mackay b Simpson	4	b Davidson	8
J.A.Flavell not out	0	not out	0
Extras (B 2, LB 4, W 1)	7	(B 5, W 2)	7
	367		**201**

1/3 2/43 3/154 4/212 5/212
6/272 7/358 8/362 9/367

1/40 2/150 3/150 4/158 5/163
6/171 7/171 8/189 9/193

Bowling: *First Innings*—Davidson 39-11-70-3; McKenzie 38-11-106-2; Mackay 40-9-71-1; Benaud 35-15-80-0; Simpson 11.4-4-23-4. *Second Innings*—Davidson 14.4-1-50-2; McKenzie 4-1-20-0; Benaud 32-11-70-6; Simpson 8-4-21-1; Mackay 13-7-33-1;

Umpires: J.G.Langridge and W.E.Phillipson

ENGLAND v AUSTRALIA 1961 (Fifth Test)

At Kennington Oval, London, 17, 18, 19, 21, 22 August

Result: Match drawn

England

Batsman	1st Innings		2nd Innings	
G.Pullar b Davidson	8	c Grout b Mackay	13
R.Subba Row lbw b Gaunt	12	and b Benaud	137
M.C.Cowdrey c Grout b Davidson	0	(5) c Benaud b Mackay	3
P.B.H.May* c Lawry b Benaud	71	c O'Neill b Mackay	33
E.R.Dexter c Grout b Gaunt	24	c Gaunt b Mackay	0
K.F.Barrington c Grout b Gaunt	53	(3) c O'Neill b Benaud	83
J.T.Murray† c O'Neill b Mackay	27	c Grout b Benaud	40
G.A.R.Lock c Grout b Mackay	3	c Benaud b Mackay	0
D.A.Allen not out	22	not out	42
J.B.Statham b Davidson	18	not out	9
J.A.Flavell c Simpson b Davidson	14		
Extras (B 1, LB 2, W 1)	4	(B 6, LB 3, W 1)	10
	256	(8 wkts)	**370**

1/18 2/20 3/20 4/67 5/147
6/193 7/199 8/202 9/238

1/33 2/33 3/83 4/90
5/262 6/283 7/283 8/355

Bowling: *First Innings*—Davidson 34.1-8-83-4; Gaunt 24-3-53-3; Benaud 17-4-35-1; Mackay 39-14-75-2; Simpson 4-2-6-0. *Second Innings*—Davidson 29-7-67-0; Gaunt 22-7-33-0; Mackay 68-21-121-5; Benaud 51-18-113-3; Simpson 2-0-13-0; O'Neill 4-1-13-0; Harvey 1-1-0-0.

Australia

Batsman		Runs
W.M.Lawry c Murray b Statham		0
R.B.Simpson b Allen		40
R.N.Harvey lbw b Flavell		13
N.C.O'Neill c sub (M.J.Stewart) b Allen		117
P.J.P.Burge b Allen		181
B.C.Booth c Subba Row b Lock		71
K.D.Mackay c Murray b Flavell		5
A.K.Davidson lbw b Statham		17
R.Benaud* b Allen		6
A.T.W.Grout† not out		30
R.A.Gaunt b Statham		3
Extras (B 10, LB 1)		11
		494

1/0 2/15 3/88 4/211 5/396
6/401 7/441 8/455 9/472

Bowling: Statham 38.2-10-75-3; Flavell 31-5-105-2; Dexter 24-2-68-0; Allen 30-6-133-4; Lock 42-14-102-1.

Umpires: C.S.Elliott and F.S.Lee

AUSTRALIA v ENGLAND 1962-63 (Second Test)

At Melbourne Cricket Ground, 29, 31 December, 1, 2, 3 January

Result: England won by 7 wickets

Australia

Batsman	First Innings		Second Innings	
W.M.Lawry	c Smith b Trueman	52	b Dexter	57
R.B.Simpson	c Smith b Coldwell	38	b Trueman	14
N.C.O'Neill	c Graveney b Statham	19	c Cowdrey b Trueman	0
R.N.Harvey	b Coldwell	0	run out	10
P.J.P.Burge	lbw b Titmus	23	b Statham	14
B.C.Booth	c Barrington b Titmus	27	c Trueman b Statham	103
A.K.Davidson	c Smith b Trueman	40	c Smith b Titmus	17
K.D.Mackay	lbw b Titmus	49	lbw b Trueman	9
R.Benaud*	c Barrington b Titmus	36	c Cowdrey b Trueman	4
G.D.McKenzie	b Trueman	16	b Trueman	0
B.N.Jarman†	not out	10	not out	11
Extras	(B 2, LB 4)	6	(B 4, LB 5)	9
		316		248

1/62 2/111 3/112 4/112 5/155
6/164 7/237 8/289 9/294

1/30 2/30 3/46 4/69 5/161
6/193 7/212 8/228 9/228

Bowling: *First Innings*—Trueman 23-1-83-3; Statham 22-2-83-1; Coldwell 17-2-58-2; Barrington 6-0-23-0; Dexter 6-1-10-0; Titmus 15-2-43-4; Graveney 3-1-10-0. *Second Innings*—Trueman 20-1-62-5; Statham 23-1-52-2; Coldwell 25-2-60-0; Titmus 14-4-25-1; Dexter 9-2-18-1; Barrington 5-0-22-0.

England

Batsman	First Innings		Second Innings	
Rev.D.S.Sheppard	lbw b Davidson	0	run out	113
G.Pullar	b Davidson	11	c Jarman b McKenzie	5
E.R.Dexter*	c Simpson b Benaud	93	run out	52
M.C.Cowdrey	c Burge b McKenzie	113	not out	58
K.F.Barrington	lbw b McKenzie	35	not out	0
T.W.Graveney	run out	41		
F.J.Titmus	c Jarman b Davidson	15		
A.C.Smith†	not out	6		
F.S.Trueman	c O'Neill b Davidson	6		
J.B.Statham	b Davidson	1		
L.J.Coldwell	c Benaud b Davidson	1		
Extras	(B 4, LB 4, NB 1)	9	(B 5, LB 3, NB 1)	9
		331	(3 wkts)	237

1/0 2/19 3/194 4/254 5/255
6/292 7/315 8/324 9/327

1/5 2/129 3/223

Bowling: *First Innings*—Davidson 23.1-4-75-6; McKenzie 29-3-95-2; Mackay 6-2-17-0; Benaud 18-3-82-1; Simpson 7-1-34-0; O'Neill 5-1-19-0. *Second Innings*—Davidson 19-2-53-0; McKenzie 20-3-58-1; Benaud 14-1-69-0; Mackay 9-0-34-0; Simpson 2-0-10-0; Booth 0.2-0-4-0.

Umpires: C.J.Egar and W.Smyth

AUSTRALIA v ENGLAND 1962-63 (First Test)

At Woolloongabba, Brisbane, 30 November, 1, 3, 4, 5 December

Result: Match drawn

Australia

Batsman	First Innings		Second Innings	
W.M.Lawry	c Smith b Trueman	5	c Sheppard b Titmus	98
R.B.Simpson	c Trueman b Dexter	50	c Smith b Dexter	71
N.C.O'Neill	c Statham b Trueman	19	lbw b Statham	56
R.N.Harvey	b Statham	39	c Statham b Dexter	57
P.J.P.Burge	c Dexter b Trueman	6	not out	47
B.C.Booth	c Dexter b Titmus	112	not out	19
A.K.Davidson	c Trueman b Barrington	23		
K.D.Mackay	not out	86		
R.Benaud*	c Smith b Knight	51		
G.D.McKenzie	c and b Knight	2		
B.N.Jarman†	c Barrington b Knight	4		
Extras	(B 5, LB 1, NB 1)	7	(B 4, LB 10)	14
		404	(4 wkts dec.)	362

1/5 2/46 3/92 4/101 5/140
6/194 7/297 8/388 9/392

1/136 2/216
3/241 4/325

Bowling: *First Innings*—Statham 16-1-75-1; Trueman 18-0-76-3; Knight 17.5-2-65-3; Titmus 33-8-91-1; Dexter 10-0-46-1; Barrington 12-3-44-1. *Second Innings*—Trueman 15-0-59-0; Statham 16-1-67-1; Knight 14-1-63-0; Titmus 26-3-81-1; Dexter 16-0-78-2.

England

Batsman	First Innings		Second Innings	
G.Pullar	c and b Benaud	33	c and b Davidson	56
Rev.D.S.Sheppard	c McKenzie b Benaud	31	c Benaud b Davidson	53
E.R.Dexter*	c b Benaud	70	b McKenzie	99
M.C.Cowdrey	c Lawry b Simpson	21	c and b Benaud	9
K.F.Barrington	c Burge b Benaud	78	(6) c McKenzie b Davidson	23
A.C.Smith†	c Jarman b McKenzie	21		
P.H.Parfitt	c Davidson b McKenzie	80	(6) c Jarman b McKenzie	4
F.J.Titmus	c Simpson b Benaud	21	(7) not out	3
B.R.Knight	c Davidson b McKenzie	0	(8) not out	4
F.S.Trueman	c Jarman b McKenzie	19		
J.B.Statham	not out	8		
Extras	(B 4, LB 2, W 1)	7	(B 15, LB 10, NB 2)	27
		389	(6 wkts)	278

1/62 2/65 3/145 4/169 5/220
6/297 7/361 8/362 9/362

1/114 2/135 3/191
4/257 5/257 6/261

Bowling: *First Innings*—Davidson 21-4-77-0; McKenzie 20-4-115-6; Simpson 18-6-52-1; O'Neill 1-0-5-0. *Second Innings*—Davidson 20-6-43-3; McKenzie 20-4-61-2; Benaud 27-7-71-1; Mackay 7-0-28-0; Simpson 7-0-48-0.

Umpires: C.J.Egar and E.F.Wykes

AUSTRALIA v ENGLAND 1962-63 (Third Test)

At Sydney Cricket Ground, 11, 12, 14, 15 January

Result: Australia won by 8 wickets

England

Batsman	First Innings		Second Innings	
G.Pullar	c Benaud b Simpson	53	b Davidson	0
Rev.D.S.Sheppard	c McKenzie b Davidson	3	c Simpson b Davidson	12
E.R.Dexter*	c Lawry b Benaud	32	c Simpson b Davidson	11
M.C.Cowdrey	c Jarman b Simpson	85	c Simpson b Benaud	8
K.F.Barrington	lbw b Davidson	35	b McKenzie	21
P.H.Parfitt	c Lawry b Simpson	0	c O'Neill b McKenzie	28
F.J.Titmus	c Lawry b Simpson	32	c Booth b O'Neill	6
J.T.Murray†	lbw b Davidson	0	not out	3
F.S.Trueman	b Simpson	32	c Jarman b McKenzie	9
J.B.Statham	c Benaud b Simpson	0	b Davidson	2
L.J.Coldwell	not out	2	c Shepherd b Davidson	0
Extras	(LB 3, W 2)	5	(B 2, LB 2)	4
		279		**104**

1/4 2/65 3/132 4/201 5/203 6/221 7/221 8/272 9/272

1/0 2/20 3/25 4/37 5/53 6/70 7/90 8/100 9/104

Bowling: First Innings—Davidson 24.5-7-54-4; McKenzie 15-3-52-0; Guest 16-0-51-0; Benaud 16-2-60-1; Simpson 15-3-57-5. Second Innings—Davidson 10.6-2-25-5; McKenzie 14-3-26-3; Guest 2-0-8-0; Benaud 19-10-29-1; O'Neill 7-5-7-1; Simpson 4-2-5-0.

Australia

Batsman	First Innings		Second Innings	
W.M.Lawry	c Murray b Coldwell	8	b Trueman	8
R.B.Simpson	b Titmus	91	not out	34
R.N.Harvey	c Barrington b Titmus	64	lbw b Trueman	15
B.C.Booth	c Trueman b Titmus	16	not out	5
N.C.O'Neill	b Titmus	3		
B.K.Shepherd	not out	71		
B.N.Jarman†	run out	0		
A.K.Davidson	c Trueman b Titmus	15		
R.Benaud*	c and b Titmus	15		
G.D.McKenzie	lbw b Titmus	4		
C.E.J.Guest	b Statham	11		
Extras	(B 10, LB 11)	21	(B 5)	5
		319		**(2 wkts) 67**

1/14 2/174 3/177 4/187 5/212 6/216 7/242 8/274 9/280

1/28 2/54

Bowling: First Innings—Trueman 20-2-68-0; Statham 21.2-2-67-1; Coldwell 15-1-51-1; Titmus 37-14-79-7; Barrington 8-0-43-0. Second Innings—Statham 3-0-15-0; Trueman 6-1-20-2; Dexter 3.2-0-27-0.

Umpires: L.P.Rowan and W.Smyth

AUSTRALIA v ENGLAND 1962-63 (Fourth Test)

At Adelaide Oval, 25, 26, 28, 29, 30 January

Result: Match drawn

Australia

Batsman	First Innings		Second Innings	
W.M.Lawry	b Illingworth	10	c Graveney b Trueman	16
R.B.Simpson	c Smith b Statham	0	c Smith b Dexter	71
R.N.Harvey	c Statham b Dexter	154	c Barrington b Statham	6
B.C.Booth	c Cowdrey b Titmus	34	c Smith b Dexter	77
N.C.O'Neill	c Cowdrey b Dexter	100	c Cowdrey b Trueman	23
A.K.Davidson	c Statham	46	(10) b Statham	2
B.K.Shepherd	c Trueman b Statham	10	(6) c Titmus b Dexter	13
K.D.Mackay	c Smith b Trueman	1	(7) c Graveney b Trueman	3
R.Benaud*	b Dexter	16	(8) c Barrington b Trueman	48
G.D.McKenzie	c Sheppard b Titmus	15	(9) c Smith b Statham	13
A.T.W.Grout†	not out	0	not out	16
Extras	(LB 5, W 1)	6	(B 1, LB 4)	5
		393		**293**

1/2 2/16 3/101 4/295 5/302 6/331 7/336 8/366 9/383

1/27 2/37 3/170 4/175 5/199 6/205 7/228 8/254 9/258

Bowling: First Innings—Trueman 19-1-54-1; Statham 21-5-66-3; Illingworth 20-3-85-1; Dexter 23-1-94-3; Titmus 20.1-2-88-2. Second Innings—Trueman 23.3-3-60-4; Statham 21-2-71-3; Dexter 17-0-65-3; Titmus 24-5-69-0; Illingworth 5-1-23-0.

England

Batsman	First Innings		Second Innings	
G.Pullar	b McKenzie	9	c Simpson b McKenzie	3
Rev.D.S.Sheppard	st Grout b Benaud	30	c Grout b Mackay	1
K.F.Barrington	b Simpson	63	not out	132
M.C.Cowdrey	c Grout b McKenzie	13	run out	32
E.R.Dexter*	c Grout b McKenzie	61	c Simpson b Benaud	10
T.W.Graveney	c Booth b McKenzie	22	not out	36
F.J.Titmus	not out	59		
R.Illingworth	c Grout b McKenzie	12		
A.C.Smith†	c Lawry b Mackay	13		
F.S.Trueman	c Benaud b Mackay	38		
J.B.Statham	b Mackay	1		
Extras	(B 5, LB 5)	10	(B 4, W 5)	9
		331		**(4 wkts) 223**

1/17 2/84 3/117 4/119 5/165 6/226 7/246 8/275 9/331

1/2 2/4 3/98 4/122

Bowling: First Innings—Davidson 3.4-0-30-0; McKenzie 33-3-89-5; Mackay 27.6-8-80-3; Benaud 18-3-82-1; Simpson 8-1-40-1. Second Innings—McKenzie 14-0-64-1; Mackay 8-2-13-1; Benaud 15-3-38-1; O'Neill 8-0-49-0; Simpson 10-1-50-0; Lawry 1-1-0-0; Harvey 1-1-0-0.

Umpires: C.J.Egar and A.Mackley

AUSTRALIA v ENGLAND 1962-63 (Fifth Test)

At Sydney Cricket Ground, 15, 16, 18, 19, 20 February

Result: Match drawn

England

Batsman	First Innings		Second Innings	
Rev.D.S.Sheppard	c and b Hawke	19	c Harvey b Benaud	68
M.C.Cowdrey	c Harvey b Davidson	2	(5) c Benaud b Davidson	53
K.F.Barrington	c Harvey b Benaud	101	c Grout b McKenzie	94
E.R.Dexter*	c Simpson b O'Neill	47	st Grout b Benaud	6
T.W.Graveney	c Harvey b McKenzie	14	(6) c and b Davidson	3
R.Illingworth	c Grout b Davidson	27	(2) c Hawke b Benaud	18
F.J.Titmus	c Grout b Hawke	34	not out	12
F.S.Trueman	c Harvey b Benaud	30	c Harvey b McKenzie	8
A.C.Smith†	b Simpson	6	c Simpson b Davidson	1
D.A.Allen	c Benaud b Davidson	14		
J.B.Statham	not out	17		
Extras	(B 4, LB 6)	10	(B 1, LB 4)	5
		321	(8 wkts dec.)	268

1/5 2/39 3/129 4/177 5/189 6/224 7/276 8/286 9/293

1/40 2/137 3/145 4/239 5/247 6/249 7/257 8/268

Bowling: *First Innings*—Davidson 25.6-4-43-3; McKenzie 27-4-57-1; Hawke 20-1-51-2; Benaud 34-9-71-2; Simpson 18-4-51-1; O'Neill 10-0-38-1. *Second Innings*—Davidson 28-1-80-3; McKenzie 8-0-39-2; Hawke 9-0-38-0; Benaud 30-8-71-3; Simpson 4-0-22-0; Harvey 3-0-13-0.

Australia

Batsman	First Innings		Second Innings	
W.M.Lawry	c Smith b Trueman	11	not out	45
R.B.Simpson	c Trueman b Titmus	32	b Trueman	0
B.C.Booth	b Titmus	11	(5) b Allen	0
N.C.O'Neill	c Graveney b Allen	73	c Smith b Allen	17
P.J.P.Burge	lbw b Titmus	103	(6) not out	52
R.N.Harvey	c sub (P.H.Parfitt) b Statham	22	(3) b Allen	28
A.K.Davidson	c Allen b Dexter	15		
R.Benaud*	c Graveney b Allen	57		
G.D.McKenzie	c and b Titmus	0		
N.J.N.Hawke	c Graveney b Titmus	14		
A.T.W.Grout	not out	0		
Extras	(B 6, LB 5)	11	(B 4, LB 6)	10
		349	(4 wkts)	152

1/28 2/50 3/71 4/180 5/231 6/271 7/299 8/303 9/347

1/0 2/39 3/70 4/70

Bowling: *First Innings*—Trueman 11-0-33-1; Statham 18-1-76-1; Dexter 7-1-24-1; Titmus 47.2-9-103-5; Allen 43-15-87-2; Illingworth 5-1-15-0. *Second Innings*—Trueman 3-0-6-1; Statham 4-1-8-0; Dexter 4-1-11-0; Allen 19-11-26-3; Titmus 20-7-37-0; Barrington 8-3-22-0; Graveney 4-0-24-0; Illingworth 10-5-8-0.

Umpires: C.J.Egar and L.P.Rowan

AUSTRALIA v SOUTH AFRICA 1963-64 (First Test)

At Woolloongabba, Brisbane, 6, 7, 9 (no play), 10, 11 December

Result: Match drawn

Australia

Batsman	First Innings		Second Innings	
W.M.Lawry	c R.G.Pollock b Barlow	43	not out	87
R.B.Simpson	c Waite b P.M.Pollock	12	c sub (K.C.Bland) b Partridge	34
N.C.O'Neill	c Barlow b P.M.Pollock	82	not out	19
P.J.P.Burge	run out	13		
B.C.Booth	c Barlow b P.M.Pollock	169		
R.Benaud*	lbw b Goddard	43		
G.D.McKenzie	c P.M.Pollock b Goddard	39		
T.R.Veivers	c Goddard b P.M.Pollock	14		
A.T.W.Grout	c Seymour b P.M.Pollock	6		
I.Meckiff	b P.M.Pollock	7		
A.N.Connolly	not out	1		
Extras	(B 1, LB 6)	6	(LB 4)	4
		435	(1 wkt dec.)	144

1/39 2/73 3/88 4/208 5/310 6/394 7/415 8/427 9/434

1/83

Bowling: *First Innings*—P.M.Pollock 22.6-0-95-6; Partridge 25-3-87-0; Barlow 9-0-71-1; Seymour 11-0-39-0; Pithey 23-6-85-0; Goddard 24-6-52-2. *Second Innings*—P.M.Pollock 6-0-26-0; Partridge 17-1-50-1; Goddard 7-0-34-0; Pithey 5-0-30-0.

South Africa

Batsman	First Innings		Second Innings	
T.L.Goddard*	c Meckiff b Benaud	52	not out	8
E.J.Barlow	b Benaud	114	c Simpson b McKenzie	0
P.R.Carlstein	c and b Benaud	0	not out	1
R.G.Pollock	b McKenzie	25		
D.T.Lindsay	lbw b Benaud	17		
J.H.B.Waite†	lbw b Connolly	66		
P.L.van der Merwe	b O'Neill	17		
D.B.Pithey	c Meckiff b Veivers	18		
P.M.Pollock	lbw b Benaud	8		
M.A.Seymour	b Simpson	10		
J.T.Partridge	not out	3		
Extras	(B 3, LB 5, NB 8)	16	(B 4)	4
		346	(1 wkt)	13

1/74 2/78 3/120 4/157 5/239 6/272 7/321 8/325 9/335

1/1

Bowling: *First Innings*—McKenzie 23-1-88-1; Meckiff 1-0-8-0; Connolly 19-4-46-1; Veivers 34-15-48-1; Benaud 33-10-68-5; Simpson 18.5-5-52-1; O'Neill 7-0-20-1. *Second Innings*—McKenzie 3.3-1-3-1; Connolly 1-0-2-0; Benaud 2-1-4-0.

Umpires: C.J.Egar and L.P.Rowan

AUSTRALIA v SOUTH AFRICA 1963-64 (Third Test)

At Sydney Cricket Ground, 10, 11, 13, 14, 15 January

Result: Match drawn

Australia

R.B.Simpson* c Goddard b P.M.Pollock	58	lbw b Halse	31
W.M.Lawry b Partridge	23	c R.G.Pollock b Goddard	89
N.C.O'Neill c Goddard b Halse	3	c Barlow b Partridge	88
P.J.P.Burge b Partridge	36	c Waite b P.M.Pollock	13
B.C.Booth b Partridge	75	b Partridge	16
B.K.Shepherd c Waite b P.M.Pollock	0	c Waite b Partridge	11
R.Benaud c Bland b P.M.Pollock	43	c D.B.Pithey b P.M.Pollock	90
G.D.McKenzie c Goddard b Partridge	3	c van der Merwe b Partridge	76
N.J.N.Hawke c Goddard b P.M.Pollock	2	not out	6
A.T.W.Grout† c Partridge b P.M.Pollock	1	c Bland b Partridge	8
A.N.Connolly not out	3		
Extras (B 5, LB 6, NB 1, W 1)	13	(B 8, LB 8, NB 5, W 1)	22
	260	(9 wkts dec.)	450

1/59 2/66 3/108 4/128 5/129 6/229 7/238 8/248 9/256

1/58 2/198 3/235 4/235 5/259 6/264 7/424 8/436 9/450

Bowling: *First Innings*—P.M.Pollock 18-2-83-5; Partridge 19.6-2-84-4; Goddard 10-1-24-0; Halse 11-1-36-1; Bland 2-0-7-0; Barlow 2-0-9-0. *Second Innings*—P.M.Pollock 24-0-129-2; Partridge 32.5-4-123-5; Halse 15-2-58-1; Bland 1-0-7-0; Barlow 1-0-5-0; D.B.Pithey 16-1-86-0; Goddard 11-3-20-1.

South Africa

T.L.Goddard* c Connolly b Benaud	80	lbw b Simpson	84
E.J.Barlow c Grout b Connolly	6	c Simpson b Hawke	35
A.J.Pithey c Grout b Hawke	9	not out (6)	53
R.G.Pollock c McKenzie b Connolly	122	c Grout b Hawke	42
J.H.B.Waite† b McKenzie	8		
P.L.van der Merwe b McKenzie	0	not out (7)	13
K.C.Bland c McKenzie b Benaud	51	c Benaud b O'Neill (5)	85
D.B.Pithey c Lawry b Benaud	10	b McKenzie (3)	7
P.M.Pollock c Grout b Hawke	1		
J.T.Partridge b McKenzie	7		
C.G.Halse not out	1		
Extras (B 3, LB 4)	7	(B 2, LB 5)	7
	302	(5 wkts)	326

1/10 2/58 3/137 4/162 5/162 6/244 7/277 8/278 9/300

1/57 2/67 3/141 4/201 5/291

Bowling: *First Innings*—McKenzie 19-2-66-2; Hawke 18-1-56-2; Simpson 9-2-32-0; Benaud 24.1-4-55-3; O'Neill 3-0-16-0. *Second Innings*—McKenzie 14-2-61-1; Connolly 13-0-41-0; Benaud 30-8-61-0; Hawke 19-5-43-2; O'Neill 16-1-59-1; Simpson 23-8-48-1; Booth 1-0-3-0; Shepherd 1-0-3-0.

Umpires: C.J.Egar and L.P.Rowan

AUSTRALIA v SOUTH AFRICA 1963-64 (Second Test)

At Melbourne Cricket Ground, 1, 2, 3, 4, 6 January

Result: Australia won by 8 wickets

South Africa

T.L.Goddard* c Grout b McKenzie	17	lbw b Hawke	8
E.J.Barlow c Connolly b McKenzie	109	run out	54
A.J.Pithey lbw b Connolly	21	c Grout b Connolly	76
R.G.Pollock c Simpson b McKenzie	16	c Martin b Connolly	2
J.H.B.Waite† c Grout b Hawke	14	b McKenzie	77
P.L.van der Merwe st Grout b Martin	14	c Grout b Martin	31
K.C.Bland run out	50	c and b Martin	22
D.B.Pithey c Grout b McKenzie	0	c Martin b Hawke	4
P.M.Pollock c Simpson b Martin	14	(10) b Hawke	0
M.A.Seymour not out	7	(11) not out	11
J.T.Partridge run out	9	(9) b McKenzie	12
Extras (LB 3)	3	(B 2, LB 3, NB 2, W 2)	9
	274		306

1/26 2/74 3/100 4/129 5/179 6/201 7/201 8/256 9/256

1/35 2/83 3/83 4/213 5/233 6/273 7/282 8/282 9/282

Bowling: *First Innings*—McKenzie 19-1-82-4; Hawke 20-2-77-1; Connolly 18-2-62-1; Martin 16-3-44-2; Veivers 5-1-6-0. *Second Innings*—McKenzie 25-1-81-2; Connolly 18-2-49-2; Hawke 19-1-53-3; Martin 27-4-83-2; Simpson 12-2-31-0.

Australia

W.M.Lawry c sub (P.R.Carlstein) b Partridge	157	b Partridge	20
I.R.Redpath b Partridge	97	c van der Merwe b Barlow	25
R.B.Simpson* b P.M.Pollock	23	not out	55
P.J.P.Burge c Bland b P.M.Pollock	96	not out	26
B.K.Shepherd c D.B.Pithey b Barlow	3		
A.T.W.Grout† c Waite b P.M.Pollock	19		
T.R.Veivers c Waite b Partridge	2		
G.D.McKenzie c Partridge b Seymour	24		
N.J.N.Hawke b Barlow	17		
J.W.Martin c D.B.Pithey b Partridge	0		
A.N.Connolly not out	9		
Extras (B 1, LB 2, NB 6)	9	(B 5, LB 2, NB 2, W 1)	10
	447	(2 wkts)	136

1/219 2/222 3/270 4/291 5/301 6/340 7/357 8/413 9/439

1/33 2/75

Bowling: *First Innings*—P.M.Pollock 20.5-1-98-3; Partridge 34.4-4-108-4; Bland 11-2-35-0; Goddard 21-2-70-0; D.B.Pithey 5-1-20-0; Seymour 19-2-56-1; Barlow 7.6-0-51-2. *Second Innings*—Partridge 17-1-49-1; Barlow 11-0-49-1; Goddard 1-1-0-0; D.B.Pithey 6-0-18-0; Bland 2-0-6-0; van der Merwe 0.1-0-4-0.

Umpires: C.J.Egar and L.P.Rowan

AUSTRALIA v SOUTH AFRICA 1963-64 (Fourth Test)

At Adelaide Oval, 24, 25, 27, 28, 29 January
Result: South Africa won by 10 wickets

Australia

Batsman	1st innings		2nd innings	
R.B.Simpson* b Goddard	78	c Lindsay b Halse	34	
W.M.Lawry c Partridge b P.M.Pollock	14	c Goddard b P.M.Pollock	38	
N.C.O'Neill c Goddard b P.M.Pollock	0	c Partridge b Halse	66	
P.J.P.Burge c Halse b P.M.Pollock	91	run out	20	
B.C.Booth c Lindsay b Goddard	58	lbw b P.M.Pollock	24	
B.K.Shepherd lbw b Goddard	70	c Lindsay b Barlow	78	
R.Benaud b Partridge	7	b Barlow	34	
G.D.McKenzie c Lindsay b Goddard	12	c and b Barlow	4	
A.T.W.Grout† c P.M.Pollock b Goddard	0	(10) c Pithey b Halse	23	
N.J.N.Hawke not out	0	(9) c Carlstein b Seymour	0	
R.A.Gaunt run out	1	not out	2	
Extras (B 1, LB 8, NB 5)	14	(LB 4, NB 3, W 1)	8	
	345		331	

1/35 2/37 3/141 4/225 5/279 6/290 7/333 8/333 9/344
1/72 2/81 3/125 4/178 5/210 6/301 7/301 8/302 9/310

Bowling: First Innings—P.M.Pollock 21-1-96-3; Partridge 22-4-76-1; Halse 13-1-54-0; Seymour 12-2-38-0; Goddard 24.6-4-60-5; Bland 1-0-7-0. Second Innings—P.M.Pollock 14-1-73-2; Partridge 17-3-76-0; Goddard Halse 13.3-0-50-3; Seymour 19-1-54-1; Barlow 5-2-6-3.

South Africa

Batsman	1st innings	2nd innings
T.L.Goddard* b Hawke	34	not out ... 34
E.J.Barlow lbw b Hawke	201	not out ... 47
A.J.Pithey c Grout b Hawke	0	
R.G.Pollock b Hawke	175	
K.C.Bland c Grout b Gaunt	33	
P.R.Carlstein c Benaud b Gaunt	37	
D.T.Lindsay† b Simpson	41	
P.M.Pollock c Benaud b Hawke	21	
M.A.Seymour c Simpson b Hawke	3	
J.T.Partridge b McKenzie	6	
C.G.Halse not out	19	
Extras (B 7, LB 8, NB 7, W 3)	25	(W 1) ... 1
	595	(0 wkts) 82

1/70 2/70 3/411 4/437 5/500 6/501 7/559 8/568 9/575

Bowling: First Innings—McKenzie 30.1-2-156-1; Gaunt 24-2-115-2; Hawke 39-5-139-6; Benaud 20-1-101-0; Simpson 10-1-59-1. Second Innings—Gaunt 4-0-22-0; McKenzie 4-0-22-0; Hawke 6-0-20-0; Benaud 3-1-17-0.

Umpires: C.J.Egar and L.P.Rowan

AUSTRALIA v SOUTH AFRICA 1963-64 (Fifth Test)

At Sydney Cricket Ground, 7, 8, 10, 11, 12 February
Result: Match drawn

Australia

Batsman	1st innings		2nd innings	
W.M.Lawry b Halse	13	c Waite b P.M.Pollock	12	
R.B.Simpson* c Lindsay b Partridge	28	lbw b Partridge	31	
N.C.O'Neill b P.M.Pollock	21	(7) b P.M.Pollock	6	
P.J.P.Burge b Partridge	56	c Partridge b Seymour	39	
B.C.Booth not out	102	c sub (P.R.Carlstein) b Seymour	87	
B.K.Shepherd lbw b Partridge	1	c Bland b Goddard	12	
R.Benaud b Goddard	11	c sub (P.R.Carlstein) b Seymour	3	
T.R.Veivers b Partridge	43	c Barlow b Goddard	39	
G.D.McKenzie b Partridge	0	c Bland b P.M.Pollock	0	
N.J.N.Hawke c Lindsay b Partridge	0	(11) not out	16	
A.T.W.Grout† c Waite b Partridge	29	(10) c Barlow b Partridge	14	
Extras (LB 2, NB 5)	7	(B 5, LB 4, NB 2)	11	
	311		270	

1/42 2/44 3/103 4/142 5/144 6/179 7/263 8/263 9/265
1/29 2/49 3/132 4/152 5/181 6/189 7/207 8/209 9/225

Bowling: First Innings—P.M.Pollock 22-5-75-1; Partridge 31.1-6-91-7; Halse 14-3-40-1; Goddard 16-1-67-1; Barlow 9-1-31-0. Second Innings—P.M.Pollock 11-1-35-3; Partridge 32-5-85-2; Halse 7-0-22-0; Barlow 1-0-8-0; Seymour 38-9-80-3; Goddard 24.7-10-29-2.

South Africa

Batsman	1st innings	2nd innings
T.L.Goddard* c Grout b Veivers	93	not out ... 44
E.J.Barlow c Benaud b O'Neill	5	not out ... 32
A.J.Pithey c Grout b McKenzie	49	
R.G.Pollock c and b Veivers	17	
K.C.Bland c Booth b Benaud	126	
J.H.B.Waite† c Simpson b McKenzie	19	
D.T.Lindsay c sub (A.N.Connolly) b Benaud	65	
P.M.Pollock c Lawry b Benaud	6	
M.A.Seymour c Benaud b McKenzie	0	
J.T.Partridge lbw b Benaud	6	
C.G.Halse not out	10	
Extras (B 4, LB 4, NB 6, W 1)	15	
	411	(0 wkts) 76

1/18 2/142 3/157 4/182 5/223 6/341 7/365 8/368 9/389

Bowling: First Innings—McKenzie 37-4-110-3; Hawke 22-4-69-0; O'Neill 2-0-2-1; Benaud 49-10-118-4; Veivers 35-5-97-2. Second Innings—McKenzie 4-0-16-0; Hawke 4-0-16-0; Veivers 8-0-19-0; Benaud 8-0-19-0.

Umpires: C.J.Egar and L.P.Rowan

ENGLAND v AUSTRALIA 1964 (First Test)

At Trent Bridge, Nottingham, 4, 5, 6 (no play), 8, 9 June

Result: Match drawn

England

G.Boycott c Simpson b Corling	48	lbw b McKenzie	17
F.J.Titmus c Redpath b Hawke	16	c O'Neill b McKenzie (1)	68
E.R.Dexter* c Grout b Hawke	9	b McKenzie (3)	33
M.C.Cowdrey b Hawke	32	lbw b Corling (4)	33
K.F.Barrington c Lawry b Veivers	22	c and b Veivers	19
P.J.Sharpe not out	35	c Hawke b Veivers (5)	19
J.M.Parks† c Booth b Veivers	15	c Grout b McKenzie (7)	4
F.S.Trueman c Simpson b Veivers	0	lbw b McKenzie (8)	3
D.A.Allen c Grout b McKenzie	21	not out	0
L.J.Coldwell not out	0	c Parks b Coldwell	0
J.A.Flavell		c Booth b Corling (9)	7
Extras (B 5, LB 11, NB 2)	18	(B 2, LB 2, NB 3, W 1)	8

1/38 2/70 3/90 4/135 5/141 (8 wkts dec.) 216
6/164 7/165 8/212

1/90 2/95 3/147 (9 wkts dec.) 193
4/174 5/179 6/180 7/186 8/187
9/193

Bowling: *First Innings*—McKenzie 28-7-53-1; Corling 23-7-48-3; Hawke 35-15-68-3; Veivers 16-2-39-3. *Second Innings*—McKenzie 24-5-53-5; Hawke 19-5-53-0; Corling 15.5-4-54-2; Veivers 8-0-25-2.

Australia

W.M.Lawry c Barrington b Coldwell	11	run out	3
I.R.Redpath b Trueman	6	c Parks b Flavell	2
N.C.O'Neill b Allen	26	retired hurt	24
P.J.P.Burge lbw b Trueman	31	not out	4
B.C.Booth run out	0	not out	6
R.B.Simpson* c Barrington b Titmus	50		
T.R.Veivers c Trueman b Flavell	8		
G.D.McKenzie c Parks b Coldwell	4		
N.J.N.Hawke not out	10		
A.T.W.Grout† c Parks b Coldwell	13		
G.E.Corling b Trueman	3		
Extras (LB 1, NB 5),	6	(NB 1)	1

1/8 2/37 3/57 4/61 5/91 168
6/118 7/137 8/141 9/165

1/3 2/25 (2 wkts) 40

Bowling: *First Innings*—Trueman 20.3-3-58-3; Coldwell 22-3-48-3; Allen 16-8-22-1; Flavell 16-3-28-1; Titmus 4-1-6-1. *Second Innings*—Trueman 5-0-28-0; Flavell 4.2-0-11-1.

Umpires: J.S.Buller and C.S.Elliott

ENGLAND v AUSTRALIA 1964 (Second Test)

At Lord's, London, 18 (no play), 19 (no play), 20, 22, 23 June

Result: Match drawn

Australia

W.M.Lawry b Trueman	4	c Dexter b Gifford	20
I.R.Redpath c Parfitt b Coldwell	30	lbw b Titmus	36
N.C.O'Neill c Titmus b Dexter	26	c Parfitt b Trueman	22
P.J.P.Burge lbw b Dexter	1	c Parfitt b Titmus	59
B.C.Booth lbw b Trueman	14	not out	2
R.B.Simpson* c Parfitt b Trueman	54	not out	15
T.R.Veivers b Gifford	10		
G.D.McKenzie b Trueman	14		
A.T.W.Grout† c Dexter b Gifford	5		
N.J.N.Hawke not out	0		
G.E.Corling b Trueman	18		
Extras (B 8, LB 5, NB 5)		(B 8, LB 4, NB 2)	14

1/8 2/46 3/58 4/84 5/84 176
6/88 7/132 8/163 9/167

1/35 2/76 3/143 4/148(4 wkts) 168

Bowling: *First Innings*—Trueman 25-8-48-5; Coldwell 23-7-51-1; Gifford 12-6-14-2; Dexter 7-1-16-2; Titmus 17-6-29-0. *Second Innings*—Trueman 18-6-52-1; Coldwell 19-4-59-0; Dexter 3-0-5-0; Gifford 17-9-17-1; Titmus 17-7-21-2.

England

E.R.Dexter* b McKenzie	2	
J.H.Edrich c Redpath b McKenzie	120	
M.C.Cowdrey c Burge b Hawke	10	
K.F.Barrington lbw b McKenzie	5	
P.H.Parfitt lbw b Corling	20	
P.J.Sharpe lbw b Hawke	35	
J.M.Parks† c Simpson b Hawke	12	
F.J.Titmus b Corling	15	
F.S.Trueman b Corling	8	
N.Gifford c Hawke b Corling	5	
L.J.Coldwell not out	6	
Extras (LB 7, NB 1)	8	

1/2 2/33 3/42 4/83 5/138 246
6/170 7/227 8/229 9/235

Bowling: McKenzie 26-8-69-3; Corling 27.3-9-60-4; Hawke 16-4-41-3; Veivers 9-4-17-0; Simpson 21-8-51-0.

Umpires: J.S.Buller and J.F.Crapp

ENGLAND v AUSTRALIA 1964 (Fourth Test)

At Old Trafford, Manchester, 23, 24, 25, 27, 28 July
Result: Match drawn

England

	not out	0
	not out	4
	(0 wkts)	4

Australia

W.M.Lawry run out		106
R.B.Simpson* c Parks b Price		311
I.R.Redpath lbw b Cartwright		19
N.C.O'Neill b Price		47
P.J.P.Burge c Price b Cartwright		34
B.C.Booth c and b Price		98
T.R.Veivers c Edrich b Rumsey		22
A.T.W.Grout† c Dexter b Rumsey		0
G.D.McKenzie not out		0
N.J.N.Hawke		
G.E.Corling		
Extras (B 1, LB 9, NB 9)		19

1/201 2/233 3/318 4/382 5/604 (8 wkts dec.) 656
6/646 7/652 8/656

Bowling: *First Innings*—Rumsey 35.5-4-99-2; Price 45-4-183-3; Cartwright 77-32-118-2; Titmus 44-14-100-0; Dexter 4-0-12-0; Mortimore 49-13-122-0; Boycott 1-0-3-0. *Second Innings*—Barrington 1-0-4-0; Titmus 1-1-0-0.

England

G.Boycott b McKenzie		58
J.H.Edrich c Redpath b McKenzie		6
E.R.Dexter* b Veivers		174
K.F.Barrington lbw b McKenzie		256
P.H.Parfitt c Grout b McKenzie		12
J.M.Parks† c Hawke b Veivers		60
F.J.Titmus c Simpson b McKenzie		9
J.B.Mortimore c Burge b McKenzie		12
T.W.Cartwright b McKenzie		4
J.S.E.Price b Veivers		1
F.E.Rumsey not out		3
Extras (B 5, LB 11)		16

1/15 2/126 3/372 4/417 5/560 611
6/589 7/594 8/602 9/607

Bowling: McKenzie 60-15-153-7; Corling 46-11-96-0; Hawke 63-28-95-0; Simpson 19-4-59-0; Veivers 95.1-36-155-3; O'Neill 10-0-37-0.

Umpires: J.S.Buller and W.F.Price

ENGLAND v AUSTRALIA 1964 (Third Test)

At Headingley, Leeds, 2, 3, 4, 6 July
Result: Australia won by 7 wickets

England

G.Boycott c Simpson b Corling	38	c Simpson b Corling		4
J.H.Edrich c Veivers b McKenzie	3	c Grout b McKenzie		32
E.R.Dexter* c Grout b McKenzie	66	(5) c Redpath b Veivers		17
K.F.Barrington b McKenzie	29	lbw b Veivers		85
P.H.Parfitt b Hawke	32	(3) c Redpath b Hawke		6
K.Taylor c Grout b Hawke	9	(8) b Veivers		15
J.M.Parks† c Redpath b Hawke	68	(6) c Booth b McKenzie		23
F.J.Titmus c Burge b McKenzie	3	(9) c Cowper b Corling		14
F.S.Trueman c Cowper b Hawke	4	(10) not out		12
N.Gifford not out	1	(7) b McKenzie		5
J.A.Flavell c Redpath b Hawke	5	b McKenzie		15
Extras (LB 9, NB 1)	10	(B 6, LB 6, NB 2, W 1)		

1/17 2/74 3/129 4/138 5/163		268
6/215 7/232 8/260 9/263		
1/13 2/88 3/145 4/156 5/169		229
6/184 7/192 8/199 9/212		

Bowling: *First Innings*—McKenzie 26-7-74-4; Hawke 31.3-11-75-4; Corling 24-7-50-1; Veivers 17-3-35-0; Simpson 5-0-24-0. *Second Innings*—McKenzie 28-8-53-3; Corling 17.5-6-52-3; Hawke 13-1-28-1; Veivers 30-12-70-3; Simpson 1-0-11-0.

Australia

W.M.Lawry run out	78	c Gifford b Titmus		1
R.B.Simpson* b Gifford	24	c Barrington b Titmus		30
I.R.Redpath b Gifford	20	not out		58
P.J.P.Burge c sub (A.Rees) b Trueman	160	b Titmus		8
B.C.Booth st Parks b Titmus	4	not out		12
R.M.Cowper b Trueman	2			
T.R.Veivers c Parks b Titmus	8			
G.D.McKenzie b Titmus	0			
N.J.N.Hawke c Parfitt b Trueman	37			
A.T.W.Grout† lbw b Titmus	37			
G.E.Corling not out	1			
Extras (B 1, LB 8, NB 6, W 2)	17	(B 1, LB 1)		2

1/50 2/124 3/129 4/154 5/157		389
6/178 7/178 8/283 9/372		
1/3 2/45 3/64	(3 wkts)	111

Bowling: *First Innings*—Trueman 24.3-2-98-3; Flavell 29-5-97-0; Gifford 34-15-62-2; Dexter 19-5-40-0; Titmus 50-24-69-4; Taylor 2-0-6-0. *Second Innings*—Trueman 7-0-28-1; Titmus 27-19-25-2; Gifford 20-5-47-0; Dexter 3-0-9-0.

Umpires: C.S.Elliott and W.F.Price

ENGLAND v AUSTRALIA 1964 (Fifth Test)

At Kennington Oval, London, 13, 14, 15, 17, 18 (no play) August

Result: Match drawn

England

Batsman	First Innings	Runs	Second Innings	Runs
G.Boycott	b Hawke	30	c Redpath b Simpson	113
R.W.Barber	b Hawke	24	lbw b McKenzie	29
E.R.Dexter*	c Booth b Hawke	23	c Simpson b McKenzie	25
M.C.Cowdrey	c Grout b McKenzie	20	(5) not out	93
K.F.Barrington	c Simpson b Hawke	47	(6) not out	54
P.H.Parfitt	b McKenzie	3		
J.M.Parks†	c Simpson b Corling	10		
F.J.Titmus	c Grout b Hawke	8	(4) b McKenzie	56
F.S.Trueman	c Redpath b Hawke	14		
T.W.Cartwright	c Grout b McKenzie	0		
J.S.E.Price	not out	0		
Extras	(LB 3)	3	(B 6, LB 4, NB 1)	11
		182	(4 wkts)	381

1/44 2/61 3/82 4/111 5/117 6/141 7/160 8/173 9/174

1/80 2/120 3/200 4/255

Bowling: First Innings—McKenzie 26-6-87-3; Corling 14-2-32-1; Hawke 25.4-8-47-6; Veivers 6-1-13-0. Second Innings—McKenzie 38-5-112-3; Corling 25-4-65-0; Hawke 39-8-89-0; Veivers 47-15-90-0; Simpson 14-7-14-1.

Australia

Batsman	Dismissal	Runs
R.B.Simpson*	c Dexter b Cartwright	24
W.M.Lawry	c Trueman b Dexter	94
N.C.O'Neill	c Parfitt b Cartwright	11
P.J.P.Burge	lbw b Titmus	25
B.C.Booth	c Trueman b Price	74
I.R.Redpath	b Trueman	45
A.T.W.Grout†	not out	20
T.R.Veivers	not out	67
G.D.McKenzie	c Cowdrey b Trueman	0
N.J.N.Hawke	c Cowdrey b Trueman	14
G.E.Corling	c Parfitt b Trueman	0
Extras	(B 4, LB 1)	5
		379

1/45 2/57 3/96 4/202 5/245 6/279 7/343 8/343 9/367

Bowling: Trueman 33.3-6-87-4; Price 21-2-67-1; Cartwright 62-23-110-3; Titmus 42-20-51-1; Barber 6-1-23-0; Dexter 13-1-36-1.

Umpires: J.F.Crapp and C.S.Elliott

INDIA v AUSTRALIA 1964-65 (First Test)

At Corporation Stadium, Madras, 2, 3, 4, 6, 7 October

Result: Australia won by 139 runs

Australia

Batsman	First Innings	Runs	Second Innings	Runs
W.M.Lawry	b Nadkarni	62	c sub (R.F.Surti) b Nadkarni	41
R.B.Simpson*	st Indrajitsinhji b Durani	30	run out	77
N.C.O'Neill	b Durani	40	b Nadkarni	0
P.J.P.Burge	b Nadkarni	20	lbw b Nadkarni	60
B.C.Booth	lbw b Nadkarni	8	c Indrajitsinhji b Durani	29
J.W.Martin	c Indrajitsinhji b Kripal Singh	20	(8) c Nadkarni b Ranjane	39
I.R.Redpath	c Hanumant Singh b Nadkarni	10	(6) c Indrajitsinhji b Nadkarni	0
T.R.Veivers	b Kripal Singh	0	(7) c Pataudi b Nadkarni	74
G.D.McKenzie	not out	8	c Sardesai b Ranjane	27
A.T.W.Grout†	c Jaisimha b Nadkarni	0	c Hanumant Singh b Nadkarni	12
N.J.N.Hawke	b Kripal Singh	0	not out	1
Extras	(LB 6, NB 7)	13	(B 15, LB 11, NB 11)	37
		211		397

1/66 2/127 3/139 4/161 5/174 6/203 7/203 8/203 9/209

1/91 2/91 3/175 4/228 5/232 6/237 7/301 8/374 9/392

Bowling: First Innings—Ranjane 7-0-30-0; Jaisimha 4-1-13-0; Durani 21-5-68-2; Kripal Singh 18-5-43-3; Borde 4-2-13-0; Nadkarni 18-6-31-5. Second Innings—Ranjane 12-1-53-2; Jaisimha 9-2-13-0; Nadkarni 54.4-21-91-6; Durani 40-9-102-1; Kripal Singh 38-13-91-0; Borde 5-2-10-0.

India

Batsman	First Innings	Runs	Second Innings	Runs
M.L.Jaisimha	lbw b McKenzie	29	b McKenzie	0
K.S.Indrajitsinhji†	c Grout b Hawke	4	b Hawke	0
D.N.Sardesai	b McKenzie	0	c Redpath b Martin	14
V.L.Manjrekar	c Grout b Martin	33	c Simpson b O'Neill	40
Hanumant Singh	c Grout b Martin	0	(6) c O'Neill b Veivers	94
Nawab of Pataudi, jr*	not out	128	(7) b McKenzie	1
C.G.Borde	c Simpson b McKenzie	49	(8) b McKenzie	0
S.A.Durani	c Grout b McKenzie	5	(10) c O'Neill b Veivers	10
R.G.Nadkarni	lbw b Hawke	3	c Simpson b Hawke	20
A.G.Kripal Singh	b McKenzie	0	(5) b McKenzie	1
V.B.Ranjane	c Redpath b McKenzie	2	not out	13
Extras	(B 13, LB 9, NB 1)	23	(B 11, LB 2)	13
		276		193

1/12 2/13 3/55 4/56 5/76 6/218 7/232 8/249 9/256

1/0 2/0 3/23 4/24 5/117 6/130 7/130 8/168 9/191

Bowling: First Innings—McKenzie 32.3-8-58-6; Hawke 33-13-55-2; Redpath 2-1-1-0; Simpson 12-3-23-0; Martin 26-11-63-2; Booth 10-4-14-0; Veivers 10-2-20-0; O'Neill 7-3-19-0. Second Innings—McKenzie 20-9-33-4; Hawke 17-7-26-2; Martin 16-4-43-1; Veivers 10-4-18-2; Simpson 5-3-9-0; Booth 3-0-10-0; 10-2-20-0; O'Neill 9-3-41-1.

Umpires: M.V.Nagendra and S.Roy

INDIA v AUSTRALIA 1964-65 (Second Test)

At Brabourne Stadium, 10, 11, 12, 14, 15 October
Result: India won by 2 wickets

Australia

W.M.Lawry c Indrajitsinhji b Durani	16	lbw b Chandrasekhar	68
R.B.Simpson* b Chandrasekhar	27	c Hanumant Singh b Surti	20
B.C.Booth b Chandrasekhar	1	(5) st Indrajitsinhji b Nadkarni	74
P.J.P.Burge c Chandrasekhar b Borde	80	b Chandrasekhar	0
R.M.Cowper lbw b Nadkarni	20	(3) c Indrajitsinhji b Nadkarni	81
T.R.Veivers c Borde b Chandrasekhar	67	lbw b Chandrasekhar	0
B.N.Jarman† c Durani b Surti	78	b Chandrasekhar	0
J.W.Martin c Nadkarni b Chandrasekhar	0	c Surti b Nadkarni	16
G.D.McKenzie b Nadkarni	17	c Surti b Nadkarni	4
A.N.Connolly not out	0	not out	0
N.C.O'Neill absent ill	-	absent ill	-
Extras (B 7, LB 4, NB 3)	14	(B 4, LB 7)	11
	320		274

1/35 2/36 3/53 4/142 5/146   1/59 2/121 3/121 4/246 5/247 274
6/297 7/303 8/304 9/320   6/247 7/257 8/265 9/274

Bowling: First Innings—Surti 18-1-70-1; Jaisimha 8-1-20-0; Durani 20-5-78-1; Chandrasekhar 26-10-50-4; Nadkarni 24.5-6-65-2; Borde 7-0-23-1. Second Innings—Surti 21-5-77-1; Jaisimha 11-4-18-0; Chandrasekhar 30-11-73-4; Durani 15-3-48-0; Nadkarni 20.4-10-33-4; Borde 2-0-14-0.

India

D.N.Sardesai c Simpson b Connolly	3	lbw b McKenzie	56
M.L.Jaisimha b Veivers	66	c Jarman b Connolly	0
S.A.Durani c Jarman b Simpson	12	(8) c Cowper b Simpson	31
V.L.Manjrekar c Cowper b Veivers	59	(6) c Simpson b Connolly	39
Hanumant Singh b Veivers	14	b McKenzie	11
Nawab of Pataudi, jr* c McKenzie b Veivers	86	(7) c Burge b Connolly	53
C.G.Borde c Simpson b Martin	4	(9) not out	30
R.F.Surti c Jarman b Connolly	21	(5) c Booth b Veivers	10
R.G.Nadkarni c Jarman b Martin	34	(4) c Simpson b Veivers	0
K.S.Indrajitsinhji† c sub(R.Redpath)b Connolly	23	not out	3
B.S.Chandrasekhar not out	1		
Extras (B 4, LB 8, NB 6)	18	(B 15, LB 8)	23
	341	(8 wkts)	256

1/7 2/30 3/142 4/149 5/181   1/4 2/70 3/71 4/99 (8 wkts) 256
6/188 7/255 8/293 9/331   5/113 6/122 7/215 8/224

Bowling: First Innings—McKenzie 22-2-49-0; Connolly 22.3-5-66-3; Martin 34-11-72-2; Simpson 13-1-40-1; Veivers 48-20-68-4; Cowper 13-3-28-0. Second Innings—McKenzie 21-6-43-2; Connolly 18-8-24-3; Simpson 24-12-34-1; Veivers 43.4-12-82-2; Martin 14-2-35-0; Cowper 4-0-14-0; Booth 4-3-1-0.

Umpires: H.E.Choudhury and S.K.Raghunatha Rao

INDIA v AUSTRALIA 1964-65 (Third Test)

At Eden Gardens, Calcutta, 17, 18, 20, 21 (no play), 22 (no play) October
Result: Match drawn

Australia

W.M.Lawry b Durani	50	not out	47
R.B.Simpson* lbw b Surti	67	c Hanumant Singh b Surti	71
R.M.Cowper c Nadkarni b Durani	4	not out	14
P.J.P.Burge c Hanumant Singh b Durani	4		
B.C.Booth b Durani	0		
I.R.Redpath not out	32		
T.R.Veivers c Pataudi b Durani	2		
B.N.Jarman† b Durani	1		
G.D.McKenzie st Indrajitsinhji b Surti	0		
R.H.D.Sellers b Surti	0		
A.N.Connolly c Hanumant b Chandrasekhar	0		
Extras (B 1, LB 8, NB 5)	14	(B 6, NB 5)	11
	174	(1 wkt)	143

1/97 2/104 3/109 4/109 5/145 174   1/115
6/165 7/167 8/167 9/169

Bowling: First Innings—Surti 21-7-38-3; Jaisimha 5-3-2-0; Durani 28-11-73-6; Chandrasekhar 28.5-15-39-1; Nadkarni 2-0-8-0. Second Innings—Surti 10-2-37-1; Jaisimha 2-1-4-0; Durani 18-3-59-0; Chandrasekhar 8-3-27-0; Nadkarni 8-6-5-0.

India

D.N.Sardesai c Veivers b Booth	42
M.L.Jaisimha c Booth b Simpson	57
S.A.Durani c Simpson b Veivers	12
V.L.Manjrekar lbw b Veivers	9
Hanumant Singh c Burge b Veivers	5
Nawab of Pataudi, jr* b Simpson	2
R.G.Nadkarni b McKenzie	24
C.G.Borde not out	68
R.F.Surti c Sellers b Simpson	9
K.S.Indrajitsinhji† st Jarman b Booth	2
B.S.Chandrasekhar b Simpson	1
Extras (B 4)	4
	235

1/60 2/97 3/119 4/127 5/129 235
6/133 7/166 8/187 9/196

Bowling: McKenzie 13-1-31-1; Connolly 8-4-10-0; Veivers 52-18-81-3; Booth 18-10-33-2; Cowper 6-0-14-0; Simpson 28-12-45-4.

Umpires: S.P.Pan and B.Satyaji Rao

PAKISTAN v AUSTRALIA 1964-65 (Only Test)

At National Stadium, Karachi, 24, 25, 27, 28, 29 October
Result: Match drawn

Pakistan

Batsman	Dismissal (1st)	R		Dismissal (2nd)	R
Khalid Ibadulla	c Redpath b McKenzie	166		c Redpath b McKenzie	3
Abdul Kadir†	run out	95		hit wkt b Veivers	26
Saeed Ahmed	c Redpath b Martin	7	(4)	c sub (R.H.D.Sellers) b Martin	35
Javed Burki	hit wkt b McKenzie	8	(5)	c Grout b Cowper	62
Hanif Mohammad*	c and b McKenzie	0	(6)	c McKenzie b Booth	40
Shafqat Rana	c Grout b McKenzie	15	(7)	lbw b McKenzie	24
Nasim-ul-Ghani	c Redpath b Hawke	0	(8)	c Grout b Veivers	22
Majid Khan	lbw b Martin	0		not out	21
Intikhab Alam	c Grout b McKenzie	53	(3)	c and b Simpson	36
Asif Iqbal	c Booth b McKenzie	41			
Pervez Sajjad	not out	3			
Extras	(B 9, LB 12, NB 3)	24		(B 1, LB 6, NB 3)	10
		414		(8 wkts dec.)	279

1/249 2/266 3/284 4/296 5/296
6/301 7/302 8/334 9/383

1/13 2/65 3/81 4/118 5/202 6/224 7/236 8/279

Bowling: *First Innings*—McKenzie 30-9-69-6; Hawke 20-2-84-1; Martin 36-11-106-2; Veivers 16-5-33-0; Simpson 30-8-69-0; Booth 5-2-15-0; Redpath 1-0-14-0. *Second Innings*—McKenzie 25-5-62-2; Hawke 6-2-20-0; Martin 17-4-42-1; Veivers 30-16-44-2; Simpson 20-5-47-1; Booth 13-4-18-1; Cowper 11-3-36-1.

Australia

Batsman	Dismissal (1st)	R		Dismissal (2nd)	R
W.M.Lawry	hit wkt b Majid Khan	7		c Khalid Ibadulla b Majid Khan	22
R.B.Simpson*	c Pervez Sajjad b Saeed Ahmed	153		c Khalid Ibadulla b Nasim	115
I.R.Redpath	lbw b Intikhab Alam	19		not out	40
P.J.P.Burge	c Majid Khan b Pervez Sajjad	54		not out	28
B.C.Booth	c Asif Iqbal b Majid Khan	15			
R.M.Cowper	b Asif Iqbal	16			
T.R.Veivers	st Abdul Kadir b Saeed Ahmed	25			
J.W.Martin	b Asif Iqbal	26			
A.T.W.Grout†	c Asif Iqbal b Saeed Ahmed	0			
G.D.McKenzie	lbw b Intikhab Alam	2			
N.J.N.Hawke	not out	8			
Extras	(B 12, LB 8, NB 7)	27		(LB 14, NB 8)	22
		352		(2 wkts)	227

1/10 2/78 3/194 4/228 5/257
6/315 7/315 8/315 9/320

1/54 2/173

Bowling: *First Innings*—Majid Khan 30-9-55-2; Asif Iqbal 23.5-5-68-2; Pervez Sajjad 22-5-52-1; Intikhab Alam 28-5-83-2; Nasim-ul-Ghani 4-0-17-0; Saeed Ahmed 19-5-41-3; Khalid Ibadulla 7-3-9-0. *Second Innings*—Majid Khan 16-3-42-1; Asif Iqbal 12-4-28-0; Pervez Sajjad 8-2-17-0; Intikhab Alam 16-3-48-0; Nasim-ul-Ghani 12-3-48-0; Saeed Ahmed 13-6-28-0; Khalid Ibadulla 2-0-14-0; Javed Burki 2-1-3-0; Shafqat Rana 1-0-1-0.

Umpires: Daud Khan and Shujauddin

AUSTRALIA v PAKISTAN 1964-65 (Only Test)

At Melbourne Cricket Ground, 4, 5, 7, 8 December
Result: Match drawn

Pakistan

Batsman	Dismissal (1st)	R		Dismissal (2nd)	R
Abdul Kadir†	c Chappell b McKenzie	0	(7)	c Jarman b Hawke	35
Mohammad Ilyas	run out	6		lbw b McKenzie	3
Saeed Ahmed	c Chappell b Hawke	80		c Chappell b McKenzie	24
Javed Burki	c Simpson b McKenzie	29		b Hawke	47
Hanif Mohammad*	c McKenzie b Sincock	104		st Jarman b Veivers	93
Nasim-ul-Ghani	b McKenzie	27		b Sincock	10
Asif Iqbal	c McKenzie b Hawke	1	(8)	c Jarman b Hawke	15
Intikhab Alam	c Shepherd b Hawke	13	(9)	c Simpson b Hawke	61
Afaq Hussain	not out	8	(10)	not out	13
Arif Butt	c Chappell b Sincock	7	(1)	c Jarman b McKenzie	12
Farooq Hamid	b Sincock	0		b McKenzie	3
Extras	(B 4, LB 4, NB 1, W 3)	12		(B 5, LB 2, NB 1, W 2)	10
		287			326

1/0 2/18 3/112 4/127 5/225
6/226 7/255 8/275 9/287

1/6 2/37 3/46 4/130 5/152
6/198 7/229 8/267 9/323

Bowling: *First Innings*—McKenzie 22-5-66-3; Hawke 21-1-69-3; Sincock 17.6-0-67-3; Simpson 9-1-29-0; Chappell 15-2-49-0; Veivers 3-2-3-0. *Second Innings*—McKenzie 24.4-1-74-4; Hawke 21-2-72-4; Sincock 28-5-102-1; Chappell 11-2-31-0; Veivers 12-4-37-1.

Australia

Batsman	Dismissal (1st)	R		Dismissal (2nd)	R
R.B.Simpson*	b Arif Butt	47		c Hanif b Arif Butt	1
W.M.Lawry	c Hanif b Arif Butt	41		run out	19
I.M.Chappell	c Hanif b Farooq Hamid	11			
B.K.Shepherd	sub(Ghulam Abbas)b Asif Iqbal	55	(3)	not out	43
B.C.Booth	c Hanif b Arif Butt	57			
R.M.Cowper	c Intikhab Alam b Saeed Ahmed	83			
T.R.Veivers	c Hanif b Arif Butt	88	(4)	not out	16
B.N.Jarman†	b Asif Iqbal	33			
D.J.Sincock	b Arif Butt	7			
G.D.McKenzie	b Arif Butt	1			
N.J.N.Hawke	not out	24			
Extras	(B 6, LB 3, NB 14, W 1)	24		(B 2, LB 4, NB 1, W 2)	9
		448		(2 wkts)	88

1/81 2/105 3/105 4/200 5/233
6/372 7/418 8/434 9/446

1/12 2/55

Bowling: *First Innings*—Farooq Hamid 19-1-82-1; Asif Iqbal 19-1-90-2; Arif Butt 21.3-1-89-6; Afaq Hussain 9-1-45-0; Intikhab Alam 10-0-51-0; Saeed Ahmed 10-0-31-1; Nasim-ul-Ghani 4-0-36-0. *Second Innings*—Farooq Hamid 4-0-25-0; Arif Butt 5.5-0-29-1; Asif Iqbal 2-0-25-0.

Umpires: C.J.Egar and W.Smyth

WEST INDIES v AUSTRALIA 1964-65 (First Test)
At Sabina Park, Kingston, Jamaica, 3, 4, 5, 6, 8 March
Result: West Indies won by 179 runs

West Indies

C.C.Hunte c Grout b Philpott	41	c Simpson b Mayne	81
S.M.Nurse c Grout b Hawke	15	run out	17
R.B.Kanhai c Philpott b McKenzie	17	c and b Philpott	16
B.F.Butcher b Mayne	39	c Booth b Philpott	71
G.S.Sobers* lbw b Simpson	30	(6) c Simpson b Philpott	27
J.S.Solomon c Grout b Mayne	0	(7) c Simpson b Mayne	76
J.L.Hendriks† b Philpott	11	(8) b O'Neill	30
A.W.White not out	57	(9) st Grout b Philpott	3
W.W.Hall b Hawke	9	(10) b Mayne	16
C.C.Griffith b Mayne	6	(11) not out	1
L.R.Gibbs b Mayne	6	(5) b Mayne	5
Extras (B 4, LB 3, W 1)	8	(B 20, LB 7, NB 2, W 1)	30
	239		373

1/48 2/70 3/82 4/149 5/149   1/50 2/78 3/194 4/211 5/226
6/149 7/181 8/211 9/229   6/247 7/311 8/314 9/372

Bowling: *First Innings*—McKenzie 20-2-70-1; Hawke 14-4-47-2; Mayne 17-2-43-4; Philpott 14-2-56-2; Simpson 4-2-15-1. *Second Innings*—McKenzie 33-7-56-0; Hawke 18-5-25-0; Mayne 23.4-5-56-4; Philpott 47-10-109-4; Simpson 15-2-36-0; Cowper 9-1-27-0; O'Neill 7-0-34-1.

Australia

W.M.Lawry lbw b Hall	19	b Griffith	17
R.B.Simpson* c Kanhai b Hall	11	c Hendriks b Hall	16
R.M.Cowper c Nurse b Hall	26	(4) lbw b Hall	2
N.C.O'Neill c Butcher b White	40	(5) c Nurse b Gibbs	22
B.C.Booth b Griffith	2	(6) b Griffith	56
G.Thomas b Griffith	23	(7) b Hall	15
P.I.Philpott c White b Hall	22	(8) c Kanhai b Sobers	9
N.J.N.Hawke not out	45	(3) b Solomon	33
A.T.W.Grout† c Nurse b Hall	5	lbw b Hall	2
G.D.McKenzie b White	0	c Hall b White	20
L.C.Mayne b Sobers	9	not out	11
Extras (B 2, LB 8, NB 5)	15	(NB 13)	13
	217		216

1/32 2/39 3/42 4/80 5/96   1/39 2/40 3/43 4/75 5/144
6/136 7/176 8/192 9/193   6/167 7/180 8/184 9/192

Bowling: *First Innings*—Hall 24-0-60-5; Griffith 20-2-59-2; Sobers 20.4-7-30-1; Gibbs 16-8-19-0; White 15-4-34-2. *Second Innings*—Hall 19-5-45-4; Griffith 14-3-36-2; Gibbs 9-1-21-1; Sobers 17-2-64-1; Solomon 5-0-23-1; White 14.5-8-14-1.

Umpires: O.Davies and D.Sang Hue

WEST INDIES v AUSTRALIA 1964-65 (Second Test)
At Queen's Park Oval, Port-of-Spain, Trinidad, 26, 27, 29, 30 March, 1 April
Result: Match drawn

West Indies

C.C.Hunte c Simpson b McKenzie	89	b Philpott	53
B.A.Davis c Simpson b McKenzie	54	c Simpson b O'Neill	58
R.B.Kanhai c Grout b Cowper	27	c McKenzie b Philpott	53
B.F.Butcher run out	117	c Thomas b Mayne	47
G.S.Sobers* run out	69	lbw b Simpson	24
J.S.Solomon not out	31	c Booth b Simpson	48
J.L.Hendriks† c Philpott b O'Neill	2	c Grout b Hawke	22
A.W.White c Grout b Philpott	7	lbw b Hawke	4
W.W.Hall c Booth b O'Neill	4	c Mayne b Simpson	37
C.C.Griffith b O'Neill	12	not out	18
L.R.Gibbs st Grout b O'Neill	1	c Booth b Simpson	1
Extras (B 4, LB 9, NB 1, W 2)	16	(B 11, LB 8, NB 2)	21
	429		386

1/116 2/164 3/205 4/365 5/372   1/91 2/166 3/166 4/236 5/266
6/380 7/393 8/404 9/425   6/323 7/327 8/328 9/382

Bowling: *First Innings*—McKenzie 36-9-94-2; Hawke 23-4-50-0; Mayne 17-0-65-0; Philpott 36-10-82-1; Booth 2-0-5-0; Simpson 8-1-28-0; Cowper 12-1-48-1; O'Neill 17.4-3-41-4; *Second Innings*—McKenzie 21-5-62-0; Mayne 11-2-37-1; Hawke 21-4-42-2; Philpott 28-4-57-2; O'Neill 24-6-65-1; Simpson 36.5-5-83-4; Booth 5-1-14-0; Cowper 1-0-5-0.

Australia

W.M.Lawry c Davis b Griffith	1
R.B.Simpson* b Griffith	30
R.M.Cowper run out	143
N.C.O'Neill c Sobers b Hall	36
B.C.Booth c Hendriks b Griffith	117
G.Thomas c Hendriks b Hall	61
P.I.Philpott c Sobers b Gibbs	19
N.J.N.Hawke c Hall b Sobers	39
A.T.W.Grout† c Hendriks b Sobers	35
G.D.McKenzie c Butcher b Sobers	13
L.C.Mayne not out	1
Extras (B 8, LB 3, NB 10)	21
	516

1/15 2/60 3/288 4/306 5/372
6/415 7/431 8/489 9/511

Bowling: Hall 35-6-104-2; Griffith 33-5-81-3; Sobers 27.5-5-75-3; Gibbs 66-22-129-1; White 52-15-104-0; Hunte 2-1-2-0.

Umpires: C.Z.Bain and R.Gosein

WEST INDIES v AUSTRALIA 1964-65 (Third Test)

At Bourda, Georgetown, British Guiana, 14, 15, 17, 19, 20 April
Result: West Indies won by 212 runs

West Indies

Batsman	1st Innings		2nd Innings	
C.C.Hunte	c McKenzie b Philpott	31	c Grout b Hawke	38
B.A.Davis	b Hawke	28	b McKenzie	17
R.B.Kanhai	b Hawke	89	b McKenzie	0
B.F.Butcher	run out	49	b Hawke	18
S.M.Nurse	c and b Hawke	42	st Grout b Philpott	6
G.S.Sobers*	c Grout b Hawke	45	c Simpson b Philpott	42
J.S.Solomon	c Grout b Hawke	0	c Simpson b Philpott	17
J.L.Hendriks†	not out	31	c Grout b Hawke	2
W.W.Hall	c Mayne b Hawke	7	not out	20
C.C.Griffith	lbw b O'Neill	19	c Thomas b Philpott	13
L.R.Gibbs	b O'Neill	2	b Hawke	1
Extras	(B 7, LB 1, NB 3, W 1)	12	(LB 3, NB 2, W 1)	6
		355		180

1/56 2/68 3/203 4/210 5/290 6/290 7/297 8/309 9/353
1/31 2/31 3/62 4/69 5/125 6/129 7/146 8/146 9/176

Bowling: *First Innings*—McKenzie 23-2-92-0; Hawke 32-8-72-6; Mayne 12-1-54-0; Philpott 26-5-75-1; O'Neill 6.2-1-26-2; Simpson 7-1-23-0; Cowper 1-0-1-0. *Second Innings*—McKenzie 21-7-53-2; Hawke 20.4-7-43-4; Simpson 17-9-19-0; Mayne 2-1-6-0; Philpott 16-3-49-4; O'Neill 1-0-4-0.

Australia

Batsman	1st Innings		2nd Innings	
R.B.Simpson*	b Sobers	7	b Griffith	23
W.M.Lawry	run out	20	b Gibbs	22
R.M.Cowper	c Hendriks b Gibbs	41	st Hendriks b Gibbs	30
N.C.O'Neill	b Griffith	27	c Sobers b Gibbs	16
P.I.Philpott	c Butcher b Sobers	5	(8) c Sobers b Gibbs	6
B.C.Booth	c Sobers b Gibbs	37	(5) c Hendriks b Gibbs	0
G.Thomas	b Hall	8	(6) st Hendriks b Solomon	5
N.J.N.Hawke	c Sobers b Hall	0	(7) c Hendriks b Sobers	14
A.T.W.Grout†	run out	19	b Sobers	8
G.D.McKenzie	not out	3	b Gibbs	6
L.C.Mayne	b Gibbs	5	not out	0
Extras	(LB 1, NB 6)	7	(B 4, LB 4, NB 6)	14
		179		144

1/11 2/68 3/71 4/85 5/116 6/127 7/130 8/170 9/171
1/31 2/88 3/91 4/104 5/109 6/115 7/130 8/130 9/144

Bowling: *First Innings*—Hall 13-2-43-2; Sobers 12-2-38-2; Griffiths 14-2-40-1; Gibbs 25.5-9-51-3; . *Second Innings*—Hall 2-1-1-0; Griffiths 6-1-30-1; Sobers 19-7-39-2; Gibbs 22.2-9-29-6; Solomon 9-2-31-1.

Umpires: G.E.Gomez and H.B.D.Jordan

WEST INDIES v AUSTRALIA 1964-65 (Fourth Test)

At Kensington Oval, Bridgetown, Barbados, 5, 6, 7, 8, 10, 11 May
Result: Match drawn

Australia

Batsman	1st Innings		2nd Innings	
W.M.Lawry	c Sobers b Solomon	210	retired hurt	58
R.B.Simpson*	b Hall	201	c Nurse b Sobers	5
R.M.Cowper	b Sobers	102	c and b Hall	4
N.C.O'Neill	c Kanhai b Gibbs	51	not out	74
B.C.Booth	b Gibbs	5	c Sobers b Gibbs	17
G.Thomas	not out	27	b Gibbs	1
B.K.Shepherd	lbw b Hall	4		
N.J.N.Hawke	not out	8		
P.I.Philpott				
A.T.W.Grout†				
G.D.McKenzie				
Extras	(B 10, LB 12, NB 18, W 2)	42	(B 11, LB 3, NB 1, W 1)	16
	(6 wkts dec.)	650	(4 wkts dec.)	175

1/382 2/522 3/583 4/604 5/615 (6 wkts dec.) 650 6/631
1/7 2/13 3/160 4/175

Bowling: *First Innings*—Hall 27-3-117-2; Griffith 35-3-131-0; Sobers 37-7-143-1; Gibbs 73-17-168-2; Solomon 14-1-42-1; Hunte 3-1-7-0. *Second Innings*—Hall 8-0-31-0; Sobers 20-11-29-1; Gibbs 18.2-3-61-2; Griffith 7-0-38-0.

West Indies

Batsman	1st Innings		2nd Innings	
C.C.Hunte	c Simpson b McKenzie	75	c Grout b McKenzie	81
B.A.Davis	b McKenzie	8	c sub (D.J.Sincock) b Philpott	68
R.B.Kanhai	c Hawke b McKenzie	129	lbw b McKenzie	1
B.F.Butcher	c Simpson b O'Neill	9	c Booth b Philpott	27
S.M.Nurse	b Hawke	201	lbw b Hawke	0
G.S.Sobers*	c Grout b McKenzie	55	(6) lbw b Hawke	34
J.S.Solomon	c McKenzie b Hawke	1	(5) not out	6
J.L.Hendriks†	retired hurt	4	not out	
W.W.Hall	c Simpson b Hawke	3		
C.C.Griffith	run out	54		
L.R.Gibbs	not out	3		
Extras	(B 13, LB 12, NB 5, W 1)	31	(B 19, LB 3, NB 1, W 2)	25
		573	(5 wkts)	242

1/13 2/99 3/299 4/445 5/448 6/453 7/474 8/539 9/573
1/145 2/146 3/183 4/216 5/217

Bowling: *First Innings*—McKenzie 47-11-114-4; Hawke 49-11-135-3; Philpott 45-17-102-0; O'Neill 26-13-60-1; Simpson 15-3-44-0; Cowper 21-6-64-0; Booth 6-2-17-0; Shepherd 3-1-6-0. *Second Innings*—McKenzie 24-6-60-2; Hawke 15-4-37-1; Philpott 24-7-74-2; Cowper 8-4-19-0; Booth 5-1-12-0; Simpson 9-4-15-0.

Umpires: H.B.D.Jordan and C.P.Kippins

WEST INDIES v AUSTRALIA 1964-65 (Fifth Test)

At Queen's Park Oval, Port-of-Spain, Trinidad, 14, 15, 17 May

Result: Australia won by 10 wickets

West Indies

Batsman	First innings	Runs	Second innings	Runs
C.C.Hunte	c Grout b Hawke	1	not out	60
B.A.Davis	c McKenzie b Hawke	4	lbw b Hawke	8
R.B.Kanhai	c Hawke b Cowper	121	b Hawke	9
B.F.Butcher	lbw b Hawke	2	c Cowper b Sincock	26
S.M.Nurse	b McKenzie	9	lbw b Hawke	1
G.S.Sobers*	b Sincock	18	b McKenzie	8
W.V.Rodriguez	c and b Sincock	9	st Grout b Sincock	1
D.W.Allan†	run out	11	c Cowper b McKenzie	7
W.W.Hall	b Philpott	29	b McKenzie	8
C.C.Griffith	c Sincock b Philpott	11	b McKenzie	0
L.R.Gibbs	not out	0	b McKenzie	0
Extras	(B 4, LB 2, NB 1, W 2)	9	(B 2, W 1)	3
Total		224		131

1/2 2/18 3/26 4/64 5/100 6/114 7/162 8/202 9/217

1/12 2/22 3/63 4/66 5/131 6/92 7/103 8/131 9/131

Bowling: McKenzie 14-0-43-1; Hawke 13-3-42-3; Sincock 15-1-79-2; Philpott 7.3-0-25-2; Cowper 6-0-26-1. Second Innings—McKenzie 17-7-33-5; Hawke 18-0-64-3; Sincock 10-0-31-2.

Australia

Batsman	First innings	Runs	Second innings	Runs
W.M.Lawry	c Allan b Griffith	3	not out	18
R.B.Simpson*	b Griffith	72	not out	34
R.M.Cowper	lbw b Sobers	69		
B.C.Booth	lbw b Griffith	0		
G.Thomas	c Allan b Griffith	38		
B.K.Shepherd	c sub (C.A.Davis) b Gibbs	38		
N.J.N.Hawke	b Griffith	3		
P.I.Philpott	c Griffith b Gibbs	10		
A.T.W.Grout†	c Griffith b Gibbs	14		
D.J.Sincock	not out	17		
G.D.McKenzie	b Griffith	8		
Extras	(B 12, LB 3, NB 6, W 1)	22	(B 4, NB 6, W 1)	11
Total		294	(0 wkts)	63

1/5 2/143 3/143 4/167 5/222 6/230 7/248 8/261 9/270

Bowling: First Innings—Hall 14-2-46-0; Griffith 20-6-46-6; Gibbs 44-17-71-3; Rodriguez 13-2-44-0; Sobers 37-13-54-1. Second Innings—Griffith 6-0-19-0; Hall 4-0-7-0; Gibbs 4-2-7-0; Sobers 2-0-7-0; Rodriguez 1-0-8-0; Kanhai 1-0-4-0.

Umpires: H.B.D.Jordan and C.P.Kippins

AUSTRALIA v ENGLAND 1965-66 (First Test)

At Woolloongabba, Brisbane, 10 11 (no play), 13, 14, 15 December

Result: Match drawn

Australia

Batsman	How out	Runs
W.M.Lawry	c Parks b Higgs	166
I.R.Redpath	b Brown	17
R.M.Cowper	c Barrington b Brown	22
P.J.P.Burge	b Brown	0
B.C.Booth*	c and b Titmus	16
K.D.Walters	c Parks b Higgs	155
T.R.Veivers	not out	56
N.J.N.Hawke	not out	6
P.I.Philpott		
A.T.W.Grout†		
P.J.Allan		
Extras	(LB 2, NB 3)	5
Total	(6 wkts dec.)	443

1/51 2/90 3/90 4/125 5/312 6/431

Bowling: Brown 21-4-71-3; Higgs 30-6-102-2; Titmus 38-9-99-1; Allen 39-12-108-0; Barber 5-0-42-0; Barrington 4-0-16-0.

England

Batsman	First innings	Runs	Second innings	Runs
R.W.Barber	c Walters b Hawke	5	c Veivers b Walters	34
G.Boycott	b Philpott	45	not out	63
J.H.Edrich	c Lawry b Philpott	32	c Veivers b Philpott	37
K.F.Barrington	b Hawke	53	c Booth b Cowper	38
M.J.K.Smith*	b Allan	16	not out	10
J.M.Parks†	c Redpath b Philpott	52		
F.J.Titmus	st Grout b Philpott	60		
D.A.Allen	c Cowper b Walters	3		
D.J.Brown	b Philpott	3		
K.Higgs	lbw b Allan	4		
W.E.Russell	not out	0		
Extras	(B 4, NB 3)	7	(B 2, LB 2)	4
Total		280	(3 wkts)	186

1/5 2/75 3/86 4/115 5/191 6/221 7/232 8/253 9/275

1/46 2/114 3/168

Bowling: First Innings—Allan 21-6-58-2; Hawke 16-7-44-2; Walters 10-1-25-1; Philpott 28.1-3-90-5; Cowper 7-4-7-0; Veivers 11-1-49-0. Second Innings—Allan 3-0-25-0; Hawke 10-2-16-0; Walters 5-1-22-1; Philpott 14-1-62-1; Veivers 12-0-37-0; Cowper 6-0-20-1.

Umpires: C.J.Egar and L.P.Rowan

AUSTRALIA v ENGLAND 1965-66 (Second Test)

At Melbourne Cricket Ground, 30, 31 December, 1, 3, 4 January

Result: Match drawn

Australia

Batsman	1st inns		2nd inns	
R.B.Simpson*	c Edrich b Allen	59	c Barrington b Knight	67
W.M.Lawry	c Cowdrey b Allen	88	c Smith b Barber	78
P.J.P.Burge	b Jones	5	(4) c Edrich c Boycott	120
R.M.Cowper	c Titmus b Jones	99	(3) lbw b Jones	5
B.C.Booth	lbw b Jones	23	b Allen	10
K.D.Walters	c Parks b Knight	22	c and b Barrington	115
T.R.Veivers	run out	19	st Parks c Boycott	3
P.I.Philpott	b Knight	10	b Knight	2
A.T.W.Grout†	c Barber b Knight	11	c Allen b Barrington	16
G.D.McKenzie	not out	12	run out	2
A.N.Connolly	c Parks b Knight	0	not out	0
Extras	(B 2, LB 7, NB 1)	10	(B 1, LB 3, NB 3, W 1)	8
		358		**426**

1/93 2/109 3/203 4/262 5/297
6/318 7/330 8/342 9/352

1/93 2/141 3/163 4/176
5/374 6/382 7/385 8/417 9/426

Bowling: First Innings—Jones 24-4-92-3; Knight 26.5-2-84-4; Titmus 31-7-93-0; Allen 20-4-55-2; Barber 6-1-24-0. *Second Innings*—Jones 20-1-92-1; Knight 21-4-61-2; Titmus 22-6-43-0; Allen 18-3-48-1; Barber 17-0-87-1; Barrington 7.4-0-47-2; Boycott 9-0-32-2; Smith 2-0-8-0.

England

Batsman	1st inns		2nd inns	
G.Boycott	c McKenzie b Walters	51	not out	5
R.W.Barber	c Grout b McKenzie	48	not out	0
J.H.Edrich	c and b Veivers	109		
K.F.Barrington	c Burge b Veivers	63		
M.C.Cowdrey	c Connolly b Cowper	104		
M.J.K.Smith*	c Grout b McKenzie	41		
J.M.Parks†	c Cowper b McKenzie	71		
B.R.Knight	c Simpson b McKenzie	1		
F.J.Titmus	not out	56		
D.A.Allen	c Grout b Connolly	2		
I.J.Jones	b McKenzie	11		
Extras	(B 4, LB 5, W 2)	11		
		558	(0 wkts)	**5**

1/98 2/110 3/228 4/333 5/409
6/443 7/447 8/540 9/551

Bowling: First Innings—McKenzie 35.2-3-134-5; Connolly 37-5-125-1; Philpott 30-2-133-0; Walters 10-2-32-1; Simpson 16-4-61-0; Veivers 12-3-46-2; Cowper 3-0-16-1. *Second Innings*—Connolly 1-0-3-0; McKenzie 1-0-2-0.

Umpires: C.J.Egar and W.Smyth

AUSTRALIA v ENGLAND 1965-66 (Third Test)

At Sydney Cricket Ground, 7, 8, 10, 11 January

Result: England won by an innings and 93 runs

England

G.Boycott	c and b Philpott	84
R.W.Barber	b Hawke	185
J.H.Edrich	c and b Philpott	103
K.F.Barrington	c McKenzie b Hawke	1
M.C.Cowdrey	c Grout b Hawke	0
M.J.K.Smith*	c Grout b Hawke	6
D.J.Brown	c Grout b Hawke	1
J.M.Parks†	c Grout b Hawke	13
F.J.Titmus	c Grout b Walters	14
D.A.Allen	not out	50
I.J.Jones	b Hawke	16
Extras	(B 3, LB 8, NB 2, W 2)	15
		488

1/234 2/303 3/309 4/309 5/317
6/328 7/358 8/395 9/433

Bowling: McKenzie 25-2-113-0; Hawke 33.7-6-105-7; Walters 10-1-38-1; Philpott 28-3-86-2; Sincock 20-1-98-0; Cowper 6-1-33-0.

Australia

Batsman	1st inns		2nd inns	
W.M.Lawry	c Parks b Jones	0	c Cowdrey b Brown	33
G.Thomas	c Titmus b Brown	51	c Cowdrey b Titmus	25
R.M.Cowper	st Parks b Allen	60	c Boycott b Titmus	0
P.J.P.Burge	c Parks b Brown	6	run out	1
B.C.Booth*	c Cowdrey b Jones	8	b Allen	27
D.J.Sincock	c Parks b Brown	29	(7) c Smith b Allen	27
K.D.Walters	st Parks b Allen	23	(6) not out	35
N.J.N.Hawke	c Barber b Brown	0	(9) c Smith b Titmus	2
A.T.W.Grout†	b Brown	0	(10) c Smith b Allen	3
G.D.McKenzie	c Cowdrey b Barber	24	(11) c Barber b Titmus	12
P.I.Philpott	not out	5	(8) lbw b Allen	4
Extras	(B 7, LB 8)	15	(B 3, LB 1)	4
		221		**174**

1/0 2/81 3/91 4/105 5/155
6/174 7/174 8/174 9/203

1/46 2/50 3/51 4/86 5/86
6/119 7/131 8/135 9/140

Bowling: First Innings—Jones 20-6-51-2; Brown 17-1-63-5; Boycott 3-1-8-0; Titmus 23-8-40-0; Barber 2.1-1-2-1; Allen 19-5-42-2. *Second Innings*—Jones 7-0-35-0; Brown 11-2-32-1; Titmus 17.3-4-40-4; Allen 20-8-47-4; Barber 5-0-16-0.

Umpires: C.J.Egar and L.P.Rowan

AUSTRALIA v ENGLAND 1965-66 (Fourth Test)

At Adelaide Oval, 28, 29, 31 January, 1 February

Result: Australia won by an innings and 9 runs

England

G.Boycott c Chappell b Hawke	22	lbw b McKenzie	12
R.W.Barber b McKenzie	0	c Grout b Hawke	19
J.H.Edrich c Simpson b McKenzie	5	Simpson b Hawke	1
K.F.Barrington lbw b Walters	60	c Chappell b Hawke	102
M.C.Cowdrey run out	38	c Grout b Stackpole	35
M.J.K.Smith* b Veivers	29	c McKenzie b Stackpole	16
J.M.Parks† c Stackpole b McKenzie	49	run out	16
F.J.Titmus lbw b McKenzie	33	c Grout b Hawke	53
D.A.Allen c Simpson b McKenzie	2	not out	5
D.J.Brown c Thomas b McKenzie	1	c and b Hawke	0
I.J.Jones not out	0	c Lawry b Veivers	8
Extras (LB 2)	2	(LB 2, NB 8)	10
	241		**266**

1/7 2/25 3/33 4/105 5/150   241
6/178 7/210 8/212 9/222

1/23 2/31 3/32 4/114 5/123   266
6/163 7/244 8/253 9/257

Bowling: *First Innings*—McKenzie 21.7-4-48-6; Hawke 23-2-69-1; Walters 14-0-50-1; Stackpole 5-0-30-0; Chappell 4-1-18-0; Veivers 13-3-24-1. *Second Innings*—McKenzie 18-4-53-1; Hawke 21-6-54-5; Walters 9-0-47-0; Chappell 22-4-53-0; Stackpole 14-3-33-2; Veivers 3.7-0-16-1.

Australia

R.B.Simpson* c Titmus b Jones	225
W.M.Lawry b Titmus	119
G.Thomas b Jones	52
T.R.Veivers c Parks b Jones	1
P.J.P.Burge c Parks b Jones	27
K.D.Walters c Parks b Brown	0
I.M.Chappell c Edrich b Jones	17
K.R.Stackpole c Parks b Jones	43
N.J.N.Hawke not out	20
A.T.W.Grout b Titmus	4
G.D.McKenzie lbw b Titmus	1
Extras (B 4, LB 3)	7
	516

1/244 2/331 3/333 4/379 5/383   516
6/415 7/480 8/501 9/506

Bowling: Jones 29-3-118-6; Brown 28-4-109-1; Boycott 7-3-33-0; Titmus 37-6-116-3; Allen 21-1-103-0; Barber 4-0-30-0.

Umpires: C.J.Egar and L.P.Rowan

AUSTRALIA v ENGLAND 1965-66 (Fifth Test)

At Melbourne Cricket Ground, 11, 12, 14, 15 (no play), 16 February

Result: Match drawn

England

G.Boycott c Stackpole b McKenzie	17	lbw b McKenzie	1
R.W.Barber run out	17	b McKenzie	20
J.H.Edrich c McKenzie b Walters	85	b McKenzie	3
K.F.Barrington c Grout b Walters	115	not out	32
M.C.Cowdrey c Grout b Walters	79	not out	11
M.J.K.Smith* c Grout b Walters	0		
J.M.Parks† run out	89		
F.J.Titmus not out	42		
B.R.Knight c Grout b Hawke	13		
D.J.Brown c and b Chappell	12		
I.J.Jones not out	4		
Extras (B 9, LB 2, NB 1)	12	(LB 2)	2
	(9 wkts dec.) 485		**(3 wkts) 69**

1/36 2/41 3/219 4/254 5/254   485
6/392 7/419 8/449 9/474

1/6 2/21 3/34   69

Bowling: *First Innings*—McKenzie 26-5-100-1; Hawke 35-5-109-1; Simpson 5-1-20-0; Stackpole 10-2-43-0; Veivers 15-3-78-0; Chappell 17-4-70-1. *Second Innings*—McKenzie 6-2-17-3; Hawke 4-1-22-0; Walters 2-0-16-0; Stackpole 3-0-10-0; Chappell 2-0-2-0.

Australia

W.M.Lawry c Edrich b Jones	108
R.B.Simpson* b Brown	4
G.Thomas c Titmus b Jones	19
R.M.Cowper b Knight	307
K.D.Walters c and b Barber	60
I.M.Chappell c Parks b Jones	19
K.R.Stackpole b Knight	9
T.R.Veivers b Titmus	4
N.J.N.Hawke not out	0
A.T.W.Grout†	
G.D.McKenzie	
Extras (B 6, LB 5, NB 2)	13
	(8 wkts dec.) 543

1/15 2/36 3/248 4/420 5/481   543
6/532 7/543 8/543

Bowling: Brown 31-3-134-1; Jones 29-1-145-3; Knight 36.2-4-105-2; Titmus 42-12-86-1; Barber 16-0-60-1.

Umpires: C.J.Egar and L.P.Rowan

SOUTH AFRICA v AUSTRALIA 1966-67 (First Test)

At New Wanderers, Johannesburg, 23, 24, 26, 27, 28 December

Result: South Africa won by 233 runs

South Africa

T.L.Goddard	c Taber b Hawke	5	c Simpson b Hawke	13
E.J.Barlow	c Taber b McKenzie	13	c Taber b Renneberg	50
A.Bacher	c Cowper b McKenzie	5	run out	63
R.G.Pollock	c McKenzie b Renneberg	5	b Cowper	90
K.C.Bland	lbw b McKenzie	0	c Simpson b Chappell	32
H.R.Lance	hit wkt b McKenzie	44	c Simpson b McKenzie	70
D.T.Lindsay†	c Taber b Renneberg	69	c Chappell b Stackpole	182
P.L.van der Merwe*	c Taber b Simpson	19	c Chappell b Simpson	76
R.Dumbrill	c Chappell b Simpson	19	c Taber b Chappell	29
P.M.Pollock	c Taber b McKenzie	6	st Taber b Simpson	2
A.H.McKinnon	not out	0	not out	0
Extras	(B 11, W 3)	14	(B 7, LB 5, W 1)	13
		199		**620**

1/14 2/31 3/31 4/35 5/41   1/29 2/87 3/178 4/228 5/268
6/151 7/156 8/190 9/199   6/349 7/570 8/614 9/620

Bowling: *First Innings*—McKenzie 21.5-6-46-5; Hawke 8-1-25-1; Renneberg 16-3-54-2; Chappell 2-0-16-0; Veivers 9-1-13-0; Cowper 6-0-21-0; Simpson 4-1-10-0. *Second Innings*—McKenzie 39-4-118-1; Hawke 14.2-1-46-1; Renneberg 32-8-96-1; Chappell 21-3-91-2; Veivers 18-3-59-0; Cowper 16-2-56-1; Simpson 16.1-3-66-2; Stackpole 21-6-75-1.

Australia

R.B.Simpson*	c Goddard b P.M.Pollock	65	run out	48
W.M.Lawry	c Lindsay b Goddard	98	b McKinnon	27
I.R.Redpath	c Lindsay b Barlow	41	c van der Merwe b Barlow	21
R.M.Cowper	c Lindsay b Barlow	0	c Lindsay b Goddard	1
K.R.Stackpole	c Lindsay b Barlow	0	b Goddard	9
I.M.Chappell	c Lindsay b Goddard	37	c Lindsay b Dumbrill	34
T.R.Veivers	b Lance	18	c Lindsay b Goddard	55
H.B.Tabert†	c Lindsay b McKinnon	13	b Goddard	7
G.D.McKenzie	run out	16	c sub (M.J.Procter) b Goddard	34
N.J.N.Hawke	not out	18	c sub (M.J.Procter) b Goddard	13
D.A.Renneberg	c Goddard b McKinnon	9	not out	2
Extras	(LB 5, NB 3, W 2)	10	(LB 6, NB 2, W 2)	10
		325		**261**

1/118 2/204 3/207 4/207 5/218   1/62 2/97 3/98 4/110 5/112
6/267 7/267 8/294 9/299   6/183 7/210 8/212 9/248

Bowling: *First Innings*—P.M.Pollock 25-6-74-1; Dumbrill 18-3-55-0; Goddard 26-11-39-2; Lance 17-6-35-1; McKinnon 27.2-9-73-2; Barlow 17-3-39-3. *Second Innings*—P.M.Pollock 18-3-33-0; Dumbrill 16-6-43-1; Goddard 32.5-14-53-6; Lance 3-0-6-0; McKinnon 30-14-64-1; Barlow 15-1-47-1; R.G.Pollock 3-1-5-0.

Umpires: L.M.Baxter and H.C.Kidson

SOUTH AFRICA v AUSTRALIA 1966-67 (Second Test)

At Newlands, Cape Town, 31 December, 2, 3, 4, 5 January

Result: Australia won by 6 wickets

Australia

R.B.Simpson*	c Lance b Barlow	153	c Goddard b P.M.Pollock	18
W.M.Lawry	lbw b P.M.Pollock	10	c P.M.Pollock b Goddard	39
I.R.Redpath	lbw b McKinnon	54	not out	69
R.M.Cowper	c van der Merwe b Goddard	36	c Lindsay b Goddard	4
I.M.Chappell	c Lindsay b Lance	49	b McKinnon	7
T.R.Veivers	lbw b P.M.Pollock	30	not out	35
K.R.Stackpole	c Lindsay b Barlow	134		
G.D.Watson	c Lance b Barlow	50		
G.D.McKenzie	c and b Barlow	11		
H.B.Tabert	not out	2		
D.A.Renneberg	b Barlow	2		
Extras	(B 2, LB 7, W 2)	11	(LB 5, NB 3)	8
		542		**180** (4 wkts)

1/21 2/138 3/216 4/310 5/316   1/49 2/81 3/98 4/119
6/6/368 7/496 8/537 9/538

Bowling: *First Innings*—P.M.Pollock 22-4-84-2; Dumbrill 11-2-36-0; Goddard 42-15-79-1; Barlow 33.3-9-85-5; Pithey 22-5-59-0; McKinnon 38-16-93-1; Lance 20-1-95-1. *Second Innings*—P.M.Pollock 12-2-42-1; Goddard 29.1-10-67-2; Barlow 2-1-1-0; McKinnon 22-5-62-1.

South Africa

T.L.Goddard	c Stackpole b McKenzie	7	lbw b Simpson	37
E.J.Barlow	c Redpath b McKenzie	19	run out	17
A.Bacher	b McKenzie	0	c Simpson b McKenzie	4
R.G.Pollock	c Taber b Simpson	209	b Simpson	4
H.R.Lance	c Simpson b Chappell	2	run out	53
D.T.Lindsay†	c and b Renneberg	5	c Simpson b Cowper	81
P.L.van der Merwe*	c Cowper b Simpson	50	lbw b Chappell	18
D.B.Pithey	c Taber b McKenzie	4	c Redpath b Renneberg	55
R.Dumbrill	c Chappell b McKenzie	6	(10) b McKenzie	1
P.M.Pollock	c Stackpole b Veivers	41	(9) not out	75
A.H.McKinnon	not out	6	b McKenzie	8
Extras	(LB 4)	4	(B 5, LB 9)	14
		353		**367**

1/12 2/12 3/41 4/66 5/85   1/45 2/60 3/60 4/64 5/183
6/197 7/242 8/258 9/343   6/211 7/245 8/331 9/345

Bowling: *First Innings*—McKenzie 33-10-65-5; Renneberg 18-6-51-0; Watson 11-2-27-0; Chappell 13-4-51-1; Simpson 24-9-59-2; Veivers 8.1-2-32-1; Cowper 6-0-28-0; Stackpole 14-2-36-0. *Second Innings*—McKenzie 39.3-11-67-3; Renneberg 18-6-51-1; Chappell 39-17-71-1; Simpson 39-12-99-2; Veivers 7-2-21-0; Cowper 10-2-21-1; Stackpole 8-4-11-0.

Umpires: G.Goldman and H.C.Kidson

SOUTH AFRICA v AUSTRALIA 1966-67 (Fourth Test)

At New Wanderers, Johannesburg, 3, 4, 6, 7 (no play), 8 February
Result: Match drawn

Australia

Batsman	First Innings	R		Second Innings	R
W.M.Lawry	c Bacher b Trimborn	17		b Procter	2
R.B.Simpson*	c du Preez b Goddard	24		c Bacher b Procter	28
I.R.Redpath	c Lindsay b Barlow	14	(4)	c Trimborn b P.M.Pollock	46
R.M.Cowper	c Trimborn b Procter	25	(5)	b du Preez	16
I.M.Chappell	lbw b Goddard	0	(6)	not out	13
K.R.Stackpole	b Goddard	4	(7)	c Goddard b du Preez	5
T.R.Veivers	c Lindsay b Procter	19	(8)	c Lindsay b Goddard	21
G.D.Watson	c Lance b Procter	17	(9)	b Goddard	0
G.D.McKenzie	c R.G.Pollock b Procter	11	(10)	not out	0
H.B.Tabert	c Trimborn b P.M.Pollock	4	(3)	lbw b Goddard	14
D.A.Renneberg	not out	0			
Extras	(LB 6, NB 1, W 1)	8		(LB 2, NB 1)	3
		143		(8 wkts)	148

1/33 2/59 3/59 4/59 5/69
6/103 7/108 8/139 9/139

1/11 2/41 3/58 4/94
5/116 6/125 7/148 8/148

Bowling: *First Innings*—P.M.Pollock 12.1-3-21-1; Procter 18-7-32-4; Goddard 19-6-36-3; Trimborn 10-3-21-1; Barlow 11-6-25-1. *Second Innings*—P.M.Pollock 14-6-24-1; Procter 17-6-38-2; Goddard 16.3-9-23-3; Trimborn 7-3-14-0; Barlow 7-3-20-0; du Preez 14-6-22-2; Lance 3-1-4-0.

South Africa

Batsman	Dismissal	R
T.L.Goddard	c Stackpole b Renneberg	47
E.J.Barlow	c Taber b Renneberg	4
A.Bacher	c Taber b Watson	22
R.G.Pollock	c Taber b Cowper	22
H.R.Lance	lbw b Watson	30
D.T.Lindsay†	c Simpson b Renneberg	131
M.J.Procter	lbw b Simpson	16
P.L.van der Merwe*	c Taber b Renneberg	12
J.H.du Preez	c Simpson b Renneberg	0
P.M.Pollock	not out	34
P.H.J.Trimborn	not out	11
Extras	(LB 3)	3
	(9 wkts dec.)	332

1/8 2/39 3/86 4/120 5/177
6/210 7/266 8/272 9/299

Bowling: McKenzie 39-7-96-0; Renneberg 25-3-97-5; Watson 20-4-67-2; Cowper 15-7-36-1; Simpson 6-0-33-1.

Umpires: J.G.Draper and H.C.Kidson

SOUTH AFRICA v AUSTRALIA 1966-67 (Third Test)

At Kingsmead, Durban, 20, 21, 23, 24, 25 January
Result: South Africa won by 8 wickets

South Africa

Batsman	First Innings	R		Second Innings	R
E.J.Barlow	c and b McKenzie	0		c Redpath b McKenzie	22
T.L.Goddard	b Cowper	19		c Taber b Cowper	33
A.Bacher	c Taber b McKenzie	47		not out	60
R.G.Pollock	c Redpath b Cowper	2		not out	67
H.R.Lance	c Taber b Cowper	13			
D.T.Lindsay†	c Chappell b Hawke	137			
M.J.Procter	b Renneberg	1			
P.L.van der Merwe*	run out	42			
D.B.Pithey	b Hawke	15			
P.M.Pollock	not out	12			
P.H.J.Trimborn	run out	2			
Extras	(B 3, LB 2, NB 5)	10		(LB 2, NB 1)	3
		300		(2 wkts)	185

1/0 2/53 3/57 4/83 5/90
6/94 7/197 8/286 9/287

1/52 2/58

Bowling: *First Innings*—McKenzie 31-7-93-2; Hawke 18-1-69-2; Renneberg 21-4-58-1; Cowper 37-14-57-3; Redpath 4-0-13-0. *Second Innings*—McKenzie 20-7-36-1; Hawke 14-6-22-0; Renneberg 11-1-27-0; Cowper 17-9-29-1; Simpson 4-0-21-0; Chappell 7-0-39-0; Stackpole 2-0-8-0.

Australia

Batsman	First Innings	R		Second Innings	R
R.B.Simpson*	c Lindsay b Procter	6		lbw b Trimborn	94
W.M.Lawry	c Lindsay b Barlow	44		c Lindsay b Lance	34
I.R.Redpath	c Barlow b Goddard	7		c Barlow b P.M.Pollock	80
R.M.Cowper	c Goddard b Trimborn	19		c Lindsay b Lance	40
K.R.Stackpole	c Lindsay b Barlow	24	(7)	c R.G.Pollock b P.M.Pollock	35
T.R.Veivers	b Goddard	6		c Lindsay b Procter	0
I.M.Chappell	run out	6	(5)	c R.G.Pollock b Procter	25
G.D.McKenzie	lbw b Procter	17		b Procter	8
H.B.Tabert	c Bacher b Barlow	4	(10)	c Trimborn b Procter	0
N.J.N.Hawke	not out	9	(9)	b Goddard	5
D.A.Renneberg	b Procter	0		not out	0
Extras	(LB 1, NB 5)	6		(B 4, LB 4, NB 5)	13
		147			334

1/14 2/37 3/45 4/74 5/88
6/96 7/132 8/137 9/137

1/94 2/159 3/224 4/266 5/266
6/317 7/320 8/334 9/334

Bowling: *First Innings*—P.M.Pollock 13-4-35-0; Procter 14-4-27-3; Trimborn 14-3-35-1; Goddard 17-6-26-2; Barlow 11-4-18-3. *Second Innings*—P.M.Pollock 19-5-58-2; Procter 29.1-7-71-4; Trimborn 28-9-47-1; Goddard 27-15-23-1; Barlow 14-5-28-0; Pithey 28-12-55-0; Lance 15-4-39-2.

Umpires: J.G.Draper and H.C.Kidson

SOUTH AFRICA v AUSTRALIA 1966-67 (Fifth Test)

At St George's Park, Port Elizabeth, 24, 25, 27, 28 February

Result: South Africa won by 7 wickets

Australia

Batsman	First Innings		Second Innings	
R.B.Simpson*	c Lindsay b P.M.Pollock	12	lbw b Goddard	35
W.M.Lawry	run out	0	c Bacher b Barlow	25
I.M.Chappell	c Bacher b Procter	11	lbw b Barlow	15
I.R.Redpath	c du Preez b P.M.Pollock	26	lbw b P.M.Pollock	28
R.M.Cowper	c Lindsay b Trimborn	60	b Barlow	54
K.R.Stackpole	c R.G.Pollock b Goddard	24	c Lindsay b Trimborn	19
J.W.Martin	lbw b Goddard	0	c Lindsay b Goddard	20
G.D.Watson	c Barlow b Goddard	0	b P.M.Pollock	9
G.D.McKenzie	c Trimborn b du Preez	14	c R.G.Pollock b Trimborn	29
H.B.Tabert	c Bacher b Procter	20	c Goddard b Trimborn	30
D.A.Renneberg	not out	0	not out	0
Extras	(NB 6, W 1)	6	(LB 2, NB 11, W 1)	14
Total		**173**		**278**

1/4 2/17 3/27 4/89 5/137
6/137 7/137 8/137 9/173

1/50 2/74 3/79 4/144 5/166
6/207 7/207 8/229 9/268

Bowling: *First Innings*—P.M.Pollock 17-2-57-2; Procter 15.1-3-36-2; Trimborn 18-4-37-1; Goddard 10-3-13-3; Barlow 4-2-9-0; Lance 8-4-15-0; du Preez 2-2-0-1. *Second Innings*—P.M.Pollock 15-0-42-2; Procter 16-3-59-0; Trimborn 10.1-4-12-3; Goddard 36-12-63-3; Barlow 5-3-52-2; Lance 5-2-7-0; du Preez 8-4-29-0.

South Africa

Batsman	First Innings		Second Innings	
T.L.Goddard	c Taber b McKenzie	74	c Taber b McKenzie	59
E.J.Barlow	lbw b McKenzie	46	c Chappell b McKenzie	15
A.Bacher	c Taber b McKenzie	3	c Martin b Chappell	40
R.G.Pollock	b Cowper	105	not out	33
H.R.Lance	c Renneberg b Simpson	21	not out	28
D.T.Lindsay†	c Redpath b McKenzie	1		
M.J.Procter	hit wkt b McKenzie	0		
P.L.van der Merwe*	lbw b Watson	8		
P.M.Pollock	c Lawry b Cowper	13		
J.H.du Preez	lbw b Cowper	0		
P.H.J.Trimborn	not out	0		
Extras	(B 1, LB 3, W 1)	5	(LB 1, NB 1, W 2)	4
Total		**276**	(3 wkts)	**179**

1/112 2/124 3/125 4/175 5/201
6/201 7/226 8/271 9/271

1/28 2/109 3/118

Bowling: *First Innings*—McKenzie 35-13-65-5; Renneberg 19-6-44-0; Watson 18-3-58-1; Cowper 19.3-9-27-3; Martin 17-1-64-0; Simpson 8-2-13-1. *Second Innings*—McKenzie 17-5-38-2; Renneberg 12-1-38-0; Watson 3-0-10-0; Cowper 12-4-26-0; Martin 5-0-25-0; Simpson 5-0-10-0; Chappell 7.1-2-28-1.

Umpires: J.G.Draper and H.C.Kidson

AUSTRALIA v INDIA 1967-68 (First Test)

At Adelaide Oval, 23, 25, 26, 27, 28 December

Result: Australia won by 146 runs

Australia

Batsman	First Innings		Second Innings	
R.B.Simpson*	c and b Abid Ali	55	b Surti	103
W.M.Lawry	c Engineer b Abid Ali	42	c Engineer b Kulkarni	0
A.P.Sheahan	lbw b Prasanna	81	lbw b Prasanna	35
R.M.Cowper	c Engineer b Abid Ali	92	b Abid Ali	108
I.R.Redpath	c Borde b Prasanna	0	(7) lbw b Surti	34
I.M.Chappell	c Borde b Prasanna	2	(5) b Surti	13
B.N.Jarman†	b Abid Ali	34	(6) c and b Surti	17
G.D.McKenzie	c Borde b Abid Ali	5	run out	28
J.W.Gleeson	lbw b Abid Ali	1	not out	18
A.N.Connolly	not out	7	c sub (R.B.Desai) b Surti	0
D.A.Renneberg	b Chandrasekhar	1	run out	0
Extras	(B 2, LB 10, NB 3)	15	(B 5, LB 6, NB 2)	13
Total		**335**		**369**

1/99 2/109 3/227 4/227 5/235
6/311 7/319 8/324 9/330

1/0 2/61 3/233 4/263 5/263
6/295 7/322 8/364 9/365

Bowling: *First Innings*—Kulkarni 5-0-25-0; Surti 7-0-30-0; Abid Ali 17-2-55-6; Nadkarni 17-2-68-0; Chandrasekhar 27.1-3-72-1; Prasanna 17-2-60-3; Subramanya 2-0-10-0. *Second Innings*—Kulkarni 4-1-12-1; Surti 20.1-6-74-5; Abid Ali 16-2-61-1; Nadkarni 9.4-3-24-0; Chandrasekhar 13-1-67-0; Prasanna 25-2-109-1; Subramanya 1-0-9-0.

India

Batsman	First Innings		Second Innings	
F.M.Engineer†	c Jarman b McKenzie	89	run out	19
D.N.Sardesai	c Redpath b Renneberg	1	c Jarman b Renneberg	11
A.L.Wadekar	st Jarman b Connolly	28	c Jarman b Renneberg	0
C.G.Borde*	lbw b Simpson	69	b Renneberg	12
R.F.Surti	b Simpson	70	c Redpath b Gleeson	53
R.G.Nadkarni	lbw b Gleeson	3	(8) b McKenzie	15
S.Abid Ali	c and b Connolly	33	(6) lbw b Renneberg	33
V.Subramanya	b Connolly	7	(7) run out	75
E.A.S.Prasanna	c Lawry b McKenzie	1	not out	18
U.N.Kulkarni	lbw b Connolly	0	(11) c Chappell b Renneberg	2
B.S.Chandrasekhar	not out	1	(10) c Simpson b Gleeson	0
Extras	(NB 5)	5	(B 3, LB 8, NB 2)	13
Total		**307**		**251**

1/19 2/80 3/129 4/250 5/259
6/272 7/287 8/288 9/291

1/24 2/24 3/46 4/49 5/104
6/159 7/209 8/232 9/236

Bowling: *First Innings*—McKenzie 15-1-70-2; Renneberg 6-0-45-1; Connolly 12.4-1-54-4; Gleeson 13-4-36-2; Chappell 10-1-41-0; Simpson 12-2-42-1; Cowper 3-0-14-0. *Second Innings*—McKenzie 17-2-91-1; Renneberg 14.2-2-39-5; Connolly 3-0-21-0; Gleeson 16-4-38-2; Chappell 5-0-24-0; Simpson 5-0-25-0.

Umpires: C.J.Egar and L.P.Rowan

AUSTRALIA v INDIA 1967-68 (Second Test)

At Melbourne Cricket Ground, 30 December, 1, 2, 3 January
Result: Australia won by an innings and 4 runs

India

D.N.Sardesai b McKenzie	1		b McKenzie	5
F.M.Engineer† c Connolly b McKenzie	9		c Chappell b Renneberg	42
S.Abid Ali c Jarman b McKenzie	4	(8)	lbw b Cowper	21
A.L.Wadekar c Connolly b McKenzie	6	(3)	c Sheahan b Simpson	99
R.F.Surti lbw b Simpson	30	(4)	c Jarman b McKenzie	43
C.G.Borde c Redpath b McKenzie	0		c Redpath b Renneberg	6
Nawab of Pataudi, jr* c Jarman b Renneberg	75		c Redpath b Simpson	85
V.Subramanya b McKenzie	5	(9)	lbw b McKenzie	10
E.A.S.Prasanna c Chappell b Renneberg	14	(5)	c Chappell b Simpson	21
R.B.Desai not out	13		c Simpson b Connolly	14
B.S.Chandrasekhar c Jarman b McKenzie	0		not out	0
Extras (B 8, LB 2, NB 6)	16		(B 1, LB 4, NB 1)	6
	173			**352**

1/2 2/10 3/18 4/25 5/25   173
6/47 7/72 8/146 9/162

1/11 2/66 3/182 4/194 5/217   352
6/227 7/276 8/292 9/346

Bowling: *First Innings*—McKenzie 21.4-2-66-7; Renneberg 15-4-37-2; Connolly 13-3-33-0; Gleeson 5-0-9-0; Chappell 1-0-7-0; Simpson 2-0-5-1. *Second Innings*—McKenzie 19-2-85-3; Renneberg 14-1-98-2; Connolly 11.7-2-48-1; Gleeson 14-5-37-0; Chappell 4-0-14-0; Simpson 14-3-44-3; Cowper 8-2-20-1.

Australia

R.B.Simpson* b Surti	109
W.M.Lawry st Engineer b Prasanna	100
A.P.Sheahan c Engineer b Surti	24
R.M.Cowper b Prasanna	12
I.M.Chappell c Wadekar b Surti	151
I.R.Redpath run out	26
B.N.Jarman† b Prasanna	65
G.D.McKenzie c sub (B.S.Bedi) b Prasanna	0
J.W.Gleeson c Borde b Prasanna	13
A.N.Connolly c sub (B.S.Bedi) b Prasanna	5
D.A.Renneberg not out	8
Extras (B 3, LB 10, NB 3)	16
	529

1/191 2/233 3/246 4/274 5/329   529
6/463 7/463 8/500 9/508

Bowling: Desai 12-0-63-0; Surti 29.3-4-150-3; Abid Ali 20-0-106-0; Chandrasekhar 7-0-35-0; Prasanna 34-6-141-6; Subramanya 3-0-18-0.

Umpires: C.J.Egar and L.P.Rowan

AUSTRALIA v INDIA 1967-68 (Third Test)

At Woolloongabba, Brisbane, 19, 20, 22, 23, 24 January
Result: Australia won by 39 runs

Australia

W.M.Lawry* c Bedi b Nadkarni	64	c Engineer b Surti	45
I.R.Redpath c Wadekar b Prasanna	41	lbw b Prasanna	79
R.M.Cowper b Nadkarni	51	b Surti	25
A.P.Sheahan st Engineer b Surti	58	c Surti b Bedi	26
I.M.Chappell b Surti	17	b Prasanna	27
K.D.Walters c Wadekar b Kulkarni	93	not out	62
B.N.Jarman† lbw b Prasanna	18	c and b Prasanna	9
E.W.Freeman b Surti	15	c Surti b Prasanna	8
J.W.Gleeson run out	14	c Abid Ali b Surti	1
A.N.Connolly c Pataudi b Kulkarni	0	b Prasanna	0
D.A.Renneberg not out	6	c Surti b Prasanna	12
Extras (B 1, LB 1, NB 4)	6	(B 1, LB 10, NB 1)	12
	379		**294**

1/76 2/148 3/160 4/215 5/239   379
6/250 7/277 8/323 9/378

1/116 2/136 3/162 4/196   294
5/240 6/266 7/284 8/293 9/294

Bowling: *First Innings*—Kulkarni 8.2-1-37-2; Surti 26-2-102-3; Prasanna 38-6-114-2; Bedi 23-4-71-0; Abid Ali 2-0-9-0; Nadkarni 14-5-34-2; Jaisimha 1-0-6-0. *Second Innings*—Kulkarni 4-0-22-0; Surti 16-4-59-3; Prasanna 33.4-9-104-6; Bedi 14-4-44-1; Abid Ali 1-0-6-0; Nadkarni 15-5-47-0.

India

F.M.Engineer† c Gleeson b Freeman	2	c Jarman b Renneberg	0
S.Abid Ali c Redpath b Freeman	2	c Jarman b Connolly	47
A.L.Wadekar c Jarman b Renneberg	1	c Connolly b Cowper	11
R.F.Surti c Cowper b Chappell	52	b Cowper	64
Nawab of Pataudi, jr* lbw b Freeman	74	b Walters	48
M.L.Jaisimha c Lawry b Cowper	74	c Gleeson b Cowper	101
C.G.Borde c and b Connolly	12	c Redpath b Cowper	63
R.G.Nadkarni b Cowper	17	lbw b Gleeson	2
E.A.S.Prasanna c Walters b Cowper	24	b Gleeson	4
B.S.Bedi not out	7	c Lawry b Gleeson	0
U.N.Kulkarni c Cowper b Connolly	12	not out	1
Extras (B 6, LB 4, NB 2)	12	(B 4, LB 6, NB 4)	14
	279		**355**

1/2 2/5 3/9 4/137 5/139   279
6/165 7/209 8/268 9/270

1/17 2/48 3/61 4/154 5/191   355
6/310 7/313 8/323 9/333

Bowling: *First Innings*—Renneberg 10-1-40-1; Freeman 21-1-56-3; Walters 6-0-22-0; Connolly 15-4-43-2; Gleeson 15-7-20-0; Cowper 15-5-31-3; Chappell 18-4-55-1. *Second Innings*—Renneberg 7-0-43-1; Freeman 8-2-29-0; Walters 11-2-33-1; Connolly 18-6-51-1; Gleeson 21-6-50-3; Cowper 39.6-8-104-4; Chappell 5-1-31-0.

Umpires: C.J.Egar and L.P.Rowan

AUSTRALIA v INDIA 1967-68 (Fourth Test)

At Sydney Cricket Ground, 26, 27, 29, 30, 31 January
Result: Australia won by 144 runs

Australia

Batsman	First innings	R	Second innings	R
W.M.Lawry*	c Engineer b Prasanna	66	c sub (V.Subramanya) b Nadkarni	52
R.M.Cowper	b Abid Ali	32	st Engineer b Prasanna	165
A.P.Sheahan	c and b Bedi	72	(4) c Wadekar b Jaisimha	22
K.D.Walters	not out	94	(5) run out	5
L.R.Joslin	c Wadekar b Prasanna	7	(6) c Abid Ali b Bedi	2
R.B.Simpson	b Bedi	7	(3) run out	20
I.M.Chappell	run out	0	lbw b Prasanna	2
B.N.Jarman†	c Engineer b Surti	4	run out	0
E.W.Freeman	lbw b Kulkarni	11	c sub (R.C.Saxena) b Prasanna	8
N.J.N.Hawke	c Engineer b Kulkarni	1	c Abid Ali b Prasanna	4
J.W.Gleeson	lbw b Prasanna	14	not out	4
Extras	(B 2, LB 4, NB 3)	9	(B 1, LB 1, NB 1)	3
Total		**317**		**292**

1/61 2/136 3/219 4/228 5/239
6/242 7/256 8/275 9/277

1/111 2/166 3/222 4/240
5/243 6/260 7/271 8/278 9/286

Bowling: *First Innings*—Kulkarni 17-0-73-2; Surti 11-1-64-1; Abid Ali 15-1-58-1; Jaisimha 2-0-9-0; Bedi 21-4-42-2; Prasanna 20.6-5-62-3. *Second Innings*—Kulkarni 8-0-31-0; Surti 8-1-49-0; Abid Ali 2-0-7-0; Jaisimha 1-0-2-1; Bedi 21-5-66-1; Prasanna 29.3-4-96-4; Nadkarni 16-3-38-1.

India

Batsman	First innings	R	Second innings	R
F.M.Engineer†	c Chappell b Walters	17	c Simpson b Gleeson	37
S.Abid Ali	hit wkt b Gleeson	78	c Simpson b Cowper	81
A.L.Wadekar	c and b Cowper	49	lbw b Cowper	18
R.F.Surti	b Simpson	29	c Chappell b Simpson	26
Nawab of Pataudi, jr*	c Simpson b Freeman	51	c Chappell b Simpson	6
M.L.Jaisimha	c Jarman b Simpson	0	c Gleeson b Cowper	6
R.G.Nadkarni	c Sheahan b Simpson	0	(8) c Sheahan b Simpson	6
E.A.S.Prasanna	c Cowper b Freeman	26	(9) b Simpson	0
C.G.Borde	lbw b Freeman	0	(7) c Simpson b Cowper	4
B.S.Bedi	c Simpson b Freeman	8	b Simpson	2
U.N.Kulkarni	not out	1	not out	1
Extras	(B 4, LB 2, NB 3)	9	(LB 3)	3
Total		**268**		**197**

1/56 2/111 3/178 4/178 5/175
6/184 7/236 8/236 9/267

1/83 2/120 3/145 4/164 5/175
6/180 7/193 8/193 9/195

Bowling: *First Innings*—Hawke 18-2-51-0; Freeman 18.1-2-86-4; Walters 4-0-20-1; Gleeson 12-3-40-1; Cowper 12-5-21-1; Simpson 20-10-38-3; Chappell 1-0-3-0. *Second Innings*—Hawke 6-2-22-0; Freeman 4-0-26-0; Walters 3-1-11-0; Gleeson 12-4-27-1; Simpson 23-5-59-5.

Umpires: C.J.Egar and L.P.Rowan

ENGLAND v AUSTRALIA 1968 (First Test)

At Old Trafford, Manchester, 6, 7, 8, 10, 11 June
Result: Australia won by 159 runs

Australia

Batsman	First innings	R	Second innings	R
W.M.Lawry*	c Boycott b Barber	81	c Pocock b d'Oliveira	16
I.R.Redpath	lbw b Snow	8	lbw b Snow	8
R.M.Cowper	b Snow	0	c and b Pocock	37
K.D.Walters	lbw b Barber	81	lbw b Pocock	86
A.P.Sheahan	c d'Oliveira b Snow	88	c Graveney b Pocock	8
I.M.Chappell	run out	73	c Knott b Pocock	9
B.N.Jarman†	c and b Higgs	12	b Pocock	41
N.J.N.Hawke	c Knott b Snow	5	c Edrich b Pocock	0
G.D.McKenzie	c Cowdrey b d'Oliveira	0	c Cowdrey b d'Oliveira	0
J.W.Gleeson	c Knott b Higgs	0	c Snow b Barber	2
A.N.Connolly	not out	0	run out	2
Extras	(LB 7, NB 2)	9	(B 2, LB 9)	11
Total		**357**		**220**

1/29 2/29 3/173 4/174 5/326
6/341 7/351 8/353 9/357

1/24 2/24 3/106 4/122 5/140
6/211 7/211 8/214 9/214

Bowling: *First Innings*—Snow 34.5-9-97-4; Higgs 35.3-11-80-2; d'Oliveira 25-11-38-1; Pocock 22.5-5-77-0; Barber 11-0-56-2. *Second Innings*—Snow 17-2-51-1; Higgs 23-8-41-0; d'Oliveira 5-3-7-1; Pocock 33-10-79-6; Barber 10-1-31-1.

England

Batsman	First innings	R	Second innings	R
J.H.Edrich	run out	49	c Jarman b Cowper	38
G.Boycott	c Jarman b Cowper	35	c Redpath b McKenzie	11
M.C.Cowdrey*	c Lawry b McKenzie	2	c Jarman b McKenzie	11
T.W.Graveney	c McKenzie b Cowper	0	c Jarman b Gleeson	33
D.L.Amiss	c Cowper b McKenzie	0	b Cowper	0
R.W.Barber	c Sheahan b McKenzie	20	c Cowper b Hawke	46
B.L.d'Oliveira	b Connolly	9	not out	87
A.P.E.Knott†	c McKenzie b Cowper	9	lbw b Connolly	4
J.A.Snow	not out	4	c Lawry b Connolly	2
K.Higgs	lbw b Cowper	2	c Jarman b Gleeson	0
P.I.Pocock	c Redpath b Gleeson	6	lbw b Gleeson	10
Extras	(B 9, LB 3, W 3)	15	(B 5, LB 6)	11
Total		**165**		**253**

1/86 2/87 3/89 4/90 5/97
6/120 7/137 8/137 9/144

1/13 2/25 3/91 4/91 5/105
6/185 7/214 8/218 9/219

Bowling: *First Innings*—McKenzie 28-11-33-3; Hawke 15-7-18-0; Connolly 28-15-26-1; Gleeson 6.3-2-21-1; Cowper 26-11-48-4; Chappell 1-0-4-0. *Second Innings*—McKenzie 18-3-52-2; Hawke 8-4-15-1; Connolly 13-4-35-2; Gleeson 30-14-44-3; Cowper 39-12-82-2; Chappell 2-0-14-0.

Umpires: J.S.Buller and C.S.Elliott

ENGLAND v AUSTRALIA 1968 (Second Test)

At Lord's, London, 20, 21, 22, 24, 25 June
Result: Match drawn

England

J.H.Edrich	c Cowper b McKenzie	7
G.Boycott	c Sheahan b McKenzie	49
C.Milburn	c Walters b Gleeson	83
M.C.Cowdrey*	c Cowper b McKenzie	45
K.F.Barrington	c Jarman b Connolly	75
T.W.Graveney	c Jarman b Connolly	14
B.R.Knight	not out	27
A.P.E.Knott†	run out	33
J.A.Snow	not out	0
D.J.Brown		
D.L.Underwood		
Extras	(B 7, LB 5, NB 5, W 1)	18
	(7 wkts dec.)	351

1/10 2/142 3/147 4/244 5/271
6/330 7/351

Bowling: McKenzie 45-18-111-3; Hawke 35-7-82-0; Connolly 26.3-8-55-2; Cowper 8-2-40-0; Gleeson 27-11-43-1.

Australia

W.M.Lawry*	c Knott b Brown	0	c Brown b Snow	28
I.R.Redpath	c Cowdrey b Brown	4	b Underwood	53
R.M.Cowper	c Graveney b Snow	8	c Underwood b Barrington	32
K.D.Walters	c Cowdrey b Snow	26	b Underwood	0
A.P.Sheahan	c Knott b Knight	6	not out	
I.M.Chappell	lbw b Knight	7	not out	12
N.J.N.Hawke	c Cowdrey b Knight	2		
G.D.McKenzie	b Brown	5		
J.W.Gleeson	c Cowdrey b Brown	14		
B.N.Jarman†	retired hurt	0		
A.N.Connolly	not out	0		
Extras	(LB 2, NB 4)	6	(NB 2)	2
		78	(4 wkts)	127

1/1 2/12 3/23 4/46 5/52
6/58 7/63 8/78 9/78

1/66 2/93 3/97 4/115

Bowling: First Innings—Snow 9-5-14-1; Brown 14-5-42-5; Knight 10.4-5-16-3. Second Innings—Snow 12-5-30-1; Brown 19-9-40-0; Knight 16-9-35-0; Underwood 18-15-8-2; Barrington 2-0-12-1.

Umpires: J.S.Buller and A.E.Fagg

ENGLAND v AUSTRALIA 1968 (Third Test)

At Edgbaston, Birmingham, 11 (no play), 12, 13, 15, 16 July
Result: Match drawn

England

J.H.Edrich	c Taber b Freeman	88	c Cowper b Freeman	64
G.Boycott	lbw b Gleeson	36	c Taber b Connolly	31
M.C.Cowdrey*	b Freeman	104		
K.F.Barrington	lbw b Freeman	0		
T.W.Graveney	b Connolly	96	(3) not out	39
B.R.Knight	c Chappell b Connolly	6	(4) b Connolly	1
A.P.E.Knott†	b McKenzie	4	(5) not out	4
R.Illingworth	lbw b Gleeson	27		
D.J.Brown	b Connolly	0		
J.A.Snow	c Connolly b Freeman	19		
D.L.Underwood	not out	14		
Extras	(B 4, LB 6, NB 4, W 1)	15	(LB 2, NB 1)	3
		409	(3 wkts dec.)	142

1/80 2/188 3/189 4/282 5/293
6/323 7/374 8/374 9/376

1/57 2/131 3/134

Bowling: First Innings—McKenzie 47-14-115-1; Freeman 30.5-8-78-4; Connolly 35-8-84-3; Gleeson 46-19-84-2; Cowper 7-1-25-0; Walters 7-3-8-0. Second Innings—McKenzie 18-1-57-0; Freeman 9-2-23-1; Connolly 15-3-59-2.

Australia

W.M.Lawry*	retired hurt	6		
I.R.Redpath	b Brown	0	lbw b Snow	22
R.M.Cowper	b Snow	57	(1) not out	25
I.M.Chappell	b Knight	71	(3) not out	18
K.D.Walters	c and b Underwood	46		
A.P.Sheahan	b Underwood	4		
H.B.Taber†	c Barrington b Illingworth	16		
E.W.Freeman	b Illingworth	6		
G.D.McKenzie	not out	0		
J.W.Gleeson	c Illingworth b Underwood	3		
A.N.Connolly	b Illingworth	0		
Extras	(B 1, LB 10, NB 2)	13	(LB 1, NB 2)	3
		222	(1 wkt)	68

1/10 2/121 3/165 4/176 5/213
6/213 7/219 8/222 9/222

1/44

Bowling: First Innings—Snow 17-3-46-1; Brown 13-2-44-1; Knight 14-2-34-1; Underwood 25-9-48-3; Illingworth 22-10-37-3. Second Innings—Snow 9-1-32-1; Brown 6-1-15-0; Underwood 8-4-14-0; Illingworth 5.2-2-4-0.

Umpires: C.S.Elliott and H.Yarnold

ENGLAND v AUSTRALIA 1968 (Fourth Test)
At Headingley, Leeds, 25, 26, 27, 29, 30 July
Result: Match drawn

Australia

R.J.Inverarity b Snow	8	lbw b Illingworth	34
R.M.Cowper b Snow	27	st Knott b Illingworth	5
I.R.Redpath b Illingworth	92	c Edrich b Snow	48
K.D.Walters c Barrington b Underwood	42	c Graveney b Snow	56
I.M.Chappell b Brown	65	c Barrington b Underwood	81
A.P.Sheahan c Knott b Snow	38	st Knott b Illingworth	31
B.N.Jarman† c Dexter b Brown	10	st Knott b Illingworth	4
E.W.Freeman b Underwood	21	b Illingworth	10
G.D.McKenzie lbw b Underwood	5	c Snow b Illingworth	10
J.W.Gleeson not out	2	c Knott b Underwood	7
A.N.Connolly c Graveney b Underwood	0	not out	0
Extras (LB 4, NB 1)	5	(B 13, LB 8, NB 5)	26
	315		312

1/10 2/104 3/152 4/188 5/248
6/267 7/307 8/309 9/315

1/28 2/81 3/119 4/198 5/273
6/281 7/283 8/296 9/311

Bowling: *First Innings*—Snow 35-3-98-3; Brown 35-4-99-2; Illingworth 29-15-47-1; Underwood 27.4-13-41-4; Dexter 7-0-25-0. *Second Innings*—Snow 24-3-51-2; Brown 27-5-79-0; Illingworth 51-22-87-6; Underwood 45.1-22-52-2; Dexter 1-0-3-0; Barrington 6-1-14-0.

England

J.H.Edrich c Jarman b McKenzie	62	c Jarman b McKenzie	65
R.M.Prideaux c Freeman b Gleeson	64	b McKenzie	2
E.R.Dexter b McKenzie	10	b Connolly	38
T.W.Graveney* c Cowper b Connolly	37	c and b Cowper	41
K.F.Barrington b Connolly	49	not out	46
K.W.R.Fletcher c Jarman b Connolly	0	not out	23
A.P.E.Knott† lbw b Freeman	4		
R.Illingworth c Gleeson b Connolly	6		
J.A.Snow b Connolly	0		
D.J.Brown b Cowper	14		
D.L.Underwood not out	45		
Extras (B 1, LB 7, NB 3)	11	(LB 7, NB 8)	15
	302	(4 wkts)	230

1/123 2/136 3/141 4/209 5/215
6/235 7/237 8/241 9/241

1/4 2/81 3/134 4/168

Bowling: *First Innings*—McKenzie 39-20-61-2; Freeman 22-6-60-1; Gleeson 25-5-68-1; Connolly 39-13-72-5; Cowper 18-10-24-1; Chappell 4-1-6-0. *Second Innings*—McKenzie 25-2-65-1; Freeman 6-1-25-0; Gleeson 11-4-26-0; Connolly 31-10-68-2; Cowper 5-0-22-1; Chappell 5-3-6-0; Inverarity 1-0-3-0.

Umpires: J.S.Buller and A.E.Fagg

ENGLAND v AUSTRALIA 1968 (Fifth Test)
At Kennington Oval, London, 22, 23, 24, 26, 27 August
Result: England won by 226 runs

England

J.H.Edrich b Chappell	164	c Lawry b Mallett	17
C.Milburn b Connolly	8	c Lawry b Connolly	18
E.R.Dexter b Gleeson	21	b Connolly	28
M.C.Cowdrey* lbw b Mallett	16	b Mallett	35
T.W.Graveney c Redpath b McKenzie	63	run out	12
B.L.d'Oliveira c Inverarity b Mallett	158	c Gleeson b Connolly	9
A.P.E.Knott† c Jarman b Mallett	28	run out	34
R.Illingworth lbw b Connolly	8	b Gleeson	10
J.A.Snow run out	4	c Sheahan b Gleeson	13
D.L.Underwood not out	9	not out	1
D.J.Brown c Sheahan b Gleeson	2	b Connolly	1
Extras (B 1, LB 11, W 1)	13	(LB 3)	3
	494		181

1/28 2/84 3/113 4/238 5/359
6/421 7/458 8/468 9/489

1/23 2/53 3/67 4/90 5/114
6/126 7/149 8/179 9/179

Bowling: *First Innings*—McKenzie 40-8-87-1; Connolly 57-12-127-2; Walters 6-2-17-0; Gleeson 41.2-8-109-2; Mallett 36-11-87-3; Chappell 21-5-54-1. *Second Innings*—McKenzie 4-0-14-0; Connolly 22.4-2-65-4; Mallett 25-4-77-2; Gleeson 7-2-22-2.

Australia

W.M.Lawry* c Knott b Snow	135		c Milburn b Brown	4
R.J.Inverarity c Milburn b Snow	1		lbw b Underwood	56
I.R.Redpath c Cowdrey b Snow	67		lbw b Underwood	8
I.M.Chappell c Knott b Brown	10		lbw b Underwood	2
K.D.Walters c Knott b Brown	5		c Knott b Underwood	1
A.P.Sheahan b Illingworth	14		c Snow b Illingworth	24
B.N.Jarman† st Knott b Illingworth	21		b d'Oliveira	21
G.D.McKenzie b Brown	12	(9)	c Brown b Underwood	0
A.A.Mallett not out	43	(8)	c Brown b Underwood	0
J.W.Gleeson c Dexter b Underwood	19		b Underwood	5
A.N.Connolly b Underwood	3		not out	4
Extras (B 4, LB 7, NB 4)	15		(LB 4)	4
	324			125

1/7 2/136 3/151 4/161 5/185
6/188 7/237 8/269 9/302

1/4 2/13 3/19 4/29 5/65
6/110 7/110 8/110 9/120

Bowling: *First Innings*—Snow 35-12-67-3; Brown 22-5-63-3; Illingworth 48-15-87-2; Underwood 54.3-21-89-2; d'Oliveira 4-2-3-0. *Second Innings*—Snow 11-5-22-0; Brown 8-3-19-1; Underwood 31.3-19-50-7; Illingworth 28-18-29-1; d'Oliveira 5-4-1-1.

Umpires: C.S.Elliott and A.E.Fagg

AUSTRALIA v WEST INDIES 1968-69 (First Test)

At Woolloongabba, Brisbane, 6, 7, 8, 10 December
Result: West Indies won by 125 runs

West Indies

Batsman	1st innings	Runs	2nd innings	Runs
G.S.Camacho	b Gleeson	6	c Redpath b Connolly	40
M.C.Carew	run out	83	(8) not out	71
R.B.Kanhai	c Gleeson b Mallett	94	(2) c Inverarity b Gleeson	29
S.M.Nurse	c Jarman b McKenzie	25	(4) c Mallett b Gleeson	16
B.F.Butcher	c Chappell b Connolly	22	b Gleeson	1
G.S.Sobers*	c Jarman b Connolly	2	c Jarman b Gleeson	36
C.H.Lloyd	c Jarman b Connolly	7	(5) lbw b McKenzie	129
D.A.J.Holford	c Jarman b Gleeson	6	(7) c Jarman b McKenzie	4
J.L.Hendriks†	not out	15	c Jarman b Chappell	10
C.C.Griffith	c Sheahan b Connolly	8	b Gleeson	1
L.R.Gibbs	b McKenzie	17	c Inverarity b Chappell	0
Extras	(B 1, LB 6, NB 4)	11	(B 4, LB 10, NB 2)	16
		296		353

1/23 2/188 3/192 4/241 5/243
6/247 7/250 8/258 9/267

1/48 2/92 3/92 4/93 5/165
6/178 7/298 8/331 9/350

Bowling: *First Innings*—McKenzie 21-5-55-2; Connolly 19-5-60-4; Gleeson 28-7-72-2; Mallett 14-2-54-1; Chappell 4-0-10-0; Stackpole 9-3-34-0. *Second Innings*—McKenzie 16-2-55-2; Connolly 21-1-75-1; Gleeson 33-5-122-5; Mallett 4-0-32-0; Stackpole 7-1-32-0; Chappell 6-0-21-2.

Australia

Batsman	1st innings	Runs	2nd innings	Runs
I.R.Redpath	c Hendriks b Sobers	0	c Lloyd b Sobers	18
W.M.Lawry*	c Sobers b Lloyd	105	b Gibbs	9
I.M.Chappell	c Sobers b Lloyd	117	c sub (C.A.Davis) b Sobers	50
K.R.Stackpole	c Holford b Gibbs	1	b Sobers	32
A.P.Sheahan	c Nurse b Holford	14	b Sobers	34
R.J.Inverarity	c Holford b Gibbs	5	c Kanhai b Gibbs	9
B.N.Jarman†	c Sobers b Gibbs	17	st Hendriks b Sobers	4
G.D.McKenzie	c Gibbs b Holford	4	not out	38
A.A.Mallett	c Gibbs	6	lbw b Carew	19
J.W.Gleeson	not out	1	c sub (C.A.Davis) b Sobers	10
A.N.Connolly	lbw b Gibbs	0	c Holford b Sobers	0
Extras	(B 7, LB 1, NB 6)	14	(B 9, LB 7, NB 1)	17
		284		240

1/0 2/217 3/220 4/246 5/255
6/257 7/263 8/283 9/284

1/27 2/29 3/66 4/137 5/161
6/165 7/165 8/220 9/238

Bowling: *First Innings*—Sobers 14-5-30-1; Griffith 12-1-47-0; Gibbs 39.4-7-88-5; Holford 25-6-88-2; Lloyd 8-1-17-2; *Second Innings*—Sobers 33.6-12-73-6; Lloyd 2-0-7-0; Gibbs 30-6-82-3; Holford 14-1-31-0; Carew 9-1-30-1.

Umpires: C.J.Egar and L.P.Rowan

AUSTRALIA v WEST INDIES 1968-69 (Second Test)

At Melbourne Cricket Ground, 26, 27, 28, 30 December
Result: Australia won by an innings and 30 runs

West Indies

Batsman	1st innings	Runs	2nd innings	Runs
G.S.Camacho	c Chappell b McKenzie	0	lbw b Gleeson	11
R.C.Fredericks	c Redpath b McKenzie	76	c Freeman b Gleeson	47
M.C.Carew	c Gleeson b McKenzie	7	(8) b Stackpole	33
S.M.Nurse	c Jarman b Freeman	22	(5) c Stackpole b Gleeson	74
B.F.Butcher	lbw b Gleeson	42	(7) c Jarman b McKenzie	0
G.S.Sobers*	b McKenzie	19	lbw b McKenzie	67
R.B.Kanhai	c Sheahan b McKenzie	5	(4) c Redpath b Freeman	4
C.A.Davis	b McKenzie	18	(9) c Redpath b Gleeson	10
J.L.Hendriks†	c Chappell b McKenzie	0	(10) c Redpath b Gleeson	3
R.M.Edwards	not out	9	(3) run out	21
L.R.Gibbs	b McKenzie	0	not out	0
Extras	(B 1, LB 1)	2	(B 7, NB 3)	10
		200		280

1/0 2/14 3/42 4/135 5/158
6/170 7/177 8/177 9/200

1/23 2/76 3/85 4/85 5/219
6/219 7/243 8/246 9/278

Bowling: *First Innings*—McKenzie 28-5-71-8; Connolly 12-2-34-0; Freeman 7-0-32-1; Gleeson 25-8-49-1; Stackpole 1-0-12-0. *Second Innings*—McKenzie 20-2-88-2; Connolly 19-7-35-0; Freeman 11-1-31-1; Gleeson 26.4-9-61-5; Chappell 9-1-36-0; Stackpole 13-9-19-1.

Australia

Batsman	Dismissal	Runs
I.R.Redpath	c Hendriks b Edwards	7
W.M.Lawry*	c Carew b Davis	205
I.M.Chappell	b Sobers	165
K.D.Walters	c Camacho b Sobers	76
K.R.Stackpole	b Gibbs	15
A.P.Sheahan	c and b Sobers	18
B.N.Jarman†	c Butcher b Gibbs	12
E.W.Freeman	c Carew b Gibbs	2
G.D.McKenzie	b Sobers	1
J.W.Gleeson	b Gibbs	0
A.N.Connolly	not out	3
Extras	(LB 4, NB 2)	6
		510

1/14 2/312 3/435 4/453 5/488
6/501 7/505 8/506 9/506

Bowling: Sobers 33.3-4-97-4; Edwards 26-1-128-1; Davis 24-0-94-1; Gibbs 43-8-139-4; Carew 10-2-46-0.

Umpires: C.J.Egar and L.P.Rowan

AUSTRALIA v WEST INDIES 1968-69 (Third Test)

At Sydney Cricket Ground, 3, 4, 5, 7, 8 January
Result: Australia won by 10 wickets

West Indies

Batsman	Dismissal (1st)	Score	Dismissal (2nd)	Score
R.C.Fredericks	c Chappell b McKenzie	26	c Redpath b Connolly	43
M.C.Carew	c Jarman b McKenzie	30	c Jarman b Freeman	10
R.B.Kanhai	b McKenzie	17	c Chappell b McKenzie	69
B.F.Butcher	b Stackpole	28	c and b Gleeson	101
S.M.Nurse	c Redpath b Connolly	3	c Stackpole b McKenzie	17
G.S.Sobers*	b Freeman	49	c Chappell b Gleeson	36
C.H.Lloyd	c Jarman b Freeman	50	c Stackpole b Freeman	13
J.L.Hendriks†	c Stackpole b Freeman	4	(9) c Connolly b Gleeson	22
R.M.Edwards	b Connolly	10	(8) b Freeman	0
W.W.Hall	c Gleeson b McKenzie	33	st Jarman b Gleeson	5
L.R.Gibbs	not out	1	not out	1
Extras	(B 2, LB 10, NB 1)	13	(LB 3, NB 4)	7
Total		264		324

1/49 2/72 3/79 4/85 5/143 6/181 7/216 8/217 9/236

1/20 2/123 3/127 4/168 5/243 6/263 7/264 8/318 9/232

Bowling: *First Innings*—McKenzie 22.1-3-85-4; Connolly 16-1-54-2; Freeman 13-2-57-3; Walters 2-1-3-0; Gleeson 18-7-45-0; Stackpole 4-2-7-1. *Second Innings*—McKenzie 24-2-80-2; Connolly 23-7-54-1; Freeman 15-3-39-3; Gleeson 26-5-91-4; Stackpole 5-0-33-0.

Australia

Batsman	Dismissal (1st)	Score	Dismissal (2nd)	Score
W.M.Lawry*	c Carew b Edwards	29	(1) not out	21
K.R.Stackpole	c Gibbs b Hall	58	not out	21
I.M.Chappell	c Kanhai b Gibbs	33		
I.R.Redpath	st Hendriks b Carew	80		
K.D.Walters	b Gibbs	118		
A.P.Sheahan	c Lloyd b Hall	47		
B.N.Jarman†	c Fredericks b Hall	0		
E.W.Freeman	b Edwards	76		
G.D.McKenzie	run out	10		
J.W.Gleeson	not out	42		
A.N.Connolly	run out	37		
Extras	(B 5, LB 11, W 1)	17		
Total		547	(0 wkts)	42

1/68 2/95 3/153 4/235 5/345 6/349 7/387 8/418 9/474

Bowling: *First Innings*—Hall 26-2-113-3; Edwards 25-1-139-2; Sobers 21-4-109-0; Gibbs 37.6-6-124-2; Carew 12-1-45-1. *Second Innings*—Hall 2-0-8-0; Edwards 1-0-7-0; Carew 2-0-9-0; Lloyd 2-0-8-0; Kanhai 1-0-10-0.

Umpires: C.J.Egar and L.P.Rowan

AUSTRALIA v WEST INDIES 1968-69 (Fourth Test)

At Adelaide Oval, 24, 25, 27, 28, 29 January
Result: Match drawn

West Indies

Batsman	Dismissal (1st)	Score	Dismissal (2nd)	Score
R.C.Fredericks	lbw b Connolly	17	c Chappell b Connolly	23
M.C.Carew	c Chappell b Gleeson	36	c Chappell b Connolly	90
R.B.Kanhai	lbw b Connolly	11	b Connolly	80
B.F.Butcher	c Chappell b Gleeson	52	c Sheahan b McKenzie	118
S.M.Nurse	c and b McKenzie	5	lbw b Gleeson	40
G.S.Sobers*	b Freeman	110	(6) c Walters b Connolly	52
C.H.Lloyd	c Lawry b Gleeson	10	(7) c Redpath b Connolly	42
D.A.J.Holford	c McKenzie b Freeman	6	(8) c Stackpole b McKenzie	80
C.C.Griffith	b Freeman	7	(9) run out	24
J.L.Hendriks†	not out	10	(5) not out	37
L.R.Gibbs	c Connolly b Freeman	4	b McKenzie	1
Extras	(B 5, LB 2, NB 1)	8	(B 5, LB 12, NB 12)	29
Total		276		616

1/21 2/39 3/89 4/107 5/199 6/215 7/228 8/261 9/264

1/35 2/167 3/240 4/304 5/376 6/404 7/476 8/492 9/614

Bowling: *First Innings*—McKenzie 14-1-51-1; Connolly 13-3-61-2; Freeman 10.3-0-52-4; Gleeson 25-5-91-3; Stackpole 2-1-3-0. *Second Innings*—McKenzie 22.2-4-90-3; Connolly 34-7-122-5; Freeman 18-3-96-0; Gleeson 35-2-176-1; Stackpole 12-3-44-0; Chappell 14-0-50-0; Walters 1-0-6-0; Redpath 1-0-3-0.

Australia

Batsman	Dismissal (1st)	Score	Dismissal (2nd)	Score
W.M.Lawry*	c Butcher b Sobers	62	c sub (C.A.Davis) b Sobers	89
K.R.Stackpole	c Hendriks b Holford	62	c Hendriks b Gibbs	50
I.M.Chappell	c Sobers b Gibbs	76	lbw b Griffith	96
I.R.Redpath	lbw b Carew	45	run out	9
K.D.Walters	c and b Griffith	110	run out	50
A.P.Sheahan	b Gibbs	51	run out	11
E.W.Freeman	lbw b Griffith	33	run out	1
B.N.Jarman†	c Hendriks b Gibbs	3	run out	4
G.D.McKenzie	c Nurse b Holford	59	c sub (G.S.Camacho) b Gibbs	4
J.W.Gleeson	b Gibbs	17	lbw b Griffith	0
A.N.Connolly	not out	1	not out	6
Extras	(B 3, LB 6, NB 5)	14	(B 8, LB 10, NB 1)	19
Total		533	(9 wkts)	339

1/89 2/170 3/248 4/254 5/347 6/424 7/429 8/465 9/529

1/86 2/185 3/240 4/304 5/315 6/318 7/322 8/333 9/333

Bowling: *First Innings*—Sobers 28-4-106-1; Griffith 22-4-94-2; Holford 18.5-0-118-2; Gibbs 43-8-145-4; Carew 9-3-30-1; Lloyd 6-0-26-0. *Second Innings*—Sobers 22-1-107-1; Gibbs 26-7-79-2; Holford 15-1-53-0; Carew 2-0-8-0.

Umpires: C.J.Egar and L.P.Rowan

AUSTRALIA v WEST INDIES 1968-69 (Fifth Test)

At Sydney Cricket Ground, 14, 15, 16, 18, 19, 20 February

Result: Australia won by 382 runs

Australia

Batsman	First innings	R	Second innings	R
W.M.Lawry*	b Griffith	151	c Fredericks b Griffith	17
K.R.Stackpole	b Hall	20	c Carew b Hall	6
I.M.Chappell	lbw b Sobers	1	c Hendriks b Hall	10
I.R.Redpath	c Nurse b Sobers	0	b Gibbs	132
K.D.Walters	b Gibbs	242	c Fredericks b Gibbs	103
A.P.Sheahan	c Fredericks b Griffith	27	c Hendriks b Sobers	34
E.W.Freeman	c Hendriks b Griffith	56	c Carew b Sobers	15
G.D.McKenzie	b Gibbs	19	c Carew b Sobers	40
H.B.Taber†	lbw b Hall	48	not out	15
J.W.Gleeson	c Hendriks b Hall	45	not out	5
A.N.Connolly	not out	1		
Extras	(LB 2, NB 6, W 1)	9	(B 4, LB 6, NB 6, W 1)	17
Total		619	(8 wkts dec.)	394

1/43 2/51 3/51 4/387 5/435 6/453 7/483 8/543 9/614

1/21 2/36 3/40 4/250 5/301 6/329 7/329 8/388

Bowling: *First Innings*—Hall 35.7-3-157-3; Griffith 37-1-175-3; Sobers 28-9-94-2; Gibbs 40-8-133-2; Carew 10-2-44-0; Lloyd 2-1-7-0. *Second Innings*—Hall 12-0-47-2; Griffith 14-0-41-1; Gibbs 33-2-133-2; Sobers 26-3-117-3; Carew 5-0-26-0; Lloyd 2-0-13-0.

West Indies

Batsman	First innings	R	Second innings	R
R.C.Fredericks	c Taber b Connolly	39	c Taber b McKenzie	0
M.C.Carew	c Taber b Freeman	64	b Connolly	3
R.B.Kanhai	c Taber b Connolly	44	c Connolly b McKenzie	18
G.S.Sobers*	c Taber b Connolly	13	(5) c Redpath b Gleeson	113
B.F.Butcher	c Sheahan b McKenzie	10	(4) c Gleeson b Stackpole	31
C.H.Lloyd	b McKenzie	53	c Freeman b Stackpole	11
S.M.Nurse	c Stackpole b Connolly	9	b Gleeson	137
J.L.Hendriks†	c Taber b McKenzie	1	c Stackpole b McKenzie	16
C.C.Griffith	c Freeman b Gleeson	27	c Gleeson b Stackpole	15
W.W.Hall	b Gleeson	1	c Sheahan b Chappell	0
L.R.Gibbs	not out	4	not out	0
Extras	(B 2, LB 4, NB 8)	14	(B 1, LB 5, NB 2)	8
Total		279		352

1/100 2/154 3/159 4/179 5/179 6/190 7/193 8/257 9/259

1/0 2/10 3/30 4/76 5/102 6/220 7/284 8/351 9/352

Bowling: *First Innings*—McKenzie 22.6-2-90-3; Connolly 17-2-61-4; Freeman 12-2-48-1; Gleeson 19-8-53-2; Chappell 6-1-13-0. *Second Innings*—McKenzie 16-1-93-3; Connolly 18-4-72-1; Stackpole 15.2-1-84-3; Gleeson 15.2-1-84-3; Freeman 2-0-16-0; Chappell 6-0-22-1.

Umpires: C.J.Egar and L.P.Rowan

INDIA v AUSTRALIA 1969-70 (First Test)

At Brabourne Stadium, Bombay 4, 5, 7, 8, 9 November

Result: Australia won by 8 wickets

India

Batsman	First innings	R	Second innings	R
D.N.Sardesai	b McKenzie	20	c Taber b Gleeson	3
F.M.Engineer†	c Redpath b McKenzie	19	c McKenzie b Mallett	28
A.V.Mankad	b McKenzie	74	b Gleeson	8
C.G.Borde	c Chappell b McKenzie	2	c Redpath b Gleeson	18
Nawab of Pataudi*	c Lawry b Gleeson	95	c Stackpole b Gleeson	0
A.L.Wadekar	lbw b Connolly	9	c McKenzie b Stackpole	46
R.F.Surti	st Taber b Gleeson	4	lbw b Connolly	13
S.Abid Ali	c Stackpole b McKenzie	3	lbw b Connolly	2
S.Venkataraghavan	c Taber b Connolly	2	c Taber b Connolly	9
E.A.S.Prasanna	not out	12	b Mallett	3
B.S.Bedi	c McKenzie b Gleeson	7	not out	6
Extras	(B 15, LB 4, NB 5)	24	(B 4, NB 2)	6
Total		271		137

1/39 2/40 3/42 4/188 5/139 6/245 7/246 8/249 9/252

1/19 2/37 3/55 4/56 5/59 6/87 7/89 8/114 9/125

Bowling: *First Innings*—McKenzie 29-7-69-5; Connolly 31-11-55-2; Gleeson 35.4-18-52-3; Walters 6-0-13-0; Mallett 30-19-43-0; Stackpole 3-1-8-0; Chappell 1-0-7-0. *Second Innings*—McKenzie 16-4-33-0; Connolly 20-10-20-3; Gleeson 32-17-56-4; Mallett 21-9-22-2; Stackpole 1.2-1-0-1.

Australia

Batsman	First innings	R	Second innings	R
W.M.Lawry*	b Prasanna	25	b Surti	2
K.R.Stackpole	c Surti b Prasanna	103	lbw b Surti	11
I.M.Chappell	b Prasanna	31	not out	31
K.D.Walters	c Venkataraghavan b Bedi	48	not out	22
I.R.Redpath	c Wadekar b Venkataraghavan	77		
A.P.Sheahan	lbw b Venkataraghavan	14		
G.D.McKenzie	c Borde b Prasanna	16		
H.B.Taber†	c Surti b Bedi	5		
A.A.Mallett	not out	10		
J.W.Gleeson	c Borde b Prasanna	0		
A.N.Connolly	c sub (E.D.Solkar) b Bedi	8		
Extras	(B 4, NB 4)	8	(B 1)	1
Total		345	(2 wkts)	67

1/81 2/164 3/167 4/285 5/297 6/322 7/322 8/337 9/337

1/8 2/13

Bowling: *First Innings*—Abid Ali 18-3-52-0; Surti 9-2-23-0; Venkataraghavan 31-11-67-2; Bedi 62.4-33-74-3; Prasanna 49-19-121-5. *Second Innings*—Abid Ali 3-0-14-0; Surti 4-1-9-2; Bedi 9-5-11-0; Prasanna 9-3-20-0; Venkataraghavan 1-0-2-0; Mankad 0.5-0-10-0.

Umpires: I.Gopalakrishnan and S.P.Pan

INDIA v AUSTRALIA 1969-70 (Third Test)

At Feroz Shah Kotla, Delhi, 28, 29, 30 November, 2 December

Result: India won by 7 wickets

Australia

Batsman	1st innings	R	2nd innings	R
K.R.Stackpole	st Engineer b Bedi	61	b Prasanna	9
W.M.Lawry*	b Guha	6	not out	49
I.M.Chappell	b Bedi	138	c Solkar b Bedi	0
K.D.Walters	c Solkar b Prasanna	4	b Bedi	0
I.R.Redpath	c Bedi b Prasanna	6	b Bedi	4
A.P.Sheahan	b Bedi	4	c Venkataraghavan b Prasanna	15
H.B.Taber†	st Engineer b Bedi	46	c and b Prasanna	7
A.A.Mallett	b Venkataraghavan	2	(9) c Venkataraghavan b Prasanna	0
G.D.McKenzie	lbw b Prasanna	20	(8) lbw b Bedi	7
J.W.Gleeson	c Solkar b Prasanna	1	c Viswanath b Bedi	1
A.N.Connolly	not out	4	c and b Prasanna	11
Extras	(B 2, LB 1, NB 1)	4	(B 4)	4
Total		296		107

1/33 2/100 3/105 4/117 5/133 6/251 7/260 8/283 9/291

1/15 2/16 3/16 4/24 5/61 6/81 7/88 8/89 9/92

Bowling: *First Innings*—Guha 14-0-47-1; Solkar 11-1-43-0; Bedi 42-15-71-4; Prasanna 38.4-9-111-4; Venkataraghavan 14-4-20-1. *Second Innings*—Guha 2-0-7-0; Solkar 1-1-0-0; Bedi 23-11-37-5; Prasanna 24.2-10-42-5; Venkataraghavan 8-2-17-0.

India

Batsman	1st innings	R	2nd innings	R
F.M.Engineer†	b Connolly	38	c McKenzie b Mallett	6
A.V.Mankad	c Walters b Mallett	97	b Mallett	7
A.L.Wadekar	c and b Stackpole	22	(4) not out	91
G.R.Viswanath	b Gleeson	29	(5) not out	44
S.Venkataraghavan	c Walters b Mallett	0		
Nawab of Pataudi*	c Chappell b Mallett	8		
A.Roy	c Taber b Mallett	0		
E.D.Solkar	not out	13		
S.Guha	b Mallett	0		
E.A.S.Prasanna	lbw b Gleeson	1		
B.S.Bedi	b Mallett	6	(3) b Connolly	20
Extras	(B 3, LB 1, NB 5)	9	(B 9, LB 2, NB 2)	13
Total		223	(3 wkts)	181

1/85 2/124 3/176 4/177 5/197 6/202 7/207 8/207 9/208

1/13 2/18 3/61

Bowling: *First Innings*—McKenzie 12-4-22-0; Connolly 20-4-43-1; Gleeson 34-14-62-2; Mallett 32.3-10-64-6; Stackpole 10-4-23-1. *Second Innings*—McKenzie 13.4-5-19-0; Connolly 16-5-35-1; Gleeson 12-5-24-0; Mallett 29-10-60-2; Stackpole 8-4-13-0; Chappell 2-0-17-0.

Umpires: I.Gopalakrishnan and S.Roy

INDIA v AUSTRALIA 1969-70 (Second Test)

At Green Park, Kanpur, 15, 16, 18, 19, 20 November

Result: Match drawn

India

Batsman	1st innings	R	2nd innings	R
F.M.Engineer†	c and b Stackpole	77	c Gleeson b Connolly	21
A.V.Mankad	c and b Mallett	64	b McKenzie	68
A.L.Wadekar	c Mallett b Connolly	27	c Chappell b Connolly	12
G.R.Viswanath	c Redpath b Connolly	0	lbw b Mallett	137
Nawab of Pataudi*	c Redpath b McKenzie	38	lbw b McKenzie	0
A.Gandotra	c Taber b Connolly	13	c Chappell b Gleeson	8
E.D.Solkar	b Connolly	44	c Taber b McKenzie	35
S.Venkataraghavan	run out	17	not out	20
S.Guha	lbw b Mallett	6	not out	1
E.A.S.Prasanna	c McKenzie b Mallett	22		
B.S.Bedi	not out	1		
Extras	(LB 5, NB 6)	11	(LB 1, NB 9)	10
Total		320	(7 wkts dec.)	312

1/111 2/167 3/171 4/171 5/197 6/239 7/285 8/287 9/315

1/43 2/94 3/125 4/125 5/147 6/257 7/306

Bowling: *First Innings*—McKenzie 25-7-70-1; Connolly 36-13-91-4; Gleeson 29-5-79-0; Mallett 51.5-30-58-3; Walters 2-1-7-0. *Second Innings*—McKenzie 34-13-63-3; Connolly 36-7-69-2; Gleeson 35-11-74-1; Walters 3-1-7-0; Lawry 1-0-6-0.

Australia

Batsman	1st innings	R	2nd innings	R
K.R.Stackpole	run out	40	not out	37
W.M.Lawry*	c Solkar b Venkataraghavan	14	not out	56
I.M.Chappell	lbw b Prasanna	16		
K.D.Walters	b Bedi	53		
I.R.Redpath	c Guha b Solkar	70		
A.P.Sheahan	c Engineer b Guha	114		
A.A.Mallett	b Venkataraghavan	4		
G.D.McKenzie	lbw b Prasanna	0		
H.B.Taber†	c Viswanath b Venkataraghavan	1		
J.W.Gleeson	b Guha	13		
A.N.Connolly	not out	7		
Extras	(B 4, LB 7, NB 5)	16	(NB 2)	2
Total		348	(0 wkts)	95

1/48 2/56 3/93 4/140 5/271 6/287 7/290 8/297 9/331

Bowling: *First Innings*—Guha 21.2-6-55-2; Solkar 19-7-44-1; Bedi 49-21-82-1; Prasanna 39-18-71-2; Venkataraghavan 37-16-76-3; Viswanath 1-0-4-0. *Second Innings*—Guha 5-1-7-0; Solkar 12-3-37-0; Pataudi 1-0-4-0; Prasanna 15-6-17-0; Bedi 3-1-8-0; Viswanath 1-0-4-0; Mankad 1-1-0-0; Gandotra 1-0-5-0; Wadekar 1-1-0-0.

Umpires: A.M.Mamsa and B.Satyaji Rao

INDIA v AUSTRALIA 1969-70 (Fourth Test)

At Eden Gardens, Calcutta, 12, 13, 14, 16 December
Result: Australia won by 10 wickets

India

Batsman		Runs		Runs
F.M.Engineer†	c Stackpole b McKenzie	0	c Redpath b Freeman	10
A.V.Mankad	c Stackpole b McKenzie	9	c Taber b McKenzie	20
A.L.Wadekar	c Freeman b McKenzie	0	lbw b Freeman	62
G.R.Viswanath	c Taber b Mallett	54	b Freeman	5
Nawab of Pataudi*	c Chappell b Mallett	15	(6) c Connolly b Mallett	1
A.Roy	c Taber b McKenzie	18	(7) c Sheahan b Connolly	19
E.D.Solkar	c Taber b McKenzie	42	(5) lbw b Connolly	21
S.Venkataraghavan	c Stackpole b Mallett	24	b Connolly	0
E.A.S.Prasanna	run out	26	c Stackpole b Freeman	0
S.Guha	b McKenzie	4	(11) not out	4
B.S.Bedi	not out	9	(10) c Chappell b Connolly	7
Extras	(B 5, LB 1, NB 4, W 1)	11	(B 6, LB 4, NB 5)	15
		212		**161**

1/0 2/0 3/22 4/64 5/103
6/106 7/154 8/178 9/184

1/29 2/31 3/40 4/90 5/93
6/141 7/141 8/142 9/159

Bowling: *First Innings*—McKenzie 33.4-12-67-6; Freeman 17-6-43-0; Connolly 17-5-27-0; Mallett 27-9-55-3; Stackpole 2-0-9-0. *Second Innings*—McKenzie 18-4-34-1; Connolly 16.1-3-31-4; Freeman 26-7-54-4; Mallett 17-5-27-1.

Australia

Batsman		Runs		Runs
W.M.Lawry*	c Solkar b Bedi	35	not out	17
K.R.Stackpole	run out	41	not out	25
I.M.Chappell	c Wadekar b Bedi	99		
K.D.Walters	st Engineer b Bedi	56		
I.R.Redpath	c Wadekar b Bedi	0		
A.P.Sheahan	run out	32		
E.W.Freeman	c Prasanna b Bedi	29		
H.B.Taber†	b Bedi	2		
G.D.McKenzie	c Pataudi b Bedi	0		
A.A.Mallett	not out	2		
A.N.Connolly	c Guha b Solkar	31		
Extras	(B 4, LB 2, NB 2)	8		
		335	(0 wkts)	**42**

1/65 2/84 3/185 4/185 5/257
6/279 7/302 8/302 9/302

Bowling: *First Innings*—Guha 19-5-55-0; Solkar 9.1-1-28-1; Prasanna 49-15-116-0; Venkataraghavan 16-6-30-0; Bedi 50-19-98-7. *Second Innings*—Guha 3-1-25-0; Wadekar 2-0-17-0.

Umpires: S.P.Pan and J.Reuben

INDIA v AUSTRALIA 1969-70 (Fifth Test)

At Chepauk, Madras, 24, 25, 27, 28 December
Result: Australia won by 77 runs

Australia

Batsman		Runs		Runs
K.R.Stackpole	c Solkar b Venkataraghavan	37	b Amarnath	4
W.M.Lawry*	c Bedi b Prasanna	33	b Prasanna	2
I.M.Chappell	b Prasanna	4	b Amarnath	5
K.D.Walters	c Venkataraghavan b Bedi	102	c Solkar b Prasanna	1
A.P.Sheahan	c Solkar b Prasanna	1	(6) st Engineer b Prasanna	8
I.R.Redpath	c Engineer b Prasanna	33	(5) lbw b Prasanna	63
H.B.Taber†	lbw b Venkataraghavan	10	c Solkar b Prasanna	0
G.D.McKenzie	lbw b Venkataraghavan	2	lbw b Venkataraghavan	24
L.C.Mayne	c Chauhan b Venkataraghavan	10	c Viswanath b Prasanna	13
A.A.Mallett	not out	11	not out	11
A.N.Connolly	c and b Solkar	11	c Engineer b Venkataraghavan	8
Extras	(B 11, LB 2)	13	(B 8, LB 5, NB 1)	14
		258		**153**

1/60 2/69 3/78 4/82 5/184
6/219 7/225 8/243 9/245

1/4 2/12 3/15 4/16 5/24
6/24 7/57 8/107 9/140

Bowling: *First Innings*—Amarnath 7-0-21-0; Solkar 8.2-5-8-1; Bedi 26-10-45-1; Prasanna 40-13-100-4; Venkataraghavan 34-13-71-4. *Second Innings*—Amarnath 24-11-31-2; Solkar 4-2-2-0; Venkataraghavan 12.5-2-26-2; Prasanna 31-14-74-6; Bedi 9-5-6-0.

India

Batsman		Runs		Runs
C.P.S.Chauhan	c Chappell b Mallett	19	c Redpath b McKenzie	1
A.V.Mankad	c Taber b Mayne	0	c Redpath b McKenzie	10
A.L.Wadekar	c Chappell b Mallett	12	c Stackpole b Mayne	55
G.R.Viswanath	b Mallett	6	c Redpath b Mallett	59
F.M.Engineer†	c Connolly b Mallett	32	c and b McKenzie	4
Nawab of Pataudi*	c Sheahan b McKenzie	59	c Chappell b Mallett	4
E.D.Solkar	c Taber b Mallett	11	and b Mallett	12
M.Amarnath	not out	16	c Taber b Mayne	0
S.Venkataraghavan	run out	2	b Mallett	13
E.A.S.Prasanna	c Chappell b McKenzie	0	c McKenzie b Mallett	5
B.S.Bedi	absent ill	-	not out	0
Extras	(LB 5, NB 1)	6	(LB 4, NB 5)	9
		163		**171**

1/0 2/30 3/33 4/40 5/96
6/128 7/158 8/163 9/163

1/3 2/12 3/114 4/119 5/135
6/142 7/144 8/159 9/169

Bowling: *First Innings*—McKenzie 16.4-8-19-2; Mayne 7-2-21-1; Connolly 14-5-25-0; Mallett 25-7-91-5. *Second Innings*—McKenzie 24-9-45-3; Mayne 18-8-32-2; Mallett 29.2-12-53-5; Connolly 9-4-18-0; Stackpole 5-2-14-0.

Umpires: I.Gopalakrishnan and B.Satyaji Rao

SOUTH AFRICA v AUSTRALIA 1969-70 (First Test)

At Newlands, Cape Town, 22, 23, 24, 26, 27 January
Result: South Africa won by 170 runs

South Africa

Batsman	First Innings		Second Innings	
B.A.Richards	b Connolly	29	c Taber b Connolly	32
T.L.Goddard	c Taber b Walters	16	c Lawry b Mallett	17
A.Bacher*	lbw b Connolly	57	lbw b Gleeson	16
R.G.Pollock	c Chappell b Walters	49	c Walters b Connolly	50
E.J.Barlow	c Chappell b Gleeson	127	c Taber b Gleeson	16
B.L.Irvine	c Gleeson b Mallett	42	c Walters b Connolly	19
M.J.Procter	b Mallett	22	c Taber b Connolly	48
D.Gamsy†	not out	30	c Taber b Gleeson	2
P.M.Pollock	lbw b Mallett	1	b Gleeson	25
M.A.Seymour	c Lawry b Mallett	0	c Lawry b Connolly	0
G.A.Chevalier	c Chappell b Mallett	0	not out	0
Extras	(B 2, LB 5, NB 2)	9	(B 1, LB 4, NB 2)	7
		382		232

1/21 2/96 3/111 4/187 5/281
6/323 7/363 8/364 9/374

1/52 2/52 3/91 4/121 5/147
6/171 7/187 8/222 9/226

Bowling: *First Innings*—McKenzie 30-8-74-0; Connolly 29-12-62-2; Walters 8-1-19-2; Gleeson 45-17-92-1; Mallett 55.1-16-126-5. *Second Innings*—McKenzie 8-0-29-0; Connolly 26-10-47-5; Gleeson 30-11-70-4; Mallett 32-10-79-1.

Australia

Batsman	First Innings		Second Innings	
K.R.Stackpole	c Barlow b Procter	19	c Barlow b Goddard	29
W.M.Lawry*	b P.M.Pollock	2	lbw b Procter	83
I.M.Chappell	c Chevalier b P.M.Pollock	0	b Chevalier	13
K.D.Walters	c Irvine b P.M.Pollock	73	c Irvine b Procter	4
I.R.Redpath	c Barlow b Procter	8	not out	47
A.P.Sheahan	c Barlow b Chevalier	11	b Seymour	16
H.B.Tabert†	lbw b Seymour	5	lbw b Procter	15
G.D.McKenzie	c R.G.Pollock b P.M.Pollock	5 (9)	c R.G.Pollock b Chevalier	19
A.A.Mallett	c Goddard b Chevalier	19 (8)	c P.M.Pollock b Procter	5
J.W.Gleeson	b Goddard	17	b Richards	10
A.N.Connolly	not out	0	b Chevalier	25
Extras	(B 1, NB 9)	10	(B 7, LB 2, NB 5)	14
		164		280

1/5 2/5 3/38 4/39 5/58
6/92 7/123 8/134 9/164

1/75 2/130 3/131 4/136 5/161
6/188 7/198 8/228 9/239

Bowling: *First Innings*—Procter 12-4-30-2; P.M.Pollock 12-4-20-4; Goddard 19.4-9-29-1; Chevalier 11-2-32-2; Seymour 11-2-28-1; Barlow 1-0-15-0. *Second Innings*—Procter 17-4-47-4; P.M.Pollock 18-12-19-0; Goddard 32-12-66-1; Chevalier 31.1-9-68-3; Seymour 19-6-40-1; Barlow 6-2-14-0; Richards 6-1-12-1.

Umpires: G.Goldman and W.W.Wade

SOUTH AFRICA v AUSTRALIA 1969-70 (Second Test)

At Kingsmead, Durban, 5, 6, 7, 9 February
Result: South Africa won by an innings and 129 runs

South Africa

B.A.Richards	b Freeman	140
T.L.Goddard	c Lawry b Gleeson	17
A.Bacher*	b Connolly	9
R.G.Pollock	c and b Stackpole	274
E.J.Barlow	lbw b Freeman	1
B.L.Irvine	c Gleeson	13
H.R.Lance	st Taber b Gleeson	61
M.J.Procter	c Connolly b Stackpole	32
D.Gamsy†	lbw b Connolly	7
P.M.Pollock	not out	5
A.J.Traicos	not out	5
Extras	(B 1, LB 3, NB 23)	27
	(9 wkts dec.)	622

1/88 2/126 3/229 4/231 5/281
6/481 7/558 8/575 9/580

Bowling: McKenzie 25.5-3-92-0; Connolly 33-7-104-2; Freeman 28-4-120-2; Gleeson 51-9-160-3; Walters 9-0-44-0; Stackpole 21-2-75-2.

Australia

Batsman	First Innings		Second Innings	
K.R.Stackpole	c Gamsy b Goddard	29	lbw b Traicos	71
W.M.Lawry*	lbw b Barlow	15	c Gamsy b Goddard	14
I.M.Chappell	c Gamsy b Barlow	0	c Gamsy b P.M.Pollock	14
K.D.Walters	c Traicos b Barlow	4	c R.G.Pollock b Traicos	74
I.R.Redpath	c Richards b Procter	4	not out	74
A.P.Sheahan	c Traicos b Goddard	62	c Barlow b Procter	4
E.W.Freeman	c Traicos b P.M.Pollock	5	b Barlow	18
H.B.Tabert†	c and b P.M.Pollock	6	c Lance b Barlow	0
G.D.McKenzie	c Traicos b Procter	1	lbw b Barlow	4
J.W.Gleeson	not out	4	c Gamsy b Procter	24
A.N.Connolly	c Bacher b Traicos	14	lbw b Procter	0
Extras	(LB 5, NB 10)	15	(B 9, LB 8, NB 22)	39
		157		336

1/44 2/44 3/44 4/48 5/56
6/79 7/100 8/114 9/139

1/65 2/83 3/151 4/208 5/222
6/264 7/264 8/268 9/336

Bowling: *First Innings*—Procter 11-2-39-2; P.M.Pollock 10-3-31-2; Goddard 7-4-10-2; Barlow 10-3-24-3; Traicos 8.2-3-27-1; Lance 2-0-11-0. *Second Innings*—Procter 18.5-5-62-3; P.M.Pollock 21.3-4-45-1; Goddard 17-7-30-1; Barlow 31-10-63-3; Traicos 30-8-70-2; Lance 7-4-11-0; Richards 3-1-8-0.

Umpires: C.M.P.Coetzee and J.G.Draper

SOUTH AFRICA v AUSTRALIA 1969-70 (Third Test)

At New Wanderers, Johannesburg, 19, 20, 21, 23, 24 February
Result: South Africa won by 307 runs

South Africa

Batsman	1st Innings		2nd Innings	
B.A.Richards	c Taber b Connolly	65	c Taber b Mayne	35
T.L.Goddard	c Walters b Connolly	6	(9) c Taber b Connolly	2
A.Bacher*	lbw b Mayne	30	b Connolly	15
R.G.Pollock	c Taber b Freeman	52	b Freeman	87
E.J.Barlow	c Taber b Gleeson	6	(2) c Lawry b Gleeson	110
B.L.Irvine	c Stackpole b Gleeson	79	(5) c Lawry b Gleeson	73
H.R.Lance	run out	8	lbw b Gleeson	30
J.D.Lindsay†	c Stackpole b Gleeson	0	(6) b Gleeson	6
M.J.Procter	c Chappell b Walters	22	(8) not out	36
P.M.Pollock	c Taber b Walters	0	c Taber b Gleeson	1
A.J.Traicos	not out	1	lbw b Mayne	0
Extras	(LB 7, NB 2, W 1)	10	(LB 8, NB 5)	13
		279		408

1/56 2/85 3/141 4/162 5/170
6/194 7/194 8/238 9/246

1/76 2/102 3/241 4/269 5/275
6/349 7/372 8/375 9/380

Bowling: First Innings—Mayne 26-5-83-1; Connolly 30-10-49-2; Freeman 20-4-60-1; Gleeson 21.4-2-61-3; Walters 5-1-16-2. Second Innings—Mayne 18.3-1-77-2; Connolly 32-6-83-2; Freeman 19-4-77-1; Gleeson 45-15-125-5; Walters 7-1-33-0.

Australia

Batsman	1st Innings		2nd Innings	
K.R.Stackpole	c Lindsay b Procter	5	c Lindsay b Procter	1
W.M.Lawry*	c Lindsay b P.M.Pollock	1	c R.G.Pollock b Barlow	17
I.R.Redpath	lbw b Procter	0	b Goddard	66
I.M.Chappell	c Lance b Goddard	34	b Barlow	0
K.D.Walters	c Procter b P.M.Pollock	64	b Procter	15
A.P.Sheahan	b P.M.Pollock	44	b Procter	1
E.W.Freeman	c Goddard b P.M.Pollock	10	run out	18
L.C.Mayne	run out	0	c Procter b Traicos	2
H.B.Taber†	not out	26	not out	18
J.W.Gleeson	b Procter	0	b Goddard	0
A.N.Connolly	c Richards b P.M.Pollock	3	c Richards b Goddard	36
Extras	(LB 4, NB 10, W 1)	15	(NB 3, W 2)	5
		202		178

1/7 2/7 3/12 4/109 5/112
6/139 7/140 8/194 9/195

1/11 2/43 3/43 4/73 5/73
6/122 7/124 8/126 9/126

Bowling: First Innings—Procter 21-5-48-3; P.M.Pollock 23.2-10-39-5; Barlow 12-5-31-0; Goddard 26-10-41-1; Lance 3-1-5-0; Traicos 3-1-17-0. Second Innings—Procter 14-8-24-3; P.M.Pollock 15-4-56-0; Barlow 24.5-16-27-3; Goddard 24.5-16-27-3; Traicos 17-4-49-1.

Umpires: C.M.P.Coetzee and A.J.Warner

SOUTH AFRICA v AUSTRALIA 1969-70 (Fourth Test)

At St George's Park, Port Elizabeth, 5, 6, 7, 9, 10 March
Result: South Africa won by 323 runs

South Africa

Batsman	1st Innings		2nd Innings	
B.A.Richards	c Taber b Connolly	81	c Chappell b Mayne	126
E.J.Barlow	c McKenzie b Connolly	73	c Stackpole b Walters	27
A.Bacher*	run out	17	hit wkt b McKenzie	73
R.G.Pollock	c Taber b Gleeson	1	b Mayne	4
B.L.Irvine	c Redpath b Gleeson	25	c Gleeson b Mayne	102
J.D.Lindsay†	c Taber b Connolly	43	b Connolly	60
H.R.Lance	b Mayne	21	run out	19
M.J.Procter	c Taber b Connolly	26	c Mayne b Gleeson	23
P.M.Pollock	not out	4	not out	7
P.H.J.Trimborn	b Connolly	0		
A.J.Traicos	c Taber b Connolly	2		
Extras	(B 4, LB 3, NB 11)	18	(LB 9, NB 20)	29
		311	(8 wkts dec.)	470

1/157 2/158 3/159 4/183 5/208
6/259 7/294 8/305 9/305

1/73 2/199 3/213
4/279 5/367 6/440 7/440 8/470

Bowling: First Innings—McKenzie 27-7-66-0; Mayne 27-4-71-1; Connolly 28.2-9-47-6; Walters 9-1-19-0; Gleeson 32-9-90-2. Second Innings—McKenzie 20-3-72-1; Mayne 29-6-83-3; Connolly 36-3-130-1; Walters 5-2-14-1; Gleeson 30.2-5-142-1; Redpath 1-1-0-0.

Australia

Batsman	1st Innings		2nd Innings	
K.R.Stackpole	c Barlow b Procter	15	b Procter	20
W.M.Lawry*	c Lindsay b Lance	18	c Lindsay b Barlow	43
I.R.Redpath	c Trimborn b Procter	55	c Barlow b Procter	37
I.M.Chappell	c Procter b Trimborn	17	c Trimborn b Barlow	14
K.D.Walters	c Lindsay b Trimborn	1	b Procter	23
A.P.Sheahan	c Procter b P.M.Pollock	67	c Lindsay b Trimborn	46
H.B.Taber†	lbw b Barlow	3	not out	30
L.C.Mayne	b Procter	13	c Lindsay b Procter	12
G.D.McKenzie	c Barlow b P.M.Pollock	0	c Lindsay b Procter	2
J.W.Gleeson	c Lindsay b P.M.Pollock	8	b Procter	0
A.N.Connolly	not out	2	c Bacher b Trimborn	3
Extras	(LB 3, NB 9, W 1)	13	(LB 2, NB 14)	16
		212		246

1/27 2/46 3/80 4/82 5/152
6/177 7/191 8/195 9/208

1/22 2/98 3/116 4/130 5/189
6/207 7/234 8/243 9/243

Bowling: First Innings—P.M.Pollock 14-2-46-3; Procter 25.1-11-30-3; Barlow 9-1-27-1; Lance 8-1-32-1; Trimborn 17-1-47-2; Traicos 3-1-17-0. Second Innings—P.M.Pollock 1.1-0-2-0; Procter 24-11-73-6; Barlow 18-3-66-2; Lance 10-4-18-0; Trimborn 20.2-4-44-2; Traicos 14-5-21-0; Richards 3-1-6-0.

Umpires: C.M.P.Coetzee and A.J.Warner

AUSTRALIA v ENGLAND 1970-71 (First Test)

At Woolloongabba, Brisbane, 27, 28, 29 November, 1, 2 December

Result: Match drawn

Australia

Batsman	First innings		Second innings	
W.M.Lawry*	c Knott b Snow	4	c Snow b Fletcher	84
K.R.Stackpole	c Knott b Snow	207	c Knott b Shuttleworth	8
I.M.Chappell	run out	59	st Knott b Illingworth	10
K.D.Walters	b Underwood	112	c Luckhurst b Snow	7
I.R.Redpath	c Illingworth b Underwood	22	c and b Underwood	28
A.P.Sheahan	c Knott b Underwood	0	c Shuttleworth b Snow	36
R.W.Marsh†	b Snow	9	b Shuttleworth	14
T.J.Jenner	c Cowdrey b Snow	0	c Boycott b Shuttleworth	2
G.D.McKenzie	not out	3	b Shuttleworth	1
J.W.Gleeson	c Cowdrey b Snow	0	b Shuttleworth	6
A.L.Thomson	b Snow	0	not out	4
Extras	(B 7, LB 4, NB 6)	17	(B 4, LB 3, NB 7)	14
		433		214

1/12 2/163 3/372 4/418 5/418 6/421 7/422 8/433 9/433
1/30 2/47 3/64 4/137 5/152 6/193 7/199 8/201 9/208

Bowling: *First Innings*—Snow 32.3-6-114-6; Shuttleworth 27-6-81-0; d'Oliveira 16-2-63-0; Illingworth 11-1-47-0; Underwood 28-6-101-3; Cowdrey 1-0-10-0. *Second Innings*—Snow 20-3-48-2; Shuttleworth 17.5-2-47-5; d'Oliveira 7-5-7-0; Underwood 20-10-23-1; Illingworth 18-11-19-1; Fletcher 9-1-48-1; Cowdrey 2-0-8-0.

England

Batsman	First innings		Second innings	
G.Boycott	c Marsh b Gleeson	37	c and b Jenner	16
B.W.Luckhurst	run out	74	not out	20
A.P.E.Knott†	c Lawry b Walters	73		
J.H.Edrich	c Chappell b Jenner	79		
M.C.Cowdrey	c Chappell b Gleeson	28		
K.W.R.Fletcher	c Marsh b McKenzie	34		
B.L.d'Oliveira	c Sheahan b McKenzie	57		
R.Illingworth*	c Marsh b Thomson	8		
J.A.Snow	c Marsh b Walters	34		
D.L.Underwood	not out	2		
K.Shuttleworth	c Lawry b Walters	7		
Extras	(B 2, LB 7, NB 22)	31	(LB 3)	3
		464	(1 wkt)	39

1/92 2/136 3/245 4/284 5/336 6/346 7/371 8/449 9/456
1/39

Bowling: *First Innings*—McKenzie 28-5-90-2; Thomson 43-8-136-1; Gleeson 42-15-97-2; Jenner 24-5-86-1; Stackpole 4-0-12-0; Walters 5.5-0-12-3. *Second Innings*—Thomson 4-0-20-0; McKenzie 3-0-6-0; Jenner 4.6-2-9-1; Stackpole 4-3-1-0.

Umpires: T.F.Brooks and L.P.Rowan

AUSTRALIA v ENGLAND 1970-71 (Second Test)

At W.A.C.A. Ground, Perth, 11, 12, 13, 15, 16 December

Result: Match drawn

England

Batsman	First innings		Second innings	
G.Boycott	c McKenzie b Gleeson	70	st Marsh b Gleeson	50
B.W.Luckhurst	b McKenzie	131	c Stackpole b Walters	19
J.H.Edrich	run out	47	not out	115
A.P.E.Knott†	c Stackpole b Thomson	24	(8) not out	30
K.W.R.Fletcher	b Walters	22		
M.C.Cowdrey	c and b G.S.Chappell	40	(4) lbw b Gleeson	0
B.L.d'Oliveira	c Stackpole b Thomson	8	(5) c Marsh b Thomson	1
R.Illingworth*	b McKenzie	34	(6) b Gleeson	31
J.A.Snow	not out	4	(7) c Marsh b Stackpole	29
K.Shuttleworth	b McKenzie	2		
P.Lever	b McKenzie	2		
Extras	(LB 8, NB 4, W 1)	13	(B 2, LB 3, NB 7)	12
		397	(6 wkts dec.)	287

1/171 2/243 3/281 4/291 5/310 6/327 7/389 8/389 9/393
1/60 2/98 3/98 4/101 5/152 6/209

Bowling: *First Innings*—McKenzie 31.4-4-66-4; Thomson 24.4-4-118-2; G.S.Chappell 24-4-54-1; Gleeson 32-10-78-1; Walters 11-1-35-1; Stackpole 11-2-33-0. *Second Innings*—McKenzie 18-2-50-0; Thomson 25-3-71-1; Gleeson 32-11-68-3; Stackpole 15-3-43-1; Walters 7-1-26-1; G.S.Chappell 4-1-17-0.

Australia

Batsman	First innings		Second innings	
W.M.Lawry*	c Illingworth b Snow	0	not out	38
K.R.Stackpole	c Lever b Snow	5	c sub (J.H.Hampshire) b Snow	0
I.M.Chappell	c Knott b Snow	50	c sub (J.H.Hampshire) b Snow	17
K.D.Walters	c Knott b Lever	7	b Lever	8
I.R.Redpath	c and b Illingworth	171	not out	26
A.P.Sheahan	run out	2		
G.S.Chappell	c Luckhurst b Shuttleworth	108		
R.W.Marsh†	c d'Oliveira b Shuttleworth	44		
G.D.McKenzie	c Lever b d'Oliveira	7		
J.W.Gleeson	c Knott b Snow	15		
A.L.Thomson	not out	12		
Extras	(B 5, LB 4, NB 10)	19	(B 4, LB 4, NB 3)	11
		440	(3 wkts)	100

1/5 2/8 3/17 4/105 5/107 6/326 7/393 8/408 9/426
1/0 2/20 3/40

Bowling: *First Innings*—Snow 33.5-143-4; Shuttleworth 28.4-105-2; Lever 21-3-78-1; d'Oliveira 17-1-41-1; Illingworth 13-2-43-1; Boycott 1-0-7-0; Fletcher 1-0-4-0. *Second Innings*—Snow 9-4-17-2; Shuttleworth 3-1-9-0; Lever 5-2-10-0; d'Oliveira 4-2-5-0; Illingworth 4-2-12-0; Fletcher 4-0-18-0; Cowdrey 3-0-18-0.

Umpires: T.F.Brooks and L.P.Rowan

AUSTRALIA v ENGLAND 1970-71 (Third Test)

At Melbourne Cricket Ground, 31 December, 1, 2, 4, 5 January

Result: Match abandoned

Australia

W.M.Lawry*
K.R.Stackpole
I.M.Chappell
K.D.Walters
I.R.Redpath
G.S.Chappell
R.W.Marsh†
A.A.Mallett
G.D.McKenzie
J.W.Gleeson
A.N.Connolly

England

G.Boycott
B.W.Luckhurst
J.H.Edrich
M.C.Cowdrey
B.L.d'Oliveira
R.Illingworth*
A.P.E.Knott†
J.A.Snow
K.Shuttleworth
P.Lever
D.L.Underwood

Umpires: T.F.Brooks and L.P.Rowan

AUSTRALIA v ENGLAND 1970-71 (Fourth Test)

At Sydney Cricket Ground, 9, 10, 11, 13, 14 January

Result: England won by 299 runs

England

	First Innings		Second Innings	
G.Boycott	c Gleeson b Connolly	77	not out	142
B.W.Luckhurst	lbw b Gleeson	38	I.M.Chappell b McKenzie	5
J.H.Edrich	c Gleeson b G.S.Chappell	55	run out	12
K.W.R.Fletcher	c Walters b Mallett	23	c Stackpole b Mallett	8
B.L.d'Oliveira	c Connolly b Mallett	0	I.M.Chappell b G.S.Chappell	56
R.Illingworth*	b Gleeson	25	st Marsh b Mallett	53
A.P.E.Knott†	st Marsh b Mallett	6	not out	21
J.A.Snow	c Lawry b Gleeson	37		
P.Lever	c Connolly b Mallett	36		
D.L.Underwood	c G.S.Chappell b Gleeson	0		
R.G.D.Willis	not out	15		
Extras	(B 5, LB 2, NB 12, W 1)	20	(B 9, LB 4, NB 9)	22
		332	(5 wkts dec.)	319

1/116 2/130 3/201 4/205 5/208
6/219 7/262 8/291 9/291

1/7 2/35 3/48
4/181 5/276

Bowling: *First Innings*—McKenzie 15-3-74-0; Connolly 13-2-43-1; Gleeson 29-7-83-4; G.S.Chappell 11-4-30-1; Mallett 16.7-5-40-4; Walters 3-1-11-0; Stackpole 7-2-31-0. *Second Innings*—McKenzie 15-0-65-1; Connolly 14-1-38-0; G.S.Chappell 15-5-24-1; Gleeson 23-4-54-0; Mallett 19-1-85-2; Stackpole 6-1-17-0; Walters 2-0-14-0.

Australia

	First Innings		Second Innings	
W.M.Lawry*	c Edrich b Lever	9	not out	60
I.M.Chappell	c Underwood b Snow	12	c d'Oliveira b Snow	0
K.D.Walters	c Fletcher b d'Oliveira	64	c Edrich b Snow	6
I.R.Redpath	c Luckhurst b Illingworth	55	c Knott b Lever	3
G.S.Chappell	c and b Underwood	15	b Snow	2
K.R.Stackpole	c Boycott b Underwood	33	c Lever b Snow	30
R.W.Marsh†	c d'Oliveira b Underwood	8	c Willis b Snow	0
A.A.Mallett	b Underwood	4	c Knott b Willis	6
G.D.McKenzie	not out	11	retired hurt	6
J.W.Gleeson	c Fletcher b d'Oliveira	0	b Snow	0
A.N.Connolly	b Lever	14	c Knott b Snow	0
Extras	(NB 11)	11	(B 2, NB 1)	3
		236		116

1/14 2/38 3/137 4/160 5/189
6/199 7/208 8/209 9/219

1/1 2/11 3/14 4/21 5/66
6/66 7/86 8/116 9/116

Bowling: *First Innings*—Snow 14-6-23-1; Willis 9-2-26-0; Lever 8.6-1-31-2; Underwood 22-7-66-4; Illingworth 14-3-59-1; d'Oliveira 9-2-20-2. *Second Innings*—Snow 17.5-5-40-7; Lever 11-1-24-1; Willis 3-2-1-1; Underwood 8-2-17-0; d'Oliveira 7-3-16-0; Illingworth 9-5-9-0; Fletcher 1-0-6-0.

Umpires: T.F.Brooks and L.P.Rowan

AUSTRALIA v ENGLAND 1970-71 (Fifth Test)

At Melbourne Cricket Ground, 21, 22, 23, 25, 26 January

Result: Match drawn

Australia

K.R.Stackpole c Lever b d'Oliveira	30		
W.M.Lawry* c Snow b Willis	56		
I.M.Chappell c Luckhurst b Snow	111		
I.R.Redpath b Snow	72		
K.D.Walters b Underwood	55		
G.S.Chappell c Edrich b Willis	3		
R.W.Marsh† not out	92		
K.J.O'Keeffe c Luckhurst b Illingworth	27		
J.W.Gleeson c Cowdrey b Willis	5		
J.R.F.Duncan c Edrich b Illingworth	3		
A.L.Thomson not out	0		
Extras (B 10, LB 17, NB 12)	39	(9 wkts dec.)	493

1/64 2/266 3/269 4/310 5/314 (9 wkts dec.) 493
6/374 7/471 8/477 9/480

Bowling: First Innings—Snow 29-6-94-2; Lever 25-6-79-0; d'Oliveira 22-6-71-1; Willis 20-5-73-3; Underwood 19-4-78-1; Illingworth 13-0-59-2. Second Innings—Snow 12-4-21-2; Lever 12-1-53-0; Willis 10-1-42-1; Underwood 12-0-38-1.

England

G.Boycott c Redpath b Thomson	12	not out	
B.W.Luckhurst b Walters	109		
J.H.Edrich c Marsh b Thomson	9	(2) not out	
M.C.Cowdrey c and b Gleeson	13		
B.L.d'Oliveira c Marsh b Thomson	117		
R.Illingworth* lbw b Stackpole	41		
A.P.E.Knott† c Redpath b Gleeson	19		
J.A.Snow b I.M.Chappell	1		
P.Lever run out	19		
D.L.Underwood c and b Gleeson	5		
R.G.D.Willis not out	5		
Extras (B 17, LB 14, NB 11)	42	(B 1, LB 8, NB 2)	11
	392	(0 wkts)	161

1/40 2/64 3/88 4/228 5/306 392
6/340 7/354 8/362 9/379

Bowling: First Innings—Thomson 34-5-110-3; Duncan 14-4-30-0; G.S.Chappell 8-0-21-0; O'Keeffe 31-11-71-0; Gleeson 25-7-60-3; Stackpole 17.5-4-41-1; Walters 5-2-7-1. Second Innings—Thomson 11-5-26-0; Walters 7-1-14-0; Gleeson 3-1-18-0; O'Keeffe 19-3-45-0; Stackpole 13-2-28-0; G.S.Chappell 5-0-19-0.

Umpires: M.G.O'Connell and L.P.Rowan

AUSTRALIA v ENGLAND 1970-71 (Sixth Test)

At Adelaide Oval, 29, 30 January, 1, 2, 3 February

Result: Match drawn

England

G.Boycott run out	58	not out	119
J.H.Edrich c Stackpole b Lillee	130	b Thomson	40
K.W.R.Fletcher b Thomson	80	b Gleeson	5
A.P.E.Knott† c Redpath b Lillee	7		
B.L.d'Oliveira c Marsh b G.S.Chappell	47	(4) c Walters b Thomson	5
J.H.Hampshire c Lillee b G.S.Chappell	55	(5) lbw b Thomson	3
R.Illingworth* b Lillee	24	(6) not out	48
J.A.Snow b Lillee	38		
P.Lever b Thomson	5		
D.L.Underwood not out	1		
R.G.D.Willis c Walters b Lillee	4		
Extras (B 1, LB 5, NB 11, W 4)	21	(LB 4, NB 8, W 1)	13
	470	(4 wkts dec.)	233

1/107 2/276 3/289 4/289 5/385 470
6/402 7/458 8/465 9/465

1/103 2/128 (4 wkts dec.) 233
3/143 4/151

Bowling: First Innings—Thomson 29.7-6-94-2; Lillee 28.3-0-84-5; Walters 9-2-29-0; G.S.Chappell 18-1-54-2; Gleeson 19-1-78-0; Mallett 20-1-63-1; Stackpole 12-2-47-0. Second Innings—Lillee 7-0-40-0; Thomson 19-2-79-3; Walters 3-0-5-0; G.S.Chappell 5-0-27-0; Gleeson 16-1-69-1; Mallett 1-1-0-0.

Australia

K.R.Stackpole b Underwood	87	b Snow	136
W.M.Lawry* c Knott b Snow	10	c Knott b Willis	21
I.M.Chappell c Knott b Lever	28	c Willis b Underwood	104
I.R.Redpath c Lever b Illingworth	9	not out	21
K.D.Walters c Knott b Lever	8	not out	36
G.S.Chappell c Edrich b Lever	0		
R.W.Marsh† c Knott b Willis	28		
A.A.Mallett c Illingworth b Snow	28		
J.W.Gleeson c Boycott b Willis	16		
D.K.Lillee c Boycott b Lever	10		
A.L.Thomson not out	6		
Extras (LB 2, NB 3)	5	(B 2, LB 3, NB 5)	10
	235	(3 wkts)	328

1/61 2/117 3/131 4/141 5/145 235
6/163 7/180 8/219 9/221

1/65 2/267 3/271 (3 wkts) 328

Bowling: First Innings—Snow 21.4-73-2; Lever 17.1-2-49-4; Underwood 21-6-45-1; Willis 12-3-49-2; Illingworth 5-2-14-1. Second Innings—Snow 17-3-60-1; Lever 17-4-49-0; Willis 13-1-48-2; Illingworth 14-7-32-0; Underwood 35-7-85-1; d'Oliveira 15-4-28-0; Fletcher 4-0-16-0.

Umpires: T.F.Brooks and M.G.O'Connell

AUSTRALIA v ENGLAND 1970-71 (Seventh Test)

At Sydney Cricket Ground, 12, 13, 14, 16, 17 February
Result: England won by 62 runs

England

J.H.Edrich	c I.M.Chappell b Dell	30	c I.M.Chappell b O'Keeffe	57
B.W.Luckhurst	c Lillee b O'Keeffe	0	c Lillee b O'Keeffe	59
K.W.R.Fletcher	c Stackpole b O'Keeffe	33	c Stackpole b Eastwood	20
J.H.Hampshire	c Marsh b Lillee	10	c I.M.Chappell b O'Keeffe	24
B.L.d'Oliveira	b Dell	47	c I.M.Chappell b Lillee	47
R.Illingworth*	b Jenner	42	lbw b Lillee	29
A.P.E.Knott†	c Stackpole b O'Keeffe	27	b Dell	15
J.A.Snow	b Jenner	7	c Stackpole b Dell	20
P.Lever	c Jenner b O'Keeffe	4	c Redpath b Jenner	17
D.L.Underwood	not out	8	c Marsh b Dell	0
R.G.D.Willis	b Jenner	11	not out	2
Extras	(B 4, LB 4, NB 2, W 1)	11	(B 3, LB 3, NB 6)	12
		184		**302**

1/5 2/60 3/68 4/69 5/98   1/94 2/130 3/158 4/165 5/234
6/145 7/156 8/165 9/165   6/251 7/276 8/298 9/299

Bowling: *First Innings*—Lillee 13-5-32-1; Dell 16-8-32-2; Walters 4-0-10-1; G.S.Chappell 3-0-9-0; Jenner 16-3-42-3; O'Keeffe 16-3-42-3. *Second Innings*—Lillee 14-0-43-2; Dell 26.7-3-65-3; Walters 5-0-18-0; O'Keeffe 26-8-96-3; Jenner 21-5-39-1; Eastwood 5-0-21-1; Stackpole 3-1-8-0.

Australia

K.H.Eastwood	c Knott b Lever	5	b Snow	0
K.R.Stackpole	b Snow	6	b Illingworth	67
R.W.Marsh†	c Willis b Lever	4	(7) b Underwood	16
I.M.Chappell*	b Willis	25	(3) c Knott b Lever	6
I.R.Redpath	c and b Underwood	59	(4) c Hampshire b Illingworth	14
K.D.Walters	st Knott b Underwood	42	(5) c d'Oliveira b Willis	1
G.S.Chappell	b Willis	65	(6) st Knott b Illingworth	30
K.J.O'Keeffe	c Knott b Illingworth	3	sub (K.Shuttleworth) b d'Oliveira	12
T.J.Jenner	b Lever	30	c Fletcher b Underwood	4
D.K.Lillee	c Knott b Willis	6	c Hampshire b d'Oliveira	0
A.R.Dell	not out	3	not out	3
Extras	(LB 5, NB 10, W 1)	16	(B 2, LB 5)	7
		264		**160**

1/11 2/13 3/32 4/66 5/147   1/0 2/22 3/71 4/82 5/96
6/162 7/178 8/235 9/239   6/131 7/142 8/154 9/154

Bowling: *First Innings*—Snow 18-2-68-1; Lever 14.6-3-43-3; d'Oliveira 12-2-24-0; Willis 12-1-58-3; Underwood 16-3-39-2; Illingworth 11-3-16-1. *Second Innings*—Snow 2-1-7-1; Lever 12-2-23-1; d'Oliveira 5-1-15-2; Willis 9-1-32-1; Underwood 13.6-5-28-2; Illingworth 20-7-39-3; Fletcher 1-0-9-0.

Umpires: T.F.Brooks and L.P.Rowan

ENGLAND v AUSTRALIA 1972 (First Test)

At Old Trafford, Manchester, 8, 9, 10, 12, 13 June
Result: England won by 89 runs

England

G.Boycott	c Stackpole b Gleeson	8	lbw b Gleeson	47
J.H.Edrich	run out	49	c Marsh b Watson	26
B.W.Luckhurst	b Colley	14	c Marsh b Colley	0
M.J.K.Smith	lbw b Lillee	10	c Marsh b Lillee	34
B.L.d'Oliveira	b G.S.Chappell	23	c Watson b Lillee	37
A.W.Greig	lbw b Colley	57	b G.S.Chappell	62
A.P.E.Knott†	c Marsh b Lillee	18	c Marsh b Lillee	1
R.Illingworth*	not out	26	c I.M.Chappell b Lillee	14
J.A.Snow	b Colley	3	lbw b Lillee	0
N.Gifford	run out	15	c Marsh b Lillee	0
G.G.Arnold	c Francis b Gleeson	1	not out	0
Extras	(B 10, LB 9, NB 4, W 2)	25	(B 4, LB 8, NB 1)	13
		249		**234**

1/50 2/86 3/99 4/118 5/127   1/60 2/65 3/81 4/140 5/182
6/190 7/200 8/209 9/243   6/192 7/234 8/234 9/234

Bowling: *First Innings*—Lillee 29-14-40-2; Colley 33-3-83-3; G.S.Chappell 16-6-28-1; Walters 5-1-7-0; Watson 4-2-8-0; Gleeson 24.4-10-45-2; Inverarity 9-3-13-0. *Second Innings*—Lillee 30-8-66-6; Colley 23-3-68-1; G.S.Chappell 21.2-6-42-1; Watson 5-0-29-1; Gleeson 7-3-16-1.

Australia

K.R.Stackpole	lbw b Arnold	53	b Greig	67
B.C.Francis	lbw b d'Oliveira	27	lbw b Snow	6
I.M.Chappell*	c Smith b Greig	0	c Knott b Snow	7
G.S.Chappell	c Greig b Snow	24	c d'Oliveira b Arnold	23
G.D.Watson	c Knott b Arnold	2	c and b Snow	0
K.D.Walters	c Illingworth b Snow	17	b Greig	20
R.J.Inverarity	c Knott b Arnold	4	c Luckhurst b d'Oliveira	3
R.W.Marsh†	c Edrich b Arnold	8	c Knott b Greig	91
D.J.Colley	b Snow	4	c Greig b Snow	4
J.W.Gleeson	b Snow	0	b Greig	30
D.K.Lillee	not out	1	not out	0
Extras	(B 1, LB 4)	5	(W 1)	1
		142		**252**

1/68 2/69 3/91 4/99 5/119   1/9 2/31 3/77 4/78 5/115
6/124 7/134 8/137 9/137   6/120 7/136 8/147 9/251

Bowling: *First Innings*—Snow 20-7-41-4; Arnold 25-4-62-4; Greig 7-1-21-1; d'Oliveira 6-1-13-1. *Second Innings*—Snow 27-2-87-4; Arnold 20-2-59-1; Greig 19.2-7-53-4; d'Oliveira 16-4-23-1; Gifford 3-0-29-0.

Umpires: C.S.Elliott and T.W.Spencer

ENGLAND v AUSTRALIA 1972 (Second Test)

At Lord's, London, 22, 23, 24, 26 June

Result: Australia won by 8 wickets

England

G.Boycott b Massie ... 11 — b Lillee ... 6
J.H.Edrich lbw b Lillee ... 10 — c Marsh b Massie ... 6
B.W.Luckhurst b Lillee ... 1 — c Marsh b Lillee ... 4
M.J.K.Smith b Massie ... 34 — c Edwards b Massie ... 30
B.L.d'Oliveira lbw b Massie ... 32 — c G.S.Chappell b Massie ... 3
A.W.Greig c Marsh b Massie ... 54 — c I.M.Chappell b Massie ... 3
A.P.E.Knott† c Colley b Massie ... 43 — c G.S.Chappell b Massie ... 12
R.Illingworth* lbw b Massie ... 30 — c Stackpole b Massie ... 12
J.A.Snow b Massie ... 37 — c Marsh b Massie ... 0
N.Gifford c Marsh b Massie ... 3 — not out ... 16
J.S.E.Price not out ... 4 — c G.S.Chappell b Massie ... 19
Extras (LB 7, NB 2) ... 13 — (NB 4, W 1) ... 5

272   116

1/22 2/23 3/28 4/84 5/97
6/193 7/200 8/260 9/265

1/12 2/16 3/18 4/25 5/31
6/52 7/74 8/74 9/81

Bowling: *First Innings*—Lillee 28-3-90-2; Massie 32.5-7-84-8; Colley 16-2-42-0; G.S.Chappell 6-1-18-0; Gleeson 9-1-25-0. *Second Innings*—Lillee 21-6-50-2; Massie 27.2-9-53-8; Colley 7-1-8-0.

Australia

K.R.Stackpole c Gifford b Price ... 5 — not out ... 57
B.C.Francis b Snow ... 0 — c Knott b Price ... 9
I.M.Chappell* c Smith b Snow ... 56 — c Luckhurst b d'Oliveira ... 6
G.S.Chappell b d'Oliveira ... 131 — not out ... 7
K.D.Walters c Illingworth b Snow ... 1
R.Edwards c Smith b Illingworth ... 28
J.W.Gleeson c Knott b Greig ... 1
R.W.Marsh† c Greig b Snow ... 50
D.J.Colley c Greig b Price ... 25
R.A.L.Massie c Knott b Snow ... 2
D.K.Lillee not out ... 2
Extras (LB 7, NB 2) ... 9 — (LB 2) ... 2

308   (2 wkts) 81

1/1 2/7 3/82 4/84 5/190
6/212 7/250 8/290 9/290

1/20 2/51

Bowling: *First Innings*—Snow 32-13-57-5; Price 26.1-5-87-2; Greig 29-6-74-1; d'Oliveira 17-5-48-1; Gifford 11-4-20-0; Illingworth 11-4-20-0. *Second Innings*—Snow 8-2-15-0; Price 7-0-28-1; Greig 3-0-17-0; d'Oliveira 8-3-14-1; Luckhurst 0.5-0-5-0.

Umpires: D.J.Constant and A.E.Fagg

ENGLAND v AUSTRALIA 1972 (Third Test)

At Trent Bridge, Nottingham, 13, 14, 15, 17, 18 July

Result: Match drawn

Australia

K.R.Stackpole c Parfitt b Greig ... 114 — c Luckhurst b Snow ... 12
B.C.Francis c Smith b Lever ... 10 — lbw b Illingworth ... 50
I.M.Chappell* c Knott b Snow ... 34 — b Snow ... 72
G.S.Chappell c Parfitt b Snow ... 26 — c Gifford b Snow ... 7
K.D.Walters c Parfitt b Snow ... 2 — not out ... 170
R.Edwards c Knott b Snow ... 13 — (2) not out ... 7
R.W.Marsh† c d'Oliveira b Gifford ... 41
D.J.Colley c Greig b d'Oliveira ... 54 — (6)
R.A.L.Massie c Parfitt b Snow ... 0
J.W.Gleeson not out ... 6
D.K.Lillee c Knott b Greig ... 0
Extras (B 4, LB 6, NB 5) ... 15 — (LB 4, NB 1, W 1) ... 6

315   (4 wkts dec.) 324

1/16 2/98 3/157 4/165 5/189
6/227 7/289 8/298 9/315

1/15 2/139 3/285
4/295

Bowling: *First Innings*—Snow 31-8-92-5; Lever 26-8-61-1; Greig 38.4-9-88-2; d'Oliveira 18-5-41-1; Gifford 5-1-18-1. *Second Innings*—Snow 24-1-94-3; Lever 19-3-76-0; Greig 12-1-46-0; d'Oliveira 7-0-12-0; Gifford 15-1-49-0; Illingworth 15-4-41-1.

England

B.W.Luckhurst lbw b Lillee ... 23 — c G.S.Chappell b I.M.Chappell ... 96
J.H.Edrich c Marsh b Colley ... 37 — b Massie ... 15
P.H.Parfitt b Massie ... 0 — b Lillee ... 46
M.J.K.Smith c Marsh b Massie ... 17 — lbw b Lillee ... 15
B.L.d'Oliveira lbw b Lillee ... 29 — not out ... 50
N.Gifford c Marsh b Massie ... 16
A.W.Greig c Marsh b Massie ... 7 — (6) not out ... 36
A.P.E.Knott† c Marsh b Massie ... 0
R.Illingworth* not out ... 24
J.A.Snow c Marsh b Lillee ... 6
P.Lever c Walters b Colley ... 9
Extras (B 5, LB 2, NB 13, W 1) ... 21 — (B 17, LB 9, NB 2, W 4) ... 32

189   (4 wkts) 290

1/55 2/60 3/74 4/111 5/133
6/145 7/145 8/155 9/166

1/50 2/167 3/200
4/201

Bowling: *First Innings*—Lillee 29-15-35-4; Massie 30-10-43-4; Colley 23.3-5-68-2; Gleeson 6-1-22-0. *Second Innings*—Lillee 25-10-40-2; Massie 36-13-49-1; Colley 19-6-43-0; I.M.Chappell 12-5-26-1; Gleeson 30-13-49-0; G.S.Chappell 9-4-16-0; Stackpole 17-4-35-0.

Umpires: A.E.G.Rhodes and T.W.Spencer

ENGLAND v AUSTRALIA 1972 (Fourth Test)

At Headingley, Leeds, 27, 28, 29 July

Result: England won by 9 wickets

Australia

Batsman	1st innings		2nd innings	
K.R.Stackpole	c Knott b Underwood	52	lbw b Underwood	28
R.Edwards	c Knott b Snow	0	c Knott b Arnold	0
I.M.Chappell*	c and b Illingworth	26	c Knott b Arnold	0
G.S.Chappell	lbw b Underwood	12	c d'Oliveira b Underwood	13
A.P.Sheahan	c Illingworth b Underwood	0	not out	41
K.D.Walters	b Illingworth	4	c Parfitt b Underwood	3
R.W.Marsh†	c Illingworth b Underwood	1	c Knott b Underwood	0
R.J.Inverarity	not out	26	c Illingworth b Underwood	0
A.A.Mallett	lbw b Snow	20	b Illingworth	9
R.A.L.Massie	b Arnold	0	(11) b Illingworth	18
D.K.Lillee	c Greig b Arnold	0	(10) b Underwood	7
Extras	(LB 2, NB 3)	5	(LB 12, NB 4)	16
		146		**136**

1/10 2/79 3/93 4/93 5/97 6/98 7/98 8/145 9/146

1/5 2/7 3/31 4/51 5/63 6/69 7/69 8/93 9/111

Bowling: *First Innings*—Arnold 9.5-2-28-2; Snow 13-5-11-2; Greig 10-1-25-0; Illingworth 21-11-32-2; Underwood 31-16-37-4; d'Oliveira 2-1-8-0. *Second Innings*—Arnold 6-1-17-2; Snow 10-2-26-0; Underwood 21-6-45-6; Illingworth 19.1-5-32-2.

England

Batsman	1st innings		2nd innings	
B.W.Luckhurst	c G.S.Chappell b Mallett	18	not out	12
J.H.Edrich	c I.M.Chappell b Mallett	45	lbw b Lillee	4
P.H.Parfitt	c Marsh b Lillee	2	not out	0
K.W.R.Fletcher	lbw b Mallett	5		
B.L.d'Oliveira	b Mallett	12		
A.W.Greig	c G.S.Chappell b Inverarity	24		
A.P.E.Knott†	st Marsh b Mallett	0		
R.Illingworth*	lbw b Lillee	57		
J.A.Snow	st Marsh b Inverarity	48		
D.L.Underwood	c I.M.Chappell b Inverarity	5		
G.G.Arnold	not out	1		
Extras	(B 19, LB 15, NB 8, W 4)	46	(LB 3, NB 2)	5
		263	(1 wkt)	**21**

1/43 2/52 3/66 4/76 5/108 6/108 7/128 8/232 9/246

1/7

Bowling: *First Innings*—Lillee 26.1-10-39-2; Massie 14-4-34-0; Mallett 52-20-114-5; Inverarity 33-19-26-3; I.M.Chappell 3-2-1-0; G.S.Chappell 2-0-3-0. *Second Innings*—Lillee 5-2-7-1; Mallett 5-1-9-0.

Umpires: D.J.Constant and C.S.Elliott

ENGLAND v AUSTRALIA 1972 (Fifth Test)

At Kennington Oval, London, 10, 11, 12, 14, 15, 16 August

Result: Australia won by 5 wickets

England

Batsman	1st innings		2nd innings	
B.Wood	c Marsh b Watson	26	lbw b Massie	90
J.H.Edrich	lbw b Lillee	8	b Lillee	18
P.H.Parfitt	b Lillee	51	b Lillee	18
J.H.Hampshire	c Inverarity b Mallett	42	c I.M.Chappell b Watson	20
B.L.d'Oliveira	c G.S.Chappell b Mallett	4	c I.M.Chappell b Massie	43
A.W.Greig	c Stackpole b Mallett	16	c Marsh b Lillee	29
R.Illingworth*	c G.S.Chappell b Lillee	0	b Lillee	31
A.P.E.Knott†	c Marsh b Lillee	92	b Lillee	63
J.A.Snow	c Marsh b Lillee	3	c Stackpole b Mallett	14
G.G.Arnold	b Inverarity	22	lbw b Mallett	4
D.L.Underwood	not out	3	not out	0
Extras	(LB 8, NB 8, W 1)	17	(B 11, LB 8, NB 7)	26
		284		**356**

1/25 2/50 3/133 4/142 5/145 6/145 7/159 8/181 9/262

1/56 2/81 3/114 4/194 5/205 6/270 7/271 8/333 9/356

Bowling: *First Innings*—Lillee 24.2-7-58-5; Massie 27-5-69-0; Watson 12-4-23-1; Mallett 23-4-80-3; G.S.Chappell 2-0-18-0; Inverarity 4-0-19-1. *Second Innings*—Lillee 32.2-8-123-5; Massie 32-10-77-2; Watson 19-8-32-1; Mallett 23-7-66-2; Inverarity 15-4-32-0.

Australia

Batsman	1st innings		2nd innings	
G.D.Watson	c Knott b Arnold	13	lbw b Arnold	6
K.R.Stackpole	b Snow	18	c Knott b Greig	79
I.M.Chappell*	c Snow b Arnold	118	c sub (R.G.D.Willis) b Underwood	37
G.S.Chappell	c Greig b Illingworth	113	lbw b Underwood	16
R.Edwards	b Underwood	79	lbw b Greig	1
A.P.Sheahan	c Hampshire b Underwood	5	not out	44
R.W.Marsh†	b Underwood	44	not out	43
R.J.Inverarity	c Greig b Underwood	28		
A.A.Mallett	run out	5		
R.A.L.Massie	b Arnold	4		
D.K.Lillee	not out	1		
Extras	(LB 8, NB 7, W 1)	16	(LB 6, NB 10)	16
		399	(5 wkts)	**242**

1/24 2/34 3/235 4/296 5/310 6/310 7/383 8/387 9/399

1/16 2/132 3/136 4/137 5/171

Bowling: *First Innings*—Arnold 35-11-87-3; Snow 34.5-5-111-1; Greig 18-9-25-0; d'Oliveira 9-4-17-0; Underwood 38-16-90-4; Illingworth 17-4-53-1. *Second Innings*—Arnold 13-5-26-1; Snow 25.3-10-49-2; Greig 6-1-21-0; Underwood 35-11-94-2; Illingworth 8.5-2-26-0; Parfitt 2-0-10-0.

Umpires: A.E.Fagg and A.E.G.Rhodes

AUSTRALIA v PAKISTAN 1972-73 (First Test)

At Adelaide Oval, 22, 23, 24, 26, 27 December
Result: Australia won by an innings and 114 runs

Pakistan

Sadiq Mohammad c G.S.Chappell b Massie	11	c and b Mallett	81
Talat Ali retired hurt	7	(11) c Edwards b Mallett	0
Zaheer Abbas c Marsh b Lillee	7	c Marsh b O'Keeffe	0
Majid Khan c Sheahan b Massie	11	c I.M.Chappell b Mallett	11
Mushtaq Mohammad c G.S.Chappell b Lillee	3	lbw b Mallett	32
Saeed Ahmed c Marsh b Massie	36	(2) lbw b Mallett	39
Asif Iqbal c Marsh b Massie	16	(6) c G.S.Chappell b Mallett	6
Intikhab Alam* c Edwards b Lillee	64	(7) c G.S.Chappell b Lillee	30
Wasim Bari† c Redpath b Mallett	72	(8) c O'Keeffe b Mallett	0
Salim Altaf not out	17	(9) not out	9
Asif Masood c Marsh b Lillee	0	(10) c Marsh b Mallett	1
Extras (B 4, LB 3, NB 2, W 4)	13	(B 3, LB 4, NB 3, W 1)	11
	257		**214**

1/30 2/30 3/33 4/74 5/95
6/104 7/208 8/255 9/257

1/88 2/89 3/111 4/162 5/162
6/182 7/182 8/211 9/214

Bowling: *First Innings*—Lillee 20.3-7-49-4; Massie 24.3-7-70-4; G.S.Chappell 11-2-29-0; Mallett 12-3-52-1; O'Keeffe 8-1-44-0. *Second Innings*—Lillee 15-3-53-1; Massie 9-3-26-0; G.S.Chappell 4-0-21-0; Mallett 23.6-6-59-8; O'Keeffe 14-1-44-1.

Australia

A.P.Sheahan b Asif Masood	44
I.R.Redpath c Wasim Bari b Asif Masood	2
I.M.Chappell* c Asif Iqbal b Majid Khan	196
G.S.Chappell lbw b Salim Altaf	28
R.Edwards lbw b Asif Masood	89
J.Benaud lbw b Salim Altaf	24
R.W.Marsh† b Mushtaq Mohammad	118
K.J.O'Keeffe b Mushtaq Mohammad	40
A.A.Mallett c sub (Sarfraz Nawaz) b Majid Khan	0
D.K.Lillee c Saeed Ahmed b Mushtaq Mohammad	14
R.A.L.Massie not out	12
Extras (B 2, LB 12, NB 4)	18
	585

1/3 2/103 3/158 4/330 5/390
6/413 7/533 8/534 9/566

Bowling: Asif Masood 19-1-110-3; Salim Altaf 25-1-83-2; Asif Iqbal 14-0-76-0; Intikhab Alam 18-2-115-0; Saeed Ahmed 3-0-28-0; Majid Khan 20-1-88-2; Mushtaq Mohammad 11.2-0-67-3.

Umpires: M.G.O'Connell and N.Townsend

AUSTRALIA v PAKISTAN 1972-73 (Second Test)

At Melbourne Cricket Ground, 29, 30 December, 1, 2, 3 January
Result: Australia won by 92 runs

Australia

I.R.Redpath c Saeed Ahmed b Intikhab Alam	135	c Wasim Bari b Salim Altaf	6
A.P.Sheahan run out	23	c Sarfraz Nawaz b Asif Masood	127
I.M.Chappell* c Wasim Bari b Sarfraz Nawaz	66	st Wasim Bari b Majid Khan	9
G.S.Chappell not out	116	(4) run out	62
J.Benaud c Sarfraz Nawaz b Intikhab Alam	13	(5) c Wasim Bari b Salim Altaf	142
R.W.Marsh† c Wasim Bari b Sarfraz Nawaz	74	(3) c Asif Iqbal b Asif Masood	3
K.J.O'Keeffe		b Sarfraz Nawaz	24
A.A.Mallett		c Wasim Bari b Sarfraz Nawaz	8
M.H.N.Walker		run out	11
J.R.Thomson		not out	19
D.K.Lillee		c Mushtaq Ahmed b Intikhab Alam	2
Extras (B 1, LB 6, NB 7)	14	(LB 3, NB 9)	12
	(5 wkts dec.) 441		**425**

1/60 2/183 3/273 4/295 5/441
1/18 2/51 3/288 4/298 5/305
6/375 7/391 8/392 9/418

Bowling: *First Innings*—Asif Masood 17-0-97-0; Salim Altaf 9-0-49-0; Sarfraz Nawaz 22.5-4-100-2; Intikhab Alam 16-0-101-2; Majid Khan 21-2-80-0. *Second Innings*—Asif Masood 12-0-59-2; Salim Altaf 14-0-50-2; Sarfraz Nawaz 22-2-99-2; Intikhab Alam 15.6-3-70-1; Majid Khan 17-1-61-1; Mushtaq Ahmed 7-0-33-0.

Pakistan

Sadiq Mohammad lbw b Lillee	137	c Marsh b Walker	5
Saeed Ahmed c G.S.Chappell b Walker	50	c Mallett b Lillee	6
Zaheer Abbas run out	51	run out	25
Majid Khan c Marsh b Walker	158	c Marsh b Lillee	47
Mushtaq Mohammad c Marsh b O'Keeffe	60	run out	13
Asif Iqbal c Lillee b Mallett	7	c Redpath b Walker	37
Intikhab Alam* c Sheahan b Mallett	68	c I.M.Chappell b Mallett	48
Wasim Bari† b Mallett	7	b Walker	0
Salim Altaf not out	13	b O'Keeffe	10
Sarfraz Nawaz not out	0	run out	8
Asif Masood		not out	1
Extras (B 12, LB 7, NB 3, W 1)	23		
	(8 wkts dec.) 574		**200**

1/128 2/323 3/395 4/416 5/429
6/519 7/541 8/572

1/11 2/15 3/80 4/83 5/128
6/138 7/138 8/161 9/161

Bowling: *First Innings*—Lillee 16.6-1-90-1; Thomson 17-1-100-0; Walker 24-1-112-2; Mallett 38-4-124-3; O'Keeffe 23-1-94-1; I.M.Chappell 5-0-21-0; Redpath 1-0-10-0. *Second Innings*—Lillee 11-1-59-2; Thomson 2-0-10-0; Walker 14-3-39-3; Mallett 17.5-3-56-1; O'Keeffe 9-4-10-1; I.M.Chappell 3-0-16-0; G.S.Chappell 1-0-10-0.

Umpires: J.R.Collins and P.R.Enright

AUSTRALIA v PAKISTAN 1972-73 (Third Test)

At Sydney Cricket Ground, 6, 7, 8, 10, 11 January
Result: Australia won by 52 runs

Australia

K.R.Stackpole	c Wasim Bari b Sarfraz Nawaz	28	c Intikhab Alam b Salim Altaf	9
I.R.Redpath	run out	79	c Nasim-ul-Ghani b Sarfraz Nawaz	18
I.M.Chappell*	lbw b Sarfraz Nawaz	43	c Wasim Bari b Sarfraz Nawaz	27
G.S.Chappell	b Majid Khan	30	(6) lbw b Sarfraz Nawaz	6
R.Edwards	c Wasim Bari b Salim Altaf	69	(4) lbw b Salim Altaf	3
K.D.Walters	b Asif Iqbal	19	(5) lbw b Salim Altaf	6
R.W.Marsh†	c Wasim Bari b Salim Altaf	15	c Zaheer Abbas b Salim Altaf	0
M.H.N.Walker	c Majid Khan b Sarfraz Nawaz	5	c Mushtaq b Sarfraz Nawaz	16
J.R.Watkins	not out	3	c Zaheer Abbas b Intikhab Alam	36
D.K.Lillee	b Sarfraz Nawaz	2	(11) not out	2
R.A.L.Massie	b Salim Altaf	2	(10) c Sadiq Mohammad b Mushtaq	42
Extras	(B 18, LB 8, NB 9, W 4)	39	(B 10, LB 3, NB 8)	21
		334		184

1/56 2/138 3/196 4/220 5/271 6/315 7/324 8/327 9/329
1/29 2/31 3/34 4/44 5/70 6/73 7/94 8/101 9/184

Bowling: *First Innings*—Asif Masood 18-1-80-0; Salim Altaf 21.5-3-71-3; Sarfraz Nawaz 19-3-53-4; Majid Khan 18-1-66-1; Intikhab Alam 2-0-13-0; Asif Iqbal 2-0-11-1. *Second Innings*—Asif Masood 3-0-15-0; Salim Altaf 20-5-60-4; Sarfraz Nawaz 21-7-56-4; Intikhab Alam 4-2-9-1; Asif Iqbal 2-0-10-0; Mushtaq Ahmed 3.1-0-13-1.

Pakistan

Sadiq Mohammad	c G.S.Chappell b Lillee	30	c Edwards b Massie	6
Nasim-ul-Ghani	c Redpath b G.S.Chappell	64	b Lillee	5
Zaheer Abbas	c Marsh b Massie	14	c Redpath b Lillee	47
Majid Khan	b Massie	0	lbw b Walker	12
Mushtaq Mohammad	c Walker b G.S.Chappell	121	c Marsh b Lillee	15
Asif Iqbal	c Marsh b G.S.Chappell	65	c Marsh b Walker	5
Intikhab Alam*	c Marsh b G.S.Chappell	5	c Watkins b Walker	8
Wasim Bari†	b G.S.Chappell	1	c Edwards b Walker	0
Salim Altaf	c Marsh b Walker	12	c Massie b Walker	0
Sarfraz Nawaz	b G.S.Chappell	12	c Redpath b Walker	1
Asif Masood	not out	1	not out	3
Extras	(B 12, LB 10, NB 3, W 6)	31	(LB 2, NB 1, W 1)	4
		360		106

1/56 2/79 3/83 4/131 5/270 6/279 7/280 8/336 9/349
1/7 2/11 3/52 4/83 5/88 6/93 7/95 8/95 9/103

Bowling: *First Innings*—Lillee 10-2-34-1; Massie 28-6-123-3; Walker 16-2-65-1; G.S.Chappell 18.6-5-61-5; Walters 9-3-25-0; Watkins 6-1-21-0; I.M.Chappell 1-1-0-0. *Second Innings*—Lillee 18.6-5-68-3; Massie 7-4-19-1; Walker 16-8-15-6.

Umpires: T.F.Brooks and J.R.Collins

WEST INDIES v AUSTRALIA 1972-73 (First Test)

At Sabina Park, Kingston, Jamaica, 16, 17, 18, 20, 21 February
Result: Match drawn

Australia

K.R.Stackpole	c Rowe b Holder	142
I.R.Redpath	c Kanhai b Gibbs	60
I.M.Chappell*	not out	38
G.S.Chappell	not out	14
Extras	(LB 2, NB 4)	6
	(2 wkts dec.)	260

1/161 2/230

K.R.Stackpole	b Foster	44
I.R.Redpath	b Gibbs	46
I.M.Chappell*	c Dowe b Inshan Ali	19
G.S.Chappell	c Kallicharran b Gibbs	42
R.Edwards	c and b Gibbs	63
K.D.Walters	c Kanhai b Gibbs	72
R.W.Marsh†	hit wkt b Dowe	97
K.J.O'Keeffe	not out	19
M.H.N.Walker		
J.R.Hammond		
D.K.Lillee		
Extras	(B 6, LB 12, NB 7, W 1)	26
	(7 wkts dec.)	428

1/66 2/106 3/128 4/179 5/271 6/365 7/428

Bowling: *First Innings*—Holder 26-5-55-0; Dowe 21-3-96-1; Foster 44-18-84-1; Gibbs 41-14-85-4; Inshan Ali 25-5-82-1. *Second Innings*—Holder 19-5-34-1; Dowe 21-4-72-0; Foster 22-7-71-0; Gibbs 15-4-40-1; Inshan Ali 4-0-28-0; Fredericks 1-0-9-0.

West Indies

R.C.Fredericks	c O'Keeffe b Walker	31	c Marsh b G.S.Chappell	21
G.A.Greenidge	b Walker	0		
L.G.Rowe	c Stackpole b Walker	76	c G.S.Chappell b Hammond	4
A.I.Kallicharran	c Marsh b Hammond	50	not out	7
R.B.Kanhai*	c Marsh b Hammond	84		
M.L.C.Foster	b Walker	125	(5) not out	18
T.M.Findlay†	c Marsh b Walker	12	(2) c Marsh b G.S.Chappell	13
Inshan Ali	c Marsh b Walker	10		
V.A.Holder	lbw b Hammond	12		
L.R.Gibbs	c O'Keeffe b Hammond	5		
U.G.Dowe	not out	5		
Extras	(LB 9, NB 9)	18	(B 1, NB 2, W 1)	4
		428	(3 wkts)	67

1/16 2/49 3/165 4/165 5/375 6/385 7/400 8/417 9/423
1/35 2/36 3/42

Bowling: *First Innings*—Lillee 26-4-112-0; Walker 39-10-114-6; Hammond 28.5-5-79-4; O'Keeffe 18-1-71-0; I.M.Chappell 11-3-30-0; G.S.Chappell 2-0-4-0. *Second Innings*—Lillee 6-1-20-0; Walker 6-3-8-0; Hammond 10-4-17-1; G.S.Chappell 10-4-18-2; Walters 1-1-0-0.

Umpires: R.Gosein and D.Sang Hue

WEST INDIES v AUSTRALIA 1972-73 (Second Test)
At Kensington Oval, Bridgetown, Barbados, 9, 10, 11, 13, 14 March
Result: Match drawn

Australia

K.R.Stackpole c Kanhai b Holder	1		b Foster	53
I.R.Redpath c Kanhai b Boyce	6		c Greenidge b Gibbs	20
I.M.Chappell* run out	72		not out	106
G.S.Chappell c Murray b Holder	106			
R.Edwards c Murray b Boyce	15			
K.D.Walters c Kanhai b Gibbs	1	(4)	not out	102
R.W.Marsh† c Rowe b Willett	78			
K.J.O'Keeffe b Willett	21			
J.R.Hammond lbw b Boyce	0			
T.J.Jenner not out	10			
M.H.N.Walker b Gibbs	0			
Extras (NB 14)	14		(B 1, LB 6, NB 12)	19
	324		(2 wkts dec.)	300

1/2 2/19 3/148 4/189 5/194   1/79 2/108
6/218 7/264 8/283 9/320

Bowling: *First Innings*—Holder 21-5-49-2; Boyce 22-5-68-3; Foster 15-4-35-0; Willett 37-11-79-2; Gibbs 37-11-79-2. *Second Innings*—Holder 21-5-52-0; Boyce 18-4-54-0; Foster 13-4-29-1; Willett 28-15-45-0; Gibbs 25-10-55-1; Fredericks 1-0-3-0; Greenidge 7-0-24-0; Kanhai 6.1-1-19-0.

West Indies

R.C.Fredericks lbw b Hammond	98		not out	22
G.A.Greenidge lbw b Walker	9		not out	10
L.G.Rowe c Stackpole b Walker	16			
A.I.Kallicharran b Walker	14			
R.B.Kanhai* lbw b I.M.Chappell	105			
M.L.C.Foster b Jenner	12			
D.L.Murray† c Redpath b Jenner	90			
K.D.Boyce lbw b Walker	10			
E.T.Willett c Stackpole b Jenner	0			
V.A.Holder b Walker	1			
L.R.Gibbs not out	0			
Extras (B 13, LB 5, NB 14, W 4)	36		(LB 2, NB 1, W 1)	4
	391		(0 wkts)	36

1/19 2/77 3/118 4/162 5/179
6/344 7/385 8/386 9/391

Bowling: *First Innings*—Hammond 31-9-114-1; Walker 51.4-20-97-5; G.S.Chappell 22-11-37-0; Jenner 28-9-65-3; O'Keeffe 10-3-18-0; Walters 2-0-7-0; I.M.Chappell 8-3-17-1. *Second Innings*—Hammond 4-1-10-0; Walker 4-3-1-0; O'Keeffe 6-2-15-0; Stackpole 5-3-6-0.

Umpires: H.B.D.Jordan and D.Sang Hue

WEST INDIES v AUSTRALIA 1972-73 (Third Test)
At Queen's Park Oval, Port-of-Spain, Trinidad, 23, 24, 25, 27, 28 March
Result: Australia won by 44 runs

Australia

K.R.Stackpole c Foster b Boyce	0		c Fredericks b Boyce	18
I.R.Redpath run out	66		c Kanhai b Willett	44
G.S.Chappell c Kallicharran b Gibbs	56	(4)	c and b Gibbs	1
K.D.Walters c Fredericks b Inshan Ali	112	(5)	c Gibbs b Willett	32
R.Edwards lbw b Boyce	12	(6)	b Gibbs	14
I.M.Chappell* c and b Inshan Ali	8	(3)	c Fredericks b Willett	97
R.W.Marsh† b Inshan Ali	14		b Inshan Ali	8
K.J.O'Keeffe run out	37		c Kallicharran b Gibbs	7
T.J.Jenner lbw b Gibbs	0		b Gibbs	6
M.H.N.Walker b Gibbs	2	(11)	not out	23
J.R.Hammond not out	2	(10)	c Kanhai b Gibbs	19
Extras (B 10, LB 7, NB 6)	23		(B 5, LB 7)	12
	332			281

1/1 2/108 3/181 4/240 5/257   1/31 2/96 3/99 4/156 5/185
6/262 7/312 8/321 9/321   6/208 7/231 8/231 9/248

Bowling: *First Innings*—Boyce 18-4-54-2; Lloyd 7-3-13-0; Gibbs 38-11-79-3; Willett 19-3-62-0; Inshan Ali 41.1-11-89-3; Foster 6-2-12-0. *Second Innings*—Boyce 10-1-41-1; Lloyd 3-1-11-0; Gibbs 45-14-102-5; Willett 28-15-33-3; Inshan Ali 21-2-82-1.

West Indies

R.C.Fredericks c I.M.Chappell b Jenner	16		c Redpath b Stackpole	76
M.L.C.Foster lbw b Jenner	25	(6)	c G.S.Chappell b O'Keeffe	34
A.I.Kallicharran c G.S.Chappell b Jenner	53		c Marsh b Walker	91
C.H.Lloyd c and b G.S.Chappell	20	(5)	c Stackpole b O'Keeffe	15
R.B.Kanhai* c Redpath b O'Keeffe	56	(4)	b G.S.Chappell	14
D.L.Murray† lbw b Hammond	40	(2)	c Redpath b Walker	7
K.D.Boyce c Marsh b O'Keeffe	12		c I.M.Chappell b O'Keeffe	11
Inshan Ali c Marsh b Walker	15		b Walker	2
E.T.Willett not out	4		b O'Keeffe	0
L.R.Gibbs c O'Keeffe b Jenner	6		not out	0
L.G.Rowe absent hurt	-		absent hurt	-
Extras (B 17, LB 11, NB 4, W 1)	33		(B 19, LB 13, NB 7)	39
	280			289

1/33 2/44 3/100 4/149 5/206   1/39 2/141 3/177 4/219 5/268
6/230 7/265 8/267 9/280   6/274 7/281 8/288 9/289

Bowling: *First Innings*—Walker 30-8-55-1; Hammond 7-3-7-1; Jenner 38.3-7-98-4; O'Keeffe 28-10-62-2; G.S.Chappell 14-8-16-1; Stackpole 2-0-8-0; I.M.Chappell 2-1-1-0. *Second Innings*—Walker 25-6-43-3; Hammond 6-3-12-0; Jenner 15-2-46-0; O'Keeffe 24.1-5-57-4; G.S.Chappell 32-10-65-1; Stackpole 11-4-27-1.

Umpires: R.Gosein and D.Sang Hue

WEST INDIES v AUSTRALIA 1972-73 (Fourth Test)

At Bourda, Georgetown, Guyana, 6, 7, 8, 10, 11 April

Result: Australia won by 10 wickets

West Indies

Batsman	First Innings		Second Innings	
R.C.Fredericks	c I.M.Chappell b Walters	30	c Marsh b Hammond	6
G.A.Greenidge	b Walters	22	b Hammond	24
A.I.Kallicharran	run out	13	c Walker b Hammond	8
C.H.Lloyd	b Hammond	178	c Marsh b Hammond	3
R.B.Kanhai*	c O'Keeffe b Hammond	57	lbw b Walker	23
C.A.Davis	lbw b Walker	16	c Marsh b Walker	16
D.L.Murray†	c I.M.Chappell b Hammond	1	c Marsh b Walker	3
K.D.Boyce	c Edwards b Walters	23	c G.S.Chappell b Walters	10
E.T.Willett	lbw b Walters	12	not out	3
V.A.Holder	not out	9	b Walters	3
L.R.Gibbs	b Walters	1	b Walker	7
Extras	(B 5, LB 6, NB 2, W 2)	15	(LB 3)	3
		366		109

1/55 2/56 3/90 4/277 5/307 6/310 7/337 8/347 9/356

1/12 2/30 3/39 4/42 5/77 6/82 7/91 8/95 9/100

Bowling: *First Innings*—Hammond 33-6-110-3; Walker 38-11-77-1; G.S.Chappell 16-4-56-0; Walters 18.2-1-66-5; O'Keeffe 8-1-27-0; Jenner 7-0-15-0; I.M.Chappell 1-1-0-0. *Second Innings*—Hammond 16-4-38-4; Walker 23.3-4-45-2; Walters 13-3-23-2.

Australia

Batsman	First Innings		Second Innings	
K.R.Stackpole	lbw b Boyce	1	not out	76
I.R.Redpath	c Fredericks b Holder	22	not out	57
I.M.Chappell*	b Gibbs	109		
G.S.Chappell	b Willett	51		
K.D.Walters	c Murray b Gibbs	81		
R.Edwards	c Murray b Boyce	13		
R.W.Marsh†	lbw b Willett	23		
K.J.O'Keeffe	b Gibbs	5		
T.J.Jenner	c Kallicharran b Boyce	10		
J.R.Hammond	run out	1		
M.H.N.Walker	not out	2		
Extras	(B 9, LB 7, NB 3, W 4)	23	(LB 2)	2
		341	(0 wkts)	135

1/5 2/36 3/157 4/229 5/262 6/306 7/316 8/334 9/336

Bowling: *First Innings*—Holder 35-6-64-1; Boyce 24.4-6-69-3; Davis 6-0-15-0; Willett 27-3-88-2; Gibbs 36-15-67-3; Lloyd 7-1-15-0. *Second Innings*—Holder 7-2-21-0; Boyce 8-1-33-0; Davis 3-2-5-0; Willett 6-2-20-0; Gibbs 5-4-9-0; Lloyd 5-1-15-0; Kanhai 5-1-15-0; Greenidge 4-0-15-0.

Umpires: C.P.Kippins and D.Sang Hue

WEST INDIES v AUSTRALIA 1972-73 (Fifth Test)

At Queen's Park Oval, Port-of-Spain, Trinidad, 21, 22, 23, 25, 26 April

Result: Match drawn

Australia

Batsman	First Innings		Second Innings	
I.R.Redpath	c Fredericks b Gibbs	36	c Boyce b Foster	24
R.Edwards	c Fredericks b Jumadeen	74	c Kallicharran b Inshan Ali	14
I.M.Chappell*	c Kallicharran b Inshan Ali	56	c Kallicharran b Gibbs	37
G.S.Chappell	c Fredericks b Gibbs	41	c Fredericks b Gibbs	31
K.D.Walters	c Fredericks b Gibbs	70	c Murray b Gibbs	27
J.Benaud	c and b Inshan Ali	8	c Davis b Inshan Ali	36
R.W.Marsh†	c Inshan Ali b Jumadeen	56	not out	21
K.J.O'Keeffe	b Inshan Ali	37	c Lloyd b Gibbs	0
T.J.Jenner	not out	27	not out	11
J.R.Hammond	not out	6		
M.H.N.Walker				
Extras	(B 5, LB 1, NB 2)	8	(B 13, LB 2, NB 1, W 1)	17
	(8 wkts dec.)	419	(7 wkts dec.)	218

1/50 2/159 3/169 4/280 5/281 6/293 7/379 8/395

1/37 2/49 3/101 4/114 5/157 6/195 7/197

Bowling: *First Innings*—Boyce 10-3-21-0; Lloyd 12-6-19-0; Davis 5-0-22-0; Gibbs 52-15-114-3; Jumadeen 40-8-89-2; Inshan Ali 44-4-124-3; Foster 8-3-15-0; Fredericks 2-0-7-0. *Second Innings*—Lloyd 3-0-16-0; Davis 5-0-16-0; Gibbs 32-12-66-4; Jumadeen 18-5-32-0; Inshan Ali 19-2-68-2; Foster 3-1-3-0.

West Indies

Batsman	First Innings		Second Innings	
R.C.Fredericks	c Edwards b Jenner	73	c Marsh b Hammond	8
M.L.C.Foster	c Marsh b Walker	29	c I.M.Chappell b Walker	19
C.A.Davis	c Marsh b Walker	25	b Benaud	24
A.I.Kallicharran	c Hammond b Jenner	32	c O'Keeffe b Benaud	26
R.B.Kanhai*	b Jenner	3	(6) not out	16
C.H.Lloyd	c Redpath b Walker	59	(7) not out	22
D.L.Murray†	c Marsh b Walker	34	(5) c I.M.Chappell b Jenner	7
K.D.Boyce	b Jenner	31		
Inshan Ali	c G.S.Chappell b Walker	0		
R.R.Jumadeen	not out	11		
L.R.Gibbs	c Hammond b Jenner	6		
Extras	(B 6, LB 4, NB 5, W 1)	16	(B 10, NB 3)	13
		319	(5 wkts)	135

1/48 2/88 3/151 4/171 5/180 6/270 7/271 8/271 9/303

1/25 2/30 3/81 4/86 5/96

Bowling: *First Innings*—Hammond 21-4-76-0; Walker 37-10-75-5; G.S.Chappell 7-2-21-0; Walters 3-2-5-0; Jenner 32.2-9-90-5; O'Keeffe 11-1-36-0. *Second Innings*—Hammond 15-8-25-1; Walker 17-8-24-1; G.S.Chappell 6-2-11-0; Jenner 17-7-33-1; O'Keeffe 10-5-17-0; Benaud 4-1-12-2.

Umpires: R.Gosein and D.Sang Hue

AUSTRALIA v NEW ZEALAND 1973-74 (First Test)

At Melbourne Cricket Ground, 29, 30 December, 1, 2 January
Result: Australia won by an innings and 25 runs

Australia

Batsman	Dismissal	Runs
K.R.Stackpole	c Parker b Shrimpton	122
A.P.Sheahan	c Wadsworth b D.R.Hadlee	28
I.M.Chappell*	c R.J.Hadlee b Shrimpton	54
G.S.Chappell	c Wadsworth b Congdon	60
K.D.Walters	c Wadsworth b D.R.Hadlee	79
I.C.Davis	c Wadsworth b D.R.Hadlee	15
R.W.Marsh†	c Parker b D.R.Hadlee	6
K.J.O'Keeffe	not out	40
G.J.Gilmour	b Congdon	52
A.A.Mallett		
A.R.Dell		
Extras	(LB 4, NB 1, W 1)	6
Total	**(8 wkts dec.)**	**462**

1/75 2/203 3/212 4/304 5/345 6/363 7/381 8/462

Bowling: R.J.Hadlee 25-4-104-0; Andrews 19-2-100-0; D.R.Hadlee 20-2-102-4; O'Sullivan 22-3-80-0; Shrimpton 7-0-39-2; Congdon 8.5-1-31-2.

New Zealand

Batsman	First Innings	Runs	Second Innings	Runs
G.M.Turner	c Gilmour b Dell	6	absent hurt	–
J.M.Parker	c I.M.Chappell b O'Keeffe	27	(1) c I.M.Chappell b Walters	23
M.J.F.Shrimpton	c Marsh b Gilmour	16	b Walters	22
B.F.Hastings	b O'Keeffe	1	c Marsh b Mallett	22
B.E.Congdon*	st Marsh b Mallett	31	c Marsh b Mallett	14
J.F.M.Morrison	c Marsh b Gilmour	44	(6) c Marsh b Walters	16
K.J.Wadsworth†	c G.S.Chappell b Gilmour	80	(2) c Stackpole b Mallett	30
R.J.Hadlee	c Marsh b Gilmour	9	(7) c I.M.Chappell b O'Keeffe	6
D.R.Hadlee	run out	2	(8) c and b O'Keeffe	37
D.R.O'Sullivan	c Davis b Mallett	6	(9) c and b Mallett	8
B.Andrews	not out	0	(10) not out	5
Extras	(B 8, LB 5, NB 2)	15	(B 8, LB 9)	17
Total		**237**		**200**

1/19 2/47 3/51 4/56 5/100 6/189 7/215 8/230 9/237
1/37 2/54 3/83 4/109 5/113 6/134 7/150 8/188 9/200

Bowling: First Innings—Dell 22-7-54-1; Gilmour 22.4-7-5-4; G.S.Chappell 4-2-4-0; Mallett 16.7-2-46-2; O'Keeffe 14-4-40-2; I.M.Chappell 1-0-3-0. Second Innings—Dell 5-0-9-0; Gilmour 3-0-16-0; G.S.Chappell 7-3-18-0; Mallett 24-4-63-4; O'Keeffe 29.6-12-51-2; Walters 13-4-26-3.

Umpires: T.F.Brooks and J.R.Collins

AUSTRALIA v NEW ZEALAND 1973-74 (Second Test)

At Sydney Cricket Ground, 5, 6, 7 (no play), 9, 10 (no play) January
Result: Match drawn

New Zealand

Batsman	First Innings	Runs	Second Innings	Runs
J.M.Parker	c Marsh b Walker	108	c Marsh b G.S.Chappell	11
J.F.M.Morrison	c G.S.Chappell b Walters	28	c Davis b I.M.Chappell	117
M.J.F.Shrimpton	b Walters	0	c and b Walters	28
B.E.Congdon*	c Marsh b Walters	4	b Gilmour	17
B.F.Hastings	c Marsh b Walker	16	b G.S.Chappell	83
J.V.Coney	c Stackpole b O'Keeffe	45	c Davis b G.S.Chappell	11
K.J.Wadsworth†	c Marsh b Walters	54	(7) c G.S.Chappell b Gilmour	2
D.R.Hadlee	c and b G.S.Chappell	14	(6) not out	18
R.J.Hadlee	c I.M.Chappell b G.S.Chappell	17	(9) run out	1
D.R.O'Sullivan	not out	3	(8) lbw b Gilmour	1
B.Andrews	c Marsh b Gilmour	17		
Extras	(LB 2, NB 4)	6	(B 4, LB 11, W 1)	16
Total		**312**	**(9 wkts dec.)**	**305**

1/78 2/78 3/90 4/112 5/193 6/221 7/268 8/292 9/293
1/23 2/94 3/120 4/244 5/255 6/276 7/282 8/292 9/305

Bowling: First Innings—Gilmour 18.6-3-70-1; Walker 22-2-71-2; G.S.Chappell 19-2-76-2; Walters 11-0-39-4; Mallett 8-0-31-0; O'Keeffe 8-2-20-1. Second Innings—Gilmour 21.2-1-70-3; G.S.Chappell 16-3-54-3; Walters 11-0-54-1; Mallett 14-1-65-0; O'Keeffe 10-0-40-0; I.M.Chappell 3-0-6-1.

Australia

Batsman	First Innings	Runs	Second Innings	Runs
A.P.Sheahan	c Coney b Andrews	7	not out	14
K.R.Stackpole	c Morrison b R.J.Hadlee	8	lbw b R.J.Hadlee	2
I.M.Chappell*	c Hastings b D.R.Hadlee	45	lbw b R.J.Hadlee	6
G.S.Chappell	c Coney b Andrews	0	not out	8
K.D.Walters	c Coney b D.R.Hadlee	41		
I.C.Davis	c Andrews b R.J.Hadlee	29		
R.W.Marsh†	c Wadsworth b D.R.Hadlee	10		
K.J.O'Keeffe	c Wadsworth b R.J.Hadlee	9		
G.J.Gilmour	c Wadsworth b Congdon	3		
A.A.Mallett	lbw b R.J.Hadlee	0		
M.H.N.Walker	not out	2		
Extras	(LB 5, NB 3)	8		
Total		**162**	**(2 wkts)**	**30**

1/20 2/20 3/21 4/98 5/115 6/133 7/150 8/157 9/160
1/10 2/22

Bowling: First Innings—R.J.Hadlee 9.4-2-33-4; Andrews 9-1-40-2; D.R.Hadlee 13-3-52-3; Congdon 13-2-29-1. Second Innings—R.J.Hadlee 4.3-0-16-2; Andrews 4-0-14-0.

Umpires: P.R.Enright and M.G.O'Connell

AUSTRALIA v NEW ZEALAND 1973-74 (Third Test)

At Adelaide Oval, 26, 27, 28, 30 (no play), 31 January
Result: Australia won by an innings and 57 runs

Australia

K.R.Stackpole c Parker b D.R.Hadlee	15
A.J.Woodcock c Coney b Cairns	27
I.M.Chappell* c R.J.Hadlee b Cairns	22
G.S.Chappell b Congdon	42
K.D.Walters b O'Sullivan	94
I.C.Davis c Congdon b O'Sullivan	15
R.W.Marsh† st Wadsworth b O'Sullivan	132
K.J.O'Keeffe lbw b R.J.Hadlee	85
A.A.Mallett c Wadsworth b O'Sullivan	11
A.G.Hurst c Hastings b O'Sullivan	16
G.Dymock not out	0
Extras (B 3, LB 6, NB 9)	18
	477

1/21 2/67 3/73 4/173 5/221 6/232 7/400 8/452 9/472

Bowling: R.J.Hadlee 28-3-102-1; D.R.Hadlee 21-2-76-1; Cairns 21-4-73-2; O'Sullivan 35.5-4-148-5; Congdon 15-1-60-1.

New Zealand

J.M.Parker c Marsh b Dymock	0	c I.M.Chappell b Dymock	22
G.M.Turner lbw b Hurst	20	c O'Keeffe b Dymock	34
J.F.M.Morrison c I.M.Chappell b O'Keeffe	40	c I.M.Chappell b O'Keeffe	4
B.F.Hastings c Woodcock b O'Keeffe	23	c Stackpole b Dymock	7
B.E.Congdon* run out	23	not out	71
J.V.Coney c Marsh b Dymock	8	b Dymock	17
K.J.Wadsworth† lbw b I.M.Chappell	48	c Marsh b O'Keeffe	16
D.R.Hadlee c G.S.Chappell b Mallett	29	c G.S.Chappell b Mallett	0
R.J.Hadlee c I.M.Chappell b Mallett	20	c Marsh b O'Keeffe	15
D.R.O'Sullivan b O'Keeffe	2	c I.M.Chappell b Dymock	4
B.L.Cairns not out	4	c I.M.Chappell b Mallett	0
Extras (B 4, LB 4, NB 3)	11	(B 2, LB 8, NB 2)	12
	228		202

1/2 2/35 3/84 4/89 5/107 6/110 7/176 8/209 9/214
1/56 2/65 3/65 4/73 5/105 6/130 7/143 8/170 9/197

Bowling: First Innings—Hurst 19-3-56-1; Dymock 19-5-44-2; Walters 1-0-2-0; Mallett 23-6-46-2; O'Keeffe 24.3-9-55-3; I.M.Chappell 1-0-4-1. Second Innings—Hurst 10-2-17-0; Dymock 27-7-58-5; Walters 3-0-17-0; Mallett 21.5-9-47-2; O'Keeffe 28-12-51-3.

Umpires: J.R.Collins and P.R.Enright

NEW ZEALAND v AUSTRALIA 1973-74 (First Test)

At Basin Reserve, Wellington, 1, 2, 3, 5, 6 March
Result: Match drawn

Australia

K.R.Stackpole b Webb	10	b Collinge	27
I.R.Redpath c Coney b Hadlee	19	c Howarth b Congdon	93
I.M.Chappell* c Wadsworth b Webb	145	c Hadlee b Howarth	121
G.S.Chappell not out	247	c Wadsworth b Collinge	133
I.C.Davis c Wadsworth b Hadlee	16	c Wadsworth b Howarth	8
K.D.Walters c Howarth b Collinge	32	c Morrison b Hadlee	8
R.W.Marsh† lbw b Congdon	22	c Collinge b Congdon	17
K.J.O'Keeffe		c Howarth b Congdon	2
M.H.N.Walker		not out	22
A.A.Mallett		not out	4
G.Dymock			
Extras (B 1, LB 4, NB 15)	20	(B 4, LB 4, NB 16, W 1)	25
(6 wkts dec.)	511	(8 wkts)	460

1/13 2/55 3/319 4/359 5/431 6/511
1/67 2/208 3/294 4/318 5/359 6/414 7/433 8/433

Bowling: First Innings—Webb 21-1-114-2; Collinge 24-3-103-1; Hadlee 27-7-107-2; Howarth 21-0-113-0; Congdon 12.5-0-54-1. Second Innings—Webb 19-3-90-0; Collinge 19-3-60-2; Hadlee 21-2-106-1; Howarth 25-3-97-2; Congdon 13-1-60-3; Coney 2-0-13-0; Hastings 2-0-6-0.

New Zealand

G.M.Turner c Redpath b O'Keeffe	79
J.M.Parker lbw b Walker	10
J.F.M.Morrison b Walker	66
B.E.Congdon* c Davis b Mallett	132
B.F.Hastings c I.M.Chappell b Dymock	101
J.V.Coney c G.S.Chappell b Walker	13
K.J.Wadsworth† b Dymock	5
D.R.Hadlee c Davis b O'Keeffe	9
R.O.Collinge run out	2
H.J.Howarth not out	29
M.G.Webb c O'Keeffe b Dymock	12
Extras (B 10, LB 5, NB 11)	26
	484

1/28 2/136 3/169 4/398 5/409 6/423 7/423 8/430 9/437

Bowling: Walker 41-11-107-3; Dymock 35-7-77-3; Walters 8-1-39-0; Mallett 41-8-117-1; O'Keeffe 33-9-83-2; G.S.Chappell 7-0-27-0; I.M.Chappell 4-0-8-0.

Umpires: D.E.A.Copps and F.R.Goodall

NEW ZEALAND v AUSTRALIA 1973-74 (Third Test)
At Eden Park, Auckland, 22, 23, 24 March
Result: Australia won by 297 runs

Australia

K.R.Stackpole c Parker b R.J.Hadlee	0		c Congdon b Collinge	0
I.R.Redpath c Wadsworth b Collinge	13		not out	159
I.M.Chappell* c Turner b Collinge	37		lbw b Collinge	35
G.S.Chappell c Howarth b Collinge	0		c Wadsworth b Howarth	38
I.C.Davis c Hastings b Collinge	0		c Parker b Howarth	5
K.D.Walters not out	104		c Parker b Congdon	5
R.W.Marsh† c Hastings b Collinge	45		c R.J.Hadlee b Howarth	47
K.J.O'Keeffe c Morrison b Congdon	1		c Burgess b Collinge	32
G.J.Gilmour c Morrison b Congdon	1		b R.J.Hadlee	4
M.H.N.Walker c Burgess b Congdon	7		b R.J.Hadlee	0
A.A.Mallett c Turner b Congdon	7		c Parker b Collinge	6
Extras (B 4, LB 1, NB 2)	7		(B 4, LB 4, NB 6, W 1)	15
	221			**346**

1/0 2/32 3/37 4/37 5/64   1/2 2/69 3/118 4/132 5/143
6/150 7/154 8/162 9/191   6/230 7/315 8/330 9/330

Bowling: *First Innings*—R.J.Hadlee 9-1-45-1; Collinge 18-4-82-5; D.R.Hadlee 9-0-41-0; Congdon 10.2-0-46-4. *Second Innings*—R.J.Hadlee 9-1-50-2; Collinge 16.4-0-84-4; D.R.Hadlee 7-0-48-0; Howarth 28-5-83-3; Congdon 19-1-66-1.

New Zealand

G.M.Turner c G.S.Chappell b Mallett	41		c I.M.Chappell b Walker	72
J.M.Parker lbw b Gilmour	11		c Marsh b Gilmour	34
J.F.M.Morrison c Marsh b Walker	9		c Marsh b Gilmour	0
B.E.Congdon* lbw b Gilmour	4		c Marsh b Walker	4
B.F.Hastings b Gilmour	0		lbw b Walker	1
M.G.Burgess c Marsh b Gilmour	7		c Stackpole b Walker	6
K.J.Wadsworth† c Marsh b Gilmour	0		c G.S.Chappell b Mallett	21
H.J.Howarth c Gilmour b Mallett	0	(10)	not out	3
D.R.Hadlee b Mallett	4	(8)	c Walters b Mallett	1
R.J.Hadlee c I.M.Chappell b Mallett	13	(9)	b O'Keeffe	4
R.O.Collinge not out	8		c I.M.Chappell b O'Keeffe	4
Extras (B 4, LB 1, NB 10)	15		(B 3, LB 2, NB 3)	8
	112			**158**

1/16 2/28 3/34 4/40 5/62   1/107 2/107 3/112 4/115
6/62 7/63 8/72 9/102   5/116 6/127 7/145 8/147 9/147

Bowling: *First Innings*—Walker 10-4-11-1; Gilmour 15-3-64-5; Mallett 5.2-0-22-4. *Second Innings*—Walker 19-8-39-4; Gilmour 16-0-52-2; Mallett 13-6-51-2; O'Keeffe 5-1-8-2.

Umpires: D.E.A.Copps and W.R.C.Gardiner

NEW ZEALAND v AUSTRALIA 1973-74 (Second Test)
At Lancaster Park, Christchurch, 8, 9, 10, 12, 13 March
Result: New Zealand won by 5 wickets

Australia

K.R.Stackpole b Collinge	4		c Wadsworth b Collinge	9
I.R.Redpath c and b Collinge	71		c Howarth b R.J.Hadlee	58
I.M.Chappell* b R.J.Hadlee	20		b Collinge	1
G.S.Chappell c Howarth b Congdon	25		c Coney b R.J.Hadlee	6
I.C.Davis lbw b R.J.Hadlee	5		c Congdon b R.J.Hadlee	50
K.D.Walters b R.J.Hadlee	6		lbw b D.R.Hadlee	65
R.W.Marsh† b Congdon	38		c and b D.R.Hadlee	4
K.J.O'Keeffe c Wadsworth b Congdon	3		not out	23
M.H.N.Walker not out	18		c Howarth b D.R.Hadlee	4
A.A.Mallett b Collinge	1	(11)	c Wadsworth b R.J.Hadlee	11
G.Dymock c Congdon b D.R.Hadlee	13	(10)	c Wadsworth b D.R.Hadlee	0
Extras (B 1, LB 6, NB 12)	19		(B 16, LB 4, NB 8)	28
	223			**259**

1/8 2/45 3/101 4/120 5/128   1/12 2/26 3/33 4/139 5/142
6/181 7/190 8/194 9/196   6/160 7/232 8/238 9/239

Bowling: *First Innings*—R.J.Hadlee 14-2-59-3; Collinge 21-4-70-3; Congdon 11-2-33-3; D.R.Hadlee 12.2-2-42-1. *Second Innings*—Collinge 9-0-37-2; R.J.Hadlee 18.4-3-71-4; D.R.Hadlee 20-2-75-4; Congdon 9-3-26-0; Howarth 11-2-22-0.

New Zealand

G.M.Turner c Stackpole b G.S.Chappell	101		not out	110
J.M.Parker lbw b Dymock	18		c Marsh b Walker	26
J.F.M.Morrison c Marsh b G.S.Chappell	12		lbw b Walker	0
B.E.Congdon* c I.M.Chappell b Walker	8		run out	2
B.F.Hastings c Marsh b Walker	19		b Mallett	46
J.V.Coney c Marsh b Dymock	15		c Marsh b G.S.Chappell	14
K.J.Wadsworth† c Marsh b Mallett	24		not out	9
D.R.Hadlee c Marsh b Dymock	11			
R.J.Hadlee lbw b Walker	23			
H.J.Howarth c I.M.Chappell b Walker	0			
R.O.Collinge not out	1			
Extras (B 4, LB 8, NB 11)	23		(B 4, LB 14, NB 5)	23
	255		(5 wkts)	**230**

1/59 2/90 3/104 4/136 5/171   1/51 2/55 3/62 4/177
6/213 7/220 8/241 9/242   5/206

Bowling: *First Innings*—Walker 19.6-5-60-4; Dymock 24-6-59-3; G.S.Chappell 20-2-76-2; Walters 7-1-34-0; Mallett 3-1-3-1. *Second Innings*—Walker 28-10-50-2; Dymock 25-5-84-0; G.S.Chappell 17.6-5-38-1; Mallett 13-4-35-1.

Umpires: J.B.R.Hastie and R.L.Monteith

AUSTRALIA v ENGLAND 1974-75 (First Test)
At Woolloongabba, Brisbane, 29, 30 November, 1, 3, 4 December
Result: Australia won by 166 runs

Australia

I.R.Redpath b Willis	5	b Willis	25
W.J.Edwards c Amiss b Hendrick	4	c Knott b Willis	5
I.M.Chappell* c Greig b Willis	90	c Fletcher b Underwood	11
G.S.Chappell c Fletcher b Underwood	58	b Underwood	71
R.Edwards c Knott b Underwood	32	c Knott b Willis	53
K.D.Walters c Lever b Willis	3	not out	62
R.W.Marsh† c Denness b Hendrick	14	not out	46
T.J.Jenner c Lever b Willis	12		
D.K.Lillee c Knott b Greig	15		
M.H.N.Walker not out	41		
J.R.Thomson run out	23		
Extras (LB 4, NB 8)	12	(B 1, LB 7, NB 6, W 1)	15
	309	**(5 wkts dec.)**	**288**

1/7 2/10 3/110 4/197 5/202   1/15 2/39 3/59
6/205 7/228 8/229 9/257   4/173 5/190

Bowling: *First Innings*—Willis 21.5-3-56-4; Lever 16-1-53-0; Hendrick 19-3-64-2; Greig 16-2-70-1; Underwood 20-6-54-2. *Second Innings*—Willis 15-3-45-3; Lever 18-4-58-0; Hendrick 13-2-47-0; Underwood 26-6-63-2; Greig 13-2-47-0.

England

D.L.Amiss c Jenner b Thomson	7	c Walters b Thomson	25
B.W.Luckhurst c Marsh b Thomson	1	c I.M.Chappell b Lillee	3
J.H.Edrich c I.M.Chappell b Thomson	48	b Thomson	6
M.H.Denness* lbw b Walker	6	c Walters b Thomson	27
K.W.R.Fletcher b Lillee	17	c G.S.Chappell b Jenner	19
A.W.Greig c Marsh b Lillee	110	b Thomson	2
A.P.E.Knott† c Jenner b Walker	12	b Thomson	19
P.Lever c I.M.Chappell b Walker	4	c Redpath b Lillee	14
D.L.Underwood c Redpath b Walters	25	c Walker b Jenner	30
R.G.D.Willis not out	13	not out	0
M.Hendrick c Redpath b Walker	4	b Thomson	18
Extras (B 5, LB 2, NB 8, W 3)	18	(B 8, LB 3, NB 5, W 2)	18
	265		**166**

1/9 2/10 3/33 4/57 5/130   1/18 2/40 3/44 4/92 5/94
6/162 7/168 8/226 9/248   6/94 7/115 8/162 9/163

Bowling: *First Innings*—Lillee 23-6-73-2; Thomson 21-5-59-3; Walker 24.5-2-73-4; Walters 6-1-18-1; Jenner 6-1-24-0. *Second Innings*—Lillee 12-2-25-2; Thomson 17.5-3-46-6; Jenner 16-5-45-2; Walker 9-4-32-0; Walters 2-2-0-0.

Umpires: R.C.Bailhache and T.F.Brooks

AUSTRALIA v ENGLAND 1974-75 (Second Test)
At W.A.C.A. Ground, Perth, 13, 14, 15, 17 December
Result: Australia won by 9 wickets

England

D.Lloyd c G.S.Chappell b Thomson	49		c G.S.Chappell b Walker	35
B.W.Luckhurst c Mallett b Walker	27		c Mallett b Lillee	23
M.C.Cowdrey b Thomson	22	(7)	lbw b Thomson	41
A.W.Greig c Mallett b Walker	23	(2)	c G.S.Chappell b Thomson	32
K.W.R.Fletcher c Redpath b Lillee	4		c Marsh b Thomson	0
M.H.Denness* c G.S.Chappell b Lillee	2	(3)	c Redpath b Thomson	20
A.P.E.Knott† c Redpath b Walters	51	(6)	c G.S.Chappell b Lillee	18
F.J.Titmus c Redpath b Walters	10		c G.S.Chappell b Mallett	61
C.M.Old c G.S.Chappell b I.M.Chappell	7		c Thomson b Mallett	43
G.G.Arnold run out	1		c Mallett b Thomson	0
R.G.D.Willis not out	4		not out	0
Extras (NB 5, W 3)	8		(LB 4, NB 11, W 1)	16
	208			**293**

1/44 2/99 3/119 4/128 5/132   1/62 2/106 3/124 4/124 5/154
6/132 7/194 8/201 9/202   6/156 7/219 8/285 9/293

Bowling: *First Innings*—Lillee 16-4-48-2; Thomson 15-6-45-2; Walker 20-5-49-2; Mallett 10-3-35-0; Walters 2.3-0-13-2; I.M.Chappell 2-0-10-1. *Second Innings*—Lillee 22-5-59-2; Thomson 25-4-93-5; Walker 24-7-76-1; Walters 9-4-17-0; Mallett 11.1-4-32-2.

Australia

I.R.Redpath st Knott b Titmus	41	not out	12
W.J.Edwards c Lloyd b Greig	30	lbw b Arnold	0
I.M.Chappell* c Knott b Arnold	25	not out	11
G.S.Chappell c Greig b Willis	62		
R.Edwards b Arnold	115		
K.D.Walters c Fletcher b Willis	103		
R.W.Marsh† c Lloyd b Titmus	41		
M.H.N.Walker c Knott b Old	19		
D.K.Lillee b Old	11		
J.R.Thomson c Knott b Old	0		
A.A.Mallett not out	11		
Extras (B 7, LB 14, NB 2)	23		
	481	**(1 wkt)**	**23**

1/64 2/101 3/113 4/192 5/362   1/4
6/416 7/449 8/462 9/462

Bowling: *First Innings*—Willis 22-0-91-2; Arnold 27-1-129-2; Old 22.6-3-85-3; Greig 9-0-69-1; Titmus 28-3-84-2. *Second Innings*—Willis 2-0-8-0; Arnold 1.7-0-15-1.

Umpires: R.C.Bailhache and T.F.Brooks

AUSTRALIA v ENGLAND 1974-75 (Third Test)

At Melbourne Cricket Ground, 26, 27, 28, 30, 31 December

Result: Match drawn

England

Batsman	1st Innings		2nd Innings	
D.L.Amiss	c Walters b Lillee	4	c I.M.Chappell b Mallett	90
D.Lloyd	c Mallett b Thomson	14	c and b Mallett	44
M.C.Cowdrey	lbw b Thomson	35	c G.S.Chappell b Lillee	8
J.H.Edrich	c Marsh b Mallett	49	c Marsh b Thomson	4
M.H.Denness*	c Marsh b Mallett	8	c I.M.Chappell b Thomson	2
A.W.Greig	run out	28	c G.S.Chappell b Lillee	60
A.P.E.Knott†	b Thomson	52	c Marsh b Thomson	4
F.J.Titmus	c Mallett b Lillee	10	b Mallett	0
D.L.Underwood	c Marsh b Walker	9	c I.M.Chappell b Mallett	4
R.G.D.Willis	c Walters b Thomson	13	b Thomson	15
M.Hendrick	not out	8	not out	0
Extras	(LB 2, NB 9, W 1)	12	(B 2, LB 9, W 2)	13
		242		**244**

1/4 2/34 3/110 4/110 5/141 6/157 7/176 8/213 9/232

1/115 2/134 3/152 4/156 5/158 6/165 7/178 8/182 9/238

Bowling: *First Innings*—Lillee 20-2-70-2; Thomson 22.4-4-72-4; Walker 24-10-36-1; Walters 7-2-15-0; Mallett 15-3-37-2. *Second Innings*—Lillee 17-3-55-2; Thomson 17-1-71-4; Walker 11-0-45-0; Mallett 24-6-60-4.

Australia

Batsman	1st Innings		2nd Innings	
I.R.Redpath	c Knott b Greig	55	run out	39
W.J.Edwards	c Denness b Willis	29	lbw b Greig	0
G.S.Chappell	c Greig b Willis	2	(4) lbw b Titmus	61
R.Edwards	c Cowdrey b Titmus	1	(5) c Lloyd b Titmus	10
K.D.Walters	c Lloyd b Greig	36	(6) c Denness b Greig	32
I.M.Chappell*	lbw b Willis	36	(3) lbw b Willis	0
R.W.Marsh†	c Knott b Titmus	44	c Knott b Greig	40
M.H.N.Walker	c Knott b Willis	30	not out	23
D.K.Lillee	run out	0	c Denness b Greig	14
A.A.Mallett	run out	2	not out	0
J.R.Thomson	b Willis	2		
Extras	(B 2, LB 2)	4	(B 6, LB 9, NB 4)	19
		241	(8 wkts)	**238**

1/65 2/67 3/68 4/121 5/126 6/173 7/237 8/237 9/238

1/4 2/5 3/106 4/120 5/121 6/171 7/208 8/235

Bowling: *First Innings*—Willis 21.7-4-61-5; Hendrick 2.6-1-8-0; Underwood 22.6-2-0; Greig 24-2-63-2; Titmus 22-11-43-2. *Second Innings*—Willis 14-2-56-1; Greig 18-2-56-4; Underwood 19-7-43-0; Titmus 29-10-64-2.

Umpires: R.C.Bailhache and T.F.Brooks

AUSTRALIA v ENGLAND 1974-75 (Fourth Test)

At Sydney Cricket Ground, 4, 5, 6, 8, 9 January

Result: Australia won by 171 runs

Australia

Batsman	1st Innings		2nd Innings	
I.R.Redpath	hit wkt b Titmus	33	c sub (C.M.Old) b Underwood	105
R.B.McCosker	c Knott b Greig	80		
I.M.Chappell*	c Knott b Arnold	53	(2) c Lloyd b Willis	5
G.S.Chappell	c Greig b Arnold	84	(3) c Lloyd b Arnold	144
R.Edwards	b Greig	15	not out	17
K.D.Walters	lbw b Arnold	1	(4) b Underwood	5
R.W.Marsh†	b Greig	30	(6) not out	7
M.H.N.Walker	c Greig b Arnold	30		
D.K.Lillee	b Arnold	8		
A.A.Mallett	lbw b Greig	31		
J.R.Thomson	not out	24		
Extras	(LB 4, NB 11, W 1)	16	(LB 2, NB 3, W 1)	6
		405	(4 wkts dec.)	**289**

1/96 2/142 3/199 4/251 5/255 6/305 7/310 8/332 9/368

1/15 2/235 3/242 4/280

Bowling: *First Innings*—Willis 18-2-80-0; Arnold 29-7-86-5; Greig 22.7-2-104-4; Underwood 13-3-54-0; Titmus 16-2-65-1. *Second Innings*—Willis 11-1-52-1; Arnold 22-3-78-1; Greig 12-1-64-0; Underwood 12-1-65-2; Titmus 7.3-2-24-0.

England

Batsman	1st Innings		2nd Innings	
D.L.Amiss	c Mallett b Walker	12	c Marsh b Lillee	37
D.Lloyd	c Thomson b Lillee	19	c G.S.Chappell b Thomson	26
M.C.Cowdrey	c McCosker b Thomson	22	c I.M.Chappell b Walker	1
J.H.Edrich*	c Marsh b Walters	50	not out	33
K.W.R.Fletcher	c Redpath b Walker	24	c Redpath b Thomson	11
A.W.Greig	c G.S.Chappell b Thomson	9	st Marsh b Mallett	54
A.P.E.Knott†	b Thomson	82	c Redpath b Mallett	10
F.J.Titmus	c Marsh b Walters	22	c Thomson b Mallett	4
D.L.Underwood	c Walker b Lillee	27	c and b Walker	5
R.G.D.Willis	b Thomson	2	b Lillee	12
G.G.Arnold	not out	3	c G.S.Chappell b Mallett	14
Extras	(B 15, LB 7, W 1)	23	(B 13, LB 3, NB 5)	21
		295		**228**

1/36 2/46 3/69 4/108 5/123 6/180 7/240 9/273 9/285

1/68 2/70 3/74 4/103 5/136 6/156 7/158 8/175 9/201

Bowling: *First Innings*—Lillee 19.1-2-66-2; Thomson 19-3-74-4; Walker 23-2-77-2; Mallett 1-0-8-0; Walters 7-2-26-2; I.M.Chappell 4-0-21-0. *Second Innings*—Lillee 21-5-65-2; Thomson 23-7-74-2; Walker 16-5-46-2; Mallett 16.5-9-21-4; I.M.Chappell 3-2-1-0.

Umpires: R.C.Bailhache and T.F.Brooks

AUSTRALIA v ENGLAND 1974-75 (Fifth Test)
At Adelaide Oval, 25 (no play), 26, 27, 29, 30 January
Result: Australia won by 163 runs

Australia

I.R.Redpath	c Greig b Underwood	21	b Underwood	52
R.B.McCosker	c Cowdrey b Underwood	35	c Knott b Arnold	11
I.M.Chappell*	c Knott b Underwood	0	c Knott b Underwood	41
G.S.Chappell	lbw b Underwood	5	c Greig b Underwood	18
K.D.Walters	c Willis b Underwood	55	not out	71
R.W.Marsh†	c Greig b Underwood	6	c Greig b Underwood	55
T.J.Jenner	b Underwood	74	not out	14
M.H.N.Walker	run out	41		
D.K.Lillee	b Willis	26		
A.A.Mallett	not out	23		
J.R.Thomson	b Arnold	5		
Extras	(B 4, LB 4, NB 5)	13	(LB 4, NB 6)	10
		304	(5 wkts dec.)	**272**

1/52 2/52 3/58 4/77 5/84
6/164 7/241 8/259 9/295

1/16 2/92 3/128
4/133 5/245

Bowling: *First Innings*—Willis 10-0-46-1; Arnold 12.2-3-42-1; Underwood 29-3-113-7; Greig 10-0-63-0; Titmus 7-1-27-0. *Second Innings*—Willis 5-0-27-0; Arnold 20-1-71-1; Underwood 26-5-102-4; Titmus 13-1-53-0; Greig 2-0-9-0.

England

D.L.Amiss	c I.M.Chappell b Lillee	0	c Marsh b Lillee	0
D.Lloyd	c Marsh b Lillee	4	c Walters b Walker	5
M.C.Cowdrey	c Walker b Thomson	26	c Mallett b Lillee	3
M.H.Denness*	c Marsh b Thomson	51	c Jenner b Lillee	14
K.W.R.Fletcher	c I.M.Chappell b Thomson	40	lbw b Lillee	63
A.W.Greig	c Marsh b Lillee	19	lbw b Walker	20
A.P.E.Knott†	c Lillee b Mallett	5	not out	106
F.J.Titmus	c G.S.Chappell b Mallett	11	lbw b Jenner	20
D.L.Underwood	c Lillee b Mallett	0	c I.M.Chappell b Mallett	0
G.G.Arnold	b Lillee	0	b Mallett	0
R.G.D.Willis	not out	11	b Walker	3
Extras	(LB 2, NB 3)	5	(B 3, LB 3, NB 1)	7
		172		**241**

1/0 2/8 3/10 4/33 5/76
6/144 7/212 8/213 9/217

1/2 2/19 3/66 4/90 5/130
6/147 7/155 8/156 9/161

Bowling: *First Innings*—Lillee 12.5-2-49-4; Thomson 15-1-58-3; Walker 5-1-18-0; Jenner 5-0-28-0; Mallett 9-4-14-3. *Second Innings*—Lillee 14-3-69-4; Walker 20-3-89-3; Mallett 25-10-36-2; Jenner 15-4-39-1; I.M.Chappell 1-0-1-0.

Umpires: R.C.Bailhache and T.F.Brooks

AUSTRALIA v ENGLAND 1974-75 (Sixth Test)
At Melbourne Cricket Ground, 8, 9, 10, 12, 13 February
Result: England won by an innings and 4 runs

Australia

I.R.Redpath	c Greig b Lever	1	c Amiss b Greig		83
R.B.McCosker	c Greig b Lever	0	c Cowdrey b Arnold		76
I.M.Chappell*	c Knott b Old	65	c Knott b Greig		50
G.S.Chappell	c Denness b Lever	1	b Lever		102
R.Edwards	c Amiss b Lever	0	c Knott b Arnold		18
K.D.Walters	c Edrich b Old	12	b Arnold		3
R.W.Marsh†	b Old	29	c Denness b Lever		1
M.H.N.Walker	not out	20	c and b Greig		17
D.K.Lillee	c Knott b Lever	12	not out	(11)	0
A.A.Mallett	b Lever	7	c Edrich b Greig	(9)	0
G.Dymock	c Knott b Greig	0	c Knott b Lever	(10)	0
Extras	(B 2, LB 1, NB 2)	5	(B 9, LB 5, NB 5, W 4)		23
		152			**373**

1/0 2/5 3/19 4/23 5/50
6/104 7/115 8/141 9/149

1/111 2/215 3/248 4/289
5/297 6/306 7/367 8/373 9/373

Bowling: *First Innings*—Arnold 6-2-24-0; Lever 11-2-38-6; Old 11-0-50-3; Greig 8.7-1-35-1. *Second Innings*—Arnold 23-6-83-3; Lever 16-1-65-3; Old 18-1-75-0; Underwood 18-5-39-0; Greig 31.7-7-88-4.

England

D.L.Amiss	lbw b Lillee	0
M.C.Cowdrey	c Marsh b Walker	7
J.H.Edrich	c I.M.Chappell b Walker	70
M.H.Denness*	c and b Walker	188
K.W.R.Fletcher	c Redpath b Walker	146
A.W.Greig	c sub (T.J.Jenner) b Walker	89
A.P.E.Knott†	c Marsh b Walker	5
C.M.Old	b Dymock	0
D.L.Underwood	b Walker	11
G.G.Arnold	c Marsh b Walker	0
P.Lever	not out	6
Extras	(B 4, LB 2, NB 1)	7
		529

1/4 2/18 3/167 4/359 5/507
6/507 7/508 8/514 9/514

Bowling: Lillee 6-2-17-1; Walker 42.2-7-143-8; Dymock 39-6-130-1; Walters 23-3-86-0; Mallett 29-8-96-0; I.M.Chappell 12-1-50-0.

Umpires: R.C.Bailhache and T.F.Brooks

ENGLAND v AUSTRALIA 1975 (First Test)

At Edgbaston, Birmingham, 10, 11, 12, 14 July

Result: Australia won by an innings and 85 runs

Australia

R.B.McCosker b Arnold	59
A.Turner c Denness b Snow	37
I.M.Chappell* c Fletcher b Snow	52
G.S.Chappell lbw b Old	0
R.Edwards c Gooch b Old	56
K.D.Walters c Old b Greig	14
R.W.Marsh† c Fletcher b Arnold	61
M.H.N.Walker c Knott b Snow	7
J.R.Thomson c Arnold b Underwood	49
D.K.Lillee c Knott b Arnold	3
A.A.Mallett not out	3
Extras (B 1, LB 8, NB 9)	18
	359

1/80 2/126 3/135 4/161 5/186
6/265 7/286 8/332 9/343

Bowling: Arnold 33-3-91-3; Snow 33-6-86-3; Old 33-7-111-2; Greig 15-2-43-1; Underwood 7-3-10-1.

England

J.H.Edrich lbw b Lillee	34	c Marsh b Walker	5
D.L.Amiss c Thomson b Lillee	4	c sub (G.J.Gilmour) b Thomson	5
K.W.R.Fletcher c Mallett b Walker	6	c Walters b Lillee	51
M.H.Denness* c G.S.Chappell b Walker	3	b Thomson	8
G.A.Gooch c Marsh b Walker	0	c Marsh b Thomson	0
A.W.Greig c Marsh b Walker	8	c Marsh b Walker	7
A.P.E.Knott† b Lillee	14	c McCosker b Thomson	38
D.L.Underwood b Lillee	10	(10) b Mallett	3
C.M.Old c G.S.Chappell b Walker	13	(8) c Walters b Lillee	7
J.A.Snow lbw b Lillee	0	(9) c Marsh b Thomson	34
G.G.Arnold not out	0	not out	6
Extras (LB 3, NB 1, W 5)	9	(LB 5, NB 2, W 2)	9
	101		173

1/9 2/24 3/46 4/46 5/54
6/75 7/78 8/87 9/97
1/7 2/18 3/20 4/52 5/90
6/100 7/122 8/151 9/167

Bowling: First Innings—Lillee 15-8-15-5; Thomson 10-3-21-0; Walker 17.3-5-48-5; Mallett 3-1-8-0. Second Innings—Lillee 20-8-45-2; Walker 24-9-47-2; Thomson 18-8-35-5; Mallett 13.2-6-34-1.

Umpires: H.D.Bird and A.E.Fagg (A.S.M.Oakman and T.W.Spencer deputised)

ENGLAND v AUSTRALIA 1975 (Second Test)

At Lord's, London, 31 July, 1, 2, 4, 5 August

Result: Match drawn

England

B.Wood lbw b Lillee	6	c Marsh b Thomson	52
J.H.Edrich lbw b Lillee	9	c Thomson b Mallett	175
D.S.Steele b Thomson	50	c and b Walters	45
D.L.Amiss lbw b Lillee	0	c G.S.Chappell b Lillee	10
G.A.Gooch c Marsh b Lillee	6	b Mallett	31
A.W.Greig* c I.M.Chappell b Walker	96	c Walters b I.M.Chappell	41
A.P.E.Knott† lbw b Thomson	69	not out	22
R.A.Woolmer c Turner b Mallett	33	b Mallett	31
J.A.Snow c Walker b Mallett	11		
D.L.Underwood not out	0		
P.Lever lbw b Walker	4		
Extras (B 3, LB 1, NB 23, W 4)	31	(LB 18, NB 9, W 2)	29
	315	(7 wkts dec.)	436

1/10 2/29 3/31 4/49 5/145
6/222 7/288 8/309 9/310
1/111 2/215
3/249 4/315 5/380 6/387 7/436

Bowling: First Innings—Lillee 20-4-84-4; Thomson 24-7-92-2; Walker 21.4-7-52-2; Mallett 22-4-56-2. Second Innings—Lillee 33-10-80-1; Thomson 29-8-73-1; Walker 37-8-95-0; Mallett 36.4-10-127-3; I.M.Chappell 10-2-26-1; Walters 2-0-6-1.

Australia

R.B.McCosker c and b Lever	29	lbw b Steele	79
A.Turner lbw b Snow	9	c Gooch b Greig	21
I.M.Chappell* c Knott b Snow	2	lbw b Greig	86
G.S.Chappell lbw b Snow	4	not out	73
R.Edwards lbw b Woolmer	99	not out	52
K.D.Walters c Greig b Lever	2		
R.W.Marsh† c Amiss b Greig	3		
M.H.N.Walker b Snow	5		
J.R.Thomson b Underwood	17		
D.K.Lillee not out	73		
A.A.Mallett lbw b Steele	14		
Extras (LB 5, NB 6)	11	(B 4, LB 14)	18
	268	(3 wkts)	329

1/21 2/29 3/37 4/54 5/56
6/64 7/81 8/133 9/199
1/50 2/169 3/222

Bowling: First Innings—Snow 21-4-66-4; Lever 15-0-83-2; Woolmer 13-5-31-1; Greig 15-5-47-1; Underwood 13-5-29-1; Steele 0.4-0-1-1. Second Innings—Snow 19-3-82-0; Lever 20-5-55-0; Greig 26-6-82-2; Underwood 31-14-64-0; Woolmer 3-1-3-0; Steele 9-4-19-1; Wood 1-0-6-0.

Umpires: W.E.Alley and T.W.Spencer

ENGLAND v AUSTRALIA 1975 (Third Test)

At Headingley, Leeds, 14, 15, 16, 18, 19 (no play) August
Result: Match drawn

England

Batsman	1st Innings		2nd Innings	
B.Wood	lbw b Gilmour	9	lbw b Walker	25
J.H.Edrich	c Mallett b Thomson	62	b Mallett	35
D.S.Steele	c Walters b Thomson	73	c G.S.Chappell b Gilmour	92
J.H.Hampshire	lbw b Gilmour	14	(7) c G.S.Chappell b Thomson	0
K.W.R.Fletcher	c Mallett b Lillee	8	(4) c G.S.Chappell b Lillee	14
A.W.Greig*	run out	51	(5) c and b Mallett	49
A.P.E.Knott†	lbw b Gilmour	14	(8) c Thomson b Lillee	31
P.H.Edmonds	not out	13	(9) c sub (A.Turner) b Gilmour	8
C.M.Old	b Gilmour	5	(6) st Marsh b Mallett	10
J.A.Snow	c Walters b Gilmour	0	c Marsh b Gilmour	9
D.L.Underwood	c G.S.Chappell b Gilmour	0	not out	0
Extras	(B 4, LB 15, NB 9, W 11)	39	(B 5, LB 2, NB 9, W 2)	18
Total		**288**		**291**

1/25 2/137 3/159 4/189 5/209
6/268 7/269 8/284 9/284

1/55 2/70 3/103 4/197 5/209
6/210 7/272 8/276 9/285

Bowling: *First Innings*—Lillee 28-12-53-1; Thomson 22-8-53-2; Gilmour 20-5-72-3; Walker 18-4-54-0; I.M.Chappell 2-0-4-0. *Second Innings*—Lillee 20-5-48-2; Gilmour 31.2-10-85-6; Thomson 20-6-67-1; Walker 15-4-36-1; Mallett 19-4-50-3.

Australia

Batsman	1st Innings		2nd Innings	
R.B.McCosker	c Hampshire b Old	0	not out	95
R.W.Marsh†	b Snow	25	b Underwood	25
I.M.Chappell*	b Edmonds	35	lbw b Old	35
G.S.Chappell	c Underwood b Edmonds	13	c Steele b Edmonds	13
R.Edwards	lbw b Edmonds	19		
K.D.Walters	lbw b Edmonds	19	(5) not out	25
G.J.Gilmour	c Greig b Underwood	6		
M.H.N.Walker	c Old b Edmonds	0		
J.R.Thomson	c Steele b Snow	16		
D.K.Lillee	b Snow	11		
A.A.Mallett	not out	9		
Extras	(LB 5, NB 3, W 1)	9	(B 4, LB 8, NB 2)	14
Total		**135**	(3 wkts)	**220**

1/8 2/53 3/78 4/78 5/81
6/96 7/104 8/107 9/128

1/55 2/161 3/174

Bowling: *First Innings*—Snow 18.5-7-22-3; Old 11-3-30-1; Greig 3-0-14-0; Wood 5-2-10-0; Underwood 19-12-22-1; Edmonds 20-7-28-5. *Second Innings*—Old 17-5-61-1; Snow 15-6-21-0; Underwood 15-4-40-1; Edmonds 17-4-64-1; Greig 9-3-20-0.

Umpires: D.J.Constant and A.E.Fagg

ENGLAND v AUSTRALIA 1975 (Fourth Test)

At Kennington Oval, London, 28, 29, 30 August, 1, 2, 3 September
Result: Match drawn

Australia

Batsman	1st Innings		2nd Innings	
R.B.McCosker	c Roope b Old	127	not out	25
A.Turner	c Steele b Old	2	c Woolmer b Greig	8
I.M.Chappell*	c Greig b Woolmer	192		
G.S.Chappell	c Knott b Old	0	not out	4
R.Edwards	c Edrich b Snow	44	(3) c Old b Underwood	2
K.D.Walters	b Underwood	65		
R.W.Marsh†	c and b Greig	32		
M.H.N.Walker	c Steele b Greig	13		
J.R.Thomson	c Old b Greig	0		
D.K.Lillee	not out	28		
A.A.Mallett	not out	5		
Extras	(LB 5, NB 17, W 2)	24	(LB 1)	1
Total	(9 wkts dec.)	**532**	(2 wkts)	**40**

1/7 2/284 3/286 4/356 5/396
6/441 7/477 8/477 9/501

1/22 2/33

Bowling: *First Innings*—Old 28-7-74-3; Snow 27-4-74-1; Woolmer 18-3-38-1; Edmonds 38-7-118-0; Underwood 44-13-96-1; Greig 24-5-107-3; Steele 2-1-1-0. *Second Innings*—Old 2-0-7-0; Snow 2-1-4-0; Edmonds 6.1-2-14-0; Underwood 2-0-5-1; Greig 5-2-9-1.

England

Batsman	1st Innings		2nd Innings	
B.Wood	b Walker	32	lbw b Thomson	22
J.H.Edrich	lbw b Walker	12	b Lillee	96
D.S.Steele	b Lillee	39	c Marsh b Lillee	66
G.R.J.Roope	c Turner b Walker	0	b Lillee	77
R.A.Woolmer	c Mallett b Thomson	5	lbw b Walters	149
A.W.Greig*	c Marsh b Lillee	17	c Marsh b Lillee	15
A.P.E.Knott†	lbw b Walker	9	c Marsh b Walters	64
P.H.Edmonds	c Marsh b Thomson	4	(9) run out	7
C.M.Old	not out	25	(8) c I.M.Chappell b Walters	0
J.A.Snow	c G.S.Chappell b Thomson	30	c and b Walters	0
D.L.Underwood	c G.S.Chappell b Thomson	0	not out	3
Extras	(LB 3, NB 12, W 3)	18	(B 2, LB 15, NB 17, W 5)	39
Total		**191**		**538**

1/45 2/78 3/83 4/96 5/103
6/125 7/131 8/147 9/190

1/77 2/209 3/209 4/331 5/371
6/522 7/522 8/533 9/533

Bowling: *First Innings*—Lillee 19-7-44-2; Thomson 22.1-7-50-4; Walker 25-7-63-4. *Second Innings*—Lillee 52-18-91-4; Thomson 30-9-63-1; Walker 46-15-91-0; Mallett 64-31-95-0; I.M.Chappell 17-6-52-0; G.S.Chappell 12-2-53-0; Walters 10.5-3-34-4; Edwards 2-0-20-0.

Umpires: H.D.Bird and T.W.Spencer

AUSTRALIA v WEST INDIES 1975-76 (First Test)

At Woolloongabba, Brisbane, 28, 29, 30 November, 2 December

Result: Australia won by 8 wickets

West Indies

Batsman	First Innings		Second Innings	
R.C.Fredericks	c Marsh b Gilmour	46	c Marsh b Gilmour	7
C.G.Greenidge	lbw b Lillee	0	c McCosker b Gilmour	0
L.G.Rowe	run out	28	(4) c I.M.Chappell b Jenner	107
A.I.Kallicharran	c Turner b Lillee	4	b Mallett	101
I.V.A.Richards	c Gilmour b Lillee	0	(5) run out	12
C.H.Lloyd*	c Marsh b Gilmour	7	(7) c Redpath b Jenner	0
D.L.Murray†	c Mallett b Gilmour	66	(8) c and b Mallett	55
M.A.Holding	c G.S.Chappell b Gilmour	34	c Turner b Lillee	19
Inshan Ali	c Redpath b Thomson	12	(3) b Lillee	24
A.M.E.Roberts	c I.M.Chappell b Mallett	3	lbw b Lillee	3
L.R.Gibbs	not out	11	not out	4
Extras	(LB 1, NB 2)	3	(B 4, LB 15, NB 14, W 5)	38
		214		370

1/3 2*63 3/70 4/70 5/81
6/99 7/171 8/199 9/199

1/6 2/12 3/50 4/248 5/248
6/269 7/275 8/346 9/348

Bowling: First Innings—Lillee 11-0-84-3; Thomson 10-0-69-1; Gilmour 12-1-42-4; Jenner 4-1-15-0; Mallett 0.5-0-1-1. Second Innings—Lillee 16-3-72-3; Gilmour 11-4-26-2; Thomson 18-3-89-0; Mallett 21.4-6-70-2; Jenner 20-2-75-2.

Australia

Batsman	First Innings		Second Innings	
I.R.Redpath	run out	39	b Gibbs	26
A.Turner	b Roberts	81	not out	74
I.M.Chappell	lbw b Gibbs	41	not out	109
G.S.Chappell*	c Greenidge b Roberts	123	(1) c Murray b Roberts	2
R.B.McCosker	c Kallicharran b Inshan Ali	1		
R.W.Marsh†	c Murray b Gibbs	48		
G.J.Gilmour	c Lloyd b Gibbs	13		
T.J.Jenner	not out	6		
D.K.Lillee	b Roberts	1		
J.R.Thomson	lbw b Gibbs	4		
A.A.Mallett	c Fredericks b Gibbs	0		
Extras	(LB 5, NB 4)	9	(B 5, LB 2, NB 1)	8
		366	(2 wkts)	219

1/99 2/142 3/178 4/195 5/317
6/350 7/354 8/361 9/366

1/7 2/60

Bowling: First Innings—Roberts 25-2-85-3; Holding 20-4-81-0; Gibbs 38-7-102-5; Inshan Ali 10-0-57-0; Lloyd 6-1-22-0. Second Innings—Roberts 14-2-47-1; Holding 10-0-46-0; Gibbs 20-8-48-1; Inshan Ali 10-0-57-0; Fredericks 2-0-12-0; Kallicharran 0.2-0-1-0.

Umpires: R.C.Bailhache and T.F.Brooks

AUSTRALIA v WEST INDIES 1975-76 (Second Test)

At W.A.C.A. Ground, Perth, 12, 13, 14, 16 December

Result: West Indies won by an innings and 87 runs

Australia

Batsman	First Innings		Second Innings	
R.B.McCosker	lbw b Roberts	0	c Rowe b Roberts	13
A.Turner	c Gibbs b Roberts	23	c Murray b Roberts	0
I.M.Chappell	b Holding	156	c sub (C.G.Greenidge) b Roberts	20
G.S.Chappell*	c Murray b Julien	13	c Rowe b Roberts	43
I.R.Redpath	c Murray b Julien	33	lbw b Roberts	0
R.W.Marsh†	c Julien b Boyce	23	c Murray b Roberts	39
G.J.Gilmour	c Julien b Gibbs	45	c Fredericks b Roberts	3
M.H.N.Walker	c Richards b Holding	1	c sub (C.G.Greenidge) b Julien	3
D.K.Lillee	not out	12	c Lloyd b Julien	4
J.R.Thomson	b Holding	0	b Julien	9
A.A.Mallett	b Holding	0	not out	18
Extras	(B 12, LB 5, NB 6)	23	(B 13, LB 2, NB 2)	17
		329		169

1/0 2/37 3/70 4/149 5/189
6/277 7/285 8/329 9/329

1/0 2/25 3/45 4/45 5/124
6/128 7/132 8/142 9/146

Bowling: First Innings—Roberts 13-1-65-2; Boyce 12-2-53-1; Holding 18.7-1-88-4; Julien 12-0-51-2; Gibbs 14-4-49-1. Second Innings—Roberts 14-3-54-7; Holding 10.6-1-53-0; Julien 10.1-1-32-3; Boyce 2-0-8-0; Gibbs 3-1-3-0; Fredericks 1-0-2-0.

West Indies

Batsman	First Innings	
R.C.Fredericks	c G.S.Chappell b Lillee	169
B.D.Julien	c Mallett b Gilmour	25
L.G.Rowe	c Marsh b Thomson	19
A.I.Kallicharran	c I.M.Chappell b Walker	57
I.V.A.Richards	c Gilmour b Thomson	12
C.H.Lloyd*	b Gilmour	149
D.L.Murray†	c Marsh b Lillee	63
M.A.Holding	c Marsh b Thomson	0
K.D.Boyce	not out	49
A.M.E.Roberts	b Walker	0
L.R.Gibbs	run out	13
Extras	(B 2, LB 16, NB 11)	29
		585

1/91 2/134 3/258 4/297 5/461
6/461 7/522 8/548 9/548

Bowling: Lillee 20-0-123-3; Thomson 17-0-128-3; Gilmour 14-0-103-2; Walker 17-1-99-2; Mallett 26-4-103-0; I.M.Chappell 1.4-1-0-0.

Umpires: R.R.Ledwidge and M.G.O'Connell

AUSTRALIA v WEST INDIES 1975-76 (Third Test)
At Melbourne Cricket Ground, 26, 27, 28, 30 December
Result: Australia won by 8 wickets

West Indies

Batsman	First Innings	Runs	Second Innings	Runs
R.C.Fredericks	c McCosker b Thomson	59	b G.S.Chappell	26
C.G.Greenidge	c Marsh b Thomson	3	c Marsh b Walker	8
L.G.Rowe	c I.M.Chappell b Thomson	0	c Marsh b Lillee	8
A.I.Kallicharran	c Marsh b Thomson	20	c Marsh b Lillee	32
I.V.A.Richards	b Lillee	41	c Marsh b Thomson	36
C.H.Lloyd*	c G.S.Chappell b Thomson	24	c Lillee b Mallett	102
D.L.Murray†	c Walker b Lillee	18	c Marsh b Lillee	22
B.D.Julien	c Mallett b Lillee	24	b Walker	27
V.A.Holder	b Walker	24	run out	15
A.M.E.Roberts	c Marsh b Lillee	6	c Mallett b I.M.Chappell	5
L.R.Gibbs	not out	0	not out	0
Extras	(LB 4, NB 22, W 1)	27	(B 8, LB 4, NB 14)	26
		224		**312**

1/22 2/22 3/91 4/103 5/108 6/167 7/172 8/199 9/218
1/14 2/48 3/48 4/99 5/151 6/229 7/278 8/288 9/297

Bowling: First Innings—Lillee 14-2-56-4; Thomson 11-1-62-5; Walker 13-1-46-1; Cosier 4-0-15-0; Mallett 5-1-18-0. Second Innings—Lillee 15-1-70-3; Walker 19-1-74-2; G.S.Chappell 7-1-23-1; I.M.Chappell 5.2-3-7-1; Thomson 9-0-51-1; Mallett 14-0-61-1.

Australia

Batsman	First Innings	Runs	Second Innings	Runs
I.R.Redpath	b Roberts	102	(3) c sub (K.D.Boyce) b Julien	9
A.Turner	b Roberts	21	b Roberts	21
R.B.McCosker	c Murray b Julien	4	(1) not out	22
I.M.Chappell	c Kallicharran b Gibbs	35	not out	13
G.S.Chappell*	c Murray b Julien	52		
G.J.Cosier	c Kallicharran b Roberts	109		
R.W.Marsh†	c and b Gibbs	56		
M.H.N.Walker	c Murray b Roberts	1		
D.K.Lillee	c Richards b Holder	25		
J.R.Thomson	lbw b Julien	44		
A.A.Mallett	not out	3		
Extras	(B 5, LB 6, NB 22)	33	(LB 1, NB 3)	4
		485	(2 wkts)	**55**

1/49 2/61 3/151 4/188 5/302 6/390 7/392 8/415 9/471
1/23 2/36

Bowling: First Innings—Roberts 32-2-126-4; Holder 27-2-123-1; Julien 28.3-8-5-120-3; Gibbs 30-9-81-2; Richards 1-0-2-0. Second Innings—Roberts 3-0-19-1; Julien 3-0-13-1; Greenidge 1-1-0-0; Rowe 1-0-6-0; Kallicharran 0.7-0-13-0.

Umpires: R.C.Bailhache and J.R.Collins

AUSTRALIA v WEST INDIES 1975-76 (Fourth Test)
At Sydney Cricket Ground, 3, 4, 5, 7 January
Result: Australia won by 7 wickets

West Indies

Batsman	First Innings	Runs	Second Innings	Runs
R.C.Fredericks	c I.M.Chappell b Thomson	48	c Turner b Gilmour	24
B.D.Julien	not out	46	(9) lbw b Walker	8
A.I.Kallicharran	c Redpath b Thomson	9	(2) c Walker b Thomson	7
L.G.Rowe	b Walker	67	c Marsh b Thomson	7
I.V.A.Richards	c I.M.Chappell b G.S.Chappell	44	(3) c Thomson b Gilmour	2
C.H.Lloyd*	c Turner b Walker	51	c Thomson b Gilmour	19
D.L.Murray†	c Thomson b Walker	32	b Thomson	50
K.D.Boyce	c and b Mallett	16	c Redpath b Thomson	0
M.A.Holding	hit wkt b Thomson	2	(5) b Thomson	9
A.M.E.Roberts	c Marsh b Walker	4	b Walker	2
L.R.Gibbs	c Marsh b G.S.Chappell	5	not out	0
Extras	(B 5, LB 14, NB 3, W 9)	31		
		355		**128**

1/44 2/87 3/160 4/213 5/233 6/259 7/321 8/321 9/346
1/23 2/32 3/33 4/47 5/52 6/95 7/95 8/120 9/126

Bowling: First Innings—Thomson 25-5-117-3; Gilmour 13-2-54-0; Walker 21-8-70-4; Cosier 3-1-13-0; Mallett 13-4-50-1; G.S.Chappell 4.2-0-10-2; I.M.Chappell 1-0-10-0. Second Innings—Thomson 15-4-50-6; Gilmour 12-4-40-2; Walker 9.3-3-31-2; G.S.Chappell 2-0-5-0; Mallett 1-0-2-0.

Australia

Batsman	First Innings	Runs	Second Innings	Runs
I.R.Redpath	c Murray b Holding	25	b Boyce	28
A.Turner	c Lloyd b Boyce	53	c Murray b Holding	15
G.N.Yallop	c Murray b Julien	16	not out	16
I.M.Chappell	c Murray b Holding	4	c sub (C.G.Greenidge) b Kallicharran	9
G.S.Chappell*	not out	182	not out	6
G.J.Cosier	b Holding	28		
R.W.Marsh†	c Gibbs b Julien	38		
G.J.Gilmour	run out	20		
M.H.N.Walker	c Lloyd b Roberts	8		
J.R.Thomson	c Richards b Roberts	0		
A.A.Mallett	lbw b Roberts	13		
Extras	(B 3, LB 8, NB 5, W 2)	18	(LB 4, W 4)	8
		405	(3 wkts)	**82**

1/70 2/93 3/103 4/103 5/202 6/319 7/348 8/377 9/377
1/45 2/51 3/67

Bowling: First Innings—Roberts 20.6-3-94-3; Holding 21-2-79-3; Boyce Gibbs 18-3-52-0; Julien 15-2-87-2. Second Innings—Roberts 4-1-12-0; Holding 7-0-33-1; Boyce 4-0-14-1; Kallicharran 2-1-7-1; Gibbs 1-0-4-0; Richards 0.1-0-4-0.

Umpires: T.F.Brooks and R.R.Ledwidge

AUSTRALIA v WEST INDIES 1975-76 (Fifth Test)

At Adelaide Oval, 23, 24, 26, 27, 28 January
Result: Australia won by 190 runs

Australia

Batsman	1st Innings		2nd Innings	
I.R.Redpath	b Gibbs	103	c Lloyd b Gibbs	65
A.Turner	b Boyce	26	c Richards b Gibbs	136
G.N.Yallop	c Richards b Holder	47	lbw b Holder	43
I.M.Chappell	lbw b Holder	42	run out	23
G.S.Chappell*	c Richards b Holder	48	not out	48
G.J.Cosier	c Murray b Holder	37		
R.W.Marsh†	b Roberts	24	(6) c Murray b Holder	1
G.J.Gilmour	c Holding b Gibbs	95	(7) c Fredericks b Holder	0
A.A.Mallett	c Fredericks b Holding	5	(8) c Murray b Gibbs	11
J.R.Thomson	c Murray b Holder	6		
D.K.Lillee	not out	16		
Extras	(B 1, LB 9, NB 2, W 1)	13	(LB 7, NB 11)	18
		418	(7 wkts dec.)	345

1/43 2/171 3/190 4/199 5/259 6/272 7/327 8/355 9/362

1/148 2/253 3/261 4/302 5/318 6/318 7/345

Bowling: *First Innings*—Roberts 12-1-54-1; Holding 22-3-126-1; Boyce 7-0-40-1; Holder 21-1-108-5; Gibbs 26-4-77-2. *Second Innings*—Roberts 4-0-24-0; Holding 14-0-55-0; Boyce 5-0-22-0; Holder 23-2-115-3; Gibbs 32.5-5-106-3; Fredericks 1-0-5-0.

West Indies

Batsman	1st Innings		2nd Innings	
R.C.Fredericks	lbw b Gilmour	0	lbw b Lillee	10
I.V.A.Richards	c Yallop b Thomson	30	b Lillee	101
L.G.Rowe	run out	7	c G.S.Chappell b Thomson	15
A.I.Kallicharran	lbw b Thomson	76	c Redpath b Mallett	67
C.H.Lloyd*	lbw b Lillee	6	b Mallett	5
D.L.Murray†	c Mallett b Lillee	18	c Marsh b Thomson	6
K.D.Boyce	not out	95	c sub (M.H.N.Walker) b Mallett	69
M.A.Holding	c Mallett b Thomson	8	c I.M.Chappell b Gilmour	10
V.A.Holder	lbw b Thomson	0	c Marsh b Gilmour	7
A.M.E.Roberts	c Redpath b I.M.Chappell	17	c and b Gilmour	0
L.R.Gibbs	b Gilmour	3	not out	0
Extras	(LB 1, NB 13)	14	(B 1, LB 2, NB 5, W 1)	9
		274		299

1/0 2/21 3/50 4/78 5/110 6/149 7/171 8/171 9/239

1/23 2/55 3/182 4/189 5/212 6/216 7/265 8/285 9/299

Bowling: *First Innings*—Thomson 11-0-68-4; Gilmour 8.2-1-37-2; Lillee 10-0-68-2; Cosier 5-0-23-0; Mallett 5-0-37-0; I.M.Chappell 2-0-23-1; G.S.Chappell 1-0-4-0. *Second Innings*—Lillee 14-0-64-2; Thomson 13-2-66-2; Gilmour 10.4-1-44-3; G.S.Chappell 5-0-21-0; Mallett 20-3-91-3; I.M.Chappell 1-0-4-0.

Umpires: T.F.Brooks and M.G.O'Connell

AUSTRALIA v WEST INDIES 1975-76 (Sixth Test)

At Melbourne Cricket Ground, 31 January, 1, 2, 4, 5 February
Result: Australia won by 165 runs

Australia

Batsman	1st Innings		2nd Innings	
I.R.Redpath	c Holding b Gibbs	101	c sub (C.G.Greenidge) b Holder	70
A.Turner	c Gibbs b Holder	30	lbw b Boyce	21
R.B.McCosker	b Boyce	21	not out	109
I.M.Chappell	b Holder	21	c Holder b Boyce	31
G.S.Chappell*	c Boyce b Fredericks	68	not out	54
G.N.Yallop	c Holding b Boyce	57		
R.W.Marsh†	b Holding	7		
G.J.Gilmour	lbw b Gibbs	9		
A.A.Mallett	lbw b Boyce	16		
J.R.Thomson	lbw b Holder	0		
D.K.Lillee	not out	19		
Extras	(B 4, LB 11, NB 7)	22	(B 5, LB 9, NB 1)	15
		351	(3 wkts dec.)	300

1/44 2/92 3/96 4/220 5/250 6/261 7/277 8/317 9/323

1/53 2/132 3/190

Bowling: *First Innings*—Boyce 17.2-1-75-3; Holding 16-4-51-1; Holder 20-2-86-3; Lloyd 7-2-20-0; Fredericks 6-0-29-1; Gibbs 24-4-68-2. *Second Innings*—Boyce 19-2-74-2; Holding 1-0-2-0; Holder 18-1-81-1; Lloyd 4-1-14-0; Fredericks 3-1-14-0; Gibbs 26-3-62-0; Richards 7-0-38-0.

West Indies

Batsman	1st Innings		2nd Innings	
R.C.Fredericks	c Thomson b Gilmour	22	b Thomson	6
I.V.A.Richards	c Marsh b Lillee	50	c G.S.Chappell b Lillee	98
L.Baichan	c G.S.Chappell b Gilmour	3	b Thomson	20
A.I.Kallicharran	b Gilmour	4	c McCosker b Lillee	44
C.H.Lloyd*	c Redpath b Lillee	37	not out	91
L.G.Rowe	c Marsh b Gilmour	6	c Redpath b Mallett	6
D.L.Murray†	c Marsh b Lillee	1	c Marsh b Lillee	5
K.D.Boyce	lbw b Gilmour	0	c G.S.Chappell b Mallett	11
M.A.Holding	lbw b Lillee	9	c Gilmour b Mallett	4
V.A.Holder	not out	14	b Thomson	22
L.R.Gibbs	c Marsh b Lillee	2	c Marsh b Thomson	0
Extras	(LB 5, NB 6, W 1)	12	(B 6, LB 10, NB 3)	19
		160		326

1/44 2/49 3/53 4/99 5/110 6/113 7/118 8/140 9/151

1/6 2/53 3/170 4/175 5/186 6/199 7/226 8/238 9/326

Bowling: *First Innings*—Thomson 9-0-51-0; Lillee 11.3-0-63-5; Gilmour 10-3-34-5. *Second Innings*—Thomson 12.5-0-80-4; Lillee 18-1-112-3; Gilmour 7-1-26-0; G.S.Chappell 2-0-6-0; I.M.Chappell 2-0-10-0; Mallett 13-1-73-3.

Umpires: T.F.Brooks and M.G.O'Connell

AUSTRALIA v PAKISTAN 1976-77 (First Test)

At Adelaide Oval, 24, 26, 27, 28, 29 December

Result: Match drawn

Pakistan

Batsman	1st innings		2nd innings	
Majid Khan	c McCosker b Thomson	15	lbw b Lillee	47
Mudassar Nazar	c Marsh b Gilmour	13	c Marsh b Gilmour	22
Zaheer Abbas	c Walters b O'Keeffe	85	c Davis b Lillee	101
Mushtaq Mohammad*	c McCosker b Thomson	18	c Marsh b Lillee	37
Javed Miandad	b O'Keeffe	15	b Gilmour	54
Asif Iqbal	c Marsh b O'Keeffe	0	not out	152
Imran Khan	b Chappell	48	b O'Keeffe	0
Salim Altaf	c Davis b Chappell	16	c Turner b Lillee	21
Wasim Bari†	run out	21	lbw b Lillee	0
Sarfraz Nawaz	c Marsh b Lillee	29	c Lillee b O'Keeffe	0
Iqbal Qasim	not out	1	run out	4
Extras	(LB 6, NB 5)	11	(B 14, LB 1, NB 8)	23
		272	(8 wkts dec.)	**466**

1/19 2/56 3/98 4/140 5/152
6/157 7/220 8/221 9/271

1/58 2/92 3/182 4/236 5/293
6/298 7/368 8/378 9/379

Bowling: First Innings—Lillee 19-1-104-1; Thomson 8.5-2-34-2; Gilmour 14.2-1-55-1; Walters 3-0-12-0; O'Keeffe 19-5-42-3; Chappell 7-2-14-2. Second Innings—Lillee 47.7-10-163-5; Chappell 11-3-31-0; O'Keeffe 53-12-166-3; Cosier 5-1-11-0; Walters 2-1-5-0; Gilmour 14-1-67-1.

Australia

Batsman	1st innings		2nd innings	
I.C.Davis	c Mushtaq b Javed Miandad	105	b Sarfraz Nawaz	0
A.Turner	c Zaheer Abbas b Imran Khan	33	c Sarfraz Nawaz b Javed Miandad	48
R.B.McCosker	b Mushtaq Mohammad	65	c Wasim Bari b Iqbal Qasim	42
G.S.Chappell*	c Zaheer Abbas b Javed Miandad	52	c Mushtaq b Iqbal Qasim	70
K.D.Walters	c Javed Miandad b Sarfraz Nawaz	107	c Wasim Bari b Iqbal Qasim	51
G.J.Cosier	c Asif Iqbal b Javed Miandad	33		
R.W.Marsh†	b Mushtaq Mohammad	36	(7) not out	25
G.J.Gilmour	c Iqbal Qasim b Mushtaq Mohammad	3	(8) not out	13
K.J.O'Keeffe	not out	—	(6) b Iqbal Qasim	5
D.K.Lillee	c Majid Khan b Mushtaq Mohammad	0		
J.R.Thomson	absent hurt	—		
Extras	(LB 4, NB 13)	17	(B 1, LB 3, NB 3)	7
		454	(6 wkts)	**261**

1/63 2/188 3/244 4/278 5/366
6/445 7/451 8/451 9/454

1/0 2/92 3/100 4/101
5/219 6/228

Bowling: First Innings—Sarfraz Nawaz 24-3-75-1; Salim Altaf 15-0-71-0; Imran Khan 22-2-92-1; Iqbal Qasim 14-0-56-0; Javed Miandad 25-3-85-3; Mushtaq Mohammad 19.4-2-58-4. Second Innings—Sarfraz Nawaz 8-1-24-1; Imran Khan 5-0-25-0; Mushtaq Mohammad 9-1-50-0; Javed Miandad 21-6-71-1; Iqbal Qasim 30-6-84-4.

Umpires: R.C.Bailhache and M.G.O'Connell

AUSTRALIA v PAKISTAN 1976-77 (Second Test)

At Melbourne Cricket Ground, 1, 2, 3, 5, 6 January

Result: Australia won by 348 runs

Australia

Batsman	1st innings		2nd innings	
I.C.Davis	c Imran Khan b Asif Iqbal	56	c Asif Iqbal b Iqbal Qasim	88
A.Turner	b Asif Iqbal	82	lbw b Imran Khan	5
R.B.McCosker	lbw b Asif Iqbal	0	st Wasim Bari b Iqbal Qasim	105
G.S.Chappell*	c Wasim Bari b Iqbal Qasim	121	c Majid Khan b Imran Khan	67
K.D.Walters	st Wasim Bari b Iqbal Qasim	42	b Imran Khan	0
G.J.Cosier	c Asif Masood b Majid Khan	168	b Imran Khan	8
R.W.Marsh†	lbw b Iqbal Qasim	0	st Wasim Bari b Iqbal Qasim	13
G.J.Gilmour	st Wasim Bari b Iqbal Qasim	0	not out	7
K.J.O'Keeffe	not out	28	(9) b Imran Khan	6
D.K.Lillee				
M.H.N.Walker				
Extras	(B 3, LB 7, NB 7, W 1)	18	(B 2, LB 11, NB 3)	16
	(8 wkts dec.)	**517**	(8 wkts dec.)	**315**

1/134 2/134 3/151 4/227 5/398
6/400 7/400 8/517

1/6 2/182 3/223
4/226 5/244 6/301 7/301 8/315

Bowling: First Innings—Imran Khan 22-0-115-0; Salim Altaf 17-2-117-0; Asif Masood 13-1-79-0; Asif Iqbal 16-3-52-3; Javed Miandad 2-0-15-0; Iqbal Qasim 21-5-111-4; Majid Khan 1.6-0-10-1. Second Innings—Salim Altaf 6-1-28-0; Imran Khan 25.5-2-122-5; Iqbal Qasim 25-2-119-3; Majid Khan 2-0-12-0; Mushtaq Mohammad 3-0-18-0.

Pakistan

Batsman	1st innings		2nd innings	
Majid Khan	c Marsh b Lillee	76	b Lillee	35
Sadiq Mohammad	c McCosker b O'Keeffe	105	c Walters b Gilmour	0
Zaheer Abbas	b Gilmour	90	lbw b Walker	58
Mushtaq Mohammad*	lbw b Lillee	9	c Chappell b Lillee	4
Javed Miandad	lbw b Lillee	5	c Turner b O'Keeffe	10
Asif Iqbal	c sub (K.J.Hughes) b Gilmour	35	lbw b Lillee	6
Imran Khan	c Marsh b Lillee	5	c and b O'Keeffe	28
Salim Altaf	c Chappell b Lillee	0	b O'Keeffe	0
Wasim Bari†	lbw b Lillee	0	c Walker b O'Keeffe	2
Iqbal Qasim	run out	1	c Marsh b Lillee	1
Asif Masood	not out	0	not out	0
Extras	(LB 2, NB 5)	7	(B 1, LB 6)	7
		333		**151**

1/113 2/241 3/270 4/285 5/292
6/303 7/303 8/303 9/332

1/4 2/86 3/99 4/104 5/120
6/124 7/128 8/136 9/145

Bowling: First Innings—Lillee 23-4-82-6; Gilmour 16.1-2-78-2; Walker 22-1-93-0; O'Keeffe 21-4-63-1; Cosier 2-0-10-0. Second Innings—Lillee 14-1-53-4; Gilmour 3-0-19-1; Walker 9-2-34-1; O'Keeffe 18.1-5-38-4.

Umpires: T.F.Brooks and M.G.O'Connell

AUSTRALIA v PAKISTAN 1976-77 (Third Test)

At Sydney Cricket Ground, 14, 15, 16, 18 January
Result: Pakistan won by 8 wickets

Australia

Batsman	1st Innings		2nd Innings	
I.C.Davis	b Sarfraz Nawaz	20	c Haroon Rashid b Imran Khan	25
A.Turner	c Wasim Bari b Sarfraz Nawaz	0	c Majid Khan b Sarfraz Nawaz	11
R.B.McCosker	c Mushtaq b Imran Khan	8	c Wasim Bari b Imran Khan	8
G.S.Chappell*	c Zaheer Abbas b Imran Khan	28	c Wasim Bari b Sarfraz Nawaz	5
K.D.Walters	c Wasim Bari b Imran Khan	2	c Wasim Bari b Imran Khan	38
G.J.Cosier	c Wasim Bari b Imran Khan	50	c Wasim Bari b Sarfraz Nawaz	4
R.W.Marsh†	c and b Imran Khan	14	run out	41
G.J.Gilmour	c Javed Miandad b Sarfraz Nawaz	32	c Zaheer Abbas b Imran Khan	0
K.J.O'Keeffe	c Asif Iqbal b Imran Khan	1	c Haroon Rashid b Imran Khan	7
D.K.Lillee	lbw b Javed Miandad	14	c Zaheer Abbas b Imran Khan	27
M.H.N.Walker	not out	34	not out	3
Extras	(B 5, NB 3)	8	(B 7, NB 4)	11
		211		180

1/3 2/26 3/28 4/38 5/100
6/125 7/138 8/146 9/159

1/32 2/41 3/51 4/61 5/75
6/99 7/99 8/115 9/177

Bowling: First Innings—Sarfraz Nawaz 16-4-42-3; Imran Khan 26-6-102-6; Asif Iqbal 2-1-2-0; Iqbal Qasim 4-3-2-0; Javed Miandad 1.2-0-2-1. Second Innings—Sarfraz Nawaz 15-3-77-0; Imran Khan 19.7-3-63-6; Iqbal Qasim 2-1-2-0; Javed Miandad 5-0-27-0.

Pakistan

Batsman	1st Innings		2nd Innings	
Majid Khan	b Walker	48		
Sadiq Mohammad	c Cosier b Walker	25	not out	26
Zaheer Abbas	c Turner b Lillee	5	c Marsh b Lillee	0
Mushtaq Mohammad*	c Turner b Lillee	9	c Walters b Lillee	4
Haroon Rashid	c Marsh b Gilmour	57	not out	0
Asif Iqbal	b Gilmour	120		
Javed Miandad	c Walters b Walker	64		
Imran Khan	c Turner b Gilmour	0		
Sarfraz Nawaz	c Turner b Walker	13		
Wasim Bari†	c Walters b Lillee	5		
Iqbal Qasim	not out	0		
Extras	(B 6, LB 6, NB 2)	14	(B 1, NB 1)	2
		360	(2 wkts)	32

1/42 2/51 3/77 4/111 5/205
6/320 7/322 8/339 9/360

1/1 2/22

Bowling: First Innings—Lillee 22.3-0-114-3; Gilmour 16-1-81-3; Walker 29-4-112-4; Walters 4-1-7-0; O'Keeffe 11-2-32-0. Second Innings—Lillee 4-0-24-2; Walker 3.2-1-6-0.

Umpires: T.F.Brooks and R.R.Ledwidge

NEW ZEALAND v AUSTRALIA 1976-77 (First Test)

At Lancaster Park, Christchurch 18, 19, 20, 22, 23 February
Result: Match drawn

Australia

Batsman	1st Innings		2nd Innings	
A.Turner	b Chatfield	3	lbw b D.R.Hadlee	20
I.C.Davis	c G.P.Howarth b R.J.Hadlee	34	c Lees b R.J.Hadlee	22
R.B.McCosker	c Parker b D.R.Hadlee	37	not out	77
G.S.Chappell*	c Turner b R.J.Hadlee	44	c Parker b H.J.Howarth	0
G.J.Cosier	b R.J.Hadlee	23	run out	2
K.D.Walters	c H.J.Howarth b D.R.Hadlee	250	not out	20
R.W.Marsh†	c Parker b H.J.Howarth	2		
G.J.Gilmour	b Chatfield	101		
K.J.O'Keeffe	run out	8		
D.K.Lillee	c R.J.Hadlee b Chatfield	19		
M.H.N.Walker	not out	10		
Extras	(B 7, LB 10, NB 4)	21	(LB 10, NB 3)	13
		552	(4 wkts dec.)	154

1/9 2/76 3/78 4/112 5/205
6/208 7/425 8/454 9/504

1/37 2/67 3/68
4/82

Bowling: First Innings—R.J.Hadlee 29-1-155-3; Chatfield 31-4-125-3; D.R.Hadlee 24.5-1-130-2; Congdon 7-0-27-0; H.J.Howarth 19-2-94-1. Second Innings—R.J.Hadlee 13-4-41-1; Chatfield 11-1-34-0; D.R.Hadlee 8-0-28-1; H.J.Howarth 10-0-37-1; Congdon 1-0-1-0.

New Zealand

Batsman	1st Innings		2nd Innings	
G.M.Turner*	c Turner b O'Keeffe	15	c and b O'Keeffe	36
G.P.Howarth	c Marsh b O'Keeffe	42	c Marsh b Gilmour	28
B.E.Congdon	c Gilmour b Walker	23	not out	107
J.M.Parker	c Marsh b O'Keeffe	34	c McCosker b Walker	21
M.G.Burgess	c Marsh b Walker	66	c McCosker b Walker	39
G.N.Edwards	c Gilmour b O'Keeffe	34	c Marsh b Walker	15
W.K.Lees†	c Marsh b Lillee	14	c Marsh b Lillee	3
R.J.Hadlee	c Marsh b O'Keeffe	3	c Cosier b Walker	15
H.J.Howarth	b Walker	61	b Lillee	0
D.R.Hadlee	not out	37	not out	8
E.J.Chatfield	b Lillee	5		
Extras	(LB 9, NB 12, W 2)	23	(LB 12, NB 8, W 1)	21
		357	(8 wkts)	293

1/60 2/65 3/91 4/189 5/193
6/220 7/223 8/265 9/338

1/70 2/70 3/128 4/218
5/238 6/245 7/245 8/260

Bowling: First Innings—Lillee 31.2-6-119-2; Walker 26-7-66-3; Gilmour 10-0-48-0; O'Keeffe 28-5-101-5. Second Innings—Lillee 18-1-70-2; Walker 25-4-65-4; Gilmour 10-0-48-1; O'Keeffe 20-4-56-1; Chappell 11-0-33-0.

Umpires: D.E.A.Copps and F.R.Goodall

NEW ZEALAND v AUSTRALIA 1976-77 (Second Test)

At Eden Park, Auckland, 25, 26, 27 February, 1 March

Result: Australia won by 10 wickets

New Zealand

G.M.Turner* c Marsh b Walker ... 4 — c Walters b Lillee ... 23
G.P.Howarth c McCosker b Lillee ... 59 — c Turner b Lillee ... 2
B.E.Congdon c Marsh b Lillee ... 25 — c McCosker b Lillee ... 1
J.M.Parker c Cosier b Lillee ... 20 — c Turner b Walker ... 5
M.G.Burgess c Marsh b Walters ... 1 — b Walker ... 38
G.N.Edwards† c Lillee b Gilmour ... 51 — c Marsh b Lillee ... 0
R.J.Hadlee c McCosker b Lillee ... 44 — b Chappell ... 81
B.L.Cairns b Chappell ... 2 — c Lillee b Walker ... 7
H.J.Howarth b Walker ... 5 — lbw b Lillee ... 6
P.J.Petherick c Marsh b Lillee ... 4 — b Lillee ... 4
E.J.Chatfield not out ... 0 — not out ... 7
Extras (LB 7, NB 7) ... 14 — (B 4, LB 2, NB 1) ... 7
229 — **175**

1/6 2/63 3/112 4/113 5/121 — 1/10 2/12 3/23 4/31 5/31
6/177 7/202 8/211 9/228 — 6/136 7/162 8/163 9/169

Bowling: *First Innings*—Lillee 17.3-4-51-5; Walker 24-6-60-2; Gilmour 7-0-56-1; Chappell 13-4-8-1; Walters 4-1-20-1; O'Keeffe 1-1-0-0. *Second Innings*—Lillee 15.7-2-72-6; Walker 17-4-70-3; Gilmour 1-0-11-0; Chappell 9-4-15-1.

Australia

I.C.Davis b Chatfield ... 13 — not out ... 13
A.Turner c Edwards b Cairns ... 30 — not out ... 20
R.B.McCosker c Edwards b Cairns ... 84
G.S.Chappell* run out ... 58
G.J.Cosier c and b Cairns ... 21
K.D.Walters c Hadlee b Chatfield ... 16
R.W.Marsh† lbw b Hadlee ... 4
G.J.Gilmour b Chatfield ... 64
K.J.O'Keeffe c Congdon b Hadlee ... 32
D.K.Lillee not out ... 23
M.H.N.Walker c Turner b Chatfield ... 9
Extras (B 9, LB 9, NB 5) ... 23 — (LB 1, NB 1) ... 2
377 — **(0 wkts) 28**

1/31 2/56 3/171 4/202 5/217
6/221 7/245 8/338 9/364

Bowling: *First Innings*—Hadlee 28-2-147-2; Chatfield 27.1-3-100-4; Cairns 28-9-69-3; Congdon 5-1-8-0; H.J.Howarth 5-1-16-0; Petherick 4-2-14-0. *Second Innings*—Hadlee 2-0-11-0; Chatfield 1.5-0-15-0.

Umpires: D.E.A.Copps and W.R.C.Gardner

AUSTRALIA v ENGLAND 1976-77 (Centenary Test)

At Melbourne Cricket Ground, 12, 13, 14, 16, 17 March

Result: Australia won by 45 runs

Australia

I.C.Davis lbw b Lever ... 5 — c Knott b Greig ... 68
R.B.McCosker b Willis ... 4 — (10) c Greig b Old ... 25
G.J.Cosier c Fletcher b Lever ... 10 — (4) c Knott b Lever ... 4
G.S.Chappell* b Underwood ... 40 — (3) b Old ... 2
D.W.Hookes c Greig b Old ... 17 — (6) c Fletcher b Underwood ... 56
K.D.Walters c Greig b Willis ... 4 — (5) c Knott b Greig ... 66
R.W.Marsh† c Knott b Old ... 28 — not out ... 110
G.J.Gilmour c Greig b Old ... 4 — b Lever ... 16
K.J.O'Keeffe c Brearley b Underwood ... 0 — (2) c Willis b Old ... 14
D.K.Lillee not out ... 10 — (9) c Amiss b Old ... 25
M.H.N.Walker b Underwood ... 2 — not out ... 8
Extras (B 4, LB 2, NB 8) ... 14 — (LB 10, NB 15) ... 25
138 — **(9 wkts dec.) 419**

1/11 2/13 3/23 4/45 5/51 — 1/33 2/40 3/53 4/132 5/187 6/244 7/277 8/353
6/102 7/114 8/117 9/136 — 9/407

Bowling: *First Innings*—Lever 12-1-36-2; Willis 8-0-33-2; Old 12-4-39-3; Underwood 11.6-2-16-3. *Second Innings*—Lever 21-1-95-2; Willis 22-0-91-0; Old 27.6-2-104-4; Greig 14-3-66-2; Underwood 12-2-38-1.

England

R.A.Woolmer c Chappell b Lillee ... 9 — lbw b Walker ... 12
J.M.Brearley c Hookes b Lillee ... 12 — lbw b Lillee ... 43
D.L.Underwood c Chappell b Walker ... 7 — (10) b Lillee ... 7
D.W.Randall c Marsh b Lillee ... 4 — (3) c Cosier b O'Keeffe ... 174
D.L.Amiss c O'Keeffe b Walker ... 4 — (4) b Chappell ... 64
K.W.R.Fletcher c Marsh b Walker ... 4 — (5) c Marsh b Lillee ... 1
A.W.Greig* b Walker ... 18 — (6) c Cosier b O'Keeffe ... 41
A.P.E.Knott† lbw b Lillee ... 15 — (7) lbw b Lillee ... 42
C.M.Old c Marsh b Lillee ... 3 — (8) c Chappell b Lillee ... 2
J.K.Lever c Marsh b Lillee ... 11 — (9) lbw b O'Keeffe ... 4
R.G.D.Willis not out ... 1 — not out ... 5
Extras (B 2, LB 2, NB 2, W 1) ... 7 — (B 8, LB 4, NB 7, W 3) ... 22
95 — **417**

1/19 2/30 3/34 4/40 5/40 — 1/28 2/113 3/279 4/290 5/346
6/61 7/65 8/78 9/86 — 6/369 7/380 8/385 9/410

Bowling: *First Innings*—Lillee 13.3-2-26-6; Walker 15-3-54-4; O'Keeffe 1-0-4-0; Gilmour 5-3-4-0. *Second Innings*—Lillee 34.4-7-139-5; Walker 22-4-83-1; Gilmour 4-0-29-0; Chappell 16-7-29-1; O'Keeffe 33-6-108-3; Walters 3-2-7-0.

Umpires: T.F.Brooks and M.G.O'Connell

ENGLAND v AUSTRALIA 1977 (First Test)

At Lord's, London, 16, 17, 18, 20, 21 June
Result: Match drawn

England

D.L.Amiss b Thomson	4	b Thomson	0
J.M.Brearley* c Robinson b Thomson	9	c Robinson b O'Keeffe	49
R.A.Woolmer run out	79	c Chappell b Pascoe	120
D.W.Randall c Chappell b Walker	53	(7) c McCosker b Thomson	0
A.W.Greig b Pascoe	1	(4) c O'Keeffe b Pascoe	91
G.D.Barlow c McCosker b Walker	1	(5) lbw b Pascoe	5
A.P.E.Knott† c Walters b Thomson	8	(6) c Walters b Walker	8
C.M.Old c Marsh b Walker	9	c Walters b Walker	0
J.K.Lever b Pascoe	8	c Marsh b Thomson	3
D.L.Underwood not out	11	not out	12
R.G.D.Willis b Thomson	17	c Marsh b Thomson	0
Extras (B 1, LB 3, NB 7, W 1)	12	(B 5, LB 9, NB 2, W 1)	17
	216		**305**

1/12 2/13 3/111 4/121 5/134   216
6/155 7/171 8/183 9/189

1/0 2/132 3/224 4/263 5/286   305
6/286 7/286 8/286 9/305

Bowling: *First Innings*—Thomson 20.5-5-41-4; Pascoe 23-7-53-2; Walker 30-6-66-3; O'Keeffe 10-3-32-0; Chappell 3-0-12-0. *Second Innings*—Thomson 24.4-3-86-4; Pascoe 26-2-96-3; Walker 35-13-56-2; O'Keeffe 15-7-26-1; Chappell 12-2-24-0.

Australia

R.D.Robinson b Lever	11	c Woolmer b Old	4
R.B.McCosker b Old	23	b Willis	1
G.S.Chappell* c Old b Willis	66	c Lever b Old	24
C.S.Serjeant c Knott b Willis	81	(6) c Amiss b Underwood	3
K.D.Walters c Brearley b Willis	53	c sub (A.G.E.Ealham) b Underwood	10
D.W.Hookes c Brearley b Old	11	(4) c and b Willis	50
R.W.Marsh† lbw b Willis	1	not out	6
K.J.O'Keeffe c sub (A.G.E.Ealham) b Willis	12	not out	8
M.H.N.Walker c Knott b Willis	4		
J.R.Thomson b Willis	6		
L.S.Pascoe not out	3		
Extras (LB 7, NB 17, W 1)	25	(NB 8)	8
	296		**(6 wkts) 114**

1/25 2/51 3/135 4/238 5/256   296
6/264 7/265 8/284 9/290

1/5 2/5 3/48 4/64 5/71   (6 wkts) 114
6/102

Bowling: *First Innings*—Willis 30.1-7-78-7; Lever 19-5-61-1; Underwood 25-6-42-0; Old 35-10-70-2; Woolmer 5-1-20-0. *Second Innings*—Willis 10-1-40-2; Lever 5-2-4-0; Underwood 10-3-16-2; Old 14-0-46-2.

Umpires: H.D.Bird and W.L.Budd

ENGLAND v AUSTRALIA 1977 (Second Test)

At Old Trafford, Manchester, 7, 8, 9, 11, 12 July
Result: England won by 9 wickets

Australia

R.B.McCosker c Old b Willis	2	c Underwood b Willis	0
I.C.Davis c Knott b Old	34	c Lever b Willis	12
G.S.Chappell* c Knott b Greig	44	b Underwood	112
C.S.Serjeant lbw b Lever	14	c Woolmer b Underwood	8
K.D.Walters c Greig b Miller	88	lbw b Greig	10
D.W.Hookes c Knott b Lever	5	c Brearley b Miller	28
R.W.Marsh† c Amiss b Miller	36	c Randall b Underwood	1
R.J.Bright c Greig b Lever	12	c and b Underwood	0
K.J.O'Keeffe c Knott b Willis	12	not out	24
M.H.N.Walker b Underwood	14	c Greig b Underwood	6
J.R.Thomson not out	27	c Randall b Underwood	1
Extras (LB 15, NB 12)	27	(LB 1, NB 14, W 1)	16
	297		**218**

1/4 2/80 3/96 4/125 5/140   297
6/238 7/246 8/272 9/272

1/0 2/30 3/74 4/92 5/146   218
6/147 7/147 8/202 9/212

Bowling: *First Innings*—Willis 21-8-45-2; Lever 25-8-60-3; Old 20-3-57-1; Underwood 20.2-7-53-1; Greig 13-4-37-1; Miller 10-3-18-2. *Second Innings*—Willis 16-2-56-2; Lever 4-1-11-0; Old 8-1-26-0; Underwood 32.5-13-66-6; Greig 12-6-19-1; Miller 9-2-24-1.

England

D.L.Amiss c Chappell b Walker	11	not out	28
J.M.Brearley* c Chappell b Thomson	6	c Walters b O'Keeffe	44
R.A.Woolmer c Davis b O'Keeffe	137	not out	0
D.W.Randall lbw b Bright	79		
A.W.Greig c and b Walker	76		
A.P.E.Knott† c O'Keeffe b Thomson	39		
G.Miller c Marsh b Thomson	6		
C.M.Old c Marsh b Walker	37		
J.K.Lever b Bright	10		
D.L.Underwood b Bright	10		
R.G.D.Willis not out	1		
Extras (B 9, LB 9, NB 7)	25	(LB 3, NB 7)	10
	437		**(1 wkt) 82**

1/19 2/23 3/165 4/325 5/348   437
6/366 7/377 8/404 9/435

1/75   (1 wkt) 82

Bowling: *First Innings*—Thomson 38-11-73-3; Walker 54-15-131-3; Bright 35.1-12-69-3; O'Keeffe 36-11-114-1; Chappell 6-1-25-0. *Second Innings*—Thomson 8-2-24-0; Walker 7-0-17-0; Bright 5-2-6-0; O'Keeffe 9.1-4-25-1.

Umpires: W.E.Alley and T.W.Spencer

ENGLAND v AUSTRALIA 1977 (Third Test)

At Trent Bridge, Nottingham, 28, 29, 30 July, 1, 2 August

Result: England won by 7 wickets

Australia

	First Innings		Second Innings	
R.B.McCosker	c Brearley b Hendrick	51	c Brearley b Willis	107
I.C.Davis	c Botham b Underwood	33	c Greig b Willis	9
G.S.Chappell*	b Botham	19	b Hendrick	27
D.W.Hookes	c Hendrick b Willis	17	lbw b Hendrick	42
K.D.Walters	c Hendrick b Botham	11	c Randall b Greig	28
R.D.Robinson	c Brearley b Greig	11	lbw b Underwood	34
R.W.Marsh†	lbw b Botham	0	c Greig b Willis	0
K.J.O'Keeffe	not out	48	not out	21
M.H.N.Walker	c Hendrick b Botham	0	b Willis	17
J.R.Thomson	c Knott b Botham	21	b Willis	0
L.S.Pascoe	c Greig b Hendrick	20	c Hendrick b Underwood	0
Extras	(B 4, LB 2, NB 6)	12	(B 1, LB 5, NB 17, W 1)	24
		243		309

1/79 2/101 3/131 4/133 5/153
6/153 7/153 8/155 9/196

1/18 2/60 3/154 4/204 5/240
6/240 7/250 8/307 9/308

Bowling: First Innings—Willis 15-0-58-1; Hendrick 21.2-6-46-2; Botham 20-5-74-5; Greig 15-4-35-1; Underwood 11-5-18-1. Second Innings—Willis 26-6-88-5; Hendrick 32-14-56-2; Botham 25-5-60-0; Greig 9-2-24-1; Underwood 27-15-49-2; Miller 5-2-5-0; Woolmer 3-3-0-0.

England

	First Innings		Second Innings	
J.M.Brearley*	c Hookes b Pascoe	15	b Walker	81
G.Boycott	c McCosker b Thomson	107	not out	80
R.A.Woolmer	lbw b Pascoe	0		
D.W.Randall	run out	13	(5) not out	19
A.W.Greig	b Thomson	11	(4) b Walker	0
G.Miller	c Robinson b Pascoe	13		
A.P.E.Knott†	c Davis b Thomson	135	(3) c O'Keeffe b Walker	2
I.T.Botham	b Walker	25		
D.L.Underwood	b Pascoe	7		
M.Hendrick	b Walker	1		
R.G.D.Willis	not out	2		
Extras	(B 9, LB 7, NB 16, W 3)	35	(B 2, LB 2, NB 2, W 1)	7
		364	(3 wkts)	189

1/34 2/34 3/52 4/64 5/82
6/297 7/326 8/357 9/357

1/154 2/156 3/158

Bowling: First Innings—Thomson 31-6-103-3; Pascoe 32-10-80-4; Walker 39.2-12-79-2; Chappell 8-0-19-0; O'Keeffe 11-4-43-0; Walters 3-0-5-0. Second Innings—Thomson 16-6-34-0; Pascoe 22-6-43-0; O'Keeffe 19.2-2-65-0; Walker 24-8-40-3.

Umpires: H.D.Bird and D.J.Constant

ENGLAND v AUSTRALIA 1977 (Fourth Test)

At Headingley, Leeds, 11, 12, 13, 15 August

Result: England won by an innings and 85 runs

England

J.M.Brearley*	c Marsh b Thomson	0
G.Boycott	c Chappell b Pascoe	191
R.A.Woolmer	c Chappell b Thomson	37
D.W.Randall	lbw b Pascoe	20
A.W.Greig	b Thomson	43
G.R.J.Roope	c Walters b Thomson	34
A.P.E.Knott†	lbw b Bright	57
I.T.Botham	b Bright	0
D.L.Underwood	c Bright b Pascoe	6
M.Hendrick	c Robinson b Pascoe	4
R.G.D.Willis	not out	5
Extras	(B 5, LB 9, NB 22, W 3)	39
		436

1/0 2/82 3/105 4/201 5/275
6/398 7/398 8/412 9/422

Bowling: Thomson 34-7-113-4; Walker 48-21-97-0; Pascoe 34.4-10-91-4; Bright 26-9-66-2; Chappell 10-2-25-0.

Australia

	First Innings		Second Innings	
R.B.McCosker	run out	27	c Knott b Greig	12
I.C.Davis	lbw b Hendrick	0	c Knott b Greig	19
G.S.Chappell*	c Brearley b Hendrick	4	c Greig b Willis	36
D.W.Hookes	lbw b Botham	24	lbw b Hendrick	21
K.D.Walters	c Hendrick b Botham	4	lbw b Woolmer	15
R.D.Robinson	c Greig b Hendrick	20	b Hendrick	20
R.W.Marsh†	c Knott b Botham	2	c Randall b Hendrick	63
R.J.Bright	not out	9	c Greig b Hendrick	5
M.H.N.Walker	c Knott b Botham	7	b Willis	30
J.R.Thomson	b Botham	0	b Willis	0
L.S.Pascoe	b Hendrick	0	not out	0
Extras	(LB 3, NB 2, W 1)	6	(B 1, LB 4, NB 18, W 4)	27
		103		248

1/8 2/26 3/52 4/57 5/66
6/77 7/87 8/100 9/100

1/31 2/35 3/63 4/97 5/130
6/167 7/179 8/244 9/245

Bowling: First Innings—Willis 5-0-35-0; Hendrick 15.3-2-41-4; Botham 11-3-21-5. Second Innings—Willis 14-7-32-3; Hendrick 22.5-6-54-4; Greig 20-7-64-2; Botham 17-3-47-0; Woolmer 8-4-8-1; Underwood 8-3-16-0.

Umpires: W.E.Alley and W.L.Budd

ENGLAND v AUSTRALIA 1977 (Fifth Test)

At Kennington Oval, London, 25 (no play), 26, 27, 29, 30 August

Result: Match drawn

England

J.M.Brearley*	c Marsh b Malone	39	c Serjeant b Thomson ... 4
G.Boycott	c McCosker b Walker	39	not out ... 25
R.A.Woolmer	lbw b Thomson	15	c Marsh b Malone ... 6
D.W.Randall	c Marsh b Malone	3	not out ... 20
A.W.Greig	c Bright b Malone	0	
G.R.J.Roope	b Thomson	38	
A.P.E.Knott†	c McCosker b Malone	6	
J.K.Lever	lbw b Malone	3	
D.L.Underwood	b Thomson	20	
M.Hendrick	b Thomson	15	
R.G.D.Willis	not out	24	
Extras	(LB 6, NB 5, W 1)	12	(W 2) ... 2
		214	**(2 wkts) 57**

1/86 2/88 3/104 4/104 5/106 6/122 7/130 8/169 9/174

1/5 2/16

Bowling: *First Innings*—Thomson 23.2-3-87-4; Malone 47-20-63-5; Walker 28-11-51-1; Bright 3-2-1-0. *Second Innings*—Thomson 5-1-22-1; Malone 10-4-14-1; Walker 8-2-14-0; Bright 3-2-5-0.

Australia

C.S.Serjeant	lbw b Willis	0
R.B.McCosker	lbw b Willis	32
G.S.Chappell*	c and b Underwood	39
K.J.Hughes	c Willis b Hendrick	1
D.W.Hookes	c Knott b Greig	85
K.D.Walters	b Willis	4
R.W.Marsh†	lbw b Hendrick	57
R.J.Bright	lbw b Willis	16
M.H.N.Walker	not out	78
M.F.Malone	b Lever	46
J.R.Thomson	b Willis	17
Extras	(B 1, LB 6, NB 3)	10
		385

1/0 2/54 3/67 4/84 5/104 6/184 7/236 8/252 9/352

Bowling: Willis 29.3-5-102-5; Hendrick 37-5-93-2; Lever 22-6-61-1; Underwood 35-9-102-1; Greig 8-2-17-1.

Umpires: D.J.Constant and T.W.Spencer

AUSTRALIA v INDIA 1977-78 (First Test)

At Woolloongabba Cricket Ground, Brisbane, 2, 3, 4, 6 December

Result: Australia won by 16 runs

Australia

P.A.Hibbert	c Kirmani b Amarnath	13	lbw b Madan Lal ... 2
G.J.Cosier	c Madan Lal b Amarnath	19	c Prasanna b Madan Lal ... 0
A.D.Ogilvie	lbw b Viswanath b Bedi	5	b Chandrasekhar ... 46
C.S.Serjeant	c Gavaskar b Bedi	0	b Amarnath ... 0
R.B.Simpson	c Gavaskar b Bedi	7	c Viswanath b Amarnath ... 89
P.M.Toohey	st Kirmani b Bedi	82	c Bedi b Chandrasekhar ... 57
A.L.Mann	lbw b Madan Lal	19	c Amarnath b Madan Lal ... 29
S.J.Rixon	c Amarnath b Bedi	9	c Kirmani b Madan Lal ... 6
W.M.Clark	c Gavaskar b Chandrasekhar	4	b Madan Lal ... 12
J.R.Thomson	b Chandrasekhar	3	not out ... 41
A.G.Hurst	not out	0	run out ... 26
Extras	(B 3, LB 1, W 1)	5	(B 6, LB 11, NB 2) ... 19
		166	**327**

1/24 2/33 3/33 4/43 5/49 6/90 7/107 8/112 9/132

1/0 2/6 3/7 4/100 5/184 6/233 7/237 8/246 9/277

Bowling: *First Innings*—Amarnath 13-4-43-2; Madan Lal 10-3-27-1; Bedi 13.7-3-55-5; Prasanna 4-2-2-0; Chandrasekhar 6-1-34-2. *Second Innings*—Madan Lal 19-2-72-5; Amarnath 8-1-24-2; Bedi 18.5-2-71-0; Prasanna 20-4-59-0; Chandrasekhar 26-4-82-2.

India

S.M.Gavaskar	c Cosier b Clark	3	c Rixon b Clark ... 113
D.B.Vengsarkar	hit wkt b Thomson	48	b Clark ... 1
M.Amarnath	lbw b Clark	0	c Rixon b Thomson ... 47
G.R.Viswanath	c Hurst b Mann	45	c Ogilvie b Thomson ... 35
B.P.Patel	c Serjeant b Clark	13	lbw b Thomson ... 3
A.V.Mankad	c Rixon b Thomson	0	b Hurst ... 21
S.Madan Lal	b Clark	4	c Rixon b Clark (8) ... 2
S.M.H.Kirmani†	c Ogilvie b Thomson	11	c Serjeant b Hurst (7) ... 55
E.A.S.Prasanna	c Thomson b Mann	23	c Hibbert b Clark ... 8
B.S.Bedi	not out	2	not out ... 0
B.S.Chandrasekhar	lbw b Mann	4	c Rixon b Thomson ... 13
Extras	(NB 4)	4	(LB 6, NB 7) ... 13
		153	**324**

1/11 2/15 3/90 4/108 5/110 6/112 7/119 8/149 9/151

1/7 2/88 3/147 4/151 5/196 6/243 7/251 8/275 9/318

Bowling: *First Innings*—Thomson 16-1-54-3; Clark 18-5-46-4; Hurst 7-0-31-0; Cosier 3-1-6-0; Mann 6-0-12-3. *Second Innings*—Thomson 19.7-1-76-4; Clark 26-1-101-4; Hurst 15-3-50-2; Simpson 4-0-22-0; Mann 15-3-52-0; Cosier 5-1-10-0.

Umpires: T.F.Brooks and M.G.O'Connell

AUSTRALIA v INDIA 1977-78 (Third Test)

At Melbourne Cricket Ground, 30, 31 December, 2, 3, 4 January

Result: India won by 222 runs

India

Batsman	First Innings		Second Innings	
S.M.Gavaskar	c Serjeant b Gannon	118	c Rixon b Thomson	0
C.P.S.Chauhan	run out	20	c Mann b Clark	0
M.Amarnath	(7) b Cosier	41	c Simpson b Clark	72
G.R.Viswanath	lbw b Clark	54	c Rixon b Thomson	59
D.B.Vengsarkar	c Cosier b Clark	6	b Thomson	37
A.V.Mankad	b Clark	38	c Clark b Gannon	44
S.M.H.Kirmani†	c Thomson b Mann	29	lbw b Simpson	29
K.D.Ghavri	(3) c Simpson b Clark	6	b Gannon	6
E.A.S.Prasanna	c Rixon b Gannon	11	b Clark	0
B.S.Bedi	not out	12	not out	2
B.S.Chandrasekhar	lbw b Cosier	0	b Clark	0
Extras	(LB 1, NB 7)	8	(LB 3, NB 4)	7
Total		343		256

1/40 2/89 3/187 4/198 5/265 6/286 7/294 8/315 9/343

1/0 2/3 3/105 4/174 5/180 6/234 7/254 8/254 9/256

Bowling: *First Innings*—Thomson 16-2-78-3; Clark 19.2-2-73-4; Gannon 14-2-47-2; Cosier 12-3-25-0; Simpson 3-1-11-1; Mann 5-1-15-0. *Second Innings*—Clark 29-3-96-4; Gannon 22-4-88-2; Cosier 12.7-2-58-2; Thomson 18-4-47-0; Mann 4-0-24-1; Simpson 3-0-22-0.

Australia

Batsman	First Innings		Second Innings	
J.Dyson	b Ghavri	0	lbw b Bedi	12
G.J.Cosier	c Chauhan b Chandrasekhar	67	b Chandrasekhar	34
A.D.Ogilvie	lbw b Ghavri	6	c Chauhan b Bedi	0
C.S.Serjeant	b Chandrasekhar	85	b Chandrasekhar	17
R.B.Simpson	c Mankad b Chandrasekhar	2	lbw b Chandrasekhar	4
P.M.Toohey	c Viswanath b Bedi	14	c Chauhan b Chandrasekhar	14
A.L.Mann	c Gavaskar b Bedi	11	c Gavaskar b Chandrasekhar	18
S.J.Rixon†	lbw b Chandrasekhar	11	c and b Chandrasekhar	12
W.M.Clark	lbw b Chandrasekhar	3	c Ghavri b Bedi	33
J.R.Thomson	c Ghavri b Chandrasekhar	0	c and b Bedi	7
J.B.Gannon	not out	0	not out	3
Extras	(B 6, LB 7, NB 1)	14	(B 6, LB 4)	10
Total		213		164

1/0 2/18 3/122 4/124 5/166 6/178 7/202 8/211 9/211

1/42 2/42 3/52 4/60 5/77 6/98 7/115 8/122 9/151

Bowling: *First Innings*—Ghavri 9-0-37-2; Gavaskar 2-0-7-0; Bedi 15-2-71-2; Chandrasekhar 14.1-2-52-6; Prasanna 10-1-32-0. *Second Innings*—Ghavri 4-0-29-0; Amarnath 3-0-10-0; Prasanna 8-4-5-0; Bedi 16.1-5-58-4; Chandrasekhar 20-3-52-6.

Umpires: R.A.French and M.G.O'Connell

AUSTRALIA v INDIA 1977-78 (Second Test)

At W.A.C.A. Ground, Perth, 16, 17, 18, 20, 21 December

Result: Australia won by 2 wickets

India

Batsman	First Innings		Second Innings	
S.M.Gavaskar	c Rixon b Clark	4	b Clark	127
C.P.S.Chauhan	c Gannon b Simpson	88	c Ogilvie b Thomson	32
M.Amarnath	c Gannon b Thomson	90	c Rixon b Simpson	100
G.R.Viswanath	b Thomson	38	c Rixon b Clark	1
D.B.Vengsarkar	c Rixon b Clark	49	c Hughes b Gannon	9
B.P.Patel	c Rixon b Thomson	3	b Gannon	27
S.M.H.Kirmani†	c Rixon b Thomson	38	lbw b Gannon	2
S.Venkataraghavan	c Simpson b Gannon	37	c Hughes b Gannon	14
S.Madan Lal	b Gannon	43	b Thomson	3
B.S.Bedi	b Gannon	3	not out	0
B.S.Chandrasekhar	not out	0	not out	0
Extras	(B 1, NB 8)	9	(B 1, LB 4, NB 10)	15
Total		402	(9 wkts dec.)	330

1/14 2/163 3/224 4/229 5/235 6/311 7/319 8/383 9/391

1/47 2/240 3/244 4/283 5/287 6/289 7/327 8/328 9/330

Bowling: *First Innings*—Thomson 24-1-101-4; Clark 17-0-95-2; Gannon 16.6-1-84-3; Mann 11-0-63-0; Simpson 11-0-50-1. *Second Innings*—Thomson 21.5-3-65-2; Gannon 18-2-77-4; Clark 18-1-83-2; Mann 8-0-49-0; Simpson 8-2-41-1.

Australia

Batsman	First Innings		Second Innings	
J.Dyson	c Patel b Bedi	53	c Vengsarkar b Bedi	4
C.S.Serjeant	c Kirmani b Madan Lal	13	c Kirmani b Madan Lal	12
A.D.Ogilvie	b Bedi	27	(4) b Bedi	47
P.M.Toohey	st Kirmani b Bedi	0	(5) c Amarnath b Bedi	83
R.B.Simpson*	c Vengsarkar b Venkataraghavan	176	(6) run out	39
S.J.Rixon†	c Kirmani b Amarnath	50	(8) lbw b Bedi	23
K.J.Hughes	c Patel b Bedi	28	lbw b Madan Lal	0
A.L.Mann	c Vengsarkar b Bedi	7	(3) c Kirmani b Bedi	105
W.M.Clark	c Patel b Chandrasekhar	15	not out	5
J.R.Thomson	c Amarnath b Venkataraghavan	0	not out	6
J.B.Gannon	not out	0		
Extras	(LB 25)	25	(B 8, LB 10)	18
Total		394	(8 wkts)	342

1/19 2/61 3/65 4/149 5/250 6/321 7/341 8/388 9/388

1/13 2/33 3/172 4/195 5/295 6/296 7/330 8/330

Bowling: *First Innings*—Madan Lal 15-1-54-1; Amarnath 16-2-57-1; Chandrasekhar 33.6-6-114-1; Bedi 31-6-89-5; Venkataraghavan 23.4-55-2. *Second Innings*—Madan Lal 11-0-44-2; Amarnath 3-0-22-0; Bedi 30.2-6-105-5; Chandrasekhar 15-0-67-0; Venkataraghavan 28-9-86-0.

Umpires: R.A.Bailhache and R.A.French

AUSTRALIA v INDIA 1977-78 (Fourth Test)

At Sydney Cricket Ground, 7, 8, 9, 11, 12 January
Result: India won by an innings and 2 runs

Australia

J.Dyson lbw b Chandrasekhar	26		c and b Chandrasekhar	6
G.J.Cosier b Amarnath	17		b Bedi	68
P.M.Toohey run out	4	(6)	c sub (S.Madan Lal) b Ghavri	85
C.S.Serjeant c Ghavri b Bedi	4		b Prasanna	1
R.B.Simpson c Kirmani b Chandrasekhar	38		lbw b Prasanna	33
K.J.Hughes b Bedi	17	(3)	c Vengsarkar b Bedi	19
A.L.Mann b Bedi	0		c and b Prasanna	0
S.J.Rixon† lbw b Chandrasekhar	17		c Viswanath b Chandrasekhar	11
W.M.Clark c Gavaskar b Chandrasekhar	0		b Prasanna	10
J.R.Thomson not out	1		b Ghavri	16
J.B.Gannon c Amarnath b Prasanna	0		not out	0
Extras (LB 5, NB 2)	7		(B 5, LB 6, NB 3)	14
	131			263

1/29 2/34 3/46 4/61 5/84
6/84 7/125 8/125 9/130
1/26 2/87 3/88 4/106 5/171
6/171 7/194 8/221 9/257

Bowling: *First Innings*—Ghavri 7-1-25-0; Amarnath 7.4-2-14-1; Chandrasekhar 15-3-30-4; Bedi 13-3-49-3; Prasanna 7.4-2-14-1. *Second Innings*—Ghavri 12.7-3-42-2; Amarnath 5-3-9-0; Chandrasekhar 24-3-85-2; Bedi 28-8-62-2; Prasanna 29-11-51-4.

India

S.M.Gavaskar c Rixon b Thomson	49
C.P.S.Chauhan c Mann b Clark	42
M.Amarnath c Gannon b Clark	9
G.R.Viswanath b Thomson	79
D.B.Vengsarkar b Thomson	48
A.V.Mankad b Thomson	16
S.M.H.Kirmani† b Cosier	42
K.D.Ghavri c Serjeant b Thomson	64
E.A.S.Prasanna not out	25
B.S.Bedi not out	1
B.S.Chandrasekhar	
Extras (LB 9, NB 12)	21
(8 wkts dec.)	396

1/97 2/102 3/116 4/241 5/261
6/263 7/344 8/395

Bowling: Thomson 27-8-83-4; Clark 21-3-66-2; Gannon 20-4-65-0; Mann 20-0-101-0; Simpson 4-0-34-0; Cosier 9-1-26-2

Umpires: R.A.Bailhache and T.F.Brooks

AUSTRALIA v INDIA 1977-78 (Fifth Test)

At Adelaide Oval, 28, 29, 30 January, 1, 2, 3 February
Result: Australia won by 47 runs

Australia

G.M.Wood st Kirmani b Chandrasekhar	39		c Vengsarkar b Bedi	8
W.M.Darling c Vengsarkar b Chandrasekhar	65		b Bedi	56
G.N.Yallop c Gavaskar b Amarnath	121		b Bedi	24
P.M.Toohey c Gavaskar b Chandrasekhar	60		c Kirmani b Prasanna	10
R.B.Simpson c Viswanath b Ghavri	100		lbw b Ghavri	51
G.J.Cosier b Ghavri	1		st Kirmani b Bedi	34
S.J.Rixon† b Bedi	32		run out	13
B.Yardley c and b Ghavri	22		c Vengsarkar b Ghavri	26
J.R.Thomson c Ghavri b Chandrasekhar	24	(11)	c Amarnath b Ghavri	3
W.M.Clark b Chandrasekhar	0	(9)	lbw b Ghavri	1
I.W.Callen not out	22	(10)	not out	4
Extras (B 4, LB 14, NB 1)	19		(B 5, LB 15, NB 3, W 3)	26
	505			256

1/89 2/110 3/230 4/334 5/337
6/406 7/450 8/457 9/458
1/17 2/84 3/95 4/107 5/172
6/210 7/214 8/240 9/248

Bowling: *First Innings*—Ghavri 22-2-93-3; Amarnath 12-0-45-1; Bedi 34-1-127-1; Prasanna 10-1-48-0; Chandrasekhar 29.4-0-136-5; Gaekwad 5-0-37-0. *Second Innings*—Ghavri 10.5-2-45-4; Amarnath 4-0-12-0; Prasanna 34-7-68-1; Bedi 20-3-53-4; Chandrasekhar 14-0-52-0.

India

S.M.Gavaskar c Toohey b Thomson	7	c Rixon b Callen	29
C.P.S.Chauhan c Cosier b Clark	15	c Wood b Yardley	32
M.Amarnath c Cosier b Thomson	0	c Callen b Yardley	86
G.R.Viswanath c Rixon b Callen	89	c Simpson b Clark	73
D.B.Vengsarkar c Rixon b Callen	44	c Toohey b Yardley	78
A.D.Gaekwad c Rixon b Callen	27	c and b Yardley	12
S.M.H.Kirmani† run out	48	b Clark	51
K.D.Ghavri c Simpson b Clark	3	c sub (K.J.Hughes) b Callen	23
E.A.S.Prasanna not out	15	not out	10
B.S.Bedi c sub (K.J.Hughes) b Clark	6	c Cosier b Callen	16
B.S.Chandrasekhar c and b Clark	2	c Rixon b Simpson	2
Extras (B 4, LB 1, NB 8)	13	(B 6, LB 11, NB 16)	33
	269		445

1/23 2/23 3/23 4/159 5/166
6/216 7/226 8/249 9/263
1/40 2/79 3/210 4/256 5/323
6/348 7/415 8/417 9/442

Bowling: *First Innings*—Thomson 3.3-1-12-2; Clark 20.7-6-62-4; Callen 22-0-83-3; Cosier 4-3-4-0; Yardley 23-6-62-0; Simpson 9-0-33-0. *Second Innings*—Callen 33-5-108-3; Clark 29-6-79-2; Yardley 43-6-134-4; Simpson 23.4-6-70-1; Cosier 13-6-21-0.

Umpires: R.A.French and M.G.O'Connell

WEST INDIES v AUSTRALIA 1977-78 (First Test)

At Queen's Park Oval, Port-of-Spain, Trinidad, 3, 4, 5 March
Result: West Indies won by an innings and 106 runs

Australia

Batsman	First Innings	Runs	Second Innings	Runs
G.M.Wood	c Haynes b Croft	2	lbw b Roberts	32
C.S.Serjeant	c Murray b Croft	3	lbw b Garner	40
G.N.Yallop	c Richards b Croft	2	b Roberts	81
P.M.Toohey	b Garner	20	absent hurt	–
R.B.Simpson*	lbw b Garner	0	b Parry	14
G.J.Cosier	c Greenidge b Croft	46	(4) lbw b Garner	19
S.J.Rixon†	run out	1	(6) lbw b Roberts	0
B.Yardley	c Murray b Roberts	2	(7) not out	7
J.R.Thomson	c Austin b Roberts	0	(8) b Parry	4
W.M.Clark	b Garner	0	(9) b Roberts	0
J.D.Higgs	not out	0	(10) b Roberts	2
Extras	(B 4, LB 6, NB 4)	14	(B 6, LB 1, NB 2, W 1)	10
		90		**209**

1/7 2/10 3/16 4/23 5/45 6/75 7/75 8/84 9/90
1/59 2/90 3/149 4/194 5/194 6/194 7/200 8/201 9/209

Bowling: *First Innings*—Roberts 12-4-26-2; Croft 9.1-5-15-4; Garner 15-7-35-3. *Second Innings*—Roberts 16.3-3-56-5; Croft 13-1-55-0; Garner 17-5-39-2; Parry 17-1-49-2.

West Indies

Batsman	Dismissal	Runs
C.G.Greenidge	b Yardley	43
D.L.Haynes	c Rixon b Higgs	61
I.V.A.Richards	lbw b Thomson	39
A.I.Kallicharran	b Yardley	127
C.H.Lloyd*	b Thomson	86
R.A.Austin	c sub (T.J.Laughlin) b Thomson	2
D.L.Murray†	c Rixon b Higgs	21
D.R.Parry	b Yardley	0
A.M.E.Roberts	st Rixon b Higgs	7
J.Garner	c Cosier b Higgs	0
C.E.H.Croft	not out	4
Extras	(LB 9, NB 6)	15
		405

1/87 2/143 3/143 4/313 5/324 6/385 7/385 8/391 9/391

Bowling: Thomson 21-6-84-3; Clark 16-3-41-0; Higgs 24.5-3-91-4; Simpson 16-2-65-0; Yardley 19-1-64-3; Cosier 13-2-45-0.

Umpires: R.Gosein and D.Sang Hue

WEST INDIES v AUSTRALIA 1977-78 (Second Test)

At Kensington Oval, Bridgetown, Barbados, 17, 18, 19 March
Result: West Indies won by 9 wickets

Australia

Batsman	First Innings	Runs	Second Innings	Runs
W.M.Darling	c Richards b Haynes	4	c Murray b Croft	8
G.M.Wood	lbw b Roberts	69	run out	56
G.N.Yallop	c Austin b Croft	47	c Lloyd b Garner	14
C.S.Serjeant	c Murray b Parry	4	c Murray b Roberts	2
R.B.Simpson*	c Murray b Croft	9	c Murray b Roberts	17
G.J.Cosier	c Murray b Roberts	1	(7) c Croft b Roberts	8
S.J.Rixon†	lbw b Garner	16	(5) c Lloyd b Roberts	0
B.Yardley	b Garner	74	(6) b Garner	43
J.R.Thomson	b Garner	12	c Richards b Garner	11
W.M.Clark	b Garner	0	lbw b Garner	0
J.D.Higgs	not out	4	not out	0
Extras	(B 3, LB 4, NB 3)	10	(B 1, LB 8, NB 10)	19
		250		**178**

1/13 2/105 3/116 4/134 5/135 6/149 7/161 8/216 9/216
1/21 2/62 3/69 4/80 5/95 6/99 7/154 8/167 9/173

Bowling: *First Innings*—Roberts 18-2-79-1; Croft 18-3-47-4; Garner 16.1-2-65-4; Parry 12-4-44-1; Austin 1-0-5-0. *Second Innings*—Roberts 18-5-50-4; Croft 15-4-53-1; Garner 15-3-56-4.

West Indies

Batsman	First Innings	Runs	Second Innings	Runs
C.G.Greenidge	c Cosier b Thomson	8	not out	80
D.L.Haynes	c Rixon b Higgs	66	c Yardley b Higgs	55
I.V.A.Richards	c Clark b Thomson	23		
A.I.Kallicharran	c Yardley b Thomson	8		
C.H.Lloyd*	c Serjeant b Clark	42		
R.A.Austin	c Serjeant b Clark	20		
D.L.Murray†	c Darling b Thomson	60		
D.R.Parry	c Serjeant b Simpson	27	(3) not out	3
A.M.E.Roberts	lbw b Thomson	4		
J.Garner	not out	5		
C.E.H.Croft	lbw b Thomson	3		
Extras	(LB 3, NB 19)	22	(LB 2, W 1)	3
		288		**(1 wkt) 141**

1/16 2/56 3/71 4/154 5/172 6/198 7/263 8/269 9/282
1/131

Bowling: *First Innings*—Thomson 13-1-77-6; Clark 24-3-77-2; Cosier 9-4-24-0; Higgs 16-4-46-1; Simpson 7-1-30-1; Yardley 2-0-12-0. *Second Innings*—Thomson 6-1-22-0; Clark 7-0-27-0; Higgs 13-4-34-1; Yardley 10.5-2-55-0.

Umpires: R.Gosein and S.E.Parris

WEST INDIES v AUSTRALIA 1977-78 (Third Test)

At Bourda, Georgetown, Guyana, 31 March, 1, 2, 4, 5 April
Result: Australia won by 3 wickets

West Indies

A.E.Greenidge	lbw b Thomson	56
A.B.Williams	lbw b Clark	10
H.A.Gomes	b Clark	4
A.I.Kallicharran*	b Thomson	0
I.T.Shillingford	c Clark b Laughlin	3
D.A.Murray†	c Ogilvie b Clark	21
S.Shivnarine	c Rixon b Thomson	53
N.Phillip	c Yardley b Simpson	15
V.A.Holder	c Laughlin b Clark	1
D.R.Parry	not out	21
S.T.Clarke	b Thomson	6
Extras	(LB 2, NB 13)	15
		205

1/31 2/36 3/48 4/77 5/84
6/130 7/165 8/166 9/193

Bowling: *First Innings*—Thomson 16.2-1-57-4; Clark 24-6-64-4; Cosier 2-1-1-0; Simpson 8-1-34-1. *Second Innings*—Thomson 20-2-83-1; Clark 34.4-4-124-4; Yardley 30-6-96-3; Simpson 19-4-70-1; Cosier 6-1-14-1; Laughlin 7-1-33-0.

Australia

W.M.Darling	c Greenidge b Phillip	15	c Williams b Clarke	0
G.M.Wood	lbw b Holder	50	run out	126
A.D.Ogilvie	c and b Phillip	4	b Holder	0
G.J.Cosier	lbw b Clarke	9	(6) b Phillip	0
C.S.Serjeant	b Clarke	0	csub (S.F.A.F.Bacchus) bPhillip	124
R.B.Simpson*	run out	67	(4) c Murray b Clarke	4
T.J.Laughlin	c Greenidge b Parry	21	(8) c and b Parry	24
S.J.Rixon†	c Holder b Phillip	54	(7) not out	39
B.Yardley	b Clarke	33	not out	15
J.R.Thomson	c and b Phillip	3		
W.M.Clark	not out	2		
Extras	(LB 12, NB 15, W 1)	28	(B 8, LB 4, NB 16, W 2)	30
		286	(7 wkts)	362

1/28 2/36 3/77 4/85 5/90
6/142 7/237 8/256 9/268

1/11 2/13 3/22 4/273
5/279 6/290 7/338

Bowling: *First Innings*—Phillip 18-0-76-4; Clarke 22-3-57-3; Holder 17-1-40-1; Gomes 3-0-8-0; Parry 15-2-39-1; Shivnarine 8-0-38-0. *Second Innings*—Clarke 27-5-83-3; Phillip 19-2-65-2; Holder 20-3-55-0; Parry 17-1-61-1; Shivnarine 18-2-68-0.

Umpires: R.Gosein and C.F.Vyfhuis

WEST INDIES v AUSTRALIA 1977-78 (Fourth Test)

At Queen's Park Oval, Port-of-Spain, Trinidad, 15, 16, 17, 18 April
Result: West Indies won by 198 runs

West Indies

A.E.Greenidge	c Wood b Clark	6	c Thomson b Yardley	69
A.B.Williams	c Yallop b Higgs	87	c Yallop b Simpson	24
D.A.Murray†	c Wood b Yardley	4	lbw b Clark	4
H.A.Gomes	c Simpson b Clark	30	c Simpson b Higgs	14
A.I.Kallicharran*	c Yallop b Clark	92	c and b Clark	27
S.F.A.F.Bacchus	b Higgs	9	c Wood b Yardley	7
S.Shivnarine	c Simpson b Thomson	10	c Serjeant b Simpson	11
D.R.Parry	st Rixon b Higgs	22	c Serjeant b Simpson	65
N.Phillip	c Rixon b Thomson	3	c Serjeant b Yardley	46
V.A.Holder	b Thomson	7	c Wood b Yardley	0
R.R.Jumadeen	not out	0	b Simpson	2
Extras	(B 7, LB 1, NB 12, W 2)	22	(B 1, LB 13, NB 7)	21
		292		290

1/7 2/16 3/111 4/166 5/185
6/242 7/258 8/262 9/291

1/36 2/51 3/79 4/134 5/151
6/151 7/204 8/273 9/280

Bowling: *First Innings*—Thomson 23-8-64-3; Clark 24-6-65-3; Yardley 18-5-48-1; Higgs 16.5-2-53-3; Simpson 15-4-40-0. *Second Innings*—Thomson 15-1-76-0; Clark 21-4-62-2; Simpson 14-2-45-3; Higgs 21-7-46-1; Yardley 30.2-15-40-4.

Australia

G.M.Wood	c Murray b Phillip	16	lbw b Holder	17
W.M.Darling	c Jumadeen b Holder	10	b Phillip	6
P.M.Toohey	c Williams b Parry	40	c Bacchus b Jumadeen	17
G.N.Yallop	c Murray b Jumadeen	75	c Kallicharran b Parry	18
C.S.Serjeant	st Murray b Jumadeen	49	c Bacchus b Jumadeen	4
R.B.Simpson*	lbw b Holder	36	lbw b Jumadeen	6
S.J.Rixon†	c Murray b Holder	21	not out	13
B.Yardley	c Williams b Holder	22	b Parry	3
J.R.Thomson	b Holder	4	b Parry	1
W.M.Clark	b Holder	0	b Parry	0
J.D.Higgs	not out	17	b Parry	4
Extras	(B 4, LB 2, NB 11)	17	(LB 2, NB 3)	5
		290		94

1/23 2/43 3/92 4/193 5/204
6/254 7/275 8/275 9/289

1/9 2/42 3/44 4/60 5/72
6/76 7/80 8/86 9/88

Bowling: *First Innings*—Phillip 17-0-73-1; Holder 13-4-28-6; Jumadeen 24-4-83-2; Parry 30-5-77-1; Shivnarine 6-1-12-0. *Second Innings*—Phillip 7-0-24-1; Holder 11-3-16-1; Jumadeen 15-3-34-3; Parry 10.4-4-15-5.

Umpires: R.Gosein and C.F.Vyfhuis

WEST INDIES v AUSTRALIA 1977-78 (Fifth Test)

At Sabina Park, Kingston, Jamaica, 28, 29, 30 April, 2, 3 May

Result: Match drawn

Australia

Batsman	1st innings		2nd innings	
G.M.Wood	c Parry b Phillip	16	c Bacchus b Jumadeen	90
A.D.Ogilvie	c Shivnarine b Holder	0	st Murray b Parry	43
P.M.Toohey	c Williams b Holder	122	st Murray b Jumadeen	97
G.N.Yallop	c sub (H.G.Gordon) b Shivnarine	57	not out	23
C.S.Serjeant	b Holder	26	not out	32
R.B.Simpson*	c Murray b Foster	46		
T.J.Laughlin	c sub (H.G.Gordon) b Jumadeen	35		
S.J.Rixon†	not out	13		
B.Yardley	b Jumadeen	7		
J.R.Thomson	c Murray b Jumadeen	4		
J.D.Higgs	c Foster b Jumadeen	0		
Extras	(LB 5, NB 11, W 1)	17	(B 5, LB 8, NB 7)	20
Total		343	(3 wkts dec.)	305

1/0 2/38 3/171 4/217 5/266
6/308 7/324 8/335 9/343

1/65 2/245 3/246 (3 wkts dec.) 305

Bowling: *First Innings*—Phillip 32-5-90-1; Holder 31-8-68-3; Parry 5-0-15-0; Jumadeen 38.4-6-72-4; Foster 32-10-68-1; Shivnarine 9-2-13-1. *Second Innings*—Phillip 17-1-64-0; Holder 18-2-41-0; Jumadeen 23-2-90-2; Parry 18-3-60-1; Foster 7-1-22-0; Shivnarine 3-1-8-0.

West Indies

Batsman	1st innings		2nd innings	
A.B.Williams	c Serjeant b Laughlin	17	c Wood b Yardley	19
S.F.A.F.Bacchus	c Yardley b Thomson	5	c Simpson b Thomson	21
D.A.Murray†	c Wood b Laughlin	12	(6) b Yardley	10
H.A.Gomes	b Thomson	115	(3) c Rixon b Higgs	115
A.I.Kallicharran*	c Ogilvie b Laughlin	6	lbw b Higgs	126
M.L.C.Foster	c Rixon b Laughlin	8	(4) run out	5
S.Shivnarine	st Rixon b Higgs	53	c Yallop b Yardley	27
D.R.Parry	lbw b Higgs	4	c Serjeant b Yardley	0
N.Phillip	c Rixon b Simpson	26	not out	26
V.A.Holder	lbw b Laughlin	24	c Rixon b Higgs	6
R.R.Jumadeen	not out	4	not out	0
Extras	(LB 1, NB 5)	6	(B 14, LB 2, NB 1)	17
Total		280	(9 wkts)	258

1/13 2/28 3/41 4/47 5/63
6/159 7/173 8/219 9/276

1/42 2/38 3/43 4/59 (9 wkts) 258
5/88 6/179 7/181 8/242 9/258

Bowling: *First Innings*—Thomson 22-4-61-2; Laughlin 25.4-4-101-5; Yardley 14-4-27-0; Simpson 10-0-38-1; Higgs 19-3-47-2. *Second Innings*—Thomson 15-1-53-1; Laughlin 10-1-34-0; Higgs 28.4-10-67-3; Yardley 29-17-35-4; Simpson 11-4-44-0; Yallop 3-1-8-0.

Umpires: R.Gosein and W.Malcolm

AUSTRALIA v ENGLAND 1978-79 (First Test)

At Woolloongabba, Brisbane, 1, 2, 3, 5, 6 December

Result: England won by 7 wickets

Australia

Batsman	1st innings		2nd innings	
G.M.Wood	c Taylor b Old	7	lbw b Old	19
G.J.Cosier	run out	1	b Willis	5
P.M.Toohey	b Willis	1	lbw b Botham	1
G.N.Yallop*	c Gooch b Willis	7	c and b Willis	102
K.J.Hughes	c Taylor b Botham	4	c Edmonds b Willis	129
T.J.Laughlin	c sub (J.K.Lever) b Willis	33	lbw b Old	5
J.A.Maclean†	not out	17	lbw b Miller	15
B.Yardley	c Taylor b Willis	17	c Brearley b Miller	16
R.M.Hogg	c Taylor b Botham	36	b Botham	16
A.G.Hurst	c Taylor b Botham	0	b Botham	0
J.D.Higgs	b Old	1	not out	0
Extras	(LB 1, NB 6)	7	(B 9, LB 5, NB 22)	36
Total		116		344

1/2 2/5 3/14 4/22 5/24
6/26 7/53 8/113 9/113

1/0 2/2 3/49 4/219 5/228
6/261 7/310 8/339 9/339

Bowling: *First Innings*—Willis 14-2-44-4; Old 9.7-1-24-2; Botham 12-1-40-3; Gooch 1-0-1-0; Edmonds 1-1-0-0. *Second Innings*—Willis 27.6-3-69-3; Botham 26-5-93-3; Old 17-1-60-2; Miller 34-12-52-2; Edmonds 12-1-27-0.

England

Batsman	1st innings		2nd innings	
G.Boycott	c Hughes b Hogg	13	run out	16
G.A.Gooch	c Laughlin b Hogg	2	c Yardley b Hogg	2
D.W.Randall	c Laughlin b Hurst	75	not out	74
R.W.Taylor†	lbw b Hurst	20		
J.M.Brearley*	c Maclean b Hogg	6	(4) c Maclean b Yardley	13
D.I.Gower	c Maclean b Hurst	44	(5) not out	48
I.T.Botham	c Maclean b Hurst	49		
G.Miller	lbw b Hogg	27		
P.H.Edmonds	c Maclean b Hogg	1		
C.M.Old	not out	29		
R.G.D.Willis	c Maclean b Hurst	8		
Extras	(B 7, LB 4, NB 1)	12	(B 12, LB 3, NB 2)	17
Total		286	(3 wkts)	170

1/2 2/38 3/111 4/120 5/120
6/215 7/219 8/226 9/266

1/19 2/37 3/74

Bowling: *First Innings*—Hurst 27.4-6-93-4; Hogg 28-8-74-6; Laughlin 22-6-54-0; Yardley 7-1-34-0; Cosier 1-1-0-0; Higgs 6-2-9-0. *Second Innings*—Hogg 12.5-2-35-1; Hurst 10-4-17-0; Yardley 13-1-41-1; Laughlin 3-0-6-0; Higgs 12-1-43-0; Cosier 3-0-11-0.

Umpires: R.A.French and M.G.O'Connell

AUSTRALIA v ENGLAND 1978-79 (Second Test)

At W.A.C.A. Ground, Perth, 15, 16, 17, 19, 20 December

Result: England won by 166 runs

England

G.Boycott lbw b Hurst	77	lbw b Hogg	23
G.A.Gooch c Maclean b Hogg	1	lbw b Hogg	43
D.W.Randall c Wood b Hogg	0	c Cosier b Yardley	45
J.M.Brearley* c Maclean b Dymock	17	c Maclean b Hogg	0
D.I.Gower b Hogg	102	c Maclean b Hogg	12
I.T.Botham lbw b Hurst	11	c Wood b Yardley	30
G.Miller b Hogg	40	c Toohey b Yardley	25
R.W.Taylor† c Hurst b Yardley	12	(9) c Maclean b Hogg	2
J.K.Lever c Cosier b Hurst	14	(8) c Maclean b Hurst	10
R.G.D.Willis c Yallop b Hogg	2	not out	3
M.Hendrick not out	7	b Dymock	1
Extras (B 6, LB 9, NB 8, W 3)	26	(LB 6, NB 8)	14
	309		**208**

1/3 2/3 3/41 4/199 5/219
6/224 7/253 8/295 9/300

1/58 2/93 3/93 4/135 5/151
6/176 7/201 8/201 9/206

Bowling: *First Innings*—Hogg 30.5-9-65-5; Dymock 34-4-72-1; Hurst 26-7-70-3; Yardley 23-1-62-1; Cosier 4-2-14-0. *Second Innings*—Hogg 17-5-43-1; Yardley 16-1-41-3.

Australia

G.M.Wood lbw b Lever	5	c Taylor b Lever	64
W.M.Darling run out	25	c Boycott b Lever	5
K.J.Hughes b Willis	16	c Gooch b Willis	12
G.N.Yallop* b Willis	3	c Taylor b Hendrick	3
P.M.Toohey not out	81	c Taylor b Hendrick	0
G.J.Cosier c Gooch b Willis	4	lbw b Miller	47
J.A.Maclean† c Gooch b Miller	0	c Brearley b Miller	1
B.Yardley c Taylor b Hendrick	12	c Botham b Lever	7
R.M.Hogg c Taylor b Willis	18	b Miller	0
G.Dymock b Hendrick	11	not out	6
A.G.Hurst c Taylor b Willis	5	b Lever	5
Extras (LB 7, NB 2, W 1)	10	(LB 3, NB 4, W 4)	11
	190		**161**

1/8 2/34 3/38 4/60 5/78
6/79 7/100 8/128 9/185

1/8 2/36 3/58 4/58 5/141
6/143 7/143 8/147 9/151

Bowling: *First Innings*—Lever 7-0-20-1; Botham 11-2-46-0; Willis 18.5-5-44-5; Hendrick 14-1-39-2; Miller 16-6-31-1. *Second Innings*—Willis 12-1-36-1; Lever 8.1-2-28-4; Botham 11-1-54-0; Hendrick 8-3-11-2; Miller 7-4-21-3.

Umpires: R.C.Bailhache and T.F.Brooks

AUSTRALIA v ENGLAND 1978-79 (Third Test)

At Melbourne Cricket Ground, 29, 30 December, 1, 2, 3 January

Result: Australia won by 103 runs

Australia

G.M.Wood c Emburey b Miller	100	b Botham	34
W.M.Darling run out	33	c Randall b Miller	21
K.J.Hughes c Taylor b Botham	0	c Gower b Botham	48
G.N.Yallop* c Hendrick b Botham	41	c Taylor b Miller	16
P.M.Toohey c Randall b Miller	32	c Botham b Emburey	20
A.R.Border c Brearley b Hendrick	29	run out	0
J.A.Maclean† b Botham	8	c Hendrick b Emburey	10
R.M.Hogg c Randall b Miller	0	b Botham	1
G.Dymock b Hendrick	0	c Brearley b Hendrick	6
A.G.Hurst b Hendrick	0	(11) not out	0
J.D.Higgs not out	1	(10) st Taylor b Emburey	0
Extras (LB 8, NB 6)	14	(B 4, LB 6, NB 1)	11
	258		**167**

1/65 2/65 3/126 4/189 5/247
6/250 7/250 8/251 9/252

1/55 2/81 3/101 4/136 5/136
6/152 7/157 8/167 9/167

Bowling: *First Innings*—Willis 13-2-47-0; Botham 20.1-4-68-3; Hendrick 23-3-50-3; Emburey 14-1-44-0; Miller 19-6-35-3. *Second Innings*—Willis 7-0-21-0; Botham 15-4-41-3; Hendrick 14-4-25-1; Miller 14-5-39-2; Emburey 21.2-12-30-3.

England

G.Boycott b Hogg	1	lbw b Hurst	38
J.M.Brearley* lbw b Hogg	1	c Maclean b Dymock	0
D.W.Randall lbw b Hurst	13	lbw b Hogg	2
G.A.Gooch c Border b Dymock	25	lbw b Hogg	40
D.I.Gower lbw b Dymock	29	lbw b Dymock	49
I.T.Botham c Darling b Higgs	22	c Maclean b Higgs	10
G.Miller b Hogg	7	c Hughes b Higgs	1
R.W.Taylor† b Hogg	1	c Maclean b Hogg	5
J.E.Emburey b Hogg	0	not out	7
R.G.D.Willis c Darling b Dymock	19	c Yallop b Hogg	3
M.Hendrick not out	6	b Hogg	0
Extras (B 6, LB 4, NB 9)	19	(B 10, LB 7, NB 6, W 1)	24
	143		**179**

1/2 2/3 3/40 4/52 5/81
6/100 7/101 8/101 9/120

1/1 2/6 3/71 4/122 5/163
6/163 7/167 8/171 9/179

Bowling: *First Innings*—Hogg 17-7-30-5; Hurst 12-2-24-1; Dymock 15.6-4-38-3; Higgs 19-9-32-1. *Second Innings*—Hogg 17-5-36-5; Dymock 18-4-37-2; Hurst 11-1-39-1; Higgs 16-2-29-2; Border 5-0-14-0.

Umpires: R.A.French and M.G.O'Connell

AUSTRALIA v ENGLAND 1978-79 (Fourth Test)

At Sydney Cricket Ground, 6, 7, 8, 10, 11 January
Result: England won by 93 runs.

England

Batsman	First Innings	R	Second Innings	R
G.Boycott	c Border b Hurst	8	lbw b Hogg	0
J.M.Brearley*	b Hogg	17	b Border	53
D.W.Randall	c Wood b Hurst	0	lbw b Hogg	150
G.A.Gooch	c Toohey b Higgs	18	c Wood b Higgs	22
D.I.Gower	c Maclean b Hurst	7	c Maclean b Hogg	34
I.T.Botham	c Yallop b Hogg	59	c Wood b Hogg	6
G.Miller	c Maclean b Hurst	4	lbw b Hogg	17
R.W.Taylor†	c Border b Higgs	10	not out	21
J.E.Emburey	c Wood b Higgs	7	c Darling b Higgs	14
R.G.D.Willis	not out	7	c Toohey b Higgs	7
M.Hendrick	b Hurst	10	c Toohey b Higgs	0
Extras	(B 1, LB 1, NB 8, W 2)	12	(B 5, LB 3, NB 14)	22
Total		**152**		**346**

1/18 2/18 3/35 4/51 5/66
6/70 7/94 8/98 9/141

1/0 2/111 3/169 4/237 5/267
6/292 7/307 8/334 9/334

Bowling: *First Innings*—Hogg 11-3-36-2; Dymock 13-1-34-0; Hurst 10.6-2-28-5; Higgs 18-4-42-3. *Second Innings*—Hogg 28-10-67-4; Dymock 17-4-35-0; Hurst 19-3-43-0; Higgs 59.6-15-148-5; Border 23-11-31-1.

Australia

Batsman	First Innings	R	Second Innings	R
G.M.Wood	b Willis	0	c Gooch b Hendrick	27
W.M.Darling	c Botham b Miller	91	c Emburey b Miller	13
K.J.Hughes	c Emburey b Willis	48	c Emburey b Miller	15
G.N.Yallop*	c Botham b Hendrick	44	c and b Hendrick	1
P.M.Toohey	c Gooch b Botham	1	b Miller	5
A.R.Border	not out	60	not out	45
J.A.Maclean†	lbw b Emburey	12	c Botham b Miller	0
R.M.Hogg	run out (9)	6	c Botham b Emburey	0
G.Dymock	b Botham (8)	5	b Emburey	0
J.D.Higgs	c Botham b Hendrick	11	lbw b Emburey	3
A.G.Hurst	run out	0	b Emburey	0
Extras	(B 2, LB 3, NB 11)	16	(LB 1, NB 1)	2
Total		**294**		**111**

1/1 2/126 3/178 4/179 5/210
6/235 7/245 8/276 9/290

1/38 2/44 3/45 4/59 5/74
6/76 7/85 8/85 9/105

Bowling: *First Innings*—Willis 9-2-33-2; Botham 28-3-87-2; Hendrick 24-4-50-2; Miller 13-2-37-1; Emburey 29-10-57-1; Gooch 5-1-14-0. *Second Innings*—Willis 2-0-8-0; Hendrick 10-3-17-2; Emburey 17.2-7-46-4; Miller 20-7-38-3.

Umpires: R.C.Bailhache and R.A.French

AUSTRALIA v ENGLAND 1978-79 (Fifth Test)

At Adelaide Oval, 27, 28, 29, 31 January, 1 February
Result: England won by 205 runs

England

Batsman	First Innings	R	Second Innings	R
G.Boycott	c Wright b Hurst	6	c Hughes b Hurst	49
J.M.Brearley*	c Wright b Hogg	2	lbw b Carlson	9
D.W.Randall	c Carlson b Hurst	4	c Yardley b Hurst	15
G.A.Gooch	c Hughes b Hogg	1	b Carlson	18
D.I.Gower	lbw b Hurst	9	lbw b Higgs	21
I.T.Botham	c Wright b Higgs	74	c Yardley b Hurst	7
G.Miller	lbw b Hogg	31	c Wright b Hurst	64
R.W.Taylor†	run out	4	c Wright b Hogg	97
J.E.Emburey	b Higgs	4	b Hogg	42
R.G.D.Willis	c Darling b Hogg	24	c Wright b Hogg	12
M.Hendrick	not out	0	not out	3
Extras	(B 1, LB 4, NB 2, W 3)	10	(B 1, LB 16, NB 4, W 2)	23
Total		**169**		**360**

1/10 2/12 3/16 4/18 5/27
6/80 7/113 8/136 9/147

1/31 2/57 3/97 4/106 5/130
6/132 7/267 8/336 9/347

Bowling: *First Innings*—Hogg 10.4-1-26-4; Hurst 14-1-65-3; Carlson 9-1-34-0; Higgs 3-1-9-2. *Second Innings*—Hogg 27.6-7-59-3; Hurst 37-9-97-4; Carlson 27-8-41-2; Yardley 20-6-60-0; Higgs 28-4-75-1; Border 3-2-5-0.

Australia

Batsman	First Innings	R	Second Innings	R
W.M.Darling	c Willis b Botham	15	b Botham	18
G.M.Wood	c Randall b Emburey	35	run out	9
K.J.Hughes	c Emburey b Hendrick	4	c Gower b Hendrick	46
G.N.Yallop*	b Hendrick	0	b Hendrick	36
A.R.Border	c Taylor b Botham	11	b Willis	11
P.H.Carlson	c Taylor b Botham	0	c Gower b Hendrick	21
B.Yardley	b Botham	28	c Brearley b Willis	0
K.J.Wright†	lbw b Emburey	29	c Emburey b Miller	0
R.M.Hogg	lbw b Willis	0	b Miller	2
J.D.Higgs	run out	16	not out	3
A.G.Hurst	not out	17	b Willis	13
Extras	(B 1, LB 3, NB 5)	9	(LB 1, NB 10)	11
Total		**164**		**160**

1/5 2/10 3/22 4/24 5/72
6/94 7/114 8/116 9/133

1/31 2/36 3/115 4/120 5/121
6/121 7/124 8/130 9/147

Bowling: *First Innings*—Willis 11-1-55-1; Hendrick 19-1-45-2; Botham 11.4-0-42-4; Emburey 12-7-13-2. *Second Innings*—Willis 12-3-41-3; Hendrick 14-6-19-3; Botham 14.4-3-37-1; Miller 18-3-36-2; Emburey 9-5-16-0.

Umpires: R.C.Bailhache and M.G.O'Connell

AUSTRALIA v ENGLAND 1978-79 (Sixth Test)

At Sydney Cricket Ground, 10, 11, 12, 14 February
Result: England won by 9 wickets

Australia

G.M.Wood c Botham b Hendrick	15	c Willis b Miller ... 29
A.M.J.Hilditch run out	3	c Taylor b Hendrick ... 1
K.J.Hughes c Botham b Willis	16	c Gooch b Emburey ... 7
G.N.Yallop* c Gower b Botham	121	c Taylor b Miller ... 17
P.M.Toohey c Taylor b Botham	8	c Gooch b Emburey ... 0
P.H.Carlson c Gooch b Botham	2	c Botham b Emburey ... 0
B.Yardley c Emburey	7	not out ... 61
K.J.Wright† st Taylor b Emburey	3	c Boycott b Miller ... 5
R.M.Hogg c Emburey b Miller	9	b Miller ... 7
J.D.Higgs not out	9	c Botham b Emburey ... 2
A.G.Hurst b Botham	0	c and b Miller ... 4
Extras (LB 3, NB 2)	5	(B 3, LB 6, NB 1) ... 10
	198	**143**

1/18 2/19 3/67 4/101 5/109   1/8 2/28 3/48 4/48 5/48
6/116 7/124 8/159 9/198   6/82 7/114 8/130 9/136

Bowling: *First Innings*—Willis 11-4-48-1; Hendrick 12-2-21-1; Botham 9.7-1-57-4; Emburey 18-3-48-2; Miller 9-3-13-1; Boycott 1-0-6-0. *Second Innings*—Willis 3-0-15-0; Hendrick 7-3-22-1; Emburey 24-4-52-4; Miller 27.1-6-44-5.

England

G.Boycott c Hilditch b Hurst	19	c Hughes b Higgs ... 13
J.M.Brearley* c Toohey b Higgs	46	not out ... 20
D.W.Randall lbw b Hogg	7	not out ... 0
G.A.Gooch st Wright b Higgs	74	
D.I.Gower c Wright b Higgs	65	
I.T.Botham c Carlson b Yardley	23	
G.Miller lbw b Hurst	18	
R.W.Taylor† not out	36	
J.E.Emburey c Hilditch b Hurst	0	
R.G.D.Willis b Higgs	10	
M.Hendrick c and b Yardley	0	
Extras (B 3, LB 5, NB 2)	10	(NB 2) ... 2
	308	**(1 wkt) 35**

1/37 2/46 3/115 4/182 5/233   1/31
6/247 7/270 8/280 9/306

Bowling: *First Innings*—Hogg 18-6-42-1; Hurst 20-4-58-3; Yardley 25-2-105-2; Carlson 10-1-24-0; Higgs 30-8-69-4. *Second Innings*—Yardley 5.2-0-21-0; Higgs 5-1-12-1.

Umpires: A.R.Crafter and D.G.Weser

AUSTRALIA v PAKISTAN 1978-79 (First Test)

At Melbourne Cricket Ground, 10, 11, 12, 14, 15 March
Result: Pakistan won by 71 runs.

Pakistan

Majid Khan c Wright b Hogg	1	b Border ... 108
Mohsin Khan c Hilditch b Hogg	14	c and b Hogg ... 14
Zaheer Abbas b Hogg	11	b Hogg ... 59
Javed Miandad b Hogg	19	c Wright b Border ... 16
Asif Iqbal c Wright b Clark	9	lbw b Hogg ... 44
Mushtaq Mohammad* c Wright b Hurst	36	c sub (J.D.Higgs) b Sleep ... 28
Wasim Raja b Hurst	13	c Wright b Hurst ... 28
Imran Khan c Wright b Hurst	33	c Clark b Hurst ... 28
Sarfraz Nawaz c Wright b Sleep	35	lbw b Hurst ... 1
Wasim Bari† run out	0	not out ... 8
Sikander Bakht not out	5	
Extras (B 2, LB 7, NB 10, W 1)	20	(B 4, LB 6, NB 9) ... 19
	196	**(9 wkts dec.) 353**

1/2 2/22 3/28 4/40 5/83   1/30 2/165 3/204
6/99 7/122 8/173 9/177   4/209 5/261 6/299 7/330 8/332
   9/353

Bowling: *First Innings*—Hogg 17-4-49-4; Hurst 20-4-55-3; Clark 17-4-56-1; Sleep 7.7-2-16-1. *Second Innings*—Hogg 19-2-75-3; Hurst 19.5-1-115-3; Clark 21-6-47-0; Sleep 8-0-62-1; Border 14-5-35-2.

Australia

G.M.Wood not out	5	(6) c Wasim Bari b Sarfraz Nawaz ... 0
A.M.J.Hilditch c Javed Miandad b Imran Khan	3	b Sarfraz Nawaz ... 62
A.R.Border b Imran Khan	20	b Sarfraz Nawaz ... 105
G.N.Yallop* b Imran Khan	25	run out ... 8
K.J.Hughes run out	19	c Mohsin Khan b Sarfraz Nawaz ... 84
D.F.Whatmore lbw b Sarfraz Nawaz	43	(1) b Sarfraz Nawaz ... 15
P.R.Sleep c Wasim Bari b Imran Khan	10	b Sarfraz Nawaz ... 0
K.J.Wright† c Imran Khan b Wasim Raja	9	not out ... 1
W.M.Clark c Mushtaq Mohammad b Wasim Raja	9	b Sarfraz Nawaz ... 0
R.M.Hogg run out	0	lbw b Sarfraz Nawaz ... 0
A.G.Hurst c and b Sarfraz Nawaz	0	c Wasim Bari b Sarfraz Nawaz ... 0
Extras (B 1, LB 5, NB 8, W 2)	16	(B 13, LB 13, NB 9) ... 35
	168	**310**

1/11 2/53 3/63 4/97 5/109   1/49 2/109 3/128 4/305 5/305
6/140 7/152 8/167 9/167   6/306 7/308 8/309 9/310

Bowling: *First Innings*—Imran Khan 18-8-26-4; Sarfraz Nawaz 21.6-6-39-2; Sikander Bakht 10-1-29-0; Mushtaq Mohammad 7-0-35-0; Wasim Raja 5-0-23-2. *Second Innings*—Imran Khan 27-9-73-0; Sarfraz Nawaz 35.4-7-86-9; Sikander Bakht 7-0-29-0; Mushtaq Mohammad 11-0-42-0; Wasim Raja 3-0-11-0; Majid Khan 9-1-34-0.

Umpires: R.C.Bailhache and C.E.Harvey

AUSTRALIA v PAKISTAN 1978-79 (Second Test)

At W.A.C.A. Ground, Perth, 24, 25, 26, 28, 29 March

Result: Australia won by 7 wickets

Pakistan

	First Innings		Second Innings	
Majid Khan	c Hilditch b Hogg	0	c sub (T.J.Laughlin) b Hogg	0
Mudassar Nazar	c Wright b Hurst	5	c Hilditch b Hurst	25
Zaheer Abbas	c Wright b Hurst	29	c Wright b Hogg	18
Javed Miandad	not out	129	c Wright b Hurst	19
Haroon Rashid	c Border b Hurst	4	c Yardley b Dymock	47
Asif Iqbal	run out	35	not out	134
Mushtaq Mohammad*	run out	23	lbw b Yardley	1
Imran Khan	c Wright b Dymock	27	c Wright b Hurst	15
Sarfraz Nawaz	c Wright b Hurst	27	c Yardley b Hurst	3
Wasim Bari†	c Hilditch b Dymock	0	c Whatmore b Hurst	0
Sikander Bakht	b Dymock	0	run out	0
Extras	(LB 3, NB 5, W 3)	11	(B 3, LB 8, NB 12)	23
		290		285

1/0 2/27 3/41 4/49 5/90 / 1/0 2/35 3/68 4/86 5/152
6/176 7/224 8/276 9/277 / 6/153 7/245 8/263 9/263

Bowling: First Innings—Hogg 19-2-88-1; Hurst 23-4-61-4; Dymock 21.6-4-65-3; Yardley 14-2-52-0. Second Innings—Hogg 20-5-45-2; Hurst 24.7-2-94-5; Dymock 23-5-72-1; Yardley 14-3-42-1; Border 4-0-9-0.

Australia

	First Innings		Second Innings	
W.M.Darling	lbw b Mudassar Nazar	75	run out	79
A.M.J.Hilditch	c Majid Abbas b Imran Khan	41	handled the ball	29
A.R.Border	c Majid Khan b Javed Miandad	85	not out	66
K.J.Hughes*	lbw b Sikander Bakht	9		
J.K.Moss	c Wasim Bari b Mudassar Nazar	22		
D.F.Whatmore	c Asif Iqbal b Imran Khan	15	not out	38
K.J.Wright†	c Wasim Bari b Mudassar Nazar	16		
B.Yardley	b Sarfraz Nawaz	19	(4) run out	1
G.Dymock	not out	5		
R.M.Hogg	b Imran Khan	3		
A.G.Hurst	c Wasim Bari b Sarfraz Nawaz	16		
Extras	(B 3, LB 4, NB 13, W 1)	21	(LB 13, NB 10)	23
		327	(3 wkts)	236

1/96 2/143 3/161 4/219 5/246 / 1/87 2/153 3/155
6/273 7/297 8/301 9/304

Bowling: First Innings—Imran Khan 32-5-105-3; Sarfraz Nawaz 35.1-7-112-2; Sikander Bakht 10.5-1-33-1; Mudassar Nazar 16-2-48-3; Javed Miandad 2-0-8-1. Second Innings—Imran Khan 17-1-81-0; Sarfraz Nawaz 19-1-85-0; Mudassar Nazar 10.1-2-35-0; Javed Miandad 2-0-12-0.

Umpires: A.R.Crafter and M.G.O'Connell

INDIA v AUSTRALIA 1979-80 (First Test)

At Chidambaram Stadium, Chepauk, Madras, 11, 12, 14, 15, 16 September

Result: Match drawn

Australia

	First Innings		Second Innings	
A.M.J.Hilditch	c Venkataraghavan b Kapil Dev	4	lbw b Doshi	55
G.M.Wood	lbw b Doshi	33	c Chauhan b Kapil Dev	2
A.R.Border	run out	162	b Venkataraghavan	50
K.J.Hughes*	c Venkataraghavan b Doshi	100	lbw b Venkataraghavan	36
G.N.Yallop	c Yajurvindra Singh b Doshi	18	run out	8
D.F.Whatmore	c Venkataraghavan b Doshi	20	c Chauhan b Doshi	8
K.J.Wright†	b Venkataraghavan	20	b Venkataraghavan	5
G.Dymock	lbw b Kapil Dev	16	not out	28
R.M.Hogg	c Kapil Dev b Doshi	3	not out	8
A.G.Hurst	c Kirmani b Doshi	0		
J.D.Higgs	not out	1		
Extras	(B 1, LB 7, NB 4, W 1)	13	(B 11, LB 4, NB 3)	18
		390	(7 wkts)	212

1/8 2/75 3/297 4/318 5/339 / 1/2 2/103 3/123 4/127
6/352 7/369 8/375 9/376 / 5/146 6/156 7/175

Bowling: First Innings—Kapil Dev 25.4-3-95-2; Yajurvindra Singh 9.1-29-0; Ghavri 20-4-49-0; Venkataraghavan 46-16-101-1; Doshi 43-10-103-6. Second Innings—Kapil Dev 9-3-30-1; Ghavri 17.4-8-23-0; Venkataraghavan 45-10-77-3; Doshi 42-15-64-2.

India

	First Innings	
S.M.Gavaskar*	c Wood b Hogg	50
C.P.S.Chauhan	c Wright b Higgs	26
S.M.H.Kirmani†	c Border b Hogg	57
G.R.Viswanath	c Hughes b Higgs	17
D.B.Vengsarkar	c Whatmore b Higgs	65
Yashpal Sharma	lbw b Higgs	52
Yajurvindra Singh	c Wright b Yallop	15
Kapil Dev	c Hurst b Higgs	83
K.D.Ghavri	not out	23
D.R.Doshi	c Hogg b Higgs	3
S.Venkataraghavan	lbw b Higgs	4
Extras	(B 2, LB 5, NB 23)	30
		425

1/80 2/89 3/122 4/221 5/240
6/281 7/371 8/394 9/417

Bowling: Hogg 22-1-85-2; Hurst 23-8-51-0; Higgs 41.3-12-143-7; Dymock 24-6-65-0; Border 14-4-30-0; Yallop 6-1-21-1.

Umpires: M.V.Gothaskar and Swaroop Kishen

INDIA v AUSTRALIA 1979-80 (Third Test)

At Green Park, Kanpur, 2, 3, 4, 6, 7 October
Result: India won by 153 runs

India

Batsman	First Innings		Second Innings	
S.M.Gavaskar*	lbw b Dymock	76	c Whatmore b Yardley	12
C.P.S.Chauhan	c and b Hogg	58	c Yardley b Dymock	84
D.B.Vengsarkar	lbw b Hogg	52	c Whatmore b Dymock	20
G.R.Viswanath	c sub (P.R.Sleep) b Dymock	44	c Whatmore b Yardley	52
Yashpal Sharma	b Hogg	0	c Wright b Dymock	0
Kapil Dev	c Hughes b Border	5	b Dymock	10
S.M.H.Kirmani†	c Whatmore b Hogg	4	b Dymock	45
K.D.Ghavri	c Whatmore b Dymock	5	c sub (P.R.Sleep) b Hogg	25
N.S.Yadav	lbw b Dymock	0	c Whatmore b Dymock	18
S.Venkataraghavan	c Border b Dymock	1	not out	4
D.R.Doshi	not out	0	b Dymock	0
Extras	(B 5, LB 6, NB 15)	26	(B 11, LB 9, NB 21)	41
		271		**311**

1/114 2/201 3/206 4/214 5/231 6/239 7/246 8/246 9/256
1/24 2/48 3/161 4/163 5/177 6/256 7/261 8/302 9/311

Bowling: *First Innings*—Dymock 35-7-99-5; Hogg 26-3-66-4; Yardley 20-6-54-0; Higgs 7-4-23-0; Border 3-2-3-1. *Second Innings*—Dymock 28.4-5-67-7; Hogg 19-4-49-1; Yardley 40-15-82-2; Higgs 22-7-68-0; Border 2-1-4-0.

Australia

Batsman	First Innings			Second Innings	
A.M.J.Hilditch	c Chauhan b Ghavri	1		b Doshi	23
B.Yardley	c Yashpal Sharma b Ghavri	29	(8)	lbw b Kapil Dev	5
A.R.Border	c Viswanath b Venkataraghavan	24	(6)	b Yadav	8
K.J.Hughes*	b Yadav	50		lbw b Kapil Dev	1
G.N.Yallop	hit wkt b Kapil Dev	89	(3)	c Kirmani b Ghavri	15
K.J.Wright†	lbw b Kapil Dev	6	(7)	b Yadav	11
D.F.Whatmore	c Gavaskar b Doshi	14	(5)	b Yadav	33
W.M.Darling	c Kirmani b Ghavri	59	(2)	st Kirmani b Yadav	4
G.Dymock	run out	11		lbw b Kapil Dev	6
R.M.Hogg	b Yadav	10		lbw b Kapil Dev	8
J.D.Higgs	not out	3		not out	8
Extras	(LB 2, NB 6)	8		(B 1, LB 2, NB 2)	5
		304			**125**

1/1 2/51 3/75 4/168 5/175 6/192 7/246 8/263 9/294
1/13 2/32 3/37 4/49 5/74 6/93 7/104 8/106 9/112

Bowling: *First Innings*—Kapil Dev 27-5-78-2; Ghavri 23.3-5-65-3; Venkataraghavan 18-6-56-1; Doshi 16-5-32-1; Yadav 25-3-65-2. *Second Innings*—Kapil Dev 16.2-5-30-4; Ghavri 11-0-28-1; Venkataraghavan 9-4-13-0; Doshi 12-5-14-1; Yadav 12-0-35-4.

Umpires: S.N.Hanumantha Rao and Mohammad Ghouse

INDIA v AUSTRALIA 1979-80 (Second Test)

At Karnataka State C.A. Stadium, Bangalore, 19, 20, 22, 23, 24 September
Result: Match drawn

Australia

Batsman	First Innings			Second Innings	
A.M.J.Hilditch	c sub (Arun Lal) b Yadav	62		lbw b Yadav	3
W.M.Darling	b Kapil Dev	7			
A.R.Border	c Yadav b Doshi	44		b Yadav	19
K.J.Hughes*	c Ghavri b Kapil Dev	86		not out	13
G.N.Yallop	c Viswanath b Yadav	12		not out	6
B.Yardley	c and b Ghavri	47			
G.M.Wood	c Kirmani b Ghavri	18	(2)	c Viswanath b Yadav	30
K.J.Wright†	not out	16			
R.M.Hogg	lbw b Venkataraghavan	19			
J.D.Higgs	lbw b Yadav	1			
A.G.Hurst	b Yadav	0			
Extras	(B 5, LB 6, NB 10)	21		(LB 5, NB 1)	6
		333		(3 wkts)	**77**

1/21 2/99 3/137 4/159 5/258 6/294 7/294 8/332 9/333
1/13 2/53 3/62

Bowling: *First Innings*—Kapil Dev 25-4-89-2; Ghavri 19-5-68-2; Venkataraghavan 20-6-43-1; Yadav 22.5-5-49-4. *Second Innings*—Kapil Dev 3-2-1-0; Ghavri 3-1-9-0; Doshi 8-4-11-0; Venkataraghavan 8-2-18-0; Yadav 15.4-4-32-3.

India

Batsman	First Innings	
S.M.Gavaskar*	c Hilditch b Yardley	10
C.P.S.Chauhan	c Hilditch b Yardley	31
D.B.Vengsarkar	lbw b Yardley	112
S.M.H.Kirmani†	st Wright b Higgs	30
G.R.Viswanath	not out	161
Yashpal Sharma	c Border b Yardley	37
Kapil Dev	not out	38
K.D.Ghavri		
N.S.Yadav		
S.Venkataraghavan		
D.R.Doshi		
Extras	(B 12, LB 8, NB 17, W 1)	38
	(5 wkts dec.)	**457**

1/22 2/61 3/120 4/279 5/372

Bowling: Hogg 32-6-118-0; Hurst 29-3-93-0; Yardley 44-16-107-4; Higgs 37-9-95-1; Yallop 2-0-6-0.

Umpires: P.R.Punjabi and K.B.Ramaswami

INDIA v AUSTRALIA 1979-80 (Fourth Test)

At Feroz Shah Kotla, Delhi, 13, 14, 16, 17, 18 October

Result: Match drawn

India

Batsman	Dismissal	Runs
S.M.Gavaskar*	lbw b Higgs	115
C.P.S.Chauhan	c Whatmore b Dymock	19
D.B.Vengsarkar	st Wright b Higgs	26
G.R.Viswanath	st Wright b Higgs	131
Yashpal Sharma	not out	100
Kapil Dev	c Whatmore b Dymock	29
M.V.Narasimha Rao	c Wright b Dymock	5
S.M.H.Kirmani†	b Dymock	35
K.D.Ghavri	not out	8
N.S.Yadav		
D.R.Doshi		
Extras	(B 6, LB 12, NB 24)	42

1/38 2/108 3/267 4/338 5/395 (7 wkts dec.) 510
6/415 7/467

Bowling: Dymock 42.2-8-135-4; Hogg 33-8-91-0; Yallop 5-0-21-0; Border 4-2-5-0; Higgs 47-11-150-3; Sleep 13-1-66-0.

Australia

Batsman	First Innings	Runs	Second Innings	Runs
A.M.J.Hilditch	c Kirmani b Yadav	29	c Kirmani b Ghavri	85
W.M.Darling	c Kirmani b Kapil Dev	19	c Kirmani b Kapil Dev	7
A.R.Border	c Narasimha Rao b Kapil Dev	24	c Narasimha Rao b Ghavri	46
K.J.Hughes*	c Kirmani b Kapil Dev	18	c and b Ghavri	40
D.F.Whatmore	lbw b Yadav	77	(6) lbw b Kapil Dev	54
P.R.Sleep	c Chauhan b Narasimha Rao	17	(7) c sub (Arun Lal) b Chauhan	64
G.N.Yallop	c Chauhan b Narasimha Rao	21	(5) b Doshi	25
K.J.Wright†	not out	55	b Yadav	15
G.Dymock	c Kirmani b Kapil Dev	0	not out	31
R.M.Hogg	b Kapil Dev	0	run out	0
J.D.Higgs	lbw b Doshi	11	c Vengsarkar b Viswanath	7
Extras	(B 4, LB 4, NB 19)	27	(B 13, LB 9, NB 16, W 1)	39

1/32 2/72 3/93 4/116 5/160 298
6/225 7/228 8/242 9/246

1/20 2/147 3/156 4/205 5/241 413
6/318 7/344 8/395 9/395

Bowling: First Innings—Ghavri 22-8-58-0; Kapil Dev 32-7-82-5; Doshi 13.3-5-29-1; Yadav 27-10-56-2; Narasimha Rao 12-1-46-2. Second Innings—Ghavri 30-8-74-3; Kapil Dev 20-7-48-2; Doshi 34-11-69-1; Yadav 36-10-101-1; Narasimha Rao 19-3-50-0; Gavaskar 4-1-10-0; Chauhan 5-1-11-1; Viswanath 3.3-0-11-1.

Umpires: P.R.Punjabi and K.B.Ramaswami

INDIA v AUSTRALIA 1979-80 (Fifth Test)

At Eden Gardens, Calcutta 26, 27, 28, 30, 31 October

Result: Match drawn

Australia

Batsman	First Innings	Runs	Second Innings	Runs
A.M.J.Hilditch	c Kirmani b Kapil Dev	0	b Ghavri	29
G.N.Yallop	c Gavaskar b Yadav	167	lbw b Kapil Dev	4
A.R.Border	lbw b Kapil Dev	54	st Kirmani b Doshi	6
K.J.Hughes*	lbw b Kapil Dev	92	not out	64
D.F.Whatmore	b Kapil Dev	4	c Vengsarkar b Doshi	4
W.M.Darling	st Kirmani b Doshi	39	c Gavaskar b Yadav	7
B.Yardley	not out	61	c Narasimha Rao b Yadav	12
K.J.Wright†	lbw b Doshi	0	not out	12
G.Dymock	lbw b Doshi	3		
R.M.Hogg	c Yashpal Sharma b Doshi	0		
J.D.Higgs	lbw b Kapil Dev	1		
Extras	(B 7, LB 7, NB 7)	21	(B 9, LB 4)	13
		442	(6 wkts dec.)	151

1/0 2/97 3/303 4/311 5/347 442
6/396 7/396 8/418 9/426

1/21 2/39 3/53 (6 wkts dec.) 151
4/62 5/81 6/115

Bowling: First Innings—Kapil Dev 32-9-74-5; Ghavri 24-3-85-0; Yadav 42-8-135-1; Narasimha Rao 8-0-24-0; Doshi 43-10-92-4; Chauhan 4-0-11-0. Second Innings—Kapil Dev 11-3-33-1; Ghavri 13.3-5-39-1; Yadav 11-6-16-2; Doshi 22-6-50-2.

India

Batsman	First Innings	Runs	Second Innings	Runs
S.M.Gavaskar*	lbw b Hogg	14	c Hilditch b Dymock	25
C.P.S.Chauhan	c Border b Higgs	39	c Wright b Dymock	50
D.B.Vengsarkar	c Hughes b Yardley	89	c Wright b Dymock	2
G.R.Viswanath	c Wright b Yardley	96	lbw b Dymock	7
Yashpal Sharma	c Wright b Hogg	22	not out	85
M.V.Narasimha Rao	run out	10	not out	20
Kapil Dev	c Hughes b Dymock	30		
S.M.H.Kirmani†	not out	13		
K.D.Ghavri	c Wright b Yardley	1		
N.S.Yadav	c Wright b Yardley	0		
D.R.Doshi	b Dymock	0		
Extras	(B 12, LB 9, NB 8, W 4)	33	(B 4, LB 7)	11
		347	(4 wkts)	200

1/21 2/132 3/256 4/290 5/290 347
6/305 7/341 8/342 9/346

1/52 2/54 3/70 4/123 (4 wkts) 200

Bowling: First Innings—Dymock 26.4-8-56-2; Hogg 26-2-103-2; Yardley 42-11-91-4; Higgs 28-12-56-1; Border 2-0-8-0; Yallop 1-1-0-0. Second Innings—Dymock 25-7-63-4; Hogg 8.2-1-26-0; Yardley 13-1-47-0; Higgs 16-3-51-0; Yallop 1-0-2-0.

Umpires: S.N.Hanumantha Rao and Swaroop Kishen

INDIA v AUSTRALIA 1979-80 (Sixth Test)

At Wankhede Stadium, Bombay, 3, 4, 6, 7 November
Result: India won by an innings and 100 runs

India

S.M.Gavaskar* c Hughes b Border	123
C.P.S.Chauhan b Dymock	73
D.B.Vengsarkar c Whatmore b Border	6
G.R.Viswanath c and b Higgs	10
S.M.H.Kirmani† not out	101
Yashpal Sharma c Whatmore b Hogg	8
M.Amarnath hit wkt b Hogg	2
Kapil Dev c Whatmore b Higgs	17
K.D.Ghavri c sub (G.D.Porter) b Dymock	86
N.S.Yadav not out	0
D.R.Doshi	
Extras (B 3, LB 12, NB 17)	32

1/192 2/222 3/231 4/240 5/272 (8 wkts) dec 458
6/281 7/327 8/454

Bowling: Dymock 31-5-95-2; Hogg 28-14-53-2; Higgs 29-4-116-2; Border 27-7-60-2; Sleep 28-7-79-0; Whatmore 5-2-11-0; Yallop 1-0-12-0.

Australia

A.M.J.Hilditch run out	13	b Kapil Dev	9
G.N.Yallop c Kapil Dev b Yadav	60	c Amarnath b Ghavri	4
A.R.Border c Vengsarkar b Yadav	23	b Doshi	61
K.J.Hughes* c Vengsarkar b Doshi	14	c Ghavri b Kapil Dev	80
D.F.Whatmore lbw b Doshi	6	lbw b Kapil Dev	0
W.M.Darling c sub (R.M.H.Binny) b Yadav	16	retired hurt	0
P.R.Sleep b Yadav	1	c Kapil Dev b Doshi	0
K.J.Wright† not out	11	lbw b Doshi	3
G.Dymock c Chauhan b Doshi	7	c Viswanath b Yadav	5
R.M.Hogg c Amarnath b Doshi	5	not out	3
J.D.Higgs b Doshi	0	b Kapil Dev	4
Extras (B 1, LB 2, NB 7)	10	(LB 12, NB 10)	22
	160		198

1/28 2/77 3/110 4/118 5/124   1/11 2/17 3/149 4/154 5/159
6/125 7/144 8/145 9/158   6/176 7/183 8/187 9/198

Bowling: First Innings—Kapil Dev 8-0-26-0; Ghavri 8-1-30-0; Doshi 19.5-4-43-5; Yadav 21-7-40-4; Amarnath 5-1-11-0. Second Innings—Kapil Dev 14.1-5-39-4; Ghavri 10-0-28-1; Doshi 25-6-60-3; Amarnath 2-1-1-0; Yadav 22-9-48-1.

Umpires: J.D.Ghosh and Mohammad Ghouse

AUSTRALIA v WEST INDIES 1979-80 (First Test)

At Woolloongabba, Brisbane, 1, 2, 3, 4, 5 December
Result: Match drawn

Australia

B.M.Laird c Murray b Garner	92	c sub (M.D.Marshall) b Garner.	75
R.B.McCosker c Kallicharran b Croft	14	b Holding	33
A.R.Border c Murray b Garner	1	c Richards b Garner	7
G.S.Chappell* c King b Roberts	74	b Croft	124
K.J.Hughes† not out	3	not out	130
D.W.Hookes c Holding b Croft	43	b Roberts	37
R.W.Marsh† c Murray b Garner	3	c Kallicharran b King	19
R.J.Bright b Holding	13	not out	2
D.K.Lillee lbw b Garner	0		
R.M.Hogg b Roberts	8		
J.R.Thomson not out	0		
Extras (B 1, LB 4, NB 12)	17	(B 2, LB 11, NB 6, W 2)	21
	268	(6 wkts dec.)	448

1/19 2/26 3/156 4/174 5/228   1/40 2/55 3/179
6/242 7/246 8/252 9/268   4/297 5/371 6/442

Bowling: First Innings—Roberts-18.1-5-50-2; Holding 16-3-53-1; Croft 25-6-80-3; Garner 22-5-55-4; King 5-1-13-0. Second Innings—Roberts-27-5-70-1; Holding 30-4-94-1; Croft 28-3-106-1; Garner 41-13-75-2; King 22-6-50-1; Kallicharran 18-0-32-0.

West Indies

C.G.Greenidge c Marsh b Lillee	34		c McCosker b Thomson	0
D.L.Haynes c Marsh b Thomson	42		lbw b Hogg	4
I.V.A.Richards c Marsh b Lillee	140			
A.I.Kallicharran c Marsh b Thomson	38		not out	10
L.G.Rowe b Chappell	50	(3)	b Hogg	3
C.L.King c Marsh b Lillee	0	(5)	not out	8
D.L.Murray*† c McCosker b Thomson	21			
A.M.E.Roberts run out	7			
J.Garner lbw b Lillee	60			
M.A.Holding b Bright	11			
C.E.H.Croft not out	2			
Extras (B 5, LB 3, NB 28)	36		(B 5, NB 9, W 1)	15
	441		(3 wkts)	40

1/68 2/93 3/198 4/317 5/317   1/2 2/15 3/16
6/341 7/365 8/365 9/385

Bowling: First Innings—Lillee 29.1-8-104-4; Hogg 25-6-55-0; Thomson 24-4-90-3; Chappell 12-2-25-1; Bright 32-9-97-1; Border 5-1-19-0; Hookes 5-2-15-0. Second Innings—Lillee 2-0-3-0; Hogg 5-2-11-2; Thomson 3-2-3-1; Bright 4-3-8-0.

Umpires: R.C.Bailhache and A.R.Crafter

AUSTRALIA v ENGLAND 1979-80 (First Test)

At W.A.C.A. Ground, Perth, 14, 15, 16, 18, 19 December

Result: Australia won by 138 runs

Australia

J.M.Wiener run out	11	c Randall b Underwood	58
B.M.Laird lbw b Botham	0	c Taylor b Underwood	33
A.R.Border lbw b Botham	4	c Taylor b Willis	115
G.S.Chappell* c Boycott b Botham	19	st Taylor b Underwood	43
K.J.Hughes c Brearley b Underwood	99	c Miller b Botham	4
P.M.Toohey c Underwood b Dilley	19	c Taylor b Botham	3
R.W.Marsh† c Taylor b Botham	42	c Gower b Botham	4
R.J.Bright c Taylor b Botham	17	lbw b Botham	12
D.K.Lillee c Taylor b Botham	18	c Willey b Dilley	19
G.Dymock b Botham	5	not out	20
J.R.Thomson not out	1	b Botham	8
Extras (B 4, LB 3, NB 2)	9	(B 4, LB 5, NB 7, W 2)	18
	244		**337**

1/2 2/17 3/20 4/88 5/127   1/91 2/100 3/168 4/183 5/191
6/186 7/219 8/219 9/243   6/204 7/225 8/303 9/323

Bowling: *First Innings*—Dilley 18-1-47-2; Botham 35-9-78-6; Willis 23-7-47-0; Underwood 13-4-33-1; Miller 11-2-30-0. *Second Innings*—Dilley 18-3-50-1; Botham 45.5-14-98-5; Willis 26-7-52-1; Underwood 41-14-82-3; Miller 10-1-36-0; Willey 1-0-1-0.

England

D.W.Randall c Hughes b Lillee	0	lbw b Dymock	1
G.Boycott lbw b Lillee	0	not out	99
P.Willey c Chappell b Dymock	9	lbw b Dymock	12
D.I.Gower c Marsh b Lillee	17	c Thomson b Dymock	23
G.Miller c Hughes b Thomson	25	c Chappell b Thomson	8
J.M.Brearley* c Marsh b Lillee	64	(7) c Marsh b Bright	11
I.T.Botham c Toohey b Thomson	15	(6) c Marsh b Lillee	18
R.W.Taylor† b Chappell	14	b Lillee	15
G.R.Dilley not out	38	c Marsh b Dymock	16
D.L.Underwood lbw b Dymock	13	c Wiener b Dymock	0
R.G.D.Willis b Dymock	11	c Chappell b Dymock	0
Extras (LB 7, NB 15)	22	(LB 3, NB 8, W 1)	12
	228		**215**

1/1 2/12 3/14 4/41 5/74   1/8 2/26 3/64 4/75 5/115
6/90 7/123 8/185 9/203   6/141 7/182 8/211 9/211

Bowling: *First Innings*—Lillee 28-11-73-4; Dymock 29.1-14-52-3; Chappell 11-6-5-1; Thomson 21-3-70-2; Bright 2-0-6-0. *Second Innings*—Lillee 23-5-74-2; Dymock 17.2-4-34-6; Thomson 11-3-30-1; Bright 23-11-30-1; Wiener 8-3-22-0; Border 2-0-7-0.

Umpires: M.G.O'Connell and D.G.Weser

AUSTRALIA v WEST INDIES 1979-80 (Second Test)

At Melbourne Cricket Ground, 29, 30, 31 December, 1 January

Result: West Indies won by 10 wickets

Australia

J.M.Wiener lbw b Garner	40	c Murray b Croft	24
B.M.Laird c Lloyd b Holding	16	c Garner b Holding	69
A.R.Border c Richards b Garner	17	lbw b Holding	15
G.S.Chappell* c Murray b Garner	19	c Murray b Roberts	22
K.J.Hughes c Rowe b Holding	4	lbw b Roberts	70
P.M.Toohey c Roberts b Holding	10	c Murray b Croft	7
R.W.Marsh† c Kallicharran b Holding	0	b Croft	7
D.K.Lillee c Lloyd b Croft	12	c and b Roberts	0
G.Dymock c Kallicharran b Croft	7	c Lloyd b Garner	17
R.M.Hogg c Greenidge b Croft	14	c Holding b Garner	11
J.D.Higgs not out	0	not out	0
Extras (B 9, LB 4, NB 2, W 2)	17	(B 2, LB 10, NB 5)	17
	156		**259**

1/38 2/69 3/97 4/108 5/112   1/43 2/88 3/121 4/187 5/205
6/118 7/123 8/133 9/143   6/228 7/228 8/233 9/258

Bowling: *First Innings*—Roberts 14-1-39-0; Holding 14-3-40-4; Croft 13.3-4-27-3; Garner 15-7-33-3. *Second Innings*—Roberts 21-1-64-3; Holding 23-7-61-2; Croft 22-2-61-3; Garner 20.4-2-56-2.

West Indies

C.G.Greenidge c Higgs b Dymock	48	not out	9
D.L.Haynes c Hughes b Lillee	29	not out	9
I.V.A.Richards c Toohey b Dymock	96		
A.I.Kallicharran c Laird b Higgs	39		
L.G.Rowe b Lillee	26		
C.H.Lloyd* c Marsh b Dymock	40		
D.L.Murray† b Dymock	24		
A.M.E.Roberts lbw b Lillee	54		
J.Garner c Dymock b Higgs	29		
M.A.Holding not out	1		
C.E.H.Croft lbw b Higgs	0		
Extras (LB 4, NB 7)	11	(LB 4)	4
	397	(0 wkts)	**22**

1/46 2/156 3/215 4/226 5/250   6/305 7/320 8/390 9/396

Bowling: *First Innings*—Lillee 36-7-96-3; Hogg 6-0-59-0; Dymock 31-2-106-4; Higgs 34.4-4-122-3; Chappell 5-2-3-0. *Second Innings*—Lillee 3-0-9-0; Dymock 3-0-5-0; Hughes 1-1-0-0; Toohey 0.2-0-4-0.

Umpires: A.R.Crafter and C.E.Harvey

AUSTRALIA v ENGLAND 1979-80 (Second Test)

At Sydney Cricket Ground, 4, 5, 6, 8, 9 January
Result: Australia won by 6 wickets

England

Batsman	1st innings	R	2nd innings	R
G.A.Gooch	b Lillee	18	c G.S.Chappell b Dymock	4
G.Boycott	b Dymock	8	c McCosker b Pascoe	18
D.W.Randall	c G.S.Chappell b Lillee	0	(6) c Marsh b G.S.Chappell	25
P.Willey	c Wiener b Dymock	8	(3) b Pascoe	3
J.M.Brearley*	c Pascoe b Dymock	7	(4) c Marsh b Pascoe	19
D.I.Gower	b Chappell	3	(7) not out	98
I.T.Botham	c G.S.Chappell b Pascoe	27	(8) c Wiener b G.S.Chappell	0
R.W.Taylor†	c Marsh b Lillee	10	(9) b Lillee	8
G.R.Dilley	not out	22	(10) b Dymock	4
R.G.D.Willis	c Wiener b Dymock	4	(11) c G.S.Chappell b Lillee	1
D.L.Underwood	c Border b Lillee	12	(5) c Border b Dymock	43
Extras	(NB 5)	5	(B 1, LB 10, NB 2, W 1)	14
Total		**123**		**237**

1/10 2/13 3/31 4/38 5/41 6/74 7/75 8/90 9/98
1/6 2/21 3/29 4/77 5/105 6/156 7/174 8/211 9/218

Bowling: *First Innings*—Lillee 13.3-4-40-4; Dymock 17-6-42-4; Pascoe 9-4-14-1; G.S.Chappell 4-1-19-1; Higgs 1-0-3-0. *Second Innings*—Lillee 24.3-4-63-2; Dymock 28-8-48-3; Pascoe 23-3-76-3; G.S.Chappell 21-10-36-2.

Australia

Batsman	1st innings	R	2nd innings	R
R.B.McCosker	c Gower b Willis	1	c Taylor b Underwood	41
J.M.Wiener	run out	22	b Underwood	13
I.M.Chappell	c Brearley b Gooch	42	c Botham b Underwood	9
G.S.Chappell*	c Taylor b Underwood	3	not out	98
K.J.Hughes	c Taylor b Botham	18	c Dilley b Willis	47
A.R.Border	c Gooch b Botham	15	not out	2
R.W.Marsh†	c Underwood b Gooch	7		
D.K.Lillee	c Brearley b Botham	5		
G.Dymock	c Taylor b Botham	4		
L.S.Pascoe	not out	10		
J.D.Higgs	b Underwood	2		
Extras	(B 2, LB 12, W 2)	16	(LB 8, W 1)	9
Total		**145**	(4 wkts)	**219**

1/18 2/52 3/71 4/92 5/100 6/114 7/121 8/129 9/132
1/31 2/51 3/98 4/203

Bowling: *First Innings*—Botham 17-7-29-4; Willis 11-3-30-1; Underwood 13.2-3-39-2; Dilley 5-1-13-0; Willey 1-0-2-0; Gooch 11-4-16-2. *Second Innings*—Botham 23.3-12-43-0; Willis 12-2-26-1; Underwood 26-6-71-3; Dilley 12-0-33-0; Willey 4-0-17-0; Gooch 8-2-20-0.

Umpires: R.C.Bailhache and W.J.Copeland

AUSTRALIA v WEST INDIES 1979-80 (Third Test)

At Adelaide Oval, 26, 27, 28, 29, 30 January
Result: West Indies won by 408 runs

West Indies

Batsman	1st innings	R	2nd innings	R
C.G.Greenidge	lbw b Lillee	6	st Marsh b Mallett	76
D.L.Haynes	c Lillee b Mallett	28	c Marsh b Pascoe	27
I.V.A.Richards	c Marsh b Lillee	76	b Border	74
A.I.Kallicharran	c I.M.Chappell b Mallett	9	b Mallett	106
L.G.Rowe	c Lillee b Dymock	40	c Marsh b Dymock	43
C.H.Lloyd*	lbw b Lillee	121	(7) c Marsh b Dymock	40
D.L.Murray†	c Marsh b Dymock	9	(8) c G.S.Chappell b Dymock	28
A.M.E.Roberts	b Lillee	9	(9) c G.S.Chappell b Dymock	8
J.Garner	c Hughes b Lillee	16	(10) c Laird b Dymock	1
M.A.Holding	b Pascoe	9	(11) not out	1
C.E.H.Croft	not out	1	(6) c Border b Pascoe	12
Extras	(B 2, NB 7)	9	(B 1, LB 10, NB 21)	32
Total		**328**		**448**

1/11 2/115 3/115 4/126 5/239 6/252 7/300 8/303 9/326
1/48 2/184 3/213 4/299 5/331 6/398 7/417 8/443 9/446

Bowling: *First Innings*—Lillee 24-3-78-5; Dymock 25-7-74-2; Pascoe 15.3-1-90-1; Mallett 27-5-77-2. *Second Innings*—Lillee 26-6-75-0; Dymock 33.5-7-104-5; Pascoe 25-3-93-2; Mallett 38-7-134-2; Border 4-2-10-1.

Australia

Batsman	1st innings	R	2nd innings	R
J.M.Wiener	c Haynes b Holding	3	c Murray b Roberts	8
B.M.Laird	c Garner b Croft	52	lbw b Garner	36
I.M.Chappell	c Greenidge b Roberts	0	c Murray b Holding	4
G.S.Chappell*	c Garner b Roberts	34	lbw b Croft	31
K.J.Hughes	c Lloyd b Croft	54	lbw b Garner	11
A.R.Border	b Roberts	5	c Greenidge b Roberts	24
R.W.Marsh†	c Murray b Croft	16	not out	23
D.K.Lillee	c Haynes b Holding	10	c Kallicharran b Croft	0
G.Dymock	c Rowe b Croft	0	c Richards b Holding	2
A.A.Mallett	c Rowe b Garner	5	b Holding	12
L.S.Pascoe	not out	5	b Holding	5
Extras	(B 1, LB 14, NB 7)	22	(LB 2, NB 5, W 2)	9
Total		**203**		**165**

1/23 2/26 3/26 4/83 5/110 6/127 7/165 8/188 9/189
1/12 2/21 3/71 4/83 5/98 6/130 7/131 8/135 9/159

Bowling: *First Innings*—Roberts 16.5-5-43-3; Holding 15-5-31-2; Garner 18-4-43-1; Croft 22-4-57-4. *Second Innings*—Roberts 15-5-30-2; Holding 13-2-40-4; Garner 11-3-39-2; Croft 11-1-47-2.

Umpires: M.W.Johnson and M.G.O'Connell

AUSTRALIA v ENGLAND 1979-80 (Third Test)

At Melbourne Cricket Ground, 1, 2, 3, 5, 6 February

Result: Australia won by 8 wickets

England

G.A.Gooch	run out	99	b Mallett	51
G.Boycott	c Mallett b Dymock	44	b Lillee	7
W.Larkins	c G.S.Chappell b Pascoe	25	lbw b Pascoe	3
D.I.Gower	lbw b Lillee	0	b Pascoe	11
P.Willey	lbw b Pascoe	1	c Marsh b Lillee	2
I.T.Botham	c Marsh b Lillee	8	not out	119
J.M.Brearley*	not out	60	(7) c Border b Pascoe	10
R.W.Taylor†	b Lillee	23	(6) c Border b Lillee	32
D.L.Underwood	c I.M.Chappell b Lillee	3	b Pascoe	0
J.K.Lever	b Lillee	22	c Marsh b Lillee	12
R.G.D.Willis	c G.S.Chappell b Lillee	4	c G.S.Chappell b Pascoe	2
Extras	(B 1, LB 2, NB 14)	17	(B 2, LB 12, NB 10)	24
		306		**273**

1/116 2/170 3/175 4/177 5/177
6/192 7/238 8/242 9/298

1/25 2/46 3/64 4/67 5/88
6/92 7/178 8/179 9/268

Bowling: *First Innings*—Lillee 33.1-9-60-6; Dymock 28-6-54-1; Mallett 33-9-104-0; Pascoe 32-7-71-2. *Second Innings*—Lillee 33-6-78-5; Dymock 11-2-30-0; Mallett 14-1-45-1; Pascoe 29.5-3-80-4; Border 4-0-16-0.

Australia

R.B.McCosker	c Botham b Underwood	33	lbw b Botham	33
B.M.Laird	c Gower b Underwood	74	c Boycott b Underwood	25
I.M.Chappell	c and b Underwood	75	not out	26
K.J.Hughes	c Underwood b Botham	15		
A.R.Border	c and b Lever	63		
G.S.Chappell*	c Larkins b Lever	114	(4) not out	40
R.W.Marsh†	c Botham b Lever	17		
D.K.Lillee	c Willey b Lever	8		
G.Dymock	b Botham	19		
A.A.Mallett	lbw b Botham	25		
L.S.Pascoe	not out	1		
Extras	(B 13, LB 12, NB 7, W 1)	33	(LB 8, NB 2)	10
		477	**(2 wkts)**	**103**

1/52 2/179 3/196 4/219 5/345
6/411 7/421 8/432 9/465

1/20 2/42

Bowling: *First Innings*—Lever 53-15-111-4; Botham 39.5-15-105-3; Willis 21-4-61-0; Underwood 53-19-131-3; Willey 13-2-36-0. *Second Innings*—Lever 7.4-3-18-0; Botham 12-5-24-1; Willis 5-3-8-0; Underwood 14-2-49-1.

Umpires: R.C.Bailhache and P.M.Cronin

PAKISTAN v AUSTRALIA 1979-80 (First Test)

At National Stadium, Karachi, 27, 28, 29 February, 2 March

Result: Pakistan won by 7 wickets

Australia

B.M.Laird	lbw b Imran Khan	6	c Javed Miandad b Iqbal Qasim	23
G.N.Yallop	c Taslim Arif b Tauseef Ahmed	12	c Majid Khan b Iqbal Qasim	16
K.J.Hughes	c Majid Khan b Tauseef Ahmed	85	st Taslim Arif b Tauseef Ahmed	8
G.S.Chappell*	st Taslim Arif b Iqbal Qasim	20	c Taslim Arif b Tauseef Ahmed	13
D.W.Hookes	c Majid Khan b Iqbal Qasim	0	lbw b Iqbal Qasim	0
A.R.Border	lbw b Iqbal Qasim	30	not out	58
R.W.Marsh†	c Haroon Rashid b Tauseef Ahmed	13	c Mudassar Nazar b Iqbal Qasim	1
G.R.Beard	b Imran Khan	9	b Iqbal Qasim	4
R.J.Bright	c Majid Khan b Iqbal Qasim	15	c Majid Khan b Iqbal Qasim	5
D.K.Lillee	not out	12	lbw b Iqbal Qasim	0
G.Dymock	c Wasim Raja b Tauseef Ahmed	3	b Tauseef Ahmed	0
Extras	(B 8, LB 9, NB 3)	20	(B 4, LB 5, NB 2, W 1)	12
		225		**140**

1/8 2/39 3/93 4/93 5/161
6/177 7/181 8/199 9/216

1/38 2/51 3/55 4/59 5/89
6/90 7/106 8/108 9/139

Bowling: *First Innings*—Imran Khan 16-4-28-2; Sarfraz Nawaz 13-4-20-0; Mudassar Nazar 2-0-6-0; Iqbal Qasim 30-12-69-4; Tauseef Ahmed 30.2-9-64-4; Majid Khan 2-0-13-0; Wasim Raja 2-0-5-0. *Second Innings*—Sarfraz Nawaz 7-2-7-0; Mudassar Nazar 2-0-4-0; Iqbal Qasim 42-22-49-7; Tauseef Ahmed 34-11-62-3; Majid Khan 1-1-0-0; Wasim Raja 4-1-6-0.

Pakistan

Taslim Arif	c Marsh b Bright	58	b Bright	8
Haroon Rashid	b Bright	6	b Bright	10
Zaheer Abbas	c Lillee b Bright	8	not out	18
Javed Miandad*	c Border b Chappell	40	b Bright	21
Wasim Raja	c sub (G.F.Lawson) b Chappell	0		
Majid Khan	c Border b Bright	89		
Mudassar Nazar	c Border b Bright	29		
Imran Khan	c Border b Chappell	9		
Sarfraz Nawaz	c Chappell b Bright	17		
Iqbal Qasim	not out	14		
Tauseef Ahmed	b Bright	0		
Extras	(LB 12, NB 10)	22	(LB 3, NB 4)	7
		292	**(3 wkts)**	**64**

1/34 2/44 3/120 4/121 5/134
6/210 7/238 8/266 9/292

1/17 2/26 3/60

Bowling: *First Innings*—Lillee 28-4-76-0; Dymock 5-2-5-0; Bright 46.5-17-87-7; Beard 17-8-39-0; Chappell 20-3-49-3; Yallop 2-0-14-0. *Second Innings*—Lillee 11-2-22-0; Dymock 2-0-9-0; Bright 11-5-24-3; Beard 1.1-0-14-0.

Umpires: Mahboob Shah and Shakoor Rana

PAKISTAN v AUSTRALIA 1979-80 (Second Test)

At Iqbal Stadium, Faisalabad 6 (no play), 7, 8, 10, 11 March
Result: Match drawn

Australia

J.M.Wiener b Ehteshamuddin	5
B.M.Laird c Taslim Arif b Sarfraz Nawaz	0
K.J.Hughes c Ehteshamuddin b Tauseef Ahmed	88
G.S.Chappell* lbw b Sarfraz Nawaz	235
G.N.Yallop b Wasim Raja	172
A.R.Border run out	4
R.W.Marsh† lbw b Tauseef Ahmed	71
G.R.Beard c Sarfraz Nawaz b Tauseef Ahmed	13
R.J.Bright b Wasim Raja	5
D.K.Lillee lbw b Wasim Raja	0
G.Dymock not out	0
Extras (B 11, LB 10, NB 3)	24
	617

1/1 2/21 3/200 4/417 5/434 6/561 7/585 8/592 9/612

Bowling: Sarfraz Nawaz 49-13-119-2; Ehteshamuddin 18-2-59-1; Iqbal Qasim 56-11-156-0; Tauseef Ahmed 33-3-77-3; Wasim Raja 30-6-100-3; Majid Khan 22-2-66-0; Javed Miandad 3-0-16-0.

Pakistan

Taslim Arif† not out	210
Haroon Rashid lbw b Dymock	21
Zaheer Abbas run out	19
Javed Miandad* not out	106
Wasim Raja	
Majid Khan	
Mudassar Nazar	
Sarfraz Nawaz	
Iqbal Qasim	
Ehteshamuddin	
Tauseef Ahmed	
Extras (B 7, LB 4, NB 15)	26
	(2 wkts) 382

1/87 2/159

Bowling: Lillee 21-4-91-0; Dymock 20-5-49-1; Bright 33-9-71-0; Border 3-2-3-0; Beard 15-4-30-0; Hughes 8-1-19-0; Laird 2-1-3-0; Chappell 6-3-5-0; Wiener 5-1-19-0 Marsh 10-1-51-0; Yallop 3-0-15-0.

Umpires: Javed Akhtar and Khalid Aziz

PAKISTAN v AUSTRALIA 1979-80 (Third Test)

At Gaddafi Stadium, Lahore 18, 19, 21, 22, 23 March
Result: Match drawn

Australia

J.M.Wiener b Iqbal Qasim	93	c Mudassar Nazar b Imran Khan	4
B.M.Laird b Tauseef Ahmed	17	c Taslim Arif b Tauseef Ahmed	63
K.J.Hughes b Iqbal Qasim	1	c Iqbal Qasim b Imran Khan	0
G.S.Chappell* lbw b Imran Khan	56	b Iqbal Qasim	57
G.N.Yallop lbw b Iqbal Qasim	3	c and b Wasim Raja	34
A.R.Border not out	150	st Javed Miandad b Azhar Khan	153
R.W.Marsh† lbw b Iqbal Qasim	8	run out	13
G.R.Beard lbw b Imran Khan	39	c sub (Sultan Rana) b Taslim Arif	49
R.J.Bright not out	26	not out	10
D.K.Lillee		not out	1
G.Dymock			
Extras (B 4, LB 6, NB 4)	14	(LB 4, NB 3)	7
(7 wkts dec.)	407	(8 wkts)	391

1/50 2/53 3/136 4/153 5/204 6/218 7/298

1/4 2/7 3/115 4/149 5/192 6/223 7/357 8/390

Bowling: *First Innings*—Imran Khan 28-7-86-2; Sarfraz Nawaz 28-6-67-0; Mudassar Nazar 6-1-16-0; Iqbal Qasim 39-10-90-4; Tauseef Ahmed 21-3-81-1; Wasim Raja 14-3-45-0; Azhar Khan 2-1-1-0; Javed Miandad 2-0-5-0; Majid Khan 2-0-2-0. *Second Innings*—Imran Khan 12-3-30-2; Sarfraz Nawaz 14-5-42-0; Mudassar Nazar 2-0-20-0; Iqbal Qasim 34-8-111-1; Tauseef Ahmed 26-3-72-1; Wasim Raja 9-1-42-1; Azhar Khan 1-0-1-1; Javed Miandad 4-0-14-0; Majid Khan 9-3-24-0; Taslim Arif 5-0-28-1.

Pakistan

Mudassar Nazar c Yallop b Lillee	59
Taslim Arif† c Marsh b Bright	31
Iqbal Qasim c Marsh b Lillee	5
Azmat Rana c Chappell b Beard	49
Javed Miandad* c Marsh b Bright	14
Wasim Raja c Border b Lillee	55
Majid Khan not out	110
Azhar Khan b Bright	14
Imran Khan c Chappell b Bright	56
Sarfraz Nawaz st Marsh b Bright	5
Tauseef Ahmed	
Extras (LB 4, NB 17, W 1)	22
	(9 wkts dec.) 420

1/37 2/53 3/133 4/161 5/177 6/270 7/299 8/410 9/420

Bowling: Lillee 42-9-114-3; Dymock 24-6-66-0; Bright 56-14-172-5; Beard 10-5-26-1; Chappell 8-3-20-0.

Umpires: Amanullah Khan and Khizer Hayat

ENGLAND v AUSTRALIA 1980 (Centenary Test)

At Lord's, London, 28, 29, 30 August, 1, 2 September

Result: Match drawn

Australia

G.M.Wood st Bairstow b Emburey	112	lbw b Old	8
B.M.Laird c Bairstow b Old	24	c Bairstow b Old	6
G.S.Chappell* c Gatting b Old	47	b Old	59
K.J.Hughes c Athey b Old	117	lbw b Botham	84
G.N.Yallop lbw b Hendrick	2		
A.R.Border not out	56	(5) not out	21
R.W.Marsh† not out	16		
R.J.Bright			
D.K.Lillee			
A.A.Mallett			
L.S.Pascoe			
Extras (B 1, LB 8, NB 2)	11	(B 1, LB 8, NB 2)	11
1/64 2/150 3/260 4/267 5/320 (5 wkts dec.)	385	1/15 2/28 3/139 (4 wkts dec.)	189
		4/189	

Bowling: *First Innings*—Old 35-9-91-3; Hendrick 30-6-67-1; Botham 22-2-89-0; Embury 38-9-104-1; Gooch 8-3-16-0; Willey 1-0-7-0. *Second Innings*—Old 20-6-47-3; Hendrick 15-4-53-0; Emburey 9-2-35-0; Botham 9.2-1-43-1.

England

G.A.Gooch c Bright b Lillee	8	lbw b Lillee	16
G.Boycott c Marsh b Lillee	62	not out	128
C.W.J.Athey c Lillee	9	c Laird b Pascoe	1
D.I.Gower b Lillee	45	b Mallett	35
M.W.Gatting lbw b Pascoe	12	not out	51
I.T.Botham c Wood b Pascoe	0		
P.Willey lbw b Pascoe	5		
D.L.Bairstow lbw b Pascoe	6		
J.E.Emburey lbw b Pascoe	3		
C.M.Old not out	24		
M.Hendrick c Border b Mallett	5		
Extras (B 6, LB 8, NB 12)	26	(B 3, LB 2, NB 8)	13
1/10 2/41 3/137 4/151 5/158	205	1/19 2/43 3/124 (3 wkts)	244
6/163 7/164 8/173 9/200			

Bowling: *First Innings*—Lillee 15-4-43-4; Pascoe 18-5-59-5; Chappell 2-0-2-0; Bright 21-6-50-0; Mallett 7.2-3-25-1. *Second Innings*—Lillee 19-5-53-1; Pascoe 17-1-73-1; Bright 25-9-44-0; Mallett 21-2-61-1.

Umpires: H.D.Bird and D.J.Constant

AUSTRALIA v NEW ZEALAND 1980-81 (First Test)

At Woolloongabba, Brisbane, 28, 29, 30 November

Result: Australia won by 10 wickets

New Zealand

J.G.Wright c Marsh b Pascoe	29	c Walters b Lillee	1
B.A.Edgar c Marsh b Lawson	20	c Hughes b Lillee	51
P.E.McEwan c Border b Lillee	6	c Hughes b Lillee	0
G.P.Howarth* c and b Higgs	65	c Wood b Lillee	4
J.M.Parker b Pascoe	52	c Dyson b Lawson	4
M.G.Burgess c Chappell b Pascoe	0	c Wood b Lillee	2
I.D.S.Smith† c Hughes b Lillee	7	c Hughes b Pascoe	7
R.J.Hadlee c Marsh b Higgs	10	(9) not out	51
B.L.Cairns c Border b Higgs	0	(10) c Border b Lillee	0
J.G.Bracewell not out	6	(8) c Border b Lawson	0
B.P.Bracewell b Higgs	0	b Pascoe	8
Extras (LB 18, NB 7, W 5)	30	(B 4, LB 4, NB 5, W 1)	14
1/64 2/71 3/76 4/193 5/193	225	1/6 2/9 3/14 4/30 5/34	142
6/209 7/209 8/210 9/221		6/58 7/61 8/114 9/114	

Bowling: *First Innings*—Lillee 18-7-36-2; Pascoe 19-4-41-3; Lawson 12-2-39-1; Chappell 4-1-18-0; Higgs 16.1-3-59-4; Walters 1-0-2-0. *Second Innings*—Lillee 15-1-53-6; Pascoe 13.1-2-30-2; Lawson 8-0-26-2; Higgs 5-1-19-0.

Australia

G.M.Wood c Parker b J.G.Bracewell	111	not out	32
J.Dyson lbw b Cairns	30	not out	24
G.S.Chappell* c McEwan b Cairns	35		
K.J.Hughes c Wright b Hadlee	9		
A.R.Border run out	36		
K.D.Walters b Cairns	17		
R.W.Marsh† b Hadlee	8		
D.K.Lillee c Parker b Cairns	24		
G.F.Lawson c sub (S.L.Boock) b Hadlee	16		
L.S.Pascoe b Cairns	5		
J.D.Higgs not out	1		
Extras (B 1, LB 7, NB 5)	13	(B 2, LB 2, NB 3)	7
1/80 2/145 3/160 4/225 5/235	305	(0 wkts)	63
6/250 7/258 8/299 9/299			

Bowling: *First Innings*—Hadlee 37-8-83-3; B.P.Bracewell 22-8-71-0; Cairns 38.5-11-87-5; J.G.Bracewell 18-5-51-1. *Second Innings*—Hadlee 6-0-28-0; B.P.Bracewell 3-3-0-0; Cairns 7.3-3-16-0; J.G.Bracewell 5-0-12-0.

Umpires: R.C.Bailhache and M.W.Johnson

AUSTRALIA v NEW ZEALAND 1980-81 (Second Test)

At W.A.C.A. Ground, Perth, 12, 13, 14 December

Result: Australia won by 8 wickets

New Zealand

Batsman	1st		2nd
J.G.Wright b Pascoe	10	(2) c Marsh b Hogg	3
B.A.Edgar c Border b Lillee	0	(1) c Hughes b Pascoe	0
J.M.Parker c Chappell b Hogg	3	(4) c Hughes b Hogg	18
P.E.McEwan c Marsh b Lillee	8	(5) c Marsh b Lillee	16
J.V.Coney b Hogg	71	(6) c Marsh b Higgs	0
M.G.Burgess* c Hughes b Lillee	43	(7) lbw b Higgs	18
W.K.Lees† c Marsh b Pascoe	5	(8) not out	25
R.J.Hadlee c Hughes b Pascoe	23	(9) c Chappell b Higgs	0
J.G.Bracewell lbw b Lillee	6	(3) run out	16
B.L.Cairns c Pascoe b Lillee	13	c Border b Higgs	6
G.B.Troup not out	0	c Marsh b Lillee	6
Extras (LB 3, NB 9, W 2)	14	(LB 12, NB 5, W 2)	19
	196		121

1/6 2/13 3/24 4/28 5/116   1/0 2/27 3/38 4/63 5/64
6/133 7/171 8/177 9/196   6/73 7/115 8/115 9/121

Bowling: *First Innings*—Lillee 23.5-5-63-5; Hogg 16-5-29-2; Pascoe 20-3-61-3; Chappell 7-3-5-0; Higgs 5-1-13-0; Walters 2-0-11-0. *Second Innings*—Lillee 15.1-7-14-2; Hogg 10-2-25-2; Pascoe 10-1-30-1; Chappell 3-1-7-0; Higgs 8-2-25-4; Walters 2-1-1-0.

Australia

Batsman	1st		2nd
G.M.Wood c Bracewell b Hadlee	0	(2) c Lees b Hadlee	0
J.Dyson c Bracewell b Cairns	28	(1) not out	25
G.S.Chappell* c Cairns b Troup	12	c Lees b Hadlee	13
K.J.Hughes c Lees b Hadlee	3	not out	16
A.R.Border b Cairns	10		
K.D.Walters c Coney b Hadlee	55		
R.W.Marsh† c Coney b Hadlee	91		
D.K.Lillee c and b Hadlee	8		
R.M.Hogg b Cairns	3		
L.S.Pascoe not out	30		
J.D.Higgs c Coney b Cairns	7		
Extras (B 3, LB 4, NB 10, W 1)	18	(LB 1)	1
	265		(2 wkts) 55

1/0 2/22 3/25 4/50 5/68   1/3 2/31
6/156 7/176 8/187 9/244

Bowling: *First Innings*—Hadlee 27-8-87-5; Troup 22-5-57-1; Cairns 28.1-7-88-4; Bracewell 4-1-15-0. *Second Innings*—Hadlee 11.1-4-20-2; Troup 1-0-1-0; Cairns 5-2-17-0; Bracewell 5-0-16-0.

Umpires: A.R.Crafter and D.G.Weser

AUSTRALIA v NEW ZEALAND 1980-81 (Third Test)

At Melbourne Cricket Ground, 26, 27, 28, 29, 30 December

Result: Match drawn

Australia

Batsman	1st		2nd
G.M.Wood c Lees b Hadlee	0	(2) c Lees b Hadlee	21
J.Dyson b Troup	13	(1) lbw b Cairns	16
G.S.Chappell* c Coney b Hadlee	42	b Hadlee	78
K.J.Hughes c Parker b Hadlee	51	b Hadlee	30
A.R.Border c Cairns b Coney	45	c Lees b Hadlee	9
K.D.Walters b Coney	107	run out	2
R.W.Marsh† c Parker b Coney	1	lbw b Cairns	0
D.K.Lillee b Cairns	27	c Coney b Bracewell	8
R.M.Hogg run out	0	b Hadlee	12
L.S.Pascoe b Cairns	0	not out	0
J.D.Higgs not out	6	b Hadlee	0
Extras (B 7, LB 13, NB 6, W 3)	29	(B 6, LB 4, NB 2)	12
	321		188

1/0 2/32 3/75 4/159 5/190   1/25 3/64 4/111 5/131
6/192 7/261 8/261 9/261   6/131 7/149 8/185 9/188

Bowling: *First Innings*—Hadlee 39-8-89-3; Troup 26-5-54-1; Cairns 35-6-83-2; Bracewell 9-0-38-0; Coney 12.3-6-28-3. *Second Innings*—Hadlee 27.2-7-57-6; Troup 11-3-31-0; Cairns 33-13-65-2; Bracewell 15-5-22-1; Coney 1-0-1-0.

New Zealand

Batsman	1st		2nd
J.G.Wright c Chappell b Higgs	44	c Wood b Hogg	4
B.A.Edgar lbw b Higgs	25	run out	21
G.P.Howarth* b Hogg	65	lbw b Chappell	20
J.M.Parker c Marsh b Pascoe	56	lbw b Chappell	1
M.G.Burgess lbw b Pascoe	49	(6) not out	10
J.V.Coney not out	55	(5) lbw b Hogg	3
J.G.Bracewell c Chappell b Pascoe	0		
W.K.Lees† lbw b Hogg	4	(7) b Lillee	7
R.J.Hadlee c Border b Hogg	9	(8) not out	5
B.L.Cairns lbw b Higgs	18		
G.B.Troup c Hughes b Hogg	1		
Extras (B 13, LB 12, NB 10)	35	(B 2, LB 8, NB 2, W 1)	13
	317		(6 wkts) 128

1/27 2/32 3/157 4/163 5/247   1/50 2/96 3/97 4/101 5/101 6/121
6/247 7/264 8/280 9/316

Bowling: *First Innings*—Lillee 21-4-49-0; Hogg 26.2-9-60-4; Higgs 29-6-87-3; Pascoe 26-6-75-3; Border 4-1-6-0; Chappell 2-0-5-0. *Second Innings*—Lillee 13-3-30-1; Hogg 8-1-14-2; Higgs 12-4-24-0; Pascoe 11-1-35-0; Border 2-1-5-0; Chappell 7-4-7-2; Hughes 1-1-0-0.

Umpires: R.C.Bailhache and A.R.Crafter

AUSTRALIA v INDIA 1980-81 (First Test)

At Sydney Cricket Ground, 2, 3, 4 January

Result: Australia won by an innings and 4 runs

India

S.M.Gavaskar* c Marsh b Lillee	0	(2)	c Marsh b Hogg		10
C.P.S.Chauhan c Border b Pascoe	20	(1)	c Walters b Pascoe		36
D.B.Vengsarkar c Marsh b Lillee	22		c Marsh b Pascoe		34
G.R.Viswanath b Hogg	26		st Marsh b Higgs		24
Yashpal Sharma c Marsh b Pascoe	6		c Walters b Lillee		4
S.M.Patil retired hurt	65		c Wood b Lillee		4
Kapil Dev c Marsh b Pascoe	22	(8)	c sub (S.F.Graf) b Higgs		19
S.M.H.Kirmani† c Walters b Lillee	27	(7)	not out		43
R.M.H.Binny c Marsh b Pascoe	3		lbw b Lillee		0
K.D.Ghavri c Wood b Lillee	7		c Hogg b Higgs		21
D.R.Doshi not out	0		c Lillee b Higgs		0
Extras (LB 1, NB 2)	3		(B 2, LB 3, W 1)		6
	201				**201**

1/0 2/36 3/62 4/70 5/78   1/21 2/74 3/92 4/110 5/120
6/145 7/183 8/186 9/201   6/126 7/144 8/144 9/201

Bowling: *First Innings*—Lillee 20.2-3-86-4; Hogg 14-1-51-1; Pascoe 19-6-61-4. *Second Innings*—Lillee 18-2-79-3; Hogg 9-1-24-1; Pascoe 11-2-35-2; Higgs 18-8-45-4; Walters 6-3-12-0.

Australia

G.M.Wood c Kirmani b Kapil Dev	9
J.Dyson c Gavaskar b Kapil Dev	0
G.S.Chappell* c Kapil Dev b Ghavri	204
K.J.Hughes c Kirmani b Kapil Dev	24
A.R.Border c Kirmani b Kapil Dev	31
K.D.Walters c Viswanath b Ghavri	67
R.W.Marsh† c Binny b Ghavri	12
D.K.Lillee c Doshi b Ghavri	5
R.M.Hogg not out	26
L.S.Pascoe c Doshi b Ghavri	7
J.D.Higgs b Kapil Dev	19
Extras (B 4, LB 3, NB 9, W 3)	19
	406

1/3 2/14 3/95 4/169 5/341
6/355 7/363 8/366 9/376

Bowling: Kapil Dev 36.1-7-97-5; Ghavri 30-7-107-5; Binny 15-1-70-0; Doshi 27-0-103-0; Chauhan 1-0-10-0.

Umpires: M.W.Johnson and R.V.Whitehead

AUSTRALIA v INDIA 1980-81 (Second Test)

At Adelaide Oval, 23, 24, 25, 26, 27 January

Result: Match drawn

Australia

J.Dyson c Gavaskar b Kapil Dev	28	(2)	lbw b Ghavri		28
G.M.Wood c Doshi b Yadav	125	(1)	c Patil b Doshi		3
G.S.Chappell* c Chauhan b Doshi	36		st Kirmani b Doshi		52
K.J.Hughes c Yashpal Sharma b Yadav	213		b Kapil Dev		53
A.R.Border c Gavaskar b Kapil Dev	57		b Doshi		7
K.D.Walters c Viswanath b Yadav	20		not out		33
R.W.Marsh† run out	0		c Kirmani b Yadav		23
B.Yardley c Viswanath b Doshi	12		c Vengsarkar b Yadav		2
D.K.Lillee c Kapil Dev b Doshi	2		not out		10
R.M.Hogg c and b Yadav	11				
L.S.Pascoe not out	1				
Extras (LB 13, NB 7, W 1)	21		(B 2, LB 5, NB 3)		10
	528			(7 wkts dec.)	**221**

1/84 2/152 3/234 4/363 5/393   1/5 2/74 3/118
6/399 7/435 8/461 9/505   4/138 5/165 6/204 7/208

Bowling: *First Innings*—Kapil Dev 32-5-112-2; Ghavri 27-4-106-0; Doshi 48-6-146-3; Yadav 42.4-6-143-4. *Second Innings*—Kapil Dev 17-3-55-1; Ghavri 11-2-37-1; Doshi 33-11-49-3; Yadav 29-6-70-2.

India

S.M.Gavaskar* b Pascoe	23		c Chappell b Pascoe		5
C.P.S.Chauhan c Marsh b Lillee	97		c Marsh b Pascoe		11
N.S.Yadav c Chappell b Yardley	16	(10)	not out		0
G.R.Viswanath lbw b Hogg	3		b Pascoe		16
D.B.Vengsarkar lbw b Lillee	2	(3)	c Chappell b Border		37
S.M.Patil lbw b Hogg	174	(5)	lbw b Lillee		9
Yashpal Sharma c Marsh b Lillee	47	(6)	lbw b Yardley		13
Kapil Dev c Border b Lillee	2	(7)	c Marsh b Lillee		7
S.M.H.Kirmani† b Pascoe	6	(8)	c Marsh b Chappell		14
K.D.Ghavri c Wood b Yardley	3	(9)	not out		7
D.R.Doshi not out	6				
Extras (B 11, LB 10, NB 17, W 2)	40		(B 7, LB 1, NB 8)		16
	419			(8 wkts)	**135**

1/77 2/112 3/115 4/130 5/238   1/13 2/16 3/44 4/57
6/385 7/393 8/399 9/409   5/90 6/103 7/126 8/128

Bowling: *First Innings*—Lillee 34-10-80-4; Hogg 28-6-100-2; Yardley 44.4-16-90-2; Pascoe 17-2-62-2; Chappell 6-2-14-0; Walters 3-0-21-0; Border 4-1-11-0; Hughes 1-0-1-0. *Second Innings*—Lillee 19-7-38-2; Hogg 3-0-11-0; Pascoe 11-2-32-3; Yardley 24-13-25-1; Chappell 9-6-4-1; Border 9-5-9-1.

Umpires: A.R.Crafter and R.V.Whitehead

AUSTRALIA v INDIA 1980-81 (Third Test)

At Melbourne Cricket Ground, 7, 8, 9, 10, 11 February
Result: India won by 59 runs

India

Batsman	First Innings		Second Innings	
S.M.Gavaskar*	c Hughes b Pascoe	10	lbw b Lillee	70
C.P.S.Chauhan	c Yardley b Pascoe	0	c Yardley b Lillee	85
D.B.Vengsarkar	c Border b Lillee	12	c Marsh b Pascoe	41
G.R.Viswanath	c Chappell b Yardley	114	b Lillee	30
S.M.Patil	c Hughes b Lillee	23	c Chappell b Yardley	36
Yashpal Sharma	c Marsh b Lillee	4	b Pascoe	9
Kapil Dev	c Hughes b Pascoe	5	(8) b Yardley	0
S.M.H.Kirmani†	c Marsh b Lillee	25	(7) run out	9
K.D.Ghavri	run out	0	not out	11
N.S.Yadav	not out	20	absent hurt	—
D.R.Doshi	c Walters b Yardley	7	(10) b Lillee	7
Extras	(B 1, LB 8, NB 9, W 6)	24	(B 11, LB 8, NB 7)	26
Total		**237**		**324**

1/0 2/22 3/43 4/91 5/99 — 237
6/115 7/164 8/190 9/230
1/165 2/176 3/243 4/245 5/260 — 324
6/296 7/296 8/308 9/324

Bowling: First Innings—Lillee 25-6-65-4; Pascoe 22-11-29-3; Chappell 5-2-9-0; Yardley 13-3-45-2; Higgs 19-2-65-0. Second Innings—Lillee 32.1-5-104-4; Pascoe 29-4-80-2; Yardley 31-11-65-2; Higgs 15-3-41-0; Border 2-0-8-0.

Australia

Batsman	First Innings		Second Innings	
J.Dyson	c Kirmani b Kapil Dev	16	c Kirmani b Ghavri	3
G.M.Wood	c Doshi b Ghavri	10	st Kirmani b Doshi	10
G.S.Chappell*	c and b Ghavri	76	b Ghavri	0
K.J.Hughes	c Chauhan b Yadav	24	b Doshi	16
A.R.Border	b Yadav	124	c Kirmani b Kapil Dev	9
K.D.Walters	st Kirmani b Doshi	78	(6) not out	18
R.W.Marsh†	c sub (K.Azad) b Doshi	45	(7) b Kapil Dev	3
B.Yardley	lbw b Doshi	0	(8) b Kapil Dev	7
D.K.Lillee	c and b Patil	19	(5) b Kapil Dev	4
L.S.Pascoe	lbw b Patil	3	run out	6
J.D.Higgs	not out	1	lbw b Kapil Dev	0
Extras	(B 12, LB 6, NB 5)	23	(LB 5, NB 2)	7
Total		**419**		**83**

1/30 2/32 3/81 4/189 5/320 — 419
6/356 7/356 8/413 9/413
1/11 2/11 3/18 4/40 5/50 — 83
6/55 7/61 8/69 9/79

Bowling: First Innings—Kapil Dev 19-7-41-1; Doshi 52-14-109-3; Ghavri 39-4-110-2; Yadav 32-6-100-2; Chauhan 2-0-8-0; Patil 12.3-4-28-2. Second Innings—Kapil Dev 16.4-4-28-5; Doshi 22-9-33-2; Ghavri 8-4-10-2; Patil 2-0-5-0.

Umpires: M.W.Johnson and R.V.Whitehead

ENGLAND v AUSTRALIA 1981 (First Test)

At Trent Bridge, Nottingham, 18, 19, 20, 21 June
Result: Australia won by 4 wickets

England

Batsman	First Innings		Second Innings	
G.A.Gooch	c Wood b Lillee	10	c Yallop b Lillee	6
G.Boycott	c Border b Alderman	27	c Marsh b Alderman	4
R.A.Woolmer	c Wood b Lillee	0	c Marsh b Alderman	0
D.I.Gower	c Yallop b Lillee	26	c sub (M.F.Kent) b Lillee	28
M.W.Gatting	lbw b Hogg	52	lbw b Alderman	15
P.Willey	c Border b Alderman	10	lbw b Lillee	13
I.T.Botham*	b Alderman	1	c Border b Lillee	33
P.R.Downton†	c Yallop b Alderman	8	lbw b Alderman	13
G.R.Dilley	b Hogg	34	c Marsh b Alderman	13
R.G.D.Willis	c Marsh b Hogg	0	c Chappell b Lillee	1
M.Hendrick	not out	6	not out	9
Extras	(LB 6, NB 4, W 1)	11	(LB 8, NB 1)	9
Total		**185**		**125**

1/13 2/13 3/57 4/67 5/92 — 185
6/96 7/116 8/159 9/159
1/12 2/12 3/13 4/39 5/61 — 125
6/94 7/109 8/113 9/125

Bowling: First Innings—Lillee 13-3-34-3; Alderman 24-7-68-4; Hogg 11.4-1-47-3; Lawson 8-3-25-0. Second Innings—Lillee 16.4-2-46-5; Alderman 19-3-62-5; Hogg 3-1-8-0.

Australia

Batsman	First Innings		Second Innings	
G.M.Wood	lbw b Dilley	0	(2) c Woolmer b Willis	8
J.Dyson	c Woolmer b Willis	5	(1) c Downton b Dilley	38
G.N.Yallop	lbw b Hendrick	13	c Gatting b Botham	6
K.J.Hughes*	lbw b Willis	7	lbw b Dilley	22
T.M.Chappell	lbw b Hendrick	17	not out	20
A.R.Border	c and b Botham	63	b Dilley	20
R.W.Marsh†	c Boycott b Willis	19	lbw b Dilley	0
G.F.Lawson	c Gower b Botham	14	not out	5
D.K.Lillee	c Downton b Dilley	12		
R.M.Hogg	c Boycott b Dilley	0		
T.M.Alderman	not out	12		
Extras	(B 4, LB 8, NB 4, W 1)	17	(B 1, LB 6, NB 6)	13
Total		**179**	(6 wkts)	**132**

1/0 2/21 3/21 4/33 5/64 — 179
6/89 7/110 8/147 9/153
1/20 2/40 3/77 4/80 — (6 wkts) 132
5/122 6/122

Bowling: First Innings—Dilley 20-7-38-3; Willis 30-14-47-3; Hendrick 20-7-43-2; Botham 16.5-6-34-2. Second Innings—Dilley 11.1-4-24-4; Willis 13-2-28-1; Hendrick 20-7-33-0; Botham 10-1-34-1.

Umpires: W.E.Alley and D.J.Constant

ENGLAND v AUSTRALIA 1981 (Second Test)

At Lord's, London, 2, 3, 4, 6, 7 July
Result: Match drawn

England

G.A.Gooch	c Yallop b Lawson	44
G.Boycott	c Alderman b Lawson	17
R.A.Woolmer	c Marsh b Lawson	21
D.I.Gower	c Marsh b Lawson	27
M.W.Gatting	lbw b Bright	59
P.Willey	c Border b Alderman	82
J.E.Emburey	run out	31
I.T.Botham*	lbw b Lawson	0
R.W.Taylor†	c Hughes b Lawson	0
G.R.Dilley	not out	7
R.G.D.Willis	c Wood b Lawson	5
Extras	(B 2, LB 3, NB 10, W 3)	18
		311

Second innings: G.A.Gooch lbw b Lawson 20; G.Boycott c Marsh b Lillee 60; R.A.Woolmer lbw b Alderman 9; D.I.Gower c Alderman b Lillee 89; M.W.Gatting c Wood b Bright 16; P.Willey (7) c Chappell b Bright 12; I.T.Botham* (6) b Bright 0; R.W.Taylor† b Lillee 9; G.R.Dilley (8) not out 27; Extras (B 2, LB 8, NB 13) 23; (8 wkts dec.) 265

1/60 2/65 3/134 4/187 5/284 6/293 7/293 8/293 9/298 — 311
1/31 2/55 3/178 4/217 5/217 6/217 7/242 8/265

Bowling: First Innings—Lillee 35.4-7-102-0; Alderman 30.2-7-79-1; Lawson 43.1-14-81-7; Bright 15-7-31-1. *Second Innings*—Lillee 26.4-8-82-3; Alderman 17-2-42-1; Lawson 19-6-51-1; Bright 36-18-67-3.

Australia

G.M.Wood	c Taylor b Willis	44
J.Dyson	c Gower b Botham	7
G.N.Yallop	b Dilley	1
K.J.Hughes*	c Willis b Emburey	42
T.M.Chappell	c Taylor b Dilley	2
A.R.Border	c Gatting b Botham	64
R.W.Marsh†	lbw b Dilley	47
R.J.Bright	lbw b Emburey	33
G.F.Lawson	lbw b Willis	5
D.K.Lillee	not out	40
T.M.Alderman	c Taylor b Willis	5
Extras	(B 6, LB 11, NB 32, W 6)	55
		345

Second innings: G.M.Wood (2) not out 44; J.Dyson (1) lbw b Dilley 7; G.N.Yallop c Botham b Willis 1; K.J.Hughes* lbw b Dilley 3; T.M.Chappell c Taylor b Botham 4; A.R.Border not out 28; Extras (NB 2, W 1) 3; (4 wkts) 90

1/62 2/69 3/81 4/81 5/167 6/244 7/257 8/268 9/314 — 345
1/2 2/11 3/17 4/62

Bowling: First Innings—Willis 27.4-9-50-3; Dilley 30-8-106-3; Botham 26-8-71-2; Gooch 10-4-28-0; Emburey 25-12-35-2. *Second Innings*—Willis 12-3-35-1; Dilley 7.5-1-18-2; Botham 8-3-10-1.

Umpires: D.O.Oslear and K.E.Palmer

ENGLAND v AUSTRALIA 1981 (Third Test)

At Headingley, Leeds, 16, 17, 18, 20, 21 July
Result: England won by 18 runs

Australia

J.Dyson	b Dilley	102
G.M.Wood	lbw b Botham	34
T.M.Chappell	c Taylor b Willey	27
K.J.Hughes*	c and b Botham	89
R.J.Bright	b Dilley	7
G.N.Yallop	c Taylor b Botham	58
A.R.Border	lbw b Botham	8
R.W.Marsh	b Botham	28
G.F.Lawson	c Taylor b Botham	13
D.K.Lillee	not out	3
T.M.Alderman	not out	0
Extras	(B 4, LB 13, NB 12, W 3)	32
		(9 wkts dec.) 401

Second innings: J.Dyson (2) c Taylor b Willis 34; G.M.Wood (1) c Taylor b Botham 10; T.M.Chappell c Taylor b Willis 8; K.J.Hughes* c Botham b Willis 0; R.J.Bright (8) b Willis 19; G.N.Yallop (5) c Gatting b Willis 0; A.R.Border (6) b Old 0; R.W.Marsh (7) c Dilley b Willis 4; G.F.Lawson c Taylor b Willis 1; D.K.Lillee c Gatting b Willis 17; T.M.Alderman not out 0; Extras (LB 3, NB 14, W 1) 18; 111

1/55 2/149 3/196 4/220 5/332 6/354 7/357 8/396 9/401 — 401
1/13 2/56 3/58 4/58 5/65 6/68 7/74 8/75 9/110

Bowling: First Innings—Willis 30-8-72-0; Old 43-14-91-0; Dilley 27-4-78-2; Botham 39.2-11-95-6; Willey 13-2-31-1; Boycott 3-2-2-0. *Second Innings*—Botham 7-3-14-1; Dilley 2-0-11-0; Willis 15.1-3-43-8; Old 9-1-21-1; Willey 3-1-4-0.

England

G.A.Gooch	lbw b Alderman	2
G.Boycott	b Lawson	12
J.M.Brearley*	c Marsh b Alderman	10
D.I.Gower	c Marsh b Lawson	24
M.W.Gatting	lbw b Lillee	15
P.Willey	b Lawson	8
I.T.Botham	c Marsh b Lillee	50
R.W.Taylor†	c Marsh b Lillee	5
G.R.Dilley	c and b Lillee	13
C.M.Old	c Border b Alderman	0
R.G.D.Willis	not out	1
Extras	(B 6, LB 11, NB 11, W 6)	34
		174

Second innings: G.A.Gooch c Alderman b Lillee 0; G.Boycott lbw b Alderman 46; J.M.Brearley* c Alderman b Lillee 14; D.I.Gower c Border b Alderman 9; M.W.Gatting lbw b Alderman 1; P.Willey c Dyson b Lillee 33; I.T.Botham not out 149; R.W.Taylor† c Bright b Alderman 1; G.R.Dilley b Alderman 56; C.M.Old b Lawson 29; R.G.D.Willis c Border b Alderman 2; Extras (B 5, LB 3, NB 5, W 3) 16; 356

1/12 2/40 3/42 4/84 5/87 6/112 7/148 8/166 9/167 — 174
1/0 2/18 3/37 4/41 5/105 6/133 7/135 8/252 9/319

Bowling: First Innings—Lillee 18.5-7-49-4; Alderman 19-4-59-3; Lawson 13-3-32-3. *Second Innings*—Lillee 25-6-94-3; Alderman 35.3-6-135-6; Lawson 23-4-96-1; Bright 4-0-15-0.

Umpires: D.G.L.Evans and B.J.Meyer

ENGLAND v AUSTRALIA 1981 (Fourth Test)

At Edgbaston, Birmingham, 30, 31 July, 1, 2 August
Result: England won by 29 runs

England

Batsman	Dismissal	Runs		Dismissal	Runs
G.Boycott	c Marsh b Alderman	13		c Marsh b Bright	29
J.M.Brearley*	c Border b Lillee	48		lbw b Lillee	13
D.I.Gower	c Hogg b Alderman	0		c Border b Bright	23
G.A.Gooch	c Marsh b Bright	21		b Bright	21
M.W.Gatting	c Alderman b Lillee	21		b Bright	39
P.Willey	b Bright	16		b Bright	5
I.T.Botham	b Alderman	26		c Marsh b Lillee	3
J.E.Emburey	b Hogg	3	(9)	not out	37
R.W.Taylor†	b Alderman	0	(10)	lbw b Alderman	8
C.M.Old	not out	11	(8)	c Marsh b Alderman	23
R.G.D.Willis	c Marsh b Alderman	13		c Marsh b Alderman	2
Extras	(B 1, LB 5, NB 10, W 1)	17		(LB 6, NB 9, W 1)	16
Total		189			219

1/29 2/29 3/60 4/101 5/126
6/145 7/161 8/161 9165

1/18 2/52 3/89 4/98 5/110
6/115 7/154 8/167 9/217

Bowling: *First Innings*—Lillee 18-4-61-2; Alderman 23.1-8-42-5; Hogg 16-3-49-1; Bright 12-4-20-2. *Second Innings*—Lillee 26-9-51-2; Alderman 22-5-65-3; Hogg 10-3-19-0; Bright 34-17-68-5.

Australia

Batsman	Dismissal	Runs		Dismissal	Runs
G.M.Wood	run out	38	(2)	lbw b Old	2
J.Dyson	b Old	1	(1)	lbw b Willis	13
A.R.Border	c Taylor b Old	2		c Gatting b Emburey	40
R.J.Bright	lbw b Botham	27	(8)	lbw b Botham	0
K.J.Hughes*	lbw b Old	47	(4)	c Emburey b Willis	5
G.N.Yallop	b Emburey	30	(5)	c Botham b Emburey	30
M.F.Kent	c Willis b Emburey	46	(6)	b Botham	10
R.W.Marsh†	b Emburey	2	(7)	b Botham	4
D.K.Lillee	b Emburey	18		c Taylor b Botham	3
R.M.Hogg	run out	0		not out	0
T.M.Alderman	not out	3		b Botham	0
Extras	(B 4, LB 19, NB 21)	44		(B 1, LB 2, NB 11)	14
Total		258			121

1/5 2/14 3/62 4/115 5/166
6/203 7/220 8/253 9/253

1/2 2/19 3/29 4/87 5/105
6/114 7/114 8/120 9/121

Bowling: *First Innings*—Willis 19-3-63-0; Old 21-8-44-3; Emburey 26.5-12-43-4; Botham 20-1-64-1. *Second Innings*—Willis 20-6-37-2; Old 11-4-19-1; Emburey 22-10-40-2; Botham 14-9-11-5.

Umpires: H.D.Bird and D.O.Oslear

ENGLAND v AUSTRALIA 1981 (Fifth Test)

At Old Trafford, Manchester, 13, 14, 15, 16, 17 August
Result: England won by 103 runs

England

Batsman	Dismissal	Runs		Dismissal	Runs
G.A.Gooch	lbw b Lillee	10		b Alderman	5
G.Boycott	c Marsh b Alderman	10		lbw b Alderman	37
C.J.Tavare	c Alderman b Whitney	69		c Kent b Alderman	78
D.I.Gower	c Yallop b Whitney	23		c Bright b Lillee	1
J.M.Brearley*	lbw b Alderman	2	(6)	c Marsh b Alderman	3
M.W.Gatting	c Border b Lillee	32	(5)	lbw b Alderman	11
I.T.Botham	c Bright b Lillee	0		c Marsh b Whitney	118
A.P.E.Knott†	c Border b Alderman	13		c Dyson b Lillee	59
J.E.Emburey	c Border b Alderman	1		c Kent b Whitney	57
P.J.W.Allott	not out	52		c Hughes b Bright	14
R.G.D.Willis	c Hughes b Lillee	11		not out	5
Extras	(LB 6, W 2)	8		(B 1, LB 12, NB 3)	16
Total		231			404

1/19 2/25 3/57 4/62 5/109
6/109 7/131 8/137 9/175

1/7 2/79 3/80 4/98 5/104
6/253 7/282 8/356 9/396

Bowling: *First Innings*—Lillee 24.1-8-55-4; Alderman 29-5-88-4; Whitney 17-3-50-2; Bright 16-6-30-0. *Second Innings*—Lillee 46-13-137-2; Alderman 52-19-109-5; Whitney 27-6-74-2; Bright 26.4-12-68-1.

Australia

Batsman	Dismissal	Runs		Dismissal	Runs
G.M.Wood	lbw b Allott	19	(2)	c Knott b Allott	6
J.Dyson	c Botham b Willis	0	(1)	run out	5
K.J.Hughes*	lbw b Willis	4		lbw b Botham	43
G.N.Yallop	c Botham b Willis	0		b Emburey	114
M.F.Kent	c Knott b Emburey	52		c Brearley b Emburey	2
A.R.Border	c Gower b Botham	11	(6)	not out	123
R.W.Marsh†	c Botham b Willis	1		c Knott b Willis	47
R.J.Bright	c Knott b Botham	22		c Knott b Willis	5
D.K.Lillee	c Gooch b Botham	13		c Botham b Allott	28
M.R.Whitney	b Allott	0		c Gatting b Willis	0
T.M.Alderman	not out	2		lbw b Botham	0
Extras	(NB 6)	6		(LB 9, NB 18, W 2)	29
Total		130			402

1/20 2/24 3/24 4/24 5/58
6/59 7/104 8/125 9/126

1/7 2/24 3/119 4/198 5/206
6/296 7/322 8/373 9/378

Bowling: *First Innings*—Willis 14-0-63-4; Allott 6-1-17-2; Botham 6.2-1-28-3; Emburey 4-0-16-1. *Second Innings*—Willis 30.5-2-96-3; Allott 17-3-71-2; Botham 36-16-86-2; Emburey 49-9-107-2; Gatting 3-1-13-0.

Umpires: D.J.Constant and K.E.Palmer

ENGLAND v AUSTRALIA 1981 (Sixth Test)
At Kennington Oval, London, 27, 28, 29, 31 August, 1 September
Result: Match drawn

Australia

G.M.Wood c Brearley b Botham	66			
M.F.Kent c Gatting b Botham	54			
K.J.Hughes* hit wkt b Botham	31		lbw b Hendrick	6
G.N.Yallop c Botham b Willis	26		b Hendrick	35
A.R.Border not out	106		c Tavare b Emburey	84
D.M.Wellham b Willis	24		lbw b Botham	103
R.W.Marsh† c Botham b Willis	12		c Gatting b Botham	52
R.J.Bright c Brearley b Botham	3		b Botham	11
D.K.Lillee b Willis	11		not out	
T.M.Alderman b Botham	0			
M.R.Whitney b Botham	4	(10)	c Botham b Hendrick	0
Extras (B 4, LB 6, NB 4, W 1)	15		(B 1, LB 8, NB 7, W 1)	17
	352		(9 wkts dec.)	344

1/120 2/125 3/169 4/199 5/260 6/280 7/303 8/319 9/320
1/26 2/36 3/41 4/104 5/205 6/291 7/332 8/343 9/344

Bowling: *First Innings*—Willis 31-6-91-4; Hendrick 31-2-58-0; Botham 47-13-125-6; Emburey 23-2-82-4. *Second Innings*—Willis 10-0-41-0; Botham 42-9-128-4; Hendrick 29.2-6-82-4; Emburey 23-3-76-1.

England

G.Boycott c Yallop b Lillee	137		lbw b Lillee	0
W.Larkins c Alderman b Lillee	34		c Alderman b Lillee	24
C.J.Tavare c Marsh b Lillee	24		c Kent b Whitney	8
M.W.Gatting b Lillee	53		c Kent b Lillee	56
J.M.Brearley* c Bright b Alderman	0	(6)	c Hughes b Alderman	51
P.W.G.Parker c Kent b Alderman	0	(5)	c Kent b Alderman	13
I.T.Botham c Yallop b Lillee	3		lbw b Alderman	16
A.P.E.Knott† b Lillee	36		not out	70
J.E.Emburey lbw b Lillee	0		not out	5
R.G.D.Willis b Alderman	3			
M.Hendrick not out	0			
Extras (LB 9, NB 12, W 3)	24		(B 2, LB 5, NB 9, W 2)	18
	314		(7 wkts)	261

1/61 2/131 3/246 4/248 5/248 6/256 7/293 8/293 9/302
1/0 2/18 3/88 4/101 5/127 6/144 7/237

Bowling: *First Innings*—Lillee 31.4-4-89-7; Alderman 35-4-84-3; Whitney 23-3-76-0; Bright 21-6-41-0. *Second Innings*—Lillee 20-3-78-1; Alderman 19-6-60-2; Whitney 11-4-46-1; Bright 27-12-50-0; Yallop 8-2-17-0.

Umpires: H.D.Bird and B.J.Meyer

AUSTRALIA v PAKISTAN 1981-82 (First Test)
At W.A.C.A. Ground, Perth, 13, 14, 15, 16, 17 November
Result: Australia won by 286 runs

Australia

B.M.Laird c Wasim Bari b Imran Khan	85	(2)	c Wasim Bari b Imran Khan	27
G.M.Wood lbw b Sikander Bakht	49	(1)	b Iqbal Qasim	33
G.S.Chappell* lbw b Imran Khan	6		b Imran Khan	22
K.J.Hughes b Sarfraz Nawaz	6		c Majid Khan b Imran Khan	14
G.N.Yallop c and b Iqbal Qasim	106		c Imran Khan b Sikander Bakht	20
A.R.Border c Wasim Bari b Sarfraz Nawaz.	38		c Mudassar Nazar b Sikander Bakht	3
R.W.Marsh† c Iqbal Qasim b Sikander Bakht.	37		c Mansoor Akhtar b Wasim Raja	16
B.Yardley c Wasim Bari b Imran Khan	47		st Wasim Bari b Iqbal Qasim.	9
D.K.Lillee c Wasim Bari b Wasim Raja	22		not out	16
J.R.Thomson b Imran Khan	4		not out	2
T.M.Alderman not out	5			0
Extras (B 1, LB 9, NB 14, W 1)	25		(LB 5, NB 12, W 1)	18
	(8 wkts dec.) 424			180

1/92 2/105 3/192 4/262 5/327 6/360 7/412 8/416
1/45 2/81 3/89 4/113 5/119 6/136 7/154 8/165 9/180

Bowling: *First Innings*—Imran Khan 31.4-8-66-4; Sarfraz Nawaz 27-10-43-2; Sikander Bakht 21-4-47-2; Iqbal Qasim 3-1-6-1; Wasim Raja 1-1-0-1. *Second Innings*—Imran Khan 39-12-90-3; Sarfraz Nawaz 16-4-43-2; Sikander Bakht 23-3-79-2; Iqbal Qasim 26-4-81-2; Wasim Raja 20-3-58-1; Javed Miandad 1-0-2-0; Mudassar Nazar 2-1-1-0.

Pakistan

Mudassar Nazar c Marsh b Lillee	0		lbw b Alderman	5
Rizwan-uz-Zaman lbw b Alderman	0		c Marsh b Alderman	8
Mansoor Akhtar c Marsh b Alderman	6		c Hughes b Thomson	36
Javed Miandad* c Hughes b Alderman	6		b Yardley	79
Majid Khan c Marsh b Lillee	3		c Marsh b Yardley	0
Wasim Raja c Thomson b Lillee	4		c Hughes b Yardley	48
Imran Khan c Yardley b Lillee	4		c Alderman b Yardley	31
Sarfraz Nawaz c Marsh b Alderman	26		c and b Yardley	9
Wasim Bari† c Marsh b Lillee	1		c Border b Yardley	20
Iqbal Qasim c Alderman b Thomson	5		c Alderman b Lillee	4
Sikander Bakht not out	3		not out	0
Extras (NB 4)	4		(LB 1, NB 15)	16
	62			256

1/1 2/1 3/14 4/17 5/21 6/25 7/25 8/26 9/57
1/8 2/27 3/96 4/99 5/174 6/198 7/229 8/236 9/254

Bowling: *First Innings*—Lillee 9-3-18-5; Alderman 10.2-2-36-4; Thomson 2-1-4-1. *Second Innings*—Lillee 20-3-78-1; Alderman 16-4-43-2; Thomson 12-4-35-1; Yardley 25.5-5-84-6.

Umpires: A.R.Crafter and M.W.Johnson

AUSTRALIA v PAKISTAN 1981-82 (Second Test)

At Woolloongabba, Brisbane, 27, 28, 29, 30 November, 1 December

Result: Australia won by 10 wickets

Pakistan

Mudassar Nazar	c Marsh b Lillee	36	c Laird b Lillee	33
Mohsin Khan	c Border b Chappell	11	c Marsh b Lillee	43
Majid Khan	c Chappell b Lillee	29	c Chappell b Yardley	15
Javed Miandad*	b Lillee	20	lbw b Lillee	38
Zaheer Abbas	b Lillee	80	lbw b Yardley	0
Wasim Raja	c Laird b Lillee	43	b Lillee	36
Imran Khan	c Marsh b Alderman	0	c Wellham b Yardley	3
Ijaz Faqih	b Yardley	34	c Chappell b Thomson	21
Sarfraz Nazar	c Border b Alderman	7	c Alderman b Yardley	13
Wasim Bari	c Marsh b Thomson	1	not out	4
Sikander Bakht	not out	1	b Thomson	2
Extras	(B 12, LB 1, NB 12, W 1)	26	(B 2, LB 3, NB 9, W 1)	15
		291		**223**

1/40 2/60 3/105 4/111 5/236   1/72 2/90 3/115 4/115 5/177
6/237 7/245 8/263 9/285   6/178 7/189 8/216 9/219

Bowling: *First Innings*—Lillee 20-3-81-5; Alderman 25-6-74-2; Thomson 15-2-52-1; Yardley 15-1-51-1; Border 1-0-1-0. *Second Innings*—Lillee 19-4-51-4; Chappell 3-1-6-1; Yardley 15-3-43-2; Thomson 15-3-37-0; Alderman 15-3-37-0; Thomson 24-4-77-4.

Australia

G.M.Wood	c Mudassar Nazar b Wasim Raja	72	(2) not out	0
B.M.Laird	c Zaheer Abbas b Ijaz Faqih	44	(1) not out	3
G.S.Chappell*	c Zaheer Abbas b Sikander	201		
A.R.Border	b Imran Khan	36		
K.J.Hughes	b Imran Khan	28		
D.M.Wellham	b Imran Khan	36		
R.W.Marsh†	c Zaheer Abbas b Imran Khan	27		
B.Yardley	b Sarfraz Nawaz	2		
D.K.Lillee	b Sarfraz Nawaz	14		
J.R.Thomson	not out	22		
T.M.Alderman	not out	5		
Extras	(B 1, LB 5, NB 17, W 2)	25		
	(9 wkts dec.)	**512**	(0 wkts)	**3**

1/109 2/149 3/219 4/298 5/429 (9 wkts dec.) 512
6/448 7/469 8/470 9/492

Bowling: *First Innings*—Imran Khan 40-6-92-4; Sarfraz Nawaz 35-4-121-2; Sikander Bakht 24-2-81-1; Ijaz Faqih 22-1-76-1; Wasim Raja 17-0-68-1; Mudassar Nazar 2-0-10-0; Javed Miandad 3-0-18-0; Majid Khan 9-1-21-0. *Second Innings*—Imran Khan 1.2-1-2-0; Sikander Bakht 1-0-1-0.

Umpires: A.R.Crafter and M.W.Johnson

AUSTRALIA v PAKISTAN 1981-82 (Third Test)

At Melbourne Cricket Ground, 11, 12, 13, 14, 15 December

Result: Pakistan won by an innings and 82 runs

Pakistan

Mudassar Nazar	c Lillee b Yardley	95
Mohsin Khan	c Thomson b Yardley	17
Majid Khan	c Wood b Yardley	74
Javed Miandad*	lbw b Yardley	62
Zaheer Abbas	c and b Yardley	90
Wasim Raja	c Laird b Yardley	50
Imran Khan	not out	70
Sarfraz Nawaz	c Yardley b Chappell	8
Wasim Bari†	b Yardley	8
Iqbal Qasim	not out	16
Sikander Bakht		
Extras	(B 1, LB 5, NB 12)	18
	(8 wkts)	**500**

1/40 2/181 3/201 4/329 5/363
6/443 7/444 8/456

Bowling: Lillee 36.3-9-104-0; Alderman 27-8-62-0; Thomson 25-2-85-0; Yardley 66-16-187-7; Border 4-1-16-0; Chappell 9-2-17-1; Hughes 3-1-2-0; Laird 1-0-9-0.

Australia

B.M.Laird	lbw b Iqbal Qasim	35	(2) c Sarfraz Nawaz b Iqbal Qasim	52
G.M.Wood	c Mohsin Khan b Sarfraz Nawaz	100	(1) c Wasim Bari b Sarfraz Nawaz	0
G.S.Chappell*	c Wasim Bari b Wasim Raja	22	c Javed Miandad b Sarfraz Nawaz	0
A.R.Border	run out	7	run out	1
K.J.Hughes	c and b Iqbal Qasim	34	c Majid Khan b Iqbal Qasim	11
D.M.Wellham	c Mudassar Nazar b Sarfraz Nawaz	26	b Sarfraz Nawaz	13
R.W.Marsh†	c Mudassar Nazar b Imran Khan	31	c Mohsin Khan b Iqbal Qasim	21
B.Yardley	b Iqbal Qasim	20	b Imran Khan	0
D.K.Lillee	lbw b Imran Khan	2	c Wasim Bari b Iqbal Qasim	4
J.R.Thomson	not out	3	b Imran Khan	17
T.M.Alderman	lbw b Imran Khan	1	not out	4
Extras	(B 4, LB 6, NB 3)	13	(B 1)	1
		293		**125**

1/75 2/118 3/127 4/173 5/232   1/1 2/9 3/13 4/29 5/77
6/235 7/286 8/288 9/289   6/78 7/79 8/92 9/121

Bowling: *First Innings*—Imran Khan 24.1-7-41-3; Sarfraz Nawaz 14-3-43-2; Wasim Raja 37-7-73-1; Iqbal Qasim 55-17-104-3; Sikander Bakht 2-0-9-0; Majid Khan 2-0-10-0. *Second Innings*—Imran Khan 14.1-5-21-2; Sarfraz Nawaz 15-10-11-3; Wasim Raja 13-2-34-0; Iqbal Qasim 24-11-44-4; Majid Khan 4-1-5-0; Javed Miandad 2-0-9-0.

Umpires: R.C.Bailhache and R.A.French

AUSTRALIA v WEST INDIES 1981-82 (First Test)

At Melbourne Cricket Ground, 26, 27, 28, 29, 30 December
Result: Australia won by 58 runs

Australia

Batsman	First Innings		Second Innings	
B.M.Laird	c Murray b Holding	4	(2) lbw b Croft	64
G.M.Wood	c Murray b Roberts	3	(1) c Murray b Garner	46
G.S.Chappell*	c Murray b Holding	0	c Murray b Garner	6
A.R.Border	c Murray b Holding	4	b Holding	66
K.J.Hughes	not out	100	b Holding	8
D.M.Wellham	c sub (A.L.Logie) b Croft	17	lbw b Holding	2
R.W.Marsh†	c Richards b Garner	21	c Murray b Holding	2
B.Yardley	b Garner	21	b Garner	13
D.K.Lillee	c Gomes b Holding	1	c Murray b Holding	0
G.F.Lawson	b Holding	2	not out	0
T.M.Alderman	c Murray b Croft	10	c Murray b Holding	1
Extras	(B 1, LB 6, NB 8)	15	(B 5, LB 4, NB 4, W 1)	14
Total		**198**		**222**

1/4 2/5 3/8 4/26 5/59 1/82 2/106 3/139 4/184 5/190
6/115 7/149 8/153 9/155 6/199 7/215 8/218 9/220

Bowling: First Innings—Holding 17-3-45-5; Roberts 15-6-40-1; Garner 20-6-59-2; Croft 16.1-3-39-2. Second Innings—Holding 21.3-5-62-6; Roberts 18-4-31-0; Garner 18-5-37-3; Croft 20-2-61-1; Richards 5-0-17-0.

West Indies

Batsman	First Innings		Second Innings	
D.L.Haynes	c Border b Lillee	1	c Lillee b Yardley	28
S.F.A.F.Bacchus	c Wood b Alderman	1	lbw b Alderman	0
C.E.H.Croft	lbw b Lillee	0	(11) not out	0
I.V.A.Richards	b Lillee	2	(3) b Alderman	0
C.H.Lloyd*	c Alderman b Yardley	29	(4) c Border b Lawson	19
H.A.Gomes	c Chappell b Lillee	55	(5) b Yardley	24
P.J.L.Dujon	c Hughes b Lillee	41	(6) c Marsh b Yardley	43
D.A.Murray†	not out	32	(7) c Marsh b Yardley	10
A.M.E.Roberts	c Marsh b Lillee	18	(8) lbw b Lillee	10
M.A.Holding	c and b Alderman	2	(9) lbw b Lillee	7
J.Garner	c Laird b Lillee	7	(10) lbw b Lillee	0
Extras	(B 1, LB 3, NB 9)	13	(B 1, LB 10, NB 9)	20
Total		**201**		**161**

1/3 2/5 3/6 4/10 5/62 1/4 2/4 3/38 4/80 5/88
6/134 7/147 8/174 9/183 6/116 7/150 8/154 9/154

Bowling: First Innings—Lillee 26.3-3-83-7; Alderman 18-3-54-2; Lawson 9-2-28-0; Chappell 2-2-0-0; Yardley 7-2-23-1. Second Innings—Lillee 27.1-8-44-3; Alderman 9-3-23-2; Lawson 17-3-36-1; Yardley 21-7-38-4.

Umpires: R.C.Bailhache and A.R.Crafter

AUSTRALIA v WEST INDIES 1981-82 (Second Test)

At Sydney Cricket Ground, 2, 3, 4, 5, 6 January
Result: Match drawn

West Indies

Batsman	First Innings		Second Innings	
C.G.Greenidge	c Laird b Lillee	66	c Yardley b Lillee	8
D.L.Haynes	lbw b Thomson	15	lbw b Lillee	51
I.V.A.Richards	c Marsh b Lillee	44	c Border b Alderman	22
H.A.Gomes	c Chappell b Yardley	126	c Border b Yardley	43
C.H.Lloyd*	b Thomson	40	c Hughes b Yardley	57
P.J.L.Dujon	c and b Yardley	44	c and b Yardley	48
D.A.Murray†	c Marsh b Lillee	13	c Laird b Yardley	1
M.A.Holding	lbw b Lillee	9	c Dyson b Yardley	5
S.T.Clarke	c Laird b Thomson	14	c Dyson b Yardley	5
J.Garner	c Marsh b Yardley	1	b Yardley	0
C.E.H.Croft	not out	0	not out	4
Extras	(LB 3, NB 9)	12	(LB 1, NB 5, W 5)	11
Total		**384**		**255**

1/37 2/128 3/133 4/229 5/325 1/29 2/52 3/112 4/179 5/208
6/346 7/363 8/379 9/380 6/225 7/231 8/246 9/255

Bowling: First Innings—Lillee 39-6-119-4; Alderman 30-9-73-0; Thomson 20-1-93-3; Yardley 26.2-3-87-3; Border 1-1-0-0. Second Innings—Lillee 20-6-50-2; Alderman 12-2-46-1; Thomson 15-3-50-0; Yardley 31.4-6-98-7.

Australia

Batsman	First Innings		Second Innings	
B.M.Laird	c Dujon b Garner	14	(4) c Murray b Croft	38
G.M.Wood	c Murray b Holding	63	b Gomes	7
J.Dyson	lbw b Holding	28	(2) not out	127
G.S.Chappell*	c Dujon b Holding	12	(3) c Murray b Croft	0
T.M.Alderman	b Clarke	0		
K.J.Hughes	b Garner	16	(5) lbw b Gomes	13
A.R.Border	not out	53	(6) not out	9
R.W.Marsh†	c Holding b Gomes	17		
B.Yardley	b Holding	45		
D.K.Lillee	c Garner b Holding	4		
J.R.Thomson	run out	8		
Extras	(B 1, LB 2, NB 2, W 2)	7	(B 2, LB 1, NB 3)	6
Total		**267**		**(4 wkts) 200**

1/38 2/108 3/111 4/112 5/128 1/104 2/104 3/149 4/169
6/141 7/172 8/242 9/246

Bowling: First Innings—Holding 29-9-64-5; Clarke 16-4-51-1; Garner 20-4-52-2; Croft 20-7-53-0; Gomes 9-1-19-1. Second Innings—Holding 19-6-31-0; Clarke 16-9-25-0; Garner 12-3-27-0; Croft 27-5-58-2; Richards 13-3-33-0; Gomes 15-7-20-2.

Umpires: R.A.French and M.W.Johnson

AUSTRALIA v WEST INDIES 1981-82 (Third Test)

At Adelaide Oval, 30, 31 January, 1, 2, 3 February

Result: West Indies won by 5 wickets

Australia

B.M.Laird c Dujon b Roberts	2	(2)	c Dujon b Croft	78
G.M.Wood c Garner b Roberts	5	(1)	c and b Holding	6
J.Dyson c Dujon b Holding	1		c Lloyd b Garner	10
K.J.Hughes c Greenidge b Holding	5	(5)	c Bacchus b Garner	84
G.S.Chappell* c Garner b Holding	61	(7)	lbw b Holding	7
A.R.Border c Dujon b Roberts	78	(4)	c Dujon b Roberts	126
R.W.Marsh† c Dujon b Holding	39	(6)	c Haynes b Holding	38
B.Yardley b Croft	8		b Garner	6
D.K.Lillee b Roberts	2		c Dujon b Garner	1
J.R.Thomson not out	18		c Bacchus b Garner	0
L.S.Pascoe b Holding	10		not out	0
Extras (B 1, LB 2, NB 5, W 1)	9		(B 7, LB 10, NB 13)	30
	238			386

1/3 2/8 3/8 4/17 5/122
6/193 7/206 8/209 9/210

1/10 2/35 3/201 4/267 5/362
6/373 7/383 8/383 9/383

Bowling: *First Innings*—Holding 25-5-72-5; Roberts 19-7-43-4; Croft 23-4-60-1; Garner 17-4-44-0; Gomes 7-3-10-0. *Second Innings*—Holding 29-9-70-3; Roberts 24-7-64-1; Croft 32-4-90-1; Garner 35-15-56-5; Gomes 14-1-38-0; Richards 18-3-38-0.

West Indies

C.G.Greenidge c Border b Thomson	8		c Marsh b Thomson	52
D.L.Haynes c Marsh b Thomson	26		c Marsh b Thomson	4
I.V.A.Richards c Laird b Yardley	42		b Pascoe	50
H.A.Gomes not out	124		b Pascoe	21
S.F.A.F.Bacchus c Laird b Pascoe	0	(6)	c Lillee b Pascoe	27
C.H.Lloyd* c Marsh b Thomson	53	(5)	not out	77
C.E.H.Croft b Thomson	0			
P.J.L.Dujon† c Thomson b Yardley	51	(7)	not out	0
A.M.E.Roberts c sub (D.W.Hookes) b Yardley	42			
M.A.Holding b Yardley	3			
J.Garner c Wood b Yardley	12			
Extras (B 4, LB 7, NB 14, W 3)	28		(LB 2, NB 5, W 1)	8
	389		4/176(5 wkts)	239

1/12 2/72 3/85 4/92 5/194
6/194 7/283 8/365 9/369

1/7 2/107 3/114 4/176(5 wkts) 239
5/235

Bowling: *First Innings*—Lillee 4.5-3-4-0; Thomson 29-1-112-4; Yardley 40.5-10-132-5; Pascoe 30-3-94-1; Border 5-0-19-0. *Second Innings*—Lillee 4-0-17-0; Thomson 19.1-4-62-2; Yardley 16-0-68-0; Pascoe 22-3-84-3.

Umpires: R.C.Bailhache and M.W.Johnson

NEW ZEALAND v AUSTRALIA 1981-82 (First Test)

At Basin Reserve, Wellington, 26 (no play), 27, 28 February, 1 (no play), 2 March

Result: Match drawn

New Zealand

B.A.Edgar lbw b Alderman	55
J.G.Wright c Chappell b Yardley	38
J.F.M.Morrison b Thomson	15
G.P.Howarth* not out	58
J.V.Coney lbw b Yardley	1
M.D.Crowe run out	9
R.J.Hadlee b Thomson	21
I.D.S.Smith† c Chappell b Yardley	11
B.L.Cairns not out	19
M.C.Snedden	
E.J.Chatfield	
Extras (B 5, LB 19, NB 11, W 4)	39
(7 wkts dec.)	266

1/86 2/120 3/149 4/162 5/186
6/212 7/246

Bowling: Thomson 26-13-35-2; Alderman 44-20-93-1; Lillee 15-5-32-0; Chappell 8-2-18-0; Yardley 23-10-49-3.

Australia

G.M.Wood b Cairns	41
B.M.Laird not out	27
J.Dyson not out	12
G.S.Chappell*	
K.J.Hughes	
A.R.Border	
R.W.Marsh†	
B.Yardley	
D.K.Lillee	
J.R.Thomson	
T.M.Alderman	
Extras (LB 2, NB 3)	5
(1 wkt)	85

1/65

Bowling: Hadlee 7-2-15-0; Snedden 8-1-24-0; Cairns 11-4-20-1; Chatfield 8-5-7-0; Crowe 4-1-14-0.

Umpires: F.R.Goodall and S.J.Woodward

NEW ZEALAND v AUSTRALIA 1981-82 (Third Test)
At Lancaster Park, Christchurch, 19, 20, 21, 22 March
Result: Australia won by 8 wickets

Australia

B.M.Laird c Smith b Troup	12	(2) c Edgar b Snedden	31
G.M.Wood c Hadlee b Snedden	64	(1) c Coney b Hadlee	15
J.Dyson c Crowe b Hadlee	1	not out	14
G.S.Chappell* c Smith b Coney	176	not out	3
K.J.Hughes b Hadlee	12		
A.R.Border b Snedden	6		
R.W.Marsh† c Cairns b Hadlee	23		
B.Yardley c Cairns b Hadlee	8		
J.R.Thomson b Hadlee	25		
D.K.Lillee c and b Hadlee	7		
T.M.Alderman not out	1		
Extras (B 2, LB 8, NB 8)	18	(B 2, LB 2, NB 2)	6
	353	**(2 wkts)**	**69**

1/50 2/57 3/82 4/128 5/145 6/237 7/256 8/340 9/352
1/24 2/60

Bowling: *First Innings*—Hadlee 28.5-5-100-6; Troup 11-1-53-1; Snedden 18-2-89-2; Cairns 21-3-74-0; Coney 8-2-15-1; Morrison 3-0-4-0. *Second Innings*—Hadlee 8-2-10-1; Snedden 4-0-15-1; Cairns 9-1-28-0; Coney 1-0-2-0; Morrison 2-1-6-0; Wright 1-0-2-0; Crowe 0.3-0-0-0.

New Zealand

B.A.Edgar c Dyson b Alderman	22	c Marsh b Alderman	11
J.G.Wright c Marsh b Lillee	13	b Alderman	141
J.F.M.Morrison lbw b Thomson	8	lbw b Chappell	4
G.P.Howarth* c Alderman b Thomson	9	c Wood b Border	41
J.V.Coney b Lillee	0	b Border	9
M.D.Crowe c Marsh b Lillee	0	b Yardley	9
R.J.Hadlee c Marsh b Thomson	40	c Alderman b Yardley	0
I.D.S.Smith† b Thomson	0	c Wood b Yardley	0
B.L.Cairns run out	0	lbw b Yardley	16
M.C.Snedden b Alderman	3	b Border	20
G.B.Troup not out	32	not out	8
Extras (B 8, LB 2, NB 11, W 1)	22	(B 4, LB 7, NB 9, W 2)	22
	149		**272**

1/33 2/57 3/57 4/57 5/67 6/82 7/82 8/87 9/149
1/21 2/36 3/129 4/133 5/162 6/166 7/166 8/215 9/249

Bowling: *First Innings*—Thomson 21-5-51-4; Alderman 19.2-3-63-2; Lillee 12-6-13-3. *Second Innings*—Alderman 23-5-66-2; Chappell 18-5-30-1; Thomson 19-5-54-0; Yardley 27-7-80-4; Border 10.3-4-20-3.

Umpires: F.R.Goodall and D.A.Kinsella

NEW ZEALAND v AUSTRALIA 1981-82 (Second Test)
At Eden Park, Auckland, 12, 13, 14, 15, 16 March
Result: New Zealand won by 5 wickets

Australia

B.M.Laird c Smith b Troup	38	(2) lbw b Hadlee	39
G.M.Wood c Smith b Cairns	9	(1) c Snedden b Cairns	100
J.Dyson b Snedden	33	b Cairns	33
K.J.Hughes c Smith b Troup	0	b Cairns	17
G.S.Chappell* run out	32	c Edgar b Hadlee	24
A.R.Border run out	0	c Howarth b Morrison	38
R.W.Marsh† b Troup	33	c Crowe b Hadlee	3
B.Yardley b Hadlee	25	c Coney b Hadlee	0
J.R.Thomson lbw b Hadlee	13	lbw b Hadlee	4
D.K.Lillee c Crowe b Troup	9	c Smith b Morrison	5
T.M.Alderman not out	0	not out	0
Extras (LB 2, NB 16)	18	(B 4, LB 5, NB 8)	17
	210		**280**

1/19 2/75 3/76 4/120 5/120 6/131 7/173 8/187 9/203
1/106 2/167 3/196 4/202 5/241 6/254 7/254 8/260 9/277

Bowling: *First Innings*—Hadlee 20-7-38-2; Troup 18.3-3-82-4; Cairns 17-7-38-1; Snedden 12-5-26-1; Howarth 1-0-8-0. *Second Innings*—Hadlee 28-9-63-5; Troup 15-4-31-0; Cairns 44-10-85-3; Snedden 8-2-22-0; Howarth 4-2-4-0; Coney 4-1-6-0; Morrison 35-16-52-2.

New Zealand

B.A.Edgar c and b Yardley	161	c Lillee b Yardley	29
J.G.Wright c Yardley b Lillee	4	c Laird b Alderman	4
J.F.M.Morrison b Lillee	11	c Marsh b Lillee	8
G.P.Howarth* run out	56	c Chappell b Yardley	19
J.V.Coney b Yardley	73	(6) not out	5
M.D.Crowe c Wood b Lillee	2		
R.J.Hadlee c Chappell b Yardley	25	not out	6
I.D.S.Smith† lbw b Yardley	5		
B.L.Cairns c Lillee b Alderman	14	(5) b Border	34
M.C.Snedden not out	18		
G.B.Troup c Border b Alderman	4		
Extras (B 4, LB 7, NB 2, W 1)	14	(LB 4)	4
	387	**(5 wkts)**	**109**

1/15 2/35 3/122 4/276 5/291 6/326 7/345 8/352 9/366
1/4 2/17 3/44 4/97 5/103

Bowling: *First Innings*—Thomson 23-8-52-0; Alderman 24.3-5-59-2; Lillee 39-7-106-3; Yardley 56-22-142-4; Border 3-0-11-0; Chappell 5-2-3-0. *Second Innings*—Alderman 7-0-30-1; Lillee 13-5-32-1; Yardley 7.4-2-40-2; Border 2-1-3-1.

Umpires: B.A.Bricknell and S.J.Woodward

PAKISTAN v AUSTRALIA 1982-83 (First Test)

At National Stadium, Karachi, 22, 23, 24, 26, 27 September

Result: Pakistan won by 9 wickets

Australia

G.M.Wood c Wasim Bari b Imran Khan	0		csub (Salim Malik)b Abdul Qadir.	17
B.M.Laird run out	32		c Mansoor Akhtar b Imran Khan.	3
J.Dyson b Iqbal Qasim	87		b Abdul Qadir	6
K.J.Hughes* c Wasim Bari b Iqbal Qasim	54	(5)	c Wasim Bari b Iqbal Qasim	14
A.R.Border not out	55	(4)	csub (Salim Malik)b Abdul Qadir	8
G.M.Ritchie c Haroon Rashid b Abdul Qadir.	4		b Iqbal Qasim	17
R.W.Marsh† b Tahir Naqqash	19		lbw b Imran Khan	32
B.Yardley c Javed Miandad b Tahir Naqqash.	0		lbw b Abdul Qadir	0
R.J.Bright c Haroon Rashid b Tahir Naqqash.	2		not out	32
G.F.Lawson c Wasim Bari b Tahir Naqqash	0		run out	11
J.R.Thomson st Wasim Bari b Abdul Qadir	14		c Wasim Bari b Iqbal Qasim	18
Extras (B 4, LB 10, NB 2, W 1)	17		(B 2, LB 19)	21
	284			**179**

1/0 2/71 3/169 4/202 5/211 284
6/249 7/249 8/255 9/255

1/10 2/29 3/32 4/45 5/72 179
6/72 7/73 8/137 9/160

Bowling: *First Innings*—Imran Khan 23-3-38-1; Tahir Naqqash 16-3-61-4; Mudassar Nazar 13-0-33-0; Abdul Qadir 21.4-1-80-2; Iqbal Qasim 26-10-55-2. *Second Innings*—Imran Khan 12-5-17-2; Tahir Naqqash 7-3-17-0; Abdul Qadir 26-7-76-5; Iqbal Qasim 21.5-6-48-2.

Pakistan

Mohsin Khan handled the ball	58		not out	14
Mansoor Akhtar c Bright b Thomson	32		not out	26
Haroon Rashid c Laird b Yardley	82	(3)		
Javed Miandad b Lawson	32			
Zaheer Abbas c Marsh b Lawson	91			
Mudassar Nazar not out	52	(2)	c Border b Thomson	5
Imran Khan* c Yardley b Bright	1			
Tahir Naqqash st Marsh b Bright	15			
Wasim Bari† b Bright	0			
Abdul Qadir run out	29			
Iqbal Qasim not out	25		(NB 2)	2
Extras (B 4, LB 8, NB 12, W 1)	25			
	(9 wkts dec.) **419**		(1 wkt) **47**

1/43 2/168 3/188 4/277 5/328 419
6/329 7/351 8/353 9/404

1/5 47

Bowling: *First Innings*—Thomson 29-5-103-1; Lawson 39-10-93-2; Bright 36-8-96-3; Yardley 23-2-98-1; Border 1-0-4-0. *Second Innings*—Thomson 3-1-16-1; Bright 5-0-14-0; Yardley 3-1-9-0; Hughes 0.1-0-6-0.

Umpires: Khizer Hayat and Mahboob Shah

PAKISTAN v AUSTRALIA 1982-83 (Second Test)

At Iqbal Stadium, Faisalabad, 30 September, 1, 2, 4, 5 October

Result: Pakistan won by an innings and 3 runs

Pakistan

Mohsin Khan c Marsh b Lawson	76
Mudassar Nazar c Hughes b Border	79
Mansoor Akhtar c Marsh b Lawson	111
Javed Miandad c Laird b Lawson	6
Zaheer Abbas b Sleep	126
Haroon Rashid c Laird b Lawson	51
Imran Khan* not out	24
Tahir Naqqash not out	15
Wasim Bari†	
Abdul Qadir	
Iqbal Qasim	
Extras (B 4, LB 1, NB 8)	13
	(6 wkts dec.) **501**

1/123 2/181 3/201 4/356 5/428 (6 wkts dec.) 501
6/482

Bowling: Thomson 23-5-79-0; Lawson 33-6-97-4; Sleep 36-3-158-1; Bright 41-15-107-0; Border 11-3-47-1.

Australia

B.M.Laird lbw b Abdul Qadir	8		c Mudassar Nazar b Abdul Qadir.	60
G.M.Wood c Wasim Bari b Mudassar Nazar	49	(7)	c Wasim Bari b Iqbal Qasim	22
J.Dyson c Mudassar Nazar b Iqbal Qasim	23	(2)	c Iqbal Qasim b Abdul Qadir	43
A.R.Border c Javed Miandad b Imran Khan.	9	(3)	c Haroon Rashid b Abdul Qadir	31
K.J.Hughes* c Imran Khan b Abdul Qadir.	11	(4)	lbw b Abdul Qadir	7
G.M.Ritchie run out	34	(5)	not out	106
P.R.Sleep lbw b Imran Khan	0	(6)	c Mohsin Khan b Abdul Qadir	29
R.W.Marsh† b Abdul Qadir	0		run out	8
R.J.Bright c Haroon Rashid b Abdul Qadir	0		csub (Salim Malik)b Iqbal Qasim	0
G.F.Lawson c Zaheer Abbas b Iqbal Qasim	14		lbw b Abdul Qadir	0
J.R.Thomson not out	1		st Wasim Bari b Abdul Qadir	11
Extras (B 8, LB 6, NB 3, W 2)	19		(LB 7, NB 5, W 1)	13
	168			**330**

1/20 2/82 3/96 4/113 5/123 168
6/123 7/124 8/124 9/167

1/73 2/125 3/133 4/162 5/218 330
6/290 7/309 8/309 9/310

Bowling: *First Innings*—Imran Khan 14-6-16-2; Tahir Naqqash 15-4-21-0; Abdul Qadir 42-14-76-4; Iqbal Qasim 24.5-11-28-2; Mudassar Nazar 7-2-8-1. *Second Innings*—Imran Khan 10-5-20-0; Tahir Naqqash 9-1-25-0; Abdul Qadir 50.5-12-142-7; Iqbal Qasim 46-18-97-2; Mudassar Nazar 9-3-26-0; Zaheer Abbas 3-0-5-0; Javed Miandad 1-0-2-0.

Umpires: Khizer Hayat and Mahboob Shah

PAKISTAN v AUSTRALIA 1982-83 (Third Test)

At Gaddafi Stadium, Lahore, 14, 15, 16, 18, 19 October
Result: Pakistan won by 9 wickets

Australia

G.M.Wood c Javed Miandad b Abdul Qadir	85	(2) c Mudassar Nazar b Jalaluddin	30
B.M.Laird lbw b Abdul Qadir	28	(1) lbw b Tahir Naqqash	6
J.Dyson b Jalaluddin	10	b Tahir Naqqash	51
A.R.Border lbw b Imran Khan	9	lbw b Imran Khan	6
K.J.Hughes* b Tahir Naqqash	29	st Wasim Bari b Abdul Qadir	39
G.M.Ritchie lbw b Imran Khan	26	lbw b Imran Khan	18
R.W.Marsh† c sub (Iqbal Sikander) b Imran Khan	1	c Mudassar Nazar b Jalaluddin	12
B.Yardley c Haroon Rashid b Jalaluddin	40	b Imran Khan	21
G.F.Lawson not out	57	c sub (Iqbal Sikander) b Imran Khan	9
J.R.Thomson lbw b Jalaluddin	0	not out	5
T.M.Alderman b Imran Khan	7	c Zaheer Abbas b Imran Khan	0
Extras (B 1, LB 13, NB 5, W 5)	24	(B 4, LB 5, NB 8)	17
	316		**214**

1/85 2/120 3/140 4/140 5/197
6/202 7/203 8/264 9/264

1/21 2/55 3/64 4/138 5/157
6/170 7/189 8/203 9/214

Bowling: *First Innings*—Imran Khan 24.2-10-45-4; Tahir Naqqash 18-4-65-1; Mudassar Nazar 6-1-17-0; Jalaluddin 19-4-77-3; Abdul Qadir 37-7-86-2; Zaheer Abbas 2-0-5-0. *Second Innings*—Imran Khan 20-6-35-4; Tahir Naqqash 16-3-39-2; Mudassar Nazar 2-0-5-0; Jalaluddin 16-8-15-2; Abdul Qadir 35-7-102-2; Zaheer Abbas 1-0-1-0.

Pakistan

Mohsin Khan b Border	135	lbw b Lawson	14
Mudassar Nazar lbw b Lawson	23	not out	39
Abdul Qadir c Laird b Yardley	1	(3) not out	2
Mansoor Akhtar lbw b Lawson	12		
Javed Miandad c Hughes b Alderman	138		
Zaheer Abbas c Yardley b Alderman	52		
Haroon Rashid c Ritchie b Thomson	15		
Imran Khan* not out	39		
Tahir Naqqash not out	7		
Wasim Bari†			
Jalaluddin			
Extras (B 3, LB 13, NB 27, W 2)	45	(B 4, LB 5)	9
	(7 wkts dec.) **467**		(1 wkt) **64**

1/92 2/93 3/119 4/269 5/392
6/402 7/442

1/55

Bowling: *First Innings*—Thomson 19-1-73-1; Lawson 35-4-91-2; Alderman 34-4-144-2; Yardley 27-6-102-1; Border 4-1-12-1. *Second Innings*—Thomson 5-0-24-0; Lawson 7-1-21-1; Alderman 3-0-10-0.

Umpires: Javed Akhtar and Shakoor Rana

AUSTRALIA v ENGLAND 1982-83 (First Test)

At W.A.C.A. Ground, Perth, 12, 13, 14, 16, 17 November
Result: Match drawn

England

G.Cook c Dyson b Lillee	1	c Border b Lawson	7
C.J.Tavare c Hughes b Yardley	89	c Chappell b Yardley	9
D.I.Gower c Dyson b Alderman	72	lbw b Lillee	28
A.J.Lamb c Marsh b Yardley	46	c Marsh b Lawson	56
I.T.Botham c Marsh b Lawson	12	b Lawson	0
D.W.Randall c Wood b Yardley	78	b Lawson	115
G.Miller c Marsh b Lillee	30	c Marsh b Yardley	0
D.R.Pringle b Lillee	0	not out (8)	47
R.W.Taylor† not out	29	b Yardley (9)	31
R.G.D.Willis* c Lillee b Yardley	26	b Lawson (7)	0
N.G.Cowans b Yardley	4	lbw b Chappell	36
Extras (B 7, LB 9, NB 6, W 2)	24	(B 5, LB 11, NB 11, W 2)	29
	411		**358**

1/14 2/109 3/189 4/204 5/304
6/323 7/342 8/357 9/406

1/10 2/51 3/77 4/80 5/151
6/228 7/242 8/292 9/292

Bowling: *First Innings*—Lillee 38-13-96-3; Alderman 43-15-84-1; Lawson 29-6-89-1; Chappell 3-0-11-0; Yardley 42.4-15-107-5. *Second Innings*—Lillee 33-12-89-1; Lawson 32-5-108-5; Chappell 2.3-1-8-1; Yardley 41-10-101-3; Border 7-2-21-0; Hookes 1-0-2-0.

Australia

G.M.Wood c and b Willis	29	c Taylor b Willis	0
J.Dyson lbw b Miller	52	c Cowans b Willis	12
A.R.Border c Taylor b Botham	8	not out	32
G.S.Chappell* c Lamb b Willis	117	not out	22
K.J.Hughes c Willis b Miller	62		
D.W.Hookes lbw b Miller	56		
R.W.Marsh† c Cook b Botham	0		
G.F.Lawson b Miller	50		
B.Yardley c Lamb b Willis	17		
D.K.Lillee not out	2		
T.M.Alderman			
Extras (B 4, LB 1, NB 25, W 1)	31	(LB 1, NB 6)	7
	(9 wkts dec.) **424**		(2 wkts) **73**

1/63 2/76 3/123 4/264 5/311
6/311 7/374 8/414 9/424

1/2 2/22

Bowling: *First Innings*—Willis 31.5-4-95-3; Botham 40-10-121-2; Cowans 13-2-54-0; Pringle 10-1-37-0; Miller 33-11-70-4; Cook 4-2-16-0. *Second Innings*—Willis 6-1-23-2; Botham 6-1-23-2; Cowans 3-1-15-0; Pringle 2-0-3-0; Miller 4-3-8-0; Lamb 1-1-0-0.

Umpires: A.R.Crafter and M.W.Johnson

AUSTRALIA v ENGLAND 1982-83 (Second Test)

At Woolloongabba, Brisbane, 26, 27, 28, 30 November, 1 December
Result: Australia won by 7 wickets

England

C.J.Tavare c Hughes b Lawson	1	c Marsh b Lawson	13
G.Fowler c Yardley b Lawson	7	c Marsh b Thomson	83
D.I.Gower c Wessels b Lawson	18	c Marsh b Thomson	34
A.J.Lamb c Marsh b Lawson	72	c Wessels b Thomson	12
I.T.Botham c Rackemann b Yardley	40	(6) c Marsh b Thomson	15
D.W.Randall c Lawson b Rackemann	37	(5) c Yardley b Thomson	4
G.Miller c Marsh b Lawson	0	c Marsh b Lawson	60
R.W.Taylor† c Lawson b Rackemann	1	c Hookes b Lawson	3
E.E.Hemmings not out	15	b Lawson	18
R.G.D.Willis* c Thomson b Yardley	1	not out	10
N.G.Cowans c Marsh b Lawson	10	c Marsh b Lawson	5
Extras (B 2, NB 14, W 1)	17	(B 8, LB 8, NB 35, W 1)	52
	219		**309**

1/8 2/13 3/63 4/141 5/152
6/152 7/178 8/191 9/195
1/54 2/144 3/165 4/169 5/194
6/204 7/226 8/285 9/295

Bowling: *First Innings*—Lawson 18.3-4-47-6; Rackemann 21-8-61-2; Thomson 8-0-43-0; Yardley 17-5-51-2. *Second Innings*—Lawson 35.3-11-87-5; Rackemann 12.2-3-35-0; Thomson 31-6-73-5; Yardley 40.4-21-50-0; Chappell 6-2-8-0; Hookes 2-0-4-0.

Australia

K.C.Wessels b Willis	162	b Hemmings	46
J.Dyson b Botham	1	retired hurt	4
A.R.Border c Randall b Willis	0	c Botham b Hemmings	15
G.S.Chappell* run out	53	c Lamb b Cowans	8
K.J.Hughes c Taylor b Botham	0	not out	39
D.W.Hookes c Taylor b Botham	28	not out	66
R.W.Marsh† c Taylor b Botham	11		
B.Yardley c Tavare b Willis	53		
G.F.Lawson c Hemmings b Willis	6		
C.G.Rackemann b Willis	4		
J.R.Thomson not out	5		
Extras (B 2, LB 8, NB 8)	18	(B 2, LB 5, NB 5)	12
	341	(3 wkts)	**190**

1/4 2/11 3/94 4/99 5/130
6/171 7/271 8/310 9/332
1/60 2/77 3/83

Bowling: *First Innings*—Willis 29.4-3-66-5; Botham 22-1-105-3; Cowans 6-0-36-0; Hemmings 33.3-6-81-0; Miller 19.3-4-35-1. *Second Innings*—Willis 4-1-24-0; Botham 15.5-1-70-0; Cowans 9-1-31-1; Hemmings 29-9-43-2; Miller 3-0-10-0.

Umpires: R.C.Bailhache and M.W.Johnson

AUSTRALIA v ENGLAND 1982-83 (Third Test)

At Adelaide Oval, 10, 11, 12, 14, 15 December
Result: Australia won by 8 wickets

Australia

K.C.Wessels c Taylor b Botham	44	(2) c Taylor b Botham	1
J.Dyson c Taylor b Botham	44	(1) not out	37
G.S.Chappell* c Gower b Willis	115	(4) not out	26
K.J.Hughes run out	88		
G.F.Lawson c Botham b Willis	2	(3) c Randall b Willis	14
A.R.Border c Taylor b Pringle	26		
D.W.Hookes c Botham b Hemmings	37		
R.W.Marsh† c Hemmings b Pringle	3		
B.Yardley c Gower b Botham	38		
R.M.Hogg not out	14		
J.R.Thomson c and b Botham	3		
Extras (LB 6, NB 18)	24	(NB 5)	5
	438	(2 wkts)	**83**

1/76 2/138 3/264 4/270 5/315
6/355 7/359 8/391 9/430
1/3 2/37

Bowling: *First Innings*—Willis 25-8-76-2; Botham 36.5-5-112-4; Pringle 33-5-97-2; Miller 14-2-33-0; Hemmings 48-17-96-1. *Second Innings*—Willis 8-1-17-1; Botham 10-2-45-1; Pringle 1.5-0-11-0; Hemmings 4-1-5-0.

England

C.J.Tavare c Marsh b Hogg	0	c Wessels b Thomson	0
G.Fowler c Marsh b Lawson	11	c Marsh b Lawson	37
D.I.Gower c Marsh b Lawson	60	b Hogg	114
A.J.Lamb c Marsh b Lawson	82	c Chappell b Yardley	8
I.T.Botham c Wessels b Thomson	35	c Dyson b Yardley	58
D.W.Randall b Lawson	0	c Marsh b Lawson	17
G.Miller c Yardley b Hogg	7	lbw b Lawson	17
R.W.Taylor† c Chappell b Yardley	2	(9) not out	3
D.R.Pringle not out	1	(8) c Marsh b Thomson	9
E.E.Hemmings b Thomson	0	c Wessels b Lawson	0
R.G.D.Willis* b Thomson	1	c Marsh b Lawson	10
Extras (LB 5, NB 11)	16	(B 7, LB 15, NB 15, W 3)	31
	216		**304**

1/1 2/21 3/140 4/181 5/181
6/194 7/199 8/213 9/213
1/11 2/90 3/118 4/247 5/247
6/272 7/277 8/289 9/290

Bowling: *First Innings*—Lawson 18-4-56-4; Hogg 14-2-41-2; Thomson 14.5-3-51-3; Yardley 21-7-52-1. *Second Innings*—Lawson 24-6-66-5; Hogg 19-5-53-1; Thomson 13-3-41-2; Yardley 37-12-90-2; Border 8-2-14-0; Hookes 3-1-9-0.

Umpires: R.A.French and M.W.Johnson

AUSTRALIA v ENGLAND 1982-83 (Fourth Test)

At Melbourne Cricket Ground, 26, 27, 28, 29, 30 December

Result: England won by 3 runs

England

Batsman	First Innings		Second Innings	
G.Cook	c Chappell b Thomson	10	c Yardley b Thomson	26
G.Fowler	c Chappell b Hogg	4	b Hogg	65
C.J.Tavare	c Yardley b Thomson	89	b Hogg	0
D.I.Gower	c Marsh b Hogg	18	c Marsh b Lawson	3
A.J.Lamb	c Dyson b Yardley	83	c Marsh b Hogg	26
I.T.Botham	c Wessels b Yardley	27	c Chappell b Thomson	46
G.Miller	c Border b Yardley	10	lbw b Lawson	14
D.R.Pringle	c Wessels b Hogg	9	c Marsh b Lawson	42
R.W.Taylor†	c Marsh b Yardley	1	lbw b Thomson	37
R.G.D.Willis*	not out	6	not out	8
N.G.Cowans	c Lawson b Hogg	3	b Lawson	10
Extras	(B 3, LB 6, NB 12, W 3)	24	(B 2, LB 9, NB 6)	17
		284		**294**

1/11 2/25 3/56 4/217 5/227
6/259 7/262 8/268 9/278

1/40 2/41 3/45 4/128 5/129
6/160 7/201 8/262 9/280

Bowling: *First Innings*—Lawson 17-6-48-0; Hogg 23.3-6-69-4; Yardley 27-9-89-4; Thomson 13-2-49-2; Chappell 1-0-5-0. *Second Innings*—Lawson 21.4-6-66-4; Hogg 22-5-64-3; Yardley 15-2-67-0; Thomson 21-3-74-3; Chappell 1-0-6-0.

Australia

Batsman	First Innings		Second Innings	
K.C.Wessels	b Willis	47	b Cowans	14
J.Dyson	lbw b Cowans	21	c Tavare b Botham	31
G.S.Chappell*	c Lamb b Cowans	0	c sub (I.J.Gould) b Cowans	2
K.J.Hughes	b Willis	66	c Taylor b Miller	48
A.R.Border	b Botham	2	not out	62
D.W.Hookes	c Taylor b Pringle	53	(6) c Willis b Cowans	68
R.W.Marsh†	b Willis	53	(5) lbw b Cowans	13
B.Yardley	b Miller	9	b Cowans	0
G.F.Lawson	c Fowler b Miller	0	c Cowans b Pringle	7
R.M.Hogg	not out	8	lbw b Botham	4
J.R.Thomson	b Miller	1	c Miller b Botham	21
Extras	(LB 8, NB 19)	27	(B 5, LB 9, NB 3, W 1)	18
		287		**288**

1/55 2/55 3/83 4/89 5/180
6/261 7/276 8/276 9/278

1/37 2/39 3/71 4/171 5/173
6/190 7/190 8/202 9/218

Bowling: *First Innings*—Willis 15-2-38-3; Botham 18-3-69-1; Cowans 16-0-69-2; Pringle 15-2-40-1; Miller 15-5-44-3. *Second Innings*—Willis 17-0-57-0; Botham 25.1-4-80-2; Cowans 26-6-77-6; Pringle 12-4-26-1; Miller 16-6-30-1.

Umpires: A.R.Crafter and R.V.Whitehead

AUSTRALIA v ENGLAND 1982-83 (Fifth Test)

At Sydney Cricket Ground, 2, 3, 4, 6, 7 January

Result: Match drawn

Australia

Batsman	First Innings		Second Innings	
K.C.Wessels	c Willis b Botham	19	(2) lbw b Botham	53
J.Dyson	c Taylor b Hemmings	79	(1) c Gower b Willis	2
G.S.Chappell*	lbw b Willis	35	c Randall b Hemmings	11
K.J.Hughes	c Cowans b Botham	29	c Botham b Hemmings	137
D.W.Hookes	c Botham b Hemmings	17	lbw b Miller	19
A.R.Border	c Miller b Hemmings	89	c Botham b Cowans	83
R.W.Marsh†	c and b Miller	3	c Taylor b Miller	41
B.Yardley	b Cowans	24	c Botham b Hemmings	0
G.F.Lawson	c and b Botham	6	not out	13
J.R.Thomson	c Lamb b Botham	0	c Gower b Miller	12
R.M.Hogg	not out	0	run out	0
Extras	(B 3, LB 8, W 2)	13	(LB 7, NB 4)	11
		314		**382**

1/39 2/96 3/150 4/173 5/210
6/219 7/262 8/283 9/291

1/23 2/38 3/82 4/113 5/262
6/350 7/357 8/358 9/382

Bowling: *First Innings*—Willis 20-6-57-1; Cowans 21-3-67-1; Botham 30-8-75-4; Hemmings 27-10-68-3; Miller 17-7-34-1. *Second Innings*—Willis 10-2-33-1; Cowans 13-1-47-1; Botham 10-0-35-1; Hemmings 47-16-116-3; Miller 49.3-12-133-3; Cook 2-1-7-0.

England

Batsman	First Innings		Second Innings	
G.Cook	c Chappell b Hogg	8	lbw b Lawson	2
C.J.Tavare	b Lawson	0	lbw b Yardley	16
D.I.Gower	c Chappell b Lawson	70	(4) c Hookes b Yardley	24
A.J.Lamb	b Lawson	0	(5) c and b Yardley	29
D.W.Randall	b Thomson	70	(6) b Thomson	44
I.T.Botham	c Wessels b Thomson	5	(7) lbw b Thomson	32
G.Miller	lbw b Thomson	34	(8) c Marsh b Thomson	21
R.W.Taylor†	lbw b Thomson	0	(9) not out	28
E.E.Hemmings	c Border b Yardley	29	(3) c Marsh b Yardley	95
R.G.D.Willis*	c Border b Thomson	1		
N.G.Cowans	not out	0		
Extras	(B 4, LB 4, NB 12)	20	(B 1, LB 10, NB 11, W 1)	23
		237	(7 wkts)	**314**

1/8 2/23 3/24 4/146 5/163
6/169 7/170 8/220 9/232

1/3 2/55 3/104 4/155
5/196 6/260 7/361

Bowling: *First Innings*—Lawson 20-2-70-3; Hogg 16-2-50-1; Thomson 14.5-2-50-5; Yardley 14-4-47-1. *Second Innings*—Lawson 15-1-50-1; Hogg 13-6-25-0; Thomson 12-3-30-2; Yardley 37-6-139-4; Border 16-3-36-0; Chappell 1-0-6-0; Hookes 2-1-5-0.

Umpires: R.A.French and M.W.Johnson

SRI LANKA v AUSTRALIA 1982-83 (Only Test)

At Asgiriya Stadium, Kandy, 22, 23, 24, 26 April
Result: Australia won by an innings and 38 runs

Australia

K.C.Wessels c Dias b de Silva		141
G.M.Wood c Ratnayake b Ranatunga		4
G.N.Yallop lbw b de Mel		98
G.S.Chappell* lbw b de Mel		66
D.W.Hookes not out		143
A.R.Border not out		47
R.D.Woolley†		
T.G.Hogan		
B.Yardley		
D.K.Lillee		
R.M.Hogg		
Extras (LB 11, NB 3, W 1)		15

1/43 2/213 3/290 4/359 (4 wkts dec.) 514

Bowling: de Mel 23-3-113-2; Ratnayake 28-4-108-0; Ranatunga 19-2-72-1; de Silva 44-7-122-1; Guneratne 17-1-84-0.

Sri Lanka

S.Wettimuny c Woolley b Lillee	0		b Hogan	96
E.R.N.S.Fernando c Woolley b Hogg	0		c Woolley b Lillee	3
R.L.Dias c Border b Lillee	4		b Hogan	10
L.R.D.Mendis* c Hookes b Yardley	74	(5)	c Border b Yardley	6
R.S.Madugalle c and b Yardley	9	(6)	b Yardley	0
A.Ranatunga c Lillee b Yardley	90	(7)	b Hogan	32
D.S.de Silva c Hogan b Yardley	26	(8)	c Woolley b Hogan	5
A.L.F.de Mel c Hookes b Hogan	29	(9)	c Yallop b Hogan	0
R.G.de Alwis† c Border b Yardley	3	(10)	run out	9
R.J.Ratnayake c Woolley b Border	14	(4)	run out	30
R.P.W.Guneratne not out	0		not out	1
Extras (B 4, LB 5, NB 12, W 1)	22		(B 6, LB 7, NB 1)	14
	271			**205**

1/1 2/5 3/9 4/46 5/142   1/17 2/59 3/120 4/151 5/155
6/220 7/224 8/247 9/270   6/155 7/162 8/164 9/191

Bowling: First Innings—Lillee 19-3-67-2; Hogg 12-4-31-1; Chappell 1-0-2-0; Yardley 25-7-88-5; Hogan 11-1-50-1; Border 4.5-0-11-1. Second Innings—Lillee 11-3-40-1; Hogg 3-2-7-0; Yardley 26-6-78-2; Hogan 25.2-6-66-5.

Umpires: C.E.B.Anthony and H.C.Felsinger

AUSTRALIA v PAKISTAN 1983-84 (First Test)

At W.A.C.A. Ground, Perth, 11, 12, 13, 14 November
Result: Australia won by an innings and 9 runs

Australia

K.C.Wessels c Wasim Bari b Azeem Hafeez	12	c Border b Rackemann	24
W.B.Phillips c Tahir Naqqash b Moh'd Nazir	159	c Chappell b Rackemann	27
G.N.Yallop b Azeem Hafeez	141	c Marsh b Rackemann	65
K.J.Hughes b Abdul Qadir	16	lbw b Rackemann	46
A.R.Border c Wasim Raja b Azeem Hafeez	32	c Marsh b Lawson	30
G.S.Chappell* c Azeem Hafeez b Abdul Qadir	17	c Marsh b Lawson	4
R.W.Marsh† c Wasim Bari b Azeem Hafeez	24	c Marsh b Lawson	7
G.F.Lawson c Mohammad Nazir b Abdul Qadir	9	c Marsh b Rackemann	26
D.K.Lillee c Wasim Raja b Azeem Hafeez	0	run out	18
R.M.Hogg not out	7	c Border b Hogg	18
C.G.Rackemann		not out	0
Extras (LB 9, NB 7, W 3)	19	(B 4, LB 7, NB 20, W 2)	33

1/34 2/293 3/321 4/369 5/386 (9 wkts dec.) 436   1/62 2/63 3/188 4/197 5/206 298
6/404 7/424 8/424 9/436   6/218 7/257 8/267 9/281

Bowling: Tahir Naqqash 22-6-76-0; Azeem Hafeez 27.3-5-100-5; Mudassar Nazir 15-1-39-0; Mohammad Nazir 29-5-91-1; Abdul Qadir 32-4-121-3.

Pakistan

Mohsin Khan c Marsh b Hogg	8
Mudassar Nazar c Phillips b Lillee	1
Qasim Omar c Yallop b Rackemann	48
Javed Miandad c Phillips b Hogg	0
Zaheer Abbas* c Phillips b Hogg	0
Wasim Raja c Chappell b Rackemann	14
Wasim Bari† c Chappell b Rackemann	0
Tahir Naqqash not out	29
Abdul Qadir b Rackemann	5
Mohammad Nazir c Chappell b Rackemann	16
Azeem Hafeez c Border b Lawson	1
Extras (LB 3, NB 4)	7
	129

1/7 2/13 3/15 4/15 5/65
6/68 7/90 8/105 9/124

Bowling: First Innings—Lillee 13-3-26-1; Hogg 12-4-20-3; Rackemann 8-0-32-5; Lawson 7.2-0-48-1. Second Innings—Lillee 29-6-56-0; Hogg 21.1-2-72-1; Rackemann 26-6-86-6; Lawson 13-1-53-2; Chappell 9-1-20-0.

Umpires: M.W.Johnson and P.J.McConnell

AUSTRALIA v PAKISTAN 1983-84 (Second Test)

At Woolloongabba, Brisbane, 25, 26, 27, 28, 29 (no play) November
Result: Match drawn

Pakistan

	First Innings		Second Innings	
Mohsin Khan	c Chappell b Lawson	2	b Lawson	37
Mudassar Nazar	c Marsh b Lawson	24	c Wessels b Rackemann	18
Qasim Omar	c Hughes b Lawson	17	not out	11
Javed Miandad	c Marsh b Hogg	6	c Phillips b Rackemann	5
Zaheer Abbas*	c Border b Lawson	56	not out	3
Wasim Raja	c Hughes b Rackemann	27		
Wasim Bari†	c Border b Rackemann	0		
Abdul Qadir	b Rackemann	13		
Rashid Khan	not out	2		
Azeem Hafeez	b Lawson	1		
Mohammad Nazir	c Marsh b Hogg	6		
Extras	(LB 3, NB 2, W 1)	6	(LB 6, NB 2)	8
		156	(3 wkts)	**82**

1/10 2/39 3/46 4/62 5/124
6/128 7/128 8/146 9/147

1/57 2/59 3/74

Bowling: First Innings—Lawson 17.1-1-49-5; Hogg 15-2-43-2; Lillee 8-1-33-0. Second Innings—Lawson 10-3-24-1; Hogg 3-0-11-0; Rackemann 8-1-31-2; Lillee 2-0-10-0.

Australia

K.C.Wessels	c Qasim Omar b Azeem Hafeez	35
W.B.Phillips	b Rashid Khan	46
G.N.Yallop	c Wasim Bari b Rashid Khan	33
K.J.Hughes	c Mohammad Nazir b Azeem Hafeez	53
A.R.Border	c Wasim Bari b Rashid Khan	118
G.S.Chappell*	not out	150
R.W.Marsh†	b Azeem Hafeez	1
G.F.Lawson	b Abdul Qadir	49
D.K.Lillee		
R.M.Hogg		
C.G.Rackemann		
Extras	(B 2, LB 6, NB 15, W 1)	24
	(7 wkts dec.)	**509**

1/56 2/120 3/124 4/232 5/403
6/406 7/509

Bowling: Azeem Hafeez 37-7-152-3; Rashid Khan 43-10-129-3; Mudassar Nazar 16-2-47-0; Abdul Qadir 32-5-112-1; Mohammad Nazir 24-6-50-0; Wasim Raja 3-0-11-0.

Umpires: R.A.French and M.W.Johnson

AUSTRALIA v PAKISTAN 1983-84 (Third Test)

At Adelaide Oval, 9, 10, 11, 12, 13 December
Result: Match drawn

Australia

	First Innings		Second Innings	
K.C.Wessels	c Zaheer Abbas b Abdul Qadir	179	(2) c Wasim Bari b Sarfraz Nawaz	2
W.B.Phillips	c Wasim Bari b Azeem Hafeez	12	(1) c Mudassar Nazar b Abdul Qadir	54
G.N.Yallop	c Qasim Omar b Sarfraz Nawaz	68	c Javed Miandad b Abdul Qadir	14
K.J.Hughes	c Wasim Bari b Azeem Hafeez	30	c Mudassar Nazar b Azeem Hafeez	106
A.R.Border	not out	117	lbw b Azeem Hafeez	66
G.S.Chappell*	c Wasim Bari b Sarfraz Nawaz	6	run out	4
R.W.Marsh†	c Mohsin Khan b Sarfraz Nawaz	2	retired hurt	33
T.G.Hogan	run out	2	c Qasim Omar b Salim Malik	8
G.F.Lawson	c Wasim Bari b Azeem Hafeez	4	not out	7
D.K.Lillee	c Sarfraz Nawaz b Azeem Hafeez	25	not out	4
R.M.Hogg	c Javed Miandad b Azeem Hafeez	5		
Extras	(LB 7, NB 4, W 4)	15	(B 3, LB 4, NB 4, W 1)	12
		465	(7 wkts)	**310**

1/21 2/163 3/219 4/353 5/376
6/378 7/383 8/394 9/451

1/3 2/44 3/121 4/216
5/228 6/293 7/305

Bowling: First Innings—Azeem Hafeez 38.2-8-167-5; Sarfraz Nawaz 42-7-105-3; Abdul Qadir 20-1-96-1; Mudassar Nazar 10-2-45-0; Mohammad Nazir 9-0-37-0; Mohsin Khan 3-0-8-0. Second Innings—Sarfraz Nawaz 30-8-69-1; Azeem Hafeez 19-4-50-2; Abdul Qadir 47-9-132-2; Mohammad Nazir 27-14-39-0; Javed Miandad 3-0-10-0; Mohsin Khan 1-1-0-0; Salim Malik 1-0-3-1; Qasim Omar 1-1-0-0.

Pakistan

Mohsin Khan	c Phillips b Lawson	149
Mudassar Nazar	c Marsh b Lillee	44
Qasim Omar	c Marsh b Lillee	113
Javed Miandad	lbw b Lawson	131
Zaheer Abbas*	c Yallop b Hogg	46
Salim Malik	c Lawson b Hogan	77
Sarfraz Nawaz	c Yallop b Lillee	32
Abdul Qadir	b Lillee	10
Wasim Bari†	c Marsh b Lillee	0
Mohammad Nazir	not out	5
Azeem Hafeez	c Wessels b Lillee	5
Extras	(B 1, LB 4, NB 4)	12
		624

1/73 2/306 3/314 4/371 5/557
6/590 7/604 8/612 9/613

Bowling: Lawson 37-7-127-2; Hogg 34-3-123-1; Lillee 50.2-8-171-6; Hogan 37-8-107-1; Chappell 32-6-82-0; Border 1-0-9-0.

Umpires: A.R.Crafter and R.A.French

AUSTRALIA v PAKISTAN 1983-84 (Fourth Test)

At Melbourne Cricket Ground, 26, 27, 28, 29, 30 December

Result: Match drawn

Pakistan

Batsman	First Innings	R	Second Innings	R
Mohsin Khan	lbw b Lillee	152	c Hughes b Lillee	3
Mudassar Nazar	c Marsh b Lawson	7	lbw b Matthews	35
Qasim Omar	b Maguire	23	b Lawson	9
Javed Miandad	c Marsh b Maguire	27	lbw b Lillee	11
Zaheer Abbas	run out	44	b Matthews	50
Salim Malik	c Maguire b Lawson	35	(6) b Lillee	14
Imran Khan*	c Marsh b Lillee	83	(8) not out	72
Sarfraz Nawaz	c Hughes b Maguire	22		
Abdul Qadir	c Lawson b Matthews	45	(9) not out	11
Wasim Bari†	not out	6		
Azeem Hafeez	c Maguire b Matthews	7	(5) b Lawson	12
Extras	(LB 11, NB 8)	19	(B 10, LB 9, W 2)	21
Total		**470**	**(7 wkts)**	**238**

1/13 2/64 3/112 4/244 5/294
6/321 7/349 8/457 9/459

1/3 2/18 3/37 4/73
5/81 6/160 7/213

Bowling: *First Innings*—Lawson 38-8-125-2; Lillee 38-11-113-2; Maguire 29-7-111-3; Matthews 28.4-7-95-2; Chappell 7-3-15-0. *Second Innings*—Lawson 21-8-47-2; Lillee 29-7-71-3; Maguire 12-3-26-0; Matthews 21-8-48-2; Border 5-3-9-0; Chappell 8-3-13-0; Marsh 2-0-3-0; Wessels 2-1-2-0.

Australia

Batsman		R
K.C.Wessels	c Wasim Bari b Azeem Hafeez	11
W.B.Phillips	lbw b Azeem Hafeez	35
G.N.Yallop	c Wasim Bari b Sarfraz Nawaz	268
K.J.Hughes	lbw b Azeem Hafeez	94
A.R.Border	lbw b Abdul Qadir	32
G.S.Chappell*	c Salim Malik b Abdul Qadir	5
R.W.Marsh†	c Mudassar Nazar b Abdul Qadir	0
G.R.J.Matthews	lbw b Sarfraz Nawaz	75
G.F.Lawson	c Mudassar Nazar b Abdul Qadir	0
J.N.Maguire	c Wasim Bari b Abdul Qadir	4
D.K.Lillee	not out	2
Extras	(B 15, LB 9, NB 3, W 2)	29
Total		**555**

1/21 2/70 3/273 4/342 5/354
6/354 7/539 8/540 9/553

Bowling: Sarfraz Nawaz 51-12-106-2; Azeem Hafeez 35-8-115-3; Abdul Qadir 54.3-12-166-5; Mudassar Nazar 20-0-76-0; Javed Miandad 5-0-16-0; Zaheer Abbas 22-5-42-0; Salim Malik 2-1-10-0.

Umpires: A.R.Crafter and P.J.McConnell

AUSTRALIA v PAKISTAN 1983-84 (Fifth Test)

At Sydney Cricket Ground, 2, 3, 4, 5, 6 January

Result: Australia won by 10 wickets

Pakistan

Batsman	First Innings	R	Second Innings	R
Mohsin Khan	c Border b Lillee	14	c Chappell b Lawson	1
Mudassar Nazar	c Chappell b Lawson	84	b Lawson	21
Qasim Omar	c Border b Lillee	15	c Marsh b Lawson	26
Abdul Qadir	c Hughes b Lawson	4	(9) c Marsh b Lillee	5
Javed Miandad	c Lillee b Matthews	16	c Marsh b Lawson	60
Zaheer Abbas	c Yallop b Lawson	61	(4) c Marsh b Hogg	33
Salim Malik	c Lillee b Lawson	5	(5) c Marsh b Hogg	10
Imran Khan*	c Yallop b Lawson	54	(6) c Chappell b Lillee	7
Sarfraz Nawaz	lbw b Lillee	5	(7) c Phillips b Lillee	20
Wasim Bari†	not out	7	(8) c Phillips b Lillee	20
Azeem Hafeez	c Marsh b Lillee	4	not out	2
Extras	(B 2, LB 7)	9	(LB 4, NB 1)	5
Total		**278**		**210**

1/18 2/57 3/67 4/131 5/150
6/158 7/254 8/267 9/267

1/5 2/47 3/56 4/104 5/132
6/163 7/163 8/173 9/191

Bowling: *First Innings*—Lillee 31.2-10-65-4; Hogg 18-1-61-0; Chappell 8-0-25-0; Lawson 25-5-59-5; Matthews 18-4-59-1. *Second Innings*—Lillee 29.5-5-88-4; Lawson 20-7-48-4; Matthews 7-4-17-0; Hogg 14-2-53-2.

Australia

Batsman	First Innings	R	Second Innings	R
K.C.Wessels	c Wasim Bari b Azeem Hafeez	3	not out	14
W.B.Phillips	c Salim Malik b Sarfraz Nawaz	37	not out	19
G.N.Yallop	c Wasim Bari b Mudassar Nazar	30		
G.S.Chappell*	lbw b Mudassar Nazar	182		
K.J.Hughes	lbw b Sarfraz Nawaz	76		
A.R.Border	c Wasim Bari b Mudassar Nazar	64		
G.R.J.Matthews	not out	22		
R.W.Marsh†	not out	15		
G.F.Lawson				
R.M.Hogg				
D.K.Lillee				
Extras	(LB 15, NB 9, W 1)	25	(NB 2)	2
Total	**(6 wkts dec.)**	**454**	**(0 wkts)**	**35**

1/11 2/66 3/83 4/254 5/407
6/436

Bowling: *First Innings*—Sarfraz Nawaz 53-13-132-2; Azeem Hafeez 36-7-121-1; Mudassar Nazar 31-9-81-3; Abdul Qadir 54.3-12-166-5. *Second Innings*—Sarfraz Nawaz 3-1-7-0; Azeem Hafeez 2.4-0-28-0.

Umpires: R.A.French and M.W.Johnson

WEST INDIES v AUSTRALIA 1983-84 (First Test)

At Bourda, Georgetown, Guyana, 2, 3, 4, 6, 7 March

Result: Match drawn

Australia

Batsman	First Innings	Runs	Second Innings	Runs
S.B.Smith	c Dujon b Garner	3	(2) c Dujon b Garner	12
K.C.Wessels	c Lloyd b Garner	4	(1) c Lloyd b Daniel	20
G.M.Ritchie	c Davis b Harper	78	lbw b Garner	3
K.J.Hughes*	b Garner	18	c Haynes b Daniel	0
A.R.Border	b Garner	5	run out	54
D.W.Hookes	c Dujon b Harper	32	b Garner	10
W.B.Phillips†	c Greenidge b Harper	16	b Daniel	76
G.F.Lawson	c Richards b Harper	11	not out	35
T.G.Hogan	not out	42	lbw b Davis	18
T.M.Alderman	lbw b Garner	1	(11) not out	3
R.M.Hogg	lbw b Garner	52	(10) b Davis	6
Extras	(B 2, LB 3, NB 11, W 1)	17	(B 10, LB 15, NB 11)	36
Total		279	(9 wkts)	273

1/6 2/23 3/55 4/63 5/139 6/166 7/180 8/181 9/182

1/37 2/41 3/42 4/50 5/60 6/185 7/209 8/249 9/263

Bowling: *First Innings*—Garner 27.2-10-75-6; Daniel 12-3-60-0; Davis 19-2-45-0; Harper 24-7-56-4; Gomes 15-1-35-0; Richards 5-2-3-0. *Second Innings*—Garner 24-5-67-3; Daniel 27-4-86-3; Davis 14-3-35-2; Harper 15-4-27-0; Gomes 11-2-25-0; Richards 6-2-8-0.

West Indies

Batsman	First Innings	Runs	Second Innings	Runs
C.G.Greenidge	c Wessels b Lawson	16	not out	120
D.L.Haynes	lbw b Hogg	60	not out	103
R.B.Richardson	lbw b Lawson	19		
I.V.A.Richards	c Phillips b Hogg	8		
H.A.Gomes	c Border b Hogan	10		
C.H.Lloyd*	c Phillips b Alderman	36		
P.J.L.Dujon†	c Phillips b Hogan	21		
R.A.Harper	b Hogan	10		
J.Garner	not out	16		
W.W.Davis	c Ritchie b Hogan	11		
W.W.Daniel	lbw b Lawson	4		
Extras	(LB 3, NB 16)	19	(B 10, LB 13, NB 4)	27
Total		230	(0 wkts)	250

1/29 2/72 3/93 4/110 5/154 6/181 7/191 8/203 9/225

Bowling: *First Innings*—Lawson 20.4-4-59-3; Alderman 21-3-61-1; Hogg 12-0-48-2; Hogan 25-9-56-4. *Second Innings*—Hogg 13-0-56-0; Alderman 11-0-43-0; Lawson 18-0-54-0; Hogan 19-2-74-0.

Umpires: D.M.Archer and D.J.Narine

WEST INDIES v AUSTRALIA 1983-84 (Second Test)

At Queen's Park Oval, Port-of-Spain, Trinidad, 16, 17, 18, 20, 21 March

Result: Match drawn

Australia

Batsman	First Innings	Runs	Second Innings	Runs
K.C.Wessels	c Gomes b Garner	4	lbw b Garner	4
W.B.Phillips†	c Dujon b Garner	4	run out	0
G.M.Ritchie	b Garner	1	b Small	26
K.J.Hughes*	c Dujon b Garner	24	lbw b Marshall	33
A.R.Border	not out	98	not out	100
D.W.Hookes	c Dujon b Garner	23	(6) c Richardson b Gomes	21
D.M.Jones	c and b Richards	48	(7) b Richards	5
G.F.Lawson	c and b Daniel	14	(8) b Marshall	20
T.G.Hogan	c Greenidge b Daniel	0	(9) c Logie b Daniel	38
R.M.Hogg	c Marshall b Daniel	11	(5) c Garner b Richards	9
T.M.Alderman	c Richardson b Garner	1	not out	21
Extras	(B 6, LB 4, NB 17)	27	(B 6, LB 1, NB 14, W 1)	22
Total		255	(9 wkts)	299

1/4 2/7 3/16 4/50 5/85 6/185 7/233 8/233 9/253

1/1 2/35 3/41 4/114 5/115 6/153 7/162 8/196 9/238

Bowling: *First Innings*—Garner 28.1-9-60-6; Marshall 19-4-73-0; Small 10-3-24-0; Gomes 10-0-33-0; Richards 10-4-15-1. *Second Innings*—Marshall 22-3-73-2; Garner 15-4-35-1; Small 14-2-51-1; Daniel 9-3-11-1; Richards 25-5-65-2; Gomes 27-5-53-1; Logie 0.1-0-4-0.

West Indies

Batsman	Innings	Runs
C.G.Greenidge	c Phillips b Hogg	24
D.L.Haynes	run out	53
R.B.Richardson	c Wessels b Alderman	23
I.V.A.Richards*	c Phillips b Alderman	76
H.A.Gomes	c and b Lawson	3
A.L.Logie	lbw b Hogan	97
P.J.L.Dujon†	c Phillips b Hogan	130
M.D.Marshall	lbw b Lawson	10
J.Garner	not out	24
W.W.Daniel	not out	6
M.A.Small		
Extras	(B 7, LB 12, NB 1, W 2)	22
Total	(8 wkts dec.)	468

1/35 2/93 3/124 4/129 5/229 6/387 7/430 8/462

Bowling: Lawson 32-3-132-2; Hogg 31-2-103-1; Alderman 35-9-91-2; Hogan 28-3-123-2.

Umpires: D.M.Archer and C.E.Cumberbatch

WEST INDIES v AUSTRALIA 1983-84 (Third Test)

At Kensington Oval, Bridgetown, Barbados, 30, 31 March, 1, 3, 4 April
Result: West Indies won by 10 wickets

Australia

S.B.Smith c Dujon b Marshall	10	(2)	b Marshall	7
G.M.Wood c Dujon b Holding	68	(1)	lbw b Garner	20
G.M.Ritchie c and b Harper	57		c Haynes b Marshall	0
K.J.Hughes* c Lloyd b Holding	20		c Lloyd b Holding	25
A.R.Border c Richardson b Marshall	38	(6)	c Dujon b Holding	8
D.W.Hookes c Dujon b Garner	30	(7)	b Holding	9
T.G.Hogan b Garner	40	(5)	c Richardson b Holding	2
W.B.Phillips† c Dujon b Garner	120		b Marshall	1
G.F.Lawson b Baptiste	10		c Harper b Marshall	2
R.M.Hogg c Garner b Harper	3		not out	5
T.M.Alderman not out	2		b Marshall	0
Extras (B 14, LB 8, NB 9)	31		(B 1, LB 6, NB 11)	18
	429			97

1/11 2/114 3/158 4/171 5/223 1/13 2/13 3/63 4/65 5/68
6/263 7/307 8/330 9/366 6/80 7/85 8/85 9/92

Bowling: *First Innings*—Garner 33.5-6-110-3; Marshall 26-2-83-2; Holding 30-5-94-2; Baptiste 17-5-34-1; Harper 43-9-86-2. *Second Innings*—Marshall 15.5-1-42-5; Garner 8-4-9-1; Holding 15-4-24-4; Harper 2-1-1-0; Baptiste 3-0-14-0.

West Indies

C.G.Greenidge run out	64	not out	10
D.L.Haynes b Hogg	145	not out	11
R.B.Richardson not out	131		
I.V.A.Richards b Lawson	6		
E.A.E.Baptiste b Lawson	11		
P.J.L.Dujon† b Alderman	2		
C.H.Lloyd* b Hogg	76		
M.D.Marshall b Hogg	10		
R.A.Harper b Hogg	19		
J.Garner c Phillips b Hogg	9		
M.A.Holding c Smith b Hogg	0		
Extras (LB 25, NB 11)	36		
	509	(0 wkts)	21

1/132 2/277 3/289 4/313 5/316
6/447 7/465 8/493 9/509

Bowling: *First Innings*—Lawson 33.2-4-150-2; Alderman 42.4-6-152-1; Hogg 32.4-4-77-6; Hogan 34-8-97-0; Border 3-1-8-0. *Second Innings*—Lawson 2-1-3-0; Alderman 1.4-0-18-0.

Umpires: D.M.Archer and L.H.Barker

WEST INDIES v AUSTRALIA 1983-84 (Fourth Test)

At Recreation Ground, St John's, Antigua, 7, 8, 9, 11 April
Result: West Indies won by an innings and 36 runs

Australia

W.B.Phillips c Dujon b Garner	5	(2)	b Garner	22
G.M.Ritchie c Holding b Marshall	6	(1)	c Dujon b Garner	23
A.R.Border c Dujon b Baptiste	98		c Greenidge b Baptiste	19
K.J.Hughes* c Marshall b Harper	24		c Richards b Marshall	29
D.M.Jones b Harper	1		c Dujon b Garner	11
D.W.Hookes c Richardson b Baptiste	51		c Greenidge b Holding	29
R.D.Woolley† c Dujon b Baptiste	13		lbw b Marshall	8
T.G.Hogan c Harper b Holding	14		c Baptiste b Garner	6
G.F.Lawson b Holding	4		not out	17
J.N.Maguire not out	15		b Marshall	0
C.G.Rackemann b Holding	12		b Garner	0
Extras (B 5, LB 4, NB 10)	19		(B 19, LB 7, NB 10)	36
	262			200

1/14 2/14 3/67 4/78 5/202 1/50 2/57 3/97 4/116 5/150
6/208 7/217 8/224 9/246 6/167 7/176 8/185 9/185

Bowling: *First Innings*—Marshall 18-2-70-1; Garner 18-5-34-1; Holding 19.5-3-42-3; Harper 19-4-58-2; Baptiste 17-2-42-3; Richards 5-0-7-0. *Second Innings*—Marshall 17-5-51-3; Garner 20.5-2-63-5; Holding 14-2-22-1; Baptiste 8-2-14-1; Harper 6-0-24-0.

West Indies

C.G.Greenidge c Ritchie b Lawson	0
D.L.Haynes b Lawson	21
R.B.Richardson c Woolley b Rackemann	154
I.V.A.Richards c Woolley b Rackemann	178
P.J.L.Dujon† c Hughes b Rackemann	28
C.H.Lloyd* c Jones b Rackemann	38
M.D.Marshall c Hookes b Maguire	6
E.A.E.Baptiste b Maguire	6
R.A.Harper c Ritchie b Maguire	27
J.Garner c Hogan b Rackemann	10
M.A.Holding not out	3
Extras (B 13, LB 13, NB 1)	27
	498

1/0 2/43 3/351 4/390 5/405
6/426 7/442 8/468 9/491

Bowling: Lawson 29-4-125-2; Rackemann 42.4-8-161-5; Maguire 44-9-121-3; Hogan 30-9-65-0.

Umpires: D.M.Archer and A.E.Weekes

WEST INDIES v AUSTRALIA 1983-84 (Fifth Test)

At Sabina Park, Kingston, Jamaica, 28, 29, 30 April, 2 May
Result: West Indies won by 10 wickets

Australia

Batsman	First Innings		Second Innings	
W.B.Phillips†	c Dujon b Garner	12	b Garner	2
S.B.Smith	c Greenidge b Marshall	9	absent hurt	–
A.R.Border	c Dujon b Marshall	41	not out	60
G.M.Ritchie	c Dujon b Marshall	5	b Holding	8
K.J.Hughes*	c Harper b Holding	19	c Greenidge b Marshall	23
D.W.Hookes	b Harper	36	c Dujon b Marshall	7
G.R.J.Matthews	st Dujon b Harper	7	(2) b Holding	7
T.G.Hogan	c and b Garner	25	(7) b Marshall	10
G.F.Lawson	c Harper b Garner	15	(8) b Marshall	4
R.M.Hogg	not out	1	(9) b Marshall	14
J.N.Maguire	c b Baptiste	9	(10) b Garner	0
Extras	(B 8, LB 3, NB 8, W 1)	20	(B 17, LB 4, NB 4)	25
		199		160

1/22 2/23 3/34 4/32 5/113
6/124 7/142 8/181 9/190

1/7 2/15 3/27 4/89 5/109
6/125 7/131 8/159 9/160

Bowling: *First Innings*—Marshall 18-4-37-3; Garner 17-4-42-3; Holding 12-2-43-1; Baptiste 11-3-40-1; Harper 20-8-26-2. *Second Innings*—Marshall 23-3-51-5; Garner 16.4-6-28-2; Holding 11-4-20-2; Baptiste 6-3-11-0; Harper 9-2-25-0; Richards 2-0-4-0.

West Indies

Batsman	First Innings		Second Innings	
C.G.Greenidge	c Ritchie b Hogan	127	not out	32
D.L.Haynes	b Hogan	60	not out	15
R.B.Richardson	c Phillips b Lawson	0		
I.V.A.Richards	run out	2		
C.H.Lloyd*	c Phillips b Lawson	20		
P.J.L.Dujon†	c Phillips b Maguire	23		
M.D.Marshall	c Hookes b Maguire	19		
E.A.E.Baptiste	c Lawson b Maguire	27		
R.A.Harper	c Phillips b Maguire	0		
J.Garner	c Phillips b Lawson	7		
M.A.Holding	not out	0		
Extras	(B 1, LB 11, NB 8)	20	(B 2, LB 3, NB 3)	8
		305	(0 wkts)	55

1/162 2/169 3/174 4/213 5/228
6/260 7/274 9/297

Bowling: *First Innings*—Lawson 30-6-93-1; Hogg 16-2-67-0; Hogan 30-8-68-2; Maguire 16.4-2-57-4; Matthews 2-0-10-0. *Second Innings*—Lawson 5-0-24-0; Hogg 5.2-0-18-0; Maguire 1-0-8-0.

Umpires: D.M.Archer and L.H.Barker

AUSTRALIA v WEST INDIES 1984-85 (First Test)

At W.A.C.A. Ground, Perth, 9, 10, 11, 12 November
Result: West Indies won by an innings and 112 runs

West Indies

Batsman		Runs
C.G.Greenidge	c Rackemann b Alderman	30
D.L.Haynes	c Yallop b Hogg	56
R.B.Richardson	b Alderman	0
H.A.Gomes	b Hogg	127
I.V.A.Richards	c Phillips b Alderman	10
C.H.Lloyd*	c Phillips b Alderman	139
P.J.L.Dujon†	c Phillips b Alderman	1
M.A.Holding	c Wood b Alderman	1
M.D.Marshall	c Hughes b Hogg	21
J.Garner	c Phillips b Hogg	17
C.A.Walsh	not out	9
Extras	(B 1, LB 1, NB 4)	6
		416

1/83 2/83 3/89 4/104 5/104
6/186 7/335 8/337 9/387

Bowling: Lawson 24-3-79-0; Rackemann 28-3-106-0; Hogg 32-6-101-4; Alderman 39-12-128-6.

Australia

Batsman	First Innings		Second Innings	
K.C.Wessels	c Holding b Garner	13	(2) c Lloyd b Garner	0
J.Dyson	c Lloyd b Marshall	0	(1) b Marshall	30
G.M.Wood	c Lloyd b Garner	6	c Richardson b Walsh	56
A.R.Border	c Dujon b Holding	15	c Haynes b Marshall	6
K.J.Hughes*	c Marshall b Holding	4	lbw b Marshall	37
G.N.Yallop	c Greenidge b Holding	2	c Haynes b Walsh	1
W.B.Phillips†	c Marshall b Holding	22	c Dujon b Garner	16
G.F.Lawson	c Dujon b Marshall	1	not out	38
R.M.Hogg	b Holding	0	b Marshall	0
C.G.Rackemann	c Richardson b Holding	0	b Garner	0
T.M.Alderman	not out	0	c Richardson b Holding	23
Extras	(B 4, LB 2, NB 7)	13	(LB 7, NB 14)	21
		76		228

1/1 2/18 3/28 4/40 5/46
6/53 7/58 8/63 9/63

1/4 2/94 3/107 4/107 5/124
6/166 7/168 8/168 9/169

Bowling: *First Innings*—Marshall 15-5-25-2; Garner 7-0-24-2; Holding 9.2-3-21-6. *Second Innings*—Marshall 21-4-68-4; Garner 16-5-52-3; Holding 11.3-1-53-1; Walsh 20-4-43-2; Gomes 1-0-1-0; Richards 1-0-4-0.

Umpires: A.R.Crafter and P.J.McConnell

AUSTRALIA v WEST INDIES 1984-85 (Second Test)

At Woolloongabba, Brisbane, 23, 24, 25, 26, 27 November
Result: West Indies won by 8 wickets

Australia

	1st		2nd	
J.Dyson c Dujon b Holding	13	(2)	c Dujon b Marshall	21
K.C.Wessels b Garner	0	(1)	c Gomes b Walsh	61
G.M.Wood c Marshall b Walsh	20		c Richardson b Holding	3
A.R.Border c Lloyd b Marshall	17		c sub (R.A.Harper) b Holding	24
K.J.Hughes* c Marshall b Garner	34		lbw b Holding	4
D.C.Boon c Richardson b Marshall	11		c Holding b Marshall	51
W.B.Phillips† c Dujon b Walsh	44	(8)	c sub (R.A.Harper) b Holding	54
G.F.Lawson b Garner	14	(9)	c Richards b Marshall	14
T.M.Alderman c Lloyd b Walsh	0	(7)	c Richardson b Marshall	1
R.G.Holland c Dujon b Garner	6		b Marshall	0
R.M.Hogg not out	0		not out	21
Extras (B 7, LB 1, NB 11)	16		(B 4, LB 5, NB 8)	17
	175			**271**

1/1 2/33 3/33 4/81 5/97 1/88 2/88 3/99 4/106 5/131
6/102 7/122 8/136 9/173 6/212 7/236 8/236 9/271

Bowling: *First Innings*—Garner 18.4-5-67-4; Marshall 14.4-5-39-2; Holding 6.2-2-9-1; Walsh 16-5-55-3. *Second Innings*—Marshall 34-7-82-5; Garner 20-4-80-0; Holding 30-7-92-4; Walsh 5-2-7-1; Richards 1-0-1-0.

West Indies

	1st		2nd	
C.G.Greenidge c Border b Lawson	44	(1)	b Lawson	7
D.L.Haynes b Alderman	21	(2)	c Alderman b Hogg	5
R.B.Richardson c Phillips b Alderman	138	(3)	not out	9
H.A.Gomes b Holland	13	(4)	not out	3
I.V.A.Richards c Boon b Lawson	6			
P.J.L.Dujon† c Phillips b Holland	14			
C.H.Lloyd* c Hughes b Alderman	114			
M.D.Marshall b Lawson	57			
M.A.Holding b Lawson	1			
J.Garner not out	0			
C.A.Walsh c Phillips b Lawson	0			
Extras (B 2, LB 6, NB 8)	16		(LB 2)	2
	424		(2 wkts)	**26**

1/36 2/99 3/129 4/142 5/184 1/6 2/18
6/336 7/414 8/423 9/424

Bowling: *First Innings*—Lawson 30.4-8-116-5; Alderman 29-10-107-3; Hogg 21-3-71-0; Holland 27-5-97-2; Border 5-0-25-0. *Second Innings*—Lawson 5-0-10-1; Hogg 4.1-0-14-1.

Umpires: A.R.Crafter and M.W.Johnson

AUSTRALIA v WEST INDIES 1984-85 (Third Test)

At Adelaide Oval, 7, 8, 9, 10, 11 December
Result: West Indies won by 191 runs

West Indies

	1st		2nd	
C.G.Greenidge c Hogg b Lawson	95		lbw b Lawson	4
D.L.Haynes c Hughes b Hogg	0		c Wood b Lawson	50
R.B.Richardson c Border b Lawson	8	(4)	lbw b Hogg	3
H.A.Gomes c Rixon b Lawson	60	(5)	not out	120
I.V.A.Richards c Rixon b Lawson	42	(6)	c Rixon b Hogg	42
C.H.Lloyd* b Lawson	78	(7)	c Rixon b Lawson	6
P.J.L.Dujon† b Lawson	77	(8)	c Boon b Holland	32
M.D.Marshall c Rixon b Lawson	9			
R.A.Harper c Rixon b Lawson	9	(3)	c Rixon b Hogg	26
J.Garner not out	8			
C.A.Walsh b Holland	0			
Extras (B 5, LB 4, NB 3)	12		(LB 2, NB 7)	9
	356		(7 wkts dec.)	**292**

1/4 2/25 3/157 4/157 5/172 1/4 2/39 3/45
6/322 7/331 8/348 9/355 4/121 5/218 6/225 7/292

Bowling: *First Innings*—Lawson 40-7-112-8; Hogg 28-7-75-1; Alderman 19-8-38-0; Holland 30.2-5-109-1; Wessels 5-0-13-0. *Second Innings*—Lawson 24-6-69-3; Hogg 21-2-77-3; Holland 18.1-1-54-1; Alderman 12-1-66-0; Border 4-0-24-0.

Australia

	1st		2nd	
G.M.Wood c Greenidge b Harper	41	(7)	c Dujon b Harper	19
J.Dyson c Dujon b Walsh	8	(2)	lbw b Marshall	5
K.C.Wessels b Marshall	98	(1)	c Dujon b Harper	70
S.J.Rixon† c Richards b Marshall	0	(6)	lbw b Harper	16
K.J.Hughes c Dujon b Garner	0	(4)	b Marshall	2
A.R.Border* c Garner b Marshall	21	(3)	b Marshall	18
D.C.Boon c Dujon b Marshall	12	(5)	c Harper b Garner	9
G.F.Lawson c Dujon b Garner	49		c Dujon b Marshall	2
R.G.Holland c Haynes b Walsh	2		not out	7
R.M.Hogg not out	7		b Harper	7
T.M.Alderman c Richardson b Marshall	10		b Marshall	0
Extras (B 2, LB 8, NB 26)	36		(B 7, LB 7, NB 4)	18
	284			**173**

1/28 2/91 3/91 4/122 5/138 1/22 2/70 3/78 4/97 5/126
6/145 7/232 8/241 9/265 6/150 7/153 8/153 9/170

Bowling: *First Innings*—Marshall 26-8-69-5; Garner 26-5-61-2; Walsh 24-8-88-2; Harper 21-4-56-1. *Second Innings*—Marshall 15.5-4-38-5; Garner 16-2-58-1; Walsh 4-0-20-0; Harper 15-6-43-4.

Umpires: A.R.Crafter and M.W.Johnson

AUSTRALIA v WEST INDIES 1984-85 (Fourth Test)
At Melbourne Cricket Ground, 22, 23, 24, 26, 27 December
Result: Match drawn

West Indies

First Innings

Batsman		R
C.G.Greenidge	c Bennett b Lawson	10
D.L.Haynes	c Border b Lawson	13
R.B.Richardson	b McDermott	51
H.A.Gomes	c Matthews b McDermott	68
I.V.A.Richards	c Hughes b Matthews	208
P.J.L.Dujon†	b McDermott	0
C.H.Lloyd*	c Lawson b Matthews	19
M.D.Marshall	c Rixon b Hogg	55
R.A.Harper	c and b Hogg	5
J.Garner	lbw b Lawson	8
C.A.Walsh	not out	18
Extras	(B 1, LB 11, NB 12)	24
Total		**479**

1/27 2/30 3/153 4/154 5/154 6/362 8/376 9/426

Second Innings

Batsman		R
Greenidge	lbw b Lawson	1
Haynes	b McDermott	63
Richardson	b Lawson	3
Gomes	c Bennett b McDermott	18
Richards	lbw b McDermott	0
Lloyd	not out	49
Marshall	not out	34
Extras	(B 4, LB 9, NB 5)	18
Total	**(5 wkts dec.)**	**186**

1/2 2/12 3/63 4/63 5/100

Bowling: First Innings—Lawson 37-9-108-3; Hogg 27-7-96-2; McDermott 27-2-118-3; Bennett 20-0-78-0; Matthews 14.3-2-67-2. Second Innings—Lawson 19-4-54-2; Hogg 14-3-40-0; McDermott 21-6-65-3; Bennett 3-0-12-0; Wessels 1-0-2-0.

Australia

First Innings

Batsman		R
A.M.J.Hilditch	b Harper	70
G.M.Wood	lbw b Garner	12
K.C.Wessels	c Dujon b Marshall	90
K.J.Hughes	c Dujon b Walsh	0
A.R.Border*	c Richards b Walsh	35
G.R.J.Matthews	b Marshall	5
S.J.Rixon†	c Richardson b Marshall	0
M.J.Bennett	not out	22
G.F.Lawson	c Walsh b Garner	8
C.J.McDermott	b Marshall	0
R.M.Hogg	lbw b Marshall	19
Extras	(B 5, LB 7, NB 22, W 1)	35
Total		**296**

1/38 2/161 3/163 4/220 5/238 6/238 7/240 8/253 9/253

Second Innings

Batsman		R
Hilditch	b Gomes	113
Wood	c Dujon b Garner	5
Wessels	b Garner	0
Hughes	lbw b Garner	0
Border	c Dujon b Richards	41
Matthews	b Harper	2
Rixon	c Richardson b Harper	17
Bennett	not out	3
Lawson	b Walsh	0
Hogg	not out	0
Extras	(B 6, LB 2, NB 9)	17
Total	**(8 wkts)**	**198**

1/17 2/17 3/128 4/128 5/131 6/162 7/198 8/198

Bowling: First Innings—Marshall 31.5-6-86-5; Garner 24-6-74-2; Walsh 21-5-57-2; Harper 14-1-58-1; Richards 1-0-9-0. Second Innings—Marshall 20-4-36-0; Garner 19-1-49-3; Walsh 18-4-44-1; Harper 22-4-54-2; Richards 6-2-7-1; Gomes 2-0-7-1.

Umpires: P.J.McConnell and S.G.Randell

AUSTRALIA v WEST INDIES 1984-85 (Fifth Test)
At Sydney Cricket Ground, 30, 31 December, 1, 2, 3 January
Result: Australia won by an innings and 55 runs

Australia

Batsman		R
A.M.J.Hilditch	c Dujon b Holding	2
G.M.Wood	c Haynes b Gomes	45
K.C.Wessels	b Holding	173
G.M.Ritchie	run out	37
A.R.Border*	c Greenidge b Walsh	69
D.C.Boon	b Garner	49
S.J.Rixon†	c Garner b Holding	20
M.J.Bennett	c Greenidge b Garner	23
G.F.Lawson	not out	5
C.J.McDermott	c Greenidge b Walsh	4
R.G.Holland		
Extras	(B 7, LB 20, NB 17)	44
Total	**(9 wkts dec.)**	**471**

1/12 2/126 3/338 4/342 5/350 6/392 7/450 8/463 9/471

Bowling: Marshall 37-2-111-0; Garner 31-5-101-2; Holding 31-7-74-3; Walsh 38.2-1-118-2; Gomes 12-2-29-1; Richards 7-2-11-0.

West Indies

First Innings

Batsman		R
C.G.Greenidge	c Rixon b McDermott	18
D.L.Haynes	c Wessels b Holland	34
R.B.Richardson	b McDermott	2
H.A.Gomes	c Bennett b Holland	28
I.V.A.Richards	c Wessels b Holland	15
C.H.Lloyd*	c Wood b Holland	33
P.J.L.Dujon†	c Hilditch b Bennett	22
M.D.Marshall	st Rixon b Holland	0
M.A.Holding	c McDermott b Bennett	0
J.Garner	c Rixon b Holland	0
C.A.Walsh	not out	1
Extras	(LB 3, NB 7)	10
Total		**163**

1/26 2/34 3/72 4/103 5/106 6/160 7/160 8/160 9/161

Second Innings

Batsman		R
Greenidge	b Holland	12
Haynes	lbw b McDermott	3
Richardson	c Wood b Bennett	26
Gomes	c Wood b Lawson	8
Richards	b Bennett	58
Lloyd	c Border b McDermott	72
Dujon	c and b Holland	8
Marshall	not out	32
Holding	c Wessels b Holland	0
Garner	c Rixon b Bennett	8
Walsh	c Bennett b Holland	4
Extras	(B 2, LB 12, NB 8)	22
Total		**253**

1/7 2/31 3/46 4/93 5/153 6/180 7/234 8/241 9/244

Bowling: First Innings—Lawson 9-1-27-0; McDermott 9-0-34-2; Bennett 22.5-7-45-2; Holland 22-7-54-6. Second Innings—Lawson 6-1-14-1; McDermott 12-0-56-2; Bennett 33-9-79-3; Holland 33-8-90-4.

Umpires: R.C.Isherwood and M.W.Johnson

ENGLAND v AUSTRALIA 1985 (First Test)

At Headingley, Leeds, 13, 14, 15, 17, 18 June

Result: England won by 5 wickets

Australia

G.M.Wood lbw b Allott	14	(2)	c Lamb b Botham		3
A.M.J.Hilditch c Downton b Gooch	119	(1)	c Robinson b Emburey		80
K.C.Wessels c Botham b Emburey	36		b Emburey		64
A.R.Border* c Botham b Cowans	32		c Downton b Botham		8
D.C.Boon lbw b Gooch	14		b Cowans		22
G.M.Ritchie b Botham	46		b Emburey		1
W.B.Phillips† c Gower b Emburey	30		c Lamb b Botham		91
C.J.McDermott b Botham	18	(10)	c Gooch b Emburey		6
S.P.O'Donnell lbw b Botham	0	(8)	c Downton b Botham		24
G.F.Lawson c Downton b Allott	0	(9)	c Downton b Emburey		15
J.R.Thomson not out	4		not out		2
Extras (LB 13, NB 1, W 4)	18		(B 4, LB 3, W 1)		8
	331				**324**

1/23 2/155 3/201 4/229 5/229 1/5 2/144 3/151 4/159 5/160
6/284 7/326 8/326 9/327 6/192 7/272 8/307 9/318

Bowling: *First Innings*—Cowans 20-4-78-1; Allott 22-3-74-2; Botham 29.1-8-86-3; Gooch 21-4-57-2; Emburey 6-1-23-2. *Second Innings*—Botham 33-7-107-4; Allott 17-4-57-0; Emburey 43.4-14-82-5; Cowans 13-2-50-1; Gooch 9-3-21-0.

England

G.A.Gooch lbw b McDermott	5	lbw b O'Donnell	28
R.T.Robinson c Boon b Lawson	175	b Lawson	21
D.I.Gower* c Phillips b McDermott	17	c Border b O'Donnell	5
M.W.Gatting c Hilditch b McDermott	53	c Phillips b Lawson	12
A.J.Lamb b O'Donnell	38	not out	31
I.T.Botham b Thomson	60	b O'Donnell	12
P.Willey c Hilditch b Lawson	36	not out	3
P.R.Downton† c Border b McDermott	54		
J.E.Emburey b Lawson	21		
P.J.W.Allott c Boon b Thomson	12		
N.G.Cowans not out	22		
Extras (B 5, LB 16, NB 14, W 5)	40	(LB 7, NB 3, W 1)	11
	533	(5 wkts)	**123**

1/14 2/50 3/186 4/264 5/344 1/44 2/59 3/71 4/83
6/417 7/422 8/462 9/484 5/110

Bowling: *First Innings*—Lawson 26-4-117-3; McDermott 32-2-134-4; Thomson 34-3-166-2; O'Donnell 27-8-77-1; Border 3-0-16-0; Wessels 3-2-2-0. *Second Innings*—McDermott 4-0-20-0; Lawson 16-4-51-2; O'Donnell 15.4-5-37-3; Thomson 3-0-8-0.

Umpires: B.J.Meyer and K.E.Palmer

ENGLAND v AUSTRALIA 1985 (Second Test)

At Lord's, London, 27, 28, 29 June, 1, 2 July

Result: Australia won by 4 wickets

England

G.A.Gooch lbw b McDermott	30		c Phillips b McDermott		17
R.T.Robinson lbw b McDermott	6		b Holland		12
D.I.Gower* c Border b McDermott	86	(5)	c Phillips b McDermott		22
M.W.Gatting lbw b Lawson	14	(6)	not out		75
A.J.Lamb c Phillips b Lawson	47	(7)	c Holland b Lawson		9
I.T.Botham c Ritchie b Lawson	5	(8)	c Border b Holland		85
P.R.Downton† c Wessels b McDermott	21	(9)	c Boon b Holland		0
J.E.Emburey lbw b O'Donnell	33	(3)	b Lawson		20
P.H.Edmonds c Border b McDermott	21	(10)	c Boon b Holland		1
N.A.Foster c Wessels b McDermott	3	(11)	c Border b Holland		0
P.J.W.Allott not out	1	(4)	b Lawson		0
Extras (B 1, LB 4, NB 17, W 1)	23		(B 1, LB 12, NB 3, W 4)		20
	290				**261**

1/26 2/51 3/99 4/179 5/184 1/32 2/34 3/38 4/57 5/77
6/211 7/241 8/273 9/283 6/98 7/229 8/229 9/261

Bowling: *First Innings*—Lawson 25-2-91-3; McDermott 29.2-5-70-6; O'Donnell 22-3-82-1; Holland 23-6-42-0. *Second Innings*—McDermott 20-2-84-2; Lawson 23-0-86-3; Holland 32-12-68-5; O'Donnell 5-0-10-0.

Australia

G.M.Wood c Emburey b Allott	8	(2) c Lamb b Botham	6
A.M.J.Hilditch b Foster	14	(1) c Lamb b Botham	0
K.C.Wessels lbw b Botham	11	run out	28
A.R.Border* c Gooch b Botham	196	(5) not out	41
D.C.Boon c Downton b Botham	4	(6) b Edmonds	1
G.M.Ritchie lbw b Botham	94	(4) b Allott	2
W.B.Phillips† c Edmonds b Botham	21	c Edmonds b Emburey	29
S.P.O'Donnell c Lamb b Edmonds	48	not out	9
G.F.Lawson not out	5		
C.J.McDermott run out	9		
R.G.Holland b Edmonds	0		
Extras (LB 10, NB 4, W 1)	15	(LB 11)	11
	425	(6 wkts)	**127**

1/11 2/24 3/80 4/101 5/317 1/0 2/9 3/22 4/63 5/65
6/347 7/398 8/414 9/425 6/116

Bowling: *First Innings*—Foster 23-1-83-1; Allott 30-4-70-1; Botham 24-2-109-5; Edmonds 24.5-5-85-2; Gooch 3-1-11-0; Emburey 19-3-57-0. *Second Innings*—Botham 15-0-49-2; Allott 7-4-8-1; Edmonds 16-5-35-1; Emburey 8-4-24-1.

Umpires: H.D.Bird and D.G.L.Evans

ENGLAND v AUSTRALIA 1985 (Third Test)

At Trent Bridge, Nottingham, 11, 12, 13, 15, 16 July
Result: Match drawn

England

Batsman	First Innings	Second Innings
G.A.Gooch	c Wessels b Lawson ... 70	c Ritchie b McDermott ... 48
R.T.Robinson	c Border b Lawson ... 38	not out ... 77
D.I.Gower*	c Phillips b O'Donnell ... 166	c Phillips b McDermott ... 17
M.W.Gatting	run out ... 74	not out ... 35
A.J.Lamb	lbw b Lawson ... 17	
I.T.Botham	c O'Donnell b McDermott ... 38	
P.R.Downton†	c Ritchie b McDermott ... 0	
A.Sidebottom	c O'Donnell b Lawson ... 2	
J.E.Emburey	not out ... 16	
P.H.Edmonds	b Holland ... 12	
P.J.W.Allott	c Border b Lawson ... 7	
Extras	(LB 12, NB 3, W 1) ... 16	(B 1, LB 16, NB 2) ... 19
	456	(2 wkts) 194

1/55 2/171 3/358 4/365 5/416 6/416 7/419 8/419 9/443
1/79 2/107

Bowling: First Innings—Lawson 39.4-10-103-5; McDermott 35-3-147-2; O'Donnell 29-4-104-1; Holland 26-3-90-1. Second Innings—Lawson 13-4-32-0; McDermott 16-2-42-2; Holland 28-9-69-0; O'Donnell 10-2-26-0; Ritchie 1-0-10-0.

Australia

G.M.Wood c Robinson b Botham		172
A.M.J.Hilditch lbw b Allott		47
R.G.Holland lbw b Sidebottom		10
K.C.Wessels c Downton b Emburey		33
A.R.Border* c Botham b Edmonds		23
D.C.Boon c and b Emburey		15
G.M.Ritchie b Edmonds		146
W.B.Phillips† b Emburey		2
S.P.O'Donnell c Downton b Botham		46
G.F.Lawson c Gooch b Botham		18
C.J.McDermott not out		0
Extras (B 6, LB 7, NB 12, W 2)		27
		539

1/87 2/128 3/205 4/234 5/263 6/424 7/437 8/491 9/539

Bowling: Botham 34.2-3-107-3; Sidebottom 18.4-3-107-3; Sidebottom 18.4-3-65-1; Allott 18-4-55-1; Edmonds 66-18-155-2; Emburey 55-15-129-3; Gooch 8.2-2-13-0; Gatting 1-0-2-0.

Umpires: D.J.Constant and T.Whitehead

ENGLAND v AUSTRALIA 1985 (Fourth Test)

At Old Trafford, Manchester, 1, 2, 3, 5, 6 August
Result: Match drawn

Australia

Batsman	First Innings	Second Innings
K.C.Wessels	c Botham b Emburey ... 34	(3) c and b Emburey ... 50
A.M.J.Hilditch	c Gower b Edmonds ... 49	(1) b Emburey ... 40
D.C.Boon	c Lamb b Botham ... 61	(5) b Emburey ... 7
A.R.Border*	st Downton b Edmonds ... 8	not out ... 146
G.M.Ritchie	c and b Edmonds ... 4	(6) b Emburey ... 31
W.B.Phillips†	c Downton b Botham ... 36	(7) not out ... 39
G.R.J.Matthews	b Botham ... 4	(2) c and b Edmonds ... 17
S.P.O'Donnell	b Edmonds ... 45	
G.F.Lawson	c Downton b Botham ... 4	
C.J.McDermott	lbw b Emburey ... 0	
R.G.Holland	not out ... 5	
Extras	(LB 3, NB 3, W 1) ... 7	(B 1, LB 6, NB 3) ... 10
	257	(5 wkts) 340

1/71 2/97 3/118 4/122 5/193 6/198 7/211 8/223 9/224
1/38 2/85 3/126 4/138 5/213

Bowling: First Innings—Botham 23-4-79-4; Agnew 14-0-65-0; Allott 13-1-29-0; Emburey 24-7-41-2; Edmonds 15.1-4-40-4. Second Innings—Botham 15-3-50-0; Allott 6-2-4-0; Edmonds 54-12-122-1; Emburey 51-17-99-4; Agnew 9-2-34-0; Gatting 4-0-14-0; Lamb 1-0-10-0.

England

G.A.Gooch lbw b McDermott		74
R.T.Robinson c Border b McDermott		10
D.I.Gower* c Hilditch b McDermott		47
M.W.Gatting c Phillips b McDermott		160
A.J.Lamb run out		67
I.T.Botham c O'Donnell b McDermott		20
P.R.Downton† b McDermott		23
J.E.Emburey not out		31
P.H.Edmonds b McDermott		1
P.J.W.Allott b McDermott		7
J.P.Agnew not out		2
Extras (B 7, LB 16, NB 17)		40
		(9 wkts dec.) 482

1/21 2/142 3/148 4/304 5/339 6/430 7/448 8/450 9/470

Bowling: Lawson 37-7-114-0; McDermott 36-3-141-8; Holland 38-7-101-0; O'Donnell 21-6-82-0; Matthews 9-2-21-0.

Umpires: H.D.Bird and D.R.Shepherd

ENGLAND v AUSTRALIA 1985 (Sixth Test)

At Kennington Oval, London, 29, 30, 31 August, 2, 3 September

Result: England won by an innings and 94 runs

England

Batsman	Dismissal	Runs
G.A.Gooch	c and b McDermott	196
R.T.Robinson	b McDermott	3
D.I.Gower*	c Bennett b McDermott	157
M.W.Gatting	c Border b Bennett	4
J.E.Emburey	c Wellham b Lawson	9
A.J.Lamb	c McDermott b Lawson	1
I.T.Botham	c Phillips b Lawson	12
P.R.Downton†	b McDermott	16
R.M.Ellison	c Phillips b Gilbert	3
P.H.Edmonds	lbw b Lawson	12
L.B.Taylor	not out	1
Extras	(B 13, LB 11, NB 26)	50
Total		**464**

1/20 2/371 3/376 4/403 5/405
6/418 7/425 8/447 9/452

Bowling: Lawson 29.2-6-101-4; McDermott 31-2-108-4; Gilbert 21-2-96-1; Bennett 32-8-111-1; Border 2-0-8-0; Wessels 3-0-16-0.

Australia

Batsman	Dismissal	Runs		Dismissal	Runs
G.M.Wood	lbw b Botham	22	(2)	b Botham	6
A.M.J.Hilditch	c Gooch b Botham	17	(1)	c Gower b Taylor	9
K.C.Wessels	b Emburey	12		c Botham b Botham	7
A.R.Border*	b Edmonds	38		c Botham b Ellison	58
D.M.Wellham	c Downton b Ellison	13		lbw b Ellison	5
G.M.Ritchie	not out	64		c Downton b Ellison	6
W.B.Phillips†	b Edmonds	18		c Downton b Botham	10
M.J.Bennett	c Robinson b Ellison	12		c and b Taylor	11
G.F.Lawson	c Botham b Taylor	14		c Downton b Ellison	7
C.J.McDermott	run out	25		c Botham b Ellison	2
D.R.Gilbert	b Botham	1		not out	0
Extras	(LB 3, W 2)	5		(B 4, NB 4)	8
Total		**241**			**129**

1/35 2/52 3/56 4/101 5/109
6/144 7/171 8/192 9/235

1/13 2/16 3/37 4/51 5/71
6/96 7/114 8/127 9/129

Bowling: First Innings—Botham 20-3-64-3; Taylor 13-1-39-1; Ellison 18-5-35-2; Emburey 19-7-48-1; Edmonds 14-2-52-2. Second Innings—Botham 17-3-44-3; Taylor 11.3-1-34-2; Ellison 17-3-46-5; Emburey 1-0-1-0.

Umpires: H.D.Bird and K.E.Palmer

ENGLAND v AUSTRALIA 1985 (Fifth Test)

At Edgbaston, Birmingham, 15, 16, 17, 19, 20 August

Result: England won by an innings and 118 runs

Australia

Batsman	Dismissal	Runs		Dismissal	Runs
G.M.Wood	c Edmonds b Botham	19	(2)	c Robinson b Ellison	10
A.M.J.Hilditch	c Downton b Edmonds	39	(1)	c Ellison b Botham	10
K.C.Wessels	c Downton b Ellison	83		c Downton b Ellison	10
A.R.Border*	c Edmonds b Ellison	45	(5)	b Ellison	2
G.M.Ritchie	c Botham b Ellison	8	(6)	c Lamb b Emburey	20
W.B.Phillips†	c Robinson b Ellison	15	(7)	c Gower b Edmonds	59
S.P.O'Donnell	c Downton b Taylor	1	(8)	b Botham	11
G.F.Lawson	run out	53	(9)	c Gower b Edmonds	3
C.J.McDermott	c Gower b Ellison	35	(10)	c Edmonds b Botham	8
J.R.Thomson	not out	28	(11)	not out	4
R.G.Holland	c Edmonds b Ellison	0	(4)	lbw b Ellison	0
Extras	(LB 4, NB 4, W 1)	9		(B 1, LB 3, NB 1)	5
Total		**335**			**142**

1/44 2/92 3/189 4/191 5/207
6/208 7/218 8/276 9/335

1/10 2/32 3/32 4/35 5/36
6/113 7/117 8/120 9/137

Bowling: First Innings—Botham 27-1-108-1; Taylor 26-5-78-1; Ellison 31.5-9-77-6; Edmonds 20-4-47-1; Emburey 9-2-21-0. Second Innings—Botham 14.1-2-52-3; Taylor 13-4-27-0; Ellison 9-3-27-4; Edmonds 15-9-13-2; Emburey 13-5-19-1.

England

Batsman	Dismissal	Runs
G.A.Gooch	c Phillips b Thomson	19
R.T.Robinson	b Lawson	148
D.I.Gower*	c Border b Lawson	215
M.W.Gatting	not out	100
A.J.Lamb	c Wood b McDermott	46
I.T.Botham	c Thomson b McDermott	18
P.R.Downton†		
J.E.Emburey		
R.M.Ellison		
P.H.Edmonds		
L.B.Taylor		
Extras	(B 7, LB 20, NB 22)	49
Total	(5 wkts dec.)	**595**

1/38 2/369 3/463 4/572 5/592

Bowling: Lawson 37-1-135-2; McDermott 31-2-155-2; Thomson 19-1-101-1; Holland 25-4-95-0; O'Donnell 16-3-69-0; Border 6-1-13-0.

Umpires: D.J.Constant and D.R.Shepherd

AUSTRALIA v NEW ZEALAND 1985-86 (First Test)

At Woolloongabba, Brisbane 8, 9, 10, 11, 12 November

Result: New Zealand won by an innings and 41 runs

Australia

Batsman		Runs			Runs
K.C.Wessels	lbw b Hadlee	70	(2)	c Brown b Chatfield	3
A.M.J.Hilditch	c Chatfield b Hadlee	0	(1)	c Chatfield b Hadlee	12
D.C.Boon	c Coney b Hadlee	31		c Smith b Chatfield	1
A.R.Border*	c Edgar b Hadlee	1		not out	152
G.M.Ritchie	c M.D.Crowe b Hadlee	8		c Coney b Snedden	20
W.B.Phillips†	b Hadlee	34		b Hadlee	
G.R.J.Matthews	b Hadlee	2		c Coney b Hadlee	115
G.F.Lawson	c Hadlee b Brown	8	(9)	c Brown b Chatfield	7
C.J.McDermott	c Coney b Hadlee	9	(8)	c and b Hadlee	5
D.R.Gilbert	not out	0		c Chatfield b Hadlee	10
R.G.Holland	c Brown b Hadlee	0		b Hadlee	6
Extras	(B 9, LB 5, NB 2)	16		(LB 3, NB 3)	
		179			**333**

1/1 2/70 3/72 4/82 5/148
6/150 7/159 8/175 9/179

1/14 2/16 3/16 4/47 5/67
6/264 7/272 8/291 9/333

Bowling: First Innings—Hadlee 23.4-4-52-9; Chatfield 18-6-29-0; Snedden 11-1-45-0; M.D.Crowe 5-0-14-0; Brown 12-5-17-1; Coney 7-5-8-0. Second Innings—Hadlee 28.5-9-71-6; Chatfield 32-9-75-3; Snedden 19-3-66-1; M.D.Crowe 9-2-19-0; Brown 25-5-96-0; Coney 3-1-3-0.

New Zealand

Batsman		Runs
B.A.Edgar	c Phillips b Gilbert	17
J.G.Wright	lbw b Matthews	46
J.F.Reid	c Border b Gilbert	108
M.D.Crowe	b Matthews	188
J.V.Coney*	c Phillips b Lawson	22
J.J.Crowe	c Holland b Matthews	35
V.R.Brown	not out	36
R.J.Hadlee	c Phillips b McDermott	54
I.D.S.Smith†	not out	2
M.C.Snedden		
E.J.Chatfield		
Extras	(B 2, LB 11, NB 32)	45
	(7 wkts dec.)	**553**

1/36 2/85 3/309 4/362 5/427
6/471 7/549

Bowling: Lawson 36.5-8-96-1; McDermott 31-3-119-1; Gilbert 39-9-102-2; Matthews 31-5-110-3; Holland 22-3-106-0; Border 0.1-0-0-0; Wessels 1-0-7-0.

Umpires: A.R.Crafter and R.A.French

AUSTRALIA v NEW ZEALAND 1985-86 (Second Test)

At Sydney Cricket Ground, 22, 23, 24, 25, 26 November

Result: Australia won by 4 wickets

New Zealand

Batsman		Runs		Runs
J.G.Wright	c O'Donnell b Bright	38	c and b Matthews	43
B.A.Edgar	c Border b Holland	50	c and b Holland	52
J.F.Reid	c Kerr b Holland	7	b Matthews	19
M.D.Crowe	run out	8	b Holland	0
J.V.Coney*	c Border b Holland	8	b Holland	7
J.J.Crowe	b Holland	13	c and b Holland	6
V.R.Brown	lbw b Holland		b Bright	15
I.D.S.Smith†	c Hookes b Bright	28	c and b Bright	12
R.J.Hadlee	lbw b Bright	5	lbw b Gilbert	26
J.G.Bracewell	not out	83	not out	2
S.L.Boock	lbw b Gilbert	37	c Boon b Bright	3
Extras	(B 6, LB 8, NB 2)	16	(B 1, LB 4, NB 3)	8
		293		**193**

1/79 2/92 3/109 4/112 5/128
6/128 7/161 8/166 9/169

1/100 2/106 3/107 4/119
5/131 6/137 7/162 8/163 9/190

Bowling: First Innings—Gilbert 20.3-6-41-1; O'Donnell 6-2-13-0; Bright 34-12-87-2; Matthews 17-3-32-0; Holland 47-19-106-6. Second Innings—Gilbert 9-2-22-1; O'Donnell 5-4-4-0; Holland 41-16-68-4; Matthews 30-11-55-2; Bright 17.5-3-39-3.

Australia

Batsman		Runs		Runs
W.B.Phillips†	b Bracewell	31	c Bracewell b Boock	63
R.B.Kerr	lbw b Hadlee	7	c Wright b Bracewell	7
D.C.Boon	lbw b Hadlee	0	c Reid b Bracewell	81
A.R.Border*	b Bracewell	20	st Smith b Bracewell	11
G.M.Ritchie	c J.J.Crowe b Hadlee	89	c M.D.Crowe b Hadlee	13
D.W.Hookes	run out	0	not out	38
G.R.J.Matthews	c Smith b Hadlee	50	lbw b Hadlee	32
S.P.O'Donnell	not out	20	not out	2
R.J.Bright	lbw b Boock	1		
D.R.Gilbert	c Smith b Hadlee	0		
R.G.Holland	st Smith b Boock	0		
Extras	(B 5, LB 2, NB 2)	9	(B 3, LB 9, NB 1)	13
		227	(6 wkts)	**260**

1/19 2/22 3/48 4/71 5/71
6/186 7/224 8/225 9/226

1/27 2/132 3/144
4/163 5/192 6/258

Bowling: First Innings—Hadlee 24-2-65-5; M.D.Crowe 5-2-15-0; Bracewell 25-9-51-2; Boock 29.5-14-53-2; Brown 13-3-35-0; Coney 1-0-1-0. Second Innings—Hadlee 27.1-10-58-2; M.D.Crowe 2-1-7-0; Bracewell 30-7-91-3; Boock 22-4-49-1; Brown 7-0-28-0; Coney 9-1-15-0.

Umpires: M.W.Johnson and B.E.Martin

AUSTRALIA v NEW ZEALAND 1985-86 (Third Test)

At W.A.C.A. Ground, Perth, 30 November, 1, 2, 3, 4 December

Result: New Zealand won by 6 wickets

Australia

Batsman	First Innings		Second Innings	
W.B.Phillips†	c Smith b Chatfield	37	c M.D.Crowe b Coney	44
R.B.Kerr	c Smith b Chatfield	17	b Hadlee	34
D.C.Boon	c Bracewell b Hadlee	12	c J.J.Crowe b Hadlee	50
A.R.Border*	c Smith b Hadlee	12	b Bracewell	36
G.M.Ritchie	lbw b Coney	83	lbw b Coney	21
D.W.Hookes	c Bracewell b Coney	6	c Bracewell b Coney	11
G.R.J.Matthews	b Hadlee	14	b Hadlee	12
G.F.Lawson	c J.J.Crowe b Hadlee	3	not out	11
C.J.McDermott	b Chatfield	11	c Crowe b Hadlee	4
D.R.Gilbert	not out	0	b Hadlee	10
R.G.Holland	c Crowe b Hadlee	0	not out	—
Extras	(LB 6, NB 2)	8	(B 2, LB 5, NB 9)	16
		203		**259**

1/38 2/63 3/78 4/85 5/85 6/114 7/131 8/159 9/190

1/3 2/28 3/109 4/195 5/207 6/214 7/234 8/251 9/255

Bowling: *First Innings*—Hadlee 26.5-6-65-5; Cairns 14-1-50-0; Chatfield 16-6-33-3; Coney 21-11-43-2; Bracewell 6-3-6-0. *Second Innings*—Hadlee 39-11-90-6; Cairns 26-6-59-0; Chatfield 30-9-47-1; Bracewell 28.5-8-47-2; Coney 8-5-9-1.

New Zealand

Batsman	First Innings		Second Innings	
J.G.Wright	c Phillips b Lawson	20	(2) b Gilbert	35
B.A.Edgar	c Hookes b McDermott	74	(1) c Border b Matthews	16
J.F.Reid	b Gilbert	7	c Phillips b Gilbert	28
M.D.Crowe	lbw b McDermott	71	not out	42
J.V.Coney*	c Phillips b Lawson	19	b Gilbert	16
J.J.Crowe	lbw b Holland	17	not out	2
R.J.Hadlee	c Hookes b Holland	26		
I.D.S.Smith†	c Matthews b Lawson	12		
J.G.Bracewell	not out	28		
B.L.Cairns	c Ritchie b Holland	0		
E.J.Chatfield	c Phillips b Lawson	3		
Extras	(B 1, LB 7, NB 14)	22	(B 7, LB 7, NB 11)	25
		299	(4 wkts)	**164**

1/43 2/55 3/184 4/191 5/215 6/253 7/256 8/273 9/276

1/47 2/77 3/121 4/149

Bowling: *First Innings*—Lawson 47-12-79-4; McDermott 33-9-66-2; Gilbert 31-9-75-1; Holland 40-12-63-3; Matthews 5-3-6-0; Hookes 1-0-2-0. *Second Innings*—Lawson 21-7-35-0; Gilbert 23-5-48-3; McDermott 13-1-27-0; Matthews 9-3-13-1; Holland 8-1-27-0.

Umpires: R.C.Isherwood and P.J.McConnell

AUSTRALIA v INDIA 1985-86 (First Test)

At Adelaide Oval, 13, 14, 15, 16, 17 December

Result: Match drawn

Australia

Batsman	First Innings		Second Innings	
W.B.Phillips†	c Yadav b Kapil Dev	11		
D.C.Boon	c Vengsarkar b Kapil Dev	123	(1) not out	11
G.R.Marsh	c Sharma b Binny	5	(2) not out	2
A.R.Border*	b Kapil Dev	49		
G.M.Ritchie	c Kirmani b Kapil Dev	128		
D.W.Hookes	b Yadav	34		
G.R.J.Matthews	lbw b Kapil Dev	18		
R.J.Bright	not out	5		
C.J.McDermott	lbw b Kapil Dev	0		
B.A.Reid	c Gavaskar b Kapil Dev	2		
M.G.Hughes	c Vengsarkar b Kapil Dev	0		
Extras	(LB 4, NB 2)	6	(LB 3, NB 1)	4
		381	(0 wkts)	**17**

1/19 2/35 3/124 4/241 5/318 6/374 7/375 8/375 9/381

Bowling: *First Innings*—Kapil Dev 38-6-106-8; Binny 24-7-56-1; Sharma 19-3-70-0; Yadav 27-6-66-1; Shastri 38-11-70-0; Amarnath 3-0-9-0. *Second Innings*—Kapil Dev 3-1-3-0; Sharma 2-0-9-0; Yadav 2-1-2-0; Shastri 1-1-0-0.

India

S.M.Gavaskar	not out	166
K.Srikkanth	c Ritchie b McDermott	51
C.Sharma	c Phillips b Reid	54
D.B.Vengsarkar	c Phillips b Hughes	7
M.Azharuddin	c Phillips b Reid	17
M.Amarnath	c Marsh b McDermott	37
R.J.Shastri	b Reid	42
Kapil Dev*	lbw b Bright	38
R.M.H.Binny	c Phillips b McDermott	38
S.M.H.Kirmani†	c Boon b Reid	7
N.S.Yadav	c Hughes b Hookes	41
Extras	(B 2, LB 7, NB 12, W 1)	22
		520

1/95 2/131 3/171 4/187 5/247 6/273 7/333 8/409 9/426

Bowling: McDermott 48-14-131-3; Hughes 38-6-123-1; Reid 53-22-113-4; Bright 44-15-80-1; Matthews 17-2-60-0; Hookes 2-0-4-1.

Umpires: A.R.Crafter and S.G.Randell

AUSTRALIA v INDIA 1985-86 (Second Test)
At Melbourne Cricket Ground, 26, 27, 28, 29, 30 December
Result: Match drawn

Australia

Batsman	First Innings		Second Innings	
W.B.Phillips†	b Yadav	7	(7) c Srikkanth b Yadav	13
D.C.Boon	lbw b Shastri	14	c and b Kapil Dev	19
G.R.Marsh	c Sivaramakrishnan b Yadav	30	(1) c Sivaramakrishnan b Shastri	19
A.R.Border*	c and b Sivaramakrishnan	11	(3) st Kirmani b Yadav	163
D.W.Hookes	b Shastri	42	(4) c Srikkanth b Shastri	5
S.R.Waugh	c Kapil Dev b Sivaramakrishnan	13	(5) b Shastri	0
G.R.J.Matthews	not out	100	(6) c Azharuddin b Sivaramakrishnan	16
R.J.Bright	b Shastri	28	lbw b Kapil Dev	20
C.J.McDermott	c Kapil Dev b Shastri	1	c and b Shastri	2
B.A.Reid	c Srikkanth b Kapil Dev	1	c Sivaramakrishnan b Yadav	13
D.R.Gilbert	c Kirmani b Yadav	4	not out	10
Extras	(B 5, LB 6)	11	(B 11, LB 16, NB 1)	28
		262		308

1/22 2/26 3/41 4/90 5/109 6/127 7/193 8/195 9/216

1/32 2/54 3/54 4/84 5/126 6/161 7/202 8/205 9/231

Bowling: First Innings—Kapil Dev 23-6-38-1; Binny 3-0-11-0; Shastri 37-13-87-4; Yadav 27.5-10-64-3; Sivaramakrishnan 13-2-51-2. Second Innings—Kapil Dev 22-7-53-2; Amarnath 3-0-9-0; Shastri 47-13-92-4; Yadav 38.5-15-84-3; Sivaramakrishnan 13-1-43-1.

India

Batsman	First Innings		Second Innings	
S.M.Gavaskar	b Gilbert	6	b Reid	8
K.Srikkanth	lbw b Gilbert	86	c Bright b Reid	38
M.Amarnath	c Phillips b Reid	45	not out	3
D.B.Vengsarkar	c and b Matthews	75	not out	1
M.Azharuddin	b Matthews	37		
R.J.Shastri	c Phillips b Waugh	49		
Kapil Dev*	c Hookes b Reid	55		
R.M.H.Binny	c Matthews b Reid	0		
S.M.H.Kirmani†	c Phillips b Waugh	35		
L.Sivaramakrishnan	c Phillips b Reid	15		
N.S.Yadav	not out	6		
Extras	(B 4, LB 15, NB 17)	36	(B 4, LB 1, NB 4)	9
		445	(2 wkts)	59

1/15 2/116 3/172 4/246 5/291 6/370 7/372 8/420 9/425

1/39 2/57

Bowling: First Innings—McDermott 15-5-52-0; Gilbert 22-1-81-2; Reid 38.2-11-100-4; Bright 31-8-76-0; Matthews 31-7-81-2; Waugh 11-5-36-2. Second Innings—McDermott 6-1-17-0; Gilbert 4-0-9-0; Reid 8-1-23-2; Bright 7-4-5-0.

Umpires: R.A.French and R.C.Isherwood

AUSTRALIA v INDIA 1985-86 (Third Test)
At Sydney Cricket Ground, 2, 3, 4, 5, 6 January
Result: Match drawn

India

S.M.Gavaskar	b Holland	172
K.Srikkanth	b Reid	116
M.Amarnath	c Bright b Gilbert	138
Kapil Dev*	b Gilbert	42
D.B.Vengsarkar	not out	37
M.Azharuddin	not out	59
R.J.Shastri		
S.M.H.Kirmani†		
C.Sharma		
L.Sivaramakrishnan		
N.S.Yadav		
Extras	(B 5, LB 9, NB 22)	36
	(4 wkts dec.)	600

1/191 2/415 3/485 5/540

Bowling: Gilbert 37-3-135-2; Reid 34-8-89-1; Bright 41-7-121-0; Holland 21-6-113-1; Matthews 29-2-95-0; Waugh 7-0-33-0.

Australia

Batsman	First Innings		Second Innings	
D.C.Boon	b Kapil Dev	131	(2) run out	25
G.R.Marsh	c Gavaskar b Shastri	92	(1) lbw b Yadav	28
A.R.Border*	c Sharma b Shastri	71	(7) c Sivaramakrishnan b Yadav	4
G.M.Ritchie	c Kapil Dev b Yadav	14	(3) not out	17
W.B.Phillips†	c Srikkanth b Shastri	14	c Srikkanth b Shastri	22
G.R.J.Matthews	c Amarnath b Yadav	40	c Kapil Dev b Yadav	17
S.R.Waugh	c Sivaramakrishnan b Yadav	8	(4) lbw b Shastri	0
R.J.Bright	c Kirmani b Shastri	3	not out	0
D.R.Gilbert	c Azharuddin b Yadav	1		
B.A.Reid	st Kirmani b Yadav	4		
R.G.Holland	not out	1		
Extras	(LB 14, NB 3)	17	(B 3, LB 2, NB 1)	6
		396	(6 wkts)	119

1/217 2/258 3/277 4/302 5/369 6/387 7/388 8/390 9/395

1/57 2/57 3/60 4/87 5/111 6/115

Bowling: First Innings—Kapil Dev 25-8-65-1; Shastri 57-21-101-4; Yadav 62.3-21-99-5; Sivaramakrishnan 22-2-79-0; Sharma 13-2-38-0. Second Innings—Kapil Dev 7-3-11-0; Yadav 33-22-19-3; Sharma 3-0-11-0; Shastri 25-12-36-2; Sivaramakrishnan 9-0-37-0.

Umpires: P.J.McConnell and S.G.Randell

NEW ZEALAND v AUSTRALIA 1985-86 (First Test)

At Basin Reserve, Wellington, 21, 22, 23, 24, 25 (no play) February

Result: Match drawn

Australia

D.C.Boon c Smith b Troup	70
G.R.Marsh c Coney b Chatfield	43
W.B.Phillips b Gillespie	32
A.R.Border* lbw b Hadlee	13
G.M.Ritchie b Troup	92
G.R.J.Matthews c Rutherford b Coney	130
S.R.Waugh c Smith b Coney	11
T.J.Zoehrer† c sub (J.G.Bracewell) b Coney	18
C.J.McDermott b Hadlee	2
B.A.Reid not out	0
S.P.Davis c and b Hadlee	0
Extras (B 2, LB 9, NB 9, W 4)	24
	435

1/104 2/143 3/166 4/166 5/379
6/414 7/418 8/435 9/435

Bowling: Hadlee 37.1-5-116-3; Chatfield 36-10-96-1; Troup 28-6-86-2; Coney 18-7-47-3.

New Zealand

T.J.Franklin c Border b McDermott	0
B.A.Edgar c Waugh b Matthews	38
J.F.Reid c Phillips b Reid	32
S.R.Gillespie c Border b Reid	28
M.D.Crowe b Matthews	19
K.R.Rutherford c sub (R.J.Bright) b Reid	65
J.V.Coney* not out	101
R.J.Hadlee not out	72
I.D.S.Smith†	
G.B.Troup	
E.J.Chatfield	
Extras (B 2, LB 6, NB 15, W 1)	24
	(6 wkts) 379

1/0 2/57 3/94 4/115 5/138 6/247

Bowling; McDermott 25.3-5-80-1; Davis 25-4-70-0; Reid 31-6-104-3; Matthews 37-10-107-2; Border 4-3-1-0; Waugh 4-1-9-0.

Umpires: F.R.Goodall and S.J.Woodward

NEW ZEALAND v AUSTRALIA 1985-86 (Second Test)

At Lancaster Park, Christchurch, 28 February, 1, 2, 3, 4 March

Result: Match drawn

Australia

G.R.Marsh b Hadlee	28	(2) lbw b Bracewell	15
D.C.Boon c Coney b Hadlee	26	(1) c Coney b Troup	6
W.B.Phillips c Smith b Chatfield	1	b Hadlee	25
A.R.Border* b Chatfield	140	not out	114
G.M.Ritchie lbw b Hadlee	4	c Smith b Bracewell	11
G.R.J.Matthews c Smith b Hadlee	6	c sub (J.J.Crowe) b Hadlee	3
S.R.Waugh lbw b Hadlee	74	c Smith b Bracewell	1
T.J.Zoehrer† c Coney b Hadlee	30	c Rutherford b Bracewell	13
R.J.Bright c Smith b Bracewell	21	not out	21
D.R.Gilbert b Hadlee	15		
B.A.Reid not out	1		
Extras (B 1, LB 9, NB 8)	18	(LB 6, NB 3, W 1)	10
	364		(7 wkts dec.) 219

1/57 2/58 3/58 4/64 5/74 1/15 2/32 3/76
6/251 7/319 8/334 9/358 4/120 5/129 6/130 7/166

Bowling: *First Innings*—Hadlee 44.4-8-116-7; Troup 34-4-104-0; Chatfield 36-13-56-2; Coney 9-0-28-0; Bracewell 27-9-46-1; Crowe 2-1-4-0. *Second Innings*—Hadlee 25-4-47-2; Troup 15-0-50-1; Chatfield 17-6-29-0; Bracewell 33-12-77-4; Reid 1-1-0-0; Coney 3-1-10-0.

New Zealand

B.A.Edgar lbw b Reid	8	c and b Matthews	9
J.G.Wright c Zoehrer b Gilbert	10	not out	4
J.F.Reid c Zoehrer b Waugh	2	not out	0
M.D.Crowe c Waugh b Reid	137		
K.R.Rutherford lbw b Gilbert	0		
J.V.Coney* c Reid b Waugh	98		
R.J.Hadlee c Zoehrer b Reid	22		
I.D.S.Smith† b Waugh	20		
J.G.Bracewell c Marsh b Reid	0		
G.B.Troup lbw b Waugh	2		
E.J.Chatfield not out	30	(NB 3)	3
Extras (B 6, LB 8, NB 16)	30		
	329		(1 wkt) 16

1/17 2/29 3/29 4/48 5/124 1/13
6/190 7/263 8/311 9/311

Bowling: *First Innings*—Reid 34.3-8-90-4; Gilbert 26-4-106-2; Waugh 23-6-56-4; Bright 18-6-51-0; Matthews 6-1-22-0. *Second Innings*—Gilbert 7-4-9-0; Reid 4-0-7-0; Matthews 3-3-0-1.

Umpires: B.L.Aldridge and F.R.Goodall

NEW ZEALAND v AUSTRALIA 1985-86 (Third Test)

At Eden Park, Auckland, 13, 14, 15, 16, 17 March

Result: New Zealand won by 8 wickets

Australia

D.C.Boon c Coney b Hadlee	16	(2)	not out	58
G.R.Marsh c Coney b Hadlee	118	(1)	lbw b Hadlee	0
W.B.Phillips c Smith b Bracewell	62		c Bracewell b Chatfield	15
A.R.Border* c Smith b Chatfield	17	(5)	b Bracewell	6
T.J.Zoehrer† c Coney b Robertson	9	(4)	lbw b Chatfield	1
G.M.Ritchie c Smith b Chatfield	56		lbw b Chatfield	1
G.R.J.Matthews c Smith b Bracewell	5		st Smith b Bracewell	4
S.R.Waugh c Reid b Bracewell	1		b Bracewell	0
R.J.Bright c Smith b Hadlee	5		b Bracewell	0
C.J.McDermott lbw b Bracewell	9		b Bracewell	6
B.A.Reid not out	0		c Hadlee b Bracewell	8
Extras (B 2, LB 11, NB 3)	16		(LB 4)	4
	314			**103**

1/25 2/193 3/225 4/225 5/278
6/293 7/294 8/301 9/309

1/0 2/28 3/35 4/59 5/62
6/71 7/71 8/71 9/85

Bowling: *First Innings*—Hadlee 31-12-60-3; Robertson 24-6-91-1; Chatfield 29-10-54-2; Crowe 3-2-4-0; Bracewell 43.3-19-74-4; Coney 5-0-18-0. *Second Innings*—Hadlee 20-7-48-1; Chatfield 18-9-19-3; Bracewell 22-8-32-6.

New Zealand

J.G.Wright c Zoehrer b McDermott	56		c Boon b Matthews	59
B.A.Edgar lbw b Matthews	24		b Reid	1
K.R.Rutherford b Matthews	0		not out	50
M.D.Crowe lbw b Matthews	0		not out	23
J.F.Reid c Zoehrer b Bright	16			
J.V.Coney* c Border b McDermott	93			
R.J.Hadlee b Reid	33			
I.D.S.Smith† b Waugh	3			
J.G.Bracewell c Boon b Bright	4			
G.K.Robertson st Zoehrer b Matthews	12			
E.J.Chatfield not out	1			
Extras (B 7, LB 8, NB 1)	16		(B 18, LB 4, NB 5)	27
	258		(2 wkts)	**160**

1/73 2/73 3/73 4/103 5/107
6/170 7/184 8/203 9/250

1/6 2/106

Bowling: *First Innings*—McDermott 17-2-47-2; Reid 19-2-63-1; Matthews 34-15-61-4; Bright 22-4-58-2; Waugh 5-1-14-1. *Second Innings*—McDermott 14-3-29-0; Reid 12.4-2-30-1; Matthews 31-8-46-1; Bright 23-12-29-0; Waugh 4-1-4-0.

Umpires: R.L.McHarg and S.J.Woodward

INDIA v AUSTRALIA 1986-87 (First Test)

At Chidambaram Stadium, Chepauk, Madras, 18, 19, 20, 21, 22 September

Result: A tie

Australia

D.C.Boon c Kapil Dev b Sharma	122	(2)	lbw b Maninder Singh	49
G.R.Marsh c Kapil Dev b Yadav	22	(1)	b Shastri	11
D.M.Jones b Yadav	210		c Azharuddin b Maninder Singh	24
R.J.Bright c Shastri b Yadav	30			
A.R.Border* c Gavaskar b Shastri	106	(4)	b Maninder Singh	27
G.M.Ritchie run out	13	(5)	c Pandit b Shastri	28
G.R.J.Matthews c Pandit b Yadav	44	(6)	not out	27
S.R.Waugh not out	12	(7)	not out	2
T.J.Zoehrer†				
C.J.McDermott				
B.A.Reid				
Extras (B 1, LB 7, NB 6, W 1)	15		(LB 1, NB 1)	2
	(7 wkts dec.) **574**		(5 wkts dec.)	**170**

1/48 2/206 3/282 4/460 5/481
6/544 7/573

1/31 2/81 3/94
4/125 5/165

Bowling: *First Innings*—Kapil Dev 18-5-52-0; Sharma 16-1-70-1; Maninder Singh 39-8-135-0; Yadav 49.5-9-142-4; Shastri 47-8-161-1; Srikkanth 1-0-6-0. *Second Innings*—Sharma 6-0-19-0; Kapil Dev 1-0-5-0; Shastri 14-2-50-2; Maninder Singh 19-2-60-3; Yadav 9-0-35-0.

India

S.M.Gavaskar c and b Matthews	8		c Jones b Bright	90
K.Srikkanth c Ritchie b Matthews	53		c Waugh b Matthews	39
M.Amarnath run out	1		c Boon b Matthews	51
M.Azharuddin c and b Bright	50		c Ritchie b Bright	42
R.J.Shastri c Zoehrer b Matthews	62	(7)	not out	48
C.S.Pandit c Waugh b Matthews	35	(5)	b Matthews	39
Kapil Dev* c Border b Matthews	119	(6)	c Bright b Matthews	1
K.S.More† c Zoehrer b Waugh	4	(9)	lbw b Bright	0
C.Sharma c Zoehrer b Reid	30	(8)	c McDermott b Bright	23
N.S.Yadav c Border b Bright	19		b Bright	8
Maninder Singh not out	0		lbw b Matthews	0
Extras (B 1, LB 9, NB 6)	16		(B 1, LB 3, NB 2)	6
	397			**347**

1/62 2/65 3/65 4/142 5/206
6/220 7/245 8/330 9/387

1/55 2/158 3/204 4/251 5/253 347
6/291 7/331 8/334 9/344

Bowling: *First Innings*—McDermott 14-2-59-0; Reid 18-4-93-1; Matthews 28.2-3-103-5; Bright 23-3-88-2; Waugh 11-2-44-1. *Second Innings*—McDermott 5-0-27-0; Reid 10-2-48-0; Matthews 39.5-7-146-5; Bright 25-3-94-5; Border 3-0-12-0; Waugh 4-1-16-0.

Umpires: D.N.Dotiwalla and V.Vikramraju

INDIA v AUSTRALIA 1986-87 (Second Test)
At Feroz Shah Kotla, Delhi, 26 (no play), 27 (no play), 28 (no play), 29, 30 September
Result: Match drawn

Australia

D.C.Boon c Maninder Singh b Shastri		67
D.M.Jones c Pandit b Shastri		29
G.R.Marsh c Pandit b Sharma		11
S.R.Waugh not out		39
T.J.Zoehrer† not out		52
A.R.Border*		
G.M.Ritchie		
G.R.J.Matthews		
R.J.Bright		
C.J.McDermott		
D.R.Gilbert		
Extras (LB 2, NB 3, W 4)		9
	(3 wkts dec.)	207

1/34 2/110 3/118

Bowling: Kapil Dev 14-5-27-0; Sharma 8-1-34-1; Shastri 21.4-4-44-2; Maninder Singh 19-4-54-0; Yadav 13-1-46-0

India

S.M.Gavaskar b Gilbert		0
K.Srikkanth run out		26
M.Azharuddin c Zoehrer b Waugh		24
D.B.Vengsarkar not out		22
C.S.Pandit† not out		26
M.Amarnath		
R.J.Shastri		
Kapil Dev*		
C.Sharma		
N.S.Yadav		
Maninder Singh		
Extras (LB 5)		5
	(3 wkts)	103

1/9 2/57 3/59

Bowling: McDermott 6-1-24-0; Gilbert 11-1-44-1; Waugh 6-0-29-1; Boon 2-1-5-0; Jones 1-1-0-0.

Umpires: V.K.Ramaswamy and P.D.Reporter

INDIA v AUSTRALIA 1986-87 (Third Test)
At Wankhede Stadium, Bombay, 15, 16, 17, 18, 19 October
Result: Match drawn

Australia

G.R.Marsh c Gavaskar b Kulkarni	101	(2)	b Shastri	20
D.C.Boon c Gavaskar b Kulkarni	47	(1)	c More b Shastri	40
D.M.Jones c sub(L.Sivaramakrishnan) b Yadav.	35		not out	73
A.R.Border* st More b Maninder Singh	46		not out	66
G.M.Ritchie run out	31			
G.R.J.Matthews b Yadav	20			
S.R.Waugh b Yadav	6			
T.J.Zoehrer† c and b Maninder Singh	21			
R.J.Bright lbw b Kulkarni	8			
D.R.Gilbert c sub(L.Sivaramakrishnan) b Yadav.	1			
B.A.Reid not out	2			
Extras (B 5, LB 12, NB 10)	27		(B 5, LB 5, NB 7)	17
	345		(2 wkts)	216

1/76 2/151 3/241 4/252 5/295   1/64 2/70
6/304 7/308 8/340 9/340

Bowling: *First Innings*—Kulkarni 23-2-85-3; Kapil Dev 6-1-16-0; Shastri 42-16-68-0; Yadav 41.4-8-84-4; Maninder Singh 33-10-72-2; Srikkanth 2-0-3-0. *Second Innings*—Kapil Dev 6-1-24-0; Maninder Singh 20-6-31-0; Shastri 30-8-60-2; Yadav 23-7-52-0; Kulkarni 6-0-29-0; Srikkanth 3-0-10-0.

India

S.M.Gavaskar c Ritchie b Matthews		103
K.Srikkanth c Marsh b Bright		24
K.S.More† c Jones b Matthews		15
M.Amarnath c sub(M.R.J.Veletta) b Matthews		35
D.B.Vengsarkar not out		164
M.Azharuddin c sub(M.R.J.Veletta) b Matthews		10
R.J.Shastri not out		121
Kapil Dev*		
N.S.Yadav		
R.R.Kulkarni		
Maninder Singh		
Extras (B 9, LB 15, NB 21)		45
	(5 wkts dec.)	517

1/53 2/119 3/194 4/205 5/219

Bowling: Reid 32-5-81-0; Gilbert 24-3-75-0; Matthews 52-8-158-4; Bright 38-6-109-1; Border 10-3-29-0; Waugh 14-2-41-0.

Umpires: Ghosh and R.B.Gupta

AUSTRALIA v ENGLAND 1986-87 (First Test)

At Woolloongabba, Brisbane, 14, 15, 16, 18, 19 November

Result: England won by 7 wickets

England

Batsman	First Innings		Second Innings	
B.C.Broad c Zoehrer b Reid	8		not out	35
C.W.J.Athey c Zoehrer b C.D.Matthews	76		c Waugh b Hughes	1
M.W.Gatting* b Hughes	61		c G.R.J.Matthews b Hughes	12
A.J.Lamb lbw b Hughes	40		lbw b Reid	9
D.I.Gower c Ritchie b C.D.Matthews	51		not out	15
I.T.Botham c Hughes b Waugh	138			
C.J.Richards† b C.D.Matthews	0			
J.E.Emburey c Waugh b Hughes	8			
P.A.J.DeFreitas c C.D.Matthews b Waugh	40			
P.H.Edmonds not out	9			
G.R.Dilley c Boon b Waugh	0			
Extras (B 3, LB 19, NB 3)	25		(B 2, NB 3)	5
	456		**(3 wkts)**	**77**

1/15 2/116 3/198 4/198 5/316 6/324 7/351 8/443 9/451

1/6 2/25 3/40

Bowling: *First Innings*—Reid 31-4-86-1; Hughes 36-7-134-3; C.D.Matthews 35-10-95-3; Waugh 21-3-76-3; G.R.J.Matthews 11-2-43-0. *Second Innings*—C.D.Matthews 4-0-11-0; Hughes 5.3-0-28-2; Reid 6-1-20-1; G.R.J.Matthews 7-1-16-0.

Australia

Batsman	First Innings		Second Innings	
G.R.Marsh c Richards b Dilley	56	(2)	b DeFreitas	110
D.C.Boon c Broad b DeFreitas	10	(1)	lbw b Botham	14
T.J.Zoehrer† lbw b Dilley	38	(8)	not out	16
D.M.Jones lbw b DeFreitas	18	(3)	st Richards b Emburey	18
A.R.Border* c DeFreitas b Edmonds	7	(4)	c Lamb b Emburey	23
G.M.Ritchie c Edmonds b Dilley	41	(5)	lbw b DeFreitas	45
G.R.J.Matthews not out	56	(6)	c and b Dilley	13
S.R.Waugh c Richards b Dilley	0	(7)	b Emburey	28
C.D.Matthews c Gatting b Botham	11		lbw b Emburey	0
M.G.Hughes b Botham	0		b DeFreitas	0
B.A.Reid c Richards b Dilley	3		c Broad b Emburey	2
Extras (B 2, LB 8, NB 6, W 2)	18		(B 5, LB 6, NB 2)	13
	248			**282**

1/27 2/97 3/114 4/126 5/159 6/198 7/204 8/239 9/239

1/24 2/44 3/92 4/205 5/224 6/262 7/266 8/266 9/275

Bowling: *First Innings*—DeFreitas 16-5-32-2; Dilley 25.4-7-68-5; Emburey 34-11-66-0; Edmonds 12-6-12-1; Botham 16-1-58-2; Gatting 1-0-2-0. *Second Innings*—Botham 12-0-34-1; Dilley 19-6-47-1; Emburey 42.5-14-80-5; DeFreitas 17-2-62-3; Edmonds 24-8-46-0; Gatting 2-0-2-0.

Umpires: A.R.Crafter and M.W.Johnson

AUSTRALIA v ENGLAND 1986-87 (Second Test)

At W.A.C.A. Ground, Perth, 28, 29, 30 November, 2, 3 December

Result: Match drawn

England

Batsman	First Innings		Second Innings	
B.C.Broad c Zoehrer b Reid	162		lbw b Waugh	16
C.W.J.Athey b Reid	96		c Border b Reid	
A.J.Lamb c Zoehrer b Reid	0	(4)	lbw b Reid	2
M.W.Gatting* c Waugh b C.D.Matthews	14	(3)	b Waugh	70
D.I.Gower c Waugh b G.R.J.Matthews	136		c Zoehrer b Waugh	48
I.T.Botham c Border b Reid	0		c G.R.J.Matthews b Reid	6
C.J.Richards† c Waugh b C.D.Matthews	133		c Lawson b Waugh	15
P.A.J.DeFreitas lbw b C.D.Matthews	11		b Waugh	15
J.E.Emburey not out	5		not out	4
P.H.Edmonds				
G.R.Dilley				
Extras (B 4, LB 15, NB 13, W 3)	35		(B 2, LB 11, NB 4)	17
	(8 wkts dec.)	**592**	**(8 wkts dec.)**	**199**

1/223 2/227 3/275 4/333 5/339 6/546 7/585 8/592

1/8 2/47 3/50 4/123 5/140 6/172 7/190 8/199

Bowling: *First Innings*—Lawson 41-8-126-0; C.D.Matthews 28.1-4-112-3; Reid 40-8-115-4; Waugh 24-4-90-0; G.R.J.Matthews 34-3-124-1; Border 2-0-6-0. *Second Innings*—Reid 21-3-58-3; Lawson 9-1-44-0; Waugh 21.3-4-69-5; C.D.Matthews 2-0-15-0.

Australia

Batsman	First Innings		Second Innings	
G.R.Marsh c Broad b Botham	15	(2)	lbw b Emburey	49
D.C.Boon b Dilley	2	(1)	c Botham b Dilley	0
S.R.Waugh c Botham b Emburey	71			
D.M.Jones c Athey b Edmonds	27	(3)	run out	69
A.R.Border* c Richards b Dilley	125	(4)	c Lamb b Edmonds	16
G.M.Ritchie c Botham b Edmonds	33	(5)	not out	24
G.R.J.Matthews c Botham b Dilley	45	(6)	not out	14
T.J.Zoehrer† lbw b Dilley	29			
G.F.Lawson b DeFreitas	13			
C.D.Matthews c Broad b Emburey	10			
B.A.Reid not out	2			
Extras (B 9, LB 9, NB 11)	29		(B 9, LB 6, NB 10)	25
	401		**(4 wkts)**	**197**

1/4 2/64 3/114 4/128 5/198 6/279 7/334 8/360 9/385

1/0 2/126 3/145 4/152

Bowling: *First Innings*—Botham 22-4-72-1; Dilley 24.4-4-79-4; Emburey 43-9-110-2; DeFreitas 24-4-67-1; Edmonds 21-4-55-2. *Second Innings*—Dilley 15-1-53-1; Botham 7.2-4-13-0; DeFreitas 13.4-2-47-0; Emburey 28-11-41-1; Edmonds 27-13-25-1; Gatting 5-3-3-0; Lamb 1-1-0-0.

Umpires: R.A.French and P.J.McConnell

AUSTRALIA v ENGLAND 1986-87 (Third Test)

At Adelaide Oval, 12, 13, 14, 15, 16 December

Result: Match drawn

Australia

G.R.Marsh b Edmonds	43	(2)	c and b Edmonds	
D.C.Boon c Whitaker b Emburey	103	(1)	lbw b DeFreitas	
D.M.Jones c Richards b Dilley	93		c Lamb b Dilley	2
A.R.Border* c Richards b Edmonds	70		not out	100
G.M.Ritchie c Broad b DeFreitas	36		not out	46
G.R.J.Matthews not out	73			
S.R.Waugh not out	79			
P.R.Sleep				
G.C.Dyer†				
B.A.Reid				
M.G.Hughes				
Extras (LB 2, NB 15)	17		(B 3, LB 7, NB 2)	12

1/113 2/185 3/311 4/333 5/368 (5 wkts dec.) 514   1/1 2/8 3/77 (3 wkts dec.) 201

Bowling: *First Innings*—Dilley 32-3-111-1; DeFreitas 32-4-128-1; Emburey 46-11-117-1; Edmonds 52-14-134-2; Gatting 9-1-22-0. *Second Innings*—Dilley 21-8-38-1; DeFreitas 16-5-36-1; Emburey 22-6-50-0; Edmonds 29-7-63-1; Gatting 2-1-4-0.

England

B.C.Broad c Marsh b Waugh	116	not out	15
C.W.J.Athey b Sleep	55	c Dyer b Hughes	12
M.W.Gatting* c Waugh b Sleep	100	b Matthews	0
A.J.Lamb c Matthews b Hughes	14	not out	9
D.I.Gower lbw b Reid	38		
J.E.Emburey c Dyer b Reid	49		
J.J.Whitaker c Matthews b Reid	11		
C.J.Richards† c Jones b Sleep	29		
P.A.J.DeFreitas not out	4		
P.H.Edmonds c Border b Sleep	13		
G.R.Dilley b Reid	0		
Extras (B 6, LB 12, NB 4, W 4)	26	(B 2, LB 1)	3

1/112 2/273 3/283 4/341 5/341   1/21 2/22 (2 wkts) 39
6/361 7/422 8/439 9/454 455

Bowling: *First Innings*—Hughes 30-8-82-1; Reid 28.4-8-64-4; Sleep 47-14-132-4; Matthews 23-1-102-0; Border 1-0-1-0; Waugh 19-4-56-1. *Second Innings*—Hughes 7-2-16-1; Waugh 3-1-10-0; Matthews 8-4-10-1; Sleep 5-5-0-0.

Umpires: A.R.Crafter and S.G.Randell

AUSTRALIA v ENGLAND 1986-87 (Fourth Test)

At Melbourne Cricket Ground, 26, 27, 28 December

Result: England won by an innings and 14 runs

Australia

G.R.Marsh c Richards b Botham	17	(2)	run out	60
D.C.Boon c Botham b Small	7	(1)	c Gatting b Small	8
D.M.Jones c Gower b Small	59		c Gatting b DeFreitas	21
A.R.Border* c Richards b Botham	15		c Emburey b Small	34
S.R.Waugh c Botham b Small	10		b Edmonds	49
G.R.J.Matthews c Botham b Small	14		b Emburey	0
P.R.Sleep c Richards b Small	0		run out	6
T.J.Zoehrer† b Botham	5		c Athey b Edmonds	1
C.J.McDermott c Richards b Botham	0		b Emburey	1
M.G.Hughes c Richards b Botham	2		c Small b Edmonds	8
B.A.Reid not out	2		not out	0
Extras (B 1, LB 1, NB 7, W 1)	10		(LB 3, NB 2, W 1)	6
	141			194

1/16 2/44 3/80 4/108 5/118   1/13 2/48 3/113 4/153 5/153
6/118 7/129 8/133 9/137   6/175 7/180 8/185 9/189

Bowling: *First Innings*—Small 22.4-7-48-5; DeFreitas 11-1-30-0; Emburey 4-0-16-0; Botham 16-4-41-5; Gatting 1-0-4-0. *Second Innings*—DeFreitas 12-1-44-1; Small 15-3-40-2; Botham 7-1-19-0; Edmonds 19.4-5-45-3; Emburey 20-5-43-2.

England

B.C.Broad c Zoehrer b Hughes	112
C.W.J.Athey lbw b Reid	21
M.W.Gatting* c Hughes b Reid	40
A.J.Lamb c Zoehrer b Reid	43
D.I.Gower c Matthews b Sleep	7
I.T.Botham c Zoehrer b McDermott	29
C.J.Richards† c Marsh b Reid	3
P.A.J.DeFreitas c Matthews b McDermott	7
J.E.Emburey c and b McDermott	22
P.H.Edmonds lbw b McDermott	19
G.C.Small not out	21
Extras (B 6, LB 7, NB 11, W 1)	25
	349

1/56 2/163 3/198 4/251 5/273
6/273 7/277 8/289 9/319

Bowling: McDermott 26.5-4-83-4; Hughes 30-3-94-1; Reid 28-5-78-4; Waugh 8-4-16-0; Sleep 28-4-65-1.

Umpires: A.R.Crafter and R.A.French

AUSTRALIA v ENGLAND 1986-87 (Fifth Test)

At Sydney Cricket Ground, 10, 11, 12, 14, 15 January
Result: Australia won by 55 runs

Australia

Batsman	1st innings		2nd innings	
G.R.Marsh	c Gatting b Small	24	(2) c Emburey b Dilley	14
G.M.Ritchie	lbw b Dilley	6	(1) c Botham b Edmonds	13
D.M.Jones	not out	184	c Richards b Emburey	30
A.R.Border*	c Botham b Edmonds	34	b Edmonds	49
D.M.Wellham	c Richards b Small	17	c Lamb b Emburey	1
S.R.Waugh	c Richards b Small	9	c Athey b Emburey	73
P.R.Sleep	c Richards b Small	10	c Lamb b Emburey	10
T.J.Zoehrer†	c Gatting b Small	12	lbw b Emburey	1
P.L.Taylor	c Emburey b Edmonds	11	c Lamb b Emburey	42
M.G.Hughes	c Botham b Edmonds	16	b Emburey	5
B.A.Reid	b Dilley	4	not out	1
Extras	(B 12, LB 4, NB 8, W 2)	26	(B 5, LB 7)	12
		343		**251**

1/8 2/58 3/149 4/184 5/184
6/200 7/232 8/271 9/338

1/29 2/31 3/106 4/110 5/115
6/141 7/145 8/243 9/248

Bowling: *First Innings*—Dilley 23.5-5-67-2; Small 33-11-75-5; Botham 23-10-42-0; Emburey 30-4-62-0; Edmonds 34-5-79-3; Gatting 1-0-2-0. *Second Innings*—Dilley 15-4-48-1; Small 8-2-17-0; Edmonds 43-16-79-2; Emburey 46-15-78-7; Botham 3-0-17-0; Gatting 2-2-0-0.

England

Batsman	1st innings		2nd innings	
B.C.Broad	lbw b Hughes	6	c and b Sleep	17
C.W.J.Athey	c Zoehrer b Hughes	5	b Sleep	31
M.W.Gatting*	lbw b Reid	0	(5) c and b Waugh	96
A.J.Lamb	c Zoehrer b Taylor	24	c Waugh b Taylor	3
D.I.Gower	c Wellham b Taylor	72	c Marsh b Border	37
I.T.Botham	c Marsh b Taylor	16	c Wellham b Taylor	0
C.J.Richards†	c Wellham b Reid	46	(3) b Sleep	38
J.E.Emburey	b Taylor	69	b Sleep	22
P.H.Edmonds	c Marsh b Taylor	3	lbw b Sleep	0
G.C.Small	b Taylor	14	c Border b Reid	0
G.R.Dilley	not out	4	not out	2
Extras	(B 9, LB 3, NB 2, W 2)	16	(B 8, LB 6, NB 3, W 1)	18
		275		**264**

1/16 2/17 3/17 4/89 5/119
6/142 7/213 8/219 9/270

1/24 2/91 3/91 4/102 5/102
6/233 7/257 8/257 9/262

Bowling: *First Innings*—Hughes 16-3-58-2; Reid 25-7-74-2; Waugh 6-4-6-0; Taylor 26-7-78-6; Sleep 21-6-47-0. *Second Innings*—Hughes 12-3-32-0; Reid 19-8-32-1; Sleep 35-14-72-5; Taylor 29-10-76-2; Border 13-6-25-1; Waugh 6-2-13-1.

Umpires: P.J.McConnell and S.G.Randell

AUSTRALIA v NEW ZEALAND 1987-88 (First Test)

At Woolloongabba, Brisbane, 4, 5, 6, 7 December
Result: Australia won by 9 wickets

New Zealand

Batsman	1st innings		2nd innings	
K.R.Rutherford	c Veletta b Reid	0	c Dyer b McDermott	2
J.G.Wright	c Dyer b Hughes	38	lbw b Reid	15
A.H.Jones	b McDermott	4	c Border b Reid	45
M.D.Crowe	c Waugh b Hughes	67	c Jones b Hughes	23
J.J.Crowe*	lbw b Waugh	16	lbw b Reid	12
D.N.Patel	c Dyer b McDermott	8	c Dyer b Hughes	62
R.J.Hadlee	c Boon b Hughes	8	c Marsh b McDermott	24
J.G.Bracewell	c Veletta b McDermott	11	c Dyer b McDermott	0
I.D.S.Smith†	lbw b Reid	2	c Veletta b Reid	9
D.K.Morrison	c Waugh b McDermott	0	c Dyer b Waugh	2
E.J.Chatfield	not out	0	not out	0
Extras	(B 1, LB 7, NB 11, W 4)	23	(B 6, LB 1, NB 9, W 1)	17
		186		**212**

1/0 2/28 3/80 4/133 5/143
6/153 7/175 8/180 9/181

1/18 2/20 3/66 4/103 5/104
6/142 7/142 8/152 9/204

Bowling: *First Innings*—Reid 25-10-40-2; McDermott 22.2-6-43-4; Hughes 18-5-40-3; Waugh 22-9-35-1; Sleep 6-1-20-0. *Second Innings*—Reid 25-6-53-4; McDermott 21-2-79-3; Hughes 17-7-57-2; Waugh 2-1-2-1; Sleep 14-5-14-0.

Australia

Batsman	1st innings		2nd innings	
G.R.Marsh	c Bracewell b Hadlee	25	(2) not out	31
D.C.Boon	run out	143	(1) lbw b Bracewell	24
D.M.Jones	b Hadlee	2	not out	38
A.R.Border*	lbw b Morrison	9		
M.R.J.Veletta	c Rutherford b Bracewell	4		
S.R.Waugh	c Jones b Morrison	21		
P.R.Sleep	c and b Bracewell	39		
G.C.Dyer†	lbw b Hadlee	8		
C.J.McDermott	c Wright b Morrison	22		
M.G.Hughes	c Smith b Morrison	5		
B.A.Reid	not out	8		
Extras	(B 3, LB 5, NB 9, W 2)	19	(LB 1, NB 2, W 1)	4
		305	(1 wkt)	**97**

1/65 2/72 3/110 4/131 5/219
6/219 7/250 8/286 9/291

1/37

Bowling: *First Innings*—Hadlee 31-5-95-3; Morrison 28-7-86-4; Chatfield 34-11-58-0; Bracewell 24.5-3-58-2. *Second Innings*—Hadlee 8-3-14-0; Morrison 8-0-32-0; Bracewell 13-3-32-1; Patel 3.1-0-18-0.

Umpires: A.R.Crafter and M.W.Johnson

AUSTRALIA v NEW ZEALAND 1987-88 (Second Test)

At Adelaide Oval, 11, 12, 13, 14, 15 December
Result: Match drawn

New Zealand

J.J.Crowe* c Veletta b Reid	0	c Boon b May	19
J.G.Wright c Waugh b May	45	b McDermott	8
A.H.Jones run out	150	c Border b Sleep	64
M.D.Crowe c sub (M.G.Hughes) b Sleep	137	c Border b Sleep	8
D.N.Patel c Marsh b McDermott	35	c Boon b May	40
E.J.Gray c Boon b McDermott	23	c Border b May	14
R.J.Hadlee c and b Jones	36	(9) not out	3
J.G.Bracewell c Sleep b McDermott	32		
I.D.S.Smith† not out	8	(8) c Dyer b Sleep	5
M.C.Snedden c Veletta b McDermott	0	(7) not out	8
D.K.Morrison			
Extras (B 3, LB 7, NB 8, W 1)	19	(B 2, LB 4, NB 7)	13

1/0 2/128 3/341 4/346 5/398 (9 wkts dec.) 485   1/16 2/57 3/77 4/139 (7 wkts) 182
6/405 7/473 8/481 9/485   5/153 6/170 7/179

Bowling: *First Innings*—Reid 7-0-21-1; McDermott 45.5-10-135-4; Waugh 31-11-71-0; May 54-13-134-1; Sleep 34-5-109-1; Jones 3-1-5-1. *Second Innings*—McDermott 10-3-29-1; Waugh 10-4-17-0; Sleep 32-14-61-3; May 30-10-68-3; Jones 3-2-1-0.

Australia

G.R.Marsh c Gray b Hadlee	30
D.C.Boon b Hadlee	6
D.M.Jones c Smith b Hadlee	0
A.R.Border* st Smith b Bracewell	205
S.R.Waugh lbw b Snedden	61
P.R.Sleep c Smith b Morrison	62
M.R.J.Veletta c sub (K.R.Rutherford) b Bracewell	10
G.C.Dyer† run out	60
C.J.McDermott lbw b Hadlee	18
T.B.A.May not out	14
B.A.Reid c Smith b Hadlee	5
Extras (B 2, LB 13, NB 9, W 1)	25

1/29 2/29 3/85 4/201 5/355 496
6/380 7/417 8/451 9/489

Bowling: Hadlee 42-16-68-5; Morrison 22-0-89-1; Bracewell 48-8-122-2; Snedden 32-6-89-1; Gray 44-10-102-0; Patel 7-3-11-0.

Umpires: R.C.Bailhache and S.G.Randell

AUSTRALIA v NEW ZEALAND 1987-88 (Third Test)

At Melbourne Cricket Ground, 26, 27, 28, 29, 30 December
Result: Match drawn

New Zealand

P.A.Horne c Dyer b Dodemaide	7	c Boon b Dodemaide	27
J.G.Wright c Waugh b McDermott	99	b Sleep	43
A.H.Jones c Dyer b McDermott	40	run out	20
M.D.Crowe c Veletta b McDermott	82	c Border b Dodemaide	79
J.J.Crowe* lbw b McDermott	6	c Boon b Sleep	25
D.N.Patel b McDermott	6	c Dyer b Dodemaide	38
J.G.Bracewell c Dyer b Whitney	9	(8) c Veletta b Dodemaide	1
R.J.Hadlee c Dodemaide b Whitney	11	(7) lbw b Sleep	29
I.D.S.Smith† c Jones b Whitney	44	c Dyer b Dodemaide	12
D.K.Morrison c Border b Whitney	0	b Dodemaide	0
E.J.Chatfield not out	6	not out	1
Extras (B 1, LB 4, NB 8)	13	(B 2, LB 8, NB 1)	11

1/32 2/119 3/187 4/221 5/223 317   1/73 2/76 3/158 4/178 5/220 286
6/254 7/254 8/280 9/294   6/272 7/272 8/281 9/285

Bowling: *First Innings*—McDermott 35-8-97-5; Whitney 33.3-6-92-4; Dodemaide 20-4-48-1; Waugh 12-1-31-0. *Second Innings*—McDermott 10-3-43-0; Whitney 20-5-45-0; Dodemaide 28.3-10-58-6; Sleep 26-5-107-3; Jones 8-3-23-0.

Australia

D.C.Boon lbw b Hadlee	10	(2) c M.D.Crowe b Morrison	54
G.R.Marsh c sub (K.R.Rutherford) b Hadlee	13	(1) c Bracewell b Hadlee	23
D.M.Jones c Smith b Hadlee	4	c M.D.Crowe b Chatfield	8
A.R.Border* c J.J.Crowe b Bracewell	31	lbw b Hadlee	43
M.R.J.Veletta lbw b Hadlee	31	c Patel b Bracewell	39
S.R.Waugh c Jones b Bracewell	55	c Patel b Chatfield	10
P.R.Sleep lbw b Morrison	90	lbw b Hadlee	20
G.C.Dyer† run out	21	c Smith b Hadlee	4
A.I.C.Dodemaide c Smith b Morrison	50	lbw b Hadlee	3
C.J.McDermott b Morrison	33	not out	10
M.R.Whitney not out	0	not out	2
Extras (LB 8, NB 11)	19	(B 1, LB 9, NB 4)	14

1/24 2/30 3/31 4/78 5/121 357   1/45 2/59 3/103 4/147 (9 wkts) 230
6/170 7/213 8/293 9/354   5/176 6/209 7/209 8/216 9/227

Bowling: *First Innings*—Hadlee 44-11-109-5; Morrison 27.4-5-93-2; Chatfield 30-10-55-0; Bracewell 32-8-69-2; Patel 12-6-23-0. *Second Innings*—Hadlee 31-9-67-5; Morrison 16-2-54-1; Chatfield 21-6-41-2; Bracewell 24-5-58-1.

Umpires: A.R.Crafter and R.A.French

AUSTRALIA v ENGLAND 1987-88 (Bicentennial Test)
At Sydney Cricket Ground, 29, 30, 31 January, 1, 2 February
Result: Match drawn

England

B.C.Broad	b Waugh	139
M.D.Moxon	b Sleep	40
R.T.Robinson	c Veletta b Dodemaide	43
M.W.Gatting*	c Dyer b Waugh	13
C.W.J.Athey	c and b Taylor	37
D.J.Capel	c Sleep b Taylor	21
J.E.Emburey	st Dyer b Sleep	23
B.N.French†	st Dyer b Taylor	47
N.A.Foster	c Border b Taylor	19
E.E.Hemmings	not out	8
G.R.Dilley	b Waugh	13
Extras	(B 4, LB 9, NB 8, W 1)	22
		425

1/93 2/192 3/245 4/262 5/313
6/314 7/346 8/387 9/410

Bowling: McDermott 35-8-65-0; Dodemaide 36-10-98-1; Taylor 34-10-84-4; Waugh 22.5-5-51-3; Sleep 45-8-114-2.

Australia

D.C.Boon	c French b Foster	12	(2)	not out	184
G.R.Marsh	c French b Capel	5	(1)	c Athey b Emburey	56
D.M.Jones	c Emburey b Hemmings	56		c Moxon b Capel	24
A.R.Border*	c Broad b Capel	2		not out	48
M.R.J.Veletta	c Emburey b Hemmings	22			
S.R.Waugh	c French b Dilley	27			
P.R.Sleep	c Athey b Foster	41			
G.C.Dyer†	lbw b Dilley	0			
P.L.Taylor	c French b Hemmings	20			
A.I.C.Dodemaide	not out	12			
C.J.McDermott	c Foster b Dilley	1			
Extras	(LB 10, NB 5, W 1)	16		(B 3, LB 7, NB 6)	16
		214		(2 wkts)	328

1/18 2/25 3/34 4/82 5/116 1/162 2/218
6/147 7/153 8/183 9/209

Bowling: First Innings—Dilley 19.1-4-54-3; Foster 19-6-27-2; Emburey 30-10-57-0; Capel 6-3-13-2; Hemmings 22-3-53-3. Second Innings—Foster 15-6-27-0; Capel 17-4-38-1; Dilley 13-1-48-0; Hemmings 52-15-107-0; Emburey 38-5-98-1.

Umpires: A.R.Crafter and P.J.McConnell

AUSTRALIA v SRI LANKA 1987-88 (Only Test)
At W.A.C.A. Ground, Perth, 12, 13, 14, 15 February
Australia won by an innings and 108 runs

Australia

G.R.Marsh	b Labrooy	53
D.C.Boon	b Ratnayeke	64
D.M.Jones	lbw b Labrooy	102
A.R.Border*	b Ratnayeke	88
M.R.J.Veletta	c de Alwis b Ratnayeke	21
S.R.Waugh	c Labrooy b Amalean	20
G.C.Dyer†	c Ramanayake b Amalean	38
P.L.Taylor	c Amalean b Ratnayeke	18
A.I.C.Dodemaide	not out	16
C.J.McDermott	c de Alwis b Amalean	4
M.G.Hughes	b Amalean	8
Extras	(LB 12, NB 6, W 5)	23
		455

1/120 2/133 3/289 4/346 5/346
6/380 7/418 8/434 9/443

Bowling: Ratnayeke 40-6-98-4; Labrooy 36-5-108-2; Ramanayake 17-2-58-0; Amalean 22.2-1-97-4; Kaluperuma 13-0-62-0; Ranatunga 8-2-18-0; de Silva 1-0-2-0.

Sri Lanka

D.S.B.P.Kuruppu	c Marsh b McDermott	19	c Dyer b Dodemaide	3
R.S.Mahanama	c Dyer b Dodemaide	41	run out	28
S.M.S.Kaluperuma	lbw b McDermott	0	c and b Hughes	6
P.A.de Silva	lbw b Waugh	6	lbw b Dodemaide	7
A.Ranatunga	c and b Waugh	55	lbw b Dodemaide	45
R.S.Madugalle*	c Border b Dodemaide	6	c Waugh b Hughes	7
J.R.Ratnayeke	c Marsh b McDermott	24	c Dyer b Dodemaide	38
R.G.de Alwis†	c Dyer b Waugh	9	c Waugh b Hughes	8
C.P.H.Ramanayake	c Dyer b Waugh	9	c Veletta b Hughes	0
G.F.Labrooy	c Dyer b Dodemaide	4	b Hughes	4
K.N.Amalean	not out	7	not out	0
Extras	(B 1, LB 6, NB 14, W 2)	23	(LB 6, NB 1)	7
		194		153

1/51 2/51 3/60 4/93 5/107 1/36 2/42 3/42 4/66 5/83
6/147 7/148 8/181 9/182 6/110 7/130 8/131 9/153

Bowling: First Innings—McDermott 20-3-50-3; Hughes 18-2-61-0; Dodemaide 22.3-6-40-3; Waugh 20-7-33-4; Taylor 2-1-3-0. Second Innings—McDermott 4-2-8-0; Hughes 21-7-67-5; Dodemaide 19.1-7-58-4; Waugh 8-4-14-0.

Umpires: R.C.Bailhache and P.J.McConnell

PAKISTAN v AUSTRALIA 1988-89 (First Test)

At National Stadium, Karachi, 15, 16, 17, 19, 20 September

Result: Pakistan won by an innings and 188 runs

Pakistan

Batsman		Runs
Mudassar Nazar b Reid		0
Ramiz Raja c Healy b Reid		9
Shoaib Mohammad b Waugh		94
Javed Miandad* c Boon b Reid		211
Tauseef Ahmed c Boon b May		35
Salim Malik c Boon b May		45
Ijaz Ahmed c Boon b Reid		12
Aamer Malik not out		17
Salim Yousuf† c Wood b May		5
Abdul Qadir c Marsh b May		8
Iqbal Qasim		
Extras (B 16, LB 12, NB 5)		33
	(9 wkts dec.)	469

1/0 2/21 3/217 4/284 5/398
6/428 7/444 8/457 9/469

Bowling: Reid 41-10-109-4; Dodemaide 29-13-35-0; Waugh 26-3-94-1; May 40.5-10-97-4; Taylor 16-2-73-0; Border 17-7-33-0.

Australia

Batsman	1st Innings	R	2nd Innings	R
G.R.Marsh	b Iqbal Qasim	8	lbw b Tauseef Ahmed	17
D.C.Boon	b Abdul Qadir	14	(3) b Iqbal Qasim	4
D.M.Jones	lbw b Iqbal Qasim	3	(4) c Ijaz Ahmed b Abdul Qadir	4
G.M.Wood	c Iqbal Qasim b Tauseef Ahmed	23	(5) lbw b Iqbal Qasim	15
A.R.Border*	c Aamer Malik b Iqbal Qasim	4	(6) b Iqbal Qasim	18
S.R.Waugh	lbw b Iqbal Qasim	54	(7) st Salim Yousuf b Iqbal Qasim	13
P.L.Taylor	not out	0	(2) c Ijaz Ahmed b Aamer Malik	2
I.A.Healy†	c Ijaz Ahmed b Mudassar Nazar	26	c Shoaib Moh'd b Mudassar Nazar	21
A.I.C.Dodemaide	c Ijaz Ahmed b Salim Malik	8	st Salim Yousuf b Tauseef Ahmed	2
T.B.A.May	c Salim Yousuf b Abdul Qadir	6	lbw b Abdul Qadir	0
B.A.Reid	lbw b Iqbal Qasim	0	not out	8
Extras	(B 12, LB 7)	19	(B 6, LB 6)	12
		165		116

1/19 2/23 3/40 4/48 5/54   1/4 2/10 3/15 4/46 5/50
6/64 7/106 8/139 9/162   6/80 7/93 8/104 9/104

Bowling: First Innings—Mudassar Nazar 10-3-15-1; Aamer Malik 2-0-6-0; Iqbal Qasim 39-24-35-5; Abdul Qadir 37-16-54-2; Tauseef Ahmed 26-15-28-1; Shoaib Mohammad 2-1-1-0; Salim Malik 6-4-7-1. Second Innings—Mudassar Nazar 3-0-5-0; Aamer Malik 2-2-0-1; Iqbal Qasim 25-14-49-4; Abdul Qadir 13-4-34-3; Tauseef Ahmed 21.4-13-16-2.

Umpires: Khizer Hayat and Mahboob Shah

PAKISTAN v AUSTRALIA 1988-89 (Second Test)

At Iqbal Stadium, Faisalabad, 23, 24, 25, 27, 28 September

Result: Match drawn

Pakistan

Batsman	1st Innings	R	2nd Innings	R
Mudassar Nazar	c Marsh b Reid	9	c Border b May	27
Ramiz Raja	lbw b Dodemaide	0	c Boon b Waugh	32
Shoaib Mohammad	b Dodemaide	11	st Healy b May	74
Javed Miandad*	c Boon b May	43	lbw b Reid	107
Salim Malik	b Dodemaide	0	c Border b Reid	10
Ijaz Ahmed	b Reid	122	c Healy b Reid	0
Salim Yousuf†	c Boon b Dodemaide	62	not out	66
Abdul Qadir	b Reid	6	(10) c Reid b May	13
Tauseef Ahmed	not out	35	(8) c Waugh b Dodemaide	2
Iqbal Qasim	c and b Sleep	16	(9) lbw b Reid	28
Salim Jaffer	lbw b Sleep	0		
Extras	(B 2, LB 6, NB 4)	12	(LB 6, NB 13)	19
		316	(9 wkts dec.)	378

1/4 2/20 3/24 4/25 5/144   1/64 2/64 3/236
6/255 7/255 8/267 9/316   4/264 5/265 6/269 7/274 8/344 9/378

Bowling: First Innings—Reid 31-8-92-3; Dodemaide 34-6-87-4; Waugh 11-3-36-0; Sleep 5.5-1-24-2; May 19-3-58-1; Border 6-1-11-0. Second Innings—Reid 30-6-100-4; Dodemaide 20-4-48-1; Waugh 18-6-44-1; May 34.4-7-126-3; Sleep 13-4-51-0; Border 1-0-3-0.

Australia

Batsman	1st Innings	R	2nd Innings	R
D.C.Boon	b Mudassar Nazar	13	c Mudassar Nazar b Tauseef Ahmed	15
G.R.Marsh	b Tauseef Ahmed	51	b Abdul Qadir	9
D.M.Jones	lbw b Abdul Qadir	16	not out	21
G.M.Wood	lbw b Salim Jaffer	32	(5) not out	2
A.I.C.Dodemaide	c Ijaz Ahmed b Mudassar Nazar	19		
A.R.Border*	not out	113		
S.R.Waugh	st Salim Yousuf b Tauseef Ahmed	1		
P.R.Sleep	b Tauseef Ahmed	12		
I.A.Healy†	c Iqbal Qasim b Salim Jaffer	12		
T.B.A.May	c sub (Moin-ul-Atiq) b Abdul Qadir	14	(4) c and b Shoaib Mohammad	19
B.A.Reid	c Salim Yousuf b Iqbal Qasim	1		
Extras	(B 4, LB 15, NB 2, W 1)	22	(B 1)	1
		321	(3 wkts)	67

1/24 2/65 3/122 4/122 5/167   1/18 2/30 3/65
6/170 7/204 8/256 9/318

Bowling: First Innings—Salim Jaffer 29-7-69-2; Mudassar Nazar 17-4-39-2; Abdul Qadir 34-5-84-2; Tauseef Ahmed 35-10-73-3; Iqbal Qasim 14.5-4-37-1. Second Innings—Salim Jaffer 2-0-8-0; Mudassar Nazar 2-0-5-0; Abdul Qadir 10-1-34-1; Tauseef Ahmed 11-4-17-1; Shoaib Mohammad 1-0-2-1.

Umpires: Mahboob Shah and Tariq Ata

PAKISTAN v AUSTRALIA 1988-89 (Third Test)

At Gaddafi Stadium, Lahore, 7, 8, 9, 10, 11 October
Result: Match drawn

Australia

D.C.Boon c Shoaib Mohammad b Salim Jaffer	43	c Javed Miandad b Salim Jaffer	28
G.R.Marsh st Salim Yousuf b Iqbal Qasim	64	not out	84
D.M.Jones lbw b Tauseef Ahmed	0	lbw b Salim Jaffer	0
A.R.Border* c Salim Yousuf b Tauseef Ahmed	75	c Salim Yousuf b Tauseef Ahmed	20
G.M.Wood lbw b Mudassar Nazar	15		
P.L.Taylor st Salim Yousuf b Abdul Qadir	29	(5) not out	25
S.R.Waugh c Ijaz Ahmed b Iqbal Qasim	59		
I.A.Healy† lbw b Abdul Qadir	0		
A.I.C.Dodemaide c Iqbal Qasim b Abdul Qadir	14		
T.B.A.May not out	13		
B.A.Reid c Mudassar Nazar b Tauseef Ahmed	8		
Extras (B 4, LB 12, NB 4)	20	(LB 4)	4
	340	**(3 wkts dec.)**	**161**

1/87 2/88 3/155 4/200 5/231 6/241 7/241 8/294 9/331

1/71 2/71 3/108

Bowling: *First Innings*—Salim Jaffer 33-9-82-1; Mudassar Nazar 15-6-23-1; Abdul Qadir 37-10-88-3; Tauseef Ahmed 50-20-85-3; Iqbal Qasim 22-6-42-2; Shoaib Mohammad 1-0-4-0. *Second Innings*—Salim Jaffer 14-2-60-2; Mudassar Nazar 3-0-8-0; Tauseef Ahmed 17-2-48-1; Abdul Qadir 4-1-26-0; Iqbal Qasim 3-0-15-0.

Pakistan

Mudassar Nazar c Boon b May	27	c Border b Taylor	27
Ramiz Raja c Healy b Reid	64	c Boon b May	21
Shoaib Mohammad run out	13	lbw b May	3
Javed Miandad* c Healy b Reid	27	c Border b May	24
Salim Malik c and b Dodemaide	26	c Healy b Taylor	13
Ijaz Ahmed lbw b Dodemaide	23	c Taylor b Dodemaide	15
Salim Yousuf† c Healy b Reid	1	c Waugh b Taylor	2
Abdul Qadir lbw b Dodemaide	18	st Healy b Taylor	6
Iqbal Qasim lbw b May	14	not out	10
Tauseef Ahmed c Boon b May	3	not out	1
Salim Jaffer not out	0		
Extras (LB 6, NB 11)	17	(B 6, LB 1, NB 2)	9
	233	**(8 wkts)**	**153**

1/80 2/104 3/118 4/172 5/172 6/173 7/206 8/228 9/232

1/36 2/48 3/86 4/107 5/123 6/125 7/131 8/147

Bowling: *First Innings*—Reid 23-3-53-3; Waugh 18-4-34-0; Dodemaide 26-6-56-3; May 27.2-6-73-3; Taylor 4-2-11-0. *Second Innings*—Dodemaide 12-5-20-1; Waugh 5-1-8-0; May 35-20-39-3; Taylor 28-9-78-4; Border 4-3-1-0.

Umpires: Khizer Hayat and Salim Badar

AUSTRALIA v WEST INDIES 1988-89 (First Test)

At Woolloongabba, Brisbane, 18, 19, 20, 21 November
Result: West Indies won by 9 wickets

Australia

G.R.Marsh c Logie b Ambrose	27	(2) lbw b Ambrose	2
D.C.Boon lbw b Marshall	10	(1) c Dujon b Marshall	12
M.R.J.Veletta b Hooper	37	c Hooper b Walsh	10
G.M.Wood c Greenidge b Ambrose	6	(5) lbw b Walsh	0
A.R.Border* c Dujon b Ambrose	4	(6) c Haynes b Ambrose	41
S.R.Waugh lbw b Marshall	4	(4) c Haynes b Marshall	90
I.A.Healy† c Logie b Walsh	27	c Ambrose b Marshall	28
A.I.C.Dodemaide c Richards b Walsh	22	c Richards b Marshall	7
C.J.McDermott c Logie b Walsh	2	not out	32
C.D.Matthews c Dujon b Walsh	1	c sub (K.L.T.Arthurton) b Walsh	32
T.B.A.May not out	4	c Hooper b Ambrose	5
Extras (B 1, LB 5, NB 16, W 1)	23	(B 4, LB 5, NB 21)	30
	167		**289**

1/19 2/52 3/64 4/76 5/86 6/126 7/138 8/140 9/150

1/14 2/16 3/65 4/65 5/157 6/199 7/212 8/212 9/270

Bowling: *First Innings*—Marshall 18-3-39-2; Patterson 3.1-1-5-0; Ambrose 16.5-5-30-3; Walsh 18.3-3-62-4; Hooper 12-2-24-1; Richards 1-0-1-0. *Second Innings*—Marshall 26-2-92-4; Ambrose 26.1-5-78-3; Walsh 19-3-61-3; Richards 11-4-26-0; Hooper 4-0-23-0.

West Indies

C.G.Greenidge b May	80	c Healy b Dodemaide	16
D.L.Haynes c Healy b Waugh	40	not out	30
R.B.Richardson lbw b Dodemaide	81	not out	7
C.L.Hooper c Border b Waugh	1		
I.V.A.Richards* c McDermott b May	68		
A.L.Logie c Border b May	19		
P.J.L.Dujon† c May b McDermott	27		
M.D.Marshall c Border b McDermott	11		
C.E.L.Ambrose not out	19		
C.A.Walsh lbw b McDermott	0		
B.P.Patterson lbw b Dodemaide	0		
Extras (B 5, LB 9, NB 28, W 6)	48	(LB 4, NB 3, W 3)	10
	394	**(1 wkt)**	**63**

1/135 2/156 3/162 4/270 5/307 6/359 7/361 8/389 9/393

1/43

Bowling: *First Innings*—McDermott 28-3-99-3; Matthews 21-3-62-0; May 29-6-90-3; Waugh 18-2-61-2; Border 1-0-8-0. *Second Innings*—McDermott 4-0-12-0; Matthews 3.5-1-18-0; Dodemaide 5.2-1-15-1; Waugh 6-0-14-0.

Umpires: A.R.Crafter and P.J.McConnell

AUSTRALIA v WEST INDIES 1988-89 (Second Test)

At W.A.C.A. Ground, Perth, 2, 3, 4, 5, 6 December

Result: West Indies won by 169 runs

West Indies

Batsman		1st		2nd
C.G.Greenidge	b Lawson	40	lbw b Hughes	0
D.L.Haynes	lbw b Hughes	11	c Healy b Hughes	100
R.B.Richardson	c Boon b Hughes	66	c Healy b Hughes	48
C.L.Hooper	c Boon b Lawson	26	c Dodemaide b Hughes	64
I.V.A.Richards*	c Dodemaide b Lawson	146	lbw b Hughes	5
A.L.Logie	c Waugh b May	93	b Hughes	30
P.J.L.Dujon†	c Veletta b May	32	c Dodemaide b Hughes	9
M.D.Marshall	c Veletta b Hughes	4	c Healy b Dodemaide	23
C.E.L.Ambrose	c Healy b Hughes	8	c Wood b Hughes	15
C.A.Walsh	not out	0	not out	17
B.P.Patterson	c Dodemaide b Hughes	1	not out	6
Extras	(B 1, LB 12, NB 9)	22	(B 14, LB 9, NB 9)	32
		449	**(9 wkts dec.)**	**349**

1/16 2/82 3/126 4/180 5/343
6/421 7/426 8/440 9/448

1/0 2/103 3/216 (9 wkts dec.) 349
4/236 5/246 6/259 7/300 8/310
9/341

Bowling: *First Innings*—Lawson 32-7-97-3; Hughes 36.1-7-130-5; Dodemaide 17-1-79-0; Waugh 28-3-90-0; May 10-3-40-2. *Second Innings*—Hughes 37-9-87-8; Dodemaide 24-2-101-1; Waugh 23-1-70-0; May 14-1-68-0.

Australia

Batsman		1st			2nd
G.R.Marsh	c Richardson b Walsh	30	(2)	c Logie b Marshall	6
D.C.Boon	c Logie b Ambrose	80	(1)	b Patterson	4
M.R.J.Veletta	run out	11		c Dujon b Marshall	13
G.M.Wood	c Richardson b Ambrose	111		c Greenidge b Walsh	42
A.R.Border*	c Dujon b Ambrose	6		b Ambrose	26
S.R.Waugh	c Dujon b Ambrose	91		c Hooper b Patterson	26
I.A.Healy†	lbw b Marshall	8		c Logie b Ambrose	52
A.I.C.Dodemaide	not out	7		lbw b Ambrose	11
T.B.A.May	c Richards b Ambrose	2		not out	8
G.F.Lawson	retired hurt	0		absent injured	
M.G.Hughes			(10)	c Logie b Ambrose	0
Extras	(B 5, LB 9, NB 35)	49		(B 5, LB 4, NB 37)	46
	(8 wkts dec.)	**395**			**234**

1/83 2/139 3/152 4/167 5/367
6/374 7/388 8/395

1/14 2/14 3/46 4/93 5/138
6/140 7/190 8/232 9/234

Bowling: *First Innings*—Marshall 23-4-84-1; Patterson 23-3-90-0; Ambrose 23.3-3-72-5; Richards 14-0-43-0; Hooper 5-0-29-0. *Second Innings*—Marshall 12-0-50-2; Patterson 14-2-58-2; Ambrose 17-1-66-3; Walsh 15-1-46-1; Hooper 5-2-5-1.

Umpires: R.C.Bailhache and T.A.Prue

AUSTRALIA v WEST INDIES 1988-89 (Third Test)

At Melbourne Cricket Ground, 24, 26, 27, 28, 29 December

Result: West Indies won by 285 runs

West Indies

Batsman		1st			2nd
C.G.Greenidge	c Healy b Alderman	49		not out	36
D.L.Haynes	c Boon b McDermott	17		b Alderman	23
R.B.Richardson	c Taylor b Alderman	26		c and b Waugh	122
C.L.Hooper	c Border b McDermott	38		lbw b Alderman	4
I.V.A.Richards*	c Border b Waugh	12	(6)	lbw b Waugh	63
A.L.Logie	lbw b Alderman	10	(10)	c Border b Waugh	17
P.J.L.Dujon†	c Healy b Waugh	26	(5)	c Wood b Alderman	46
M.D.Marshall	c Jones b Waugh	7	(7)	c Alderman b Waugh	19
C.E.L.Ambrose	lbw b McDermott	44	(8)	c Marsh b McDermott	5
C.A.Walsh	not out	30	(9)	c Marsh b Waugh	6
B.P.Patterson	lbw b Alderman	13		not out	3
Extras	(B 1, LB 4, NB 2)	8		(LB 1, NB 16)	17
		280		**(9 wkts dec.)**	**361**

1/68 2/68 3/114 4/137 5/147
6/166 7/185 8/199 9/256

1/38 2/92 3/191 (9 wkts dec.)
4/284 5/317 6/324 7/324 8/335
9/356

Bowling: *First Innings*—Hughes 14-3-52-0; Alderman 32.1-9-68-4; McDermott 19-3-62-3; Waugh 21-3-77-3; Taylor 7-3-16-0. *Second Innings*—Hughes 24-8-71-0; Alderman 36-12-78-3; Waugh 24-5-92-5; McDermott 26-3-78-1; Border 1-1-0-0; Taylor 9-1-41-0.

Australia

Batsman		1st			2nd
D.C.Boon	run out	23	(2)	lbw b Marshall	1
G.R.Marsh	b Patterson	36	(1)	b Patterson	20
D.M.Jones	b Ambrose	28		c sub (R.A.Harper) b Ambrose	18
G.M.Wood	c Haynes b Patterson	12		c Ambrose b Walsh	7
A.R.Border*	b Ambrose	0		c Haynes b Patterson	20
S.R.Waugh	c Greenidge b Ambrose	42		c sub (R.A.Harper) b Ambrose	3
I.A.Healy†	lbw b Patterson	4		c Hooper b Walsh	8
P.L.Taylor	c Greenidge b Ambrose	14		not out	18
C.J.McDermott	c Marshall b Patterson	28		c sub (K.L.T.Arthurton) b Patterson	0
M.G.Hughes	not out	21		c Dujon b Patterson	4
T.M.Alderman	b Walsh	3		c Dujon b Patterson	0
Extras	(B 2, LB 14, NB 15)	31		(B 4, LB 5, NB 6)	15
		242			**114**

1/40 2/103 3/117 4/117 5/155
6/161 7/186 8/190 9/234

1/7 2/30 3/56 4/58 5/64
6/75 7/104 8/104 9/114

Bowling: *First Innings*—Marshall 30-8-68-0; Ambrose 27-7-60-4; Walsh 17.3-3-49-1; Patterson 20-2-49-4. *Second Innings*—Marshall 9-3-12-1; Patterson 15.1-3-39-5; Ambrose 13-5-21-2; Walsh 16-7-21-2; Richards 4-1-12-0.

Umpires: A.R.Crafter and P.J.McConnell

AUSTRALIA v WEST INDIES 1988-89 (Fourth Test)

At Sydney Cricket Ground, 26, 27, 28, 29, 30 January
Result: Australia won by 7 wickets

West Indies

Batsman	1st Innings		2nd Innings	
C.G.Greenidge	c Waugh b P.L.Taylor	56	c and b Hughes	4
D.L.Haynes	c Boon b Hohns	75	c M.A.Taylor b Border	143
R.B.Richardson	c P.L.Taylor b Border	28	c Hughes b P.L.Taylor	22
C.L.Hooper	c Marsh b Border	0	c Jones b Hohns	35
I.V.A.Richards*	c Boon b Border	11	c Jones b Hohns	4
A.L.Logie	b Border	0	c P.L.Taylor b Hohns	6
P.J.L.Dujon†	c Hughes b Border	18	run out	9
R.A.Harper	c P.L.Taylor b Border	17	lbw b Border	12
M.D.Marshall	c Marsh b Border	9	c P.L.Taylor b Border	3
C.E.L.Ambrose	c Jones b P.L.Taylor	1	c Boon b Border	5
C.A.Walsh	not out	4	not out	7
Extras	(B 1, NB 3, W 1)	5	(B 1, NB 4, W 1)	6
		224		**256**

1/90 2/144 3/156 4/174 5/174 6/174 7/199 8/213 9/220

1/17 2/56 3/167 4/188 5/198 6/225 7/232 8/244 9/247

Bowling: First Innings—Alderman 10-2-17-0; Hughes 10-3-28-0; Taylor 25.2-8-65-2; Hohns 24-8-49-1; Border 26-10-46-7; Waugh 4-0-18-0. Second Innings—Hughes 18-6-29-1; Alderman 2-0-6-0; Waugh 3-0-10-0; Taylor 29-4-91-1; Hohns 34-11-69-3; Border 18.4-3-50-4.

Australia

Batsman	1st Innings		2nd Innings	
G.R.Marsh	c Dujon b Marshall	2	(2) b Richards	23
M.A.Taylor	b Ambrose	25	(1) c Haynes b Ambrose	3
D.C.Boon	c Dujon b Walsh	149	c Harper b Marshall	10
D.M.Jones	b Richards	29	not out	24
A.R.Border*	b Marshall	75	not out	16
S.R.Waugh	not out	55		
I.A.Healy†	c Logie b Marshall	11		
P.L.Taylor	lbw b Marshall	0		
T.V.Hohns	b Marshall	0		
M.G.Hughes	c Dujon b Walsh	12		
T.M.Alderman	run out	9		
Extras	(B 6, LB 14, NB 14)	34	(B 3, LB 1, NB 2)	6
		401	(3 wkts)	**82**

1/14 2/43 3/114 4/284 5/335 6/355 7/357 8/357 9/388

1/3 2/16 3/55

Bowling: First Innings—Marshall 31-16-29-5; Ambrose 33-5-78-1; Harper 37-9-86-0; Walsh 22.5-5-48-2; Hooper 37-10-72-0; Richards 31-1-68-1. Second Innings—Marshall 8-2-17-1; Ambrose 7-1-16-1; Hooper 10.3-2-24-0; Walsh 3-0-9-0; Richards 7-2-12-1.

Umpires: L.J.King and T.A.Prue

AUSTRALIA v WEST INDIES 1988-89 (Fifth Test)

At Adelaide Oval, 3, 4, 5, 6, 7 February
Result: Match drawn

Australia

Batsman	1st Innings		2nd Innings	
G.R.Marsh	c Dujon b Ambrose	21	(2) c Dujon b Ambrose	79
M.A.Taylor	run out	3	(1) run out	36
D.C.Boon	c Richardson b Ambrose	34	not out	55
D.M.Jones	run out	216	lbw b Richards	6
A.R.Border*	b Marshall	64	(6) not out	6
S.R.Waugh	c Dujon b Walsh	12	(5) run out	8
I.A.Healy†	lbw b Walsh	0		
T.V.Hohns	c Hooper b Walsh	9		
T.B.A.May	c Richardson b Ambrose	24		
M.G.Hughes	not out	72		
M.R.Whitney	c Dujon b Patterson	2		
Extras	(LB 18, NB 40)	58	(B 11, LB 13, NB 10)	34
		515	(4 wkts dec.)	**224**

1/7 2/64 3/75 4/289 5/311 6/311 7/333 8/383 9/497

1/98 2/176 3/187 4/213

Bowling: First Innings—Marshall 23-3-67-1; Patterson 30.5-1-130-1; Ambrose 26-4-93-3; Walsh 33-5-120-3; Hooper 3-0-14-0; Richards 25-1-73-0. Second Innings—Marshall 12-2-30-0; Ambrose 15-2-44-1; Walsh 13-2-26-0; Patterson 8-1-29-0; Richards 24-3-64-1; Hooper 3-1-7-0.

West Indies

Batsman	1st Innings		2nd Innings	
C.G.Greenidge	b Whitney	12	c Boon b May	104
D.L.Haynes	run out	83	c Healy b Whitney	15
R.B.Richardson	c Jones b Whitney	106	c Border b Whitney	22
C.L.Hooper	c Healy b Whitney	2	b May	0
I.V.A.Richards*	c Boon b Whitney	69	not out	68
A.L.Logie	c Healy b Hohns	21	not out	2
P.J.L.Dujon†	b Hohns	28		
M.D.Marshall	c Marsh b Whitney	0		
C.E.L.Ambrose	c Boon b Whitney	9		
C.A.Walsh	c Healy b Whitney	4		
B.P.Patterson	not out	9		
Extras	(B 6, LB 10, NB 10)	26	(B 3, LB 7, NB 11, W 1)	22
		369	(4 wkts)	**233**

1/19 2/186 3/190 4/231 5/293 6/315 7/315 8/331 9/346

1/21 2/87 3/89 4/212

Bowling: First Innings—Hughes 15-0-86-0; Whitney 30-6-89-7; May 16-6-42-0; Waugh 3-0-17-0; Hohns 47.4-9-106-2; Border 16-2-13-0. Second Innings—Hughes 9-5-20-0; Whitney 20-4-60-2; Waugh 9-3-23-0; Hohns 15-3-56-0; May 23-3-60-2; Border 5-3-4-0.

Umpires: R.J.Evans and P.J.McConnell

ENGLAND v AUSTRALIA 1989 (First Test)

At Headingley, Leeds, 8, 9, 10, 12, 13 June

Result: Australia won by 210 runs

Australia

Batsman	First Innings	Runs	Second Innings	Runs
G.R.Marsh	lbw b DeFreitas	16	(2) c Russell b Foster	6
M.A.Taylor	lbw b Foster	136	(1) c Broad b Pringle	60
D.C.Boon	c Russell b Foster	9	lbw b DeFreitas	43
A.R.Border*	c Foster b DeFreitas	66	not out	60
D.M.Jones	c Russell b Newport	79	not out	40
S.R.Waugh	not out	177		
I.A.Healy†	c and b Newport	16		
M.G.Hughes	c Russell b Foster	71		
G.F.Lawson	not out	10		
G.D.Campbell				
T.M.Alderman				
Extras	(LB 13, NB 7, W 1)	21	(B 2, LB 5, NB 5, W 9)	21
Total	(7 wkts dec.)	601	(3 wkts dec.)	230

1/44 2/57 3/174 4/273 5/411 6/441 7/588

1/14 2/97 3/129

Bowling: *First Innings*—DeFreitas 45.3-8-140-2; Foster 46-14-109-3; Newport 39-5-153-2; Pringle 33-5-123-0; Gooch 9-1-31-0; Barnett 6-0-32-0. *Second Innings*—Foster 19-4-65-1; DeFreitas 18-2-76-1; Pringle 12.5-1-60-1; Newport 5-2-22-0.

England

Batsman	First Innings	Runs	Second Innings	Runs
G.A.Gooch	lbw b Alderman	13	lbw b Hughes	68
B.C.Broad	b Hughes	37	lbw b Alderman	7
K.J.Barnett	lbw b Alderman	80	c Taylor b Alderman	34
A.J.Lamb	c Boon b Alderman	125	c Boon b Alderman	4
D.I.Gower*	c Healy b Lawson	26	c Healy b Lawson	34
R.A.Smith	lbw b Alderman	66	c Border b Lawson	0
D.R.Pringle	lbw b Campbell	6	c Border b Alderman	0
P.J.Newport	c Boon b Lawson	36	c Marsh b Alderman	8
R.C.Russell†	c Marsh b Lawson	15	c Healy b Hughes	2
P.A.J.DeFreitas	lbw b Alderman	1	(11) b Hughes	21
N.A.Foster	not out	2	(10) not out	1
Extras	(B 5, LB 7, NB 10, W 1)	23	(B 4, LB 3, NB 5)	12
Total		430		191

1/35 2/81 3/195 4/243 5/323 6/338 7/392 8/421 9/424

1/17 2/67 3/77 4/134 5/134 6/153 7/153 8/166 9/170

Bowling: *First Innings*—Alderman 37-7-107-5; Lawson 34.5-6-105-3; Campbell 14-0-82-1; Hughes 28-7-92-1; Waugh 6-2-27-0; Border 2-1-5-0. *Second Innings*—Alderman 20-7-44-5; Lawson 11-2-58-2; Campbell 10-0-42-0; Hughes 9.2-2-36-3; Border 5-3-4-0.

Umpires: J.W.Holder and D.R.Shepherd

ENGLAND v AUSTRALIA 1989 (Second Test)

At Lord's, London, 22, 23, 24, 26, 27 June

Result: Australia won by 6 wickets

England

Batsman	First Innings	Runs	Second Innings	Runs
G.A.Gooch	c Healy b Waugh	60	lbw b Alderman	0
B.C.Broad	lbw b Alderman	18	b Lawson	20
K.J.Barnett	c Boon b Hughes	14	c Jones b Alderman	3
M.W.Gatting	c Boon b Hughes	0	lbw b Alderman	22
D.I.Gower*	b Lawson	57	c Border b Hughes	106
R.A.Smith	c Hohns b Lawson	32	b Alderman	96
J.E.Emburey	b Alderman	0	(8) not out	36
R.C.Russell†	not out	64	(7) c Boon b Lawson	29
N.A.Foster	c Jones b Hughes	16	lbw b Alderman	4
P.W.Jarvis	c Marsh b Hughes	6	lbw b Alderman	5
G.R.Dilley	c Border b Alderman	7	c Boon b Hughes	24
Extras	(LB 9, NB 3)	12	(B 6, LB 6, NB 2)	14
Total		286		359

1/31 2/52 3/58 4/131 5/180 6/185 7/191 8/237 9/253

1/0 2/18 3/28 4/84 5/223 6/274 7/300 8/304 9/314

Bowling: *First Innings*—Alderman 20.5-4-60-3; Lawson 27-8-88-2; Hughes 23-6-71-4; Waugh 9-3-49-1; Hohns 7-3-9-0. *Second Innings*—Alderman 38-6-128-6; Lawson 39-10-99-2; Hughes 24-8-44-2; Border 9-3-23-0; Hohns 13-6-33-0; Waugh 7-2-20-0.

Australia

Batsman	First Innings	Runs	Second Innings	Runs
G.R.Marsh	c Russell b Dilley	3	(2) b Dilley	1
M.A.Taylor	lbw b Foster	62	(1) c Gooch b Foster	27
D.C.Boon	c Gooch b Dilley	94	not out	58
A.R.Border*	c Smith b Emburey	35	c sub (R.J.Sims) b Foster	1
D.M.Jones	lbw b Foster	27	c Russell b Foster	0
S.R.Waugh	not out	152	not out	21
I.A.Healy†	c Russell b Jarvis	3		
M.G.Hughes	c Gooch b Emburey	30		
T.V.Hohns	b Emburey	21		
G.F.Lawson	c Broad b Emburey	74		
T.M.Alderman	lbw b Emburey	8		
Extras	(LB 11, NB 8)	19	(B 3, LB 4, NB 4)	11
Total		528	(4 wkts)	119

1/6 2/151 3/192 4/221 5/235 6/265 7/331 8/381 9/511

1/9 2/51 3/61 4/67

Bowling: *First Innings*—Dilley 34-3-141-2; Foster 45-7-129-3; Jarvis 31-3-150-1; Emburey 42-12-88-4; Gooch 6-2-9-0. *Second Innings*—Dilley 10-2-27-1; Foster 18-3-39-3; Emburey 3-0-8-0; Jarvis 9.2-0-38-0.

Umpires: H.D.Bird and N.T.Plews

ENGLAND v AUSTRALIA 1989 (Third Test)

At Edgbaston, Birmingham, 6, 7, 8, 10, 11 July

Result: Match drawn

Australia

Batsman	First Innings	Runs	Second Innings	Runs
G.R.Marsh	lbw b Botham	42	(2) b Jarvis	42
M.A.Taylor	st Russell b Emburey	43	(1) c Botham b Gooch	51
D.C.Boon	run out	38	not out	22
A.R.Border*	b Emburey	8		
D.M.Jones	c sub (I.Folley) b Fraser	157		
S.R.Waugh	b Fraser	43		
I.A.Healy†	b Fraser	2	(4) not out	33
M.G.Hughes	c Botham b Dilley	2		
T.V.Hohns	c Gooch b Dilley	40		
G.F.Lawson	b Fraser	12		
T.M.Alderman	not out	0		
Extras	(LB 20, NB 17)	37	(B 4, LB 4, NB 2)	10
		424	(2 wkts)	158

1/88 2/94 3/105 4/201 5/272 6/289 7/299 8/391 9/421

1/81 2/109

Bowling: First Innings—Dilley 31-3-123-2; Jarvis 23-4-82-0; Fraser 33-8-63-4; Botham 26-5-75-1; Emburey 29-5-61-2. Second Innings—Dilley 10-4-27-0; Fraser 12-0-29-0; Jarvis 6-1-20-1; Emburey 20-8-37-0; Gooch 14-5-30-1; Curtis 3-0-7-0.

England

Batsman	First Innings	Runs
G.A.Gooch	lbw b Lawson	8
T.S.Curtis	lbw b Hughes	41
D.I.Gower*	lbw b Alderman	8
C.J.Tavare	c Taylor b Alderman	2
K.J.Barnett	c Healy b Waugh	10
I.T.Botham	b Hughes	46
R.C.Russell†	c Taylor b Hohns	42
J.E.Emburey	c Boon b Lawson	26
A.R.C.Fraser	run out	12
G.R.Dilley	not out	11
P.W.Jarvis	lbw b Alderman	22
Extras	(B 1, LB 2, NB 11)	14
		242

1/17 2/42 3/47 4/75 5/75 6/171 7/171 8/185 9/215

Bowling: Alderman 26.3-6-61-3; Lawson 21-4-54-2; Waugh 11-3-38-1; Hughes 22-4-68-2; Hohns 16-8-18-1.

Umpires: H.D.Bird and J.W.Holder

ENGLAND v AUSTRALIA 1989 (Fourth Test)

At Old Trafford, Manchester, 27, 28, 29, 31 July, 1 August

Result: Australia won by 9 wickets

England

Batsman	First Innings	Runs	Second Innings	Runs
G.A.Gooch	b Lawson	11	c Alderman b Lawson	13
T.S.Curtis	b Lawson	22	c Boon b Alderman	0
R.T.Robinson	lbw b Lawson	0	lbw b Lawson	12
R.A.Smith	c Hohns b Hughes	143	c Healy b Alderman	1
D.I.Gower*	lbw b Hohns	35	c Marsh b Lawson	15
I.T.Botham	b Hohns	1	lbw b Alderman	4
R.C.Russell†	lbw b Lawson	5	not out	128
J.E.Emburey	lbw b Hohns	39	b Alderman	64
N.A.Foster	c Border b Lawson	2	b Alderman	6
A.R.C.Fraser	lbw b Lawson	2	c Marsh b Hohns	3
N.G.B.Cook	not out	2	c Healy b Hughes	5
Extras	(LB 2)		(LB 6, NB 5, W 2)	13
		260		264

1/23 2/57 3/57 4/132 5/140 6/147 7/158 8/232 9/252

1/10 2/25 3/27 4/28 5/38 6/59 7/201 8/223 9/255

Bowling: First Innings—Alderman 25-13-49-0; Lawson 33-11-72-6; Hughes 17-6-55-1; Hohns 22-7-59-3; Waugh 6-1-23-0. Second Innings—Lawson 31-8-81-3; Alderman 27-7-66-5; Hohns 26-15-37-1; Hughes 14.4-2-45-1; Border 8-2-12-0; Waugh 4-0-17-0.

Australia

Batsman	First Innings	Runs	Second Innings	Runs
M.A.Taylor	st Russell b Emburey	85	(2) not out	37
G.R.Marsh	c Russell b Botham	47	(1) c Robinson b Emburey	31
D.C.Boon	b Fraser	12	not out	10
A.R.Border*	c Russell b Foster	80		
D.M.Jones	b Botham	69		
S.R.Waugh	c Curtis b Fraser	92		
I.A.Healy†	lbw b Foster	0		
T.V.Hohns	c Gower b Cook	17		
M.G.Hughes	b Cook	3		
G.F.Lawson	b Fraser	17		
T.M.Alderman	not out	6		
Extras	(B 5, LB 7, NB 6, W 1)	19	(NB 3)	3
		447	(1 wkt)	81

1/135 2/143 3/154 4/274 5/362 6/362 7/413 8/423 9/423

1/62

Bowling: First Innings—Foster 34-12-74-2; Fraser 36.5-4-95-3; Emburey 45-9-118-1; Cook 28-6-85-2; Botham 24-6-63-2. Second Innings—Foster 5-2-5-0; Fraser 10-0-28-0; Emburey 13-3-30-1; Cook 4.5-0-18-0.

Umpires: J.H.Hampshire and B.J.Meyer

ENGLAND v AUSTRALIA 1989 (Fifth Test)

At Trent Bridge, Nottingham, 10, 11, 12, 14 August

Result: Australia won by an innings and 180 runs

Australia

G.R.Marsh	c Botham b Cook	138
M.A.Taylor	st Russell b Cook	219
D.C.Boon	st Russell b Cook	73
A.R.Border*	not out	65
D.M.Jones	c Gower b Fraser	22
S.R.Waugh	c Gower b Malcolm	0
I.A.Healy†	b Fraser	5
T.V.Hohns	not out	19
M.G.Hughes		
G.F.Lawson		
T.M.Alderman		
Extras	(B 6, LB 23, NB 29, W 3)	61
	(6 wkts dec.)	602

1/329 2/430 3/502 4/543 5/553 6/560

Bowling: Fraser 52.3-18-108-2; Malcolm 44-2-166-1; Botham 30-4-103-0; Hemmings 33-9-81-0; Cook 40-10-91-3; Atherton 7-0-24-0.

England

T.S.Curtis	lbw b Alderman	2	(2)	lbw b Alderman	6
M.D.Moxon	c Waugh b Alderman	0	(5)	b Alderman	18
M.A.Atherton	c and b Hohns	0	(3)	c and b Hohns	47
R.A.Smith	c Healy b Alderman	101		b Hughes	26
D.I.Gower*	c Healy b Lawson	11	(1)	b Lawson	5
R.C.Russell†	c Healy b Lawson	20		b Lawson	1
E.E.Hemmings	b Alderman	38		lbw b Hughes	35
A.R.C.Fraser	b Hohns	29		b Hughes	-
I.T.Botham	c Waugh b Hohns	12		absent hurt	
N.G.B.Cook	not out	2	(9)	not out	7
D.E.Malcolm	c Healy b Hughes	9	(10)	b Hughes	5
Extras	(LB 18, NB 13)	31		(B 3, LB 6, NB 6, W 1)	16
		255			167

1/1 2/14 3/14 4/37 5/119 6/172 7/214 8/243 9/244

1/5 2/13 3/67 4/106 5/114 6/120 7/134 8/160 9/167

Bowling: First Innings—Alderman 19-2-69-5; Lawson 21-5-57-2; Hohns 18-8-48-2; Hughes 7.5-0-40-1; Waugh 11-4-23-0. Second Innings—Alderman 16-6-32-2; Lawson 15-3-51-2; Hughes 12.3-1-46-3; Hohns 12-3-29-2.

Umpires: N.T.Plews and D.R.Shepherd

ENGLAND v AUSTRALIA 1989 (Sixth Test)

At Kennington Oval, London, 24, 25, 26, 28, 29 August

Result: Match drawn

Australia

G.R.Marsh	c Igglesden b Small	17	(2)	lbw b Igglesden	4
M.A.Taylor	c Russell b Igglesden	71	(1)	c Russell b Small	48
D.C.Boon	c Atherton b Small	46		run out	37
A.R.Border*	c Russell b Capel	76		not out	51
D.M.Jones	c Gower b Small	122		b Capel	50
S.R.Waugh	b Igglesden	14		not out	7
I.A.Healy†	c Russell b Pringle	44			
T.V.Hohns	c Russell b Pringle	30			
M.G.Hughes	lbw b Pringle	21			
G.F.Lawson	b Pringle	2			
T.M.Alderman	not out	6			
Extras	(B 1, LB 9, NB 9)	19		(B 2, LB 7, NB 13)	22
		468		(4 wkts dec.)	219

1/48 2/130 3/149 4/345 5/347 6/386 7/409 8/447 9/453

1/7 2/100 3/101 4/189

Bowling: First Innings—Small 40-8-141-3; Igglesden 24-2-91-2; Pringle 24.3-6-70-4; Capel 16-2-66-1; Cook 25-5-78-0; Atherton 1-0-10-0; Gooch 2-1-2-0. Second Innings—Small 20-4-57-1; Igglesden 13-1-55-1; Capel 8-0-35-1; Pringle 16-0-53-0; Cook 6-2-10-0.

England

G.A.Gooch	lbw b Alderman	0	c and b Alderman	10
J.P.Stephenson	c Waugh b Alderman	25	lbw b Alderman	11
M.A.Atherton	c Healy b Hughes	12	b Lawson	14
R.A.Smith	b Lawson	11	not out	77
D.I.Gower*	c Healy b Alderman	79	c Waugh b Lawson	7
D.J.Capel	lbw b Alderman	4	c Taylor b Hohns	17
R.C.Russell†	c Healy b Alderman	12	not out	0
D.R.Pringle	c Taylor b Hohns	27		
G.C.Small	c Jones b Lawson	59		
N.G.B.Cook	c Jones b Lawson	31		
A.P.Igglesden	not out	2		
Extras	(B 2, LB 7, NB 13, W 1)	23	(LB 1, NB 5, W 1)	7
		285	(5 wkts)	143

1/1 2/28 3/47 4/80 5/84 6/98 7/169 8/201 9/274

1/20 2/27 3/51 4/67 5/138

Bowling: First Innings—Alderman 27-7-66-5; Lawson 29.1-9-85-3; Hughes 23-3-84-1; Hohns 10-1-30-1; Waugh 3-0-11-0. Second Innings—Alderman 13-3-30-2; Lawson 15.1-2-41-2; Hughes 8-2-34-0; Hohns 10-2-37-1.

Umpires: H.D.Bird and K.E.Palmer

AUSTRALIA v SRI LANKA 1989-90 (First Test)

At Woolloongabba, Brisbane, 8, 9, 10, 11, 12 December

Result: Match drawn

Australia

D.C.Boon c Samarasekera b Labrooy	0	(2) lbw b Ramanayake	26
M.A.Taylor c Wickremasinghe b Ramanayake	9	(1) lbw b Ramanayake	164
T.M.Moody c Wickremasinghe b Labrooy	106	c A.Ranatunga b E.A.R.de Silva	30
A.R.Border* c A.Ranatunga b Labrooy	56		
D.M.Jones lbw b Labrooy	15	(4) c Ramanayake b P.A.de Silva	23
S.R.Waugh c A.Ranatunga b Ramanayake	60	(5) b Gurusinha	57
I.A.Healy† lbw b Gurusinha	21	(6) not out	26
M.G.Hughes run out	25	not out	23
G.F.Lawson c Wickremasinghe b Labrooy	22		
C.G.Rackemann not out	5	(7) b Gurusinha	0
T.M.Alderman c P.A.de Silva b Gurusinha	18		
Extras (B 1, LB 8, NB 21)	30	(B 5, LB 4, NB 17)	26
	367	**(6 wkts)**	**375**

1/1 2/27 3/185 4/197 5/210 6/247 7/293 8/337 9/337

1/60 2/124 3/167 4/316 5/324 6/324

Bowling: *First Innings*—Ratnayeke 8.5-1-17-0; Labrooy 31.1-5-133-5; Ramanayake 26-2-101-2; A.Ranatunga 13-1-49-0; E.A.R.de Silva 8-1-21-0; Gurusinha 8.3-1-37-2. *Second Innings*—Labrooy 24-4-69-0; Ramanayake 28-3-81-2; E.A.R.de Silva 39-8-112-1; P.A.de Silva 15-2-45-1; Gurusinha 10-2-31-2; A.Ranatunga 6-0-25-0; Mahanama 1-0-3-0.

Sri Lanka

R.S.Mahanama lbw b Alderman	5
D.Ranatunga c Waugh b Lawson	40
A.P.Gurusinha c Healy b Rackemann	43
E.A.R.de Silva b Alderman	22
P.A.de Silva c Lawson b Rackemann	167
A.Ranatunga* lbw b Hughes	25
M.A.R.Samarasekera c Moody b Rackemann	18
J.R.Ratnayeke lbw b Hughes	56
A.G.D.Wickremasinghe† c Boon b Hughes	2
G.F.Labrooy lbw b Alderman	1
C.P.H.Ramanayake not out	10
Extras (LB 23, NB 4, W 2)	29
	418

1/10 2/80 3/114 4/148 5/201 6/238 7/382 8/386 9/391

Bowling: Alderman 40-13-81-3; Lawson 33-10-51-1; Rackemann 30.3-6-88-3; Hughes 39-8-123-3; Moody 16-8-15-0; Border 7-0-36-0; Jones 1-0-1-0.

Umpires: A.R.Crafter and C.D.Timmins

AUSTRALIA v NEW ZEALAND 1989-90 (Only Test)

At W.A.C.A. Ground, Perth, 24, 25, 26, 27, 28 November

Result: Match drawn

Australia

M.A.Taylor c Wright b Morrison	9
D.C.Boon c Wright b Snedden	200
T.M.Moody c Smith b Snedden	61
A.R.Border* b Morrison	50
D.M.Jones lbw b Morrison	99
S.R.Waugh c Greatbatch b Snedden	17
I.A.Healy† c J.J.Crowe b Patel	28
M.G.Hughes c Wright b Snedden	16
G.F.Lawson b Morrison	1
C.G.Rackemann not out	15
T.M.Alderman	
Extras (B 1, LB 9, NB 13, W 2)	25
	(9 wkts dec.) 521

1/28 2/177 3/316 4/361 5/395 6/449 7/489 8/490 9/521

Bowling: Morrison 39.1-8-145-4; Cairns 12-2-60-0; Snedden 42-10-108-4; Watson 37-7-118-0; Patel 28-5-80-1.

New Zealand

J.G.Wright* b Rackemann	34	c Border b Lawson	3
R.H.Vance b Alderman	4	c Alderman b Rackemann	8
M.J.Greatbatch c Healy b Hughes	76	not out	146
M.D.Crowe lbw b Alderman	62	c Taylor b Moody	30
D.N.Patel c Boon b Hughes	0	lbw b Alderman	7
J.J.Crowe c Healy b Rackemann	7	lbw b Hughes	49
I.D.S.Smith† c Lawson b Hughes	11	c Border b Hughes	0
C.L.Cairns c Healy b Hughes	11	lbw b Hughes	28
M.C.Snedden not out	13	not out	33
D.K.Morrison c Border b Lawson	3		
W.Watson lbw b Alderman	4		
Extras (B 1, LB 6, NB 5, W 4)	16	(LB 14, NB 4)	18
	231	**(7 wkts)**	**322**

1/28 2/84 3/173 4/178 5/191 6/204 7/206 8/212 9/226

1/11 2/11 3/79 4/107 5/189 6/189 7/234

Bowling: *First Innings*—Alderman 25.4-7-73-2; Lawson 22-5-54-1; Rackemann 20-4-39-2; Hughes 20-7-51-4; Moody 4-1-6-0; Border 1-0-1-0. *Second Innings*—Alderman 32-14-59-1; Lawson 38-12-88-1; Rackemann 31-21-23-1; Hughes 36-8-92-3; Moody 17-6-23-1; Border 5-2-17-0; Jones 3-2-6-0.

Umpires: R.J.Evans and P.J.McConnell

AUSTRALIA v PAKISTAN 1989-90 (First Test)

At Melbourne Cricket Ground, 12, 13, 14, 15, 16 January

Result: Australia won by 92 runs

Australia

G.R.Marsh c Salim Yousuf b Wasim Akram	30	(2)	c Wasim Akram b Aaqib Javed	24
M.A.Taylor c Aaqib Javed b Imran Khan	52	(1)	c Aamer Malik b Tauseef Ahmed	101
D.C.Boon lbw b Wasim Akram	0		run out	21
A.R.Border* c Javed Miandad b Wasim Akram	24		lbw b Wasim Akram	62
D.M.Jones c Salim Yousuf b Imran Khan	0		lbw b Wasim Akram	0
S.R.Waugh c Salim Yousuf b Aaqib Javed	20		c Salim Yousuf b Wasim Akram	3
P.R.Sleep lbw b Wasim Akram	23		b Wasim Akram	0
I.A.Healy† c Shoaib Mohammad b Aaqib Javed	48		c Ijaz Ahmed b Wasim Akram	25
M.G.Hughes c Mansoor Akhtar b Wasim Akram	8		c Mansoor Akhtar b Wasim Akram	32
T.M.Alderman c Aamer Malik b Wasim Akram	0		not out	1
C.G.Rackemann not out	0			
Extras (LB 9, NB 9)	18		(B 2, LB 10, NB 20, W 1)	33
	223		**(8 wkts dec.) 312**	

1/90 2/90 3/98 4/98 5/131 6/148 7/201 8/223 9/223

1/73 2/116 3/204 4/216 5/220 6/220 7/260 8/305

Bowling: *First Innings*—Imran Khan 18-6-53-2; Wasim Akram 22.1-7-47-2; Waqar Younis 12-3-27-0; Tauseef Ahmed 8-1-25-0. *Second Innings*—Wasim Akram 41.4-12-98-5; Aaqib Javed 21-1-55-1; Imran Khan 8-2-21-0; Waqar Younis 22-4-68-0; Tauseef Ahmed 16-3-58-1.

Pakistan

Aamer Malik lbw b Alderman	7	(3)	c Taylor b Hughes	0
Shoaib Mohammad c Healy b Alderman	6		c Boon b Hughes	10
Mansoor Akhtar c Taylor b Rackemann	5	(2)	lbw b Alderman	14
Javed Miandad c Healy b Alderman	3		lbw b Waugh	65
Ijaz Ahmed c Taylor b Hughes	19		c Marsh b Hughes	121
Imran Khan* c Alderman b Rackemann	3		lbw b Alderman	45
Salim Yousuf† c Taylor b Hughes	16		lbw b Alderman	38
Wasim Akram c Healy b Hughes	6		c Taylor b Sleep	6
Tauseef Ahmed not out	9		not out	14
Waqar Younis lbw b Sleep	18		lbw b Alderman	4
Aaqib Javed c Healy b Rackemann	0		lbw b Alderman	0
Extras (B 1, LB 4, NB 10)	15		(B 1, LB 7, NB 9, W 2)	19
	107		**336**	

1/12 2/20 3/20 4/44 5/44 6/65 7/71 8/71 9/106

1/4 2/23 3/31 4/134 5/218 6/291 7/303 8/328 9/333

Bowling: *First Innings*—Alderman 19-6-30-3; Rackemann 21.5-8-32-3; Hughes 17-7-34-3; Sleep 8-5-6-1. *Second Innings*—Hughes 42-14-79-3; Rackemann 38-13-67-0; Alderman 33.5-6-105-5; Sleep 21-7-64-1; Waugh 3-0-13-1.

Umpires: R.J.Evans and P.J.McConnell.

AUSTRALIA v SRI LANKA 1989-90 (Second Test)

At Bellerive Oval, Hobart, 16, 17, 18, 19, 20 December

Result: Australia won by 173 runs

Australia

D.C.Boon c Mahanama b Ratnayake	41	(2)	c Ratnayake b Labrooy	0
M.A.Taylor c Tillekeratne b Ratnayake	23	(1)	c Gurusinha b P.A.de Silva	108
T.M.Moody c Gurusinha b Ratnayake	6		c Tillekeratne b Ratnayake	5
A.R.Border* c E.A.R.de Silva b Ratnayeke	24	(5)	b P.A.de Silva	85
D.M.Jones c Tillekeratne b Ratnayake	3	(6)	not out	118
S.R.Waugh c Tillekeratne b Labrooy	16	(7)	not out	134
P.R.Sleep not out	47			
I.A.Healy† c Tillekeratne b Gurusinha	17			
M.G.Hughes b E.A.R.de Silva	27	(4)	c Gurusinha b Ratnayake	30
G.D.Campbell c Mahanama b Ratnayake	6			
T.M.Alderman b Ratnayake	0			
Extras (LB 7, NB 6, W 1)	14		(B 2, LB 5, NB 22, W 4)	33
	224		**(5 wkts dec.) 513**	

1/50 2/68 3/83 4/89 5/112 6/123 7/166 8/207 9/224

1/0 2/10 3/77 4/240 5/253

Bowling: *First Innings*—Ratnayeke 15-2-39-1; Labrooy 19-3-61-1; Ratnayake 19.4-2-66-6; Ramanayake 4-0-21-0; Gurusinha 6-0-20-1; E.A.R.de Silva 9-6-10-1. *Second Innings*—Labrooy 22-3-100-1; Ratnayake 35-5-123-2; Ratnayeke 19-1-86-0; E.A.R.de Silva 21-2-83-0; P.A.de Silva 18-1-65-2; Ramanayake 10-0-49-0.

Sri Lanka

R.S.Mahanama c Healy b Sleep	85		lbw b Campbell	5
D.Ranatunga c Moody b Alderman	2		c Healy b Hughes	45
A.P.Gurusinha c Taylor b Alderman	0		c sub (R.J.Tucker) b Hughes	20
E.A.R.de Silva c Border b Campbell	2	(8)	b Campbell	50
P.A.de Silva lbw b Campbell	75	(4)	c Campbell b Sleep	72
A.Ranatunga* c Moody b Sleep	21	(5)	c Jones b Hughes	38
H.P.Tillekeratne† c Taylor b Sleep	9	(6)	c Waugh b Hughes	6
J.R.Ratnayeke c Taylor b Hughes	9	(7)	c Healy b Campbell	75
G.F.Labrooy b Hughes	11		b Hughes	5
C.P.H.Ramanayake not out	4		not out	2
R.J.Ratnayake c Border b Hughes	0		lbw b Hughes	5
Extras (LB 4, NB 3)	7		(B , LB , NB 4)	25
	216		**348**	

1/11 2/15 3/18 4/176 5/188 6/192 7/193 8/201 9/216

1/6 2/53 3/94 4/187 5/187 6/208 7/332 8/337 9/337

Bowling: *First Innings*—Alderman 23-2-71-2; Campbell 23-9-41-2; Hughes 21.4-6-68-3; Sleep 10-4-26-3; Waugh 6-3-6-0. *Second Innings*—Alderman 30-12-48-0; Campbell 33-8-102-3; Sleep 36-16-73-2; Hughes 31.4-8-88-5; Moody 2-0-9-0; Jones 4-2-5-0; Border 5-4-2-0.

Umpires: L.J.King and S.G.Randell.

AUSTRALIA v PAKISTAN 1989-90 (Second Test)
At Adelaide Oval, 19, 20, 21, 22, 23 January·
Result: Match drawn

Pakistan

Shoaib Mohammad lbw b Hughes 43   (1) c Healy b Hughes 0
Ramiz Raja c P.L.Taylor b Campbell 9   c Waugh b Hughes 2
Salim Yousuf lbw b Rackemann 38   c M.A.Taylor b Hughes 1
Javed Miandad c Healy b Campbell 52   (6) c P.L.Taylor b Hughes 21
Ijaz Ahmed c Marsh b Border 28   (4) c P.L.Taylor b Hughes 4
Salim Malik c Healy b Hughes 11   (8) not out 65
Imran Khan* c Healy b Rackemann 13   (5) b P.L.Taylor 136
Wasim Akram c Border b Campbell 52   (7) b Campbell 123
Tauseef Ahmed c Healy b Rackemann 0   c Healy b Rackemann 18
Mushtaq Ahmed c Healy b Rackemann 0   b P.L.Taylor 4
Waqar Younis not out 1
Extras (B 4, LB 4, NB 1, W 1) 10   (B 4, LB 5, NB 3, W 1) 13

257   1/0 2/2 3/7 4/22 (9 wkts dec.) 387
1/27 2/91 3/95 4/166 5/187   5/90 6/281 7/316 8/381 9/387
6/187 7/241 8/251 9/251

Bowling: *First Innings*—Hughes 18-5-63-2; Campbell 21.3-2-79-3; P.L.Taylor 12-0-57-0; Rackemann 21-3-40-4; Border 4-0-10-1. *Second Innings*—Hughes 32-9-111-5; Campbell 29-5-83-1; Rackemann 37-11-85-1; P.L.Taylor 41.5-13-94-2; Border 4-0-5-0.

Australia

G.R.Marsh c Salim Yousuf b Wasim Akram.. 13   (1) c sub(Saeed Anwar) b Mushtaq...59
M.A.Taylor lbw b Imran Khan 77   (2) c Ramiz Raja b Wasim Akram ...5
D.C.Boon lbw b Wasim Akram 29   (3) c Salim Yousuf b Waqar Younis ..8
A.R.Border* b Waqar Younis 13   (4) not out 121
D.M.Jones c Wasim Akram b Imran Khan... 116   (5) b Tauseef Ahmed 4
S.R.Waugh lbw b Wasim Akram 17   (6) c sub(Aamer Malik) b Tauseef ...27
I.A.Healy† c sub (Maqsood Rana) b Waqar Younis 12   (7) c Shoaib Mohammad b Tauseef ..2
P.L.Taylor run out 33   (8) not out 6
M.G.Hughes not out 6
G.D.Campbell lbw b Wasim Akram 0
C.G.Rackemann b Wasim Akram 0
Extras (LB 12, NB 13) 25   (LB 3, NB 3) 6

341   1/9 2/33 3/106 4/129 (6 wkts) 233
1/82 2/113 3/156 4/188 5/216   5/213 6/229
6/328 7/328 8/341 9/341

Bowling: *First Innings*—Wasim Akram 43-10-100; Waqar Younis 26-4-66-2; Mushtaq Ahmed 23-4-69-0; Imran Khan 27-6-61-2; Tauseef Ahmed 14-1-33-0. *Second Innings*—Wasim Akram 11-3-29-1; Waqar Younis 14-4-42-1; Tauseef Ahmed 32-6-80-3; Mushtaq Ahmed 25-5-72-1; Shoaib Mohammad 1-0-7-0.

Umpires: A.R.Crafter and L.J.King

AUSTRALIA v PAKISTAN 1989-90 (Third Test)
At Sydney Cricket Ground, 3 (no play), 4 (no play), 5, 6, 7 (no play), 8 February
Result: Match drawn

Pakistan

Aamer Malik c Healy b Alderman 7
Ramiz Raja c and b Hughes 0
Shoaib Mohammad lbw b Alderman 9
Javed Miandad c Jones b Hughes 49
Ijaz Ahmed c M.A.Taylor b Rackemann 8
Imran Khan* not out 82
Wasim Akram c M.A.Taylor b Alderman 10
Salim Yousuf† c Jones b Rackemann 6
Tauseef Ahmed b Alderman 0
Waqar Younis c Veletta b Hughes 16
Nadeem Ghauri b Alderman 0
Extras (B 1, LB 7, NB 4) 12

199
1/2 2/15 3/20 4/51 5/106
6/128 7/154 8/160 9/191

Bowling: Alderman 33.5-10-65-5; Hughes 31-16-70-3; Rackemann 22-8-33-2; P.L.Taylor 8-1-23-0.

Australia

M.A.Taylor not out 101
M.R.J.Veletta lbw b Waqar Younis ...9
T.M.Moody c Aamer Malik b Tauseef Ahmed. 26
A.R.Border* not out 27
D.M.Jones
S.R.Waugh
I.A.Healy†
P.L.Taylor
M.G.Hughes
C.G.Rackemann
T.M.Alderman
Extras (B 4, LB 5, NB 4) 13

(2 wkts) 176
1/33 2/106

Bowling: Wasim Akram 10-3-29-0; Imran Khan 17-2-32-0; Tauseef Ahmed 19-3-62-1; Nadeem Ghauri 8-1-20-0; Waqar Younis 9-4-21-1; Ijaz Ahmed 2-0-3-0.

Umpires: A.R.Crafter and P.J.McConnell

NEW ZEALAND v AUSTRALIA 1989-90 (Only Test)

At Basin Reserve, Wellington, 15, 16, 17, 18, 19 March
Result: New Zealand won by 9 wickets

Australia

	First Innings		Second Innings	
M.A.Taylor	lbw b Morrison	4	(2) lbw b Hadlee	5
G.R.Marsh	b Morrison	4	(1) c Rutherford b Bracewell	41
D.C.Boon	lbw b Hadlee	0	c Smith b Bracewell	12
A.R.Border*	lbw b Morrison	1	(5) not out	78
D.M.Jones	c Wright b Snedden	20	(6) lbw b Morrison	0
S.R.Waugh	b Hadlee	25	(7) c Greatbatch b Hadlee	25
I.A.Healy†	b Snedden	4	(8) c Rutherford b Bracewell	10
P.L.Taylor	c Wright b Hadlee	29	(4) c Rutherford b Bracewell	87
G.D.Campbell	lbw b Hadlee	0	b Bracewell	0
C.G.Rackemann	not out	6	b Bracewell	1
T.M.Alderman	b Hadlee	4	st Smith b Bracewell	1
Extras	(LB 6, NB 7)	13	(LB 6, NB 3)	9
Total		110		269

1/4 2/9 3/9 4/12 5/38   1/27 2/54 3/91 4/123 5/194
6/44 7/70 8/87 9/103   6/232 7/261 8/261 9/267

Bowling: *First Innings*—Hadlee 16.2-5-39-5; Morrison 10-4-22-3; Snedden 15-2-33-2; *Second Innings*—Hadlee 25-3-70-2; Morrison 24-8-58-2; Snedden 25-5-46-0; Bracewell 34-11-85-6; Jones 1-0-4-0.

New Zealand

	First Innings		Second Innings	
T.J.Franklin	c Marsh b P.L.Taylor	28	c Healy b Campbell	18
J.G.Wright*	c Healy b Alderman	36	not out	117
A.H.Jones	c and b Border	18	not out	33
M.C.Snedden	c and b Alderman	23		
M.J.Greatbatch	c Healy b P.L.Taylor	16		
K.R.Rutherford	c Healy b P.L.Taylor	12		
J.J.Crowe	lbw b Alderman	9		
R.J.Hadlee	b Campbell	18		
I.D.S.Smith†	c M.A.Taylor b Campbell	1		
J.G.Bracewell	not out	19		
D.K.Morrison	c M.A.Taylor b Alderman	12		
Extras	(B 2, LB 5, NB 3)	10	(B 2, LB 10, NB 1)	13
Total		202	(1 wkt)	181

1/48 2/89 3/89 4/111 5/123   1/53
6/150 7/151 8/152 9/171

Bowling: *First Innings*—Alderman 29-9-46-4; Rackemann 32-17-42-0; Taylor 33-19-44-3; Border 6-3-12-1. *Second Innings*—Alderman 14-8-27-0; Rackemann 15-4-39-0; P.L.Taylor 11-3-39-0; Campbell 7-2-23-1; Jones 6-3-14-0; Border 10.4-5-27-0.

Umpires: R.S.Dunne and S.J.Woodward

AUSTRALIA v ENGLAND 1990-91 (First Test)

At Woolloongabba, Brisbane, 23, 24, 25 November
Result: Australia won by 10 wickets

England

	First Innings		Second Innings	
M.A.Atherton	lbw b Reid	13	b Alderman	15
W.Larkins	c Healy b Hughes	12	lbw b Reid	0
D.I.Gower	c Healy b Reid	61	b Hughes	27
A.J.Lamb*	c Hughes b Matthews	32	lbw b Alderman	14
R.A.Smith	b Reid	7	c M.A.Taylor b Alderman	1
A.J.Stewart	lbw b Reid	4	c sub (P.E.Cantrell) b Alderman	6
R.C.Russell†	c and b Alderman	16	lbw b Waugh	15
C.C.Lewis	c Border b Hughes	20	lbw b Alderman	14
G.C.Small	not out	12	c Alderman b Hughes	15
A.R.C.Fraser	c Healy b Alderman	1	c sub (P.E.Cantrell) b Alderman	0
D.E.Malcolm	c Waugh b Hughes	5	not out	0
Extras	(B 1, LB 7, NB 3)	11	(LB 3, NB 4)	7
Total		194		114

1/23 2/43 3/117 4/123 5/134   1/0 2/42 3/46 4/60 5/78
6/135 7/167 8/181 9/187   6/84 7/93 8/112 9/114

Bowling: *First Innings*—Alderman 18-5-44-2; Reid 11-1-53-4; Hughes 19-5-39-3; Waugh 7-2-20-0; Matthews 16-8-30-1. *Second Innings*—Alderman 22-7-47-6; Reid 14-3-40-1; Hughes 12.1-5-17-2; Matthews 1-1-0-0; Waugh 4-2-7-1.

Australia

	First Innings		Second Innings	
G.R.Marsh	lbw b Fraser	9	(2) not out	72
M.A.Taylor	c Lewis b Fraser	10	(1) not out	67
D.C.Boon	lbw b Small	18		
A.R.Border*	c Atherton b Small	9		
D.M.Jones	c Small b Lewis	17		
S.R.Waugh	c Smith b Small	1		
G.R.J.Matthews	c Small b Malcolm	35		
I.A.Healy†	c Atherton b Lewis	22		
M.G.Hughes	c Russell b Fraser	9		
B.A.Reid	lbw b Lewis	0		
T.M.Alderman	not out	0		
Extras	(B 1, LB 10, NB 11)	22	(B 3, LB 2, NB 10, W 3)	18
Total		152	(0 wkts)	157

1/22 2/35 3/49 4/60 5/64
6/89 7/135 8/150 9/150

Bowling: *First Innings*—Malcolm 17-2-45-1; Fraser 21-6-33-3; Taylor 33-17-42-0; Small 16-4-34-3; Lewis 9-0-29-3. *Second Innings*—Fraser 14-2-36-0; Small 14-2-36-0; Malcolm 9-5-22-0; Lewis 6-0-29-0; Atherton 2-0-16-0.

Umpires: A.R.Crafter and P.J.McConnell

AUSTRALIA v ENGLAND 1990-91 (Second Test)

At Melbourne Cricket Ground, 26, 27, 28, 29, 30 December

Result: Australia won by 8 wickets

England

Batsman	1st innings		2nd innings	
G.A.Gooch*	lbw b Alderman	20	c Alderman b Reid	58
M.A.Atherton	c Boon b Reid	0	c Healy b Reid	4
W.Larkins	c Healy b Reid	64	c Healy b Reid	54
R.A.Smith	c Healy b Hughes	30	c Taylor b Reid	8
D.I.Gower	c and b Reid	100	c Border b Matthews	0
A.J.Stewart	c Healy b Reid	79	c Marsh b Reid	0
R.C.Russell†	c Healy b Hughes	15	c Jones b Matthews	1
P.A.J.DeFreitas	c Healy b Hughes	3	lbw b Reid	0
A.R.C.Fraser	c Jones b Alderman	24	c Taylor b Reid	0
D.E.Malcolm	c Taylor b Reid	6	lbw b Matthews	1
P.C.R.Tufnell	not out	0	not out	0
Extras	(LB 2, NB 9)	11	(B 7, LB 3, NB 6)	16
		352		**150**

1/12 2/30 3/109 4/152 5/274 6/303 7/307 8/324 9/344

1/17 2/103 3/115 4/122 5/147 6/148 7/148 8/148 9/150

Bowling: *First Innings*—Alderman 30.4-7-86-2; Reid 39-8-97-6; Hughes 29-7-83-2; Matthews 27-8-65-0; Waugh 6-2-19-0. *Second Innings*—Alderman 10-2-19-0; Reid 22-12-51-7; Hughes 9-4-26-0; Matthews 25-9-40-3; Waugh 7-6-4-0.

Australia

Batsman	1st innings		2nd innings	
G.R.Marsh	c Russell b DeFreitas	36	(2) not out	79
M.A.Taylor	c Russell b DeFreitas	61	(1) c Atherton b Malcolm	5
D.C.Boon	c Russell b Fraser	28	(4) not out	94
A.R.Border*	c Russell b Malcolm	62		
D.M.Jones	c Russell b Fraser	44		
S.R.Waugh	b Fraser	19		
G.R.J.Matthews	lbw b Fraser	12		
I.A.Healy†	c Russell b Fraser	5	(3) c Atherton b Fraser	1
M.G.Hughes	lbw b Malcolm	4		
T.M.Alderman	b Fraser	0		
B.A.Reid	not out	3		
Extras	(B 4, LB 12, NB 16)	32	(B 4, LB 12, NB 2)	18
		306	(2 wkts)	**197**

1/63 2/133 3/149 4/224 5/264 6/281 7/289 8/298 9/302

1/9 2/10

Bowling: *First Innings*—Malcolm 25.5-4-74-2; Fraser 39-10-82-6; Tufnell 21-5-62-0; DeFreitas 25.5-5-69-2; Atherton 2-1-3-0. *Second Innings*—Malcolm 23-7-52-1; Fraser 20-4-33-1; Tufnell 24-12-36-0; DeFreitas 16-3-46-0; Atherton 3-0-14-0.

Umpires: A.R.Crafter and P.J.McConnell

AUSTRALIA v ENGLAND 1990-91 (Third Test)

At Sydney Cricket Ground, 4, 5, 6, 7, 8 January

Result: Match drawn

Australia

Batsman	1st innings		2nd innings	
G.R.Marsh	c Larkins b Malcolm	13	(2) c Stewart b Malcolm	4
M.A.Taylor	c Russell b Malcolm	11	(1) lbw b Hemmings	19
D.C.Boon	c Atherton b Gooch	97	(4) c Gooch b Tufnell	29
A.R.Border*	b Hemmings	78	(5) c Gooch b Tufnell	20
D.M.Jones	st Russell b Small	60	(6) c and b Tufnell	0
S.R.Waugh	c Stewart b Malcolm	48	(7) c Russell b Hemmings	14
G.R.J.Matthews	c Hemmings b Tufnell	128	(8) b Hemmings	19
I.A.Healy†	c Small b Hemmings	35	(3) c Smith b Tufnell	69
C.G.Rackemann	b Hemmings	1	b Malcolm	9
T.M.Alderman	not out	26	c Gower b Tufnell	1
B.A.Reid	c Smith b Malcolm	0	not out	5
Extras	(B 5, LB 8, NB 8)	21	(LB 16)	16
		518		**205**

1/21 2/38 3/185 4/226 5/292 6/347 7/442 8/457 9/512

1/21 2/29 3/81 4/129 5/129 6/166 7/166 8/189 9/192

Bowling: *First Innings*—Malcolm 45-12-128-4; Small 31-5-103-1; Hemmings 32-7-105-3; Tufnell 30-6-95-1; Gooch 14-3-46-1; Atherton 5-0-28-0. *Second Innings*—Malcolm 6-1-19-2; Small 2-1-6-0; Hemmings 41-9-94-3; Tufnell 37-18-61-5; Atherton 3-1-9-0.

England

Batsman	1st innings		2nd innings	
G.A.Gooch*	c Healy b Reid	59	(6) c Border b Matthews	54
M.A.Atherton	c Boon b Matthews	105	not out	3
W.Larkins	run out	11	lbw b Border	0
R.A.Smith	c Healy b Reid	18	(5) not out	10
D.I.Gower	c Marsh b Reid	123	(2) c Taylor b Matthews	36
A.J.Stewart	lbw b Alderman	91	(4) run out	7
R.C.Russell†	not out	30		
G.C.Small	lbw b Alderman	10		
E.E.Hemmings	b Alderman	0		
P.C.R.Tufnell	not out	5		
D.E.Malcolm				
Extras	(B 1, LB 8, NB 8)	17	(LB 1, NB 2)	3
	(8 wkts dec.)	**469**	(4 wkts)	**113**

1/95 2/116 3/156 4/295 5/394 6/426 7/444 8/444

1/84 2/84 3/100 4/100

Bowling: *First Innings*—Alderman 20.1-4-62-3; Reid 35.1-9-79-3; Rackemann 25.5-5-89-0; Matthews 58-16-145-1; Border 19-5-45-0; Waugh 14-3-40-0. *Second Innings*—Alderman 4-0-29-0; Rackemann 3-0-20-0; Matthews 9-2-26-2; Border 9-1-37-1.

Umpires: A.R.Crafter and P.J.McConnell

WEST INDIES v AUSTRALIA 1990-91 (Fifth Test)

At Recreation Ground, Antigua, St John's, 27, 28, 29 April, 1, 2 May

Result: Australia won by 157 runs

Australia

Batsman	1st innings		2nd innings	
M.A.Taylor	c Dujon b Hooper	59	(2) c and b Ambrose	1
G.R.Marsh	c Richards b Patterson	6	(1) c Dujon b Ambrose	1
D.C.Boon	c Greenidge b Ambrose	0	(4) b Walsh	35
A.R.Border*	c Dujon b Hooper	59	(5) b Walsh	5
D.M.Jones	lbw b Marshall	81	(6) b Walsh	8
M.E.Waugh	not out	139	(7) lbw b Walsh	0
I.A.Healy†	c Dujon b Marshall	12	(3) c Logie b Patterson	32
P.L.Taylor	c Dujon b Ambrose	2	lbw b Marshall	4
M.G.Hughes	b Ambrose	1	c Walsh b Ambrose	13
C.J.McDermott	c Dujon b Walsh	7	c Dujon b Marshall	1
T.M.Alderman	b Walsh	0	not out	0
Extras	(B 1, LB 12, NB 18, W 6)	37	B 11, LB 7, NB 4	22
		403		**265**

1/10 2/13 3/129 4/156 5/184
6/371 7/381 8/385 9/403

1/4 2/49 3/142 4/168 5/184
6/184 7/237 8/258 9/265

Bowling: *First Innings*—Ambrose 30-6-92-3; Patterson 12-1-44-1; Walsh 22-1-54-2; Marshall 22-1-72-2; Hooper 15-2-82-2; Richards 7-0-46-0. *Second Innings*—Ambrose 16-1-64-3; Walsh 26-2-56-4; Hooper 27-6-61-0; Patterson 1-0-1-1; Marshall 13.1-3-36-2; Richards 8-0-29-0.

West Indies

Batsman	1st innings		2nd innings	
C.G.Greenidge	lbw b McDermott	6	run out	43
D.L.Haynes	lbw b McDermott	84	run out	33
R.B.Richardson	b McDermott	3	c Jones b Waugh	41
C.L.Hooper	lbw b Hughes	2	c Waugh b P.L.Taylor	35
I.V.A.Richards*	lbw b McDermott	0	c Alderman b Border	2
A.L.Logie	c Jones b P.L.Taylor	24	lbw b Alderman	61
P.J.L.Dujon†	c Jones b Hughes	33	lbw b McDermott	4
M.D.Marshall	c Healy b Waugh	28	lbw b Hughes	51
C.E.L.Ambrose	c M.A.Taylor b Hughes	8	run out	0
C.A.Walsh	not out	11	c Healy b Hughes	7
B.P.Patterson	b Hughes	2	not out	0
Extras	(LB 2, NB 11)	13	(B 5, LB 7, NB 8)	20
		214		**297**

1/10 2/22 3/35 4/46 5/114
6/136 7/186 8/195 9/206

1/76 2/92 3/142 4/145 5/182
6/193 7/271 8/271 9/271

Bowling: *First Innings*—McDermott 15-4-42-4; Alderman 7-0-42-0; Hughes 17-2-65-4; P.L.Taylor 11-2-40-1; Waugh 5-0-23-1. *Second Innings*—McDermott 17-2-55-1; Hughes 19-5-49-2; P.L.Taylor 10-0-39-1; Border 15-2-71-1; Alderman 15.4-4-63-1; Waugh 5-3-8-1.

Umpires: L.H. Barker and S.A.Bucknor

AUSTRALIA v INDIA 1991-92 (First Test)

At Woolloongabba, Brisbane, 29, 30 November, 1, 2 December

Result: Australia won by 10 wickets

India

Batsman	1st innings		2nd innings	
R.J.Shastri	c Waugh b McDermott	8	c Healy b McDermott	41
K.Srikkanth	c Boon b McDermott	13	c Boon b Hughes	0
S.V.Manjrekar	c and b Hughes	17	c Boon b Hughes	5
D.B.Vengsarkar	c Waugh b Hughes	5	lbw b Hughes	0
M.Azharuddin*	c Hughes b Whitney	10	c Boon b Hughes	12
S.R.Tendulkar	b Whitney	16	c Healy b McDermott	7
Kapil Dev	b McDermott	44	c Waugh b McDermott	25
M.Prabhakar	not out	54	c Healy b Whitney	39
K.S.More†	c Whitney b Hughes	19	lbw b McDermott	1
S.L.Venkatapathy Raju	c Healy b McD'mott	12	c Healy b Whitney	2
J.Srinath	c Healy b McDermott	21	not out	12
Extras	(B 1, LB 6, NB 13)	20	(LB 4, NB 8)	12
		239		**156**

1/21 2/24 3/50 4/53 5/67
6/83 7/141 8/186 9/206

1/0 2/14 3/14 4/32 5/47
6/87 7/136 8/140 9/142

Bowling: *First Innings*—McDermott 28.1-11-54-5; Whitney 21-2-82-2; Hughes 20-5-34-3; Waugh 1-0-6-0; P.L.Taylor 18-3-56-0. *Second Innings*—McDermott 25-7-47-4; Hughes 16-4-50-4; Whitney 17.2-3-55-2.

Australia

Batsman	1st innings		2nd innings	
G.R.Marsh	b Srinath	47		
M.A.Taylor	c Vengsarkar b V'pathy Raju	94		
D.C.Boon	c More b Prabhakar	66	(2) not out	17
A.R.Border*	b Kapil Dev	28	(1) not out	35
D.M.Jones	b Kapil Dev	0		
M.E.Waugh	c More b Srinath	11		
I.A.Healy†	lbw b Prabhakar	12		
P.L.Taylor	c Venkatapathy Raju b Srinath	31		
M.G.Hughes	b Kapil Dev	11		
C.J.McDermott	c Azharuddin b Kapil Dev	8		
M.R.Whitney	not out	7		
Extras	(LB 15, NB 9, W 1)	25	(LB 4, NB 2)	6
		340	(0 wkts)	**58**

1/95 2/217 3/244 4/244 5/265
6/278 7/280 8/301 9/316

Bowling: *First Innings*—Kapil Dev 34-9-80-4; Prabhakar 37-10-88-2; Srinath 24.4-4-59-3; Venkatapathy Raju 31-8-90-1; Tendulkar 1-0-8-0. *Second Innings*—Kapil Dev 9-0-23-0; Prabhakar 2-1-3-0; Srinath 9-5-6-0; Venkatapathy Raju 3-1-13-0; Tendulkar 1-0-5-0; Manjrekar 0.5-0-4-0.

Umpires: P.J.McConnell and S.G.Randell

WEST INDIES v AUSTRALIA 1990-91 (Fourth Test)

At Kensington Oval, Bridgetown, Barbados, 19, 20, 21, 23, 24 April
Result: West Indies won by 343 runs

West Indies

Batsman	Dismissal (1st)	Runs		Dismissal (2nd)	Runs
C.G.Greenidge	c Reid b McDermott	10	(2)	lbw b Hughes	226
D.L.Haynes	c M.E.Waugh b Hughes	28		c Healy b M.E.Waugh	40
R.B.Richardson	c Boon b McDermott	1	(4)	lbw b M.E.Waugh	99
C.L.Hooper	c Jones b Hughes	0	(5)	c Healy b M.E.Waugh	57
I.V.A.Richards*	c Hughes b McDermott	32	(6)	lbw b M.E.Waugh	25
A.L.Logie	c Taylor b Reid	11	(7)	not out	33
P.J.L.Dujon†	c Healy b Hughes	10	(8)	c M.E.Waugh b McDermott	4
M.D.Marshall	c Marsh b Reid	17	(3)	c Healy b McDermott	15
C.E.L.Ambrose	not out	19		b Reid	2
C.A.Walsh	c M.E.Waugh b McDermott	10		c Marsh b Reid	0
B.P.Patterson	c M.E.Waugh b Hughes	1		not out	4
Extras	(LB 3, NB 7)	10		(LB 19, NB 12)	31
		149		(9 wkts dec.)	536

1/17 2/21 3/22 4/72 5/89 6/96 7/103 8/125 9/148
1/129 2/153 3/352 4/454 5/470 6/512 7/522 8/525 9/525

Bowling: *First Innings*—McDermott 22-7-49-4; Reid 21-8-50-2; Hughes 16.1-2-44-4; S.R.Waugh 2-0-3-0. *Second Innings*—McDermott 37.3-8-130-2; Reid 30-4-100-2; Hughes 36-6-125-1; S.R.Waugh 28-6-77-0; M.E.Waugh 28-6-80-4; D.M.Jones 3-1-5-0.

Australia

Batsman	Dismissal (1st)	Runs		Dismissal (2nd)	Runs
M.A.Taylor	lbw b Ambrose	76	(2)	lbw b Marshall	26
G.R.Marsh	c Logie b Ambrose	0	(1)	lbw b Ambrose	12
D.C.Boon	c Hooper b Marshall	57		b Ambrose	0
A.R.Border*	b Marshall	0		c Dujon b Ambrose	29
D.M.Jones	lbw b Marshall	37	(6)	b Hooper	22
M.E.Waugh	not out	3	(7)	b Hooper	20
S.R.Waugh	c Dujon b Patterson	4		not out	2
I.A.Healy†	c Dujon b Walsh	3	(9)	lbw b Marshall	2
M.G.Hughes	c Logie b Walsh	3	(5)	c Dujon b Marshall	3
C.J.McDermott	b Walsh	2		c sub (R.I.C.Holder) b Walsh	2
B.A.Reid	b Walsh	0		b Walsh	0
Extras	(LB 2, NB 14)	16		(B 3, LB 5, NB 18)	26
		134			208

1/24 2/27 3/59 4/95 5/97 6/100 7/106 8/121 9/127
1/0 2/111 3/111 4/122 5/190 6/200 7/200 8/200 9/208

Bowling: *First Innings*—Ambrose 16-5-36-2; Patterson 13-6-22-1; Marshall 16-1-60-3; Walsh 5.1-1-14-4. *Second Innings*—Ambrose 19-7-36-3; Patterson 15-3-56-0; Walsh 14.2-3-37-2; Marshall 17-6-35-3; Hooper 19-4-28-2; Richards 3-0-8-0.

Umpires: D.M.Archer and L.H.Barker

WEST INDIES v AUSTRALIA 1990-91 (Third Test)

At Queen's Park Oval, Port-of-Spain, Trinidad, 5, 6, 8, 9, 10 April
Result: Match drawn

Australia

Batsman	Dismissal (1st)	Runs		Dismissal (2nd)	Runs
G.R.Marsh	c Hooper b Ambrose	10	(2)	lbw b Marshall	12
M.A.Taylor	c Walsh b Marshall	61	(1)	b Patterson	2
D.C.Boon	c Logie b Patterson	27		b Walsh	29
A.R.Border*	run out	43	(5)	not out	27
D.M.Jones	lbw b Patterson	21	(4)	not out	39
M.E.Waugh	lbw b Marshall	64			
S.R.Waugh	c Dujon b Walsh	26			
I.A.Healy†	c Dujon b Marshall	9			
C.J.McDermott	c Richardson b Patterson	0			
M.G.Hughes	lbw b Patterson	0			
B.A.Reid	not out	0			
Extras	(B 6, LB 14, NB 13)	33		(B 1, LB 9, NB 4)	14
		294		(3 wkts)	123

1/24 2/93 3/116 4/174 5/210 6/268 7/293 8/294 9/294
1/3 2/49 3/53

Bowling: *First Innings*—Ambrose 29-7-51-1; Patterson 26-2-50-4; Marshall 18.1-3-55-3; Walsh 30-9-45-1; Hooper 25-5-73-0. *Second Innings*—Ambrose 10-4-11-0; Patterson 7-0-27-1; Marshall 10-3-24-1; Walsh 12-6-11-1; Hooper 13-3-38-0; Richardson 1-0-2-0.

West Indies

Batsman	Dismissal	Runs
C.G.Greenidge	c M.E.Waugh b Reid	12
D.L.Haynes	b McDermott	1
R.B.Richardson	c Taylor b Hughes	30
C.L.Hooper	lbw b Hughes	12
A.L.Logie	c M.E.Waugh b Hughes	1
I.V.A.Richards*	c S.R.Waugh b Hughes	2
P.J.L.Dujon†	lbw b McDermott	70
M.D.Marshall	c McDermott b Border	12
C.E.L.Ambrose	c Border b M.E.Waugh	53
C.A.Walsh	not out	12
B.P.Patterson	b McDermott	0
Extras	(B 6, LB 7, NB 9)	22
		227

1/16 2/18 3/46 4/52 5/56 6/86 7/110 8/197 9/225

Bowling: McDermott 14.2-2-36-3; Reid 22-0-79-1; Hughes 17-5-48-4; S.R.Waugh 5-0-10-0; M.E.Waugh 6-2-9-1; Jones 1-0-4-0.

Umpires: D.M.Archer and L.H.Barker

WEST INDIES v AUSTRALIA 1990-91 (First Test)

At Sabina Park, Kingston, Jamaica, 1, 2, 3, 5 (no play), 6 March

Result: Match drawn

West Indies

Batsman	1st Innings		2nd Innings	
C.G.Greenidge	c Healy b McDermott	27	c Healy b McDermott	35
D.L.Haynes	b McDermott	8	c Healy b McDermott	84
R.B.Richardson	c Healy b Hughes	15	not out	104
C.L.Hooper	c Marsh b Hughes	0	b McDermott	31
I.V.A.Richards*	c Hughes b McDermott	11	not out	52
A.L.Logie	not out	77		
P.J.L.Dujon†	c Marsh b McDermott	59		
M.D.Marshall	lbw b McDermott	0		
C.E.L.Ambrose	c and b Waugh	33		
C.A.Walsh	lbw b Hughes	10		
B.P.Patterson	b Hughes	4		
Extras	(LB 6, NB 13, W 1)	20	(B 15, LB 6, NB 6, W 1)	28
		264	(3 wkts)	334

1/33 2/37 3/57 4/68 5/75 6/75 7/144 8/166 9/234

1/118 2/134 3/216

Bowling: First Innings—McDermott 23-3-80-5; Whitney 21-4-58-0; Hughes 21.3-4-67-4; Matthews 11-2-28-0; Waugh 6-1-25-1. Second Innings—McDermott 24-10-48-3; Whitney 17-3-55-0; Hughes 22-5-79-0; Matthews 25-2-90-0; Waugh 13-6-20-0; Border 10-3-21-0.

Australia

G.R.Marsh	c Dujon b Ambrose	69
M.A.Taylor	c Hooper b Patterson	58
D.C.Boon	not out	109
A.R.Border*	c Dujon b Ambrose	31
D.M.Jones	c and b Hooper	0
M.E.Waugh	lbw b Marshall	39
G.R.J.Matthews	c Dujon b Patterson	10
I.A.Healy†	lbw b Walsh	0
C.J.McDermott	lbw b Patterson	1
M.G.Hughes	c Hooper b Patterson	0
M.R.Whitney	b Patterson	2
Extras	(B 4, LB 23, NB 21, W 4)	52
		371

1/139 2/159 3/227 4/228 5/329 6/357 7/358 8/365 9/365

Bowling: Ambrose 30-3-94-2; Patterson 24-1-83-5; Marshall 22-3-57-1; Walsh 23-4-73-1; Hooper 21-7-37-1.

Umpires: D.M.Archer and S.A.Bucknor

WEST INDIES v AUSTRALIA 1990-91 (Second Test)

At Bourda, Georgetown, Guyana, 23, 24, 25, 27, 28 March

Result: West Indies won by 10 wickets

Australia

Batsman	1st Innings		2nd Innings		
M.A.Taylor	lbw b Patterson	0	(2)	lbw b Ambrose	15
G.R.Marsh	c Hooper b Patterson	94	(1)	b Walsh	22
D.C.Boon	c Dujon b Marshall	7		c Dujon b Marshall	2
A.R.Border*	b Marshall	47		c Dujon b Marshall	34
D.M.Jones	b Marshall	34		run out	3
M.E.Waugh	c Dujon b Patterson	71		c Richards b Ambrose	31
G.R.J.Matthews	c Dujon b Ambrose	1		c Dujon b Marshall	16
I.A.Healy†	run out	53		run out	47
C.J.McDermott	lbw b Patterson	1		c Dujon b Patterson	4
M.G.Hughes	b Ambrose	0		c Patterson b Walsh	21
M.R.Whitney	not out	1		not out	0
Extras	(B 6, LB 8, NB 23, W 2)	39		(B 17, LB 6, NB 28, W 2)	53
		348			248

1/3 2/24 3/124 4/188 5/237 6/238 7/339 8/346 9/346

1/32 2/43 3/67 4/73 5/130 6/161 7/172 8/187 9/241

Bowling: First Innings—Ambrose 31.4-9-64-2; Patterson 24-1-80-4; Walsh 24-2-81-0; Marshall 23-3-67-3; Hooper 13-3-37-0; Richards 1-0-5-0. Second Innings—Ambrose 24-5-45-2; Patterson 14-5-46-1; Walsh 23-4-55-2; Marshall 15-2-31-3; Hooper 18-6-35-0; Richards 4-2-13-0.

West Indies

Batsman	1st Innings		2nd Innings	
C.G.Greenidge	lbw b McDermott	2		
D.L.Haynes	c M.E.Waugh b Border	111	not out	5
R.B.Richardson	lbw b McDermott	182	not out	23
C.L.Hooper	c M.E.Waugh b Matthews	62		
I.V.A.Richards*	b Matthews	50		
A.L.Logie	c Healy b Border	54		
P.J.L.Dujon†	lbw b Border	29		
M.D.Marshall	not out	22		
C.E.L.Ambrose	b Border	0		
C.A.Walsh	b Border	1		
B.P.Patterson	lbw b Matthews	15		
Extras	(B 5, LB 13, NB 23)	41	(LB 2, NB 1)	3
		569	(0 wkts)	31

1/10 2/307 3/353 4/443 5/444 6/529 7/530 8/530 9/532

(0 wkts) 31

Bowling: First Innings—McDermott 36-3-114-2; Whitney 28-4-103-0; Matthews 37.5-6-155-3; Hughes 20-4-93-0; Waugh 2-0-18-0; Border 30-11-68-5. Second Innings—McDermott 4-1-10-0; Hughes 3.5-0-19-0.

Umpires: C.E.Cumberbatch and C.R.Duncan

AUSTRALIA v ENGLAND 1990-91 (Fourth Test)

At Adelaide Oval, 25, 26, 27, 28, 29 January

Result: Match drawn

Australia

Batsman		Runs		Runs
G.R.Marsh	c Gooch b Small	37	(2) c Gooch b Small	0
M.A.Taylor	run out	5	(1) run out	4
D.C.Boon	c Fraser b Malcolm	49	b Tufnell	121
A.R.Border*	b DeFreitas	12	(7) not out	83
D.M.Jones	lbw b DeFreitas	0	(4) lbw b DeFreitas	8
M.E.Waugh	b Malcolm	138	(5) b Malcolm	23
G.R.J.Matthews	c Stewart b Gooch	65	(8) not out	34
I.A.Healy†	c Stewart b DeFreitas	1		
C.J.McDermott	not out	42		
M.G.Hughes	lbw b Small	1	(6) c Gooch b Fraser	30
B.A.Reid	c Lamb b DeFreitas	5		
Extras	(B 2, LB 23, NB 4, W 2)	31	(B 1, LB 7, NB 2, W 1)	11
Total		**386**	**(6 wkts dec.)**	**314**

1/11 2/62 3/104 4/104 5/124
6/295 7/298 8/358 9/373

1/1 2/8 3/25 4/64
5/130 6/240

Bowling: *First Innings*—Malcolm 38-7-104-2; Fraser 23-6-48-0; Small 34-10-92-2; DeFreitas 26.2-6-56-4; Tufnell 5-0-38-0; Gooch 9-2-23-1. *Second Innings*—Malcolm 21-0-87-1; Small 18-3-64-1; DeFreitas 23-6-61-1; Fraser 26-3-66-1; Tufnell 16-3-28-1.

England

Batsman		Runs		Runs
G.A.Gooch*	c Healy b Reid	87	c Marsh b Reid	117
M.A.Atherton	lbw b McDermott	0	c Waugh b Reid	87
A.J.Lamb	c Healy b McDermott	0	b McDermott	53
R.A.Smith	c and b Hughes	53	(5) not out	10
D.I.Gower	c Hughes b McDermott	11	(4) lbw b Hughes	16
A.J.Stewart†	c Healy b Reid	11	c Jones b McDermott	9
P.A.J.DeFreitas	c Matthews b McDermott	45	not out	19
G.C.Small	b McDermott	1		
A.R.C.Fraser	c Healy b Reid	2		
D.E.Malcolm	c Healy b Reid	2		
P.C.R.Tufnell	not out	0		
Extras	(B 1, LB 3, NB 13)	17	(B 5, LB 9, NB 9, W 1)	24
Total		**229**	**(5 wkts)**	**335**

1/10 2/11 3/137 4/160 5/176
6/179 7/198 8/215 9/219

1/203 2/246 3/287
4/287 5/297

Bowling: *First Innings*—Reid 29-9-53-4; McDermott 26.3-3-97-5; Hughes 22-4-62-1; Waugh 4-1-13-0. *Second Innings*—Reid 23-5-59-2; McDermott 27-5-106-2; Matthews 31-7-100-0; Hughes 14-3-52-1; Waugh 1-0-4-0.

Umpires: L.J.King and T.A.Prue

AUSTRALIA v ENGLAND 1990-91 (Fifth Test)

At W.A.C.A. Ground, Perth, 1, 2, 3, 4, 5 February

Result: Australia won by nine wickets

England

Batsman		Runs		Runs
G.A.Gooch*	c Healy b McDermott	13	c Alderman b Hughes	18
M.A.Atherton	c Healy b McDermott	27	c Boon b Hughes	25
A.J.Lamb	c Border b McDermott	91	lbw b McDermott	5
R.A.Smith	c Taylor b McDermott	58	lbw b Alderman	43
D.I.Gower	not out	28	c Taylor b Alderman	5
A.J.Stewart†	lbw b McDermott	2	c Healy b McDermott	7
P.A.J.DeFreitas	c Marsh b McDermott	5	c Healy b Alderman	5
P.J.Newport	c Healy b McDermott	0	not out	40
G.C.Small	c Boon b Hughes	0	c Taylor b Hughes	4
P.C.R.Tufnell	c Healy b Hughes	0	c Healy b Hughes	8
D.E.Malcolm	c Marsh b McDermott	7	c Jones b McDermott	6
Extras	(B 1, LB 6, NB 5, W 1)	13	(B 5, LB 5, NB 6)	16
Total		**244**		**182**

1/27 2/50 3/191 4/212 5/220
6/226 7/226 8/227 9/227

1/41 2/49 3/75 4/80 5/114
6/118 7/125 8/134 9/144

Bowling: *First Innings*—Alderman 22-5-66-0; McDermott 24.4-2-97-8; Waugh 1-0-9-0; Matthews 2-0-16-0. *Second Innings*—McDermott 19.3-2-60-3; Alderman 22-3-75-3; Hughes 20-7-37-4.

Australia

Batsman		Runs		Runs
G.R.Marsh	c Stewart b Small	63	(2) not out	1
M.A.Taylor	c Stewart b Malcolm	19	(1) c Stewart b DeFreitas	12
D.C.Boon	c Stewart b Malcolm	30	not out	30
A.R.Border*	lbw b DeFreitas	17		
D.M.Jones	b Newport	34		
M.E.Waugh	c Small b Malcolm	26		
G.R.J.Matthews	not out	60		
I.A.Healy†	c Lamb b Small	42		
C.J.McDermott	b Tufnell	25		
M.G.Hughes	c Gooch b Tufnell	0		
T.M.Alderman	lbw b DeFreitas	7		
Extras	(B 2, LB 8, NB 8, W 1)	19	(LB 5, NB 1, W 2)	8
Total		**307**	**(1 wkt)**	**120**

1/1 2/44 3/90 4/113 5/161
6/168 7/230 8/281 9/283

1/39

Bowling: *First Innings*—Malcolm 30-4-94-3; Small 23-3-97-5; DeFreitas 16.5-2-57-2; Newport 14-0-56-1; Tufnell 7-1-25-2. *Second Innings*—Malcolm 9-0-40-0; Small 10-5-24-0; DeFreitas 6.2-0-29-1; Newport 6-0-22-0.

Umpires: S.G.Randell and C.D.Timmins

AUSTRALIA v INDIA 1991-92 (Second Test)

At Melbourne Cricket Ground, 26, 27, 28, 29 December
Result: Australia won by 8 wickets

India

R.J.Shastri	c Healy b Reid	23	(2) c Healy b Reid	6
K.Srikkanth	c Boon b Reid	5	lbw b Reid	6
M.Prabhakar	b Reid	0	(9) c Healy b Reid	17
S.V.Manjrekar	c Waugh b Reid	25	(3) c M.A.Taylor b McDermott	30
D.B.Vengsarkar	c Reid b Hughes	23	(4) c sub (Whitney) b McDermott	54
M.Azharuddin*	c Jones b McDermott	22	(5) c M.A.Taylor b Reid	2
S.R.Tendulkar	c Waugh b Reid	15	c Border b P.L.Taylor	40
Kapil Dev	c Hughes b McDermott	19	c Healy b Reid	12
K.S.More†	not out	67	lbw b Reid	1
S.L.Venkatapathy Raju	c Border b Hughes	31	(10) c and b McDermott	0
J.Srinath	c Border b Reid	14	(6) not out	1
Extras	(B 1, LB 8, NB 4, W 6)	19	(B 1, LB 6, NB 10)	17
		263		**213**

1/11 2/11 3/61 4/63 5/109 6/109 7/128 8/151 9/228
1/13 2/48 3/75 4/78 5/79 6/141 7/155 8/173 9/210

Bowling: First Innings—McDermott 30-6-100-2; Reid 26.2-7-66-6; Hughes 23-6-52-2; Waugh 8-1-16-0; P.L.Taylor 6-0-20-0. Second Innings—McDermott 29-8-63-3; Reid 29-9-60-6; Hughes 19-6-43-0; P.L.Taylor 11-3-40-1.

Australia

G.R.Marsh	c Vengsarkar b Kapil Dev	86	(2) lbw b Prabhakar	10
M.A.Taylor	c Tendulkar b Prabhakar	13	(1) st More b Venkatapathy Raju	60
D.C.Boon	c Srikkanth b Kapil Dev	11	not out	44
A.R.Border*	b Kapil Dev	0	not out	5
D.M.Jones	c More b Prabhakar	59		
M.E.Waugh	c More b Shastri	34		
I.A.Healy†	lbw b Kapil Dev	60		
P.L.Taylor	c More b Prabhakar	11		
M.G.Hughes	c Tendulkar b Kapil Dev	36		
B.A.Reid	c Kapil Dev b Prabhakar	3		
C.J.McDermott	not out	16		
Extras	(LB 9, NB 11)	20	(LB 3, NB 6)	9
		349	(2 wkts)	**128**

1/24 2/55 3/55 4/162 5/211 6/229 7/262 8/326 9/337
1/16 2/104

Bowling: First Innings—Kapil Dev 35-9-97-5; Prabhakar 34-7-84-4; Srinath 25-3-71-0; Venkatapathy Raju 17-3-52-0; Tendulkar 4-1-16-0; Shastri 7-1-20-1. Second Innings—Kapil Dev 12-1-30-0; Prabhakar 11-0-38-1; Srinath 8-0-28-0; Venkatapathy Raju 6-0-17-1; Shastri 3-1-12-0.

Umpires: L.J.King and T.A.Prue

AUSTRALIA v INDIA 1991-92 (Third Test)

At Sydney Cricket Ground, 2, 3, 4, 5, 6 January
Result: Match drawn

Australia

G.R.Marsh	b Banerjee	8	(2) c Pandit b Kapil Dev	4
M.A.Taylor	c Pandit b Banerjee	56	(1) c Kapil Dev b Shastri	35
D.C.Boon	not out	129	c Azharuddin b Srinath	7
M.E.Waugh	c Prabhakar b Banerjee	5	lbw b Prabhakar	18
D.M.Jones	run out	35	c Pandit b Shastri	18
A.R.Border*	c Pandit b Kapil Dev	19	not out	53
I.A.Healy†	c sub (K.Srikkanth) b Prabhakar	1	c Prabhakar b Shastri	7
M.G.Hughes	c Pandit b Prabhakar	2	c Prabhakar b Tendulkar	21
C.J.McDermott	b Prabhakar	1	c Vengsarkar b Shastri	0
S.K.Warne	c Pandit b Kapil Dev	20	not out	1
B.A.Reid	c Tendulkar b Kapil Dev	0		
Extras	(B 4, LB 14, NB 18, W 1)	37	(LB 4, NB 4, W 1)	9
		313	(8 wkts)	**173**

1/22 2/117 3/127 4/210 5/248 6/251 7/259 8/269 9/313
1/9 2/31 3/55 4/85 5/106 6/114 7/164 8/171

Bowling: First Innings—Kapil Dev 33-9-60-3; Prabhakar 39-12-82-3; Srinath 21-5-69-0; Shastri 13-1-37-0. Second Innings—Kapil Dev 19-5-41-1; Prabhakar 27-10-53-1; Srinath 12-0-28-1; Shastri 25-8-45-4; Tendulkar 1-0-2-1.

India

R.J.Shastri	c Jones b Warne	206
N.S.Sidhu	c Waugh b McDermott	0
S.V.Manjrekar	c Waugh b Hughes	34
D.B.Vengsarkar	c Waugh b McDermott	54
M.Azharuddin*	c Boon b McDermott	4
S.R.Tendulkar	not out	148
M.Prabhakar	c Taylor b Hughes	14
Kapil Dev	c Marsh b Hughes	0
C.S.Pandit†	run out	9
S.Banerjee	c Border b McDermott	3
J.Srinath	run out	1
Extras	(B 1, LB 4, NB 5)	10
		483

1/7 2/86 3/197 4/201 5/397 6/434 7/434 8/458 9/474

Bowling: McDermott 51-12-147-4; Reid 4-0-10-0; Hughes 41.4-8-104-3; Waugh 14-5-28-0; Warne 45-7-150-1; Border 13-3-39-0.

Umpires: P.J.McConnell and S.G.Randell

AUSTRALIA v INDIA 1991-92 (Fourth Test)

At Adelaide Oval, 25, 26, 27, 28, 29 January

Result: Australia won by 38 runs

Australia

Batsman	1st inns		2nd inns	
G.R.Marsh b Prabhakar	8	(2)	b Kapil Dev	5
M.A.Taylor b Tendulkar	11	(1)	c Venkatapathy Raju b Kapil Dev	100
D.C.Boon b Kapil Dev	19		run out	135
A.R.Border* c Pandit b Tendulkar	0		not out	91
D.M.Jones c Azharuddin b Venkatapathy Raju	41		c Pandit b Kapil Dev	0
M.E.Waugh lbw b Prabhakar	15		c Tendulkar b Kapil Dev	0
I.A.Healy† c Pandit b Kapil Dev	1		c Srikkanth b Kapil Dev	41
M.G.Hughes c Manjrekar b Kapil Dev	26		lbw b Srinath	23
S.K.Warne st Pandit b Venkatapathy Raju	7		c Pandit b Srinath	
C.J.McDermott b Venkatapathy Raju	0		b Venkatapathy Raju	21
M.R.Whitney not out	0		c Srinath b Venkatapathy Raju	12
Extras (LB 10, NB 7)	17		(LB 15, NB 8)	23
	145			**451**

1/13 2/36 3/39 4/50 5/77 6/81 7/117 8/141 9/145
1/10 2/231 3/277 4/277 5/277 6/348 7/383 8/383 9/409

Bowling: *First Innings*—Kapil Dev 23-11-33-3; Prabhakar 18-3-55-2; Srinath 10-2-26-0; Tendulkar 4-2-10-2; Venkatapathy Raju 11.4-7-11-3. *Second Innings*—Kapil Dev 51-12-130-5; Prabhakar 21-5-60-0; Srinath 37-13-76-2; Srikkanth 1-0-5-0; Venkatapathy Raju 56-15-121-2; Tendulkar 20-5-44-0.

India

Batsman	1st inns		2nd inns	
K.Srikkanth c Healy b McDermott	17		b McDermott	22
N.S.Sidhu c Healy b Hughes	27		lbw b Hughes	35
S.V.Manjrekar lbw b Hughes	2		run out	45
D.B.Vengsarkar c Waugh b McDermott	13	(5)	lbw b Hughes	4
M.Azharuddin* lbw b McDermott	1	(6)	c Taylor b McDermott	106
S.R.Tendulkar lbw b McDermott	6	(4)	lbw b Waugh	17
Kapil Dev c Border b Hughes	56		c Marsh b Hughes	5
M.Prabhakar lbw b Whitney	33		lbw b McDermott	64
C.S.Pandit† c Boon b McDermott	15		c Waugh b McDermott	7
S.L.Venkatapathy Raju not out	19		not out	8
J.Srinath c Healy b Whitney	21		c Warne b McDermott	3
Extras (LB 5, NB 10)	15		(B 3, LB 9, NB 5)	17
	225			**333**

1/30 2/33 3/55 4/64 5/70 6/70 7/135 8/174 9/192
1/52 2/72 3/97 4/102 5/172 6/182 7/283 8/291 9/327

Bowling: *First Innings*—McDermott 31-9-76-5; Whitney 26.2-6-68-2; Hughes 18-5-55-3; Warne 7-1-18-0; Waugh 2-1-3-0. *Second Innings*—McDermott 29.1-8-92-5; Whitney 17-3-59-0; Hughes 23-5-66-3; Waugh 12-2-36-1; Warne 16-1-60-0; Border 3-0-8-0.

Umpires: D.B.Hair and P.J.McConnell

AUSTRALIA v INDIA 1991-92 (Fifth Test)

At W.A.C.A. Ground, Perth, 1, 2, 3, 4, 5 February

Result: Australia won by 300 runs

Australia

Batsman	1st inns		2nd inns	
M.A.Taylor c Srikkanth b Kapil Dev	2	(2)	lbw b Kapil Dev	16
W.N.Phillips c More b Prabhakar	8	(1)	c Kapil Dev b Srinath	14
D.C.Boon c Sidhu b Prabhakar	107		c Kapil Dev b Prabhakar	38
A.R.Border* c Srikkanth b Kapil Dev	59	(8)	not out	20
D.M.Jones c Srikkanth b Venkatapathy Raju	7	(4)	not out	150
T.M.Moody c Vengsarkar b Prabhakar	50	(5)	c More b Kapil Dev	101
I.A.Healy† c More b Srinath	28	(6)	c More b Venkatapathy Raju	7
M.G.Hughes c Srikkanth b Srinath	24	(7)	c Tendulkar b Srinath	11
P.R.Reiffel c More b Prabhakar	31			
C.J.McDermott c Srikkanth b Prabhakar	1			
M.R.Whitney not out	1			
Extras (B 1, LB 7, NB 12)	20		(LB 4, NB 6)	10
	346		(6 wkts dec.)	**367**

1/10 2/21 3/138 4/145 5/232 6/259 7/290 8/303 9/339
1/27 2/31 3/113 4/286 5/298 6/315

Bowling: *First Innings*—Kapil Dev 40-12-103; Prabhakar 32.5-9-101-5; Srinath 25-5-69-2; Tendulkar 5-2-9-0; Venkatapathy Raju 23-6-56-1. *Second Innings*—Kapil Dev 28-8-48-2; Prabhakar 32-4-116-1; Srinath 29.3-4-121-2; Venkatapathy Raju 24-5-78-1.

India

Batsman	1st inns		2nd inns	
K.Srikkanth c Boon b McDermott	34		c Jones b Whitney	38
N.S.Sidhu c Healy b Hughes	5		c Jones b Reiffel	35
S.V.Manjrekar c Jones b Hughes	31		c Healy b Whitney	8
S.R.Tendulkar c Moody b Whitney	114		c Moody b Reiffel	5
D.B.Vengsarkar c Taylor b Hughes	1		c Moody b Whitney	4
M.Azharuddin* c Healy b McDermott	11		lbw b Whitney	24
S.L.Venkatapathy Raju c Taylor b Whitney	1	(10)	c Healy b Whitney	8
Kapil Dev c Hughes b Whitney	4	(7)	lbw b Whitney	0
M.Prabhakar c Reiffel b Whitney	0	(8)	c Healy b McDermott	3
K.S.More† c Healy b Hughes	43	(9)	c Taylor b Whitney	1
J.Srinath not out	5	(11)	not out	1
Extras (LB 14, NB 9)	23		(LB 11, NB 3)	14
	272			**141**

1/25 2/69 3/100 4/109 5/130 6/135 7/159 8/159 9/240
1/82 2/90 3/97 4/103 5/111 6/111 7/126 8/129 9/134

Bowling: *First Innings*—McDermott 21-6-47-2; Hughes 26.5-5-82-4; Reiffel 17-5-46-0; Whitney 23-4-68-4; Moody 2-0-15-0. *Second Innings*—McDermott 20-8-44-1; Hughes 12-2-25-0; Reiffel 11-2-34-2; Whitney 12.1-3-27-7.

Umpires: A.R.Crafter and T.A.Prue

SRI LANKA v AUSTRALIA 1992-93 (First Test)

At Sinhalese Sports Club Cricket Ground, Colombo, 17, 18, 19, 21, 22 August
Result: Australia won by 16 runs

Australia

M.A.Taylor	lbw b Wickramasinghe	42	(2)	c Gurusinha b Anurasiri	43
T.M.Moody	lbw b Ramanayake	1	(1)	b Ramanayake	13
D.C.Boon	c Ranatunga b Hathurusingha	32		c Ranatunga b Anurasiri	68
D.M.Jones	lbw b Hathurusingha	10		run out	57
M.E.Waugh	c Kaluw'rana b Hathurusingha	5		c Kaluwitharana b Wick'singhe	56
A.R.Border*	b Hathurusingha	3		c Gurusinha b Anurasiri	15
G.R.J.Matthews	lbw b Ramanayake	6		c Kaluwitharana b Ramanayake	64
I.A.Healy†	not out	66		lbw b Hathurusingha	12
C.J.McDermott	c Ranatunga b Ram'yake	22		lbw b Ramanayake	40
S.K.Warne	c and b Anurasiri	24		b Anurasiri	35
M.R.Whitney	c and b Wickramasinghe	13		not out	10
Extras	(LB 10, NB 19, W 3)	32		(LB 23, NB 34, W 1)	58
		256			471

1/8 2/84 3/94 4/96 5/109
6/118 7/124 8/162 9/207

1/41 2/107 3/195 4/233 5/269
6/319 7/361 8/417 9/431

Bowling: *First Innings*—Ramanayake 20-4-51-3; Wickramasinghe 18-4-69-2; Hathurusingha 22-5-66-4; Madurasinghe 10-1-21-0; Gurusinha 2-0-17-0; Anurasiri 12-2-22-1. *Second Innings*—Ramanayake 37-10-113-3; Wickramasinghe 19-0-79-1; Hathurusingha 27-7-79-1; Anurasiri 35-3-127-4; Madurasinghe 14-1-50-0.

Sri Lanka

R.S.Mahanama	c Healy b Waugh	78		c Boon b Matthews	39
U.C.Hathurusingha	c Taylor b Waugh	18		run out	36
A.P.Gurusinha	c Jones b Whitney	137		not out	31
P.A.de Silva	lbw b Matthews	6		c Border b McDermott	37
A.Ranatunga*	c Warne b Matthews	127		c Border b McDermott	0
M.S.Atapattu	b Matthews	0		b Matthews	1
R.S.Kaluwitharana†	not out	132		b Matthews	4
C.P.H.Ramanayake	c Healy b McDermott	0		lbw b Matthews	6
G.P.Wickramasinghe	c M'thews b McDermott	21	(11)	c Waugh b Warne	2
M.A.W.R.Madurasinghe	not out	5		c Matthews b Warne	0
S.D.Anurasiri			(10)	c Waugh b Warne	1
Extras	(B 2, LB 7, NB 13, W 1)	23		(B 2, LB 3, NB 2)	7
	(8 wkts dec.)	547			164

1/36 2/128 3/137 4/367 5/367
6/463 7/472 8/503

1/76 2/79 3/127 4/132 5/133
6/137 7/147 8/150 9/156

Bowling: *First Innings*—McDermott 40-9-125-2; Whitney 32-10-84-1; Moody 17-3-44-0; Waugh 17-3-77-2; Warne 22-2-107-0; Matthews 38-11-93-3; Border 4-1-8-0. *Second Innings*—McDermott 14-4-43-2; Whitney 5-2-13-0; Moody 5-2-13-0; Matthews 20-2-76-4; Waugh 2-0-6-0; Warne 5.1-3-11-3.

Umpires: K.T.Francis and T.M.Samarasinghe

SRI LANKA v AUSTRALIA 1992-93 (Second Test)

At Khettarama Stadium, Colombo, 28, 29, 30 August, 1, 2 September
Result: Match drawn

Australia

T.M.Moody	c Kaluwitharana b Liyanage	1	(2)	b Muralidharan	54
M.A.Taylor	c Jayasuriya b Hathurusingha	15	(1)	lbw b Hathurusingha	26
D.C.Boon	c Jayasuriya b Liyanage	28		c Mahanama b Anurasiri	15
D.M.Jones	lbw b Gurusinha	77		not out	100
M.E.Waugh	c Jayasuriya b Ramanayake	0		lbw b Muralidharan	0
A.R.Border*	b Liyanage	13		lbw b Anurasiri	28
G.R.J.Matthews	c Mur'haran b Ram'yake	55		c Mahanama b Anurasiri	51
I.A.Healy†	lbw b Gurusinha	0		not out	4
C.J.McDermott	lbw b Muralidharan	9			
A.I.C.Dodemaide	not out	16			
M.R.Whitney	lbw b Ramanayake	1			
Extras	(B 10, LB 14, NB 6, W 2)	32		(B 4, LB 9, NB 5)	18
		247		(6 wkts dec.)	296

1/1 2/34 3/69 4/72 5/109
6/181 7/183 8/200 9/239

1/61 2/102 3/104
4/104 5/149 6/280

Bowling: *First Innings*—Ramanayake 23.3-7-64-3; Liyanage 30-10-66-3; Hathurusingha 9-1-26-1; Gurusinha 9-2-18-2; Anurasiri 8-0-17-0; Muralidharan 17-2-32-1. *Second Innings*—Ramanayake 12-0-49-0; Liyanage 13-1-47-0; Hathurusingha 12-4-12-1; Anurasiri 44-11-66-3; Muralidharan 34-7-109-2.

Sri Lanka

R.S.Mahanama	c Moody b Dodemaide	14		lbw b McDermott	69
U.C.Hathurusingha	b Moody	67		c Moody b McDermott	49
A.P.Gurusinha	c Healy b Whitney	29		not out	8
P.A.de Silva	c Healy b McDermott	85			
A.Ranatunga*	c sub (D.R.Martyn) b D'maide	18			
S.T.Jayasuriya	c Healy b McDermott	19	(4)	not out	1
R.S.Kaluwitharana†	c sub (Martyn) b Border	1			
C.P.H.Ramanayake	b McDermott	8			
D.K.Liyanage	c Healy b McDermott	4			
S.D.Anurasiri	not out	0			
M.Muralidharan	not out	11			
Extras	(LB 6, NB 3)	9		(LB 6, NB 5)	11

1/26 2/67 3/174 4/211 5/240 (9 wkts dec.) 258
6/243 7/243 8/255 9/258

1/110 2/129 (2 wkts) 136

Bowling: *First Innings*—McDermott 20-4-53-4; Whitney 16-1-49-1; Dodemaide 25-4-74-2; Matthews 10-2-20-0; Waugh 4-0-11-0; Moody 6-1-17-1; Border 11-3-28-1. *Second Innings*—McDermott 19-7-32-2; Whitney 5-2-13-0; Matthews 21-5-59-0; Dodemaide 5-2-11-0; Border 4-0-15-0.

Umpires: I.Anandappa and W.A.U.Wickremasinghe

SRI LANKA v AUSTRALIA 1992-93 (Third Test)

At Tyronne Fernando Stadium, Moratuwa, 8, 9, 10, 12, 13 September

Result: Match drawn

Australia

T.M.Moody b Ramanayake	0	(2)	c Tillakaratne b Ramanayake	2
M.A.Taylor c Ranatunga b Anurasiri	19	(1)	c Mahanama b Liyanage	3
D.C.Boon c de Silva b Ramanayake	18		lbw b Liyanage	0
D.M.Jones lbw b Liyanage	11		c and b Anurasiri	21
M.E.Waugh b Ramanayake	0		c Tillakaratne b Liyanage	0
A.R.Border* b Ramanayake	106		lbw b Ramanayake	78
G.R.J.Matthews run out	57		b Ramanayake	96
I.A.Healy† c Jayasuriya b M.Muralidharan	71		c Jayasuriya b Liyanage	49
C.J.McDermott c Tillakaratne b Hathurusingha	10			
S.K.Warne c Gurusinha b Ramanayake	7			
A.I.C.Dodemaide not out	13	(9)	not out	2
Extras (B 3, LB 9, NB 10, W 3)	25		(LB 4, NB 15, W 1)	20
	337		(8 wkts)	271

1/0 2/42 3/46 4/57 5/58
6/185 7/252 8/283 9/302

1/6 2/6 3/6 4/9 5/60
6/132 7/261 8/271

Bowling: *First Innings*—Ramanayake 31-3-82-5; Liyanage 17-0-54-1; Hathurusingha 21-8-50-1; Anurasiri 22-2-57-1; Muralidharan 15.1-2-58-1; Jayasuriya 2-0-9-0; Gurusinha 3-0-15-0. *Second Innings*—Ramanayake 22.1-4-75-3; Liyanage 16-3-56-4; Hathurusingha 4-2-3-0; Gurusinha 1-0-5-0; Anurasiri 29-5-49-1; Muralidharan 7-1-26-0; Ranatunga 1-0-9-0; Jayasuriya 7-1-17-0; Mahanama 5-0-27-0.

Sri Lanka

R.S.Mahanama lbw b Matthews	50
U.C.Hathurusingha c Boon b McDermott	2
A.P.Gurusinha c Healy b McDermott	0
P.A.de Silva b Dodemaide	58
H.P.Tillakaratne† c Waugh b McDermott	82
A.Ranatunga* c Jones b McDermott	48
S.T.Jayasuriya c Boon b Dodemaide	2
C.P.H.Ramanayake not out	15
D.K.Liyanage c Moody b Dodemaide	1
S.D.Anurasiri b Dodemaide	0
M.Muralidharan	
Extras (LB 8, NB 5, W 3)	16
	(9 wkts dec.) 274

1/4 2/4 3/111 4/116 5/232
6/234 7/262 8/274 9/274

Bowling: McDermott 31-6-89-4; Dodemaide 23.5-9-65-4; Moody 3-0-8-0; Matthews 31-8-64-1; Warne 11-3-40-0.

Umpires: B.C.Cooray and K.T.Francis

AUSTRALIA v WEST INDIES 1992-93 (First Test)

At Woolloongabba, Brisbane, 27, 28, 29, 30 November, 1 December

Result: Match drawn

Australia

M.A.Taylor c Williams b Bishop	7	(2)	c Williams b Walsh	34
D.C.Boon c Simmons b Hooper	48	(1)	c Arthurton b Bishop	111
S.R.Waugh c Williams b Ambrose	10		c Williams b Ambrose	20
M.E.Waugh c and b Hooper	39		c Haynes b Ambrose	60
D.R.Martyn c Lara b Ambrose	36		lbw b Ambrose	15
A.R.Border* run out (Hooper/Williams)	73		c Williams b Walsh	17
G.R.J.Matthews c Arthurton b Bishop	30		lbw b Ambrose	0
I.A.Healy† c Lara b Hooper	17		c Williams b Bishop	18
M.G.Hughes c Bishop b Hooper	10		c Williams b Ambrose	1
C.J.McDermott c Hooper b Patterson	3		not out	16
B.A.Reid not out	1		c Richardson b Hooper	1
Extras (B 3, LB 4, NB 12)	19		(B 4, LB 2, NB 9)	15
	293			308

1/8 2/21 3/88 4/125 5/180
6/252 7/264 8/285 9/288

1/64 2/114 3/124 4/250 5/255
6/255 7/280 8/287 9/295

Bowling: *First Innings*—Ambrose 29.1-12-53-2; Bishop 23-3-51-2; Patterson 19-0-83-1; Walsh 0.5-0-2-0; Hooper 30.1-4-75-4; Simmons 7-2-16-0; Arthurton 3-0-6-0. *Second Innings*—Ambrose 32-8-66-5; Bishop 27-6-58-2; Hooper 28.2-8-63-1; Walsh 24-3-64-2; Patterson 7-0-44-0; Arthurton 1-0-2-0; Simmons 1-0-5-0.

West Indies

D.L.Haynes c Taylor b Reid	8		c Healy b McDermott	1
P.V.Simmons b Reid	27		c Healy b Reid	1
R.B.Richardson* c Matthews b Hughes	17		c Healy b Hughes	66
B.C.Lara st Healy b Matthews	58		c Taylor b McDermott	0
K.L.T.Arthurton not out	157		b McDermott	0
C.L.Hooper b S.R.Waugh	47		c Boon b Matthews	32
D.Williams† c Hughes b Reid	15		lbw b McDermott	0
I.R.Bishop b McDermott	5		not out	16
C.E.L.Ambrose lbw b Reid	4		c Hughes b Reid	4
B.P.Patterson c S.R.Waugh b Reid	0			
C.A.Walsh b Hughes	0	(10)	not out	0
Extras (LB 6, NB 10)	16		(LB 7, NB 6)	13
	371		(8 wkts)	133

1/25 2/50 3/58 4/170 5/265
6/293 7/307 8/321 9/331

1/2 2/2 3/3 4/9 5/95
6/96 7/123 8/128

Bowling: *First Innings*—McDermott 22-7-49-4; Reid 21-8-50-2; Hughes 16.1-2-44-4; S.R.Waugh 2-0-3-0. *Second Innings*—McDermott 37.3-8-130-2; Reid 30-4-100-2; Hughes 36-6-125-1; S.R.Waugh 28-6-77-0; M.E.Waugh 28-6-80-4; D.M.Jones 3-1-5-0.

Umpires: T.A.Prue and S.G.Randell

AUSTRALIA v WEST INDIES 1992-93 (Second Test)

At Melbourne Cricket Ground, 26, 27, 28, 29, 30 December
Result: Australia won by 139 runs

Australia

Batsman		Score		Second innings	Score
D.C.Boon c Williams b Walsh		46	(2)	b Simmons	11
M.A.Taylor c Lara b Walsh		13	(1)	b Bishop	42
S.R.Waugh c Lara b Ambrose		38	(4)	c Simmons b Bishop	1
M.E.Waugh c Williams b Ambrose		112	(5)	c Adams b Walsh	16
D.R.Martyn c Simmons b Ambrose		7	(6)	not out	67
A.R.Border* c Williams b Bishop		110	(7)	b Bishop	4
I.A.Healy† c Hooper b Walsh		24	(8)	c and b Walsh	8
M.G.Hughes not out		9	(9)	c Williams b Ambrose	15
S.K.Warne c Adams b Bishop		1	(3)	c Arthurton b Ambrose	5
C.J.McDermott b Walsh		17		c Arthurton b Simmons	4
M.R.Whitney lbw b Bishop		0		run out	13
Extras (LB 14, NB 3, W 1)		18		B 1, LB 8, NB 1	10
		395			**196**

1/38 2/100 3/104 4/115 5/319 6/362 7/364 8/369 9/394
1/22 2/40 3/41 4/73 5/90 6/102 7/121 8/154 9/167

Bowling: *First Innings*—Ambrose 35-10-70-3; Bishop 29-2-84-3; Simmons 10-2-23-0; Walsh 39-10-91-4; Hooper 36-3-95-0; Adams 4-0-18-0. *Second Innings*—Ambrose 30-9-57-2; Bishop 20-5-45-3; Walsh 21-7-42-2; Simmons 18-6-34-2; Hooper 2.4-1-9-0.

West Indies

Batsman	Score	Second innings	Score
D.L.Haynes b Hughes	7	c Healy b Hughes	7
P.V.Simmons c Boon b Hughes	6	c Boon b Warne	110
R.B.Richardson* c Healy b Hughes	15	b Warne	52
B.C.Lara lbw Whitney	52	c Boon b Whitney	4
K.L.T.Arthurton c Healy b McDermott	71	st Healy b Warne	13
C.L.Hooper c and b S.R.Waugh	3	c Whitney b Warne	0
J.C.Adams† c Boon b McDermott	47	c Taylor b McDermott	16
D.Williams† c Healy b McDermott	0	c M.E.Waugh b Warne	0
I.R.Bishop b McDermott	9	c Taylor b Warne	7
C.E.L.Ambrose c McDermott b Warne	7	not out	0
C.A.Walsh not out	0	c Hughes b Warne	6
Extras (LB 10, NB 6)	16	(B 3, LB 2, NB 1)	6
	233		**219**

1/11 2/28 3/33 4/139 5/144 6/192 7/192 8/206 9/233
1/9 2/143 3/148 4/165 5/177 6/198 7/206 8/206 9/219

Bowling: *First Innings*—McDermott 25.1-8-66-4; Hughes 19-5-51-3; Whitney 13-4-27-1; Warne 24-7-65-1; S.R.Waugh 4-1-14-1. *Second Innings*—McDermott 17-2-66-1; Hughes 18-7-41-1; Whitney 10-2-32-1; Warne 23.2-8-52-7; M.E.Waugh 3-0-23-0.

Umpires: S.G.Randell and C.D.Timmins

AUSTRALIA v WEST INDIES 1992-93 (Third Test)

At Sydney Cricket Ground, 2, 3, 4, 5, 6 January
Result: Match drawn

Australia

Batsman	Score		Second innings	Score
D.C.Boon c Murray b Adams	76	(2)	not out	63
M.A.Taylor c Murray b Bishop	20	(1)	not out	46
S.R.Waugh c Simmons b Ambrose	100			
M.E.Waugh run out	57			
D.R.Martyn b Ambrose	0			
A.R.Border* c Murray b Hooper	74			
G.R.J.Matthews c Murray b Hooper	79			
I.A.Healy† not out	36			
M.G.Hughes c Haynes b Bishop	17			
S.K.Warne c Simmons b Hooper	14			
C.J.McDermott				
Extras (B 2, LB 2, NB 23)	30		(B 1, LB 2, NB 5)	8
	(9 wkts dec.) 503			**(0 wkts) 117**

1/42 2/160 3/254 4/261 5/270 6/425 7/440 8/469 9/503

Bowling: *First Innings*—Ambrose 35-8-87-2; Bishop 36-6-137-3; Adams 15-2-56-1; Simmons 10-2-25-0. *Second Innings*—Ambrose 6-2-10-0; Bishop 4-1-9-0; Simmons 3-2-9-0; Walsh 8-3-13-0; Hooper 10-2-22-0; Adams 8-1-29-0; Arthurton 5-1-14-0; Lara 2-0-4-0; Richardson 1-0-4-0.

West Indies

Batsman	Score
D.L.Haynes b Matthews	22
P.V.Simmons c Taylor b McDermott	3
R.B.Richardson* c Warne b b Hughes	109
B.C.Lara run out	277
K.L.T.Arthurton c Healy b Matthews	47
C.L.Hooper b Warne	21
J.C.Adams not out	77
J.R.Murray† c Healy b Hughes	11
I.R.Bishop run out	1
C.E.L.Ambrose c Martyn b M.E.Waugh	16
C.A.Walsh c Healy b Hughes	0
Extras (B 4, LB 9, NB 8, W 1)	22
	606

1/13 2/31 3/324 4/448 5/481 6/537 7/573 8/577 9/603

Bowling: McDermott 33-3-119-1; Hughes 16.4-1-76-3; Matthews 59-12-169-2; S.R.Waugh 11-1-43-0; Warne 41-6-116-1; Border 14-1-41-0; M.E.Waugh 10-1-29-1.

Umpires: D.B.Hair and T.A.Prue

AUSTRALIA v WEST INDIES 1992-93 (Fourth Test)

At Adelaide Oval, 23, 24, 25, 26, 27 January

Result: West Indies won by 1 run

West Indies

D.L.Haynes st Healy b May	45	c Healy b McDermott	11
P.V.Simmons c Hughes b S.R.Waugh	46	b McDermott	10
R.B.Richardson* lbw b Hughes	2	c Healy b Warne	72
B.C.Lara c Healy b McDermott	52	c S.R.Waugh b Hughes	7
K.L.T.Arthurton c S.R.Waugh b May	0	c Healy b McDermott	0
C.L.Hooper c Healy b Hughes	2	c Hughes b May	25
J.R.Murray† not out	49	c M.E.Waugh b May	0
I.R.Bishop c M.E.Waugh b Hughes	13	c M.E.Waugh b May	6
C.E.L.Ambrose c Healy b Hughes	0	st Healy b May	1
K.C.G.Benjamin b M.E.Waugh	15	c Warne b May	0
C.A.Walsh lbw b Hughes	5	not out	0
Extras LB 11, NB 12	23	(LB 2, NB 12)	14
	252		**146**

1/84 2/99 3/129 4/130 5/134 6/189 7/206 8/206 9/247

1/14 2/49 3/63 4/65 5/124 6/137 7/145 8/146 9/146

Bowling: *First Innings*—McDermott 16-1-85-1; Hughes 21.3-3-64-5; S.R.Waugh 13-4-37-1; May 14-1-41-2; Warne 2-0-11-0; M.E.Waugh 1-0-3-1. *Second Innings*—McDermott 11-0-66-3; Hughes 13-1-43-1; S.R.Waugh 5-1-8-0; May 6.5-3-9-5; Warne 6-2-18-1.

Australia

M.A.Taylor c Hooper b Bishop	1	(2) c Murray b Benjamin	7
D.C.Boon not out	39	(1) lbw b Ambrose	0
J.L.Langer c Murray b Benjamin	20	c Murray b Bishop	54
M.E.Waugh c Simmons b Ambrose	0	c Hooper b Walsh	26
S.R.Waugh c Murray b Ambrose	42	c Arthurton b Ambrose	4
A.R.Border* c Hooper b Ambrose	19	c Haynes b Ambrose	1
I.A.Healy† c Hooper b Ambrose	0	b Walsh	0
M.G.Hughes c Murray b Hooper	43	lbw b Ambrose	1
S.K.Warne lbw b Hooper	0	lbw b Bishop	9
T.B.A.May c Murray b Ambrose	6	not out	42
C.J.McDermott b Ambrose	14	c Murray b Walsh	18
Extras (B 7, LB 3, NB 19)	29	(B 1, LB 8, NB 13)	22
	213		**184**

1/1 2/16 3/46 4/108 5/108 6/112 7/181 8/181 9/197

1/5 2/16 3/54 4/64 5/72 6/73 7/74 8/102 9/144

Bowling: *First Innings*—Ambrose 28.2-6-74-6; Bishop 18-3-48-1; Benjamin 6-0-22-1; Walsh 10-3-34-0; Hooper 13-4-25-2. *Second Innings*—Ambrose 26-5-46-4; Bishop 17-3-41-2; Benjamin 12-2-32-1; Walsh 19-4-44-3; Hooper 5-1-12-0.

Umpires: D.B.Hair and L.J.King

AUSTRALIA v WEST INDIES 1992-93 (Fifth Test)

At W.A.C.A. Ground, Perth, 30, 31 January, 1 February

Result: West Innings won by an innings and 25 runs

Australia

J.L.Langer c Murray b Bishop	10	(2) c sub (A.L.Logie) b Ambrose	1
D.C.Boon c Richardson b Ambrose	44	(1) b Bishop	52
S.R.Waugh c Murray b Bishop	13	c sub (A.L.Logie) b Bishop	0
M.E.Waugh c Murray b Ambrose	9	c Richardson b Bishop	21
D.R.Martyn c Simmons b Ambrose	13	(6) c Ambrose b Cummins	31
A.R.Border* c Murray b Ambrose	0	(7) b Bishop	0
I.A.Healy† c Lara b Ambrose	0	(8) c Murray b Bishop	27
M.G.Hughes c Arthurton b Ambrose	13	(9) c Murray b Walsh	22
S.K.Warne run out	0	(5) c Murray b Ambrose	0
J.Angel c Murray b Ambrose	2	not out	4
C.J.McDermott not out	15	c Lara b Bishop	8
Extras (LB 8, NB 6, W 1)	15	(B 1, LB 6, NB 5)	12
	119		**178**

1/27 2/58 3/85 4/90 5/90 6/100 7/102 8/104 9/104

1/13 2/14 3/66 4/67 5/95 6/95 7/130 8/162 9/170

Bowling: *First Innings*—Ambrose 18-9-25-7; Bishop 11-6-17-2; Cummins 7-0-24-0. *Second Innings*—Ambrose 21-8-54-2; Bishop 16-4-40-6; Walsh 12-2-46-1; Cummins 8-3-31-1.

West Indies

D.L.Haynes c Healy b Hughes	24
P.V.Simmons c S.R.Waugh b Angel	80
R.B.Richardson* c Langer b McDermott	47
B.C.Lara c Warne b McDermott	16
K.L.T.Arthurton c S.R.Waugh b McDermott	77
J.C.Adams b Hughes	8
J.R.Murray† c Healy b M.E.Waugh	37
I.R.Bishop c Healy b M.E.Waugh	0
A.C.Cummins c M.E.Waugh b Hughes	3
C.E.L.Ambrose not out	9
C.A.Walsh b Hughes	1
Extras (B 4, LB 10, NB 6)	20
	322

1/111 2/136 3/184 4/195 5/205 6/280 7/286 8/301 9/319

Bowling: McDermott 22-4-85-3; Hughes 25.4-6-71-4; Angel 19-4-72-1; S.R.Waugh 6-3-8-0; M.E.Waugh 6-1-21-2.

Umpires: S.G.Randell and C.D.Timmins

NEW ZEALAND v AUSTRALIA 1992-93 (First Test)

At Lancaster Park, Christchurch, 25, 26, 27, 28 February

Result: Australia won by an innings and 60 runs

Australia

D.C.Boon c Parore b Owens	15
M.A.Taylor c Crowe b Morrison	82
J.L.Langer lbw b Morrison	63
M.E.Waugh c Parore b Patel	13
S.R.Waugh lbw b Owens	62
A.R.Border* c Parore b Morrison	88
I.A.Healy† c Morrison b Owens	54
M.G.Hughes c Cairns b Patel	45
P.R.Reiffel c Greatbatch b Su'a	18
S.K.Warne not out	22
C.J.McDermott c Jones b Cairns	4
Extras (B 2, LB 6, NB 6, W 5)	19
	485

1/33 2/149 3/170 4/217 5/264
6/363 7/435 8/441 9/480

Bowling: Morrison 36-11-81-3; Su'a 33-5-106-1; Cairns 31.3-9-87-1; Owens 26-9-58-3; Patel 31-3-145-2.

New Zealand

M.J.Greatbatch c Healy b McDermott	4	c Reiffel b Hughes	0
J.G.Wright lbw b Warne	39	b McDermott	14
A.H.Jones lbw b McDermott	8	c Border b McDermott	10
M.D.Crowe* c Taylor b Hughes	15	lbw b Hughes	14
K.R.Rutherford b Warne	57	c Healy b Warne	102
C.L.Cairns c Boon b McDermott	0	c Taylor b Warne	21
A.C.Parore† c Boon b Reiffel	6	c Boon b Warne	5
D.N.Patel c McDermott b Hughes	35	b Warne	8
M.L.Su'a c Healy b Reiffel	4	b Hughes	44
D.K.Morrison not out	0	c Healy b Hughes	19
M.B.Owens lbw b Warne	14	not out	0
Extras (B 2, LB 4, NB 4, W 4)	14	(LB 2, NB 4)	6
	182		243

1/4 2/18 3/53 4/124 5/128   1/0 2/19 3/24 4/51 5/92
6/138 7/150 8/152 9/181   6/110 7/144 8/190 9/242

Bowling: First Innings—McDermott 21-4-73-3; Hughes 21-10-44-2; Reiffel 18-8-27-2; S.R.Waugh 4-2-9-0; Warne 22-12-23-3. Second Innings—Hughes 24.5-6-62-4; McDermott 19-6-45-2; Reiffel 18-3-59-0; S.R.Waugh 2-2-0-0; Warne 26-7-63-4; M.E.Waugh 5-1-12-0.

Umpires: B.L.Aldridge and C.E.King

NEW ZEALAND v AUSTRALIA 1992-93 (Second Test)

At Basin Reserve, Wellington, 4, 5, 6, 7, 8 March

Result: Match drawn

New Zealand

M.J.Greatbatch c Taylor b Reiffel	61		b McDermott	0
J.G.Wright c Healy b Hughes	72	(6)	not out	46
A.H.Jones b Reiffel	4	(2)	lbw b Warne	42
M.D.Crowe* b McDermott	98	(3)	lbw b McDermott	3
K.R.Rutherford c Healy b Hughes	32	(4)	c Healy b Reiffel	11
T.E.Blain† b Hughes	1	(5)	c Healy b Warne	51
C.L.Cairns c Border b McDermott	13		lbw b McDermott	14
D.N.Patel not out	13		c Healy b M.E.Waugh	25
D.K.Morrison c Warne b McDermott	2		not out	0
W.Watson c Taylor b Warne	3			
M.B.Owens b Warne	0			
Extras (B 7, LB 11, NB 10, W 2)	30		(B 8, LB 8, NB 1, W 1)	18
	329		(7 wkts)	210

1/111 2/120 3/191 4/287 5/289   1/4 2/9 3/30 4/101
6/306 7/308 8/314 9/329   5/131 6/154 7/202

Bowling: First Innings—McDermott-31-8-66-3; Hughes-35-9-100-3; Reiffel-23-8-55-2; S.R.Waugh-15-7-28-0; Warne-29-9-59-2; M.E.Waugh-2-1-3-0. Second Innings—McDermott-23-9-54-3; Hughes-11-5-22-0; Warne-40-25-49-2; Reiffel-16-7-27-1; Border-12-5-15-0; M.E.Waugh-8-3-12-1; Taylor-4-2-15-0; Boon-1-1-0-0.

Australia

M.A.Taylor run out	50
D.C.Boon c and b Morrison	37
J.L.Langer c Blain b Watson	24
M.E.Waugh c and b Owens	12
S.R.Waugh c Blain b Morrison	75
A.R.Border* lbw b Morrison	30
I.A.Healy† c Rutherford b Morrison	8
M.G.Hughes c Wright b Morrison	8
P.R.Reiffel lbw b Morrison	7
S.K.Warne c Greatbatch b Morrison	22
C.J.McDermott not out	7
Extras (LB 14, NB 4)	18
	298

1/92 2/105 3/128 4/154 5/229
6/237 7/251 8/258 9/271

Bowling: Morrison-26.4-5-89-7; Cairns-24-3-77-0; Watson-29-12-60-1; Owens-21-3-54-1; Patel-1-0-4-0.

Umpires: B.L.Aldridge and R.S.Dunne

NEW ZEALAND v AUSTRALIA 1992-93 (Third Test)

At Eden Park, Auckland, 12, 13, 14, 15, 16 March

Result: New Zealand won by 5 wickets

Australia

D.C.Boon	lbw b Watson	20	(2) lbw b Su'a	53
M.A.Taylor	lbw b Morrison	13	(1) st Blain b Patel	3
J.L.Langer	c Blain b Morrison	0	lbw b Patel	0
D.R.Martyn	c Blain b Watson	1	c Greatbatch b Patel	74
S.R.Waugh	c Jones b Watson	41	lbw b Patel	0
A.R.Border*	c Blain b Morrison	0	c Harris b Watson	71
I.A.Healy†	c Jones b Morrison	0	c Blain b Patel	24
M.G.Hughes	c Morrison b Patel	33	not out	31
P.R.Reiffel	c Blain b Morrison	9	b Watson	1
S.K.Warne	not out	3	c Jones b Morrison	2
C.J.McDermott	b Morrison	6	c Wright b Watson	10
Extras	(LB 7, NB 6)	13	(B 1, LB 7, NB 8)	16
		139		**285**

1/38 2/38 3/39 4/39 5/43 6/48 7/101 8/121 9/133

1/5 2/8 3/115 4/119 5/160 6/225 7/261 8/271 9/274

Bowling: First Innings—Morrison 18.4-5-37-6; Su'a 14-3-27-0; Watson 19-9-47-3; Patel 4-0-21-1. Second Innings—Morrison 33-8-81-1; Patel 34-10-93-5; Watson 19-5-43-3; Su'a 18-4-56-1; Harris 2-1-4-0.

New Zealand

J.G.Wright	c Taylor b McDermott	33	run out	33
M.J.Greatbatch	c Border b Hughes	32	b Hughes	29
A.H.Jones	c Healy b Hughes	20	b Warne	26
M.D.Crowe*	c Taylor b Waugh	31	c Langer b Warne	25
K.R.Rutherford	st Healy b Warne	43	not out	53
C.Z.Harris	c Taylor b Warne	13	lbw b Waugh	0
T.E.Blain†	c Healy b McDermott	15	not out	24
D.N.Patel	c Healy b Warne	2		
M.L.Su'a	c Waugh b Warne	3		
D.K.Morrison	not out	10		
W.Watson	lbw b Hughes	0		
Extras	(B 7, LB 10, NB 5)	22	(LB 10, NB 1)	11
		224	(5 wkts)	**201**

1/60 2/91 3/97 4/144 5/178 6/200 7/205 8/206 9/224

1/44 2/65 3/109 4/129 5/134

Bowling: First Innings—McDermott 19-6-50-2; Hughes 24.5-6-67-3; Reiffel 22-6-63-0; Warne 15-12-8-4; Waugh 14-6-19-1; Martyn 1-1-0-0. Second Innings—McDermott 12-3-38-0; Hughes 15.4-2-54-1; Reiffel 6-1-19-0; Warne 27-8-54-2; Border 6-3-11-0; Waugh 6-1-15-1.

Umpires: B.L.Aldridge and C.E.King

ENGLAND v AUSTRALIA 1993 (First Test)

At Old Trafford, Manchester, 3, 4, 5, 6, 7 June

Result: Australia won by 179 runs

Australia

M.A.Taylor	c and b Such	124	(2) lbw b Such	9
M.J.Slater	c Stewart b DeFreitas	58	(1) c Caddick b Such	27
D.C.Boon	c Lewis b Such	21	c Gatting b DeFreitas	93
M.E.Waugh	c and b Tufnell	6	b Tufnell	64
A.R.Border*	st Stewart b Such	17	c and b Caddick	31
S.R.Waugh	b Such	3	not out	78
I.A.Healy†	c Such b Tufnell	12	not out	102
B.P.Julian	c Gatting b Such	0		
M.G.Hughes	c DeFreitas b Such	2		
S.K.Warne	not out	15		
C.J.McDermott	run out	8		
Extras	(B 8, LB 8, NB 7)	23	(B 6, LB 14, NB 8)	28
		289	(5 wkts dec.)	**432**

1/128 2/183 3/221 4/225 5/232 6/260 7/264 8/266 9/267

1/23 2/46 3/155 4/234 5/252

Bowling: First Innings—Caddick 15-4-38-0; DeFreitas 23-8-46-1; Lewis 13-2-44-0; Such 33.3-9-67-6; Tufnell 28-5-78-2. Second Innings—Caddick 20-3-79-1; DeFreitas 24-1-80-1; Such 31-6-78-2; Tufnell 37-4-112-1; Hick 9-1-20-0; Lewis 9-0-43-0.

England

G.A.Gooch*	c Julian b Warne	65	handled the ball	133
M.A.Atherton	c Healy b Hughes	19	c Taylor b Warne	25
M.W.Gatting	b Warne	4	b Hughes	23
R.A.Smith	c Taylor b Warne	4	b Warne	18
G.A.Hick	c Border b Hughes	34	c Healy b Hughes	22
A.J.Stewart†	b Julian	27	c Healy b Warne	11
C.C.Lewis	c Boon b Hughes	9	c Taylor b Warne	43
P.A.J.DeFreitas	lbw b Julian	5	lbw b Julian	7
A.R.Caddick	c Healy b Warne	7	c Warne b Hughes	25
P.M.Such	not out	14	c Border b Hughes	9
P.C.R.Tufnell	c Healy b Hughes	1	not out	0
Extras	(B 6, LB 10, NB 5)	21	(LB 11, NB 4, W 1)	16
		210		**332**

1/71 2/80 3/84 4/123 5/148 6/168 7/178 8/183 9/203

1/73 2/133 3/171 4/223 5/230 6/238 7/260 8/299 9/331

Bowling: First Innings—McDermott 18-2-50-0; Hughes-20.5-5-59-4; Julian-11-2-30-2; Warne-24-10-51-4; Martyn 1-1-0-0. Second Innings—McDermott-30-9-76-0; Hughes-27.2-4-92-4; Warne-49-26-86-4; Julian-14-1-67-1.

Umpires: H.D.Bird and K.E.Palmer

ENGLAND v AUSTRALIA 1993 (Second Test)

At Lord's, London, 17, 18, 19, 20, 21 June
Result: Australia won by an innings and 62 runs

Australia

Batsman	1st Innings
M.A.Taylor st Stewart b Tufnell	111
M.J.Slater c sub (B.F.Smith) b Lewis	152
D.C.Boon not out	164
M.E.Waugh b Tufnell	99
A.R.Border* b Lewis	77
S.R.Waugh not out	13
I.A.Healy†	
M.G.Hughes	
S.K.Warne	
T.B.A.May	
C.J.McDermott	
Extras (LB 1, NB 14, W 1)	16
	(4 wkts dec.) 632

1/260 2/277 3/452 4/591

Bowling: Caddick 38-5-120-0; Foster 30-4-94-0; Such 36-6-90-0; Tufnell 39-3-129-2; Lewis 36-5-151-2; Gooch 9-1-26-0; Hick 8-3-21-0.

England

Batsman	1st Innings		2nd Innings	
G.A.Gooch* c May b Hughes	12	c Healy b Warne		29
M.A.Atherton b Warne	80	run out		99
M.W.Gatting b May	5	lbw b Warne		59
R.A.Smith st Healy b May	22	c sub (M.L.Hayden) b May		5
G.A.Hick c Healy b Hughes	20	c Taylor b May		64
A.J.Stewart† lbw b Hughes	3	lbw b May		62
C.C.Lewis lbw b Warne	0	st Healy b May		0
N.A.Foster c Border b Warne	16	c M.E.Waugh b Border		20
A.R.Caddick c Healy b Hughes	21	not out		0
P.M.Such c Taylor b Warne	7	b Warne		4
P.C.R.Tufnell not out	2	b Warne		0
Extras (LB 8, NB 9)	17	(B 10, LB 13)		23
	205			365

1/33 2/50 3/84 4/123 5/131
6/132 7/167 8/174 9/189

1/29 2/175 3/180 4/244 5/304
6/312 7/361 8/361 9/365

Bowling: First Innings—Hughes 20-5-52-4; M.E.Waugh 6-1-16-0; S.R.Waugh 4-1-5-0; May 31-12-64-2; Warne 35-12-57-4; Border 3-1-3-0. Second Innings—Hughes 31-9-75-0; M.E.Waugh 17-4-55-0; A.May 51-23-81-4; S.R.Waugh 2-0-13-0; Warne 48.5-17-102-4; Border 16-9-16-1.

Umpires: M.J.Kitchen and D.R.Shepherd

ENGLAND v AUSTRALIA 1993 (Third Test)

At Trent Bridge, Nottingham, 1, 2, 3, 5, 6 July
Result: Match drawn

England

Batsman	1st Innings		2nd Innings	
M.N.Lathwell c Healy b Hughes	20	lbw b Warne		33
M.N.Atherton c Boon b Warne	11	c Healy b Hughes		9
R.A.Smith c and b Julian	86	c Healy b Warne		50
A.J.Stewart† c M.E.Waugh b Warne	25	lbw b Hughes		6
G.A.Gooch* c Border b Hughes	38	c Taylor b Warne		120
G.P.Thorpe c S.R.Waugh b Hughes	6	not out		114
N.Hussain c Boon b Warne	71	not out	(7)	47
A.R.Caddick lbw b Hughes	15	c Boon b Julian	(6)	12
M.J.McCague c M.E.Waugh b Hughes	9			
M.C.Ilott c Taylor b May	6			
P.M.Such not out	0			
Extras (B 5, LB 23, NB 2, W 4)	34	(B 13, LB 9, NB 9)		31
	321		(6 wkts dec.)	422

1/28 2/63 3/153 4/159 5/174
6/220 7/290 8/304 9/321

1/11 2/101 3/109
4/117 5/159 6/309

Bowling: First Innings—Hughes 31-7-92-5; Julian 24-3-84-1; Warne 40-17-74-3; May 14.4-7-31-1; S.R.Waugh 8-4-12-0; M.E.Waugh 1-1-0-0. Second Innings—Hughes 22-8-41-2; Julian 33-10-110-1; May 38-6-112-0; Warne 50-21-108-3; S.R.Waugh 1-0-3-0; Border 5-0-11-0; M.E.Waugh 6-3-15-0.

Australia

Batsman	1st Innings		2nd Innings	
M.J.Slater lbw b Caddick	40	b Such	(2)	26
M.A.Taylor c Stewart b McCague	28	c Atherton b Such	(1)	28
D.C.Boon b McCague	101	c Stewart b Caddick		18
M.E.Waugh c McCague b Such	70	b Caddick		1
S.R.Waugh c McCague b McCague	13	not out	(6)	47
I.A.Healy† c Thorpe b Ilott	9	lbw b Ilott	(7)	5
B.P.Julian c Stewart b Ilott	5	not out	(8)	56
A.R.Border* c Smith b Such	38	c Thorpe b Caddick	(5)	2
M.G.Hughes b Ilott	17			
S.K.Warne not out	35			
T.B.A.May lbw b McCague	1			
Extras (B 4, LB 8, W 4)	16	(B 5, LB 5, NB 5, W 4)		19
	373		(6 wkts)	202

1/55 2/74 3/197 4/239 5/250
6/262 7/284 8/311 9/356

1/46 2/74 3/75 4/81
5/93 6/115

Bowling: First Innings—McCague 32.3-5-121-4; Ilott 34-8-108-3; Such 20-7-51-2; Caddick 22-5-81-1. Second Innings—McCague 19-6-58-0; Ilott 18-5-44-1; Such 23-6-58-2; Caddick 16-6-32-3.

Umpires: B.J.Meyer and R.Palmer

ENGLAND v AUSTRALIA 1993 (Fourth Test)

At Headingley, Leeds, 22, 23, 24, 25, 26 July
Result: Australia won by an innings and 148 runs

Australia

Batsman	Dismissal	Runs
M.J.Slater	b Ilott	67
M.A.Taylor	lbw b Bicknell	27
D.C.Boon	lbw b Ilott	107
M.E.Waugh	b Ilott	52
A.R.Border*	not out	200
S.R.Waugh	not out	157
I.A.Healy†		
P.R.Reiffel		
M.G.Hughes		
S.K.Warne		
T.B.A.May		
Extras	(B 8, LB 22, NB 9, W 4)	43
	(4 wkts dec.)	653

1/86 2/110 3/216 4/321

Bowling: McCague 28-2-110-0; Ilott 51-11-161-3; Caddick 42-5-138-0; Bicknell 50-8-155-1; Gooch 16-5-40-0; Thorpe 6-1-14-0.

England

Batsman	1st dismissal	Runs	2nd dismissal	Runs
M.N.Lathwell	c Healy b Hughes	0	b May	25
M.A.Atherton	b Reiffel	55	st Healy b May	63
R.A.Smith	c and b May	23	lbw b Reiffel	35
A.J.Stewart†	c Slater b Reiffel	5	c M.E.Waugh b Reiffel	78
G.A.Gooch*	lbw b Reiffel	59	c Taylor b Reiffel	26
G.P.Thorpe	c Healy b Reiffel	0	c Taylor b Reiffel	13
N.Hussain	b Reiffel	15	not out	18
A.R.Caddick	c M.E.Waugh b Hughes	9	lbw b Hughes	12
M.P.Bicknell	c Border b Hughes	12	lbw b Hughes	0
M.J.McCague	c Taylor b Warne	0	b Hughes	11
M.C.Ilott	not out	0	c Border b May	4
Extras	(B 2, LB 3, NB 17)	22	(B 5, LB 3, NB 11, W 1)	20
		200		305

1/0 2/43 3/50 4/158 5/158
6/169 7/184 8/195 9/200

1/60 2/131 3/149 4/202 5/256 305
6/263 7/279 8/279 9/295

Bowling: First Innings—Hughes 15.5-3-47-3; Reiffel 26-6-65-5; May 15-3-33-1; Warne 23-9-43-1; M.E.Waugh 3-0-7-0. Second Innings—Hughes 30-10-79-3; Reiffel 28-8-87-3; Warne 40-16-63-0; May 27-6-65-4; M.E.Waugh 2-1-3-0.

Umpires: H.D.Bird and N.T.Plews

ENGLAND v AUSTRALIA 1993 (Fifth Test)

At Edgbaston, Birmingham, 5, 6, 7, 8, 9 August
Result: Australia won by 8 wickets

England

Batsman	1st dismissal	Runs	2nd dismissal	Runs
G.A.Gooch	c Taylor b Reiffel	8	b Warne	48
M.A.Atherton*	b Reiffel	72	c Border b Warne	28
R.A.Smith	b M.E.Waugh	21	lbw b Warne	19
M.P.Maynard	c S.R.Waugh b May	0	c Healy b May	10
A.J.Stewart†	c and b Warne	45	lbw b Warne	5
G.P.Thorpe	c Healy b May	37	st Healy b Warne	60
N.Hussain	b Reiffel	3	c S.R.Waugh b May	0
J.E.Emburey	not out	55	c Healy b May	37
M.P.Bicknell	c M.E.Waugh b Reiffel	14	c S.R.Waugh b May	0
P.M.Such	b Reiffel	0	not out	7
M.C.Ilott	c Healy b Reiffel	3	b May	15
Extras	(B 4, LB 6, NB 7)	17	(B 11, LB 9, NB 2)	22
		276		251

1/17 2/71 3/76 4/156 5/156
6/160 7/215 8/262 9/264

1/60 2/104 3/115 4/115 5/124 251
6/125 7/229 8/229 9/229

Bowling: First Innings—Hughes 19-4-53-0; Reiffel 22.5-3-71-6; M.E.Waugh 15-4-43-1; S.R.Waugh 5-2-4-0; May 19-9-32-2; Warne 21-7-63-1. Second Innings—Hughes 18-7-24-0; Reiffel 11-2-30-0; May 48.2-15-89-5; Warne 49-23-82-5; Border 2-1-1-0; M.E.Waugh 5-2-5-0.

Australia

Batsman	1st dismissal	Runs	2nd dismissal	Runs
M.A.Taylor	run out	19	(2) c Thorpe b Such	4
M.J.Slater	c Smith b Such	22	(1) c Thorpe b Emburey	8
D.C.Boon	lbw b Emburey	0	not out	38
M.E.Waugh	c Thorpe b Ilott	137	not out	62
A.R.Border*	c Hussain b Such	3		
S.R.Waugh	c Stewart b Bicknell	59		
I.A.Healy†	c Stewart b Bicknell	80		
M.G.Hughes	b Bicknell	38		
P.R.Reiffel	b Such	20		
S.K.Warne	c Stewart b Emburey	10		
T.B.A.May	not out	3		
Extras	(B 7, LB 8, NB 2)	17	(B 3, LB 5)	8
		408	(2 wkts)	120

1/34 2/39 3/69 4/80 5/233
6/263 7/370 8/379 9/398

1/12 2/12

Bowling: First Innings—Bicknell 34-9-99-3; Ilott 24-4-85-1; Such 52.5-18-90-3; Emburey 39-9-119-2. Second Innings—Bicknell 3-0-9-0; Such 20.3-4-58-1; Emburey 18-4-31-1; Ilott 2-0-14-0.

Umpires: J.H.Hampshire and D.R.Shepherd

ENGLAND v AUSTRALIA 1993 (Sixth Test)

At The Oval, London, 19, 20, 21, 22, 23 August

Result: England won by 161 runs

England

Batsman	First Innings		Second Innings	
G.A.Gooch	c Border b S.R.Waugh	56	c Healy b Warne	79
M.A.Atherton*	lbw b S.R.Waugh	50	c Warne b Reiffel	42
G.A.Hick	c Warne b May	80	c Boon b May	36
M.P.Maynard	b Warne	20	c Reiffel b Hughes	9
N.Hussain	c Taylor b Warne	30	c M.E.Waugh b Hughes	0
A.J.Stewart†	c Healy b Hughes	76	c M.E.Waugh b Reiffel	35
M.R.Ramprakash	c Healy b Hughes	6	c Slater b Hughes	64
A.R.C.Fraser	b Reiffel	28	c Healy b Reiffel	13
S.L.Watkin	c S.R.Waugh b Reiffel	13	lbw b Warne	4
P.M.Such	c M.E.Waugh b Hughes	4	lbw b Warne	10
D.E.Malcolm	not out	0	not out	0
Extras	(LB 7, NB 9, W 1)	17	(B 5, LB 12, NB 3, W 1)	21
		380		313

1/88 2/143 3/177 4/231 5/253 6/272 7/339 8/363 9/374

1/77 2/157 3/180 4/180 5/186 6/254 7/276 8/283 9/313

Bowling: *First Innings*—Hughes 30-7-121-3; Reiffel 28.5-4-88-2; S.R.Waugh 12-2-45-2; Warne 20-5-70-2; M.E.Waugh 1-0-17-0; May 10-3-32-1. *Second Innings*—Hughes 31.2-9-110-3; Reiffel 24-8-55-3; Warne 40-15-78-3; May 24-6-53-1.

Australia

Batsman	First Innings		Second Innings	
M.A.Taylor	c Hussain b Malcolm	70	(2) b Watkin	9
M.J.Slater	c Gooch b Malcolm	4	(1) c Stewart b Watkin	12
D.C.Boon	c Gooch b Malcolm	13	lbw b Watkin	7
M.E.Waugh	c Stewart b Fraser	10	c Ramprakash b Malcolm	49
A.R.Border*	c Stewart b Fraser	48	c Stewart b Malcolm	17
S.R.Waugh	b Fraser	20	lbw b Malcolm	4
I.A.Healy†	not out	83	c Maynard b Watkin	30
M.G.Hughes	c Ramprakash b Watkin	7	c Watkin b Fraser	0
P.R.Reiffel	c Maynard b Watkin	0	c and b Fraser	30
S.K.Warne	c Stewart b Fraser	16	lbw b Fraser	37
T.B.A.May	c Stewart b Fraser	15	not out	17
Extras	(B 5, LB 6, NB 4, W 2)	17	(B 2, LB 6, NB 7, W 2)	17
		303		229

1/9 2/30 3/53 4/132 5/164 6/181 7/196 8/196 9/248

1/23 2/23 3/30 4/92 5/95 6/106 7/142 8/143 9/217

Bowling: *First Innings*—Malcolm 26-5-86-3; Watkin 28-4-87-2; Fraser 26.4-4-87-5; Such 14-4-30-0. *Second Innings*—Malcolm 20-3-84-3; Watkin 25-9-65-4; Fraser 19.1-5-44-3; Such 9-4-17-0; Hick 8-3-11-0.

Umpires: M.J.Kitchen and B.J.Meyer

AUSTRALIA v NEW ZEALAND 1993-94 (First Test)

At W.A.C.A. Ground, Perth, 12, 13, 14, 15, 16 November

Result: Match drawn

Australia

Batsman	First Innings		Second Innings	
M.A.Taylor	b Cairns	64	(2) not out	142
M.J.Slater	c Patel b Cairns	10	(1) c Blain b Patel	99
D.C.Boon	c Rutherford b Cairns	0	not out	67
M.E.Waugh	lbw b Morrison	36		
A.R.Border*	c Rutherford b Morrison	16		
S.R.Waugh	c Blain b Patel	44		
I.A.Healy†	not out	113		
P.R.Reiffel	c Jones b Watson	51		
S.K.Warne	c Patel b Cairns	11		
C.J.McDermott	b Su'a	35		
G.D.McGrath	lbw b Su'a	0		
Extras	(B 4, LB 7, NB 7)	18	(LB 6, NB 9)	15
		398	(1 wkt dec.)	323

1/37 2/37 3/100 4/129 5/164 6/198 7/291 8/329 9/398

1/198

Bowling: *First Innings*—Morrison 35-4-113-2; Cairns 28-4-113-4; Su'a 19.5-2-72-2; Patel 8-0-37-1. *Second Innings*—Morrison 25-5-80-0; Patel 39-4-144-1; Cairns 1-0-12-0; Su'a 20-0-71-0; Pocock 2-0-10-0.

New Zealand

Batsman	First Innings		Second Innings	
M.J.Greatbatch	c Healy b McGrath	18	c Healy b McGrath	0
B.A.Pocock	c Boon b McDermott	34	c Healy b McDermott	28
A.H.Jones	c Healy b M.E.Waugh	143	lbw b M.E.Waugh	45
M.D.Crowe*	c Taylor b Reiffel	42	lbw b S.R.Waugh	31
K.R.Rutherford	c Healy b McDermott	17	not out	39
D.N.Patel	c S.R.Waugh b Reiffel	20	not out	18
C.L.Cairns	c Healy b Warne	78		
T.E.Blain†	lbw b McDermott	36		
M.L.Su'a	not out	14		
D.K.Morrison	lbw b McGrath	0		
W.Watson	not out	0		
Extras	(B 1, LB 6, NB 10)	17	(LB 1, NB 4)	5
	(9 wkts dec.)	419	(4 wkts)	166

1/25 2/100 3/199 4/239 5/275 6/292 7/394 8/413 9/418

1/0 2/66 3/85 4/145

Bowling: *First Innings*—McDermott 40-10-127-3; McGrath 39-12-92-2; Reiffel 24-2-75-2; Warne 37.1-6-90-1; M.E.Waugh 13-5-18-1; S.R.Waugh 4-0-10-0; Border 2-2-0-0. *Second Innings*—McDermott 13-3-40-1; McGrath 16-6-50-1; Reiffel 7-2-25-0; M.E.Waugh 6-4-17-1; Warne 13-6-23-0; S.R.Waugh 7-2-10-1.

Umpires: D.B.Hair and A.J.McQuillan

AUSTRALIA v NEW ZEALAND 1993-94 (Second Test)

At Bellerive Oval, Hobart, 26, 27, 28, 29 November
Result: Australia won by an innings and 222 runs

Australia

M.A.Taylor	c Jones b Su'a	27
M.J.Slater	c Morrison b Patel	168
D.C.Boon	c Jones b Doull	106
M.E.Waugh	c Doull b de Groen	111
A.R.Border*	c and b Morrison	60
S.R.Waugh	not out	25
I.A.Healy†	c Doull b de Groen	1
P.R.Reiffel	not out	23
S.K.Warne		
C.J.McDermott		
T.B.A.May		
Extras	(B 7, LB 2, NB 14)	23
	(6 wkts dec.)	544

1/65 2/300 3/335 4/485
5/501 6/502

Bowling: Morrison 33-4-125-1; Su'a 24-3-102-1; Doull 21-0-99-1; de Groen 23-3-78-1; Harris 2-0-18-0.

New Zealand

M.J.Greatbatch	c May b McDermott	12	c M.E.Waugh b McDermott	0
B.A.Pocock	lbw b M.E.Waugh	9	st Healy b Warne	15
A.H.Jones	c Healy b May	47	c Border b M.E.Waugh	18
K.R.Rutherford*	c Taylor b May	17	b Warne	55
D.N.Patel	c Taylor b Warne	18	lbw b May	16
C.Z.Harris	c M.E.Waugh b May	0	b May	4
T.E.Blain†	c Warne b May	40	c and b Warne	29
M.L.Su'a	c Taylor b Warne	6	b Warne	5
D.K.Morrison	c M.E.Waugh b May	0	b Warne	0
S.B.Doull	lbw b Warne	0	c May b Warne	1
R.P.de Groen	not out	0	not out	3
Extras	(B 2, LB 1, NB 9)	12	(B 2, LB 5, NB 8)	15
		161		161

1/15 2/47 3/84 4/105 5/107   1/1 2/29 3/84 4/103 5/111
6/117 7/137 8/138 9/139   6/133 7/149 8/149 9/158

Bowling: First Innings—McDermott 15-3-29-1; Reiffel 5-1-13-0; S.R.Waugh 4-1-8-0; M.E.Waugh 9-4-7-1; May 31.3-10-65-5; Warne 18-5-36-3. Second Innings—McDermott 17-8-42-1; Reiffel 12-1-28-0; M.E.Waugh 4-0-8-1; May 25-13-45-2; Warne 19.5-9-31-6.

Umpires: D.B.Hair and W.P.Sheahan

AUSTRALIA v NEW ZEALAND 1993-94 (Third Test)

At Woolloongabba, Brisbane, 3, 4, 5, 6, 7 December
Result: Australia won by an innings and 96 runs

New Zealand

B.A.Pocock	c Healy b McDermott	0	(2) c Healy b McDermott	11
B.A.Young	c Healy b M.E.Waugh	38	(1) b Warne	53
A.H.Jones	b Warne	56	c Border b Warne	15
K.R.Rutherford*	c Boon b McDermott	36	c Warne b McGrath	86
M.J.Greatbatch	c Healy b McDermott	35	lbw b McGrath	2
C.L.Cairns	c and b Warne	5	c Healy b McGrath	16
D.N.Patel	c Boon b May	1	b Warne	3
T.E.Blain†	not out	42	(8) b Warne	18
D.K.Morrison	c Healy b Warne	0	not out	20
S.B.Doull	c Healy b McDermott	10	(7) c Taylor b Warne	24
R.P.de Groen	c Border b Warne	3	b May	6
Extras	(B 2, LB 3, NB 2)	7	(B 7, LB 12, NB 5)	24
		233		278

1/2 2/96 3/98 4/167 5/170   1/34 2/80 3/81 4/84 5/138
6/174 7/174 8/178 9/193   6/187 7/218 8/230 9/265

Bowling: First Innings—McDermott 23-11-39-4; McGrath 20-7-45-0; S.R.Waugh 3-0-13-0; M.E.Waugh 10-4-14-1; May 21-7-51-1; Warne 28.3-12-66-4. Second Innings—McDermott 25-4-63-2; McGrath 21-1-66-3; May 16-3-41-1; Warne 35-11-59-4; M.E.Waugh 6-1-30-0.

Australia

M.J.Slater	c Blain b Patel	28
M.A.Taylor	c Pocock b Doull	53
D.C.Boon	c Blain b Doull	89
M.E.Waugh	c Greatbatch b Cairns	68
A.R.Border*	c Patel b de Groen	105
S.R.Waugh	not out	147
I.A.Healy†	run out	15
S.K.Warne	not out	74
C.J.McDermott		
T.B.A.May		
G.D.McGrath		
Extras	(B 6, LB 13, NB 9)	28
	(6 wkts dec.)	607

1/80 2/102 3/227 4/277 5/436 (6 wkts dec.) 607
6/465

Bowling: Morrison 33-3-104-0; Cairns 36-7-128-1; Doull 33-5-105-2; de Groen 46-14-120-1; Patel 33-4-125-1; Jones 2-0-6-0.

Umpires: P.D.Parker and S.G.Randell

AUSTRALIA v SOUTH AFRICA 1993-94 (First Test)

At Melbourne Cricket Ground, 26, 27 (no play), 28, 29, 30 December

Result: Match drawn

Australia

M.A.Taylor	b Symcox	170
M.J.Slater	c Kirsten b Donald	32
S.K.Warne	lbw b de Villiers	0
D.C.Boon	b Matthews	25
M.E.Waugh	lbw b Matthews	84
A.R.Border*	c D.J.Richardson b Matthews	2
D.R.Martyn	b Symcox	8
I.A.Healy†	not out	7
P.R.Reiffel		
C.J.McDermott		
T.B.A.May		
Extras	(B 2, LB 7, NB 5)	14
	(7 wkts dec.)	342

1/57 2/58 3/127 4/296 5/300
6/327 7/342

Bowling: Donald 30-4-108-1; de Villiers 32-6-83-1; Matthews 24-5-68-2; Symcox 16.5-3-49-2.

South Africa

A.C.Hudson	retired hurt	64
G.Kirsten	c Taylor b Waugh	16
W.J.Cronje	c Boon b Warne	71
D.J.Cullinan	c A.R.Border b C.J.McDermott	0
J.N.Rhodes	not out	35
K.C.Wessels*	not out	63
D.J.Richardson†		
C.R.Matthews		
P.L.Symcox		
A.A.Donald		
P.S.de Villiers		
Extras	(LB 2, NB 7)	9
	(3 wkts)	258

1/49 (2/157 3/157

Bowling: First Innings—McDermott 23-5-60-1; Reiffel 21-4-55-0; Waugh 12-3-20-1; May 28-7-58-0; Warne 31-8-63-1.

Umpires: P.J.McConnell and S.G.Randell

AUSTRALIA v SOUTH AFRICA 1993-94 (Second Test)

At Sydney Cricket Ground, 2, 3, 4, 5, 6 January

Result: South Africa won by 5 runs

South Africa

A.C.Hudson	lbw b McGrath	0		c Healy b McDermott	1
G.Kirsten	st Healy b Warne	67		b McDermott	41
W.J.Cronje	c Waugh b McDermott	41		b McDermott	38
D.J.Cullinan	b Warne	9		lbw b Warne	2
J.N.Rhodes	lbw b Warne	4	(5)	not out	76
K.C.Wessels*	c and b Warne	3	(6)	b Warne	18
D.J.Richardson†	c Taylor b Warne	4	(4)	lbw b McGrath	24
P.L.Symcox	b Warne	7		c Healy b McDermott	4
C.R.Matthews	c Taylor b Warne	0		c Waugh b Warne	4
P.S.de Villiers	c Waugh b McDermott	18		lbw b Warne	2
A.A.Donald	not out	0		c Healy b Warne	10
Extras	(B 1, LB 4, NB 11)	16		(B 13, LB 1, NB 5)	19
		169			239

1/1 2/91 3/110 4/133 5/134   1/2 2/75 3/101 4/107 5/110
6/141 7/142 9/152   6/182 7/188 8/197 9/203

Bowling: First Innings—McDermott 18.1-2-42-2; McGrath 28-9-62-4; Warne 27-8-56-7; May 10-1-34-0. Second Innings—McDermott 28-9-62-4; McGrath 14-3-30-1; May 22-4-53-0; Warne 42-17-72-5; Border 3-1-8-0.

Australia

M.J.Slater	b Donald	92	(2)	b de Villiers	1
M.A.Taylor	c Richardson b Donald	7	(1)	c Richardson b de Villiers	27
D.C.Boon	b de Villiers	19		c Kirsten b de Villiers	24
M.E.Waugh	lbw b Symcox	7	(5)	lbw b Donald	11
A.R.Border*	c Richardson b de Villiers	49	(6)	b Donald	7
D.R.Martyn	c Richardson b de Villiers	59	(7)	c Hudson b Donald	6
I.A.Healy†	c Richardson b Donald	19	(8)	b de Villiers	1
S.K.Warne	c Rhodes b Symcox	11	(9)	run out	1
C.J.McDermott	c Cronje b de Villiers	6	(10)	not out	29
T.B.A.May	not out	8	(4)	lbw b de Villiers	5
G.D.McGrath	b Donald	9		c and b de Villiers	1
Extras	(B 1, LB 2, NB 3)	6		(LB 3)	3
		292			111

1/10 2/58 3/75 4/179 5/179   1/4 2/51 3/51 4/56 5/63
6/229 7/250 8/266 9/281   6/72 7/73 8/75 9/110

Bowling: First Innings—Donald 31.2-8-83-4; de Villiers 36-12-80-4; Matthews 28-11-44-0; Symcox 46-11-82-2. Second Innings—Donald 17-5-34-3; de Villiers 23.3-8-43-6; Matthews 6-5-9-0; Symcox 10-3-22-0.

Umpires: S.G.Randell and W.P.Sheahan

SOUTH AFRICA v AUSTRALIA 1993-94 (First Test)

At New Wanderers, Johannesburg, 4, 5, 6, 7, 8 March
Result: South Africa won by 197 runs

South Africa

Batsman	1st Innings		2nd Innings	
A.C.Hudson	c Healy b McDermott	17	b Warne	60
G.Kirsten	b Hughes	47	c Hughes b May	35
W.J.Cronje	c Border b May	21	c S.R.Waugh b Hughes	122
K.C.Wessels*	c Hayden b Hughes	18	c Border b Warne	50
P.N.Kirsten	b May	12	c Boon b May	53
J.N.Rhodes	c M.E.Waugh b McDermott	69	c Healy b S.R.Waugh	14
B.M.McMillan	c Boon b May	31	(8) b Warne	24
D.J.Richardson†	lbw b Warne	6	(9) c Border b Warne	20
C.R.Matthews	c Boon b Hughes	16	(10) not out	31
P.S.de Villiers	b McDermott	0	(7) b McDermott	4
A.A.Donald	not out	14	not out	15
Extras	(B 1, LB 10, NB 3)	14	(B 13, LB 4, NB 5)	22
Total		**251**	**(9 wkts dec.)**	**450**

1/21 2/70 3/103 4/116 5/126 6/126 7/194 8/203 9/249
1/76 2/123 3/258 4/289 5/324 6/343 7/366 8/403 9/406

Bowling: *First Innings*—McDermott 15.2-3-63-3; Hughes 20-6-59-3; May 22-5-62-2; S.R.Waugh 9-2-14-1; Warne 14-4-42-1. *Second Innings*—McDermott 35-3-112-1; Hughes 25-5-86-1; May 39-11-107-2; S.R.Waugh 10-3-28-1; M.E.Waugh 6-2-14-0; Warne 44.5-14-86-4.

Australia

Batsman	1st Innings		2nd Innings	
M.J.Slater	c Hudson b de Villiers	26	b de Villiers	41
M.L.Hayden	c Richardson b Donald	15	b de Villiers	5
D.C.Boon	c de Villiers b Donald	17	b Matthews	83
M.E.Waugh	run out	42	c Richardson b Donald	28
A.R.Border*	run out	34	c Kirsten b McMillan	14
S.R.Waugh	not out	45	c Richardson b Matthews	0
I.A.Healy†	b Matthews	11	c and b Donald	30
M.G.Hughes	c G.Kirsten b McMillan	7	not out	26
S.K.Warne	lbw b Matthews	15	lbw b McMillan	1
C.J.McDermott	lbw b Donald	31	b McMillan	10
T.B.A.May	lbw b de Villiers	2	c G.Kirsten b Cronje	11
Extras	(B 1, LB 1, NB 1)	3	(LB 5, NB 2)	7
Total		**248**		**256**

1/37 2/56 3/70 4/136 5/142 6/169 7/176 8/201 9/245
1/18 2/95 3/136 4/164 5/164 6/191 7/219 8/225 9/235

Bowling: *First Innings*—Donald 19-0-86-3; de Villiers 19.3-1-74-2; McMillan 14-3-46-1; Matthews 15-4-40-2. *Second Innings*—Donald 23-3-71-2; de Villiers 30-11-70-2; McMillan 19-2-61-3; Matthews 20-6-42-2; G.Kirsten 4-0-7-0; Cronje 0.3-0-0-1.

Umpires: S.B.Lambson and D.R.Shepherd

AUSTRALIA v SOUTH AFRICA 1993-94 (Third Test)

At Adelaide Oval, 28, 29, 30, 31 January, 1 February
Result: Australia won by 191 runs

Australia

Batsman	1st Innings		2nd Innings	
M.A.Taylor	b G.Kirsten	62	(2) b Snell	38
M.J.Slater	c Rhodes b Donald	53	(1) lbw b Donald	7
D.C.Boon	c de Villiers b Donald	50	c Hudson b McMillan	38
M.E.Waugh	c Snell b McMillan	2	c Richardson b Donald	12
A.R.Border*	c Richardson b McMillan	84	run out	4
S.R.Waugh	c Richardson b Donald	164	c Richardson b Snell	1
I.A.Healy†	c Rhodes b McMillan	32	not out	14
P.R.Reiffel	not out	4	not out	2
S.K.Warne	not out			
C.J.McDermott				
T.B.A.May				
Extras	(LB 9, NB 9)	18	(LB 7, NB 1)	8
Total	**(7 wkts dec.)**	**469**	**(6 wkts dec.)**	**124**

1/83 2/152 3/159 4/183 5/391 6/391 7/464
1/23 2/79 3/91 4/99 5/103 6/109

Bowling: *First Innings*—Donald 38-7-122-3; de Villiers 41-11-105-0; Snell 19-6-44-0; McMillan 30-3-89-3; Cronje 9-3-21-0; G.Kirsten 23-8-62-1; P.N.Kirsten 4-0-17-0. *Second Innings*—Donald 11-2-26-2; McMillan 11-0-33-1; Cronje 6-1-20-0; Snell 12-3-38-2.

South Africa

Batsman	1st Innings		2nd Innings	
A.C.Hudson	lbw b S.R.Waugh	90	(2) c S.R.Waugh b McDermott	2
G.Kirsten	c May b McDermott	43	(1) b Warne	7
W.J.Cronje*	c Healy b Reiffel	0	lbw b Warne	4
P.N.Kirsten	c M.E.Waugh b Warne	79	lbw b McDermott	42
J.N.Rhodes	b S.R.Waugh	5	lbw b May	4
D.J.Cullinan	b S.R.Waugh	10	(7) c Healy b McDermott	5
B.M.McMillan	lbw b S.R.Waugh	2	(8) lbw b Warne	4
D.J.Richardson†	lbw b McDermott	6	(9) c Taylor b May	10
R.P.Snell	c Healy b McDermott	10	(10) c and b Warne	1
P.S.de Villiers	run out	4	(5) c Reiffel b McDermott	30
A.A.Donald	not out	1	not out	0
Extras	(B 3, LB 10, NB 9, W 1)	23	(B 9, LB 7, NB 3, W 2)	21
Total		**273**		**129**

1/100 2/103 3/173 4/179 5/195 6/203 7/222 8/243 9/270
1/12 2/17 3/18 4/100 5/105 6/113 7/116 8/128 9/128

Bowling: *First Innings*—McDermott 27-9-49-3; Reiffel 15-4-36-1; May 25-9-57-0; Warne 44.2-15-85-1; M.E.Waugh 3-1-7-0; S.R.Waugh 18-7-26-4. *Second Innings*—McDermott 19-8-33-4; Reiffel 11-4-15-0; Warne 30.5-15-31-4; May 32-20-26-2; S.R.Waugh 6-3-4-0; Border 4-3-1-0; M.E.Waugh 3-2-3-0.

Umpires: D.B.Hair and T.A.Prue

SOUTH AFRICA v AUSTRALIA 1993-94 (Third Test)

At Kingsmead, Durban, 25, 26, 27, 28, 29 March

Result: Match drawn

South Africa

Batsman	Dismissal	Runs
A.C.Hudson	lbw b Reiffel	65
G.Kirsten	c Healy b Reiffel	41
W.J.Cronje	c S.R.Waugh b Warne	26
K.C.Wessels*	lbw b McDermott	49
P.N.Kirsten	lbw b S.R.Waugh	78
J.N.Rhodes	lbw b Warne	2
B.M.McMillan	c Slater b S.R.Waugh	84
D.J.Richardson†	c Reiffel b Warne	59
C.R.Matthews	lbw b Warne	0
P.S.de Villiers	lbw b S.R.Waugh	0
A.A.Donald	not out	0
Extras	(B 3, LB 10, NB 5)	18
Total		**422**

1/100 2/117 3/118 4/155 5/256 6/274 7/417 8/422 9/422

Bowling: McDermott 38-11-76-1; Reiffel 30-7-77-2; McGrath 41-11-78-0; Warne 55-20-92-4; S.R.Waugh 27.2-12-40-3; M.E.Waugh 11-3-38-0; Border 3-1-8-0.

Australia

Batsman	First Innings	Runs	Second Innings	Runs
M.J.Slater	c Rhodes b Matthews	20	(2) lbw b Donald	95
M.A.Taylor	lbw b Donald	1	(1) lbw b de Villiers	12
D.C.Boon	c G.Kirsten b Donald	37	c P.N.Kirsten b Donald	12
M.E.Waugh	c Richardson b Donald	43	(5) not out	113
A.R.Border*	c Rhodes b McMillan	17	(6) not out	42
S.R.Waugh	c Wessels b Matthews	64		
I.A.Healy†	b Matthews	55		
P.R.Reiffel	lbw b de Villiers	13		
S.K.Warne	c Wessels b Matthews	2	(4) c McMillan b Donald	12
C.J.McDermott	c Donald b de Villiers	6		
G.D.McGrath	not out	0		
Extras	(LB 1, NB 9, W 1)	11	(LB 6, NB 4, W 1)	11
Total		**269**	**(4 wkts)**	**297**

1/7 2/45 3/81 4/123 5/123 6/215 7/250 8/256 9/269

1/55 2/81 3/109 4/157

Bowling: *First Innings*—Donald 18-1-71-3; de Villiers 24.2-5-55-2; Matthews 29-9-65-4; McMillan 19-5-56-1; Cronje 5-1-8-0; G.Kirsten 6-1-13-0. *Second Innings*—Donald 28-8-66-3; de Villiers 24-5-69-1; McMillan 22-6-53-0; Matthews 28-12-56-0; Cronje 18-5-40-0; G.Kirsten 3-1-7-0; Rhodes 1-1-0-0.

Umpires: Mahboob Shah and C.J.Mitchley

SOUTH AFRICA v AUSTRALIA 1993-94 (Second Test)

At Newlands, Cape Town, 17, 18, 19, 20, 21 March

Result: Australia won by 9 wickets

South Africa

Batsman	First Innings	Runs	Second Innings	Runs
A.C.Hudson	run out	102	lbw b S.R.Waugh	49
G.Kirsten	run out	29	lbw b Warne	10
W.J.Cronje	b McGrath	2	c and b S.R.Waugh	19
K.C.Wessels*	c M.E.Waugh b McDermott	11	run out	9
P.N.Kirsten	lbw b Warne	70	c Taylor b Warne	3
J.N.Rhodes	lbw b McGrath	5	c Border b S.R.Waugh	27
B.M.McMillan	b Warne	74	(8) lbw b S.R.Waugh	3
D.J.Richardson†	lbw b McDermott	34	(9) c Healy b McGrath	31
C.R.Matthews	not out	7	(10) not out	0
P.S.de Villiers	c Taylor b Warne	7	(7) lbw b Warne	0
A.A.Donald	c Healy b McGrath	7	b S.R.Waugh	0
Extras	(LB 6, NB 7)	13	(B 4, LB 6, NB 3)	13
Total		**361**		**164**

1/71 2/78 3/100 4/189 5/197 6/260 7/335 8/339 9/348

1/33 2/69 3/94 4/95 5/97 6/97 7/103 8/164 9/164

Bowling: *First Innings*—McDermott 27-6-80-2; Hughes 20-1-80-0; McGrath 26.1-4-65-3; S.R.Waugh 9-3-20-0; Warne 47-18-78-3; M.E.Waugh 10-3-23-0; Border 5-2-9-0. *Second Innings*—McDermott 13-3-39-0; Hughes 5-1-12-0; Warne 30-13-38-3; McGrath 16-6-26-1; S.R.Waugh 22.3-9-28-5; Border 1-1-0-0; M.E.Waugh 3-1-11-0.

Australia

Batsman	First Innings	Runs	Second Innings	Runs
M.J.Slater	c P.N.Kirsten b de Villiers	26	(2) not out	43
M.A.Taylor	c Richardson b de Villiers	70	(1) b Donald	14
D.C.Boon	c Richardson b de Villiers	96	(3) not out	32
M.E.Waugh	c P.N.Kirsten b McMillan	45		
A.R.Border*	c Richardson b Matthews	86		
S.R.Waugh	b Matthews	61		
I.A.Healy†	c de Villiers b Matthews	0		
M.G.Hughes	lbw b Matthews	11		
S.K.Warne	c McMillan b de Villiers	1		
C.J.McDermott	c P.N.Kirsten b Matthews	1		
G.D.McGrath	not out	1		
Extras	(B 6, LB 17, NB 7, W 1)	31	(B 1, NB 2)	3
Total		**435**	**(1 wkt)**	**92**

1/40 2/145 3/153 4/244 5/310 6/418 7/418 8/430 9/434

1/30

Bowling: *First Innings*—Donald 35-10-111-0; de Villiers 44.4-12-117-4; Matthews 36-12-80-5; McMillan 29-8-82-1; G.Kirsten 4-0-13-0; Cronje 11-4-9-0. *Second Innings*—Matthews 6-1-14-0; de Villiers 6-1-20-0; Donald 5-0-23-1; McMillan 5-0-20-0; Cronje 2-0-4-0; G.Kirsten 1.1-0-10-0.

Umpires: K.E.Liebenberg and D.R.Shepherd

PAKISTAN v AUSTRALIA 1994-95 (First Test)

At National Stadium, Karachi, 28, 29, 30 September, 1, 2 October
Result: Pakistan won by 1 wicket

Australia

M.J.Slater lbw b Wasim Akram	36		lbw b Mushtaq Ahmed	23
M.A.Taylor* c and b Wasim Akram	0		c Rashid Latif b Waqar Younis	0
D.C.Boon b Mushtaq Ahmed	19		not out	114
M.E.Waugh c Zahid Fazal b M'taq Ahmed	20		b Waqar Younis	61
M.G.Bevan c Aamer Sohail b M'taq Ahmed	82		b Wasim Akram	0
S.R.Waugh b Waqar Younis	73		lbw b Wasim Akram	0
I.A.Healy† c Rashid Latif b Waqar Younis	57		c Rashid Latif b Wasim Akram	9
S.K.Warne c Rashid Latif b Aamer Sohail	22		lbw b Waqar Younis	0
J.Angel b Wasim Akram	5		c Rashid Latif b Wasim Akram	8
T.B.A.May not out	1		b Wasim Akram	1
G.D.McGrath b Waqar Younis	0		b Waqar Younis	1
Extras (B 2, LB 12, NB 8)	22		(B 6, LB 4, NB 5)	15
	337			**232**

1/12 2/41 3/75 4/95 5/216
6/281 7/325 8/335 9/335

1/1 1/2 2/49 3/171 4/174 5/174
6/213 7/218 8/227 9/229

Bowling: *First Innings*—Wasim Akram 25-4-75-3; Waqar Younis 19.2-2-75-3; Mushtaq Ahmed 24-2-97-3; Akram Raza 14-1-50-0; Aamer Sohail 5-0-19-1; Saleem Malik 1-0-7-0. *Second Innings*—Wasim Akram 22-3-64-5; Waqar Younis 18-2-69-4; Mushtaq Ahmed 21-3-51-1; Akram Raza 10-1-19-0; Aamer Sohail 7-0-19-0.

Pakistan

Saeed Anwar c M.E.Waugh b May	85	(1)	c and b Angel	77
Aamer Sohail c Bevan b Warne	36	(2)	run out	34
Zahid Fazal c Boon b May	27	(3)	c Boon b Warne	3
Saleem Malik* lbw b Angel	26	(4)	c Taylor b Angel	43
Basit Ali c Bevan b McGrath	0	(6)	lbw b Warne	12
Inzamamul Haq c Taylor b Warne	9	(8)	not out	58
Rashid Latif† c Taylor b Warne	2	(9)	lbw b S.R.Waugh	35
Wasim Akram c Healy b Angel	39	(7)	c and b Warne	4
Akram Raza b McGrath	13	(5)	lbw b Warne	2
Waqar Younis c Healy b Angel	6	(10)	c Healy b Warne	7
Mushtaq Ahmed not out	2	(11)	not out	20
Extras (LB 7, NB 4)	11		(B 4, LB 13, NB 3)	20
	256			**315** (9 wkts)

1/90 2/153 3/154 4/157 5/175
6/181 7/200 8/234 9/253

1/45 2/64 3/148 4/157 5/155
5/174 6/179 7/184 8/236 9/258

Bowling: *First Innings*—McGrath 25-6-70-2; Angel 13.1-0-54-3; May 20-5-55-2; Warne 27-10-61-3; S.R.Waugh 2-0-9-0. *Second Innings*—McGrath 6-2-18-0; Angel 28-8-92-2; Warne 36.1-12-89-5; May 18-4-67-0; M.E.Waugh 3-1-4-0.

Umpires: H.D.Bird and Khizer Hayat

PAKISTAN v AUSTRALIA 1994-95 (Second Test)

At Pindi Cricket Stadium, Rawalpindi, 5, 6, 7, 8, 9 October
Result: Match drawn

Australia

M.A.Taylor* lbw b Mohsin Kamal	69	(2)	not out	5
M.J.Slater c Inz'ul Haq b Mohsin Kamal	110	(1)	b Mohsin Kamal	1
D.C.Boon b Mushtaq Ahmed	4		not out	7
M.E.Waugh c Aamer Sohail b Mohsin Kamal	68			
M.G.Bevan lbw b Waqar Younis	70			
S.R.Waugh b Waqar Younis	98			
I.A.Healy† c Mohsin Kamal b Aamer Sohail	58			
S.K.Warne c and b Aamer Sohail	14			
J.Angel b Wasim Akram	7			
C.J.McDermott not out	9			
D.W.Fleming				
Extras (B 3, LB 3, NB 5, W 3)	14		(LB 1)	1
	521			**14** (1 wkt)

1/176 2/181 3/198 4/323 5/347
6/456 7/501 8/511 9/521

1/2

Bowling: *First Innings*—Wasim Akram 23.5-3-62-1; Waqar Younis 32-6-112-2; Mohsin Kamal 26-3-109-3; Mushtaq Ahmed 36-2-145-1; Aamer Sohail 21-3-67-2; Aamer Malik 5-2-16-0; Saleem Malik 1-0-4-0. *Second Innings*—Waqar Younis 5-3-2-1; Rashid Latif 2-0-10-0; Saeed Anwar 2-2-0-0; Mushtaq Ahmed 1-0-1-0.

Pakistan

Saeed Anwar c S.R.Waugh b McDermott	15	c Healy b M.E.Waugh	75
Aamer Sohail b Fleming	80	c Healy b McDermott	72
Zahid Fazal b Fleming	10	c Healy b M.E.Waugh	1
Saleem Malik* b McDermott	33	c Healy b Fleming	237
Aamer Malik lbw b McDermott	11	c Bevan b Fleming	65
Inzamamul Haq lbw b Warne	14	lbw b Fleming	0
Rashid Latif† c Slater b Fleming	18	c Bevan b Taylor	38
Wasim Akram not out	45	c Healy b Angel	5
Mushtaq Ahmed c Warne b McDermott	0	c S.R.Waugh b McDermott	0
Waqar Younis lbw b Fleming	13	lbw b Slater	10
Mohsin Kamal run out	2	not out	0
Extras (B 10, LB 7, NB 2)	19	(B 17, LB 13, NB 3, W 1)	34
	260		**537**

1/28 2/90 3/119 4/152 5/155
6/189 7/189 8/198 9/253

1/79 2/227 3/336 4/469 5/469
6/478 7/495 8/496 9/527

Bowling: *First Innings*—C.J.McDermott-22-8-74-4; D.W.Fleming-22-3-75-4; S.K.Warne-21.4-8-58-1; J.Angel-11-2-36-0. *Second Innings*—C.J.McDermott-33-3-86-2; D.W.Fleming-26-2-86-3; J.Angel-28-1-124-1; M.E.Waugh-16-1-63-2; S.K.Warne-25-6-56-0; M.G.Bevan-4-0-27-0; S.R.Waugh-13-2-41-0; M.J.Slater-1.1-0-4-1; D.C.Boon-3-1-9-0; M.A.Taylor-3-1-11-1.

Umpires: K.E.Liebenberg and Mahboob Shah

PAKISTAN v AUSTRALIA 1994-95 (Third Test)

At Gaddafi Stadium, Lahore, 1, 2, 3, 4, 5 November

Result: Match drawn

Pakistan

Batsman	1st Innings		2nd Innings	
Saeed Anwar	b Warne	30	(2) c Emery b McGrath	32
Aamer Sohail	c Emery b McGrath	1	(7) st Emery b Warne	105
Inzamamul Haq	lbw b May	66	c Emery b McDermott	3
Saleem Malik*	c Bevan b May	75	b Bevan	143
Ijaz Ahmed	c Boon b Warne	48	lbw b McGrath	6
Basit Ali	c Waugh b Warne	0	(1) c Emery b McGrath	2
Moin Khan†	not out	115	(6) c McDermott b May	16
Akram Raza	b Warne	0	lbw b Warne	32
Mushtaq Ahmed	b May	14	c Emery b McGrath	27
Aaqib Javed	c Waugh b Warne	2	b Warne	2
Mohsin Kamal	lbw b Warne	4	not out	0
Extras	(B 5, LB 7, NB 6)	18	(B 8, LB 16, NB 8, W 4)	36
		373		404

1/8 2/34 3/157 4/204 5/209 6/294 7/294 8/346 9/355

1/20 2/28 3/60 4/74 5/107 6/303 7/363 8/384 9/394

Bowling: First Innings—McDermott 24-4-87-0; McGrath 24-6-65-1; Warne 41.5-12-136-6; May 29-7-69-3; M.E.Waugh 2-0-4-0. Second Innings—McDermott 19-2-81-1; McGrath 25.1-1-92-4; Warne 30-2-104-3; May 25-4-60-1; Bevan 4-0-21-1; M.E.Waugh 6-0-22-0.

Australia

M.J.Slater	c Moin Khan b Mohsin Kamal	74
M.A.Taylor*	c Saeed Anwar b M'taq Ahmed	32
D.C.Boon	c Moin Khan b Akram Raza	5
P.A.Emery†	not out	8
M.E.Waugh	c Moin Khan b Mohsin Kamal	71
M.G.Bevan	c sub (Nadeem Ahmed) b M'taq Ahmed	91
J.L.Langer	c Ijaz Ahmed b Mohsin Kamal	69
S.K.Warne	c and b Mohsin Kamal	33
C.J.McDermott	c and b Mushtaq Ahmed	29
T.B.A.May	c Moin Khan b Akram Raza	10
G.D.McGrath	b Mushtaq Ahmed	3
Extras	(B 3, LB 17, NB 8, W 2)	30
		455

1/97 2/106 3/126 4/248 5/318 6/402 7/406 8/443 9/450

Bowling: Aaqib Javed 31-9-75-0; Mohsin Kamal 28-3-116-4; Mushtaq Ahmed 45.1-6-121-4; Akram Raza 45-9-123-2.

Umpires: C.J.Mitchley and Riazuddin

AUSTRALIA v ENGLAND 1994-95 (First Test)

At Woolloongabba, Brisbane, 25, 26, 27, 28, 29 November

Result: Australia won by 184 runs

Australia

Batsman	1st Innings		2nd Innings	
M.J.Slater	c Gatting b Gooch	176	(2) lbw b Gough	45
M.A.Taylor*	run out	59	(1) c Stewart b Tufnell	58
D.C.Boon	b Gough	3	b Tufnell	28
M.E.Waugh	c Stewart b Gough	140	b Tufnell	15
M.G.Bevan	c Hick b Gough	7	c Rhodes b Tufnell	21
S.K.Warne	c Rhodes b Gough	2	(8) c sub (C.White) b DeFreitas	0
S.R.Waugh	c Hick b DeFreitas	19	(6) c sub (C.White) b Tufnell	7
I.A.Healy†	c Hick b DeFreitas	7	(7) not out	45
C.J.McDermott	c Gough b McCague	2	c Rhodes b Gough	6
T.B.A.May	not out	3	not out	9
G.D.McGrath	c Gough b McCague	0		
Extras	(B 5, LB 2, NB 1)	8	(B 2, LB 9, NB 1, W 2)	14
		426	(8 wkts dec.)	248

1/99 2/126 3/308 4/326 5/352 6/379 7/407 8/419 9/425

1/109 2/117 3/139 4/174 5/183 6/190 7/191 8/201

Bowling: First Innings—DeFreitas 31-8-102-2; McCague 19.2-4-96-2; Gough 32-7-107-4; Tufnell 25-3-72-0; Hick 4-0-22-0; Gooch 9-2-20-1. Second Innings—DeFreitas 22-1-74-2; Gough 23-3-78-2; Tufnell 38-10-79-4; Hick 2-1-1-0.

England

Batsman	1st Innings		2nd Innings	
M.A.Atherton*	c Healy b McDermott	54	lbw b Warne	23
A.J.Stewart	c Healy b McDermott	16	b Warne	33
G.A.Hick	c Healy b McDermott	3	c Healy b Warne	80
G.P.Thorpe	c and b Warne	28	b Warne	67
G.A.Gooch	c Healy b May	20	c Healy b Warne	56
M.W.Gatting	lbw b McDermott	10	c Healy b McDermott	13
M.J.McCague	b McDermott	0	(10) lbw b Warne	0
S.J.Rhodes†	lbw b McDermott	4	(7) c Healy b McDermott	2
P.A.J.DeFreitas	c Healy b Warne	7	(8) b Warne	11
D.Gough	not out	17	(9) c M.E.Waugh b Warne	10
P.C.R.Tufnell	c Taylor b Warne	0	not out	2
Extras	(LB 1, NB 6)	7	(B 9, LB 5, NB 12)	26
		167		323

1/22 2/35 3/82 4/105 5/131 6/133 7/140 8/147 9/151

1/50 2/59 3/219 4/220 5/250 6/280 7/309 8/310 9/310

Bowling: First Innings—McDermott 19-3-53-6; McGrath 10-2-40-0; May 17-3-34-1; Warne 21.2-7-39-3. Second Innings—McDermott 23-4-90-2; McGrath 19-4-61-0; Warne 50.2-22-71-8; May 35-16-59-0; M.E.Waugh 7-1-17-0; Bevan 3-0-11-0.

Umpires: C.J.Mitchley and S.G.Randell

AUSTRALIA v ENGLAND 1994-95 (Second Test)

At Melbourne Cricket Ground, 24, 26, 27, 28, 29 December

Result: Australia won by 295 runs

Australia

M.J.Slater	run out	3	(2) st Rhodes b Tufnell	44
M.A.Taylor*	lbw b DeFreitas	9	(1) lbw b Gough	19
D.C.Boon	c Hick b Tufnell	41	(3) lbw b DeFreitas	131
M.E.Waugh	c Thorpe b DeFreitas	71	(4) c and b Gough	29
M.G.Bevan	c Atherton b Gough	3	(5) c sub (J.P.Crawley) b Tufnell	35
S.R.Waugh	not out	94	(6) not out	26
I.A.Healy†	c Rhodes b Tufnell	17	(7) c Thorpe b Tufnell	17
S.K.Warne	c Hick b Gough	6	(8) c DeFreitas b Gough	0
T.B.A.May	lbw b Gough	9		
C.J.McDermott	b Gough	0	(9) not out	2
D.W.Fleming	c Hick b Malcolm	16		
Extras	(LB 7, NB 3)	10	(B 1, LB 9, NB 6, W 1)	17
		279	**(7 wkts dec.)**	**320**

1/10 2/39 3/91 4/100 5/171   1/61 2/81 3/157
6/208 7/220 8/242 9/242   4/269 5/275 6/316 7/317

Bowling: *First Innings*—Malcolm 28.3-4-78-1; DeFreitas 23-4-66-2; Gough 26-9-60-4; Tufnell 28-7-59-2; Hick 2-0-9-0. *Second Innings*—Malcolm 22-3-86-0; DeFreitas 26-2-70-1; Tufnell 48-8-90-3; Gough 25-6-59-3; Hick 3-2-5-0.

England

M.A.Atherton*	lbw b Warne	44	(2) c Healy b Fleming	25
A.J.Stewart	c and b Warne	16	(7) not out	8
G.A.Hick	c Healy b McDermott	23	b Fleming	2
G.P.Thorpe	c M.E.Waugh b Warne	51	(1) c Healy b McDermott	9
G.A.Gooch	c and b McDermott	15	c Healy b McDermott	2
M.W.Gatting	c S.R.Waugh b Warne	9	(5) c Taylor b McDermott	25
D.Gough	c Healy b McDermott	20	(9) c Healy b Warne	0
S.J.Rhodes†	c M.E.Waugh b McDermott	0	(6) c M.E.Waugh b McDermott	16
P.A.J.DeFreitas	st Healy b Warne	14	(8) lbw b Warne	0
D.E.Malcolm	not out	11	c Boon b Warne	0
P.C.R.Tufnell	run out	0	c Healy b McDermott	0
Extras	(LB 7, NB 2)	9	(LB 2, NB 3)	5
		212		**92**

1/40 2/119 3/124 4/140 5/148   1/2 2/10 3/23 4/43 5/81
6/151 7/185 8/189 9/207   6/88 7/91 8/91 9/91

Bowling: *First Innings*—McDermott 24-6-72-3; Fleming 11-5-30-0; M.E.Waugh 3-1-11-0; Warne 27.4-8-64-6; May 18-5-28-0. *Second Innings*—McDermott 16.5-5-42-5; Fleming 9-1-24-2; Warne 13-6-16-3; May 4-1-8-0.

Umpires: S.A.Bucknor and S.G.Randell

AUSTRALIA v ENGLAND 1994-95 (Third Test)

At Sydney Cricket Ground, 1, 2, 3, 4, 5 January

Result: Match drawn

England

G.A.Gooch	c Healy b Fleming	1	(1) lbw b Fleming	29
M.A.Atherton*	b McDermott	88	(2) c Taylor b Fleming	67
G.A.Hick	b McDermott	2	(3) not out	98
G.P.Thorpe	lbw b McDermott	10	(4) not out	47
J.P.Crawley	c M.E.Waugh b Fleming	72		
M.W.Gatting	c Healy b McDermott	0		
A.R.C.Fraser	c Healy b Fleming	27		
S.J.Rhodes†	run out	1		
D.Gough	c Fleming b McDermott	51		
D.E.Malcolm	b Warne	29		
P.C.R.Tufnell	not out	4		
Extras	(B 8, LB 7, NB 9)	24	(LB 6, NB 7, W 1)	14
		309	**(2 wkts dec.)**	**255**

1/1 2/10 3/20 4/194 5/194   1/54 2/158
6/196 7/197 8/255 9/295

Bowling: *First Innings*—McDermott 30-7-101-5; Fleming 26.2-12-52-3; Warne 36-10-88-1; May 17-4-35-0; M.E.Waugh 6-1-10-0; Bevan 4-1-8-0. *Second Innings*—McDermott 24-2-76-0; Fleming 20-3-66-2; M.E.Waugh 2-1-4-0; Warne 16-2-48-0; May 10-1-55-0.

Australia

M.J.Slater	b Malcolm	11	(2) c Tufnell b Fraser	103
M.A.Taylor*	c and b Gough	49	(1) b Malcolm	113
D.C.Boon	b Gough	3	(3) c Hick b Gough	17
M.E.Waugh	c Rhodes b Malcolm	3	(4) lbw b Fraser	25
M.G.Bevan	c Thorpe b Fraser	8	(5) c Rhodes b Fraser	7
S.R.Waugh	b Gough	1	(6) c Rhodes b Fraser	0
I.A.Healy†	c Hick b Gough	10	(7) c Rhodes b Fraser	5
S.K.Warne	c Gatting b Fraser	0	(8) not out	36
T.B.A.May	c Hick b Gough	21	(9) not out	10
C.J.McDermott	not out	0		
D.W.Fleming	b Gough	0		
Extras	(B 6, LB 1, NB 3)	10	(B 12, LB 3, NB 12, W 1)	28
		116	**(7 wkts)**	**344**

1/12 2/15 3/18 4/38 5/39   1/208 2/239 3/245 4/282 5/286 6/289 7/292
6/57 7/62 8/65 9/116

Bowling: *First Innings*—Malcolm 13-4-34-2; Gough 18.5-4-49-6; Fraser 11-1-26-2. *Second Innings*—Malcolm 21-4-75-1; Gough 28-4-72-1; Fraser 25-3-73-5; Tufnell 35.4-9-61-0; Hick 5-0-21-0; Gooch 7-1-27-0.

Umpires: S.A.Bucknor and D.B.Hair

AUSTRALIA v ENGLAND 1994-95 (Fourth Test)

At Adelaide Oval, 26, 27, 28, 29, 30 January
Result: England won by 106 runs

England

Batsman	1st Innings		2nd Innings	
G.A.Gooch	c M.E.Waugh b Fleming	47	c Healy b McDermott	34
M.A.Atherton*	c Boon b Fleming	80	lbw b M.E.Waugh	14
M.W.Gatting	c S.R.Waugh b McIntyre	117	b M.E.Waugh	0
G.P.Thorpe	c Taylor b Warne	26	c Warne b McDermott	83
J.P.Crawley	b Warne	28	c and b M.E.Waugh	71
S.J.Rhodes†	c Taylor b McDermott	6	c Fleming b Warne	2
C.C.Lewis	c Blewett b McDermott	10	b Fleming	7
P.A.J.DeFreitas	c Blewett b McIntyre	21	c Healy b M.E.Waugh	88
A.R.C.Fraser	run out	7	c McDermott b M.E.Waugh	5
D.E.Malcolm	b McDermott	0	not out	10
P.C.R.Tufnell	not out	0	lbw b Warne	0
Extras	(B 2, LB 5, NB 2, W 2)	11	(B 6, LB 8)	14
		353		**328**

1/93 2/175 3/211 4/286 5/293 6/307 7/334 8/353 9/353
1/26 2/30 3/83 4/154 5/169 6/181 7/270 8/317 9/317

Bowling: First Innings—McDermott 41-15-66-3; Fleming 25-6-65-2; Blewett 16-4-59-0; Warne 31-9-72-2; McIntyre 19.3-3-51-2; M.E.Waugh 9-1-33-0. Second Innings—McDermott 27-5-96-2; Fleming 11-3-37-1; Warne 30.5-9-82-2; M.E.Waugh 14-4-40-5; McIntyre 8-0-36-0; Blewett 4-0-23-0.

Australia

Batsman	1st Innings		2nd Innings	
M.J.Slater	c Atherton b DeFreitas	67	(2) c Tufnell b Malcolm	5
M.A.Taylor*	lbw b Lewis	90	(1) c Thorpe b Malcolm	13
D.C.Boon	c Rhodes b DeFreitas	0	c Rhodes b Fraser	4
M.E.Waugh	c Rhodes b Fraser	39	c Gatting b Tufnell	24
S.R.Waugh	c Atherton b Lewis	19	b Malcolm	0
G.S.Blewett	not out	102	c Rhodes b Lewis	12
I.A.Healy†	c Rhodes b Malcolm	74	not out	51
S.K.Warne	c Thorpe b Fraser	7	lbw b Lewis	2
D.W.Fleming	c Rhodes b Malcolm	0	(10) lbw b Lewis	24
P.E.McIntyre	b Malcolm	0	(11) lbw b Malcolm	0
C.J.McDermott	c Crawley b Fraser	5	(9) c Rhodes b Lewis	0
Extras	(B 2, LB 7, NB 7)	16	(B 3, LB 5, NB 13)	21
		419		**156**

1/128 2/130 3/202 4/207 5/232 6/396 7/405 8/406 9/414
1/17 2/22 3/22 4/23 5/64 6/75 7/83 8/83 9/152

Bowling: First Innings—Malcolm 26-5-78-3; Fraser 28.5-6-95-3; Tufnell 24-5-64-0; DeFreitas 20-3-70-2; Lewis 18-1-81-2; Gooch 5-0-22-0. Second Innings—Malcolm 16.1-3-39-4; Fraser 12-1-37-1; DeFreitas 11-3-31-0; Lewis 13-4-24-4; Tufnell 9-3-17-1.

Umpires: P.D.Parker and S.Venkataraghavan

AUSTRALIA v ENGLAND 1994-95 (Fifth Test)

At W.A.C.A. Ground, Perth, 3, 4, 5, 6, 7 February
Result: Australia won by 329 runs

Australia

Batsman	1st Innings		2nd Innings	
M.J.Slater	c Lewis b DeFreitas	124	(2) c Atherton b Fraser	45
M.A.Taylor*	c Rhodes b Lewis	9	(1) b Fraser	52
D.C.Boon	c Ramprakash b Lewis	1	(4) c Rhodes b Malcolm	18
M.E.Waugh	c DeFreitas b Lewis	88	(5) c Rhodes b DeFreitas	1
S.R.Waugh	not out	99	(6) c Ramprakash b Lewis	80
G.S.Blewett	c Rhodes b Fraser	20	(7) c Malcolm b Lewis	115
I.A.Healy†	c Lewis b DeFreitas	12	(8) not out	11
S.K.Warne	c Rhodes b DeFreitas	11	(9) c Lewis b Malcolm	6
J.Angel	run out	0	(3) run out	0
G.D.McGrath	run out	0		
C.J.McDermott	run out	6		
Extras	(B 14, LB 4, NB 9, W 4)	31	(B 1, LB 9, NB 7)	17
		402		**345** (8 wkts dec.)

1/47 2/55 3/238 4/247 5/287 6/320 7/328 8/386 9/388
1/75 2/79 3/102 4/115 5/123 6/326 7/333 8/345

Bowling: First Innings—Malcolm 31-6-93-0; DeFreitas 29-8-91-3; Fraser 32-11-84-1; Lewis 31.5-8-73-3; Gooch 1-1-0-0; Ramprakash 11-0-43-0. Second Innings—Malcolm 23.3-3-105-2; Fraser 21-3-74-2; Lewis 16-1-71-2; DeFreitas 22-10-54-1; Ramprakash 8-1-31-0.

England

Batsman	1st Innings		2nd Innings	
G.A.Gooch	b M.E.Waugh	37	(1) c and b McDermott	4
M.A.Atherton*	c Healy b McGrath	4	(2) c Healy b McGrath	8
M.W.Gatting	b McGrath	0	(3) b McDermott	8
G.P.Thorpe	st Healy b Warne	123	(5) c Taylor b McGrath	0
J.P.Crawley	c Warne b M.E.Waugh	0	(6) c M.E.Waugh b McDermott	0
M.R.Ramprakash	b Warne	72	(7) c S.R.Waugh b M.E.Waugh	42
S.J.Rhodes†	c Healy b Angel	2	(8) not out	39
C.C.Lewis	c Blewett b McGrath	40	(9) lbw b McDermott	11
P.A.J.DeFreitas	b Angel	0	(10) c Taylor b McDermott	0
A.R.C.Fraser	c Warne b Angel	9	(4) lbw b McGrath	5
D.E.Malcolm	not out	0	(11) b McDermott	0
Extras	(B 4, LB 1, NB 3)	8	(LB 1, NB 4, W 1)	6
		295		**123**

1/5 2/5 3/77 4/77 5/235 6/246 7/246 8/247 9/293
1/4 2/17 3/26 4/26 5/27 6/27 7/95 8/121 9/123

Bowling: First Innings—Angel 22.3-7-65-3; McGrath 25-6-88-3; Blewett 4-1-9-0; M.E.Waugh 9-2-29-2; Warne 23-8-58-2; McDermott 13-5-41-0. Second Innings—McGrath 15-4-38-6; McDermott 13-4-40-3; Angel 3-0-20-0; Warne 7-3-11-0; M.E.Waugh 3-0-13-1.

Umpires: K.E.Liebenberg and S.G.Randell

WEST INDIES v AUSTRALIA 1994-95 (First Test)

At Kensington Oval, Bridgetown, Barbados, 31 March, 1, 2 April

Result: Australia won by 10 wickets

West Indies

S.C.Williams c Taylor b Julian	1	(2)	not out	20
S.L.Campbell c Healy b Reiffel	0	(1)	not out	16
B.C.Lara c S.R.Waugh b Julian	65		c Healy b McGrath	10
R.B.Richardson* c Healy b Julian	0		c S.R.Waugh b Warne	6
C.L.Hooper c Taylor b Julian	60		c Healy b McGrath	9
J.C.Adams c Warne b McGrath	16		c Reiffel b Julian	16
J.R.Murray† c Taylor b McGrath	21		b Reiffel	36
W.K.M.Benjamin c Taylor b Warne	14		not out	39
C.E.L.Ambrose c Blewett b McGrath	7		c S.R.Waugh b Warne	23
C.A.Walsh c S.R.Waugh b Warne	1		lbw b McGrath	26
K.C.G.Benjamin not out	0		c Blewett b McGrath	6
			b McGrath	4
			b Warne	5
Extras (B 3, NB 6, W 1)	10		(LB 1, NB 8)	9
	195			**189**

1/1 2/5 3/6 4/130 5/152
6/156 7/184 8/193 9/194

1/19 2/25 3/31 4/57 5/91
6/135 7/170 8/176 9/180

Bowling; First Innings—Reiffel 11-2-41-1; Julian 12-0-36-4; McGrath 12.1-1-46-3; Warne 12-2-57-2; M.E.Waugh 1-0-12-0. Second Innings—Reiffel 11-6-15-1; Julian 12-2-44-1; Warne 26.3-5-64-3; McGrath 22-6-68-5.

Australia

M.J.Slater c Taylor b W.K.M.Benjamin	18	(2)	not out	20
M.A.Taylor* c Hooper b K.C.G.Benjamin	55	(1)	not out	16
D.C.Boon c W.K.M.Benjamin b Walsh	20			
M.E.Waugh c Murray b Ambrose	40			
S.R.Waugh c Murray b K.C.G.Benjamin	65			
G.S.Blewett c Murray b Ambrose	14			
I.A.Healy† not out	74			
B.P.Julian c K.C.G.Benjamin b Hooper	31			
P.R.Reiffel b W.K.M.Benjamin	6			
S.K.Warne c Adams b Walsh	1			
G.D.McGrath b W.K.M.Benjamin	4			
Extras (LB 13, NB 5)	18		(NB 3)	3
	346		(0 wkts)	**39**

1/27 2/72 3/121 4/166 5/194
6/230 7/290 8/291 9/331

Bowling; First Innings—Ambrose 20-7-41-2; Walsh 25-5-78-2; K.C.G.Benjamin 20-1-84-2; W.K.M.Benjamin 23.2-6-71-3; Hooper 12-0-59-1. Second Innings—Walsh 3-0-19-0; K.C.G.Benjamin 2.5 1 14 0; Hooper 1-0-6-0.

Umpires: L.H.Barker and S.Venkatraghavan

WEST INDIES v AUSTRALIA 1994-95 (Second Test)

At Recreation Ground, St John's, Antigua, 8, 9, 10, 12, 13 April

Result: Match drawn

Australia

M.J.Slater c Adams b Walsh	41	(2)	c Richardson b Walsh	18
M.A.Taylor* c Walsh b Ambrose	37	(1)	c Murray b Walsh	5
D.C.Boon b Walsh	21		lbw b W.K.M.Benjamin	67
M.E.Waugh c Hooper b Walsh	4		b W.K.M.Benjamin	61
S.R.Waugh b W.K.M.Benjamin	15		not out	65
G.S.Blewett c Murray b W.K.M.Benjamin	11		c Williams b Hooper	19
I.A.Healy† c Walsh b K.C.G.Benjamin	14		c Hooper b Walsh	26
B.P.Julian b Walsh	22		run out	6
P.R.Reiffel not out	22		not out	13
S.K.Warne c Arthurton b Walsh	11			
G.D.McGrath c Murray b Walsh	0			
Extras (LB 12, NB 6)	18		(B 1, LB 9, NB 10)	20
	216		(7 wkts dec.)	**300**

1/82 2/84 3/89 4/126 5/126
6/150 7/188 9/204

1/22 2/43 3/149
4/162 5/196 6/256 7/273

Bowling; First Innings—Ambrose 14-5-34-1; Walsh 21.3-7-54-6; K.C.G.Benjamin 16-3-58-1; W.K.M.Benjamin 15-2-40-2; Hooper 2-0-18-0. Second Innings—Ambrose 19-3-42-0; Walsh 36-7-92-3; W.K.M.Benjamin 24-2-72-2; K.C.G.Benjamin 15-1-51-0; Arthurton 1-0-1-0; Hooper 9-3-16-1; Adams 4-0-16-0.

West Indies

S.C.Williams c Boon b Warne	16		not out	31
R.B.Richardson* c S.R.Waugh b Julian	37		b Reiffel	2
B.C.Lara c Boon b S.R.Waugh	88		b Julian	43
J.C.Adams lbw b Warne	22		not out	3
C.L.Hooper c Julian b S.R.Waugh	11			
K.L.T.Arthurton c Taylor b Warne	26			
J.R.Murray† lbw b Reiffel	26			
W.K.M.Benjamin c Taylor b McGrath	4			
C.E.L.Ambrose c Taylor b Reiffel	0			
C.A.Walsh b Reiffel	9			
K.C.G.Benjamin not out	5			
Extras (B 6, LB 3, NB 6, W 1)	16		(NB 1)	1
	260		(2 wkts)	**80**

1/34 2/104 3/168 4/186 5/187
6/240 7/240 8/240 9/254

1/11 2/69

Bowling; First Innings—Reiffel 17-3-53-3; Julian 10-5-36-1; Warne 28-9-83-3; McGrath 20.1-5-59-1; S.R.Waugh 6-1-20-2. Second Innings—Reiffel 6-2-12-1; Julian 5-2-15-1; Warne 7-0-18-0; McGrath 6-2-20-0; M.E.Waugh 6-2-15-0.

Umpires: S.A.Bucknor and D.R.Shepherd

WEST INDIES v AUSTRALIA 1994-95 (Third Test)

At Queen's Park Oval, Port-of-Spain, Trinidad, 21, 22, 23 April

Result: West Indies won by 9 wickets

Australia

M.A.Taylor* c Murray b K.C.G.Benjamin	2	(2) c Murray b K.C.G.Benjamin	30
M.J.Slater c Murray b Walsh	0	(1) c Richardson b Walsh	15
D.C.Boon c Richardson b Ambrose	18	c sub (S.Chanderpaul) b Walsh	9
M.E.Waugh c Murray b Ambrose	2	lbw b Ambrose	7
S.R.Waugh not out	63	c Hooper b K.C.G.Benjamin	21
G.S.Blewett c Murray b W.K.M.Benjamin	17	c Murray b K.C.G.Benjamin	2
I.A.Healy† c Richardson b Walsh	8	b Ambrose	0
B.P.Julian c Adams b K.C.G.Benjamin	0	b Ambrose	0
P.R.Reiffel c Lara b Walsh	11	c Hooper b Ambrose	6
S.K.Warne b Ambrose	0	c Hooper b Walsh	11
G.D.McGrath c Murray b Ambrose	0	not out	0
Extras (LB 6, W 1)	7	(LB 3, NB 1)	4
	128		**105**

1/2 1/2 3/14 4/37 5/62   1/26 2/52 3/56 4/85 5/85
6/95 7/98 8/121 9/128   6/85 7/87 8/87 9/105

Bowling: *First Innings*—C.E.L.Ambrose 16-5-45-5; C.A.Walsh 17-4-50-3; W.K.M.Benjamin 6-3-13-1; K.C.G.Benjamin 8-2-14-1. *Second Innings*—C.E.L.Ambrose 10.1-1-20-4; C.A.Walsh 13-4-35-3; W.K.M.Benjamin 5-0-15-0; K.C.G.Benjamin 8-1-32-3.

West Indies

S.C.Williams c Taylor b Reiffel	0	c Warne b M.E.Waugh	42
R.B.Richardson* c Healy b McGrath	2	not out	38
B.C.Lara c M.E.Waugh b McGrath	24	not out	14
J.A.Adams c M.E.Waugh b Reiffel	42		
C.L.Hooper c Reiffel b S.R.Waugh	21		
K.L.T.Arthurton c M.E.Waugh b McGrath	5		
J.R.Murray† c Healy b McGrath	13		
W.K.M.Benjamin c Slater b Warne	7		
C.A.Ambrose c Slater b McGrath	1		
C.A.Walsh c Blewett b McGrath	14		
K.C.G.Benjamin not out	1		
Extras (LB 4, NB 2)	6	(B 4)	4
	136		**(1 wkt) 98**

1/1 2/6 3/42 4/87 5/95   1/81
6/106 7/113 8/114 9/129

Bowling: *First Innings*—McGrath 21.5-11-47-6; Reiffel 16-7-26-2; Julian 7-1-24-0; S.R.Waugh 3-1-19-1; Warne 12-5-16-1. *Second Innings*—McGrath 6-1-22-0; Reiffel 6-2-21-0; Julian 3-0-16-0; Warne 3.5-0-26-0; M.E.Waugh 2-0-9-1.

Umpires: C.E.Cumberbatch and D.R.Shepherd

WEST INDIES v AUSTRALIA 1994-95 (Fourth Test)

At Sabina Park, Kingston, Jamaica, 29, 30 April, 1, 3 May

Result: Australia won by an Innings and 53 Runs

West Indies

S.C.Williams c Blewett b Reiffel	0	b Reiffel	20
R.B.Richardson* lbw b Reiffel	100	c & b Reiffel	14
B.C.Lara c Healy b Warne	65	lbw b Reiffel	0
J.C.Adams c Slater b Julian	20	c S.R.Waugh b McGrath	18
C.L.Hooper c M.E.Waugh b Julian	23	run out (6)	13
K.L.T.Arthurton c Healy b McGrath	16	(7) lbw b Warne	14
C.O.Browne† c Boon b Warne	7	(8) c Taylor b Warne	31
W.K.M.Benjamin lbw b S.R.Waugh	7	(5) lbw b Reiffel	51
C.E.L.Ambrose not out	6	st Healy b Warne	5
C.A.Walsh c Boon b S.R.Waugh	2	c Blewett b Warne	14
K.C.G.Benjamin c Healy b Reiffel	5	not out	6
Extras (B 1, LB 9, NB 9, W 1)	20	(B 8, LB 13, NB 6)	27
	265		**213**

1/0 2/103 3/131 4/188 5/220   1/37 2/37 3/46 4/98 5/134
6/243 7/250 8/250 9/254   6/140 7/166 8/172 9/204

Bowling: *First Innings*—Reiffel 13.4-2-48-3; Julian 12-3-31-2; McGrath 20-4-79-1; Warne 25-6-72-2; S.R.Waugh 11-5-14-2; M.E.Waugh 4-1-11-0. *Second Innings*—Reiffel 18-5-47-4; Julian 10-2-37-0; Warne 23.4-8-70-4; M.E.Waugh 1-0-1-0; S.R.Waugh 4-0-9-0; McGrath 13-2-28-1.

Australia

M.J.Slater c Lara b Walsh	27
M.A.Taylor* c Adams b Walsh	8
D.C.Boon c Browne b Ambrose	17
M.E.Waugh c Adams b Hooper	126
S.R.Waugh c Lara b K.C.G.Benjamin	200
G.S.Blewett b Arthurton	69
I.A.Healy† c Lara b W.K.M.Benjamin	8
B.P.Julian c Adams b Walsh	8
P.R.Reiffel b K.C.G.Benjamin	23
S.K.Warne c Lara b K.C.G.Benjamin	0
G.D.McGrath not out	3
Extras (B 11, LB 6, NB 26, W 1)	44
	531

1/17 2/50 3/73 4/304 5/417
6/433 7/449 8/522 9/522

Bowling: Ambrose 21-4-76-1; Walsh 33-6-103-3; K.C.G.Benjamin 23.5-0-106-3; W.K.M.Benjamin 24-3-80-1; Hooper 43-9-94-1; Adams 11-0-38-0; Arthurton 4-1-17-1.

Umpires: S.A.Bucknor and K.E.Liebenberg

BIBLIOGRAPHY

Arlott, John (ed), *The Great Bowlers*, Collins, London, 1969

Arlott, John, *100 Greatest Batsmen*, Macdonald Queen Anne Press, London, 1986

   The Great Captains, Pelham, London, 1971

   Fred, Eyre & Spottiswoode, London, 1971

Armstrong, Geoff, *A Century of Summers*, Ironbark Press, Sydney, 1992

   The People's Game, Ironbark Press, Sydney, 1994

Barnes, Sidney, *It Isn't Cricket*, William Kimber, London, 1953

Benaud, Richie, *Way of Cricket*, Hodder & Stoughton, London, 1961

   On Reflection, Collins, Sydney, 1984

Border, Allan, *Beyond Ten Thousand*, Swan Publishing, Nedlands, WA, 1993

Bose, Mihir, *A History of Indian Cricket*, Andre Deutsch, London, 1990

Boyle, Harry and Scott, Henry, *The Fourth Australian Team*, Wright & Co., Melbourne, 1884

Brearley, Mike, *The Art of Captaincy*, Hodder & Stoughton, London, 1985

Cashman, Richard, *The Demon Spofforth*, University of NSW Press, Sydney, 1990

Chappell, Greg and McGregor, Adrian, *Greg Chappell*, Collins, Sydney, 1985

Chappell, Ian, *Chappelli*, Hutchinson Group, Melbourne, 1976

   The Cutting Edge, Swan Publishing, Nedlands, WA, 1992

Coleman, Robert, *Seasons in the Sun*, Hargreen Publishing, Melbourne, 1993

Coward, Mike, *Cricket Beyond the Bazaar*, Allen & Unwin, Sydney, 1990

Derriman, Phil, *True to the Blue*, Richard Smart, Sydney, 1985

   Ashes from Ashes, Australian Broadcasting Commission, Sydney, 1989

Dunstan, Keith, *The Paddock that Grew*, Cassell, Melbourne, 1962

Ferguson, W.H., *Mr Cricket*, Nicholas Kaye, London, 1957

Fingleton, Jack, *Cricket Crisis*, Cassell, Melbourne, 1947

Fishman, Roland, *Calypso Cricket*, Margaret Gee Holdings, Sydney, 1991

Forsyth, Chris, *The Great Cricket Hijack*, Widescope, Melbourne, 1979

Frindall, Bill, *England Test Cricketers*, Willow Books, London, 1989

Frith, David, *The Fast Men*, Richard Smart Publishing, Sydney, 1981

    The Slow Men, Richard Smart Publishing, Sydney, 1984

    By His Own Hand, ABC Books, Sydney, 1990

Giffen, George, *With Bat and Ball*, Ward Lock, London, 1898

Growden, Greg, *A Wayward Genius*, ABC Books, Sydney, 1991

Haigh, Gideon, *The Cricket War*, Text Publishing, Melbourne, 1993

Haygarth, Arthur, Ashley-Cooper, F.S. and Lillywhite, Frederick, *MCC Scores and Biographies*, Vols 1–XVI, Longmans, London

Hill, Alan, *Hedley Verity*, Kingswood Press, Surrey, 1986

    Les Ames, Christopher Helm, London, 1990

    Herbert Sutcliffe, Simon & Schuster, London, 1991

Hutcheon, E.H., *A History of Queensland Cricket*, Queensland Cricket Association, Brisbane, 1947

James, Alfred, *The Second Australian XI's 1880–81 Tour*, privately printed, 1994

Laver, Frank, *An Australian Cricketer on Tour*, Bell & Sons, London, 1907

Lillee, Dennis, *Back to the Mark*, Hutchinson, Melbourne, 1974

McHarg, Jack, *Stan McCabe*, Collins, Sydney, 1987

    A Cricketing Life, Millennium Books, Sydney, 1990

    An Elegant Genius, ABC Books, Sydney, 1994

Mailey, Arthur, *Ten for 66 and All That*, Phoenix, London, 1958

Mallett, Ashley, *Rowdy*, Lynton Publishing, Adelaide, 1973

    Spin Out, Gary Sparke, Melbourne, 1977

    Trumper, Macmillan, Melbourne, 1985

Mant, Gilbert, *A Cuckoo in the Bodyline Nest*, Kangaroo Press, Sydney, 1992

Marsh, Rodney, *You'll Keep*, Hutchinson, Melbourne, 1975

Martin-Jenkins, Christopher, *Complete Who's Who Of Test Cricketers*, Rigby, Adelaide, 1980

Miller, Keith, *Keith Miller on Cricket*, Pelham, London, 1965

Moody, Clarence P., *Album of Noted Cricketers*, R.A. Thompson, Adelaide, 1898

    South Australian Cricket Reminiscences, R.A. Thompson, Adelaide, 1905

Moyes, A.G., *A Century of Cricketers*, Angus & Robertson, Sydney, 1950

    Australian Cricket: a history, Angus & Robertson, Sydney, 1950

Mullins, Patrick and Matthews, Brian (ed), *Cradle Days of Australian Cricket*, Macmillan Co. of Australia, 1989

Noble, M.A., *The Game's the Thing*, Cassell, Sydney, 1926

Page, Roger, *A History of Tasmanian Cricket*, Roger Page, Hobart, 1957

Pollard, Jack, *Six and Out*, Viking O'Neil, Melbourne, 1990

    Middle & Leg, Macmillan Co. of Australia, Melbourne, 1988

Australian Cricket: the game and the players, Angus & Robertson, Sydney, 1988

Australian Cricket: A History (5 vols), Angus & Robertson, Sydney 1990

The Glovemen, Kangaroo Press, Sydney, 1993

The World's Greatest Leg-Spin Bowlers, Kangaroo Press, Sydney, 1994

The Mollydookers, Five Mile Press, Melbourne, 1995

Richardson, Victor, *The Victor Richardson Story*, Rigby, Adelaide, 1946

Roebuck, Peter, *Great Innings*, Pan Books, Sydney, 1990

Rosenwater, Irving, *Sir Donald Bradman*, Batsford, London, 1978

Ross, Alan, *Ranji, Prince of Cricketers*, Collins, London, 1983

Rowan, Lou, *The Umpire's Story*, Pollard Publishing, Sydney, 1972

Scott, John, *Caught in Court*, Andre Deutsch, London, 1989

Sharpham, Peter, *Trumper*, Hodder & Stoughton, Sydney, 1985

Sissons, Ric, *The Players*, Pluto Press, Sydney, 1988

Cricket and Empire, Allen & Unwin, Sydney, 1984

Smith, Rick, *The ABC Guide to Australian Test Cricketers*, ABC Books, Sydney, 1993

Stackpole, Keith and Trengove, Alan, *Not Just For Openers*, Stockwell, Melbourne, 1974

Wakely, B.J., *Bradman the Great*, Nicholas Kaye, London, 1959

Walker, Max, *Tangles*, Barry Sparkes, Melbourne, 1976

Warner, Sir Pelham, *How We Recovered the Ashes*, Chatto & Windus, London, 1905

Weaver, Amanda, and Cashman, Richard, *Wicket Women*, University of NSW, 1991

Webster, Ray, *First-Class Cricket in Australia 1850–51 to 1941–42*, privately printed, Melbourne, 1991

Williams, Marcus, *Double Century*, Willow Publishing, London, 1985

Willis, Ronald, *Cricket's Biggest Mystery, the Ashes*, Rigby, Adelaide, 1982

Wisden Cricketers' Almanacks, Sporting Handbooks and Macdonald & Jane, London

Wynne-Thomas, Peter, *Give Me Arthur*, Arthur Barker, London, 1985

Complete Book of Cricket Tours, Guild, London, 1989

INDEX

Bold numbers refer to illustrations. All Australian players mentioned in the text have been included in the index.